Deng Xiaoping
and the Transformation
of China

Deng Xiaoping

and the

Transformation

of China

EZRA F. VOGEL

THE BELKNAP PRESS OF HARVARD UNIVERSITY PRESS

Cambridge, Massachusetts, and London, England   2011

Library of Congress Cataloging-in-Publication Data

Vogel, Ezra F.
Deng Xiaoping and the transformation of China / Ezra F. Vogel.
    p.   cm.
    Includes bibliographical references and index.
    ISBN 978-0-674-05544-5
    1. Deng, Xiaoping, 1904–1997.   2. Heads of state—China—Biography.
3. China—Politics and government—1976–2002.   I. Title.
DS778.T39V64 2011
951.05092—dc22
[B]   2011006925

To my wife, Charlotte Ikels,

and to my Chinese friends determined to help a foreigner understand

Contents

The Deng Era, 1978–1989

Challenges to the Deng Era, 1989–1992

Deng's Place in History

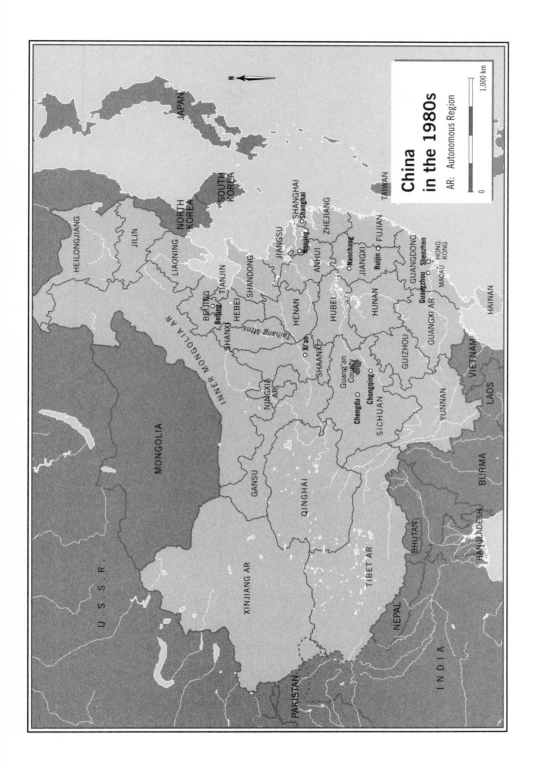

China
in the 1980s

AR: Autonomous Region

0   1,000 km

Preface: In Search of Deng

In the summer of 2000, relaxing after a leisurely outdoor supper on Cheju Island, South Korea, I told my friend Don Oberdorfer, one of America's greatest twentieth-century reporters on East Asia, that I was retiring from teaching and wanted to write a book to help Americans understand key developments in Asia. Many people said that my 1979 book, *Japan as Number One,* helped prepare some U.S. leaders in business and government for Japan's rise in the 1980s, which had shocked many in the West. What would best help Americans understand coming developments in Asia at the start of the twenty-first century? Without hesitation, Don, who had covered Asia for half a century, said, "You should write about Deng Xiaoping." After some weeks of reflection, I decided he was right. The biggest issue in Asia was China, and the man who most influenced China's modern trajectory is Deng Xiaoping. Moreover, a rich analysis of Deng's life and career could illuminate the underlying forces that have shaped recent social and economic developments in China.

Writing about Deng Xiaoping would not be easy. When carrying on underground activities in Paris and Shanghai in the 1920s, Deng had learned to rely entirely on his memory—he left no notes behind. During the Cultural Revolution, critics trying to compile a record of his errors found no paper trail. Speeches prepared for formal meetings were written by assistants and recorded, but most other talks or meetings required no notes, for Deng could give a well-organized lecture for an hour or more drawing only on his memory. In addition, like other high-level party leaders, Deng strictly observed party discipline. Even when exiled with his wife and some of his children to Jiangxi during the Cultural Revolution, he never talked with them about high-level party business, even though they were also party members.

Deng criticized autobiographies in which authors lavished praise on themselves. He chose not to write an autobiography and insisted that any evaluation of him by others "should not be too exaggerated or too high."[1] In fact, Deng rarely reminisced in public about past experiences. He was known for not talking very much *(bu ai shuohua)* and for being discreet about what he said. Writing about Deng and his era thus poses more than the usual challenges in studying a national leader.

I regret that I never had the chance to meet and talk with Deng personally. When I first went to Beijing in May 1973, as part of a delegation sponsored by the National Academy of Sciences, we met Zhou Enlai and other high officials, but we did not meet Deng. One of my strongest impressions from the trip was the buzz in high circles about the recent return of Deng to Beijing from his exile during the Cultural Revolution and the high expectation that he would play some important role that would bring great changes. What role? What changes? We Westerners speculated, but none of us could have predicted the sea change in China that was to occur over the next two decades, and how much China's future would be advanced by the efforts of this singular leader.

The closest I ever came to Deng was a few feet away at a reception at the National Gallery in Washington in January 1979. The reception was a grand gathering of American China specialists from government, academia, the media, and the business world to celebrate the formal establishment of U.S.-China relations. Many of us at the reception had known each other for years. We had often met in Hong Kong—the great gathering spot for China watchers when China was closed to most Westerners—where we would share the latest news or rumors in our efforts to penetrate the bamboo curtain. It had been a long time since some of us had last seen each other, however, and we were eager to catch up. Further, the National Gallery, where the reception was held, was not meant for speeches: the acoustics were terrible. Unable to hear a thing that Deng and his interpreter were saying through the loudspeaker, we, the gathered throng, continued talking with our fellow China-watcher friends. Those close to Deng said he was upset about the noisy, inattentive crowd, but most of us watching were impressed with how he read his speech as if delivering it to a disciplined Chinese audience sitting in reverential silence.

I have therefore come to know about Deng as a historian knows his subject, by poring over the written word. And there are many accounts of various parts of Deng's life. Despite Deng's admonitions to writers not to lavish praise, the tradition of writing an official or semi-official history to glorify one hero and downplay the role of others remains alive and well in China. Since other officials have been glorified by their secretaries or family members, the careful reader can compare these different accounts. And among party historians, there are some who have, out of a professional sense of responsibility, written about events as they actually occurred.

There will be more books about Deng written in the years ahead as additional party archives become available to the public. But I believe there will never be a better time than now for a scholar to study Deng. Many of the basic chronologies have now been compiled and released, many reminiscences have been published, and I have had an opportunity that will not be available to later historians: I met and spoke with Deng's family members, colleagues, and family members of these colleagues, who gave me insights and details not necessarily found in the written records. In all, I spent roughly twelve months in China (over several years), interviewing in Chinese those who had knowledge about Deng and his era.

The single most basic resource for studying the objective record of Deng's activities is *Deng Xiaoping nianpu* (A Chronology of Deng Xiaoping). The first publication, a two-volume, 1,383-page official summary of Deng's almost-daily meetings from 1975 until his death in 1997, was released in 2004; the second, a three-volume, 2,079-page description of his life from 1904 to 1974, was published in 2009. The teams of party historians who worked on these volumes had access to many party archives and were conscientious in reporting accurately. The chronology does not provide explanations, does not criticize or praise Deng, does not speculate, does not mention some of the most sensitive topics, and does not refer to political rivalries. Yet it is very helpful for determining whom Deng saw and when and, in many cases, what they talked about.

Many of Deng's major speeches have been compiled, edited, and published in the official *Selected Works of Deng Xiaoping*. The three-volume work provides a useful account of many of his major policies, although it is critical to interpret them in the context of national and world events at the time. Chronologies about and key speeches and writings by Chen Yun, Ye Jianying, Zhou Enlai, and others are similarly useful.

The books that offer the most in-depth understanding of Deng's personal thinking are the two by Deng Rong (Maomao), his youngest daughter, about the period before he came to power. The books draw on her own recollections, her visits with people who knew Deng, and party archives. After 1989, when Deng's health began to deteriorate after the Tiananmen incident, Deng Rong usually accompanied her father whenever he went outside of his home. Although Deng Xiaoping did not talk with members of his family about high-level politics, they knew both him and the country's situation well enough to perceive and understand his concerns and perspectives, some of which only they could see. One volume *(My Father, Deng Xiaoping)* is about Deng's life before 1949, and the other *(Deng Xiaoping and the Cultural Revolution)* describes the time when Deng Rong accompanied her parents in exile away from Beijing in Jiangxi province from 1969 to 1973. She displays obvious affection and respect for her father and presents a highly positive picture, but she also provides details that reveal much about his personal qualities and attitudes. In fact, considering the constraints of party policy and her efforts to paint a positive picture, she is remarkably frank, open, and concrete. In writing these volumes, Deng Rong was assisted by party historians, who have checked the dates, names, and events. She is continuing to write about some of Deng's activities in the early post-1949 period, but she has not written about the years after 1973, which are still more controversial. She has kindly granted me several long interviews supplementing what she has written.

There are several works in English that provided me with a good start for studying the Deng Xiaoping era before I plunged into the Chinese sources, but with the exception of Sun and Teiwes they were written before the chronologies and the reminiscences on the hundredth anniversary of his birth became available. I found especially useful the works by Richard Baum, Richard Evans, Joseph Fewsmith, Merle Goldman, Roderick MacFarquhar and Michael Schoenhals, Maurice Meisner, Qian Qichen, Robert Ross, Ruan Ming, Harrison Salisbury, Frederick Teiwes and Warren Sun, and Yu Guangyuan.

Ambassador Richard Evans, a wise and seasoned British diplomat and ambassador to Beijing from 1984 to 1988, drew on his own meetings with Deng and the resources of the British government to write *Deng Xiaoping and the Making of Modern China,* a highly literate, brief overview for the educated public that is mostly about Deng's years prior to 1973. Among Western political scientists, Richard Baum has done the most detailed study of the politics of the Deng era, which he reports in *Burying Mao.* He draws on materials from China available before his book's publication in 1994 as well as works by Hong Kong analysts. He uses Hong Kong reports with discretion, but I have chosen to rely even less on these Hong Kong sources because it is hard to trace the origins of their information and therefore to assess their reliability. In *The Deng Xiaoping Era,* Maurice Meisner, a thoughtful scholar deeply knowledgeable about Marxist theory, presents Deng in the context of Marxist theoretical issues. In preparing *Sowing the Seeds of Democracy in China: Political Reform in the Deng Xiaoping Era,* my longtime Fairbank Center colleague Merle Goldman traces the changing intellectual currents during the Deng era, drawing not only on publications but also on discussions with many of the intellectuals, especially dissidents, about whom she writes. Ruan Ming, author of *Deng Xiaoping: Chronicle of an Empire,* was a researcher at the Chinese Communist Central Party School until he was removed by party conservatives in 1983. Finding refuge in the United States, Ruan Ming presents a passionate critique of the conservative ideologues who dragged their feet on reforms.

Qian Qichen, author of *Ten Episodes in China's Diplomacy,* was foreign minister and vice premier during much of Deng's era and has written a balanced, informative work on the foreign policies of the era. Yu Guangyuan, who helped Deng prepare the text of his speech for the Third Plenum, describes this historical turning point in *Deng Xiaoping Shakes the World.* Because I helped edit the English translation of these two volumes, I had the opportunity to have supplementary discussions with the authors, both of whom, as former officials, had worked closely with Deng.

The late Harrison Salisbury, a journalist and the author of *The New Emperors: China in the Era of Mao and Deng,* was given access to several key leaders soon after Mao's death. Although some of his descriptions, such as those of Deng's relation to third-front industries, show serious misunderstandings, he was given much better access than most journalists and he relates fresh views that were not available to others at the time.

David Shambaugh, editor of *The China Quarterly* when Deng came to power, brought together a group of scholars to assess Deng and his era shortly after Deng withdrew from power in 1992. The articles were reprinted in the book *Deng Xiaoping,* edited by Shambaugh.

Frederick Teiwes and Warren Sun have done the most exhaustive reading of Chinese sources of any Western scholars for the period from 1974 to 1982 in preparation for a projected three volumes. They have published the first, spanning the years 1974 to 1976. They aim to get the basic facts straight in a highly detailed way, by carefully evaluating different interpretations of various events. Warren Sun, who has been more persistent for two decades in tracing every important fact about the era than anyone I know, later spent more than two months checking through various drafts of my manuscript, correcting errors and suggesting supplementary interpretations and key works.

Joseph Fewsmith has written the best book in English on the economic debates of the era: *The Dilemmas of Reform in China.* Robert Ross has written excellent works that examine the foreign relations issues during the period. Roderick MacFarquhar, who has spent several decades studying Chinese elite politics and the Cultural Revolution, has written a three-volume set on *The Origins of the Cultural Revolution* and, with Michael Schoenhals, *Mao's Last Revolution,* about the Cultural Revolution. I have known all these authors and talked with all of them about Deng and his era. They have been generous in supplementing what is in their publications and giving me a clearer sense of some of the important issues about which they write.

In Chinese so much has been released that even the best Chinese scholars have not been able to read all of it. Beginning in the 1990s an explosion of information became available on the Chinese Internet. I have been assisted by many research assistants, but particularly by Ren Yi and Dou Xinyuan. Ren Yi's grandfather, first party secretary of Guangdong province Ren Zhongyi, was the great reform leader of Guangdong. Dou Xinyuan, who served for many years in the Economic Commission of Guangdong, combines personal experience with a scholar's determination to get at deeper truths within historical documents. Ren and Dou each spent over a year working full-time to help me cover vast amounts of material and to try to think through how Chinese people in various positions felt and acted. Yao Jianfu, an official in the Rural Development Institute under Zhao Ziyang, also spent several weeks going over my drafts of the chapters on economics.

The Chinese Internet is an extraordinary source for tracing names, dates, and the like, but beyond these specific issues it is often difficult to distinguish fact from fantasy or interesting storytelling. When articles on the Internet present important information without detailing the source, I have tried to track down the original sources, or at least compare them with other sources before using them. In doing so, I have found that *China Vitae* in particular is a very useful English-language website on Chinese officials who are still alive.

There are a great many reminiscences by officials who worked with Deng. The three-volume collection *Huiyi Deng Xiaoping* (Remembering Deng Xiaoping) is one of the best, though a similar series is the three-volume collection *Deng Xiaoping: Rensheng jishi* (Record of the Actual Events in the Life of Deng Xiaoping). Two excellent journals that contain many articles by those who worked with Deng are *Yanhuang chunqiu* and *Bainianchao. Yanhuang chunqiu* is edited by former high-level officials who are knowledgeable and reform-minded. A different view can be found in the book *Shierge chunqiu, 1975–1987* (Twelve Springs and Autumns, 1975–1987), written by the conservative official Deng Liqun and published in Hong Kong, as well as in Deng Liqun's unpublished talks at the Contemporary China Research Institute (Dangdai Zhongguo Yanjiusuo), the research center he founded that has paved the way for many of the histories on post-1949 events.

There are also many accounts, often written by able Chinese journalists, of all the key figures of the era, including Chen Yun, Gu Mu, Hu Yaobang, Wan Li, Ye Jianying, and Zhao Ziyang, that provide varying perspectives. The best journalist's account of Deng is Yang Jisheng, *Deng Xiaoping shidai: Zhongguo gaige kaifang ershinian jishi* (The Age of Deng Xiaoping: A Record of Twenty Years of China's Reform and Opening). Official histories, like *Chen Yun zhuan* (Biography of Chen Yun), are carefully edited and based on documentary sources. Zhu Jiamu's book on Chen Yun (Zhu Jiamu, Chi Aiping, and Zhao Shigang, *Chen Yun*), although brief, benefits from Zhu's five years' service as an assistant to Chen as well as careful research. In addition to the *Deng Xiaoping nianpu,* there are also official chronologies *(nianpu)* for Chen Yun, Zhou Enlai, Ye Jianying, and a number of other officials who worked closely with Deng.

Another valuable resource is the national history *(Guoshi)* of China since 1949, seven volumes of which have already appeared, with three more forthcoming. Written by mainland scholars, including Gao Hua, Han Gang, Shen Zhihua, and Xiao Donglian, among others, this monumental work is being published by the Research Centre for Contemporary Culture, the Chinese University of Hong Kong. The volumes set a new standard of objective overall scholarship for the era.

The Chinese government has greatly increased the scope of what people can write about, but some works by well-informed insiders on the mainland are still considered too controversial to be published in Beijing. Hong Kong publishing, however, is much more open, so many of these books have been published in Hong Kong. Some of the most informative are those by Deng Liqun, Hu Jiwei, Yang Jisheng, Zhao Ziyang, and Zong Fengming. Among the reformers who have written their reminiscences is Hu Jiwei, former editor of the *Renmin ribao* (People's Daily), who authored *Cong Hua Guofeng xiatai dao Hu Yaobang xiatai* (From the Fall of Hua Guofeng to the Fall of Hu Yaobang).

Although chronologies of Hu Yaobang have not been published in the mainland, his mainland friends have published two lengthy two-volume chronologies in Hong Kong. One, edited by Sheng Ping, is *Hu Yaobang sixiang nianpu* (A Chronology of Hu Yaobang's Thought) and a second, edited by Zheng Zhongbing, is *Hu Yaobang ziliao changbian* (Materials for a Chronological Record of Hu Yaobang's Life). There is also a three-volume biography by Zhang Liqun and others—*Hu Yaobang zhuan* (A Biography of Hu Yaobang)—that remains unpublished. Hu's friends have collected four volumes of recollections, *Huainian Yaobang* (Remembering Yaobang), which have been edited by Zhang Liqun and others and published in Hong Kong. And on the mainland, Hu's daughter, under the name Man Mei, published *Sinian yiran wujin: Huiyi fuqin Hu Yaobang* (Longing without End: Memories of My Father, Hu Yaobang).

Zhao Ziyang, while under house arrest after 1989, found a way to record in his own words an account of his history and personal views, a work that has been translated into English as *Prisoner of the State: The Secret Journal of Premier Zhao Ziyang,* and edited by Bao Pu, Renee Chiang, and Adi Ignatius. After 1989, the outside person with whom Zhao spoke the most is Zong Fengming, who wrote *Zhao Ziyang, Ruanjinzhong de tanhua* (Conversations with Zhao Ziyang while under House Arrest). Zhao did not authorize the reminiscences by Zong, but he authorized and personally reviewed three recorded, highly focused conversations with journalist Yang Jisheng, published in *Zhongguo gaige niandai zhengzhi douzheng* (Political Struggle in the Period of Chinese Reform). These works, including some very critical of some of Deng's activities, offer valuable alternative perspectives to those given in the mainland publications.

I have also viewed Chinese documentaries showing Deng giving speeches, meeting people, visiting various sites, and relaxing with his family. At my direction, research assistants translated materials from the Russian.

In addition to general works on much of the Deng era, I have made use of many more specialized materials on specific subjects covered in this volume (see materials in English, Chinese, and Japanese that are included in the online bibliography and glossary at http://scholar.harvard.edu//ezravogel).

Apart from various short trips to China, when I was in Beijing for longer periods—five months in 2006, one month in 2007, several weeks in 2008, one month in 2009, and several weeks in 2010—I had an opportunity to interview in particular three categories of knowledgeable people: party historians, children of top officials, and officials who worked under Deng. Except for several English-speaking Chinese who preferred to speak in English, the interviews were conducted in Chinese without an interpreter. In particular, I have benefited from extensive interviews with Zhu Jiamu, Cheng Zhongyuan, Chen Donglin, and Han Gang, all outstanding historians specializing in party history. I also conducted interviews with two children of Deng

Xiaoping (Deng Rong and Deng Lin), two children of Chen Yun (Chen Yuan and Chen Weili), and two children of Hu Yaobang (Hu Deping and Hu Dehua). In addition, I have interviewed children of Chen Yi, Ji Dengkui, Song Renqiong, Wan Li, Ye Jianying, Yu Qiuli, and Zhao Ziyang. They are all bright, thoughtful people. Discreet and filial, they shared concrete reminiscences that gave a flavor of their parents and their parents' colleagues.

The former officials I interviewed range from those who are great admirers of Deng Xiaoping to severe critics who feel both that Deng did not fully support Hu Yaobang and the intellectuals and that he tragically missed opportunities to push for political reform. Some are well-known officials who had worked with and under Deng, including former foreign minister Huang Hua, former president Jiang Zemin, former deputy head of the Organization Department of the party Li Rui, former vice premier Qian Qichen, and former first party secretary of Guangdong Ren Zhongyi. All of these officials had retired, allowing us to have a more leisurely conversation than would have been possible while they were still working.

I also benefited from interviews with a talented group of retired officials who worked under Deng, some of whom now write articles for the journal *Yanhuang chunqiu,* including Du Daozheng, Feng Lanrui, Sun Changjiang, Wu Mengyu, Yang Jisheng, and the late Zhu Houze. Some are occasionally criticized or warned for their outspoken comments, but generally they have been given freedom to express their views. In addition, I had a chance to interview scholars at research centers and universities in China. Scholars tend to be not as well informed on inner-party workings as those who served in the government and party under Deng, even if they are party members, but they often have had opportunities to know key people and some have read broadly and researched available documents with great care.

Although there are several institutions where specialists are doing research on party history, including the Central Party School, several universities, and the Contemporary China Research Institute, the institution with the greatest number of researchers, the greatest resources, and the best access to party materials is the Central Party Literature Research Center (Zhonggong Zhongyang Wenxian Yanjiushi), which is operated under the purview of the Central Committee. Some fifteen people at this center worked on compiling *Deng Xiaoping nianpu.* In addition, about fifteen are now working on an official biography of Deng that they hope to complete within the next several years.

At Harvard, I have had the opportunity over the years to exchange views with many visiting Chinese officials and scholars, some of whom are very familiar with the politics of Beijing. A number are prominent political dissidents—very able, dedicated, and idealistic people who ran afoul of party orthodoxy in the 1980s. I particularly benefited from talks with Chen Yizi, Dai Qing, Gao Wenquan, the late Liu Binyan, Ruan Ming, and the late Wang Ruoshui. I have talked with Wang Dan, a student leader during the Tiananmen incident, and Wei Jingsheng, whose famous 1978 wall poster on Democracy Wall, "On the Fifth Modernization," led to a sentence of fifteen years' imprisonment. I have also talked with younger former officials such as Wu Guoguang, Wu Jiaxiang (who has since returned to Beijing), and Yu Qihong, all of whom worked in central party organs. And I have learned from economic specialists whom I knew in Beijing and at Harvard, particularly Fan Gang, Lu Mai, and Qian Yingyi.

In addition to those mentioned earlier, I have interviewed Bao Pu, Chris Buckley, Anson Chan, Chen Guangzhe, Chen Haosu, Chen Kaizhi, Chen Weili, Chen Xiankui, Chen Xiaolu, Chen Yuan, Chen Zhiya, Cheng Zhongyi, Chung Jae Ho, Deng Yingtao, John Dolfin, Peter Drysdale, Du Pu, Du Ruizhi, Du Runsheng, Gao Hua, Gao Shangquan, Gao Xiqing, the late Gong Yuzhi, Leo Goodstadt, He Fang, He Liliang, Hu Xiaojiang, Huang Ping, Huang Renwei, Ji Humin, Jiang Mianheng, Jin Chongji, Larry Lau, Leng Rong, Leung Chun-ying, Li Dequan, Li Jie, Li Junru, Li Pu, Li Sengping, the late Li Shenzhi, Li Xiangqian, Li Yu, Lin Jingyao, Liu Shuqing, Liu Yawei, Christine Loh, Long Yongtu, Lu Yaogang, Luo Yuan, Ma Liqun, Ma Peiwen, Charles Martin, Dede Nickerson, Chris Patten, Mario Pini, Sha Zukang, Shang Yuan, Shen Shaojie, Shen Zaiwang, Song Kehuang, Song Yiping, Sun Gang, Donald Tseng, Wan Shupeng, Wang Jian, Wang Juntao, Wang Yannan, Wang Yi, Wu Jinglian, Wu Nansheng, Xiao Donglian, Xie Mingang, Xiong Huayuan, Yan Jiaqi, Yang Chengxu, Yang Qixian, Yang Tianshi, Ye Xuanji, Ye Xuanlian, Regina Yip, Yu Xiaoxia, Zeng Yanxiu, Zhai Zhihai, Zhang Baijia, Zhang Guoxing, Zhang Xianyang, Zhang Xingxing, Zhang Xinsheng, Zhang Ying, Zhang Yunlin, Zhao Shukai, Zheng Bijian, Zheng Zhongbing, Zhou Mingwei, Zhou Muzhi, Zhou Qi, and Zhu Qizhen. I am indebted to all my Chinese friends and acquaintances who tried to help a foreigner understand. But none bears any responsibility for the views I present, which are my own best judgments from the various sources I have seen.

To get a better sense of the environment that Deng experienced, I spent several days each in locations that were important to Deng during his lifetime: his birthplace in Guang'an county in Sichuan; the Taihang Mountains in Shanxi where Deng spent eight years as a guerrilla fighter; Chongqing and Chengdu, Deng's base when he was in charge of the Southwest Bureau from 1949 to 1952; and Ruijin, Jiangxi, where he lived for several years during the early 1930s. I also visited Chen Yun's birth site in Qingpu, on the outskirts of Shanghai. In each of these places, local scholars and officials were helpful in supplementing the materials in museums, giving me a sense of Deng's role in the local setting.

I traveled to Singapore to talk with former prime minister Lee Kuan Yew, who perhaps knew Deng Xiaoping as well as any foreign leader, former prime minister Goh Chok Tong, former adviser on the Chinese coastal areas Goh Keng Swee, President S. R. Nathan, and other officials. I also had long discussions with scholars, especially Wang Gungwu, John Wong, and Zheng Yongnian. In Hong Kong I met Yang Zhenning and Edgar Cheng, who met Deng many times when traveling with his father-in-law, Y. K. Pao, the leading Hong Kong shipping magnate who had more meetings with Deng than anyone else living outside mainland China.

In Australia, I had a chance to talk with former prime minister Robert Hawke, former ambassador to Beijing Ross Garnaut, former foreign ministry official Richard Rigby, Roger Uren, and others. In addition, I traveled to Moscow, where I met Lev Deliusin who spent many years in China, headed the Oriental Institute in Moscow, and wrote a book on Deng. I have benefited especially from discussions with Alexander Pantsov, a meticulous scholar now teaching in the United States, who is knowledgeable about Russian sources on Mao and Deng, and Sergei Tikhvinsky.

My visits to England in search of greater insights on Deng led to discussions with former ambassador Sir Alan Donald, former ambassador Richard Evans, and former Hong Kong governor David Wilson—and while in Beijing, I met former British ambassador Sir Anthony Galsworthy. I also talked with former Hong Kong chief executive Tung Chee Hwa and spent many sessions with Sin Por Shiu, a member of the Hong Kong negotiating team with Beijing.

While in Japan, I talked with former prime minister Nakasone Yasuhiro; former ambassadors to Beijing, including Anami Koreshige, Kunihiro Michihiko, and Tanino Sakutaro; other former China specialists in the Japanese Foreign Ministry such as Hatakenaka Atsushi, Kato Koichi, and Shimokouji Shuji; and generalists who know a great deal about Japanese foreign policy, including Kawashima Yutaka, Togo Katsuhiko, and Watanabe Koji. I have also talked with Japanese scholars who specialize in China's relations with other countries, particularly Hirano Ken'ichiro, Kawashima Shin, Kokubun Ryosei, Mori Kazuko, Soeya Yoshihide, Takagi Seiichiro, Takahara Akio, Tanaka Akihiko, Tsuji Kogo, Yabuki Susumu, and Yamada Tatsuo. I am indebted especially to two Japanese scholars of China, Masuo Chisako and Sugimoto Takashi, who are translating this book into Japanese. Masuo, who wrote an excellent book on Deng's foreign policy, assisted me in collecting Japanese materials, including some that have been declassified by the Japanese government.

I have had the chance to talk with a number of American officials who met Deng, including former president Jimmy Carter and former vice president Walter Mondale, who had key visits with Deng in 1979; as well as Henry Kissinger and Brent Scowcroft. I also talked with Zbigniew Brzezinski and the late Michel Oksenberg, who were the key White House officials who managed the normalization talks. Edward Cox, a son-in-law of President Richard Nixon who visited Deng with the president, shared his recollections with me. I talked with several former U.S. ambassadors to Beijing, including the late Arthur Hummel, the late Jim Lilley, Winston Lord, Joe Prueher, Sandy Randt, Stapleton Roy, Jim Sasser, and the late Leonard Woodcock. Ambassador Woodcock's widow, Sharon Woodcock, kindly shared with me her husband's papers. I have also had an opportunity to talk with other China specialists who served in the White House, the State Department, or other parts of the U.S. government, particularly Mike Armacost, Chris Clarke, Richard Fisher, Chas Freeman, David Gries, Charles Hill, Don Keyser, Paul Kreisberg, Herb Levin, Ken Lieberthal, Bill McCahill, Doug Paal, Nick Platt, Alan Romberg, Stapleton Roy, Richard Solomon, Doug Spelman, Robert Suettinger, Roger Sullivan, Robert Sutter, Harry Thayer, and John Thomson. Two former students, Susan Lawrence and Melinda Liu, who spent many years reporting from Beijing, have been extraordinarily generous with their time and insights. Jan Berris of the National Committee on U.S.-China Relations has been a wonderful source of information about people and events. I have also interviewed four of Deng's interpreters: Ji Chaozhu, Shi Yanhua, Nancy Tang, and the late Zhang Hanzhi.

I have benefited from the careful reading of drafts of the entire manuscript by Paul Cohen, Joseph Fewsmith, Merle Goldman, Charlotte Ikels, Don Keyser, Andrew Nathan, Tony Saich, and David Shambaugh. I have also been fortunate to have had parts of the manuscript read carefully by John Berninghausen, Ashley Esarey, Mel Goldstein, Arthur Kleinman, Mike Lampton, Diana Lary, Susan Lawrence, Cheng Li, Edwin and Cyril Lim, Perry Link,

Bill McCahill, Lawrence Reardon, Robert Ross, Stapleton Roy, Richard Samuels, Richard Solomon, Mike Szonyi, Martin Whyte, Dalena Wright, and Ye Nan. (Those who read Chapter 18 are listed in the notes to that chapter.) A number of party historians in China were kind enough to read through an earlier draft of this manuscript that had been translated into Chinese to help correct errors and misunderstandings: Chen Donglin, Cheng Zhongyuan, Han Gang, Qi Weiping, Shen Zhihua, Xiao Yanzhong, Yang Kuisong, and Zhu Jiamu. Only I, however, can be held responsible for any errors not corrected and for those that have crept in since they read the manuscript.

I have benefited greatly from discussions with colleagues at Harvard, including William Alford, Peter Bol, Julian Chang, Paul Cohen, Tim Colton, Nara Dillon, Mark Elliott, Joe Fewsmith, Merle Goldman, Steve Goldstein, Rowena He, Sebastian Heilmann, William Hsiao, Iain Johnston, Bill Kirby, Arthur Kleinman, Rod MacFarquhar, Suzanne Ogden, Bill Overholt, Dwight Perkins, Liz Perry, Robert Ross, Tony Saich, Mike Szonyi, Tam Tai, Tu Weiming, Ning Wang, James L. Watson, John and Anne Watt, Martin Whyte, Jeff Williams, Endymion Wilkinson, and David Wolff. I have discussed issues with scholars elsewhere including John Berninghausen, Tom Bernstein, Chen Guangzhe, Deborah Davis, John Dolfin, Tom Gold, Mel Goldstein, Gui Benqing, Mike Lampton, Perry Link, Richard Madsen, Jean Oi, Jonathan Pollack, the late Lucian Pye, Dick Samuels, David Shambaugh, Susan Shirk, Dorie Solinger, Ed Steinfeld, and Andrew Walder.

I have also been assisted by Holly Angell, Deirdre Chetham, Jorge Espada, Shenpeng Gao, Elizabeth Gilbert, Anna Laura Rosow, Kate Sauer, Shi Wenying, and Zhang Ye. Like all other scholars working on post-1949 Chinese materials at Harvard, I am greatly indebted to the Fairbank Center librarian in the Fung Library, Nancy Hearst, who combines an intimate knowledge of source materials with a seemingly boundless passion to help scholars locate the information they need. She corrected my notes and proofread the manuscript several times. As China grows increasingly important in the twenty-first century, we are privileged at Harvard to have access to a special collection of materials in the Fairbank Collection of the Fung Library that are an invaluable resource for research on contemporary China. Not only are many of these materials unavailable in other Western libraries, they are inaccessible in Chinese libraries as well.

I am also indebted to Jean Hung, who has, with equal passion to help scholars, assembled and creatively organized the most complete collection of materials on this period outside mainland China, at the Universities Service

Centre of The Chinese University of Hong Kong. I was also fortunate to receive assistance from the librarians at the Carter Library in Atlanta, who helped me find and use documents from the Carter administration. My conscientious editor Earl Harbert worked line by line to make the manuscript clear to those who are not China specialists. Julie Carlson, my copyeditor, has been creative, thorough, and tireless in helping me shape the manuscript. Kathleen McDermott, editor at Harvard University Press, has been the creative, diligent, enthusiastic manager who oversaw every aspect of the publication.

My wife, Charlotte Ikels, a specialist on the anthropology of China, has been a constant intellectual companion at all stages of this work. She patiently tried her best to provide balance and spiritual support to a driven workaholic.

Although I served as a U.S. national intelligence officer for East Asia from 1993 to 1995, I have not had access to classified materials in the course of this research. All statements of fact, opinion, or analysis expressed are those of the author. The materials presented here do not reflect the official positions or views of the CIA or any other U.S. government agency. Nothing in the contents should be construed as asserting or implying U.S. government authentication of information or endorsement of the author's views. This material has been reviewed by the CIA to prevent the disclosure of classified information.

Introduction: The Man and His Mission

In March 1979 Sir Murray MacLehose, the widely respected Chinese-speaking British governor of Hong Kong, flew to Beijing to explain Hong Kong's problems. Told in advance only that he would meet a high official, MacLehose was delighted to learn after he arrived that he would be meeting Deng Xiaoping, who had just been named China's preeminent leader.[1] During an intimate meeting in the Great Hall of the People, MacLehose told Deng about the growing difficulties confronting Hong Kong. As both men well knew, the British had ruled the colony of Hong Kong since the Opium War, but the lease from China for most of the land that was now part of Hong Kong would expire in 1997. Governor MacLehose was measured and diplomatic as he talked of the need to reassure Hong Kong people deeply worried about what might happen after 1997. Deng listened attentively to Governor MacLehose's concerns and then, as they rose after their talk and moved toward the door, he beckoned to MacLehose. The governor, well over six feet tall, leaned over to hear the words of his five-foot host: "If you think governing Hong Kong is hard, you ought to try governing China."[2]

Deng was acutely aware that China was in a disastrous state. At the beginning of the previous decade, during the Great Leap Forward, more than thirty million people had died. The country was still reeling from the Cultural Revolution in which young people had been mobilized to attack high-level officials and, with Mao's support, push them aside as the country of almost one billion people was plunged into chaos. The average per capita income of Chinese peasants, who made up 80 percent of the population, was then only US$40 per year. The amount of grain produced per person had fallen below what it had been in 1957.

1

Military officials and revolutionary rebels had been moved in to replace the senior party officials who had been forced out, but they were unprepared and unqualified for the positions they had assumed. The military had become bloated and was neglecting the military tasks, while military officers in civilian jobs were enjoying the perquisites of offices without performing the work. The transportation and communication infrastructure was in disarray. The bigger factories were still operating with technology imported from the Soviet Union in the 1950s, and the equipment was in a state of disrepair.

Universities had been basically closed down for almost a decade. Educated youth had been forcibly sent to the countryside and it was becoming harder to make them stay. Yet in the cities there were no jobs for them, nor for the tens of millions of peasants wanting to migrate there. Further, the people who were already living in the cities, fearing for their jobs, were not ready to welcome newcomers.

Some officials were bold enough to suggest that the real cause of the problems China was facing was Mao Zedong himself, but Deng believed that a single person should not be held responsible for the failures of the previous two decades. "We are all to blame," he said. Mao had made huge mistakes, certainly, but in Deng's view the larger problem was the faulty system that had given rise to those mistakes. The effort to gain control of the political system down to the household had overreached, creating fear and lack of initiative. The effort to gain control of the economic system had also overreached, causing rigidities that stymied dynamism. How could China's leaders loosen things up while keeping the country stable?

For more than a decade before the Cultural Revolution, no one had greater responsibility for building and administering the old system than Deng Xiaoping. During his three and a half years in the countryside from 1969 to 1973, no one who had held high positions had thought more deeply about what went wrong with China's old system and what needed to be done than Deng Xiaoping.

In 1978, Deng did not have a clear blueprint about how to bring wealth to the people and power to the country; instead, as he confessed, repeating a widely used saying—he "groped for the stepping stones as he crossed the river."[3] But he did have a framework for thinking about how to proceed.

He would open the country wide to science, technology, and management systems, and to new ideas from anywhere in the world, regardless of the country's political system. He was aware that the new dynamos of Asia—Japan, South Korea, Taiwan, Hong Kong, and Singapore—were growing faster than any countries ever had. But Deng realized he could not simply import an entire system from abroad, for no alien system could fit the unique needs of China—which had a rich cultural heritage but was also huge, diverse, and poor. He realized what some free-market economists did not, that one could not solve problems simply by opening markets; one had to build institutions gradually. He would encourage other officials to expand their horizons, to go everywhere to learn what brings success, to bring back promising technology and management practices, and to experiment to see what would work at home. He would help pave the way by developing good relations with other countries so they would be receptive to working with China.

To provide order during this rebuilding, he believed there was only one organization that could manage the process—the Communist Party. The most experienced leaders available in China in 1978 were the party leaders who had risen to levels of responsibility in the 1950s and early 1960s. They needed to be brought back and young people had to be trained overseas and bring back the best ideas, the best science, the best technology, from anywhere. Bringing in new ways would be terribly disruptive. Even the Communist Party would have to change fundamentally its goals and its methods of operation.

As the paramount leader, Deng did not see his role as coming up with new ideas. He saw his job as managing the disruptive process of devising and implementing a new system. He would have the ultimate responsibility and he needed to make sound judgment calls. He would need to select a core of co-workers who could share responsibility for guiding the system and he would have to set up quickly an organization so they could work together effectively. He needed the best information he could get about what was actually going on in the country and what was happening abroad. He needed to provide hope without raising expectations that were unrealistic, as Mao had done in 1958. He would have to explain the situation to his officials and to the public and pace the changes so that people could accept them and the country would not split apart. Although he had considerable power, he knew he had to be sensitive to the political atmosphere among his colleagues if they were to implement what he directed. He needed to allow a measure of stability in employment and daily life even as the system underwent fundamental changes. In short, Deng faced a tall order, and an unprecedented one: at the time, no other Communist country had succeeded in reforming its economic system and bringing sustained rapid growth, let alone one with one billion people in a state of disorder.

The Man: Deng Xiaoping

Despite Deng's diminutive stature, once he became the preeminent leader, when he appeared in a room he had a commanding presence that made him a natural center of attention. More than one observer commented that it was as if the electricity in the room flowed to him. He had the concentrated intensity of someone determined to resolve important matters. He possessed the natural poise of a former wartime military commander as well as the self-assurance that came from half a century of dealing with life-and-death issues near the center of power. Having faced ups and downs, and been given time to recover with support from his wife, children, and close colleagues, he had become comfortable with who he was. When he did not know something, he readily admitted it. President Jimmy Carter commented that Deng, unlike Soviet leaders, had an inner confidence that allowed one to get directly into substantive issues. He did not dwell on what might have been or who was at fault for past errors; as in bridge, which he played regularly, he was ready to play the hand he was dealt. He could recognize and accept power realities and operate within the boundaries of what seemed possible. Once Mao was no longer alive to look over his shoulder, Deng was sufficiently sure of himself and his authority that with guests he could be relaxed, spontaneous, direct, witty, and disarmingly frank. At a state banquet in Washington in January 1979, when told by Shirley MacLaine about a Chinese intellectual who was so grateful for what he had learned about life after being sent to the country-side to raise tomatoes during the Cultural Revolution, Deng's patience was soon exhausted. He interrupted her to say, "He was lying" and went on to tell her how horrible the Cultural Revolution had been.

For someone who turned seventy-four in 1978, Deng was still vigorous and alert. He still took his morning break with a fast-paced half-hour walk around the garden of his home where he also kept his office. Many Chinese leaders, when seated next to their guest in comfortable chairs that were placed aside each other, would look straight ahead when they talked, but Deng liked to turn and look directly at the person he was talking with. He had an inquisitive mind and was a good listener. When he objected to the policies of foreign nations, foreign officials described him as feisty and "tough as nails." Having observed nations pursuing their self-interest through imperialism, colonialism, and the use of military force abroad, Deng was never naïve about what to expect from foreign leaders professing goodwill. But even when they did not like what he had to say, foreign visitors, from different social positions and different parties, from large countries and small, ended up feeling comfortable with him. They felt he was someone with whom they could do business.

Some Westerners were so impressed with Deng's directness and pragmatism that they mistakenly thought he was a capitalist at heart and that he would lead China toward a Western-style democracy. He was always ready to learn, but in the end he believed he knew better than they what was good for China and it was not capitalism and Western-style democracy.

By 1978, Deng was hard of hearing in his right ear, and it was awkward for him to take part in group meetings where various people expressed their views. He much preferred to read papers, and he spent every morning sitting by himself reading reports; his office director each day brought him fifteen newspapers and all the important reports; Deng would choose which ones to spend time on. In some ways it was easier for him to meet foreigners, for the interpreter could speak directly in his good left ear, making it natural as he exchanged views with his guests. Deng spoke Mandarin with a strong Sichuanese accent, but it was intelligible to other Mandarin speakers and did not slow him down. The responsibilities Deng faced were daunting, but it is difficult to imagine how anyone could have been much better prepared for the tasks or better suited for them by temperament and habit.

Deng had an instinctive patriotism and commitment to the Communist Party that inspired the confidence of his fellow officials. The patriotism that underlay Deng's lifelong activism had jelled at age fourteen, just when popular nationalism took hold in the country, as he took to the streets of Guang'an county where he was attending middle school. Five years later in France, disappointed with the dirty and difficult factory work assigned to Chinese and the withdrawal of the promise of opportunities to study, Deng joined the French branch of the Chinese Communist Party. He would remain a committed Communist until his death more than seven decades later.

From his five years in France and one year in the Soviet Union, Deng acquired a far better understanding of developments around the world and far more perspective on China than Mao had garnered. Deng had a chance to see industry and commerce in a modern country, and his year in the Soviet Union gave him a chance to see how the first Communist country had tackled modernization.

Already while in France, Deng had an opportunity to take part in the small groups of intellectuals considering overall strategy for the Communist youth movement. From that time on, Deng's association with the grand strategists of the Chinese revolution gave him a unique view, from "commanding heights," of how these theories took hold and influenced events on the ground. In France, Deng quit his factory jobs and did odd jobs around the tiny Chinese Communist Party office led by Zhou Enlai, who was six years older than Deng. Deng, known then as "Dr. Mimeograph" for his role in producing the simple propaganda pamphlets that publicized the leftist cause to Chinese students in France, became in effect an apprentice where he could observe how Zhou Enlai, already a leader among fellow Chinese youth, with experience in Japan and England, went about building an organization. Though one of the youngest in the group, Deng soon was on the executive committee of the Communist youth organization in Europe. At Sun Yat-sen (Zhongshan) University in Moscow where the Soviets were just beginning to train Chinese for the international communist movement, Deng was selected for Group No. 7, in which the highest level of Chinese leaders were trained for the international Communist movement. At Sun Yat-sen University Deng had an opportunity to understand how the Soviets had built their Communist movement and to learn their views on how to build a movement in China.

For his entire career, with brief interruptions, Deng had been close enough to the top seat of power that he could observe from the inside how the top leaders responded to different situations. Not long after he returned to China in 1927, he was again under Zhou Enlai, in the Shanghai underground, as the party tried to devise survival strategies while Chiang Kai-shek, their former colleague, tried to wipe them out. Not only did Deng take part in the planning to create urban insurrections, but at age twenty-five he was sent to Guangxi province to lead urban insurrections. As Mao began to build up the Jiangxi Soviet base, Deng went there where as head of the party in Ruijin county, he learned how Mao was building up his rural base. On the Long March, Deng got to attend the crucial Zunyi conference where Mao began to emerge as leader. Before the Long March had ended Deng had the opportunity to become a confidante of Mao's. Not long after Mao set up his base in northwest China, Mao entrusted Deng with major responsibilities as a political commissar, providing political leadership within the military. Later in the civil war, he was given responsibility for taking over Shanghai and guiding the transition to Communist rule and was then sent to the Southwest where he was given responsibility for leading one of the six major regions of the country.

Above all, it was at the center of power in Beijing, from 1952 to 1966, that Deng had the opportunity to work closely with Mao to consider strategies for China's development and for dealing with foreign countries. Mao had identified Deng as one of his potential successors, and Deng had taken part in

Politburo meetings and after 1956 in its Standing Committee, along with the other five highest-ranking officials in the country. Deng also became a central participant in the planning and creation of a socialist structure that featured agricultural collectivization and nationalization of industry, and played a central role in land reform in the Southwest. In 1959–1961, he had played a major part in guiding the adjustments to the socialist structure after the failures of the Great Leap Forward. In short, Deng in 1978 had half a century of experience in thinking about strategies used by China's top leaders in guiding the country.

Deng was a military leader for twelve years, and even later described himself as a soldier. He was a political commissar rather than a military commander, but he was party secretary and had responsibility for approving military actions. Working closely with a military commander, he fought first in small guerrilla activities, but then in huge battles in the civil war. During the Huai Hai military campaign in late 1948, he ended up as the party secretary of the front command, responsible for coordinating half a million soldiers in one of the largest battles in military history and one of the key turning points in the civil war.

Throughout his career, Deng was responsible for implementation rather than for theory. His responsibilities had grown from leading a small county in the Jiangxi Soviet to leading the work of several counties in the Taihang Mountains as political commissar in World War II, to leading a border area where several provinces intersected after World War II, to leading the entire Southwest after 1949, to leading the country.

In the 1950s, Deng was responsible for guiding the Chinese Communist Party's relations with other Communist parties, at a time when China had few relations with the West. After he was allowed to return from the Cultural Revolution, Deng served as an apprentice to Zhou Enlai as he accepted responsibilities for leading China's work in foreign relations.

Some say Deng had little experience in economic affairs, but economic activities were always an important responsibility of party generalists. Furthermore, from 1953–1954 Deng had served for a year as finance minister at a crucial stage as China was building its socialist economic structure.

An important part of Communist activity was always propaganda. In France, Deng had been responsible for putting out a propaganda bulletin. In the Jiangxi Soviet, after undergoing criticism, he was put in charge of propaganda for the entire soviet area, and on the Long March he again had responsibilities in the area of propaganda. As a political commissar in the military, Deng found that he was most persuasive when he was direct and gave his troops a broad perspective, connecting their efforts to the overall situation and mission.

In short, Deng had an enormous range of governing experiences at the local, regional, and national levels that he could draw on. For half a century he had been part of the broad strategic thinking of party leaders. He had held high positions in the party, in the government, and in the army. In the 1950s he had taken part in bringing in new industries and new technology from the Soviet Union, just as he would have responsibility for bringing in new industries from the West in the 1980s.

Deng was very bright, always at the top of his class. He was the youngest of eighty-four students to have passed the examinations to be sent from Sichuan to France in 1920. He had been good at one of the main tasks in his early Confucian training, learning to recite long passages of texts by memory. In the underground he had learned not to leave a paper trail, but to keep information in his mind. Deng could deliver well-thought-through and well-organized hour-long lectures without notes. Mao once called him a walking encyclopedia. Before important events, Deng liked to spend time thinking quietly by himself as he considered what to say so that when the time came, he could give clear and decisive presentations.

Deng had been hardened by seeing comrades die in battle and in intra-party purges. He had seen friends become enemies, and enemies become friends. Three times Deng had been purged, in the Jiangxi Soviet, in 1966 in the Cultural Revolution when he was subjected to blistering criticism, and in 1976. Deng had developed a steely determination. He had disciplined himself not to display raw anger and frustration and not to base his decisions on feelings but on careful analysis of what the party and country needed. Mao once described Deng as a needle inside a cotton ball, tough on the inside, soft on the outside, but many of Deng's colleagues rarely sensed a ball of cotton.[4] His colleagues did not believe he was unfair: unlike Chairman Mao, Deng was not vindictive—though when he judged that it was in the interest of the party, he would remove even those who had dedicated themselves to him and his mission.

During difficulties, Deng was sustained partly by the warm and close relations with his wife and family and by a certain inner confidence that came from overcoming past hardships. But until 1976 he was also sustained by a special relationship with the dominant figure of China's revolution, Chairman Mao. Mao destroyed many of his comrades, but he had a special relationship with Deng from the 1930s after Deng's first purge for being a part of the Mao faction. Mao twice purged Deng, but he never destroyed him. He set him aside for possible use later.

Deng's colleagues understood that he regarded ruling China as serious business, and although he could be witty, with colleagues he was usually formal. He did not take an interest in their personal lives. He was above petty concerns and instead focused on providing the firm leadership that most felt China needed, as well as a sense of direction for their shared cause. He was clear, logical, and predictable. He was known for thinking about the big issues, and for leaving details to others. He was not a micromanager.

With ordinary citizens, however, Deng was far more approachable than the godlike Chairman Mao; people spoke reverently of "Chairman Mao," but they could call Deng by his first name, "Xiaoping." Deng was also relaxed about his vices, of which, he told visitors, he had three—smoking cigarettes, drinking alcohol, and spitting into the spittoon that was placed on the floor beside him. And he enjoyed them all.

Deng was determined to do what was good for the party and the country, not what was good for his friends. After leaving his home at sixteen, Deng never again visited his parents or his hometown. He made it clear that he did not represent one locality, one faction, or one group of friends. His closest colleagues were comrades working for a common cause, not friends whose loyalty extended beyond the needs of the organization. Though he was unusually close to his wife and children, Deng kept to the code of party discipline: he never revealed high-level secrets to his family, even though his wife and four children were all party members. As a disciplined military officer, when given orders, Deng was known for charging boldly ahead, even when he knew that there would be heavy casualties.

Deng was not admired by all Chinese. Some considered him too autocratic, too ready to take charge and to disregard what others had to say. Intellectuals were unhappy with how he cracked down on outspoken people in the anti-rightist campaign of 1957. Some considered him too rash, too ready to charge ahead, too willing to impose discipline. Like any good military officer, he expected his subordinates to carry out orders. And although he welcomed what he considered constructive suggestions to resolve problems, he bristled when foreigners and political dissidents criticized the party. He vividly remembered the chaos of the civil war and the Cultural Revolution and believed that social order in China was fragile; when he judged that it was at risk, he would respond forcefully. As paramount leader, he was also prepared to undertake bold reforms and opening on his own timetable. In short, by the time he emerged as the preeminent leader, Deng was a disciplined, experienced official determined to serve the needs of his party and his country.

The Mission: Making China Rich and Strong

For almost two centuries before 1978, other leaders of China, like Deng, had been trying to find a way to make China rich and powerful.[5] The imperial system, which had been established at roughly the same time as the Roman Empire, had been extraordinarily successful. With some interruptions and modifications, it had not only enabled Chinese leaders to govern a larger population for a longer time than any other government on earth, but also produced a great civilization. In such a vast country, where it took a month to get from one end of the empire to the other, officials in the capital could not supervise closely how every town and village was implementing national laws and rules. The leaders had developed a remarkable system of selecting able officials by examination, training them, and providing some supervision while giving them great local autonomy.

By the end of the eighteenth century, rapid population growth, the expanded commercial developments in local areas, and the arrival of imperialist Western powers on the China coast were straining the imperial system. By then each of the roughly 1,500 counties had an average population of about 200,000 and was governed by a single small office. New advances in military, communications, manufacturing, and transportation technologies—gunpowder and ships, for example—gave rise to economic development and social forces that the thin layer of bureaucracy could not contain. In earlier centuries, rulers had limited the growth of local economies in an effort to keep them within the bounds of imperial control, but now rulers in Beijing struggled to adapt the imperial system to cope with the changes.

Complicating their efforts was the sheer size of China. At this point, China had the world's largest population, which had doubled in size in the previous two hundred years and was continuing to grow rapidly, and its geographical area had expanded in those years to the west and northeast. Along the coast and even along some of the land borders, the Chinese military could not stop the advance of foreigners, and civilian leaders could not halt the expanded commercial activities.

As the challenges to the system grew more severe, it remained difficult to convince the rulers in Beijing that their system, which had survived for almost two millennia, was under serious threat. Between 1861 and 1875, just at the time when Deng's frugal grandfather was saving to increase the size of the family's landholdings, a group of officials under the Tongzhi Emperor was working to overcome growing social turmoil. Failing to realize the depth of change required to cope with the new social forces at home and with the foreigners at their gates, they endeavored to keep the past on its throne. While sending troops to quell the rebellions, they sought to reinvigorate the existing institutions—by strengthening the examination system and the teaching of Confucianism, and by spending lavishly on rebuilding the palace.

The Tongzhi Emperor's successors had their faith in the traditional system shaken, above all, by their shocking military defeat at the hands of their small island neighbor, Japan, in the sea battles of 1894–1895. In 1898, with the support of China's twenty-seven-year-old emperor, reform-minded officials rushed to introduce within one hundred days some forty edicts to create a new order. They opened modern schools and universities and prepared to send people abroad to learn modern Western subjects. But whereas the Japanese had spent decades studying the West and crafting their own new systems, China's 1898 reformers had not built a political or institutional base to support reform. The Empress Dowager, threatened by the changes, placed the emperor under house arrest and stopped the reforms. She later abolished the traditional examination system, tried to modernize the military, and prepared to write a new constitution. But she too failed to forge an effective system. Instead of putting money into building naval ships, she built a marble boat and an expensive summer palace. It was not easy to change the complex and intricate imperial system with its established customs and institutions.

By the time Deng Xiaoping was born in 1904, China's last dynasty, the Qing, was already irreparably weakened by its inability to respond effectively to both interior rebellions and intrusions of foreign powers along the coast. In 1911 a small group of rebels in Wuhan who took control of the office of a Qing governor-general and military commander set off a chain reaction, bringing the imperial institutions to an abrupt end. The events of 1911 are called the "1911 Revolution," but it would be more accurate to describe them as a collapse. They were not the result of a well-organized revolutionary force but instead a response to the failure of the imperial system. Several brilliant Qing officials had thoughtfully analyzed the problems China confronted and had made creative proposals, but overall the rulers failed in their mission to adapt the imperial system to meet the challenges.

In 1911 China, unlike Japan which kept the emperor and Great Britain which kept the king, completely abolished the imperial system and created, on paper, a republic. In fact there was no effective governmental structure to replace imperial rule. Instead, after 1911, a series of leaders—Yuan Shikai,

Sun Yat-sen, Chiang Kai-shek, and Mao Zedong—all tried to build a new system to make the country rich and powerful.

Yuan Shikai, the most respected military leader at the time of the 1911 revolution, tried to unify the country militarily. But he was unable to win the support of civilian leaders and failed to overcome all the regional military leaders across the country who had taken up arms to bring order to their local areas as the imperial system had weakened.

Sun Yat-sen, who as a schoolboy had spent many years living with an elder brother in Hawaii, became a great publicist and fundraiser, first promoting the revolution and then trying to create a unified government. He has been called the father of the Chinese republic for his initial role in working with Yuan Shikai to establish a government after 1911, but he quickly lost out to Yuan Shikai. When Yuan Shikai's efforts failed, Sun in 1923 set up a government in Guangzhou that he hoped would become a national government. He formed a political party, the Guomindang (Nationalist Party) to provide political leadership, and on paper set up a national government with the outlines of a democratic structure. Sun attracted promising patriotic youth to Guangzhou, including those who later became Communist leaders—Mao Zedong, Zhou Enlai, Ye Jianying, Lin Biao—who were then also members of the Guomindang. Sun helped strengthen the base of popular nationalism, encouraged young people to go abroad to study, and promoted the mass media. But he confronted a chaotic environment and lacked both the organizational skills and the base of support necessary to build an effective political system. He died in 1925 with his dreams unfulfilled.

Chiang Kai-shek, then a young military official trained in Japan, was brought to Guangzhou by Sun Yat-sen to be commander of the newly established Whampoa (Huangpu) Military Academy. There he was to train a new national military officers' corps that would lead the military unification of the country. Chiang inherited Sun's mantle in 1925, but he had difficulties controlling growing rivalries within the Guomindang between the Communists and the right wing of the party. The rivalry grew into enmity, and in April 1927 Chiang moved peremptorily to attack and kill those who would not give up communism and declare allegiance to the Guomindang. Chiang Kai-shek was a general of considerable talent, but to govern he needed to work with the power holders—big businessmen, landlords, and warlords— who had alienated the common people. He became head of the Chinese government with the support of a shaky coalition of warlords, but he lost support as he proved unable to contain the corruption and inflation that wracked the country. He lost the ensuing civil war to the more unified Communists, who during the anti-Japanese war had built a strong party, army, and base of support by exploiting the fears of city dwellers panicked from rampant inflation and by appealing to the hopes of peasants expecting to receive their own land from redistributed landlord holdings.

Mao Zedong, a charismatic visionary, brilliant strategist, and shrewd but devious political manipulator, led the Communists to victory in the civil war and in 1949 unified the nation and eliminated most of the foreign-held territories. The military forces he had accumulated during the civil war were sufficiently strong that with the Communist Party's organizational discipline and propaganda, he was able to establish in the early 1950s a structure that penetrated far more deeply into the countryside and into urban society than had the imperial system. He built up a unified national governing structure led by the Communist Party and, with Soviet help, began to introduce modern industry. By 1956, with both peace and stability at hand, Mao might have brought wealth and power to China. But instead he plunged the country into an ill-advised utopian debacle that led to massive food shortages and millions of unnatural deaths. In his twenty-seven years of rule, Mao destroyed not only capitalists and landlords, but also intellectuals and many senior officials who had served under him. By the time he died in 1976, the country was in chaos and still mired in poverty.

When Deng ascended to power in 1978, he had many advantages that his predecessors lacked. In the mid-nineteenth century, few people had understood how deeply the new technology and developments along the coast were challenging the Chinese system. In the last years of the empire, the reformers had little idea of the institutional developments required to implement progressive new ideas. At the time of Yuan Shikai and Sun Yat-sen, there was no unified army and no governmental structure capable of uniting contenders for power. And after coming to power, Mao, who had no foreign experience, could not receive help from the West due to the Cold War.

By the time Deng came to power, Mao had already unified the country, built a strong ruling structure, and introduced modern industry—advantages that Deng could build on. Many high officials realized that Mao's system of mass mobilization was not working, that China was lagging far behind the foreign countries in science and technology, and that it needed to learn from the West. More fundamental change was called for, and Deng could rely on help from disgraced former senior officials who had been removed from power but not eliminated. These returning revolutionaries stood ready to unite under the leadership of Deng and the Communist Party, providing a ready resource of skills and energy, a useful transition to a new generation better trained in modern science, technology, and administration.

In 1978, because of the Soviet Union's aggressive behavior following the American withdrawal from Vietnam, Western countries were receptive to helping China loosen its ties with the Soviet Union. With the global expansion of trade that followed, China had access to new markets and advanced technologies—Japan, Taiwan, South Korea, Hong Kong, and Singapore—and nearby examples for how latecomers to the international scene could modernize quickly. And unlike the Communist countries of Eastern Europe, China was already completely independent from the Soviet Union, which meant that its leaders were free to make decisions based on what they believed to be China's best interests.

Yet all the favorable conditions that China enjoyed in 1978 would have been insufficient to transform the huge, chaotic civilization into a modern nation without a strong and able leader who could hold the country together while providing strategic direction. Deng was far better prepared for such a role than Yuan Shikai, Sun Yat-sen, Chiang Kai-shek, or Mao Zedong had been. It was he who would finally realize the mission that others had tried for almost two centuries to achieve, of finding a path that would make China rich and powerful.

In pursuing this mission, Deng's role changed fundamentally from one period to the next. Before 1949, he was a revolutionary, and after 1949 he became a builder helping to create a socialist state. From 1969 to 1973, during the Cultural Revolution, he used his time while banished to the countryside to reflect on the need for change. Then, during 1974–1975, while Mao was still alive, he was allowed to help bring order to China, thereby laying the groundwork for what he later achieved. When he returned to work in 1977 he became a reformer, first under Hua Guofeng, and after 1978, as preeminent leader.

While hosting a delegation of U.S. university presidents in 1974, Deng said, "I have never attended a university, but I have always considered that since the day I was born, I have been in the university of life. There is no graduation date except when I go to meet God."[6] Throughout his life, Deng kept learning and solving problems. In the process, stepping stone by stepping stone, he guided the transformation of China into a country that was scarcely recognizable from the one he had inherited in 1978.

Deng's Background

1

From Revolutionary to Builder to Reformer

1904–1969

Deng Xiaoping was born in 1904 in Paifang, Guang'an county, Sichuan. Though born to a small landlord family in a rural village, his village glorified the example of a relative, Deng Shimin, a member of the Deng extended family who had become a high official in imperial China and risen so high that he had written secret memos for China's top leaders.[1] The village was renamed "paifang" ("memorial arch") since a memorial arch had been erected in Shimin's honor after he returned there in 1774. The accomplishments of Shimin and his brothers were truly extraordinary. At a time when only a few thousand people each year passed the imperial examinations, and in a country inhabited by over 300 million people, Shimin as well as two of his brothers all passed the difficult test. In fact, Shimin went on to pass the second examination and then the third, the top level, and was appointed a high official in Beijing.[2]

In his brief autobiography, written when he was in Moscow in 1926–1927, Deng Xiaoping wrote that his father had had dreams of Xiaoping, too, becoming a high official—dreams that perhaps had been reinforced by Deng's mother, since some of her relatives had also passed examinations and become county magistrates. In imperial China, many families with a very bright child, especially families in which another relative had become an official, were willing to sacrifice to educate that child in the hope that he too might become an official, bringing honor and wealth to the family. Xiaoping was such a bright child, and although Deng Xiaoping's father, Deng Wenming, spent little time with his son, he made great efforts to further his education.

Deng Xiaoping's father participated actively in affairs beyond their village, but gave little attention to matters at home. His first wife died without children and he then married Xiaoping's mother, two years older than himself, when he was sixteen years old. She gave birth first to a daughter, then to Xiaoping, then to two more sons and another daughter, who died at age ten. Wenming added to the family a third wife who died shortly after giving birth to a son, and then a fourth wife, Xia Bogen, who gave birth to three daughters. Deng Xiaoping's father, at his peak, owned nearly forty *mou* of land (6.6 acres) and had several laborers who helped with the farm work and with raising silkworms.

Over his lifetime, Wenming's fortunes declined. He was head of the secret society, Gelaohui, in his village, but he spent most of his time in the nearby market town, Xiexing, a little more than a mile from Paifang, in the county capital six miles away, and in Chongqing. In 1914 he became head of the county police office. At one time, Wenming owned a small restaurant in Xiexing and was one of the elders supporting a school there that his son, Xiaoping, attended. But because he gambled and lost, he had to sell some of his land and almost went bankrupt, and due to bad relations with a higher official, he fled to other localities. Still, he continuously helped with Xiaoping's education.

Deng Rong reports that Deng's mother was very devoted to her son Xiaoping. Deng Xiaoping later recalled that he greatly respected his mother, who died in 1926 at age forty-two, for her efforts, with an absent husband, to look after the family. Mao Zedong was rebellious toward his father. Deng did not rebel; he was simply distant. In later years, Deng Rong would recall that her dad never talked about his own father who died in 1936.

When Deng Xiaoping was growing up, it was not clear what kind of schooling would best prepare a child for the future. The imperial examinations had been abandoned the year after Xiaoping was born, and Xiaoping was only seven years old when the 1911 Revolution brought an end to imperial officialdom. Yet the school system to replace Confucian training was just beginning. So like many of the more privileged youth in Chinese villages of the day, Xiaoping began his education at age five with standard Confucian training at the home of an educated relative in Paifang. The next year he transferred to a larger school in Xiexing, where he continued the study of the Confucian classics and cultivated his skills in memorizing texts. At the time, in Guang'an county, which had a population of over 200,000, there was only one public primary school to train promising youth in modern subjects. He must have learned these subjects well: when he was eleven, Xiaoping passed the highly competitive examinations to enter the upper primary school and with his father's financial support boarded there, in the town of Guang'an, six miles away from Paifang village. At age fourteen, he also passed the entrance examinations to Guang'an's one public junior middle school (comparable to an American high school). By age fifteen when he left that school to go to Chongqing, he had acquired a good grounding in the Confucian classics, in modern subjects including mathematics, science, history, and geography, as well as reading and writing the Chinese language.[3]

Some progressive schoolteachers heightened Deng's sense of patriotism; already, in 1919, at the tender age of fourteen, he took part in the demonstrations as part of the May Fourth Movement. The movement began when Western leaders, who were assembled at Versailles to define the shape of the postwar world, decided that the eastern portion of Shandong province, formerly a German concession, would be passed on to Japan rather than returned to China. Students at Peking University and Yenching University were outraged, and on May 4, 1919, they took to the streets of Beiping (renamed Beijing when it became the capital in 1949) to demonstrate not only against the Western powers for disregarding China, but against the Chinese government for being too weak to stand up for China's interests.

News of the May Fourth demonstrations spread quickly to universities and to some high schools throughout the country, helping to fan the flames of a new awareness of international developments and a new popular nationalism among China's educated youth. Guang'an was much more in touch with outside developments than more remote areas of China: the Qujiang River, more than a hundred meters wide as it ran through the county seat at Guang'an, was connected by two other rivers to Chongqing, some sixty miles away, and Chongqing was only five days by steamer from Shanghai. Xiaoping, a precocious teenager, joined the movement and with other students demonstrated on the streets of Guang'an. He also paraded in the anti-Japanese boycotts in Chongqing in the fall of 1919. The birth of Deng Xiaoping's personal awareness of the broader world coincided precisely with the birth of national awareness among educated youth. From this moment on, Deng's personal identity was inseparable from the national effort to rid China of the humiliation it had suffered at the hands of other countries and to restore it to a position of greatness, to make it rich and strong.[4]

Deng Xiaoping's nascent understanding of the wider world was to expand further when Deng Wenming found an opportunity for his son to go abroad for more education and training. During World War I, when many young Frenchmen were off to fight the war, there was an acute labor shortage in French factories, and tens of thousands of Chinese laborers were recruited to go there to work. At the time there were virtually no scholarships available in Western countries for bright Chinese students. An exception was offered by a national organization established even before the war by some prominent Chinese who hoped to enable Chinese students to go to France for "diligent work and frugal study"; they would work part-time to earn a living as well as attend French universities part-time to study modern science and technology. France was then known in China for its high level of culture and it became the favorite destination of Chinese students going overseas. A rich business-man from Sichuan who had studied in France established a special scholar-ship fund to enable Sichuan students to take part in the work-study program in France. A year-long preparatory school was established in Chongqing, and Xiaoping took the entrance examination, passed, and spent the 1919–1920 school year there preparing to go abroad. At the end of the year, a few schol-arships were made available to help some students travel to France. Xiaoping, never particularly skilled in foreign languages, did not pass the French-language examination; his father Wenming paid for his passage. One of Xiao-ping's classmates, an uncle three years older than him, made the journey with Xiaoping and remained his constant companion during their first months in France.

Birth of a Revolutionary: France and the Soviet Union, 1920–1927

When in 1920 the sixteen-year-old Deng Xiaoping boarded a steamer from Chongqing to Shanghai on the first leg of his journey to France, he was the youngest of eighty-four students from Sichuan to participate in the student-worker program. His journey itself would prove formative. During his week-long layover in Shanghai, Deng Xiaoping saw white people treating Chinese, in their own country, as if they were slaves. And when the refurbished cargo ship *Lebon,* which transported the group to France, stopped in Hong Kong, Vietnam, Singapore, and Ceylon (Sri Lanka), similar interactions between white masters and local laborers left a deep impression of unfairness on Xiao-ping and the other youths on board.

When the Chinese students arrived in Marseilles on October 19, the local paper reported that they wore Western-style clothes with broad-brimmed hats and pointed shoes; the students were immobile and silent, but appeared very intelligent.[5] They were bused to Paris and the next day dispersed to several middle schools that had arranged special training programs in the French language and other subjects. Deng was sent as part of a group of nineteen students to Bayeux Middle School in Normandy.

Some 1,600 Chinese student workers arrived in France between 1919 and 1921 through joint arrangements made by Chinese leaders and their French counterparts, but their arrival was ill-timed. By 1919 the young Frenchmen who had survived the war had returned to work, so jobs in France were hard to come by and inflation was severe. On January 12, 1921, less than three months after Deng and his fellow student-workers arrived in France, the Sichuan foundation, strapped for funds for a program that had quickly outgrown its resources, announced that it was breaking relations with the "diligent work, frugal study" program and that no funds would be available to students after March 15.[6] The French government urged the school at Bayeux to find a way to continue the program, but the school reported that it could not locate sufficient funds. On March 13, Deng and his eighteen Chinese fellow "worker-students" left Bayeux; three weeks later he found a job in the southern city of Creusot working at Schneider & Cie, France's largest ordnance factory.

Meanwhile, Chinese students in Paris, also deeply distressed that they could not continue their studies, demonstrated in front of the Chinese government's office in Paris, insisting that the government find some way to help them since they were acquiring scientific and technical knowledge for China's future. The Chinese government in Paris announced that it was not possible, and the French police arrested the leaders of the demonstrations. Throughout France, Chinese students, outraged that their opportunities to study had disappeared, responded by strengthening their contacts with each other and creating their own organizations to protest to both the Chinese and the French governments. Some leaders of the Chinese student demonstrations in France, such as student activist Cai Hesen and Chen Yi, who later served as mayor of Shanghai and as foreign minister, were expelled from France in the summer of 1921 for taking part in such protests.

While the Chinese student-workers in France scrounged for menial jobs that could provide them a subsistence wage, and as factory workers toiling long hours in poor working conditions, they observed rich French business families living lives of comfort far beyond what Deng had known in Sichuan.[7] The Chinese students, mostly from more affluent Chinese families, had been selected because of their academic achievements; they were among the elite selected to learn modern technologies to bring back to China. The jobs they were able to find, however, were those that French workers tried to avoid; they worked as unskilled laborers in heavy and chemical industry factories and mines. Moreover, Deng and the other Chinese workers generally began as apprentices with salaries that were even lower than those of ordinary workers.

The Chinese student-workers in France, despite their humiliating circumstances, took pride in Chinese civilization and saw themselves as future leaders. They formed their own separate communities; Deng never became fluent in French. They also split into various groups to discuss why the Chinese government was so weak and how the world had become so unjust. Some of these group members would go on to become anarchists, whereas Deng and others sought to build a movement to replace the weak and cowardly Chinese government.

Deng arrived in France three years after the Russian Revolution, and what he learned from his more studious fellow workers in discussion groups about capitalism, imperialism, and the Soviet Union gave a deeper meaning to what he had seen and experienced while traveling to, and living in, France. European imperialists were humiliating China, the bourgeois were exploiting workers, and Chinese workers were treated worse than local workers. A vanguard of elites was needed to organize movements to change the situation. Just as young Chinese in France were beginning to work in factories in late 1921, word came of the founding of the Chinese Communist Party in July of that year. The initial party was small: in 1921, there were only fifty some members of the Communist Party in China, and in 1922 there were still fewer than two hundred. Its presence, however, was to have a profound effect on the Chinese student-workers in France. In 1922 an organization was formed in France that members referred to as Communist, and in November 1922, one of the student leaders, Li Weihan, was dispatched from France to China to seek approval for affiliating this young Communist organization with the Chinese Communist Youth League. Permission was granted, and in February 1923 Deng took part in a congress of European young Communists who formally declared themselves part of the Chinese Communist Youth League; Zhou Enlai was named party secretary.[8]

The job Deng had been assigned at the Schneider ordnance factory involved using large metal pincers to pull a large mass of molten steel out of blast furnaces with flames pouring out. Deng, not yet seventeen and just five feet tall, left the job three weeks after taking it and made his way back to Paris to look for other work. (His uncle lasted at his job at Schneider a month longer.) After some weeks of searching, Deng found a temporary job in a small factory in Paris making paper flowers, then landed a steady job in Hutchison Rubber factory (which then employed about a thousand people, mostly foreigners), located in the small town of Châlette-sur-Loing. There, with a brief interruption, he worked making rubber overshoes, one of the less physically demanding jobs in the factory, from February 13, 1922, until March 7, 1923. After a brief apprenticeship, Deng, like the other workers, was paid by the piece: he thus learned to work quickly and for long periods, logging in fifty-four hours a week. On October 17, having saved some money from his job and having received a small sum from his father, he resigned from the factory and tried to enroll at a nearby college, the Collège de Châtillon-sur-Seine; it turned out, however, he did not have enough funds. Three months later he returned to work at Hutchison. After he left the company a second time, in March, the company records report that he "refused to work" and that he "would not again be given work there."[9]

After his last effort to find an opportunity to study failed, Deng devoted himself to the radical cause. While at Hutchison the second time, he took part in study groups established by cells of secret Chinese Communist members in nearby Montargis, many of whom had been his classmates at the preparatory school in Chongqing. Some of the students had been radicalized even before the Chinese Communist Party was formed. Deng was especially moved by the magazine *New Youth (Xin qingnian),* which was inspiring students in China to join the radical cause; the magazine was led by Chen Duxiu, who had two sons then among the students in France.

Deng remained in Châlette-sur-Loing until June 11, 1923, when he went to Paris to work at the tiny office of the European Communist organization. His coworkers at Hutchison and fellow radicals there and at Montargis had been mostly fellow Sichuanese, but in Paris Deng joined in the national movement with Chinese from other provinces. Upon his arrival in Paris, Deng performed miscellaneous jobs at the office under the direction of Zhou Enlai. Printing the group's ten-page mimeographed journal was a key part of his work, and Deng, skilled at handwriting, cut the stencils and came to be known as "Doctor of the Mimeograph." In February 1924, the name of the journal was changed to *Red Light (Chi guang).*[10] The journal announced the editors' opposition to warlord rule and to imperialism. Its intended readership was Chinese students in France, some of whom were still pursuing anarchism or more right-wing conservative policies. Deng worked under office director Zhou Enlai, six years his senior, who had met radicals in Japan and England, and was the natural leader among Chinese youth for his sense of strategy and his ability to get diverse people to work together. Under Zhou's tutelage, Deng acquired a broad understanding of the Communist movement, and he too became involved in devising strategies for their movement while cutting stencils for and printing *Red Light*.[11]

Having proved himself in the office, Deng was brought onto the executive committee of the Chinese Communist Youth League in Europe. At their meeting in July 1924, in accordance with a decision by the Chinese Communist Party, all of the members of this executive committee, including Deng, automatically became members of the Chinese Communist Party. At the time, the entire Chinese Communist Party, in China and France together, had fewer than a thousand members and Deng was not yet twenty years old.

The political struggles among Chinese students in France paralleled those among young political leaders in China. As soon as the Communists in China in June 1923 announced that they would join the Guomindang under the leadership of Sun Yat-sen, the young Communists in France announced that they too would join the Guomindang in Europe. Deng himself joined and by 1925 he had already become a leader of the European branch of the Guomindang.[12] In articles in *Red Light*, Deng argued against more conservative Guomindang supporters in favor of more radical revolutionary change.

Two French scholars who carefully traced the activities of Deng during these five years in France conclude: "Here in France, Deng discovered the West, Marxism, the world of work, the organizational work of the party, the place of China, social and regional diversity, and his place in the world."[13] France also affected his taste: for the rest of his life, Deng enjoyed drinking wine and coffee and eating cheese and bread. More important, by the time he left France at age twenty-one, Deng had become a hardened and experienced revolutionary leader, and his personal identity had become inseparable from that of the party and his Communist comrades. From that time until his death seven decades later, Deng's life was focused on the Chinese Communist Party.

In the spring of 1925, having proved himself able and reliable, Deng was assigned to Lyon as head of the party organization there. After demonstrators in China took to the streets on May 30, 1925, to protest that British police in Shanghai had fired into a large crowd of Chinese student demonstrators, Deng joined other Chinese students in France to protest France's continued cooperation with the oppressive Chinese government.[14] In November 1925, Deng was assigned to work in the Renault car factory in Paris, where he also carried on propaganda work in an effort to organize workers. It was in late 1925, when top Chinese student leaders of the demonstrations were deported, that Deng, then twenty-one, assumed an increasingly important role in the group, giving major speeches and chairing meetings. On January 7, 1926, Deng, alerted that he too had been targeted for arrest, escaped by train to the Soviet Union, by way of Germany.

In no country outside China did the Chinese Communist Party play a greater role than in France. After 1949, these returnees from France played a unique and important role in building the Chinese state. The French returnees were far more cosmopolitan than the vast majority of Chinese Communist leaders, including Mao, who before 1949 had never left China. Although the French returnees did not necessarily hold high positions in the revolutionary struggles from 1937–1949, from 1949–1966, as the Communists were building the country, not just Premier Zhou Enlai and Deng Xiaoping but other French returnees as well would play leading roles in economic planning (Li Fuchun), foreign affairs (Chen Yi), science and technology (Nie Rongzhen), and even united front propaganda (Li Weihan). The Communist Party abhorred factions, and the French returnees were careful not to behave as a faction, but they shared a special understanding of what China needed to do.

After escaping from Paris, Deng arrived in Moscow on January 17, 1926, and two weeks later was admitted to the first class at Sun Yat-sen University. Eight months after Sun Yat-sen died in March 1925, the Comintern had established Sun Yat-sen University in Moscow for the sole purpose of training members of the Guomindang and the Communist Party.

Within a week after his arrival in Moscow, Deng wrote a self-criticism. Like all Chinese expatriates in Moscow, he was considered a petit-bourgeois intellectual; in his self-criticism, he vowed to give up his class origins and to dedicate his life to being a disciplined, obedient member of the proletariat class. His abilities were soon recognized by officials at the university. The student body of some three hundred students was divided into thirteen groups. Deng was assigned to Group 7, the "theory group," which consisted of those students who were considered especially promising as future political leaders. His group also included Chiang Ching-kuo, son of Chiang Kai-shek, as well as two daughters and a son of the Chinese warlord Feng Yuxiang, an unusually progressive regional leader who at the time was working with and receiv-

ing funds from the Comintern. Within his group, Deng was selected by his
fellow students as the Communist Party representative.[15]

The Chinese students at Sun Yat-sen University were organized under the
leadership of a fellow student whom Deng had known in France, Ren Zhou-
xuan (better known as Ye Qing). Ren demanded strict obedience and military-
style discipline, an approach that caused a backlash among many of the Chinese students and the school leadership; in fact, by the summer of 1926, Ren
had been removed from the school. Shortly thereafter, the Comintern announced that foreign students while in the Soviet Union would not be allowed to hold meetings of the Communist parties of other countries and instead would become apprentice members of the Soviet Communist Party,
with the possibility of becoming full members within five years.

Many Chinese complained about the cancellation of meetings of the Chinese Communist Party. Not Deng. In the reports filed with the Soviet Communist Party at Sun Yat-sen University, Deng was praised for his strong sense
of discipline, for acknowledging the need to obey the leaders. He had followed the leadership of Ren, but when Ren had been removed, he followed
the leadership of the Soviet Communist Party. On November 5, near the end
of his stay, the party evaluated Deng Xiaoping: "As someone who is both disciplined and consistent, as well as capable in his studies, he has accumulated a
lot of experience from his organizational work in the Communist Youth
League Bureau and greatly matured. He takes an active part in political work.
He acts like a comrade in his relations with others. He is among the best students."[16]

In Moscow, Deng attended classes eight hours a day, six days a week. He
took a full schedule of courses that included study of works by Marx, Engels,
and Lenin, as well as classes on historical materialism, economic geography,
the history of the Soviet Communist Party, and the history of the Chinese
revolutionary movement. The Comintern, which hoped to develop good relations with potential leaders of the Chinese Communist movement, provided far better living conditions for the Chinese students than ordinary Rus-
sians enjoyed.

While Deng was studying in Moscow, the Soviet Union had not yet built
its socialist structure. The Soviet Union was still under the National Economic Policy (NEP). Under the NEP, independent farmers, small businesspeople, and even larger businesses were encouraged to prosper while the socialist economy was beginning to develop heavy industry. Foreigners, too,
were invited to invest in the Soviet Union. Deng believed, as did others at

that time, that such an economic structure—whereby private enterprise was allowed and foreign investment was encouraged, all under Communist Party leadership—promoted faster economic growth than could be achieved in capitalist economies.[17] The fundamentals of the NEP, a market economy under Communist leadership, were similar to those of the economic policies that Deng would carry out when he was in charge of China's Southwest Bureau in 1949–1952 and those that he would reintroduce in the 1980s.

Some ideas Deng espoused in Moscow, at age twenty-two, were unusually developed for someone so young, and remained unchanged throughout his life. To take just one example, in an August 12, 1926, class composition, he wrote: "Centralized power flows from the top down. It is absolutely necessary to obey the directions from above. How much democracy can be permitted depends on the changes in the surrounding environment."[18]

Resisting the Guomindang, 1927–1930

Although the training at Sun Yat-sen University was designed to last two years, on January 12, 1927, after only one year, Deng, along with some twenty young Communist political instructors, was sent by the Comintern to take advantage of an opportunity provided by the warlord Feng Yuxiang, whose base was in the Yellow River valley in Shanxi. As the split within the Guomindang between the Communists and the Guomindang right wing was growing more intense, the Communists, weak militarily compared to their right-wing Guomindang adversaries, sought military alliances to brace against a split that was beginning to seem inevitable. Feng Yuxiang, who had visited Moscow's Sun Yat-sen University while his three children were studying in Moscow, offered just such a relationship. Feng believed that Communist political instructors could help instill a purpose in his troops, and he used promising leaders like Deng to help give them a sense of what they were fighting for. When the Guomindang and the Communists split in April 1927, Feng Yuxiang, who enjoyed good relations with Deng and his Communist colleagues, realized that the Guomindang had far more military power than the tiny band of Communists and concluded he had no choice but to ally with the Guomindang. Feng bade Deng and his comrades a cordial goodbye and sent them on their way.

From Shanxi, Deng, following party orders, reported to the Communist Party headquarters in Shanghai to take part in underground work. Chiang Kai-shek, aware of the growing gulf with the Communists and fearing an attack by them, had moved first, in April 1927, to destroy the Communists, immediately killing many of their leaders. In Shanghai, the Communist Central Committee, in constant danger of exposure by former allies who were now deadly enemies, carried on underground activities. To avoid being discovered, Deng took on various disguises and honed skills that would remain with him his entire life: he never passed on clues of Communist activities to outsiders and never left a paper trail that might implicate other party members. Indeed, from this time on, he always kept the names and locations of key members in his head, not on paper.

Deng went to Shanghai with his new wife, whom he had first met as a fellow student in the Soviet Union. Soviet supervisors had observed then that Deng was fond of a young woman named Zhang Xiyuan, but unlike most of his peers who were constantly pestering women students, Deng had not made advances; instead he concentrated on his studies and party work.[19] It wasn't until Deng returned to China and met Zhang Xiyuan again at a meeting in Wuhan that the two began a brief courtship and were married. In Shanghai Deng and Zhang Xiyuan lived next door to Zhou Enlai and his wife, Deng Yingchao, with whom they shared their underground work.

On August 7, 1927, twenty-one Communist Party leaders assembled for an emergency meeting in Wuhan to respond to the widespread slaughter of Communists by the Guomindang. The twenty-two-year-old Deng, who was not a regular member of the group, served as note-taker and processed the documents. (In later Communist history, Deng was given the august title of "head of the secretariat" for his modest role of taking notes for this small band of Communists.) At that meeting he first met the tall, confident, and forceful Mao Zedong, who had not yet risen to the position of supreme leader.

In 1929, the party dispatched Deng from Shanghai to Guangxi, a poor province west of Guangdong where, at age twenty-five, he was to lead an alliance with some small local warlords and establish a Communist base. Deng's selection for this task reflected the high regard that party leaders had for his commitment to the revolution and for his ability to manage complex relations with warlords, local people, and the party center in a rapidly shifting political environment. After the party's split with the Guomindang, the party Central Committee, under orders from the Comintern, had directed local Communists to lead urban insurrections.

The small number of Communists working with Deng in their South China Bureau in Hong Kong and in Guangxi built a base of cooperation with some small local military officials in Guangxi (Li Mingrui and Yu Zuoyu) who had broken with Chiang Kai-shek and the larger, more powerful Guangxi warlords who had joined the "northern march" by which Chiang hoped to unify China. In Guangxi, Deng played an essential—if behind-the-scenes—role in achieving some short-term success. Deng and his allies managed to take over two localities, Baise and Longzhou, in western Guangxi, near the Yunnan border.

These developments are celebrated in Communist history as Communist uprisings. But when Guangxi warlord Li Zongren left the northern march and returned to the province, his far more powerful forces quickly overran Deng's forces in Baise and Longzhou. Many of Deng's allies were killed, and the rest, several hundred men of the Seventh Red Army, fled—first to the north with the help of Zhuang minority allies, and then eastward along hundreds of miles of mountains of northern Guangxi and Guangdong. In their retreat they were almost completely devastated in a series of battles with regional military forces. After one of the battles in which he was separated from his troops, Deng left the Seventh Red Army and returned to the party center in Shanghai. Upon his arrival, Deng submitted a written self-criticism of his failures in Guangxi. In it, he explained why he had left his military post, writing that the leaders of the Seventh Red Army had agreed that he should report to the party center in Shanghai, and that it was officially permissible to do so. Yet he confessed that he had exercised poor political judgment in leaving his troops while they were still in trouble. During the Cultural Revolution, he was accused of having deserted the Seventh Red Army to return to Shanghai.

In Guangxi, while in his mid-twenties, Deng received his initial military training not at a military academy like a number of his comrades, but through sharing battles with comrades who had military training and fighting experience. In his year in Guangxi, Deng had been given an enormous range of important responsibilities—building military alliances, getting provisions to the troops, escaping from better-armed warlords, and cooperating with local Zhuang minority leaders. But like all Communist urban insurrections of the time, including the far more famous Communist-led Nanchang and Guangzhou uprisings, the Guangxi uprising ended in total failure. Most leaders who cooperated with Deng were killed, either in battle or as part of internal purges within the Communist movement, whose own leadership became suspicious that they had cooperated with the enemy.

After Deng left the Seventh Red Army and returned to Shanghai, he visited his wife in a Shanghai hospital as she prepared to give birth. It was one of their last times together. Conditions in the hospital were poor; during the birth she contracted puerperal fever and she died several days later. Shortly thereafter, the infant also died. Deng was reported to have been deeply saddened by these deaths, but he returned to work immediately. Within a year of the tragedy, in Shanghai where he awaited reassignment after Guangxi, he began pairing up with a bright, free-thinking Shanghai revolutionary, Ah Jin (Jin Weiying).[20]

Jiangxi, the Long March, and the Northwest Base, 1930–1937

In Shanghai the Central Committee was slow in giving Deng a new assignment, but after some months it agreed to his request to go to the Central Soviet in Jiangxi. There, beyond the mountains, the military under Mao had captured several counties and had set up a haven, a Soviet base area with its own local government where they were carrying out land reforms. They hoped to build up their forces until they were strong enough to assault the Guomindang and the warlords. The Central Soviet stretched several hundred miles, from the beautiful but inhospitable Jinggang Mountains in the northwest region of the province to the flat farmland in the southeast. Deng was assigned to report to Ruijin county, in the southeast, where Deng and his second wife, Ah Jin, arrived in August 1931.

Within weeks after his arrival in Ruijin, Deng's immediate superiors in Jiangxi decided to make Deng the party secretary in charge of Ruijin county. He began the job at a time when the Guomindang was trying to kill off Communists and each side attempted to have spies in the other's camp. After the 1927 split with the Guomindang, Communist officials were terrified that some party members were secretly providing information to the enemy, and in fact, before Deng arrived in Ruijin, several hundred Communists in Ruijin were suspected of spying and had been jailed or executed. But Deng, who began his work after several weeks of careful investigation of the situation, concluded that the suspects had been wrongly accused. Consequently, those in prison were freed and the leader who had persecuted the local party members was himself executed. Deng's decision was very popular among the local Communists, and enabled him to maintain their strong support throughout his year in Ruijin.

In Jiangxi, Deng developed an enormous admiration for Mao Zedong, who led a small band of followers as they fled from warlords in his native

Hunan eastward across the mountainous area into the neighboring province of Jiangxi. As someone who had struggled to build and maintain a Communist base in Guangxi and failed, Deng understood the scope of Mao's achievement in building a base. Not only did Mao need to find adequate provisions, he also had to keep the enemy at bay and win the support of the local population.

While Deng was the party secretary of Ruijin, central party officials decided to establish the national capital there. Before the capital was established, a large congress of representatives from the Communist bases throughout China was held in the county. Although Deng was not one of the 610 delegates to the congress, he played a key role in laying the groundwork for the meeting and for establishing the new capital on the outskirts of the county. After a year in Ruijin, Deng was transferred to become acting head of Huichang county, south of Ruijin; there he was also responsible for Communist activities in Xunfu and Anfu counties.

Like Mao, Deng believed the Communists had to build up a rural base until they were strong enough to challenge their opponents. But central party officials accused Deng of following the defeatist policy of Luo Ming (a Fujian official), and of not being aggressive enough in attacking enemy troops. In what would later be called "Deng's first fall," he was removed from his post as head of Huichang county, and, along with three other officials (Mao's brother, Mao Zetan, and Gu Bo), subjected to severe criticism, then sent away for punishment. Indeed Deng was bitterly attacked for being the leader of a "Mao faction." Moreover, Deng's second wife, Ah Jin, joined in the attack, left Deng, and married one of his accusers, Li Weihan, whom Deng had known in France. Fortunately, another acquaintance from France, Li Fuchun, then Jiangxi provincial party secretary, brought Deng back from his several months of punishment to work as the head of Jiangxi province's propaganda department.

Deng Rong reports that friends of her father regarded him as a cheerful, fun-loving extrovert before the heavy blows of 1930–1931: the death of his first wife and child, serious criticism and demotion in the party, and divorce by his second wife. After the string of tragedies and setbacks, he became more subdued, less talkative. He couldn't know then that in the long run, being attacked and punished as the head of a "Mao faction" would prove to be a blessing for his career, because it gave Mao lasting confidence in Deng's loyalty. Even when Mao directed the radicals to attack Deng in later years, he never allowed Deng to be expelled from the party.

As the Communists built up their Soviet base, Chiang Kai-shek, worried about the Communist threat, sent his troops to encircle and destroy the Jiangxi Soviet. In four of these campaigns, the Communists were able to drive away the Guomindang, but during the fifth encirclement, the strong Guomindang routed the Communists from their base. In making their escape, the Communists embarked on what would become known as the "Long March," a brutal six-thousand-mile trek that lasted slightly over one year, until the Communists settled in a new base area in northern Shaanxi. The journey took a terrible toll on the fleeing Communists. They started the Long March with roughly 86,000 troops, but because many died on the trek and others deserted, fewer than 10,000 made it all the way to the Shaanxi-Gansu-Ningxia border area, where in October 1935 they were welcomed by a small band of local Communists. Although there is no record of contacts between Mao and Deng during the Long March, as the number of surviving troops grew smaller, Deng, who was responsible for propaganda to help sustain morale during the march, had, as his daughter writes, many opportunities to talk with Mao.

A few weeks into the Long March, a critical January 1935 meeting was held in Zunyi, Guizhou province, that gave Mao authority over the military and paved the way for him to become the top leader of the Chinese Communist Party. Deng was not a formal participant, but he was able to attend as a note-taker; although no records from the meeting remain, Deng was later given the glorious title of "secretary general" of the meeting.

During the first few weeks of the Long March, Deng was in charge of putting out a propaganda sheet called "Red Star." Within a few weeks, as transporting supplies became more burdensome, the mimeograph machine was cast aside. As a propaganda official, however, Deng continued to rally the troops orally to continue the struggle. Deng contracted typhoid on the journey and nearly died; he made the Long March, he later explained to a visitor, half on horseback, half on foot. While the Communists were establishing their base in the Northwest, the invading Japanese rather than the Guomindang became the main enemy, and an appeal to patriotism was added to the appeal against despotic landlords.

In December 1936, an opportunity emerged for the Communists when troops belonging to the warlord Zhang Xueliang kidnapped Generalissimo Chiang Kai-shek in Xi'an. To win his release, Chiang was forced to agree to a new period of cooperation between the Guomindang and the Communists to fight the Japanese. To take advantage of this new agreement, which removed the pressure from Chiang's forces, the Communists in January 1937 moved to a larger base area, located in Yan'an, in northern Shaanxi province. There, as head of the propaganda department of the First Corps, Deng guided the development of musical and drama teams in addition to delivering speeches to instruct the troops and party officials. Deng developed his characteristic approach to giving propaganda messages: he was brief and to the point, presenting the broad international situation and relating it to present responsibilities. By the time he ended, listeners had a clear notion of what their responsibilities were.

Later that year, as the Japanese moved beyond Manchuria to invade all of China, they captured all the major cities and transport routes. Only rural areas and cities in the Southwest remained under Chinese control. Skirmishes continued, but the Japanese became an army of occupation.

Attacking the Japanese, 1937–1945

After the Communists agreed to unite with the Guomindang to fight the Japanese, their forces were reorganized as the Eighth Route Army, part of the overall Chinese forces officially under the direction of Chiang Kai-shek. In fact the Guomindang and the Communists remained deeply suspicious of each other and had little contact.

The headquarters of the Communist's Eighth Route Army was located in Shanxi, a fertile area hundreds of miles east of Yan'an where the troops had access to adequate grain provisions and were close enough to Japanese forces that they could harass them with guerrilla attacks.

In 1937, Mao assigned one of his ablest generals, Liu Bocheng, as commander of the 129th Division, a major unit in the Eighth Route Army. Shortly thereafter, in January 1938, as in other units, Mao paired the commander with a political commissar: Deng Xiaoping. But unlike other political commissars, Deng was made first party secretary and Liu was named second party secretary, giving Deng added authority, including the right to make judgments about the political readiness of the troops and the surrounding communities before they engaged in a battle. Liu Bocheng was a head taller and a decade older than Deng, and blind in one eye from a battle injury. The two men would work together closely. When Deng first arrived in the Taihang Mountains where the 129th Division was located, he immediately established his authority: Liu was away on a trip and Deng took over in his absence.

From 1937 to 1949, Deng and Liu formed a team against the Japanese, and after World War II, in the civil war against the Guomindang. They worked so closely together that the name "Liu-Deng" was used as a single word. Liu was considered more kindly toward the troops than Deng, who demanded more of his charges and was ready to be bold in advancing to fight the enemy. Liu was also more reluctant than Deng to execute soldiers suspected of spying for the Guomindang.

From 1937–1945, to evade the Japanese, the base of the 129th Division occasionally moved to various spots within the Taihang Mountains in eastern Shanxi, but it always stayed no more than a day's horseback ride from the Eighth Route Army headquarters so that the leaders could easily attend important meetings. From wherever they were located, they occasionally carried out guerrilla attacks on the better-armed Japanese forces, concentrating greater numbers on small groups of the enemy that was stretched to maintain control of the towns and major transport lines. Yan'an was a large enough base, and far enough from the enemy, that Mao had time to indulge his interests in history, philosophy, and poetry even as he worked on developing Communist theory and an overall strategy. By contrast, Deng, as political commissar in the smaller base in the Taihang Mountains located closer to Japanese lines, had little time for theory. He was responsible for practical issues in dealing with the local population. In effect, during those eight years Deng became the top political official on the Shanxi side of the Taihang Mountain area, with responsibility for developing a self-sufficient economy to produce adequate food for the tens of thousands of local people and troops, and enough commercial crops to support the local industries that made cloth and other daily goods. Deng was also in charge of recruiting soldiers for the regular army and evaluating the political implications of military actions, tasks that he had learned well while in Guangxi. As part of his efforts to spur the area's economy, Deng devised a system of taxation to encourage local production. He wrote: "people should be taxed according to the average production of recent years and any amount exceeding that average should entirely belong to the producer."[21] To keep the local militias that supported the regular army ready to attack the Japanese, he traveled secretly within the region.[22]

In 1939, on one of his two trips back to Yan'an, Deng married Zhuo Lin, one of three bright, leftist daughters of a well-to-do businessman famous for making Yunnan ham, who was later killed during land reform. At a time when fewer than 1 percent of people in Zhuo Lin's age group had attended a university and an educated woman was a rarity, the sisters had all studied at universities, where they had joined the revolution. Zhuo Lin in particular was admitted to the highly competitive Peking University, where she studied physics. She once commented that Deng stood out from most Communist officers, whom she thought were not well educated.

The simple, rustic wedding of Deng and Zhuo Lin, who was twelve years his junior, took place in front of Mao's cave in the presence of Mao, Liu Shaoqi, Li Fuchun, and a handful of others. Although there is no reliable record of what were probably many meetings between Mao and Deng in northwest China, they clearly had bonded by the time of Deng's wedding. Mao later referred approvingly to Deng's suffering in Jiangxi (for having been a member of the "Mao faction"), and he was undoubtedly impressed not only by Deng's abilities and readiness to take action, but also by his deep respect for Mao's early achievement in establishing a Communist base in rural China, which Deng himself had tried and failed to accomplish.

Deng and Zhuo Lin eventually had three daughters (Lin, Nan, and Rong, all named for trees) and two boys (Pufang and Zhifang). Except for separations when Deng was fighting in dangerous areas, the two remained together until Deng's death fifty-eight years later, making theirs one of the more stable families among the Communist leadership. Although Deng was not close to his own father, his wife and children were a haven for Deng as he faced the pressures of his weighty responsibilities. Their intimacy did not extend to political matters, since he did not share high-level party discussions with his family.

The Civil War, 1946–1949

After World War II ended, Deng was in fact the highest-ranked Communist official in Jin-Ji-Lu-Yu, a border region of several million people that spanned four provinces—Hebei, Shanxi, Shandong, and Henan. There in the mountainous areas, away from the urban areas where Guomindang troops were located, he helped prepare troops for the inevitable war with the Guomindang. A key responsibility was to identify and cultivate promising young Communist organizers, two of whom, Zhao Ziyang and Wan Li, would play a large role after 1978.

Scarcely a year after the end of World War II, and shortly after the civil war between the Guomindang and the Communists broke out, Liu Bocheng and Deng were ordered to lead their troops southwest to the Dabie Mountains located on the edge of the large plains of central China. Mao's immediate goal in ordering the move was to help pull Guomindang troops away from the Northwest, where they were threatening the Communist headquarters in Yan'an. Beyond that, however, Mao was hoping to establish a base on the edge of the central plain where, throughout Chinese history, final showdowns between contending forces had usually taken place. The march to the Dabie Mountains was certain to involve heavy casualties, because the Liu-Deng forces lacked supplies, including warm clothing for the harsh winter, and because enemy forces were strong in the region.

Deng, ever the tough, disciplined soldier, did not hesitate to charge ahead, despite the certainty of heavy losses. Many of the Liu-Deng troops were indeed killed or died from the cold or from food shortages, and the surviving soldiers remained in a precarious position, vulnerable to attacks by the enemy and to further losses from the cold and lack of provisions. Despite these difficulties, the remnant forces and newly recruited troops, as Mao had envisioned, were able to establish a base overlooking the central plain. Unlike the guerrilla fighting in World War II, in the civil war massive armies on the two sides engaged in large pitched battles. This base would prove critical for the forthcoming Huai Hai campaign, one of the three decisive campaigns in the civil war.

The Huai Hai campaign, which lasted from early November 1948 to January 1949, was one of the largest campaigns in military history, involving roughly 600,000 Guomindang troops, some led by very able generals, and about 500,000 Communist troops. The Communists also mobilized over a million peasants to carry food and other supplies to the troops, and requisitioned more than 700,000 draft animals to help with transport. The Communist strategy of engaging the Guomindang north of the Yangtze River to fight a war of annihilation, so that they could then cross the wide Yangtze River with less resistance, was proposed by the able general Su Yu, deputy to Chen Yi, then commander of the East China Army (later the Third Field Army). Although Deng kept in close touch with Yan'an during the Huai Hai campaign, Mao gave far more leeway to his local Communist commanders to make their own decisions than Chiang Kai-shek gave to his generals. Already at this time Chiang Kai-shek was keenly worried about the superior morale of the Communist troops who, as poor peasants, expected that their families would be given their own land after victory. After his troops were defeated by the Communists in the northeast on the eve of the Huai Hai campaign, Chiang became pessimistic about the outcome of the war.[23]

The East China Army, led by Su Yu, was larger and, during the initial battles of the campaign, more successful in routing its opponents than were the
Liu-Deng troops, which were under siege by larger enemy forces. The Liu-
Deng forces, then called the Central Plain Army (soon to be renamed the
Second Field Army) charged into battle but suffered heavy casualties and required the assistance of troops and artillery from Su Yu's East China Army
forces. In the final stages of the Huai Hai campaign, Mao ordered the establishment of a "front" organization that unified all 500,000 Communist
troops under Deng as general secretary.

Deng's leadership during the Huai Hai campaign was not without controversy. Liu Bocheng, worried about the safety of his troops, sought to build
more trenches for protection from the superior Guomindang firepower, but
Deng insisted on charging ahead. Deng was later criticized for exposing his
troops to greater danger, causing more casualties than necessary early in the
campaign, as well as for not digging more of these defensive trenches.

In the last stages of the campaign, however, the half million Communist
forces, unified under Deng as the general secretary of the front command,
prevailed. The campaign was a great moral victory as well as a military victory, and from then on Chiang's forces remained on the defensive as the
Communists pushed southward and westward. In fact, after the Huai Hai
campaign, the Guomindang had difficulty assembling large forces to resist
these Communist advances. The Communist army easily overcame the resistance to crossing the broad Yangtze River and continued its rapid march
southward and westward. In 1984, Deng, when asked by Prime Minister Nakasone what was the happiest time of his life, replied that it was the three
years when they overcame the dual obstacles of smaller numbers of troops
and poorer equipment to win victory in the civil war. He particularly highlighted the crossing of the Yangtze River.[24]

As the Communist troops advanced, taking over cities one by one, some of
the troops remained behind in each city and town, both to set up the Military Control Commission that would administer the city and to begin the
transition to Communist rule. After the Communist military victory in
Shanghai, Deng was for several weeks personally in charge of the Military
Control Commission that took over the various branches of the Shanghai
government. Communist Party members, who until then had kept their
membership secret, as well as "progressive" youth in Shanghai who favored
the Communists, assisted in the takeover. Deng met with various local leaders, explained Communist policies, and selected and assigned subordinates

to provide additional local support beyond the brief transition. He also expanded the recruitment of new party members to provide leadership in the Shanghai area. The local citizenry, alienated from the Guomindang because of its well-known corruption and the rampant inflation, generally welcomed the Communists, but it would take several years to overcome the damage and chaos generated by the civil war. After guiding the transition to Communist rule in Shanghai, Deng left Shanghai and rejoined his forces as they marched into the Southwest.

Establishing Communist Rule in the Southwest, 1949–1952

It took the Communists more than two years, from 1947 when they captured the northeast, until 1949, to gain control of the entire country. As they took over each of the six major regions of China, they set up a regional bureau to rule that region; until 1952 the six regional bureaus together had the major responsibility of ruling the country while the central party and government were gradually built up in Beijing. To establish these bases of Communist rule, Mao usually chose leaders for a region who were from that region. Liu Bocheng, like Deng, was from Sichuan, by far the largest province in the Southwest. In wartime, the political commissar was expected to yield to the commander, but in peacetime, the commander was expected to yield to the commissar. Deng Xiaoping was thus made first secretary of the Southwest Bureau, representing the last of the six major regions, with its population of 100 million, to come under Communist control. Deng was to remain in this position until 1952, when major regional leaders, and their responsibilities, were transferred to Beijing.

While first secretary of the Southwest Bureau, Deng was in charge of pacifying the area, managing the transition of governance from the Guomindang to the Communists, recruiting and training party members to lead the government and society, overcoming the chaos of the wartime years, and guiding the region's overall economic development.[25] As the Communist Party extended its roots into society, Deng took on responsibility for every aspect of public life—security, the economy, industry and commerce, transportation and communication, culture and education, and health.

Pacifying the countryside was more difficult in the Southwest than in some other regions because Guomindang supporters had remained there since World War II, when it had been their headquarters, and because for Guomindang soldiers the Southwest was the end of the line, where they either deserted or blended into the local populations. Some continued to resist Communist rule, passively or actively. To ensure that these troublemakers were rounded up or pacified at last, General He Long and his First Field Army came from the Northwest region to reinforce commander Liu Bocheng's troops. The last province to come under Communist control was Tibet. In 1951 Deng drew from troops based in both the Southwest and the Northwest to gain control and establish order there. The Tibetans did not have strong military forces, and their losses in western Sichuan before the invasion made the military conquest of Tibet relatively easy.

Deng realized that long-term success or failure in the Southwest depended on his ability to recruit and retain talented subordinates. He drew heavily on the political commissars from the Second Field Army, who had experience in keeping up the morale of the troops and managing relations between the troops and the local population, to staff high party and government positions, while allowing many government officials who had served under the Guomindang to remain if they were prepared to cooperate with the Communists. He then supervised his subordinates as they recruited and trained able youth to staff the local party and government.

Deng gave great attention to gaining the cooperation and support of the people in the region. In speeches and in articles in the press, Deng explained Communist rule to local government officials and the people. He also organized the recruitment and training of officials to administer the land reform that would wipe out the landlord class and pass control of the land to the tillers. Unlike Ye Jianying in south China, who was criticized for being too soft on local landlords, Deng was praised by Mao for his success in land reform by attacking landlords, killing some of the landlords with the largest holdings, allocating their land to peasants, and mobilizing local peasants to support the new leadership.

Deng also pushed hard to realize the project that he regarded as the most crucial for development of the Southwest, one that Deng's father and his acquaintances had envisioned a generation earlier: construction of a railway between the region's two largest cities, Chongqing and Chengdu. The task was formidable, given the primitive construction equipment then available. Nonetheless Deng and the workers persevered, and in 1952, just before Deng left the Southwest to take up his position in Beijing, he proudly joined the celebration for the completed railway project.

Building Socialism, 1952–1959

In 1952, when regional leaders were transferred to the central government that now ruled the country, Deng was appointed vice premier in the central government. Not long thereafter, Mao wrote a note indicating that government documents going to the party center should first be cleared by Deng Xiaoping. It was a measure of Mao's deep confidence in Deng and in the central role Deng had in coordinating activities from the time of his arrival in Beijing. In 1956 Deng was made secretary general of the party, the key position for administering the daily work of the party, and a member of the Standing Committee of the Politburo. He took part in meetings with Mao to discuss the establishment of the First Five-Year Plan and to plan for "socialist transformation," which involved organizing individual farms into collectives, collectivizing small enterprises, and nationalizing large enterprises.

In 1953, when Bo Yibo lost his position as finance minister because Mao complained that he had been too soft in assessing taxes on the capitalists, Mao appointed Deng to replace him. Deng's year as finance minister coincided with the first year of the First Five-Year Plan; he thus supervised the political process of negotiating with the provinces to determine how much grain and how much tax revenue each would pass on to higher levels and how much the government would disburse to the various provinces. Deng did not make final decisions, but at a time when the country was very poor, he had to make judgments with great consequences and report to Mao and Zhou about the capacity of the provinces to meet grain quotas and to pay taxes.[26] In those days Mao often met with his top officials; Deng attended meetings with him as often as several times a month. In 1953, Deng and Chen Yun (see Key People in the Deng Era, p. 717) went to Mao to inform him of the biggest personnel problem facing China in its early years of Communist rule: the threat that Gao Gang might split the party. Mao heeded their warning, and Deng and Chen Yun played a central role in managing the case.[27]

While playing the central role in leading the daily work of the party, Deng could see firsthand how Mao weighed the issues facing China and how he made decisions affecting the country. In his later years Mao was to commit devastating errors, yet he remained a brilliant political leader with deep insight and bold strategies. In addition, as Kissinger was later to consider Premier Zhou Enlai one of the greatest leaders he ever encountered, Deng could see how this great master, whom he had known well in Paris and Shanghai, dealt with foreign relations and with managing overall government activity. By taking part in top-level meetings with both Mao and Zhou, Deng had an opportunity to learn how China's two greatest leaders of their generation assessed the major issues facing the country. Further, as a participant in the building of new organizations, Deng had the chance to see the logic of major decisions and to consider the broader framework of fundamental changes, experiences that would serve him well as he endeavored to rebuild China's economic and political framework in the 1980s.

Mao in 1960 split with the Soviet Union and kept China a closed country, but he spent a great deal of time considering how to deal with the great powers. Deng, as vice premier in the government from 1952 to 1955, was included in discussions on foreign relations. As general secretary of the party from 1956 to 1966, he dealt with relations with other Communist parties (not with non-Communist countries), at a time when most of China's important foreign relationships were with these Communist countries. In February 1956, for instance, he was the political leader of the Chinese delegation to Moscow for the 20th Soviet Party Congress, when Khrushchev denounced Stalin. Like other foreign comrades attending the congress, Deng was not allowed to attend the session in which Khrushchev made his speech, but he was allowed to read the text of that speech the next day. Deng, who was shrewd enough to recognize immediately that the speech had not just domestic but also international implications, assigned two interpreters to work all night to translate the speech, even as he also carefully avoided addressing the content of the speech until Mao decided how to respond. He therefore returned to Beijing and reported on the speech to Mao (who was vulnerable to many of the same criticisms made of Stalin), and Mao made the decisions about how to proceed.[28] Deng was immediately aware that the massive criticism of Stalin would affect those who worked with Stalin and weaken the authority of the Soviet Communist Party.

From September 15–27, 1956, after China's agriculture and handicrafts had been collectivized and its industry had been nationalized, the Chinese Communist Party held its 8th Party Congress, the first party congress to be held since the 7th Party Congress in 1945 that had set out the tasks on the eve of the civil war. The congress was comprehensive and carefully prepared; it offered a vision of a party with responsibility for governing a great nation. The early stage of socialism had arrived, five-year plans had been introduced, the bourgeois and landlord classes no longer existed, and class warfare had ended. Zhou Enlai, Deng, and others hoped that the party could thereafter concentrate on strengthening regular procedures and advancing orderly economic growth.[29]

Deng played a central role at the 8th Party Congress; he was promoted to general secretary of the party, making him, as a member of the Politburo Standing Committee, one of the top six leaders of the party (after Mao, Liu Shaoqi, Zhou Enlai, Zhu De, and Chen Yun). His 1954 position of secretary general had been one of an office manager, albeit a strong one who was deeply involved in the decision-making process for all major decisions. In 1956, however, as general secretary—a position he continued to hold until the Cultural Revolution—he became the leader in charge of daily party work. He was responsible for supervising the party leadership organs in Beijing and in dealing with provincial party leaders. Under Mao's overall leadership, Liu Shaoqi, as first vice chairman of the party, provided guidance to the Standing Committee of the Politburo, which made the decisions that were then implemented by Deng.

When Deng traveled with Mao to Moscow in November 1957, Mao was extremely pleased with Deng's fierce and effective arguments with Mikhail Suslov, the great Soviet theorist. Toward the end of the meetings in Moscow, Mao pointed to Deng and said, "See that little man there? He's highly intelligent and has a great future ahead of him."[30] As Khrushchev recalled, "Mao regarded him as the most up-and-coming member of the leadership."[31]

Beginning in the spring of 1957, many intellectuals and leaders of the minority parties, who had been encouraged to speak out in the campaign to "let a hundred flowers bloom and a hundred schools of thought contend," surprised Mao with the depth of their criticism. Mao lashed back at those "bourgeois intellectuals" who could not erase their class origins even though capitalism had already been eliminated. In the summer of 1957, Mao launched the "anti-rightist campaign" to discredit all those who had been so critical of the party. During the campaign, which Mao tapped Deng to manage, Mao led a vicious attack on some 550,000 intellectual critics branded as rightists. Deng, who during the Hundred Flowers period had told local party officials to listen to criticism and not to fight back, was disturbed that some intellectuals had arrogantly and unfairly criticized officials who were trying to cope with their complex and difficult assignments. During the anti-rightist campaign, Deng strongly supported Mao in defending the authority of the party and in attacking the outspoken intellectuals. These attacks, and Deng's role in them, would not be forgotten by China's intellectual elite.

The anti-rightist campaign destroyed many of China's best scientific and technical minds and alienated many others. Critics who might have restrained Mao from launching his Great Leap Forward, a utopian ill-conceived and brutally implemented effort to transform the economy and society of China within only a few years, were too frightened to speak out. Beginning with the Great Leap Forward, Mao consulted his officials less often than previously. Many loyal Maoists were also silenced.

Deng, the implementer, had always been more practical and realistic than Mao, the philosopher, poet, and dreamer, but Mao valued Deng and others like Lin Biao in part because they would freely express their views to him, while speaking little in public. Deng, like many other party loyalists, aware of Mao's unwillingness to tolerate dissent during the Great Leap Forward, restrained himself from criticizing Mao. Furthermore, he and others believed that Mao's decisions during the civil war and during the unification of the country had so often proved correct that they should suspend their doubts and just carry out his orders. Deng Xiaoping later told his daughter Deng Rong that he regretted not doing more to stop Mao from making such grievous errors.

The misguided Great Leap Forward caused devastation throughout China. Starvation was widespread. After peasants were organized in huge communes with mess halls so that more of them could work on large poorly planned construction projects or in the fields, they could see that those who performed no work were fed as well as the others and they lost any incentive to work, causing a great drop in the size of the harvests; many mess halls ran out of food.

Environmental degradation was also a problem. Local areas that were encouraged to build "backyard furnaces" deforested their own natural areas to find firewood and exhausted their own people in producing substandard metal. Large new construction sites also depleted supplies of cement, leaving little for better-planned projects, and local party secretaries, pressured to make unrealistic promises for grain production, later drained local storehouses to meet promises of grain delivery to higher levels, even though their own people were starving from lack of grain. Although it is impossible to measure the number of fatalities from famine over the three worst years, 1959 to 1961, statistics compiled by mainland officials estimate that about 16 to 17 million people died from unusual causes, and estimates by foreign analysts run as high as 45 million.[32]

Until 1959, Deng was an obedient official carrying out Mao's plans for the Great Leap Forward. As the disastrous effects of the utopian experiment became apparent, however, Deng had the unenviable task of containing the chaos and providing direction to local party officials trying to cope. Deng's daily work schedule generally included relaxing with his family in the evenings, but during the turmoil of the Great Leap Forward it was difficult to find time to rest. In the summer of 1959, a year after the launch of the Great Leap Forward, Deng slipped and broke his leg while playing billiards. Doctors testified that he would not be able to return to work for some months; some knowledgeable insiders believe Deng purposefully avoided the meetings because he knew he would be asked to support Mao's unrealistic efforts to keep the Great Leap alive and he wanted to avoid being put in such a position.

Deng's perspective had changed by the time his medical leave of absence began.[33] After returning to work several months later, he continued to follow Mao's orders and declare his loyalty to Mao. But the disasters of the Great Leap Forward had widened the gap between the unreconstructed romantic visionary and the pragmatic implementer. Although complying with Mao's orders, Deng expanded his range of freedoms by not seeking Mao's direction as much as he had earlier. And in 1960–1961 Deng played an active role in making realistic adjustments in industry, agriculture, education, and other sectors to retrench from the excesses of the Great Leap. At the time, Mao did not criticize these realistic adjustments, but later he complained that when he was talking, Deng would sit in the back of the room and not listen. Mao grumbled that the officials under him were treating him like a departed ancestor, offering respect but not listening to what he said.

As much as the gaps between the revolutionary romantic and the pragmatic implementer over domestic issues caused strains in the early 1960s, Mao remained totally supportive of Deng in the strong role he then played in China's dispute with the Soviet Union. Deng led the Chinese delegation to the Soviet Union in August 1960 and again in October–November 1960, arguing for more freedom for China within the Communist movement. He also supervised preparations on the Chinese side for the exchange of nine nasty letters with the Soviet Union. In July 1963, Mao was so impressed with Deng's performance in the bitter exchange with Mikhail Suslov—an interaction so acrimonious that it weakened the international Communist movement—that he did Deng the rare honor of going to the Beijing airport to welcome him home. Indeed, Mao's confidence in Deng surrounding the anti-

Soviet dispute helped keep their relationship strong despite the awkwardness of their differences on domestic policy.[34]

After Nikita Khrushchev was overthrown in a coup by his colleagues in October 1964, Mao, already concerned about underlings who did not whole-heartedly follow his wishes, talked more about cultivating successors and became even more insistent in his demands for total personal loyalty. In February 1965 Mao sent his wife Jiang Qing to stir up criticism of party officials not fully supporting Mao's revolutionary views, and in mid-May 1966 he launched the Cultural Revolution attack on "those in authority pursuing the capitalist road." For Mao a "capitalist roader" was someone who was thinking and acting independently, not fully following his leadership. Mao mobilized the Red Guards and older rebels to attack those in positions of authority. By skillfully splitting high officials from one another and relying on Lin Biao to control the army, Mao was able to remove vast numbers of senior officials from positions of leadership and to send them away for physical labor and reeducation.

Fueling much of Mao's anger was public dissension over his pursuit of the Great Leap Forward. He was furious, for instance, that Liu Shaoqi in the 1962 meeting of seven thousand officials had blamed Mao for the failures of the Great Leap and had refused to accept full responsibility for his own initial support; consequently Mao was determined to remove him from office. Mao was also upset that after that meeting, Deng continued to work closely with Liu Shaoqi. Therefore in 1966 when Mao attacked Liu Shaoqi, he targeted Deng, too, as the "number-two person in authority pursuing the capitalist road."[35]

Mao's attack was vindictive and fierce. Beginning in late 1966, day after day for months, the media blasted out criticisms of Liu Shaoqi and Deng Xiaoping. Liu Shaoqi, who had been vice chairman of the party and Mao's designated successor, died under house arrest in Kaifeng without needed medical care and away from his family while his wife languished in prison.

In 1967, Mao had Deng and his wife placed under house arrest in their home in Zhongnanhai (the compound next to Tiananmen where the top party officials lived and worked). After their children were sent away that same year, they had no contact with the outside world and for two years had no news of their children. They spent their time reading newspapers and books and listening to the radio; they swept the front walk every day. Their situation was far better than many officials being criticized. In Zhongnanhai they were protected from assaults by the Red Guards, they were allowed to keep their cook and an orderly, and they could withdraw funds from their salaries to buy necessities. Mao was teaching Deng a lesson about personal loyalty but he was keeping open the option of using him at a later time.

Deng's children were not similarly protected. They were assaulted by Red Guards and pressed to give information about the crimes of their father. Lin, the oldest daughter, was under attack at her art academy while Pufang and Nan were subjected to attacks at Peking University, where they were studying physics. In 1967, the two younger children, Rong and Zhifang (and Deng's stepmother Xia Bogen) were sent away to live in ordinary crowded workers' housing in Beijing and allowed no contact with their parents. There Red Guards would sometimes barge unannounced into their home, forcing them to stand with heads bowed while the Red Guards grilled them for information about the crimes of their father, shouted at them, pasted slogans on their walls, and occasionally smashed things. Later, the three sisters and Zhifang were all sent off to perform labor in the countryside.

In 1968 a "special case team" was established to investigate the "crimes" of Deng Xiaoping. The team questioned those who knew Deng and investigated his desertion from the Seventh Red Corps; his continuing good relations with Peng Dehuai, whom Mao had criticized; and other crimes. As part of the investigation, Deng was made to write his history since age eight, listing all his personal connections. He was fortunate that early on he had learned to leave no notes and that his work had never brought him into close contact with Guomindang officials. At the 9th Party Congress in 1969, Jiang Qing demanded that Deng be expelled, but Mao refused and continued to protect him from the radicals.

In 1969, after the first military clash with the Soviet Union, Mao directed that a number of high-level leaders be sent to the countryside so that if the Soviets were to invade, they could organize local resistance. Accordingly, Zhu De and Dong Biwu were sent to Guangdong; Ye Jianying to Hunan; Nie Rongzhen and Chen Yi to Henan; and Chen Yun, Wang Zhen, and Deng Xiaoping to different parts of Jiangxi. In fact, when they arrived in the countryside, they did not play any role in organizing local defense preparations. Some astute Beijing observers believe that Lin Biao, worried about possible rivals, used the danger of Soviet attack to persuade Mao to exile other high-level officials in Beijing who might have threatened his power. Indeed, after Lin Biao died in 1971, the leaders in the regions were allowed to return to Beijing.

By the time Deng left for Jiangxi, he was already convinced that China's problems resulted not only from Mao's errors but also from deep flaws in the system that had produced Mao and had led to the disastrous Great Leap Forward and Cultural Revolution. In 1949 when the Communists took over, Deng, who had been a revolutionary, became a builder, helping to establish a new political system and a socialist structure. By the time he left for Jiangxi, he was already beginning to think about what kind of reforms China needed. By then he had accumulated an extraordinary depth of experience at the highest levels in the military, the government, and the party, spanning all major domestic and foreign policy issues, on which to base his ruminations about how China should proceed with reforms.

Deng's Tortuous Road to the Top

1969–1977

2

Banishment and Return

1969–1974

On October 26, 1969, Deng Xiaoping, along with his wife, Zhuo Lin, and his stepmother, Xia Bogen, left Zhongnanhai, where they had lived for more than a decade. They were taken by special plane to Nanchang in Jiangxi province where Deng was to engage in physical labor and be reeducated in Mao Zedong Thought. They were allowed to take along personal belongings and several cases of books. Deng's request to see Mao before leaving was not granted, but he was told he could write letters to Wang Dongxing, head of the party's General Office, and it was reasonable to expect that Wang Dongxing would show the letters to Mao. As he boarded the plane, Deng had no way of knowing how long he would remain in Jiangxi.

In Jiangxi, Deng was not allowed to see classified materials or to have contact with officials other than specially designated local officials, but he was permitted to remain a party member, which gave him hope that Mao would someday allow him to return to work. In April 1969, shortly before he left Beijing, after he completed his self-criticism, Deng and his family were no longer treated as class enemies, even though Mao still insisted that Deng needed reeducation. A conversation with Wang Dongxing on the eve of Deng's departure from Beijing offered another ray of hope: Wang Dongxing told Deng that he and his wife could eventually return to their original home in Zhongnanhai, which would remain vacant during their absence. All of this must have offered him hope, for when he arrived in Nanchang, Deng told the local representatives of the special team investigating his case: "I'll be coming out eventually. I can still work for the party for another ten years."[1] As it happened, when Deng returned to Beijing he served the party for almost twenty more years.

Before Deng was sent to Jiangxi, Zhou Enlai phoned local Jiangxi officials with directions for preparing Deng's living arrangements. To ensure security against attacks by radicals, the Deng family was to be located in a military compound. The home was to be near the city of Nanchang, where they could have quick access to transport if necessary. There was to be a factory nearby where Deng and Zhuo Lin could engage in manual labor. Local officials chose the two-story house previously occupied by the superintendent of the Nanchang Infantry School. Deng was to live on the second floor with his family, while security and other officials lived on the first floor. By the standards of the day, the house was appropriate for a high official: modest, but comfortable and adequate. As it turned out, the house was only several miles from the site of the much celebrated Nanchang Uprising, the birthplace of the People's Liberation Army (PLA), where on August 1, 1927, the Communists (including Zhou Enlai, Zhu De, Chen Yi, Liu Bocheng, He Long, and many other later leaders) had engaged in their first armed resistance against the Guomindang.

Once settled in their home in Jiangxi, each day Deng and Zhuo Lin rose at 6:30 a.m. In his military years, Deng had begun each day by dumping a bucket of cold water over his head. In Jiangxi, Deng doused a small hand towel in icy water, then washed his head and face with it, believing this would help build resistance to the cold weather. As part of their reeducation program, Deng and Zhuo Lin then engaged in an hour of supervised compulsory reading of the works of Chairman Mao. Deng did not discuss politics with local officials except during their instructions on Mao Zedong Thought.

After breakfast, Deng and Zhuo Lin walked to the small county tractor-repair station, where they worked in the morning. Deng was employed as a machinist performing low-level manual tasks, much as he had done in the French factories half a century earlier. The repair station was located only a kilometer from the house, and local people had made a special secure path from the home to the station so that Deng and Zhuo Lin could walk to and from work each day without encountering other people.[2] Fellow workers were aware of Deng's identity, but Deng told them simply to call him "Old Deng," the familiar term for a senior colleague. While at work, Deng did not talk with the workers about anything beyond the immediate work and his local living arrangements.

At home, Deng's stepmother, Xia Bogen, prepared their food and was in charge of keeping house. After lunch, Deng and Zhuo Lin took naps, then read from among the books they had brought with them—some classic Chinese history books, novels like *Dream of the Red Chamber* and *Water Margin,* and translations of Russian and French literature. Television was not yet available, but they listened to the evening news on Central People's Radio and at 10 p.m. read in bed for an hour before going to sleep. After their children finally arrived, one by one, they brought news of the outside world. When Pufang arrived in the summer of 1971, he repaired a radio so they could listen to shortwave broadcasts.

In addition to their factory work, Deng and Zhuo Lin worked in their vegetable garden. Deng also helped at home by washing the floor and splitting firewood.[3] Deng's and Zhuo Lin's salaries were lower than their previous ones, and their life was spartan. Xia Bogen raised chickens so they could have eggs and meat. Deng cut down on his smoking to one pack every several days: he gave up smoking in the morning while in the factory and smoked only a few cigarettes each afternoon and evening. He also gave up wine, except for one glass of inexpensive local wine at lunch.[4] Once they arrived, daughters Deng Lin and Deng Nan, who still received meager salaries from their work units, shared their salaries with their unemployed siblings.

As distressed as Deng was about the Cultural Revolution and what it meant for China, for himself and for his family, according to Deng Rong— who was with her parents much of the last two years they were in Jiangxi— her father "never let his emotions run away with him. He did not become depressed; he never gave up hope."[5] In this way he was unlike some of his compatriots. Marshal Chen Yi, for instance, mayor of Shanghai from 1949 to 1958 and foreign minister from 1958 to 1972—whom Deng knew in France and as a partner in the Huai Hai campaign—became depressed and listless while enduring his forced rustication in Henan.[6]

Li Shenzhi, once an assistant to Zhou Enlai, later an official at the Chinese Academy of Social Sciences and an adviser who accompanied Deng on his trip to the United States, said that Mao did not realize how much Deng had changed as a result of his time in Jiangxi.[7] Upon his return to Beijing, Deng would do what was necessary to work under Mao, but he had come to the conclusion that China needed deeper changes and he had a clearer view about what directions he believed China should take.

Time to Ponder

Whatever Mao intended for Deng in Jiangxi, it proved to be an opportunity for Deng to gain distance from the intense political turmoil in Beijing when those under suspicion were preoccupied with how to defend against the next unpredictable and potentially devastating attack. Like Churchill, de Gaulle, Lincoln, and other national leaders who fell from high positions and then spent time in the wilderness before returning to high office, Deng found that the time away from daily politics enabled him to achieve clarity about major, long-term national goals. It is hard to imagine that after 1977 Deng could have moved so deftly and forcefully had he not had a considerable length of time to ponder the nature of the reforms that China needed and how to achieve them. Just as Mao drew on his time in isolated Yan'an to consider overall strategies to pursue when the Communists took over the country, so Deng used his time in Jiangxi to consider directions he would pursue to achieve reform. But Mao in Yan'an, in formulating his policies, held daily discussions with his comrades and his assistants and with their help wrote essays. Deng in Jiangxi thought through things alone and kept his ideas to himself.

The withdrawal to Jiangxi enabled Deng quickly to regain his emotional calm. Although Deng did not easily display his feelings, his daughter Deng Rong reports that he was in fact an emotional person. She reports that her father, who had lost weight and seemed tired during the three years he was under attack in Beijing, in Jiangxi began to gain weight and regain his health. For many years he had taken sleeping pills, and during the Cultural Revolution he increased his dosage. On January 1, 1970, scarcely two months after he arrived in Jiangxi, he stopped taking sleeping pills altogether.[8] Deng Rong reports that each afternoon while in Jiangxi, her father would take a walk of about five thousand paces, some forty times around the house on a garden path. She reports that he would "circle the house with quick steps . . . deep in thought. . . . He walked around and around, day after day, year after year."[9] The prospect that he would again play an important role in Beijing gave purpose to his ruminations. Although Deng did not talk about high-level party business with his wife and children, his wife and daughter Deng Rong, living with him every day and knowing a great deal about Beijing politics, could observe his moods and sense his concerns.[10] Deng Rong reports they could tell that as her father paced about he was thinking especially about his future and China's future, and about what he would do after he returned to Beijing.[11]

There was no way to anticipate when Deng would return to Beijing, what responsibilities Mao might give him, nor the precise circumstances China would face at that time. He could reflect on how he might regain Mao's favor to return to office and he could go over in his mind all the dramatic life-and-death struggles of people with whom he had worked. But he could also think about some fundamentals—about how the party could deal with the legacy of Mao, who was already in his last years, and how he could maintain the people's respect for the party while allowing Mao's successors to pursue a different direction. From his vast personal connections with all the party leaders, Deng could evaluate the roles the various leaders might play. He could consider how to realize the goal of four modernizations that Zhou Enlai had enunciated and that he and his closest associates had already worked so hard to realize.

One of the first things China needed to do was to restore order after the disastrous Cultural Revolution. Deng Pufang was the last of Deng Xiaoping's five children to be allowed to visit in Jiangxi. In 1968, Deng Pufang had been under such constant torment from the Red Guards that he fell from a high window and broke his spine. Initially, hospitals were afraid to treat him since his father was being criticized and his condition grew worse. He was finally admitted to Beijing No. 3 Hospital, where doctors found that he had fractured his spine and suffered compound fractures of his chest vertebra; he was also running a high fever. At the hospital, Pufang went in and out of consciousness for three days. Doctors kept him alive but did not perform the surgery that would have prevented the severe paralysis that was to leave him with no sensation from the chest down and with no control over his urinary and bowel functions. He was then transferred to Peking University Hospital, but still the surgery that would have helped his condition was not performed. Pufang's sisters Deng Rong and Deng Nan moved near the hospital so they could take turns caring for him. In mid-1969 when Deng Nan was allowed to visit her parents while they were still in Beijing, she told them what had happened to Pufang. Deng Rong reports that when her parents learned of their son's permanent paralysis, Zhuo Lin cried for three days and nights while Deng sat in silence, smoking cigarettes one after another.[12]

When Pufang, who had been the closest of all the children to his father, was finally allowed to join his parents in Jiangxi in June 1971, because he could not move his body on his own, he was given a room on the first floor of the home so he could be easily moved. He was also required to rest on a hard bed and his body had to be rotated every two hours to avoid sores. Deng Xiaoping, with help from Deng Rong, Zhuo Lin, and Xia Bogen, was responsible for rotating him during the day. Deng also helped to wash and massage him. When a foreigner would later raise the topic of the Cultural Revolution, Deng passionately described it as a disaster.

Mao was so powerful as a personality and as a leader—with his enormous contributions, ruthless devastation of good comrades, and brilliant use of stratagems—that it was difficult for anyone to be neutral about him. It was especially difficult for Deng, whose life had been so deeply intertwined with Mao's. Deng had great admiration for Mao's spectacular achievements and served him faithfully for almost four decades. Yet Mao's policies had devastated the country. And Mao had launched the Red Guards to attack not only Deng as the nation's number-two enemy but also, by extension, the entire Deng family. It would have been inhuman not to feel betrayed, and Deng was very human. Deng had to consider how to get along with Mao if given a chance to return to high office. The question for Deng became not only how to work with Mao while he was still alive—since as long as Mao was alive, Mao would still dominate—but also how to maximize any decision-making leeway that Mao might tolerate. When Deng was sent to Jiangxi, Mao was already seventy-five years old and not well. He would not live forever. It was essential to begin to think through how to handle Mao's reputation and what directions to pursue after he departed from the scene.

Having been in Moscow in 1956 when Khrushchev denounced Stalin, Deng was fully aware that Khrushchev's emotional attack had devastated the Soviet Communist Party and all those who had worked with Stalin. Although the Chinese press was filled with criticisms of Deng that portrayed him as China's Khrushchev, long before he was sent to Jiangxi Deng had already decided that he would not be China's Khrushchev. The question was how to manage the awe and respect that Mao evoked from the masses, the fury of those whose careers and lives had been ruined by Mao, and the awareness among many party officials of the severity of Mao's errors. How could Deng preserve the party's aura of providing correct leadership and avoid tainting those who had worked with Mao, even as he changed Mao's economic and social policies?

All evidence points to Deng's having resolved in his own mind by the time he returned from Jiangxi the basic approach he would take for dealing with the problem. Chinese leaders should praise Mao and keep him on a pedestal. But they also should interpret Mao's teachings not as a rigid ideology, but as a successful adaptation to the conditions of the time—an interpretation that would give Mao's successors the leeway to adapt to new conditions.

By the time Deng was sent to Jiangxi, he could already sense the dawning of a sea change in China's relationship with the West. Ever since the Korean War, and even in the early 1960s when Deng had supervised the exchange of nine hostile letters with the Soviet Union, China had remained closed to the West. But given the threatening Brezhnev doctrine of September 1968 that justified interfering in the internal affairs of Communist countries when their basic system was threatened, and the fighting with the Soviets along the Ussuri River, China needed the cooperation of other countries against the Soviet threat. When Mao asked four marshals—Chen Yi, Nie Rongzhen, Xu Xiangqian, and Ye Jianying—to recommend a response to the dangers from the Soviet Union, they responded, as they knew Mao wanted them to, by suggesting that China initiate overtures with the West.

While in Jiangxi, Deng could receive newspapers and, after Pufang arrived, listen to foreign radio broadcasts. In 1970 Deng learned that China and Canada had normalized relations. He immediately understood what Kissinger later admitted U.S. officials did not understand at the time: Mao's invitation to Edgar Snow to attend the National Day celebrations in 1970 signaled a readiness to expand relations with the United States. In 1971 Deng, still in Jiangxi, learned that Beijing had replaced Taiwan as representative of China in the United Nations, that eleven additional countries had formally recognized China, and that Kissinger had visited Beijing to prepare for Nixon's 1972 visit. The next year he learned that Japan had formally recognized China.

Knowing how assistance from the Soviet Union had helped upgrade China's economy and technology in the 1950s, Deng would naturally begin to think about how to expand this opening to the West to help modernize China. He would think through how to manage the domestic conservative opposition as China opened up and how to preserve a political structure that was both strong and flexible.

One Asian country that had already benefited from closer ties to the West was Japan, and by the time Deng left for Jiangxi, he knew that Japan was completing a decade-long period of double-digit increases in personal income—while China, behind closed doors, had fallen only further behind. The West's willingness to transfer technological know-how and equipment had been central to Japan's modernization. How could China develop a relationship with the United States so that it could reap similar benefits?

By 1969 other Asian countries were also beginning to take off economically, including not only South Korea, but also places with ethnic Chinese populations—Taiwan, Hong Kong, and Singapore. Some Chinese, seeing how far China had fallen behind Europe, expressed doubts that the Chinese tradition was compatible with modernization. But if people who were ethnically and culturally Chinese could modernize, why couldn't China grow just as quickly?

Deng's time in Jiangxi strengthened his convictions about how far behind China was and how much it needed to change. His experiences gave him insights into the extent of the Great Leap's failure that other party leaders, who were continually reading exaggerated reports of local achievements, had difficulty evaluating. Deng Rong reports, for example, that when Pufang arrived in Jiangxi in June 1971, her father, looking for something helpful that Pufang could do, asked his fellow workers if they had any radios to repair. A worker replied that there was no way any of the workers made enough money to buy radios. Deng Rong commented that her father was sick at heart to learn that after twenty years of socialism a worker's family still could not even afford a radio.[13]

Other insights came by way of Deng's children's experiences. All of the children, except for Deng Pufang who was paralyzed, were sent to the countryside to engage in manual labor and to be reeducated. When Deng Rong returned to Jiangxi from her assignment in the northern Shaanxi countryside, she told her family that the rural areas still lacked toilets and pig pens. Further, all of the children reported to their parents that the peasants did not have enough to eat or wear. They described the devastation of the economy and the destruction of the party organization that Deng had worked so hard to build. Deng, obviously moved by what he was hearing, listened to his children but said nothing.[14]

The first friends allowed to visit the Deng family in Jiangxi were three children of Li Jingquan, who were permitted a five-day visit during the Spring Festival of 1972. Li Jingquan had served as a deputy political commissar under Deng in the Southwest Military Region and had succeeded Deng as head of the Southwest Bureau in 1952. At the time of their visit, Li's three children were working in Jiangxi, Li Jingquan's original home province. They told Deng that their father had been attacked and removed from his post and that their mother had been driven to suicide. Deng, who had always sought to learn the truth, took great interest in the details of the struggles under the Red Guards in the Southwest and in the observations about the rural area where one of the three Li children had been sent. He made almost no comment at the time except to say that the people in the countryside needed more education.[15] By the time Deng left Jiangxi, he had no illusions about the seriousness of China's problems and about the depth of change that was needed.

Deepening Family Bonds

For several years after Deng was attacked during the Cultural Revolution, his five children were all subjected to frequent criticism by the Red Guards. Deng Lin and Deng Nan were attacked in their work units, and the others were attacked in their schools. When they ventured from their home, they were likely to be recognized, detained, and verbally assaulted by the Red Guards. The family was close even before the Cultural Revolution, but when the children came under attack they bonded even more tightly, never wavering in their belief that their father was innocent and that they would endure this terrible experience as a united family. Deng was acutely aware that his children had suffered because of him. With officials outside the family, Deng remained a comrade, and party policies took precedence over personal relations. But Deng's relations with Zhuo Lin and their children were not contingent on policy; they had a deep loyalty and affection, and they were always in it together. Deng never broke off relations with any of his children, and none of them ever broke off relations with him. He also maintained close friendships with the household help—the driver, the cook, the orderly, and the director of his personal office, Wang Ruilin. Indeed, Wang Ruilin, except when separated from Deng from 1966 to 1972, served as Deng's office director from 1952, when Wang was just twenty years old, until Deng's death in 1997. He was regarded by Deng as more like a family member than a comrade.

During the Cultural Revolution, problems for the children began with the October 1, 1966, editorial criticizing the number-two person following the "capitalist road"—for although Deng's name was not mentioned, it was clear that he was the target. His three daughters immediately knew that the charges were false, and they never provided any new information to the Red Guards or anyone else that could be used as evidence against their father.[16] Zhuo Lin later praised all the children for not denouncing their father even when pressured to do so.

Most of the letters Deng wrote from Jiangxi were requests that their children be allowed to visit, that they be given work assignments closer to Nanchang, and that Pufang receive the medical care he needed. Deng Rong reports that never in his life had Deng written so many letters as he did on behalf of his children.[17] The letters, which Deng assumed would be shown to Mao, also provided a way of reminding Mao that Deng was in Jiangxi and was ready to accept any assignment he was given, but the letters themselves were all about the children. There were sometimes long delays before responses came from Beijing, but eventually all of Deng's children were allowed to visit Deng in Jiangxi, for at least two weeks each. Deng Rong was allowed to stay much longer. In December 1969, first Rong and then Zhifang were allowed to stay during the agricultural winter break, but they were sent back to their rural brigades when the spring planting was about to begin. Next to visit were Nan and her husband; she was then working for the Science and Technology Commission and the two were allowed to visit for the New Year holiday season in 1971. While in Jiangxi, Nan gave birth to a girl, Deng's first grandchild. Lin, the eldest, was also allowed to visit during the New Year break. These visits were possible because Mao still felt closer to Deng than to Liu Shaoqi and other officials.

Of the five children, Pufang was best informed about higher-level political developments.[18] Pufang's presence in Jiangxi gave his father an opportunity to hear more details of the students' political struggles and to get a sense of the political situation in Beijing. Later on, people who knew Deng would say that although he did not let personal emotions influence his decisions in meting out punishments for most people, he was especially severe in insisting that Nie Yuanzi be imprisoned for ten years for launching the political attacks at Peking University that culminated in Pufang's paralysis and the death of some sixty people at the university.

After the Cultural Revolution and even after Deng's death in 1997, all five children, along with their spouses and children, kept their residences in the same compound. Pufang devoted himself to the cause of the handicapped but also engaged in business. Nan went into science administration and rose to become vice minister of the Science and Technology Commission. At Deng's request his daughter Rong studied medicine in Nanchang, not far from where Deng was living, and Zhifang, who took up physics, also studied in Nanchang. Rong later served in the Chinese embassy in Washington for two years beginning in 1980, doing consular work and promoting cultural exchanges. As part of this effort, she became the family historian, led a foundation to promote exchanges with leaders of other countries, and helped sponsor concerts of Western music. For eight years Zhifang studied in the United States, receiving a Ph.D. in physics from the University of Rochester.

He then joined a company engaged in importing and exporting technology and later branched out into real estate and communications equipment. After 1994 Deng Xiaoping was no longer mentally alert; it is reported that Zhuo Lin, upset when Zhifang was criticized for corruption, took drugs to attempt suicide. She was saved and in the end Zhifang was not punished.

By the time Deng returned from Jiangxi, in 1973, his hearing was becoming more difficult, and he did not join in regular group conversations with his children and grandchildren. He did, however, take great joy in watching the grandchildren and in watching television. To the extent he did take part in conversations with the children speaking directly into his ear, his children offered their observations and their opinions, but Rong reports that their father had sufficient confidence in his own experiences and judgments that he was rarely influenced by their opinions.[19]

Lin Biao's Crash and Deng's Letter to Mao

In the late 1950s and early 1960s, Mao regarded Marshal Lin Biao and Deng as two of the most promising candidates for succeeding him.[20] Indeed, in the fall of 1965, Zhou Enlai told a confidante, Wang Jiaxiang, that Mao was considering two possible successors: Lin Biao and Deng Xiaoping.[21] It is understandable, then, that the two saw each other as rivals for Mao's highest blessing.

Deng Rong said that her father got along with all ten marshals except one, Lin Biao. Mao himself noticed the conflict; Deng reports that in 1966 Mao summoned him and asked him to meet with Lin Biao and to cooperate with him. Deng agreed to the meeting, but the talk failed to resolve the problems between the two; it led them to go their separate paths.[22] In 1966, Mao chose Lin Biao as his "comrade-in-arms" and as his successor, thereby also ensuring the cooperation of the PLA, which Lin had led since 1959 when he replaced Peng Dehuai. Even so, in 1967, Mao confided privately that if Lin Biao's health were to fail, he would bring Deng back.[23]

Lin Biao, a reclusive hypochondriac after his head injury in World War II, was aware of the risks in getting close to Mao and three times he refused the position before Mao in effect ordered him to take it. Once he became Mao's "comrade-in-arms," Lin was filled with anxiety about his relations with the mercurial Mao—and for good reason. By 1970, the ever-distrustful Mao suspected that Lin Biao might be planning to usurp power while he was still alive. Consequently, in the late summer of 1971 Mao began preparing to push him aside, meeting first with leading military officials under Lin Biao to ensure their loyalty. In early September 1971, as Mao was returning by train from Hangzhou to Beijing, the train stopped in Shanghai. Especially cautious about personal security given his heightened suspicions of Lin, Mao did not get off the train but had Wang Hongwen, a former rebel leader who had become deputy head of the Shanghai Revolutionary Committee, and Xu Shi-you, the head of the Nanjing Military Region who was close to Lin Biao, board the train. Mao secured their support and told them he would deal with the problem of Lin Biao when he returned to Beijing. On September 12, as soon as Lin Biao's son, Lin Liguo, heard that Mao was back in Beijing, the Lin family became concerned; Lin Liguo hired a pilot and their plane took off that very evening, carrying Lin Biao, his wife, Lin Liguo, and a small group of followers toward the Soviet Union. But the plane never made it to its destination; it crashed in Mongolia and there were no survivors.[24]

Deng first learned of the plane crash from his son Deng Pufang, who had heard the news on his shortwave radio. Yet he waited almost two months, until the news became official, before he took any action. On November 6, when the announcement of the crash reached down to county levels, Deng and Zhuo Lin, along with some eighty workers in the factory where they worked, were told to listen to a two-hour reading of the Central Committee documents concerning Lin Biao's crimes. Because he was hard of hearing, Deng was allowed to sit in the front row and to take home a copy of the documents to review. After Lin Biao's death, many assumed that Mao would soon be calling on Deng Xiaoping to assume a major position. Deng must have thought so too. Two days after he heard the official report on Lin, even though he had been told not to send any more letters to Wang Dongxing, Deng was emboldened to send off a letter to Chairman Mao.[25]

Deng knew well what kind of letter would be most appealing to Mao. So in addition to asking Mao to let his two youngest children live near him in Jiangxi, he wrote:

The revelations about Lin Biao were very sudden. I was shocked and angered to learn of the despicable crimes. . . . Had it not been for the brilliant leadership of the Chairman and the Central Committee and the early exposure and quick disposition, the plot might have succeeded. . . . In keeping with your instructions I have been reforming myself through labor and study. . . . I have no requests for myself, only that some day I may be able to do a little work for the Party. Naturally, it would be some sort of technical job. . . . I am longing for a chance to pay back by hard work a bit of what I owe.[26]

Despite the humility of his statement, Deng was aware that Mao would be unlikely to place a bold seasoned leader like himself in anything less than a high position.

For some months, Deng did not receive a reply and even when Deng did hear back, Mao had not yet made a decision as to whether or when to allow Deng to return, let alone what position he would be asked to fill. Mao was exhausted and what energy he had was devoted not to preparing his post-Lin team but to making preparations for the Nixon visit of February 1972.

Mao Turns to Zhou and Party Elders, September 1971–May 1973

Had Mao been able to control the pacing of his plan to depose Lin Biao, he would have prepared his replacement. The sudden plane crash, however, upset Mao's plans to win acceptance in high party circles for his decision to depose Lin. When the person whom Mao had embraced as his successor and "closest comrade-in-arms" was suddenly recast, after his still-mysterious death, as a renegade trying to usurp power, even ordinary people had questions about Mao's judgment. Mao, sick and depressed, scarcely rose from his bed for two months.[27] Afterward he did gradually begin to get up, but on February 12, 1972, he fainted. His lung problems had already affected his heart. They also made sleeping difficult due to frequent coughing, so Mao slept on a sofa. Though he could not move easily, at least at some points, on the big issues, his mind remained clear.[28]

Officials who had suffered under Mao and who grieved over the disasters he had perpetrated understood that the cult of Mao was so powerful that the country would be thrown into even greater chaos if Mao were attacked directly. In December 1958, when his errors in charging ahead during the Great Leap Forward had become all too obvious, Mao had made policy concessions and granted other leaders more leeway to make decisions—even as he maneuvered to remain at the helm. After Lin's death, Mao again made concessions in policies and gave others more decision-making authority, but remained in charge.

Mao needed to move quickly to establish a new post-Lin party leadership and the 10th Party Congress was not scheduled until 1974—five years after the 9th Party Congress. Mao, however, put the new leadership structure in place in less than two years, enabling him to hold the 10th Party Congress in August 1973, one year ahead of the scheduled date. To make this happen, Mao had to reach beyond his closest inner circle, for although he could rely on his wife, Jiang Qing, and her associates to criticize others, they lacked the experience, good judgment, and the ability to gain the cooperation of others to govern the country. Mao had no realistic choice but to turn to experienced senior officials, most of whom had been victims of his Cultural Revolution. They had risen to their positions before the Cultural Revolution at least in part because of their proven abilities to lead, and Mao once again needed their seasoned managerial skills.[29] When Zhou Enlai reported to Mao on the fate of many of these senior officials, Mao said he had been unaware that many had been so badly treated.

At this point, there was in fact only one person in place who could manage the party and the government and who, due to deeply ingrained attitudes, would not threaten Mao's power: Zhou Enlai. Of the five people who had been on the Politburo Standing Committee in August 1970, Lin Biao was dead, his ally Chen Boda was in prison, and Kang Sheng was incapacitated by cancer, thus leaving only Mao and Zhou. With so few alternatives, Mao allowed Zhou Enlai more leeway to restore order to the party and the government; he assigned Zhou to chair not only the Politburo, but also the government and the party structure.

Some observers thought Zhou Enlai would have been jubilant over the death of Lin Biao, but in fact Zhou was deeply upset. Zhou was known to have powerful control over his own emotions, but shortly after Lin Biao's crash, when he explained the country's difficult predicament to Vice Premier Ji Dengkui (see Key People in the Deng Era, p. 730), he not only wept but had to pause to try to regain control; despite his efforts, he continued sobbing as he spoke. It is said that Zhou cried only three times in his life: when he was belatedly told of his father's death; after the death of Ye Ting, a fellow revolutionary from the 1920s; and after the death of Lin Biao.

There were probably several reasons for Zhou's emotional reaction to Lin's death. Zhou knew that despite Lin's reputation as a radical, he had been pragmatic, concerned about order, and, for Zhou, easy to work with. In addition, Zhou, who had exhausted himself for decades trying to manage affairs under Mao, grieved for the country, which after the devastation of the Great Leap Forward and Cultural Revolution was now confronting yet another upheaval. He was acutely aware that any move forward would be a monumental task.[30]

Some believed that Zhou also wept for himself. Until that point, he had been able to avoid the suspicion and wrath of Mao that had led to the death of two number twos, Liu Shaoqi and Lin Biao. He had managed to remain number three, but now he was number two, and he knew Mao would be suspicious. Indeed, within two years Mao would attack him.

In addition to relying on Zhou, Mao called on Ye Jianying, a respected senior military statesman who was not personally ambitious, to bring order to the military. Without fanfare, Mao also began to allow some of the others who had been pushed aside in 1966–1967 to return to work. While resting during the two months after Lin Biao's crash, on several occasions Mao acknowledged that many senior officials had suffered too much. He explained this mistake by claiming that he had wrongly heeded allegations made by Lin Biao.[31]

On November 14, 1971, two months after Lin's crash, there were more signs of Mao's shift in perspective. On that day, he received a delegation that included Marshal Ye Jianying, who was already beginning to rebuild the army leadership structure. In a gesture that was an encouraging signal to high-ranking victims of the Cultural Revolution, Mao pointed to Ye Jianying and said to the delegation, "Don't call him part of the February Counter-Current [when three vice premiers and four marshals in February 1967 had criticized and tried to stop the Cultural Revolution]."[32] He further said that the unrest had been directed by Lin Biao and that the term "February Counter-Current" should no longer be used.[33] In this way, Mao tried to distance himself from the 1967 attacks on those accused of taking part in the "February Counter-Current." He also issued directives to correct the treatment of Tan Zhenlin, Chen Zaidao, and other leading officials who had been criticized in 1967.

The memorial service held on January 10, 1972, for Marshal Chen Yi provided Mao an excellent opportunity to reconnect with some senior officials who had suffered during the Cultural Revolution. A few hours before the memorial service was to take place, Mao let it be known that he would attend. It was his first public appearance since the Lin Biao crash four months earlier. Chen Yi, Deng's partner in the Huai Hai campaign, the first mayor of Shanghai during the early days after the Communist takeover, and a one-time foreign minister, was one of the nation's most beloved leaders. Years later, his statue, erected on the Bund in Shanghai, would symbolize the public's high regard for him. Yet during the Cultural Revolution, he was brutally attacked. Although he did finally receive medical care at a military hospital, it was too late: he died from a lack of proper medical attention. Further, many of China's leading military leaders had visited Chen Yi during his last days and knew well how Mao's Cultural Revolution had contributed to his death.

At the memorial service, Mao bowed three times to show his respect for Chen Yi and said, "Comrade Chen Yi was a good man, a good comrade. . . . If Lin Biao had succeeded in his plot, he would have destroyed all of us veterans." Thus Mao passed on responsibility for the mistreatment of Chen Yi to his one-time "closest comrade-in-arms." Mao, dressed in pajamas, covered by an overcoat, on a cold day, was obviously ill and his legs wobbly. His frailty and message were compelling for those attending the service. What better way for Mao to pave the way for reconciliation with the victims of the Cultural Revolution attacks than by coming in such a condition to offer apologies and pay his respects to a favorite comrade?

All of the Chinese high officials knew that Chen Yi would not have been criticized without Mao's approval. But for the time being, they were willing to accept the fiction that it was Lin Biao who had caused Chen's problems. They could not expect Mao to acknowledge his errors, and it was in their interest to take advantage of Mao's changed stance toward his old comrades. Mao put politics before economics, but he never gave up wanting to improve the nation's economy. Moreover, he may have had an extraordinary emotional hold over the Chinese people, but he still needed competent party leaders. Even the leaders whom Mao had retained throughout the Cultural Revolution recognized that, for stability and growth, the country would need the firm hand of those officials who had served before the Cultural Revolution. By 1972, Mao was ready to bring back these experienced senior officials— and to start returning to their barracks the military officers, most of whom had been ineffective in the civilian positions they had occupied during Lin Biao's tenure in the late 1960s. Soon thereafter, in March 1972, Zhou Enlai submitted a list of more than four hundred senior officials to the party Organization Department to be rehabilitated, and Mao promptly approved their return.[34] In 1975, and again in 1978, these senior officials would play a key role in helping Deng to restore order and unity.

In May 1972, Zhou was diagnosed with bladder cancer, but for the remainder of 1972 and into early 1973, he continued his heavy work schedule.[35] During the chaotic period after Lin Biao's crash, Zhou had used his unparalleled close relations with other officials to keep the country from falling more deeply into chaos.[36] Extremely knowledgeable and virtually tireless in spite of early stage cancer, Zhou continued to find ways for people of diverse backgrounds to work together. In situations requiring delicate personal diplomacy, no one could achieve more than Zhou.[37]

Zhou continued to seek Mao's approval on major appointments and sensitive issues, and he tried to make decisions that Mao would support. But Mao's withdrawal and recognition that a readjustment was required allowed Zhou to resolve a larger range of issues more forcefully than before. He threw himself into managing the relationships among senior officials, restoring order to the economy, curbing leftist excesses in the countryside, and expanding diplomatic contacts with the West.[38] He even made it possible for the distinguished physicist and president of Peking University, Zhou Peiyuan, to put forth plans to promote theoretical research.[39] These efforts by Zhou Enlai to craft order from chaos foreshadowed the broader initiatives that Deng Xiaoping would launch in 1975. It should have come as no surprise, then, that Mao's criticism of Zhou in late 1973 foreshadowed his criticism of Deng in early 1976.

Unlike Deng, who focused on the important and put aside the less important, Zhou Enlai, with his amazing command of details, dealt with matters both large and small. When Mao gave him the leeway, he used his prodigious memory to show extraordinary consideration to many who had been victimized in the Cultural Revolution. Those victims and their families remained enormously grateful to Zhou Enlai for saving their lives and easing their pain. Zhou extended this same interest to Deng Xiaoping and his family. In December 1972, when Zhou felt Mao would allow it, he prodded Wang Dongxing to speed up the process of giving Deng an assignment.

Zhou's attempts to help the victims of the Cultural Revolution, however, were limited by his fear of enraging Mao. His concern seems to have been well founded. After a Politburo meeting in 1956, Zhou upset Mao when he told him privately that he could not in good conscience support some of his economic policies. After being criticized then, Zhou went to extraordinary lengths for the next fifteen years to give Mao no reason to doubt his total commitment to carry out the Chairman's wishes.[40] Even so, in January 1958, Mao exploded at Zhou, saying Zhou was only fifty meters away from being a rightist, an accusation that led Zhou to back down.

Zhou had exhausted himself during the Cultural Revolution by painfully carrying out Mao's directives, while also trying to shield those whom he felt he could protect.[41] He was a virtuoso at balancing these competing interests in an emotionally charged environment. Perhaps no one was better than Zhou in intuiting what Mao was thinking but did not say. Some lionize Zhou for his combination of political skills, tireless dedication to the party and country, unfailing poise and gentlemanly demeanor, and devotion to assisting victims. Many who knew the situation well believed that Zhou did everything he could to moderate Mao's excesses. Not everyone, however, felt that Zhou Enlai was a hero. Chen Yi's family members, for example, were upset that Zhou did not protect Chen Yi, and families of other victims who had not received help from Zhou expressed similar sentiments. Still others considered him an accomplice who was in a pact with the devil, implementing the Cultural Revolution with all its horrors. Is it not possible, some asked, that the horrors would have ended sooner had Zhou Enlai not prevented the regime from falling apart?

Regardless of one's views on Zhou and the Cultural Revolution, it was clear that no one else could have so skillfully managed what was then high on Mao's agenda—the opening of relations with the United States. Zhou first met U.S. Secretary of State Henry Kissinger on July 9, 1971, just two months before Lin Biao's crash. In October 20–26, 1971, only a month after the crash, Kissinger returned to Beijing to plan for the visit, which took place the following February. Kissinger later wrote that he considered Zhou to be one of the two or three most impressive men he had ever met. John Holdridge, a Kissinger aide, described Kissinger's mood before meeting Zhou as the anticipation of one of the world's two grand chess masters on his way to the championship match.[42]

Mao and Zhou, Nixon and Kissinger

In 1969 China and the United States, which had been trading partners for two centuries, World War II allies for four years, and Cold War enemies for two decades, began to consider rekindling a diplomatic relationship. Mao, concerned about the risk of Soviet invasion after the 1969 border clashes, had for the first time since the Korean War decided to increase contacts with the West, and had assigned Zhou Enlai to carry on the negotiations. Nixon, who was looking for a way to resolve the Vietnam conflict and was seeking long-term cooperation against the Soviet Union, assigned Henry Kissinger to be Zhou's counterpart in negotiating the new overtures to China. Kissinger's dramatic trip from Pakistan to Beijing in 1971, to prepare for the Nixon visit, and the Nixon visit in February 1972 were breathtaking events that helped set the stage for the rapid expansion of U.S.-China contacts during the Deng era.

Deng had nothing to do with the 1966–1969 deterioration in Sino-Soviet relations that had led to the 1969 conflict. But he had led the team that drafted the famous nine polemical letters to Moscow from 1961 to 1963, and he had personally delivered the last major Chinese speech in Moscow in 1963 that had capped those angry exchanges. Deng also had nothing to do with the opening to the United States that took place while he was still in Jiangxi, although by late 1973 he was at Zhou's side, helping to carry on negotiations. No, Deng's contributions would come later.

Restoring Deng Slowly, January 1972–April 1973

Not until February 1973, sixteen months after Lin Biao's death, did Mao invite Deng Xiaoping to return to Beijing. Having criticized Deng so severely in 1966, Mao could not expect others to be ready to accept Deng quickly, and he had not yet decided how to use him. Deng had been attacked so vehemently for taking the "capitalist road" that it was a challenge for Mao to explain to others why he would welcome him back. Mao's strategy was to explain that Deng, the highly respected general secretary, had been "mistreated by Lin Biao." At the memorial service for Chen Yi in January 1972, Mao said to Chen Yi's family that Deng was different from Liu Shaoqi: his situation was less serious. Zhou Enlai then suggested to Chen Yi's family that they should let Mao's appraisal of Deng be more widely known.[43] When word of Mao's comments reached Deng, it was the first indication that Mao had received his letter of September 1971. More hints were coming, however. In early April 1972, Deng was informed by the Jiangxi Provincial Revolutionary Committee that, in line with his wishes expressed in the letter to Mao, his youngest son, Zhifang, had been admitted to Jiangxi College of Science and Technology and his youngest daughter, Rong, would be allowed to enter Jiangxi Medical University.[44]

With these positive signals, on April 26, 1972, Deng was emboldened to write to Wang Dongxing, explaining that since his two children had gone off to college, he wondered if he might be allowed to hire someone to help Zhuo Lin and him to look after Pufang. He concluded the letter saying, "As for myself, I am still awaiting instructions from you allowing me to do a few more years of work."[45] Deng received no direct response or communication, but within a month the salaries of both Deng and Zhuo Lin were restored to their original levels.[46]

Deng Rong later wrote that these signs that Deng's political situation had improved were enormously encouraging for the entire family. The extent to which the Deng family waited for any positive signal reveals how completely Mao Zedong, even when he was sick and disheartened by Lin Biao's crash, could control the fate of the people under him. Indeed, Chen Yun had been allowed to return to Beijing from Jiangxi on April 22, 1972, yet Mao kept Deng in Jiangxi for almost another year.

On August 3, 1972, after several months with no response from Mao or Wang Dongxing, Deng again wrote to Mao, trying to clear up the doubts that he suspected Mao might be harboring about him. Deng began by writing that he had just heard the reports given to all workers in his factory about the crimes of Lin Biao and Chen Boda. He reported that although Lin was a shrewd general, on the Long March he had once teamed up secretly with Peng Dehuai against Mao and recalled that Lin Biao had refused Mao's request to lead the army during the Korean War. Deng confessed that Lin Biao was better than he was at understanding Mao's wishes, but that he could not agree with the way Lin had simplified Mao's thinking by stressing only three articles, because more of Mao's works should be used. Deng also wrote that both Lin Biao and Chen Boda would be happy only if Deng were dead, and Deng therefore thanked Mao for protecting him during the Cultural Revolution. Deng had no compunctions about telling Mao what he thought Mao wanted to hear.

In his letter, Deng reinforced the message that everything he wrote in his self-criticism of June and July 1968 was correct. In addition to explaining again his error in leaving the Guangxi troops in 1931, he also admitted that there were weaknesses in his performance as general secretary of the party because he sometimes failed to seek Chairman Mao's opinion. In 1960–1961 he had not been able to eliminate his capitalist thinking. He had also failed to implement effectively Chairman Mao's decision to build up the "third front" by moving defense-related industries inland. And he did not in a timely fashion ask Chairman Mao's permission before making reports. Deng acknowledged that it had been correct for the Cultural Revolution to have revealed his errors. In the letter he also tried to relieve Mao's worries about one critical issue: he wrote that he would never reverse the verdicts on people criticized during the Cultural Revolution. He also indicated that he would return to the Chairman's proletarian revolutionary line.[47]

This message from Deng was apparently what Mao was waiting to hear. On August 14, 1972, only a few days after receiving Deng's reassurances, Mao wrote Premier Zhou Enlai, instructing him to arrange Deng's return to

Beijing. Mao reiterated that Deng's case was different from that of Liu Shaoqi. Deng had never surrendered to the enemy and he was never suspected of passing on secrets to the Guomindang. In addition, Deng had supported General Liu Bocheng in battle and had made many other contributions to the party and the country.[48] The very day Zhou received Mao's memo, he circulated it to the Central Committee.[49] But because Jiang Qing, Mao's wife, dragged her feet on bringing Deng back, at that point no action was taken.[50]

In September 1972, Deng, sensing he might be allowed more freedom, asked for and received permission to visit the old Jiangxi Soviet base areas, including Ruijin. It was the first time he left his house in three years. He visited for five days, and was hosted with the same courtesy given a provincial leader. Deng also received permission to spend two days visiting Wang Rui-lin, his office director since 1952, who was then in Jinxian county, Jiangxi, performing physical labor at a "May 7 Cadre School" for reeducating officials. Later, when Deng returned to Beijing, Wang was allowed to return as well, to serve Deng as before. On December 18, 1972, Zhou Enlai asked Wang Dongxing and Ji Dengkui why Mao's August instruction regarding Deng had not been carried out, and on December 27, after checking with Mao, they responded that Deng could return to Beijing at last.[51] The next month, in January 1973, Bai Dongcai, party secretary of the Jiangxi Provincial Revolutionary Committee, brought Deng the good news, and on February 20, after workers from Deng's factory came to bid him farewell, Deng and his family were driven by car to Yingtan, where they boarded a train for Beijing.[52] As he left Jiangxi, Deng said, "I can still work for twenty years."[53] Indeed, it was not until nineteen years and eight months later, after the 14th Party Congress, that Deng would retire from the political stage.

Deng Returns to Beijing, 1973

When a person who had been criticized was to take on an important position in the Chinese leadership, it was standard practice first to hint that he was once again in good favor: that way, others would have an easier time accepting the new appointment. After Deng returned from Jiangxi on February 22, 1973, he was not immediately given an assignment, even though his appearance in Beijing implied that he would again play a major role. As word of his return began to spread, Deng visited some old acquaintances but for some weeks he still did not attend any formal meetings or assume any responsibilities, nor did he meet with either Mao or Zhou.

Mao gave Zhou the task of convening a series of Politburo meetings to discuss Deng's future. Members of the Cultural Revolution Small Group—as well as Zhang Chunqiao, a potential rival for succeeding Zhou as premier, and Zhang Chunqiao's supporter Jiang Qing—strongly opposed Deng's being given a major role. But Mao insisted that Deng should return to work and participate in regular party meetings.[54] At the end of the deliberations, the Politburo proposed that Deng be assigned to the *yewuzu,* the leadership group under Zhou Enlai and vice head Li Xiannian that had maintained regular government functions during the chaos of the Cultural Revolution, and that he be allowed to attend regular weekly party meetings.[55] On March 9 Zhou forwarded to Mao a document summarizing these decisions, Mao approved it, and the document was distributed to Deng and party committees down to the county level and to military officials down to the regimental level.[56]

Deng's first meeting with Zhou after his return to Beijing occurred on the evening of March 28, 1973, and was also attended by Li Xiannian (see Key People in the Deng Era, p. 731) and Jiang Qing. Immediately after the meeting, Zhou reported to Mao that Deng was in good spirits and in good health, and seemed ready to return to work. The very next afternoon, Mao met with Deng for the first time in six years, telling Deng, "Work hard. Stay healthy." Deng responded that he had remained healthy because he had faith in the Chairman and had been awaiting his call.[57] That evening, Zhou, at Mao's behest, chaired a Politburo meeting during which it was announced that Deng would be made vice premier and take part in foreign affairs activities. Deng was not yet to be made a regular member of the Politburo, but he was to attend its meetings when important matters were to be discussed. Zhou sent a letter to Mao summarizing the Politburo discussions, Mao approved it, and Deng formally took on the position.[58]

Deng's first official appearance after 1968 was on April 12, 1973, at a banquet for Prince Norodom Sihanouk of Cambodia. There he was introduced as vice premier. Deng and others acted as if his attendance were perfectly natural, though some remained reserved as they greeted him. Following his appearance there was a great buzz among officials and foreign correspondents about what role Deng might play.[59]

Clearly, Mao wanted Deng to be given important work. During 1973, as we will see, Deng gradually became a more prominent leader, first by being allowed to attend high-level meetings, then by being apprenticed to Zhou Enlai, next by becoming a member of the Central Committee at the August

10th Party Congress, and then, in December, after proving his loyalty to Mao, by becoming a member of the Politburo and a member of the Central Military Commission (CMC).

As an apprentice to Zhou Enlai, beginning in April 1973 Deng would accompany Zhou when greeting guests from Cambodia, Mexico, Japan, North Korea, Mali, Nepal, Congo, Philippines, France, Canada, Australia, and elsewhere at the airport, welcoming them and then seeing them off. He did attend some of the meetings with foreigners, but as yet he still was not responsible for carrying out any discussions with them.[60]

Mao Cultivates Wang Hongwen, 1973–1974

Mao, like all other senior Chinese leaders, devoted great attention to cultivating young leaders as successors. After the death of Lin Biao and with Mao's own health declining, the issue of a successor became more pressing. Mao drew on his deep knowledge of how Chinese leaders throughout the centuries had dealt with succession when crafting his own strategy. That is, Mao kept his options open: while giving hints and signs of his intent, he continued to observe, maintain his own authority, and ensure that he could always change his mind. Between 1971 and September 1972, Mao brought three promising young officials to Beijing to work at the party center: first Hua Guofeng, then Wang Hongwen and Wu De. By late 1972 he had singled out as especially promising Wang Hongwen—a young, strong rebel with a fierce loyalty to Mao and the Communist Party. Mao liked Wang's worker background, his service as a soldier, and his bold confident leadership style (see Key People in the Deng Era, p. 738).

Mao knew that Wang Hongwen did not have the knowledge or background to lead the government, but he believed that Wang's proven radical commitment and leadership potential made him a prime candidate to become a high-level party leader. Indeed, Mao began to lean toward the idea of keeping Wang as a party leader while at the same time finding someone else to replace Zhou Enlai as head of the government.

Mao Makes Deng an Apprentice to Zhou

Throughout Chinese history, as emperors aged and their energy declined, they often stopped seeing a broad range of officials and narrowed their contacts to an inner cabinet of fawning eunuchs. After Lin Biao's death, Mao similarly rarely saw any officials, including Deng, and relied primarily on three women to keep him posted about the outside world: Zhang Yufeng, an assistant who lived at his residence, and the "two ladies," that is, Tang Wensheng ("Nancy"), his interpreter, and Wang Hairong, Mao's "niece" (actually his cousin's granddaughter). Mao had met Zhang Yufeng when she was assigned to be an assistant on his special train. She was attractive, intellectually sophisticated, and politically astute, although she did not have the depth of experience to understand all the complexities of high-level politics. The "two ladies" had originally been sent by the Ministry of Foreign Affairs to assist Mao when meeting foreign guests. Mao conversed with them before and after he met the foreign visitors, and the two gradually acquired a broader role as go-betweens with the outside world. Whatever their personal views, they had no choice but to be thoroughly loyal to Mao in their dealings with outsiders, who came to regard them as representatives of Mao's leftism. When Mao was attacking Zhou Enlai, for instance, the two ladies were responsible for conveying Mao's views. This situation posed a serious problem for their relationship with Zhou when Mao became critical of Zhou, for the two ladies became in effect Mao's mouthpiece in dealing with Zhou, and they were expected to report to Mao any possible problems in his behavior. By 1973, Mao, suffering from Lou Gehrig's disease, had difficulty holding his head up straight and mumbled. In February 1972 he once fell unconscious, but he was still able to meet Nixon nine days later. Mao was preoccupied with stories from Chinese history and literature. But on issues he cared about, like major personnel appointments, his reputation, and managing relationships, he was as shrewd, devious, and cunning as ever. On those issues, he remained firmly in charge and made calculating use of go-betweens.

Beyond planning their successors, aged emperors also tended to focus on ensuring their historical legacy. Mao had always been concerned about his place in history. In 1945, when he went to meet Chiang Kai-shek, Mao wrote what would become one of his most famous poems. In it he asked: Who was the greatest leader in Chinese history? Was it one of the great emperors Qin Shihuang, Han Wudi, Tang Taizong, or Song Taizu? Mao's answer: "To find the greatest leader one must look to the present." In megalomania and lust for power, Mao ranked high among world leaders. At his zenith, Mao was involved in a broad range of activities, but with his health waning and his years numbered, Mao began to focus even more on his place in history and on successors who would honor his legacy.

Mao also ranked high among world leaders in paranoid suspicions of others plotting to usurp power, but it was not unreasonable to worry that if Zhou Enlai were to survive him, he might abandon Mao's commitment to class struggle and the continuing revolution and reduce the glorification of Mao in the official history of the era.[61] For his extraordinary skills and prodigious memory in managing government activities and foreign relations, Zhou was by then almost indispensable, especially to China's emerging relationship with the United States and other Western countries. It was well known in high circles that Mao did not like Zhou, but he needed him. Zhou Enlai had developed a large number of internal spies who worked under him in Shanghai in the 1930s and whose identity remained secret; they remained intensely loyal to Zhou, and Mao was cautious about removing someone who commanded such a large secret network of supporters. Zhou Enlai, unlike Liu Shaoqi and Lin Biao, had taken extraordinary care over the years not to threaten Mao's power. Nonetheless, by 1973, although it could not be said publicly, it was not difficult for Mao to discern that among many high-level officials, Zhou was thought of as the good leader—the one who struggled to keep order, show consideration for others, and rein in the wild schemes of the bad leader.

Mao's problem with Zhou was less a concern that Zhou might try to seize power, and more that Zhou's reputation might rise at the expense of his own and that Zhou might be too soft on the United States. These problems would be especially severe if Zhou were to survive him. Consequently, when Nancy Tang and Wang Hairong reported to Mao the lavish praise that the foreign press was heaping on "Zhou Enlai's foreign policy" for improving U.S.-China relations, Mao was livid.[62] It should be known as Mao's foreign policy, not Zhou's. Starting around this time, then, Mao began finding ways to weaken Zhou's reputation and to ensure that the person who took over Zhou's work as his cancer advanced would be loyal to Mao, not to Zhou.[63]

Regardless of Mao's megalomania, eccentricities, and policy errors, his underlings acknowledged that in addition to being a brilliant national strategist he had a good eye for talent. The one political leader other than Zhou Enlai who in Mao's eyes had proven that he could skillfully manage a host of complex issues, including foreign relations, was Deng Xiaoping.[64] Deng had worked closely with Zhou since their time in France half a century earlier, when Zhou had supervised his work. But Deng had bonded with Mao in the Jiangxi Soviet in the early 1930s and risen over the years because he was Mao's man, not because he was Zhou's man.[65] In 1973, Zhou managed a broad range of extraordinarily complex foreign policy issues. Deng thus had much to learn from Zhou Enlai when he became his apprentice in the spring of 1973. Mao, having been disappointed that Deng had grown distant from him and too close to Liu in the early 1960s, had reason to wonder whether Deng, if given an important position, would be less responsive to Mao than he had been in the years immediately before the Cultural Revolution and more responsive to Zhou. Was there a danger that Deng might criticize the Cultural Revolution, replace Mao's key appointments, and leave to history an evaluation of Mao that emphasized his errors?[66] Throughout 1973, then, Mao observed Deng very closely.

The 10th Party Congress, August 1973

The 10th Party Congress, held August 24–28, 1973, was the first high-level large meeting since 1949 at which Mao, already seriously ill, did not personally make a speech. The First Plenum, held as usual immediately after the congress to announce the personnel appointments, was the last Central Committee meeting that Mao would attend. During the congress Mao could scarcely stand, and waited until the participants had left the hall before he himself departed so they would not see how difficult it was for him to move. Mao retained the power to set the overall direction and to approve important personnel appointments, but with Mao's illness, participants could not help but think about succession.

At the congress, Wang Hongwen, then thirty-eight years old, was catapulted to leadership, making it clear to leaders at home and abroad that Mao had chosen him to be the leading candidate to succeed him as head of the party.[67] Wang's importance had already become obvious to party leaders two months earlier, when Wang had been named head of the Election Preparatory Committee that would nominate the new members of the Central Committee. He had also been put in charge of preparing a new constitution and at the congress he delivered the report on it, a responsibility that Deng had held at the 8th Party Congress in 1956, when he was the promising candidate to succeed Mao as party leader.[68] At the First Plenum, Wang Hongwen was also named vice chairman of the party, ranking him third in command behind Mao and Zhou. Other leaders, foreign diplomats, and the foreign press also began to treat him as Mao's likely successor.[69]

Deng's role at the party congress could not compare with Wang's. He was readmitted as a member of the Central Committee, but he played no leadership role. Compared to a usual party congress, this 10th Party Congress was rushed in order to provide the new leadership structure after the death of Lin Biao and the elimination of his closest followers. The congress lacked the comprehensive overview of issues discussed at the 8th Party Congress of 1956 and even of the 9th Party Congress, where Lin Biao played the key role. It lasted five days compared to the twenty-four days of the 9th Party Congress, and the two major speeches, by Wang Hongwen and Zhou Enlai, together lasted less than one hour, far shorter than a typical party congress speech.[70] This congress represented the end of the Lin Biao era with a new Central Committee membership but not yet a new program. The congress focused on three topics—criticism of Lin Biao, the rectification campaign following the fall of Lin, and the 1973 economic plan.[71] Almost half of Zhou Enlai's political report criticized Lin Biao. The economic plan, however, was not discussed in detail because the economy was still in a chaotic state and the leadership did not have time to make a detailed presentation of the remaining two years, 1974 and 1975, of the current five-year plan.

Perhaps the most important change at the party congress was the return to the Central Committee of so many senior officials, for they would provide the backbone of support for Deng when he was given more power at the end of 1973. They replaced the many military officials who had been brought in at the 9th Party Congress led by Lin Biao. Among the 191 members of the new Central Committee, some forty were senior officials who had been brought back after being criticized during the Cultural Revolution.[72] Among those whom Mao allowed to return were vice premier Tan Zhenlin, one of the commanders under Deng Xiaoping's front command during the Huai Hai campaign, who in February 1967 had boldly objected to the Cultural Revolution; Wang Zhen; and Deng Xiaoping. Already by mid-July Deng, who until then was only allowed to sit in on meetings with foreigners, had begun participating in the discussions.[73]

Mao's decision to elevate a rebel leader as young and inexperienced as Wang Hongwen was an outrage to senior officials. On August 21, during the last Politburo meeting prior to the congress, senior officials dared to raise objections to Wang Hongwen's appointment. General Xu Shiyou spoke for less daring senior officials when he said that one vice chairman, Zhou Enlai, was enough. When pressured, Xu responded that Kang Sheng and Marshal Ye Jianying could be added.[74] In the end, however, Mao persisted; Wang Hongwen was appointed and so was Kang Sheng, who had played a sinister role in selecting high officials for attack during the Cultural Revolution. The other two vice chairman, however, Zhou Enlai and Marshal Ye Jianying, could provide experienced and moderate leadership.

Although Zhou Enlai was allowed to present the political report to the congress, it was drafted by two of Jiang Qing's supporters, Zhang Chunqiao and Yao Wenyuan, who had also drafted key documents for the 9th Party Congress. Therefore, while the documents criticized Lin Biao, they basically affirmed the radical outcome of the 9th Party Congress, when Lin Biao was in charge. Indeed, Politburo membership after the 10th Party Congress was still dominated by the radicals. There were four radicals on the new twenty-one-member Politburo—Wang Hongwen, Zhang Chunqiao, Jiang Qing, and Yao Wenyuan; they were not working together as a team but their views were similar and later they became infamous as the "Gang of Four." Other Politburo members—including Wu De, Chen Xilian, and Ji Dengkui—although less radical, still leaned toward the left. Mao tried to balance the senior officials who were returned to the Central Committee with "mass representatives," peasants and worker representatives. Even if, as Mao acknowledged, "their intellectual level was a little lower," they could be counted on to support the radicals who favored continuing the revolution.

Deng was not yet given responsibilities to go with his new position, but to shrewd political observers it was clear that Mao was beginning to think of Deng and Wang Hongwen working together. Mao sent them together on an inspection trip so they would get to know each other.[75]

Mao Attacks Zhou Enlai, November–December 1973

In February 1973, when Henry Kissinger met Mao for the first time, he found Mao upset with the United States for cooperating with the Soviet Union at the expense of China. By November of that year, when Kissinger again went to Beijing, Mao not only complained about U.S. cooperation with the Soviet Union but also about Zhou Enlai for being too soft in dealing with the United States. During the summer months, Mao complained bitterly that the United States was "standing on China's shoulders," using China to get agreements with the Soviet Union. Mao's suspicions heightened further in June 1973 when Brezhnev visited the United States and met with Nixon in San Clemente, California, to celebrate ratification of the Treaty for the Prevention of Nuclear War. Immediately after Brezhnev's U.S. visit, the Chinese delivered a formal note to the White House complaining that by helping the Soviets present a posture of peace, the U.S. was enabling the Soviet Union to mask its expansionism.[76] Mao suspected that the United States and the Soviet Union were forging an agreement that would leave the Soviet Union free to aim its weapons toward China without any response from the United States.

Mao accused Zhou Enlai and the Ministry of Foreign Affairs of being too conciliatory toward the United States, allowing China to be used to improve relations with the Soviet Union. Mao was also upset that the United States was doing nothing to weaken ties with Taiwan or to normalize relations with China. Nixon had promised to normalize relations with China in 1976 and now, whatever the explanation (that the Watergate investigation weakened Nixon's power so he could not get normalization through Congress), the United States was using China to improve relations with the Soviet Union.

When Kissinger arrived in Beijing in November 1973, he found Zhou's power much reduced by Mao. Zhou was so sensitive to accusations of being a Confucian (being too moderate, not fighting for China's national interests) that when Kissinger said China was still influenced by Confucius, Zhou flew into a rage, the only time that Kissinger recalls Zhou becoming angry in all their dozens of hours of meetings. Clearly Zhou was under pressure, and the two ladies would report his behavior to Mao. By the time Kissinger arrived, the United States had just appointed a new high-level ambassador, Leonard Unger, to Taiwan and had agreed to supply Taiwan with new military technology. Mao was furious.

In November, after the first day of discussions between Zhou and Kissinger, Zhou and Nancy Tang reported to Mao. Zhou told Mao of Kissinger's suggestion that Washington might be able to win Congressional approval to advance toward normalization of the U.S.-China relationship if the Chinese could be somewhat more flexible than in the Japan formula and allow Washington to maintain closer relations with Taiwan. Nancy Tang chimed in at that point, telling Mao that it sounded like a "two-China policy."[77] (Zhou later confessed to Kissinger that "when we were with the Chairman, I dared not explain the statement, but she dared to make an explanation.") When Mao heard that Zhou was seriously listening to Kissinger's proposals allowing the United States to keep a stronger relationship with Taiwan as well as with the mainland, Mao, the elemental patriot, was furious at Zhou.

Kissinger told Zhou that "the growth of Chinese nuclear capability was unacceptable to the Soviet Union."[78] Kissinger also proposed the establishment of a hotline so the United States and China would immediately exchange information in case of possible Soviet action ("to lessen the vulnera-bility of your forces and to increase the warning time"). Zhou told Kissinger that if an agreement were reached on the sharing of intelligence, "it would be of great assistance to China" and on the last morning of Kissinger's visit (No-vember 14) they exchanged drafts of documents about the sharing of intelli-gence.[79]

To Mao, hearing reports of Kissinger's discussion with Zhou, the proposal had overtones of the Soviet Union's proposal in the late 1950s to provide a collective defense for China, which had led Mao to break off relations with the Soviet Union for fear of granting powers to the Soviet Union that would have compromised Chinese sovereignty. Now, in Mao's view, Zhou was ready to grant the United States power over intelligence-gathering that would com-promise China's independence.

Jiang Qing, sensitive to Mao's moods and always seeking opportunities to criticize Zhou Enlai, saw her moment and launched an attack on Zhou for being too eager to yield to the United States. She called him a capitulation-ist.[80] Mao, who wanted a firmer backbone in China's foreign policy, was ready to allow a vigorous attack on Zhou Enlai.

From November 25 to December 5, 1973, immediately after Kissinger's visit, Mao organized a series of Politburo struggle sessions against Zhou Enlai in the Great Hall of the People. After Lin Biao's death, Mao had taken little interest in the details of daily work, but he micromanaged the criticism of Zhou by selecting who would attend, outlining what they would say, and setting the overall tone of the meetings. In his view Zhou was close to be-ing a rightist capitulationist.[81] All of the Politburo members were required to publicly criticize him. Zhou wrote a detailed self-criticism, but Mao judged it inadequate, demanding that Zhou compose another one that condemned his own actions even more strongly. After the November 1973 meetings, Kissinger was able to visit Zhou, but never again, as Zhou made clear to Kissinger, was he allowed to negotiate with him.

Mao Passes Responsibilities to Deng, December 1973

After Kissinger's November visit, for dealing with the United States Mao turned to the person who had proved absolutely firm in standing up to the Soviet Union: Deng Xiaoping. In December 1973 Deng was directed to at-tend the Politburo meetings to criticize Zhou. Zhou had been like an elder brother to Deng in France, in the underground in Shanghai, and in their work in Beijing in the early 1950s. Yet Mao had reason to hope that Deng would choose to side with him rather than with Zhou. During the rectification campaign of the 1940s, Deng had been on Mao's side while Zhou had not. Deng had bonded with Mao since being accused of leading the Mao clique in 1931, and he had been promoted in the 1950s by Mao. After 1956, when Deng had become general secretary of the party, his relations with Zhou were sometimes awkward regarding party matters: Zhou, who remained senior in rank, had to report to and receive instructions from Deng, who managed daily party affairs.[82] And during the Cultural Revolution, Zhou did not defend Deng.[83]

Deng knew very well that what he said at the meetings to criticize Zhou would be reported to Mao by the two ladies. Near the end of the meetings, Deng said to Zhou, "You are only one step away from the Chairman. Others could hope for such a position, but it would be unattainable; for you it is attainable. I hope you will take this as an adequate warning."[84] On the surface Deng's words may not have seemed vicious, but in the context they were damning. In effect, Deng had implied that there was a danger Zhou might try to upstage Mao and usurp his role. When the two ladies reported Deng's comments to Mao, Mao was thrilled, and immediately invited Deng in for a talk.

Several days later, Mao called a meeting of the Politburo, asking the members to make Deng a full member as well as a member of the CMC. This was the first time in history that Mao had rushed through such an appointment without having it cleared by a plenary session of the Central Committee.[85] Zhou officially remained on as premier, but Deng began attending his meetings with foreign officials. Indeed, although he was still physically able seven months later to take the plane flight and possibly represent China in May 1974 at the United Nations, Mao chose Deng to attend in his stead. And after Zhou entered the hospital on June 1, 1974 for surgery, Deng began hosting the visits with foreign dignitaries.[86]

Firming up the Military, 1971–1974

After Lin Biao's death in the plane crash en route to the Soviet Union, Mao needed to ensure that his military leadership was loyal and united. Before the plane crash, Mao had already taken precautions to firm up support against Lin Biao. In August 1971, for instance, Mao took a personal tour of military bases in central and south China and talked openly of differences with

Lin Biao. He also replaced a number of military leaders, which weakened Lin's base of support.[87] Immediately after the crash, the four military officers on the Politburo—Huang Yongsheng, Wu Faxian, Li Zuopeng, and Qiu Huizuo—were given ten days to declare their distance from Lin. Those who failed to do so were arrested within a matter of days and released in the late 1980s.

Just as Mao turned to Lin Biao in 1959 to unify the military after he had removed Peng Dehuai, so too did he need someone after Lin's death to strengthen the military's central command. Mao turned first to Marshal Ye Jianying, who was widely respected in the military, had no enemies, and, being a decade older than Lin Biao, had no leadership ambitions (see Key People in the Deng Era, p. 740). At the end of 1973, however, when Mao began to rely on Deng Xiaoping to manage U.S. relations with a firmer hand, he turned to Deng to help strengthen control over the military as well.

Not long after the 10th Party Congress, Mao reportedly tested Wang Hongwen and Deng by asking what might happen after his death. Wang replied that the Chairman's revolutionary line would continue. Deng, acutely aware of the power of the commanders in the military regions, said that warlords might emerge and the country might sink into crisis. Mao thought Deng gave the better answer, and by the end of the year the military commanders had been rotated yet again.[88]

Also shortly after the 10th Party Congress, Mao learned that when Lin Biao was still alive, Li Desheng, a military leader who had recently risen to be a party vice chairman, had signed a letter of loyalty to Lin that in Mao's view went further than necessary. It was a great shock to Mao. Fearing that other regional commanders might have been too close to Lin Biao, Mao decided to rotate them; to reduce the risk that they might organize people in their new posts, they were transferred without their staff.

After discovering other letters of loyalty by military leaders to Lin Biao, Mao also became more suspicious of the political leadership in Beijing that had worked with Lin and decided to bring to Beijing new regional officials who had not worked closely with the former "comrade in arms" who proved unfaithful. Because Deng had spent his time in Jiangxi while Lin Biao was at the helm, Mao knew that Deng could not possibly have had close relations with Lin. He also knew that two of the key military leaders—Li Desheng, who was being sent to the Shenyang Military Region, and Chen Xilian, who was brought in to take the most sensitive position, head of the Beijing Military Region—had both served in Deng's Second Field Army. Mao could be confident that Deng would keep them in check.

Soon after the rotation of the regional military commanders, then, Mao announced that a military officer, Deng Xiaoping, would be a member of the Politburo and of the CMC. As Mao put it, "I am thinking of making him secretary general of the Politburo. If you don't like that title, we'll call him chief-of-counsels."[89] Deng, always more concerned about actual authority than titles, politely refused those titles. Mao knew that the senior military officers would be relieved by Deng's appointment, not only because he had military credentials, but also because they knew he would not take part in any vindictive purges. So although Deng had to show his loyalty to Mao by severely criticizing the eight military commanders who had been influenced by Lin, the experienced senior officials knew Deng did this because he was required to do so. After his appointment, it was not entirely clear whether Marshal Ye outranked Deng or Deng outranked Marshal Ye, but each was deferential to the other and they cooperated effectively in working with the regional commanders.

While curbing Lin Biao's influence in the military, Mao also launched a political campaign among the general public to criticize those who had been close to Lin. It was discovered that Lin Biao had written notes in the margins of things he had read, showing he had great respect for Confucius; the campaign against him and someone else accused of being too Confucian, Zhou Enlai, was therefore called "Criticize Lin, criticize Confucius" *(pi-Lin, pi-Kong)*. The campaign began with editorials on January 1, 1974, and continued throughout the first half of 1974. It initially targeted Li Desheng and others in the military who appeared to be too close to Lin Biao. By late January, however, Jiang Qing was using the campaign to criticize Zhou Enlai. In addition to criticizing Lin Biao and Confucius, it took aim at "the duke of Zhou." Zhou was damaged, but he weathered the storm. He continued on as premier and even chaired meetings during which he was being criticized, though he was removed from sensitive negotiations with the United States.

At the end of the campaign in August 1974, Mao the instigator became Mao the magnanimous. He blamed the two ladies for acting like little generals when criticizing Zhou Enlai, and he criticized Jiang Qing for overdoing the criticisms in the campaign to criticize Lin Biao and Confucius. He went as far as to tell Jiang Qing that she should stop attacking people and that she did not represent his views. She was wrong, Mao asserted, to declare that Zhou's problems were so serious as to be called an eleventh-line struggle, and she was wrong to have accused Zhou of being impatient to seize authority.[90]

At a July 17, 1974, Politburo meeting, Mao warned Jiang Qing, Wang Hongwen, Zhang Chunqiao, and Yao Wenyuan that they should not be a "Gang of Four." It was the first time the term was used to describe these four radical members of the Politburo Standing Committee. Although these four had not operated as a tightly organized and well-planned clique, they had played a central role in attacking Zhou.

The name "Gang of Four" would catch on—as would the idea that they were dangerous. As Jiang Qing continued to attack Zhou and senior officials, she and the other three in turn became the target of intellectuals and senior officials who attacked this Gang of Four. It was not yet possible, however, to push back against the one who made it possible for the Gang of Four to launch their attacks, Chairman Mao. Indeed it was only in private conversations that some brave people, with friends they thoroughly trusted, would hold up four fingers and wiggle their thumbs, indicating that it was not just a Gang of Four but there was a fifth as well: Mao Zedong.

While under criticism, Zhou Enlai's cancer continued to advance. On June 1, 1974, he entered the No. 301 Hospital for an operation and remained living there in an attractive suite of rooms for much of the time until his death in January 1976. Zhou was seasoned enough to know that Deng's criticism in late 1973 had been made under pressure from Mao. By early 1974 Zhou and Deng were working together closely on foreign policy issues, with Deng in effect serving as acting premier under the personal guidance of the hospitalized Zhou, who officially kept his post.[91] Deng may have been returned to office by Mao, not by Zhou, but in 1974 and 1975 Zhou and Deng were once again collaborating as closely as they had in France, in the Shanghai underground, and in Beijing before the Cultural Revolution.

Deng knew that Mao wanted him also to work with Jiang Qing, and he tried to do so. But as Zhou became weaker, Jiang Qing began to worry about Mao's willingness to give more responsibilities to Deng and began redirecting her criticisms toward him.[92] Jiang Qing was right that Deng was rising in prominence within the party. The most striking sign of Mao's growing trust in Deng was Deng's selection as the first Chinese leader to make a major presentation at the U.N. General Assembly.

Deng's Historic U.N. Address

In the spring of 1974, Deng was elevated to international prominence when Mao designated him to make the presentation for China at the Sixth Special Session of the U.N. General Assembly. Since 1971, when mainland China had replaced Taiwan in the China seat at the United Nations, no Chinese leader had addressed the General Assembly.

Months earlier it was expected that the maiden speech by a Chinese representative would focus on economic issues. The Ministry of Foreign Trade, not the Ministry of Foreign Affairs, was assigned to prepare the speech for a Chinese leader and Li Qiang, in charge of trade policy, was to make the presentation. Shortly before the event, when it become apparent that the United Nations would focus on China's international relations, responsibility for preparing the speech was handed over to the Ministry of Foreign Affairs.

In making the decision to send Deng to New York, Mao took into consideration that Zhou was too soft to be a reliable representative. Wang Hongwen, with his lack of seasoning, would have been an embarrassment. Above all, Mao wanted a senior leader who would stand up to the United States.

To put his plan into action, Mao, the wire puller, had Wang Hairong and Nancy Tang approach their ministry, the Ministry of Foreign Affairs, to ask that Deng be made head of the delegation to the United Nations. The ministry quickly obliged. Jiang Qing, unaware that Mao had been behind the decision to send Deng to the United Nations, bitterly opposed the selection. She knew that the visit would strengthen Deng's influence at home and abroad and that Deng, whose firm resolve had inspired the nickname the "steel factory," might well place limits on her activities.[93] On March 27, 1974, Mao, who by this time was living apart from Jiang Qing, warned her by letter not to attack Deng's selection because he himself had made it. Except for Jiang Qing, the Politburo unanimously supported the selection of Deng as head of the Chinese delegation.[94]

Mao's decision to send Deng to the United Nations was made at the last minute. Foreign Minister Qiao Guanhua was given scarcely a week to prepare the speech. When Qiao, who was thoroughly familiar with Mao's views, completed a draft of the speech, he sent it to Mao, who wrote, "Good. Approved."[95] Qiao's speech, which Deng read to the United Nations, basically represented Mao's new view of the world as one in which nations were allied not by their commitment to the Communist revolution, but by their economic development: he described them as first-world, second-world, and third-world countries. Against this background, Mao, through Qiao and Deng, described how although he had hoped the United States would join China to oppose the Soviet Union, recent setbacks—notably, the Brezhnev visit to Washington—convinced him that the United States and the Soviet Union were scheming together. Mao was now hoping to unite the developed countries of the second world and the developing countries of the third world against the two superpowers.

Officially, Foreign Minister Qiao, the sophisticated, knowledgeable diplomat whose family was rich enough to have supported his university training in philosophy in Germany, was head of the delegation. Knowledgeable people at home and abroad, however, understood that Deng held the real power. Chinese leaders saw the trip to the United Nations as a major breakthrough, a coming-out party in the council of nations. Though ill, Zhou Enlai and an estimated two thousand others went to the airport to send off the delegation. Zhou also joined the large crowd at the airport that welcomed the delegation back on April 6.[96]

Deng's speech to the United Nations was received with an unusually long period of applause. Because of its size and potential, China was seen as a rallying force among the developing countries. The delegates of the developing countries were especially pleased with Deng's statement that China would never become a tyrant and that if it were to ever oppress or exploit others, then the rest of the world, especially the developing countries, should expose China as a "social imperialist" country and, in cooperation with the Chinese people, overthrow the government.

While at the United Nations, Deng held side meetings with leaders from various countries. He was cautious in answering questions and making comments because he had witnessed Mao's severe criticism of Zhou and he had had only a week to prepare for the visit. Instead, he referred the difficult questions to Foreign Minister Qiao Guanhua. Personally, Deng was well received by other foreign leaders and by the foreign press.[97] Since the basic ideas in his speech about the third world came from Mao and because Americans were not happy to be linked with the Soviets, the speech is not among Deng's speeches included in his *Selected Works*.[98]

In New York, Deng and Kissinger met for the first time a few days after the speech. At their initial meeting, Kissinger was somewhat taken aback by Deng's direct, blunt style. Deng was courteous but he had a tough message from Mao: knowing how Zhou Enlai had been criticized for being soft on the United States, he ensured he would not be made vulnerable to such charges. Deng conveyed Mao's displeasure at the United States for standing on China's shoulders to reach détente with the Soviet Union through agreements on missile control. He also repeated Mao's view that the Soviet Union's strategy was to "feint toward the East" in order to strike the West, that is, that the United States should be on its guard against the Soviet Union. The Soviet Union, Deng told Kissinger, was then anti-Chinese but its real target was the West.[99] Deng also expressed the fear that the United States no longer regarded the Soviets as its key adversary and might encourage China to fight the Soviet Union, thereby weakening both socialist adversaries.[100] Kissinger later compared Deng's direct style with the subtle, polished, and urbane manner of Zhou Enlai. Noting Deng's unfamiliarity with some of the global issues raised in the discussion, his frequent references to Mao, and his passing questions on to Qiao Guanhua, Kissinger said that Deng seemed to be on a "training mission." Deng's cautious manner in 1974 was to be in striking contrast to his confidence in meetings with foreigners beginning in mid-1978 after he was more experienced in meeting foreign leaders and Mao was no longer alive to receive reports of Deng's comments.

Kissinger also observed that compared to Mao and Zhou, who sought to improve relations with the United States primarily for security reasons, Deng focused on domestic developments and was already thinking about what improved relations with the United States could do for China's modernization.[101] Kissinger later came to have high regard for Deng's abilities in representing China.[102]

Zhou's name was never mentioned by any member of the Chinese delegation to the United Nations. In fact, several friendly references from Kissinger to Deng concerning Zhou went unacknowledged. When Deng said that Confucius was conservative and that to emancipate people's thinking, Confucius needed to be criticized, Kissinger asked if that view had any practical relevance for contemporary individuals. Deng replied that criticism of a conservative ideology does in fact have implications for those individuals who represent those ideologies.[103] The message, though indirect, was loud and clear. Deng was not assisting Zhou but replacing him.[104]

On Sunday, when Deng's schedule in New York allowed some free time, his staff inquired what he would like to do. Without hesitation, Deng said, "Visit Wall Street." To Deng, Wall Street was the symbol not only of American capitalism but also of American economic might. Deng had an instinct for finding the source of real power and wanting to understand it. Although Wall Street was closed on Sundays, Deng still had his staff take him there, so at least he could get an impression of the place.[105] Deng was allotted only a few dollars to spend on the trip, and his personal office director, Wang Ruilin, was sent off to buy some thirty-nine-cent toys at Woolworth's for Deng's grandchildren. Tang Minzhao, Nancy Tang's father (who was also the editor of a leftist Chinese-language newspaper in New York), with his own funds purchased for Deng a doll that could cry, suck, and pee. When Deng took it home, it was a great hit.[106]

Deng flew home from New York by way of Paris, where he stayed several days in the Chinese embassy. It was his first visit to France since leaving there in 1926. While there, he enjoyed coffee and croissants, as he had half a century earlier. For security reasons, he was not allowed to walk around the city. His staff tried to locate the places where he had lived, but they found no trace. Before flying home Deng bought two hundred croissants and some cheese, which, upon his return, he divided up and distributed to Zhou Enlai, Deng Yingchao (Zhou Enlai's wife), Li Fuchun, Nie Rongzhen, and other fellow revolutionaries who had been with him in France in the 1920s.

Mao considered Deng's visit to the United Nations a great success and continued to assign him the major role in welcoming foreign visitors. Mao allowed Wang Hongwen to sit in on meetings with foreign visitors, but he did not participate actively in the discussions. In fact, before 1973, Wang had never met any foreigners.[107]

On June 1, only a few weeks after Deng's speech at the United Nations in New York, Zhou Enlai entered the hospital for another operation and stopped meeting foreigners. At this point Deng met most of his foreign visitors in one of the provincial rooms in the Great Hall of the People, and they were housed in the gracious Diaoyutai guest facilities. Like Zhou, he entertained guests in a style that had caused Kissinger to comment, only half-jokingly, "I come from a country undeveloped in hospitality."

In the fall of 1974, Deng met with officials from all major continents, including from countries as diverse as Japan, Pakistan, Iran, Yemen, Congo, Romania, Yugoslavia, Vietnam, North Korea, Turkey, Germany, France, Canada, and the United States. The meetings included political leaders, business leaders, journalists, scientists, and athletes. Certain themes came up repeatedly in his discussions. In particular, he was interested in how Japanese leaders had led Japan's economic development and how Japan had modernized its science and technology.

With some foreign leaders, Deng engaged in broad discussions on world affairs, especially in the context of the competition between the Soviet Union and the United States. He strongly approved of efforts by the European countries to strengthen cooperation with each other and with the United States, which he saw as a bulwark against the Soviet Union, and he expressed skepticism about the ability to contain Soviet military growth by arms control agreements. He encouraged Turkey to resolve its problems with Greece, to avoid letting the "big fishermen," the Soviet Union and the United States, take advantage of the conflict between the fish. He explained that China had difficulties with the Soviet Union because Khrushchev had tried to exert too much control over China. He also made clear to U.S. businesspeople that economic exchanges could progress more rapidly with formal diplomatic relations, and that in turn would depend on the United States ending its formal relations with Taiwan.

The Americans he met included George H. W. Bush, then head of the U.S. Liaison Office in China; Senators Mike Mansfield and Henry Jackson; and a delegation of university presidents.[108] He exchanged views with Mansfield and Jackson, kindred souls, on how to resist Soviet advances. When he met the university presidents, he told them that scholarly exchanges would continue and increase.[109]

Mao Calls for Stability and Unity

Mao was a bold revolutionary who could ignore realities in the short run, but even he could not be impervious to serious problems forever. He had overpowered resistance to the Great Leap Forward, but in late 1958 and again after 1960, he had allowed some adjustments to deal with the disaster. By 1974, the chaos from the Cultural Revolution was so widespread that even he realized that something needed to be done. The economy was not really moving ahead and by mid-1974 reports were coming in that the campaign to criticize Lin Biao and Confucius had created even further disorder. Steel production had declined, and railway transport was down. Mao, thinking about his legacy, did not want to be remembered as the one who left the economy in a disastrous state.

In August 1974 Mao called the regional military commanders and the heads of their political departments to his residence in Wuhan's Donghu Meiling (East Lake in the Plum Mountain Range), one of his favorite locations. He told them that "The Great Proletarian Cultural Revolution has already gone on for eight years. Now it is time for stability. The whole party and the whole army should now unite."[110] Mao was mercurial, but in late

1974 he consistently supported the need for unity and stability. When he met Zhou Enlai in December 1974, Mao approved the use of the expression "stability and unity" *(anding tuanjie)* as a keynote for the Second Plenum that was to be held January 8–10, 1975.

The Implementer and the Watchdog Clash

By late 1974, it was becoming clear that Mao wanted Deng to play a major role in restoring stability and unity.[111] On October 4, 1974, Mao announced that he was appointing Deng Xiaoping first vice premier of the State Council. The appointment reflected Mao's satisfaction with Deng's performance; it was the first clear indication to party leaders that Mao intended for Deng to take over Zhou's responsibilities as premier.

Mao's decision to wind down the turmoil of the Cultural Revolution and appoint Deng to bring stability and unity was as disturbing to Jiang Qing and her radicals as it was exhilarating to pragmatic senior officials. Mao asked Wang Hongwen, as head of daily party work, to announce the appointment, but Wang stalled long enough to convey the news to Jiang Qing, which gave her time to prepare a response. Other high-level political leaders knew that Jiang Qing and Wang Hongwen were promoting Zhang Chunqiao for the position. But Jiang Qing was unsuccessful in her attempt to persuade Mao to change his mind about Deng's appointment. Two days later, after delaying the announcement more than he should have, Wang had no choice but to follow Mao's order and announce Deng's promotion.[112]

Even though Mao had sent Jiang Qing off to live separately, until the end his life he regarded her as faithful to his cause of promoting the revolution and the only one both tough and determined enough to stand up to other high-level party officials, including the most resolute of them all, Deng Xiaoping. Yet Mao was upset at signs that she was scheming to seize power after his death. As recently as 1972, he had been unhappy that she had spent a week talking with an American scholar, Roxane Witke, who was planning to publish a book about her (just as Mao had talked to Edgar Snow to publicize his personal rise to power).[113]

The issue of Deng's promotion further soured their relationship. In her later recollections, Jiang Qing said that when Deng first returned in the spring of 1973, the problems between Mao and herself were not as serious as they later would become. This may have been due in part to Mao: in mid-

1974 as Mao sought to restore unity and stability, he told Jiang Qing to calm down and Wang Hongwen not to pay so much attention to her.

Two weeks after Deng was formally named vice premier, Jiang Qing, always on the lookout for ways to arouse Mao's suspicions of Deng, chanced upon a newspaper article that praised the Chinese-built ship the *Fengqinglun*. At this point, Deng, eager to increase foreign trade, had supported the Ministry of Transportation's conclusion that China was not yet up to producing large transport ships and that in the short run, to increase trade, it was necessary to purchase foreign vessels. Jiang Qing, drawing on the newspaper article she read, wrote comments to praise the 10,000-ton *Fengqinglun* and to protest that Zhou Enlai and Deng were wasting the country's money buying foreign ships. Further, she declared that Deng's interest in buying the foreign ships showed that he, as well as officials in the Ministry of Transportation, had a comprador mentality and worshipped things foreign. Domestic vessels, she wrote, are just as good: "We can build even 10,000-ton ships like the *Fengqinglun*."[114]

The next volley came at a Politburo meeting on October 17, when Jiang Qing again attacked Deng, this time verbally, for supporting the purchase of foreign ships, and for being a slave to the West. China, she repeated, could produce its own excellent ships. Deng was ordinarily able to keep his cool, but under Jiang Qing's continued attacks, he lost it. Deng, who was then also angry at Jiang Qing for trying to promote her ally Yang Chengwu to be chief of staff, replied angrily that when he had traveled abroad a half-century earlier, he had traveled on a 40,000-ton ship made in the West and that even then a ship of that size was not unusual. In short, China was far behind in shipping and Jiang Qing was out of touch. After Deng exploded, at Li Xiannian's urging, he left the room, red-faced with anger.[115] Deng later confessed to Zhou Enlai that Jiang Qing had attacked him seven or eight times during Politburo meetings and he could no longer stand it.[116]

The day after Deng's October 17 outburst at the Politburo meeting, Wang Hongwen, on behalf of the Politburo, flew to Changsha. Echoing Jiang Qing's comments, he tried to raise doubts in Mao's mind about Deng's abilities to play such an important leadership role. The meeting, however, only increased Mao's doubts about whether Wang was the best person for his job.[117] Two days later, on October 20, when Mao met Danish prime minister Poul Hartling in Changsha, Deng Xiaoping was invited to join the reception.

By this time, the two ladies, Wang Hairong and Tang Wensheng, had briefed Mao on the confrontation between Jiang Qiang and Deng Xiaoping in Beijing. Mao was furious at Jiang Qing, who was clearly continuing to carry on political attacks when he wanted her to quiet down.[118] During the next month Mao criticized Jiang for interfering, for criticizing government documents (like the decision to buy foreign ships), for issuing documents without consultation, and for trying to form her own leadership team against the wishes of the majority. Alluding to characters in a play by Xi Xiangji, Mao told Jiang to act like a kind old lady, not a scheming matchmaker. Mao did not dismiss her. She had proved to be a determined ally in attacking whomever Mao wanted to be attacked, and he might again need those skills. At least for the moment, however, as he began to prepare for the forthcoming 4th National People's Congress, he held her back while encouraging Deng to take on a greater role.[119]

3

Bringing Order under Mao

1974–1975

In December 1974, Zhou Enlai left his hospital bed and flew to Changsha to meet Mao. The two men were convening to decide on appointments for the key leadership positions in Beijing, and because they knew that neither had long to live, their work had great urgency. Following a major cancer operation on June 1, Zhou Enlai was so frail he could not carry on his daily work, and his plane carrying him to Changsha was like a small hospital, with doctors on board.[1] Mao, suffering from heart trouble and from amyotrophic lateral sclerosis (ALS, also known as Lou Gehrig's disease), had been told that he had less than two years to live. His eyesight had deteriorated and his slurred speech was difficult to understand. But despite their health problems, both of the leaders' minds remained clear. Mao and Zhou, despite their differences, shared a commitment to choosing leaders for the party and the government who would continue their life's work.

In Changsha they were joined by Wang Hongwen, then thirty-nine, who was in charge of the daily work of the party. Although it was not formally stated, the expectation was that if those whom they selected performed well, they would continue to serve after Mao and Zhou had left the scene. The party appointments they decided on were to be officially approved at the Second Plenum, scheduled for January 8–10, 1975, and the government appointments were to be officially approved at the National People's Congress (NPC) that would be held immediately thereafter. Zhou's physical condition prevented him from long daily sessions, so the three stretched their meetings out over five days, with ample time for rest. They met daily from December 23 to December 27, except on December 26, Mao's eighty-first birthday, when Mao and Zhou met alone.

In preparation for the meetings in Changsha, Zhou had consulted with government leaders for several weeks, winnowing down the list of names of those they considered best for the top positions. After Zhou and his staff worked through three drafts of the list of proposed appointments and the agenda for the NPC, the final versions, which were forwarded to Mao a few days before their meetings, became the basis for discussion.

Mao, though aged and infirm, still possessed the power to shake up the country. In December 1974, however, his top priority was stability and unity. His sharp attacks on Zhou during the campaign to criticize Lin Biao and Confucius had ended, and the two towering leaders now worked together as before.[2] In their meetings, Mao expressed his continued dedication to the revolution, but in fact he approved the selection of experienced officials whom Zhou and his underlings in Beijing considered most able to lead the government and guide the economy.[3] Buoyed by Mao's support for high officials who would provide a more stable political environment—one that would promote orderly economic growth—Zhou Enlai returned to Beijing exhausted, but exhilarated.

The Mao-Zhou Succession Plan, December 1974

Before Mao and Zhou met, it was already assumed that Wang Hongwen would remain as first vice chairman of the party. They also agreed that major responsibility for leading government work would officially be assigned to Deng Xiaoping. Deng had capably filled in for Zhou after his June 1 operation, and Mao announced his support for Deng to be the first vice premier in October. At the NPC meeting, it would become official. In addition to his major responsibility for leading the government, Deng was to be promoted to high positions in both the party and the military.

Wang Hongwen and Deng Xiaoping would formally carry on the work as top leaders in the party and government, but they remained in effect apprentices to Mao and Zhou, who retained the titles of chairman and premier until their deaths. Wang and Deng would continue to receive directions from the two senior leaders, and Mao retained the power to replace them at any time if he was dissatisfied with their performance.

On January 5, 1975, then, Central Committee Document No. 1, the first document of the year, listed Mao as chairman of the party and the Central Military Commission (CMC) and named Deng as vice chairman of the CMC and chief of the General Staff. At the Second Plenum of the 10th

Party Congress, held January 8–10, Wang Hongwen was confirmed as the first vice chairman of the party Central Committee (ranked after Mao and Zhou), and Deng was named a vice chairman of the party Central Committee and a member of the Standing Committee of the Politburo. And at the NPC meeting, held January 13–17, 1975, Deng officially became first vice premier.

To Mao, the team of Wang and Deng was a promising combination. Wang, a former rebel leader completely beholden to Mao and with no independent power base, could be counted on to lead the party along Mao's revolutionary path and would display ample respect for Mao's personal legacy. Deng, meanwhile, with his wide knowledge, experience, and proven leadership abilities, would direct foreign affairs and the complex work of the government.

Anyone who knew Wang and Deng realized that Wang, with so little experience in high positions, would in fact wield far less power than Deng, who had mastered the workings of the party and government during his ten years as general secretary and who was not bashful in exercising power. But by placing Wang Hongwen in the higher position, and by giving responsibility for propaganda to the radicals, led by Jiang Qing, whatever tendencies Deng might have had to depart from Mao's legacy (like those he had displayed in the early 1960s) could be kept under control. Mao had criticized Jiang Qing for her excesses and her ambition, but he knew that she was tough and thoroughly reliable in supporting his propaganda line.[4] Furthermore the radicals, under Jiang Qing and with the help of Yao Wenyuan, took charge of the party newspaper, the *People's Daily,* and its theoretical journal, *Red Flag,* while Zhang Chunqiao, also a radical, took charge of the Political Department of the People's Liberation Army.[5]

Zhou's Farewell, January 1975

On January 13, 1975, when the NPC convened for its first meeting since January 1965, Mao remained in Changsha. Zhou, drawn and pale from late-stage cancer, in his last major public appearance, presented the government's work report. Behind the scenes, Deng had supervised preparation of Zhou's speech. So as not to exhaust Zhou, Deng had told the drafters to keep it to fewer than five thousand characters, much shorter than a typical work report. Deng, acutely aware of Mao's remaining power and determination, filled the report with Cultural Revolution rhetoric. In the speech, Zhou praised the Cultural Revolution and its models, Dazhai and Daqing, and said, at one point, "Our primary task is to deepen, broaden, and persevere in the movement to criticize Lin Biao and Confucius"—a moment that must have struck the audience as especially poignant because Zhou himself was one of the main targets in that campaign.[6]

When he finished speaking, the NPC members, many of whom had been tearful during Zhou's painful performance, gave him a standing ovation for several minutes. This emotional response showed their respect for a dying leader who had dedicated his life to the party and the country, who had served with such distinction and had protected so many of them during the Cultural Revolution, but yet had suffered unfairly at the hands of Mao. Looking forward, many hoped that the devastation of the Cultural Revolution would soon be over, and that the country could finally take on the task that Zhou had first enunciated eleven years earlier and again spelled out in his report—achieving the four modernizations (of agriculture, industry, national defense, and science and technology) by the end of the century.[7]

On February 1, 1975, at a smaller meeting of leaders of the various ministries and commissions associated with the State Council, Zhou explained that in the future he would no longer attend their meetings. "The Chairman directed that the first vice premier is Deng Xiaoping. The Chairman said that Deng is an able person with a strong political ideology and a rare talent. . . . I cannot ordinarily take part in these meetings. In the future, I asked Deng Xiaoping to chair such meetings." In fact, for almost a year, beginning with his trip to the U.N. meetings in May 1974, Deng had been hosting foreign visitors and performing other duties as a substitute for Zhou Enlai, but in February 1975 authority was firmly passed to Deng, allowing him to take full charge as long as Mao was not too upset. Deng, respectful of Zhou, often visited Zhou in the hospital and explained with appropriate modesty that he was helping the premier because of his illness.[8] In fact, Deng had taken charge.

Consolidating Party Leadership Teams

For Deng, the issue in 1975 was how to retain Mao's support while restoring order and setting China on a path for growth. To help himself stay on Mao's good side, Deng paid great attention to his favorite themes. He repeatedly praised Marxism-Leninism and Mao Zedong Thought and avoided criticism of the Cultural Revolution. In early 1975, too, Deng creatively combined several of Mao's expressions to support his own agenda. The "three direc- tives," which Mao himself had never linked, were first presented together in a speech Deng gave on May 29, 1975. They were, first, to oppose revisionism; second, to promote stability and unity; and third, to improve the national economy.[9] The inclusion of the first statement, about revisionism, provided public reassurance to Mao that Deng was determined not to follow the bour- geois path for which he had been criticized during the Cultural Revolution. But it was also meant as sugar for helping the medicine go down. For by em- phasizing in the same breath Mao's support for stability and unity, and for improving the national economy, Deng made it difficult for Mao to oppose the rather dramatic steps he was taking to both stabilize and reinvigorate a China weary from the excesses of the Cultural Revolution.

With Mao's "three directives" as cover, warrior Deng, boldly swinging his broad sword and axe *(dadao kuofu)*, set out to eliminate chaos and to put the country on a path to modernization. The problems he faced were monu- mental. Like leaders of other countries after a civil war, he had to unite the perpetrators and victims of the Cultural Revolution. Meanwhile, the Chinese economy was stagnant, planning was in disorder, and statistical reports were unreliable. Agricultural production was not enough to feed the population, let alone produce industrial crops like cotton and flax. Transportation sys- tems had broken down, keeping resources in one locality from reaching the industrial producers in other localities. The military, overstretched from the countless political struggles and its limitless responsibilities running civilian work units throughout the country, had neglected training and fallen far be- hind possible adversaries in terms of military technology: China simply was not prepared for armed conflict. And because Chinese intellectuals had been decimated during the Cultural Revolution, virtually no technical specialists had been trained for an entire decade. Deng thus lacked the trained man- power needed to guide the work on the four modernizations.

Since 1941, Mao had used "rectification" *(zhengfeng)* campaigns to bring unity to the Communist Party. The campaigns were a powerful weapon for attacking those who were not sufficiently committed to Mao's personal leadership and what he stood for. During lengthy inquisitions, the victims were required to give detailed protestations of loyalty that would convince colleagues of their sincerity. Psychological pressures on those being criticized were enormous, and the results were ugly: some were killed or sent to engage in physical labor, and others, unable to stand the intense pressure, committed suicide. The discipline gained through such rectification during the 1940s and early 1950s had been critical for enabling the Communists to defeat the Guomindang during the civil war and unify the country. The rectification campaigns after 1956, however, were so severe that they had alienated many intellectuals and party members who previously had been loyal.

The term Deng used in 1975 to describe his efforts to achieve unity was *zhengdun* (consolidation), a term long used in the Chinese Communist military that Zhou Enlai had adapted in 1972 to describe an initiative similar to Deng's. Among soldiers, *zhengdun* described how after a battle or a campaign, the surviving troops in various units would regroup to prepare for the next battle. A key part of regrouping was identifying and empowering a new leadership team in each unit, to replace those who had been injured or killed. During consolidation, errors in the previous battles were criticized but the main focus was on rebuilding the supply lines and reorganizing the leadership to face the next battle.

In 1975, in carrying out consolidation, it was not easy to prevent lower-level officials from reverting to the more vicious attacks they had come to know during the rectification campaigns—especially when they found opportunities to settle accounts with those who had earlier destroyed their friends and relatives. Deng sought to end the cycle of retribution in political campaigns of the previous twenty-five years; he continued to reiterate that the purpose was not to settle old scores but to regroup to prepare for a new round of challenges.

The key to organizing an effective national government, Deng believed, was not changing laws and rules but locating and empowering a team of leaders in every administrative unit. To provide capable direction based on good grassroots information, it was essential that, at each level, officials would choose able and reliable leaders for the next level below. In Deng's view, for organizational reliability, a team of leaders was better than a single leader, no matter how able. Something might happen to one leader, but if there were a small team, then others would be ready to take over if problems arose. Ideally, these leadership team members would not only be able to provide overall leadership when needed but would also develop specialized knowledge in the areas to which they were assigned—for example, industry, culture, or political-legal work. In larger units as many as seven or eight leaders might constitute the team, in smaller units perhaps only two or three. The leaders would be given great leeway in how they went about their work as long as they met the goals set by the next higher-level units.

During his work in 1975, Deng made identifying team leaders in units throughout the country a top priority. Until October 1975, Deng enjoyed Mao's full support in this effort, which at times included clamping down on former revolutionaries and replacing them with experienced officials who had been attacked during the early years of the Cultural Revolution. In late 1974 and 1975, Mao supported the rehabilitation of more than six hundred leading senior officials.

Taking a long-term view, in late 1975 Deng began to improve the educational system so that at some point in the future, new officials would be chosen based on their knowledge and ability to manage, not just on whom they knew. By necessity, this was a distant dream. The system Deng inherited in 1975 was in shambles and many of the most able officials had not had any opportunity to study. Their experiences were so varied that even standardized tests could not be useful. It would take another decade before schools and universities would produce enough graduates so that one's level of education could be a useful criterion for selecting team leaders, even for mid-level units. Instead, for many years the government had to continue to rely primarily on personal evaluations for the selection of officials.

For the official chosen or not chosen, the stakes were high. Those chosen received not only employment but also perquisites and honor, as well as improved job prospects and the possibility of better housing and education for their families. Moreover, given the divisive legacy of the Cultural Revolution, the process of selecting team officials was contentious. To make the system more meritocratic, Deng would have to start at the top with proven senior officials who would choose team leaders, who in turn would pick those at the next level down, all the way down to the lowest levels. Deng began his consolidation with the military.[10]

Consolidating the Military

When he was named chief of the General Staff, Deng wasted no time in getting to work on what he considered the most important steps toward consolidation in the PLA: restoring discipline, downsizing, improving training, and establishing a new team of leaders in each unit. On January 25, 1975, with Mao's full support, Deng called together officials at the regimental level and above. Former political commissar Deng did not mince words as he spelled out what was wrong with the military. The PLA had become overextended as it took on civilian functions during the Cultural Revolution. In addition, many officials had become "bloated, disorganized, arrogant, extravagant, and lazy" *(zhong, san, jiao, she, duo)*. A lack of discipline at the top, Deng said, had resulted in factionalism. Officers had become arrogant because of their power over civilians during the Cultural Revolution and many used this power to enjoy luxurious housing, expensive banquets, and lavish entertainment, as well as to shower extravagant gifts on their friends. High officials had become lazy in attending to the problems at lower levels, lax in carrying out orders, and reluctant to undertake bold initiatives.[11] Consequently, the military, despite its huge size, was in a poor position to defend the country. Many military units behaved like the groups of guerrillas on separate mountaintops during the anti-Japanese struggle.[12]

Deng, the "steel factory," made it clear how he would treat those who disobeyed orders to end factionalism: "People guilty of factionalism," he said, "will all be transferred out. We won't leave a single officer or enlisted man." This threat, he made clear, included people at the very top. He vowed to "carry it out no matter how many would be involved. . . . We are the PLA. Our job is to fight."[13] Many still involved in factionalism had taken part in Red Guard and revolutionary rebel activity, but he did not attack them for having taken part in those organizations in the past. The important thing was what they were doing now. Whatever the past battles, all those who were ready to work with their new leaders were welcome.

Fortunately for Deng and Marshal Ye, their effort to restore discipline and plain living in the military was supported by a solid majority of the eleven members on the Standing Committee of the CMC. The CMC, officially restored on February 5, 1975, provided leadership over the daily work of military affairs. The radicals on the Standing Committee (Wang Dongxing, Wang Hongwen, and Zhang Chunqiao) were completely outnumbered by the supporters of Deng and Marshal Ye.

With the support of the Standing Committee and with Mao's approval, the two leaders continued to bring back many of the 25,000 former military officers whom Deng said had been falsely accused during the Lin Biao period. Deng directed that those people wrongly accused should be allowed to return to work and receive necessary medical treatment. Investigations, he said, should be carried out quickly and without publicity.[14]

Before he took on his new responsibilities, Deng had clearly been thinking about what it would take to modernize the military. On January 14, 1975, after scarcely a week in his new position, Deng directed his staff to begin working on five- and ten-year visions for upgrading military equipment and munitions.[15] The conceptual plans would address repairing and upgrading old equipment and manufacturing missing parts, areas badly neglected during the Cultural Revolution, as well as the development of missiles and other modern equipment.[16]

Like Mao, Deng bristled as he talked about the growing threat of the Soviet Union after the United States pulled out of Vietnam. He worried about the loss of public support in the United States for remaining firm against the Soviets. He worried that President Ford, who had replaced President Nixon in August 1974, lacked Nixon's deep understanding of strategic issues and his sure-footed readiness to respond to any new Soviet threat. Because the United States would not press the Soviet Union, the Soviets were left free to advance in Asia, where a million Soviet troops were already stationed not far from the Chinese border.

Knowing that the United States was the only power capable of pressuring the Soviet Union on a broad scale, Deng, in all his meetings with American officials, pressed them to take a stronger stance against the Soviets. Mao did not need to worry that Deng would be as soft as Zhou Enlai in dealing with the United States. When Deng met Kissinger in April and November 1974, he not only called attention to the Soviet Union's aggressive actions, but kept needling Kissinger for being too timid in responding to the Soviet threat.[17] In fact, Deng instructed his foreign ministry officials, particularly Foreign Minister Huang Hua, to complain to the Americans at every meeting that the United States was not standing firm enough against the Soviet Union.

The military issue that occupied most of Deng's time in 1975 was downsizing. The huge size of the military strained the budget; more than six million people were serving in the military, over 20 percent more than in 1966.[18] China needed to reduce the number of less-educated senior officers and train a new, better-educated generation of leaders to handle modern technologies. Downsizing was a critical first step for the long-range development of a modern sustainable military. But Deng knew he could not undertake a disruptive downsizing if war were imminent. Although Mao had said that war was inevitable, and Deng did not yet challenge this view, Deng did say that China could reduce the risk of a conflict occurring over the next several years.[19]

No military issue aroused more serious resistance than downsizing, and a leader without Deng's military stature and toughness would have found the task nearly impossible. Every year, many soldiers who completed their terms in the military were unable to find civilian jobs. New market opportunities were not yet available and the government budget was limited. Placement services were in shambles, too, causing groups of discharged veterans to protest that they had not been given appropriate work assignments.

The essence of Deng's approach to downsizing was to develop new tables of organization that reduced the targeted number of soldiers to be allotted to the various units throughout the military. As early as January 14, 1975, at a forum of officials from the General Staff Department, Deng announced that new tables of organization were to be drawn up. When the new tables of organization were completed, the air force and navy did not lose slots, but the army did. In addition, the number of positions for technical specialists was not reduced. In some locations troop numbers could be substantially reduced but in sensitive regions like Xinjiang, the targeted number of soldiers was increased.[20] After the new tables were completed, the units were responsible for managing the concrete reductions within their units, selecting who was to be retained and who was to be discharged.[21] As always when dealing with controversial issues, Deng not only issued directives but also presented his rationale: he explained that with a limited national budget, the only way China could find money to invest in modern weapon systems was to cut personnel costs. Even those who worried that they themselves might be retired found it difficult to disagree with Deng's logic.

Deng tried to reduce the resistance to downsizing by strengthening the effort to find work for those who would be pushed to retire. Positions in local party or government units or state enterprises were sought for the retiring senior officers. Ordinary soldiers, meanwhile, were to be assigned primarily to the countryside as commune officials, with some transferred to factories.[22] Government officials were assigned responsibility for finding jobs for veterans within their respective localities.

Deng used an enlarged CMC meeting—held June 24 to July 15, 1975 after a four-year postponement due to Lin Biao's defection—to seek support for his downsizing plan. Some officers made special appeals to avoid reductions in their sectors, but few changes were made.[23] The meeting set the target of reducing military positions by 1.6 million, including by some 600,000 officers, within three years.[24]

Once the new organization tables had been drawn up, the military began selecting the leadership teams at each level. Deng set the tone for what this new leadership should look like, saying that the selected officers should be able to use new technologies to improve both their conventional equipment and their advanced weapons, as well as to conduct scientific analyses to enhance their command and administrative skills. Additional training and maneuvers were needed to enhance the quality of officers and to help them develop strategies appropriate to future conditions. Able political officers who could respond to the personal concerns of their troops and improve relations with the public were also needed.[25] Although China's weapons were badly outdated and few funds were available, Deng wanted to make the best use of the funds they had. From July 20 to August 4—that is, immediately after the enlarged CMC meeting—leading officials from more than four hundred major defense industry factories met to review their responsibilities in line with the new priorities for upgrading technologies.[26]

A few weeks after the enlarged CMC meeting, the new membership of the CMC was announced. Mao still allowed the radicals to dominate propaganda work. Zhang Chunqiao, the most experienced official among the Gang of Four, was head of the General Political Department of the PLA. But Deng remained chief of the General Staff, Marshal Ye retained leadership of the CMC, and most of the Standing Committee members of the CMC were experienced military officials who could work with Deng and Ye: Nie Rongzhen, Su Yu, Chen Xilian, and Liang Biye.

Deng and his allies were effective in controlling the radicals. During the enlarged CMC meeting, the highest-ranking radicals, Wang Hongwen and Zhang Chunqiao, made no public presentations. The Gang of Four tried but failed to gain control of personnel appointments and to obtain dossiers they could later use to attack their opponents. Zhang Chunqiao had leverage over propaganda, but he never controlled the personnel decisions. And Deng and Marshal Ye, who enjoyed far more support in the military than Zhang, determined the agenda and played the major role in guiding appointments at the lower levels.[27]

Deng also revived military training programs. Most of the 101 training institutions that existed in 1966 had been closed down during the Cultural Revolution. Some were in such bad shape that they were not fit to reopen. At others, however, the faculty, although no longer teaching, had remained living in the school compounds. Now experienced faculty members still able to teach were invited to revise their teaching materials and reopen their classrooms.

Compared to the schools, the high-level military technology research centers had been protected during the Cultural Revolution. (Even some civilian research centers had been protected by being placed under the National De-fense Technology Commission.) But without support from universities and new graduates, without civilian research centers to provide related support, and without access to foreign technology, Chinese military technologies had fallen farther behind those used by their potential adversaries. The research centers needed revamping, and by 1975 Marshal Ye had persuaded Zhang Aiping, an able high general experienced in organizing military research, to return from the sidelines and help in this effort.

In two research and development centers, factionalism was so serious as to require special attention—the No. 2 Ministry of Machine Building, which focused on nuclear development, and the No. 7 Ministry of Machine Build-ing, which was devoted to ballistic missile technologies. In 1974, three at-tempts to fire intercontinental ballistic missiles (ICBMs) had all failed. The failures made it easy to win political support to criticize the current leader-ship of those ministries, but support for the radicals was not dead.[28] Followers of the Gang of Four, still active in a factory under one of these ministries, put up posters denouncing Zhang Aiping for his emphasis on production.

On May 19, the day after Deng returned from his state visit to France, Deng joined Nie Rongzhen, China's leading official concerned with military technology (and one of Deng's comrades since their days in France in the 1920s), at a meeting at the No. 7 Ministry of Machine Building. In his speech, Deng, with steely resolve, said that the government would no longer tolerate factionalism. Leaders had until June 30 to eliminate all factions; by July 1 everyone should be working together. If not, the government would not be polite: punishments would be meted out.

With approval from Mao and Zhou Enlai, Deng and Marshal Ye saw that the two troubled ministries carried out consolidation, eliminating workers still taking part in factions and setting up a new leadership team to organize research.[29] During the last quarter of 1975 and into 1976, as part of the downsizing, some 464,000 positions were officially removed from the orga-nization tables. No one was surprised when some people in those positions found ways to continue working in their jobs. But Marshal Ye and Deng did all they could to see that their plans for downsizing were implemented and that new leadership teams were selected that would be able, when the time came, to incorporate modern technologies into their departments and groups.[30]

In short, Deng and Marshal Ye, with the support of Chairman Mao and a solid majority on the CMC, were able in 1975 to make considerable progress in restoring discipline, downsizing, and paving the way for improving the education and technical levels of their troops.

Strategic Civilian Consolidation: Xuzhou Railway Center

For his civilian breakthrough in consolidation, Deng chose to focus on a project that would quickly both increase production and inspire others. Ever since his guerrilla days, he had believed in fighting small battles that he was sure to win, as a way of encouraging his troops as they prepared for larger battles. In 1975, many of the factories criticized for failing to meet production targets complained that they lacked adequate supplies. Transportation was an obvious bottleneck. Could a success in transportation provide an early victory that would both increase production and demonstrate possibilities for success in other areas?

In the mid-1970s, China lacked a modern highway system, so goods overwhelmingly were transported by rail. In his quest to improve transportation, then, Deng chose to focus his attention on Xuzhou, a railway junction in northwest Jiangsu, where a major east-west railway, the Long-Hai, crossed a major north-south railway, the Jin-Pu. During the twenty-one months prior to March 1975, the Xuzhou Railway Bureau had never once met its quota for loading or dispatching railway cars. Since January 1967, there had been almost continuous fighting there between rebel factions.

The situation in 1975 looked both ugly and entrenched. Gu Binghua, a rebel leader who headed the Xuzhou Railway Bureau, had access to arms and stubbornly resisted outside attempts at control. Since 1966 Gu and the rebels occupied the Materials Bureau building next to the railway station, which they treated as their personal storehouse for materials and supplies. When Public Security Bureau officials arrested some workers, Gu's allies forcefully detained the officials. Gu's allies were even brazen enough to take over the Xuzhou municipal party offices and detain city party officials.[31]

Mao strongly supported Deng's efforts to bring order to the railways, in part because he had personally experienced a railway delay due to the turmoil. On February 3, 1975, Mao was supposed to travel from Changsha to Hangzhou by special train, but security officials could not ensure its safety, so the trip was put off until February 8.[32] Wang Hongwen, former rebel leader, was now ready to put down the rebels. He supported a crackdown at Xuzhou: as deputy head of the Shanghai Revolutionary Committee, he knew that Shanghai needed supplies by rail.

The support of Mao and Wang allowed Deng to move quickly and force-fully in Xuzhou. By this time Wan Li (see Key People in the Deng Era, p. 736) was on board as minister of railways. One of Deng's first steps, which he took even before his new position began in January 1975, was to recommend that Wan Li, who had a great reputation for breaking through bottlenecks, be appointed minister of railways. Mao had earlier praised Wan Li for the excellent job he did in overcoming obstacles when he was in charge of the construction projects around Tiananmen Square, including the Great Hall of the People, the Museum of Chinese History, and the Museum of the Chinese Revolution.[33] Indeed, the characters for Wan Li's name mean 10,000 *li* (one *li* is half a kilometer), and Mao had joked that Wan Li was a man who could run 10,000 *li*. When Mao and Zhou met in Changsha in December 1974, they had quickly approved his appointment.

When Wan Li took up his new post in January 1975, Deng told him to improve the situation in the railways "as fast as possible by the most effective means."[34] Deng asked Wan Li, as new minister of railways, to prepare a report immediately on the Xuzhou problem, and ten days after he became vice premier, Deng received Wan Li to hear it. Wan Li reported that the key problem was factionalism and that the issues were so complex that they would take six months to resolve. Deng responded that the situation was too serious to wait that long.

Several weeks later, on February 6, Deng summoned Ji Dengkui and Wang Zhen to hear Wan Li's plans to resolve the Xuzhou issue more quickly. At this meeting, General Wang Zhen, rough, ready, and loyal to Deng, offered to send in troops. Wan Li reported that many officials in Xuzhou, worried that an oral directive might soon be reversed, had requested a written order from the central government granting him the authority to crack down on the revolutionary rebels who controlled the Xuzhou railway junction. Deng ordered that such a document be drawn up immediately.

From February 25 until March 5 the party secretaries in charge of industry and transport from all twenty-nine provincial-level governments (including the autonomous regions and the cities directly under the central government) were gathered together in Beijing to respond to Deng's call to draw up a written document to prepare to break through the railway bottlenecks. The participants agreed that the Xuzhou problems were the most serious and should be dealt with first. They hoped that by the second quarter of the year freight traffic on the railways would be flowing smoothly.[35] Immediately after the meeting and drawing on these discussions, Central Party Document No. 9

(that is, the ninth of the important documents promulgated that year), was issued, titled "The Decision of the Central Committee of the Communist Party of China on Improving Railway Work."[36] This document, approved by Mao, provided a systematic analysis of the problems and outlined the solution. Above all, it showed that the leadership in Beijing, including Chairman Mao, fully backed Wan Li's efforts in Xuzhou.

Document No. 9 resolved the nightmare of overlapping jurisdictions by centralizing all political and military authority for Xuzhou in the hands of Wan Li and the Ministry of Railways. Until this point, operation of the Xuzhou railway junction, in the northwest corner of Jiangsu close to the borders of Shandong, Anhui, and Henan provinces, had involved officials from all four provinces, who handled various parts of the operation, from security to railway management and railway maintenance.

Document No. 9 further decreed that factions were to be abolished and that railway ministry officials would be held responsible for any accidents. Anyone found to be opposing these measures (those engaged in factional activities, work stoppages, or destruction of property) was to be punished immediately. Deng captured the ideological high ground by declaring that anyone who resisted the leadership of the Ministry of Railways—even those who had joined radical groups—was to be labeled "bourgeois" for pursuing an individualistic path of resisting organizational discipline. In addition, anyone who destroyed railway property was to be labeled a "counter-revolutionary" and punished severely and quickly.[37]

Deng Xiaoping's speech at the end of the conference of provincial secretaries[38] was brief and to the point. It showed his firmness of purpose and was presented in a way that made it difficult for Mao to disagree even though Deng was constraining some revolutionaries. He quoted Mao by saying it was necessary "to make revolution, promote production, and other work and to ensure preparedness in the event of war." If there were a war, transportation would be essential and at present the system did not function properly. To reassure those leaders who feared that they would continue to be attacked for paying too much attention to the economy, as they had been during the Cultural Revolution, Deng said, "Some comrades nowadays only dare to make revolution but not to promote production. They say that the former is safe but the latter is dangerous. This is utterly wrong." He made it clear that Mao now supported the focus on the economy: "How can we give a boost to the economy? Analysis shows that the weak link at the moment is the railways."[39]

Since railways were to be the model for civilian consolidation, Deng personally plunged into the details of the national railway problem. He stated that the estimated loading capacity nationally was 55,000 rail cars per day, but only a little more than 40,000 cars were being loaded daily. "The present number of railway accidents is alarming. There were 755 major ones last year, some of them extremely serious." (By comparison, in 1964 there had been only eighty-eight accidents.) Discipline was poor and rules and regulations were not enforced: "Train conductors go off to eat whenever they like, and therefore the trains frequently run behind schedule," for instance, and rules against consuming alcohol on duty were not strictly observed. In addition, "if we don't take action now [against bad elements who speculate, engage in profiteering, grab power and money] . . . how much longer are we going to wait? . . . Persons engaging in factionalism should be reeducated and their leaders opposed." To those participating in factions but who correct their mistakes, Deng said, "[We can] let bygones be bygones, but if they refuse to mend their ways, they will be sternly dealt with." Meanwhile, "active factionalists must be transferred to other posts," and if a factional ringleader refuses to be transferred, "stop paying his wages until he submits." Switching to a more positive tone, Deng proclaimed, "I think the overwhelming majority" supports the decision. Railway workers are "among the most advanced and best organized sections of the Chinese working class. . . . If the pros and cons are clearly explained to them, the overwhelming majority of railway personnel will naturally give their support. . . . [and] the experience gained in handling the problems in railway work will be useful to the other industrial units."[40] This was vintage Deng. Paint the broad picture, tell why something needed to be done, focus on the task, cover the ideological bases, and seek public support for replacing officials who were not doing their jobs.

To implement Deng's plan, the day after the meeting concluded, Wan Li held a mass meeting of all the units under the jurisdiction of the Ministry of Railways in the Beijing area. A summary of the key points in Document No. 9 and Deng's speech were distributed to the participants. The next day, in a telephone conference of railway units around the country, local officials were briefed on the significance of the document and Deng's speech. Wang Zhen spoke on the phone, saying he would be sending work teams from the Ministry of Railways to areas where blockages seemed serious. Officials knew that General Wang Zhen's work teams would include troops ready to use force if necessary.[41] Sending work teams from higher levels had been a basic approach for imposing national policies on local areas ever since land reform.

Armed with national support for cracking down on railway stoppages, including a written document, on March 9 Wan Li, accompanied by a work team from Beijing, met party and government leaders of Jiangsu province and Xuzhou City.[42] Upon his arrival, it was announced that Gu Binghua, the leader of the Xuzhou Railway Bureau, whom Deng had criticized by name four days earlier, had been arrested on a warrant personally approved by Deng.[43] Wan Li knew that if Gu had not been arrested, some officials, still intimidated by Gu, would be cautious about sticking their necks out to criticize him. He also knew that others would still be frightened, as Deng had said in his speech, of being labeled rightists. An experienced revolutionary leader, Wan Li knew that for people to feel secure in denouncing Gu, a mass meeting would have to be held that displayed overwhelming support and that showed prominent people publicly denouncing Gu. The issuance of Document No. 9 was critical because it made clear that his crackdown was not just an expression of one leader who might soon be transferred but had the full support of the central party and government.

The day after he arrived in Xuzhou, then, Wan Li spoke at a huge ("10,000 person") meeting for employees and their families in the Xuzhou Railway Bureau. He spelled out the content of Document No. 9 and urged them to make the bureau a model for promoting the smooth flow of transportation by the end of the month. The next day, at the Xuzhou gymnasium, Wan Li and others addressed a large meeting of Xuzhou City party officials. Wan Li passed on Chairman Mao's three directives as highlighted by Deng and repeated Mao's call for "stability and unity." After Wan Li spoke at another mass meeting, this time of maintenance workers, their leaders guaranteed that freight would flow smoothly.[44]

After Gu's arrest, his closest associates continued to resist until they too were arrested. Wan Li and the work team from Beijing, like other work teams sent down to manage such occasions, distinguished between large-scale troublemakers, who were arrested or at least removed from their office, and those who with "education" could still cooperate with the new leadership team. Lower-level leaders were told to disband the factions and admit their errors; many did and were allowed to stay on. Then, in small groups, each individual declared that he or she would not take part in factions and would help ensure the smooth flow of freight.[45]

To strengthen support for the new leadership strategy, to help put the area's tumultuous history behind them, and to assure the local public that followers of the radical left would not easily return, past verdicts on some six thousand people in the Xuzhou area who had been persecuted early during the Cultural Revolution were declared unjust and those people still under detention were freed. Apologies were offered to the relatives of those who had been killed in the factional fighting and living victims were compensated.[46] Employment opportunities were found for many who had been unjustly punished.[47] To motivate railway workers to meet their targets, Wan Li encouraged the local leadership team to help improve the workers' living situations. After Wan Li met with the newly selected leadership teams, he and his work team left Xuzhou, just twelve days after their arrival, leaving the local leadership team to follow up and send reports. By the end of March the average number of railway cars handled per day in Xuzhou had increased from 3,800 to 7,700 and those loaded per day had doubled from 700 to 1,400.[48]

In introducing new programs throughout the country, Communist leaders talked of moving from the point *(dian)* to the line *(xian)*, and from the line to the whole surface *(mian)*. Deng, after having made a great breakthrough in Xuzhou, built on that "point" experience to consolidate other railway centers and then to use the railway experience to consolidate other sectors. By late March, officials had moved from Xuzhou to railway centers in Nanjing and then elsewhere in Jiangsu.[49] Deng first concentrated his efforts on the railway centers that exhibited serious problems, at Taiyuan, Kunming, and Nanchang. When he heard that a Taiyuan vice party secretary was interfering with progress in opening rail transport in his locality, Deng directed that the case be investigated immediately. If such a report was confirmed, the vice party secretary and any superiors who supported him were to be transferred by the end of the month.[50]

Wan Li continued to travel to railway trouble spots and followed up with visits to all the railway car factories—in Loyang, Taiyuan, Chengdu, and Liuzhou—to ensure the availability of railway equipment. On April 22, when Deng accompanied Kim Il Sung to Nanjing, Wan Li went to Nanjing to report to Deng on the progress on the railways.[51] In other railway bottlenecks, Wan Li followed the same strategy used in Xuzhou: he met with small groups to hear reports on local conditions, publicized Document No. 9, reiterated Mao's commitment to stability and unity, and held mass meetings to get a broad public commitment to the changes, an effort that, if necessary, was backed by force. New leadership teams were selected and put in place. Not surprisingly, those who were replaced had been revolutionary rebels.

From June 30 to July 7, a work meeting was held in Beijing under Wan Li's leadership to summarize the experiences of the previous few months following issuance of Document No. 9. Clearly the changes had been a great success. Wan Li reported that nationwide in the second quarter, rail freight transport had increased by 19.8 percent over the first quarter and in the same period some 18.4 percent more rail passenger cars were in use.[52]

Deng could not spend as much time on other cases as he did on resolving the Xuzhou railway blockages, but the case illustrates Deng's approach to overcoming chaos and the example others were to follow: he did what he could to make sure Mao remained on his side; he relied on officials with a proven record of success; he provided documents, held large mass meetings, and assigned troops to assure local people that there would be no easy return to Cultural Revolution policies; he arrested those who blocked progress; and he supervised the establishment of new leadership teams. Further, he did all this quickly and with a firm hand.

Extending the Xuzhou Model to Coal and Steel

After the great victory in Xuzhou, Deng used the Xuzhou model to drive consolidation elsewhere. On March 25, Deng had Wan Li report on progress in Xuzhou not to railway officials, but to a large meeting of all State Council employees. Deng usually listened quietly during such reports, but he became so intense that several times he interrupted Wan Li to amplify his comments.

Officials under Deng thus moved from attacking factionalism in Xuzhou to attacking factionalism in all of Xuhai prefecture, where Xuzhou was located, then in the rest of Jiangsu province. In 1975, Jiangsu was one of the most troubled provinces in the nation. By the end of 1974, national GNP had increased, but Jiangsu productivity had decreased by 3 percent. Wan Li was given support to move beyond railways to carry out overall consolidation in Jiangsu province, as he had in Xuzhou, by attacking factionalism and selecting new officials who seemed promising to bring order and growth. Within three months, Wan Li was reporting substantial progress in consolidating a new leadership in Jiangsu, and on June 2, Beijing issued Document No. 12, which in effect adapted Document No. 9 to report on progress made in Xuzhou, Haizhou, and other parts of Jiangsu. Deng praised the report, saying that Jiangsu's experience could be used as a guide for other localities.[53] Indeed, from Jiangsu, the reforms moved on to Zhejiang. Although Zhejiang posed special problems because rebel resistance remained strong there, by

July 17 those problems essentially had been resolved, and Document No. 16, based on the Zhejiang experience, was drawn up as a model for consolidation in other provinces.[54]

On July 4, Deng outlined the tasks of extending consolidation from the points and lines to the whole surface, from railways and local governments to other sectors—first, coal and steel; next to other industries and other forms of transportation; then to commerce, finance, and agriculture; and finally from the economic sector to culture and education, from defense technology to technology in general, and from the military to local government.

The key to China's energy supply was coal, which was used to heat buildings, generate electricity, and power factories. Distribution was essential: roughly 40 percent of the total freight carried by the railways consisted of coal. But when during the Cultural Revolution transportation systems lagged, coal simply piled up near the coal mines and there was no incentive to mine more.

By mid-1975, as the railway bottlenecks began to be opened, Beijing began to pay more attention to coal production. Indeed, when Document No. 9 appeared, Deng encouraged Xu Jinqiang, minister of mining, to use the prospect of improved transportation to spur increases in coal mining. In the spring of 1975, Xu focused his attention on coal mines with access to rail transportation: in Shaanxi, Hebei, Henan, Anhui, and the Northeast.

Under Deng's leadership, Xu waged war on factionalism, focusing on provinces where the problems seemed especially severe. These mines, which provided about 40 percent of the coal for eastern China, played a key role in supplying steel plants in those provinces. Consolidation made a huge difference to their productivity: coal production expanded rapidly in the second quarter of 1975, so that by the end of the first half of the year, 55.5 percent of the new annual coal-transport quota had been achieved.[55]

During this time, improvements were also made in the production of fertilizer, light industrial goods, and electric power. Steel manufacturing, however, continued to lag. Steel production had peaked in 1973 at 25.3 million tons, but fell to 21.1 million tons in 1974, as a result of the disruptive campaign to criticize Lin Biao and Confucius. In early 1975 the annual target was set at 26 million tons.[56] At the State Council meeting that Deng chaired on March 25, after Wan Li reported on how to use the Xuzhou example in other sectors, Deng said that "solving the steel problem must now occupy the top position in our work."[57]

In a speech at a forum on steel that same month, Vice Premier Yu Qiuli declared bluntly: "There have been twenty-six years since the founding of our nation. We have invested over 50 billion yuan, we employ over 3 million people [in the steel industry] and we are still scarcely producing 20 million tons a year." Yu stated that to increase steel production the government needed, first, to assure the long-term transportation of coal and to have the needed supply of heavy oil and electricity; second, to mobilize the masses and place in responsible positions good managers who understood the technology; and third, to deal with the weak links, especially the four large steel plants at Angang, Wugang, Baogang, and Taigang. If people did not perform their jobs, they were to be fired. They should "shit or get off the pot hole" *(buyao zhan maokeng bu lashi).*[58]

In early May, Vice Premier Li Xiannian assembled the party secretaries of twelve leading steel plants and of the local governments supervising these plants for a forum on the steel industry.[59] There the leaders of steel plants that did not meet their targets had to explain to a critical audience why they were still underperforming. They explained that the officials who had been criticized during the campaign against Lin Biao and Confucius feared making political errors. They were afraid that there would be a reversion to Mao's policies and that they would be punished for promoting economic expansion and productivity rather than emphasizing politics.

On May 21, three days after he returned from his week-long state visit to France, Deng chaired a forum sponsored by the State Council to discuss the steel problem.[60] Deng could not discuss openly the underlying worry of many officials—that Mao might change his mind and again attack those who were paying close attention to the economy, as the Gang of Four was urging him to do. In March and April 1975, articles by Zhang Chunqiao and Yao Wenyuan publicly attacked "empiricism," the focus on economic production, and the neglect of ideology. What Deng knew but could not say publicly at the time was that Mao had reassured him on April 18 and had written a note on an article by Yao Wenyuan on April 23 that further confirmed both his current opposition to such attacks on empiricism and his solid support of Deng's efforts to achieve order.

What Deng did say at the May State Council forum was, "Now that transportation has been restored, it exposes our problems in metallurgy, electric power, and other specific sectors. Each ministry must calculate again how to resolve the most difficult long-term problems. The core of our next phase should be how to resolve the steel problem."[61] Gu Mu began to speak to the group about the seriousness of the steel problem, but Deng interrupted: "He didn't put it strongly enough. If we continue in the way we are going, it will be a disaster." He went on, "Gu Mu said it shouldn't be a problem to increase 2.5 million tons a year. I say it shouldn't be a problem to increase 3 million tons a year. . . . It doesn't matter what your rank is, you can't always be afraid of this and that. Among officials, a major problem is 'fear itself.' Some are afraid of stroking the tiger's rear end. We will support you."[62]

Deng explained that it didn't matter if they were forty- or even fifty-year veterans. "If there is a faction, we don't care if it's at a tiger's rear end or a lion's rear end. We aren't afraid of stroking it. . . . If people transferred out because of factionalism form factions again, they will be transferred again. If necessary we will transfer them 360 days a year. We will give you until July 1. . . . If necessary, we will transfer you to Urumqi [in the far West where most officials dreaded being sent]. If the wife threatens divorce, maybe then he will listen."[63] He added, "We have to be very strict . . . those who deserve it will be attacked in criticism sessions. You can't just stand around and wait. In the railways people took solid steps, but here I don't see many people like that." And, he continued, "Perhaps some of you will commit errors. We need to find people who aren't afraid of being knocked down, who dare to accept responsibility. We want in the leadership teams those who dare to struggle. I myself am like a young Uighur girl with lots of braids [vulnerable to being yanked, that is, criticized]." Deng said that a large plant like Angang was complicated to run, but that senior managers should not be concerned only with the minutiae of keeping the technology going day to day. Instead, "We need a group with overall responsibility for production."[64]

In his remarks at a meeting on the steel industry on May 29, Deng stressed the need for a strong leadership team in every enterprise. He focused on the eight large steel plants that produced half the steel in China, complaining that each of the top four steel mills—Angang, Wugang, Taigang, and Baogang—was behind in meeting its targets. The biggest problem, Deng said, was at the huge steel complex at Angang, where the key issue was leaders who were soft, lazy, and disorganized (*ruan, lan, san*).[65]

On June 4, 1975, Document No. 13, which was analogous to Document No. 9 on the railways, was issued and distributed to the local authorities to deal with the steel issue. The document, which had been cleared by the Politburo and approved by Mao, reiterated a target output of 26 million tons for 1975. The State Planning Commission set up a small group from various ministries that would answer directly to the State Council and would guarantee that the steel quota would be met. Ministries concerned with electricity, coal, transport, electric power, and petroleum represented in this group were expected to assure that necessary supplies were available to the steel plants. Provincial and municipal party committees were told to exercise leadership over the steel plants and to make sure they were meeting their targets.[66]

To implement the directives of Document No. 13, the major steel factories all organized mass meetings, some with as many as 40,000 people in attendance.[67] At the top, the small group under the State Council met weekly to review individual plans and to ensure that targets were being met.[68] By August 1, however, when the small group was holding a conference to assess steel production, participants were acknowledging difficulties in meeting their previously high targets. One setback was the sudden illness of Yu Qiuli, who had boldly led the effort to promote steel in the spring, but was unable to provide his usual firm leadership after he became ill during the summer. Officials were still afraid that if they neglected leftist politics in favor of production they might later be in trouble. Indeed, the Gang of Four was then criticizing Deng for making just such an error.

In 1975, China produced 23.9 million tons of steel—a significant increase over the 21.1 million tons produced in 1974, but still short of the goal of 26 million tons. Deng accepted the improvement and declared victory. But from December 15 to December 23, 1975, when criticism of Deng was already beginning in small circles at the top, Gu Mu chaired a meeting of provincial-level officials responsible for steel production to discuss the problems. Despite the bravado at the meeting, top officials already knew that in the new political atmosphere, with Deng Xiaoping under siege, local officials had become more cautious about continuing their single-minded efforts to increase production. Indeed, in 1976—after Deng fell from power for the third time and was removed from all his positions—production fell to 20.5 million tons.

The improvement in Chinese steel production in 1975 was infinitesimal compared with Japan's steel production at the time, as Deng would see for himself three years later when he was shown a modern Japanese steel plant that by itself produced several times as much steel as all of China's increased steel production in 1975. In fact, Deng's 1975 efforts marked his last attempt to increase steel production by political mobilization. After he visited a large modern Japanese steel plant in October 1978, he took a very different approach to increasing steel production, focusing on science and technology instead of consolidation. The payoff for that revised strategy would be huge. In the 1980s, with imported modern steel technology from Japan, China's steel production would leap from 37.2 million tons in 1982 to 61.2 million tons in 1989, and then to 101 million tons in 1996, when China became the world's largest steel producer.[69] By 2010 as steel plants with modern technology were being duplicated in various localities, China, without political mobilization, would produce 600 million tons per year, almost thirty times what it had produced in 1975.

Zhejiang and the Fall of Wang Hongwen

In 1975 Mao supported Deng's effort to select new leadership teams that could get people who had formerly fought against one another to work together. No province was then more divided and in need of such efforts to bring unity than Zhejiang.[70] In 1974 all provinces except Jiangsu and Zhejiang had recorded economic growth as a result of the partial restoration of order. Zhejiang was a populous, relatively advanced coastal province with a large industrial base. Yet its problems continued into the first quarter of 1975 when industrial production fell 20 percent below that of the first quarter of 1974 and provincial revenue was down 28.5 percent. Due to efforts by Deng, Wan Li, and others, compared to the previous year, industrial production in the first eight months of 1975 across the nation rose by an average 17 percent. But in Zhejiang it was down by 6 percent.[71]

Mao took a special interest in Zhejiang when, on February 8, 1975, he moved from Changsha to the beautiful West Lake area of Hangzhou, in Zhejiang province, and remained there until mid-April, when he returned to Beijing to host North Korean leader Kim Il Sung. While in Hangzhou, Mao had ample opportunity to talk with Zhejiang provincial officials, particularly Tan Qilong, a senior party official, and Tie Ying, a senior military official, who had been attacked during the Cultural Revolution. In his current mood to restore order, Mao found them able leaders. Conversely, while in Hangzhou he formed a negative impression of Weng Senhe, the former rebel leader who had been supported by Wang Hongwen in 1973 and 1974. The problems in Zhejiang had grown worse during the campaign to criticize Lin Biao and Confucius in 1974, when Wang Hongwen had supported the rebels and Tan Qilong had been unable to bring them under control. The falling out between Mao and Wang Hongwen had already begun in 1974, for when Wang flew to Changsha on October 18, 1974, Mao was displeased that he was following Jiang Qing too closely.

By the spring of 1975, Mao's doubts about Wang Hongwen had grown. The seriousness of the problems in Zheijiang was receiving attention in Beijing and Wang Hongwen, who was assigned to meet with Zhejiang leaders to resolve the problems in November 1974 and March 1975, failed in his assignment. In a series of Politburo meetings from April 27 to June 3, Wang Hongwen was criticized, along with Jiang Qing, in part for his inability to resolve the Zhejiang problems. Wang undertook a self-criticism.[72]

After Wang was arrested in October 1976 as a member of the Gang of Four, he was criticized as an incompetent radical, bold and coarse, who had begun to enjoy the high life of fancy banquets and elegant clothes. In fact Wang did make a serious effort to carry out his responsibilities leading the daily work of the party; indeed, some who knew him felt that he should not have been implicated in crimes committed by the others in Gang of Four. But in Beijing, a city of many proven officials with great experience, Wang, a young upstart who suddenly catapulted ahead of more experienced and more skilled officials, failed to win the respect needed to provide high-level leadership.

In late June 1975, it was announced that Wang Hongwen would temporarily give up his responsibilities leading the daily work of the Central Committee in Beijing to take an assignment in Shanghai and then in Zhejiang. Mao supported the recommendation by Zhou Enlai and Deng Xiaoping that Wang Hongwen be sent to Zhejiang as part of a work team led by Vice Premier Ji Dengkui to deal with the problems there. Wang was sent, in effect, for training and reform and was in the awkward position of joining Ji in criticizing the Zhejiang rebels whom he previously had supported. His presence was helpful in resolving the Zhejiang problem because the radicals whom he had supported could see that even Wang Hongwen, with his august titles and radical credentials, was unable to help them.[73]

The work that Ji Dengkui did in Zhejiang was similar to what Wan Li did in Xuzhou. Ji and his work team met with local officials to understand the problems, held mass meetings, selected a new leadership team led by Tan Qilong and Tie Ying, and used formal documents to support their efforts. Although Deng was centrally involved, Mao, having just been in Zhejiang and having talked with those who would now take charge, played a more active role in resolving the Zhejiang problem than the Xuzhou problem. Zhou Enlai, whose family had originally come from Zhejiang and who took a deep interest in Zhejiang affairs, was also consulted.

In Ji Dengkui's last days in Zhejiang, he worked with the leaders on the drafts of what would become Document No. 16, which would do for Zhejiang what Document No. 9 had done for the railways and Document No. 13 had done for the steel industry. On June 14, 1975, Ji Dengkui, Wang Hongwen, Tan Qilong, and Tie Ying flew to Beijing with the draft of the document. The next day Deng Xiaoping chaired a meeting to review the draft and make decisions about the leadership in Zhejiang province and Hangzhou City. Tie Ying sat to Deng's left to make sure that Deng, increasingly hard of hearing in his right ear, could follow the discussions.[74] On the next day, the document was forwarded to Mao who approved it as well as the personnel decisions, and on the following day Document No. 16 was issued.

The consolidation in Zhejiang, whereby Mao and the central leadership came down firmly on the side of enforcing unity, achieved its goals of restoring order and a semblance of cohesion in the most troubled province. Tan Qilong, who in his talks apologized for his weak leadership in the previous year, was greatly buoyed by the support from the highest levels and with the help of Beijing gained firm control over the rebels. At the end of 1975 Zhejiang officials announced that industrial production in the second half of 1975 was 4 percent higher than it had been in the first half of the year.[75]

Mao did not shake the party by suddenly announcing that Wang Hongwen was relieved of his official position. Wang kept his titles another half-year after the trip to Zhejiang and until then the general public knew nothing of his fall from grace—but Mao never returned him to his leadership post in Beijing.

Promotions for Deng

The first clear hint that Mao intended to give Deng even more responsibilities came on April 18, 1975, when Mao invited Deng to join his meeting with Kim Il Sung. Mao said to Kim, "I won't speak to you about political matters. I will let him talk to you about that. That person is named Deng Xiaoping. He can wage war, he can oppose revisionism. Red Guards attacked him, but now there are no problems. At that time, he was knocked down for some years, but now he is back again. We need him."[76]

During the Kim visit, Mao talked briefly with Deng alone. Deng raised his concerns about the growing attacks on "empiricism" by Jiang Qing, Zhang Chunqiao, Yao Wenyuan, and others. Fearful about Deng's growing influence with Mao due to his success in bringing order and economic progress, they had begun attacking him for paying too much attention to economic matters and too little attention to underlying principles, an argument that had previously appealed to Mao. But in April 1975, Mao reassuringly told Deng that these criticisms were excessive, noting that "in our party not many people understand Marxism-Leninism. Some people believe they understand it, but actually they don't understand it. . . . This issue should be discussed by the Politburo."[77] To knowledgeable insiders, the implications of Mao's comments were perfectly clear: the "some people," the Gang of Four, had overstretched; and now they were vulnerable to criticism.

Indeed the Politburo took up the issue soon thereafter, at a session to discuss Mao's April 25 criticisms of the Gang of Four's writings attacking empiricism. At the Politburo meeting, Marshal Ye Jianying criticized Jiang Qing and other members of the Gang of Four for attacking empiricism. As a result, Jiang Qing was forced to engage in a self-criticism. Immediately after the meeting, Wang Hongwen, who supported Jiang Qing in trying to block the growing power of Deng, wrote to Mao complaining that Zhou Enlai's characteristic pessimism about the state of affairs was now being expressed by others on his behalf.[78] It was clear to everyone reading his note that the primary "other" was Deng. But at this point, Mao's confidence in Deng was unwavering.

Late at night on May 3, Mao called a Politburo meeting at his home. For Mao to chair a Politburo meeting was a signal that he had unusually strong views that required discussion, for he had long before passed on responsibility for these high-level meetings to others. Zhou Enlai, making a great effort, left his hospital bed to come to the meeting, the first time he had met with Mao since December. Zhou lived eight more months but this would be the last time the two leaders would spend time together. Mao was still physically able to visit Zhou in the hospital, but he chose not to do so.

At the May 3 meeting, Mao criticized Jiang Qing and others who attacked "empiricism" without also attacking dogmatism. Mao never cut off his relations with Jiang Qing, but at this meeting he was very severe with her. He declared "Don't behave like a 'Gang of Four.' Why are you acting that way? Why aren't you uniting with the more than 200 Central Committee members? . . . You must unite and not split. You should be open and aboveboard and not carry on hidden plots." Mao added: "If you have opinions, you should discuss them in the Politburo. When you publish things, they should be in the name of the party center, not your personal name. You should not use my name, I haven't sent you materials." Then, pointing to Deng, he said, "You are the representative of Mao Zedong." This was also to be the last time that Mao would attend a Politburo meeting.[79]

At the Politburo meeting, Deng, Marshal Ye, and others added their own voices to Mao's, further criticizing "the Gang of Four." They said that Mao's directive on May 3 was very important; it instructed them to practice Marxism-Leninism, not revisionism; to seek unity and not to separate from the mainstream; and the party should be open and aboveboard and not hatch secret plots. They also criticized Jiang Qing for exaggerating the differences with Zhou Enlai and for using the campaign to criticize Lin Biao and Confucius as a way to attack Marshal Ye.

On May 27 and June 3, Deng for the first time replaced Wang Hongwen as chair of a Politburo meeting. At the June 3 meeting, Jiang Qing and Wang Hongwen were forced to carry out self-criticisms.[80] Deng told Mao about it a few days later, when he joined Mao for the visit of President Marcos of the Philippines, and Mao expressed his approval for his conduct of the meeting, for he had not been overly harsh with Jiang Qing. Deng had proved to Mao that he would do what Mao wished and would continue working with her.

Mao never completely shut out Wang Hongwen, who would assist Hua Guofeng in officiating at Mao's funeral, but in fact after his trip to Zhejiang, Wang did not play a role in party deliberations. When Wang was sent off to Zhejiang, he suggested that Mao ask either Marshal Ye or Deng to take his place in chairing party meetings. When Marshal Ye declined, writing to Mao on July 1 that he was too old and that Deng should lead the daily work of the party, Mao immediately approved. On July 2 Marshal Ye wrote the official document announcing that Deng would now, in addition to leading the government as de facto premier and the military as vice chairman of the CMC, lead the daily work of the party. Topping it all off, around this time Mao also gave him a new assignment in the area of foreign policy: Deng was to become the first Chinese Communist official to make a state visit to a Western country.

Breakthrough to the West: The French Connection

From May 12 to May 17, 1975, during the first state visit of a Chinese Communist leader to a Western country—France—Deng had an opportunity to begin preparations for helping China learn from the West, just as it had learned from the Soviet Union in the 1950s.[81] Deng's selection by Mao for this important trip aroused the suspicion of the Gang of Four, who correctly saw it as one more sign of Deng's increasing power. The trip certainly had a great influence on Deng as a leader. In contrast to his fleeting trip through France the year before, Deng's visit would offer him an opportunity to learn in some detail how much the country he had known half a century earlier had been transformed, and to consider what China might need to do to achieve the four modernizations.

Why France? A year earlier Mao had put forth his theory of the "three worlds," which presented the developed European countries as part of the second world—that is, countries that China should join with to resist the two dominant powers, the Soviet Union and the United States. Of all the second-world countries, France had taken the most initiative to build good relations with China. It had normalized diplomatic relations with China in 1962, when few Western countries were willing to do so. In September 1973, too, President Pompidou had made a formal and well-received visit to Beijing, the first such visit by the head of a European country. So in 1975, when France offered a formal invitation for a state visit, China welcomed the opportunity to both return Pompidou's overture and signal that it was rousing itself after the self-imposed isolation of the Cultural Revolution.

During his 1975 visit to France, Deng was received by President Giscard D'Estaing and Prime Minister Jacques Chirac. Chirac later recalled that Deng was straightforward, warm-hearted, and well-informed about international relations.[82] While touring the country, Deng showed his personal appreciation of French life as he traveled to Lyon and Paris to visit some of the places he had seen while there half a century earlier.

Deng's key foreign policy message to France was a request for continuing support from the West as they together resisted the most aggressive dominant power, the Soviet Union. Deng expressed doubts about the value of détente with the Soviet Union and praised the unity of the Western Europeans, who were standing fast against the Soviets. But for Deng, learning about modernization was at least as important as tackling foreign policy issues. He visited agricultural and industrial sites, and held discussions about increasing trade between France and China. For the first time Deng toured modern Western factories, where he saw the remarkable changes in France since he had left fifty years earlier, and where he was struck by how far China had fallen behind. The ripple effects of this learning experience and of the successful state visit were far-reaching. Just three years later, Chinese economic officials led by Gu Mu would follow up on Deng's visit and play a crucial role in both awakening party leaders to economic and diplomatic opportunities overseas and building support for opening China even more to the West.

4

Looking Forward under Mao

1975

When in 1975 Mao tapped Deng to replace Wang Hongwen as chair of party meetings, the party was still in disarray from the struggles of the Cultural Revolution. Deng's new position in the party structure allowed him to make major strides in rebuilding the party throughout the country. The first step in renovation beyond Beijing was at the provincial level, and three months later the process would extend further, down to county and commune levels.[1] Two days after Marshal Ye's July 2 letter announcing Deng's appointment to head party affairs, Deng addressed a party center "theoretical study group" attended by provincial party leaders; the meeting focused on unifying and then rebuilding the party.

In his presentation, Deng, knowing he was on a short leash from Mao, drew heavily on Mao's teachings, or at least "Mao's three important instructions," the selection of Mao's teachings that Deng had packaged together to fit his current goals. Deng's objectives were, first, to reassure Mao that he would fight against revisionism, and then to focus on political stability and unity while boosting the economy. In his efforts to unify the party Deng drew on Mao's efforts at the 7th Party Congress, held in 1945 at the end of World War II. At that congress, the first one that Deng attended, Mao had stressed the need to unify various guerrilla-warfare units that had been spread out engaging the Japanese. Deng, making the connection to the earlier period, explained that just as "our mountaintop" mentality developed naturally when guerrillas were fighting from different locations, so too did factionalism develop naturally during the Cultural Revolution. And, Deng concluded, the party needed once again to overcome factionalism and heed Mao's call for unity made at the 7th Party Congress.[2] Members "not guilty of crimes" who cooperated with consolidation and gave up factionalism, including former radicals, would be treated favorably.

While taking care not to challenge Mao's sensitivities, Deng moved boldly and strategically to select those who could contribute to governing the country rather than to making a revolution. Although he did not explicitly vow to clean the party of "leftists" or "radicals," he did criticize "sectarianism" (leftists clinging to their factions) more than "revisionism" (rightists). Leadership, Deng declared, should be in the hands of officials who had ten or more years of experience. Without explicitly objecting to those who had risen through the ranks of the Red Guards, he thus excluded those who risen since 1965, namely during the Cultural Revolution, when some had "helicoptered up" quickly to high positions. Deng also called for a reexamination of those who had entered the party without proper scrutiny of their qualifications; again without specifically saying so, this directive focused on the 16 million new party members added between 1966 and 1975 when procedures were chaotic, rather than on the 18 million who were admitted before the Cultural Revolution.[3] In essence, those weeded out for "lacking qualifications" were those who retained factional allegiances. Mao did not challenge Deng's efforts, thereby implicitly acknowledging that at that point the country did need more stable leadership.

A central task in party rebuilding was the removal of military officers from leadership in civilian institutions, where they had been placed by Lin Biao. On August 8, 1975, Deng directed that the army, with few exceptions, should be withdrawn from all civilian positions. Many in the military were then serving as parts of "revolutionary committees" that would at some point be transformed into regular government offices. In late 1975 many of the troops were sent back to the barracks.

On May 5, 1975, immediately after Mao had chaired his last Politburo meeting, Deng again visited Zhou Enlai in the hospital. Deng was aware that he was beginning to deal with issues close to Mao's heart and he knew that Zhou Enlai was the one person who had even more experience than he did in dealing with Mao's changing moods. Zhou warned Deng to proceed cautiously and to deal with specific issues step by step, rather than to undertake overall consolidation. As much as Deng respected Zhou and acknowledged the risk that Mao might withdraw his support, Deng was bolder than Zhou and determined to move ahead with overall consolidation by attacking the big long-term issues he considered necessary to promote the four modernizations.[4]

Deng was not yet talking about reform, but while building the party structure that could later carry out reform he was also beginning to consider the content of future reforms. To do this he needed to expand his personal brain trust—writers, theorists, and strategists operating outside the regular bureaucracy who could help him think through the big issues. Shortly after Mao asked Deng to take over leadership of the daily work of the party, Deng sought and received Mao's approval to expand his personal brain trust into a formal party structure, the Political Research Office. It was placed under the State Council, but in fact Deng continued to provide personal leadership and Hu Qiaomu, former head of the brain trust, remained to guide the work.

The Political Research Office

On January 6, 1975, the day after Deng took office as vice premier, he had called in Hu Qiaomu and suggested to him that he, Wu Lengxi, Hu Sheng, Li Xin, and others form a small group of writers to deal with theoretical issues.[5] Acutely aware of Mao's sensitivities on theoretical issues, Deng and Hu chose people highly regarded by Mao and selected topics to work on that were dear to Mao's heart: the "three worlds," the character of the Soviet Union, the crisis of capitalism, and critiques of revisionism and imperialism. From the beginning, Deng spent a great deal of time and energy to find ideological arguments acceptable to Mao, to permit himself to have maximum freedom to pursue policies that he felt beneficial to the party and country. As the small brain trust that had been assembled in January expanded its membership in the Political Research Office beginning in July, Deng could work on issues he personally regarded as important (and that Mao would not object to), especially science and technology, and industrial development.

Although the Political Research Office was much smaller than the U.S. White House and was not responsible for implementation, it shared a similar purpose—to act, in effect, as an inner cabinet, a small group of independent advisers directly responsible to Deng who could help him define an overall strategy and draft public announcements. Deng had far greater control over the Political Research Office than over the party bureaucracy, which was too large and diverse to be his personal instrument.

In addition to their informal exchanges, members met every two weeks.

They divided their work into three main areas: theory (Marxist theory and Maoism), domestic issues, and international relations. Initially there were only six senior members (Hu Qiaomu, Wu Lengxi, Li Xin, Xiong Fu, Hu Sheng, and Yu Guangyuan), but soon a seventh was added (Deng Liqun—see Key People in the Deng Era, p. 722). Even at its peak, only forty-one staff members, including support staff, worked in the Political Research Office. A number of the members had been part of Deng's Diaoyutai group, which had worked on the famous nine letters to the Soviet Union in 1962–1963. All the office members were recognized as senior party intellectuals, creative strategists, and good writers. Wu Lengxi, Li Xin, Xiong Fu, Hu Sheng, and Hu Qiaomu had a great deal of experience guiding propaganda work under Mao, but Hu Qiaomu, like Deng Liqun and Yu Guangyuan, also had a strong theoretical background and broad intellectual training.

Deng worked closely with the office members when preparing major speeches and documents. He provided the political direction and laid out the ideas to be incorporated into the drafts they prepared, but he relied on their expertise to ensure that the speeches and documents were faithful to the historical record and consistent with Mao's past writings and Marxist theory. Deng personally read the drafts of important speeches and documents, then met with the writers to go over them. On especially important issues, the documents were then passed on to Mao before they were released, and after Deng received Mao's comments, he would check personally that Mao's views had been incorporated properly.[6] Even though Deng had an unusual relationship with Mao, he, like others, worried that the mercurial Mao might find some document unacceptable and let loose his fury in attacks like those at the peak of the Cultural Revolution.

Despite Deng's general authority over party affairs, Mao allowed the Gang of Four to retain control over propaganda in order to prevent Deng from veering from Mao's intended message. In fact, Jiang Qing had her own special writing group, which met at Peking University and at the Beijing City party offices and which was constantly looking for opportunities to criticize documents coming from Deng's Political Research Office.

Jiang Qing's propaganda work and Deng's responsibilities, including culture, science, and technology, inevitably overlapped. To Deng, consolidation in the cultural sphere required a fundamental reorientation—one that involved winning back intellectuals who had been alienated by the Cultural Revolution and putting them in positions where they could contribute to China's modernization. The Political Research Office thus played a key role in 1975 in strengthening institutions that promoted science, particularly the Chinese Academy of Sciences (CAS).[7]

One of the most disputed areas between Jiang Qing and Deng was over the compilation and editing of the fifth and final volume of Mao's selected works; it became a battleground for how to define Mao's legacy. One reason Deng had invited Li Xin into his brain trust was because as former secretary to Kang Sheng he had retained control over many of Mao's papers; Li Xin's presence in the Political Research Office strengthened the case for keeping the compilation of the fifth volume under Deng's control. Yet even though Hu Qiaomu, Li Xin, Wu Lengxi, and others on the Political Research Office staff prepared papers for the fifth volume, they conducted their work in a separate office, under the umbrella of a different organization.

One document considered for inclusion in volume 5, Mao's speech "On the Ten Great Relationships," emerged as a major point of contention. In this speech, originally given on April 25, 1956, after collectivization and nationalization of enterprises had been completed, Mao made a number of points that Deng could use to support programs he was promoting in 1975. Mao said that in peaceful times China should reduce military and defense expenses and channel resources to support economic development in the coastal regions, and that the leaders should learn from the strong points of all nations. Deng requested Mao's permission to republish that speech. When Mao reviewed the drafts of that speech prepared for republication, he suggested some changes, which Deng made. When Deng returned the revised draft to Mao, his cover letter suggested that because the speech had implications for their current domestic and international work, it might be useful to publish it soon, even before volume 5 as a whole was published.[8] Mao returned the draft once again with the comment that it should be sent to the Politburo members for discussion. Not surprisingly, the Gang of Four objected to its republication, and Mao never approved its distribution to the general public. On December 26, 1976, shortly after Mao had died and the Gang of Four had been arrested, the speech was finally republished.[9]

The Political Research Office officially halted its work in December 1975, after Deng lost Mao's support. In its five months of activity, it had held only thirteen meetings of the entire staff.[10] In this brief time, it had spearheaded Deng's efforts to develop a long-term road map describing the changes needed in the remainder of the century to achieve the four modernizations. It played a critical role in preparing for the revival of higher education, widening the range of acceptable cultural activities, and promoting science, including social science. In 1976 it would be criticized for its role in producing the "three poisonous weeds": (1) The Twenty Articles on Industry, (2) The Outline Report on the Work of the CAS, and (3) The Discussion of Overall Principles. The office played a major but not exclusive role in shaping the first two documents, and the third was produced entirely within the office.

The Twenty Articles on Industry

With his new broader responsibilities, Deng called together officials from all the major economic ministries. From June 16 until August 1, participants met at a State Council theoretical forum on planning work *(Guowuyuan ji-hua gongzuo wuxuhui)* where they discussed the long-term goals for the economy.[11] The forum's planners, from the State Planning Commission, created an agenda that avoided the contentions that inevitably arose in discussions of five-year plans that specified where resources would come from and the size of allocations to specific sectors and projects. Although work on the Ten-Year Economic Vision, the Five-Year Plan (1976–1980), and the 1976 Annual Plan had begun even before the forum opened, the final decisions on these plans were shaped by the long-term goals set by the forum.

The discussions at this State Council forum centered particularly on industry. In the recovery from the Great Leap Forward, Deng had supervised the drafting of the Seventy Articles on Industry in 1961, which provided an overall framework for the structure and goals of the industrial system. This forum addressed similar issues, and although the number of articles varied in different drafts, the last version in 1975 contained twenty articles.

Because statistical systems and reporting were still in disarray in 1975, participants in various fields first exchanged what information they had about the economic situation. During the forum's first two weeks, plenary sessions were held during which leading economic officials heard reports from all the major sectors of the economy. Participants in each sector could see from these reports how much their sectoral goals had to be balanced with the needs and capacities of the other sectors. Beginning on July 2, Gu Mu divided the forum into various working groups to deal with problems in theory, organization, and several key sectors. At the end of the month, the meeting resumed as a whole and pulled together the participants' conclusions in the "Twenty Articles on Industry."

By 1975, officials had heard about the takeoff of the four little dragons

(South Korea, Taiwan, Hong Kong, and Singapore), all capitalist countries that were growing more rapidly than the Soviet Union and the socialist countries in Eastern Europe. At that time, however, it was still taboo to openly praise capitalism, because doing so would raise questions about the value of China's sacrifices over many years and even about whether the Chinese Communist Party should remain in power. Instead Marxism-Leninism and Maoism remained the official creed for justifying high-level decision-making.

After the disruptions of the Great Leap Forward and the Cultural Revolution, however, leaders' enthusiasm for modernizing the country by relying heavily on willpower, as they had during the Great Leap Forward, had virtually disappeared. Most participants believed that to grow economically China needed to return to the sober planning of the 1950s before the Great Leap Forward and of the early 1960s during the recovery from the Leap. Participants believed that China should rely on a planning system because of its huge population, shortage of land, and its limited resources. Whereas less crowded countries with smaller populations could enjoy the benefits of lavish consumption despite the waste that comes from open markets, party leaders believed China had to establish priorities and control profits and wasteful consumption. Furthermore, given the risk that Mao might oppose even this sober planning, participants justified it as Mao's way. Invitations to the forum announced that its purpose was to discuss "Mao's theory of speeding up modernization." And after the forum, the Ten-Year Economic Vision that emerged was labeled "Mao's plans for modernization."[12]

In acknowledging the need for China to raise its sights, Deng was ahead of the other leaders. His travels to New York and France and his frequent meetings with foreign officials had given him a far clearer sense than most officials of how much other countries had been transformed and how far China had fallen behind. To catch up, China needed fundamental changes.

Some years after Mao's death, Deng could boldly explain that China must borrow ideas from capitalist countries, and that doing so would not threaten its sovereignty or rule by the Communist Party. But Deng had been criticized during the Cultural Revolution for being too bourgeois, and in 1975 there was not yet a consensus about opening markets and learning from capitalist countries. So he did what he could to push at the margins. He promoted an expansion of foreign technology imports. He accepted the view of fellow officials that China should not borrow money from foreigners, but the country could make "delayed payments" when foreigners sent goods or capital to China.[13] In addition, Deng supported giving material incentives to workers by offering to pay not according to need, but "according to work." Even these modest efforts to modify the old system, however, frightened some conservative officials, who continued to argue fiercely about the need to adhere strictly to the principles of Mao Zedong.

Deng did not attend the forum, but he read the summary reports of the discussions and on August 18, after the first draft of the "Twenty Articles on Industry" was completed, he gave his views on the major issues presented. He acknowledged that agricultural production had to be increased before industry could be expanded and he agreed that industry should provide machinery to the communes to help raise agricultural production. At the time, Chinese industry was in no position to sell manufactured goods abroad. To pay for a planned expansion of technology imports to improve China's production capacity, Deng was prepared to sell petroleum, coal, and handicrafts. Some of the early imports would be mining equipment so that China could expand the production of coal and petroleum. Overall, Deng stressed the importance of science and technology and of improving enterprise management and the quality of products. He wanted new rules and laws, better enforcement, and organizational discipline. He also confirmed his support for giving extra pay to those who did difficult or hazardous work.[14] The drafters revised their document to take Deng's views into account.

On September 5, representatives from some twenty leading state enterprises were invited to review the drafts of the "Twenty Articles on Industry" and offer their views.[15] One round of revision was completed on October 25, which happened to be the same day that Mao Yuanxin first passed on Mao's criticism of Deng at a Politburo meeting. Although the drafters had taken care to call the plans "Mao's plans," on October 29 Zhang Chunqiao complained that the twenty articles used quotations by Mao only from before the Cultural Revolution. Hu Qiaomu quickly turned out a new draft that incorporated phrases Mao had used during the Cultural Revolution. (He later blamed himself for failing to anticipate that problem, which triggered Mao's criticisms and gave Mao an excuse for dismissing Deng.) Members of the Gang of Four had not been included in the discussions on the economic issues, but early in 1976, once the issues had been politicized, they joined in the criticism, calling it one of the three "poisonous weeds" that had encouraged material incentives and neglected mass mobilization.

While the twenty articles on industry were taking shape, the Ten-Year Economic Vision was also being drawn up in preparation for a planning meeting to be convened in November. On October 5, Deng personally chaired the initial State Council meeting to discuss the draft of the Ten-Year Economic Vision that had been drawn together quickly. Deng approved the draft and on October 27 forwarded it to Mao, who gave permission to distribute it to those central and provincial officials responsible for the economy.[16]

On November 1, with Mao's approval, a National Planning Conference was convened focusing on the Fifth Five-Year Plan (1976–1980) and the 1976 Annual Plan. Officials from various localities suggested possible revisions to the Ten-Year Economic Vision, some of which were incorporated into the revisions of the document. Meanwhile, discussions of the five-year and annual plans continued, and by the end of December the drafts were passed to Mao.[17]

The newly formulated five-year and annual plans represented a clear victory for the cautious planners, who had been struggling for years to overcome the chaos in planning work and finally had achieved their goal.[18] But divisions had emerged between these cautious planners and the conceptualizers who had created the more ambitious Ten-Year Economic Vision, divisions that would become even more acute in the 1980s.

The Chinese Academy of Sciences

In June 1975 Deng turned his attention to rebuilding China's scientific establishment. During the Cultural Revolution, one out of every 250 scientific personnel at the CAS, where the vast majority of high-level scientists were concentrated, had been persecuted to death; in the CAS Shanghai branch the figure was one out of every 150 scientists. Even in the small number of civilian research units that remained open, work was disrupted.[19] In 1965, on the eve of the Cultural Revolution, there had been some 106 research centers under CAS, with 24,714 scientific and research personnel.[20] In 1975, by contrast, CAS had been reduced to thirteen research institutes, two research offices, and about 2,000 employees, of whom 1,800 were officials or researchers and 200 were lower-level support staff. Many of the scientists who had been sent to the countryside had not yet returned. On June 29, Deng told Hu Qiaomu that the Political Research Office should spearhead the consolidation of CAS, which would include selecting new leaders and preparing to resume the publication of scientific works. Accordingly, the consolidation of China's scientific institutions began at CAS, then spread to many other institutions.

Deng himself decided that the man on the ground at CAS, directing the actual consolidation work, should be Hu Yaobang (see Key People in the Deng Era, p. 726). In mid-July Hua Guofeng, on behalf of Deng and the party center, explained to Hu the party's hope that CAS would play an important role in the four modernizations. Hu was to investigate current conditions at the academy, report his findings to the party center, and then draw up a plan for reorganization.[21] Only after consolidation had been achieved at CAS would it be carried out at other scientific institutions—those under the direction of the national defense ministries, economic ministries, and local governments. Consolidation of schools and publications would follow.

Hu Yaobang, heading a team of three, arrived at CAS on July 18 with his mandate to carry out consolidation. He declared that the Cultural Revolution was over at CAS and that the propaganda teams of workers and the military should leave. Former employees of CAS who had been sent to the countryside could now return to their offices and resume their work. Researchers would be allowed access to needed research materials, including foreign publications.[22]

A few weeks later, Hu Yaobang held a series of meetings with members of CAS and representatives of key ministries to discuss China's science and technology needs for the next decade. These meetings marked the first step toward drawing up the ten-year vision in science. From August 15 to August 22, Hu met with the relevant party officials to discuss the reorganization of CAS and the selection of key leaders. He announced that China's goal was to achieve the four modernizations, including scientific modernization, by the end of the century.[23] Throughout September Hu met with leaders in each of the various institutes to discuss how to overcome specific obstacles in their work. Before going to each institute, he reviewed thoroughly the materials related to the institute and met with people familiar with the work conducted there.

To those who had suffered, Hu could relate his personal experiences, both as a victim and a survivor. Shortly after he joined the Communist movement as a teenager, he had been sentenced to death for questionable associations; he also suffered during the Cultural Revolution before being allowed to return to party work in Beijing. The scientists returning to their jobs could relate to Hu and came to trust him: here was someone who understood their suffering because he too had suffered. Moreover, by careful study, he had come to understand the specific problems at each institute and he believed completely in the scientific mission of CAS.

Hu also helped to resolve problems in the personal lives of CAS personnel, in part by improving living conditions and bringing back family members from the countryside. In fact, he guided the officials at each institute in drawing up a list of all former employees who had been sent to the countryside for labor and "study" and he found ways to cut through the official red tape to bring them back to Beijing. He was not afraid to speak out and fight for their cause, and when he gave talks at an institute, it always was a dramatic moment. He soon became a hero to the Chinese scientific community.

When Hu Yaobang met with Deng Xiaoping on September 26 to update him on the progress at CAS, Deng strongly endorsed Hu's efforts.[24] On October 4, Hu Yaobang was formally named first deputy head of the "Communist party small group" at CAS. From his new position, Hu appointed within each institute separate leadership teams for the party, for scientific work, and for supplies and support. He showed respect for the specialists and made it clear that they would be allowed to make decisions about the content of their work.[25] When Deng began to be criticized late in the year, Hu was in the process of naming new administrative heads of the various institutes. At that point, the climate changed and progress stalled.

While plans were being made for the consolidation of CAS and the birth of an independent Chinese Academy of Social Sciences (CASS), Hu Yaobang was following Deng's directions to help pull together the ten-year vision for the development of science that would be under CAS. Because the plan was being drawn up in great haste, Hu drew heavily on the existing twelve-year vision (1956–1967) that had been approved in 1956. A first draft of the new vision was completed on August 11, just before Hu began his series of meetings at the CAS institutes. It affirmed the progress made during the first seventeen years (1949–1966), which had produced some 150,000 scientific and technical specialists who later were criticized by the Gang of Four as "bourgeois" scientists. The drafters of the plan tried to cover their political bases by quoting Mao's 1962 statement that China needed to continue its class struggle. The emphasis of the document, however, was on providing stable work conditions to promote the "struggle for production and scientific experimentation."[26] The document discussed the technology needed to meet demands in agriculture, industry, and the military, but it also addressed strategies for developing cutting-edge computer, laser, remote sensing, and bionic technologies, as well as plans for conducting basic scientific research in nuclear energy, particle physics, and other areas.[27]

Reviewing the document, Deng was concerned about Mao's probable reactions; he directed Hu Yaobang and the drafters to take the scattered references to Mao and put them together in one place to make clear that the document was in keeping with Mao's general views. While emphasizing the successes during the first seventeen years, the drafters were told to tread lightly over the problems encountered since. Deng also said that the document should be shortened.

Deng asked Hu Qiaomu to oversee these revisions, and on August 26, Hu wrote a memo to the drafters regarding Deng's views and then supervised the editing, with the hope that the results would be more acceptable to Mao. A fourth draft, completed on September 2, discussed China's scientific progress not during the first seventeen years but during the entire twenty-six years of the People's Republic, thus avoiding criticism of the Cultural Revolution. The document announced that the aim was to realize "Mao's goal of four modernizations" by 2000, and to catch up or even surpass world scientific levels. Scientists, it read, must continue to reform themselves and to unite with workers and peasants. Action clauses specified how scientists were to take the lead in opening new areas for basic research as part of their mandate to support the four modernizations. Finally, to achieve Mao's goals, the report stated, large numbers of outstanding scientific specialists with advanced training would be required. The document noted that although they must not assume that all things foreign were good, when appropriate, the Chinese should be open to learning from foreigners.[28]

At the State Council meeting on September 26 to discuss the report, as Hu Yaobang was making the presentation, Deng interrupted frequently. When Hu Yaobang talked about reaching world scientific levels, Deng emphasized that China had to be modest about its present levels because the nation had fallen far behind other countries in science and technology. Deng continued to interrupt, reflecting his passion to revive science in China—a step that, as he repeated, was essential for achieving the four modernizations. Deng stressed the need to support the small number of really brilliant scientists, even if they were unusual characters. It was important to solve their housing problems and other problems of daily life: their children should be placed in good kindergartens, and any spouses still in the countryside should be allowed to return to Beijing. Deng said that when he was in the Soviet Union in the 1950s he had learned that the basic work on the Soviet atomic bomb had been done by three young men, all in their thirties and forties. In contrast, Deng complained that the brilliant semiconductor scientist Huang Kun had not been given a good position, and he said that if Peking University did not want him, he should be made head of a semiconductor institute where the party secretary would support his work.

Deng continued that although he had never become fluent in either French or Russian, Chinese scientists had to learn foreign languages so they could read foreign reports. They also had to learn scientific theory and if they did not understand math, physics, and chemistry, regardless of their degrees, they would not be able to handle scientific work. He defended those scientists who had tried to keep their studies going during the Cultural Revolution, despite having been criticized, saying that they were "a lot better than those who fight factional battles," who "occupy the pot hole without taking a shit" and "hold back the wheels of progress."[29]

Deng complained that some were even afraid to use the word "expert." In his view, China should cherish its experts. It needed to introduce automation into its factories and to support talented scientists who could make it happen. Aware of the continuing ideological criticism of "bourgeois intellectuals," Deng stressed that scientists were members of the working class. He directed that after the ten-year plan for the development of science was revised, it should be sent to Mao and to the members of the Politburo.[30]

Rarely was Deng as passionate as he was at this meeting on science. Not only did he interrupt frequently but he fervently argued that scientific research must take the lead among the four modernizations.[31] But taking the lead would not require a complete reorganization, Deng insisted. Rather than change as many as 45,000 officials in the science sector, as some had proposed, changing only 5,000 would be sufficient. The key was the leadership team at each level. Why should people be kept in their posts if they don't know a specialty and don't yearn to get something done? Why can't China promote people with high levels of knowledge to become heads of research centers? The challenges were immense, and the key was to rely on scientists and leaders in their early forties and older who had been trained before the Cultural Revolution. Indeed, Deng said that China's educational system, in which some colleges were operating at the level of high schools in the West, faced a crisis that could hold back the entire modernization effort.[32]

By September 28, Hu Qiaomu had incorporated Deng's comments into a fifth draft. The report gave the necessary praise for Marxism-Leninism and Mao Zedong Thought, but boldly stated that political theory could not be used as a substitute for science. This fifth draft was the first to be shown to

Mao. Just at that time, at Mao's request, his nephew Mao Yuanxin was visiting him in Beijing. Mao complained to his nephew about Deng and his consolidation efforts at Tsinghua University. Mao was also furious about the document on science; he zeroed in on one sentence that Hu Qiaomu had inserted in the final draft quoting Mao as saying that "science and technology constitute a force of production" *(kexue jishu shi shengchan li)*. Mao insisted that he had never said that.[33]

Just at that time, Deng's plans for the development of the social sciences were coming to fruition. Deng was personally focused on reviving the natural sciences, but he also accepted the need for revitalized work in philosophy and the social sciences. Considering the minefield of political sensitivities in this area, Deng showed courage when he argued that the social sciences were important enough to deserve a separate academy. On August 30, 1975, Hu Qiaomu, with Deng's support, issued State Council Directive No. 142 establishing the philosophy and social science departments of CAS. In that document, Hu laid out plans for developing an independent academy that would later be known as the CASS. Deng also declared that institutes in the social sciences should gradually resume issuing publications, starting with a more general journal intended for nonspecialist audiences that would set out a theoretical basis for their work. To reduce the danger of attack by the Gang of Four, and possibly by Mao as well, Deng ordered that all articles submitted to the journal should first be cleared by the Political Research Office, which would scrutinize them for any comments likely to provoke the radicals. In his letter announcing the publication, Hu Qiaomu took the precaution of announcing that it would follow Marxism-Leninism and Mao Zedong Thought.

Hu Qiaomu completed his letter on social science and philosophy work on October 4, and the next day Deng passed it on to Mao, who approved the document, including publication of the first issue of the new journal *The Ideological Frontline (Sixiang zhanxian)* on October 6. Shortly thereafter, a forum was held to discuss the journal. After the criticism of Deng in the Politburo on October 25, however, plans for the journal were stopped. The articles never saw the light of day. Hu Qiaomu made an effort to continue the project, but on January 17, 1976, the Political Research Office, under pressure from Mao, issued a statement saying that it would no longer be responsible for supervising philosophy and the social sciences.[34] The great enterprise of restoring China's social sciences aborted before it really began.

A Mini "Hundred Flowers" in the Arts and Culture

Deng had to be particularly careful about fostering any sort of change in the cultural sphere because Mao was especially sensitive and mercurial about controlling the arts. During the Cultural Revolution, Mao had allowed Jiang Qing to keep a tight grip on all cultural affairs: no dramas were performed except her model Peking operas, virtually all periodicals ceased publication, and only a handful of short stories and novels were printed. Bookstores sold collections of Mao's works, tales of revolutionary heroes, a small number of school textbooks, and a few books on elementary technology. But there were virtually no customers. Many intellectuals, too, had been sent away to rusticate at "May 7th Cadre Schools," where they took part in physical labor, studied Mao Zedong Thought, and joined in mutual criticism and self-criticism; they were not given the opportunity to read novels and short stories.

In 1975, however, the mercurial Mao, aware of how few stories and dramas were being produced, complained to Deng that "model Peking operas aren't enough . . . if people make a little mistake, they are criticized. There is no sign of a hundred flowers. Others aren't allowed to express their opinions. This is not good. People are afraid to write articles, they are afraid to write plays, and there are no novels, no poems or songs."[35] With Mao's permission, Deng immediately directed that Mao's views be printed and distributed within the party. On that same day, July 9, Deng, while acknowledging that he himself was unfamiliar with culture and the arts, called a meeting of the senior members of the Political Research Office and told them to collect publications in the fields of culture, science, and education so they could see to what extent Mao's policy of encouraging a hundred flowers to bloom was being implemented. Their judgment that there was indeed a dearth of cultural activity paved the way for a modest expansion of the range of what was considered permissible in Chinese culture and the arts.[36]

A few days before he first complained to Deng about the lack of cultural vitality, Mao had asked a secretary to send a letter to the Politburo to declare that Zhou Yang—in effect the ranking cultural czar before the Cultural Revolution—should be released because "locking up leaders in the cultural sphere is not a good way to deal with them." On July 12, Zhou Yang's wife received word that her husband had been freed, and soon other prominent people once associated with Zhou Yang were also released. A few days later Mao told Jiang Qing that he wanted to see a broader range of works in the arts and greater leniency for writers. When writers have problems in ideology, he advised, an effort should be made to "cure the patient."[37]

Yet Mao allowed the Gang of Four to retain authority over cultural institutions, including the Propaganda Department, the Ministry of Culture, the Political Department of the army, the *People's Daily*, and *Red Flag*. In essence, then, beginning in July 1975 Mao allowed a tug-of-war between the Gang of Four—who remained alert to any criticism of Mao, real or implied—and Deng Xiaoping, who with the support of Hu Qiaomu was promoting a mini-hundred-flowers policy. Every hint that Mao dropped for widening the sphere of permissible activities was quickly followed up by Deng and Hu Qiaomu, who nevertheless proceeded carefully to avoid crossing boundaries that might arouse Mao's concerns.

Not surprisingly, the reentry of Zhou Yang continued to be a source of conflict between the two sides. On July 27 Mao announced that Zhou Yang's problems were not so serious as to be called contradictions between the people and the enemy. The very next day Deng had Mao's statement widely distributed. But the Gang of Four still managed to prevent Zhou Yang's salary and positions from being fully restored. In the tug-of-war, Jiang Qing also blocked Zhou Yang from receiving a special invitation for the National Day celebrations on October 1. When Mao later found out, he complained angrily.[38]

Other skirmishes erupted over films. Hu Qiaomu came across some documents that showed how the Gang of Four had suppressed a film celebrating workers and some senior leaders, especially Yu Qiuli, whom Jiang Qing disliked. Hu Qiaomu guided the scriptwriter in writing a letter to Mao asking for release of the film. Hu advised the author that the letter should not be emotional but instead should report verifiable, unbiased information that would still lead to the conclusion that the movie should be shown. The scriptwriter took Hu's advice; his letter made clear that in making the film, he had followed Mao's directives about literary works issued at the Yan'an Forum on Literature and the Arts. In particular, the film showed the contributions of workers, and workers took pride in the film and warmly welcomed it.[39]

A great breakthrough in expanding the range of cultural freedom occurred on July 25 when Mao viewed the film *The Pioneers (Chuangye)*, which lionized Yu Qiuli and the team of workers who had developed the Daqing oilfield and had long been praised by Mao. Hu Qiaomu, judging that Mao would be sympathetic since he had strongly praised the work at Daqing, directed that information about the case be collected. On July 25, Mao, who had just recovered from an eye operation that greatly improved his vision, saw the movie and was in a very good mood.[40] His speech was not clear, so Mao scrawled out his views in several lines of big characters, between five and twelve characters per page, stretched out over six pages. He wrote, "This film doesn't have many errors. I suggest it be shown. It doesn't need overall criticism. To say it has ten errors is a great exaggeration and not beneficial for the party's policy on literature and the arts."

The next day Mao's letter was delivered to Deng Xiaoping while he was holding a meeting of the Political Research Office. Deng interrupted the session to read the letter aloud. Mao wrote that the Ministry of Culture had been too crude, had blocked the showing of a good film, and had obstructed further showings, going against the hundred flowers policy. Deng immediately publicized Mao's letter, setting off great excitement in literature and art circles. The incident marked the first public criticism of the Gang of Four's cultural policy since the beginning of the Cultural Revolution. Hu Qiaomu, worried about retaining Mao's support, cautioned the scriptwriter not to brag about his success in public; his wife was also advised to send a letter to Mao to express her appreciation.[41]

Deng lost no time in taking advantage of this breakthrough. He approved another letter to Mao about the movie *The Glow above the Sea (Haixia)*, based on the novel *The Island Militiawoman (Haidao nü minbing)*. From then on, Hu Qiaomu, Deng Liqun, and even Deng Xiaoping personally helped writers and musicians prepare letters to Mao that might lead Mao to approve greater freedom in the cultural sphere, and in a number of cases they succeeded.

Although it was known that Mao greatly respected Lu Xun, who is widely considered the greatest Chinese writer of the twentieth century, throughout the 1970s Jiang Qing blocked plans to publish Lu Xun's letters and correspondence. In the freer atmosphere of mid-1975, however, a breakthrough seemed possible. Lu Xun's son, Zhou Haiying, also with advice from Hu Qiaomu, drafted a letter to Mao asking permission to publish his father's works. Hu passed the letter to Deng Xiaoping, who forwarded it to Mao. Mao responded: "I agree with Comrade Zhou Haiying's opinion. Print the letter and send it to the Politburo members. Have a discussion, make a decision, and immediately carry it out." By 1980, all sixteen volumes of Lu Xun's works, including the annotations and notes, had been published.[42]

In the months after July 1975, Mao's support for expanding cultural affairs left the Gang of Four on the defensive. Wang Hongwen was in Shanghai and Zhejiang quieting down rebels. Yao Wenyuan complained that after being sent to Shanghai, he was, like any ordinary citizen, "hopping onto the crowded bus for work."[43] Jiang Qing remained in Beijing, but was on a short leash. She could not stop those who appealed to Mao one by one to expand China's cultural offerings.

Journals resumed publication more slowly than novels. In the summer of 1975, it was announced that the magazine *People's Literature (Renmin wenxue)*, which had been closed down in 1966, would soon resume publication. Predictably, the Gang of Four worked to prevent this from occurring—and when thwarted, tried to gain as much influence as possible over the magazine's content. Deng Xiaoping led the struggle for *People's Literature* against the Gang of Four, but after he was criticized beginning in October, the conservative Ministry of Culture gained the upper hand. By the time the first issue appeared in January 1976, Deng had no control over the content of the magazine.[44]

Zhou Rongxin and the Effort to Revive Higher Education

In the summer of 1975, Deng, his education minister Zhou Rongxin, and several others made a valiant effort to begin the restoration of Chinese higher education. A few universities had remained open during the Cultural Revolution, but they did not remain genuine institutions of higher learning. On July 21, 1968, Mao had directed that universities shorten the time they took to educate students and enroll instead peasants and workers who, after receiving their training, would return to the production line. In June 1970, it was announced that workers, farmers, and soldiers, rather than academics, should take charge of the universities. Factories were attached to all universities so that students could spend part of their time working there. And on August 13, 1971, official directives were issued stating that admission to universities would be by recommendation, not by examination.[45] These changes had a devastating effect on higher education in China. In May 1973, when U.S. scientists visited Peking University, the premier university in China, they concluded that science training there was at about the level offered by a U.S. technical junior college.[46]

Deng's efforts to revive higher education began, in part, with the knowledge that Mao and other radicals would find it difficult to oppose the opening of military universities. During the Cultural Revolution, many personnel from the best military science and technology university, Harbin Military

Industrial University, had been transferred to Changsha. There they had been absorbed into Changsha Industrial University, which had been given leeway to raise its standards.[47] A small number of promising intellectuals had been allowed to enter this school and other military universities as a way of cloaking their research as military-related even before civilian institutions resumed their normal operations.

The situation for most other intellectuals was bleak. Shortly after Nixon visited China in 1972, Zhou Peiyuan, the leading academic administrator at Peking University, was asked to report to Zhou Enlai on the state of Chinese science. Zhou Peiyuan was bold enough to report that in all thirty-two areas of science, China had fallen seriously behind.[48] Further, a brief glimmer of hope that academics could resume their normal work had ended on New Year's 1975 with the outbreak of Mao's "Criticize Lin [Biao], criticize Confucius" (pi-Lin, pi-Kong) campaign.[49] Advances in science would be forced to wait.

Zhou Enlai returned from his December 1974 talks with Mao with renewed hope of reviving higher education. During that meeting Zhou Enlai had yielded in allowing candidates proposed by the Gang of Four to lead China's ministries for culture and physical education, but he was prepared to fight to enable his candidate Zhou Rongxin to lead education, and received Mao's agreement. Zhou Rongxin, no relation to Zhou Enlai, had mostly been involved in party work, but he had studied at the anti-Japanese university in Yan'an and in 1961 had served briefly as a vice minister of education. In this position, Zhou Rongxin had begun making plans for genuine university education, but Mao did not approve and his plans were aborted the following year.

After his appointment as minister of education in January 1975, Zhou Rongxin again began planning to restore higher education.[50] To reduce the risk of Mao's opposition, he was careful to reiterate the importance of theoretical study, which included Marxism-Leninism and Chairman Mao's directives on education. But he also pursued genuine reform. From May through September the Ministry of Education, under Zhou Rongxin's direction, sponsored many public forums to discuss educational matters. In addition, the ministry published the journal Educational Revolution Bulletin (Jiaoyu geming tongxun) in which Zhou Rongxin gave voice to those with genuine experience in higher education.[51] He dared to say that in their one year of university study, workers, peasants, and soldiers could not learn as much as students who had previously studied there for three years. He also boldly asserted that the workers, peasants, and soldiers studying at university who would simply return to their rural cooperatives could not fill China's need for trained officials and for scientific and technical specialists.[52]

Deng Xiaoping fully supported Zhou Rongxin. In a talk on September 26, 1975, Deng declared that all countries that modernized, no matter what their social system, required skilled people with high levels of education and training, and that Chinese universities had fallen to the level of high schools elsewhere. During the previous year, when a visiting delegation of U.S. university presidents had cautiously told Deng that in their view Chinese higher education had serious problems, Deng replied, to their surprise, that he completely agreed with them and said he wanted them to convey their views to other party officials as well.[53]

At a rural work forum from September 27 to October 4, Deng once again spoke out about improving China's institutes of higher learning. He said that to meet Mao's goal of achieving the four modernizations, China would need officials who had received a higher education. He also explained that the primary responsibility of the university was to educate and that in order for the faculty to teach well, their status would have to be improved.[54] Years later, such comments would seem like common sense, but given the political climate of the time, Deng was courageous; he risked incurring Mao's wrath.

In 1975 Deng went so far as to suggest that students should be allowed to go directly from high school to university without the usual two-year interruption for physical labor. Actually, Chinese-American Nobel laureate Lee Tsung-Dao had suggested this to Zhou Enlai when they met in October 1972 and even Mao had approved of the idea when Lee Tsung-Dao raised it with him on May 30, 1974. In November 1975, however, this notion, then called "Premier Zhou's directive," was attacked as part of Deng's supposed efforts to bring back "bourgeois officials" and to carry out a "rightist reversal of verdicts."[55] While Mao remained alive, Deng was not able to achieve his goal of allowing universities to resume normal operations.

Meanwhile, with Deng's encouragement, Zhou Rongxin began drawing up a document to guide educational policy. A third draft was completed on November 12, after the criticism of Deng had begun. Yet the essential core of the document remained unchanged: persons trained from 1949 to 1966 would have the value of their educations affirmed (they would not be disparaged as "bourgeois intellectuals"); high-level specialized training was to be resumed; the amount of time spent in high school and university training would be increased; and overall educational standards were to be raised. Two days later, on November 14, Zhou Rongxin was summoned to a Politburo meeting where he was bitterly attacked for his proposals.[56]

The criticism of Zhou Rongxin was even more severe than the criticism of Deng. In December 1975 Zhou Rongxin was subject to continuous criticism until he fell ill and had to be taken to the hospital. Even so, he was taken from the hospital and subjected to more than fifty additional criticism sessions. Finally, at a criticism meeting on the morning of April 12, 1976, Zhou Rongxin fainted and before dawn the next day, at age fifty-nine, he passed away.[57] For a time, Chinese educational reform also died.

Prelude to Mao's Dismissal of Deng, Fall 1975

In his later years, Mao spent less time on the details of governing and more time indulging his interests in literature and history, albeit with an eye to their relevance to current politics. Before his eye operation on July 23, 1975, Mao, scarcely able to see, had others read to him. Beginning on May 29, 1975, a classics professor from Peking University, Ms. Lu Di, came to read him classic stories and to discuss them with him. On August 14, she recorded Mao's views on the Chinese classic story of the righteous rebels in *Water Margin,* including his view that their experiences had contemporary relevance.[58] Mao's views were passed on to Yao Wenyuan, who seized the opportunity to join Jiang Qing in criticizing Zhou Enlai and Deng Xiaoping for behaving like the rebel leader Song Jiang, a capitulationist who had lost his revolutionary fervor.[59]

At a meeting of the Political Research Office on August 21, Deng Xiaoping, sensing trouble and trying to keep it under control, announced that the discussion of *Water Margin* was strictly a literary issue, to be discussed only in literary circles.[60] But Mao had a different view and allowed the discussion to get broad public attention. Mao was already concerned that Deng, like Zhou, was eager to recall many senior political figures who would then turn their backs on the Cultural Revolution. It would be difficult to stop Mao's suspicions from escalating.[61] The question of how Deng might treat Mao's reputation after his death was too sensitive to discuss directly; they brought it up indirectly, by discussing how Khrushchev had savaged Stalin's reputation. Deng's critics warned that he could end up being China's Khrushchev. If Deng removed Mao's rebels under the guise of "opposing factionalism" and allowed bureaucrats to return, might they not seek revenge—against both

Mao and those rebels who had attacked them—by sullying Mao's reputation?

Jiang Qing, always looking for a chance to attack Deng that would appeal to Mao, pounced on the opportunity presented by Mao's description of *Water Margin*. From August 23 to September 5, a series of articles appeared in *Guangming Daily, People's Daily, Red Flag,* and other papers, warning against the negative example of the rebel leader Song Jiang in *Water Margin.* Jiang Qing also began speaking out more forcefully against Deng and others who had been making changes. On September 15, she used a large political conference on the Dazhai agricultural model to deliver an hour-long diatribe in which she drew analogies from *Water Margin* and complained that some high officials were trying to push Mao aside.

Mao, however, who since the fall of 1974 in his effort to achieve stability and unity had generally restrained Jiang Qing, felt that she had misused the conference on rural issues and had gone too far in her comments. When Nancy Tang showed him a copy of Jiang's speech, Mao declared that it was "bullshit" *(fang pi)* and "way off the mark" *(wenbu duiti),* blocked its publication, and announced that Jiang Qing should quiet down.[62] Many high officials suspected that Mao had been growing uncomfortable with the continued criticism of former revolutionary rebels and the return of so many senior officials, but for the moment the *Water Margin* campaign trailed off.

Meanwhile, on September 20, 1975, Zhou Enlai, feeling the pressure from the *Water Margin* campaign, locked himself in a small hospital room before surgery and reviewed the entire transcript of the records about an event when as an underground worker in 1931 he was suspected of allowing information to be passed to the Guomindang.[63] As he went into the operating room Zhou said to his wife, Deng Yingchao, "I am loyal to the party. I am loyal to the people. I am not one who surrenders." She passed his remarks on to Wang Dongxing to deliver to Mao.[64] It seems that Zhou, like Mao, would spend his last months filled with concern about his reputation in the party.

The Clash over Tsinghua University, Fall 1975

After his successful eye operation on July 23, 1975, Mao began reading documents that he had not been able to read before. As he read, he became increasingly concerned that Deng was moving too fast, going beyond what was necessary to restore order.[65] By October, Mao had begun to focus on Tsinghua University, which had been dear to his heart since 1969 when he had declared it, along with Peking University and six factories, a national model. During 1975 Mao had restrained himself as Deng criticized one group after another that Mao had supported earlier in the Cultural Revolution; in the case of Tsinghua University, however, Deng had gone too far.[66]

Although none of Deng's generation of top political leaders had graduated from university, Deng and many bright Communists of his era, like Zhou Enlai, Ye Jianying, Hu Yaobang, and Zhao Ziyang, but unlike Mao, were instinctively comfortable with intellectuals and believed deeply that their help was essential to modernization. Deng knew Mao's sensitivities about "bourgeois intellectuals," but in late 1975, having gained confidence by retaining Mao's support as he consolidated in other areas, Deng charged boldly into the lion's den—into Tsinghua University—even though he knew Mao had a special attachment to the place.

The Tsinghua leaders in 1975, Party Secretary Chi Qun and Deputy Party Secretary Xie Jingyi, had arrived at Tsinghua early in the Cultural Revolution as revolutionary rebels who were part of the "worker propaganda teams." Chi Qun, a soldier who had become deputy head of the propaganda section of the 8341 Central Guards Regiment Unit that guarded Zhongnanhai, was sent to Tsinghua in 1968 by Wang Dongxing. A committed radical, he rose to the position of party secretary of the university. His comrade-in-arms at Tsinghua was Ms. Xie Jingyi. From 1958 to 1968 Xie Jingyi had been a confidential secretary (jiyao mishu) for Chairman Mao, who, using the familiar term for juniors, referred to her as "little Xie" (Xiao Xie). "Little Xie" rose to become one of the party secretaries of Beijing City, as well as a deputy secretary at Tsinghua. Chi Qun and Xie Jingyi, supported by the radicals, were regarded by Tsinghua University intellectuals as oppressive ideologues.

In August 1975, as Deng was expanding his targets for consolidation, Liu Bing, a deputy party secretary at Tsinghua, became more optimistic. A former subordinate of Hu Yaobang in the Communist Youth League, Liu was persuaded by Tsinghua intellectuals to send a letter to Mao that spelled out how Chi Qun was leading a degenerate "bourgeois" lifestyle and poisoning the atmosphere at the university. In his letter, Liu Bing wrote that Chi Qun did not look at documents and refused to meet people or otherwise carry out his work responsibilities. Chi Qun was often drunk and ill-tempered, cursing people, flying into a rage, and smashing cups and glasses. He was also guilty of sexual harassment. When Liu Bing consulted with Hu Yaobang about the appropriate channels to get the letter to Mao, Hu suggested that he first give the letter to Deng. Deng promptly and courageously forwarded the letter to Mao.

Mao did not answer Liu Bing nor did he say anything about it to Deng, but Chi Qun was made aware of the letter and immediately held a high-level party meeting to criticize "those within the Tsinghua Party Committee supporting the 'revisionist' line," namely, Liu Bing and his supporters. Not long thereafter, Liu Bing drafted a second letter, this time focusing on the political problems of Chi Qun. Party Secretary Chi Qun, he wrote, with the support of Xie Jingyi, was obstructing the circulation of Deng's speeches and Minister of Education Zhou Rongxin's directives. (Zhou Rongxin had announced that students no longer needed to spend one-third of their time in physical labor, that the number of peasant and worker students with low academic credentials would be reduced, and that the focus would be on educating science and technical specialists.) Deng was advised by Li Xin and others not to forward Liu's second letter because of Mao's sensitivities about his two model universities, but Deng was undeterred; he forwarded it on to Mao.[67]

On October 19, Mao summoned Li Xiannian, Wang Dongxing, and others to a meeting, but Deng was not included. The Chairman told them that Liu Bing's "motive in writing the letters was impure. He wants, Mao said, to overthrow Chi Qun and Little Xie. The spearhead in the letter is aimed at me . . . in 1968 Little Xie led 30,000 workers into Tsinghua." Mao asked why Liu Bing had not sent the letters directly and instead sent them by way of Deng. He told them, "Tell Xiaoping that he should pay attention and not fall into the trap of being partial to Liu Bing."[68] In line with Mao's directives, on October 23 Deng chaired an enlarged meeting of the Politburo, where he passed on Mao's instructions. High officials from the Beijing Party Committee in turn passed on Mao's instructions to the Tsinghua Party Committee.

It was at this point that Mao took up the quotation in the fifth draft of the ten-year vision for the development of science under the CAS that he had objected to. It had quoted Mao as saying that "science and technology constitute a force of production." After Mao looked it over, he said that he had not said that. To say that, he argued, would make science and technology as important as class struggle, an idea he could not accept. In Mao's view, "class struggle is the key link." After being called to task by Mao, Deng told Hu Qiaomu, who had been responsible for the draft document, to go back to the sources. When Hu Qiaomu checked, he found that Mao was correct—he had never uttered that expression. Hu Qiaomu had simply come across a similar idea in Mao's works, and, as an editor, made slight alterations in the wording.[69] Mao had allowed Deng to undo much of the damage done by the Cultural Revolution while clinging to the fig leaf of a belief that the Cultural Revolution was good. Now Deng was attacking the fig leaf. If while Mao was alive, Deng was already altering what Mao said and attacking Mao's favorites at Tsinghua University, what might Deng do after Mao died?

Mao's New Messenger, Mao Yuanxin, October 1975–April 1976

As Mao's suspicions about Deng's disregard for his own views deepened, his suspicions about his two go-betweens, the two ladies (Nancy Tang and his distant relative Wang Hairong), also intensified. They were becoming too close to Deng.[70] They had been behaving, Mao said, like "rats on a sinking ship."[71] Mao was fading, Deng was rising, and the two ladies could no longer be counted on to be loyal to the sinking ship. Indeed, Deng continued to meet with them occasionally even after he fell into disfavor with Mao.[72]

Because of Nancy Tang's central role in the 1972 visit by President Richard Nixon, Mao allowed her to interpret during the visit of Julie Nixon and David Eisenhower a few weeks later, on January 1 and 2, 1976.[73] But that was the last time she interpreted for Mao. Weeks before, Mao had already begun to rely on another messenger, his nephew Mao Yuanxin (see Key People in the Deng Era, p. 733).

When he became Mao's messenger, Mao Yuanxin was a mature, experienced official, eager to carry out Mao's instructions. He stopped at Mao's residence in Beijing on September 27, 1975, en route to Xinjiang (where his father had been a Communist martyr) to celebrate the twentieth anniversary of the establishment of the Xinjiang Uighur Autonomous Region on September 30. As he had done before, he gave his uncle a detailed account of events in the Northeast. He said that opinion there was divided between those who thought the Cultural Revolution had been 70 percent successful and those who thought it had been 70 percent a failure. The negative critics, he said, were even more vocal than the critics of ultra-leftism who had emerged in 1972 after Lin Biao's death.

After taking part in the celebrations in Xinjiang, Yuanxin returned for a week to the Northeast to wrap up his affairs, then moved to Beijing to serve as his uncle's full-time liaison. Mao Yuanxin was still in awe of his uncle and he shared his radical perspective. As an experienced official and Mao's nephew, Yuanxin carried far more authority in his role as go-between than the two ladies had. He also played a far more active role than they ever did as his uncle began to orchestrate an almost daily campaign to criticize Deng.

Some of Deng's supporters later claimed that Mao Yuanxin made Mao suspicious of Deng; he may have increased Mao's suspicions by, for example, calling attention to how Deng made some changes in the documents Mao had approved before they were distributed. But in fact Mao was already suspicious of Deng when Yuanxin arrived.[74] Other officials were convinced that Yuanxin sometimes inserted his own views when reporting Mao's instructions.

Whether or not he heightened the problems between Mao and Deng, as Deng's supporters complain, Yuanxin did have a radical perspective and he had worked with Chi Qun in Liaoning in late 1974. The two had teamed together to promote the "Chaoyang model," which was designed to promote political education by providing colleges with course material adapted to the needs of rural officials.[75] Yuanxin thus personally agreed with Chi Qun about the importance of political education at Tsinghua University and, like Chi Qun, opposed the new emphasis on academic quality by Liu Bing, Deng, and Zhou Rongxin.

Mao Launches Criticism of Deng, November 1975

On October 31, Deng, aware of Mao's growing dissatisfaction with his work, requested a meeting with Mao. Mao saw him the next day and criticized him for supporting Liu Bing.[76] But he also provided some reassurance: responding to Deng's request for an appraisal of the work of the Central Committee during the previous few months, Mao said that the policies were "correct," and he went on to acknowledge the achievements of consolidation.[77] In the several confrontations with Jiang Qing that had flared over the previous few months, Mao had invariably supported Deng, and Deng, while realizing he was taking some risks, hoped Mao would continue to do so. As it turned out, Deng had overestimated how much support he would receive from Mao in the weeks ahead.

When Mao Yuanxin met with Mao the next day, he reported to his uncle that Deng rarely talked about the achievements of the Cultural Revolution, seldom criticized Liu Shaoqi's revisionist line, and hardly ever praised the campaign to criticize Lin Biao and Confucius that had also targeted Zhou Enlai. Mao Yuanxin added that Deng rarely mentioned class struggle and concentrated solely on improving production. And finally, speaking to Mao's deepest fears, he told his uncle there was a danger that Deng would restore the pre–Cultural Revolution structure.[78] After that meeting between Mao and his nephew, tensions between Deng and Mao escalated rapidly.

Deng tried on several occasions to see Mao privately "to receive instructions," but after his meeting with Mao on November 1, Mao always refused to see him. If Deng were to tell him in private that he approved of the Cultural Revolution, then after Mao's death he could deny what he said. Party historians who have seen the relevant documents are convinced that Mao wanted Deng's approval of the Cultural Revolution to be on the record, heard by other people, or committed in writing so that Deng could never publicly deny it. When Mao met his nephew on November 2, for instance, he told Mao Yuanxin to meet Deng that same day, in the presence of two other officials, to tell him Mao's views.

Although Deng's daughter Deng Rong does not record the date, she relates a meeting at their house between her father and Mao Yuanxin that quite likely occurred that evening.[79] She writes that one evening Yuanxin, at his uncle's behest, came to their house to talk with Deng. Deng's daughter did not know what went on during their private conversation behind closed doors, but she could tell that Mao Yuanxin had come "to fuss" and that her father "didn't waver." She concludes, "The talk between Papa and Mao Yuanxin went badly." When Mao Yuanxin left, she writes, "Papa did not see him out."[80] Mao Yuanxin is reported to have begun his job as Mao's messenger with some diffidence toward the senior party officials, including Deng. But when he spoke with the full support of Mao Zedong behind him, he acquired some authority. It is easy to imagine that Deng, proud of his many personal accomplishments, convinced of his rectitude, and reluctant to affirm the Cultural Revolution, would have been less than enthusiastic about being criticized by someone half his age.

The two people selected by Mao to join Mao Yuanxin and Deng Xiaoping at the meeting on the next day were Wang Dongxing and Chen Xilian, both of whom shared Mao's commitment to the Cultural Revolution. Deng knew Mao Yuanxin would report back to Mao, but he did not waver. He presented his views forthrightly: "You [Mao Yuanxin] said that the party center consolidation has followed the revisionist line and that in all areas we have not carried out the Chairman's line. That's not right. As for what line I have been carrying out in the three months since I have been leading the work of the Central Committee, as for whether conditions throughout the country are a bit better or a bit worse, one can evaluate by the actual results." Deng, aware that he was in deep trouble with Mao, added that he was willing to undergo a self-criticism.[81]

After the meeting, on the same day that Yuanxin reported to his uncle that Deng had not tamely accepted criticism, Mao told his nephew that they should immediately convene a meeting of eight people: the same four (Deng, Mao Yuanxin, Wang Dongxing, and Chen Xilian), along with Zhang Chunqiao (one of the Gang of Four) and three key vice premiers—Li Xiannian, Ji Dengkui, and Hua Guofeng—who had guided economic and government work during the Cultural Revolution. Mao said, "It doesn't matter if there is some quarreling. The next stage will be for the Politburo to meet." Earlier, Mao had said the Cultural Revolution was 90 percent good, but in preparation for this meeting Mao settled for a lower hurdle: Deng and the other officials must acknowledge that the Cultural Revolution was 70 percent good, and "if one Politburo meeting doesn't resolve the issue, it can meet a second time and a third time."[82]

The group of eight met the next day, November 4, and that same evening Yuanxin again reported to Mao the results of their meeting. Mao Yuanxin had urged Deng to accept the Cultural Revolution as basically good and to agree that class struggle was still the "key link." Instead, Deng avoided giving Mao's nephew a direct answer. Mao was clearly displeased with Deng's response, but he said to his nephew that they were undertaking criticism of Deng not to remove him but to help him correct his errors. Mao then directed his nephew to warn Zhang Chunqiao, a member of the Gang of Four, not to mention a word about these proceedings to Jiang Qing, who always was ready to criticize Deng publicly.[83] After Mao Yuanxin reported to his uncle, Mao directed that the group of eight should meet again, and they did so. Later that day, November 7, Yuanxin reported to his uncle that there had been no progress in getting Deng to budge.

The strategy that Mao followed next was to gradually enlarge the number of participants and ratchet up the pressure until Deng would give a clear commitment of support for the Cultural Revolution. Accordingly, Mao directed Yuanxin to assemble all seventeen people on the Politburo, including Jiang Qing. The Politburo members were to criticize by name those who had supported Deng in the fields of culture and science and technology: Hu Qiaomu, Hu Yaobang, Li Chang, and Zhou Rongxin. Deng's daughter Deng Rong writes that launching attacks on these people whom Deng had supported was a way of putting greater pressure on Deng, who knew that his refusal to yield would create serious problems for his associates. As explained earlier, Minister of Education Zhou Rongxin, once president of Zhejiang University and a long-time staff assistant to Zhou Enlai and to Chen Yun, had been speaking out boldly about raising the educational levels to assist modernization and even about reducing the role of political education.[84] On November 8, in a further blow to Deng, Zhang Chunqiao, who was responsible for supervising the field of education, told Zhou Rongxin to engage in a self-criticism for encouraging students to study while ignoring China's political struggles.

Parallel to the Politburo meetings criticizing Deng and his colleagues were large public denunciations of Deng's allies for their elitist views on education. At the time, Deng's name was not yet mentioned publicly. But on November 13, Mao, unhappy about Deng's failure to respond at the initial meetings, wrote out specific instructions for the Politburo meetings to "help" Deng.

Two days later, Deng, acutely aware of the seriousness of Mao's criticism and quite likely thoroughly aware of Mao's disillusionment with Wang Hongwen, wrote to Mao suggesting that Wang Hongwen, who had completed his assignment in Zhejiang, replace him in leading the daily work of the Central Committee. Mao replied the same evening that for the time being Deng Xiaoping should continue to chair the meetings. Mao did not invite Wang Hongwen to resume his former responsibilities, and two months later he named Hua Guofeng as acting vice chairman.

On November 16 and 17, the Politburo again met to criticize Deng and his key supporters in the fields of education and science. Like Zhou Enlai, Deng had the stamina to chair, at Mao's insistence, a meeting at which he was the target of criticism. Mao Yuanxin made the key presentation criticizing Deng for his failure to follow Mao's directives affirming the Cultural Revolution, class struggle, and Mao's educational policies. Jiang Qing, who was by then allowed to attend the criticism sessions, and her radical allies added their voices to the criticism. During the meeting, Deng made no comments beyond the minimum necessary to serve as chair. After allowing his attackers to present their case, from the chair Deng called on those being criticized—Hu Yaobang, Hu Qiaomu, Zhou Rongxin, Li Chang, and Liu Bing—to explain their positions. But when asked at the end of the meeting to summarize the discussion, Deng declined, saying that he was hard of hearing.[85]

The proceedings against Deng escalated rapidly during the first half of November and reached a climax on November 20, when the discussion turned into an overall evaluation of the Cultural Revolution. Again at Mao's direction, Deng chaired the meeting. Deng rarely asked others for advice, but in the days before this meeting, under continued pressure, Deng consulted with Zhou Enlai, Ye Jianying, and Chen Yun. He struggled to find a way to side-step an affirmation of the Cultural Revolution in a way that Mao would find the least objectionable. When pressed by the Politburo members to agree on a formula affirming the Cultural Revolution, Deng, following a suggestion by Ji Dengkui, said: "During the Cultural Revolution. . . . I was in the Peach Blossom Grove. I didn't even know what happened in the Han dynasty, to say nothing of what followed later during the Wei and Jin dynasties." This clever allusion, one that Mao himself had used only a week earlier, referred to a well-known story, "The Peach Blossom Grove" by Tao Yuanming, in which the people in the grove admit that because they were closed off, they were in no position to know what was happening in the wider world.[86] Deng's effort to dodge the issue did not satisfy Mao, who wanted a clear affirmation of the Cultural Revolution. Mao and Deng had reached an impasse.

For more than four decades, Deng had followed Mao's orders and had said what Mao wanted to hear. As a target of attack during the Cultural Revolution and with his eldest son paralyzed, Deng undoubtedly had strong personal feelings about the Cultural Revolution, but he had long separated those feelings from his work on national policy, following Mao's lead without complaint. Why, when he clearly understood Mao's intention, did Deng fail to comply this time? Deng knew that Mao was growing weaker and no longer had the commanding presence to control events as he had earlier; indeed, he did not have long to live. But the answer seems to lie in Deng's estimate of what was needed for China's future. Bo Yibo later said that if Deng had affirmed the Cultural Revolution, he could not have restored order, would not have been able to "seek the true path from facts," and would not have been able to launch a new reform policy and liberate people's thinking.[87] That is, if Deng had approved of the policies of the Cultural Revolution, he would have undone much of the consolidation work and, because he would have been on record as supporting the earlier failed policies, he would have been unable to do what he considered necessary to move the country forward. Some rebels whom he had removed would have returned to power, making his tasks even more difficult, especially in education and science. If Deng was to be given a role in governing after Mao's death, he would need to distance himself from class struggle, to continue the consolidation policies, and to gain full cooperation from those who suffered during the Cultural Revolution and believed it had been a disaster.

If Deng had followed the advice of Zhou Enlai or Chen Yun, he would have bent to Mao's pressure and probably avoided being removed from office. But Deng did not yield. Deng Rong recalls that when, earlier that year, her father began pressing for consolidation, he expected to be criticized and purged, and that he was mentally prepared.[88] As painful and uncertain as Deng's fate was at the time, when he returned in 1977 his efforts to distance himself from Mao gave him far greater room to maneuver than if he had yielded in 1975.

Mao and Deng both drew a line in the sand, but in preparing for a large meeting to be held on November 24, 1975, each still acted with some restraint. Mao was aware of the great progress that had been achieved during the year under Deng's leadership, and he approved of much of what Deng had done. He knew that no one else could have provided as much stability as Deng, and that he had no good replacement for him. Furthermore, President Gerald Ford was expected to visit China between December 1 and December 5. Because Zhou Enlai was gravely ill, the previous month Deng had worked with Henry Kissinger to prepare for the Ford visit, and Mao knew of no other party leader versed in foreign policy who could so forcefully and skillfully present China's views on sensitive issues such as U.S. support for Taiwan, the U.S. delay in recognizing China, and U.S. détente with the Soviet Union.

During his first meeting with Ford in early December, Deng used a story from the popular novel *Romance of the Three Kingdoms (Sanguo yanyi)* to describe the danger that the United States might concede too much to the Soviet Union. He said that after Cao Cao, emperor of the Wei Kingdom, won the war, the losing general Liu Bei offered to work for him. Cao Cao, suspicious of Liu Bei's loyalty, said, "Liu Bei is like an eagle, which when it is hungry will work for you, but when it is well fed, will fly away."[89] In other words, giving the Soviet Union what it wanted would not work, for once it had what it wanted, it would pursue its own interests. One has to wonder, too, whether Deng, in telling the story, identified with Liu Bei, whose loyalty was being called into question by his leader and who might fly from his leader's grasp.

When he met Ford, Mao acknowledged that China had little weaponry to fight the Soviet Union, only empty cannons, but he confessed: "With regard to cursing, we have some ability."[90] To ratchet up the pressure on Deng, Mao allowed Jiang Qing and her radicals to make full use of that ability. Deng knew that Mao still had the power to determine his fate and that he would also have to work with other leaders who still respected Mao, despite the errors of the Cultural Revolution. The planned meeting on November 24, scripted by Mao but to be chaired by Deng, would remind senior officials about correct party policy. Three days before the meeting, Deng wrote Mao detailing his suggestions on how he might conduct the meeting, and the next day Mao wrote back approving of his suggestions. Mao also directed that some younger officials be invited, since they too needed to have a correct understanding of policy. Both Mao and Deng knew, however, that most of the "young officials" were former rebels, some of whom might well exercise their ability to curse Deng. Mao soon reconsidered his decision, and the next day he wrote that there was no rush to educate young officials. That could be saved for a later meeting.[91] In attacking Deng, Mao avoided going all out— for now.

At the November 24 meeting to "sound the alert" *(da zhaohu)*, more than 130 senior officials assembled to receive instructions on how to "avoid making new mistakes," namely, how to stop following the path that Deng had been pursuing. In accordance with Mao's directions for conducting the meeting, Deng read Mao's letter out loud. In it, Mao criticized Liu Bing for trying to overthrow Chi Qun and Xie Jingyi, and said that Liu Bing's letter was in fact aimed at Mao who supported Chi and Xie. Deng's name was not mentioned, but because he was the one who had forwarded Liu Bing's letter to Mao, it was obvious to those assembled that Mao was criticizing Deng. At that meeting, when called on to give his response to Mao's letter, Deng tried to walk a narrow line, not affirming the Cultural Revolution but still following Mao's directions. He said that Mao wanted officials to take the correct attitude toward the Cultural Revolution and that Mao's saying that "class struggle is the key link" was the fundamental tenet of the party.[92] In effect, he acknowledged what Mao had said was party policy, but did not say he agreed with it. The written summary of the meeting was approved by Mao and on November 26 it was sent to high-level party officials and military officers throughout the country. Even though Deng's name was not mentioned, readers understood he was in deep trouble.[93]

Criticism of Deng Expands, December 1975–January 8, 1976

After the November 26 summary of the November 24 meeting was distributed, the Politburo held a series of additional meetings over the next two months to criticize Deng for his "rightist reversal of verdicts," which had allowed too many senior officials to return to work. Mao assigned Deng to continue chairing the meetings at which he was the main target of attack. Deng did open and close the meetings, but otherwise he sat silently while Jiang Qing and her radicals heaped criticism on him and his policies. *Red Flag, People's Daily*, and other media followed up with further criticism. The four who steadfastly supported Deng during these criticisms (referred to as the "four protective Buddhist deities" [*jingang*])—Hu Yaobang, Wan Li, Zhou Rongxin, and Zhang Aiping—were attacked for supporting Deng's efforts to reverse the verdicts. The Political Research Office and the senior officials there, including Hu Qiaomu, Deng Liqun, and Yu Guangyuan, were also attacked during criticism sessions for their errors in supporting Deng.[94]

On December 18, Mao Yuanxin forwarded to his uncle the materials critical of Deng, Zhou Enlai, and Ye Jianying that he had been collecting since October, with help from the party committees in Liaoning province, Shanghai, and at Tsinghua and Peking universities, where the radical critics had a strong base. Mao Yuanxin attached a memo asking permission to release the evidence and Mao immediately gave his approval.[95] Two days later, the materials were forwarded to high officials in the party and military.[96] On the same day, Deng made a brief "self-criticism" without a written text.[97] He recalled that when he had taken office in early 1975, production was stagnating in a number of industries and there was serious factional strife. To deal with the problems of factional strife Deng had focused first on the railways, where the problems were quickly resolved. Using the same methods, he then turned to the steel industry to increase production. He said his failures were due not to his eight years of absence during the Cultural Revolution but to his attitude toward the Cultural Revolution. His "self-criticism" was actually, as his daughter points out, a defense of his policies, which he still believed to be correct.[98]

In hopes of improving his relations with Mao, the next day Deng sent Mao a personal letter, enclosing a transcript of his verbal self-criticism and adding that it was only a preliminary version and that he welcomed Mao's advice on what he should do next. Not surprisingly, Mao regarded Deng's self-criticism as inadequate, and instead of sending him a reply, he expanded the campaign against him.[99] Immediately after the 1976 New Year, Wang Dongxing called Deng to make sure he had read the New Year's editorial approved by Mao. It declared that achieving stability and unity did not mean neglecting class struggle. Deng understood what Mao expected and he immediately composed by hand another self-criticism, which he submitted on January 3, 1976. He repeated in writing what he had said on December 20,

adding only that before enunciating policies he had sometimes failed to receive Mao's approval. When criticized by Jiang Qing and her radicals during
the sessions that followed, Deng stood his ground. He would rather take their
punishment than declare that class struggle should continue to be China's
central objective. Five days after Deng submitted his self-criticism, Zhou Enlai passed away. Immediately thereafter Deng was replaced by Hua Guofeng.

The Interlude with Kissinger and President Ford

In the meantime, Deng had been given time off from criticism sessions to
carry on negotiations with Henry Kissinger and later with President Gerald
Ford. During three days of lengthy meetings with Kissinger to prepare the
Ford visit, from October 20–22, Deng and Kissinger exchanged views on
global developments. Deng scarcely let Kissinger make his initial presentation before pressing him with pointed questions: How much grain are you
selling to the Soviet Union? How much modern U.S. equipment and technology are you passing on to the Soviet Union? What is your assessment of
the Helsinki Conference (in which the United States was promoting détente
between Western Europe and the Communist bloc)? Deng then spelled out
the experience of Chamberlain and Daladier trying to appease Hitler on the
eve of World War II. The lesson: because Britain and France gave a weak response to Hitler's initial forays, Hitler attacked to the West. To stop a threat,
one needs to make a firm response, he advised, and the United States is now
giving a weak response. The Soviet Union, he said, is now stronger than the
United States and Western Europe combined. The Soviet Union has two
weaknesses: it needs grain and technology, and the United States is helping
with both, helping resolve its weaknesses and thus increasing the risk of a
Soviet attack.[100] Zhou had been accused of being a capitulationist, but when
attendees at this session would report to Mao, it would be hard to find evidence that Deng could be seen in a similar light.

In the long conversations with Kissinger covering global affairs, Deng kept
returning to the dangers of a Soviet advance following the U.S. withdrawal
from Vietnam. Throughout their discussions, Deng kept up the pressure on
Kissinger for the United States to respond more vigorously to the Soviet
threat, and Kissinger attempted to explain how much the United States was
doing to counter the Soviet threat. Deng was intense and feisty, but he remained within the bounds of diplomatic courtesy.

Deng sat in on Kissinger's meeting with Mao, and Mao, like Deng, focused on the U.S. failure to respond adequately to the Soviet challenge. In his report on his meetings with Deng and Mao, Kissinger reported to President Ford that the discussions during his visit signaled a troublesome cooling of the U.S.-China relationship, linked to China's perception that the United States was fading in the face of Soviet advance. Kissinger concluded that China, disappointed with the U.S. response, was ready to rely on its own strength to defend itself against the Soviet Union.[101]

It was a measure of Deng's toughness under pressure that even during long negotiation sessions, he remained intensely focused on the discussions. Neither Kissinger nor any of his staff had any notion that Deng was then under severe political pressure from Mao. In fact, Kissinger concluded from the meeting that because Mao was very sick and incapable of detailed or sustained work, now "Deng is the key official."[102]

On November 4, the day Deng first faced criticism at the meeting of eight, Foreign Minister Qiao Guanhua called in the head of the U.S. Liaison Office, George H. W. Bush, to request that President Gerald Ford postpone the visit planned for December. But the United States requested the trip go ahead as planned, and on November 13, China confirmed that the trip would take place. Deng was President Ford's main host, welcoming him at the airport one week after he had been the target of attack in the presence of 130 high officials. Deng hosted a welcoming banquet, gave the farewell luncheon, and carried on three lengthy negotiating sessions, in addition to joining Mao when Mao met with Ford.

Chinese officials had not expected much from the Ford visit. They had regarded Nixon as a well-informed reliable leader in the face of Soviet pressure, and now Ford, still recovering from Watergate, was weak and new to the position. Nixon had vowed to normalize relations with China in 1976, and they knew before the visit that Ford would not go ahead with normalization plans. Ford was less experienced than Nixon in foreign affairs. Indeed, in pressing the United States to take stronger action against the Soviet Union, Deng said to Ford in their first long session, "I hope I will not offend you, but in the dealings with the Soviet Union, perhaps we are a little more experienced than you."[103] He pressed his views about the Soviet Union as he had done with Kissinger six weeks earlier. China, he said, was prepared to go it alone in defending against the Soviet Union; even though it was a poor country without technology it was prepared to "dig tunnels and prepare millet" to feed the troops. While complaining about U.S. weakness in responding to the Soviets, Deng gave no indication that China would be prepared to increase its own military budget.

Yet Deng and Mao were more cordial to President Ford than they had been to Kissinger six weeks earlier. Deng told Ford: "We believe in having deep exchanges. . . . It does not matter if we have different views or even if we quarrel sometimes." In addition to pressing the United States on Soviet questions, Deng was his charming but feisty self in pushing the United States on U.S.-China relations, trade, cultural exchanges, and U.S. policy toward Taiwan.[104] Deng also found President Ford far more knowledgeable about world affairs and far firmer in his anti-Soviet attitudes than he had expected. He told George Bush a week later that the results of his visit with Ford were also far greater than expected.[105]

The criticism sessions against Deng resumed immediately after Ford returned to the United States, yet still no one on the U.S. side was aware that Deng was then being criticized. A week after the Ford visit, when Deng gave a farewell luncheon for George H. W. Bush, who was completing his work as head of the U.S. Liaison Office and returning to the United States, Bush described the luncheon meeting as "relaxed and convivial."[106]

Mao's meeting with President Ford on December 2, 1975, was the last time that Deng was invited by Mao to join him in meeting a foreign guest. It was also the last time that Deng saw Mao. Deng was allowed to meet President Nixon's daughter Julie and her husband David Eisenhower on January 1, and on the next day to host a U.S. Congressional delegation led by Margaret Heckler.[107] But Zhou Enlai died less than a week later and this was the last time Deng would meet foreign guests until his return in 1977.

Deng's Initiatives Placed in Cold Storage

Once Mao's nephew, Mao Yuanxin, conveyed his uncle's criticism of Deng to the Politburo on October 25, 1975, all forward movement on party building, science, education, and culture came to a halt. The lower-level units did not learn of Mao's criticism of Deng immediately, but as the weeks passed, they sensed that their efforts to get approval for changes were being stymied at higher levels. By January 1976 Deng was no longer around to support them.

Deng's efforts from May through October 1975 to look forward, to lay the groundwork for long-term progress in party building, economics, science, technology, and culture, were frozen but they were not dead. The economic plans drawn up under Deng in 1975 remained the basis for the 1976–1980 Fifth Five-Year Plan. The Gang of Four printed out the three "three poisonous weeds" and conducted a campaign to criticize them. Those who read them could not publicly express their appreciation for them, but in 1977 they were dusted off and became known as the "three fragrant flowers," serving as the basis for the programs in the years ahead. The plans to establish an independent academy of social sciences, for example, were stopped in late 1975, but implemented in 1977 when the academy was established. The Political Research Office by late 1975 was moribund, but many of the writers it had assembled played a role in writing the documents for the Third Plenum of 1978 and for the reforms that followed.

In the military, the campaign to criticize Deng never gained real traction: outside the Political Work Department of the PLA, the Gang of Four found very little support. Within the military, the most noticeable effect was a slowing of the recall of senior officials who had been criticized during the Cultural Revolution and a delay in the reopening of military schools. In 1977 officials were again being recalled and military schools were being reopened.[108]

Deng's fall had a dramatic short-term impact on higher education. Plans to raise educational standards and reduce political education were halted. Momentum for rebuilding the CAS was lost, and boundaries for acceptable activity in literature and art were narrowed. A chill once again came over writers, musicians, and artists.

In the political realm, too, activity in reversing the verdicts on senior party officials slowed. Some of Deng's closest supporters, particularly Hu Yaobang and Hu Qiaomu, were attacked and removed from office, and lower-level officials who served under them also lost their jobs.

In 1975, Mao had been willing to bend to bring order, stability, and economic growth, but in the end Deng pushed further than Mao could tolerate. In his last months of life, Mao had the power to yank the leash, to remove Deng and have him criticized. Yet Mao no longer had the strength or the support to control the thinking of officials below him. In the short run, Deng was out. But his firmness in refusing to renounce what he had supported in late 1975 stood him in good stead beginning in 1977, when he returned and took out of cold storage the people and programs that he had created and encouraged in 1975.

5

Sidelined as the Mao Era Ends

1976

Within a single year, between December 1975 and September 1976, four senior Chinese leaders passed away. First Kang Sheng, the master internal spy who had done the dirty work for Mao in arranging the killing of hundreds of officials accused of betraying the revolution, died in December 1975. Then Premier Zhou Enlai passed away during the morning of January 8, 1976. Zhu De, founder of the Red Army and an early military leader, died in July 1976. And Chairman Mao, who towered above all others, expired in September 1976. With their deaths and the arrest of the Gang of Four in October 1976, the era when a godlike revolutionary could shake an entire nation came to an end.

The Death of Zhou Enlai

When Zhou passed away before Mao, it allowed Mao to shape the nature of Zhou's funeral arrangements—and he used the occasion to try to dampen the public memory of Zhou, offering what was by party standards only minimal recognition of Zhou's service. But Mao's tactic backfired. Instead of being placated, many Chinese people were upset that Zhou, who had earned their respect and admiration, was not given the posthumous recognition they felt he deserved.

The afternoon of the day Zhou died, the Politburo met to plan arrangements for the funeral, and at 6:30 p.m., Deng, still officially vice premier, sent to Mao the draft of the announcement of Zhou's death, prepared by the Politburo, along with a message asking for his approval. Early the next morn-

157

ing Mao approved the draft announcement and did not object to the selection of 107 people for the funeral committee, headed by Mao, Wang Hongwen, Ye Jianying, Deng Xiaoping, and Zhu De.[1] Mao even permitted Deng to present the eulogy, and Zhou was to be cremated at Babaoshan, the cemetery for revolutionary heroes.

But Mao did not attend the funeral service. Three days before the service was to be held at the Great Hall of the People, Mao scoffed to his bodyguard Wang Dongxing, "Why do I have to go to the service?" He instructed his personal assistant Zhang Yufeng to explain simply that he was unable to be there (even though, just a few weeks later, Mao was well enough to meet former president Nixon for a full hour and forty minutes).[2] Mao did send a memorial wreath for Zhou, but he did not take part in any other expression of grief.

During Zhou's last months, Mao had been similarly distant. By September 1975 Zhou's weight had dropped from his usual 143 pounds to a mere 88 pounds.[3] Deng, Ye Jianying, and other close associates frequently visited Zhou in his hospital suite, even when Zhou was not able to talk. On January 5, Deng, Li Xiannian, and several other leaders went to be with Zhou during his final operation.[4] Mao, though far more mobile than Zhou, never once visited him in the hospital. Mao also tried to dampen foreigners' celebration of Zhou. Deng, at 4:00 p.m. on the day of Zhou's death, reported to Mao that many representatives of foreign countries were asking to pay their respects. When Deng met the Albanian ambassador later that day, he announced, in accord with Mao's direction, that foreign ambassadors in Beijing could take part in expressing their condolences and that leaders of various countries could express their condolences to the Chinese embassy in their own country, but no foreign delegations were to be sent to Beijing.[5]

By contrast, and in spite of Mao's coolness, among the general public the announcement of Zhou's death on radios and loudspeakers precipitated a huge national expression of grief. In the public eye, Zhou had suffered from unfair treatment since 1973. The spontaneous outpouring was comparable to that in the United States in 1945 when Franklin Roosevelt died and in 1963, when Jack Kennedy was shot. The Chinese people, aware of how emaciated Zhou had appeared at the National People's Congress the year before, were not surprised, but they were frightened that no one else could defend the country against the madness that Mao and the Gang of Four had perpetrated. Some leaders who had suffered during the Cultural Revolution remained deeply upset that Zhou had been so willing to collaborate with Mao, but in the public eye, Zhou had saved them from Mao's excesses.[6] Many feared what might follow now that Zhou was no longer around to defend them.

On January 11, Beijing residents, who had heard only by word of mouth that Zhou's funeral procession would take place that day, gathered at Tiananmen Square to pay their respects. Late in the afternoon, a hearse with Zhou's body, followed by one hundred black limousines, passed through the square on the way to Babaoshan, the cemetery for revolutionary heroes in the Western Hills where his body was to be cremated. Despite the freezing weather, an estimated one to two million people lined the streets.[7] Anxious mourners, upset at the rumor that the Politburo had ordered Zhou's cremation against his will, blocked the procession of vehicles until Zhou's widow Deng Yingchao assured them that Zhou himself had asked to be cremated.[8]

On January 12, the *People's Daily* carried a photograph of Zhou draped in the party flag, indicating that mourning was permitted.[9] Hundreds of thousands of people went to the Imperial City's Hall of the Ancestors to visit the wooden casket that contained Zhou's cremated remains. The wearing of black armbands was prohibited, but supplies of black cloth used to make armbands and white silk paper to make chrysanthemums for mourning sold out in Beijing.[10] By January 12 an estimated two million people had taken wreaths and eulogies to the Monument to the People's Heroes in Tiananmen Square.[11]

At the Politburo meeting on January 12, Zhang Chunqiao suggested that Marshal Ye Jianying present the eulogy that the Politburo was preparing for the January 15 memorial service. Only a month earlier, Marshal Ye had presented the eulogy for Kang Sheng, but he chose to give to Deng the opportunity to deliver Zhou's eulogy, even though Deng was being subjected to severe criticism at the time, and the other Politburo members agreed.[12] Mao had the power to stop Deng from delivering the eulogy, but it would have been awkward to reject the Politburo's decision. He chose instead to allow Deng to present the eulogy, formally prepared under the Politburo's direction.

At the memorial ceremony, Deng, speaking on behalf of the Central Committee, gave the eulogy before five thousand carefully selected attendees. Ji Chaozhu, who often interpreted for Deng as well as for Zhou, recalled that while Deng rarely displayed any emotion, "when Deng began by saying, 'our premier,' his voice broke. Everyone was sobbing."[13] Deng's life had been closely intertwined with Zhou's for half a century, and both of them had suffered under Mao whom they had served with dedication for many decades. This would be Deng's last public appearance until the spring of 1977.

The eulogy read by Deng praised Zhou, but the content prepared under the Politburo's direction would be difficult for Mao or the Gang of Four to disagree with. According to the eulogy, Zhou had contributed to the Communist Party, to the undefeated PLA, to the victory of the New Democratic Revolution, to the creation of the new socialist China, and to the great unity of workers, peasants, and minority groups. He had made indelible contributions to the dictatorship of the proletariat and in foreign relations had carried out the revolutionary foreign policy line of Chairman Mao. Throughout his life, Comrade Zhou had been loyal to Marxism-Leninism and Mao Zedong Thought. He always saw the big picture, he respected party discipline, and he was good at uniting with the great majority of officials. He was modest, prudent, and unassuming, setting an example by his hardworking conduct and plain living. In addition, Deng concluded, he had waged a heroic revolutionary struggle against his illness.[14]

Immediately after the memorial ceremony, the official period of mourning was declared over. Although the bare facts of the memorial service and of Deng's eulogy were printed in the newspapers, in contrast to the usual practice when dealing with the death of a revolutionary hero, virtually nothing about Zhou's career made it into print nor was there an official estimate of the crowds that had paid homage in Tiananmen Square or along the funeral procession. Many people were upset about this glossing over of Zhou's death, not only because it failed to provide a fitting commemoration to someone they admired, but also because of what it signified—that Zhou's and Deng's enemies were in a strong political position and would pursue policies quite different from Zhou's.[15]

After the memorial service, Zhou's widow, Deng Yingchao, was granted her request to accompany the ashes to the airport. There workmen carried the ashes onto a plane, to be dispersed in the skies over the Chinese land to which Zhou had dedicated his life.[16]

Deng's Fall and the Selection of Hua Guofeng, January 1976

The Zhou Enlai memorial activities interrupted the Politburo sessions attacking Deng for only a few days. Mao, dissatisfied with Deng's two self-criticisms, had directed the day before Zhou's memorial service that both of these self-criticisms be printed and distributed to the Politburo for further consideration.[17] For Deng, the meaning was ominous. At the Politburo meeting on January 20 when Deng made his third self-criticism, he again requested an opportunity to meet Mao. Jiang Qing demanded to know why, and Deng replied that he wanted to talk personally to the Chairman about the seriousness of his errors, to hear personally the Chairman's criticisms and directions, and to present some problems he had had in his work.[18] Mao, however, made no exception to his usual practice of refusing to meet anyone who had become a target of his criticism. He chose not to hear from Deng in private what he could later easily retract.[19]

Upon hearing that he would not have a private audience with Mao, Deng composed a handwritten letter to Mao that in effect announced his resignation, and he gave it to Mao Yuanxin to deliver to Mao. He wrote, "Chairman, I beg that you approve my request to be relieved of my duties leading the daily work of the party center.[20] For the past two months I have been criticized. I fear my continuing to work will weaken the efforts of the Central Committee and that I will make further errors. I will follow the decisions of the Chairman and the Central Committee."[21]

The day after he received Deng's letter, Mao met with his nephew to hear his report on Deng's conduct at their meeting the day before. In Mao Yuanxin's view, Deng's self-criticism still had not gone far enough. Yuanxin also reported to Mao that the three vice premiers, Hua Guofeng, Ji Dengkui, and Chen Xilian, had requested that someone be named acting premier. (These three younger provincial leaders had been brought into the Politburo in 1973 with the expectation that they would later be leading candidates for higher positions.) Mao immediately replied that Hua should be given responsibility for leading the daily work of the party.[22]

To foreigners and even to the Chinese general public, Hua Guofeng was a new face, but Mao had known Hua for two decades. He first met Hua in 1955 when Hua was prefectural party secretary in Xiangtan, Hunan, Mao's home prefecture. Hua was then a strong supporter of Mao's rapid agricultural collectivization and Mao formed a positive impression of him. Over the two decades Mao had known Hua, Hua had firmly supported Mao in each political campaign and had risen in status after each one of them. He proved a reliable supporter after Mao's controversial criticism of Peng Dehuai in 1959, and after his criticism of Lin Biao after Lin's crash. Other Beijing leaders had a chance to know Hua after he was elevated to the Politburo in 1973 (see Key People in the Deng Era, p. 729). Wang Hongwen had been too strong-willed and failed to get people to work together; Hua enjoyed better relations with officials of different political views. He had been a senior official even before the Cultural Revolution so he could be acceptable to officials returning to work. He was also acceptable to members of the Gang of Four, who were optimistic that he would be pliable and easy to manipulate.

On the same day Mao told Mao Yuanxin that Hua was to be acting premier, Jiang Qing and Zhang Chunqiao arranged a meeting of the party committees at Tsinghua and Peking universities where Deng was publicly criticized by name for the first time. Chi Qun, the official at Tsinghua whom Deng's followers had criticized, took the lead in organizing more public meetings attacking Deng.[23]

There was a logic to Mao's timing of the public criticism of Deng and his withdrawal from public life. In 1975 the general public had accepted Deng as the leader and had approved of the job he was doing. If Hua were to be accepted as the new leader and not troubled by the presence of Deng, it would be better to remove Deng from the public scene and to take his public reputation down a notch.

The Chinese public and the foreign press learned that Hua was acting premier on January 26 from the *People's Daily.* The news was presented not in banner headlines that might have aroused opposition; instead, in an innocuous report that Hua had hosted a trade delegation from Romania, he was listed with his new title, acting premier.[24] On January 28, Mao formally asked Hua to be responsible for the daily work of the party center.[25] And on February 2, two weeks after Deng had submitted his resignation, the party center announced to high-level party members throughout the country that Hua, with the unanimous approval of the Politburo, had been appointed acting premier.[26] Meanwhile, Deng had dropped out of sight. After submitting his resignation, Deng did not return to work until the summer of 1977.[27]

Mao knew that Hua Guofeng was not as outstanding as Deng Xiaoping, Zhou Enlai, or Chen Yun, but he had no other official of the appropriate age and experience who better fulfilled his requirements. Mao, at least for the moment, had abandoned Deng, but he had not abandoned his search for unity and stability, and Hua (unlike Wang Hongwen) had no enemies and avoided factionalism. Indeed, Hua was the kind of person Deng himself looked for when he was considering which lower-level officials to promote— he was a pragmatic problem-solver who rose step by step. Although Hua lacked knowledge of Marxist-Leninist theory and experience in foreign affairs, Mao hoped he could grow into those areas.

Perhaps most important to Mao, Hua Guofeng, a beneficiary of the Cultural Revolution, could be counted on not to denounce it. Unlike Deng, Hua did not have his own base of support and so his claim to leadership would depend entirely on his selection by Mao. Mao could be confident that Hua would uphold his reputation and his legacy.[28]

But Hua, who had not been tested in a high position, was made only acting premier: Mao still wanted to observe him before making a permanent change. In January 1975 Mao, confident of Deng's demonstrated leadership, had given him formal titles in the military, the party, and the government. In January 1976, by contrast, Hua was not even given a position on the Standing Committee of the Politburo nor was he made a party vice chairman. Furthermore, he was not yet given any important position in the military. Mao did, however, give Hua responsibility for chairing Politburo meetings and for providing overall leadership for the daily work of the party and the government. One of Hua's initial duties was to lead the campaign opposing the "rightist reversal of verdicts" that would criticize Deng Xiaoping's effort to bring back many senior officials.

The Unsuccessful Public Campaign against Deng

Even after he removed Deng from his high positions and began preparations to denounce him in public, Mao limited the attacks on Deng. In his talk on January 21, after choosing Hua Guofeng, Mao said that the differences with Deng were still contradictions among the people, which were not as serious as contradictions with the enemy, and that he would later consult again about Deng's work situation. For now, Deng's work would be reduced but he could continue to work. He would not be beaten to death. Mao had not completely given up on Deng, but he chose to proceed with the public campaign to criticize him. Mao also worked to loosen Deng's hold on the military, so as to make it more difficult for Deng to try to unite with the military against Mao.

Already on January 18, just two days before Deng sent Mao his letter of resignation, a crowd estimated at 7,000 to 8,000 officials in the national defense science sector were assembled in the Peasants Gymnasium *(Xiannongtan tiyuguan)* to criticize the "rightist reversal of verdicts." General Zhang Aiping, who had worked closely with Deng on national defense science and who had already been roundly criticized and even called a Taiwan spy by Jiang Qing, sent word that he was unable to appear at the gathering because of illness. In his brief message, he explained that he was personally responsible for the decisions he had made and that those working under him had played no role in those decisions.[29]

General Zhang wasn't the only one feeling ill as the political climate rapidly turned against Deng and his associates. Aside from Zhang Aiping, the other three "protective Buddhist deities" and their closest associates were also attacked—Hu Yaobang and his colleagues promoting science, Wan Li and his colleagues working on the railways, and Zhou Rongxin and his education colleagues were all subject to attack. Two months later Zhou Rongxin died. On February 2, it was announced that because Marshal Ye Jianying was ill, Chen Xilian would lead the work of the Central Military Commission (CMC). Chen Xilian had worked closely with Mao's nephew Mao Yuanxin in Liaoning, and Mao Yuanxin could serve as go-between, ensuring that Mao's interests in the military would be upheld. On February 16, the party center approved a CMC report announcing that at the enlarged CMC conference the previous summer Deng and Marshal Ye had made serious errors, so circulation of their speeches would be discontinued. Once this notice was published, the participation of Deng and Marshal Ye in CMC work stopped.[30] Mao would not run any risk that Deng and Marshal Ye, under criticism, might try to unite with the military leaders against Mao.

Mao Yuanxin took the lead in organizing a conference sponsored by the Central Committee, at which provincial-level leaders and leaders of the large military regions joined in criticizing Deng. During this conference, held from late February to early March, many regional leaders first heard about Mao's criticisms of Deng Xiaoping, based on materials collected by Mao Yuanxin. Mao had complained to his nephew that Deng's linking of Mao's "three directives" (to resist revisionism, encourage unity and stability, and boost the national economy) had neither been cleared by the Politburo nor reported to Mao. Mao had also protested that Deng's use of the "white cat, black cat theory" ("it doesn't matter if the cat is black or white as long as it catches the mouse") did not make any distinction between imperialism and Marxism-Leninism; it reflected bourgeois thinking. Zhang Chunqiao chimed in that Deng was a representative of the monopoly capitalist class and that he was a revisionist at home and a capitulationist abroad.

At some earlier criticisms of Deng, his name was not mentioned, but at this meeting, Hua Guofeng mentioned Deng by name and criticized his "revisionist" line. Yet Hua, like Mao, placed limits on the anti-Deng campaign:

there would not be any big-character posters criticizing Deng, nor would any criticisms be broadcast. On March 3 a summary of Mao's and Hua's criticisms of Deng was circulated to all levels of the party.[31]

Jiang Qing was, as usual, less restrained. She called a meeting on March 2 for leaders from twelve provinces, at which she tried to escalate the seriousness of Deng's errors, calling him a "counter-revolutionary" and a "fascist." To Mao, this was going too far. He criticized her for calling the meeting without consulting him and forbade her from sending out announcements reporting on the results of the meeting. On March 21, when the *People's Daily* asked whether the "person pursuing the capitalist road [Deng] who is trying to reverse verdicts . . . will have a genuine change of heart," officials in Beijing understood: Mao, still hoping Deng might change, was giving him another chance.[32] Deng, however, showed no signs of softening his stance. On April 5 it would become clear that the campaign to criticize Deng had not won the hearts and minds of the public.

Demonstrating for Zhou and Deng: Tiananmen Square, April 5, 1976

The Qing Ming (Annual Grave Sweeping) festival is held every year in China to remember the dead. In the weeks before the 1976 festival, which was scheduled for April 5, the Gang of Four began to anticipate that some people would use the occasion to launch demonstrations to remember Zhou Enlai. They were right to be concerned. In Beijing, not only officials and students but also many ordinary people, upset that Zhou Enlai in January had not been properly memorialized, were indeed planning to show their respect for him on April 5.

On March 25, a few days before the festival, Shanghai's *Wenhui bao*, a newspaper dominated by the Gang of Four, published an article criticizing Deng and his "backer," another person "taking the capitalist road," whom everyone understood to mean Zhou Enlai. In this case, the Gang of Four proved to have a poor grasp of public opinion, for the article attempting to dampen support for Zhou Enlai backfired. Angry former Red Guards turned the skills they had acquired in attacking Jiang Qing's enemies against Jiang Qing herself. In Shanghai, large crowds immediately surrounded the offices of the newspaper to demand an explanation.

At Nanjing University, too, then three hours from Shanghai by train, posters immediately went up condemning *Wenhui bao,* and demonstrations spread from the university to the main streets of the city. People carried wreaths from the center of Nanjing to lay at the Yuhuatai Memorial, which had been erected to commemorate the 100,000 Communists killed by the Nationalists. Later, the Gang of Four mobilized their supporters to remove the wreaths and block further demonstrations. They did manage to keep news of the Nanjing events out of the official media, but they were unable to stop informal reports from spreading to other cities.[33]

On March 26, the day after the demonstrations in Nanjing, Deng Xiaoping was brought to an enlarged Politburo meeting to be criticized as the head of the reviled capitalists in the party. He was also accused of forming a faction designed to seize power and, ultimately, to restore capitalism.[34] Deng was in effect warned that he too would be held responsible for any demonstrations on April 5.

Just four days later, on March 30, the first wreaths honoring Zhou in Beijing began to appear at the Monument to the People's Heroes in Tiananmen Square. Poems and essays honoring Zhou Enlai were posted, and speeches praising Zhou and attacking the Gang of Four began to attract crowds. Other posters expressed support for Deng Xiaoping, and some people placed little bottles on the street, because the Chinese word for "little bottle" is pronounced "xiao ping."

The party leadership in Beijing, attempting to head off any larger outpouring of emotions, announced that work units could commemorate Zhou within their units but Tiananmen Square was to remain orderly. Patrols were sent to block any demonstrations. Beijing municipal officials estimated that by Saturday, April 3, some one million Chinese had visited the square, with several hundred thousand there at peak times and never fewer than tens of thousands at other times during the day.[35] The party leadership in Beijing sent out an urgent order: "Do not go to Tiananmen to lay wreaths. . . . The laying of wreaths is an outmoded custom."[36] But news spread by word of mouth, and on Sunday, April 4, there was a tremendous outpouring of people (estimated at more than two million) to pay tribute to Zhou Enlai, to oppose the Gang of Four, and to express support for Deng.

To avoid giving Jiang Qing any further excuse to attack him, Deng forbade his family members from going to the square, where poems, posters, white chrysanthemums, and wreaths were accumulating.[37] Groups gathered to hear speakers risking possible arrest by loudly expressing both their devotion to Zhou and their readiness to sacrifice their lives to defeat the Gang of Four, which was plotting to seize power. People in the square came from all walks of life: officials, students, workers, and peasants.[38] A few of the boldest speakers were arrested. Roger Garside, a British embassy official who personally observed these developments, commented,

> As a memorial for Zhou, this people's ceremony was more moving than any state funeral I have seen. As a political demonstration, it was utterly unlike anything I had ever seen in China . . . the crowds were acting out of conviction . . . expressing thoughts and feelings that had been flowing underground for years. . . . There was . . . anger at what had been done to the legacy of Zhou . . . a spirit of revolt against Mao. . . . apprehension for the future of China and defiance of those who would certainly seek to punish the demonstrators. . . . The Mandate had been removed from Mao.[39]

On the evening of April 4, the Politburo met in the Fujian Room of the Great Hall of the People to discuss how to respond to events in the square. Politburo members Marshal Ye and Li Xiannian, who were sympathetic to the demonstrators, were on sick leave, and Deng Xiaoping was not present. Hua Guofeng chaired the meeting and Mao Yuanxin attended. At the meeting, Wu De, chairman of the Beijing Party Committee and head of the Beijing Revolutionary Committee (which had overall responsibility for maintaining public order in Beijing), reported that 2,073 wreaths had been presented on behalf of over 1,400 work units. At one location, the pile of wreaths was more than six meters wide. Wu De also reported that some of the demonstrators had been planning these activities for some time and that they had been influenced by Deng Xiaoping. Jiang Qing, in her attempt to stop the demonstrations, declared that Qing Ming was over and that before dawn all the wreaths should be cleared away and sent to the Babaoshan Revolutionary Cemetery in Beijing. Hua Guofeng directed Wu De to find a way to implement her request.[40]

On Monday, April 5, before dawn, some two hundred trucks from Beijing municipality arrived at Tiananmen Square. Workers tossed the wreaths onto the trucks and hauled them away. After sunrise, crowds began to swell to over 100,000 people. As they realized what had happened, they grew increasingly angry and began yelling, "Return our wreaths. Return our comrade-in-arms." The defiant crowds assaulted the Great Hall of the People, burned cars, smashed bicycles, struck a foreign cameraman, and assaulted a small building used by the militia.

That afternoon, the Politburo met again. Deng Xiaoping, who had not attended Politburo meetings for some time, was brought in to receive criticism. Zhang Chunqiao first attacked Deng by saying he was like Imre Nagy, the fiery leader of the Hungarian revolt of 1956.[41] Mao Yuanxin passed on critical messages from Mao, some written, some oral, with Deng all the while remaining silent. Wang Hongwen then delivered to the Politburo Mao's order to prepare 100,000 militiamen to put down the demonstrators—but Ni Zhifu, in charge of the militia, replied that at most only 30,000 were available, with Wu De adding that they would be no match for the large numbers of protesters in the square.

Next, Zhang Chunqiao said that Wu De should make a broadcast to the protesters. Wu De therefore wrote out a brief message to be broadcast and showed it to Hua Guofeng and the other Politburo members, who approved it. The broadcast would not refer to the causes of the protests, but instead direct attention to a small group of counter-revolutionaries in the square who were turning the memorial into a political movement by attacking Mao and the Central Committee. It would also refer to the unrepentant person taking the capitalist road who had promoted the rightist reversal of verdicts instead of uniting behind Mao and the party. Because counter-revolutionaries are misusing the incident, the broadcaster would say, the revolutionary masses should immediately evacuate the square.

At 6:30 p.m. on April 5, the Politburo tapes were broadcast in the square. The next day, in the print version of Wu De's announcement that appeared in the *People's Daily*, Deng's name—which had been absent from the broadcast—was inserted, specifically identifying him as the unrepentant "capitalist roader."[42]

The plan approved by the Politburo called for the militia to move in at 8:00 p.m., but at that time Wu Zhong, the commander of the Beijing Garrison who was on the scene, judged that too many protesters remained in the square. He explained to Hua Guofeng and Chen Xilian, who continued to phone him, that it was too soon for the militia to clear the area. At 10:30 p.m., the floodlights were turned on and Wu De's tape was played again, telling the demonstrators to leave the square. Finally, at 11:00 p.m. when Wu Zhong reported by phone to Wu De that only about a thousand protesters remained, Wu De gave permission to bring in the militia. More than a hundred people who resisted were arrested. Although the police did not use fire-arms, they did use clubs and dozens of people were injured; pools of blood remained on the streets after the area was cleared.[43] But no deaths were re-ported.

A few hours later, before dawn on April 6, some members of the Politburo met to review the incident. They concluded that the demonstrations had been planned and organized, and therefore they constituted a plot against the state. That afternoon, Mao Yuanxin met with Mao to discuss the nature of the incident, and the Chairman approved broadcasting that it had been a plot. There is no evidence that Mao personally believed that Deng was the "black hand" who had organized the demonstrations (as was publicly an-nounced), but he did believe that if Deng were to remain in power, he would lead the party down the wrong path.[44] By that evening, Jiang Qing had al-ready met with Mao and again demanded that Deng be removed from the party, but Mao still did not agree.[45]

Gao Wenqian, who at the time was working in the party archives, reports that for Mao the news of what happened in Tiananmen on April 5 was "more than distressing. . . . At the very site where millions of young Red Guards had shouted 'long live' to him . . . the same multitudes . . . [were] roaring in protest against his rule. . . . The judgment of history, he knew, would be ex-ceedingly harsh. [He] was suddenly overwhelmed by fear and depression."[46] China had not yet introduced voting, even in the villages, but the April 5 demonstrations had made it clear, at least in Beijing where the political con-sciousness was by far the highest, that Mao had lost the popular mandate, that Zhou Enlai was the public's hero, and that Deng Xiaoping had enough public support to become the preeminent leader.

The Removal of Deng and the Elevation of Hua, April 1976

On the morning of April 7, when Mao Yuanxin reported the latest develop-ments to Mao, Mao gave him written directions about how to proceed at the Politburo meeting scheduled for later that day. When the Politburo met, Mao Yuanxin took out the note from Mao and showed it to the others. It read: "It was in the capital, it was at Tiananmen, there was burning and hit-ting. The nature of the movement has changed." In short, the movement had become counter-revolutionary. Contradictions were no longer among the people; they were more serious: they were between the party and the enemy trying to bring down the party. Mao Yuanxin also conveyed to the Politburo

Chairman Mao's two proposals: first, that Hua Guofeng, the acting premier, be made premier and first vice chairman of the party; and second, that Deng, who until that time had not been officially removed from his positions in the government, party, or military, be stripped of all his positions. Yet even at this point Mao placed limits on the treatment of Deng: he also directed that Deng be "allowed to remain in the party to see how he behaves." When Mao's proposals were conveyed, the Politburo fell silent, and then approved them. Once Mao spoke, there was never any question about the outcome.

Mao completely removed Deng from power. And yet, when Wang Dongxing first informed Mao that Jiang Qing might be mobilizing the masses to attack Deng, Mao directed that Wang Dongxing move Deng to a safe place not far from his children, and that Deng's location be kept secret from the Gang of Four.[47]

By giving Hua full power and by removing Deng from all official positions, Mao cleared the way for Hua to lead the country. From Mao's perspective, Hua had made no major errors during his months as acting premier, and Mao had no better choice who would be loyal to Mao's reputation and who had the potential to get along with radicals and senior officials. He had also shown great strength in putting down the April 5 demonstrations.

Knowledgeable officials in Beijing believe that until April 5, Mao had left open the possibility that Deng and Hua might share leadership positions, but after such a level of popular support for Deng it was just not possible: Hua would have been overwhelmed by Deng. By allowing Deng to remain in the party, Mao left open the possibility that Deng might again serve the country, though not anytime soon. That evening, at 8:00 p.m. there was a public announcement that Hua Guofeng had been named first vice chairman of the party as well as premier.[48]

Top officials in the party organized demonstrations in various cities throughout the country to show their loyalty to Hua Guofeng. Demonstrations were also organized at work units and universities. At Peking University, for example, all students were told to assemble to listen to an announcement at 8:00 p.m. on April 7. At the appointed time, loudspeakers throughout the campus bellowed out congratulations to Hua Guofeng for his new appointment as first vice chairman and premier, then announced a huge schoolwide meeting featuring representatives from each department at the university. At that meeting, those representatives denounced Deng and supported Hua, though observers noted that they carefully followed their scripts, without showing nearly the same enthusiasm as did the demonstrators in Tiananmen Square on April 4 and 5.[49]

Although Hua rarely met Mao, when they met at the April 30 visit to Beijing by Prime Minister Muldoon of New Zealand, Mao took out a piece of paper and scrawled this message to Hua: "Go slowly, don't be in a rush. Act according to the past directions. With you in charge, I am at ease" *(Manman lai, buyao zhaoji, zhao guoqu fangzhen ban, ni banshi, wo fangxin).*[50] Hua did not publicize the last part of the message at the time, but there is no doubt of its authenticity and of Mao's meaning.[51] Mao had chosen Hua as his successor. Mao's judgment that Hua would remain loyal to him and his policies was to prove correct, but his hope that Hua could unite the radicals and the pragmatists was not realized. Within days after Mao's death, Hua would conclude that it was impossible to work with Jiang Qing and her fellow radicals. Mao also wished that Hua, with support from some senior leaders like Marshal Ye and Li Xiannian, might provide long-term leadership, but these hopes, too, never came to fruition.

Deng after April 7, 1976

On April 8, 1976, the day he was removed from all his posts, Deng passed to Wang Dongxing a letter to be delivered to Mao. In his letter, Deng made it clear that he remained faithful to party discipline, writing, "I fully support the party center's decision concerning Comrade Hua Guofeng assuming the positions of first vice chairman and premier." Aware that Jiang Qing had tried to remove him from the party, Deng added, "I express my deep appreciation to the Chairman and to the party center for allowing me to remain in the party."[52]

Yet Deng was forbidden to take part in high-level party discussions and public meetings. He was not allowed to participate in any of the funeral activities for Zhu De, commander of the Red Army, after he died on July 6, or for Chairman Mao, after he died on September 9.[53] At the Politburo meeting on the night of Mao's death, Jiang Qing again tried to remove Deng from the party, although her efforts were repulsed by Hua Guofeng, who faithfully followed Mao's orders, as well as by Marshal Ye.[54]

The pressure from the criticism and isolation were heavy burdens, even for one as hardened as Deng Xiaoping, and some others would prove less sturdy. After April 5 the criticism sessions against Zhou Rongxin intensified; even

Wu De, who led the clearing of Tiananmen Square, acknowledged that the Gang of Four and Chi Qun had "struggled him to death."[55]

Mao not only protected Deng and allowed him to keep his party membership, but he offered him some special consideration. On June 10, for example, Deng passed a letter to Wang Dongxing, to be forwarded to Hua Guofeng and Mao, indicating that his wife had been hospitalized for an eye disease and it would make a big difference if a family member could remain with her in the hospital. Mao gave his permission. On June 30, too, Deng received notification that he could return to his old home on Kuang Street from his temporary residence on Dong Jiaomin Lane. Even in his last days, Mao never completely gave up on Deng.

Nine days after the Deng family moved back home, there was a catastrophic earthquake, centered in Tangshan several hundred miles from Beijing, that according to official figures resulted in 242,000 deaths. The tremors shook Beijing badly and caused structural damage to an estimated one-third of Beijing's buildings. As in imperial times, some regarded the natural disaster as a sign that the heavens were dissatisfied with the top leadership. Deng and his family, like many others, camped out in the yard outside their residence until their fear that the building might collapse subsided. After moving back into their home, from April 1976 until when Deng returned to work in the spring of 1977, Deng's life centered, as it had in Jiangxi for over three years, on his family and the news he received from the radio and newspapers.

The Political Balance after April 7, 1976

The selection of Hua Guofeng as premier and first vice chairman meant that for the first time Hua had a higher political rank than any of the Gang of Four. Hua had tried to maintain good relations with all of the gang, but they moved to a different drummer: in short, they were radical propagandists, and he was a pragmatic problem-solver. Moreover, Hua's promotions made the Gang of Four regard him as a serious rival.

Hua, a modest middle-level official suddenly filling huge shoes, took a cautious approach in the charged political atmosphere. Many senior officials supported him because at least in the short run they saw no alternative for holding the country together, because he pursued moderate policies, and because he reached out to them to get their cooperation.

Until April 7, Mao retained enough power and energy to orchestrate high-level politics, but he was aware that others did not expect him to live more than a year. As he had observed, the rats were abandoning the sinking ship. When he met former president Nixon on February 23, he had said, referring to the six factories and two schools dear to his heart, "I've only been able to change a few places in the vicinity of Beijing."[56] High officials continued to respect him for his early achievements, but they were discerning in deciding how much to follow him. He could no longer translate his aura into power to mobilize the country as he had in 1958 and 1966–1967.

Mao chose Hua, but the two had had very little direct contact before or after April 7, when Mao gave him a clearer mandate to lead. Until then, even from his sickbed, Mao actively orchestrated the criticisms of Deng and selected the future leadership core. After April 7, and especially after his first heart attack on May 11, however, Mao lacked the energy and even the vision to take an active role in tutoring Hua. Jiang Qing, in contrast, remained highly energized, criticizing Deng and other senior officials. She endeavored to deepen her networks, located primarily in the propaganda apparatus of both the civilian and military hierarchies, intimidating those afraid to cross someone who might gain power after Mao's death.

In May 1976, General Wang Zhen, one of Marshal Ye's most trusted friends, visited Ye at his home in the military compound in the Western Hills. There Wang Zhen raised the question of how to respond to the Gang of Four. Very few dared to say then what many knew—that it was really a Gang of Five led by Chairman Mao. Indeed it is reported that when Wang Zhen cautiously asked Marshal Ye's views of the Gang of Four, Ye, concerned about the possibility of bugging, replied by opening the four fingers of his right hand and moving the thumb down to the palm, indicating they should wait until Mao had passed away. Even if that story is apocryphal, it is believed by many people in Beijing and is consistent with Marshal Ye's actions.

Mao Yuanxin had played a central role as Mao's messenger in orchestrating the criticism of Deng and the rise of Hua Guofeng, but after April 5, as Mao Zedong took a less active role, Mao Yuanxin's role as messenger became less important.

Although Hua assumed higher formal positions on April 7, he did not gain control over the bureaucracy to exercise power in the way that Deng had. To the extent that Hua had a policy perspective that guided his actions, it did not depart greatly from Deng's practice of using pragmatic means to work toward the four modernizations. Higher-level decisions remained in limbo and the bureaucracy, while waiting uncertainly for the new structure of power that would follow Mao, continued its daily work without clear overall direction.

The Death of Mao, September 9, 1976

On May 11, scarcely one month after the Tiananmen demonstrations, Mao suffered a heart attack (myocardial infarction). He remained conscious, but was seriously weakened. Until then, Mao had continued to receive Politburo documents and to give final approval on Politburo decisions before they were distributed and implemented. But after May 11, he no longer looked at documents. On June 26, Mao suffered a second heart attack, on September 2 a third, and on September 9, at 12:10 a.m., he died. Hua, who automatically became acting chairman of the party, immediately called together the Politburo members who met in the wee hours of the morning to approve the wording of the official announcement of Mao's death that would be released at 4:00 p.m. that same day.

The death of Mao brought on national state-led mourning. The larger-than-life man who had dominated the party for over forty years and the nation for twenty-seven years had passed away, and ordinary people who knew almost nothing about politics wept as they paid their respects to the leader they had been taught to revere. Even those who demonstrated on April 5 worried about the future of China and even how it might affect their personal lives. Would China return to the chaos of 1966–1969? Would the government fall apart and force the nation into civil war?

However much high-level officials harbored similar concerns, in the short term they plunged into their work to stay atop all the immediate arrangements—the preparation for ceremonies, the treatment of the corpse, the wording of announcements, the liaison with diverse groups at home and abroad, and the preservation of security in the capital. The 377-member funeral committee, headed by Hua Guofeng, was announced immediately; the list was a defining moment for ranking the overall positions of officials and their contributions to the party and the country.

For the elaborate ceremonies in both Beijing and the provinces, political juggling was temporarily put aside while all worked together to pay respects to Mao's memory. Leaders at all levels took their assigned places, reaffirming their positions in the political hierarchy. Hua Guofeng was firmly in charge, and he was later given high marks for his overall management of the mourning activities. Daily memorial services were held in the Great Hall of the People from September 11 to September 17.

On September 18, following protocol, Wang Hongwen, who had been removed from actual work but not from his formal position, was allowed to chair the memorial proceedings. But the pride of place was given to Hua Guofeng who delivered the memorial speech in Tiananmen Square, praising Mao as the "greatest Marxist of our time" while an estimated one million listeners attended to pay their respects. On that same day, the whistles of all factories and trains in the country blew a three-minute tribute. Hua also announced that following an autopsy, Mao's body would be preserved and displayed. Later, a mausoleum was erected in Tiananmen Square where viewers lined up outside before being allowed to enter and take their turn viewing his body. It was a blow to Deng Xiaoping and the officials with whom he had worked closely during 1975—Hu Qiaomu, Zhang Aiping, Wan Li, and Hu Yaobang—that they were excluded from the community of party leaders paying their respects to Mao. Deng, nonetheless, erected in his home a special altar where he and his family paid their own private tribute to Mao.[57]

Once the memorial activities had ended, high-level political leaders resumed their maneuvering to define and control the images presented to the public, positioning themselves for the struggles that were sure to come.

The Arrest of the Gang of Four

Jiang Qing told her Western biographer Roxane Witke, "Sex is engaging in the first rounds, but what sustains interest in the long run is power."[58] She proudly announced after Mao's death that she had been his most faithful dog, but she might have added "attack" before "dog" to indicate her specialty: she was unrivaled in her fearlessness in destroying targets that Mao identified. The educated public, aware of her origins, privately derided her as a courtesan and a second-class actress who had risen improperly. She lacked the confidence and grace of someone who had risen to power naturally; instead she displayed the haughtiness of one who had elbowed her way to the top. She was regarded as rude and inconsiderate even by people who worked for her. She displayed the elemental anger of someone who had been shunned by senior party officials since the 1940s; by serving Mao, she acquired the power to deliver payback, and she did so ruthlessly. A symbol of Mao's worst side, she was easily the most hated figure in China. Starting in 1974, when Mao began to seek national unity and stability, Mao treated her as a loose cannon in need of some restraint, but he remained appreciative of her loyalty, concerned about her welfare, and protective lest he need to call on her again.

There was no indication that Mao ever intended Jiang Qing to be a high-level leader, and when she revealed such ambitions, he restrained her. Once Mao had formally designated Hua as first vice chairman and premier, the possibility of her getting a top position, or playing an important role in the leadership in fact disappeared, although her ambitions did not.

Jiang Qing never acquired the vision, the organizational skills, or the ability to get the positive cooperation from other power holders that was needed to be a real contender for power. She had burned too many bridges, destroyed too many high officials, and alienated too many colleagues. She lacked the self-restraint to be part of a loyal opposition. She lacked support among senior party officials, who were far more skilled in organizing; within the military she had virtually no support outside the Political Department.

During Mao's last year, Jiang Qing endeavored to deepen her base, working through the civilian propaganda apparatus and the Political Department of the PLA as she continued Mao's revolutionary class struggle against the bourgeoisie. She kept in touch with the radicals in the Shanghai militia who had access to arms. Generals did not worry that she would win in a military showdown—they were concerned that some military officers might be intimidated into cooperating with her and that she might stir up so many radicals as to create long-term struggles and chaos, which would only slow China's progress.

Jiang Qing realized that her best hope was to find or perhaps to alter some document of Mao's that would allow her to secure more power and define Mao's legacy. Immediately after Mao's death, Jiang Qing went to Mao's personal assistant Zhang Yufeng day after day, demanding that all of Mao's documents be turned over to her. She did receive some documents and kept them in her possession for a few days, but when Hua Guofeng insisted that all of Mao's papers were to be held by Wang Dongxing, she reluctantly passed them over. She then began pressing Ji Dengkui to gain access to archives of materials originally collected and controlled by Lin Biao, which were being housed at Lin's former home at Maojiawan.[59]

The day after Hua's memorial address, Jiang Qing requested an immediate meeting of the Politburo Standing Committee, which included her allies Wang Hongwen and Zhang Chunqiao, without the presence of Marshal Ye, to discuss the handling of Mao's documents.[60] Hua, feeling he had no choice, called the meeting that afternoon. Jiang Qing brought with her Yao Wenyuan and Mao Yuanxin. At the meeting, she demanded that Mao Yuanxin, who had managed Mao's papers during the last ten months of his life, be kept in charge of his uncle's materials while he prepared a report on them. Others disagreed, and because the meeting reached no decision, the materials remained at the party center.[61]

Jiang Qing also attempted to extend her control in the propaganda apparatus, which she had controlled at the zenith of her power in the earlier days of the Cultural Revolution. In addition, she tried to mobilize youth, telling them to persist in class struggle and in their attacks on bureaucratism. In a speech at Tsinghua University on October 1, Jiang Qing encouraged young people to take an oath to fight to the end.

When Hua heard that at some meetings the Gang of Four had told allies to expect good news on October 7, 8, or 9, he concluded that he needed to act urgently. Although there was no real evidence that Jiang Qing had planned a coup, there were other ominous signs. On October 4, Chi Qun swore an oath of loyalty to Jiang Qing. And the October 4 edition of the *Guangming Daily* featured an article written by "Liang Xiao" (a pen name used by the radicals at the two universities, Peking University and Tsinghua University), declaring that the struggle against capitalists inside the party must be carried through to the end. Concerned about these developments, Marshal Ye went that same day to consult Wang Dongxing and Hua Guofeng, who were already worried that the Gang of Four might soon carry out some kind of action.[62]

No one doubted that Jiang Qing was part of the "I live, you die" political tradition, prepared to fight to the end. Any decision to arrest the Gang of Four would require the bold leadership of Acting Chairman Hua Guofeng and the cooperation of both Marshal Ye, vice chairman of the CMC, and Wang Dongxing, head of the Palace Guard (which protected the party center). All saw eye to eye and moved quickly. Immediately after Mao's death, Marshal Ye, then minister of defense as well as vice chairman of the CMC, had pledged to Hua his wholehearted support to keep the post-Mao transition smooth. Several days after Mao's death, Hua sent Li Xiannian to sound out Ye on how to deal with the Gang of Four, and Li and Ye agreed that fast action was called for. When Wang Dongxing would later describe the preparations for the arrest of the Gang of Four, he would say that Hua Guofeng and Ye Jianying were the strategists, and that he simply implemented their directions.[63]

Marshal Ye sought to make the arrests in a way that would prevent a clash between military forces, which could create further instability. Because the Gang of Four had their own guards at Diaoyutai where they lived, that meant avoiding a confrontation there. But timing was also critical. The three partners in planning (Hua, Ye, and Wang Dongxing) realized that they must take the initiative before the Gang of Four did. After they saw the October 4 editorial and heard that the Gang of Four were telling their allies to expect good news as early as October 9, Hua, Ye, and Wang Dongxing prepared to move swiftly and decisively. Meanwhile, one by one Wang Dongxing was selecting a small number of men in his guard unit on whom he could rely.

On the afternoon of October 5, Marshal Ye talked separately with Hua and Wang Dongxing. They decided that on the next day, October 6, Hua would call a Politburo Standing Committee meeting on short notice (as was often done) to be held at 8:00 p.m. in Huairen Hall of Zhongnanhai. The stated agenda would include three important issues: publication of volume 5 of Mao's *Selected Works,* planning for the Mao Memorial Hall, and policies on the use of Mao's former residence in Zhongnanhai. Usually Politburo Standing Committee meetings were only attended by Hua, Ye, Wang Hongwen, and Zhang Chunqiao. With these items on the agenda, Wang and Zhang would not want to miss the meeting. And because Yao Wenyuan was centrally involved in publication of volume 5 of Mao's *Selected Works,* it was natural to invite him to join this discussion as well, even though he was not a member of the Standing Committee.

On the night of October 6, although Wang Dongxing's small group of special forces was already inside, everything outside the building appeared normal. Just before 8:00 p.m., Wang Hongwen strode into the building and was suddenly grabbed by the guards. He yelled angrily, "I've come for a meeting, what are you doing?" The guards wrestled him to the floor and carried him to the main hall, where Hua Guofeng stood up to say, "Wang Hongwen, you have committed anti-party and anti-socialist crimes. The party center is placing you in confinement for investigation." While Wang was taken away from the main hall, Zhang Chunqiao, carrying his briefcase, arrived exactly on time. About to enter the main hall, he too was arrested by guards and handcuffed; Hua Guofeng announced he would be interrogated for his crimes, and he submitted without resistance. When Yao Wenyuan arrived, he was immediately arrested just outside the building.

Meanwhile, a small group of special forces attached to the Central Committee office building went to Jiang Qing's residence and told her that she was being held for special examination. She replied that she needed to go to the restroom, so a female member of the special forces accompanied her. Upon returning, she was escorted to a car and driven away. Within thirty-five minutes, with no firing of guns and no bloodshed, the threat from the Gang of Four was eliminated.[64]

At around the same time, Hua and Ye had also sent special teams to the broadcasting studios, to New China News Agency (Xinhua), to the *People's Daily*, and to other publications to make certain that followers of the Gang of Four were given no public voice and that no news would spread until the key followers of the gang had been arrested. The day after the gang's arrests took place, Xie Jingyi of the Beijing Municipal Party Committee and Chi Qun of Tsinghua University were placed in protective custody.[65]

To get around the problem of the Gang of Four being Politburo members who would resist formalizing Hua Guofeng's position as the top leader—a position that Jiang Qing had coveted for herself—Marshal Ye convened a meeting of the Politburo without the Gang of Four, at his home in the Western Hills. The meeting began at 10:00 p.m. on the evening of the gang's arrest, and continued until 4:00 a.m. At the meeting, the participants unanimously chose Hua as chairman of both the party and the CMC. They also discussed what cautionary steps were needed to avoid disruptions by followers of the Gang of Four.[66] In addition, immediately after the Politburo meeting, it was announced that volume 5 of Mao's *Selected Works*, which Deng and the Gang of Four had struggled so hard to control, would be published under the direction of Hua Guofeng, giving Hua the critical opportunity to define Mao's legacy.[67]

The greatest risk of disorder from Gang of Four followers came from the armed militia forces in Shanghai.[68] Indeed, Ye, Hua, and the others kept the gang's arrest secret until they were certain the Shanghai problem was under control. Xu Shiyou, former longtime commander of the Nanjing Military Region with jurisdiction over the Shanghai area, flew to Beijing where he assured the leaders that the military was fully prepared in case fighting were to break out in Shanghai. There was good cause for concern. Two days after the arrest of the Gang of Four, the gang's followers in Shanghai began to suspect that something terrible had happened because they couldn't reach the gang, and they began to prepare for armed resistance.

Beijing countered this threat by sending senior leaders led by General Su Zhenhua to Shanghai to quiet things down. While there, the leaders also invited Ma Tianshui and other followers of Jiang Qing from Shanghai to Beijing for a meeting, where unbeknownst to them, they would become hostages. By October 14, those remaining in Shanghai who were still planning to resist realized that high-level party officials, as well as the public, were overwhelmingly opposed to armed resistance. Seeing the hopelessness of their situation, they yielded without a fight.[69]

Meanwhile, security officials had been reaching decisions about which former subordinates of the Gang of Four were most dangerous. On the day after the Gang of Four was arrested, thirty of the gang's most loyal followers in Beijing were taken into custody. Security officials continued to observe those still considered security risks.[70] Mao Yuanxin was also arrested.

The sudden release of the news of the arrest of the Gang of Four thrilled and relieved a public weary of continued struggles and afraid of their return. The public announcement was made on October 18, and huge, spontaneous public celebrations erupted. Foreign correspondents observing the events reported extraordinary excitement as the masses poured onto the streets of all major cities to celebrate.[71]

Chairman Hua Seeks Party Support

Yet within the party there were doubts as to whether the Gang of Four should be arrested and even whether Mao had actually chosen Hua to be his successor. Mao had never announced publicly that Hua Guofeng was his successor. High-level officials knew that Mao would never have arrested the Gang of Four and even some who disliked the Gang of Four felt that Mao's wishes should be followed.

In an effort to solidify support for Hua's rule, Marshal Ye and Li Xiannian supported Hua Guofeng at a meeting that brought together leading central, provincial, and military officials in a meeting in Beijing. They enumerated the crimes of the Gang of Four and explained the need for arresting them. Most high officials agreed with the need to arrest the Gang of Four and acknowledged that Hua, Marshal Ye, and Wang Dongxing had acted wisely and courageously in the way they carried it out.

It was at this meeting that Hua revealed for the first time the scrawled note that Mao had given to him on April 30 during the visit of New Zealand's prime minister, Robert Muldoon: "with you in charge, I am at ease."[72] The revelation helped persuade the regional party secretaries that Mao had indeed chosen Hua. At the meeting Hua received declarations of approval for his selection as chairman of the party and the CMC. The confrontation between Hua and the Gang of Four would be told and retold as a great struggle between good and evil—between the party pursuing the correct path and a gang plotting against the party. Like many stories recorded in Chinese historical documents, the victor was seen as virtuous and the loser as villainous. But this time, as in 1949, there was genuine and widespread popular support for the victor.

To further solidify his position, Hua chose to continue the criticism of Deng and to delay his return. On October 26, Hua announced that in addition to criticizing the Gang of Four, the party would also continue its criticism of Deng Xiaoping.[73] The party's criticism was not as extreme as that initiated by the Gang of Four, but it continued for several months. Hua was not ready to welcome Deng back. Deng was too experienced, too confident, and too ready to take charge. Marshal Ye also thought that Hua needed time to establish himself as a strong leader and that Deng should return somewhat later. It wasn't until near the end of 1976 that Marshal Ye, Li Xiannian, and other senior officials began advocating that Deng be brought back to work.[74]

Deng, always ready to accept power realities, was one of the first leaders to express support for Hua Guofeng. On October 7, Deng Rong's husband, He Ping, heard through Marshal Ye's family about the arrest of the Gang of Four. He rushed home by bicycle to report the good news to Deng and his family, who thus learned about the arrest even before it was made public.[75] On October 10, Deng wrote a letter that was delivered to Wang Dongxing to pass on to Hua Guofeng. In the letter, Deng congratulated the party under the leadership of Comrade Hua for its decisive action and great victory over those who had been plotting to seize power. He wrote, "I sincerely support the decision of the party center on the appointment of Comrade Hua Guofeng as chairman of the Central Committee and of the Central Military Affairs Commission. . . . Comrade Guofeng is the most appropriate successor to Mao. . . . How jubilant this makes us feel."[76]

On December 10, two months after the arrest of the Gang of Four, Deng was admitted to the No. 301 Military Hospital with a prostate problem, and on December 14, the party center passed a resolution that Deng again be permitted to read party documents. The first batch of materials he received in the hospital was "Evidence of the Crimes of the Anti-Party Faction Activities of Wang Hongwen, Zhang Chunqiao, Jiang Qing, and Yao Wenyuan." It was to be the first of several batches of such materials that Deng would be given in order to secure his support for Hua's arrest of the Gang of Four. After reading the first batch, Deng said there was plenty of evidence to justify the actions taken and he did not need to see more.[77] Even so, while Deng was still in the hospital Hua Guofeng personally briefed him on issues concerning the Gang of Four.[78]

By this time, other leaders had begun to assume that at some point Deng would return to work. Some leaders thought he might be assigned a role like the one Mao had conceived for him in 1974 when he replaced Zhou Enlai in leading government work and was paired with Wang Hongwen. Perhaps Deng Xiaoping would use his immense experience and skills to handle government work under party head Hua Guofeng. Others thought Deng might play a more limited role, handling foreign affairs, and still others thought he might at some point take over party responsibilities completely as he had in mid-1975. On January 6, 1977, a decision was made that Deng would return to work. It turned out, however, that Hua Guofeng would have another six months to establish himself before Deng returned to work.

The End of Radical Maoism

The scholar Joseph Levenson describes the fate of Confucianism in the late imperial period: when it lost its vitality, Confucianism was still celebrated in the temples and museums, which people visited to pay homage, but it had lost its connection to people's daily lives. Similarly, after Mao's death and the arrest of the Gang of Four, Mao was still enshrined, and multitudes continued to visit the Mao Mausoleum in the center of Tiananmen Square. But radical Maoism, with its mass movements and class warfare, was no longer a part of the daily experience of the Chinese people.

This process of separating radical Maoism from the people's daily lives had in fact already begun under Mao when in 1974 he announced his support for national stability and unity. It continued under the leadership of Deng in 1975 and under Hua in early 1976. With the arrest of the Gang of Four, radical Maoism finally lost its last powerful advocates. The spontaneous celebrations after the announcement of the arrest of the Gang of Four, in addition to the outpouring on April 5, 1976, were powerful, visible symbols of the public's s animus against the radical Maoism that had brought such chaos and destruction.

The trial of the Gang of Four took shape as a giant national rite in which radical Maoism was blamed not on Mao but on the Gang of Four. In truth, many people, including some of the officials who were now celebrating the arrest and trial of the gang, had once shared the vision of radical Maoism and had even taken part in the efforts to realize the vision. Even so, the demise of the Gang of Four marked the end of an era, of hopes to reshape the world through continuing revolution and class struggle. The relief and excitement of the Chinese people at this turn of events was to translate into a deep base of support for pragmatic policies underlying reform and opening.

6

Return under Hua

1977–1978

Shortly after Hua was named premier and first vice chairman of the party in April 1976, Thomas Gates, head of the U.S. Liaison Office in Beijing, met with him for an hour and forty-five minutes. Gates's staff wrote an assessment of Hua based on that meeting, which Gates signed, that proved remarkably prescient. It concluded that Hua was "an intelligent, colorless individual whose hallmark is caution. He handles his material well enough, but he gave off no sparks of unusual intellect or charisma. Hua came across as an ideal transition figure who is unlikely to take any dramatic steps in either internal or external affairs. . . . I doubt Hua has the vision or the leadership qualities necessary to make it over the long term. . . . I think new and better qualified leadership will arise . . . and the colorless Mr. Hua, having fulfilled his historical purpose, will be forced to step aside."[1] Chinese officials would never have said so publicly, but officials at the U.S. Liaison Office undoubtedly sensed that some of them held similar views.

In keeping with a long-standing tradition in Chinese political history writing, which glorifies the victor and denigrates the vanquished, Deng has been credited with launching opening and reform, and Hua has been blamed for following everything Mao decided and directed. It is true that Hua's rise to the highest level of leadership was a stretch for someone who had spent his career in a province and had little experience in Beijing, had no experience in foreign affairs, and had only limited experience in military affairs. In his first year of meetings with foreign leaders, Hua, cautious about making mistakes, understandably fell back on general statements of policy, vague platitudes, and safe slogans. Hua was bright and had been a good official, but he could not compare to Deng in overall ability and leadership qualities. In addition, he did not support the full-scale return of senior officials who had been brought back to work under Deng's leadership, and he could not have provided the sure-footed bold leadership and achieved the good relations with foreign countries that Deng achieved.

But many underestimated Hua and his commitment to reform. Later official histories understate Hua's willingness to depart from the ways of Mao, as well as his support for the policy of opening China to the West. During his interregnum, which lasted from Mao's death in September 1976 until the Third Plenum in December 1978, Hua in fact not only arrested the Gang of Four but abandoned radical Maoism, reduced the roles of ideology and political campaigns, focused on modernization more than class struggle, and regularized the scheduling of party meetings that had been held irregularly under Mao. Hua also sent delegation after delegation abroad to learn about modern technology. He—not Deng—launched China's special economic zones, which experimented with efforts to bring in foreign direct investment. Hua did try to delay Deng's return to office in 1977, but he did not undo the progress that Deng had made in 1975, and he supported the later changes that Deng introduced after returning in 1977. He not only promoted the rapid opening of the country, but even suffered sharp criticism for carrying it too far in his "Western-led Leap Forward" *(yang yuejin).*[2]

Hua's Authority: Official, Not Personal

Hua Guofeng's claim to authority and power stemmed entirely from his selection by Mao and from the official positions he held in the party and governmental bureaucracies. But in China, in 1976, the underpinnings for formal institutional authority were still weak. Mao's dominance of the top positions in the party, the military, and the government during his twenty-seven-year rule had made it more difficult for others to challenge him, but the core of Mao's power remained personal. His authority came not from his official positions, but from his extraordinary success in leading the revolution to military victory, his mastery of the uses of power, his grandiose visions, and the hope and awe he inspired in his people—with the help of a disciplined party and a controlled media.

Hua lacked Mao's and Deng's heroic revolutionary past, their grand appreciation of history, their sure-footed sense of how to respond to issues, and their confidence and poise. He was knowledgeable about many different aspects of party work; he had been minister of public security; and since 1971 (when he was invited to attend Politburo meetings) and 1973 (when he was elevated to full membership on the Politburo), he had had ample opportunity to learn about national politics. But his personal accomplishments, breadth of perspective, and overall stature among the people of China could not compare with those of the seasoned old revolutionaries—Deng Xiaoping, Ye Jianying, Chen Yun, and Li Xiannian.

After Mao's death, the Politburo had given Hua the appropriate titles—chairman of the party, premier, chairman of the Central Military Commission (CMC)—to enable him to govern. Ye and his colleagues announced that the party should increase the importance of formal institutions that did not depend on the personality of one person. Earlier, in the mid-1950s, as China had begun to build a stable structure, organizations had developed predictable procedures; and again in the early 1960s, after the Great Leap disasters, and in 1975 under Deng, they returned to regular procedures that limited leaders from making arbitrary decisions.[3] But there was still a long way to go before these regular procedures and emerging government organizations would acquire the same force of law that they had in many Western countries. Instead, when Chinese officials at lower levels read documents that came from higher levels of power, they realized that in a crisis the top officials could create new documents, each undoing the content of the last.

In late 1976 and early 1977, Marshal Ye and Wang Dongxing endeavored to build up a cult of personality for Hua to enhance his weak personal base of power. Hua's extraordinary victory in arresting the Gang of Four, the lone achievement that raised him above ordinary good officials, was widely celebrated, and in the months after October 1976, hundreds of books and articles appeared lauding Hua's leadership.[4] Poems and songs celebrating his leadership were composed and widely distributed, and his picture appeared throughout the country, paired with that of Mao. Television was not yet widespread in China, but radio messages, piped through loudspeakers in work units and rural villages, celebrated his great abilities at the helm.

The promotion of Hua, however, stirred up reactions. Senior party revolutionary leaders who had gone to battle for their country looked down on young upstarts like Hua, who had entered the party after 1938, and found his glorification excessive and presumptuous. Furthermore, many influential party leaders were reluctant to again worship an individual, fearing that doing so would inhibit inner-party democracy. By late 1978, Hua was on the defensive for having allowed the publicity about his own achievements to reach such heights. He had failed to convince others that he had a personal claim to power that went beyond his appointed positions of leadership.

Hua's modest leadership style was a natural response to his situation in Beijing, but even in Hunan he had a reputation for being cautious and timid compared to other officials of the same rank.[5] Others felt comfortable working with him because they knew he would not boldly challenge them. Indeed, except for the Gang of Four and their followers whom he considered beyond the pale, Hua made an effort to get along with everyone.

When the Communists took power in 1949, Mao and his colleagues had already spent almost two decades planning what to do after they took power, but Hua had little time to prepare. The former revolutionaries who had built the country and created policies from scratch held far broader perspectives than did Hua and others of his generation, who grew up learning how to implement rather than create programs and policies. Until early 1976, when Hua was suddenly elevated to replace Wang Hongwen as the leading candidate to succeed Mao, he was unprepared for top leadership. Even after becoming acting premier in January 1976, Hua was so busy dealing with urgent issues—the death of Zhou, the April 5 Tiananmen incident, the death of Mao, the arrest of the Gang of Four—that he had little time to consider broad strategic issues. After October 1976, Hua, confronted with such huge problems, like an earnest young emperor ascending the throne, welcomed the advice of two senior counselors, Marshal Ye and Li Xiannian. Both were ready to guide him.

Hua had known Marshal Ye and Li Xiannian long before 1976, but he had not been particularly close to them until they bonded to form a small trusted circle, operating in secret to plan the arrest of the Gang of Four. Ye and Li, like Hua, did not suffer deeply during the Cultural Revolution, and they remained relatively free of the passion and animus of the senior officials who had been removed and persecuted. Marshal Ye had been shunted aside before the Cultural Revolution and therefore was not one of the power holders whom Mao had attacked. Li was part of the *yewuzu,* the group of officials who attended to the more routine government activities like running the economy while the political battles of the Cultural Revolution raged around them. Hua, Ye, and Li had all worked well with senior officials before the Cultural Revolution, and all three proved able to collaborate with the beneficiaries of the Cultural Revolution as well as with the senior officials.

Marshal Ye and Li were not among the radicals who attacked others, nor were they on the forefront of those demanding greater democracy and bolder experimentation in the economic sphere. Instead, they were ready to help Hua navigate pragmatically and safely in the uncharted post-Mao period. In particular, Marshall Ye could pave the way for Hua in his relations with the military and Li Xiannian could guide Hua on economic issues.

Hua Balances Mao's Legacy with China's Opening

From the time of Mao's death, Hua was under pressure to show the hardcore radicals that he was following Mao's legacy. They could see that Hua, while claiming to be a follower of Mao, was not pursuing political campaigns and class warfare. Reports in the Western press that after Mao's death China was beginning a process of "de-Maoization" created even more of a burden on Hua to show that he was staying true to Mao's legacy.

The arrest of the Gang of Four was enormously popular with most party officials and with the Chinese public, but radicals who saw themselves as following the real Mao were upset about it. They knew that until his death Mao had tried to ensure a place for the Gang of Four among the top party leadership. This dissonance put Hua and his senior advisers, Marshal Ye and Li Xiannian, on the defensive; they strained to prove that the arrest of the Gang of Four was consistent with carrying out Mao's legacy. Hua collected materials that spelled out the crimes of the gang and, in three batches of material he had distributed, made the case that their arrest was consistent with Mao's views.

Ever since Mao's death, Hua had asserted that he was following Mao's legacy and continuing his policies. But some ideologues and hardcore followers of Mao continued to criticize him for straying from Mao's party line. To answer such critiques, Hua directed his supporters to prepare a theoretical article to show his commitment to the Maoist legacy. The resulting article appeared on February 7, 1977, as an editorial in the *People's Daily, Red Flag,* and the PLA newspaper *Jiefangjun bao.* The editorial declared that whatever policies Mao supported, and whatever instructions Mao gave, should still be followed. The editorial became known as the "two whatevers," Hua's banner for showing that he was fully committed to Mao's legacy.[6] Hua apparently had not anticipated that it would become a target for those who believed that China needed to distance itself from the policies that Mao had pursued during the last two decades of his life.

For Hua to provide overall national leadership for a new era, he needed to convene a party congress, much as Mao had done in 1956 (the 8th Party

Congress); Lin Biao had done in 1969 (the 9th Party Congress); and Mao had done yet again in 1973, after Lin Biao's demise (the 10th Party Congress). It takes many months to formulate economic plans, achieve consensus on policies in major spheres, and prepare the documents needed for a party congress. Hua began the work almost immediately after Mao's death and convened the 11th Party Congress on August 12–18, 1977. The Fifth National People's Congress (NPC), designed to provide overall government leadership, followed in March 1978.

To hold the party congress so soon after taking the reins of power, Hua had to leave many issues unresolved. Ideology and party platitudes were used to cover up disagreements about policy in Hua's four-hour speech to the 11th Party Congress. Yet there were real problems that needed the leaders' attention, and Hua tried to address at least some of them. Following Zhou Enlai and Deng, he continued the focus on the four modernizations. For his closest economic advisers he chose "builders" who were ready to quickly expand new construction projects and imports of industrial plants from abroad, rather than economic planners and finance officials who were more cautious. (For more on "builders" and "cautious planners," see Chapter 15.) He relied especially on Yu Qiuli, the great leader of the Daqing oilfield, to lead the effort to update Deng's ten-year vision with even loftier goals. He also relied heavily on Gu Mu, the head of the State Construction Commission who in December 1974 had been chosen by Mao and Zhou Enlai to be vice premier.

In foreign affairs, Hua began as an amateur. When he met Singapore's prime minister Lee Kuan Yew in Beijing in the spring of 1976, Hua, unaware of the details of Chinese policy, responded to comments and questions with platitudes and slogans. After succeeding Mao, however, Hua made a serious effort to get up to speed on foreign policy issues: by the time he led a delegation to Yugoslavia, Romania, and Iran in August 1978, he was far better informed than he had been in 1976.

In contrast to Deng who was on a leash from Chairman Mao when he traveled abroad in 1974 and 1975, Hua traveled to Yugoslavia and Romania in 1978 as China's top leader, on the first trip abroad by China's top leader since 1957 (when Mao had traveled to Moscow). Upon his return, Hua reported on what China could learn from Yugoslavia and Romania: those countries accepted foreign currency, had joint ventures with foreign companies, carried on compensation trade (countertrade in which investments are repaid from their profits), and brought in foreign technology—all without any loss of sovereignty. Hua commented that the factories he had seen in

Eastern Europe, while not as large as those in China, were far more efficient. The conclusion was obvious: China should follow the examples of Eastern Europe and bring in more foreign technology.

On the problem of improving rural organization, an area in which he did have considerable personal experience, Hua not only sought to retain the socialist structure of communes and production teams, but also organized several conferences to study Dazhai, the national model village for collective agriculture, where extraordinarily large groups were put to work and agricultural engineering projects like large-scale irrigation canals were extolled. Hua's main hope for improving agriculture overall lay in technology. Like Deng, Hua wanted to make up for lost time and move ahead quickly, but he had less experience in judging the institutional developments required to make such progress. His push to achieve a technological breakthrough in agricultural mechanization within four years (by 1980) was naïvely optimistic.

After Deng became the top official in December 1978, Hua underwent a self-criticism for having tried to push ahead too quickly without considering China's shortage of foreign currency, its inability to absorb so much technology so quickly, and its budget imbalances. Some of the criticism may have been warranted: for instance, Hua encouraged Yu Qiuli to consider developing within a few years ten oilfields as large as Daqing, a totally unrealistic goal. But in his overall aim to move China ahead quickly and hasten the import of foreign technologies, Hua was like many other leaders, including Deng Xiaoping.

It is often said that China's policy of opening to the outside world—including its readiness to learn from other countries and eagerness to bring in foreign technology—originated under Deng's leadership at the Third Plenum in December 1978. These efforts were, in fact, all begun under the leadership of Hua Guofeng in 1977, and the policies Hua advanced were not original. Hua and Deng both promoted policies that many party officials regarded as necessary to set China on a new path.

Maneuvering over Deng's Return, October 1976–April 1977

The question of whether Deng should return to work and, if so, with what responsibilities, loomed large from the moment the Gang of Four was arrested. Party leaders agreed that Deng was a rare talent, and senior officials who had returned to work regarded him as their proven leader. As soon as

Mao's death was announced, the media in Hong Kong and the West began speculating about an impending power struggle between Deng and Hua. Within China at the time, however, no one seriously challenged Mao's right to name his successor or Hua's right to be chairman of the party. There was a consensus that, at least for the time being, Hua had the right to keep the positions that Mao had selected for him.

In the months after Mao died, those in elite party circles wondered: should Deng be brought back to perform the work of premier under Chairman Hua Guofeng, as Zhou had served under Mao—and as Deng, in the first half of 1974, had served under Wang Hongwen—or should he become the dominant leader? Hua's senior advisers, Marshal Ye and Li Xiannian, supported Deng's return to work at some point and in some position, but under Hua's leadership. Soon after the arrest of the Gang of Four, Li Xiannian went to visit Deng in the CMC villa in the Western Hills, where Deng was then living, and encouraged him to be prepared to come back.[7] Marshal Ye and Li, the kingmakers, repeated to others their support for Deng's return.[8]

Hua never said specifically that Deng should not be allowed to return to work, but on October 26, 1976, scarcely two weeks after the arrest of the Gang of Four, Hua directed that criticism of Deng and his efforts to allow more senior officials to return (the so-called rightist reversal of verdicts) should continue.[9]

By the Central Party Work Conference in March 1977, however, Hua's encouragement of the criticism of Deng had ended. In response to the complaints of many officials that Deng had been unfairly accused of being responsible for the April 5 demonstrations, Hua directed that the Propaganda Department no longer raise the topic of the April 5 demonstrations. He also acknowledged that the vast majority of those who had taken part in the April 5 protests were not counter-revolutionary and that Deng had not been involved in planning the incident.

On December 12, 1976, there was another breakthrough for Deng. Marshal Ye received a letter from his longtime colleague Geng Biao, then head of the party's International Liaison Department. With his letter, Geng Biao enclosed a batch of documents showing that the Gang of Four had doctored evidence for the report on the April 5 incident, thus deceiving Mao and the party center. Ye immediately told his subordinates that this new evidence was important and that the verdict on the April 5 incident should be reversed.[10] Two days after Marshal Ye received these materials, Deng was again permitted to see party documents. By this point, it was assumed by many that Deng's return was simply a matter of time, even though Marshal Ye had said that the time was not yet ripe. On January 6, 1977, the question of Deng's return was discussed at a Politburo meeting and it was decided that he would be returning to serve in some position.

When Hua's "two whatevers" editorial, entitled "Study the Documents Well and Grasp the Key Link [that is, class struggle]" *(Xuehao wenjian zhua-zhu gang)* appeared on February 7, 1977, it immediately became a point of contention among high-level officials. If all the policies that Mao had approved and all Mao's directives were to be followed, then the judgment that the April 5 demonstrations were counter-revolutionary and the removal of Deng could not be reconsidered. The "two whatevers" editorial galvanized Hua's critics, and the question of whether Deng should return became a focus of the debate. Hu Jiwei, chief editor of the *People's Daily,* later said that the "two whatevers" editorial blocked the return to work of Deng and other senior officials, the reversal of verdicts on those who had taken part in the April 5 Tiananmen incident, and the dismissal of charges against others who had suffered from unjust, fake, and incorrect judgments.[11] Among those who were galvanized into action against the "two whatevers" was Deng Liqun, who took the issue to Wang Zhen, who in turn brought it to the attention of the Politburo.[12]

Following custom, a Central Party Work Conference was scheduled before the planned party congress to permit freer discussions and to create a consensus that those attending the party congress could unanimously support. The famous Central Party Work Conference held the next year, from November to December 1978, was the turning point that strengthened Deng's position and solidified support for the "reform and opening" agenda that would be approved at the Third Plenum in December 1978. At the March 10–22, 1977, Central Party Work Conference, in preparation for the 11th Party Congress to be held that August, opponents of the "two whatevers" spoke out.

In calling the work conference, held at the Jingxi Hotel, a few blocks from Zhongnanhai, Hua Guofeng announced that the agenda for the conference would be: (1) tackling the next steps in dealing with the Gang of Four, (2) mapping out the 1977 economic plan, and (3) planning the party's work for the second half of 1977, including the holding of the party congress.[13]

This conference became the first such broad discussion held among leading party officials since Mao's death just six months earlier. But in contrast to the later Central Party Work Conference of November 1978, the atmosphere in March 1977 was constrained by those who felt that it was too soon to have a frank discussion of Mao's errors. Even so, there was widespread agreement on some issues: changing the main focus of party activity from the Cultural Revolution to the four modernizations, maintaining the leadership of the Communist Party, upholding the banners of Marxism-Leninism and Mao Zedong Thought, and making increased use of foreign capital and technology.

But there remained a visceral divide between senior officials who had suffered humiliation and physical hardship during the Cultural Revolution and those who had benefited from the political upheavals. Many leaders who had risen in the Cultural Revolution by attacking others rallied behind the campaign against the "rightist reversal of verdicts" to avoid ceding power to those who had been attacked. Senior officials who had returned to work earlier were often more ready to work for the return of their friends who had still not been allowed to come back.

The balance between these two groups had increasingly tilted toward the senior officials ever since 1972 when Mao himself had begun to allow a reversal of verdicts. Already by January 1975 at the Fourth NPC, ten officials who had suffered severely during the Cultural Revolution assumed ministerial positions.[14] This trend continued. As many as 59 of the 174 full members of the Central Committee of the 10th Party Congress in 1973 who were still alive in August 1977 (many of whom had been beneficiaries of the Cultural Revolution) were not chosen to serve on the Central Committee of the 11th Party Congress. Of the 201 officials who were chosen to serve on the Central Committee of the 11th Party Congress in 1977, all but 19 were senior officials who had joined the party before 1949.[15] By contrast, the situation on the Politburo changed more slowly. The Standing Committee of the Politburo was composed of the four people who had played the key role in the arrest of the Gang of Four, but on the issue of Deng's return only Marshal Ye and Li Xiannian supported it, whereas Hua Guofeng and Wang Dongxing dragged their feet.

In his lengthy address to the Central Party Work Conference in March 1977, Hua Guofeng said: "Criticizing Deng and attacking the rightist reversal of verdicts were decided by our Great Leader Chairman Mao Zedong. It is necessary to carry out these criticisms."[16] Implying that Deng would not have fully supported Chairman Mao, he added a cutting remark: "We should learn the lessons from Khrushchev."[17] Everyone knew that Deng was often attacked as "China's Khrushchev," the one who might imitate Khrushchev's all-out attack on Stalin. Hua, in an effort to further sustain Mao's legacy, and aware of the negative reaction to the handling of the April 5 demonstrations, also told the conference participants not to discuss those demonstrations. But Hua did not have the commanding authority that Mao had: Chen Yun and Wang Zhen, both widely respected and with far more seniority and personal authority than Hua, still dared to express different views in their small groups at the conference that supported Deng's return.

Chen Yun, sober, prudent, totally dedicated to the party, and highly respected for his enormous contributions to the party, made a strong statement to the Southwest group to which he was assigned, advocating the return of Deng. As usual, Chen prepared his presentation carefully. He had Hu Qiaomu write a draft of his statement, and before he presented it he met with Wang Zhen and others at Geng Biao's home to identify any possible problems in the presentation. In the report, Chen Yun stated, "Comrade Deng Xiaoping had nothing to do with the Tiananmen incident. In response to the needs of the Chinese revolution and the Chinese Communist Party, I hear that some comrades in the party center have proposed that Comrade Deng Xiaoping return and take part in the leadership work of the party center. This is completely correct, it is completely necessary, and I completely support it."[18]

In another small group, "Bearded Wang" (Wang Zhen), crusty and rustic but loyal, blunt, and even endearing to many of the party faithful, also spoke out in favor of Deng's return. By quoting comments Mao had once made praising Deng, he made it extremely awkward for the Maoists to oppose what he said. Quoting Mao, he said that Deng's political thinking was strong, he had rare talent, he was an able warrior, and he firmly opposed revisionism. Wang Zhen went on to say that in leading the work of the party and State Council in 1975, Deng had carried out Mao's line and had achieved great successes. He had spearheaded the fight against the Gang of Four. And now, Wang said, the whole party, the whole army, and all the people warmly wish for him to return early to the leadership of the party.[19]

In the small group discussions, many supported the comments by Chen Yun and Wang Zhen, but Wang Dongxing controlled the final editing of the reports of the conference, and Chen's and Wang's comments and the ensuing discussions were not included. Wang Dongxing told them that if they revised their comments, they could be included in the summaries for publication. Chen Yun and Wang Zhen, with qualifications due to their long service to the party that far exceeded those of Wang Dongxing, replied that if their views were not included in the minutes, then so be it. Though not included in the official summaries, their comments, unaltered, were widely circulated inside and outside the conference.[20]

During the conference, Hua made some conciliatory comments to the many delegates who passionately wanted to reverse the verdicts on the April 1976 Tiananmen incident. He acknowledged that it was the Gang of Four who had suppressed the masses from mourning Zhou Enlai's death in April 1976, that Deng Xiaoping had played no part in the Tiananmen incident, and that it had been reasonable for the masses to flock to Tiananmen. Nonetheless, Hua still called the event a counter-revolutionary incident and said that a small number of participants were counter-revolutionaries. He also said that the rightist reversal of verdicts—which everyone knew Deng had favored—should be attacked.[21]

In response to the widespread support at the work conference for Deng's return, Hua said, "When the rain falls, a channel for transporting the water is formed automatically" *(shuidao qucheng),* and "when the gourd is ripe, it falls off the vine" *(guashu diluo).* His meaning was clear: when nature was ready, a way for Deng to return to work would become apparent, but they shouldn't try to rush it. As a concession to Deng's supporters, however, Hua said that at the Third Plenum (of the 10th Party Congress) and at the 11th Party Congress (to be held that summer), it would be appropriate to make a formal decision on Deng's return.

In this shifting political landscape, Hua sought to reinforce his interpretation of Mao's thought by controlling the editing of Mao's writings to be included in volume 5 of Mao's *Selected Works.* On April 7, the Central Committee released Hua Guofeng's guide on how to read the volume, which approved a passage of Mao's urging the pursuit of revolution to the end. A week later, on April 15 under Hua Guofeng's imprimatur, volume 5 of Mao's *Selected Works* was published.[22] Neither the guide nor the publication of volume 5 itself, however, would stop the growing support for Deng's return to a high-level position.

Deng made it clear, meanwhile, that he would not support Hua's "two whatevers." On April 10, in a letter to Hua Guofeng, Marshal Ye, and the rest of the Central Committee, Deng laid out his views on the controversial editorial. He said that from generation to generation we should use a "correct" and "comprehensive" understanding of Mao's thought to guide the Chinese party, army, and people.[23] By using this clever formulation, Deng accepted the authority of Mao, while asserting, in effect, that Hua Guofeng was not the only one who had the authority to interpret Mao's views; rather, any par-

ticular issue had to be seen in a broader context, and those senior party leaders who had worked with Mao far longer and more closely than Hua had
were in a better position to judge Mao's views in this "broader context." Deng
then thanked the Central Committee for clearing his name from involvement in the Tiananmen incident. He wrote that as for his personal work assignment, "what I do and when it is appropriate for me to start work, I will
completely follow the considerations and the arrangements decided by the
Party Center." Deng suggested that his letter, as well as his October 10, 1976,
letter to Hua Guofeng supporting Hua's leadership, be circulated within the
party.[24]

By the time Hua received Deng's letter, he realized that he had to respond
to the rising level of support for Deng's return. Accordingly, he sent Wang
Dongxing and Li Xin, high-ranking party officials loyal to him, to negotiate
with Deng on issues concerning his return.[25] By this time, because Hua
Guofeng had affirmed the positive role of the April 1976 demonstrations,
Deng was telling close friends that he was confident that the Tiananmen
demonstrations would soon be considered a revolutionary movement.[26] In
this context, Deng was in no mood to support the request by Wang Dongxing and Li Xin that in preparation for his return he affirm the "two whatevers." If the "two whatevers" were to become doctrine, Deng told them, it
would be difficult to explain the reason for the reversal of judgments on him
and on the Tiananmen Square demonstrations.[27]

Deng went on to explain that it would not do to take what Mao did on
one occasion and to make that the explanation for something Mao did in a
different place and time. Mao himself admitted he made errors; anyone who
does things makes mistakes. If what a person did was 70 percent correct, that
is very good. If after my death people say that what I did was 70 percent correct, Deng said, that would be quite good.[28]

It was expected that in order to return to work, Deng would write a letter
that would be made public showing that he accepted Hua Guofeng's leadership. Deng went along with this request, writing in his letter, "Not only is
Hua Guofeng the most appropriate person to succeed Mao in terms of his
politics and his ideology, but at his age . . . he can provide stability for at least
fifteen or twenty years."[29] On April 14, after Deng had made minor revisions
to the letter, Hua Guofeng approved its distribution to party members, and
on May 3, it was circulated throughout the party down to the county level,
and within the army down to the regimental level.[30] Hua had delayed Deng's

return as long as he reasonably could, but in the end, with Deng's written acceptance of his leadership, Hua yielded to the atmosphere among the powerful senior officials who wanted Deng back.

Although Deng's return would not become official until the July plenum, circulation of his letter praising the leadership of Hua, in effect, constituted a notification to the mid-levels of the party and above that in the near future Deng would be returning to work.[31] Party members expressed high expectations that Deng as a tested leader would play a major role in keeping order and bringing about modernization. Party members also whispered privately about what the foreign press speculated about more openly: the future of the relationship between Hua and Deng.

By May 12, it was understood that Deng would be returned to all his former positions, which would entail taking responsibility for military and foreign affairs. As before, he would be vice premier. Deng also volunteered to take special responsibility for science, technology, and education, for he considered science to be the most crucial of the four modernizations, the one that would drive the other three (industry, agriculture, and national defense). After his offer was accepted, Deng invited Fang Yi and Li Chang to his home, where they discussed what they could do to promote science and technology.[32] Given the prevailing mood in China, Deng would have to begin by overcoming some lingering anti-intellectual views. He told Fang Yi and Li Chang that they must emphasize that people who worked with their minds would be considered members of the politically respected working class.[33]

On May 24, preparing for his return, Deng invited his confidantes Wang Zhen and Deng Liqun to his house to talk about reviving his writing group and also about promoting science, technology, and education. Deng still valued the small writing group he had assembled in the Political Research Office, and he wanted to have a preliminary discussion with some of its former members about how to organize his writing team. Deng Liqun was one of the few who during the campaign to attack Deng Xiaoping had absolutely refused to join in the criticism and had suffered the consequences by being sent to labor in the countryside. He brought with him a letter from Hu Qiaomu, former head of Deng's writing group, apologizing for having joined in the criticism of Deng. Deng did not look at the letter. Instead he told Deng Liqun to return it, that Hu's criticism was not a problem: Hu Qiaomu had merely repeated what was generally known and that was understandable; there was no need to apologize for such gestures. Deng went on to praise Hu

Qiaomu's editing of Mao's speech "On the Ten Great Relationships" (included in volume 5 of Mao's *Selected Works*). He said he would welcome him back to the writing group.

After Marshal Ye and Deng conferred, the two vice chairmen of the CMC agreed to share responsibility for military affairs. Deng resumed working on the issues he had addressed in 1975: promoting downsizing, bringing in better-trained recruits, improving training and discipline, and upgrading military science and technology so that the military would be prepared for modern warfare. In his addresses to military groups, these remained central themes, but he also addressed broad political issues: "seek the true path from facts."[34] But he spent far less time on military affairs than on science, technology, and education.

Nor did Deng spend much time on foreign affairs. He agreed to take part in important policy decisions but said he did not want to be responsible for the day-to-day direction of foreign affairs; it was, he said, too tiring. Deng added that he really wanted to work on science, technology, and education, which he considered the most critical areas for modernization.

Deng estimated that China's science and technology lagged two decades behind that of the rest of the world; for example, he mentioned that China at that time had about 200,000 people working in science and technology, whereas the United States had 1.2 million. To catch up, Deng said, China would need to acknowledge that it was far behind and begin to develop its own talent. Resuming the policies he supported in 1975, Deng said China must use examinations to select the brightest elementary and secondary school students and give them the best training in the best universities and training schools.[35]

By offering to take responsibility for science and technology, Deng was also making it clear that in the near future he would not challenge Hua in his core political areas. But to develop science, Deng did not hesitate to touch on political questions that remained sensitive. In contrast to Maoists who insisted that politics must come before expertise, Deng dared to declare that scientists with little interest in politics could still be useful, and that the military also needed to educate talented people.[36]

Deng's Return

On July 17, the Third Plenum of the 10th Party Congress passed "The Decision Concerning the Return of Comrade Deng Xiaoping to Work." Formally, the decision required the final approval of the party congress that followed one month later, but at the plenum, Deng was officially returned to all the positions he had held before April 5, 1976: member of the Central Committee, member of the Standing Committee of the Politburo, vice chairman of the party, vice chairman of the CMC, vice premier, and chief-of-staff of the PLA. Of the five members on the Standing Committee, Deng ranked third, behind Hua Guofeng and Marshal Ye but ahead of Li Xiannian and Wang Dongxing.[37]

In what was in effect his acceptance speech, on July 21 Deng declared, "As for my return to work, one can take one of two approaches. One is to be an official, one is to accomplish something." No one was surprised at Deng's choice: he wanted to accomplish something. Yet given Mao's lingering aura in the months after his death, Deng still had to be cautious in charting his course. Deng first repeated the mantra: "Marxism-Leninism and Mao Zedong Thought constitute the guiding ideology of the party." Only then did he go on to address what he wanted to accomplish: first, improvement in the treatment of intellectuals, and second, party building. He repeated his argument for flexibility in drawing lessons from Mao. Some, he said, had distorted Mao's ideas by taking certain statements made in one context and claiming that they applied to other situations. But Mao had different solutions at different times, and one must have a correct and comprehensive understanding of Mao to apply his prescriptions correctly in each circumstance. Deng also argued that the Chinese leadership should promote inner-party democracy.[38] Four years later, after Deng had consolidated his power, critics would say that Deng was no longer as enthusiastic about inner-party democracy and had centralized power in his own hands.

On July 23, two days after Deng's speech, the *People's Daily, Red Flag,* and the PLA newspaper *Jiefangjun bao* announced his new assignments in an editorial that stated, "This meeting's decision to return Deng to his positions inside and outside the party embodies the hopes of the broad masses of party members and the public."[39] The outpouring of emotion at Tiananmen Square on April 5, 1976, and the discussions at the Central Party Work Conference confirmed that this was no exaggeration. The first time Deng appeared in public after returning to work was on July 30, at a soccer match between mainland China and Hong Kong. As the loudspeaker announced his entrance into the Worker's Stadium, Deng received an extraordinarily lengthy standing ovation.[40] The public clearly felt secure under his steady hand and, based on his achievements in 1975, hopeful.

The participants at the 11th Party Congress, held August 12–18, 1977, welcomed Deng back, but some Maoists were uneasy with his return, and there was not yet a clear consensus on how to view Mao's legacy or on what concrete policies to pursue. Party leaders, trying to paper over differences and convey unity, resorted to slogans that affirmed the legacy of Mao and spoke in general terms about the goal of modernization. The Cultural Revolution was declared over, but its value was affirmed; the revolution led by the proletariat would continue to criticize rightism even as China sought new technology from abroad. In small group meetings, some members expressed dissatisfaction with Hua's leadership, as reflected in his four-hour-long speech that used platitudes to gloss over differences. To be sure, these criticisms were excluded from the written record of the congress.[41]

Deng accommodated to the political atmosphere by repeating platitudes that would reassure those who still clung to Mao. In his brief closing address on August 18, Deng said that the congress "ushers in a new period in the development of our socialist revolution and socialist construction. We must revive and carry forward the mass line." But he also tried to create some room for flexibility. He added, "We must revive and carry forward the practice of seeking the true path from facts, the fine tradition and style which Chairman Mao fostered."[42] By including Mao's "true path," Deng confirmed his loyalty to Mao, but his emphasis on "seeking the true path from facts" gave him room to adapt policy to the needs of the current situation and to argue that concrete messages from Mao did not automatically apply to all situations.

Deng also provided reassurance that he would work under the leadership of Chairman Hua. Using a military analogy, Deng said he would look after the "rear services," and his listeners understood that this meant he would be assisting the commander, Hua Guofeng. In particular, he would take charge of science and education "to help Chairman Hua Guofeng and Ye Jianying."[43] Deng would not threaten the leadership of Hua Guofeng, at least for the moment.

Deng Micromanages Science, Technology, and Education

A few weeks after the party congress, Deng, in an address to Ministry of Education officials, said, "Although I realized it would be a tough job to be in charge of scientific and educational work, I volunteered for the post. China's four modernizations will get nowhere . . . if we don't make a success of such work."[44] Deng was ready to continue the work he had begun in 1975, with the help of Hu Yaobang, to win back the goodwill of scientists. In 1977, to a visiting Chinese-American scientist, Deng remarked that if he were not soon "called to meet Marx" (in the afterlife) he intended to work on science and education for ten years. He said that he hoped to see a few results within five years, more within ten years, and major transformations within fifteen years.[45]

Deng realized that China badly needed to raise the average literacy rate as well as the public's knowledge of science and technology, but he focused his attention at the high end: on basic research to achieve scientific breakthroughs that would drive the other three modernizations in industry, agriculture, and national defense. In his view, "China must catch up with the most advanced countries in the world."[46]

Deng met again and again with the Chinese-American Nobel prize winners Lee Tsung-Dao, Yang Zhenning, and Samuel Ting. The central question was always the same: What can China do to raise its level of science? Deng had an almost magical faith in the role that science would play in China's renewal, and he approved projects accordingly. When asked why he wanted China to spend so much money on a nuclear accelerator so early in its modernization effort, he replied that China must look ahead to develop Chinese science.

In 1957 Deng had been Mao's right-hand man in implementing the attack on intellectuals, but he did not instinctively dislike them as Mao did. Mao, who denigrated them as "bourgeois intellectuals," time and again found ways to humiliate them and to send them to be educated by performing physical labor. Deng never had an opportunity to study at a university, but he had once been on track to receive a higher education and made his best effort to enter a French university. His wife had studied physics at China's premier university, Peking University, and three of his five children had also studied physics at Peking University, and one studied medicine and the other art because she was considered too sickly for the demanding program in science. Moreover, Deng had come to see that the attacks on intellectuals had devastated Chinese science and technology, which would be essential for China's modernization. After he returned to work in 1973, Deng never again attacked intellectuals as he did in 1957. Other leaders sometimes talked of "bourgeois intellectuals," but not Deng. Science, Deng said, had no class character: it could be used by all classes and by all countries despite their different political and economic systems.

Deng soon laid out his agenda for upgrading China's scientific level:

We should select several thousand of our most qualified personnel within the scientific and technological establishment and create condi-

tions that will allow them to devote their undivided attention to research. Those who have financial difficulties should be given allowances
and subsidies. Some now have their children and aged parents living
with them, earn well under 100 yuan a month, and must spend a lot of
time doing housework. They can't even find a quiet place to read in the
evening. How can this state of affairs be allowed to continue? The political requirements set for these people must be appropriate; they should
love the motherland, love socialism, and accept the leadership of the
party. . . . We must create within the party an atmosphere of respect for
knowledge and respect for trained personnel. The erroneous attitude of
not respecting intellectuals must be opposed. All work, be it mental or
manual, is labor.[47]

Deng thought it was a terrible waste to send young intellectuals off to do
physical labor when they should be advancing Chinese science. Although he
did not use the term, in fact he believed in a meritocratic elite. He sought to
attract the best and the brightest and to provide the conditions that would
allow them to achieve the most for China.

Deng encountered massive resistance in his efforts to promote an educational and scientific elite. When he complained about the treatment of intellectuals, Deng was shrewd enough not to talk about the role of Chairman
Mao, who in fact was ultimately responsible for those policies; instead he focused on the Gang of Four. Deng said China must avoid the Gang of Four's
destructive habits of being a "hat company," that is, one that puts "hats" (political labels) on intellectuals, and a "stick company," that is, one that uses
sticks to beat intellectuals.[48]

Before Deng returned, many conservatives still argued that the educational
policies in Communist China's first seventeen years (1949 to 1966) should
be criticized as "bourgeois." On the eve of Deng's return to work, at the June
1977 Ministry of Education's All-China Higher Education Admission Work
Forum (Quanguo gaodeng xuexiao zhaosheng gongzuotanhui) in Taiyuan,
Shanxi, participants had engaged in lively debates over whether to base future policy on Cultural Revolution policies or on earlier ones—and ended
the discussion by choosing the Cultural Revolution policies as their guide.[49]
Deng clearly had plenty of work to do.

As Deng aged, he began to reduce his work schedule, but in 1977, when
he returned to work at age seventy-two, Deng was energized and threw himself into his work. Deng ordinarily dealt with broad issues, and he was a mi-

cromanager only when he considered an issue to be of the highest priority. In 1977–1978 he considered science and education to be that important. When he initially addressed the task, he said, "Over the next eight to ten years, we should bend all our efforts to educational work. For my part, I intend to pay close attention to it, keeping an eye on the leading comrades in the educational departments."[50]

Deng made the rounds of party leaders in various regions, attacking the radicals' views of intellectuals and making concrete suggestions for how to cultivate a new appreciation of their potential to help China move forward. For several days beginning on July 27, within a week after the end of the plenum that officially gave him responsibility to work in the area of science, Deng held a series of talks with the president of the Chinese Academy of Sciences, Fang Yi, the vice president of the academy, Li Chang, and Minister of Education Liu Xiyao in which he laid out his agenda to speed up China's modernization in the sciences. Deng said plans thus far were insufficient. They should draw up a list of China's most knowledgeable scientists in various specialties and make sure that they were given adequate facilities and living conditions so they could concentrate on their work. The 1964 and 1965 graduates who still did not have appropriate work should receive better assignments.[51] In addition, Deng continued, Chinese scholars who go abroad to study should be given incentives to return, and if they decline to return, they should still be considered patriots and invited to come back and give lectures. Scholars should collect textbooks from abroad to update their teaching materials, which must be concise and to the point. And the Ministry of Education should make a list of the schools with the highest standards and ensure that students with the highest entrance exam scores attend them. Deng also said that defense scientific work must be part of the overall planning for science, and officials should not be afraid if there were some duplication with other science work.[52]

Commander Deng, the micromanager, had taken charge, and as he explained to the officials who would carry out his orders in these areas, "We don't want to fire empty shells."[53] Despite Deng's energetic presentations, opposition remained strong enough that at the Forum on Science and Education Work, at which some thirty famous scientists and educators met from August 3 to 8, 1977, Deng felt it necessary to attack again the prevailing assessment that education was a "bourgeois" failure. No longer would practical technicians be extolled at the expense of theorists. As Deng envisioned it, some scientists could be selected from productive units, but most of the pioneers on the cutting edge of science and technology would have to come from the universities. In order to produce good scientists, elementary schools should build a strong basis in math and foreign languages. Universities, meanwhile, should reduce the number of factories they operate and increase their laboratories.[54]

Deng believed that some of China's most capable young people should go abroad for advanced study, and he made efforts to establish programs for Chinese to study abroad. He expressed confidence that China—which had invented the compass, the printing press, and explosives—had plenty of smart people. But China had fallen far behind and must now learn from the West. To learn from abroad, China could buy written materials from other countries (for Chinese textbook development), send scholars to study overseas, and invite foreign scientists to visit China.

By September, after two months of pushing the Ministry of Education officials to take action, Deng was still frustrated. Mao had once commented that in the military the troops were afraid of Deng. Now Commander Deng aimed his big guns at the Ministry of Education: "The Ministry of Education should take the initiative. So far you have not done so. . . . You are overcautious and afraid of making further 'mistakes' if you follow my advice. . . . We need to have specific policies and measures. . . . You should work freely and boldly and think independently instead of always looking over your shoulder. . . . Those comrades who are in favor of the policies of the party center should get on with the job, and those who aren't should switch to other lines of work."[55] Deng added that the ministry needed some twenty to forty people "about the age of forty whose duty it is to make the rounds of the schools. . . . Like commanders going down to the companies, they should sit in on classes as pupils, familiarize themselves with the real situation, supervise the implementation of plans and policies, and then report back . . . we can't afford to be satisfied with idle talk."[56]

By advocating policies fervently supported by the scholarly community, Deng won back some of the goodwill among intellectuals that he had lost in 1957 as a leader of the anti-rightist campaign. This goodwill was important for Deng's public image, for many of these same intellectuals drafted documents and wrote speeches for the Propaganda Department and the media. Even though they worked within the limits set by the political leaders, they still had opportunities to subtly shape the documents and speeches that appeared in print and on radio and television. It did not hurt for Deng to have their support.

Return of the University Entrance Exam

A crucial issue for Deng and for everyone else in China regarding the quality of education was the revival of the university entrance examinations. Long before Deng returned to work, he believed that students should be selected for the better educational institutions not on the basis of "proper class background" and "proper political thinking" (Mao's criteria), but on the basis of academic merit, as determined by competitive entrance examinations. During the 1950s, children had been tested in school, but the results were played down since officials did not want to embarrass the children of peasants and workers who had scored poorly in comparison to the children of landlords and the bourgeoisie, who had benefited from better educational opportunities before 1949.

As some universities began to reopen in the early 1970s on a small scale, they accepted young people from the "proper classes"—workers, peasants, and soldiers—based not on exam scores but on recommendations from members of their work units. It was too blatant, of course, to recommend one's one own children, but one official could write a recommendation for another's child and then the favor could be returned. Even students from "good class backgrounds" who did well on the examinations were upset when others with better connections and lesser ability were admitted in their stead. The system of recommendations had become thoroughly corrupt.

Deng, arguing that class background was no longer an issue since the bourgeois and landlord classes no longer existed, felt strongly that the sooner entrance examinations were reintroduced at every level from elementary school through higher education, the sooner China's leadership could start improving education. Deng especially wanted to restore the "unified entrance examinations for institutions of higher learning" that had been terminated during the Cultural Revolution. But by the opening session of the Forum on Science and Education on August 3, 1977, plans were already under way for universities to reopen that fall and to enroll students based on recommendations. Would it be possible to introduce entrance examinations in just a few weeks, before the fall semester began? When the issue came up at the forum, Deng turned to Minister of Education Liu Xiyao and asked him if he thought it were possible. From the moment Minister Liu responded yes, Deng was prepared to move heaven and earth to hold the university entrance examinations in 1977. Indeed, before the forum ended, Deng announced, "We will end the system of recommendations, and will accept applications directly from high school. This is a good way to begin producing people of talent more quickly and to achieve results faster."[57] Accomplishing such a huge turnaround in such a brief time frame would not be easy. Deciding which subjects would be tested, selecting faculty to prepare the content of the tests, announcing the examination plans, holding the examinations for millions, organizing and completing the grading, and determining which universities would be reopened and how many students they would take was a staggering task. Inevitably, universities opened some months later than expected, and not everything went smoothly, but they did reopen.

The Higher Education Enrollment Commission had never convened twice in the same year—until 1977. On August 13, within a week after Deng issued his decision, the Second All-China Higher Education Enrollment Work Conference was convened to plan for the fall enrollments. At this work conference, Deng explained further one of his policy changes: "In the past . . . I too stressed the advantages of having secondary school students do physical labor for two years after graduation. Facts have shown, however, that after a couple of years of labor, the students have forgotten half of what they learned at school. This is a waste of time."[58] He directed that 20 to 30 percent of those accepted to university that year would be admitted directly from high school, and that in the future most students would be admitted that way. Respect for labor could be taught to students without interrupting their education. Deng also gave his official order for unified entrance exams to be held in 1977, which some officials complained would be difficult or even impossible to accomplish so soon. Impatient, Deng countered that the policy was set. The examinations would be held in 1977. There would be no changes.[59] A summary document was prepared on the basis of the conference, discussed and approved by the Politburo on October 5, ratified by the State Council on October 12, and published in the *People's Daily* on October 21, with directions to students on how to sign up for the exam.[60]

Some 5,780,000 people who had reached college age within the last decade, many of whom were still working in the countryside, took the test that fall, but there were then only 273,000 slots at the universities. In 1977 and 1978, then, only some 5.8 percent of those who took the examinations could actually be enrolled.[61] For the first time since the Communists ruled China, class background was not a factor in selecting those to be admitted to university. Enrollment was entirely based on merit as measured by examination scores.

It was a strain for the universities to prepare for the students, even by the end of the year when they finally opened. Worker propaganda teams still quartered at the universities had to be moved out. University facilities in disrepair had to be patched up. Teachers, who for years had not been allowed to devote themselves to professional activities, had to put together their curricula and prepare teaching materials for their courses. The first students on the scene complained that at the hastily revamped universities, both the living conditions and academic experience left something to be desired. They were, as some students themselves phrased it, "students of the 1980s using texts of the 1970s, taught by faculty from the 1960s."

The system Deng introduced in 1977 has continued ever since, creating a cascade of positive results for China. As in Japan, South Korea, Taiwan, and Singapore, Chinese university entrance examinations raised the quality of both university applicants and recruits entering the workforce.[62] In particular, after entrance examinations were introduced at all levels, ambitious parents began preparing their one child (since urban families were allowed to have only one child) in math, science, and foreign languages so they could be admitted to a top elementary school, a top secondary school, and a top university. Primary and secondary schools, too, began preparing their students to take examinations as they moved up the educational ladder, and universities began preparing some of their ablest students to go on to higher education in the West.

Those who were left behind—the lost generations of youth sent to the countryside during the Cultural Revolution who did not pass the examinations, and those who scored only high enough to attend ordinary schools rather than the select top schools—were not necessarily happy with the new system. But many of those who passed the examinations, as well as those who care about quality of education—including parents, faculty, and employers—remain enormously grateful to Deng Xiaoping for hastening the return of entrance examinations and for his decisive support of quality education.

Promoting Science

Soon after he returned to work in 1977, Deng said, "I have a persistent feeling that at present things are not going well in science and education."[63] Despite Hu Yaobang's yeoman efforts in 1975, many intellectuals had not been allowed to return to useful work, and conflicts between scientists criticized for their bourgeois lifestyles and their young rebel accusers remained intense. For the scientists, as for university faculty, living conditions remained terrible.

Scientific researchers were almost exclusively doing their work at research institutes, and worker propaganda teams and troops that had been sent to the universities during the Cultural Revolution to support the left and to criticize "bourgeois intellectuals" still occupied the campuses and gave directions to scientists. Deng found the situation untenable. He stated that "the problems with the worker propaganda teams must be settled. They and the troops sent in to support the left should all be withdrawn. There will be no exceptions."[64]

Deng also responded to the continuing complaints of scientists that their professional work should be directed by someone familiar with the content. He directed that scientific institutes be reorganized with three top leaders at each institute. The party leader would manage overall policy, but the basic work of the institute would be under the direction of a leader trained in science. A third leader would be in charge of "rear services," with responsibility for improving the living conditions and for ensuring that the scientists had adequate supplies to carry on their work. Aware that intellectuals were upset that they still had to spend so much time engaged in physical labor and political education, Deng established a new rule that at least five-sixths of the scientists' work week was to be spent on basic research.

Because the State Science and Technology Commission had been abolished more than a decade earlier, in 1977 there was still no overall administrative structure to oversee science. Which fields were to receive priority? How would people be trained to meet the needs of various fields? In 1975 Deng had relied on a small group within the Chinese Academy of Sciences to draft documents for the development of science. But now, in 1977, Deng directed that the State Science and Technology Commission be reestablished to coordinate developments in science and to draw up a seven-year science plan to replace the portions of the Sixth Five-Year Plan (1980–1985) devoted to science. The documents that Deng had directed to be drawn up in 1975—and had been dubbed by radicals as "three poisonous weeds"—were dusted off, and the work completed in 1975 provided a basis for the new plans.

Deng may have started with 1975 plans, but his dreams for China had grown in the intervening years. Deng believed that China's increased contact with the outside world, compared to that in 1975, meant that planners could and should set higher goals for the development of science. To guide his ambitious new strategy, Deng continued to make good use of advice from outstanding Chinese-American scientists and to work closely with Fang Yi, the Politburo member with overall responsibility for science. Fang Yi and the Science and Technology Commission were put in charge of guiding the development of science in industry, in the military, and in other sectors, but they focused primarily on basic research conducted within universities and independent scientific institutes, particularly the Chinese Academy of Sciences and the newly established Chinese Academy of Social Sciences.[65]

Although Deng was more focused on the natural sciences than the social sciences, he believed that the social sciences, including economics, philosophy, Marxist theory, and knowledge of different societies, were also necessary to guide modernization. In May 1977 Hua had approved the plan, developed under Deng's direction in 1975, to establish an independent Chinese Academy of Social Sciences (CASS). By the time it came into being in the fall of 1977 with some two thousand members, Deng had returned and he arranged that its first head be Hu Qiaomu who had outlined the plans for its development in 1975. CASS acquired the status of an independent ministry directly under the State Council.[66] Its independence from the Ministry of Education enabled it to be relatively free of pressures to impart propaganda and allowed scholars to concentrate on research rather than the more routine task of passing on the current state of knowledge.

Tentative plans for the new seven-year plan for scientific development, to include some 108 major projects, were presented to a large conference held from March 18–31, 1978. In his opening address, Deng said that science and technology were a "force of production"—the same comment that had got him into trouble with Mao in late 1975 for regarding science as important as the class struggle. He continued by drawing on what he had learned from the Chinese-American scientists. He announced that the world was experiencing nothing short of a revolution in science and technology, with entirely new fields opening up: polymers, nuclear energy, electronic computers, semiconductors, astronautics, and lasers. In a move typical for Deng, he then reassured and reminded his Marxist-leaning audience that labor power has always included knowledge of science and technology, and that scientific developments were universal and could be used by all of mankind. Deng acknowledged that some scientists would be needed for applied fields like engineering, which would foster advances in such areas as industrial automation. But Deng's focus was on science, and he again stressed the need to learn from advanced science abroad.[67]

Deng's speech reflects the juggling act that Deng needed to perform, fighting political battles while working with specialists to develop concrete plans for development of the field. Even as he supervised the selection of projects and the plans for specific institutes, he had to continue to struggle against the perceptions of the old Maoist leadership; he argued that science was important enough to be considered a force of production, that mental labor would be regarded as labor, and that scientists would be allowed to devote themselves to their professional work without distractions from political activities. Although he did not use the words, his answer to the old debate about which is more important, red or expert, was definitely "expert." He was ready to fight the political battles to allow the experts to pursue what was most important to realize the four modernizations.

After resuming his position as vice chairman of the CMC in July 1977, officially Deng ranked under Chairman Hua Guofeng, but as chief of the General Staff he exercised responsibility for guiding military planning.[68] Moreover, with his long years of military leadership, he sought to maintain personal control over the military and not let it slip into Hua's hands. Like Mao, Deng expected strict obedience from his military leaders and he was prepared to be strict in enforcing compliance; the troops had no difficulty understanding that Deng had more power over the military than Hua.

"Practice" Challenges the "Two Whatevers"

When the Central Party School reopened in 1977, it quickly became a center for progressive party scholars and students. Scholars conducting research on party theory and history began work in March 1977, and the school opened to its first group of students in October. In the first class there were 807 students, including approximately a hundred middle-aged and older officials who had been selected by their ministries or provinces as especially promising and so were sent to study in an "advanced group" for six months.[69]

There was a special excitement among the first few groups of students, who expected to land important positions upon graduation. Most of the one hundred students in the advanced group had suffered during the Cultural Revolution and wanted both to analyze what had gone wrong during the previous two decades and to discuss their visions for China's future. To be sure, there were limits to what they could criticize and what they could propose. But within the limits, the students were open to a wide range of new ideas, and their enthusiasm was shared by faculty and researchers, who also were eager to help define the theoretical and policy directions for the new era.[70]

The desire to explore new ideas was thoroughly supported by Hu Yaobang. Although Hua Guofeng was officially president of the Central Party School and Wang Dongxing was officially first vice president, Hu Yaobang, a vice president, came to the school more often than they and took a lively interest in the students, the staff, and their ideas. He encouraged fresh thinking, and the staff and students responded warmly to his encouragement. The Central Party School soon became a center for creative new thinking within the party, a place where senior officials could occasionally break away from their daily work to explore new ideas with the staff and students.

On July 15, even before the first group of students had arrived at the Central Party School, Hu Yaobang's staff began a series of papers called *Theoretical Trends (Lilun dongtai)*. Intended to be read by a small group of high officials, the series explored new ideas and interpretations in a format that gave it more freedom than other party publications: a brief, numbered paper on a given topic would be released every few days. The papers were not circulated outside the inner circle, but they attracted great interest because they expressed the cutting edge of new thinking acceptable to the party.

On May 10, 1978, paper 60, "Practice Is the Sole Criterion for Judging Truth," appeared in *Theoretical Trends*.[71] The article had been in gestation for several months and was based on drafts written by Hu Fuming, a young philosophy faculty member at Nanjing University; Sun Changjiang, of the Central Party School's Theory Research Office; and Yang Xiguang, a student at the Central Party School in the fall of 1977.[72] In early 1978 Yang Xiguang became the editor of *Guangming Daily* and, always alert to ideas that would be new to his readers, on May 11, reprinted "Practice Is the Sole Criterion for Judging Truth," with the protective byline "specially invited commentators." On May 12, *People's Daily* and the PLA newspaper *Jiefangjun bao* reprinted it, and it was quickly picked up and reprinted in many regional papers as well.

The article argued that the only way to evaluate truth was by the broad social experience of the people. Marxism is not an unchanging body of thinking; instead Marxism must continually be reinterpreted as a result of experience. The basic principle of Marxism encompasses the combination of theory and practice. Under certain circumstances errors will be made in perceptions of the truth, but if experience reveals errors, changes should be made: in this way new experiences and practices will bring about new theories. If the existing formulas of Marxism-Leninism and Mao Zedong Thought are limited or cause disasters, they should be changed.[73]

After the article appeared, it immediately aroused great interest. Some readers were full of praise, but Wang Dongxing, the Politburo Standing Committee member responsible for overseeing propaganda work, and Wu Lengxi, former editor of the *People's Daily*, were furious. Wang Dongxing had exploded just a week earlier when an article entitled "Pay According to the Work Performed" *(anlao fenpei)* had appeared, demanding to know which Central Committee had authorized that article (only later did he find out that Deng Xiaoping and his staff had supported it).

Hu Yaobang and other liberal officials had taken advantage of an arrangement whereby papers from *Theoretical Trends* by "specially invited commentators" could be printed in newspapers without the usual surveillance by Wang Dongxing and his staff.[74] Otherwise, Wang Dongxing and his conservative staff would have weeded out such an article before it was published in newspapers. Wang Dongxing and Wu Lengxi accurately perceived that the article encouraged questioning the orthodoxy of Mao Zedong that they believed in. If class struggle and continuing revolution caused disasters, it followed that they should be abandoned. Wang Dongxing and Wu Lengxi also correctly perceived that the article, by criticizing "ossified dogmatism" and "godlike worship," was an attack on the "two whatevers" and implicitly on those responsible for it, Hua Guofeng and Wang Dongxing. Wang Dongxing argued that without a common creed, the party would not be able to maintain unity, and he phoned Hu Yaobang personally, complaining that he permitted the publication of such an article.[75]

Deng Xiaoping later told Hu Yaobang that when the article "Practice Is the Sole Criterion for Judging Truth" first came out, he did not notice it, but when the controversy became heated, he looked it up and read it. The article, he said, was a good one and it accorded with Marxism-Leninism. He praised the theoretical group that Hu Yaobang had assembled to work on *Theoretical Trends* and said it should continue its work. Deng reassured Hu, who sought to keep good relations with Hua Guofeng and other leaders, by saying that some struggle over the issue was unavoidable because of the other leaders' support for the "two whatevers." Deng's support gave Hu Yaobang great encouragement at a critical time in the course of the debate. Without it, Hu and many others might have lost heart and yielded.[76]

The two articles, "Practice" (of May 1978) and the "two whatevers" (of February 1977), became two magnetic poles, attracting those with two different perspectives. The controversy between the two exposed and sharpened the divide between those who supported Hua Guofeng and feared the consequences of loosening the traditional orthodoxy and those who supported Deng in pushing away from what they saw as stultifying dogma. The argument was phrased in ideological terms, but the passion of the two sides stemmed from the underlying politics. In Chinese Communist circles, it is taboo to criticize a leader openly and directly. But beneficiaries of the Cultural Revolution generally supported Hua Guofeng, and targets of the Cultural Revolution generally supported Deng Xiaoping.

The article "Practice Is the Sole Criterion for Judging Truth" became a vehicle to rally the growing number of officials who believed that Hua Guofeng was not up to the task of leading China, but who dared not say so publicly. It also helped to draw military leaders to the side of Deng Xiaoping, including the secretary general of the CMC, Luo Ruiqing, one of the earliest targets of the Cultural Revolution and an unusually strong and able leader who had worked with Deng for many years.[77] In the following months, as the debate heated up over the two articles, it increasingly became a political struggle between those who praised "Practice Is the Sole Criterion" and believed that Deng would be the best top leader, and those who upheld the "two whatevers" and supported Hua Guofeng. A showdown seemed inevitable.

Creating the Deng Era

1978–1980

7

Three Turning Points

1978

In Japan, the historical turning point that set the nation on the road to modernization was the Iwakura Mission. From December 1871 to September 1873, fifty-one Meiji government leaders traveled by ship and rail to fifteen different countries. The mission was composed of officials from all major sectors—industry, agriculture, mining, finance, culture, education, the military, and the police—and was led by Iwakura Tomomi, a court noble who had become one of the top leaders of the Meiji government. When the group left home, Japan was essentially a closed country; the Japanese knew little about the outside world. But as the members of the mission visited other countries' factories, mines, museums, parks, stock exchanges, railways, farms, and shipyards, their eyes were opened to ways that Japan could remake itself, not only with new technologies, but also with new organizational strategies and ways of thinking. The trip created a shared awareness among the mission members of just how far behind Japan was from the advanced countries and a common perspective about how to introduce change. Rather than becoming discouraged by what they saw, the officials returned home energized, excited by future prospects for Japan and eager to send additional teams abroad to study in more detail.

In China no single group of officials traveled together for such a long period as the Iwakura Mission, but from 1977 to 1980 many separate study tours by senior officials had a similar influence on Chinese thinking. Deng's pioneering 1975 five-day visit to France, when he took along high-level officials in industry, transport, management, and science who made observations in their respective fields, set a precedent. Deng returned from the trip a believer in study tours and began encouraging other groups to go abroad. He complained that other officials did not know how far behind China was and he was confident a trip would open their eyes. Hua Guofeng, who had led a delegation to visit Eastern Europe, also returned a supporter of trips abroad to observe modern countries.

For centuries, individual Chinese had gone to the West and returned with ideas for China. Wang Tao, for example, a nineteenth-century translator, returned from London and wrote avidly about what China could learn from the West about modernization.[1] What was different in the late 1970s was that key officials in positions of responsibility traveled together and, with the firm support of Deng and Hua, were later in positions that enabled them to implement what they had learned on a large scale.

After Deng returned from France and Mao and Jiang Qing had died, officials who long suppressed their desires to travel abroad had a new opportunity. Officials who for decades had warned the public about the horrors of capitalism vied with one another to observe capitalist countries firsthand. Retired senior officials sought overseas trips to capitalist countries as rewards for their dedicated years of service to communism and their suffering during the Cultural Revolution. It took some months after Mao's death and the arrest of the Gang of Four to make arrangements for foreign travel, but by 1978, when such preparations had been completed, many high-level officials had their first opportunities to take part in foreign study tours. In that year, some thirteen officials of the rank of vice premier or its equivalent took some twenty trips abroad, visiting a total of fifty countries.[2] Hundreds of ministers, governors, first party secretaries, and their staff took part as well. Like the Japanese officials on the Iwakura Mission, Chinese officials returned exhilarated by what they had seen, excited about new steps China could take, and ready to send additional teams abroad to study in more detail.

In late 1978, Deng, summarizing the effect of the trips, happily reported, "Recently our comrades had a look abroad. The more we see, the more we realize how backward we are."[3] Deng considered this recognition so essential for building support for reform that on December 2, 1978, he told those drafting his speech that would launch his reform and opening policy that "the basic point is: we must acknowledge that we are backward, that many of our ways of doing things are inappropriate, and that we need to change."[4] The study tours reinforced the growing conviction among many high officials that Deng's perception was correct: China must embark on a new path.

The highest-level delegations that China sent abroad in 1978 were four study tours organized in the spring of that year, one each to Eastern Europe, Hong Kong, Japan, and Western Europe. From March 9 to April 6, 1978, a study tour headed by Li Yimang, deputy head of the International Liaison Department of the Communist Party, with Qiao Shi and Yu Guangyuan as deputy heads, visited Yugoslavia and Romania.[5] From their visits to factories, farms, and science and technology units, the group returned home with some concrete suggestions about what China might do.[6] But more importantly, after the trip, Chinese leaders stopped calling Yugoslavia "revisionist," the derogatory term Mao had used to criticize the departure of the socialist countries from the true path of socialism. Furthermore, the Chinese Communist Party reestablished relations with the Yugoslav Communist Party.[7] These changes expanded the range of reforms China could consider; it was now possible to draw from the experiences of the Eastern European economic reformers without being accused of committing ideological impurities.

From April to May 1978, officials from the State Planning Commission and the Ministry of Foreign Trade visited Hong Kong to evaluate its potential for assisting Chinese developments in finance, industry, and management. The officials explored the possibility of setting up in Bao'an county, Guangdong province, across the border from Hong Kong, an export processing zone—a place where materials could be brought from abroad to be manufactured by Chinese laborers and then exported without any tariffs or other restrictions. Within a few months, the State Council formally approved the establishment of such an area, which later would become the Shenzhen Special Economic Zone (SEZ). At the time, Guangdong was suffering from a real security problem: tens of thousands of young people each year were escaping to Hong Kong. When told of the problem during a visit to Guangdong in 1977, Deng explained that the solution lay not in tightening border security with more fencing and more border patrols but in improving the economy of Guangdong so young people would not feel that they had to flee to Hong Kong to find jobs.

After the State Planning Commission delegation returned from its visit to Hong Kong, Beijing formed a Hong Kong and Macao Affairs Office under the State Council, and in December 1978, Li Qiang, vice minister of foreign trade, stopped in Hong Kong to strengthen relations between Beijing and the Hong Kong colonial government. While there, Li urged Governor Murray MacLehose to take measures so that Hong Kong could play a major role in the modernization of China; he also invited the governor to visit Beijing.

Before the State Council visit to Hong Kong, contacts between Hong Kong and the mainland were highly restricted. The visit paved the way for Hong Kong to become a major conduit to China for capital and knowledge about global economic developments.

Chinese leaders were interested in Japan not simply because it was a source for modern industrial technology, but also because it offered successful strategies for managing the overall modernization process. A delegation headed by Lin Hujia, deputy head of the Shanghai Revolutionary Committee (in effect the vice mayor of Shanghai), visited Japan from March 28 to April 22, 1978. The group included representatives from the State Planning Commission, the Ministry of Commerce, the Ministry of Foreign Trade, and the Bank of China. Japan was of special interest because it had dealt successfully with problems similar to those that China was then facing. At the end of World War II, the Japanese economy had fallen into a disastrous state. Under strong central government leadership after the war, however, the Japanese economy had progressed rapidly and caught up with the West. On the way, Japan had also moved from a wartime system with tight economic control, centralized economic planning, rationing, and price controls to a much freer, more dynamic civilian economy in which consumer industries were major drivers of industrial growth.

Upon its return to China, the Lin Hujia delegation reported to the Politburo on Japanese economic progress since World War II: the Japanese had boldly introduced foreign technologies, made use of foreign capital, and vigorously developed education and scientific research. The Lin Hujia mission reported that the Japanese government and business community were prepared to provide aid and technology for Chinese development. Among other projects, the delegation recommended to the Politburo that a ten-million-ton steel plant be built. Although a later deterioration in Sino-Japanese relations led the Chinese government to play down Japan's role in China's resurgence, this delegation, as well as the Deng visit to Japan the following October, helped facilitate substantial Japanese contributions of capital, technology, and industrial management.

Of all the study tours in 1978, the one that had by far the greatest impact on Chinese development was the study tour led by Gu Mu to Western Europe from May 2 to June 6. It ranks with the November 1978 Central Party Work Conference and the December 1978 Third Plenum as one of the three major turning points in China's reform and opening.

Gu Mu's Trip and the Modernization Forum, May–September 1978

Gu Mu, second only to Li Xiannian and Yu Qiuli in leading the economy, led a high-level delegation to Western Europe—France, Switzerland, Germany, Denmark, and Belgium—from May 2 to June 6, 1978. Although the group was briefed before the trip, the members had very little background knowledge of the West. What these highly respected officials saw and learned in Europe, and how they articulated the new possibilities for China at the state forum that followed the visit, made their observations extraordinarily influential. Unlike Deng's five-day trip to France in 1975, which had focused on foreign relations and had included only brief visits to enterprises, the five-week Gu Mu tour, which consisted of a team of officials with a broad base of expertise, delved deeply into possible technologies and ideas that China might make use of. Gu Mu recalled that on the eve of the trip, when Deng met with him to give his instructions, he said, "Have broad contacts, make detailed investigations, and carry on deep research into the issues. . . . Look at how they manage their economic activities. We ought to study the successful experiences of capitalist countries and bring them back to China."[8]

The twenty members of Gu Mu's delegation had been appointed by Hua Guofeng.[9] No fewer than six of those traveling were of ministerial rank, including the vice ministers of agriculture and water power and the director of the State Planning Commission of Guangdong. They had been selected, as the members of the Iwakura Mission had been, because they were expected upon their return to lead various sectors of the economy.[10]

Vice Premier Gu Mu, an experienced and widely respected economic bureaucrat, had been a top leader in economic circles since coming from Shanghai to Beijing in 1954 as deputy head of the State Construction Commission. During the Cultural Revolution, he had risen to become second only to Li Xiannian in leading the economic work in the *yewuzu* to provide overall economic direction. He had worked not only on economic planning, but also on science and technology. Though Deng initially had some doubts about Gu Mu because he had become more important during the Cultural Revolution, as Deng observed that Gu Mu was an effective pragmatic official who supported modernization, these doubts were quickly cast aside. Gu Mu managed to maintain good relations both with senior officials who returned and with those who had risen during the Cultural Revolution. In fact, Gu Mu was sufficiently respected that following the European study tour he was given the leading role in guiding the development of foreign trade and in developing the SEZs.

When the Gu Mu study mission set out, it was not yet clear when relations with the United States would be normalized. But China had already normalized relations with all five European countries that the group visited, and the heads of state of all those countries had sent high-level delegations to China in the 1970s. As China's first state-level delegation to most of these Western European nations, Gu Mu's group was received at the highest levels. Except for the Belgian ambassador in Beijing who was ill, all the other ambassadors in Beijing flew home to accompany the delegation as it toured their respective countries.[11]

Given that China was just beginning to emerge from a Cold War mindset, the members of the Gu Mu delegation had been prepared to be treated as enemies. Despite the informative briefings to prepare them for the trip, the friendliness and openness of their hosts took them by surprise. At that time most Chinese factories and many other facilities were clothed in secrecy, and were not even open to ordinary Chinese, so the Chinese were shocked at the willingness of the Europeans to open for inspection factories, offices, shops, and virtually any other facility they asked to see.[12]

The group visited fifteen cities in five countries. They observed ports and rode on ships and trains as well as in automobiles. They visited electric power plants, farms, factories, markets, research institutes, and living areas. The group divided into subgroups for some visits, in total touring over eighty different locations.[13] They were briefed as they traveled and collected materials from places they visited.[14] Because they were focused on economic issues, they met mostly economic specialists, but they also met diplomats, politicians, and military officials. They viewed factories making silicon chips, optical equipment, and chemicals. They had little time for sightseeing but they did visit Karl Marx's birthplace in Trier, paying homage to their Communist origins while observing Germany's success with capitalism.[15] They were impressed with the levels of mechanization and automation and with the overall productivity of the workers. They were stunned by the use of computers at a Swiss power plant and at the Charles de Gaulle Airport, where takeoffs and landings were guided electronically. For the first time, at the Port of Bremen, the Chinese representatives saw modern containers lifted onto ships. Agricultural productivity was higher than they had ever imagined. They concluded, as Deng had several years earlier, that China needed to concentrate on learning about science and technology.[16]

The members of the group had expected to see evidence of exploitation of laborers, so they were stunned by the high standard of living of ordinary workers. Wang Quanguo, head of the State Planning Commission of Guangdong province, summarized their impressions as follows: "In a little over one month of inspection, our eyes were opened. . . . Everything we saw and heard startled every one of us. We were enormously stimulated. . . . We thought capitalist countries were backward and decadent. When we left our country and took a look, we realized things were completely different."[17] Delegation members were also taken aback by the willingness of Europeans to lend them money and to offer them modern technology. At one banquet alone, a group of Europeans announced they were prepared to lend as much as US$20 billion.[18] The group was surprised as well by how the European countries gave local governments the freedom to handle their own finances, to collect their own taxes, and to make decisions about their own affairs. The group returned from abroad believing that Chinese finance was far too centralized, with not enough leeway given to more locally based party leaders.[19]

Upon their return to China, the Gu Mu delegation was scheduled to report immediately about the trip to a meeting of the Politburo, chaired by Hua Guofeng, that began at 3 p.m. Politburo members were so excited that that they decided to continue the discussions over dinner and did not conclude the meeting until 11 p.m.[20] Those who heard the Gu Mu reports were surprised to learn how enormous the gap was between China and the outside world. Some Chinese leaders suspected reports about the West, but they knew and respected the members of the Gu Mu delegation, whose credibility was unquestioned. After all the years of fearing the West, they were even more surprised that Europeans were such warm and gracious hosts and were so open and willing to extend loans and technology. Knowing his colleagues' suspicions of capitalists, Gu Mu explained that the Europeans were eager to invest because their factories were operating below capacity and they hoped to sell China their goods and technologies. Gu Mu suggested a number of possible ways that foreigners could assist China in improving production —compensation trade, joint production, and foreign investment—and suggested that China should carefully examine all these possibilities. Lest there be any doubt that Gu Mu might have been exaggerating his accounts, the top officials most familiar with foreign developments—Marshal Ye, Nie Rongzhen, and Li Xiannian—all praised Gu Mu for his objectivity and for the clarity of his presentation. Very impressed, the Politburo members agreed that China should move immediately to take advantage of these opportunities.[21] For if other countries can import capital and materials and carry on the processing of goods for export, "Why can't we?"[22]

Over the next few weeks the delegation organized their materials which they presented as an official written report to the Politburo on June 30. Deng Xiaoping, who chose not to spend his time attending Politburo meetings that he had trouble hearing, met with Gu Mu individually. When they met, Deng said that China should move as quickly as possible to follow all of Gu Mu's suggestions, including borrowing money from abroad.[23] To begin with, Chinese leaders decided to concentrate on textiles; cloth was in such short supply in China that all clothing purchases then required the use of ration coupons. Increasing the supply of cloth would quickly demonstrate to the public the value of opening to the outside and would gain support for further reform and opening. Moreover, because there were grain shortages, it would not be easy to expand rapidly the cotton crop to increase the supply of cloth. Instead, then, Gu Mu advocated quickly introducing factories that would produce synthetic fibers as needed and, like in Japan, Taiwan, South Korea, and Hong Kong, allow textile and apparel industries to drive the takeoff of light industry in China.[24]

China's new willingness to work with capitalist countries as a result of the Gu Mu trip required not only rethinking specific industrial plans, but also revising government rules and bureaucratic procedures to allow foreign firms to operate in China. Suspicions that Western capitalists would take advantage of China's ignorance of international practices did not disappear, but Chinese officials still pushed ahead. They considered new questions touching on all aspects of the economy: Which firms in China would be allowed to work with foreigners? How could they best guard against foreigners taking advantage of them? How would foreign trade be integrated with the Chinese planning system? How should they decide which localities and which sectors should receive the incoming loans and technology?

In the more leisurely days of Meiji Japan, the Iwakura Mission had taken more than a decade to produce its twelve-volume *Opinions on Industry* to guide industrial development. By contrast, after the Gu Mu trip, it took just several weeks for the delegation to complete its reports and for Chinese economic leaders to organize appropriate units to discuss the implications of what they had learned.

As soon as the reports were completed, the State Council convened the Forum on Principles to Guide the Four Modernizations *(Sihua jianshe de wuxuhui)*, which lasted from July 6 to September 9, to consider how to take advantage of the new opportunities for borrowing technology and capital from the West. At the opening session, Gu Mu presented a lengthy report of what they had learned from the trip and added some personal impressions.[25] The meetings were chaired by Li Xiannian, who was still the highest official in charge of the economy. Participants were told not to focus on errors of the past, but to think of what the country should do in the future. Deng Xiaoping, who was busy with managing education, science, technology, and foreign relations, did not attend, but he followed reports of the sessions and, at the end, read the draft final reports and made suggestions for revision.[26]

Unlike work conferences in which participants are closeted in a hotel for several days, the forum was conducted in a series of twenty-three morning sessions spread over two months. Hua Guofeng, who rarely attended State Council meetings, regarded these gatherings as so important that he took part in thirteen of the twenty-three morning sessions.[27] In the afternoons, the officials returned to their regular work units to report on the morning discussions and to prepare their units' written responses to the issues raised. The forum allowed some sixty representatives of the key economic ministries and commissions to present the overall activities and plans of their units. This way, each unit could get a sense of what all the other units were thinking without becoming involved in arguments about the precise allocations and production targets; such details would be discussed at later planning meetings.

At the closing session on September 9, Li Xiannian, who had led the economy when it was virtually closed to the outside, announced the beginning of a new age of openness for China. In his concluding report to the forum, he explained that China could no longer remain a closed economy, that it must import foreign technologies, equipment, capital, and management experience in order to accelerate its development. Li further stated that if the Chinese took full advantage of the present favorable conditions, China could achieve a high degree of modernization in the twentieth century. To achieve this goal, he declared that between 1978 and 1985 China should import US$18 billion worth of goods and equipment.[28]

In mid-1978, the forum participants were just beginning to learn about the global economic system, and China was not yet ready to begin experimenting with markets. But in the relatively free atmosphere, the participants could raise all the big issues about markets, decentralization, prices, foreign trade, micromanagement, and macromanagement that would be addressed in greater detail during the ensuing two decades. Of these, two of the most pressing were: How could China expand foreign trade and the role of foreigners without losing control? And how could China provide incentives to individuals, local areas, and foreigners but still retain overall control of the national planning system?

The ten-year vision that was shaped by the discussions at the forum reflected the optimism and excitement that had grown out of the Gu Mu trip. Some assumptions—for instance, that China could pay for imports of new plants and equipment with petroleum exports—were to prove completely unrealistic. Excited by the unprecedented new opportunities, ambitious but inexperienced officials who wanted the country to make up for the two lost decades conceived visions that would exceed their capacities. Yet although they were excessively optimistic, officials at the forum did not abandon government controls. Foreigners were not given full, unfettered access to the Chinese economy. Instead, foreigners' contacts with the Chinese economy were mediated through special units of the government involved with foreign trade, where Chinese officials with linguistic skills and some knowledge of foreigners guarded China's interests.

The optimistic forum participants were in no mood to listen to the champion of the sober cautious officials, Chen Yun. Although Chen Yun had not been an official since being pushed aside by Mao in 1962, no one knew better how the excessive optimism of the Great Leap Forward had devastated the economy and no one had been bolder in trying to temper the optimism at that time. Toward the end of the forum, Chen Yun, who had been informed of some of the forum discussions, told his former underling Li Xiannian that the forum should be extended for a few more days in order to hear other points of view.[29] Chen said, "It is correct to borrow money from foreign countries . . . but to borrow so much at once—we can't manage it. Some comrades only look at the conditions abroad and have not looked at the realities in our country. Our industrial base cannot compare with theirs, our technical capacity is not up to theirs. They only see that we can borrow money . . . if we don't do it in a balanced way, and just rely on loans from abroad, it will not be reliable."[30] Forum participants were eager to move ahead, and Hua did not extend the meeting to consider other views.

Deng did not participate in the forum, but he followed the proceedings and did nothing to restrain the optimism. When told of the decision to borrow US$18 billion worth of technology and goods, Deng casually said, "Why not US$80 billion?" Zbigniew Brzezinski, who had met Deng two months before the forum convened, accurately observed Deng's mood (see Chapter 11). Deng, he told President Carter, was in a hurry.

Lighting the Spark, September 13–20, 1978

When Mao was planning to ignite the Chinese revolution, he wrote a famous essay declaring that a single spark can start a prairie fire. Echoing this thought, Hu Yaobang said that Deng's trip to the Northeast (September 13–19, 1978) helped light the spark for a fire that would forge dramatic changes in China, changes reflected at the Central Party Work Conference held later that fall.[31] He might have added that the changes included the elevation of Deng Xiaoping as paramount leader. Deng Xiaoping himself later recalled that there were three occasions when he went to the regions to "light a spark" for reform and opening. The first occasion was in Guangzhou in November 1977, when he and Ye Jianying met with PLA officials and civilians to liven up the Guangdong economy.[32] The second was in Sichuan in February 1978, on a stopover between visits to Burma and Nepal, when he met Zhao Ziyang to discuss the promotion of rural and urban reforms. (While in Sichuan, Deng mocked those who said that if a farmer has three ducks he is socialist, but if he has five ducks he is a capitalist.[33] They should liberate their thinking from this rigid dogma, Deng argued; socialism is not poverty.) The third was on this trip to the Northeast, on his way back from attending the thirtieth anniversary celebrations of the founding of the North Korean Workers' Party.

During this last spark-lighting trip, Deng spent several days in China's three northeastern provinces (Heilongjiang, Jilin, and Liaoning, called "Manchuria" by the Japanese) and then Tangshan and Tianjin, where he championed a bolder departure from Maoism than Hua Guofeng's "two whatevers." By the time Deng visited the Northeast, the struggle between the article "Practice Is the Sole Criterion for Judging Truth," which first appeared three months earlier, and the "two whatevers" had begun to heat up. Just a few weeks earlier, Zhang Pinghua, Hua Guofeng's Propaganda Department head, had made the rounds of the Northeast urging officials to support the "two whatevers." (Zhang was to become one of the first officials whom Deng replaced after he gained more power at the Third Plenum; Hu Yaobang took his place.) Deng's Northeast tour, then, was in effect a way of answering arguments made by Zhang Pinghua and stirring up support for a bolder effort to expand reform and opening. In Beijing, Chairman Hua controlled the propaganda apparatus, so to avoid causing a direct confrontation, Deng spoke in Beijing with some caution. Away from Beijing, however, he could address larger audiences and speak with less reserve. He spoke informally so that he did not have to go through a bureaucratic process of getting official clearance for formal speeches. In his presentations, Deng did not attack Hua Guofeng directly, but he did criticize the "two whatevers" and supported "Practice," presenting indirectly his case against Hua. Politically savvy Chinese officials observing Deng concluded that by making the case for "Practice" against the "two whatevers," he was gathering support in his competition with Hua for the preeminent position in the party. It was logical for Deng to begin by lighting a spark in the Northeast because there he had his base of supporters—in particular Ren Zhongyi in Liaoning province, Wang Enmao in Jilin province, and Li Desheng, commander of the Shenyang Military Region— who were among the first to declare support for "Practice."

At a gathering of Jilin provincial party officials, Deng criticized advocates of the "two whatevers" for not conveying "Mao's true spirit, which is to seek the true path from facts." Deng said Marxism-Leninism did not tell the Chinese revolutionaries to surround the cities from the countryside: Mao had succeeded militarily because he adapted Marxism-Leninism to China's particular conditions at the time. Similarly, Deng argued, when foreigners had refused to sell their goods to China, conditions were not yet ripe for developing foreign trade, but conditions had since become favorable for improving economic relations with foreign countries. The Gang of Four may have denounced improving relations with foreigners as a "national betrayal," but the correct way to hold high the banner of Mao Zedong Thought would be to adapt to such changes and promote foreign trade.[34]

In Liaoning, Deng said that Chinese leaders, including himself, must admit that they had let down the wonderful Chinese people who had been very patient. The politically sophisticated understood, so Deng did not have to add: "Who was in charge when 'we' let down the Chinese people? Who was not making any changes to correct those errors? How could anyone believe that everything Mao said was correct?" Instead, Deng said: "Our nation's system . . . is basically taken from the Soviet Union. It is backward, deals with issues superficially, duplicates structures, and advances bureaucratism. . . . If we can't grow faster than the capitalist countries then we can't show the superiority of our system." It took no huge leap to conclude that Deng believed Hua was not doing enough to change the structure and to lay a solid foundation for economic growth.

In the Northeast Deng also wanted to firm up his support in the military. Li Desheng, the highest military official in the Northeast who was commander of the Shenyang Military Region, had served under Deng in the Second Field Army. Deng had ample opportunity to talk with Li, who accompanied Deng as he visited factories, farms, and military units.[35] At the time, Deng was concerned about the personal loyalty of another high-level military official who was stationed in the Northeast at the port of Dalian, Admiral Su Zhenhua. Su had served under Deng in the Second Field Army, but he had not proved very loyal; when officials were called upon to attack Deng in 1976 he had been more critical of Deng than Deng judged necessary. In April 1978 when a destroyer accidentally exploded in Zhanjiang harbor causing many deaths, Deng held Su Zhenhua, as the highest-ranking naval official in the country and the military representative on the Politburo, responsible. Shortly after being criticized, Su was notified that Hua Guofeng would stop in the Northeast on the way back from his trip to North Korea. Aware of the rivalry between Deng and Hua Guofeng and unhappy about being criticized, Su Zhenhua offered to hold a naval exercise with some 120 ships as part of the welcoming ceremony when Hua arrived in Dalian. When Deng heard that Su was planning to give such a display of support for Hua, he was furious and used his leverage over the military to have the military exercise cancelled. During his visit to the Northeast, Deng wanted to make sure that there were no remnants of military support for Hua Guofeng. To achieve this, he worked closely with his loyal former underling Li Desheng as they traveled together.

Deng repeated to his audiences that the criticism of the Gang of Four should end and the focus should be on doing what was necessary to increase production. Deng was prepared to start working to increase production and the audiences had no doubt that he stood ready to take on greater responsibilities as well.

Central Party Work Conference, November 10–December 15, 1978

In official Communist Party histories, the Third Plenum of the 11th Party Congress, December 18–22, 1978, is acknowledged as the meeting that launched Deng's policies of "reform and opening." In fact, the plenum was merely a formal ratification of what had been resolved in the lively discussions at the Central Party Work Conference held from November 10 to December 15. Coming two years after Mao's death and the arrest of the Gang of

Four, the conference took place at a time when various perspectives could be discussed afresh with less concern about being improperly disrespectful of Mao. As the meeting came to an end, Deng praised the conference, which marked a return to the party's tradition of democratic discussions, in which people could speak frankly about what they really believed. He said it was the best such discussion at a party meeting since 1957 (when the Hundred Flowers campaign had encouraged freer expression).[36] Some thought it was the best meeting since the 7th Party Congress of 1945, while others thought it ranked alongside the Yan'an rectification campaign of 1941–1942.[37]

The Central Party Work Conference was called by Chairman Hua Guofeng, who in his initial presentations gave little indication that he understood what was in store for him. When he opened the meeting on November 10, he said that the meeting would focus on agriculture and the national development plan for 1979–1980, and would serve as a follow-up to the Forum on Principles to Guide the Four Modernizations. His plan for the conference was fully consistent with what Deng had advocated the previous year at the PLA conference in Guangdong: they should end the criticism of the Gang of Four and concentrate on the four modernizations. Yet two days after its opening, Hua's plans for the conference were derailed by broader political discussions.

Neither Hua Guofeng nor Deng Xiaoping had anticipated how completely and how rapidly the political climate would change. A few weeks earlier Deng had outlined his speech for the conference and had tasked Hu Qiaomu and Yu Guangyuan to help to flesh it out.[38] But after Deng returned from Southeast Asia on November 14 and heard reports of the changed atmosphere in Beijing, he asked his speechwriters to draft an entirely different speech for him.[39]

Marshal Ye, who quickly realized how much the changed atmosphere had weakened the support for Hua Guofeng, advised Hua on November 11 to begin preparing a speech showing that he, too, accepted the changes. The crucial drama took place between November 11 and November 25. By the time Deng joined the conference on November 15, its focus had already shifted from economics to politics, and the political winds were blowing against Hua and his "two whatevers." Some senior party leaders would later remark that just as the Zunyi conference had been the decisive turning point in Mao's rise to the chairmanship, so this work conference proved the decisive event in the rise of Deng.[40]

The work conference brought together 210 top party officials. Attendees

included many who held important party, military, and government positions, including the heads of all major branches of party work, two top
party leaders from each provincial-level unit, and respected senior officials no
longer on the front line. It also included other party members who could
help provide a broad theoretical perspective. In his opening presentation,
Chairman Hua Guofeng announced that they had originally planned to meet
for twenty days, but more time might be needed. In the end, the meeting
lasted for thirty-six days. Attendees closeted themselves in the Jingxi [Capital
West] Hotel, within walking distance of Zhongnanhai, so that discussions
could continue in the evenings and on weekends, in and out of the formal
sessions.[41] The format of the meetings—which included both plenary and
small group sessions—and the closeting of the participants in the Jingxi Hotel
were identical to the setup and procedures used at the Central Party Work
Conference of March 1977, but twenty months later the political climate was
totally different.

The format of the meeting encouraged participation by all those present.
Except for the four plenary sessions, the participants were divided in six regional small groups (North, Northeast, East, Central-South, Southwest, and
Northwest), in which each participant was expected to express his views.
Each day a written summary report of the small group meetings was passed
on to all participants; when a group wanted to express its views for the report,
members voted with a show of hands.[42] Although Deng, like other Politburo
Standing Committee members, did not take part in the small group meetings, he followed the daily reports very closely.[43]

By the beginning of the conference, Hua realized that many participants
were dissatisfied with the "two whatevers," with the harsh criticism of those
who had taken part in the April 5 demonstrations, and by his unwillingness
to reverse the verdicts on more senior officials who had been criticized during
the Cultural Revolution.[44] The April 5 demonstrations were a particularly
touchy issue, and Hua had still not gone far enough to satisfy many of the
participants. As early as March 1977 at the earlier Central Party Work Conference, Hua had acknowledged that most of those who had gone to Tiananmen Square on April 5 had done so to praise Zhou Enlai, but even so,
the demonstration was still labeled a "counter-revolutionary incident." Most
conference participants in November 1978 found these injustices upsetting.[45]
Hua repeated that Deng had not been involved in the April 5, 1976 incident,
but many senior officials believed that Deng had been improperly removed
and replaced by Hua as a result of those events. The evaluation of the inci-

dent to some extent was an evaluation of Deng, and many were insisting that there be a new evaluation of the incident in which it would be labeled a "revolutionary movement."[46]

By focusing in his initial speeches on the four modernizations, Hua hoped to sidestep the political differences and talk about economic issues, for which there was a high level of consensus. Hua's opening speech was carefully crafted to go a considerable distance toward accommodating his critics. While not saying explicitly that he was abandoning the "two whatevers," he did not even mention the "two whatevers." Instead, after outlining the agenda for the conference, Hua made clear he was ready to accept foreign loans, foreign technology, and foreign goods as part of an economic plan, none of which Mao had authorized. He did not directly say he was rejecting political campaigns, but he said that he had carefully considered whether to initiate a campaign to mobilize people from the top to the bottom of society; he said he had concluded that this would take time and energy that would be better spent working on the pressing issues that the country faced. In addition, Hua told the conference that he had directed that people should not be paraded through the streets in mass criticism sessions.[47] Even many of the attendees who sought more reform and a more rapid return of the senior officials acknowledged that Hua, although not directly criticizing the Cultural Revolution and the class struggle, was making a serious effort to end some of its worst excesses. Deng Xiaoping would have found it difficult to disagree with the main thrust of Hua's comments.

Hua managed to keep control through the second plenary session on the afternoon of November 13, when Vice Premier Ji Dengkui made his presentation on agriculture. Most attendees had at some time been responsible for the rural areas at the basic levels; they had seen firsthand the starvation after the Great Leap Forward. Although the Communists had risen to power with the support of peasants, they were keenly aware that tens of millions of peasants had starved to death under their mistaken policies, that serious food shortages continued to exist, and that scarce foreign currency was being used to import grain. The leaders assembled had been forced to deal with the results of these disasters, facing starving peasants and distraught lower-level officials. The party could not escape responsibility for having implemented these bad decisions, even though the main responsibility for the painful mistakes was placed on Lin Biao and the Gang of Four. Officials were increasingly willing to say privately what they did not yet say publicly: that some of the responsibility should be placed on Mao.[48]

Against this backdrop, Ji Dengkui's speech offered attendees a sense that honesty and openness were returning to agricultural policy-making. Steering away from the inflated, optimistic, empty rhetoric of the Mao era, Ji made a frank and comprehensive statement stressing the seriousness of the problems. He acknowledged that China's agricultural policies had changed too often and too unpredictably and often did not conform to local conditions. Participants knew the party had to resolve the food shortages that still existed, and Ji Dengkui proposed that the agricultural problems be resolved by increasing investment, improving the supply of seeds and chemical fertilizer, doubling the loans available to farmers, and increasing the purchase price of grain by 30 percent.[49]

But Ji's openness and Hua's gestures of conciliation were not enough for what was rapidly becoming a frank discussion reflecting deep convictions that had not yet been aired at large party meetings. And one of those convictions was that Hua was no longer able to provide the top leadership the party needed. Not long after the sessions began, participants in the Central-South small group, for example, declared unanimously that they supported "Practice Is the Sole Criterion for Judging Truth."[50] And by November 11, the second day of the work conference and the first day of small group discussions, many of the participants were in revolt against the efforts of Hua Guofeng and Wang Dongxing to block the further reversal of verdicts; they wanted to clear the names of respected departed officials and to bring back their former colleagues.

On November 11, three highly respected officials, Chen Zaidao, Li Chang, and Lu Zhengcao, spoke out in their small groups on the need to reverse more verdicts. The atmosphere was so electric by the end of the day that Marshal Ye advised Hua Guofeng either to accept the changed mood or prepare to be left behind.[51] All the participants, including Hua, knew well how, in 1964, Khrushchev had been pushed out of the Soviet leadership in a coup led by Brezhnev and other officials.

On November 12, nine other people spoke out in their small groups on the need to reverse the verdicts that Hua and Wang Dongxing had refused to change. Chen Yun was the most influential of those and some accounts of the conference mistakenly credit his speech, which Hu Qiaomu had helped polish, for changing the atmosphere, but in fact the atmosphere had already changed before his speech; others had made the point in their small group meetings before he did. Chen Yun's speech, however, did offer comprehensive up-to-date data by drawing on personnel records. Because of Chen Yun's leadership in personnel work dating back almost four decades, his speech carried more weight. As he addressed the Northeast small group, Chen Yun rejected Hua Guofeng's effort to focus on economic issues, countering that to engage the enthusiasm of officials and to succeed in economic work, the party had to first deal with unresolved political controversies. In particular, they must clear the names of five groups of people who had been criticized unfairly:

1. The sixty-one members of a "renegade group," led by Bo Yibo, who had been criticized during the Cultural Revolution.[52]
2. Those accused of voluntarily surrendering to the enemy to secure their release from prison in 1940; they deserved to have their party membership restored.
3. Tao Zhu, Wang Heshou, and others who had been imprisoned in 1937 and were without basis criticized for revealing, under pressure, information about their colleagues.
4. Marshal Peng Dehuai, already deceased, who should be treated with honor and whose remains should be buried in the Babaoshan Cemetery for Revolutionary Heroes.
5. Those involved in the April 5, 1976, Tiananmen incident, which should be treated as a popular mass movement.

Chen Yun added that Kang Sheng, who during the Cultural Revolution had attacked and destroyed the careers and lives of many outstanding party leaders, though deceased, should be held responsible for his crimes.[53]

It is not difficult to imagine that Chen Yun spoke with some passion: his grievances ran deep. In particular, Hua Guofeng had not restored him to a high position and Wang Dongxing had refused to print his speech at the March 1977 Central Party Work Conference arguing that Deng Xiaoping should be allowed to return to work. But his was not the only speech infused with strong emotion: a torrent of previously suppressed anger was released by speakers in all of the groups against officials like Hua Guofeng and Wang Dongxing who had blocked the return of good officials unjustly accused. Those who spoke out could identify with those who were not yet being allowed to return, for many knew what it was to suffer humiliation and physical abuse. In each of the six small groups, speaker after speaker demanded the rehabilitation of officials unjustly accused and the posthumous condemnation of Kang Sheng, who had been responsible for so many deaths and whose former secretary, Li Xin, was even at that moment assisting Wang Dongxing in preventing the reversal of verdicts. It was this passion that fueled the dissatisfaction with Hua and Wang Dongxing.

While the Central Party Work Conference was still in its opening days, the atmosphere at the conference was reflected in actions taken by the Beijing Party Committee, which was responsible for preserving security in the city of Beijing. On October 9, Lin Hujia had become first party secretary of the Beijing Municipal Party Committee, replacing Wu De, who had supervised the arrests on April 5, 1976. As soon as he was appointed, Lin and the Beijing Party Committee began considering when and how to free those still not exonerated for their role in the April 5 demonstrations; even before the work conference they had begun preparing drafts of possible announcements.

Lin Hujia was also a participant at the Central Party Work Conference and head of the North China small group. On November 13, fully aware of the changed atmosphere following Marshal Ye's meeting with Hua and Chen Yun's speech, Lin called an enlarged meeting of the Beijing Party Committee; after the meeting, on behalf of the Beijing Party Committee, he released an announcement that went well beyond Hua's concession that the April 5 demonstrations were not counter-revolutionary. It read: "On the spring grave-sweeping festival [Qingming] of 1976, the masses of people gathered at Tiananmen Square to mourn our beloved Zhou. . . . They were gripped by a deep hatred of the crimes of the 'Gang of Four' who brought calamity to the country. This action . . . is entirely a revolutionary action. All the comrades persecuted for their involvement shall be rehabilitated and have their reputations restored."[54]

Beijing Daily, which was directly under the leadership of the Beijing Party Committee and was now headed by Lin Hujia, immediately published the announcement. Furthermore, three media officials who were attending the Central Party Work Conference—Zeng Tao, president of the New China News Agency (Xinhua) (NCNA), Hu Jiwei, the editor of *People's Daily*, and Yang Xiguang, editor of *Guangming Daily*, all of whom were also vice heads of the Propaganda Department—boldly decided to publicize the contents of the *Beijing Daily* article in their respective publications. The next day, November 15, *People's Daily* and *Guangming Daily* printed the news release from the *Beijing Daily* with the banner headline, "Beijing Municipal Party Committee Announces Tiananmen Is a Revolutionary Action." The NCNA immediately released an announcement that not only were the masses engaging in revolutionary action, but the incident itself was revolutionary. On

November 16, *People's Daily* and *Guangming Daily* reprinted the NCNA announcement.

Ordinarily such an important political announcement required Politburo approval, but the three bold editors, sensing the changing political mood, took the risky step of acting without higher-level permission.[55] When Hu Yaobang complained that the three had not told even him beforehand, let alone the Politburo, Zeng Tao answered that they thought that if Hu Yaobang had been asked, he would have had to shoulder a heavy responsibility for this decision. It was better for them to accept responsibility and just publish it.[56]

The publication of the announcement caused a flurry of excitement at the conference. Lin Hujia was understandably concerned that he might be criticized for his bold action. On November 16, after the article appeared in the two papers, he called one of the editors to ask who had authorized their headlines. Upon hearing that the editors had simply decided to print what was already in the *Beijing Daily,* Lin said that he would take responsibility for the article in the *Beijing Daily,* but that the other two must assume responsibility for the headlines in their papers. Lin Hujia—worried that Hua Guofeng might be angry—also phoned Hua to explain and ask for understanding. To his great surprise, Hua did not complain about the announcement's publication.[57] In fact, on November 18, three days after the appearance of the newspaper articles, Hua went so far as to write in his own calligraphy the title page for *Collection of Tiananmen Poems,* a new book extolling those who had taken part in the April 5 demonstrations. A photograph of Hua signing the title page was carried in the press. The ever curious and politically sensitive public in Beijing understood immediately: Hua Guofeng accepted a complete reversal of the judgment on the Tiananmen incident. He was already following Marshal Ye's advice to adapt to the changing atmosphere so he would not be left behind.[58]

On November 25, Hua Guofeng delivered his scheduled presentation. It was not a self-criticism but rather a statement that he accepted the dominant views of party members and was ready to continue to serve, even if that meant representing views completely different from those he had earlier espoused. He accepted that the April 5 Tiananmen incident was an authentic patriotic revolutionary movement and that the people involved should all be rehabilitated.

Hua admitted that after Mao's death, he had been wrong to criticize the "rightist reversal of verdicts" that had led to criticism of Deng. And he advised that the criticisms of those accused of resisting the Cultural Revolution in February 1967 ("the February counter-current") be reversed and their reputations restored. Peng Dehuai's ashes were to be placed in the Babaoshan Cemetery for Revolutionary Heroes. The case against Tao Zhu would be reversed. The label given to Yang Shangkun, that he was a conspirator against the party, would be removed and he could take part in regular "party life" meetings and receive a new assignment. Kang Sheng was to be criticized.

Hua acknowledged that political problems should be resolved on the basis of the facts and in accordance with the principle that practice is the sole criterion for judging truth.[59] Hua acknowledged as well that most conference participants felt that Ji Dengkui's comments on agriculture did not go far enough. In his speech, Hua no longer pointed to Dazhai as a model. Hua's address was warmly welcomed by the conference participants.[60] He followed up with another address on December 13, in which he acknowledged that he had personally made errors.

By yielding to the changed political climate and completely reversing himself on a number of issues, Hua avoided a fight.[61] As he put it, he acted to preserve party unity. But many believe that with the decisive change of atmosphere that had been building up over the summer and fall and that had crystallized during the first three days of the work conference, Hua had no real option. As it was, Hua was allowed to remain as chairman of the party, premier, and chairman of the Central Military Commission (CMC).

When a new policy line was introduced, it was expected that the chief supporters of the former line (now referred to as the "incorrect line") would engage in self-criticisms and declare their support for the new "correct line." But some of Hua's close associates did not move so quickly and deftly as he did. Wang Dongxing, then vice chairman of the Communist Party and director of the General Office of the party who controlled the handling of the "special cases" and supervised propaganda work, had resolutely opposed rehabilitating large numbers of officials and breaking free of Maoist ideology. Senior officials were convinced that as Mao's loyal bodyguard he had acquired positions beyond his ability and that his great contribution in arresting the Gang of Four had permitted him to remain in a position that he did not deserve in the first place and from which he was blocking progress. After Hua accepted the dominant party atmosphere on November 25, two participants felt sufficiently confident of the changing winds that they criticized Wang Dongxing by name and without prior consultation. They chastised him for blocking the return of senior officials, for opposing "Practice Is the Sole Criterion for Judging Truth," for upholding the "two whatevers," and for denigrating Deng Xiaoping. Others joined in the attack on someone whom many regarded as the biggest obstacle to rehabilitating the wrongly accused officials and to breaking free of the rigid Maoist ideology.

Wang Dongxing refused to offer an oral self-criticism, but on December 13, at the end of the work conference, he presented a written version.[62] He acknowledged that he had made mistakes in the handling of the special cases: "I did not pay due attention to the work to redress some framed, false, and wrong verdicts, and I did not act promptly and failed to do the work well." Wang also agreed that the materials from the Central Group on the Examination of Special Cases and the Special Group on the Examination of the May 16 Special Cases would be handed over to the Organization Department, following the decision of the party center: "The posts I hold exceed my ability . . . I sincerely request that the party Central Committee remove me from these posts."[63] Wu De and Li Xin were also criticized, and shortly after the Third Plenum, Zhang Pinghua was replaced. The staff writers Wu Lengxi, Xiong Fu, and Hu Sheng—who had sided with Hua Guofeng and the "two whatevers"—were subject to serious though milder criticism.

Hua Guofeng and Wang Dongxing remained for the time being members of the Politburo Standing Committee, and three of Hua's allies—Wu De, Ji Dengkui, and Chen Xilian—stayed on the Politburo. Deng, as the emerging preeminent leader, made some changes in work assignments, but decided that those serving on the Politburo and its Standing Committee who had made self-criticisms need not be removed.[64] Deng chose to avoid a confrontation and to avoid conveying to the public, both at home and abroad, that a power struggle was going on.

The Central Party Work Conference not only set in motion the replacement of Hua by Deng; it served as a forum for high-level officials to review past errors more openly and consider new policies for the future. In the small group discussions, speaker after speaker related his personal experiences in dealing with the disastrous food shortages and supported the need for more national inputs to solve the problem once and for all. For many leaders, these discussions provided a personal catharsis, as they acknowledged publicly the failures they had not yet faced so directly, failures that had caused the vast suffering and deaths that they had seen personally. Even if they laid primary blame on higher officials, they could not completely escape responsibility; for many officials it was a trauma from which they never fully recovered.

One of the boldest speeches on agriculture was given by Hu Yaobang in the Northwest group. He argued that Ji Dengkui's proposals were insufficient to resolve the rural problems and still reflected shackled thinking. Further, Hu boldly contended that the union of political and economic activities in a single local unit, the commune, was not working. To solve the problem, the party had to find a way to strengthen the initiative of peasants and local officials. Hu said that if the collective was mismanaged and did not capture the enthusiasm of the peasants, it could not be effective.[65] Here Hu was articulating his colleagues' widespread support for decentralizing the rural production team to smaller subgroups. But no one, not even Hu Yaobang or Wan Li (who was then experimenting in Anhui with smaller work groups below the production team), then discussed the possibility of contracting down to the household level and of abolishing the communes. They knew that having such discussions among the party elite would be highly controversial and would undermine the authority of the local party officials still trying to make the collectives work.[66]

Participants in the small groups also discussed economic issues. Liang Lingguang, minister of light industry (and later governor of Guangdong), stressed the importance of political stability. He reminded others that the three periods of relatively rapid growth—the early years after 1949, the First Five-Year Plan period (1953–1957), and the period of adjustment after the Great Leap Forward (1961–1965)—were all times of political stability. Liang also argued that a higher priority should be given to improving light industry, so that it could better meet daily household needs. He was somewhat ahead of his time in arguing that markets needed to play a greater role. In his view, new production technologies should be imported and to increase exports, taxes on exports had to be reduced.[67]

Toward the end of the work conference, participants began turning to another question dear to all their hearts: who should be added to the Central Committee, the Politburo, and the Standing Committee? The work conference had no authority to make personnel decisions, but most of those who would later make such decisions were in attendance. Since Deng did not want to remove members of the Politburo or its Standing Committee, participants acknowledged that in the short run the Politburo would become somewhat larger so as to allow the entry of new members. It was understood that as people retired or were found unfit, the size of the Politburo would again be reduced. Participants accepted Deng's view that new members should have a proven record of "boldly making things happen *(gan zuo)*."[68] The Northwest small group recommended, with a show-of-hands vote, that Chen Yun, Deng

Yingchao, Hu Yaobang, and Wang Zhen be added to the Politburo.[69] At the formal meetings that followed the work conference, these recommendations were officially confirmed.

There was widespread recognition at the conference that in an era when economics was the top priority, the wisest and most experienced specialist in economics, Chen Yun, should be given a high position. Chen Yun, thoroughly aware of Deng's broader experience in two critical areas where he lacked experience, foreign affairs and the military, said that for the paramount position, Deng was the only appropriate person.[70] But participants enthusiastically recommended that Chen Yun be made a vice chairman of the party.

What united Deng and Chen Yun at the time of the work conference was their determination to reverse the verdicts on senior officials and allow them to return to work. Deng became in effect the spokesperson for a collective leadership, especially in foreign affairs, and along with Marshal Ye he already held informal authority in the military. But Chen Yun acquired authority over personnel issues and within weeks took responsibility for economic concerns. In overall political status—that is, in determining political direction and selecting key personnel—Chen Yun was Deng's equal.

Deng Prepares for Reform and Opening

When Deng returned to Beijing from Southeast Asia on the fifth day of the work conference, Marshal Ye briefed him on the changed political climate and advised him to prepare for his new responsibilities. At this point, the highly respected Marshal Ye, whose seniority dated back to 1927 when he had taken part in the Guangzhou uprising, and who never wanted the responsibilities of power, emerged as "kingmaker." Marshal Ye believed deeply that the errors of the Great Leap Forward and the Cultural Revolution had been caused by the excessive concentration of power in the hands of one person. He urged both Hua Guofeng and Deng to work together in leading the party and the country. When Ye met with Deng, Deng agreed that they should strengthen the collective leadership and limit the publicity given to a single person.[71] Hua too had accepted Marshal Ye's advice to yield on the content of party policy and to accept Deng as the preeminent party spokesperson. Without any public celebration, then, Deng accepted Marshal Ye's advice to prepare for his new role, even as Hua Guofeng retained his formal titles as head of the party, the government, and the military.

To prepare for his new responsibilities, Deng had to reassure his colleagues and to revise the speeches he was preparing to give at the closing session of the work conference and at the Third Plenum. Deng met with the members of the Politburo Standing Committee and again reassured his colleagues, who were aware of his differences with Mao, that he would not become China's Khrushchev: Chairman Mao had made extraordinary contributions to the party and the party should not launch an attack on Mao like Khrushchev's attack on Stalin. He also reassured them that the country would remain united under the banner of Mao Zedong Thought. Observing the eager optimism generated at the work conference, which he had followed by reading the daily summaries, Deng, the experienced elder statesman, cautioned his juniors against the dangers of becoming "giddy with success." He warned that China would not be able to resolve all its problems quickly and they should not arbitrarily try to force quick resolutions. He also noted that it might take some time to turn around previous decisions on particular cases, such as that on Peng Dehuai and that on the leaders of the February 1967 "counter-current."[72] Some difficult problems could be resolved only by the next generation. Wanting to avoid reopening the wounds from the Cultural Revolution, he recommended further study. He counseled again, as he had many times before: look first at the big picture, then think about the smaller pictures; seek first to understand the broader truth, then consider the specific truths. Deng declared that before China could begin to bring in investment and technology from abroad, it would first need domestic stability. Only with stability could China realize the four modernizations.[73] It was vitally important, then, to avoid giving the Chinese public and the outside world any impression that there was a power struggle in China. Deng's comments to the Politburo Standing Committee were accepted as the views of the party. They were printed and distributed to conference participants a few days after the work conference.[74]

Since he would now become the preeminent leader, Deng had to redraft the speeches he was slated to give at the closing session of the work conference and at the Third Plenum. By December 2, a few days after Hua had yielded on all major points of policy, Deng called in Hu Yaobang and Yu Guangyuan, committed reformers, who would oversee preparation of his speech for the closing session of the work conference, a speech that might be the most important of his life. He was then busy finalizing negotiations with the United States on normalization of relations and making military preparations for a strong response to Vietnam's expected attack on Cambodia. But

Deng had been considering the issues he would address in the speech since at least 1969–1973 when he had been banished to Jiangxi. Hu Yaobang and Yu Guangyuan would be assisted by the actual drafters of the speech and, as usual, Hu Qiaomu was to supply the final polishing.[75]

Rarely did Deng write out notes for a speech, but for this meeting on December 2 he took out three pages of notes with some 1,600 Chinese characters (about eight hundred words) and explained to those responsible for the draft what he expected in terms of the speech's style, content, and outline. He told the writers that he wanted the speech to be brief and clear. He wanted short, concise sentences because they would be more forceful. He wanted to make clear how backward China was and how much it needed to change. On December 5, after he read the first draft, Deng gave the speechwriters detailed line-by-line comments. When he met them to review new drafts on December 9 and December 11, he again went through the same detailed process.

In the speech, Deng did not present new policies, for he had not had the time nor the staff to prepare them. Instead, he gave the assembled party leaders an overview of his approach for the new era. The speech reflected his perspective on the big issues that he was then wrestling with: how to encourage fresh thinking while minimizing resistance from conservative officials, how to show respect for Mao while departing from Mao's policies, how to present optimistic visions while preventing later disappointments, how to maintain stability while opening up the economy, and how much freedom to give local officials while still maintaining national priorities.

In his notes for the first meeting with his speechwriters, Deng had listed seven topics: (1) emancipating our minds, (2) promoting inner-party democracy and the legal system, (3) reviewing the past to guide the future, (4) overcoming excessive bureaucracy, (5) allowing some regions and enterprises to get rich first, (6) clarifying assignments of responsibility, and (7) tackling new problems. At the second meeting, Deng told his speechwriters that he had decided to combine the last several topics into one so that the final draft would address four themes.

On the afternoon of December 13, at the closing session of the Central Party Work Conference, Deng began his speech by announcing his themes: "Today, I mainly want to discuss one question, namely 'how to emancipate our minds, seek the true path from facts, and unite as one, in looking to the future.'" Deng praised the work conference as the best and most open discussion the party had convened since 1957. People, he said, must be allowed to express their views about the real situation. "Centralism can be correct only when there is a full measure of democracy. At present, we must lay particular stress on democracy, because for quite some time . . . there was too little democracy. . . . The masses should be encouraged to offer criticisms. . . . There is nothing to worry about even if a few malcontents take advantage of democracy to make trouble . . . the thing to be feared most is silence." Deng did not then or at any other time advocate unlimited free speech. In fact, by November 29, a few days after some people began posting their views on a wall not far from Tiananmen Square, Deng had already stated that some opinions posted on "Democracy Wall" were incorrect.

To praise Mao while still giving himself room to depart from some of his policies, Deng said, "Without [Mao's] outstanding leadership, [we] would still not have triumphed even today. . . . Chairman Mao was not infallible or free from shortcomings . . . at an appropriate time they should be summed up and lessons should be drawn from them . . . however, there is no need to do so hastily." He repeated his view that Mao had committed errors, that he himself had made errors, and that any leader who tries to accomplish things makes errors. Deng expressed the prevailing view at high levels that China's two huge disasters, the Great Leap and the Cultural Revolution, were caused by a system that allows one person to dominate without any input from other voices. China therefore needed to develop a legal system so that a single individual, no matter how able, will not dominate. If laws are initially imperfect and incomplete, they can be made fair and just, step by step, over time.

Deng's strategy for achieving modernization stood in stark contrast to Mao's reliance on spiritual appeals to advance the Great Leap Forward. As Deng said: "Initiative cannot be aroused without economic means. A small number of advanced people might respond to moral appeal, but such an approach can only be used for a short time."[76] Instead, Deng argued, China must create an internal structure that will reward those who advance science, technology, and productivity with promotions and a comfortable way of life. In particular, Deng advocated giving more flexibility to local officials, who would then take more initiative.

Deng declared that the theory of collective responsibility had meant, in practice, "that no one is responsible." He advocated assigning responsibilities to individuals and acknowledged that to do so, one must also give individuals power. When in 1975 he had said that lower officials must dare to think and dare to act, officials worried that Mao might reverse these policies; in 1978, when he repeated the phrase, those listening to his speech did not have to worry about a possible policy reversal: they felt empowered to try to help the country, even if they might make some mistakes along the way.

Deng supported reversing verdicts made during the Cultural Revolution: "Our principle is that every wrong should be corrected." But he was adamantly opposed to people "settling accounts" against those who in the past had attacked them or their friends or relatives. To avoid cycles of retaliation, injustices should be settled promptly without leaving loose ends. "But," he said, "to go into every detail is neither possible nor necessary." People should not dwell on the Cultural Revolution, which he knew could only be divisive, but let time clarify it: "stability and unity are of prime importance." People who had engaged in beating, smashing, looting, and factionalism could not be placed in important positions, but many who committed errors and then engaged in sincere self-criticisms should be given new opportunities. Deng made a point of mentioning, however, that the party would be stricter with those who made mistakes in the future.[77]

Deng tried to anticipate some of the problems that would arise with the new policies and to diffuse the hard feelings of those who would be unhappy about them. He knew that inequalities would increase—that given the speed of change that was to come, and the many needs of the Chinese, "some will get rich first." But, he said, others will have their opportunity later, and those who get rich first should help those who are initially left behind. He warned that problems would probably emerge that would be unfamiliar to him and other party leaders, but that the overall interests of the party and the state had to remain the priority: they must all "keep on learning."[78]

Although he did not yet get into specifics, Deng stood ready to allow some markets, and told his colleagues not to fear that they would cause economic chaos. He acknowledged that there would be frictions between those responsible for overall planning and local officials determined to exercise more autonomy. Conflicts of interest might be more serious than before, but, he argued, the long-term development of productive forces would help ease such problems.[79]

To prepare for the many changes to come, Deng recommended that the party officials study three subjects in particular: economics, science and technology, and management. And he specified how officials would be evaluated: the party committee in an economic unit would be judged mainly by the unit's adoption of advanced methods of management; by its progress in making technical innovations; by increases in productivity; and by its profits, measured in part by the personal income of its workers and the collective benefits it provides. The participants were eager for more specific guidance in this new environment. Although members ordinarily dispersed after the last major speech of a work conference, after Deng's speech, the attendees agreed to extend the conference for two more days so that the small groups from the various regions could continue to discuss how they could implement the new directions Deng had described.[80]

Many ideas expressed in Deng's speech seem to a Western business manager like common sense; some of them even had roots in policies carried out in China before 1949 as well as in the more stable years of the early 1950s and early 1960s. But for those leading China in 1978, Deng's ideas represented a fundamental departure from the Mao era. Listeners had reason to hope that China's painful period of mass mobilization, class warfare, hardline ideology, hero worship, intensive collectivization, and all-encompassing economic planning would at last be brought under control.

The Third Plenum, December 18–22, 1978

The Third Plenum of the Eleventh Party Congress began on Monday, December 18, at the Jingxi Hotel, where the work conference had ended the previous Friday. Slightly over half the participants at the plenum had also taken part in the work conference, but the plenum also included all the members of the Central Committee—who held the key positions in the party, government, and the military—whereas the work conference had included other prominent party leaders selected because they could help provide a broad theoretical perspective. Those attending the plenum who had not attended the work conference assembled on the Monday morning and afternoon before the others arrived to read the conference speeches by Deng Xiaoping, Marshal Ye, and Hua Guofeng so that they could all share the same perspective. There followed three days of formal plenary sessions and small group meetings led by the same leaders of the work conference.

The Third Plenum in a sense was a celebration of the spirit of the work conference, a formal approval of the new directions in a ceremony that announced the results of the work conference to the Chinese public and to the rest of the world. Plenums are identified by the number of the party congress that they follow, but the changes wrought by the Third Plenum of the 11th Congress were so momentous that when a Chinese person says simply, "the Third Plenum," listeners know exactly to which third plenum he or she is referring. In the minds of the Chinese public, the Third Plenum marked the beginning of "Deng's reform and opening" that was to transform China. Although reform and opening had in fact begun under Hua, they were realized under the leadership of Deng.

As agreed at the time of the work conference, Hua Guofeng retained his titles: chairman of the party, premier of the government, and chairman of the Central Military Commission (CMC). Deng retained his titles: vice chairman of the party, vice premier of the government, and vice chairman of the CMC. But the foreign press and diplomatic community, like the Chinese public, soon understood that in fact Vice Premier Deng Xiaoping had become the paramount leader. As early as November 23, two days before Hua's November 25 speech, journalists in Hong Kong explained to Robert Novak, a visiting American columnist, that "Deng, only a vice premier, now runs the authoritarian government of China."[81]

The person who gained most at the Third Plenum was Chen Yun. Prior to the plenum, he was not even on the Politburo, but at the plenum he became a member of the Standing Committee of the Politburo and vice chairman of the Central Committee. At its last plenary session, the Central Commission for Discipline Inspection was formally established, to which Chen Yun was named first secretary. Chen, rather than Wang Dongxing, was empowered to give final approval on any cases considered for a reversal of verdicts. It was understood that many cases of senior officials would be reversed in the months and years ahead, enabling them to return to work.

Ordinarily the highest official at a plenum presents a thematic report, but with Hua as the titular head and Deng as the preeminent leader, it was not easy to decide who should give it. Plenum organizers resolved the awkward situation by eliminating such a report, but in fact they treated Deng's speech, given earlier at the work conference, as the work that set the tone for the direction of the party. Although Hua presided at the final session, participants focused on the two real powers sitting next to each other in front of the assembled Central Committee who would lead China in the years ahead—Deng and Chen Yun. Ren Zhongyi, co-head of the Northeast small group, said that just as the Zunyi conference represented the triumph of Mao Zedong Thought over dogmatism, so the Third Plenum represented the triumph of the good tradition of party democratic discussion over the "two whatevers."[82] In his closing speech, Chen Yun made a different parallel, commenting that just as the rectification campaign in Yan'an had provided unity enabling the party to lead the country after 1949, so the work conference had provided the unity needed to lead the country to achieve the four moderni-zations.[83]

Succession without Coronation

In the annals of world political history, it would be difficult to find another case where a person became top leader of a major nation without formal pub-lic recognition of the succession. Before the work conference, Deng was vice chairman of the party, vice premier, and vice chairman of the CMC. After he became the preeminent leader at the Third Plenum, he was still vice chair-man of the party, vice premier, and vice chairman of the CMC. Not only was Deng not given a coronation or an inauguration, there was not even a public announcement that he had risen to the top position. What peculiar combina-tion of circumstances had created such an unusual situation and what were the consequences?

At the time of the Third Plenum, Chinese leaders wanted to avoid giving the impression to the Chinese public and to the rest of the world that China was undergoing a power struggle. Hua Guofeng had just come to power in 1976, and the top leaders feared that an abrupt change of leadership could lead to domestic instability and hamper China's efforts to attract foreign cap-ital and technologies. Over the next thirty months, Deng did in fact push Hua Guofeng aside and become the unrivaled top leader, but he did so step by step, in a relatively orderly process that did not upset the Chinese public and the world at large.

High-level officials who chose not to give Deng any new titles were also concerned about the dangers of concentrating the nation's power in the hands of one person. They believed that the disasters of the Great Leap Forward and the Cultural Revolution had resulted from the arbitrary exercise of such un-checked power by Mao, who had held all formal positions. Had Hua Guo-feng remained leader, this would not have been a worry. While Hua was in charge, Marshal Ye and others had been concerned not that he had too much power, but that he had too little power to govern effectively. With Deng Xiaoping, however, there was reason to be concerned. He was so confident, so decisive, so sure-footed that they worried he might become too much like his mentor, Mao Zedong. They decided, then, not to give him all the titles and to balance his power with that of an equal, Chen Yun. The strange ar-rangement of giving Deng authority without formal recognition worked because everyone knew what was going on, and because Deng himself was more interested in real power than in any formal job title. He readily accepted his responsibilities on an informal basis, without demanding public display.

From the Third Plenum in December 1978 until December 1979, when Deng began to push aside Hua Guofeng for the good of the party and the country, Deng and Hua spoke respectfully of each other in public. They both wanted to modernize and strengthen the country and they both were prepared to be pragmatic and flexible. Yet during 1979, when Hua was still chairman and Deng was wielding his informal authority, the relationship between the two men was especially awkward. In a showdown, Deng's informal authority would trump Hua's formal authority, but Deng, like his colleagues, tried to avoid any public dissension. Hua continued to chair meetings; he represented the party and the government in public meetings; and not only was he a member of the Politburo Standing Committee, but also several of his allies were members as well. Hua also enjoyed the support of two senior counselors, Marshal Ye and Li Xiannian, who wanted a collective leadership and feared a dictatorship. In 1979 Hua was, in Western terms, a weak chairman of the board who could not dominate, but who still had allies and whose views could not be ignored. Deng did not then tower above Hua as the preeminent leader, and he had not yet put in place his personal team and his own governing structure. But Deng had the power, the leverage, and the political skill to weaken Hua's power base. By mid-1979, Deng, who sought tighter control and a more effective governing structure, began to move step by step to weaken Hua and then push him aside.

While the Third Plenum was elevating Deng, within a few hundred yards of Zhongnanhai demonstrators were putting up wall posters that both directly and indirectly supported Deng Xiaoping by criticizing Lin Biao and the Gang of Four; some even dared to criticize Mao himself. Before long, some wall posters were even criticizing the Communist Party and Deng Xiaoping. These wall posters were not just a thorn in Deng's side; they also forced him to deal with an issue that was to plague him throughout his years as the top leader: How much freedom should be allowed? Where and how should party and government set the limits on public expressions of dissent?

8

Setting the Limits of Freedom

1978–1979

The Cultural Revolution was in fact an "anti-culture revolution" for it did more to attack the old culture than to create a new one. Red Guards used historical analogies and stories not only to attack present-day officials, but also to criticize virtually all novels, stories, plays, and essays. As the Cultural Revolution drew to a close with Mao's death and the arrest of the Gang of Four, many Chinese who had for years been silenced by terror passionately sought a chance to speak out. Some wanted to attack their tormenters, others strove to defend themselves, and still others wanted simply to give voice to the suffering that they and their families had endured.

A number of party leaders saw an opportunity to take advantage of this pent-up anger and direct it against their own enemies. Others with no political purpose wanted to express their personal feelings. Yet party leaders who thought about the whole system, including Deng Xiaoping, worried that if "too much" freedom were allowed and protestors could organize, the country might again fall into chaos as it had during the Cultural Revolution. Tens of millions had suffered or had relatives who had suffered from political campaigns or starvation. Hostility was strong not only against local leaders who oppressed the local people, but against higher-level officials who had been part of the system that had caused such suffering. In Deng's view, the society was so large, the population so diverse, the people so poor, the mutual hostilities so great, and the lack of common agreement about a code of behavior so pronounced that some measure of authority imposed from above was needed. How much could the boundaries of freedom be expanded without risking that Chinese society would devolve into chaos, as it had before 1949 and during the Cultural Revolution? This question remained a central and divisive one throughout Deng's years of rule.

Party leaders had no agreed-on way to judge when the tide of public criticism might threaten the breakdown of order. Consequently, they found it difficult to avoid disagreement among themselves about where to draw the line and how to maintain it. Officials responsible for science, higher education, youth affairs, and united front work, reflecting the views of the people with whom they worked, generally advocated more freedom of expression. Those responsible for maintaining public security remained cautious and advocated greater restrictions of freedom. And leaders in the propaganda apparatus were of two minds: some of them, well-educated in the humanities and social sciences, sought more freedom both for themselves as well as for others. But in carrying out their jobs, many became petty tyrants as they transmitted and enforced the limits.

Meanwhile, the people who dared to test the boundaries of acceptable public discussion generally did not have a landlord or bourgeois family background. Nonparty intellectuals from those "bad class backgrounds" who had been terrorized and intimidated for decades were also not at the forefront in complaining publicly. Instead, those who pushed the boundaries in the post-Mao era were usually bold youth, party members, veterans, or people who had friends or relatives in powerful positions who might protect them.

In principle, Deng supported the expansion of freedom and he was prepared to be pragmatic. Yet because he bore ultimate responsibility for maintaining public order, when he had serious doubts about whether order could be maintained, he moved swiftly to tighten control. After the Third Plenum, Deng, sensing the broad public support for ending the Cultural Revolution and for launching a new era of reform and opening, allowed two important discussions to take place that expanded freedom of expression for the Chinese people. One, open to the public, began spontaneously on a wall near Tiananmen Square that came to be known as "Xidan Democracy Wall," and was then replicated in Chinese cities throughout the country. The other was a party-sponsored discussion closed to outsiders. It brought together some intellectuals and leading officials responsible for party policies in the cultural area to explore guidelines for their work in the new era.

Democracy Wall, November 1978–March 1979

For decades it had been a Chinese custom to post official notices and newspapers on bulletin boards in villages, towns, urban neighborhoods, and at public gathering places such as bus stops. In Beijing, perhaps no space received more attention than the bulletin boards posted along a wall several hundred yards west of Tiananmen, at a place called Xidan. The huge, gray brick wall was about twelve feet high and two hundred yards long. Next to the wall was one of the busiest bus stops in the city, where many different bus lines dropped off and took on passengers. During the Cultural Revolution, Xidan Wall had been covered with posters denouncing those party leaders—including Liu Shaoqi and Deng Xiaoping—accused of following "the capitalist road." And around the time of the April 5, 1976 demonstrations, the wall was filled with posters denouncing the Gang of Four, praising Zhou Enlai, and supporting Deng Xiaoping.

On November 19, 1978, scarcely a week after the Central Party Work Conference opened, and in the context of a new political atmosphere, an entire issue of the Communist Youth League journal, not yet available in newsstands, appeared page by page on the wall. The Communist Youth League, a training ground for possible Communist Party members, stood at the forefront of the public's effort to expand freedoms. A few months earlier its journal had been one of the first to receive permission to renew publication after having been closed down during the Cultural Revolution. With encouragement from Hu Yaobang, Youth League officials sent the first issue to the printers; it was scheduled to appear on September 11. But when Wang Dongxing, who was responsible for supervising propaganda, saw the planned publication, he immediately ordered it withdrawn. Wang Dongxing complained that the publication not only lacked any poems by Mao, but it even criticized the practice of worshipping Mao.

The staff members of the journal, however, were not easily deterred. On September 20, only a few days later, copies were distributed to the newsstands.[1] As soon as they arrived on the newsstands, Wang Dongxing had all the copies collected, withdrawn from circulation, and banned from any further distribution. It was this first issue, which had been withdrawn from sale and distribution, that appeared on Xidan Wall on November 19, four days after the decision of the Beijing Party Committee to reverse the verdicts on the demonstrations of April 5, 1976.

The posters attracted enormous attention. Some of the articles posted from the Youth League journal passionately demanded a reversal of verdicts of young people who remained in prison as a result of the April 5 demonstrations. Other articles spoke against the "two whatevers" and raised questions not only about Lin Biao and the Gang of Four, but even about Mao. "Just ask yourself," one article read, "Without Mao's support could Lin Biao have achieved power? Just ask yourself: Didn't Chairman Mao know that Jiang Qing was a traitor? If Chairman Mao had not agreed, could the Gang of Four have achieved their aim of striking down Deng Xiaoping?"[2] It is not difficult to see why Wang Dongxing, former bodyguard and loyal defender of Mao, was upset by these criticisms.

Following the posting of the Youth League journal, a few brave souls began posting other messages, many of which criticized the crackdown on April 5, 1976. At first, some who walked by the wall were afraid even to look at the postings, let alone put up new ones. But as days passed and no one was punished, and especially after rumors spread that Deng supported the freedom to put up posters, people became emboldened. After the decade of the Cultural Revolution when information had been tightly controlled, many people were simply curious. Others, knowing that in the past any "incorrect" view might lead to punishment, humiliation, or banishment to the countryside, remained terror-stricken. Nevertheless, there was a buzz of excitement around Xidan Wall as new postings continued to appear.

Some people posted poems, brief personal accounts, or philosophical essays. Some big-character posters were written with large brushes; some poems and essays were written by pen on notebook paper. Many were written by youths, offspring of high-level officials who had a closer view of the changed atmosphere at the Central Party Work Conference, which was being held at the same time. Some were posted by other young people who were inspired by their newfound freedom but, having lived in a closed society, lacked the experience and wisdom to inform or temper their judgments. Under the terror of the Cultural Revolution, individuals could not test their ideas, and larger movements were unable to hone their strategies. In addition, advocates of freedom and democracy, like their critics, were not experienced or well informed about foreign developments. As they began to question Mao Zedong Thought and Marxist theory and to discover that other countries were far more advanced economically than China, some expressed an almost naïve faith in Western democracy.[3] Others wrote that all they had been taught—Marxism-Leninism and Mao Zedong Thought—was wrong. The wall became known as "Xidan Democracy Wall," or simply "Democracy Wall." At its peak, hundreds of thousands of viewers stopped by the wall each day. Similar walls appeared in other cities throughout the country.

The postings were passionately written, with some authors, fearing possible retribution, using pseudonyms, and others using their real names as a way of seeking redress. Some living far from large cities traveled long distances to post their grievances. Many who had been tortured or whose relatives had been killed during the Cultural Revolution took their chance to tell their stories at last. Those with relatives and friends still in the countryside, in prison, or under house arrest called for the freeing of the victims. Relatives of the accused who had died wanted their family reputations restored, so they could lift themselves out of lives of misery. Of the 17 million youths who had been sent to the countryside since 1967, only about 7 million had been allowed to return to the cities.[4] Many of the complaints came from those who had lost their opportunities for a higher education or for a good job and were living impoverished lives in the countryside. Others, with greater political sophistication, alluded to current debates in party circles and gave voice to the attacks on the "two whatevers" and to the demands for re-evaluating the April 5 incident.

On November 26, the day after Hua Guofeng addressed the work conference and publicly backed away from the "two whatevers," Deng Xiaoping told Sasaki Ryosaku, the head of the Japanese Democratic Socialist Party, "The writing of big-character posters is permitted by our constitution. We have no right to negate or criticize the masses for promoting democracy and putting up big-character posters. The masses should be allowed to vent their grievances."[5] He rhetorically asked, "What is wrong with allowing people to express their views?"[6] In addition, Marshal Ye and Hu Yaobang both expressed support for the people posting their opinions.

On that same afternoon, when John Fraser of the *Toronto Globe and Mail* went with the American columnist Robert Novak to see Xidan Democracy Wall, word circulated among the hundreds who surrounded them that Novak would see Deng the following day. Onlookers gave Fraser, who could speak Chinese, some questions for Novak to ask Deng Xiaoping, and Fraser agreed to report back to the onlookers the next evening. At the appointed time and place, when Fraser returned, there were thousands waiting to hear Deng's responses. When Fraser reported that Peng Dehuai's official reputation would soon be restored, they cheered. When he announced that Deng had declared the wall to be a good thing, they shouted with joy and relief.[7]

As the crowds gathered daily at the wall, brimming with excitement, individual Chinese, starved for information and eager to speak with foreigners, bombarded the foreigners with naïve but deeply sincere questions about democracy and human rights in other countries: Who in your country decides what appears in newspapers and what is heard on broadcasts?[8] Foreign correspondents, who had been trying for years to get people to express their opinions, eagerly reported to their home countries on the candid conversations and vibrant atmosphere at Democracy Wall. Although the official Chinese press did not pass on the messages appearing on Xidan Wall to the Chinese public, through the Voice of America and BBC these conversations were beamed back into China.

Although the crowds at Xidan Wall remained quite orderly, after several weeks some people began posting politically charged messages demanding democracy and the rule of law. Public security officials in Beijing reported some scuffles around the wall and expressed worries that the growing crowds posed a threat to order. In his conversation with Sasaki in late November, Deng had already warned that some postings were not conducive to stability, unity, and the realization of the four modernizations. Nevertheless, as the Third Plenum was drawing to a close, after a month of postings on Democracy Wall, China's top leaders were still willing to support the freedom to post one's views. In his closing speech at the Central Party Work Conference, for example, Marshal Ye said that the conference was a model of democracy in the party and that Xidan Democracy Wall was "a model of democracy among the people."[9]

On December 13, shortly before the Central Party Work Conference ended, Deng took aside Yu Guangyuan, a staff member in his Political Research Office and one of the drafters of Deng's speech for the Third Plenum, and asked him to prepare a speech supporting Xidan Democracy Wall. He said to Yu: "What is the harm of a little opposition?"[10] Although *People's Daily* did not report the events at Xidan, staff members at the newspapers who supported the wall published a bold editorial on January 3, 1979. It declared, "Let the people say what they wish. The heavens will not fall. . . . If people become unwilling to say anything, that would be too bad . . . the suffocation of democracy produces bad results."[11]

By mid-January the comments on the wall were becoming increasingly political. On January 14, a column of people held banners that announced that they were "persecuted people from all over China." Declaring "We want democracy and human rights," they marched from Tiananmen Square to the gates of Zhongnanhai, where the most powerful party officials lived and worked. The marchers tried to enter the gates, but were stopped by armed soldiers. Roger Garside, a British diplomat who observed the protestors, described them as "the angriest group of people I have ever met."[12]

Other groups began to print magazines and distribute them for free to people who came to view the wall. On January 17, a group of protestors calling themselves the "China Human Rights Association" printed a nineteen-point declaration that demanded freedom of speech, the right to evaluate party and state leaders, open publication of the national budget, permission for outsiders to sit in on meetings of the National People's Congress, free contact with foreign embassies, and the right of educated youth to be reassigned.[13] These angry protests took place a few days before Deng was to leave for the United States, but Deng did not impose restraint. He knew that if he clamped down on Democracy Wall just before leaving for the United States, his actions would be reported in the Western press and could affect the success of his trip. When Deng returned from the United States and Japan on February 8, however, he did not ask Yu Guangyuan to see a copy of the speech he had prepared for Deng in support of Democracy Wall. More importantly, Deng never delivered it.[14] By March, more essays had been posted attacking the basic system of Communist Party rule. Emboldened by the absence of government restraint, people began to criticize the entire Communist Party, the political system, and even Deng Xiaoping.

On March 25, Wei Jingsheng, a zoo employee and former soldier, took a bold step beyond the old boundaries. He posted a fundamental critique of the Communist Party system and called for "The Fifth Modernization—Democracy." Wei had not attended university and the piece was not a sophisticated analysis of democracy. But what Wei lacked in sophistication, he made up for in passion. He had a Tibetan girlfriend whose father had been jailed and whose mother had committed suicide after being jailed and humiliated. Wei himself had been assigned to work in a remote area of Xinjiang and was troubled by the people he saw begging for food. He sought to understand why so many people had died when some officials were living such comfortable lives. He accused the party of using the slogan the "Four Modernizations" to mask a system of class struggle that in fact remained unchanged. He asked, "Do the people enjoy democracy nowadays? No. Is it that the people do not want to be their own masters? Of course they do. . . . The People have finally learned what their goal is. They have a clear orientation and a real leader—the banner of democracy."[15] With these public declarations, Wei Jingsheng immediately became a sensation in the global media, which elevated him to the status of a leading Chinese spokesperson for a new democratic system.

It was around this time that China's attack on Vietnam had ended and

Deng could devote more attention to domestic matters, including Democracy Wall and the Theory Work Conference (for the attack on Vietnam, see Chapter 18). By then Democracy Wall had proved to be of great value to Deng politically: it had allowed people to give vent to their objections to the "two whatevers," to the handling of the April 5 demonstrations, and to the errors of Chairman Mao, thus providing Deng more political room to follow a new path without having to take part in the attacks himself.

In theory, Deng may have found democracy attractive as he was just taking over the reins of power; he encouraged more democratic discussion within the party. But when protestors attracted huge crowds and resisted basic rule by the Communist leadership, Deng moved decisively to suppress the challenge. As one provincial first party secretary later said, Deng's view of democracy was like Lord Ye's view of dragons. "Lord Ye loved looking at a book with pretty pictures of dragons *(Yegong haolong)*, but when a real dragon appeared, he was terrified." Although Hua was chairman of the party and premier, it was Deng who decided to curb the criticisms. On March 28, Beijing city government officials, reflecting the changing political climate and Deng's personal views, issued a regulation declaring that "slogans, posters, books, magazines, photographs, and other materials which oppose socialism, the dictatorship of the proletariat, the leadership of the Communist Party, Marxism-Leninism and Mao Zedong Thought are formally prohibited."[16]

As in imperial days, order was maintained by a general decree and by publicizing severe punishment of a prominent case to deter others. Deng's crackdown continued with the arrest of Wei Jingsheng on March 29, just four days after Wei's article on democracy had appeared on Democracy Wall. With Wei's arrest, the number of people going to view the wall suddenly dropped and only a few brave people continued to put up posters. The best-informed foreign estimate of the number of arrests in Beijing in the following weeks is thirty—infinitesimal compared to the hundreds of thousands arrested in 1957 or during the Cultural Revolution. No deaths were recorded.[17] Remaining posters were moved to a much less traveled spot at Yuetan Park, well beyond easy walking distance from Xidan. Articles began to appear in the press criticizing some of the postings on the wall. At Yuetan Park, officials were assigned to request the name and work unit of anyone who wished to hang a poster.[18] Wall posters were not officially prohibited at Xidan until December 1979, but by the end of March, Democracy Wall had ended. Yu Guangyuan reported that Hu Yaobang, as an obedient official, publicly supported Deng's decision, but officials who attended the opening sessions of the Theory Work Conference could see that Hu Yaobang personally believed that granting more freedoms would not endanger public order.

When the wall was closed down, few among the general public dared to protest.[19] Although many in the party firmly supported Deng's action as necessary to prevent the chaos that had characterized the Cultural Revolution, other party officials, including many intellectuals, were deeply disturbed by Deng's decision.[20] In Yu Guangyuan's view, Deng's change from approving of the wall in mid-December to closing it down three months later was one of the key turning points in China after the death of Mao.[21]

Conference on Theoretical Principles, Part One

In late September 1978, Marshal Ye, concerned about the divisive battles between the advocates of the "two whatevers" and those who favored "Practice Is the Sole Criterion for Judging Truth," proposed holding a conference to create common basic principles to guide party work in the fields of culture and education.[22] Impressed with the success of the work conference on the economy, Ye believed that a free discussion of theoretical principles would unify party leaders as they entered a new era. On December 13, at the close of the Central Party Work Conference and with the approval of other leaders, Hua Guofeng formally announced plans to hold the Conference on Theoretical Principles.[23]

The first part of the conference was held from January 18 to February 15, with a five-day break after January 26 for the Spring Festival. It was convened by the party Propaganda Department and the Chinese Academy of Social Sciences (CASS).[24] By the time the concrete plans for the conference had been completed, there was general agreement among the elite leaders that "Practice Is the Sole Criterion for Judging Truth" had won out over the "two whatevers." Hu Yaobang had just become head of the Propaganda Department, and Wang Dongxing, the leader of the more conservative forces, had undertaken a self-criticism. Those in charge of planning for the conference were largely cosmopolitan liberal leaders in the propaganda field. At a plenary session opening the conference, Hu Yaobang described the purpose of the conference: to review propaganda work over the past three decades and to outline how the party should support the greater opening of the country and implementation of the four modernizations. Hu praised the great progress that had been made in liberating thought following the fall of the Gang of Four—two years of progress that had been aided in recent months by the leadership of Deng, who had advocated seeking the true path from facts. Hu Yaobang also explained that during this first part of the conference, which would last until mid-February, the participants would be divided into five small groups.[25] During the second part, a larger group of more than four hundred leaders of propaganda units from all over the country would make plans to implement the consensus reached during this first part.

Hu Yaobang selected as chairmen of the small groups mostly liberal, open-minded intellectuals who worked at newspapers and in universities, think tanks, and propaganda departments. Although some of the participants, such as Wu Lengxi and Hu Sheng, were more conservative in their thinking, four of the five section leaders—Hu Jiwei, Yu Guangyuan, Wu Jiang, and Zhou Yang—had played active roles in the earlier discussion on "Practice Is the Sole Criterion for Judging Truth," which was an indirect attack on the rigidities of Maoist orthodoxy, and the fifth member, Tong Dalin, was a liberal close to Yu Guangyuan.[26] Although two of the most senior officials present, Zhou Yang and Lu Dingyi, had held the highest positions in the propaganda apparatus at the time of the 1957 anti-rightist campaign, they later expressed serious regrets about this campaign against intellectuals and subsequently became strong advocates of greater freedom. Participants at the conference came from all over the country, and following the meeting in Beijing, many local areas held their own similar conferences.[27]

As the conference began, Democracy Wall was in full bloom. But whereas Xidan Democracy Wall was a mass movement with no formal organization or planning, the Conference on Theoretical Principles was carefully orchestrated from start to finish. In addition, the poster writers and onlookers at Xidan were casual strangers who met one another occasionally at the wall, but the 160 participants at the Conference on Theoretical Principles were carefully selected party members who interacted almost daily for a month. Their talks were more polished and reflected broader understanding of party history and world developments than the postings at Democracy Wall. Even so, the two venues had common roots: the heartfelt desire to create a more open intellectual atmosphere in the new era. There were other connections between the two venues. Wang Ruoshui, a deputy editor of *People's Daily* and a participant at the Conference on Theoretical Principles, was assigned to report on the happenings at Xidan Democracy Wall; after going there to observe, he reported back to conference participants that Democracy Wall seemed vital and peaceful, and that the posted comments seemed sincere.[28]

Other participants at the conference conveyed similar views based on their observations at Democracy Wall.

In guiding the Conference on Theoretical Principles, Hu Yaobang made an effort to retain the support of both Hua Guofeng and Deng Xiaoping. He cleared his speech at the opening plenary session with Hua Guofeng and in it praised the successes achieved under Hua's leadership. Deng was busy planning his trip to the United States and the attack on Vietnam, but on January 27, the day before he was to depart for the United States, when Hu reported to Deng plans for the conference, Deng told him that no one had yet clarified what kind of democracy was appropriate for China and that careful thought should be given to this question. Deng told Hu Yaobang to organize twenty or thirty staff members to help clarify the relevant issues and to prepare an essay of twenty- to thirty-thousand characters on the practice of democracy to be delivered on the sixtieth anniversary of the May Fourth demonstrations. Deng said the essay should show that socialist democracy would surpass bourgeois democracy.[29]

The atmosphere at the Conference on Theoretical Principles was epitomized by the treatment of Wu Lengxi, the former editor of *People's Daily* who had been a critic of "Practice Is the Sole Criterion for Judging Truth." Wu was ordered to write a self-criticism, and when his first self-criticism was judged insufficient, he wrote another. Liberals were gaining in power but they used the same techniques of criticism and self-criticism to achieve unity that had previously been used to support the radical cause. Participants at the conference reminded Wu that Deng Xiaoping had clearly told him on August 23, 1978, that the editing of volume 5 of Mao's *Selected Works* should express the spirit of "Practice Is the Sole Criterion for Judging Truth." Wu confessed that because he had not wanted to damage Mao's reputation, he had supported the "two whatevers." He acknowledged that he should do more to "liberate his thinking."[30]

Participants responded eagerly to Hu Yaobang's opening speech at the conference, which encouraged them to liberate their thinking and to speak without inhibition.[31] The new mood burst the boundaries of restraint, allowing unprecedented levels of candor in criticism of party affairs. Participants were free to criticize past errors of the Maoist period and to consider a broader range of ideas as new boundaries for what was acceptable were drawn. Wang Ruoshui, deputy editor of *People's Daily*, powerfully argued on behalf of more freedom in a talk examining the question of how Mao and a small group of his followers could lead the entire population to the disastrous Great Leap Forward; he pointed to the attack on intellectuals in 1957 that had left them terrified to speak out and therefore unable to prevent Mao from committing horrible errors. A professor of philosophy at People's University went so far as to call the Gang of Four a "fascist dictatorship." Yan Jiaqi, later head of the Political Science Institute of the CASS, recommended limited terms of office for all officials to prevent a recurrence of such disasters.[32]

From the beginning of the conference, however, some of the participants were worried that they might get in trouble if the political tides turned and the top leaders became more conservative. One participant said that unlike the 1957 "hundred flowers" period, there should be legal guarantees so that people will not be punished for speaking out.[33]

As usual at such conferences, printed summaries of the sessions were distributed to top leaders who did not attend the sessions, and as they read the reports, several high-level leaders complained that the theorists at the meeting had gone too far. At the same time, Hong Kong and foreign journalists began writing about "de-Maoization," which put pressure on Chinese leaders to demonstrate that they were not guilty of this charge. Some Chinese leaders even feared that China's theorists were in danger of following the path of Khrushchev, whose de-Stalinization program had weakened the Soviet party's authority.[34] Indeed, senior party officials began to complain that the views expressed at the conference were dangerously close to criticizing virtually everything that had occurred during the Mao era. Some veterans who had held important positions in the Mao era worried that they too might be tarred with the growing criticism of Mao, and some began to raise questions about whether Hu Yaobang and others at the conference were being "revisionist," anti-Mao, and anti-party.

The gap between certain senior party officials, on the one hand, and the outspoken people at Democracy Wall and the Conference on Theoretical Principles, on the other, was proving too large to bridge.[35] Chen Yun, Li Xiannian, and others who had supported Deng at the Third Plenum in December 1978 began to express fears that the criticism of the party was going so far as to threaten their ability to maintain discipline and order. Hu Yaobang, sensing the growing danger of a conservative reaction, warned conference participants that the criticisms by some individuals had exceeded the bounds of good judgment and loyal party behavior. At a journalists' conference in the Propaganda Department on February 28, Hu Yaobang said that although

Mao had made errors, "we must objectively acknowledge the great contributions of Chairman Mao."[36] These comments, however, were not enough to stop the party conservatives from continuing to criticize him and the conference.

Conference on Theoretical Principles, Part Two

On March 16, the day Chinese troops left Vietnam after a month-long war, Deng addressed a meeting of party leaders. Now that his visit to the United States and the attack on Vietnam were behind him, he could refocus on basic domestic political issues. He assured participants that general conditions were good for national stability and unity, but he warned that there were some worrisome threats. Consequently, it was necessary to firmly hold high the banner of Mao Zedong. Otherwise there was a danger, he warned, that the party itself would be attacked, which would denigrate the People's Republic of China and mar an entire period of Chinese history. In order to preserve stability and unity, Deng insisted that the party set aside for now the evaluation of some historical issues, such as the Cultural Revolution. The newspapers, cautioned China's paramount leader, should give this issue careful attention.[37]

Having read the reports of the small group sessions at the first part of the Conference on Theoretical Principles, Deng agreed with the other party leaders who complained that the party theorists had gone too far in criticizing Mao and the party. Just as Mao after the campaign to let a hundred flowers bloom in 1957 felt that intellectuals had gone too far in their criticism, so Deng in 1979 felt intellectuals had again overstepped. But learning the negative lesson from Mao's 1957 counterattacks, Deng did not want to overreact and lose the support of intellectuals. Meanwhile, those who supported Democracy Wall and the spirit of the first part of the theory conference complained privately that the summary reports, written under the supervision of conservatives Deng Liqun and Hu Qiaomu, had exaggerated the level of criticism of the party in order to provoke Deng Xiaoping into breaking with those who wanted a more democratic discussion.[38] Deng Xiaoping was especially upset at Wang Ruoshui, deputy editor of *People's Daily*, who not only criticized Mao, but also allowed his views to be published in Hong Kong. Like other high-level officials, Deng insisted that differences of opinion among party leaders were not to be made public.

To help prepare his speech for the conference, Deng turned again to Hu Qiaomu, who had attended the first part of the conference. Deng's meeting with Hu Qiaomu, Hu Yaobang, and others on March 27 to go over the draft of his speech took place two days after the posting of Wei Jingsheng's essay on democracy that had so alarmed senior party officials. Although Deng wanted to allow more freedom than during the Mao era, he also wanted to establish principles that would draw a firm boundary about what kinds of political commentaries were acceptable and unacceptable. He told Hu Qiaomu, Hu Yaobang, and the other drafters of his speech that four basic principles should be presented to clarify the boundaries of freedom.[39] Although his speech was prepared within only a few days, it not only set the tone for part two of the conference, but also served for decades as the guide for deciding whether or not a given article or book or movie was politically acceptable.

Four Cardinal Principles, March 30, 1979

In his influential major address, Deng laid out the four cardinal principles (*jiben yuanze*) to draw the line between what was acceptable and what was unacceptable. Writings should not challenge: (1) the socialist path, (2) the dictatorship of the proletariat, (3) the leadership of the Communist Party, and (4) Marxism-Leninism and Mao Zedong Thought. Deng continued to acknowledge that in some areas China could learn from the capitalist countries. He also recognized that a socialist country can make serious errors and suffer setbacks, such as those caused by Lin Biao and the Gang of Four. But he denied that China's problems stemmed from socialism; in his view, they resulted instead from the long pre-Communist history of feudalism and imperialism. China's socialist revolution had already narrowed the gap with the capitalist countries and would continue to do so. Moreover, a dictatorship of the proletariat would continue to be needed to counter forces hostile to socialism and to socialist public order—including counter-revolutionaries, enemy agents, and criminals—even as China allowed the practice of "socialist democracy," which remained essential for modernization. Like modernization, Deng said, democratization could advance step by step.[40]

If anything was sacred for Deng, it was the Chinese Communist Party. He instinctively bristled at criticism of the party and emphasized that public criticism of the party would not be tolerated. He acknowledged that "Comrade Mao, like any other man, had his defects and made errors" but he argued that Mao Zedong Thought is the "crystallization of the experience of the Chinese people's revolutionary struggle for over half a century." History, he said, is not made by one person, but people can respect one person.[41] The unleashing of popular criticism at Democracy Wall and at the Conference on Theoretical Principles helped Deng weaken the hold of Maoist orthodoxy, which accepted a literal interpretation of everything Mao had said, and justified criticism of party errors during the previous two decades. But Deng still positioned himself personally not as one who led the attack on Mao, but rather as one who defended the greatness of Mao.

Marshal Ye's goal of unifying party thinking was not achieved because the gap between the hopes of the liberal intellectuals and the fears of the stalwart conservatives proved too large to bridge with a gentlemanly consensus based on open discussions.[42] In the end, Deng attempted to impose unity from above—with an authoritative statement underpinned by the power of the state. As a reluctant witness to the divisions within the party, Deng was convinced that China was not yet ready to achieve national unity without some measure of coercion. After Deng's speech on March 30, the conference broke up into twelve small groups where the participants discussed for three days how to implement Deng's message.

On April 3 in his closing speech at the conference, Hu Yaobang, a disciplined party member, expressed his full support for Deng's position on the four cardinal principles.[43] But those who had heard Hu Yaobang during the first part of conference knew that he personally would have preferred a more open society and that he believed the nation would not be thrown into disorder if different views could be expressed more freely.[44] Although Deng and Hu shared a commitment to modernization and continued to work together, their differences on where to draw the lines of freedom continued to fester, eventually leading to Deng's decision in 1987 to remove Hu from his position.

As reasoned as Deng's speech seemed to party leaders, to intellectuals the underlying message was disturbing: the boundaries of freedom were narrowed. Democracy Wall did not officially close down, but the chilling effect of Deng's speech—along with the arrest of Wei Jingsheng and the intimidation of people who continued to hang posters—brought an end to Democracy Wall and to hopes for a genuine hundred flowers in the cultural field. Those who had hoped for more freedom could not easily forget the heady moments of exuberance at Democracy Wall and the thoughtful intellectual explorations at the theory work conference. Intellectuals at the CASS and elsewhere were silenced, but many were not persuaded of the wisdom of the new policy.

The new, more conservative line emanating from Deng's four cardinal principles rippled across the media, as conference participants and others struggled to adapt to the new political reality. A *People's Daily* editorial of May 5 stated, "Some people think that democracy means they can do whatever they want. . . . What we advocate is democracy under the guidance of centralism."[45] Lower-level officials issued propaganda based on the new narrower lines about what was permissible.[46] Many intellectuals were deeply disappointed at the limitations on their freedom, but Deng's reaction was far more restrained than Mao's attack on intellectuals had been in 1957. Deng knew he needed their cooperation to achieve modernization. Following his enunciation of the four cardinal principles, intellectuals became more cautious about criticizing the party in public, but only a relatively small number of intellectuals were criticized, humiliated, or removed from their positions. Some of the best-known critics were allowed to travel and stay abroad from where they continued to speak out.[47] Indeed, the long-term trend between 1978 and 1992 was toward expanding the space for free discussion. Though upset at the sometimes clumsy and arbitrary efforts to enforce the boundaries of free expression, the general public, as well as intellectuals, continued to seek opportunities to push back the boundaries that constrained their freedom. It was impossible to set the boundaries of free expression once and for all. To allow new ideas to be tried out and to secure the cooperation of intellectuals, Deng needed to allow a larger measure of freedom than was permitted before 1978.

At the end of October 1979, at the Fourth Congress of Literature and the Arts, Deng managed to articulate this delicate balance of freedom and control in such a way that retained the support or at least the passive acceptance of most intellectuals while rebuffing any attacks he judged might threaten party authority. When preparing his speech to the Congress on Literature and the Arts, Deng's staff showed a draft copy to Zhou Yang, the cultural czar in the 1950s who in the late 1970s had become a champion of greater freedom for intellectuals. Zhou Yang advised Deng not to give a long speech; following Zhou Yang's suggestion, Deng gave a short, simple greeting of congratulations in which he praised the creativity of Chinese people in the arts, affirmed their progress in the 1950s, criticized the restrictions on freedoms imposed by Lin Biao and Jiang Qing, and said he looked forward to continued advances in the cultural sphere. His speech received warm and enthusiastic applause from people in the literary world, even from those who remained upset at his speech on the four cardinal principles.[48] Unlike Mao in 1957,

Deng in 1979 did not lose the support of mainstream intellectuals. Many who complained privately about the arbitrariness of government restrictions continued to work actively for the four modernizations. But throughout his rule and until he stepped down in 1992, Deng would face a continuing tug-of-war over the boundaries of freedom.[49] On June 4, 1989, this tug-of-war would lead to tragedy.

9

The Soviet-Vietnamese Threat

1978–1979

In mid-1977, when Deng once again became responsible for China's national security and foreign affairs, he faced two overriding concerns: defending China against threats from the Soviet Union and Vietnam, and laying the groundwork to enlist foreign help for China's modernization.[1] To reduce the danger from the Soviet military, he sought to firm up relations with China's neighbors and to block Soviet advances. For help with modernization, he turned to Japan and the United States. In pursuing these goals, for fourteen months beginning in January 1978 Deng undertook a whirlwind tour of more countries than he had visited in his entire lifetime. During these trips he improved relations with China's continental neighbors, opened China far more widely than it had been opened at any time since 1949, and set China on an irreversible course of active participation in international affairs and in the worldwide exchange of ideas. In five trips abroad, he visited Burma (renamed Myanmar after 1989), Nepal, North Korea, Japan, Malaysia, Thailand, Singapore, and the United States. During these fourteen months, Deng also concluded a Treaty of Peace and Friendship with Japan, negotiated the normalization of relations with the United States, and led China into a war in Vietnam.

Deng Inherits the Foreign Policy Mantle

When Deng returned to party work in the summer of 1977, he did not seek responsibility for foreign affairs. At one point he even said that he preferred not to take on the job because it was taxing. But China needed Deng to manage foreign affairs. Not only had he been at Mao's or Zhou Enlai's side in meeting foreign leaders for almost three decades, but he himself had been in charge of foreign affairs from mid-1973 to the end of 1975, under the tutelage of both Mao and Zhou. His colleagues recognized that after Zhou Enlai's death, no other leader could compare with Deng in terms of knowledge of foreign affairs, strategic thinking, personal relationships with foreign leaders, and skill in building goodwill abroad while firmly defending China's interests. Diplomats like Huang Hua, who replaced Qiao Guanhua as foreign minister in December 1976, had extensive knowledge of other countries and of past negotiations.[2] But China's diplomats lacked the confidence to make important political judgments and the stature to meet top foreign leaders as equals.

Foreign policy had long been a central focus of the top Communist Party leaders. Mao and Zhou in particular had been towering world-class strategists, confident in dealing with the world's other leaders as equals. Though China remained relatively closed before 1978, Mao and Zhou gave foreign affairs a great deal of attention, and they both took personal responsibility for guiding policy. When Mao met foreigners, he exuded imperial confidence and talked of philosophy, history, and literature, as well as of the raw dynamics of world power. When Zhou met with foreigners at home and abroad, he was erudite, elegant, charming, nuanced, considerate of his guests, and ready to discuss details as well as to paint the big picture.

Like Mao and Zhou, Deng possessed an instinctive national loyalty, a strategic vision, and an underlying toughness in pursuing national interests. When meeting foreigners, Deng, like Mao and Zhou, not only covered an agenda, but also tried to size up his visitor's character and objectives. Deng, however, was more systematic—as well as more direct and straightforward—than Mao or Zhou in focusing on the major issues of concern to China. Before meeting a foreign guest, he did not receive an oral briefing; he wanted to read a memo from his staff about the visitor, the purpose of the trip, and what topics should be covered. As with Mao and Zhou, the foreign visitors often met a Chinese diplomat first, and the diplomat could pass to Deng a memo about the visitors' concerns before Deng met them.

Foreign diplomats in Beijing respected Deng greatly and saw in him someone with whom they could work. He became a favorite of foreign visitors for his wit, intensity, disarming frankness, and desire to solve problems. George H. W. Bush, who saw him often in 1975 when he headed the U.S. Liaison Office in Beijing, once said, "He had an intense demeanor and talked with a bluntness that left no doubt about his meaning."[3] Huang Hua, who sat in on many sessions with Mao, Zhou Enlai, and Deng when they met foreign leaders, said of Deng, "He was good at grasping major issues, understanding and expounding briefly the essence of a problem in a profound way, and making judgments and decisions in a resolute and straightforward way."[4]

Unlike Mao, who harbored visions of grandeur for China that exceeded its power and leverage, Deng remained realistic in acknowledging China's weaknesses and backwardness. But Deng also had an underlying confidence: he knew that he was representing an enormous country with an extraordinarily long history as a great civilization, and he drew strength not only from his own success in overcoming personal challenges, but also from his broad knowledge of domestic and international affairs. Unlike some Soviet leaders, he did not attempt to impress foreigners from more modern countries, even if they towered over him. Instead, Deng engaged foreign leaders as partners in solving problems and soon got down to the issues at hand. Lacking any psychological hang-ups, he could firmly resist, without becoming defensive or nasty, any foreign pressures that he judged were not in keeping with China's interests.

Deng had not always displayed such confidence. When he first visited New York in 1974 to speak to the United Nations, Deng sounded cautious and uncomfortably formal, for he knew that his staff would report back to Mao what he said and did. Deng continued to be careful during 1975, because on all important foreign policy issues he still needed to obtain Mao's final approval. As even Deng acknowledged, Zhou Enlai's knowledge and experience far surpassed his own. After Mao and Zhou died, however, Deng could negotiate with foreign leaders without worrying about the views of others. When he returned to take charge of foreign affairs in mid-1977 Deng continued the policies he had been carrying out in 1975. But foreign officials who met Deng after July 1977 found him more spontaneous and confident, more willing to express his opinions on a broad range of foreign policy issues.

From July 1977 until late 1979, in his conversations with foreign leaders Deng spoke respectfully of "Chairman Hua." But from the time Deng returned in 1977, these foreign guests harbored no doubts that Deng was the one in charge of foreign policy. He functioned not only as China's negotiator, but also as its grand strategist. And although he read the reports from diplomats, for important decisions he relied more heavily on his own seasoned judgment. Deng could be relaxed, with a sure-footed understanding of how the topic at hand related to overall strategy and confidence in his own ability to deal with his counterparts. Over time Deng developed his own characteristic style in conducting meetings with foreigners. He would begin with a few witty remarks to welcome his foreign guests and then shift to focus on the main issues he wanted to address, making his points directly, clearly, and forcefully.

The Soviet Union as the Main Enemy

In his strategic analysis, Deng's starting point was the same as Mao's: identify the main enemy, cultivate allies against the main enemy, neutralize the enemy's allies, and draw them away from the enemy. By 1969, it was clear that the Soviet Union had replaced the United States as China's main enemy. In July of that year, President Nixon, in Guam, announced that the United States would not become involved in a land war in Asia. Also, following border clashes between China and the Soviet Union in March and August, Sino-Soviet relations remained very tense.

After the U.S. troops pulled out of Vietnam in 1975, the Soviet Union and Vietnam took advantage of the opportunity to fill the vacuum created by the U.S. troop withdrawal, and in Deng's view, increasingly threatened China's interests. Deng concluded that the Soviet Union was determined to replace the United States as the dominant global power, and that the Vietnamese were aiming to become the dominant power in Southeast Asia. Therefore, China should form a "single line" *(yi tiaoxian),* uniting with other countries at the same latitude—the United States, Japan, and northern Europe—against the Soviet Union. Meanwhile, China would also endeavor to pull other countries like India away from the Soviet Union's side.

When Deng returned to work in 1977, the Soviet Union and Vietnam appeared increasingly menacing to him as they cooperated to extend their power in Southeast Asia. Vietnam had allowed the Soviet Union to use the ports that the United States had modernized and left behind at Danang and Cam Ranh Bay. This cooperation would give the Soviet Union the freedom to move its ships into the entire area, from the Indian Ocean to the Pacific. Missile bases in Vietnam were also constructed and held Soviet missiles aimed at China, with Soviet personnel and electronic equipment on the bases to provide technical assistance. And the Soviet Union kept massive numbers of troops along China's northern border, a situation that seemed more threatening because, to the west, India was cooperating with the Soviet Union, and the Soviet Union was poised to invade Afghanistan. Meanwhile Vietnam had already taken over Laos and was preparing to invade China's ally, Cambodia. Deng, like players of the Chinese board game *weiqi* (in Japanese, *go*), thought of these developments in terms of countries staking out different locations and winning by surrounding the enemy. To Deng, China was in danger of being encircled.

Of all of these developments, the alliance between Vietnam and the Soviets appeared to Deng to be the most threatening to China, and Vietnam appeared to be the location where bold Chinese actions could have the greatest impact in preventing Soviet encirclement. Deng said that Vietnam, after expelling the American troops, was beginning to act like a proud peacock showing off its tail. In May 1978, when Brzezinski met with Deng to discuss plans for normalization, he was surprised at Deng's vehemence in denouncing Vietnamese perfidy. Other diplomats who met Deng Xiaoping in 1978 observed that whenever the topic of Vietnam came up, he became viscerally angry.[5]

Deng's Relationship with Vietnam

Toward Vietnam, Deng felt a sense of personal as well as national betrayal because China had sacrificed for Vietnam during the American attacks, and because he had had deep personal ties with Vietnamese for five decades. Half a century earlier, when Deng was a worker-student in France, he had worked with Vietnamese allies in the anti-colonial struggle against France. There is no evidence that Deng met Ho Chi Minh in France even though both were there at the same time, but he definitely met Ho in Yan'an in the late 1930s. Zhou Enlai did know Ho in France, and also as a colleague at the Whampoa Military Academy in the mid-1920s. When Deng was assigned to Guangxi in the late 1920s, he passed through Vietnam several times, where he was aided by underground Vietnamese Communists. In the 1940s and early 1950s, Deng and Vietnamese Communists were fellow revolutionaries fighting for Communist victories, but after 1954, they were fellow government officials striving to protect their national interests.

The connections with General Wei Guoqing, one of Deng's former underlings, also ran deep. Wei had served under Deng in Guangxi and in the Huai Hai campaign, and was a member of the Zhuang minority from the area of Guangxi where Deng had established his revolutionary base in 1929. Deng explained to Singapore's prime minister Lee Kuan Yew that in 1954 when the

Vietnamese were fighting the French, the Vietnamese lacked experience in large-scale combat and General Wei Guoqing from China had played a key role in guiding the fighting at Dien Bien Phu; the Vietnamese had wanted to retreat, but Wei Guoqing refused. Air defenses in the northern part of Vietnam, too, were manned by Chinese fighters.

Deng understood the complexities of the relations between China and Vietnam as national interests shifted and were reinterpreted through new lenses. He knew that over the centuries, Vietnamese patriots had regarded the Chinese as their main enemy because of Chinese invasions and occupation. He understood that Vietnam was trying to maximize aid from both China and the Soviet Union at a time when each endeavored to pull Vietnam closer. He also realized that although China considered the contributions of General Wei Guoqing and the Chinese volunteers to have been critical to the victory at Dien Bien Phu, the Vietnamese were still bitter about China's failure to support their efforts to unify their country at the 1954 Geneva Peace Treaty discussions.[6] Deng was acutely aware that Ho Chi Minh, in his last will and testament written in 1965, declared that Vietnam should be the dominant power in Indochina, a statement the Chinese did not agree with.[7] And he knew that Vietnam had been upset that China, starting in 1972, had begun to sacrifice its relations with Vietnam in order to gain better relations with the United States.

But China had also been very generous in helping North Vietnam fight the United States. When Vietnam's party secretary Le Duan visited Beijing from April 18 to April 23, 1965, seeking help during the stepped-up U.S. air attacks on North Vietnam, President Liu Shaoqi told Le Duan that whatever the Vietnamese needed, the Chinese would attempt to supply. During that visit, Deng met Le Duan upon his arrival at the airport, joined Liu Shaoqi in meetings with him, and then saw him off at the airport.[8] Afterward, the Chinese set up a small group under the State Council to coordinate China's aid to North Vietnam; it represented some twenty-one branches of government, including military, transport, construction, and rear services. According to Chinese records, from June 1965 to August 1973 China dispatched a total of 320,000 "volunteers" to Vietnam to help with anti-aircraft weaponry, machinery repair, road and railway construction, communications, airport repair, mine sweeping, rear services, and other activities. At their peak, there were 170,000 Chinese troops in Vietnam at one time. China reported some four thousand Chinese casualties during the war, but some Chinese scholars estimate that this figure is in the tens of thousands. In 1978 Deng reported to

Singapore's prime minister Lee Kuan Yew that while the Americans were in Vietnam, China had shipped goods to Vietnam that were worth over US$10 billion at the time, even more aid than China had provided to North Korea during the Korean War.[9] As the Chinese expanded their support for Vietnam, they sent in their own engineering and construction troops, anti-aircraft artillery, and additional supplies.[10]

In 1965 Deng, on behalf of the Chinese government, offered to greatly increase China's aid to Vietnam if the Vietnamese would end their relationship with the Soviets, but Vietnam refused. Instead, when U.S. bombing attacks in Vietnam increased, Vietnam turned increasingly to the country with the high technology and modern weapons it needed for defense—the Soviet Union—and the Soviets, in turn, used their increasing leverage to pressure Vietnam to lean to the Soviet side in the Sino-Soviet dispute.

The gap between China and Vietnam widened in the mid-1960s when Vietnam stopped criticizing "Soviet revisionism," and when China showed its displeasure with Vietnam's closer ties with the Soviets by pulling a military division out of Vietnam. In 1966, when Zhou Enlai and Deng met Ho Chi Minh, Deng and Zhou were keenly aware of Vietnamese complaints that Chinese troops were acting like the arrogant Chinese invaders who had appeared frequently in Vietnam's long history. Deng argued that the 100,000 troops were there solely to guard against the possibility of a Western invasion, and Zhou offered to withdraw them.[11] But Vietnam did not request their withdrawal, and China continued to supply substantial amounts of ammunition, weapons, and equipment.

Ho Chi Minh, who spoke excellent Chinese and had spent many years in China, worked hard to maintain good working relations with China as well as with the Soviet Union. But after his death in September 1969, Sino-Vietnamese relations deteriorated, Chinese aid was reduced, and China eventually pulled its troops out of Vietnam.[12] When the Chinese improved relations with the United States after Nixon's visit in 1972 and then reduced aid to Vietnam, the Vietnamese viewed this as a sign of Chinese betrayal of Vietnam's war against the United States.[13]

After the Americans pulled out of Vietnam, the Soviets were generous in supplying large-scale aid to rebuild the war-torn country. In contrast, on August 13, 1975, a few months after the Americans left Vietnam, Zhou Enlai, hospitalized and pale from cancer, told the top Vietnamese planner, Lê Thanh Nghi, that China would not be able to give much aid for Vietnam's reconstruction. China was exhausted from the Cultural Revolution and its economy was not in good shape. "You Vietnamese," Zhou said, "should let us have a respite and regain our strength." But in the same month, other Chinese officials welcomed the Cambodian deputy premiers and promised them US$1 billion of aid over the next five years.[14] By then, the Soviet Union was working closely with Vietnam and China was working with Cambodia to prevent Vietnam from dominating all of Indochina. Deng later told Singapore's prime minister Lee Kuan Yew that China had stopped giving aid to Vietnam not because it was difficult to match the amount of Soviet aid, but because Vietnam sought hegemony in Southeast Asia. The Soviet Union stood ready to support and profit from Vietnam's ambitions, whereas China did not.

One month later, in September 1975, Vietnam's highest official, First Party Secretary Le Duan, led a delegation to Beijing with the hope of avoiding a complete break in relations with China. Vietnamese leaders wanted to receive some Chinese aid, in part to achieve a measure of independence from the Soviet Union. Deng, hosting the visit under the watchful eyes of Mao, shared Le Duan's goal of avoiding a rupture in their relationship. Deng met the Vietnamese delegation at the airport, spoke at the welcoming banquet, continued discussions with Le Duan, and sent the delegation off at the railway station.[15] He was able to sign an agreement on September 25 that provided Vietnam with a small loan and a modest amount of supplies.[16] Had Deng then remained in office after 1975, he might have been able to patch over the long history of Vietnamese hostility toward China and the current differences, but after Deng was weakened, the Gang of Four took a much tougher stance, demanding that Vietnam renounce Soviet "hegemonism."[17] Such demands by the Chinese radicals proved too much for Le Duan, who refused to sign a joint communiqué and left Beijing without giving the customary return banquet.[18]

A month later, Le Duan landed in Moscow where he received the promise of long-term aid that he was seeking. Vietnam would have preferred not to be overly dependent on the Soviet Union, but it badly needed help to rebuild the country. Le Duan, lacking leverage from China (or elsewhere) to resist Soviet demands, signed agreements supporting Soviet foreign policy positions.[19] These Soviet-Vietnamese agreements further polarized Vietnamese relations with China and led China to strengthen its relations with Cambodia.[20]

In early 1977 the Vietnamese ambassador in Beijing said that if Deng were to return to power, he would approach issues more pragmatically and relations between China and Vietnam would improve. To the extent that China

had a foreign policy after Deng was removed in 1975, it was filled with revolutionary slogans, lacking in perspective, and delivered without finesse.[21] The
radicals had virtually broken Chinese ties with Vietnam and pushed Vietnam
closer to the Soviet Union. On November 9, 1975, shortly after Deng lost
control of foreign policy, Vietnam announced a political consultative conference to prepare for reunification of North and South Vietnam. Other Communist countries sent congratulatory messages, but China did not. Three days
after the conference, China's *Guangming Daily*, reversing Deng's prior acknowledgment that the dispute over the Spratly Islands remained unresolved,
published a strong statement declaring that the Spratly Islands were part of
the "sacred territory" of China.[22] (After Deng was formally dismissed in April
1976, one of the criticisms against him was that he had supported negotiations with Vietnam over the Spratly Islands.[23]) And in 1976, in response to
Vietnamese requests, the Eastern European countries, North Korea, and the
Soviet Union all promised aid to Vietnam, but China did not. The radicals
had undone the efforts by Deng and Le Duan to keep the relationship alive.

After Mao's death and the arrest of the Gang of Four, there was a brief in-
terlude when Chinese and Vietnamese leaders explored the possibility of improving ties. On October 15, 1976, just days after the gang was arrested,
Vietnamese officials, hoping that China might now pursue a more fraternal
policy and offer some help for their next five-year plan, sent a request to Beijing for economic assistance. But the request went unanswered, and in December 1976, when twenty-nine fraternal Communist parties sent delegates
to Hanoi for the Vietnamese Party Congress, China, under Hua Guofeng's
leadership, did not even reply to the invitation to attend. In February 1977,
five months before Deng returned to power, Beijing simply reiterated to a
visiting Vietnamese delegation that no aid would be forthcoming.[24]

Prelude to the Sino-Vietnamese Conflict

Had Deng not been purged in late 1975, he might have been able to avoid
the complete break between China and Vietnam. But when Deng returned
to work in July 1977, he confronted a changed situation in which Soviet-
Vietnamese cooperation had increased and China's relationship with both
the Soviet Union and Vietnam had deteriorated badly.

In March and May 1977, a few months before Deng returned to work,
Vietnamese general Vo Nguyen Giap was in Moscow, where he concluded an
agreement with the Soviets in which the two sides would expand military

cooperation.[25] The Soviet Union had begun to send personnel to naval bases in Danang and Cam Ranh Bay, with the prospect that soon Soviet ships would have access to the entire Chinese coast. Furthermore, the clashes between Vietnamese forces and the Cambodians and Chinese along their respective borders had become larger in scale and more frequent. Vietnam had been hesitant about joining the Council for Mutual Economic Assistance (COMECON), the trade organization of Communist countries, because it would require the Vietnamese to give up some of their cherished economic independence, but on June 28, 1977, the Vietnamese, with an economy badly in need of reconstruction and no other sources of economic help, agreed to join.[26]

Meanwhile ethnic Chinese had begun fleeing Vietnam. After taking over South Vietnam in 1975, the Vietnamese Communist leaders had begun the immense tasks of collectivizing and nationalizing its economy. In the process they began attacking the 1.5 million ethnic Chinese in South Vietnam, many of whom were small businesspeople opposed to collectivization. If Vietnam were to invade Cambodia or if border clashes with China were to become more serious, Vietnamese leaders feared that the ethnic Chinese might turn against them. The Vietnamese launched a huge campaign that rounded up massive numbers of ethnic Chinese and sent them to detention centers—causing many others to flee the country. The Chinese government demanded that Vietnam desist mistreating the ethnic Chinese in Vietnam, but the Vietnamese officials paid no attention. By the time Deng had returned in July 1977, the campaign that eventually expelled an estimated 160,000 ethnic Chinese from Vietnam was well under way.[27] In retaliation, in May 1978, after Deng had returned to work, China suspended work on twenty-one aid projects benefiting Vietnam.[28] As Deng later explained, by that time China did not believe that more aid would have been enough to pull Vietnam away from the Soviet Union.[29]

Deng, like Mao and Zhou Enlai, thought in terms of decades. In 1978 the threat was not one of imminent invasion of China but the larger danger that if the Soviet Union were to continue to expand its use of bases in Vietnam, it could lead to Soviet and Vietnamese encirclement of China. In explaining the situation to Westerners, Deng referred to Vietnam as the Cuba of Asia—a base by China's side from which the Soviets could position their ships, their planes, and their missiles. Scarcely a decade earlier, in 1962, the Soviet Union had withdrawn its missiles from Cuba because the Americans had threatened to use their superior military power. But the Soviet Union's military was far superior to China's. If the Soviets installed missiles in Vietnam, it would be difficult at best for China to force the Soviets to withdraw them. Deng believed that it was urgent to strengthen cooperation with other countries to resist Soviet-Vietnamese expansion before the bases became strong.

During his fourteen months of travel, Deng visited only one Communist country, North Korea, and seven non-Communist countries. He first visited several countries that had good relationships with China and that could help shore up China's security along its borders. Of his five trips abroad, the first three were made to countries along China's continental borders. Like traditional Chinese rulers, Deng sought to pacify China's borders but he also sought the cooperation of those countries in resisting Soviet and Vietnamese advances.

He then visited Japan and the United States, the two countries that could be the most helpful to China as it pursued the four modernizations and that also had great military strength to possibly help restrain the Soviet Union and Vietnam. Europe was another major area of the world that could help with modernization, but Europe's cooperation had already been assured with Deng's 1975 visit to France. Follow-up arrangements with Europe could be managed by Gu Mu's delegation; they did not require another trip by Deng.

Visits to Burma and Nepal, January and February 1978

Deng's first foreign visit after assuming responsibility for foreign affairs was to the two countries to China's south and west, both with long common borders, Burma and Nepal. China's common border with Burma extended almost 1,350 miles, and the border with Nepal almost 850 miles. Deng did not aim to sign any particular agreement with either nation. The wild Red Guards had frightened all of China's neighbors, so to develop good cooperative relations would first require some fence mending. With better relations, the countries on China's borders would be more likely to cooperate in resisting Soviet efforts to expand its influence in the region.

Despite recent memories of the Red Guards, Burma and Nepal already had relatively good relations with China. For his visit to Burma, for example, Deng could draw on almost two decades of friendly relations relatively unaffected by the Cultural Revolution. China and Burma had resolved their border issues in 1960. And after Ne Win's 1962 coup, Burma remained relatively isolated from most countries, but China had maintained close relations, which included helping Burma with the construction of electric power plants and other infrastructure projects. Zhou Enlai had visited Burma no fewer than nine times, and by 1977 former general Ne Win, who ruled from 1962 until 1981, had visited China twelve times.[30] In 1969, China and Burma signed a Treaty of Friendship and Cooperation, and in 1977, Deng Yingchao, Zhou Enlai's widow, visited Burma and Deng Xiaoping himself twice hosted Ne Win in Beijing. During one of those visits, Deng urged Ne Win to strengthen relations with China's client state, Cambodia, which was already under pressure from Vietnam. A week after Ne Win's visit to Beijing, Ne Win became the first head of state to visit Cambodia.

In his presentations in Burma, Deng was careful to refer to Chairman Hua Guofeng respectfully; he even reiterated China's policy that class struggle was the key link, something that he would drop from his comments later in the year, as the mood in the party began to shift away from Maoism and as Deng's personal stature rose. Deng believed that when visiting other countries he should not only see political leaders, but also show appreciation for the country's culture and society as a way of forming deeper bonds. In Burma, he talked with key leaders of various social groups and showed respect for the local culture by visiting famous Buddhist temples and other sites. Since Buddhism was also widespread in China, there were obviously cultural links through Buddhism. His remarks stressed the long history of friendship between Burma and China, and he spoke of their common views about countering Soviet and Vietnamese influence in Southeast Asia.

Ne Win expressed concern about China's continuing ties with Communist insurgents in Burma and other parts of Southeast Asia, which China was not yet ready to break. This problem was to limit the extent of China-Burmese cooperation, but Deng's visit was followed by an increase in cultural exchanges and, in the following year, an agreement on economic and technical cooperation. Even more importantly, although appearing to maintain its policy of nonalignment, Burma tilted further toward China in the struggle against Soviet and Vietnamese hegemony.[31]

Like Burma, Nepal gave Deng a warm welcome. During the 1950s and 1960s Nepal had tried to maintain a neutral position between Indian and Chinese interests, but in the 1970s, when Indira Gandhi took a tough line toward Nepal, Nepal's King Birendra turned to China for support. China supported Nepal's efforts to establish a zone of peace, and it expanded aid to Nepal, opened direct air links, and agreed to exchange visits of senior officials. By June 1976, King Birendra had visited both Sichuan and Tibet.

In Nepal, Deng visited temples, museums, and various historical sites. He spoke of the two millennia of Sino-Nepali friendship and reaffirmed support for King Birendra's zone of peace. Deng said that all nations desire independence, and he urged that countries in the third world cooperate in resisting imperialism, colonialism, and domination by outside powers. Deng asserted that the rivalry between the two superpowers had created serious instability in South Asia, but that conditions there still remained unfavorable to the superpowers, and China would continue to help Nepal safeguard its national independence. He not only avoided criticizing India, but also composed his message in Nepal in a way that might well appeal to India: China would assist all nations in the region trying to pursue an independent policy. Deng was paving the way for improved relations with India, which he hoped might help pull it away from the Soviet Union.[32]

In January 1978 Deng did not yet have a full mandate to depart sharply from Maoist thinking. As in Burma, he talked not only of rallying behind the party center, headed by Chairman Hua Guofeng, but also of implementing Chairman Mao's "revolutionary line" and his policies in foreign affairs.[33] It would take some months before a new Beijing consensus would allow Deng to bid farewell to class struggle. But the visits to Burma and Nepal went well and helped to strengthen those countries' cooperation with China.

North Korea, September 8–13, 1978

Once Vietnam had aligned itself with the Soviet Union, it became even more important for China to maintain good relations with the other sizeable Communist country in Asia, North Korea, and not allow it to become another "Cuba in Asia." Fluent in Chinese, Kim Il Sung had lived in China for a total of nearly twenty years before returning to Korea in 1945. After returning to North Korea, he continued to maintain close relations with Mao and Zhou Enlai who, during the Korean War, sent large numbers of troops ("volunteers") to assist North Korea and to provide logistic support from Northeast China. North Korea, like Vietnam, had skillfully used the Sino-Soviet rivalry to get aid from both, although it generally leaned toward China.

In his relations with North Korea, Deng benefited from having helped, as finance minister in 1953, to launch an aid program for rebuilding North Korea after the Korean War, and from having hosted Kim Il Sung in April 1975.[34] North Korea's capital was closer to Beijing than the capital of any other country, and North Korea's relations with China were closer than its relations with the Soviet Union. The first foreign official whom Deng received after returning to work in mid-1977 was the North Korean ambassador to China.[35] In 1978, Hua Guofeng visited four countries and Deng visited seven; only one country hosted both of them: North Korea. As two Communist powers, China and North Korea maintained both party-to-party and military-to-military relations, as well as government-to-government relations, and China made use of all those channels, The generals on the two sides who had fought together during the Korean War frequently met, and the International Liaison Department of the Chinese Communist Party kept up contacts with its North Korean counterparts.

China's decision to expand relations with the United States—the major power aiding its enemy, South Korea—would be deeply upsetting to the North Koreans. Deng's forthcoming visit to Korea's longtime enemy, Japan, which was also aiding South Korean economic development, would be a grave concern as well. Deng had wrestled with the question of how best to control the damage to relations with North Korea as he opened relations with Japan and the United States. Deng did not want North Korea to turn more to the Soviet Union. So he decided that it was better to give the North Koreans a full explanation beforehand than to surprise them later.

To warm up the relationship, Deng made a special effort to show respect to North Korea in the ways it appreciated most. North Korea was small, but it had visions of grandeur, and one way it measured its grandeur was by the number and rank of officials from abroad attending its National Day celebrations. As the Cultural Revolution was ending in China and foreign leaders resumed visits to Beijing, Kim Il Sung undertook "invitation diplomacy," informing the heads of third-world countries scheduled to visit China that they would also be welcome to visit North Korea. In 1977 only four high-level visitors accepted Kim's invitation: Ye Jianying, representing China, and representatives from East Germany, Yugoslavia, and Cambodia.[36] Kim received them royally. Prince Sihanouk from Cambodia was given his own palatial residence, and when East German leader Erich Honecker visited, he received the biggest welcome of his lifetime.[37]

For the thirtieth anniversary of the founding of the North Korean government on September 10, 1978, Kim Il Sung went to great lengths to encourage high-level foreign leaders to attend the celebrations. Deng honored Kim by spending five days in North Korea. He was the highest-ranking official from any country to attend. In public gatherings during the week, Kim, pleased that such a high-level Chinese official had accepted his invitation, always placed Deng next to himself.[38]

In North Korea, Kim met Deng several times, both privately and publicly. Deng explained China's serious economic problems and its need to modernize. At the time, North Korea's industrial development constituted a higher share of GNP than China's did, but Kim was beginning to fall behind South Korea's burgeoning industrial takeoff. As Deng told Kim, "The world's cutting-edge technology must be the starting point for our modernization. Recently, when our comrades have gone abroad to take a look, the more we have seen, the more we realize we are backward." China needed access to the most modern technology to improve its industrial capacity. This was a message that Kim, who had modernized with the help of the Soviets and China, could well understand. Deng also explained how difficult it had been to get Japan to agree to an anti-hegemony clause directed against the Soviet Union, and he briefed Kim on the progress of his secret talks on normalization with the United States.[39] He spoke, too, of the dangers of the Soviet Union, saying that to avoid war, one must prepare for war: in this way, the Soviets would remain more cautious. Deng cautioned that they must avoid appeasing the Soviet Union.[40]

Considering the policies that Deng was pursuing with the United States and Japan, his visit went remarkably well. Kim Il Sung would not join Vietnam in encircling China and instead would continue to maintain good working relations with the Chinese. In later years, Kim Il Sung assured others that Deng was his friend, and he even defended, to a group of Eastern European Communist leaders, Deng's policy of opening China economically and politically. On this 1978 trip, Deng succeeded in a very delicate mission, without which North Korea might have improved relations with the Soviet Union and distanced itself from China, which was turning to North Korea's enemies (United States and Japan).

Seeking Allies in Southeast Asia, November 5–15, 1978

Back in China, the epoch-making Central Party Work Conference was set to begin on November 10, 1978. But Deng regarded the imminent Vietnamese invasion of Cambodia as sufficiently alarming that he put aside work conference participation and normalization discussions with the United States so that he could travel to Southeast Asia for ten days to gain their understanding for China's planned response, an attack on Vietnam.

By the summer of 1978, it appeared to the Chinese that the Vietnamese were planning to invade Cambodia, and the prospect of invasion became a tripwire for Chinese action. Cambodia had become China's client state just as Vietnam had become a client of the Soviet Union. China would come to the aid of an ally to whom it had been giving aid and assistance. What was especially disturbing to the Chinese was that more Soviet "advisers" and equipment were arriving to assist the Vietnamese attack. U.S. officials estimated that between 3,500 and 4,000 Soviet advisers were in Vietnam by August 1978, and by mid-October it was reported that Soviet freighters were unloading aircraft, missiles, tanks, and munitions. By this point, Deng had had enough. He decided that first he must stand firm; the peaceful climate for modernization would have to wait. He would even cooperate with Pol Pot; Pol Pot had a terrible international reputation for his wanton killing, but in Deng's view, he was the only Cambodian with enough troops to be a useful ally against the Vietnamese.

In July, Vietnam began bombing Cambodia with as many as thirty sorties a day and in September the number increased to as many as one hundred a day.[41] In November, Chinese leaders, observing Vietnamese preparations, concluded that Vietnam would invade Cambodia in December during the dry season when it could move its tanks.[42]

Deng believed a strong military response was absolutely necessary. Deng had warned the Vietnamese, saying that France and the United States did not have the will to remain involved after their forces had suffered such heavy losses in Vietnam, but that China, its neighbor, was there to stay. The Vietnamese, however, were not heeding the warning. Deng had told Kissinger and Ford three years earlier that Hitler had invaded the West because the Western leaders had not shown that they were ready to make a strong military response. Deng believed from his long experience in dealing with the Soviets that discussions would not work. He believed that to get the Soviets to desist from expanding in Southeast Asia, he needed to take strong military action. He was ready to "teach a lesson" to the Vietnamese about the high costs of ignoring China's warnings and of providing bases for the Soviets.

As the Vietnamese were extending their power into first Laos and then Cambodia, continental Southeast Asian countries were being pressured by the Vietnamese to accommodate to its power. Southeast Asians did not welcome Vietnamese dominance, but they felt powerless against a Vietnam supported by the Soviet Union and felt they could not easily resist further Soviet expansion in their region. Deng feared that the mainland Southeast Asian countries—Malaysia, Thailand, and Singapore—would feel compelled to accommodate to Soviet-Vietnamese power to the detriment of China's long-term interests. In Deng's view it was essential to attempt to pull Southeast Asian countries away from Vietnam.

In September 1978, Vietnamese prime minister Pham Van Dong traveled to Southeast Asia to seek the understanding of Southeast Asian countries as

Vietnam prepared to invade Cambodia. Although Pham failed in his effort to sign a friendship treaty with the Association of Southeast Asian Nations (ASEAN), Southeast Asian countries were beginning to accommodate to Vietnamese power for they saw no other choice. By November, Deng had decided he had to travel to those same areas to prevent their accommodation to the growing Soviet-Vietnamese threat.

By the time he left for his Southeast Asian trip, Deng had begun military preparations to respond to a Vietnamese invasion of Cambodia, but his plans were not announced to the public. Even if Vietnam penetrated deeply into Cambodia, China would not respond favorably to Pol Pot's request to send troops to Cambodia as it had during the Korean War to help North Korea. Deng feared getting bogged down. Instead Deng decided China should "teach Vietnam a lesson" by invading, taking several county capitals to show that it could penetrate further, and then withdrawing quickly. This would also reduce the chance that the Soviet Union might send in troops to assist Vietnam. The Vietnamese would learn that the Soviet Union would not always come to its aid and that Vietnam should reduce its ambitions in the region. And by attacking Vietnam, not the Soviet Union, China would show the Soviet Union that any effort to build up its forces in the area would be very costly. Deng displayed confidence that Chinese troops, despite the toll the Cultural Revolution had taken on military training and discipline and despite their lack of battle experience, would be adequate to achieve his political goals against a more experienced and better-equipped enemy. Once Chinese troops had withdrawn, they would continue to harass Vietnamese forces along the border.

Fortunately for Deng's visit to Southeast Asia, on November 5, two days before he arrived, the Soviet Union and Vietnam cemented the pact they had been negotiating by signing a twenty-five-year treaty of peace and friendship.[43] The treaty alarmed Southeast Asian countries and made them receptive to Deng's suggestions about cooperating to resist Soviet and Vietnamese expansion. Leaders in Southeast Asia had no doubt that Deng was in charge of Chinese foreign policy and that whatever he said about foreign policy would be accepted by the other Chinese leaders.

Thailand, November 5–9, 1978

When Deng arrived on November 5, he became the first Chinese Communist leader ever to visit Thailand. Thailand's prime minister Kriangsak Chomanan welcomed Deng warmly.

Deng chose to start his Southeast Asian trip in Thailand not only because Chinese forces would need to pass through the country in order to supply Pol Pot's forces in Cambodia, but also because China enjoyed better relations with Thailand than with any other Southeast Asian country. Thailand, Malaysia, and Indonesia each had about five million ethnic Chinese, and leaders in all three countries feared that their ethnic Chinese populations might be more loyal to China than to their own country. The fear intensified during the Cultural Revolution when China began sending radio messages into those countries to encourage the local people to carry out revolution. At the time of Deng's visit, these radio appeals had not yet stopped. The problem was most acute in Indonesia, where local Chinese had joined in the resistance to Sukarno that had nearly toppled his government. (Indonesia, furious, did not normalize relations with China until 1990.) But in Thailand the ethnic Chinese were far more assimilated and the fear of ethnic Chinese becoming a fifth column was far less serious than in Malaysia or Indonesia. If Deng could successfully make his case there, then Thailand could prove helpful in persuading other Southeast Asian countries to cooperate with China and Cambodia in resisting Vietnamese expansionism.

Historically, Thailand had tried to preserve its relative independence by accommodating the wishes of stronger foreign powers—France, Great Britain, and Japan. Deng believed that if China did not assert its interests, Thailand might soon tilt toward Vietnam. Fortunately for Deng, at the time of his visit, Thai leaders—who were closely allied with the United States—sought to avoid accommodating Soviet and Vietnamese power and welcomed Chinese cooperation in resisting Vietnamese domination of the region.

To help prepare Thai public opinion before his trip and to help himself get up to speed about Thailand's concerns, Deng had several meetings with Prime Minister Kriangsak during his visit to Beijing earlier that year, and he met with a delegation of Thai journalists in Beijing in early October.[44] During Kriangsak's visit, Deng had told the prime minister of his desire to work with ASEAN and to normalize relations with Indonesia and Singapore. The two leaders shared perspectives on world issues and agreed in principle to increase cooperation against Soviet and Vietnamese domination.[45] Deng also agreed to support Kriangsak's efforts to enable ASEAN to remain a zone of peace and neutrality.[46] Perhaps most important, when Deng hosted a Sino-Thai Friendship Association delegation to Beijing in June, he urged Thailand to settle its differences with Cambodia; one month later, it was announced that in principle Thailand and Cambodia had agreed to settle their long-standing border dispute and to exchange ambassadors.[47]

When Deng met Kriangsak in Thailand in November, he again told him of his desire to work with ASEAN and to normalize relations with Indonesia and Singapore. He presented his analysis of the global ambitions of the Soviets and the regional ambitions of the Vietnamese. Soviet bases in Vietnam, he asserted, threatened not only China, but the region and the world. In a private meeting, with only a note taker and an interpreter, Deng warned Kriangsak that Vietnamese troops were preparing to invade and occupy Cambodia. Thailand, with its long border with Cambodia, would soon come under threat. Kriangsak agreed to grant China air rights to deliver supplies to Cambodia.[48]

Deng also tried to reassure Kriangsak about the loyalty of the local ethnic Chinese in Thailand. He asserted that China encouraged Chinese living overseas to become citizens of the countries where they resided. Once they had chosen the Thai nationality, they would automatically forgo their Chinese nationality. He further expressed the hope that those who became Thai nationals would abide by Thai laws, respect local customs, and live in amity with the local people, while those who chose to remain Chinese nationals would contribute to Sino-Thai friendship and to the Thai economy, culture, and public welfare.[49] Deng's confidence-building message provided a striking contrast to Mao's messages, delivered scarcely a decade earlier, encouraging people in Thailand to promote revolution. Within Thailand Mao's message appealed most to the ethnic Chinese. In his public press conference in Bangkok on November 9, Deng was less explicit about a likely conflict with Vietnam than he had been with Kriangsak in private. He stressed the necessity for Thailand and China to cooperate in dealing with those nations that seek to act like a hegemon, and especially the importance of strengthening Sino-Thai cooperation to ensure peace and security in Southeast Asia. He acknowledged that China's past relationship with the Thai Communist Party could not be ended overnight, but he said that it would not interfere with government-to-government relations. Privately, however, Deng had assured Kriangsak that China would end its support of the Communist Party of Thailand.[50] He had also explained that he would stop the Chinese clandestine radio broadcasting encouraging revolution, as soon as he had a chance to prepare the local people who had worked with China and their supporters within China. Eight months later, on July 10, 1979, the radio broadcasts came to an end.[51]

As on his other foreign trips, Deng made public appearances and took an interest in the local culture. During the visit to Thailand, which is 90 percent Buddhist, Deng was shown on television attending a Buddhist ceremony. He also met the Thai king and queen, visited sports contests and military demonstrations, and attended a ceremony supporting scientific and technical cooperation between the two countries.[52]

Malaysia, November 9–12, 1978

Malaysia proved to be a far greater challenge to Deng than Thailand. Malaysian leaders did have concerns about Vietnamese and Soviet aims in the region, but they were even more worried about the activities of the ethnic Chinese living in Malaysia. Deng, knowing this, did not expect to receive the enthusiastic reception he had received in Thailand. At best, following classic united front strategy, he hoped to neutralize Vietnam's efforts to court Malaysia and to draw Malaysia closer to China's side.

Deng's host, Prime Minister Datuk Hussein Bin Onn, had good reason to be concerned about local ethnic Chinese and their relationship with China. In the 1950s the Communist movement in the British colony of Malaya was so strong that many Malays had feared that the Communists might take over after Malaysian independence.[53] After Malaysian independence was achieved in 1963, the Malays were afraid that the ethnic Chinese, who had a strong political party, would dominate their government. To avoid this, Singapore, 75 percent ethnic Chinese and a part of Malaya, was cast out in 1965 and forced to become independent. Thereafter the Malays were a clear majority, even though ethnic Chinese still dominated the economy and the universities, and even though their powerful political party remained a constant thorn in Hussein Onn's side.

The ethnic Chinese also kept close ties to their original homeland. In May 1969 race riots erupted and lasted some two months; many local ethnic Chinese, worried about their futures, chose to keep their Chinese citizenship. When Deng visited in November 1978, the Communist Party of Malaysia was still active, most members were ethnic Chinese, and their general secretary Chin Ping sometimes took refuge in China.

Deng struck a more neutral tone with the Communist Party in Malaysia than the Vietnamese had done. Although he could not move right away to shut down the clandestine radio broadcasts, he did resolve to stop such activity (and in June 1981, at the time of the Sixth Plenum when Hua Guofeng was formally removed from his posts, China did finally shut down the clandestine Voice of Malaysia Revolution).[54] But Deng carefully avoided distancing himself too much from the Communists in Malaysia. For instance, two months before Deng visited Malaysia, even though he was a Communist, Vietnam Prime Minister Pham Van Dong had laid a ceremonial wreath at the memorial for Malay officials who had died suppressing Communist insurgents. Because Deng wanted Malaysia's support and because the Chinese Communist Party was no longer a revolutionary party, it would have been easy for Deng to do the same. But neither did he lay down a wreath, nor did he renounce the local Communist Party. Deng explained to Hussein Onn that he believed it would be difficult for China to attract and keep supporters abroad if it suddenly were to disown previous allies. He said that the Chinese government hoped to work with the Malaysian government, but the Chinese Communist Party would continue to have relations with Communist parties abroad, including Malaysia's. Datuk Hussein Bin Onn replied that Malaysia found that unacceptable, but Deng held firm.[55] He had already resigned himself to the Malaysian government not giving China its whole-hearted cooperation. And he knew he could not suddenly disown China's past policies and the people with whom China had cooperated.[56]

In 1974 when China and Malaysia established formal diplomatic relations, Zhou Enlai announced that China would not accept dual nationality. Now Deng reiterated Zhou Enlai's policy, saying that ethnic Chinese who acquired Malaysian citizenship would automatically forfeit their Chinese nationality and that China encouraged all who lived in Malaysia to follow local customs.[57] Deng was also on the defensive when pressed to discuss Pol Pot, who was anathema in Malaysia. Deng acknowledged the problems and explained that Pol Pot was the only Cambodian leader who could resist Vietnam and the country was too important strategically for China to push for a potentially destabilizing change of leadership.[58]

Deng's best hope for finding common ground with Malaysia lay in his support of the Malaysian proposal for a neutral political zone. In 1971 Malaysia's leader Tun Abdul Razak had proposed a Zone of Peace, Freedom, and Neutrality (ZOPFAN), designed to preserve local independence from the two Cold War powers. Deng praised Malaysia's initiatives in establishing a zone of peace, urging all of the ASEAN countries to close ranks and defend the ideal of a neutral zone in Southeast Asia, as a way of resisting increased efforts by Vietnam to infiltrate and expand into the area. Prime Minister Hussein Onn, who was himself worried about the threat of Vietnamese expansionism and who was aware that China was a major importer of Malaysian rubber, acknowledged Deng's point. Although he referred to Vietnam only indirectly, he agreed that foreign aggression, interference, control, and subversion were intolerable.[59]

In his talks in Malaysia, Deng made no effort to evade the problems between the two countries; rather, he was frank and forthright in acknowledging them. At the end of his visit, Hussein Onn commented on this new openness, saying that Deng's visit had been a great opportunity to develop further mutual understanding: the two rounds of discussions had been "most useful and helpful" and he expressed some confidence that "the relationship between the two countries will prosper and be strengthened in the future."[60] Given the circumstances, this was the most Deng could hope for.

Singapore, November 12–14, 1978

Deng understood that Singapore, with a population that was 75 percent ethnic Chinese, did not want to appear to its larger and stronger neighbors to be too pro-Chinese. He realized as well that as a city-state of a mere two million people, Singapore had to adapt to the power realities in the region as the Soviets and Vietnamese increased their influence. But he also knew that Prime Minister Lee Kuan Yew of Singapore had an unusual grasp of geopolitical realities and exercised great influence in ASEAN and with Western governments. He hoped, then, that Lee might help persuade ASEAN to resist Vietnam and even help persuade the United States to assist China—or at least not stand in the way—if China should enter into a conflict with Vietnam.

During Lee's previous visit to China, in May 1976, Deng was rusticating in Jiangxi, so when Deng arrived in Singapore on November 12, 1978, it was their first meeting. There was a respectful distance between the two great leaders from very different backgrounds, each aware of the other's reputation. Lee's understanding of China was derived more from academic study than from personal experience, for he had grown up in an Anglicized family and had been educated in English, not Chinese, schools, and had excelled as a law student at Cambridge University, England. In fact, although he could speak four languages, he was not completely fluent in Mandarin, and he spoke English during their meeting to signal both that he was not constrained by his ethnic background and that his first loyalty was to Singapore. Deng, meanwhile, spoke only one language, Mandarin, with a Sichuanese accent. Deng, Lee's elder by eighteen years, was the leader of a socialist country, whereas Lee was the leader of a capitalist country. Lee had to face elections, Deng faced a

Politburo. When they met, Singapore was an orderly, tidy city-state already growing rapidly, and gigantic China was poor and messy. China's population was four hundred times that of Singapore, but Singapore, as the intellectual and financial center of Southeast Asia, and with a strong leader, was far more influential than its size would suggest. Both Deng and Lee graciously tried to bridge their personal differences; briefed on Deng's habits, Lee had prepared a spittoon and offered an ashtray for Deng to smoke (with a specially constructed duct in the wall to allow the smoke to exit). Deng, however, who had been informed about Lee's views and allergies, did not spit or smoke in Lee's presence.

Deng spent the entire first two-and-a-half-hour meeting spelling out the threats from the Soviet Union and Vietnam. Without notes, he gave a tour of the geopolitical horizon, like Kissinger or Zhou Enlai might have done, that came entirely from his own synthesis and long-term historical perspectives. But what struck Lee Kuan Yew most was Deng's grim intensity and sense of urgency about the threat from the Soviet Union and Vietnam. The Soviet Union, Deng said, was spending more on armaments—20 percent of its GNP—than the United States and Europe combined. It had some 4.5 million men and women in its armed forces. And just as the Russian czars had coveted a corridor to the south, so too did the Soviet leaders now hope to push to the south, first to establish ports on the Indian Ocean and then to control the sea lanes from the Middle East. In pursuit of this goal, Deng warned, the Soviet Union had already amassed about 750 warships and was rapidly expanding its Pacific fleet. The Soviets were also seeking military bases and control over resources. But although war seemed inevitable, Deng said, China was determined to oppose the strategic deployments of the Soviet Union.

Deng went on to discuss the Vietnamese perspective. The Vietnamese had a long-cherished dream of forming an Indochinese federation to control Laos and Cambodia and to dominate Southeast Asia. The Vietnamese already controlled Laos, and considered Soviet help essential for advancing toward their immediate goal of unifying Indochina. China was considered a central obstacle. In this context, Deng explained, continued Chinese aid to Vietnam would never be enough to counter the Soviets' support for their dream of hegemony, and would only help Vietnam expand. So China had decided to cut its aid to Vietnam.[61]

When Deng, with great intensity, laid out the dangers of Soviet-Vietnamese domination, Lee pressed Deng on how China would respond to a Vietnamese invasion of Cambodia. Deng would only say that it depended how far Vietnam went. Lee surmised from this answer that if Vietnam crossed the Mekong River and went on to Phnom Penh, China would certainly respond militarily.[62]

Deng, aware that Lee was highly respected by American political leaders, expressed the hope that Lee Kuan Yew would pass on to the United States, before Deng's own visit there, the fact that China was very concerned about a possible Vietnamese invasion of Cambodia. Lee later complied.[63] Deng went on to discuss long-term prospects for relations in the region. In particular, he said that conditions were not yet ripe for China to try to pull Vietnam away from the Soviet Union, but in another eight to ten years, a better opportunity might arise. Deng's estimate proved remarkably prescient.

The following morning, on November 13, Lee laid out for Deng the various Western estimates of Soviet military power. There was no doubt that the Soviet military forces were the largest and growing. But although some experts believed that the Soviets posed an imminent threat, others were convinced that the Soviet Union was overextended. To allay Deng's worries about Singapore's willingness to welcome the Soviets to the region, Lee explained that Singapore traded mainly with Japan, the United States, Malaysia, and the European Union: only 0.3 percent of its trade was with the Soviet Union. (At the time, Singapore's trade with China constituted only 1.8 percent of its total trade.)

Lee explained that the ASEAN countries sought economic development, political stability, and national integrity. To Deng's surprise, Lee told him that the Southeast Asian countries were more worried about China than about Vietnam. Lee then described how the Southeast Asian countries worried about Chinese broadcasts encouraging revolution, especially among the ethnic Chinese, echoing the concern Deng had heard from the Thai and Malaysian leaders. Lee said that Southeast Asians were also aware that Vietnamese Prime Minister Pham Van Dong had placed a wreath on the memorial to Malaysians who had fought against the Communist insurgents, but Deng had not. To Lee's surprise, Deng then asked, "What do you and the ASEAN countries want us to do?" Lee replied, "Stop the radio broadcasts." Deng said he needed time to think about it. Lee was surprised that Deng, unlike virtually all other leaders whom he had met, was willing to change his mind when confronted with an unpleasant truth.[64] But Deng was not willing to consider laying a wreath in Malaysia for those who had killed Communists. Pham, he said, was selling his soul. Deng went on to say that the Chinese leaders have spoken honestly and if China promises something, it will carry it out.

By the time Deng left Singapore on November 14, the two leaders had developed a special relationship that, like that between Zhou Enlai and Kissinger, enabled them to communicate with mutual respect on a common wavelength. Lee and Deng had both come of age fighting colonialism, and both had lived abroad in a colonial power. Both had been bold leaders during their countries' revolutionary struggles, and both understood what it took to build order from a chaotic situation. Although Lee had received an English education, he had also studied Chinese history and could sense where Deng was coming from. They were both straightforward realists, utterly dedicated to their nations, who had risen to responsible positions at a young age and believed in the need for strong personal leadership. They understood power and thought strategically, taking into account long-term historical trends. Only one other person outside mainland China, Y. K. Pao (Yue-Kong Pao, founder of Hong Kong's World Wide Shipping Group), and no other political leader, had bonded with Deng the way Lee did. Deng had close ties with many foreign leaders, but his relationship with Lee reflected a greater depth of mutual understanding. From Deng's perspective, what made Lee and Y. K. Pao attractive was their extraordinary success in dealing with practical issues, their first-hand contacts with world leaders, their knowledge of world affairs, their grasp of long-term trends, and their readiness to face facts and speak the truth as they saw it. Lee considered Deng to be the most impressive leader he ever met—one who thought things through, and, when something went wrong, was ready to admit the mistake and set out to solve it.

Deng admired what Lee had accomplished in Singapore, and Lee admired how Deng was dealing with the problems in China. Before Deng's visit to Singapore, the Chinese press had referred to Singaporeans as the "running dogs of American imperialism." A few weeks after Deng visited Singapore, however, this description of Singapore disappeared from the Chinese press. Instead, Singapore was described as a place worth studying for its initiatives in environmental preservation, public housing, and tourism.[65] Lee and Deng would meet again, in 1980, 1985, and 1988.

Although Deng's purpose in going to Singapore had been to win support to stop the Vietnamese and Soviets in Southeast Asia, Singapore made a deep impression on Deng. When he visited New York, Paris, and Tokyo, he had not been surprised that they were all more modern than China. But Deng, who had spent two days in Singapore on his way to France in 1920, marveled at the progress that had been made there in the intervening fifty-eight years, even as China's economy and society were still mired in poverty. Deng had not yet decided what policies to pursue in China, but Singapore helped strengthen Deng's conviction of the need for fundamental reforms. As Deng once sighed, "If I had only Shanghai, I too might be able to change Shanghai as quickly. But I have the whole of China."[66]

Though Deng had read reports about Singapore, overwhelmingly his information had come from leftist sources in Singapore. To his surprise, then, he found that he was not greeted by enthusiastic throngs of ethnic Chinese and that the people had their own independent thinking and would not be subservient to China.[67] Apparently, the local Communists in Singapore, like some of their counterparts on the mainland, were so eager to convey what Beijing wanted to hear that their reports were unreliable. But Deng wanted to see and hear what was really going on. Consequently, he saw firsthand a city-state that was far more advanced and more orderly than he had expected. A year later, when the fighting with Vietnam was over, Deng commented in a speech in China on some of the good points he had observed about the factories set up by foreigners in Singapore. They pay taxes to the government, they provide work opportunities, and laborers receive income for their work. Foreign capitalists, he said, need not be so frightening.[68] Deng found orderly Singapore an appealing model for reform, and he was ready to send people there to learn about city planning, public management, and controlling corruption.

Courting the Ethnic Chinese in Southeast Asia

After returning to China, Deng continued working on the problem that had brought him to Southeast Asia, the Soviet-Vietnamese threat. But as a result of his visit, he took greater interest in the role of ethnic Chinese living outside China, both as contributors to the four modernizations in China and as good citizens who could help improve relations between China and their home countries. Deng and his colleagues began to give more attention to how ethnic Chinese abroad could supply funds and, in Deng's view even more importantly, knowledge of developments abroad to mainland China.

In the early 1950s many of those in China who had relatives living overseas lost their land, their businesses, and some had even lost their lives. Many who survived were again attacked during the Cultural Revolution. Some ethnic Chinese living abroad could never forgive the Chinese Communists for their cruelties to relatives who had remained in China. Others whose relatives had not been treated so harshly, however, responded to opportunities to make contributions to their hometown Chinese villages, efforts that were rewarded with the naming of buildings and medical facilities in their honor. Some of the relatives living oversees saw business opportunities in China. In October 1978, a few weeks before Deng's trip, in a high-level effort to heal the old wounds, Liao Chengzhi launched a large-scale attack on the former "overseas Chinese policy" of the Gang of Four. It was still too early to acknowledge that the policies that led to those persecutions had originated with Mao, but Liao's attacks on the former bad policy allowed Deng and other officials to distance themselves from the horrors of the past as they endeavored to open a new chapter.

Deng also supported the efforts for China to make amends to those mainland relatives of the ethnic Chinese overseas who had been badly treated. Some living overseas were invited back to live in their previously confiscated family homes. When that was not possible, many received some compensation for lost jobs and lost property, often in the form of better jobs, better housing, and better educational opportunities for their children. Deng realized that suspicions would not quickly disappear, but he took a long view and the policies he adopted for overseas Chinese continued during and after his years at the top. Deng wanted to keep good relations both with ethnic Chinese living overseas and with the Southeast Asian governments in the countries where they lived. When conflicts between ethnic Chinese and their Southeast Asian governments were especially acute, as in Malaysia, it was difficult for China to stand up for the fair treatment of ethnic Chinese. But because China had poor relations with Vietnam, it complained loudly about the Vietnam government's rounding up of ethnic Chinese and sending them to detention centers or expelling them, acts that caused an estimated 160,000 to flee the country.[69]

Deng's visit to Southeast Asia helped strengthen China's determination to encourage ethnic Chinese in Southeast Asia to be loyal to their country. Within two years after Deng's visit to Southeast Asia, support for the revolutionary broadcasts was ended. The Chinese Communist Party, as well as the Chinese government, endeavored to work with the Southeast Asian governments and parties in power. The change paralleled the Communists' transition at home from a revolutionary to a governing party. Even the term "overseas Chinese" fell into disfavor, for it implied that the ethnic Chinese living abroad were, in the final analysis, Chinese. They were instead described officially as "Malaysians (or Thais or Singaporeans) of Chinese ancestry."

The trip by Deng to Southeast Asia thus advanced efforts to improve relations with Southeast Asian governments; by 1990, when Indonesia and then Singapore normalized relations with China, China had thriving government, business, and cultural relationships with all of the countries of Southeast Asia. By then, all Southeast Asian countries could see the economic advantages of trade with mainland China and citizens of Chinese ancestry were regarded mainly in a positive way, as potential go-betweens bringing benefits both to China and the country where they lived.

Change through Problem-Solving

Deng's response to Vietnam's decision to invade Cambodia illustrates the process by which many changes occurred during the Deng era. Deng, the pragmatist, when confronted with a new problem first tried to understand the related issues, and only then did he decide what to do. When his actions created a new set of problems, he would tackle those one by one. Once Deng saw the threat of Soviet-Vietnamese expansionism, he decided to prepare China's military for a response, and then, when Chinese military deficiencies proved serious, he focused on improving China's military performance (see Chapter 18 for an account of China's Vietnam war). In considering how to respond to the Soviet-Vietnamese threat, Deng realized that he urgently needed the cooperation of the nearby Southeast Asian countries and thus he arranged to visit these countries to strengthen relations. But once there, he realized that to win the cooperation of these countries, he had to both phase out Chinese support to local revolutionaries and encourage the ethnic Chinese to show their loyalty to the country where they lived. To respond to the ever-increasing Soviet-Vietnamese threat, as well as to obtain support for achieving the four modernizations, Deng would also seek to deepen China's relations with the two large powers that were capable of restraining the Soviet Union, Japan and the United States.

10

Opening to Japan

1978

In his trip to Japan in October 1978, Deng sought Japanese cooperation in resisting Soviet-Vietnamese expansion. But he also knew that no country, with the possible exception of the United States, could be more helpful in its four modernizations. Japan had modern technology and effective management; it had lessons for China in how to accelerate growth, expand modern industry, and make the transition from a more regulated to a more open economy; it was located nearby; and many Japanese were prepared to be generous. Deng knew that for the relationship with Japan to work well, he would need to convince the Japanese that China was stable and prepared to be a responsible partner. Deng also knew that he had to overcome resistance from the Chinese people to working with the former enemy.

As Deng traveled to Japan, the Chinese film crews that accompanied him captured images that would help transform Chinese ideas about postwar Japan. The movies they created showed modern factories and trains as well as friendly, peaceful-looking Japanese people who welcomed their Chinese guests and proclaimed their readiness to help China. Deng knew that these images were critical for helping the Chinese public, who had learned to hate Japan, to accept the Japanese people as guests, employers, and teachers—and that this task would be at least as challenging as convincing the Japanese to supply funding, technology, and management skills. Japan had been the enemy ever since the Sino-Japanese War of 1894–1895, when Japan had taken away Taiwan and made it a Japanese colony. Some Chinese people who were over forty years old in 1978 could still recall the horrors from World War II—but all Chinese were aware, from the Chinese media or from speeches blared for three decades from loudspeakers at schools and work units, of the savage actions of some of the Japanese troops during that conflict. No propaganda had been more effective in stirring up patriotism than the searing accounts of Japanese atrocities during World War II.

Deng, the diehard pragmatist, personally had no difficulty making a cool assessment of national interests and acting accordingly. As a young man, he had passionately denounced the Japanese and other foreign imperialists. But he had been seasoned as he rose to responsible positions and observed how national interests change. Deng harbored no illusions about the dogged determination of capitalists and capitalist countries in pursuing their own interests, and in working with them he stubbornly defended China's interests. But in 1978, both Japan and the United States, alarmed by Soviet expansion, were eager to draw China farther away from the Soviet Union, and this created a window of opportunity for Deng.

For Deng to tell passionate Chinese patriots they should learn from the Japanese took political courage and determination. Fortunately, just as President Nixon had the political base to open relations with a former enemy, Communist China, because he had proved he was a passionate anti-Communist, so Deng, as a soldier who fought the Japanese for eight years, had a strong political base to take the brave step of improving relations with Japan.

Before Deng visited Japan, he first had to negotiate a treaty with Japan to pave the way. After Mao and Prime Minister Tanaka Kakuei had rushed to normalize relations between the two countries in 1972, relations between the two countries had stagnated. Mao and Tanaka had not dealt with a host of legal issues needed to establish consulates, carry on commerce, and promote exchanges of people. Before traveling to Japan, Deng needed first to address these issues.

Sino-Japanese Treaty of Peace and Friendship

When Deng returned to work in mid-1977, negotiations on a treaty to underpin Sino-Japanese relations had been dragging on for years. The key holdup was Japan's unwillingness to accept a Chinese demand that the treaty include an anti-hegemony clause, which specified that both countries agreed not to seek to dominate the region and to resist any other country that did.[1] Chinese negotiators, who wanted to draw Japan farther away from the Soviet Union, knew that the anti-hegemony clause would anger the Soviets. Japanese relations with the USSR had deteriorated after September 1976 when a Soviet pilot had defected by flying his plane to Hokkaido; the Japanese, working with the Americans to analyze the plane's capacities, had refused to return the aircraft to the Soviets. But Japan, a trading nation which then had limited capabilities for fighting militarily outside its borders, sought to avoid overly antagonizing any country, especially one with ample oil reserves after the oil shock of 1973.

The Chinese had initially proposed that the two governments negotiate a peace treaty, but Japan answered that it had already signed a peace treaty with Chiang Kai-shek who was acting on behalf of the Chinese government, and that it remained in effect. The Chinese countered with a suggestion that the two nations sign a treaty of peace and friendship, as Japan had done with many other countries. But until 1977 this approach had not solved the problem. Despite the efforts of Prime Minister Miki Takeo, who succeeded Tanaka, and Prime Minister Fukuda Takeo, who succeeded Miki in December 1976, the right-wing nationalists of Japan refused to meet the determined Chinese halfway. Deng, uncomfortable with the slow democratic process both at home or abroad, wanted to move quickly to resolve problems, but he persevered in working with the Japanese in spite of their domestic political difficulties.

As the standoff continued, Deng hosted in September and October 1977 several visiting Japanese political leaders judged to be sympathetic to China, including Nikaido Susumu and Kono Yohei, to explore possibilities for concluding a treaty.[2] Meanwhile in Japan, various business groups and local regional associations, eager for more contact with China, lobbied for greater flexibility in finding a way to conclude such a treaty.[3] Fukuda, a bright former finance ministry bureaucrat, had already received praise from other Asian leaders for the "Fukuda Doctrine," by which Japan was providing assistance to its Southeast Asian neighbors. When Fukuda reorganized his cabinet on November 28, 1977, he appointed as foreign minister Sonoda Sunao, who as an "old friend of China" (lao pengyou) was the official most likely to be able to conclude a treaty.[4] Fukuda encouraged Sonoda to negotiate with Foreign Minister Huang Hua to resolve the issues impeding the treaty's completion.[5]

From late 1977 until mid-July 1978, there were almost continuous rounds of discussions on the details of a possible treaty, but the anti-hegemony clause remained the chief sticking point. In March there were signs of progress, as Japan seemed willing to consider a slightly altered, carefully worded statement.[6] The Japanese believed that if a mitigating clause were inserted that said the treaty was not aimed at any third party, the Soviets would tolerate it.

On July 21, 1978, under Deng's guidance, formal negotiations began: the two sides held the first of what would become fourteen rounds of discussions on the treaty, and in the ensuing rounds various draft proposals were exchanged. By the beginning of August, the Japanese negotiators in Beijing were sufficiently hopeful that the Chinese would yield on the mitigating clause that Foreign Minister Sonoda personally traveled to Beijing for the negotiations. Later, the deputy head of the Japanese Treaties Division, Togo Kazuhiko, reported that Deng Xiaoping apparently made "a political decision," and that when Foreign Minister Huang Hua during the negotiations accepted the Japanese wording, "We were so happy that under the table I shook hands firmly with my boss." The mitigating clause read: "The present Treaty shall not affect the position of either Contracting Party regarding its relations with third countries."[7] The treaty was signed in Beijing on August 12, 1978, by Huang Hua and Sonoda.[8]

Why would Deng Xiaoping—after over eight months of discussions—suddenly break the diplomatic logjam and permit the Japanese to include their mitigating clause in the treaty? He was in a hurry to get on with modernization, but at the time the prospect of conflict in Vietnam gave a special urgency to moving quickly. Deng had announced two weeks earlier, on July 3, the withdrawal of all Chinese advisers from Vietnam. By then, it seemed likely to Deng that Vietnam would invade Cambodia and that if it did so, China would be forced to respond. To discourage the Soviets from entering the conflict, Deng sought to deepen relations with the major powers, Japan and the United States, as quickly as possible. As expected, the Soviets were upset with Japan over the treaty, but with the mitigating clause, they tolerated it.[9]

The Treaty of Peace and Friendship did not require that a high-level Chinese leader go to Japan to celebrate its signing. It was appropriate for China to send a high-level leader to Japan to reciprocate Tanaka Kakuei's 1972 visit to China, but for six years no Chinese leader had traveled to Japan. Deng clearly was ready to go to the island nation.

Deng's Triumphal Visit to Japan, October 19–29, 1978

In the first sixty years after World War II, three foreign leaders who visited Japan had such an electrifying effect on the Japanese public that they fundamentally changed the way the Japanese public regarded their country. In the early 1960s Robert Kennedy, brother of President John F. Kennedy, engaged groups of students and ordinary citizens in frank, lively public dialogues that went beyond what the Japanese public had ever before experienced with a foreign leader. Bobby Kennedy's vitality; his refreshing, youthful idealism; his sincere desire to serve humanity around the world; and his obvious respect for the views of others deepened Japanese understanding of the meaning of democracy at its best and strengthened Japan's goodwill toward Americans.[10]

Three decades later, in 1998, another foreign leader, President Kim Dae Jung of South Korea, made an equally dramatic impression on the Japanese when he thanked those Japanese who had helped save his life in 1973. Kim had been kidnapped and abducted by the South Korean CIA while in Tokyo, and placed in a small boat to be drowned; he was saved only by a daring rescue mission. When Kim, trying to overcome the deep Korean hostility to Japan, speaking in Japanese with obvious sincerity, said that South Korea and Japan should not look backward, but instead only forward, toward a future of peace and friendship, he touched his listeners. In public opinion polls of the Japanese and Korean people in the following months, each side revealed a far more positive attitude to the other side.

Visiting Japan between these two electrifying moments, Deng in 1978 had an equally dramatic effect on the Japanese people. In the 2,200 years of contact between China and its island neighbor, Deng was the first Chinese leader to set foot in Japan. He was also the first to meet the emperor of Japan.[11] When Deng said that despite an unfortunate period during the twentieth century the countries had enjoyed two millennia of good relations, and that he looked forward to a future of good relations, it touched the Japanese who knew how much the Chinese had suffered from Japanese aggression and who deeply wanted to express their sorrow and to extend the hand of friendship. Deng came with a spirit of reconciliation and he brought the hope that the two peoples could live together in a new era of peace and goodwill. Many felt that at last the healing, some three decades after World War II, had begun.

During Deng's trip, many Japanese expressed sorrow for the suffering they had inflicted and Japanese political leaders pledged they would never let such a tragedy occur again. Deng accepted their apologies without demanding that they spell out the horrors in more detail. To many Japanese in various spheres, helping China modernize was an expression of their repentance about Japan's past behavior as well as a way of contributing to China's prosperity, an act that would itself increase the chance that the two could live together in peace.

Virtually all Japanese households already had televisions, and the Japanese public shared the deep emotions as their leaders apologized to Deng on behalf of their nation. Although television was not widely diffused in China, film strips and photos shot in the Japanese factories that Deng visited allowed the Chinese public to see the warm welcome the Japanese were giving to Deng—as well as the new technology that showed how far behind China really was.

In 1974 and 1975, when Deng was responsible for meeting high-level foreign leaders, he saw far more visitors from Japan than from any other country. Through his personal interactions with these Japanese representatives, he had come to understand that the Japanese people, from all levels of society, shared an affinity for Chinese culture. Again and again, Japanese hosts expressed to Deng their gratitude to China as the wellspring of Japanese culture—their Buddhism, their written language, their art, and their architecture, especially in the cities that Japanese embraced as the heart of old Japan, Nara and Kyoto. During his ten days in Japan, Deng Xiaoping met people from all walks of life: government leaders, members of the ruling party and the opposition parties, representatives of big business, ordinary citizens from local communities, and members of the media. He was hosted by many of the people whom he had welcomed to Beijing in 1973–1975 and 1977–1978. He greeted them, as Chinese greet people they have seen before, as "old friends."

Deng arrived in Japan on October 19, 1978, before he became the paramount leader, but he was treated as if he already spoke for China.[12] When in Japan, Deng had a full schedule. Deng, the ex-military commander who believed in strict discipline, could not help but be impressed by the care his hosts took in arranging his visit; they paid as much attention to detail as quality-control engineers in a Japanese factory.

On the morning of October 23, Prime Minister Fukuda Takeo and four hundred Japanese formally welcomed Deng in the hall at the State Guest House and then took part in a ceremony to ratify the Treaty of Peace and Friendship. Twenty-eight ambassadors from leading countries with embassies in Tokyo attended the ceremony, but, in accordance with a request by the Chinese, the Soviet ambassador was not invited.[13]

After the ceremony, when he went to meet Prime Minister Fukuda, Deng took out a pack of Panda cigarettes and offered cigarettes to everyone, which immediately lightened the mood. Deng said, "For years I have been looking for an opportunity to visit Japan, and finally I can realize it. I am very happy to have the chance to get to know Prime Minister Fukuda." Fukuda replied, "The unusual relations between China and Japan that have existed for almost a century have come to an end. The purpose of the treaty is to establish permanent peaceful and friendly relations. The treaty is the result of decisions by Vice Premier Deng Xiaoping." When Fukuda said that he knew China only from before the war and hoped some day to have a chance to visit China again, Deng immediately replied, "On behalf of the Chinese government I invite you to visit China at a time convenient to you." His host accepted on the spot, saying, "I will definitely visit China."[14] After Fukuda spoke of strengthening their relationship, Deng laughingly said, "It's really amazing for Japan to take such a poor person [China] as a friend."[15]

After Sonoda and Huang Hua signed and exchanged the official documents, Deng unexpectedly gave a big hug to Fukuda, who looked nonplussed but quickly recovered and took it as a sign of goodwill. (Deng would do the same to Communist comrades in other countries.) Deng declared that the peace treaty, by "advancing the political, economic, cultural, technical, and other exchanges, would have . . . a positive influence on the peace and security of the Asian and Pacific area. . . . Friendly relations and cooperation are the common wish of the billion Chinese and the Japanese people, and it is the current of historical advance. . . . Let us on behalf of the people in both countries continue the friendship generation after generation."[16]

During his visit, Deng also had a two-hour lunch with the Japanese emperor at the Imperial Palace. To guarantee that the emperor will speak freely to visitors, the Japanese do not keep a record of such discussions, but Deng later reported that they had an excellent conversation. Foreign Minister Huang Hua, who was in attendance, reported that Deng had said "bygones should be bygones, and we must be forward-looking in the future and work in every field to develop relations of peace and friendship between our two countries." In noting that the emperor had used the expression "unfortunate happening," Huang Hua reported that this "amounted to an indirect apology to the Chinese for the war damage." Both the emperor and Deng expressed the view that the two countries could now enjoy a peaceful and friendly relationship that would continue forever.[17]

That afternoon, Deng had a ninety-minute talk with Fukuda, who later hosted a banquet attended by a hundred Japanese political, economic, and academic leaders, including the secretary general of the Liberal Democratic Party, Ohira Masayoshi; Fujiyama Aichiro, former foreign minister; and Nakasone Yasuhiro, a rising star who later became prime minister. In his talk at the banquet, Fukuda, after reviewing the two thousand years of close relations, declared that in "this century we suffered the distress of an unfortunate relationship." He then departed from his printed text to add, "this was indeed very regrettable," a message the Chinese recognized as an apology. Fukuda continued, "Such a thing can never be allowed again. The Treaty of Peace and Friendship is precisely meant for this, and for our vows to each other."[18] Deng replied that "although our countries have gone through an unfortunate period, in the more than 2,000 years of history of good relations, that period was really only a short instant."[19]

Deng explained to his hosts that he had come to Japan for three reasons: to exchange documents ratifying the Treaty of Peace and Friendship; to express China's appreciation to Japanese friends who in recent decades had dedicated themselves to improving Sino-Japanese relations; and like Xu Fu, to find a "secret magic drug." Japanese listeners laughed, for they were familiar with the story of Xu Fu, who, 2,200 years earlier, on behalf of Emperor Qin, had been dispatched to Japan to find a drug that would bring eternal life. Deng went on to explain that what he really meant by the "magic drug" was the secret of how to modernize. He said he wanted to learn about modern technology and management. In the good-natured banter that followed, the speaker of Japan's lower house, Hori Shigeru, remarked that the best drug would be good Sino-Japanese relations.[20] Later, when Deng was touring the Nijō Castle in Kyoto, his host said, "All the culture you see here was introduced by our ancestors who learned it from China and then gradually adapted it in our own unique way." Deng immediately responded, "Now our positions [as student and teacher] are reversed."[21]

Confident of his authority at home in Beijing and familiar with many of the people whom he was meeting, Deng could relax and share his natural charm and spontaneity. When crowds assembled to see him, Deng, aware that he was touching the hearts of his listeners, responded with the ebullience of a politician who knew he was winning over his audience.

Deng's main guide to Japan was Liao Chengzhi, with whom he had worked closely for many years in Beijing on Japanese, Hong Kong, and overseas Chinese affairs. Liao, who was four years younger than Deng, was enormously popular among the Japanese; they knew he was born in Japan, had lived there through primary school, had attended Waseda University, and for decades had hosted Japanese visitors to Beijing. Liao's father, Liao Zhongkai, had been one of the leading candidates to succeed Sun Yat-sen until 1925 when he was assassinated by rivals. Liao Chengzhi, like Deng, had participated on the Long March and had become an alternate member of the Central Committee in 1945. No Chinese leader before or since could compare to Liao in terms of his intuitive understanding of Japan, close personal friendships, and high political position within China. He was the perfect companion for Deng on his visit.

Deng was aware as he toured Japan's modern factories that good technology required effective management and that good management was in turn related to a broad national system. He expressed interest in learning from Japan's experience in moving from a government-directed closed economy in World War II to a more open dynamic economy in the 1950s. He knew that the Japanese government had played a central role in Japan's modernization while managing to escape the rigidities of socialist planning. But Deng was also fascinated by the modern technology that he saw in factories, in public transport, and in construction projects. He wanted to find a way to bring modern technology and modern management to China. And Japanese businessmen, especially those who had spent time in China before or during World War II, were prepared to be generous to China.

Deng paid courtesy calls on former prime minister Tanaka Kakuei, Speaker of the House of Representatives Hori Shigeru, and Liberal Democratic Party leader Ohira Masayoshi, then moved on to the Diet for a reception. Tanaka was then under house arrest for the Lockheed scandal and many Japanese were avoiding him. In spite of this, Deng, at his own request, was driven to Tanaka's home, where he remarked that one of the reasons he had come to Japan was to express his appreciation to old friends who had made a personal effort on behalf of improved Sino-Japanese relations. He wanted to thank former prime minister Tanaka for his contribution to friendship between the two countries and for signing the Joint Proclamation between China and Japan.[22] Deng said that although Tanaka had come to China when Deng was in the "Peach Garden" (banished to Jiangxi), "We can't forget what you did for our relationship." Deng then gave a formal invitation to Tanaka to visit China as a guest of the government. Later that day Tanaka told reporters that the union of China and Japan in the Treaty of Peace and Friendship was the best thing that had happened since the Meiji Restoration. Tanaka said that of all the foreign leaders whom he had met, Zhou Enlai had created the greatest impression, and "today in the visit of Deng Xiaoping I have the same feelings as I had when I met Zhou Enlai."[23]

By 1978, most Japanese citizens who had played a role in keeping up contacts with China in the 1950s and 1960s had passed away. In the evening of

October 24, at the Akasaka State Guest House, Deng and his wife, Zhuo Lin, welcomed the few who were still alive as well as surviving family members, primarily the widows and children of deceased politicians who had maintained relations with China during those difficult years. Deng apologized for not having time to visit each one of them personally and said that, like Zhou Enlai (who had lived in Japan from 1917 to 1919), he wanted to say to his Japanese friends that "when we drink water, we cannot forget those who dug the well." He added that even in the days before normalization, they all had believed a day would come when normal relations would be achieved. Even if some could not be there to share the joys of the day, their efforts would not be forgotten: their names would remain permanently in the records of good relations between the two countries, encouraging the two nations to continue to move forward.[24] Deng added that these individuals, as well as their widows and children, were China's friends, giving the Chinese "confidence that the good relations between the people of our two countries will be passed down from generation to generation." Deng then invited those in the audience to visit China frequently.[25] Many listeners were moved to tears.

That afternoon, Nissan's chairman Kawamata Katsuji accompanied Deng on an hour-long tour of the company's Zama plant, which had just introduced robots on the manufacturing line, making it arguably the most automated automobile factory in the world. After watching the production line and learning that the plant produced ninety-four cars per worker per year, Deng remarked that this was ninety-three cars a year better than China's best, the First Automobile Works in Changchun. When he finished touring the Nissan factory, Deng declared, "Now I understand what modernization is."[26]

On the next day, Deng met again with Prime Minister Fukuda, attended a luncheon sponsored by Keidanren, the leading Japanese business federation, and in the late afternoon held a press conference for Japanese reporters, met with Japanese residents of Chinese ancestry, and hosted a banquet. At the Keidanren luncheon, a record 320 top company executives were in attendance, surpassing the previous record of three hundred guests during Queen Elizabeth's visit.[27]

In China Deng had never held a press conference, but on that day he became the first Chinese Communist leader to hold a Western-style press conference in any location. Some four hundred reporters attended at the Japan Press Center. Deng opened with a short presentation on the dangers of countries seeking hegemony and on the importance of Japan and China working together to resist such efforts. But Deng, sensitive to the strong neutralist sentiment in Japan, insisted that the Chinese wished to resolve international issues peacefully; in fact, they needed a peaceful environment in order to modernize. At this point, Deng opened the floor for questions. When a reporter asked about ownership of the Senkaku Islands, the audience became tense, but Deng replied that the Chinese and Japanese held different views, used different names for the islands, and should put the issue aside so that later generations, who would be wiser than those present, could solve the problem. The audience was visibly relieved and impressed with Deng's wise answer. Finally, when asked about the horrible things Mao had done to his country during the Cultural Revolution, Deng answered, "These were not just Mao's mistakes, they were all our mistakes. Many of us made mistakes; we lacked experience and had poor judgment." He added, "We are very poor. We are very backward. We have to recognize that. We have a lot to do, a long way to go and a lot to learn."[28]

In answering a question about the four modernizations, Deng declared that China had set a goal of making a breakthrough by the end of the twentieth century. To achieve this, China needed the correct political atmosphere and the correct policies; the Chinese would not be like an "ugly person who tries to make herself beautiful just by putting on nice clothes." He went on to say, "We must admit our deficiencies. We are a backward country and we need to learn from Japan." When asked his impressions of his visit, he expressed appreciation for the excellent hospitality. He said that he had been received very cordially by the emperor, by the Japanese business community, and by Japanese people from different walks of life. He also said that he had had excellent talks with Fukuda and that top Chinese and Japanese leaders should meet every year. Although his trip was brief, he said, he wanted good relations between Japan and China to continue forever. The Japanese deeply wanted to hear such a message and at the end of his talk those present stood and applauded for several minutes.[29]

How could a Communist leader, holding his first press conference, score such a triumph? In part, the answer can be found in Deng's long experience in explaining problems to many different groups in China. But his success also stemmed from his familiarity with Japanese issues and opinions, his confidence in talking about Chinese policies, his frankness in acknowledging China's problems, his obvious goodwill toward Japan, and his relaxed, colorful language. In addition, there was widespread recognition among those who attended the press conference that Deng's visit to Japan was a historic moment. The Japanese people hoped that the visit, with its apologies for past injustices and pledges to help China modernize, would launch a new era in which the two nations would work together in peace.[30]

The next day, Inayama Yoshihiro, chairman of New Japan Steel and president of the Japan-China Economic Association of business leaders who traded with China, accompanied Deng on a hovercraft (a kind of speedboat not yet known in China) across Tokyo harbor to the Kimitsu Steel Factory. Kimitsu was an automated steel factory that alone produced about half as much steel as China was then producing in all of its plants together. After observing the facility, Deng immediately declared his desire to build a Chinese steel plant modeled after Kimitsu. Actually the plans for Baoshan, modeled after Kimitsu, had already begun taking shape.

From Tokyo, Deng took the *shinkansen* (bullet train) to Kyoto and also visited nearby Nara and Osaka. At a hotel in the Kansai area, Deng walked by a room with festivities and caught a glimpse of a woman in a beautiful white dress. When he asked what was going on and learned that a wedding celebration was in progress, he asked if he could see, and the happy couple, pleased that their wedding had become an international news story, happily posed for pictures with Deng to the great amusement of the onlookers.

Deng toured eighth-century Kyoto, whose city plan, art, and architecture were modeled after those of the Tang capital of Chang'an. There he met the Kyoto governor, the mayor of Kyoto city, and regional business leaders. From Kyoto he traveled by special train to Nara, which was also based on Chinese models and built even earlier than Kyoto. In Nara, he visited the great Todaiji Temple, built in the style of Southern Song temples, and lunched with Nara city officials.

From the ancient capital of Nara, Deng went to visit a state-of-the-art Matsushita electronics factory in Osaka (which also produced the Panasonic and National brands). There he met Matsushita Konosuke, who had started as a laborer making bicycle headlights in the 1920s and had grown with his enterprise until, by the time Deng arrived, it had became the world's leading electronics company. Like other Japanese business leaders, Matsushita was deeply remorseful over the great suffering that Japan had caused in China and he relayed his vision of helping to raise the living standards of the Chinese people by producing good, inexpensive television sets so that ordinary Chinese families, who at that time could not afford televisions, could buy them for their homes.[31]

At Matsushita, Deng saw the mass production of not only color televisions, but also fax machines and microwaves, neither of which had been introduced in China. Deng, who knew Matsushita's reputation, called him the "god of management" and urged him to teach the Chinese all the latest technologies. Matsushita explained to Deng what apparently Deng's advisers had not, that private companies like his earned their living by the technologies they had developed and so they would be reluctant to pass on the latest secrets. Matsushita factories went up rapidly in China, and the company did teach the Chinese technology that within a decade would help China to realize Matsushita's dream of having affordable television sets for the Chinese public.[32]

In the evening, Deng dined with Osaka government leaders and with the daughter of the late Takasaki Tatsunosuke, whom he requested to see to express his respect and appreciation for her father's contribution. Her father had worked with Liao Chengzhi to reach the 1964 Liao-Takasaki trade agreement, which had established trade offices in each country and had allowed controlled Sino-Japanese trade and exchanges of journalists even before the normalization of relations in 1972.

Japanese public television (NHK) coverage of Deng's factory visit showed an exuberant, observant, and confident Deng Xiaoping, curious and enthusiastic but not obsequious about all the superior Japanese technology he was seeing. Had he been too deferential, he would have been vulnerable to charges of fawning over things foreign. Deng must have struck the right chord, for after his trip, Chinese schoolchildren were taught that he had given the perfect answer to reporters' questions about what he thought of the *shinkansen* train. Deng had answered simply, "It is very fast"—that is, he acknowledged the value of foreign technology without sacrificing Chinese pride.

The words and actions of the Japanese leaders during Deng's trip also played well to the Japanese home audience. Even decades later, young Japanese labeled the generation of senior leaders who had hosted Deng as statesmen *(omono)*—that is, unlike their successors who had been preoccupied with financial details and petty political squabbles. The leaders who welcomed Deng (Prime Minister Fukuda, Foreign Minister Sonoda, Keidanren head Doko Toshio, business host Inayama Yasuhiro, and Matsushita Konosuke) were indeed bold planners and builders: they had guided a desolate, defeated nation with not enough to eat as it flowered into a vital nation that in 1978 was still growing rapidly. These senior Japanese leaders also had experienced World War II and knew personally what horrors Japan had caused. They knew that they never could repay China for the damages inflicted by

Japan, but they wanted to make it possible for the next generations to live in peace. They were prepared to share their experiences and their technical innovations to help China modernize in ways that went beyond their companies' profits. This was a generation of Japanese leaders to whom Deng could relate and from whom he could learn, as he worked to rebuild his country—a challenge that the Japanese had confronted as they recovered from the devastation of World War II.

Inayama, Deng's primary business host in Japan, had begun selling steel to China in 1957, and by 1971 his company was playing a major role in modernizing China's Wuhan Steel plant, making it the most modern steel factory in China. Some of Inayama's employees were unhappy that he was transferring so much technology to an outdated Soviet-style steel plant instead of building a completely new facility. Inayama responded that he was pleased to modernize the plant: when his steel company, Yawata, had opened its first factory in Japan in 1901, the iron ore had come from Wuhan, so he was happy to return a favor to the Chinese city.[33]

This was not the first time that Inayama had been criticized by subordinates for his *gaman tetsugaku* (philosophy of endurance), for being too generous to other companies and other countries even at the expense of his own company's interests. He did not want his company to lose money, but he sought to benefit society. He believed that the transfer of steel technology would benefit South Korea and China, and that such gifts to other countries could be mutually beneficial if all shared in the prosperity. He was willing to risk what Japanese called the "boomerang effect," the passing of technology to China only to find later that cheaper Chinese exports were entering Japan and destroying the domestic production base. He expressed confidence that the Chinese market was large enough to absorb the Chinese-produced steel. In the hovercraft ride to Kimitsu, Inayama and Deng chatted about being born in the same year. When Inayama asked Deng how he stayed so healthy, Deng replied, "By just being a simple soldier" *(qiuba)*.[34] Inayama later commented that Deng appreciated those Japanese who wanted to help China.

Deng expected that his trip would advance the plan to build a large, totally modern steel plant on the China coast, a project that Inayama had discussed with Vice Premier Li Xiannian the previous year. At Kimitsu, then the world's most advanced steel plant, Deng saw a new continuous-casting production line and computer-controlled technology that would become the model for China's first modern steel plant at Baoshan, just north of Shanghai. Deng said that to make Baoshan work, the Chinese needed Japanese aid to learn management skills. He added only half-jokingly, "If the student doesn't do well, that means the teacher hasn't taught him well."[35]

After visiting Japan, the term "management" took on deeper meaning for Deng, and he began to use it more often. He tried to explain to his countrymen, who believed what they had been taught under Mao about Western exploitation of workers, that the reality was really quite different: Japanese workers owned their own homes, their own cars, and electronic equipment that was unavailable in China. During his visit, Deng not only saw things that previously he had only read about; he wanted to study how Japanese organized workers to maximize their dedication and efficiency, which he summed up as "management." From his trip he concluded, "We must firmly grasp management. Just making things isn't enough. We need to raise the quality."[36] A century earlier, Chinese patriots had insisted on retaining the "Chinese spirit" while adopting Western technology. By using the neutral term "management" to refer to studying Western ways, and by keeping his unwavering commitment to socialism and the Communist Party, Deng allowed the introduction of far more than technology while reducing the resistance of Chinese conservatives. Indeed, Deng argued that socialism could also use modern management, and the Communist Party could champion it.

Japanese media reports of Deng's visit raved about the success of the trip and about the strengthening of relations between China and Japan. The reporting in China was more official in tone and more subdued, but the essence of the message was the same. In China, films and photographs of Deng's trip allowed the Chinese public to see what modern factories were like and to gauge for themselves just how far behind China was and how much work was still needed to catch up to world levels.

The Fruits of the Japan Trip

Before the end of his trip, arrangements had been made for a delegation of leading economic officials from Beijing, Tianjin, and Shanghai to follow up with a more detailed study tour of Japan. Deng Liqun served as adviser to the delegation and Yuan Baohua, deputy head of China's State Economic Planning Commission, as head. The group arrived in Japan a few days after Deng's departure and remained for a month. After the visit, the delegation produced a remarkably upbeat report that outlined how China could learn about economic management from Japan.

Mindful of its audience of Communist Party leaders steeped in their Marxist perspective, the delegation's report explained that Japan had made important adaptations to the early capitalism described by Marx. Japanese management had cleverly learned how to earn profits by providing incentives
for workers, who worked harder because they were better treated than the
exploited workers Marx had observed. After the group returned to China,
Deng Liqun took the lead in organizing new associations, including a Quality Control Association and an Enterprise Management Association, modeled on the associations that the delegation had observed in Japan. Drawing
on what they had learned, training programs for high-level economic officials
in each province were established to master some of the Japanese practices—
for instance, how to adjust prices to reflect production costs, how to set production targets not by arbitrary mandatory planning but by adapting to market demand, how to manage quality control not by inspection but through
care in the original production, and how to use indicators to evaluate the success of a manufacturing operation.[37] Chinese factories posted banners stressing the importance of studying Japanese management systems and establishing training programs.

Deng also initiated cultural exchanges that brought Japanese culture—
movies, stories, novels, and art—to China. Japanese movies, for example,
proved popular with Chinese audiences and helped increase Chinese understanding of the Japanese as a people. Deng understood that this sort of appreciation would provide a solid base for expanding economic and political
relations between the two countries. Under Deng's leadership, Chinese attitudes toward Japanese showed a striking improvement.

Deng thus made enormous progress in laying a foundation for sound Sino-
Japanese working relationships. After his trip, business relations were hampered for three years by China's retrenchment policies, which limited foreign
investment. But during most of the Deng era Japan and China continued,
despite some ups and downs, to enjoy good relations.

In fact, by December 1980, Sino-Japanese relations had already improved
sufficiently to convene the first joint cabinet-level discussions between the
two countries.[38] In addition, in that same month, Huang Hua signed an
agreement with Foreign Minister Ito Masayoshi for a long-term loan from
the Japanese Overseas Economic Cooperation Fund (OECF) on favorable
terms. From 1979 to 2007 the OECF granted more funds to China than to
any other country, a total of 2.54 trillion yen (based on the 2007 exchange
rate, this amounted to roughly US$25 billion).[39] Japanese industrial firms

set up factories throughout China, and Japan's External Trade Organization (JETRO) opened an office in Shanghai, using its broad network of contacts with Japanese firms to find companies willing to respond to Chinese requests for training programs in various sectors. During Deng's years at the helm, no country played a greater role in assisting China build its industry and infrastructure than Japan.

11

Opening to the United States

1978–1979

On the afternoon of August 22, 1977, just three days after Deng officially returned to work as a member of the Politburo Standing Committee, he met Secretary of State Cyrus Vance. Deng wanted to accomplish some things in his few years in office, and the timing of this meeting reflected the high priority he gave to normalizing relations with the United States. Hua Guofeng, China's chairman and premier, met Vance the day after Deng did, but American officials understood that the key visit was with Deng.

Ever since Nixon's visit in 1972, China had expected that normalization would follow quickly. Somehow, American politics had always interfered, and China already had been waiting impatiently for five years. Deng in particular, who was just back from eighteen months of forced retirement, was ready to move toward normalization and he had reason to hope that the Vance visit would pave the way. The Watergate episode had passed, and in February 1977 President Jimmy Carter invited Huang Zhen, head of the Chinese Liaison Office in Washington, to meet with him. He told Huang, "I hope we can see a strong movement toward normalization," and he offered to host Huang at a concert or a play.[1] In addition, just before Deng met Vance, Leonard Woodcock had arrived in Beijing to head the U.S. Liaison Office, with the understanding from President Carter himself that he would be negotiating a normalization of relations between the two countries.

Earlier, when Zhou Enlai and Mao had met with Kissinger and Nixon to improve U.S.-China relations, both sides were driven by the Soviet threat. When Deng met Vance in 1977, he too was driven by the Soviet threat. But in 1977 Deng was also beginning to consider what was needed for China to

311

modernize. He knew that Japan, South Korea, and Taiwan had relied heavily on U.S. science, technology, and education to achieve modernization. He had found that many of the patents for goods produced in Europe were held by U.S. individuals and companies, so that even technological help from Europe would require cooperation with the United States. Normalization of Sino-American relations was thus an important first step in building a relationship with the United States that would enable China to modernize.

To achieve his goal of normalizing relations with the United States, Deng was prepared to be flexible on many issues. On one issue, however—Taiwan—Deng, like Mao and Zhou, had an unshakable "principle." He would refuse to normalize relations with the United States unless the United States broke diplomatic relations with Taiwan, ended the U.S.-Taiwan Mutual Defense Treaty, and withdrew all its military forces from Taiwan. Deng expected that with the end of the Mutual Defense Treaty, Taiwan would see few options and would accept reunification; not only Deng but also many American officials expected this would happen within several years.

Cyrus Vance's "Step Backward," August 1977

Deng held high expectations for the visit of Secretary Vance, but U.S. politics again interfered. Carter had told Vance to lay the basis for an agreement with Beijing on normalization, but when Vance met President Jimmy Carter on the eve of his departure for Beijing, Carter expressed his concern about the Congressional support that was needed to pass the Panama Canal treaties (to end U.S. control over the Canal Zone). If the controversial matter of recognition of China were raised at the same time as the Panama issue was being resolved, the powerful Taiwan lobby would stir up enough opposition in Congress to derail support for the Panama Canal treaties. Carter thus believed that it was necessary to postpone the question of normalization with China until the Panama Canal treaties were concluded. Once the issue with Panama had been settled, Congressional support would be sufficient to normalize relations with China.

Vance personally believed at the time that achieving détente with the Soviet Union through the Strategic Arms Limitation Treaty (SALT) talks, a project that absorbed much of his working time, was a more urgent priority than normalizing relations with China. If the United States began the normalization process before the SALT talks were completed, it might upset the Soviet Union and, in Vance's view, potentially derail the SALT negotiations.

Moreover, since Carter was in no hurry to move ahead, Vance felt it would be worth trying to negotiate with China for a stronger governmental presence in Taiwan than the Japanese had been able to obtain when they had normalized relations with China.

Even before Vance arrived in Beijing, the Chinese began to get an inkling of the stance that Vance might take. In keeping with usual Chinese practice, Foreign Minister Huang Hua first met with Vance, then passed on Vance's concerns to Deng, who then could prepare to discuss the key issues. In his presentation to Foreign Minister Huang Hua on August 21, Vance explained that the United States hoped to move toward normalization, but it wanted to retain some government personnel on Taiwan. He also explained that the United States was interested in a peaceful settlement of the Taiwan issue.

Vance expected the Chinese to be disappointed, but he did not anticipate how upset they would be. On the following morning when Vance met Huang Hua for a second session, Huang Hua exploded with a lengthy diatribe attacking Vance's proposal that the United States would keep some official representation on Taiwan. Huang Hua went so far as to speak of "liberating Taiwan," implying that mainland Chinese forces were ready to attack if necessary.[2]

That same afternoon, when Deng met with Vance, Deng began by jokingly reminding Vance that the last time they had met was in 1975, just before he, Deng, was dismissed from all his positions for the third time. He added: "I am internationally a well-known man. It is not because I have any capability. . . . It is because I have been three times up and three times down."[3] Vance later acknowledged that during the meeting Deng had been the "embodiment of Chinese courtesy," but he was tough in criticizing the U.S. stance on Taiwan.

Deng began his discourse with a broad tour of the international political landscape that focused on the overall balance of power between the West and the Soviet Union and on their relative strength in Africa, the Middle East, and Eastern Europe. He concentrated on two issues: how to respond to the Soviet challenge and how to resolve the Taiwan issue. Deng, who had been critical of the United States for being too soft on the Soviet Union since 1974 when he had criticized Henry Kissinger for promoting détente, was especially critical of U.S. passivity toward the Soviet Union after it withdrew from Vietnam.[4] He charged that Presidential Memorandum No. 10, concerning the Soviet Union, amounted to appeasement. Letting the Soviets have control of over a third of Germany after World War II had given the Soviets effective control over the Balkans, which in turn had had a huge influence on southern Europe. Although he did not mention the board game *weiqi,* in effect Deng was telling Vance that the Soviets, who already had pieces in Yugoslavia, were beginning to place others in Austria and would move from there to other parts of Western Europe. Deng warned against continuing concessions to the Soviets: "You will end up with a Dunkirk."[5]

Concerning Taiwan, Deng referred to two documents: a summary of the presentation by President Ford in December 1975, and a statement by Kissinger that Deng asked Nancy Tang to read aloud to Vance. In these two statements, Kissinger and Ford both indicated that the United States was ready to accept the Japanese formula for normalization that would keep only unofficial American representatives in Taiwan. Deng claimed that, at present, the United States was occupying Taiwan, which was a part of China, and so was blocking Taiwan's unification with the mainland. Further, he said that the U.S. request for China not to use force to absorb Taiwan amounted to interference in the internal affairs of another country. In answer to Vance's assertion that the United States was concerned about the security of Taiwan, Deng told him that "the Chinese people themselves are more concerned about the issue pertaining to their own country than the United States." China was patient, Deng explained, but America should realize that the Chinese would not put off the resolution of this question indefinitely.[6] Deng criticized Vance's proposal for trying to maintain personnel in Taiwan as creating, in effect, a "flagless embassy."[7] But he added that if the United States still wanted to hold on to Taiwan, China would wait.[8] Deng concluded: "I would like only to point out that your present formula is a retreat from the previous state of affairs. . . . To be candid, we cannot agree to your formula. But we still look forward to further discussions." On August 28, after Vance returned to the United States, officials who had traveled with him tried to give a positive spin to the visit despite Deng's rejection of Vance's position. They told reporters that Vance had successfully conveyed the U.S. perspective. Reporter John Wallach, who listened to a government official's explanation, wrote that China was softening on the Taiwan issue. Vance, despite valiant efforts, could not stop Wallach's inaccurate report from being published and from receiving a great deal of attention.[9] Deng, not about to soften on Taiwan or to tolerate this misunderstanding, angrily denounced the Wallach report as completely inaccurate.

Deng still wanted progress on the relationship with the United States, so he tried other approaches. Believing Vance was a bad partner, he sought to involve the White House in the negotiations and have Brzezinski as his counterpart. He also went directly to the U.S. media and to the U.S. Congress to build support for normalization. At a time when China was just beginning to emerge from isolation, there was not yet a mainland China lobby to match the Taiwan lobby in the United States; in fact, the Chinese Liaison Office in Washington had scarcely begun to build a staff to work with Congress or the U.S. media. The best single channel China possessed for influencing the U.S. media and Congress was Deng himself. He made full use of U.S. curiosity about China and of his frankness, charming wit, and feistiness. On September 6, Deng hosted a high-level U.S. media delegation headed by Keith Fuller, managing editor of the Associated Press, which included Arthur O. Sulzberger, publisher of the *New York Times,* and Katharine Graham, publisher of the *Washington Post.*

In their wide-ranging discussion, Deng talked of the problems left over from Lin Biao and the Gang of Four, the need to send Chinese students abroad for advanced training to help China overcome its backwardness, and the need to provide material incentives to Chinese workers. But above all, Deng zeroed in on the Taiwan issue, declaring flatly that Vance's proposal regarding Taiwan represented a step backward that China could not accept. To normalize relations with China, the United States had to end its military pact with the Nationalist Chinese, break diplomatic relations with them, and withdraw all its troops from the island. China would strive to resolve the Taiwan issue peacefully, but the matter was entirely a domestic one and China would not accept foreign interference.[10]

On September 27, Deng saw Republican leader and future president George H. W. Bush, whom he had known since 1975, when Bush had headed the U.S. Liaison Office in Beijing. Deng repeated to Bush what he had told Vance—U.S. policy toward the Soviet Union amounted to appeasement. As reinforcement, an authoritative editorial in the *People's Daily* stated: "Certain leading figures of the U.S. monopoly bourgeoisie have forgotten the lessons of Munich."[11] Deng told Bush that in normalizing relations, China had no room to maneuver on the Taiwan issue.[12] Democratic senators Ted Kennedy and Henry M. Jackson, known to favor normalization, were also invited to visit Beijing. On January 4, 1978, Deng stressed to Kennedy that he wanted an agreement as soon as possible. The chief barrier was Taiwan and, Deng repeated, the Taiwan problem was an internal issue. As China anticipated, Kennedy, upon returning to Washington, drew on his visit with Deng to advocate speeding up normalization. On February 16, 1978, Deng met with

Senator Henry Jackson, an ally in taking a hard line toward the Soviet Union. Meanwhile, Deng and his foreign policy team kept up their criticism of U.S. appeasement of the Soviet Union and the failure of the United States to push ahead on normalization.

When Ambassador Leonard Woodcock returned to the United States for a brief trip in early 1978, he publicly expressed his impatience with the lack of progress toward normalization. Before Woodcock had accepted his assignment in Beijing, Carter had offered him a number of cabinet posts that he had turned down, and he had agreed to head the U.S. Liaison Office with the understanding that he would carry on negotiations toward normalizing relations with China. On February 1, 1978, in an address to the United Auto Workers in Washington, Woodcock said that U.S. policy toward China was based "on an obvious absurdity": since the end of World War II, the United States had recognized the Nationalist government as representing all of China, but in fact the Nationalists could only represent the small island of Taiwan. Woodcock's statement about the absurdity of U.S. policy received wide publicity, causing Woodcock to worry that he might have upset Carter, who remained concerned about the SALT talks with the Soviet Union. But when Woodcock met Carter shortly after the speech, Carter told him privately that he agreed with him.[13]

Unlike Vance, who worried about being able to move forward on the SALT talks with the Soviet Union if normalization talks with China began, Carter decided that his administration could push forward on normalization negotiations with China at the same time it conducted the SALT talks. Another potential barrier, however, had to do with relations with Vietnam. Some in the administration were advocating that the United States respond to Vietnam's desire to normalize relations with the United States, but given the growing tensions between Vietnam and China, it seemed as though the United States had to choose to hold normalization talks with either one country or the other—not both. Carter resolved the debate by saying that U.S. interests would be better served by pursuing normalization with China. Carter thus gave the go-ahead for normalization talks with China. But fearing that the Taiwan lobby in Congress could derail their discussions, he insisted they be kept secret—that is, they had to be conducted by a small group of White House officials rather than by the State Department. To prepare for discussions on normalization, Carter dispatched to Beijing a White House official whose tough stance on the Soviet Union and readiness to hasten the normalization of U.S.-China relations were similar to Deng's. He was also the very person Deng had hoped to have as his counterpart: National Security Adviser Zbigniew Brzezinski.

Zbigniew Brzezinski's "Step Forward," May 1978

In mid-November 1977, Zbigniew Brzezinski and Michel Oksenberg, his deputy for Chinese issues, had begun to explore with Chinese representatives in Washington the possibility of his visiting Beijing in early 1978. He initially announced that his goal in visiting was to hold broad consultations on global issues; the issue of normalization was not mentioned.[14] But as soon as the Chinese Liaison Office in Washington was notified of Brzezinski's interest in visiting, Deng immediately responded that China would welcome him, and he lost no time in planning the trip; Deng would receive him as soon as the United States was ready.[15] On March 17, 1978, the day after Congress passed the first Panama Canal Treaty, the Chinese Liaison Office was notified that Brzezinski was ready to make the trip, and on April 19, the day after the second and final Panama Canal Treaty was signed, a date was set.[16] President Carter authorized Brzezinski to lay the groundwork for negotiations on normalization. From Carter's perspective, the ideal time to complete such negotiations would be just after the November 1978 Congressional elections. He felt optimistic that, with the Panama Canal treaties successfully concluded, he could obtain Congressional support for both a SALT treaty with the Soviet Union and a formal agreement to normalize relations with China.

When President Carter privately told Congressional leaders from both parties about his intention to begin talks on normalization, they responded positively; they believed that doing so was in the best interest of the United States. But the issue was still politically charged. As one congressman added: if the issue became public, he would have to oppose it.[17] In his talks in Beijing, Brzezinski communicated this concern to Deng, saying, "I would like to suggest that these discussions be confidential and that no advance publicity be issued . . . [this] would minimize some of the political complications . . . in our country." Deng replied, "Please rest assured that in China there are better conditions to maintain secrecy than there are in the United States." Brzezinski agreed: "I am afraid you are absolutely right. That is why it is better to conduct . . . [the negotiations over normalization] here rather than in Washington."[18]

Though Vance was personally concerned about upsetting the Soviet Union during the continuing sensitive disarmament talks, he was a loyal official and followed Carter's instructions; he had his staff draw up a plan for U.S.-China discussions on normalizing relations. When Carter received Vance's June 13, 1978, memo on the matter he penned in his comments: "Leaks can kill the whole effort. We should limit the dispatches and negotiating information strictly. . . . Avoid any public hints of degree of progress. I don't trust: 1) Congress, 2) the White House, 3) State, or 4) Defense to keep a secret." Like the Republicans, Nixon and Kissinger before them, the Democrats—Carter, Brzezinski, and Vance—all believed that even in a democratic country, strict secrecy would be necessary.[19] And just as in Kissinger's White House days, the highly secret channel to Beijing from the White House worked to reinforce the influence of the White House National Security staff in personal and institutional rivalries relative to their State Department counterparts.[20] Deng, for his part, supported using the White House channel instead of going through the State Department.

On May 21, 1978, the first morning after arriving in Beijing, Brzezinski met with Foreign Minister Huang Hua. As Kissinger and Zhou Enlai had done before, Brzezinski and Huang Hua exchanged views on global developments, discussing key issues on each of the continents, with particular emphasis on the prevailing balance of power between the Soviet Union and the West. As Brzezinski observed in responding to Huang Hua's presentation, the two agreed on a wide range of issues, but there were some important differences: the United States did not seek to establish hegemony and accepted a world of diversity; the United States did not believe that war was inevitable; and the United States was not appeasing the Soviet Union but rather competing with the Soviets on a worldwide scale. Knowing that the results of their conversation would be passed on to Deng, whom he would be seeing later that afternoon, Brzezinski told Huang Hua that Carter had authorized him to say that the United States accepted the three Chinese conditions concerning Taiwan, but that the United States would reserve the right to announce that resolution of the issues between mainland China and Taiwan should be achieved peacefully.[21]

That afternoon, Deng met with Brzezinski for over two hours and then over dinner, as the two discussed global strategy and laying the ground for talks on normalization. Deng, knowing that Brzezinski had just arrived, graciously suggested "you must be tired," but Brzezinski replied, "I am exhilarated." Deng and Brzezinski each firmly upheld his nation's point of view, but Brzezinski later wrote, "Deng immediately appealed to me. Bright, alert, and shrewd, he was quick on the uptake, with a good sense of humor, tough, and very direct. . . . I was impressed by his sense of purpose and drive. Deng quickly got to the point. . . . The Chinese side speaks straightforwardly about their views and ideas. Deng explained that 'it is not difficult to understand China . . . Chairman Mao Zedong was a soldier, Zhou Enlai was a soldier, and I, too, am a soldier.'" (To which Brzezinski replied that Americans were also very direct.) Brzezinski was so enthusiastic about his visit with Deng that on May 26, when he reported back to Carter, Carter wrote in his diary, "Zbig . . . was overwhelmed with the Chinese. I told him he had been seduced."[22]

In his talks with Brzezinski, Deng probed to see how prepared the United States was to break relations with Taiwan. "The question remains how to make up one's mind. If President Carter has made up his mind on this issue, I think it will be easier to solve. . . . What do you think should be done in order to realize the normalization?" Brzezinski, after explaining Carter's determination to move ahead and to accept the Chinese principle regarding cutting off relations with Taiwan, proposed that the two sides begin confidential talks about normalization in June. Deng immediately accepted the proposal, while continuing to inquire about what concrete measures the United States would take to implement the three principles on Taiwan. When he said, "We look forward to the day when President Carter makes up his mind," Brzezinski replied: "I have told you before, President Carter has made up his mind."[23] Without spelling out any concrete actions the United States would take, Brzezinski repeated that the United States accepted the three principles. He went on to say that the United States planned to release a statement stressing the importance of the mainland and Taiwan resolving the Taiwan issue peacefully. Deng assured him that China did not object to the United States making such a statement, but "we cannot accept this as a condition. Taiwan is a domestic issue. It is an issue of basic sovereignty."[24] Brzezinski concluded from this that if the United States were to make such a public statement, China would not publicly oppose it. Brzezinski also informed Deng that, beginning in July, Leonard Woodcock would be prepared to enter into serious discussions with Huang Hua to explore whether normalization could be achieved on mutually acceptable terms.[25]

Deng expressed concern about the military expansion of the Soviet Union and he repeated his view that the United States was not responding with sufficient firmness. Deng talked of the growing military cooperation between the Soviet Union and Vietnam, as evidenced by Vietnamese general Vo Nguyen Giap's two recent trips to Moscow, one in March and the other in early May. Deng, convinced that it was in China's interest to have the West build up its forces in Europe, which would lead the Soviet Union to move troops from Asia to Europe, argued, as Mao and Zhou Enlai had done earlier, that the Soviets' major goals were in Europe, not Asia. Deng needled Brzezinski, pushing the United States to stand tougher in responding to Soviet actions. "Perhaps," he said, "you have a fear of offending the Soviet Union. Is that right?" Brzezinski replied, "I can assure you that my inclination to be fearful of offending the Soviet Union is rather limited." Deng pressed hard, pointing out the disadvantages to the United States of signing a SALT agreement with the Soviets, saying, "Whenever you are about to conclude an agreement with the Soviet Union, it is the product of concession on the U.S. side to please the Soviet Union." Brzezinski responded, "I would be willing to make a little bet with you as to who is less popular in the Soviet Union—you or me."[26]

Brzezinski also sought to use his visit to develop closer relationships between the bureaucracies in Beijing and Washington, and the Chinese responded positively. He brought several U.S. officials from different government departments to engage in more detailed discussions with their counterparts. Morton Abramowitz, a senior diplomat then on loan to the Defense Department, for example, met with his Chinese counterparts in defense to discuss issues such as their respective analyses of the Soviet Union.

During their meeting, Deng pressed Brzezinski on U.S. restrictions on the export of technology to China. He cited three high-tech import cases: a U.S. supercomputer, a Japanese high-speed computer with U.S. parts, and a scanner. In all three cases, the U.S. manufacturers were eager to sell, but they had been blocked by the U.S. government.

Also during the discussions, Deng alluded to his interest in visiting the United States, saying he had only about three years left as top leader. From this, Brzezinski concluded that Deng had a sense of urgency about making progress on Sino-American relations. Brzezinski, knowing that Deng would not visit the United States until normalization had been completed, showed his confidence that they would finish such talks quickly by inviting Deng to have dinner at his Washington home. Deng immediately accepted.[27]

Brzezinski also encouraged Deng to deepen China's relationship with Japan, and after the Brzezinski visit, Deng moved quickly to conclude the Sino-Japanese Treaty of Peace and Friendship. On his way home, Brzezinski did his part as well, stopping off in Japan to brief Japanese officials about U.S. plans to begin negotiations with China on normalization. When Brzezinski returned to Washington, Carter, even as he teased Brzezinski about being seduced by the Chinese, judged the visit a success. Discussions on normalization would begin soon and relations had warmed: shortly afterward, when the United States asked that Beijing cease its stream of public criticism of U.S. policies, China complied immediately.

To keep up the pressure on the United States to move quickly on normalization, only one day after Deng talked with Brzezinski, Deng told an Italian delegation that China would welcome trade and technology exchanges with the United States, but would give preferential treatment to those countries with which it had regular diplomatic relations.[28] On June 2, less than two weeks after Brzezinski met with Deng, Huang Hua in Washington told Cyrus Vance that if he wanted Deng to visit the United States, which he would do only after normalization was completed, they had to work harder, because Deng was getting older. On August 6, Deng reiterated, this time to an Austrian delegation, that China would give preference in trade to countries with which it had formal diplomatic relations.[29] And on September 27, Chai Zemin, head of the Chinese Liaison Office in Washington, told Brzezinski that the pace of the normalization negotiations was too slow.[30]

The Leap Forward in Educational Exchanges

When it became likely that relations with the United States could be normalized within a few months, Deng focused immediately on the area at the top of his American wish list: not trade, not investment, but science. To Deng, science was the most crucial factor for achieving modernization, and the United States was far ahead. Fortunately, his combination of responsibilities (foreign relations, science, technology, and education) gave him the authority to move in this area even prior to the Third Plenum. He would not send students to the United States before normalization, but as soon as relations were normalized he wanted to be prepared to send young Chinese scientists to the United States for further training.

At China's first National Science Conference in March 1978, Chinese scientists were told by the Chinese government, for the first time since the early 1950s, that they were not only permitted, but encouraged, to have contacts with fellow scientists in the West.[31] Relatives of Chinese-American scientists who had remained in China and had become targets in the numerous campaigns after 1949 were given better housing and better working conditions, and Chinese scientists were no longer labeled landlords, capitalists, or rightists. It was impossible, of course, to make up for the years of torment and broken careers, but the government gave compensation for their past suffering, and high officials in effect apologized to them (while recommending that when they met Western scientists they should not elaborate about past troubles with the Chinese government).

Deng encouraged not only Chinese-Americans but all Western scientists to visit China, and American scientists, who overwhelmingly believed in the universality of scientific research, were happy to oblige. From July 6–10, 1978, President Carter's science adviser, Frank Press, led the highest-level delegation of U.S. scientists ever to visit any foreign country. Press, formerly an MIT professor specializing in earthquake science, had been chairman of the U.S. Committee on Scholarly Communication with the People's Republic of China (CSCPRC) from 1975 to 1977, and therefore took a special interest in scholarly exchanges with China. Deng spoke to Press's delegation about China's backwardness in science and technology and expressed his concerns about American constraints on high-tech exports. He also spoke of China's need for foreign investment.[32]

In the question period following Deng's presentation, Richard Atkinson, head of the National Science Foundation, asked Deng if he feared that Chinese science students abroad might defect. Deng replied that he was not worried; Chinese students, unlike their Soviet counterparts, he said, were loyal to their country, and even those who studied abroad and did not return immediately would, in the long run, still be an asset for China. At the time, Frank Press expected that, as in the past, Chinese political leaders would continue to keep tight control over their scientists going to the United States and that they would be cautious about expanding scientific exchanges.

Frank Press was taken aback as Deng proposed that the United States immediately accept seven hundred Chinese science students, with the larger goal of accepting tens of thousands within a few years.[33] Deng was so intent on receiving a prompt answer that Press, considering this one of the most important breakthroughs in his career, called President Carter, waking him at 3 a.m. Washington time, to ask permission to agree that seven hundred Chinese students would be welcomed immediately and that far larger numbers could be accommodated within a few years. Carter, rarely awakened in the middle of the night during his presidency, responded positively, though he wondered why Press had woken him up to ask the question—he felt he had already given Press the authority to approve such requests.[34]

The Press delegation received great attention from the Chinese. The *People's Daily* rarely published speeches by foreigners, but in this case it printed Press's banquet speech stressing the advantages of globalization. And Michel

Oksenberg, Brzezinski's deputy for China policy who sat in on some fourteen meetings with Deng, said he never saw Deng more intellectually curious and more involved in articulating his vision about China's future.[35]

Indeed, with the exception of President Nixon's visit, Press received the warmest reception a U.S. delegation had received in Beijing since 1949.[36] Since Deng would not send students abroad before the two countries established normal diplomatic relations, the first group from China, some fifty students, eager but tense about whether they would later be in trouble for their American connections as their elders had been, flew off to America in early 1979 shortly after normalization. In the first five years of exchanges, some 19,000 Chinese students would go to the United States for study, and the numbers would continue to increase.

Breakthrough on Normalization, June–December 1978

Following Brzezinski's visit to China, the United States and China began secret discussions on how to structure negotiations for normalization. Both sides realized from the beginning that Taiwan was the issue that would either make or break the deal. On June 28, Vance cabled Woodcock with the U.S. proposals for normalization talks, to be presented to Foreign Minister Huang Hua: if cultural and commercial contacts were able to continue between the people of Taiwan and the people of the United States while the Chinese peacefully resolve the Taiwan question, the president was prepared to normalize relations within the framework of the three principles enunciated by China. Meetings would be held in Beijing every two weeks to discuss sequentially a series of issues that had to be resolved before normalization. Woodcock also proposed that at the regular Beijing meetings the two parties first discuss the nature of the post-normalization U.S. presence in Taiwan and the nature of formal statements announcing normalization. That is, negotiators would first deal with the easy issues to show progress; only later would they take on the more difficult issues, such as U.S. arms sales to Taiwan. Their goal was to have an agreement by December 15, several weeks after the U.S. Congressional elections.[37] The first meeting, held on July 5, was a forty-minute session during which the two sides discussed procedures and each made an initial general statement on its Taiwan position.[38]

On the Chinese side, Deng was kept informed but did not take part directly in the negotiations until the very end. Foreign Minister Huang Hua, who negotiated initially for the Chinese side, had unrivaled experience in dealing with Americans. In 1936, he had guided Edgar Snow (author of *Red Star over China*) from Beiping (renamed "Beijing," northern capital, in 1949) to meet with Mao in northern Shaanxi. Huang, a survivor who had served Mao, Zhou Enlai, and Deng, masters with very different styles, was for a time during the Cultural Revolution China's only ambassador stationed abroad. He was cautious in revealing anything beyond what he was authorized to say and he could express both Deng's anger as well as his charming goodwill. In 1971 Huang Hua went to New York as the first ambassador to the United Nations from the People's Republic of China.[39] In negotiations over normalization, he was assisted by two of the ablest Chinese diplomats experienced in dealing with the United States, Zhang Wenjin and Han Nianlong.

Both sides brought their "A" team to the table. President Carter had chosen Leonard Woodcock, labor union leader and professional mediator, to head the Beijing Liaison Office with the rank of ambassador, because Carter valued his negotiating skills and because he had strong political connections in Washington that would make it easier to win Congressional support for any agreement he might reach. Woodcock could use his personal connections with political leaders in Washington to coordinate policies that could not be easily resolved by ordinary bureaucratic procedures. Woodcock had a reputation as a tough, trusted labor negotiator and was known for his integrity and decency. Secretary Vance called Woodcock an "instinctive and brilliant diplomat" with "a photographic memory, discretion, and a verbal precision critical in these negotiations."[40] Both the State Department and the White House had sufficient confidence in Woodcock that they saw no need for a high official to engage in "shuttle diplomacy" from Washington. By the time the negotiations began, Woodcock, who had already spent a year in the Beijing Liaison Office, was also trusted by Beijing officials and readily accepted as the negotiator.

Stapleton Roy, who arrived in Beijing in June 1978 to succeed David Dean as deputy chief of mission, had grown up in Nanjing where his father was a missionary educator. He spoke Chinese, had a deep knowledge of Chinese history, and was regarded as one of the ablest of the young professionals in the State Department. In the White House, President Carter, Vice President Walter Mondale, Brzezinski, and Michel Oksenberg communicated directly with Woodcock and Roy through highly secret channels. Oksenberg, Brzezinski's deputy for China matters, a bold and broad-scale strategist, was a politically savvy China scholar with unbounded curiosity and enthusiasm. In Washington, only a handful of officials outside the White House, including

Vance and Secretary of Defense Harold Brown, were kept informed. U.S. strategy was devised at the White House with inputs from Woodcock, and the White House kept in touch with Chai Zemin of China's Liaison Office in Washington and his deputy Han Xu, but the negotiations were conducted entirely in Beijing.

Deng Xiaoping followed Huang Hua's meetings with Woodcock on July 5, July 14, August 11, September 15, and November 2; and when Huang Hua became ill, Han Nianlong's meeting with Woodcock on December 4. He then personally conducted the final negotiations with Woodcock (at 10 a.m. on December 13, 4 p.m. and 9 p.m. on December 14, and 4 p.m. on December 15). During the negotiations, Deng continued to meet U.S. officials, explaining the Chinese position and pressing for the negotiations to move ahead. On July 9, for example, four days after the first session between Woodcock and Huang Hua, Deng told a U.S. Congressional delegation headed by Congressman Lester Wolff, head of the U.S. House of Representatives Foreign Affairs Committee, that accepting the Japanese formula for maintaining a full range of private relations with Taiwan already represented a Chinese concession. Deng said that "we will do our best to create conditions to solve this question by peaceful means." He explained that "it is in both of our great interest in dealing with the Soviet Union if we can normalize relations." Deng gave the Wolff delegation absolutely no hint that negotiations had already begun.[41]

In their negotiations, the Chinese normally prefer to start with general principles, then move on to the details. At the second meeting with Woodcock on July 14, Huang Hua said that instead of dealing with one issue at a time, the Chinese side preferred that the United States first put all the major issues on the table so that the two sides could examine the whole package. In the days that followed, different views on the U.S. side in Washington were resolved by accepting Woodcock's recommendation that, in the interest of creating a good mood for further discussions, they should accept the Chinese suggestion. Both sides then prepared their positions and exchanged several papers on the key issues that needed to be resolved. At the third meeting, on August 11, the United States outlined the nature of its relations with Taiwan after normalization with the mainland: cultural, commercial, and other relations would continue, but without official U.S. government representation.

The single most difficult issue in negotiations was whether the United States would continue to sell weapons to Taiwan.[42] The United States had made it clear that it intended to continue selling weapons, but each time the issue was raised, the Chinese responded that they were bitterly opposed. Deng had hoped that if the United States agreed to stop selling arms to Taiwan, then Taiwan would feel it had no realistic choice but to reach an agreement on reunification with the mainland, and he hoped that this might happen quickly, while he was still at the helm.

In making their case, the Chinese held fast to their interpretation of the Shanghai Communiqué: that the United States supported a "one-China" (mainland only) policy. In fact, in signing the Shanghai Communiqué, Richard Nixon only acknowledged that the two sides of the Straits both maintain there is only one China, and that the United States did not challenge that view. On September 7, 1978 when Assistant Secretary of State Richard Holbrooke told Han Xu that any weapons sold to Taiwan would be defensive in nature, Han Xu responded that "the sale of weapons to Taiwan is not in conformity with the spirit of the Shanghai Communiqué."[43] On September 19, when Carter announced to Ambassador Chai Zemin, then head of the Chinese Liaison Office, that "we will continue to trade with Taiwan, including the restrained sale of some very carefully selected defensive arms," Chai replied, "For the United States to continue to sell weapons to the Chiang Clique [Chiang Ching-kuo became the dominant leader after his father died in 1975] would not be in conformity with the spirit of the Shanghai Communiqué."[44] And on October 3, when Huang Hua met Vance at the United Nations, he reiterated in his prepared statement that the continued sale of arms to the "Chiang Clique" would contravene the principles of the Shanghai Communiqué.[45]

Still, when Deng visited Tokyo in early October, he publicly announced his willingness to normalize relations with the United States so long as the agreement followed the Japanese model. Without undermining China's opposition to U.S. weapon sales to Taiwan, he said he did not object to the continuation of economic and cultural relations between the United States and Taiwan.

By late October Carter and Brzezinski began to worry that, despite their care in limiting the number of people who knew about the negotiations, the danger of leaks would increase if the issues were not resolved quickly. Brzezinski informed Chai Zemin that if China did not seize this opportunity to normalize relations, political issues would prevent any serious discussion of the issues until late 1979. Shortly thereafter, the United States announced an agreement with Taiwan to continue selling it F-5E fighter planes, but not more advanced fighters.[46]

Meanwhile, the two sides had completed most of their negotiations, and on November 2 Woodcock presented the Chinese negotiators with a draft communiqué on normalization that was to be announced on January 1. The Chinese, however, busy at home with the dramatic changes occurring at the Central Party Work Conference that began on November 10, did not respond until December 4.[47] Deng himself had been in Southeast Asia from November 5 and as soon as he returned on November 14, he plunged into the Central Party Work Conference, from which he would emerge as the paramount Chinese leader.

On November 27, two days after Hua Guofeng, at the Central Party Work Conference, had in effect acknowledged the consensus to elevate Deng to the preeminent position by accepting all the criticisms of his position, Deng welcomed one of Washington's leading newspaper columnists, Robert Novak, who had been traveling in Asia at the time. It was the first time a major Chinese leader had granted an interview to an American journalist since Zhou Enlai had met with James Reston in 1971, just before Nixon traveled to China. Deng told Novak that relations between the United States and China should be normalized quickly, not only for the sake of both countries but also for peace and stability around the world. Novak did indeed publicize the message from Deng to the American public. He concluded, "I believe Deng devoted two hours for me to send Washington the message that he wanted normalization quickly and did not have a high asking price."[48] Novak did not then know that Deng would soon be traveling to the United States and that the interview would help prepare the U.S. public for his arrival.

Woodcock's December 4 negotiating session with Han Nianlong, now acting foreign minister (replacing Huang Hua who was ill), was the first meeting since November 2. What the Chinese side knew, but the United States side did not yet know, was that on November 25, Hua Guofeng had yielded to Deng as the preeminent leader and to Deng's approach to policy. On December 4, the Chinese side was suddenly very forthcoming. Han presented Woodcock with the Chinese draft of the announcement to be issued on normalization, with only slight revisions from the American draft, and called for a January 1 deadline for its release. Han explicitly said that if the U.S. side made a statement expressing hope for a peaceful solution of the Taiwan issue, the Chinese side would not contradict it. After the discussions concluded, as Woodcock was getting ready to depart, Han said, "Finally, I would like to tell you that Vice Premier Deng would like to meet you at an early date. We will let you know the definite time."[49] In his analysis sent to Washington, Woodcock said that Han objected to arms sales to Taiwan, but concluded that this issue was unlikely to be an insurmountable obstacle to normalization. Because the U.S. side did not know precisely when the meeting with Deng would take place, Woodcock asked Stapleton Roy to cancel a planned trip and to be available on short notice to participate in the meeting with Deng.[50]

Meanwhile, in Washington on the afternoon of December 11 (already December 12 in Beijing), the day before Deng would meet with Woodcock, Brzezinski met Chai Zemin to present a revised draft of the announcement on normalization, to convey to Chai that the U.S. side wanted to meet the target date of January 1 for normalization, and to invite a Chinese leader to the United States as soon as the agreement was completed. At the time, Hua Guofeng was still officially of higher rank than Deng, and the United States assumed that China would choose to send either Hua or Deng. Brzezinski also gave Chai advance notice that there might be a U.S. summit with Brezhnev in January.[51]

Deng met Woodcock on Wednesday, December 13, in the Jiangsu Room of the Great Hall of the People. After an exchange of pleasantries, Woodcock presented Deng with four copies of a one-page draft of the proposed communiqué in English. Deng asked his interpreter to translate it orally and instead of waiting for an official translation, he took up the issues on the spot without a Chinese text. He clearly wanted to move ahead without delay. Deng asked why, since the defense treaty with Taiwan was to terminate, it would take a year to remove the U.S. military presence from Taiwan. Woodcock explained that the United States was proposing to break off diplomatic relations with Taiwan as of January 1, and the existing treaty required a one-year notice before termination—although the United States was in fact planning to withdraw its forces within four months. Deng replied that the plan was acceptable but he also hoped that the United States would be willing simply to omit all reference to Article 10 (which called attention to the one-year period before termination of military relations). He also expressed his wish that the United States not sell arms to Taiwan during this time, because if the United States did sell arms, "Chiang Ching-kuo would strut his tail feathers and this would increase the chances of conflict over the Taiwan Straits."[52]

Deng noted that the Chinese draft of the communiqué mentioned the anti-hegemony clause and the U.S. draft did not. He said that the U.S. draft was satisfactory, but he hoped that the United States would add an anti-hegemony clause for their joint declaration; otherwise it might appear to the world as if the two sides disagreed. Woodcock said he would convey Deng's views to Washington and await an answer. Deng agreed that January 1 was a good date for making the announcement.

In response to the U.S. invitation for a high-level Chinese leader to come for a visit, Deng told Woodcock, "We accept the invitation of the U.S. government to visit Washington. To be specific, I will go there."[53] That same afternoon, on December 13, knowing that the issue of normalization with the United States had been basically resolved, Deng had an important new feather in his cap as he presented his epoch-making speech to the Central Party Work Conference on reform and opening.

The next day, December 14, Woodcock and Deng were supposed to meet at 4 p.m., but instructions from Washington had not yet arrived. The small Washington team, already overwhelmed, was trying to adjust to Carter's decision to speed up the announcement of normalization to the very next day, December 15, Washington time. As the level of activity at the White House had picked up in the rush to complete all the details by January 1, other officials had become suspicious that something was going on, so Carter, hoping to head off a leak and a resulting Congressional flare-up that could derail the process, had decided to push ahead and announce normalization on December 15 instead of January 1. The formal communiqué would then be released when relations were normalized on January 1. The small team in Washington that was working secretly on these negotiations—attempting to reach a consensus among the key players, writing draft documents, planning strategies for dealing with Congress, and considering the variety of adjustments needed for commercial, military, and academic activities—was pushed to the breaking point to make this accelerated deadline. State Department China specialist Roger Sullivan, at the invitation of the White House, reported sick at the State Department for three days while he joined the frantic secret effort at the White House to help churn out all the required documents.

The U.S. team in Beijing was working at a similarly frantic pace. Three decades later when the American embassy in Beijing moved into a new building, it had a staff of over a thousand, but in 1978 there were only thirty-three Americans working in the U.S. Liaison Office in Beijing, and among them only a handful were dealing with the highly secret preparations.[54] In addition, like the Washington team, they had expected to have until January 1 to complete all the negotiations and paperwork for normalization; it would take a herculean effort to get things in order for the new December 15 deadline.

When Deng and Woodcock met at 4 p.m. on December 14, Beijing time, in the absence of instructions from Washington, they focused not on substance but only on the scheduling of normalization and on Deng's forthcoming visit to the United States. Deng accepted the U.S. request to speed up the announcement on normalization, and he agreed to begin his visit on January 28, which was one of the few dates convenient for the U.S. side. The two men then adjourned, agreeing to meet later that evening when Woodcock expected to have the instructions from Washington at last.[55]

At the 9 p.m. meeting Deng and Woodcock discussed a series of minor changes in the wording for the joint communiqué and reached agreement fairly quickly, with an understanding that Zhang Wenjin and Stapleton Roy would together go over the wording to ensure that the Chinese and English texts were both correct and compatible. Washington had accepted Woodcock's suggestion that they accept China's request for an anti-hegemony clause, since it had already been included in the Shanghai Communiqué. The atmosphere at the meeting reflected the belief on both sides that they had reached an agreement. In his report of the meeting to Washington, Woodcock wrote: "Deng was clearly elated by the outcome of our session, called this a most important matter, and asked that his personal thanks be conveyed to the president, Secretary Vance, and Dr. Brzezinski." Woodcock reported to Washington that the meeting "went extremely well."[56]

Meanwhile, in a conversation with the Chinese Liaison Office in Washington, Brzezinski was surprised to hear that Ambassador Chai Zemin still thought the United States had agreed to cancel all military sales to Taiwan—and feared that Beijing might still misunderstand Washington's determination to continue to sell arms to Taiwan.[57] The United States had agreed to Deng's request not to make new arms sales during 1979, but it intended to resume sales thereafter. As Carter, Brzezinski, and Oksenberg began to focus on how they would present the normalization agreement to Congress, they worried that Congress would fix its attention immediately on the issue of military sales to Taiwan. If Beijing still thought there would be no further military sales, when sales were announced it could set back U.S.-China relations just as they were ready to be normalized.

The stakes were high: a misunderstanding on this point, on Deng's stated unshakable "principle," could derail relations between the two countries at a critical moment. Brzezinski therefore wired Woodcock to ask if he was certain that Beijing understood that military sales would continue. Woodcock and Roy immediately prepared a cable saying that each side had put its position on arms sales clearly on the record.[58] Woodcock replied to Brzezinski that they had previously told their Chinese counterparts: "Normalization will not preclude the American people from maintaining all the commercial, cultural, and other unofficial relations with the people of Taiwan which I described to Acting Foreign Minister Han on December 4." He also wrote that Acting Foreign Minister Han did raise "emphatic objection to arms sales after normalization." Upon receiving Woodcock's message, President Carter and Brzezinski believed there was still doubt as to whether Deng clearly understood that the United States would continue selling arms after 1979. Brzezinski therefore wired Woodcock to hold another meeting with Deng to make it absolutely clear that if Congress raised questions about arms sales to Taiwan, it would be politically impossible to answer that the United States would not resume arms sales after 1979. The United States, however, would try to sell arms in moderation.[59]

Deng agreed to Woodcock's urgent request to meet again. When they met, at 4 p.m. on December 15, Beijing time, Woodcock thanked Deng for his willingness to meet on such short notice. He explained that in the spirit of total frankness, President Carter "wants to be absolutely sure that there is no misunderstanding." He then read the statement sent from the White House that explained that politics in the United States required that arms sales to Taiwan would continue. Deng, furious but controlled, said that was totally unacceptable and he raged for ten minutes. Then he bellowed, "Why has this question of the sale of arms been raised again?" Woodcock explained that they did not want the president to say something in his announcement that would surprise the Chinese. Deng continued, "Does that mean that the President, in answering questions from correspondents, will say that after January 1, 1980 the United States will continue to sell arms to Taiwan?" Woodcock answered, "We will continue to keep alive that possibility, yes." Deng said, "If that is the case, we cannot agree to it because this actually would prevent China from taking any rational formula to have a dialogue with Taiwan to solve the problem of unification of the country." Deng explained that Chiang Ching-kuo could be extremely cocky. "A peaceful solution of the Taiwan issue would be impossible and the last alternative would be the use of force."[60]

At this point in the discussion, Woodcock assured Deng that the United States would approach the problem with utmost caution. Deng countered that the Chinese side had made it clear that China would not accept continued arms sales to Taiwan and that he had raised the issue the previous day. Woodcock took responsibility, saying that perhaps he had misunderstood. Deng became so upset that Woodcock and Roy had serious doubts as to whether Deng would agree to proceed with normalization.

After almost an hour of discussion and his torrent of objections, Deng said that the problem of Taiwan was the one problem remaining unresolved: "What shall we do about it?" Woodcock responded that he thought that after normalization, with the passage of time, the American people would accept that Taiwan was part of China and they would support unification—which at the time, many American officials as well as Chinese officials expected would occur within several years. The important first task, Woodcock said, was to accomplish normalization. Deng then replied, "hao" (okay). With that word, the impasse was overcome.

As the meeting was ending, Deng cautioned that if President Carter called public attention to U.S. arms sales to Taiwan, the Chinese side would have to respond, and that any public quarrel over the issue would reduce the significance of normalization. Woodcock reassured Deng that the U.S. government would do everything possible to make the world realize that normalization was as significant as the two sides believed it to be. Deng then remarked, "OK. So we'll issue the documents as planned." With no consultation with any other Chinese officials, the decision on normalization was finalized.

There is no available record of Deng's personal calculations in making one of the most critical decisions in his life—the decision to normalize relations with the United States despite continued U.S. arms sales to Taiwan. Why did he agree to a decision he knew would thwart one of his most cherished goals, the reunification of Taiwan with the mainland during his lifetime? At the time, Deng was just emerging as the first leader among equals, and it is possible that he calculated that achieving normalization would strengthen his personal position among the Chinese leadership. Perhaps more important, Deng also knew that normalization of relations with the United States would make it far easier for China to have access to the knowledge, capital, and technology that China needed in its drive for modernization. A few weeks earlier Brzezinski had informed Chai Zemin that American politics provided a brief window of opportunity and that if they did not move quickly, the next chance would come at the end of 1979. So many years had gone by as new obstacles to normalization kept cropping up. Deng saw a good opportunity and he took it.

Another consideration high on Deng's concerns at the time was the increasing military threat from the Soviet Union to China's south. At the time, he believed there was a very real risk that the Soviet Union would advance into Vietnam and move on through Thailand and Malaysia to the Straits of Malacca. Deng believed that showing the face of Sino-American cooperation would make the Soviet Union more cautious. It would reduce the risk that the Soviet Union would respond to China's impending attack on Vietnam. Deng also knew that Brezhnev hoped to visit Washington before he did and that reaching an agreement with Woodcock would likely enable his visit to preempt Brezhnev's. Deng made a calculated decision because he did not have enough leverage to make the United States both normalize relations with China and stop arms sales to Taiwan. If he wanted normalization, he had to pay the high price of yielding on U.S. arms sales to Taiwan. He did not give up his goal of reuniting Taiwan with the mainland. After normalization he would use every opportunity to pressure Washington to reduce such sales.

The announcement of the accord was made simultaneously in Beijing and Washington. At 10 a.m. Beijing time on the morning of December 16 (and 9 p.m. in Washington the night of December 15), both sides released this joint communiqué: "The United States of America and the People's Republic of China have agreed to recognize each other and establish diplomatic relations as from January 1, 1979." President Carter made the announcement to the American public. In China, Hua Guofeng, who was still officially the top leader, held a press conference to announce the decision. When the news was broadcast in Beijing, the mood among the public as well as in party inner circles was jubilant.

The people in Taiwan, where Chiang Ching-kuo was awakened in the middle of the night to be told of the impending announcement, were as upset as the people in Beijing were euphoric. Taiwanese officials and their friends in the U.S. Congress were outraged, and other conservatives joined in criticizing U.S. officials ready to cooperate with "Communist enemies." But the image of two great nations with very different cultures extending the hand of friendship to create a peaceful world had appealed to the Americans and Chinese alike. As President Carter himself reported, "The serious opposition we had expected throughout our country and within Congress simply did not materialize. . . . The worldwide reaction was remarkably positive."[61]

Deng Visits the United States, January 28–February 5, 1979

Six weeks later, Deng—with his wife, Zhuo Lin; Woodcock and his wife, Sharon; and Deng's staff—boarded a Boeing 707 for the United States. Fellow passengers report that during the long flight, Deng spent most of his time alert and sober, not reading, not talking, but deep in thought. On some level, Deng must have felt overjoyed—he had not only successfully established formal relations with the United States, but also, on a more personal level, had returned triumphantly from a third purge to become the preeminent leader of China, and was about to become the first Chinese Communist leader to be a state guest of the United States.

Yet Deng's responsibility was heavy and his visit extremely important. Before he met a foreign guest, he would take a few minutes to order his thoughts about what he would say. Now he had to think about what he would say to many people. He would deliver some prepared speeches, but many of his talks would be improvised, without even notes. Moreover, he had already determined that China would attack Vietnam, and there was a danger the Soviets might in turn attack China. How could he secure U.S. cooperation against the Soviets without annoying President Carter, who was working toward an agreement with the USSR? What would he say to Carter about Vietnam? How could he be most effective in establishing good relations with the president, the Congress, and the American public so as to promote China's modernization? On January 9 he had told a visiting delegation led by Senator Sam Nunn that he would not discuss civil rights in the United States; he said he had some opinions critical of the way the United States exerts pressure about human rights, but he would not raise them.[62] How would he respond if there were pro-Taiwan demonstrators? How would he respond to Western TV anchormen? What would he say to the thirty-three Chinese reporters who were accompanying him and each day would be sending home news releases and TV reports for his Chinese audience? How could he keep up the pressure on the United States to reduce arms sales to Taiwan without antagonizing U.S. officials?

In preparation for Deng's arrival in Washington, Vance and his staff prepared for President Carter and other officials who would be receiving Deng briefing materials on Deng and the significance of the trip. In a thirteen-page memo, Vance called Deng "a remarkable man—impatient, feisty, self-confidently outspoken, direct, forceful, and clever." He predicted that Deng's objectives could include helping Carter to sell normalization to Congress and to the American people, broadening the U.S.-PRC relationship so that changes would become irreversible, pressing the United States to resist further Soviet expansion, and stimulating U.S. hostility to Vietnam. But the significance of the relaxation of tensions between the United States and China was even broader than these individual goals; it could "have a dramatic impact on the political and strategic landscape of Asia, and on the world."[63]

Before Deng's arrival, his trip had attracted the greatest public interest of any foreign leader's visit since Khrushchev's 1959 trip to the United States. The U.S. media were full of stories about Deng's comeback, his decision to push reform and opening to the West, his commitment to normalizing relations, and now his trip to the United States. *Time* magazine, in its January 1 issue, named Deng 1978 "Man of the Year" for his role in taking a closed Communist country onto a new open path. It acknowledged that Hua Guofeng was still the chairman, but called Deng the "architect" of China's four modernizations. *Time,* unaware of how much Hua had been wounded at the Central Party Work Conference, described Deng as the chief executive officer of China and Hua as chairman of the board.

For the American public, long curious about the mysterious, closed, ancient civilization on the other side of the world, Deng's trip provided a fascinating spectacle that attracted even more attention than Nixon's 1972 trip to China. Would this resilient, tiny leader be more like a "Communist"—rigid and ideological—or more open like Americans? U.S. businesspeople, with visions of what they might sell to China as its huge potential market opened up, vied to receive invitations to the state banquet and other meetings. And news agencies that hoped to establish bureaus in China competed for chances to be noticed by Deng and his delegation.

President Carter, like Deng, appeared subdued and serious as the trip began. His efforts to bring about peace in the Middle East, which originally had seemed so promising, had just collapsed and his popular support in the polls had dropped to around 30 percent. He had expressed concern about how the public and Congress would respond to his decision to break formal relations with Taiwan and to normalize relations with the Communist mainland. Would members of Congress, kept in the dark during the negotiations over normalization, express their annoyance at not being consulted? Among Taiwan supporters, Carter was vulnerable to charges that he had abandoned an old partner, and that he had notified Chiang Ching-kuo in such a disrespectful manner: by having U.S. officials awaken him in the wee hours to tell him that later that day the United States would announce it was breaking diplomatic relations with Taiwan and normalizing relations with the mainland.

Deng's trip had been arranged quickly; he arrived in Washington on January 28, less than six weeks after the December 15 agreement. Officials on both sides worked very hard to make the trip a success, and the visit generally went smoothly. Deng's plane landed at Andrews Air Force Base and he was taken by limousine to Blair House in the capital, where distinguished U.S. government guests were housed. Knowing of Deng's habit of using a spittoon, his American hosts placed several shiny new spittoons in Blair House. Other details had been carefully considered. During his trip Deng would not be taken to places with military equipment or other technology that could not be sold to China. Any meat served to the Chinese delegation was sliced in small portions rather than huge pieces so as to be easier to manage for officials accustomed to eating with chopsticks. Indeed, when Georgia governor George Busbee asked Deng if he had discovered anything unique about America, Deng, tongue in cheek, replied that he didn't know Americans had veal at every meal. Conscientious hosts in Washington and Atlanta, briefed on Deng's preferences, which included meat like veal, had served him veal for several dinners in a row. At his next meal, no veal was served.

U.S. hosts were worried about security, especially at open-air appearances. During the welcoming ceremony on the White House lawn, two men in the press section who yelled "Long Live Chairman Mao" were whisked away by security officers, and Deng appeared unconcerned.[64] In an era before metal detectors could screen for weapons on people at entrances to buildings, security personnel took what precautions they could. One concern was bad weather impeding the flow of the limousines. Aside from Washington, then, two of the four cities selected for the tour, Atlanta and Houston, had warm climates and the third, Seattle, had a mild climate. It was natural to select Atlanta in Carter's home state. When Woodcock had asked Deng on January 1 what he wanted to see during his trip, Deng had responded immediately that he wanted to see space exploration facilities and other advanced technologies.[65] After Houston, where he was shown NASA facilities as well as state-of-the-art oil-drilling technology, he flew to Seattle, where Boeing was producing the new jet planes that China was just beginning to purchase. Deng was interested in production, not consumption. He toured no shopping malls or private homes (except for a dinner at Brzezinski's home, with guests). In Atlanta, he visited one of Ford Motor Company's most modern plants, where he was guided by Henry Ford II, who had previously met with Deng in Beijing.

Deng had no high-ranking adviser on America to compare with Liao Chengzhi on Japan, but he had Foreign Minister Huang Hua, who had lived for several years in the United States, and Li Shenzhi, head of the Institute of American Studies of the Academy of Social Sciences in Beijing, who had conducted a serious study of American history and religion. In addition, Deng's main interpreter, Ji Chaozhu, had spent many of his childhood years in the United States and had studied at Harvard until his junior year when he returned to China in 1950.[66]

During Deng's visit to the United States, officials at the Chinese Liaison Office in Washington, which on March 1 was to become the embassy of the People's Republic of China, were so overstretched that they were not even answering the phones. Having learned English in China and with little experience in the United States, Chinese officials were overwhelmed with their responsibilities, which included security, logistics, coordination with their American hosts, preparation for toasts and speeches, and inquiries from some 950 Western press people, as well as the thirty-three representatives of Chinese news agencies. They strained to get things right.

The Chinese media gave wide coverage to Deng's visit. China then had only one television set for every 1,000 people, and most of these were located in the offices of important officials. Single sets elsewhere were often viewed simultaneously by groups of many people. Chinese cities had only one TV station, the national station. Deng's entourage included not only reporters from the leading papers and from the New China News Agency (Xinhua), but also China's leading news commentator, Zhao Zhongxiang, who while in the United States was in charge of moderating a half-hour television program that was beamed back to China at the end of each day. In addition, a Chinese film crew was busy putting together a documentary film that would be shown in China at the end of the tour. For many Chinese, Deng's trip was a chance to see America and to get a sense of the country, its modern factories, its political leaders, and ordinary American people.[67] Deng encouraged this interest, hoping that it would help Chinese viewers realize just how backward China was and how much needed to be changed.

During his first few days of public appearances, Deng remained reserved. He was formal, serious, and extremely proper, even when waving his hand. He did not hold press conferences and he revealed little of what he was feeling.

Washington, D.C.

On January 28, after landing in Washington and resting for a few hours, Deng, as he had agreed to in May, attended a small, informal dinner at the home of his anti-Soviet and pro-normalization ally, Brzezinski. Although Deng understandably seemed tired from the long flight, Brzezinski reported that he and his wife displayed excellent humor and Deng proved to be a master of quick repartee. When Brzezinski said that the Chinese and French civilizations both think of themselves as superior to all others, Deng said, "Let us put it this way. In East Asia, Chinese food is best. In Europe, French food is best."[68] When Brzezinski commented that Carter had difficulties with normalization due to the (pro-Taiwan) China lobby, and asked whether Deng had encountered similar domestic opposition, Deng in a flash responded, "Yes. I did; 17 million Chinese on Taiwan were opposed."[69]

At one point, when Deng was asked how China would respond if it were attacked by the Soviet Union, he told his listeners, including Vice President Mondale, Secretary Vance, Brzezinski, and Michel Oksenberg, that the Chinese had nuclear weapons that could take out Bratsk Dam, Novosibirsk, and possibly even Moscow. Like Mao, who had said China could survive a nuclear war and an invasion by carrying on a protracted war that wore down the invaders, Deng had thought through the worst-case scenarios. Amid the informal conversation, Deng solemnly told Brzezinski that he would like a private group meeting with the president to talk about Vietnam.[70]

The next day, January 29, Deng had morning and afternoon sessions with President Carter, a lunch hosted by Secretary Vance, and a state dinner. Carter wrote in his diary that night, "It's a pleasure to negotiate with him."[71] Deng, he wrote, listened very carefully and asked questions about Carter's comments. At their third and final session, which was held the following morning, Brzezinski reported that Carter and Deng were frank and direct; their discussions were more like those between allies than between adversaries.

At the opening session, Deng asked Carter to speak first. Carter presented his view of the international situation, emphasizing that the United States felt a responsibility to assist the people of the world to achieve a better quality of life, including political participation, liberation from persecution by their governments, and freedom from outside hegemons. When it was his turn, Deng said that Chinese leaders had always felt that the greatest dangers came from the two dominant powers, but recently they had begun to understand that the danger from the United States was less than that from the Soviet Union. Deng then became intense and deadly serious as he spoke of the looming dangers of Soviet expansionism. He acknowledged that it was not advantageous at this point for the United States and China to form an alliance, but he believed that the two should cooperate closely in resisting expansion by the Soviet Union.

Deng described Vietnam as the Cuba of the East, a Soviet base threatening China from the south. In Deng's view, the Soviets and Vietnamese had established an Asian collective-security system that endangered all nearby countries. And because "the Chinese need a long period of peace to realize their full modernization," China and the United States should coordinate activities to constrain the Soviets. It was not yet possible for China to have direct contact with South Korea, but Deng hoped as well that North and South Korea would hold talks leading to a reunification.[72] Japan, too, which Deng had visited in October, could cooperate to limit Soviet expansionism. (Just before he left for the United States, Deng had told Hedley Donovan of *Time* magazine that China should work with both Japan and the United States against the Russian polar bear.[73])

Toward the end of their afternoon meeting—the second of the three sessions, held January 29—Deng again requested a small private group meeting with Carter to discuss a confidential matter. Carter, Mondale, Vance, Brzezinski, Deng, and his interpreter then left the larger group and went into the Oval Office. There, during an hour-long meeting, in a grave but resolute manner Deng told of his plans to deliver a punitive strike in Vietnam. He explained the seriousness of the dangers posed by Soviet and Vietnamese ambitions in Southeast Asia, beginning with the Vietnamese occupation of Cambodia. Deng said it was necessary to disrupt Soviet calculations and teach the Vietnamese an appropriate, limited lesson. Carter tried to discourage Deng from attacking Vietnam, but he did not say he opposed the move. Instead he expressed concern that if China attacked Vietnam, it would be seen as an aggressor. He knew that would make it more difficult to win Congressional support for cooperation with China—especially since one of the administration's arguments for expanded relations with China had been to preserve peace.

The next day when Deng and Carter met privately to conclude discussions on the Chinese attack on Vietnam, Carter read Deng a handwritten note he had prepared overnight explaining why he advised against such a move. Among other points, Carter said that "armed conflict initiated by China would cause serious concern in the United States concerning the general character of China and the future peaceful settlement of the Taiwan Issue."[74] Deng explained why he stood behind his decision, but he assured Carter that if Chinese troops attacked, they would withdraw after ten to twenty days. Moreover, Deng insisted, the beneficial results of such a Chinese attack would be long-lasting. If China did not teach the Soviets a lesson this time, the Soviet Union would use Vietnam in the same way it had used Cuba. (Deng also predicted that the Soviets would move into Afghanistan, which in fact the Soviets did the following December.) Deng and Carter then returned to the larger group. Carter noted that Deng, having completed his truly serious business, became more relaxed and lighthearted.[75]

The United States and China were both concerned that the Soviets might enter into a conflict between Vietnam and China, and not long after Deng's visit, U.S. officials began issuing warnings about how provocative it would be if the Soviets were to begin using Vietnam's Cam Ranh Bay as a naval base.[76] Although Carter did not support the Chinese attack on Vietnam and later conveyed this to the Soviets, by the time the attack was launched in late February, Deng had achieved his goal of making the Soviets more cautious about joining the Vietnamese side, because they were now worried that the United States might retaliate in some way.

While in Washington, Deng pursued his interest in sending Chinese students to the United States. But President Carter had his own concerns related to student exchanges. He complained, first, that foreign students in China were kept separated from Chinese students. Deng explained that China did this because living conditions in Chinese universities were not good and China wanted to provide acceptable conditions for foreigners. When Carter next said that he did not want China to choose which foreign students were acceptable to study in China, Deng laughed and remarked that China was strong enough to withstand students of various backgrounds and would try not to use ideology as a basis for acceptance. He added that travel would still be limited for foreign journalists, but that there would be no censorship of their writing.

During their final meeting, Carter and Deng signed agreements on consular offices, trade, science and technology, and cultural exchanges. Deng asserted that the United States and Japan could make a contribution to world peace if they urged Taiwan to negotiate with Beijing and if the United States reduced arms sales to Taiwan. He told Carter that Beijing would go to war over Taiwan only if, over a long period of time, Taiwan refused to talk with Beijing, or if the Soviets became involved in Taiwan.[77]

Brzezinski described the state dinner for Deng as perhaps the most elegant dinner held in the four years of the Carter White House.[78] Carter himself reported that at the banquet, held on January 29, Deng's small size and exuberance made him a great favorite of his daughter, Amy, and the other children present, and that the pleasure seemed to be mutual.[79] In her description of their family life, Deng's daughter writes that her father deeply enjoyed playing with his grandchildren, even though he did not talk much.

Carter used the state banquet to engage Deng in a good-natured discussion of their different views of missionaries in China. Former Sunday-school teacher Carter, who in his youth had contributed his nickels through his church to missionaries in China, praised the role missionaries had played in China. He said that many of the missionaries who went to China were good people, and pointed to the schools and hospitals that they had established. Deng responded that too many missionaries had tried to change the Chinese way of life, and although he acknowledged that some schools and hospitals were still in operation, he also expressed his opposition to allowing missionary activities to resume. Carter then suggested that Deng allow the distribution of Bibles and freedom of worship, and when the president later visited China he felt satisfied that China had made progress in both of these areas.

Although Deng had been banished to the "Peach Garden" when Nixon visited China, he asked to meet Nixon to express his appreciation on behalf of the Chinese people for the former president's success in restoring relations between China and the United States. Carter agreed to Deng's request, allowing the two men to have a private visit. Carter also invited Nixon to the state banquet for Deng, the first time Nixon visited the White House since he had left in disgrace in August 1974.[80] After his visit, Nixon wrote a thoughtful private letter to Carter supporting Carter's decision to normalize relations and offering some ideas about the future of U.S.-China relations.[81]

A program at the Kennedy Center for the Performing Arts following the state banquet, which was broadcast on national television, was described by one official as "probably the most glittering evening of the entire Carter Administration."[82] Georgia peanut farmer Carter stood hand-in-hand with soldier Deng, each representing his country. As they were introduced to the audience, the band played "Getting to Know You."[83] And after a group of American children, including Amy Carter, sang some of Deng's favorite songs in Chinese, Deng, in a completely unscripted gesture, went up and kissed their hands. Vice President Mondale perhaps was not greatly exaggerating when he said there was not a dry eye in the hall.[84]

In his meetings with cabinet members, Deng focused on trade issues. Meeting them on January 31, Deng predicted that if China were granted most-favored-nation status, which, in fact, would mean ordinary trade relations, before long U.S. trade with the mainland (which was then about equal in value to U.S. trade with Taiwan) would expand tenfold. In his meeting with administration officials, Deng reached agreements ending the freeze on Chinese assets in the United States and on U.S. assets in China. U.S. administration officials agreed that, in addition to elevating the respective liaison offices to embassies, each country would establish two consulates in other cities. Deng discussed what needed to be done to permit direct airline flights between the two countries, and Chinese officials agreed to create a schedule for the U.S. media to set up news bureaus in China. Deng also carried on discussions about expanding academic and scientific exchanges.

Deng did not fully understand the process involved in gradually upgrading technologies nor did he fully grasp the calculations of private companies in using patents and copyrights to recoup their research and development expenses. Deng, just beginning to become aware of these complexities and filled with vaulting ambitions, simply declared that he did not want 1970s technology, but rather technology that was cutting edge.[85]

In meetings in the U.S. Senate, Deng was hosted by Senator Robert Byrd and in meetings in the House of Representatives by Speaker of the House Tip O'Neill. Deng was fascinated by O'Neill's discussion of the separation of powers, especially the ways in which the legislative and executive branches competed for power and influence. Deng took a personal liking to O'Neill, who, in response to Deng's invitation, later visited him in Beijing. But as O'Neill later wrote, Deng had absolutely no doubt that, at least for China, the separation of powers was a terribly inefficient way to run a country, something China should avoid.[86]

A key issue that came up during Deng's meetings in Congress was whether China would let people emigrate freely. Just four years earlier, Congress had passed the Jackson-Vanik amendment, which required Communist countries to allow those who wished to emigrate to do so before Congress would grant those nations normal trading relations. When members of Congress pressed Deng about whether China would let emigrants leave China freely, Deng replied, "Oh, that's easy! How many do you want? Ten million? Fifteen million?" He said this with a straight face, and members of Congress did not pursue the issue. China was given a waiver and allowed the benefits of most-favored-nation status.[87]

Despite the careful preparations, a major flaw occurred in planning the location for a reception attended by America's "China hands." The event was held in the beautiful new East Wing of the National Gallery, designed by Chinese-American architect I. M. Pei, to showcase the role of Chinese-Americans. The reception for the business, academic, and foreign policy communities interested in China was sponsored by the Foreign Policy Association, the National Gallery of Art, the National Committee on U.S.-China Relations, the Committee on Scholarly Communication with the PRC, the Asia Society, and the U.S.-China Business Council. It was a grand gathering of people from different sectors, many of whom had known each other in Hong Kong, then the main center for China watchers in government and journalism, business, and academic circles before China had begun to open. It was a festive occasion, the celebration of a day that many of the participants had been working for and waiting for. When I. M. Pei was later told about the reception, he was aghast that Deng had been asked to give a speech there, since the acoustics were not at all designed for a public address. Indeed, when Deng spoke, the reception participants, unable to hear what he was saying even with a microphone, continued casually chatting with friends. Those close to Deng knew he was upset, but he continued reading his speech without revealing any sign of discomfort, as if he were addressing disciplined party members sitting motionless at a party congress.[88]

Philadelphia, Atlanta, Houston, and Seattle

In his talks with Washington officials, Deng dealt with global strategic issues, but in his travels around the country he observed modern industry and transport as he encouraged American businesspeople to invest in China, academics to promote scholarly exchanges, and the general public to support closer relations between the two countries.[89] In his talks with businesspeople he stressed that China had many commodities that it could export to pay for the technologies he was so eager to obtain.[90] At most stops there were protestors waving Taiwanese flags. At some, boisterous American leftists protested Deng's bourgeois betrayal of the Maoist revolution. But the overwhelming mood of his audiences was supportive—a mixture of eager curiosity and goodwill.[91]

In the United States, Deng did not hold an open press conference and did not answer questions live on television. Yet U.S. reporters traveling with him were impressed with his accessibility and his continuing efforts to respond to their questions and to those of the U.S. businesspeople whom he met on the trip. He did meet the primary television networks' four anchormen.[92] And Don Oberdorfer, a distinguished diplomatic and Asian affairs reporter who traveled with Deng on his visits to the four cities, reported that Deng began to loosen up after his early days in Washington. At their stops, Deng raised his right hand and waved to crowds, then shook hands. To special friends like Senator Henry Jackson in Seattle, Deng gave bear hugs. Oberdorfer wrote of Deng, "His eyes glisten with the combination of uncertainty and fascination that is characteristic more of youth than age."[93]

When he received an honorary degree at Temple University in Philadelphia on January 31, Deng said in his speech, "Temple University is also noted for upholding academic freedom. This, I think, is an important factor for the thriving success of your university. Your conferring an honorary doctorate on me, a believer in Marxism-Leninism–Mao Zedong Thought, is ample proof of this. . . . The American people are a great people who, in the short span of two hundred years, brought into being gigantic forces of production and abundant material wealth, and made an outstanding contribution to human civilization. In the course of expanding production in the United States, a wealth of experience has been gained from which others can learn."

In Atlanta, Deng captivated President Carter's home state and dominated the media for days even though he stayed there only twenty-three hours. Addressing a luncheon of 1,400 people, he complimented the historic leaders of Atlanta who had reconstructed the city after the destruction of the Civil War.[94] He related the city's past experiences to China's current challenges: The American South had been considered a relatively backward area, "but it now has become a pacesetter. We in China are faced with the task of transforming our backwardness. . . . Your great encouragement has . . . increased our confidence."[95] Atlanta papers showed a picture of Deng's wife, Zhuo Lin, hugging Amy Carter and described her stay in Washington, when, accompanied by Mrs. Rosalynn Carter, she visited Amy's school, a children's hospital, and the pandas at the National Zoo.[96]

Woodcock recalls that in Houston, when Deng entered a replica of a spacecraft at the LBJ Space Center, "Deng was fascinated. . . . In that simulated vehicle, apparently coming in for the landing, he was so gleeful—I think he would have been willing to stay there all day."[97] And at a rodeo in Simonton, thirty-seven miles west of the city, Orville Schell reported, "Surrounded by his aides, ministers, and interpreters, pumping hands like a small-town pol, Deng . . . approaches the rail . . . a young girl on horseback gallops up and presents him with a ten-gallon hat. . . . The whistling, cheering crowd watches with delight as Deng theatrically dons his new hat. And in this one simple gesture, Deng seems not only to end thirty years of acrimony between China and America, but to give his own people permission to join him in imbibing American life and culture . . . arresting China's historic resistance to the West."[98] All over the United States, the photograph of Deng smiling beneath his ten-gallon hat became the symbol of his visit. It signaled to the U.S. public that he was not only good-humored, but, after all, less like one of "those Communists" and more like "us." The *Houston Post* headline read, "Deng avoids politics, goes Texan."[99]

In addition to touring the modern Ford and Boeing factories, oil-drilling facilities, and the Houston Space Center, Deng rode in sleek helicopters and hovercraft. By visiting modern industrial sites and the space center, Deng and his party reinforced their impressions from the visit to Japan about the scale of organizational and management changes that were needed to modernize China.[100] Pictures of Deng, along with the tall buildings and huge lines of cars on the highways, were televised throughout China.

At the end of his tour, in Seattle, Deng said, "Our two countries are neighbors on opposite shores of an ocean. The Pacific, instead of being a barrier, should henceforth serve as a link."[101] By the time Deng left Seattle for Tokyo, he had caught a cold. (As Woodcock recalled, "We were all exhilarated and exhausted.") So Foreign Minister Huang Hua substituted for him at a final breakfast meeting with reporters and editors. Just before departing, at a brief meeting held inside an airport terminal because of the cold drizzle outside, Deng, sniffling and with a fever, said, "We came to the United States with a message of friendship from the Chinese people, and we are going back laden with the warm sentiments of the American people."[102]

A Spark That Lit a Prairie Fire

In his personal diary, Jimmy Carter writes, "The Deng Xiaoping visit was one of the delightful experiences of my Presidency. To me, everything went right, and the Chinese leader seemed equally pleased."[103] Carter describes Deng as "smart, tough, intelligent, frank, courageous, personable, self-assured, friendly."[104] The president also appreciated that Deng was sensitive to American political realities and that he refrained from stressing the anti-Soviet basis of their relationship, comments that could have undone U.S. efforts to reach arms control agreements with the Soviet Union.[105]

The symbol of the trip—two nations joining hands to create a peaceful world—proved enormously appealing to both the Americans and the Chinese. To the extent that the trip's success depended on Deng's personal qualities, these included his genuine commitment to improving Chinese relations with the United States, his deep self-assurance, and his comfort with his special role. These qualities allowed him to give full play to his spontaneous frankness and sharp wit, as well as to delight in finding an appreciative audience. Some observant Chinese have noted that Deng did not exert himself in ordinary times, but when challenged, he could become fully energized, as he did in the United States.

Deng was not as colorful, flamboyant, opinionated, or boisterous as Nikita Khrushchev had been when, twenty years earlier, as leader of the Soviet Union, he had stormed the United States for thirteen days. If anything, Khrushchev had attracted even more attention. Both he and Deng were attempting to launch a new era in relations with the United States. Deng was more restrained, stuck to his script, and did not try to change his plans.[106] But Deng managed, through agreements establishing exchange programs and contacts with U.S. businesspeople, to lay deeper roots for a sustained U.S.-China relationship than Khrushchev had been able to do for U.S.-Soviet relations. American businesspeople who had heard Deng speak in the various cities immediately began to prepare for trips to China to explore business opportunities. Many of the seventeen governors who met him in Atlanta planned delegations to China with local businesspeople. Secretary of Commerce Juanita Kreps, Secretary of Agriculture Bob Bergland, and Secretary of Energy James Schlesinger also prepared to lead delegations in the months ahead to expand relations in their respective areas. Members of Congress, even many who had complained about China in the past, vied to join these and other trips to China. Five years after his visit, Khrushchev was toppled, but Deng, who remained paramount leader for over a decade after his visit, was able to witness the fruits of the seeds he had planted while in America.

On January 31, 1979, during his visit, Deng and Fang Yi, director of the State Science and Technology Commission, signed agreements with the United States to speed up scientific exchanges.[107] In early 1979, the first fifty Chinese students, promising but poorly prepared, arrived in the United States. In the year after Deng's visit, some 1,025 Chinese were in the United States on student visas, and by 1984, fourteen thousand, two-thirds of whom were studying the physical sciences, health sciences, and engineering, were attending American universities.[108] Peking and Tsinghua universities, the top universities in China, became known informally as "prep schools" for students who went to the United States for advanced training. The year 1979 may have marked a reopening of connections that had been cut off for three decades, but within only a few years the scale and scope of the exchanges would far surpass those in the years before 1949.

Thoughtful State Department officials, although thoroughly convinced of the value of restoring U.S.-China relations, expressed concern about the peaks in America's emotional response to China during Deng's visit. They worried that the U.S. administration and the U.S. media had oversold China to the American public, just as they had oversold Chiang Kai-shek during World War II, when the United States was allied with China and the American public had been unprepared for the corruption rampant within the Guomindang. After Deng's remarkable visit in 1979, enthusiastic Americans did not comprehend the continued authoritarianism of the Chinese Communist Party, the differences in national interest between their two countries, and the immense obstacles still impeding a resolution of the Taiwan issue.[109]

In China, the effect of Deng's trip was even greater than in the United States. Deng's visit changed the popular American images of China. But in China his visit helped set off a cascade of changes in the Chinese mindset and aspirations for the future. Even more than Deng's trips to Japan and Southeast Asia, the trip to America introduced the Chinese public to a modern way of life. The daily updates on Chinese television and the documentary movie that was made during Deng's visit presented a very favorable view of American life—not only of its factories, transportation, and communications, but also of families living in new housing with modern furniture and wearing fashionable clothing. A whole new way of living was presented to them, and they embraced it. Even barriers between the small number of Americans in Beijing and the Chinese broke down and suddenly visiting in each others' homes was no longer prohibited. Mao had talked of how a single spark could set off a prairie fire of revolution, but China after 1979 underwent a revolution far greater and longer lasting than the one Mao began. This massive revolution ignited from many sources, but no single spark spread more rapidly than the one resulting from Deng's visit to the United States.

Just as Americans overreacted to Deng, many Chinese also overreacted to his opening with America. Some Chinese wanted everything immediately, not realizing how much China had to change before they could enjoy the fruits of economic growth. Others rushed to embrace institutions and values that did not yet fit Chinese realities. It would not be easy to find an appropriate balance between Western and Chinese ways, but the opening brought a hybrid vitality and an intellectual renaissance that over time would remake China.

At the end of his trip to the United States in February 1979, Deng told one of his interpreters, Shi Yanhua, that with this trip, he had fulfilled his responsibility. At first, she did not understand what he meant. It was clear to his Chinese companions as well as to foreigners whom he met that he enjoyed these trips—he seemed to relish the opportunity to see the world and to receive the adulation of the crowds. But that is not why he traveled. He traveled because he had a job to do for his country. He saw it as his responsibility to improve relations with neighboring countries and to open far wider the doors to Japan and the United States, both to curb the Soviet Union and to receive assistance for China's modernization. Now, having completed his mission and fulfilled his responsibility, he could move on to other important tasks. Deng had traveled abroad five times in just fifteen months. Although he lived another eighteen years, he never again traveled outside of China.[110]

12

Launching the Deng Administration

1979–1980

When Deng emerged as the preeminent Chinese leader in December 1978, he did not yet have in place his own leadership team nor had he yet formulated a coherent vision of China's future that the public could rally behind. The leadership was shared, for the moment, with Hua Guofeng, who still held the official positions of chairman of the party and premier, and with Hua's four allies on the Politburo. In December 1978, Deng had been moved to the top of a structure that he had not created.

Deng did not care as much about titles as he did about developing an effective team and an organization that he could work with to modernize China. It would take a year to gain firm control, select his key leaders, and put them and his program into place. In the meantime, he chose to weaken and then remove Hua and his allies and to replace them with his own team and gradually develop his own agenda. As he became the preeminent leader, Deng also had to find a way to cope with the larger-than-life image of Mao that still permeated the party. While forging a new path for his administration and for the Chinese people, Deng would have to minimize the alienation of those who still revered Mao and who stood ready to accuse Deng of being the Chinese Khrushchev, the one who brought "de-Maoization" and "revisionism" to China.

In the spring of 1979, Deng sought to get tighter control over some conservatives who were worried about the bold opening Deng might undertake. Many high military and civilian officials harbored doubts about the wisdom of his attack on Vietnam and worried publicly that Deng was betraying the party and leading the country down the road to capitalism. Deng's speech on the four cardinal principles on March 30, 1979, was an important step in blunting the criticism of the conservatives. But he still needed some months to deal with the resistance before he could firmly establish his own team.

Deng had strong support, but the resistance was also palpable. On May 21, for example, there was a report in the PLA newspaper *Jiefangjun bao* that many army units were resisting carrying out the discussion of "Practice Is the Sole Criterion for Judging Truth," and that some units had reported that as many as one-third of the troops were not supportive of the overall spirit of the Third Plenum. There were reports that many soldiers supported Hua Guofeng not because of his own accomplishments, but because Mao had selected him and because he was in their view supportive of Mao's agenda.[1] Urban elites tended to be much more critical of Mao, but rural people were generally more willing to accept the Mao cult. In particular, soldiers from rural areas appreciated rural collectives that provided special support for their dependents in the villages, and many expected upon leaving the service to find employment in the collectives, a system they felt was under threat from Deng's initiatives.

To counter these conservative pressures, in the spring of 1979 Deng conducted a campaign to firm up support for "Practice Is the Sole Criterion for Judging Truth" and directed officials to conduct some "supplementary classes" *(bu ke)* to consolidate support for his reform agenda. When Deng appeared in public, he did not criticize Mao, but rather criticized Lin Biao and the Gang of Four for the problems of the era. To maintain the image of party unity, he took care not to take aim at Hua Guofeng directly but rather at the "two whatevers."

Although Chairman Hua Guofeng's power had been weakening, on June 18 he presented the government work report at the opening of the Second Session of the 5th National People's Congress (NPC). Even though at the time the listeners were unaware, this would be one of Hua's last major presentations at a party or government meeting. Shortly after that talk, Deng felt ready to move ahead in reshaping the party.

Descent from Yellow Mountain and Party Building

On July 11, 1979, Deng set out on a month-long tour of north and central China. The tour began with a climb on Anhui province's Yellow Mountain (Huang Shan). Yellow Mountain is one of China's most famous peaks, long celebrated in Chinese literature and history. On July 13, Deng began the ascent, and two days later he returned. For anyone about to turn age seventy-five, the journey was a formidable feat. The photo of a healthy-looking Deng pausing as he neared the end of his climb, with his pants rolled up and holding his walking stick, was widely circulated. When he returned to the base of the mountain, he was greeted by his ally Wan Li, first party secretary of Anhui, who had broken through the blockages on railway transport and was now paving a way to overcome the obstacles to rural reorganization. At the base of Yellow Mountain, Deng was also greeted by reporters. He told them: "As for the exam in mountain climbing, I completely passed."[2]

In Beijing, politically savvy officials understood: Deng's climb up Yellow Mountain, like Mao's famous swim in the Yangtze River, called attention to a healthy leader ready to make a vigorous push in domestic politics.[3] But Mao's July 1966 swim, orchestrated during a time of concern about the seventy-three-year-old Chairman's health, had been greatly overblown in the Chinese press: discerning readers found it difficult to believe that the elderly Mao could have achieved the world-record swimming pace that was claimed. Deng's climb, by contrast, was treated as it was, as an impressive accomplishment of an unusually healthy person ready to undertake some vigorous activities.

And what new work was Deng ready to take on? Party building—choosing high officials for key positions and selecting and training new party members. A few days after the climb, Deng gave a speech to an enlarged meeting of the Standing Committee of the Navy. The key issue facing the country, he told them, was preparing successors.[4] Deng said that China had resolved the key political and ideological issues and now needed to focus on the organizational issues—selecting and training officials. The key political goal, the achievement of the four modernizations, had been confirmed at the Third Plenum. The ideological issue had been resolved in Deng's speech on the four cardinal principles on March 30 and by Deng's assertion of Mao's ideology as interpreted by Deng—to seek the true path from facts. Now it was time to establish the criteria for selecting and training those who would form the leadership teams, first at the top and then at the lower levels, on down to the grassroots. And they would recruit and cultivate new party members. In the weeks after this speech, Deng went on to visit Shanghai, Shandong, and Tianjin, where he held several meetings designed to encourage the party committees to lay plans for cultivating talent.

Deng's choice of timing for party building followed the usual historical pattern. Since the founding of the party, once one side won a dispute and consolidated its power, its leaders would not only select high officials but also undertake a recruiting campaign to bring in those who would fit their criteria for new members. By the summer of 1979, most of the senior party officials had returned and occupied key positions, replacing the soldiers and radicals who had occupied key positions during the Cultural Revolution. Hua was sufficiently weakened by the summer of 1979 that he could no longer play a major role in party building. With Deng and his senior officials in charge, they could reach considerable agreement on the kind of officials they were seeking to cultivate.

Over the years, winners of inner-party struggles had various preferences for the kind of new members they sought—revolutionaries, soldiers, or radicals. Deng wanted for his team those who could contribute to the four modernizations. In particular, Deng was looking for officials capable of dealing with modern issues of foreign trade, finance, and technology and this in turn meant recruiting and promoting those with higher educational levels and with knowledge of science, technology, and management. As obvious as this may seem to leaders in many modern societies, in China at the time this represented a fundamental change. During Mao's era, being "red" had been more important than being "expert." Since 1949, leadership positions had mostly gone to those who were "red," those from worker and peasant backgrounds, while the educated experts from before 1949, whose families could afford their education, were labeled as coming from bourgeois and landlord classes. Deng declared that those old classes were gone, that he wanted people of ability, without regard to family background. To make way for new high-level leaders, Deng sought to remove Politburo members identified with conservative policies, beginning with four of Hua's key supporters—Wang Dongxing, Wu De, Chen Xilian, and Ji Dengkui—and he explained their removal and the selection of the new leaders in terms of what was needed to achieve modernization.

Although Deng did not announce his choices for the key positions in his administration until the end of 1979, he spent much of the year considering, consulting, and observing. Except for a handful of personal staff members and the military, Deng did not choose leaders primarily on the basis of their personal loyalty to him (see Chapter 18 for the selection of his military team). Instead, he wanted the best person in each job and he felt confident that if the person was qualified and dedicated to the party, he could cooperate with them. Deng did not confide in the people whom he appointed, even those promoted to high positions; he dealt with them in a pleasant but business-like and somewhat formal manner. They were comrades dedicated to the same cause, not personal friends. For key positions, he selected people of great talent and energy—people committed to reform and opening—who had been tested step by step, not people who had suddenly risen from much lower levels.[5]

A good judge of people, Deng spent a great deal of time considering personnel appointments. As general secretary in the decade before the Cultural Revolution, he had become familiar with many mid-level party members who, by the 1980s, had become senior leaders of the party. But for key appointments, Deng also consulted privately with other high officials to obtain their frank assessments, especially of people with whom they would work closely, before making his decision.[6]

The two highest-level members of Deng's team, Chen Yun and Li Xiannian, were not selected by him. They had such high positions that it would have been difficult to push them aside even if he had wanted to. Deng, Chen Yun, and Li Xiannian were of the same generation (born in 1904, 1905, and 1907, respectively). They had known each other long before 1949; all three had worked in Beijing under Mao and Zhou Enlai in the 1950s and early 1960s. Chen Yun and Li Xiannian could not compare with Deng as public figures, but knowledgeable officials described the power structure in the 1980s as "two and a half"—meaning that within high-level party circles, Chen Yun was regarded roughly as Deng's equal, and Li Xiannian was half a step behind. Chen Yun, though a year younger than Deng, had for twenty years beginning in the mid-1930s held a position above Deng's, and no one could match his authority in guiding the economy or in dealing with the history of personnel issues. When Chen Yun was on the sidelines from 1962 to 1978, Li Xiannian had been responsible for leading the economy under Premier Zhou Enlai.

Almost no high officials one or two decades younger than Deng had an opportunity to attend university. Deng chose for high political leadership those who respected education and had worked to educate themselves. Deng selected for his team three officials whom he was comfortable with, people he believed could lead China's modernization: Hu Yaobang (born 1915), Zhao Ziyang (born 1919), and Wan Li (born 1916). Hu Yaobang had proved capable of leading scientists at the Chinese Academy of Sciences, Zhao Ziyang had directed promising experiments in industrial reorganization in Sichuan province, and Wan Li had brought order to the railways. These three could in turn help develop young officials capable of understanding China's needs in the areas of modern science, technology, and engineering, and lead them in the implementation of innovative management techniques. Even though the three would dedicate themselves to serving Deng, they, too, were comrades dedicated to a common cause, disciplined followers implementing party policy, rather than friends. Even Wan Li, though closer to Deng than Hu or Zhao, did not consider himself a friend, but a loyal subordinate. A sixth member of the Deng team, Deng Liqun (also born in 1915), did not hold an administrative position as high as the others, but he could exercise great influence as a speechwriter and writer of internal memoranda because he had strong convictions and enjoyed the support of Chen Yun and Wang Zhen. A seventh member of the team, Hu Qiaomu (born 1912), played a special role as the guardian of orthodoxy. In an era when institutions were in flux, the personal backgrounds, characteristics, inclinations, and operating styles of these seven were critical in shaping developments during the 1980s. They were all people of high intellectual ability and broad experience who for decades had held important positions in the party.

In the Deng administration from 1980 until 1987 when Hu was removed, to use Western terms, Deng was the chairman of the board and chief executive officer and under Deng, Hu Yaobang and Zhao Ziyang were the active presidents of the two separate divisions, the party and the government. The party set the overall policies and managed personnel and propaganda at all levels from the top to the grassroots, whereas the government carried out administration at all levels. High officials held both party and government positions, and the work often overlapped, but in principle Hu and Zhao guided activities in their respective spheres, prepared documents for Deng's approval, and guided the frontline implementation—the "daily work"—in the party and government. Despite all the difficulties at the time, many fellow officials later regarded the early 1980s as a golden age when high-level officials worked together to launch and implement China's "reform and opening."

Deng was troubled by the fact that below this group of top leaders, because of the disruptions of the Cultural Revolution, there was not a well-trained next generation of experienced leaders. Deng compared the situation to the shortage of grain in late spring when the grain from the fall harvest had nearly run out and there was not yet ripe grain in the field, to meet the people's needs. China, he said, was lucky to have some senior officials who were still able to serve, but it was urgent to close the gap, to ripen the green grain on the stalks more quickly by training a successor generation from among those in their thirties and forties.

Deng asked the Party Organization Department to draw up a list of especially promising younger officials who had the potential for rising to high positions. When the list was presented later in the year, Deng and Chen Yun were dismayed to see that only 31 of the 165 people on it were university graduates. Although he did not believe that educated young people should suddenly be catapulted to the top, Deng expected that, as they proved themselves at each level, they should rise quickly.

In July 1979 Deng directed that the organization departments throughout the country, with the active participation of the top leaders at each level, aim to cultivate new talent within two or three years.[7] From September 5 to October 7, a national forum on organizational work held in Beijing was designed to follow up on Deng's efforts to cultivate talented successors. The major address at the forum was given by Hu Yaobang, who conveyed Deng's view that succession was the most pressing issue facing the country.

Deng, like other Chinese Communist leaders, talked frequently about "cultivating" *(peiyang)* successors, by which they meant, in addition to selecting and providing formal training, personal mentoring. High officials in any unit were expected to oversee the overall development of the younger people placed under them by encouraging them to read certain works, display their loyalty to the party, and accomplish something through their work.

Although key decisions on personnel would be made by the top leaders in the unit, the organization department of the party at each level played a critical role in assembling the files on each party member, carrying out training programs, and sending files on the appropriate pool of candidates to higher officials for their consideration.

While Deng was occupied with party building, he and his fellow leaders also had to confront the deep public alienation toward the party that had brought about the disasters of the Great Leap Forward and the Cultural Revolution. Until late 1979, the party leaders had not acknowledged their responsibility for these disasters, making it impossible for the party to gain credibility when it talked of other issues. It was decided at the NPC meeting in June that Marshal Ye should attempt to deal with these issues in a major address on the eve of the thirtieth anniversary of the founding of the Communist Chinese government.[8]

Marshal Ye's Thirtieth Anniversary Speech, October 1, 1979

Deng played a major role in shaping the speech that was to be delivered by Marshal Ye Jianying; he directed that the drafters should give an overall positive assessment of Chinese history since 1949 but should also present a frank recognition of the errors during the Great Leap Forward and the Cultural Revolution, which the Chinese people knew all too well from their own experience. It should offer a broad perspective on Chinese Communist Party history and provide a sense of new direction for the future. Hu Qiaomu and a staff of some twenty people helped to prepare it and it went through nine drafts that were vetted among high-level leaders, under Deng's watchful eye.[9]

Marshal Ye was the ideal person to deliver the speech. He was chairman of the NPC that was responsible for supervising government activities and the anniversary was a government occasion, not a party occasion. Further, he was widely respected, had no ambitions of own, and had managed to keep good relations with all sides including Deng and Hua Guofeng; he had never been severely criticized by Mao and was known to be close to the beloved Zhou Enlai; and he had good relations with the military. Marshal Ye was so weak physically, however, that he could only read the first few lines and the last few lines of his speech—someone else read the rest.[10]

Marshal Ye's speech, some sixteen thousand words in length, told the story of how the Chinese Communist Party had acted independently from the Soviet Union, in accord with China's own social and historical heritage, and how the Chinese Communist Party had achieved victory. Ye traced the growth of the Chinese economy and the expansion of public education. He proudly related how the party had overcome foreign aggression, but he also acknowledged that in 1957 the party had been wrong to attack so many "bourgeois rightists," wrong to boast of its own accomplishments, and wrong to have stirred up a "Communist wind" that tried to achieve such a high stage of collectivization that it had departed from reality. He affirmed that the Cultural Revolution was a serious policy error that had allowed Lin Biao, the Gang of Four, and other conspirators to attack so many good people. Ye said party efforts to build an advanced socialist system had been immature, that the party had been severely chastened by its mistakes, and that it was now working to build a "modern powerful socialist country" that would bring a great future.[11] In the speech, Ye also stressed the importance of a spiritual as well as material civilization, a theme that later would be developed more fully by Hu Yaobang.

Ye made it clear that Mao had been at the helm when the country committed the errors of the Great Leap Forward and the Cultural Revolution—the first public, though somewhat indirect, acknowledgment by a Chinese official that Mao himself bore some responsibility for errors. Ye also acknowledged that many party leaders were also responsible in part for these mistakes because of their "impatience": "We had become impatient in 1957. . . . In 1958 we departed from the principles of carrying out thoroughgoing investigation and study and of testing all innovations before popularizing them." With respect to the Cultural Revolution, he said, "We were not always able to stick to the correct principles established during our first seventeen years . . . as a result, we had to pay a very bitter price and instead of avoiding errors . . . we committed even more serious ones."[12]

Marshal Ye then offered guidance on how to draw the proper lessons from Mao's errors. After 1927, Mao had found the correct road for the Chinese revolution "by proceeding from the realities of China. . . . We Chinese Communists and the Chinese people call this development of Marxist-Leninism in the Chinese revolution 'Mao Zedong Thought.'"[13] Ye also praised the 8th Party Congress in 1956, chaired by Chairman Mao, when Mao had stated that "the large-scale turbulent class struggles of the masses characteristic of times of revolution have come to an end," and had declared that it was vitally important to "unite the entire people for economic and cultural development."[14]

The reaction to Marshal Ye's speech was very favorable. The educated public was pleased to hear that party leaders were finally facing up to their problems and moving in a realistic direction they could support. For those who had been attacked over the years, no speech could truly make up for their suffering, but the admission of party errors was a welcome if belated message, a major breakthrough in ending the empty, boastful slogans and for dealing frankly with the issues facing the country.[15]

Beginning the Evaluation of Party History

Before Marshal Ye's speech was delivered, Deng believed the speech would resolve the party's historical problems and that further discussion of Mao's role could be postponed for some years. He feared that additional discussion of Mao and his place in China's history would only extend the contentiousness that he wanted to bring to an end. It would be better simply to get on with the work. But Mao's role was so deeply embedded in a host of policy issues that many party leaders supported a further review of party history. Some feared that if Mao's ideas were not specifically criticized, political movements like the Cultural Revolution might recur. After the positive reaction to Ye's speech, Deng relented, sensing that at least some controversial issues could be discussed without splitting the country apart. He began to consult with others about how to proceed with a more detailed analysis of party history.[16]

At the 7th Party Congress, convened in 1945 as World War II was ending and the party was entering a new phase, party officials had summed up the first twenty-four years of party history in light of the new era. In 1979, as the party was coming out of the Cultural Revolution and entering another new phase, it seemed appropriate to again sum up its historical experiences. As leaders began to prepare this document, called the "Resolution on Certain Questions in the History of Our Party," discussions inevitably focused on how to evaluate Mao's role.

To prepare for this historical evaluation, Deng organized a small group with the committed reformer Hu Yaobang in charge, and two conservative defenders of party orthodoxy, Hu Qiaomu and Deng Liqun, as head and administrator, respectively, of the drafting committee.[17] As usual, Deng first met the drafters to lay out the major topics he wanted to be covered. He would meet with them fifteen more times and go over each draft, giving specific directions each time. As Hua began to lose power in mid-1979, it was easier for Deng and his allies to reach a consensus that included negative criticism of Mao, so the full evaluation would not be completed for over a year. By 1980, however, after Deng had more firmly consolidated his control and weakened Hua's base of power, Mao's errors could be addressed more directly.

Final Preparations for the New Administration, Late 1979

Hua Guofeng had been basically sidelined by the middle of 1979. In areas where Deng and Hua Guofeng had overlapping responsibility, Deng had simply moved in to take charge. Indeed, by the time U.S. Secretary of Defense Harold Brown visited Beijing in January 1980, Chairman Hua was so powerless that when he was speaking during the meetings, the other Chinese officials in attendance carried on side conversations and paid little attention, a gross violation of the respect ordinarily accorded Chinese leaders.[18]

In the latter part of October 1979, Deng met with Hu Yaobang, Yao Yilin, and Deng Liqun. They had many important issues on the table as they prepared for the Fifth Plenum, scheduled for February 1980, which may be regarded as the beginning of the Deng administration. At that plenum, Hu Yaobang and Zhao Ziyang were put in place and Hua's four key supporters

(Wang Dongxing, Wu De, Chen Xilian, and Ji Dengkui) would be removed from the Politburo. Deng also planned at the plenum to formally clear Liu Shaoqi's name.[19] In addition, the leaders needed to discuss plans for reestablishing the party Secretariat.

When these critical meetings were taking place there was no confrontation with Hua Guofeng, for at the time, following the suggestion of Deng and Li Xiannian, Hua was traveling in France, Germany, Italy, and England. He left on October 12. While Hua was away, meetings of the State Council and Politburo were chaired by Deng, and by the time Hua returned on November 10, the basic plans for the Fifth Plenum, including the planned removal of the four Hua loyalists, were in place.[20] Once Hua's supporters were removed and Zhao and Hu were in place, it would be easier to proceed with Deng's agenda on the historical resolution.

By the Fifth Plenum in February 1980, scarcely a year after the Third Plenum, Deng had consolidated his power sufficiently that he was able to set out his agenda for the 1980s, revise the structure for coordinating high-level party work, and name his team of senior officials. In American terms, the Deng administration took office in early 1980.

Deng's State of the Union Address for the 1980s

On January 16, 1980, Deng presented a major address on "The Present Situation and the Tasks before Us." It laid out his goals for the entire decade of the 1980s. It was, in effect, his state of the union address. Hua Guofeng, in his political report to the 11th Party Congress in 1977, had focused on the recent political struggles, and in his ten-year economic vision in 1978 had focused on economic issues. By contrast, Deng's brief address at the Third Plenum in 1978 was a rallying call for reform and opening. His speech in January 1980 was the first major address after Mao's death to define the overall goals for the coming decade.

Deng's logic was simple and straightforward: adopt policies that would contribute to the realization of the four modernizations:

> Modernization is at the core of all . . . major tasks, because it is the essential condition for solving both our domestic and our external problems. Everything depends on our doing the work in our own country well. The role we play in international affairs is determined by the extent of our economic growth . . . the goal of our foreign policy is a

peaceful environment for achieving the four modernizations. . . . This is a vital matter which conforms to the interests not only of the Chinese people but also of the people in the rest of the world.[21]

In his address, Deng acknowledged that "some people, especially young people, are skeptical about the socialist system, alleging that socialism is not as good as capitalism." So how should China demonstrate the superiority of socialism? "First and foremost, it must be revealed in the rate of economic growth and in economic efficiency."[22] At the time, few foreigners would have predicted that the growth rate of a country led by the Communist Party would in fact surpass the growth rate of Western countries for a whole decade, let alone three decades.

Deng was still setting down the criteria for promotions. He told his officials that if they wanted to hold important positions they needed to acquire professional qualifications. He also stated that with a strong economy, China would be in a better position to resist the hegemons and to achieve reunification with the island of Taiwan. "We must work for the return of Taiwan to the motherland, for China's reunification. We will endeavor to attain this goal in the 1980s."[23] He said that "we must surpass Taiwan, at least to a certain extent, in economic development. . . . Nothing less will do. With the success of the four modernizations and more economic growth, we will be in a better position to accomplish reunification."[24] Deng's goal of surpassing Taiwan economically and of reuniting with Taiwan within the decade was to prove overly optimistic, but within three decades, the success of Taiwan's economy was thoroughly dependent on its economic relationship with the mainland, something few could have imagined in 1980.

What was needed for China to achieve economic modernization? Deng listed four requirements: (1) a firm and consistent political message, (2) political stability and unity, (3) hard work with a pioneering spirit, and (4) a contingent of officials with both an "unswerving socialist orientation" and "professional knowledge and competence."[25] The essence of Deng's message—the need for a firm political line and a stable social order—was consistent with the four cardinal principles he had announced nine months earlier, and with the stance he would take throughout his time as preeminent leader. In his talk on January 16, 1980, he said, "There are hooligans, criminals, and counter-revolutionaries who carry on underground activities in collusion with foreign forces and the Guomindang secret service. Nor can we take too lightly the so-called democrats and other people with ulterior motives who flagrantly oppose the socialist system and Communist Party leadership. . . . It is absolutely impermissible to propagate freedom of speech, of the press, of assembly, of association in ways implying that counter-revolutionaries may also enjoy them."[26] Yet he also announced that the party would continue the policy of a hundred flowers blooming and would drop the slogan that "literature and art are subordinate to politics" because it could too easily be used as a theoretical pretext for arbitrary intervention. He warned, however, that "every progressive and revolutionary writer or artist has to take into account the social effects of his work."[27]

In an effort to lower the overly high expectations that had sprung up since December 1978, Deng talked about the hard struggle ahead and the need to preserve a pioneering spirit. Having suffered for two decades, many people had begun setting goals based more on hope than on reality. Deng remained impressed with Prime Minister Ikeda's plan to double incomes within a decade, which had stimulated Japanese growth during the 1970s. But having learned from the bitter disappointments of the Great Leap Forward when goals could not be met, Deng took care to consult not only Chinese specialists but also foreign experts from the World Bank before setting out what he considered to be a realistic goal.[28] Deng became convinced that between 1980 and 2000 China could double its income twice and therefore he popularized the slogan, "quadrupling income by 2000." When it later seemed as if that goal would be difficult to reach, he quietly began speaking of a quadrupling of GNP rather than a quadrupling of income—a goal that would be easier to achieve. He cautioned the public, however, that in the decade ahead, China would not have the resources to become a welfare state.

After the 1978 Third Plenum, Deng became acutely aware that many leading officials in the provinces, impatient to start investing and growing, were unhappy with Chen Yun's "readjustment policy" that restrained growth (see Chapter 15), but in 1980 Deng still defended that policy. Deng reminded "some comrades" who were not satisfied with the current pace of modernization how much more progress they had made in 1978–1980 compared to previous years.

In truth, when defining the ideal role for a ruling party, Deng sounded more like a Western business executive than a Maoist, when he explained that the Chinese should strive to "raise labor productivity, reduce the proportion of goods unwanted by society and the number of factory rejects, lower production costs, and increase the utilization rate of our funds."[29] In weighing the importance of whether it was more important for officials to be "red" or "expert," Deng repeated his convictions that he had already made clear: "We should make sure that the leadership of professional organizations at different levels, including the leadership of the party committees, is gradually taken over by people with professional skills." He cautioned that "some new members who joined the party during the 'Cultural Revolution' are not qualified." Deng closed his state of the union address with a ringing endorsement of the party: "Without party leadership it would be impossible to achieve anything in contemporary China."[30]

On February 29, the last day of the Fifth Plenum, Deng spelled out what he expected from the party—efficient administration. Sounding like a factory manager with a military background, he said, "Meetings should be small and short, and they should not be held at all unless the participants have prepared. . . . If you don't have anything to say, save your breath. . . . The only reason to hold meetings and to speak at them is to solve problems. . . . There should be collective leadership in settling major issues. But when it comes to particular jobs or to decisions affecting a particular sphere, individual responsibility must be clearly defined and each person should be held responsible for the work entrusted to him."[31]

Those who knew Deng were not surprised at his determination to preserve public order. Public attacks would not be tolerated: the "four big freedoms" (to speak out freely, air views fully, hold great debates, and write big-character posters), which in 1966 had given the Red Guards the right to launch their public attacks, would be abolished in the revised constitution. Deng explained what he meant by inner-party democracy: party members should speak out when they have something to say to help solve problems. Once top party leaders had listened to various views and made their decisions, the party members were to carry them out. Deng made it clear how party members who did not respond to his directives would be treated: "incompetent party members" would be removed.[32] By 1980 his views had jelled; this speech remained a cogent summary of Deng's policies throughout his time at the helm.

The Inauguration: Fifth Plenum, February 23–29, 1980

At the Fifth Plenum, February 23–29, 1980, the Central Committee formally ratified the decisions made by Deng and his allies in the last weeks of 1979. The key Politburo members who supported Hua Guofeng—Wang Dongxing, Wu De, Chen Xilian, and Ji Dengkui—were officially criticized and "resigned" from the Politburo; Chen Xilian and Ji Dengkui also lost their positions as vice premiers. Wang Dongxing and Chen Xilian were genuine radicals, but in fact Wu De and Ji Dengkui were not innately radical but experienced party leaders who had long survived by accommodating the leftist winds; their fate had been sealed by their role in the April 5, 1976, Tiananmen crackdown on those expressing respect for Zhou Enlai and Deng.

Deng's three main supporters, Hu Yaobang, Zhao Ziyang, and Wan Li, took over the key positions. Hu Yaobang became general secretary of the party. Although Hua Guofeng was nominally the premier, Zhao Ziyang became de facto premier and began leading the daily work of the State Council. Wan Li, meanwhile, became a de facto vice premier and head of the State Agricultural Commission, paving the way for the policy of allowing rural production to be contracted down to the household level. Formally, their positions as vice premiers were ratified at a meeting of the Standing Committee of the State Council in April and at a meeting of the Standing Committee of the NPC in August, when Ji Dengkui and Chen Xilian, having been removed from the Politburo in February, formally lost their positions as vice premiers.

The plenum in effect marked the inauguration of Hu Yaobang and Zhao Ziyang as leaders of the daily work of the party and government. A solid majority of Politburo members were now enthusiastic supporters of Deng's policies. This was important, not because of formal voting, which rarely takes place. Indeed, the Standing Committee of the Politburo rarely met. But the change in membership created a different political atmosphere at the top, and officials below quickly understood that their superiors would be pursuing a new policy direction. Accordingly, after the Fifth Plenum, lower-level officials scrutinized even more carefully Deng's and Hu's speeches and the documents they presented at major meetings, and no longer had to hedge their bets by paying close attention to what Hua Guofeng said.

The other high officials besides those at the very top who took office at the Fifth Plenum were senior party officials of proven ability who were also committed to reform. Deng excluded from key positions in his administration officials who had risen during the Cultural Revolution at the expense of experienced senior officials. For certain important positions within the military, he selected officials who had served under him in the Second Field Army, people with whom he had special relationships of trust. But otherwise, he had enough confidence in his own ability to lead party members of widely different backgrounds that he saw no need to require personal loyalty. He did not lead a faction but rather an entire party, minus the beneficiaries of the Cultural Revolution who had failed to make the transition to his rule.

Deng did not need to give specific directions to the Propaganda Department; propaganda officials at the Fifth Plenum, including the editors of the major media (*People's Daily*, the New China News Agency [Xinhua], *Guangming Daily*, and the party's theoretical journal, *Red Flag*) drew on Deng's presentations to write editorials and articles that reflected his views. Deng, long disciplined to bear weighty responsibilities and experienced in judging how his statements might be interpreted, was careful about what he said.

Signals from the top were studied very carefully by those below. When a provincial party secretary went to Beijing, it was common for him to talk first with a reliable acquaintance in the party Secretariat who kept abreast of Deng's current concerns. Each ministry and each province also had a small political research group, and one of its key assignments was to be fully conversant with the latest thinking of the top leaders and with the implications for their ministry or province. So many documents flowed down from above that it was impossible for lower-level officials to read every word carefully. Within each unit, the political research group worked to keep the unit's higher-level officials informed about which directives were most important, and to anticipate what Deng, General Secretary Hu Yaobang, and Premier Zhao Ziyang might do next. The leadership core in the unit then had a sense of what it had to do to stay out of trouble and how to appeal to the party center for resources.

The personnel changes in the early 1980s allowed Deng to manage routine work more efficiently and to move ahead with several programs that the Maoists would have either slowed or stopped. The logjam on reversing the verdict on Liu Shaoqi was immediately broken. From 1945 to 1966 Liu had been Mao's second in command, but then Mao had attacked Liu as a traitor and for having capitalist tendencies. Although Liu had passed away in 1969, his verdict was the most important one awaiting reversal. At the Fifth Plenum, Deng declared that such a reversal was not necessarily an attack on Mao. As it turned out, action on the reversal of Liu's verdict was a straw in the fresh wind; it helped prepare party members for the revised historical appraisal of Mao that would acknowledge his errors, and it facilitated the reversal of verdicts on other senior party officials who had worked closely with Liu.[33]

The Fifth Plenum also reestablished the party Secretariat that had been abandoned in 1966. After it was reestablished, key members of the Politburo, those responsible for leading small groups of leaders in various sectors, kept their offices there. Indeed, the Secretariat became the premier institution for coordinating the daily work of the party. Meetings were held regularly each week, and Premier Zhao Ziyang, who had his office at the State Council, would join in to provide some coordination between the party and the government.

The changes made at the Fifth Plenum helped reduce the tensions at Politburo meetings and eased the path to widespread reform. Consolidation of the new leadership made it possible for Deng, within just a few months, to direct the dissolution of local agricultural collectives and to pass responsibility for rural production down to the individual household. The plenum also paved the way for the push in late 1980 to complete the evaluation of party history and to remove Hua Guofeng from all official positions of power.

Farewell to the Mao Era and Hua Guofeng, Fall 1980–June 1981

To date, no reliable records have been released showing exactly when Deng decided to push Hua Guofeng aside. Deng's years of experience in observing how Mao removed officials and Deng's orderly step-by-step removal of Hua's power base from December 1978 to June 1981, however, make it reasonable to assume that Deng had a strategy in place. Even if he did not have in December 1978 a precise plan for removing Hua, at least by then he had considered how he might gradually reduce Hua's authority without shocking his colleagues and without open public struggles.

In attacking high-level officials, Mao had often moved to first remove their key supporters, which isolated them and made them easier to attack. Similarly, Deng removed Hua's right-hand men in February 1980, and brought in Zhao Ziyang to perform the work of the premier. By the time Hua visited Japan in May 1980 he had little power left, but his visit there helped reassure foreigners that China was not splitting apart in a power struggle.[34] In August 1980, Hua formally gave up his post of premier. Later, beginning in November 1980, at a series of Politburo meetings, despite bitter disagreements, the final decision was made to remove Hua from chairmanship of the party and the Central Military Commission (CMC), a decision that was formally announced in June 1981.

The evaluation of the history of the Chinese Communist Party, which focused on Mao, proceeded in tandem with the removal of Hua. The two efforts had a natural link: Hua had affirmed all of Mao's policies and directives, even when Mao had committed grave errors—and these errors were coming to light in the more honest appraisal of the Mao era. The evaluation of party history began shortly after Ye's 1979 National Day speech, when Deng began a broad consultative process designed to reach a party consensus on the evaluation of Mao.[35] The team that Deng set up under Hu Yaobang in the weeks after Marshal Ye's speech held its first meeting on October 30, 1979.

Deng had given the issue of how to handle Mao's legacy serious thought from at least 1956, when he was present at the 20th Party Congress in Moscow where Khrushchev had denounced Stalin. Over the years, Deng had had ample opportunity to contemplate the issue, especially during his three and a half years of rusticating in Jiangxi province during the Cultural Revolution. As a young man, he had expressed tremendous admiration for Mao, and for decades he had dedicated himself to serving Mao, only to be twice cast aside by him and subjected to humiliating public attacks. Deng's eldest son had been left paralyzed for life below the waist because of Mao's Red Guards. It would have been inhuman if Deng were not deeply resentful, and as tough as he was, Deng was very human. And yet, in his handling of the historical issue, Deng did not display any of his personal feelings.

The process of evaluating Mao was fully consistent with Deng's rational analysis of doing what was needed to retain the authority of the party, while still allowing high officials under him to depart from Mao's policies. In August 1980, when the evaluation was still in its early stages, Deng told journalist Oriana Fallaci, "We will not do to Chairman Mao what Khrushchev did to Stalin."[36] And in October 1980 when the discussions were taking place, Deng offered this guidance to the drafters: "When we write about his mistakes, we should not exaggerate, for otherwise we shall be discrediting Comrade Mao Zedong and this would mean discrediting our party and state."[37] The final document displayed enough overall respect for Mao that the authority of those who had worked closely with him, including Deng, was not endangered. Yet the resolution also had to show why those officials criticized by Mao now deserved to return to work, and to legitimatize the undoing of the high levels of collectivization and class struggle of the Mao era.

The first draft was ready in February 1980. Deng, reportedly unhappy with this early version, called in Hu Yaobang, Hu Qiaomu, and Deng Liqun to suggest that the writers (1) appraise positively Mao Zedong Thought and

Mao's historical role, (2) in the spirit of "seeking the true path from facts," make clear Mao's errors during the Cultural Revolution, and (3) reach an overall conclusion that would help people unite and look toward the future. Of the three points, the first point was "the most important, the most fundamental, the most crucial."[38] No matter how much he had personally suffered over the years from Mao's criticisms and decisions, Deng told the drafters to make it clear that the party and the people must remain firmly committed to following Mao Zedong Thought. The return of many high-level officials who had suffered under Mao and the outpouring of criticisms of Mao on Democracy Wall meant that there was plenty of support in key circles for criticism of Mao; consequently, Deng could position himself publicly as a defender of the importance of Mao without risking a return to past policies.[39] Each time he spoke out publicly, then, it was to complain that the last draft did not do enough to recognize Chairman Mao's great contributions.

On June 27, 1980, for example, Deng complained that the latest draft was too negative. Not only did he want the writers to do more to stress the positive things that Mao stood for, but he also pressed them to acknowledge that Mao's mistakes were primarily systemic and institutional. Deng accepted Hu Qiaomu's point that the drafters had no choice but to acknowledge the errors of the Great Leap Forward (in which, unlike those of the Cultural Revolution, Deng had been deeply involved). Deng insisted, however, that in dealing with the Great Leap, the drafters should begin by listing some of the positive achievements during that period and only thereafter acknowledge the weaknesses.[40]

In order to gain a broad popular consensus, one that would lead to unity rather than to polarization, Deng directed that high-level officials in both Beijing and the provinces be given a chance to comment on the draft. Thus on October 12, 1980, after the latest draft was cleared by the Politburo, the party's General Office sent it to some four thousand high-level officials who were to express their views. A summary of their views would then be sent to the drafters for further consideration.[41] In fact, including the 1,500 students at the Central Party School, an estimated 5,600 high party members joined in the discussions of the draft. Some were outspoken in demanding a more critical account. Fang Yi, a specialist in science and technology, declared that Mao had been a tyrant *(baojun)*. Tan Zhenlin, one of those who had dared to complain about the Cultural Revolution in February 1967, declared that Mao had acted against his own teachings. But when Huang Kecheng—who had been seriously criticized when his superior, Peng Dehuai, was attacked—

defended Mao's contributions, it became difficult for others to demand a more severe criticism of Mao.

Although the rounds of drafting and consultation continued, the major discussions were concluded by late November 1980. On March 24, 1981 when Deng discussed one of the later drafts with Chen Yun, Chen said that they should give more weight to Mao's pre-1949 role, which would emphasize Mao's positive achievements. Chen also suggested that they pay special attention to Mao's contributions to theory, emphasizing both Marxist-Leninist theory and Mao Zedong Thought. Deng accepted Chen Yun's views and passed them on to the drafters.[42]

The extended discussions reflected just how important high officials considered the question of Mao's reputation, since the place he would hold in history would determine both their own political futures as well as the treatment of their family members and associates. Significantly, in these evaluations, the political differences between Mao and Liu Shaoqi and between Mao and Peng Dehuai were no longer regarded as so serious as to be described as a "struggle between two lines." That gave everyone breathing room, but especially the victims' relatives and friends, who were grateful for the change in language.

The final draft of the document was full of praise for Mao Zedong Thought and for Mao's contributions as a great proletarian revolutionary, but it remained critical of Mao's role in the Great Leap Forward and the Cultural Revolution. The problems of the Great Leap Forward, for example, were "due to the fact that Comrade Mao Zedong and many leading comrades, both at the center and in the localities, had become smug about their successes, were impatient for quick results, and overestimated the role of man's subjective will and efforts." The Cultural Revolution, too, "was responsible for the most severe setback and the heaviest losses suffered by the party, the state, and the people since the founding of the People's Republic. It was initiated and led by Comrade Mao Zedong."[43] The document dealt with Mao's errors only in a general way, but Deng stated that fifteen years later, it would be possible to make another evaluation of Mao. The implication of Deng's comment seemed clear: if the party were to criticize Mao too harshly in 1980, it could be too divisive and weaken the support of the people, but years in the future, when the party could distance itself from present emotions and current personnel issues, it would be possible to make a more detailed and far franker criticism of Mao.[44]

As in the Soviet Union, where Stalin's merits were said to be 70 percent and his weaknesses 30 percent, Mao's merits too were rated at 70 percent. Mao, after all, had admitted to making errors. Deng pointed out that during the Cultural Revolution, Mao's estimates of the situation were wrong, the methods he had used were wrong, and that the combination of these mistakes had caused serious damage to the party and to China. On March 19, 1981, as the drafting of the evaluation neared an end, Deng expressed his satisfaction with the discussion of Mao's role during the Cultural Revolution.

Deng was keenly aware that just as it was imperative to reassure the Chinese public that the process of evaluating Mao and Hua was orderly and proper, so it was important to convey to the rest of the world that no disruptive "power struggle" and no "de-Maoization" was taking place in China. At this point, Deng agreed to an interview with the Italian journalist Oriana Fallaci, one of the world's best-known interviewers of high-level officials. Fallaci was known for her confrontational style, for being very well-prepared, and for asking shrewd and tough questions. Deng enjoyed the challenge. The interview on the morning of August 21, 1980, went so well that at the end Deng joked, "Let's go have lunch. My stomach is starting to lead a revolution," and he offered to meet her a second time two days later.

Two weeks before Fallaci first met Deng, Beijing had sent out a notice that the number of pictures of Mao displayed in public places and the posting of his poems could be reduced. So Fallaci began by asking if Mao's portrait would remain in Tiananmen Square. Deng answered "It will, forever." Deng explained that Mao had made mistakes but, unlike the crimes of Lin Biao and the Gang of Four, Mao's mistakes were secondary to his achievements. He explained that Mao Zedong Thought still provided important guidelines, even though Mao, in the later stages of his life, had lost touch with reality and had taken actions counter to the views that he had earlier advocated. When Fallaci asked about the mistakes of the Great Leap Forward, Deng replied that they were not Mao's alone; rather, they were mistakes for which all those who had worked with Mao must share the blame.[45] When she inquired about Mao's selection of Lin Biao, Deng said that it was feudalistic for a leader to choose his own successor. Deng's implication was unmistakable: it was also wrong for Mao to have chosen Hua Guofeng as successor. And when asked how experiences like the Cultural Revolution could be avoided in the future, Deng explained that party leaders were looking into restructuring China's institutions in order to achieve socialist democracy and uphold socialist law.[46]

Many other leaders would have become testy under Fallaci's confrontational questioning, but Deng responded easily and confidently. Later, Fallaci, reflecting on her long career, listed her two interviews with Deng as among her favorites. Foreign Minister Qian Qichen, who sat in on this and other meetings with Deng, rated Deng's performance in these two interviews as one of his most brilliant.[47]

After May 1979, Hua Guofeng did not often appear in public. In his last major presentation, at the NPC of June 18, 1980, Hua did not explicitly say that class struggle had ended, but he did say that class struggle was no longer the major contradiction and that the party should not undertake large-scale class struggles. On economic matters, his comments were in tune with party policy of the time: he supported Chen Yun's call for readjustment and stressed the importance of agriculture and light industry.[48] Some of the documents presented at that NPC, such as the "Guiding Principles," were, in effect, potent criticisms of Hua Guofeng's leadership.

At a Politburo Standing Committee meeting, members were asked whether in the document on party history it was better to use a brief six lines to summarize the period since 1976, or whether it was better to use a longer version that went into greater detail about the four years since 1976—a version that inevitably would include criticisms of Hua Guofeng. Hua was of course against spelling out the details of those four years. The participants agreed that they would first send the briefer version to other leaders for discussion and await their reactions.[49] Significant numbers of those leaders were critical of Hua Guofeng's role in blocking Deng's prompt return and they argued for the longer version. In the end, Deng agreed that the document should include a discussion of those four years, so that the reasons for Hua's removal would be clear.[50] The longer version thus became part of the final draft.[51]

In late May 1981, some seventy participants at an enlarged Politburo meeting gave final approval to the revised draft on party history. After the drafters did some fine-tuning, a polished final piece was presented to the Sixth Plenum, and approved on June 27. It was publicized throughout the country on July 1, 1981, the sixtieth anniversary of the founding of the party.[52]

The issue of whether to oust Hua from his major positions, as chairman of the party and chairman of the CMC, came to a head in a series of nine Politburo meetings held from November 10 to December 5, 1980. Those discussions were considered so sensitive that, even three decades later, most of the records of the meetings have not been made available, even to party historians. But one key document, a speech by Hu Yaobang on November 19 spelling out Hua's problems, was released to the public. In it, the main lines of argumentation were made clear.

After retirement, Hu Yaobang said that his most enjoyable years were those when he served under Hua, a comment that likely reflected his resentment for being pushed aside by Deng. Hu, in 1980, however, was assigned the task of making the case for Hua's removal. In his presentation of the history of this period, Hu began by acknowledging that the party and the people would never forget Hua's contribution in arresting the Gang of Four, although Hua had overstated his personal role in that achievement: given the political climate after the April 5 demonstrations, it had not been difficult to arrest them. Hu also said that after Mao died, Hua had continued Mao's errant policies of pursuing class struggle instead of correcting them, and he had rushed to publish volume 5 of Mao's *Selected Works* without broad consultation. When Mao was alive, Hua had sometimes disagreed with Mao and had even been criticized by him (Mao complained that Hua paid too much attention to production), but after Mao's death, Hua had used the "two whatevers" to strengthen his own power. Hu also criticized Hua for promoting a personality cult for his own self-glorification. Finally, recalling his own depression after the April 5, 1976 incident, Hu said that he was not given the opportunity to speak with Hua Guofeng from that time until February 26, 1977, and he did not feel free to visit Deng Xiaoping until March 14, 1977.

Hu reported that Chen Yun, who had not been allowed by Hua to return to work until the atmosphere of the Third Plenum demanded it, said that from Mao's death until March 1977 Hua had been very harsh in his treatment of senior officials. In particular, Hua had refused to reverse verdicts on the April 5, 1976 incident, afraid that the return of old officials would interfere with his ability to govern. Hu said that even though Marshal Ye and Li Xiannian had urged Hua on several occasions to allow Deng to return to work, and even though Chen Yun and Wang Zhen at the March 1977 work conference had agreed, Hua still had refused. Instead, Hua had relied on a tiny group of advisers, Hu said, including Wang Dongxing, Ji Dengkui, Wu De, Su Zhenhua, and Li Xin, while sometimes keeping other officials in the dark on party matters until the last minute. Hua Guofeng also tried to spur the economy to move too quickly. Hu acknowledged that this was not only Hua's error, but also Deng's and his own: indeed, at the time, only Chen Yun had recognized that the plans were too ambitious.[53]

The most serious resistance to pushing Hua aside in late 1980 came from Marshal Ye. During the party history discussions, Marshal Ye did not support the emphasis on Mao's later errors. He felt that, for the good of the country, it was essential to go further than Deng in maintaining Mao's reputation. He preferred instead to place the onus on Jiang Qing and Lin Biao. The two issues were inextricably linked for Ye: at one of the Politburo meetings, Ye recalled dramatically that when he had gone to pay his final respects to Mao shortly before his death, Mao beckoned to him. Although Mao was unable to speak, Ye understood what Mao wanted to say: Mao hoped that Ye would support Hua and help him grow into the leadership position. (Mao Yuanxin, however, who had been with Mao at the time, declared that no such incident occurred.[54]) Reportedly, Marshal Ye believed that Hua should retain his titles and that Deng should continue to carry on his work, but that officially Deng should be under Hua.

Why did Marshal Ye defend Hua Guofeng? Some speculated that Marshal Ye himself wanted to play a key role in Chinese party and governmental politics, and was supporting the man who could make that happen. But Ye was too old and weak, and not only had he never shown any sign of personal ambition, he had also for years been reluctant to manage daily affairs. More likely, as other party officials argue, Marshal Ye was concerned that Deng might become too authoritarian—that he would behave too much like Mao—and he thus sought to retain Hua as a way of constraining Deng's power and promoting inner-party democracy.

In the end, the protests of Marshal Ye and others were overcome by the majority view of the Politburo, which supported the resignation of Hua and the centralization of power in the hands of Deng and his associates. In an internal memorandum, circulated on December 5, 1980, immediately after the last in this series of Politburo meetings, the Politburo announced it would recommend to the Sixth Plenum that Hua's resignation from the chairmanship of the party and the CMC be accepted; that Hu Yaobang replace Hua as chairman of the party; and that Deng replace Hua as chairman of the CMC. Hua would remain a vice chairman of the party and a member of the Politburo.[55]

Marshal Ye was not a strong-willed person who fought for his convictions; he preferred to avoid confrontation. He accepted the Politburo's decision on Hua, and in fact engaged in a mild self-criticism for his support of Hua.[56] Indeed, once Deng became head of the CMC, Marshal Ye chose not to share this responsibility with Deng but to withdraw to his home base in Guangdong, where his son Ye Xuanping was already mayor of Guangzhou and vice governor and where he could enjoy a comfortable life. Marshal Ye was present at the beginning of the Sixth Plenum for pictures, but he did not stay for the discussions when the resolution on party history and the removal of Hua were formally passed. Later, when Marshal Ye was critically ill in 1984 and 1986, Deng did not pay a courtesy visit as he had done for Zhou. Marshal Ye died in 1986.

The Politburo resolution that finally emerged from these heated discussions was direct and forceful: "Comrade Hua Guofeng eagerly produced and accepted a new cult of personality. . . . In 1977 and 1978, Comrade Hua Guofeng promoted some leftist slogans in the realm of economic work . . . resulting in severe losses and calamities for the national economy. . . . [Although] Comrade Hua Guofeng has also done some successful work, it is extremely clear that he lacks the political and organizational ability to be chairman of the party. That he should never have been appointed chairman of the Military Affairs Commission, everyone knows."[57] Hua was finished. Although he was allowed to remain on the Politburo after the Sixth Plenum in June 1981, he was humiliated by the denunciations and rarely attended high-level party meetings.

Deng had good reason to be pleased with both the process and the results of the historical evaluation, as well as with the removal of Hua Guofeng. Hua Guofeng was removed without a public power struggle. In the historical evaluation, Deng had found a delicate balance that praised Mao enough to avoid weakening the authority of the party, while still criticizing Mao's role in the Great Leap Forward and Cultural Revolution. The broad-based consensus among high-level party leaders that Mao had made serious errors in his later years opened the way for Deng to move in directions that Mao would not have approved of, but that Deng believed would be good for China.

The Deng Era

1978–1989

13

Deng's Art of Governing

Deng would not tolerate the cult of personality that Mao happily indulged in.[1] In sharp contrast to the Mao era, virtually no statues of Deng were placed in public buildings and virtually no pictures of him hung in homes. Few songs and plays were composed to celebrate his triumphs. Deng never even became chairman of the party or premier. Students did learn about his policies and they could cite his best-known aphorisms, but they did not spend time memorizing quotations from his writings.

And yet, even without a cult or august titles—merely the positions of vice chairman of the party, vice premier, and chairman of the Central Military Commission (CMC)—Deng acquired effective control over the important levers of power. How did he accomplish this amazing feat? By fully using his reputation and moving boldly to create a well-run system capable of building a strong, prosperous country. If Mao were like an emperor above the clouds, reading history and novels and issuing edicts, Deng was more like a commanding general, checking carefully to see that his battle plans were properly staffed and implemented.

The Structure of Power

Deng worked in his home office on Kuang Street, which by car was less than ten minutes northeast of Zhongnanhai. As his hearing worsened, it was awkward for Deng to take part in group meetings. His hearing problem resulted from an untreatable, degenerative nerve disease, occasional tinnitus, which led to nerve deafness and a ringing in the ears.[2] As his hearing deteriorated in the late 1980s, a speaker had to speak loudly in his left ear. Deng also found it a better use of time to read documents than to attend meetings. He preferred to read reports of the meetings and hear about them from his office director, Wang Ruilin, who attended the meetings on his behalf and knew the views of other high officials by meeting with their office directors.

Deng kept a regular schedule. He ate breakfast at home at 8 a.m. and at 9 a.m. went into his office. Deng's wife, Zhuo Lin, and Wang Ruilin prepared materials for him to read, including some fifteen daily newspapers, reference materials with translations from the foreign press, a large stack of reports from the ministries and from provincial party secretaries, internal memoranda collected by the New China News Agency (Xinhua), and drafts of documents sent for his approval. For understanding the latest developments, Deng relied most on the summaries of major activities produced by the party Secretariat and the party General Office. Deng took no notes when he read. Documents were to be delivered to his office before 10 a.m., and he returned them the same day. He left no papers around his office, which was always clean and neat.

Chen Yun had ordered that his office director select five of the most important items for him to read each day, but Deng wanted to see the entire pile so that he could decide for himself what he would look at more carefully. After he had read the materials and made brief comments on some of them, he would pass the whole pile back to Wang and Zhuo Lin, who would pass on those with his circles of approval or his comments to the appropriate officials and place the rest in the files. Deng's circle of approval and his comments on such documents constituted his way of guiding the overall work of the party. On some documents, he simply gave final approval; other documents he sent back for more work, clarification, or with suggestions for new directions to explore.

Deng rarely met visitors during his three hours of morning reading, but for twenty to thirty minutes in the middle of the morning he would take a brisk walk around the garden next to his house. After lunch at home, he generally continued reading materials but sometimes would ask various officials to meet him in his home office. When important foreign visitors came, he would meet them in one of the rooms of the Great Hall of the People and sometimes dine with them.

Early in his career, Deng acquired a reputation for being able to distinguish between major and minor issues and to focus his efforts where they would make the biggest difference for China: devising long-term strategies, evaluating policies likely to determine the success of his long-term goals, winning the support of fellow officials and the public, and publicizing models that illustrated the policies he wished to pursue. In some important but complex areas like economics or science and technology, Deng relied on others to think through the strategies and present him with the options for the final decision. On other issues, like national security, relations with key foreign countries, and the selection of high-level officials, Deng spent more time finding out what he needed to know to devise the strategies himself. When Wang Ruilin, Deng's office director since 1952, explained Deng's views to the outside, he was very circumspect in what he said and avoided adding his own interpretation. Many officials believe that, in contrast, when Mao Yuanxin, in late 1975 and early 1976, explained his uncle's views to the outside world, he allowed his own strong convictions to color and even supplement his explanations of what Mao wanted conveyed to other officials. But Wang Ruilin avoided giving his personal interpretations of any matter concerning the party or government, even though his long relationship with Deng made him more like a member of the family. It was important to Deng that Wang Ruilin not embellish what he wanted to transmit to the outside. Sometimes, to ensure that on important matters others received his views precisely, Deng would write down his key points and then tell Wang to pass those written comments along.

General Secretary Hu Yaobang, the executive for party matters, and Premier Zhao Ziyang, the executive for government affairs, forwarded all important matters, mostly by paper and rarely in person, to Deng for a final decision. Hu Yaobang chaired the Politburo Standing Committee and regular Politburo meetings, and Zhao chaired the State Council meetings. Chen Yun and Deng rarely attended these gatherings, but instead were represented by their office directors. In his dictated memoirs, Zhao Ziyang reports that he and Hu Yaobang were more like staff assistants than decision-makers, but they were responsible for implementation. Deng did reserve the right to make final decisions, but he was ordinarily not a micromanager; rather he set the agenda and let Hu and Zhao carry out his directives as they thought best. In making the final decisions, Deng did consider the overall political atmosphere and the views of other key leaders. He was authoritarian and bold but in fact he was constrained by the overall atmosphere among Politburo members.

In 1980, the Politburo consisted of the top twenty-five party officials and two alternates. The inner core—the powerful Standing Committee—included seven members. It was understood that the younger members of the Politburo were potential candidates for membership on the Standing Committee, and that the memers of the Standing Committee would be chosen from among the Politburo members.[3] The Standing Committee in the early 1980s consisted of Deng, Chen Yun, Li Xiannian, Marshal Ye, Hua Guofeng, Hu Yaobang, and Zhao Ziyang. The elderly Marshal Ye took little part in the actual work. Chen Yun and Li Xiannian expressed their views on major issues, but the daily party decision-making was largely in the hands of Deng, Hu Yaobang, and Zhao Ziyang. Each member of the Standing Committee and a selected group of other Politburo members had an office director (*mishu,* sometimes translated as "secretary"), located at the Secretariat, who collected materials, drafted papers, processed documents, and served as liaison between the Standing Committee and the offices of other high officials. Despite differences of view, under Deng the Politburo was a relatively disciplined organization that responded to his direction.

When Hua Guofeng was in charge as chairman of the party, he held regular meetings of the Standing Committee of the Politburo. But Deng rarely called Standing Committee meetings: when Zhao once asked him why, Deng replied, "What would two deaf people [Deng and Chen Yun] talk about?" Deng aimed to have a clear assignment of responsibilities. Deng well understood that to gain control over the levers of power, it would be easier to start with a fresh organizational structure than to send one or two leading officials to an old organization that did not match his policies. After the Secretariat was reestablished it became an entirely new organization over which Deng achieved clear control. Deng located this new nerve center for the top party leadership just inside the north gate of Zhongnanhai and put his own appointee, Hu Yaobang, in charge, to lead the daily work of the party. Politburo members had offices at the Secretariat and held their regular meetings there.[4] Unlike the Communist Party General Office—a larger administrative unit responsible for drafting and distributing documents and handling communications among party units in Beijing and the provinces—the much smaller party Secretariat, which served only the highest officials, worked like an inner-party cabinet.

Hu Yaobang chaired the Secretariat meetings. Although Hu also chaired the Politburo and Standing Committee meetings, after Deng formed his own administration, the Standing Committee rarely met and the Politburo met less than once a month. Although Zhao Ziyang, as premier, sat in on the Secretariat meetings, Deng, Chen Yun, Li Xiannian, and Marshal Ye did not personally attend them; instead their office directors went in their place. Each office director had a deep understanding of the views of the person he represented, and as a group these office directors could have frank exchanges, insulated from awkward problems or tensions that might have arisen among the leaders themselves due to concerns about rank, power, or the need to save face.

Deng's perspectives helped shape the consensus, but ordinarily he did not express a final decision until an issue had been vetted through the Secretariat. Once a consensus had been reached on an important issue, documents were drawn up and circulated to the Standing Committee members, who would draw a circle to indicate approval or jot some brief comments—in which case the document would be sent back to the Secretariat for another round of drafting. In the end, Deng would figuratively "slap the table" *(pai ban)* to signify final approval of a decision or the final wording of a document.

Several high officials, mostly just below the Politburo level, were assigned to be a party secretary *(shuji)* in the Secretariat, and they all had managerial authority. Politburo members and these party secretaries were placed in charge of a "leading small group" that was responsible for coordinating work in certain areas. Peng Zhen, for example, led the leading small group on political and legal affairs; Wan Li headed the leading group on agriculture; Song Renqiong on personnel issues; Yu Qiuli on large industrial and transportation projects; Yang Dezhi on the military; Hu Qiaomu on party history and ideology; Yao Yilin on economic planning; Wang Renzhong on propaganda; Fang Yi on science and technology; Gu Mu on foreign trade and investment; and Peng Chong on work on the Yangtze delta area (around Shanghai).[5]

Other top leaders sometimes disagreed with Deng's decisions and occasionally were upset by his failure to consult with them. Early on, Deng had to contend with the views of Chen Yun, who understood the economy better than Deng and whose opinions carried great authority with the other leaders. In the military field, once Marshal Ye stepped aside, Deng did not feel inhibited by anyone else's opinions. On military and foreign policy issues, Deng, confident of his own views based on his decades of experience, rarely yielded to others—though he relied on experts for the details and the drafting of documents. Even when other leaders disagreed with decisions Deng made, they accepted party discipline and did not express contrary views in public.

Deng could engage in relaxed conversation with his office director Wang Ruilin, but his relations with Hu Yaobang and Zhao Ziyang remained more formal and he rarely saw them alone. They had considerable freedom to run their offices as they saw fit. Deng learned their views through the written documents they forwarded to him, supplemented by comments from Wang Ruilin.

Deng did occasionally meet informally with senior veterans closer to his own age, like Yang Shangkun, Wang Zhen, and Bo Yibo, all of whom he had known for several decades. The high degree of personal trust among this small group of confidants enabled Deng to get more confidential estimates of the prevailing political atmosphere and personnel issues. Deng had an especially close relationship with Yang Shangkun, who was also from Sichuan and had been in charge of the party General Office when Deng was general secretary. Yang served as Deng's trusted go-between in dealing with the military. Deng also maintained less formal relations with his personal speechwriters and document drafters, especially Hu Qiaomu and Deng Liqun, with whom he enjoyed an easier give-and-take than with Hu Yaobang or Zhao Ziyang.

Deng devoted considerable time to preparations for the annual party plenums, for they helped forge a common perspective among the more than two hundred regular members of the Central Committee and the over one hundred alternate members. He gave even more time to the preparation of party congresses, held every five years, for they helped forge a consensus among even greater numbers of delegates who planned for a longer time period. For the planning of such major meetings, Deng did work with Hu Yaobang and Zhao Ziyang to lay out his agenda of major issues to be covered, then allowed them to work with Hu Qiaomu and others in overseeing the drafting of documents and speeches. For Deng's major speeches, even after delivery there was usually another round of editing to tailor his speeches for the long-term historical record and to include them in his *Selected Works*.

Like other top officials, Deng generally spent a few weeks during the coldest months of January and February visiting warmer climates. During the summer, too, he would go to coastal Beidaihe, where top-level officials gathered for relaxation and informal conversation. But for Deng, these "vacations" were, of course, also opportunities to deal with party business. In 1984, for example, he spent his winter vacation in Guangdong and Fujian, the site of the experimental zones, to affirm their achievements and declare them models for coastal development (see Chapter 15). And in 1988, 1990, 1991, and 1992, Deng visited (among other places) Shanghai, where he promoted plans for speeding up the city's development.

In his advanced age, Deng found several ways to conserve his strength. He conducted most business through written documents, avoiding taxing meetings. Most of his phone calls were handled by Wang Ruilin. Deng required no oral briefings before meetings with foreign dignitaries, although his staff would see that he knew about some of the latest activities of the visitors. If not meeting visiting dignitaries, Deng usually ate his meals at home with his family; after supper he generally relaxed and watched TV with his children. He closely followed the news, but he also took an interest in sports, and once or twice a week he invited in people for dinner and bridge. But he did not engage in much idle conversation with his bridge partners, or even with his family.[6] Deng had a well-earned reputation, even within his family, for not being very talkative (*bu ai shuohua*).[7] Especially in his later years, Deng managed to conserve his strength so that when he met outsiders, they found him alert, lively, even intense.

When Deng gave speeches that did not require formal presentations, he could make organized presentations without notes. Typically, his only note was the topic of the speech and the group he was addressing. After he turned eighty in 1985, Deng backed away from giving lengthy speeches that required careful writing, editing, and presentation. With only a few exceptions, such as the talks from his 1992 southern journey, his speeches were no longer crafted into long symbolic documents.

Outside his immediate family, who considered him lovable, benign, and fun, Deng was not an intimate person. Colleagues and others had enormous respect for him, but they did not love him as they loved Hu Yaobang or as some loved Zhou Enlai. They knew that in a crunch Deng would do what he thought was best for the country, not necessarily what was good for those who served him. Indeed, some felt that in contrast to Zhou Enlai or Hu Yaobang, Deng treated people as useful tools. By never returning to his home village after he left at age sixteen, Deng made it clear that his personal commitment was to China as a nation, not to any locality, faction, or friend. Unlike Mao, Deng was not devious or, with only rare exceptions, vindictive. Underlings saw him as a stern, impatient, demanding but reasonable taskmaster, and they maintained a respectful distance. He was a comrade for the overall cause, not a friend whose loyalty went beyond organizational needs.[8] Mao had mercurial changes of mood, but Deng, as paramount leader, maintained a steady demeanor and consistent approach to governance.

Deng's Guidelines for Governing and Reinventing China

As a military leader during twelve years of warfare, Deng valued authority and discipline. Later, as a high civilian official participating in governing the country, Deng valued national authority because he knew how difficult it had been for Chinese leaders in the century after the Opium War to maintain the authority necessary to rule the country. As a leader in the 1950s Deng had experienced the godlike power of Mao Zedong, and he had seen what such authority could achieve. But Deng also saw how difficult it was to accomplish anything when authority dissipated as it had during the Cultural Revolution. As preeminent leader, he knew that rules alone would not make people follow him. China was not yet a country in which citizens had internalized a general respect for the law, in part because they had long seen leaders change laws at will. Deng, like his fellow Communist leaders, believed that citizens needed to be "educated" in schools and in lifelong propaganda to understand why they were expected to behave in certain ways. But the "education" needed to be supplemented by a certain awe toward the highest leaders and a vague fear of what might happen to them and their families should they dare to flout that authority.

Deng knew he could never inspire the awe that Mao once did, but he was sensitive to what could be done to preserve his own authority. By the time he had become paramount leader, he was already enjoying personal respect based on his half-century of experience as a party leader, his training by Mao and Zhou Enlai for possible successorship, and his ability to make good decisions for the country. Until 1981 the image of Mao had remained so powerful that to maintain his own authority, Deng had to show his reverence for the Chairman. But by 1981, after Deng had gained acceptance that Mao's main teaching was to "seek the true path from facts," and after the resolution on party history that acknowledged Mao's errors since 1958, Deng could maintain his authority even when he was departing from Mao's views on specific issues.

Deng embraced the notion of "inner-party democracy," by which he meant that leaders would listen to "constructive opinions" to reduce the danger of making serious errors. But once a decision was made, party members, following "democratic centralism," had to implement it.

Deng believed that economic growth would strengthen the authority of the party and his personal stature, and this assessment proved correct. When economic growth proceeded rapidly and smoothly, as in 1983–1984, Deng's authority was almost unassailable. But when economic problems became serious, such as in the late 1980s when China suffered rampant inflation, the public became frightened and Deng's stature suffered.

Deng never set out any guidelines for how to govern, but if one reads his speeches, considers the comments of his underlings, and notes what Deng actually did, it is possible to summarize some principles that underlay his pattern of rule:

SPEAK AND ACT WITH AUTHORITY. As a stern military leader for over a decade, Deng had learned to convey an air of command even when he engaged in witty conversation. Before a major presentation, he would clear his speech with other important leaders and with the guardians of orthodoxy, reinforcing his confidence that he was speaking with the voice of the party.

Once Deng announced a decision, he did not weaken his authority by admitting to errors. With foreign guests, Deng could relax, but within party circles he was cautious about putting his authority on the line, and when he did, he was decisive.

DEFEND THE PARTY. Having seen in Moscow how Nikita Khrushchev's wide-ranging attacks on Stalin in 1956 damaged the authority of the party, Deng was determined to maintain respect for the Chinese Communist Party. He reined in criticism when he judged it would undermine basic respect for the party or his leadership. If critics attracted a large following, he responded even more vigorously. When Deng judged that praise of Western ideas such as Western-style democracy implied serious criticism of the Chinese Communist Party, Deng was prepared to respond firmly to preserve the party's authority.

Unlike Mao, Deng did not subject his critics to public humiliation, but he was always tough with those whom he judged to be a threat to public order. He supported the death sentence for Jiang Qing and imprisoned critics like Wei Jingsheng. Party members who, despite their contributions, were critical of the party, like Wang Ruowang, Liu Binyan, or Fang Lizhi, were expelled from the party and dismissed from their positions. In the end, he allowed such people to travel abroad, but he prevented most from returning.

MAINTAIN A UNIFIED COMMAND STRUCTURE. Deng did not believe that a separation of powers between the executive, legislative, and judicial branches would work in China. He believed a single unified command structure was much more efficient and effective. China may have had the rudiments of a separation of power with the party congress acquiring quasi-legislative functions; the Secretariat, executive functions; and the Central Commission for Discipline Inspection a quasi-judicial function examining the behavior of party members. But under Deng, the strong single line of authority prevailed.

KEEP A FIRM GRIP ON THE MILITARY. Deng, like Mao, endeavored to retain personal as well as party control over the military. When Hua Guofeng showed signs of being too close to military leaders, Deng immediately moved to block those ties. Even after giving up his other official positions, Deng remained chairman of the CMC until November 1989. Throughout his term as preeminent leader, he worked through his loyal supporter, Yang Shangkun, to guarantee the support of the military's top brass. Deng appointed true loyalists—his former subordinates in the Second Field Army—to key positions such as head of the Beijing Garrison Command. In return, they helped ensure that no dissident group would consider challenging his authority within the party.

BUILD PUBLIC SUPPORT BEFORE PROMOTING PATH-BREAKING POLICIES. Deng tried to avoid going out on a limb to advocate policies that might arouse the resistance of many high officials and the general public. One of his most controversial moves was de-collectivizing the countryside. In 1979, Deng did not publicly support de-collectivization. He said only that where peasants were starving, they should be allowed to find a way to survive, a view that even conservative opponents could not easily criticize. Upon receiving reports that the starving peasants had dramatically increased production after they had "contracted down to the household," Deng ensured that the successes were widely publicized. Only then, in May 1980, when a substantial number of localities reported successes and there was widespread public support for the policy of contracting agricultural production down to the household, did Deng declare his own support, and even then he did so without a big public appearance. Although he was still careful to state that the household responsibility system would be permitted only where local people supported it, Deng had every reason to expect that the practice would continue to spread rapidly.

AVOID TAKING THE BLAME. When Deng's policies proved unpopular or mistaken, subordinates were ordinarily expected to take responsibility, just as Mao's errors were blamed on Lin Biao, Jiang Qing, and lower-level officials. In a country where discipline at the top still depended on personal authority, Deng, like many other high party officials, believed that it was sometimes necessary to sacrifice the pawns to ensure continued respect for the king and his throne. There were some extreme situations when Deng judged it essential to put his own authority on the line to accomplish the task at hand—for example, when attacking Vietnam in 1979. But generally, a subordinate leader was expected to shoulder the blame for things that went wrong. Some of the key problems that developed with subordinates were over the question of who should accept the blame.

SET SHORT-TERM POLICIES IN LIGHT OF LONG-TERM GOALS. Coming to power after six decades during which he had witnessed numerous changes, and leading a country proud of its 2,200 years of history, Deng found it natural to take a long-term perspective on the ups and downs of national power. Once in power, Deng did not have to face short-term elections and thus could focus on longer-term goals, such as the quadrupling of GNP between 1980 and 2000 or making the country a middle-income country by the middle of the twenty-first century. He could also offer Hong Kong and Taiwan the continuation of separate systems for at least a half-century after being absorbed into China. In making annual and five-year plans, too, Deng placed them in the perspective of his longer-term goals.

PURSUE POLICIES THAT HELP ACHIEVE LONG-TERM GOALS. Once Deng won widespread support for pursuing the four modernizations, he could then win public support for policies that helped realize that goal. Specialists were trained and hired, and older, less trained people were replaced by younger people who were better trained. Deng fought to reduce the bloated bureaucracies, both civilian and military, that were sapping resources needed to promote investment in China's modernization. Reducing the size of the military and civilian bureaucracies took a great deal of Deng's time because of powerful resistance from those who did not wish to retire. Deng also realized that many new programs had to be introduced step by step. He knew that raising educational standards, for instance, would take many decades and that he had to set benchmarks for the realization of each of the goals.

Aware that the elimination of state enterprises immediately, before new jobs were created, would create massive social and even political problems, Deng decided to postpone eliminating large numbers of noncompetitive state enterprises until more jobs were available. Realizing that the forced retirement of seniors who had fought in the revolution would create massive protests, he willingly used substantial portions of his limited budget to provide benefits to those who agreed to retire, including providing housing, recreation centers, and for some high officials, even continued use of official cars. Once these difficult transitions were complete, he began to establish a regular system with a mandatory retirement age.

Deng greatly expanded the opportunities for promising young people to receive better training, raised the status of scholars, and allowed young intellectuals to return to the urban areas from the countryside. He quickly set up training programs to allow some 4.45 million "specialists," who had been working without proper qualifications, to receive supplementary training. Personnel exchange centers *(rencai jiaoliu zhongxin)* were established and encouraged to obtain the résumés of educated personnel so as to facilitate their reassignment to places where they were most needed.[9]

Deng was willing to allow transitional measures, but he kept the long-term goals in mind. In 1981, when Chinese universities again began graduating classes after the Cultural Revolution, Deng continued the system of government placement of graduates, whereby university graduates were directed to take particular jobs in critical positions. Not until the end of the decade, when the number of graduates increased, did Deng allow some leeway for graduates to choose their own future employment.

Deng did not believe that it was possible in 1978 to foresee which institutions would be most suitable for a modernized China. So he commissioned think tanks, under Zhao Ziyang, to study the introduction of fundamentally different systems in various localities. If the trial was successful, he encouraged others to see if the same results could be repeated elsewhere.

UNCOVER EVEN THE UNPLEASANT TRUTHS. Deng believed that it was important to learn how things really were. Having been at the center of the Great Leap Forward, a tragedy exacerbated by exaggerated reporting, Deng always sought to confirm his information through several channels before deciding if it was true. Even then, he remained skeptical and welcomed opportunities to see things for himself. Deng especially listened to a select group of officials like Yang Shangkun and his office director Wang Ruilin, who would report things as they truly were. He also listened carefully to foreigners who relayed their observations of China.

Deng not only avoided overblown language about what he thought China could achieve in the long run; he also sought to dampen the unrealistic expectations of local officials and of the public at large about what could be achieved in the short term. In addition, he accepted the advice of specialists that China should not try to leapfrog into large heavy industry sectors and should instead concentrate initially on light industry.

BE BOLD. As the Chinese expression goes, Deng was ready to "move heavy things as if they were light" *(juzhong ruoqing).* Chen Yun, like Liu Bocheng, the military commander with whom Deng had worked for twelve years, had a reputation for being very cautious, "moving light things as if they were heavy." Chen Yun considered details, especially in economic matters, far more carefully than Deng did. But in Deng's view, generals who insist on gathering all the information about their enemy before they go into battle will sometimes lose their chance to strike. Deng did spend a great deal of time analyzing the potential consequences of his decisions, but on important issues, he was often ready to push ahead boldly even before all the facts were known.

PUSH, CONSOLIDATE, AND PUSH AGAIN. Deng believed that on issues where he encountered serious resistance, the most effective approach was to exert some frequent pressure, then wait for things to consolidate, and then push again.[10] In easing aside Hua Guofeng, for example, Deng applied pressure in several stages, allowing others to adjust before he pushed again. During the early 1980s, too, he believed it was not yet time to restore normal relations with the Soviet Union, but he made small advances in that direction and waited until the Soviets were overextended and thus willing to normalize relations on China's terms.

STRENGTHEN UNITY, MINIMIZE DIVISIONS. The China that Deng inherited was suffering from deep internal strife. The destruction of landlord families in the late 1940s and early 1950s and the frequent vicious political campaigns culminating in the Cultural Revolution left many "I live, you die" enmities. Moreover, the struggles had taken place within individual villages or work units, which meant that the victims or the children of the victims would often work side by side with their former assailants.

One of the most fundamental issues Deng faced on assuming office was how to dampen the passions of the families and friends of victims who were looking for opportunities to "settle accounts." He frequently used the bully pulpit to encourage people to let bygones be bygones and to get on with their work. He also frequently used the phrase *bu zhenglun* (let's avoid quarrels). He sidestepped many contentious issues by saying that solutions to the difficult problems could be left to the next generations, who would be smarter and thus better able to solve them. He also fully supported Hu Yaobang's efforts to undo the damage done during the Cultural Revolution by restoring the victims' honor or compensating those who had suffered material losses.

AVOID PUBLICIZING PAST GRIEVANCES. Deng directed that the Cultural Revolution should be discussed publicly in general terms, but that one should not go over details that would highlight personal wounds and expose, and quite likely revive, old enmities. Those officials who had been wrongly criticized during the Cultural Revolution were rehabilitated, but Deng advised bringing them back without fanfare so as to avoid stirring up old quarrels.

SIDESTEP CONSERVATIVE RESISTANCE THROUGH EXPERIMENTA-TION. Many conservative party leaders feared the formation of capitalist enterprises. But when the young people who had been forcibly sent to the countryside under Mao began streaming back into the cities, Deng and other officials became concerned that if they couldn't find jobs, massive social unrest would result. Due to current budget shortfalls, the government could not afford to expand employment in state enterprises. Thus in order to avoid massive unemployment, families were allowed to form "household enterprises" *(getihu)* in which the entrepreneur himself worked. Marx's statement in *Das Kapital* about a capitalist with eight employees exploiting his workers was interpreted to mean that working entrepreneurs who employed no more than seven others were not capitalists. Household enterprises sprouted "like bamboo shoots after the spring rain." Deng, with Chen Yun's consent, said "let's see how it goes." At first entrepreneurs were cautious about hiring more than seven workers, but as they observed the government took no action, other successful firms followed suit. Deng did not argue with them. He simply cited *"shazi guazi"* ("Simpleton's Sunflower Seeds"), the very popular toasted sunflowers produced by an illiterate farmer and his employees in Anhui. "If you put [the simpleton with his sunflower seeds] . . . out of business, it will make people anxious and that won't do anyone any good. . . . If we let him go on selling his seeds for a while, will that hurt socialism?"[11] With his clever explanation for why China should try to experiment with individual households, and a well-timed shrug at the conservatives, Deng ingeniously avoided an ideological battle, encouraged more employment, and permitted larger private enterprises.

USE APHORISMS TO EXPLAIN COMPLEX CONTROVERSIAL ISSUES. Once Deng had made a basic policy decision, he would explain it by using a popular aphorism. This shrewd but folksy touch not only made it difficult to disagree with the policy, but also made Deng himself seem personable. He was not the first high-level party leader to use the aphorisms that came to be associated with his name, but he made wide use of them. The "cat theory"—"it doesn't matter if the cat is black or white as long as it catches the mouse"—was a creative way of winning further support for diminishing the importance of Mao's ideology; it suggested that doing what worked was more important than following a particular ideology. If Deng had simply said "ideology is unimportant," he would have provoked enormous controversy, but his "cat theory" made people smile (in fact, some entrepreneurs even made and sold decorations with the cat theme). Another saying, "some people can get rich first," helped lower the expectations of many who hoped to get rich quickly after the reforms, and helped disarm those who might feel envious of those who prospered before the benefits of reform had reached everyone. It was also a promise that after some people became rich, the government would keep working to spread the wealth. "Groping for stones while crossing the river" was a creative way of encouraging experimentation and acknowledging that in a new situation they should not expect that all policies would work well.

MAKE BALANCED PRESENTATIONS THAT EXPLAIN UNDERLYING PRINCIPLES. Following well-established party practice, in major policy documents Deng aimed to present his programs as a sound middle course. He often criticized extremists, both leftists and rightists, both "feudalistic" and "bourgeois" thinkers. In addition, when presenting major policies to the public, Deng found it more effective to provide an explanation rather than to issue a direct order—to talk of the general situation and of the long-range goals that required action.

AVOID FACTIONALISM AND SELECT COMPETENT OFFICIALS. Some lower-level officials believed that it was safer to choose as work associates people with whom they shared a special connection *(guanxi)*, such as the same background, locality, or educational level. Among the Beijing elite at the time, three kinds of people were said to form easy relationships with one another: (1) those who had served as officials in the Communist Youth League, (2) "princelings," that is, children of high Communist officials who attended the same schools, and (3) those who had served as *mishu,* office directors, for high officials. Deng, however, was prepared to work with all three kinds of people if they were competent, dedicated high-level officials, and did not promote factional activities. He encouraged others to do the same.

STUDY AND SHAPE THE "ATMOSPHERE." Deng as the paramount leader enjoyed considerable flexibility in choosing policies, but even he was constrained by the political atmosphere among the highest-level officials in Beijing. When Deng moved boldly, he wanted to ensure that other high officials would fully support him. Within limits, of course, Deng could help shape the mood through his speeches, his actions, and the people whom he supported, but even when he spoke, he usually advocated broad general principles rather than specific details. The highest-level officials, those in the Politburo, knew enough about national issues that they developed their own views about what was desirable or at least acceptable. On big issues, therefore, like the handling of Mao's reputation, rural and urban de-collectivization, departure from economic planning, and allowing foreigners to travel freely within China, Deng avoided moving before he sensed that the political climate would be fully supportive.

In keeping with democratic centralism, everyone, including high-level officials, was expected to express strong support for current policies and current leaders. It was not always easy, therefore, even for a high-level official, to discern when others developed serious doubts about current policies and leaders and became convinced that changes were needed, as they were in late 1978 with respect to Hua Guofeng and his policies. Because contrary opinions on important issues of policy were not voiced openly by high-level officials, each province maintained an office in Beijing with officials who tried to discern signs of possible changes of policy, and to sense when certain actions the province was considering would be considered correct or at least tolerated. To understand the mood, even Deng needed to rely not only on his own seasoned judgment acquired from reading all the papers that came to him, but also on listening to the small number of people who dared to speak unpleasant truths to him, like Deng Liqun, Yang Shangkun, Wang Zhen, Wang Ruilin, and his own children.

What altered the atmosphere at the highest levels remained complex and subtle for it was based on tacit understandings rather than direct open discussions. Perhaps nothing was more critical in shaping changes in the high-level atmosphere than whether or not a given policy, strategy, or leader was producing results. If something was working, that policy or that person garnered support. If something was failing, however, people began to move away and to shun the failure. When economic results came in toward the end of each year, for example, they affected the evaluation of the current economic policy and of the officials responsible for the policy. Most high officials approved of trying experiments in certain localities, and when an experiment demonstrated success, Deng and others felt free to push for its adoption on a broader scale.

To be sure, views about how successful policies had been and what might work in the future were colored by the varying lenses of different officials, some more conservative and others more liberal and cosmopolitan. Deng made an effort to maintain the support or at least the acceptance of a substantial minority as well as the majority. On those issues where he sensed strong opposition—even from a small but influential minority—he would seek to find ways to win their cooperation or at least their passive acceptance before undertaking a major initiative. Otherwise he might postpone taking a firm stand until the climate became more favorable.

Ultimately, democratic centralism requires that everyone jump on the bandwagon to endorse a particular policy. With policies they considered appropriate, people were ready to sign up because they knew that if they failed to join quickly, they might suffer the consequences. For Deng, being a successful leader meant not just determining the correct strategic direction for the long run, but also knowing how to shape the atmosphere and how to time his bold steps so that they occurred when other officials and the public were ready to jump on board.

14

Experiments in Guangdong and Fujian

1979–1984

On November 11, 1977, Deng Xiaoping, in Guangdong for discussions to plan for a Central Military Commission meeting in Beijing, was briefed on the problem of young men trying to escape across the border from China into Hong Kong. Tens of thousands of youth were risking their lives each year by attempting to run or swim across the border. Until that point, Beijing had regarded the problem as a security issue. A barbed-wire fence was maintained all along the twenty-mile land border, and thousands of police and troops were assigned to patrol the area. When Chinese youth were caught trying to escape, they were housed in large detention centers. After hearing the briefing, Deng—characteristically forthright in acknowledging unpleasant realities—said the problem could not be resolved by the police or the army. The problem, he said, had arisen from the disparity of living standards on the two sides of the border; to solve it, China needed to change its policies and improve the lives of those living on the Chinese side.[1]

During Deng's meetings in Guangdong, local officials also complained about the shortage of foreign currency, which was needed to pay for foreign technology and to underwrite construction projects. Deng supported the view that to earn foreign currency they should establish two agriculture collection centers (one in Bao'an county, later part of Shenzhen, near the border with Hong Kong, and one in Zhuhai, next to the border with Macao) to collect fresh fruits and vegetables to be exported across the border. Aware that the local areas had only limited agricultural surpluses, he said that the other provinces could help supply the produce for export. He also said that Guangdong should build modern hotels and other tourist facilities to earn additional foreign currency. At the time, some local officials were trying to revive local handicrafts, but Deng did not mention the prospects for industrial exports; there were then almost no factories producing goods for export and no immediate prospects that foreign companies would be allowed to build them. Foreign investments were also not yet allowed.[2]

After Deng's visit, Beijing's interest in Guangdong's development picked up. As the government began to consider purchasing foreign technologies, officials focused on the shortage of foreign currency. Informed planners already knew that the failure to find new oilfields had ended their hopes of exporting high-priced oil after the 1973 oil shock. From April 10 to May 6, 1978, with the full support of Chairman Hua Guofeng, a delegation from the State Planning Commission in Beijing visited Guangdong to explore how to increase exports.[3] Beijing officials, under the leadership of Gu Mu, encouraged local officials in Guangdong and the neighboring province of Fujian to develop their tourist industries. They also suggested establishing export processing zones, where foreign goods and machinery would be brought in and local labor would produce goods for export.[4]

In April 1978, just as the State Planning Commission delegation was in Guangdong to encourage local initiatives, Xi Zhongxun, newly appointed as a provincial party secretary, arrived in Guangdong to help prepare for China's greater openness to the international economy. Before Xi Zhongxun left Beijing, Marshal Ye, a Guangdong native and an enthusiastic supporter of Guangdong development, had told Xi that to get wholehearted cooperation from the people of Guangdong (who were overwhelmingly Cantonese) at home and abroad, he should first reverse the verdicts on the Guangdong officials who had been accused of localism in the early 1950s.[5] By the end of 1978, Xi Zhongxun had replaced General Wei Guoqing as first secretary of the province and was following through on Marshal Ye's suggestions. In the meantime, Yang Shangkun had arrived in Guangdong as provincial party secretary to help Xi Zhongxun lay plans to transform the province. Yang worked well with Xi, assisting his preparation for the export zones and serving as a personal liaison to Deng.[6]

When Xi Zhongxun first arrived in Guangdong, he had a great deal to learn. Newly appointed after being under a political cloud, Xi began by following the official political line of the time—that is, pursuing class struggle. In one of his first meetings with local officials, he expressed Beijing's official line: the Chinese fleeing to Hong Kong were pursuing a bourgeois line and should be punished. A brave local party secretary spoke up, telling Xi that people on the Guangdong side of the border worked day and night and still did not have enough to eat, but after fleeing to Hong Kong, within a year they had all they needed. On the spot, Xi announced that the official was fired, to which the man retorted that there was no need: he had already quit. After the meeting, Xi listened to others explain the situation; they also told him about Deng's approach while visiting Guangdong the previous November. The next day at a meeting with other officials, Xi undertook a self-criticism at his own initiative and he apologized to the local official, asked him to stay on, and pledged to work to enrich the economy on the Chinese side of the border. From that moment, Xi Zhongxun became a great supporter of the province and worked tirelessly to enlist Beijing's help in improving the local economy and boosting exports.[7] Xi Zhongxun was originally from Shaanxi province, but after he retired in 1989, he chose to live in Guangdong. His son, Xi Jinping, born in 1953, was selected in 2011 to become the president of China beginning in 2012. (For more on Xi Zhongxun, see Key People in the Deng Era, p. 739.)

Upon his return to Guangdong from participating in the Third Plenum in December 1978, in which Deng became the preeminent leader, Xi Zhongxun briefed local officials on the implications of the new policies of reform and opening for Guangdong. For three decades local officials had been frustrated that Beijing—concerned about Guangdong localism, bourgeois attitudes, and security risks in a location that was so close to the open seas and the border with Hong Kong—had held back Guangdong's industrial development. Now, at last, Beijing, eager to promote exports, was willing to give Guangdong officials the opportunity for which they had been waiting: the chance to develop their own industry.

On January 6, 1979, scarcely two weeks after the Third Plenum, Xi was given the green light by Beijing to prepare a proposal seeking Beijing's formal permission for Guangdong to accept foreign investment. Unlike Deng's suggestion of November 1977, which called for agricultural produce to be exported, this proposal was for the establishment of manufacturing facilities that would make industrial products for export. Xi Zhongxun immediately convened a two-week-long meeting to prepare for the drafting of the proposal. Fujian province, across from Taiwan, was to be given the same status as Guangdong, but since Taiwan at that time did not allow trade with the mainland, Guangdong would take the lead, with the understanding that Fujian would later develop its export industries in similar ways. As Xi Zhongxun and local officials began preparing the proposal, Gu Mu was made director of the newly created ministerial-rank Special Economic Zone (SEZ) Office *(tequ bangongshi)* and was assigned to coordinate work between Guangdong and Beijing. In his new position, Gu Mu made several trips to Guangdong to assist Xi Zhongxun and other local officials in preparing for Guangdong's special status. Gu's familiarity with foreign trade and construction, the respect he enjoyed in Beijing, his commitment to reform and opening, and his skill in solving problems made him an effective go-between.[8]

On January 31, 1979, scarcely a month after the Third Plenum, Li Xiannian approved the first case of foreign investment, a proposal by the Hong Kong Merchant Steamship Group headed by Yuan Geng. To meet the strong demand in Hong Kong for scrap metal for its booming construction projects, Yuan Geng proposed destroying old Chinese ships that were no longer serviceable and selling the scrap to Hong Kong builders. For years, he had been seeking a site for such a project. Hong Kong was too crowded, so he proposed a site in Shekou, at the west end of Shenzhen in Bao'an county.

Yuan Geng's proposal was the perfect trial balloon for Guangdong's new initiative. Since the destruction of old ships did not require the erection of new factories, work could begin almost immediately. Even more important, though officially his company was considered "foreign," Yuan himself had joined the Communist Party decades earlier and he had deep experience in Guangdong and Beijing. Originally from Bao'an county (part of which later became Shenzhen), Yuan had fought there in the local Communist guerrilla forces during the civil war. After 1949, he worked in the International Liaison Department of the Communist Party in Beijing, and later headed international liaison work for the Ministry of Communications. The Hong Kong Merchant Steamship Group, descended from a late imperial government company that had been taken over by the Communists, had been placed under the Ministry of Communications, with an autonomous branch company in Hong Kong, which Yuan Geng now headed.

Yuan Geng's proposal, which Li Xiannian approved, was forwarded to Li from the Ministry of Communications, then under Minister Zeng Sheng, also a Bao'an native who had been Yuan Geng's superior in the guerrilla forces during World War II and later his superior in the Ministry of Communications. Yuan Geng had asked for a relatively small tract of land in Shekou, at the southwest tip of Shenzhen, but Li Xiannian offered a much larger one, where Yuan's business could do more than simply tear down old ships. Shekou thus became the first place in China to allow foreign direct investment and the first area where decisions about a company inside China could be made by people located outside the country. For Chinese leaders, it was a very special safe case of "foreign ownership," but it was a breakthrough nonetheless, for it opened the door for other foreign companies to seek permission to establish enterprises on the mainland. And although there were some rumblings among national planning officials, who worried that granting so many freedoms to Guangdong would interfere with overall national plans, the Guangdong officials won out with their argument that without more freedoms, they could not attract foreign companies to establish plants.

In early April 1979, Xi Zhongxun, at a party work conference in Beijing, argued that Guangdong, and other provinces as well, did not have enough autonomy to do their work effectively. He was bold enough to say that if Guangdong were a separate country, then within several years it would take off, but as it stood at the time, any change would be difficult. Other high officials were fully aware that China's economic planning had become overly centralized. Hua Guofeng, who like Deng supported granting Guangdong more independence to develop exports, assured Xi Zhongxun that Guangdong would be given the autonomy necessary to attract foreign investment.[9]

On April 17, 1979, Xi Zhongxun and his team of leaders from Guangdong brought their draft proposal to Beijing for a round of discussions with Deng Xiaoping and others before the final documents were drawn up. Xi and his colleagues, drawing on advice from Gu Mu, proposed that the entire province be allowed to implement a special policy that would give Guangdong the flexibility to adopt measures to attract foreign capital, technology, and management practices necessary to produce goods for export. China would supply the land, transport facilities, electricity, and labor needed by the factories, as well as the hotels, restaurants, housing, and other facilities needed by foreigners. Beyond the general effort to assist the provinces of Guangdong and Fujian, additional efforts, supported by the central government in Beijing, would be concentrated in three SEZs in Guangdong (Shenzhen across the border from Hong Kong, Zhuhai across the border from Macao, and Shantou [Swatow] on the northeast coast of the province) and one in Fujian (Xiamen [Amoy]).

Deng was completely supportive. He told Xi Zhongxun, "Let's call them special zones . . . since in the past the border region in Shaan-Gan-Ning (Shaanxi-Gansu-Ningxia, later headquartered in Yan'an) was called a special zone. [The party center] has no money. So we will give you a policy that allows you to charge ahead and cut through your own difficult road."[10] In saying this, Deng was responding directly to the appeal that the Guangdong delegation had made in Beijing: if you don't give us *qian* (money), then how about giving us the *quan* (authority) to raise our own funds?[11]

In his talk with Xi Zhongxun, Deng agreed that both Guangdong and Fujian should be given the flexibility to attract investments from the ethnic Chinese now outside mainland China whose ancestors hailed from these areas. On July 15, Guangdong's proposal was accepted and became Central Committee Document No. 50, granting Guangdong and Fujian a "special policy, with flexible measures" *(teshu zhengce linghuo cuoshi)* to attract foreign investment.[12] The zones were called "special districts," as Deng had suggested.[13] The four special zones were officially established on August 26, 1979. Considering the complexities of the national plans and the resistance of planning officials, it is a tribute to the determination of Deng Xiaoping, Hua Guofeng, Gu Mu, Xi Zhongxun, and other officials that the arrangements were completed only seven months after the Third Plenum.

Deng's Experiment and Its Enemies

For two decades, China had been collecting materials about the export processing zones that had already been established in some eighty countries. They had been designed to get around complex import and export rules by establishing zones where materials needed for production would come in, where local low-cost labor would produce goods that would then be exported without going through any of the usual formal import-export procedures. In China, until 1978, all efforts to establish export processing zones failed to receive the necessary political support. Beginning in 1979, the areas in Guangdong near the border with Hong Kong in effect became processing zones.

But Deng had a broader vision for the special zones in Guangdong and Fujian than merely export processing. He sought to build comprehensive metropolitan centers complete with industry, commerce, agriculture, livestock, residential housing, and tourist industries.[14] The zones would be given the flexibility to experiment with different ways of doing things. Modern management systems would not only improve Chinese enterprises, but also could be adopted by government and party units so they would become more efficient. Circular No. 41 of May 16, 1980, issued by the party center and the State Council, explained that the four special zones would "carry on systems and policies that are different from other places. The SEZs will be regulated primarily by the market."[15]

Deng could not have gotten the support to introduce such changes for the entire country, but it was far harder for conservatives to oppose experiments, for the idea of trying experiments in one locality and extending what worked had become part of the party's conventional wisdom.[16] Industrial management reforms were being tried, for example, in Sichuan, Jiangsu, and Zhejiang. But in Guangdong and Fujian, Deng allowed foreign companies to use their own labor and management systems, experiments that went far beyond those attempted elsewhere. In Shekou, experiments in voting were tried long before village elections were held elsewhere. No place was more of a laboratory than Guangdong. In the SEZs Deng encouraged experiments with markets, industry, construction, labor, finance, and foreign currency.[17] Because Guangdong was at the cutting edge, it became the target for opponents who worried that China would become capitalist, that foreign imperialists were returning, and that the socialist planning system would be destroyed. It also became the target of provinces in inner China that opposed the flow of resources to the coast.

Westerners and even some Chinese critics claimed that Deng was experimenting with capitalism without using the name, but that is not how Deng saw it. He was determined to expand markets and he personally had no ideological objections to private enterprise; he accepted competition as a driving force in commerce. But he aimed as well to keep the Chinese Communist Party firmly in control, to constrain the markets to ensure that they served public purposes, to prevent capitalists from dominating Chinese politics, to retain public ownership of land, to keep a large role for state-owned enterprises, and to maintain state economic planning. Deng said that China would not become capitalist; money, he said, would not flow into his own pockets or to those of Hua Guofeng.[18]

Even leaders too young to remember foreign "imperialists" but had learned about them from party propaganda were frightened by what powerful foreign capitalists might do. Why should China, after three decades free from foreign imperialism, now invite back the imperialists? Leaders of state and collective businesses who knew how Chinese companies had been displaced by the expansion of foreign businesses during the 1930s worried that Chinese enterprises could not compete with the better-financed and more modern foreign enterprises. Officials feared that foreign capitalists experienced in international trade harbored hidden agendas and would use international law to trick Chinese businesses and gain monopoly control in China. Deng was careful in the way he presented his ideas to the public. He joined in the criticism of those who slavishly imitated foreign systems. He was careful not to imply that foreign culture was superior, and instead expressed what Chinese could learn in a more limited way: China could study foreign "modern management." But the study of "modern management" was inclusive enough that ideas and systems could in fact be studied on a broad scale without overly upsetting patriots who believed in the superiority of Chinese culture or the "Chinese spirit."

The decision to open up Guangdong, Fujian, and other coastal provinces soon led to a fundamental shift in the location of industry from inner China to the coast. From 1966 to 1975, under Mao's policy of avoiding national security risks near China's borders, over one-half of China's investment funds had been spent in the "third front," bringing goods and people to remote areas with poor infrastructure.[19] After the attack on Vietnam in February–March 1979, however, Deng believed that the risk of foreign attack was minimal. Chinese planners were well aware that for both industrial development and international trade, the coastal areas had all the advantages of convenient transportation, a more developed infrastructure, a critical mass of specialists, and lower costs. In 1979, 12 percent of China's exports originated in Guangdong, but from the late 1980s as exports grew, roughly one-third or more of all Chinese exports each year came from Guangdong alone.[20] Deng acknowledged that people in Guangdong and Fujian might well get rich first, before other Chinese, but he proclaimed that areas that got rich first would then help other areas get rich.

Officials in Beijing who tried to keep an orderly, highly detailed national planning system faced a nightmare from Guangdong's new flexibility as they tried to keep control over the flow of goods into and out of Guangdong. As Guangdong earned more income from abroad, it could afford to pay higher prices for goods, giving incentives to localities in other provinces to pass on to Guangdong some goods needed to fulfill plans in their own province. By one calculation, no fewer than sixty-four central government units were involved in the decision to give Guangdong and Fujian more flexibility. Among the officials trying to guide local adjustments in planning in Guangdong were officials from the State Planning Commission, the Ministry of Foreign Affairs, the Ministry of Finance, the State Construction Commission, and the Ministry of Goods and Materials *(wuzibu)*.[21] In 1979, Guangdong officials persuaded Beijing leaders to agree that provincial agreements with foreign companies did not require prior permission from Beijing, even if Guangdong would have to report all such agreements to the center. Any increase in the quantity of state goods shipped to Guangdong, however, did require approval by the relevant ministries in Beijing.[22] Because the markets were constantly changing, calculation of the different types of taxes eventually became so complicated that Beijing agreed that Guangdong would make an annual lump sum payment of taxes.

To ensure that the SEZs not try political experiments, Chen Yun insisted that the term "special zones" be changed to "special economic zones." In March 1980, under pressure, Deng approved the name change.[23] Deng reassured his conservative comrades that "these are special economic districts, not special political districts."[24] But Deng did not abandon the idea that the zones would conduct broad experiments with new management techniques. In typical Deng fashion, he accepted the name change and avoided arguments, but in fact he barged ahead; he did not stop Guangdong from continuing its broad experiments.

China's Southern Gate

One possible site for a special zone was Shanghai, a city that in the 1930s was bustling with enterprises and some 300,000 foreigners, making it the most cosmopolitan city in Asia. It was then the leading center of Asian banking and commerce, far ahead of Hong Kong. As an Asian industrial center, too, only a few Japanese cities surpassed it. But in 1978, Chinese planners worried that allowing Shanghai to become an experimental zone was too risky: it was a major Chinese industrial center and contributed more revenue to the national budget than any other locality, so it would be disastrous for China if Shanghai's industry and revenue streams were to be adversely affected. Chen Yun, a native of the Shanghai area, worried that the "comprador mentality," of bending to the will of foreigners, remained alive and well in Shanghai; he opposed making Shanghai an experimental area and his view carried the day.

Guangdong and Fujian, unlike Shanghai, had very little industry that could be at risk if their experiments went awry. Because the coastal areas near Southeast Asia and Hong Kong had been considered security risks in the decades after 1949, before 1978 Beijing had limited their industrial and commercial development. In addition, if contact with the foreign capitalists were to cause spiritual pollution, the two provinces were far enough away so as to insulate the party center in Beijing. Above all, the Chinese emigrants who had settled in Southeast Asia and elsewhere overwhelmingly had come from Guangdong and Fujian and spoke the local dialects. Many still maintained close personal relations with the area and some could be prevailed upon to help with funding for the new ventures.

When Deng visited Japan in October 1978 he joked that he had come looking for the magic potion to modernize China. If there were a single magic potion for a Chinese economic takeoff, it was Hong Kong. Roughly two-thirds of the direct investment in China between 1979 and 1995 came from Hong Kong, or at least through the "southern gate" between Hong Kong and mainland China.[25] Beijing sought investments from "overseas Chinese" who lived in Southeast Asia, the United States, and elsewhere, but even more from "brethren" (*tongbao,* literally, those from the same womb), those living in territories claimed by China—Taiwan, Macao, and Hong Kong. At the time, not counting Taiwan, officials estimated that some 8.2 million descendants of Guangdong natives and some 5 million descendants of Fujian natives lived outside mainland China.[26] As the two provinces sought investment funds, these descendants would be the primary targets of money-raising efforts, although investments from elsewhere would also be welcome. Those returning to China to visit in the years after 1978 overwhelmingly came through the "southern gate" to their ancestral homes in Guangdong and Fujian. At the time, there was no direct trade between Taiwan and the mainland, and it would be almost a decade before Taiwan would allow its residents to travel there.

Once Deng allowed Guangdong to open its doors, Hong Kong became a source of investment capital, entrepreneurial dynamism, and knowledge about the outside world. Hong Kong was full of entrepreneurs, including tens of thousands who had fled there after 1948 when the Chinese Communist armies began taking over the mainland. Until 1949, Hong Kong had remained a trading center linking China and the outside world, and its economy suffered greatly when the border to China was closed after the Communist takeover. When the Communists took over China, some industrialists from Shanghai and Ningbo fled to Hong Kong where they helped build up the Hong Kong textile industry and global shipping sector. By the 1960s Hong Kong was becoming a leading international financial center. And in the 1970s talented youth who had spent their early years in Hong Kong and then gone abroad to study in England, the United States, Canada, and Australia began returning to the colony with a sophisticated understanding of modern finance, high technology, and international markets. Hong Kong in the late 1970s thus offered China something that the Soviet Union sorely lacked—a treasure trove of entrepreneurs thoroughly knowledgeable about the latest developments in the West who shared the same language and culture as their motherland, and stood ready to help.

In the early years of Deng's reforms, the door between Hong Kong and China was opened only partially and passage through the gate did not always proceed smoothly. Border checks continued and for a long time most Chinese residents had difficulty securing visas to cross the border. Many people in Hong Kong who had escaped illegally to Hong Kong, or who had left behind relatives on the mainland who had suffered miserably under the Communist regime, were simply not prepared to pass through the gate. The social differences that had grown between the mainland and rapidly changing Hong Kong in the three decades after 1949 were not easy to bridge. In the early 1980s, Hong Kong businesspeople speaking among themselves would pass on stories of the country bumpkins on the Chinese side of the gate who lived poor simple lives and knew little about the ways of the modern world. Meanwhile, those in Guangdong and Fujian who met relatives or fellow villagers visiting from Hong Kong resented their superior airs and the power that flowed from their wealth, given that they, the poorer mainland cousins, had remained in the motherland where they had suffered and sacrificed. Even mainland Chinese officials, who then were living not far above subsistence levels, were wary of the proud, well-dressed Hong Kong businesspeople, with their efficient staffs, modern equipment, and global connections. Yet many Hong Kong entrepreneurs remained eager to help their homeland and to take advantage of the nearly limitless Chinese market. Within two or three years the trickle of people, trucks, and funds passing through the southern gate became a steady stream and then a flood.

During Deng's era, mainland officials in Guangdong and Fujian, especially in the SEZs, learned valuable lessons from the cosmopolitan Hong Kongers—from their increasingly open television shows, newspapers, personal contacts, and from the factories, hotels, restaurants, and stores that they built in Guangdong. On the streets of Guangdong in the early 1980s one could distinguish by appearance and manner the stylish, well-dressed people who came from Hong Kong or elsewhere from the rustic people who had grown up on the mainland. But these differences gradually began to disappear, and by the end of the Deng era in 1992 many mainlanders in southern Guangdong were indistinguishable from the residents who had come from Hong Kong.

From 1978 through the early 1980s, the Communist organizations in

Hong Kong—such as the New China News Agency (Xinhua), the Bank of China, China Resources, the trade unions, "patriotic schools," and "patriotic" businesspeople—played a crucial role in informing mainland officials about the situation in Hong Kong. But by 1983, as Deng Xiaoping began seeing more often Hong Kong business leaders like the shipping magnate Y. K. Pao, the small community of mainland representatives in Hong Kong had largely completed their historical mission as go-betweens.

The Communists working in Hong Kong had not been part of the mainstream. They lacked the easy access to the Hong Kong elite whose cooperation Beijing now urgently needed. Chinese officials in Guangdong and Beijing began to bypass their local Hong Kong Communist comrades and go instead directly to Hong Kong's mainstream leaders. In 1982 Deng sent to Hong Kong a former provincial party secretary, Xu Jiatun, who had direct access to Deng and other high-level leaders in Beijing, to be the new head Communist representative in Hong Kong; he was to deal directly with the Hong Kong elite.

The opening of China was timed perfectly for Hong Kong factory owners in labor-intensive industries: they had begun to lose their ability to compete in international markets because a labor shortage in Hong Kong was then driving up wages and costs. The low-cost labor available on the other side of the border would not only save these owners of textile, toy, and electronics factories in Hong Kong, but also provide vastly expanded opportunities. The shift happened rapidly, sometimes astonishingly so: Hong Kong newspapers reported some cases in which Hong Kong factory workers arrived at their factories in the morning to find that all the production equipment had been removed during the night and taken to a village on the other side of the border where a new factory had been established. Hong Kong construction companies that had developed advanced building techniques during the Hong Kong construction boom in the 1960s and 1970s suddenly found limitless opportunities on the other side of the border.

Foreign businesspeople from Europe and North America who traveled to China in the 1970s and early 1980s usually entered through Hong Kong, then took the train to Guangzhou where they could fly to other destinations. Before they went to China, they were briefed by Hong Kong businesspeople, who would sometimes become either their partners or their representatives in China. Foreigners forbidden by law in their home countries to pay bribes could work through the less-constrained Hong Kong agents, who did what was necessary to pave the way with local Guangdong businesses. Taiwan businesspeople, who were prevented in the 1980s from trading with the mainland, also worked through Hong Kong partners. Deng's experiment to open the "great southern gate" between Guangdong and Hong Kong had become China's most important channel through which flowed investment, technology, management skills, and ideas about the outside world.

By the late 1980s, as China opened further, the flow extended to many other parts of China, including Beijing. The changing pattern of relationships was reflected in the dialect which Hong Kong businesspeople used in dealings with the mainland. During the early years after 1978, if there was a lingua franca between Hong Kong and Guangdong, it was Cantonese, the street language in Hong Kong and most of Guangdong. By the late 1980s, however, as other parts of China opened more widely to the outside world, Mandarin was becoming the new common language. Many Chinese settling in Shenzhen and Zhuhai were from the north and spoke Mandarin, not Cantonese. Hong Kong continued to play an important role and Cantonese continued to be used, but as Hong Kong businesspeople started interacting with partners throughout China, they began improving their Mandarin. The change in language reflected the transition from regional experimentation in Guangdong to national implementation.

The Takeoff in Guangdong and Fujian

Within three decades after Guangdong and Fujian were granted special status, Chinese exports had multiplied over one hundred times, from less than US$10 billion per year in 1978 to more than US$1 trillion, with more than one-third from Guangdong. In 1978 there were virtually no factories in Guangdong with modern assembly lines. Within three decades, a visitor to southern Guangdong would see skyscrapers, large industrial sites, apartment buildings, world-class hotels, superhighways, and traffic jams.

The entire Pearl River delta area stretching from Guangzhou to Hong Kong was transformed. In the 1980s, towns and villages in the area (formerly production brigades or communes) welcomed small manufacturers, first from Hong Kong and later from Taiwan and elsewhere, to set up factories. By the late 1980s, the entire 104-mile route from Hong Kong to Guangzhou was lined on both sides with factories.[27] In 1979, Shenzhen, just over the border from Hong Kong, was a town of some 20,000 residents, but two decades later the population of Shenzhen city, which now stretched to some of the former rural areas nearby, was approaching 10 million and still growing rapidly. Although no exact figures are available, it has been estimated that as many as 100 million migrants had flowed into the coastal areas of Guangdong by the time Deng retired in 1992; many later returned to their original homes but tens of millions stayed.

Xi Zhongxun and Yang Shangkun worked to win Beijing's approval for the measures that enabled Guangdong to take off, but the person who was Guangdong's pilot during the critical takeoff from 1980 to 1985 was first party secretary Ren Zhongyi. He was paired with Governor Liang Lingguang, the former minister of light industry, to help Guangdong develop its light industry. After Deng stepped down, just as people all over China thanked Deng for initiating the reform and opening, those in Guangdong thanked Ren Zhongyi for his bold leadership. Years later when President Hu Jintao visited Guangdong, he showed his respect for Ren Zhongyi, who had retired two decades earlier, by paying him a personal visit (for more on Ren, see Key People in the Deng Era, p. 734).

According to a circular of January 1982, Guangdong was required to submit to Beijing for approval requests for light industrial projects costing over 30 million yuan and heavy industrial projects costing over 50 million yuan.[28] When criticized by Beijing for exceeding the limits, Ren deftly dodged the accusations, reporting that the project in question was not a single project, but several that happened to be located next to each other, each of which fell under the limit. Ren's subordinates loved his willingness to work around the rules for Guangdong development and his courage in supporting them. Indeed, Ren once said that his job in Guangdong was that of an electric transformer. The electricity (Guangdong's policies and resources) came from Beijing, but he adapted and directed it to local needs. As Guangdong officials put it, "Beijing has its policies and we have our counter-policies" *(shang you zhengce, xia you duice).*

Appointed provincial leaders were rarely invited to meet the top leaders before they took up their posts, but Ren Zhongyi and Governor Liang Lingguang were invited for private meetings with Deng, as well as with Hua Guofeng, Wan Li, Chen Yun, and Marshal Ye. When he met them, Deng told them that their job was to help explore a path for the future. Deng, aware of the passions that the issue of localism had aroused in Guangdong, told Ren and Liang his views on how to treat divisive problems from the past: they should not avoid the subject entirely, but instead treat the issue in a general way, avoiding specifics. Deng said that if in their new positions they introduced the proper policies, their work would go smoothly. Deng also told them that he wanted officials in Guangdong and Fujian to provide guidelines for other localities based on their experiences. When Wan Li met them, he was bold enough to say that if Beijing's directives didn't fit the local situation, they should do what was necessary to meet local needs.[29]

Because Guangdong was a cutting-edge experiment and vulnerable to being criticized as capitalist, Ren and his staff became a target for those who feared capitalism and did not want to see the Guangdong experiment, which was proving attractive to other provinces, spread to the rest of the country. Officials under Ren were charmed by his wit and impressed with his ability to make sound strategic choices, but what most won their loyalty was his willingness to accept responsibility when criticisms came from Beijing.

Even without political pressure from Beijing, local officials found it difficult to chart an entirely new course. When they discussed building a road between Guangzhou and Shenzhen, for instance, the officials, worried about the limited budget and unable to imagine the rapid growth of motor vehicles, erred on the side of caution and decided to build a two-lane highway. Within a decade, it had to be replaced by an eight-lane expressway. Inexperience and political concerns also played a part in missteps in one of the most sensitive areas, that is, how to deal with foreign businessmen, for they wanted to attract their investments without becoming vulnerable to accusations of being soft on foreign capitalists. Initially, they did not know how to determine a reasonable amount of tax concessions, how much local infrastructure support was required and how it should be priced, and what local products could be marketed abroad. Consequently many errors were made, with some locals dragging their feet and even cheating the outside investors, and some investors cheating the locals. In addition, new factories went up faster than regulations were promulgated to control them, and the new rules did not always prove workable. As the bolder, more ambitious local leaders stepped out in front of the more cautious bureaucrats, the results not infrequently confirmed the nightmares of the conservative skeptics.

Lessons from the Experiments

In Guangdong and Fujian, local officials learned that to attract foreign factories, they had to set up "one-stop" decision centers. Early foreign investors had been frustrated by having to deal with different government bureaucracies to arrange for electricity, transportation connections, construction materials, labor supplies, and various permits. By the mid-1980s, the areas that were attracting the most foreign companies were those that had been able to reorganize and centralize decision-making so that officials could make all key decisions from one office.

Another lesson learned had to do with how much to charge the outside investors. Local governments, initially with little understanding of how to calculate costs in a market economy, often began by demanding fees that were far too high or too low by global standards. Within several years, they developed a much better sense of prices in foreign markets and began to set prices appropriately. Because the labor supply from migrants was virtually unlimited, however, the costs of labor remained far lower than in more industrialized countries.

In addition, officials in localities that competed for investment funds learned early on that if they did not allow the outside investors to earn what they considered to be reasonable returns on investment, the investors would go elsewhere. Initially, some Chinese officials, hearing of the high prices that products brought abroad, insisted on selling products to the foreigners at high prices, arguing that the Chinese laborers were being exploited by foreign capitalists. Gradually, however, Chinese officials began to accept the prices in the international markets, and found that they and their workers could benefit even if their workers earned far less than businesspeople selling their goods overseas.

Yet another learning curve had to do with reliability. If local officials wanted an outside partner who would expand his investment, they had to be reliable. When foreigners wanted assurances that if problems were to arise, there would be a fair resolution, Chinese officials signed contracts and introduced some legal procedures. Local officials found that the Chinese localities that did well over the years were those that honored the agreements. Not surprisingly, foreigners were willing to continue to invest when they found groups of local officials who were reliable and could resolve, creatively if necessary, all of the unexpected problems that arose in the early, wild years of primitive unregulated markets in China. Local managers working in foreign companies in China also learned how important it was to complete work on schedule and how to manage their various tasks efficiently. Other managerial staff learned modern accounting—how to prepare spreadsheets, how to calculate costs, and how to use calculators and then computers.

Hong Kong architects and construction companies, too, which had developed procedures for building skyscrapers during the 1960s and 1970s during the Hong Kong construction boom, began teaching their partners in Guangdong how to organize and administer such projects on the mainland. They also brought in modern construction equipment and taught local workers how to operate it.

Customer service was another area sorely in need of development. Before China's opening and its introduction of markets, Chinese state stores sold a small range of staple goods. The staff in those stores took little interest in customers; they made it clear they were not so stupid as to work hard when they were compensated so poorly. But when Hong Kong businesspeople opened the Guangzhou Hotel—the first modern hotel in Guangdong—they knew it made good business sense to bring in sales managers and service personnel from Hong Kong to teach cleanliness, efficient organization, and responsiveness to customer desires. The hotel's restaurants immediately began to attract crowds of customers, and other restaurants began to compete by offering comparable services.

The rural migrants who went to work in the factories and stores in Guangdong quickly learned to be on time and to coordinate their work with that of others. Those who were paid by the piece also learned to be more efficient as they stuffed sponges into dolls or added other parts to various consumer products. They became more careful about hand-washing and other hygienic practices. They also became more cosmopolitan as, in some cases for the first time in their lives, they met and worked with fellow workers from other regions. They learned about modern technology and current fashions, in good part from the electronic goods and clothing they produced, first for export and then for the local market. As they began to be able to afford more than just food and housing, they learned how to use televisions, washing machines, refrigerators, microwaves, and air conditioners. Young women, following fashions in Hong Kong, learned how to use cosmetics and style their hair in new ways.[30] And when these workers wrote letters home or returned to their villages, either for visits or for the long term, they became models for others who also wished to be modern.[31]

As Akio Morita, a cofounder of Sony, noted as he built factories around the world, countries without modern industry tend to preserve inefficient bureaucracies—but once modern industry introduces new standards of efficiency, those standards begin to spill over into governments. By global standards, government offices in China were still inefficient and vastly overstaffed, but once Chinese businesses became more efficient, some party leaders, including Deng, began to demand that party and government officials follow the same standards of efficiency.

Guangdong's progress cannot be explained simply by "opening markets," for many countries with open markets did not achieve the progress that Guangdong made. Instead, in Guangdong, a Communist organization that less than a decade earlier had engaged in class warfare became an effective vehicle to promote modernization. The party provided overall discipline and encouraged study and competition, and Hong Kong and Japanese enterprises were quick to offer assistance. The special policy for Guangdong and Fujian and the unique leeway given to the SEZs made these areas into incubators for developing people who would be able to function well in modern factories, stores, and offices in cosmopolitan settings. Many of the lessons learned from these enterprises spread quickly from Guangdong to other places.

Pioneers Face Conservative Political Winds

Once the experiments in Guangdong and Fujian began, officials in both areas felt under constant political pressure from Beijing. Although they had been given the responsibility for moving ahead, the vague and uncharted situation required them to be imaginative and to engage in broken field running to get their jobs done, which left them vulnerable to criticism from conservatives worried about change. Directive after directive issued from various ministries in Beijing ended with the phrase that Guangdong and Fujian were *bu liwai* (no exception). Officials in Guangdong and Fujian, then, struggled to strike the delicate and dangerous balance between doing what was needed to attract foreign investments and doing what was required to avoid being accused of selling out to foreign imperialists. How much in the way of tax incentives could they allow to persuade a foreign company to establish a factory? If a joint venture with a foreign company was allowed to make certain products, should it be allowed to make other products outside the mandate? Could some goods intended for export be sold locally?

Since there were no sharp lines between official and personal interests, it was also tempting for local officials—then still very poor—to use their official positions for personal benefit. Could they accept invitations from foreign businesspeople for free dinners? Were they allowed to accept New Year's presents of cash in little red envelopes? Could they use a company van to drive to and from work or to drop children off at school? When foreign companies, including companies in Hong Kong, were given incentives to set up plants in Guangdong, who was to know if some Guangdong people secretly set up a "fake foreign devil" *(jia yang guizi)* company in Hong Kong that could receive those tax benefits back in China? Conservative officials, always alert to opportunities to slow the rush away from planning and to calm the reformers' zeal for working with foreign businesses, had little difficulty finding activities to criticize.

Envious officials elsewhere also found opportunities to complain about what Guangdong officials were doing. Some complained to Beijing about the supplies they had to send to Guangdong and Fujian even though they were urgently needed in their home provinces. Other envious officials managed to slow down the flow of supplies needed in Guangdong: to make sure that all of the coal officially allocated to Guangdong made it there, Guangdong dispatched hundreds of officials to transshipment centers to ensure that its assigned coal was actually put on the appropriate coal cars.

Some high-level Beijing officials, aware of the collapse of party discipline during the Cultural Revolution, were deeply concerned that opportunities for making money were eroding party discipline even further. What better way to draw sharp lines than by criticizing some of the pioneers in Guangdong and Fujian? Because Chen Yun was deeply concerned about keeping the planning system functioning effectively and maintaining party discipline, other officials with similar worries went to him as their champion. In the meantime, Guangdong officials regarded him as a constant thorn in their side. All high officials except Chen Yun and Li Xiannian made at least one visit to the SEZs and praised their achievements. Chen Yun went south every winter, to Hangzhou, Shanghai, and elsewhere, but he explained that his health did not permit him to visit Guangdong.

Chen Yun, in a talk on December 12, 1981, acknowledged that it was "important to look at the positive sides of the SEZs. But," he said, "it was also necessary to look at the side-effects."[32] Ten days later, at a meeting of provincial first party secretaries, Chen Yun declared, "Four special economic zones are sufficient. We should not establish any more."[33] A month later, he said, "Now every province wants to set up special economic zones. If they are allowed to do so, foreign capitalists as well as domestic speculators at home will come out boldly and engage in speculation and profiteering. Therefore, we should not do things this way."[34] Chen Yun was also concerned by the added complexities of creating borders around zones and was particularly opposed to creating a separate SEZ currency that he feared might be more attractive to investors, thereby weakening the power of the Chinese yuan.

Chen Yun could be determined but he rarely displayed anger; one of the few times he became visibly angry was when he heard about a huge scandal that had occurred in Guangdong.[35] As chairman of the party's Central Commission for Discipline Inspection, Chen Yun vigorously pursued cases where

Guangdong officials had violated party discipline. With hundreds of thousands of party members involved in bringing in foreign goods and helping to set up factories and sell their products, smuggling, bribery, and corruption became serious problems, and Chen Yun criticized higher-level leaders in Guangdong and Fujian for not doing more to stop them.

Deng Xiaoping stayed above the fray and did not defend the officials under scrutiny, but Hu Yaobang, as general secretary of the party, kept in close touch with the regional officials responsible for promoting reform. In January 1980, when local officials came under pressure because of smuggling, Hu Yaobang went to the Zhuhai SEZ to offer support to local officials accused of not stopping it. When he received a report several months later from officials in Shekou indicating that the system of giving rewards to workers for surpassing production targets was being blocked by Beijing officials, he sent a note to Gu Mu telling him to make certain that Shekou had the freedom to carry out its work. And when Hu received a report that Beijing bureaucrats were blocking road-building in Shekou, he again wrote a note to Gu Mu telling him to clear the bureaucratic interference. Guangdong officials reported that Hu Yaobang was a fully committed supporter who tried to help in whatever way he could.

With reports of corruption in the SEZs mounting, tensions between Chen Yun and the defenders of the SEZs mounted. As disciplined party members, Chen Yun and Hu Yaobang avoided taking their disagreements public. On January 14, 1982, however, when the party Secretariat held its first lengthy discussion about the SEZs, Chen Yun attacked the widespread corruption. Without directly disagreeing with Chen Yun, Hu Yaobang concluded the discussion by saying, "The SEZs must advance, not retreat."[36]

Higher-level provincial officials serving on the Guangdong Provincial Party Committee, the Guangdong Economic Commission, and the Guangdong Discipline Inspection Commission were appointed by Beijing, but second-level provincial officials were appointed by provincial leaders. Beijing officials, concerned that the lower levels might unite and withhold information, asked that all reports about provincial colleagues, even if negative, be reported to the center. Guangdong officials who complied, however, were referred to by their local colleagues as "informers."

Two officials in Guangdong, Wang Quanguo and Xue Guangjun, had personal and professional reasons for keeping cautious planners in Beijing well informed about Guangdong's problems. Vice Governor Wang Quanguo, who was head of the Guangdong Planning Commission and who originally came from Hubei, had been passed over in the selection for governor. Ordinarily, the person chosen as governor was a member of the party's Central Committee as Wang was. But Ren Zhongyi, hoping to gain the wholehearted cooperation of the many local officials, had instead chosen as governor Vice Governor Liu Tianfu, a former member of local guerrilla forces who was not a member of the Central Committee. In 1981, when Guangdong held a meeting to promote Chen Yun's readjustment policy, Wang, in a letter to Beijing, noted that Ren Zhongyi at the meeting emphasized Deng's statements about reform and opening more than Chen Yun's remarks about retrenchment.[37]

Xue Guangjun, a member of the Guangdong Provincial Party Committee, reported to Beijing on corruption problems in Guangdong. Xue had served under Chen Yun both in the party Organization Department in Yan'an and in the Northeast during the civil war. Xue contacted Chen Yun directly and complained that Guangdong was pursuing capitalism; that problems of smuggling, bribery, and corruption were becoming increasingly serious; and that Guangdong officials were not doing enough to control the situation.[38] Work on constructing new factories had begun, but in the meantime the province was suffering from budget shortfalls and shortages of foreign currency. Beijing complained that Guangdong was lax in managing foreign exchange and in collecting and passing on to Beijing the customs fees. Guangdong, meanwhile, was complaining that it was not receiving enough coal and that Beijing had not built adequate transport facilities to meet its growing demand after the Third Plenum.[39]

When Ren Zhongyi arrived in Guangdong in October 1980, Chen Yun was vigorously promoting his readjustment policy, trying to restrain new construction so as to lessen inflationary pressures. Guangdong's efforts to expand infrastructure to attract foreign capital and investment did inevitably strain the supply of materials, leading to inflationary pressures. But Ren Zhongyi, who personally respected Chen Yun, under whom he had served in the Northeast during the civil war, saw his primary missions in Guangdong to be attracting foreign investment and contributing to Guangdong's rapid development.

"Two Summons to the Palace" (er jingong)

By late 1981, among Beijing officials, the furor over the economic crimes in Guangdong and Fujian was reaching a fever pitch. In December, Deng

Xiaoping, responding to Chen Yun's complaints about smuggling and profiteering in Guangdong, played defense. He wrote a note to Hu Yaobang saying that Beijing should send a small delegation to Guangdong both to investigate and to warn all party members about the problem. In response to Chen Yun's hard-hitting January 5, 1982 report on Guangdong smuggling, issued by the Central Discipline Inspection Commission that Chen headed, Deng wrote in the margins of the report, "With the power of a thunderbolt and the speed of lightning, grab the issue and don't let go" *(leili fengxing zhuazhu bufang)*.[40]

With his experiments now under pressure, Deng chose to spend his winter vacation, from January 20 to February 9, 1982, in Guangdong.[41] He announced that he was going to Guangdong for a rest and that he was not going to listen to official reports or talk about work. In fact, for an hour and a half he did listen intently to Ren Zhongyi, who told him exactly what was happening in Guangdong, especially in Shenzhen and Zhuhai. Deng told Ren that he believed Beijing's policy of opening to these areas was correct and "if you in Guangdong believe it to be correct, you should carry it out."[42] Deng's visit to Guangdong and his meeting with Ren showed that he cared deeply about the experiment, but Deng did not put himself on the line by publicly supporting Ren.[43]

While Deng was in Guangdong, Chen Yun in Beijing called in Yao Yilin and other planners on January 25, 1982, and reminded them of what had happened during the Great Leap Forward when China set its goals too high. Chen complained that all the provinces wanted to establish SEZs and that if they were allowed to do so, foreign capitalists and speculators would get out from their cages.[44] At the same time, Deng Liqun was stoking further criticism of the SEZs by saying the SEZs were becoming like the pre-1949 foreign settlements in the treaty port cities, which had been dominated by imperialists.

The situation came to a head when Ren Zhongyi and Liu Tianfu were directed to appear on February 13 to 15, 1982, before Beijing's Central Discipline Inspection Commission, chaired by Chen Yun. Local officials informally referred to the call to Beijing as *"jin gong"* (the summons, in imperial times, of local officials to the capital to receive criticism). The two men were told to explain their failure to stop the smuggling and corruption and warned to do better in the future.[45] As required, Ren undertook a self-criticism, though he also brought sixty-eight people from the province with him, showing that Guangdong officials were united in their efforts to promote reform and were making serious efforts to stop the smuggling. The presence of so many Guangdong officials complicated Chen Yun's task of carrying out the criticism and could not have enhanced whatever sympathy he might have felt for Ren Zhongyi. Some of the other Beijing officials at the meeting joined in the criticism, going so far as to say that a class struggle was taking place in Guangdong and the bourgeoisie were benefiting.[46] When Hu Qiaomu remarked that the situation raised broader political and ideological questions, Guangdong officials understood that the case against them was becoming very serious.

Before leaving Beijing, Ren Zhongyi consulted privately with Hu Yaobang, his key supporter in Beijing, about how to pass on Beijing's message to his subordinates and the business community in Guangdong. If he relayed the passionate attacks from the critics in Beijing, especially the discussion of class warfare, it could stifle the economic dynamism in his province. Hu Yaobang told Ren Zhongyi that Ren himself could decide what should and should not be passed on. After returning to Guangdong, Ren called an enlarged meeting of the provincial standing committee to convey Beijing's concern about the smuggling, but he did not convey the full force of Beijing's anger and he did not mention class struggle. He did say that where they had made errors, they should be corrected. Illegal activities should end. "But," he added, "we are not going to carry on campaigns or lay the blame on particular people. We will firmly oppose personal profiteering, but we will firmly support reform and opening. As first party secretary, I bear responsibility. My subordinates do not." Ren's subordinates were very grateful, for they knew that without his willingness to accept responsibility and to protect them from criticism, the experiments in Guangdong would have to be vastly scaled back.[47]

After the Beijing meeting, Chen Yun told Hu Yaobang that he was deeply disappointed with Guangdong's response. Hu then called Ren Zhongyi to tell him that they had not passed the test, and he must return for another round of criticism. Ren asked if he could bring Governor Liu Tianfu, and Hu agreed. A meeting of the party Secretariat scheduled from February 23 to February 25 was to examine Ren's failure to control smuggling, corruption, and bribery. Immediately after his arrival but before the meeting, Ren and Governor Liu Tianfu had a long talk with Hu Yaobang and Zhao Ziyang who, as friends of Guangdong's reform, explained the criticism against them. Hu told Ren Zhongyi to write a new self-criticism, which Ren agreed to do. Ren also accepted Liu Tianfu's revisions, which strengthened his self-criticism.

The formal meeting during Ren's second summons was attended by more party and government representatives than the first meeting and the criticism was more severe. An official of the Central Discipline Inspection Commission said that strange things were happening in Guangdong, and yet Guangdong officials did not seem to consider them strange. Another official said that Guangdong leaders were allowing the sheep to get out of their sight. One critic announced that the struggle against corruption was a class struggle. Ren responded to these comments by presenting his penetrating self-criticism, but he and Liu also explained the efforts Guangdong had made to deal with the problems. When Ren and Liu asked that the special policies for Guangdong not be withdrawn, Zhao Ziyang and Hu Yaobang assured them that those policies would not change, but Guangdong would have to crack down on smuggling and corruption with more vigor.[48]

This second visit to Beijing still did not resolve the problems. Following the two Beijing meetings, Gu Mu spent most of his time from April to September in Guangdong leading investigations.[49] The Central Discipline Inspection Commission also dispatched a team headed by Zhang Yun, a senior official and deputy head of the commission, for two months of further inspection. At the end of the two months, she concluded that Ren Zhongyi and others in Guangdong had made great efforts to deal with the problems.

Deng Xiaoping had been following the reports raised at the various meetings, yet avoided speaking out in public to support Guangdong and Fujian. When he read Zhang Yun's report, however, which in effect resolved the issue in favor of Guangdong, he immediately sent it on to the Politburo. The Politburo's own Document No. 50, issued on December 31, 1982, affirmed the efforts in Guangdong to deal with the economic crimes. It quoted Chen Yun's conclusion: "We must operate the SEZs, but we must continuously summarize our experiences and seek to make sure the SEZs are done well." Deng had succeeded in continuing his experiment without putting his personal authority on the line. Guangdong officials breathed a sigh of relief.[50]

Until he left office, Ren Zhongyi was under constant pressure from Beijing but he continued the reforms and kept up the rapid pace of growth.[51] In 1985, Ren reached the retirement age of seventy, and although other regional officials with comparable achievements were asked to stay on beyond retirement, Ren was honorably retired.[52] He was allowed to keep his housing and his perquisites. First Party Secretary Xiang Nan of Fujian suffered a worse fate. He was held responsible for the crimes of Jinjiang Pharmaceutical Company in Fujian, which had been found guilty of selling fake drugs. Xiang Nan had been enormously respected by reform-minded officials in Beijing for his ability and dedication to reform. But in February 1986 he was removed, forced to write a series of five humiliating self-criticisms, and given an inner-party warning by the Central Discipline Inspection Commission. Yet even though conservatives in Beijing managed to remove Ren Zhongyi and Xiang Nan, the groundbreaking policies they pursued in Guangdong and Fujian not only continued, but were expanded.

Affirming the Experiment: Fourteen Coastal Cities, 1984

Deng carefully waited for a favorable political atmosphere before expanding the policies in Guangdong and Fujian to other areas. After the Central Discipline Inspection Commission gave its stamp of approval for Guangdong's efforts at the end of December 1982, the tide of hostility began to ebb. In June 1983 Deng was able to announce, "Now, most people are saying good things about the SEZs."[53] Deng encouraged Beijing officials to travel to Shenzhen and Zhuhai to see for themselves; he knew they would be impressed by the visible progress. By then support for Deng and his policies of reform and opening in general had built up a strong momentum within the party. The problems that had led to widespread support for Chen Yun's readjustment policy had begun to disappear. Food supplies were adequate, economic growth was rapid, and budget imbalances had declined. Exports in 1984 surpassed 100 billion yuan, a 238 percent increase from 1978.[54]

On January 24, 1984, during his winter "vacation," Deng arrived in Guangdong on his special train. He spent more than two weeks visiting Guangdong and Fujian, including three of the four SEZs—Shenzhen, Zhuhai, and Xiamen—and two dynamic counties near Zhuhai, Zhongshan and Shunde.[55] Deng already had a positive view of developments in the SEZs before his trip, but he was cautious about praising them until he had listened to local reports and seen them with his own eyes. Deng was sufficiently excited by the modern skyscrapers and factories in Shenzhen that he affirmed Yuan Geng's slogan displayed on the big billboard in the center of the city: "Time is money, efficiency is our life."[56] Only after observing Shenzhen and Zhuhai and arriving in Guangzhou did he say, "The development and experience of the Shenzhen SEZ prove that our policy of establishing such zones is correct." In Shenzhen, several square kilometers of high-rise buildings, virtually unknown in China in 1978, had already given Shenzhen the appearance of a modern Western city.

Television sets were just beginning to become popular in 1984, so millions of Chinese could see on television the high-rise buildings and factories as Deng saw them. After visiting Guangdong and Fujian, Deng announced, "As for our policy of opening . . . the problem is we haven't opened enough. . . . In Shanghai we need ten more big hotels and we can rely entirely on outsiders to be the sole investors."[57] He announced that phase two of the Baoshan Steel Works could begin; there was no need to wait until the next five-year plan. Reports of the successes Deng had observed in Guangdong and Fujian helped build support for the opening of the coastal cities and the decisions on structural reform that were announced later in the year.

In saying that the "basic policies of the SEZs" were correct, Deng did not defend local officials. In effect, his message was that smuggling, bribery, and corruption were not a consequence of the policy but of its implementation, and should be stopped. Conservatives attacked the leaders in Hainan, Guangdong, and Fujian who were promoting Deng's policies, but they succeeded only in toppling the targets of their attacks, not in changing policy. Deng's concern was not with the fate of individual officials but with the plan to extend the opening to fourteen coastal cities and other areas along the coast. On this he was both vocal and successful.

On February 24, shortly after returning to Beijing, Deng called in Hu Yaobang, Zhao Ziyang, Wan Li, Yang Shangkun, Yao Yilin, Song Ping, and others to prepare the policy statements that would open the fourteen coastal cities. Reporting on the speed of construction in Shenzhen, Deng said that the construction workers were from inland cities and that their efficiency was due to a contract responsibility system whereby they were paid based on their performance. Deng stressed the advantages of the SEZs for learning about foreign technology and management skills. He reiterated that it would not be possible to pay high wages everywhere immediately, but that they should allow some areas to get rich first.[58] He also reported that because of new job opportunities in Shenzhen, many of those who had fled to Hong Kong were now returning to Shenzhen. He then instructed Yao Yilin and Song Ping to convey all of these views to Chen Yun.

Over the next two months, the party Secretariat and the State Council worked on preparing a circular, to be issued on May 4, announcing the extension of the opening policy to fourteen coastal cities, each of which would be allowed to adapt the policy to local circumstances.[59] Gu Mu, experienced in negotiating with Guangdong and Fujian, was tasked with coordinating relations between Beijing and the fourteen coastal cities. This expansion of privileges represented public acknowledgment of Guangdong's and Fujian's successes in building modern industry and accumulating foreign capital. It was also testimony to the pressure from other areas that wanted to be granted the same privileges.

To mollify officials in inner China, the circular also stated that the coastal areas would assist the inland areas by providing material and financial support and by helping to train workers. The contents of the circular were presented in such a way as to soften the objections of Chen Yun and the other more conservative officials. Chen Yun did not oppose the gradual opening of more coastal areas, but he was especially critical of new economic zones with boundaries, for they created new troublesome procedures as goods flowed between the zones and the surrounding areas.

Some other officials, too, had complained that although Guangdong was supposed to bring in high-tech factories, it had concentrated instead on low-tech, labor-intensive factories and service-sector development. Officials were very eager for China to move quickly into higher technology. To put pressure on the new areas to upgrade their technology, and to get around the moratorium on new SEZs that had been initiated in January 1982 by Chen Yun, Document No. 13 of 1984 authorized that the new zones be called Economic and Technological Development Zones and that foreign firms located there should bring in more high-tech industries.[60]

The truth is that Guangdong then lacked the technical and managerial personnel to introduce high-technology immediately, and foreign companies had invested in China to take advantage of its comparative advantage: its low labor costs. Nonetheless, to pacify the critics, the fourteen coastal Economic and Technological Development Zones were given instructions on how to set up and administer their areas, including guidelines in the "Decision on the Reform of the Economic Structure," which Deng issued at the Third Plenum of the 12th Party Congress in October of 1984. Although these documents were written in formal language, they were not taken by local officials as precise binding legal documents; instead they believed, correctly, that the instructions reflected Beijing's willingness to support a high degree of openness and flexibility in attracting and working with foreign enterprises.

Although Guangdong and Fujian officials felt relieved at the decision to open up fourteen coastal areas and took this as a vindication and affirmation of their policies, the expansion of the privileges to other areas created new problems for them—namely, increased competition. Foreigners and ethnic Chinese abroad who had been investing mostly in Guangdong and Fujian now increased investments elsewhere. As it turned out, however, there was enough foreign investment to go around. In the late 1980s, not only did the counties around the SEZs in Guangdong and Fujian flourish (albeit at a slightly lower rate of growth), but also the buildup of the SEZs within Guangdong—Shenzhen, Zhuhai, and Shantou—continued. The Shantou SEZ was expanded to include the entire island on which the SEZ was located. With the opening of Taiwan in the late 1980s, investment funds from Taiwan, Southeast Asia, and the United States increased; the Xiamen SEZ, near Taiwan, began to prosper.

Deng had great reason to be satisfied that the success of the Guangdong experiment was now spreading to other areas. In October 1984 Deng told a meeting of senior officials that he had enjoyed two major achievements that year: reaching an agreement on the future of Hong Kong, and opening the fourteen coastal cities to foreign investment.[61]

Guangdong as the New Dazhai

During the Cultural Revolution, Dazhai was Mao's great national model for moving to a higher stage of socialist agriculture. Although Guangdong was not formally designated as a model, it became well known throughout China as the de facto archetype for how to advance modernization. Officials throughout the country learned about Guangdong through reports, meetings at which Guangdong experiences were discussed, study tours, and visits by officials who had worked in or had apprenticed in Guangdong. In particular, many high-level Beijing officials who had accepted invitations to visit and enjoy Guangdong in the wintertime—invitations made to win support for the province—returned to Beijing and other northern cities and reported what they had observed in Guangdong.

Ordinary people had learned about Dazhai from the classroom and the work unit, as well as from books, propaganda classes, wall posters, loudspeakers, and visits to Dazhai. They learned about developments in Guangdong and Shenzhen mostly in their own homes from television sets that had been coming off Chinese assembly lines, mostly in Guangdong. Ordinary people went to Dazhai because they were encouraged to do so. They studied Guangdong, however, not to show that they were ideologically correct, but because they were eager to learn about what was happening there. If anything, the model was too powerful, raising hopes elsewhere long before other areas could afford to copy the Guangdong and Fujian experiments. Consequently,

Beijing did not promote the study of Guangdong, but rather tried to dampen expectations that it could be immediately copied elsewhere.

Many Western practices that had earlier been introduced into Hong Kong entered Guangdong through the southern gate, and were later passed on elsewhere in China. When Guangdong created its first toll bridge near Foshan, for example, officials there were criticized for engaging in the capitalist practice of issuing bonds to be repaid by tolls—but within a few years, the issuance of bonds and tolls had become part of the conventional wisdom about how to finance the building of large bridges and highways in China. In 1983 Guangdong also became the first province in China to eliminate set prices on many foods, such as rice and fish. The prices of these goods rose dramatically; but as people responded to the market, producing more, the prices declined. In another example, this time in the coastal city of Guangzhou, commercial taxis were introduced. Until the early 1980s virtually all automobiles in China were owned by work units and driven by chauffeurs who belonged to the work unit, but after Guangzhou purchased old Hong Kong taxis and pioneered their use on the mainland, within several years all major cities in China had launched their own commercial taxi services.

The Sixth National Games in November 1987 symbolized Guangdong's new role. They were held in a new, state-of-the-art stadium in Guangdong that featured large television screens, loudspeakers, and other technologies carefully modeled after those used in the 1984 Los Angeles Olympics. The event showcased Guangdong's advances in construction, manufacturing, and services, as well as its organizational capacities, all developed during the reform and opening. Premier Zhao Ziyang, returning to Guangdong where he had spent most of his work career, in a brief speech at the games praised Guangdong for setting a new high standard for China. Management of the National Games became a model for the Asian Games held in 1990 and the springboard for the Beijing Olympics in 2008.[62]

The pace of change in Guangdong throughout the 1980s remained well ahead of that of the rest of the country, inspiring officials in other areas of China to continue trying new approaches to modernization. Deng had made good use of Guangdong as a pacesetter for the rest of the country. In 1992, in a final gesture before he stepped down, he would return yet again to the region to make certain that the southern gate that played such a key role in the modernization of China remained wide open.

The Deng family home, where Xiaoping spent his childhood. (*Deng Xiaoping: A Pictorial Biography*, Vol. 1, Chengdu: Sichuan renmin chubanshe, 2004, p. 4)

The student-worker in France, age sixteen, March 1921. (*Deng Xiaoping,* Beijing: Central Party Literature Publishing House, 1988, p. 12)

Representatives of the 5th Congress of the European Chinese Communist Youth League in Paris. Deng is the third from the right in the last row. In the first row, the first on the left is Nie Rongzhen, the fourth from the left is Zhou Enlai and the sixth is Li Fuchun, 1924. (*Deng Xiaoping: A Pictorial Biography*, Vol. 1, Chengdu: Sichuan renmin chubanshe, 2004, p. 28)

The Huai-Hai campaign front commanders (Su Yu, Deng, Liu Bocheng, Chen Yi, Tan Zhenlin), 1948. (*Deng Xiaoping*, Beijing: Central Party Literature Publishing House, 1988, p. 146)

When the Communists took power in China, 1949. (*Deng Xiaoping: A Pictorial Biography*, Vol. 1, Chengdu: Sichuan renmin chubanshe, 2004, p. 147)

General Secretary Deng welcomes Ho Chi Minh, president of Democratic Republic of Vietnam, 1965. (*Deng Xiaoping,* Beijing: Central Party Literature Publishing House, 1988, p. 200)

Reporting to Chairman Mao, early 1960s. (*Deng Xiaoping,* Beijing: Central Party Literature Publishing House, 1988, p. 108)

At the Central Military Commission meeting in Guangzhou. From left to right: Nie Rongzhen, Lin Biao, He Long, Zhou Enlai, Luo Ruiqing, Peng Zhen, Mao Zedong, and Deng, January 1960. Lin Biao died in a plane crash in 1971; all the others but Zhou Enlai were attacked in the Cultural Revolution. (*Deng Xiaoping,* Beijing: Central Party Literature Publishing House, 1988, p. 158)

Deng's first meeting with Henry Kissinger, in New York, with Foreign Minister Qiao Guanhua, May 1974. (© Bettmann/CORBIS)

Deng becomes the first Chinese Communist leader to address the General Assembly of the United Nations, April 1974. (*Deng Xiaoping,* Beijing: Central Party Literature Publishing House, 1988, p. 25)

With Chairman Hua Guofeng when Deng was serving under him, January 1978. (AFP/Getty Images)

With Inayama Yoshihiro, chairman of New Japan Steel, visiting the Kimitsu Steel plant, which became the model for Baoshan, China's first modern steel plant, October 1978. (*Deng Xiaoping: A Pictorial Biography,* Vol. 2, Chengdu: Sichuan renmin chubanshe, 2004, p. 345)

Greeted by Prime Minister Lee Kuan Yew on arrival in Singapore, November 1978. (*Deng Xiaoping,* Beijing: Central Party Literature Publishing House, 1988, p. 207)

Lighting the sparks for reform and opening in China's Northeast, September 1978. (*Deng Xiaoping: A Pictorial Biography*, Vol. 2, Chengdu: Sichuan renmin chubanshe, 2004, p. 327)

Chen Yun and Deng Xiaoping launch reform and opening at the Third Plenum, December 1978. (*Deng Xiaoping*, Beijing: Central Party Literature Publishing House, 1988, p. 104)

Chen Yun and Deng
Xiaoping, autumn 1952.
(*Deng Xiaoping,* Beijing:
Central Party Literature
Publishing House, 1988,
p. 271)

With Ambassador Leonard Woodcock toasting the conclusion of their agreement to
normalize U.S.-China relations, prematurely, December 1978. (*Deng Xiaoping: A Pictorial
Biography,* Vol. 2, Chengdu: Sichuan renmin chubanshe, 2004, p. 357)

With President Jimmy Carter as they launch their talks, and interpreter Ji Chaozhu, January 1979. (*Thirty Years of Sino-US Relations,* Beijing: Xiyuan Publishing House, 2002, p. 49)

At the state dinner with President Carter and former president Richard Nixon on Deng's only visit to the White House after the Watergate affair, January 1979. (© CORBIS)

Donning a cowboy hat at a Texas rodeo, February 1979. (© Bettmann/CORBIS)

Ford Motor Tour, 1979. (© Bettmann/CORBIS)

Planting trees with Wan Li, who led rural reform, February 1984. (*Deng Xiaoping*, Beijing: Central Party Literature Publishing House, 1988, p. 111)

Deng views China's vast Western plains, 1981. (*Deng Xiaoping: A Pictorial Biography,* Vol. 2, Chengdu: Sichuan renmin chubanshe, 2004, p. 427)

Giving directions to General Secretary Hu Yaobang, early 1980s. (© China Features/Sygma/Corbis)

With Hong Kong Governor Sir Murray MacLehose, initiating discussions on the future of Hong Kong, January 1979. (*Deng Xiaoping: A Pictorial Biography*, Vol. 2, Chengdu: Sichuan renmin chubanshe, 2004, p. 472)

With Prime Minister Margaret Thatcher signing the Joint Declaration on the future of Hong Kong, December 1984. (*Deng Xiaoping: A Pictorial Biography*, Vol. 2, Chengdu: Sichuan renmin chubanshe, 2004, p. 478)

Going to the beach, mid-1980s. (© China Features/Sygma/Corbis)

With his immediate family on his seventieth birthday. Front row: Pufang, Zhuo Lin, Deng, Xia Bogen. Back row: Zhifang, Nan, Rong, Lin. August 1974. (*Deng Xiaoping,* Beijing: Central Party Literature Publishing House, 1988, p. 290)

Being kissed by grandson, summer 1986. (*Deng Xiaoping,* Beijing: Central Party Literature Publishing House, 1988, p. 295)

Playing bridge, late 1980s. (*Deng Xiaoping: A Pictorial Biography,* Vol. 2, Chengdu: Sichuan renmin chubanshe, 2004, p. 612)

Inspecting construction in Shenzhen, the first SEZ, with Governor Liang Lingguang of Guangdong, January 1984. (*Deng Xiaoping: A Pictorial Biography*, Vol. 2, Chengdu: Sichuan renmin chubanshe, 2004, p. 501)

With President Ronald Reagan after Reagan gave up his efforts to reestablish formal relations with Taiwan, April 1984. (*Thirty Years of Sino-US Relations*, Beijing: Xiyuan Publishing House, 2002, p. 64)

Meeting President George H. W. Bush when Fang Lizhi tried unsuccessfully to attend a reception, with interpreter Yang Jiechi, later ambassador to the United States and foreign minister, February 1989. (*Deng Xiaoping: A Pictorial Biography,* Vol. 2, Chengdu: Sichuan renmin chubanshe, 2004, p. 576)

Welcoming Mikhail and Raisa Gorbachev to Beijing despite turmoil in Tiananmen Square, May 1989. (© Jacques Langevin/Sygma/Corbis)

General Secretary Zhao Ziyang bidding farewell at Tiananmen Square; Deng did not venture out to the square during the turmoil, May 1989. (AFP/Getty Images)

Deng's "family vacation" to the South attracts onlookers, January 1992. (*Deng Xiaoping: A Pictorial Biography,* Vol. 2, Chengdu: Sichuan renmin chubanshe, 2004, p. 633)

Giving his final blessing to his successor, General Secretary Jiang Zemin, at the Fifth Plenum, 13th Party Congress, November 1989. (*Deng Xiaoping: A Pictorial Biography,* Vol. 2, Chengdu: Sichuan renmin chubanshe, 2004, p. 587)

Bidding farewell to public life at the 14th Party Congress, October 1992. (© Jacques Langevin/ Sygma/Corbis)

The UN Security Council observes a moment of silence on the passing of Deng, February 1997. (*Deng Xiaoping: A Pictorial Biography,* Vol. 2, Chengdu: Sichuan renmin chubanshe, 2004, p. 649)

15

Economic Readjustment
and Rural Reform

1978–1982

In his pursuit of economic modernization, Deng liked to say that he was groping for stones as he crossed the river. But in fact, from his five decades of experience, he had developed some strong convictions about how to get across that particular river. One was that the Communist Party should be in charge. "My father," Deng's younger son, Deng Zhifang, told an American acquaintance, "thinks Gorbachev is an idiot." Gorbachev, his father had explained, set out to change the political system first. That was a misguided policy because "he won't have the power to fix the economic problems and the people will remove him."[1] Deng also admired success and had a particular vision for achieving it for China. He wanted Chinese to scour the world to learn about successes whatever the nature of the system where they took place. He wanted to know the true situation at home; he did not want to hear exaggerated reports of progress, which had caused such deep problems during the Great Leap. He believed that people needed material incentives and had to see palpable progress to remain motivated. And he was convinced that a robust economy thrived on competition, not only among economic producers and merchants striving for profits, but also among officials trying to bring progress to their localities.

Deng realized that the path to achieving the four modernizations was very complex and he knew that he personally did not have the patience to study all the details. Consequently, Deng was not his own master strategist in economic affairs as he was in foreign policy and military affairs. In foreign policy and military affairs he consulted with others to understand the current situation and although he did read the reports of specialists, he could mull over the issues and devise strategies without consultation. On economic matters, however, he needed someone else to serve as China's economic strategist—to examine details, frame the issues, select and evaluate options, and propose possible courses of action. For these important roles, he turned first to Chen Yun and later to Zhao Ziyang. Deng, however, reserved the right to make the final decisions; he would resolve political disagreements about the major economic issues by balancing economic and other considerations. He also accepted responsibility for explaining economic policies to the public.

Builders versus Balancers, 1978–1981

When Deng became preeminent leader in December 1978, Chen Yun, who had just rejoined the top leadership team, called attention to a potential crisis looming in the economy: visions of growth had gotten out of hand, the budget was out of balance, and commitments for purchasing technology from abroad had exceeded China's foreign currency reserves, which were needed to pay for them. Among the leaders trying to provide direction for the economy in this new uncharted era, there were countless opinions about how to proceed. But as officials at the top began aggregating the various views, the different views tended to coalesce around two opposite poles. One group centered around the builders, who eagerly sought to introduce new factories and infrastructure projects; the other group, led by Chen Yun, the balancers, cautiously tried to ensure that resources were available for all the national priorities.

Beginning in 1977, some of the leading builders began selecting foreign plants to import and arranging for their installation in China. As the economy began opening, these senior project managers sought proposals from Japan and from the West, drawing from China's experiences in the 1950s introducing new industrial plants and construction projects from the Soviet Union. The builders could see how Japan and the four little dragons (Hong Kong, Singapore, South Korea, and Taiwan), by constructing new facilities with Western technology, had achieved the most rapid growth rates in the world, and they were eager to do the same. After Gu Mu's trip to Europe in 1978, hopes for importing foreign plants soared. High-level officials, mostly in the industrial and transport ministries—with support from many local leaders who wanted to build in their localities—made wish lists of types of industrial plants that they hoped to acquire for China over the next few years, then dispatched officials to Europe to select partners who could supply the technology and financing.

China's cautious balancers were concentrated in the Ministry of Finance, the State Economic Commission, the State Planning Commission, and the banks. Like their counterparts in other countries, officials who managed finance considered it their responsibility to balance the budget, ensure that enough foreign currency was available to repay foreign loans, and keep inflation under control. In drawing up China's economic plans, they strove to ensure that all the necessary materials, technologies, and personnel were available for production and construction in high-priority areas of the economy and that Chinese consumers would not face shortages.[2]

Deng Xiaoping, like Hua Guofeng, was at heart a builder who wanted to see rapid progress. He admired project managers who under adverse circumstances had been able to complete important projects that provided visible signs of progress. Deng, who had little patience with detailed calculations, considered the cautious balancers necessary, but annoying.

When Deng became China's preeminent leader, the most prominent project managers, called the "petroleum faction," had been working together since the 1950s. From 1952 to 1966 Deng had worked closely with them, for he was then vice premier with responsibility for the development of energy resources and heavy industry. Yu Qiuli, the leader of the petroleum faction, had been glorified by Mao Zedong for leading the development of the Daqing oilfield but during the Cultural Revolution he was attacked as a member of the "Deng Xiaoping faction."[3] In 1975, when Deng was in charge of the government, Yu was made head of the State Planning Commission, much to the dismay of the balancers who were accustomed to having one of their own in that important position. After Mao's death, Yu Qiuli remained at his post and Hua Guofeng turned to him to lead the work of importing industrial plants (for more on Yu Qiuli, see Key People in the Deng Era, p. 741).

Yu Qiuli and the other project managers in China during the 1960s and 1970s encountered huge difficulties. Unlike their counterparts in the advanced economies, who could count on others to supply the necessary equipment and infrastructure, Chinese project managers had to deal with untrained workers, equipment shortages, a lack of spare parts, power outages, and delays in the arrival of needed supplies. Those managers who successfully completed projects combined dedication and perseverance with sheer ingenuity in coping with so many unexpected problems.

After Mao's death, as Hua began to promote economic development, the work of these project managers increased dramatically. Officials from the State Planning Commission, State Construction Commission, and other relevant ministries were overwhelmed as they rushed about trying to set priorities among the technologies to be imported, conduct negotiations with foreign companies, select the locations for the plants, calculate what material resources would be required, and arrange for transport and personnel. In addition, because many officials were just returning after years of absence during the Cultural Revolution, they were still entangled in political struggles with incompetent officials who had been promoted during their time away: the work that Deng began in 1975 of consolidating and selecting leadership teams was not yet complete. Ever since Mao's death, project managers under Yu Qiuli had had to scramble even to create wish lists of technologies to be imported; they certainly did not have enough time to undertake careful analysis of the steps needed to import the plants and get them running.

Less than eighteen months after Mao's death, Hua Guofeng, ignoring questions raised by cautious balancers, drew from the lists compiled by Yu Qiuli's project managers, and presented to the 5th National People's Congress (NPC) a list of some 120 mega-projects.[4] The projects were expected to cost some US$12.4 billion, more than the value of all Chinese exports for the year. Hua announced that the plans called for economic growth of 10 percent or more each year.[5] In February 1978, Hua announced that these plans were in accord with his ten-year vision, which was an outgrowth of the one that Deng had introduced in 1975.[6]

One special task that Hua Guofeng assigned to Yu Qiuli was to develop new oilfields to take advantage of the high price of crude oil following the oil shock of 1973. Hua expected to produce enough oil that foreign currency from petroleum exports would pay for all of the project imports. Unfortunately, despite high hopes and strenuous exploration efforts, no major new oil fields were discovered.

In the rush to select and import projects, the wish lists of ministry and local officials soon became the basis of contracts with foreign companies. Hua Guofeng's critics later accused him of launching a "Western-led Leap Forward" (yang yuejin) and of pressuring subordinates to come up with plans hastily so as to consolidate his power by showing that he had produced economic progress. His supporters countered that Hua had done his best to bring modern industry to China quickly, under difficult circumstances.

Deng fully supported Yu Qiuli and shared his enthusiasm for importing foreign factories. In the mid-1978, the balancers, frustrated by their inability to slow down the rush to import modern projects, turned to Chen Yun for support, even though he was not then a member of the Politburo. Thus three weeks after the opening of the State Council Forum on Economic Principles, Chen Yun, who had not been invited to attend, wrote to Li Xiannian expressing his concern that some comrades were becoming overly enthusiastic about borrowing from abroad and importing plants—in his view, they had failed to first ensure that China could provide the necessary trained manpower, infrastructure, and ancillary industries to make the plans work. Chen suggested that the forum be extended in order to allow full discussion of different opinions, but the organizers chose not to do so. At the time, Chen Yun was the only high-level leader to question publicly the rosy estimates about the nation's future ability to pay for the proposed new projects.[7]

In December 1978, when senior party leaders turned to Deng to provide overall leadership, with special responsibility for foreign affairs and military issues, they turned to Chen Yun to lead the work on high-level personnel issues and economic policy. They believed that Chen Yun had consistently supplied the best economic advice and that in the new era he was the wisest person to guide the economy.

On December 10, 1978, during the meeting of the Northeast group at the Central Party Work Conference, Chen Yun voiced his concerns about the uncontrolled exuberance that had reached the highest level of party leaders. As if giving adult supervision to overly excited teenagers, Chen Yun laid out the problems in the ten-year economic vision. He spoke with authority, suggesting that he already knew he would be appointed to the Politburo. He said, "We should maintain steady progress and not get caught up in a headlong rush. . . . When materials are not available for a project, whether at the local or national level, it should not be launched."[8]

Before the Third Plenum, Deng Xiaoping had been fully supportive of the project managers, but after December 1978, when Chen Yun warned about the lack of careful planning, Deng threw his weight behind Chen. On January 6, 1979, within two weeks after the Third Plenum, Deng called in the leading project managers with whom he had worked—Yu Qiuli, Kang Shi'en, and Gu Mu—and told them that Chen had presented "some very important opinions" and that they should lower some of the planning targets. They were to avoid large foreign trade debts and when making plans they were to first check to make sure that the necessary materials were available; they were to give priority to projects likely to provide quick returns on investments and expand employment; and to avoid going into debt, they were to accumulate capital before undertaking projects.[9] In short, Deng then completely supported Chen Yun's cautious balancing. (Chen later blamed Hua for problems resulting from his excessive haste in signing contracts to import projects. Deng was not required to engage in a self-criticism for his earlier support of Hua's ambitious plans; his earlier role in agreeing with Hua to push for faster growth was simply ignored.)

Why did Deng shift course from supporting the builders to backing the balancers, led by Chen Yun? Deng recognized the importance of putting the economy on a solid base for the new era, and the summary economic data assembled in December for the past year reflected serious problems. At the time, there was only US$4 billion in foreign currency reserves and most of the foreign currency income from exports was already committed, although contracts had been signed to purchase over US$7 billion of foreign equipment.[10] Even though the imbalances would seem infinitesimal when contrasted with the foreign trade figures a decade later, they loomed large enough to worry cautious officials who were accustomed to smaller amounts and who were frightened by the leverage that such debt might give the capitalist countries. At the time, Deng was ready to unite with Chen Yun, who enjoyed great respect in the party, against Hua Guofeng. But there was another issue that influenced Deng's economic thinking at the time. He was planning to invade Vietnam a few weeks later, and that attack would be a further drain on the budget; it was prudent to cut back on commitments elsewhere.

By March 1979, Chen Yun had collected more data, done more analysis, and was ready to systematically present his proposals for cutting back on the contracts to import foreign plants and for lowering the economic targets for the next several years. Some of his proposals, and even the terminology, were remarkably similar to the retrenchment policies that he had introduced to recover from the Great Leap Forward. Rather than use the term "retrenchment," the term he used earlier, which would have sounded very negative, Chen Yun used the term "readjustment" (tiaozheng). On March 14, 1979, as the attack on Vietnam was nearing completion and they could make some estimates of its costs, Chen Yun and Li Xiannian presented a formal document proposing a two- to three-year period of readjustment. They suggested that a new structure, the Finance and Economics Commission under the State Council, be established to oversee economic planning and finance. Chen Yun was to be named chairman, and Li Xiannian, who had been in charge of the economy for the past several years, would become vice chairman, serving under his former mentor.

Chen Yun explained to his comrades that he was no longer as healthy as before and that he only had the energy to perform the most necessary tasks. He would provide overall guidance but he would rely on the people under him to do the detailed work that he had done in earlier decades. The person named secretary general of the Finance and Economics Commission, that is, the leader who would head its daily work, was the economic official whom Chen Yun most respected—Yao Yilin.

Chen Yun explained the need for the readjustment program at the Politburo meeting of March 21–23, 1979:

We have 900 million people, over 80 percent of whom are farmers. We are very poor. There are still people begging for food. We all want to modernize, but the question is what can we achieve? We need balanced development. In considering basic construction, we must first consider agriculture. We want to produce lots of steel, but we cannot possibly produce 60 million metric tons by 1985. We lack electricity, we lack transport facilities. Supplies of coal and oil are inadequate to meet needs. Some people make fun of cautious people, making it seem as if cautious people believe that the less steel we produce the better. Ridiculous. Yes, we should borrow funds and technology from abroad. But how much can we be sure that we can repay from our People's Bank? We need to ensure that we will be able to make the repayments. Officials have not done the calculations. Local industries are competing with our big national projects for materials. Five people want to eat when there is only food for three. We have made mistakes in our work; we still lack experience. I can only do my best.[11]

The essence of Chen Yun's approach to planning was balance: balance income and expenditures, loans and the ability to repay, and foreign currency income and expenditures. He also sought a balance between investment in consumer goods and producer goods, between heavy and light industry, and between industry and agriculture. In 1978, some 57 percent of China's industrial output was from heavy industry and only 43 percent from light industry.[12] Chen Yun, like many other officials, believed that China's economy had been out of balance since 1958, with food and consumer goods sacrificed for more heavy industry than the people could bear. In 1980, under Chen

Yun's direction, heavy industry grew only 1.4 percent whereas light industry grew 18.4 percent; and in 1981 heavy industry declined by 4.7 percent whereas light industry grew 14.1 percent.[13]

At the Wuxi conference, held April 5–28, 1979, shortly after the announcement of the readjustment policy, local officials and ministry officials complained of the overly tight centralization of economic planning. Chen Yun was willing to allow more flexibility for markets at lower levels, but he insisted that planning remain primary. Those who had been expecting new plants in their localities were understandably upset. As a participant from Tianjin said, reflecting the dominant mood at the meeting, "We were in high spirits. Now suddenly to propose readjustment, it is pouring a bucket of cold water on us; it is a blow to our high spirits."[14] Hu Yaobang sought a directive to reassure local officials that the party still wished to promote industrial development. Zhao Ziyang spoke out supporting readjustment, explaining that it provided the necessary conditions for later reform and development. Gu Mu, whose trip to Europe had set off the exuberance, joined in, loyally explaining the need for readjustment. Once Zhao and Gu Mu had spoken, the atmosphere at the meeting changed; local officials reluctantly approved the written report supporting readjustment.[15] Deng joined in, explaining as Zhao did that the readjustment policy was necessary to create a solid basis for future growth.

Local officials were constrained by the readjustment policies, but they found creative ways to use their counter-policies to Beijing's policies to avoid reining in investment and expenditures as much as Chen Yun sought. Chen's efforts were also hampered by his own illness. On October 24, 1979, while in Hangzhou, Chen was operated on for colon cancer and he remained in the hospital there until December 14. After returning to Beijing, Chen was admitted to the hospital from May 20 to May 29, 1980, for additional testing and recuperation. By the time Chen Yun returned to work in late 1980, the budget deficits had ballooned to become the largest since the Communists took over. The seriousness of the problem made Chen Yun more determined to clamp down and enabled him to gain support from other officials, including Deng. The deficit had grown not only due to the costs of the Vietnam War, but also because of the increase in procurement prices paid to the farmers for grain, the decline in agricultural taxes, and the costs of resettling people who had earlier been sent to the countryside and were now allowed to return to the cities. Moreover, the central government began allowing provinces and local enterprises to keep more of their own funds to stimulate local initiatives, a strategy that had reduced the total amount of taxes collected by the central government.[16] The result was a great stimulus for many provinces, but Chen Yun considered the serious budget deficits alarming and potentially disastrous.[17]

By late 1980, Chen Yun and the balancers were on the offensive and Deng supported them. At the meetings of the Standing Committee of the NPC in September, those who had been promoting rapid industrial development were accused of following the "erroneous heavy industry policy" of the Cultural Revolution.[18]

Adding to the momentum favoring the balancers, in the fall of 1980 Deng Liqun, in a series of four lectures at the Central Party School on Chen Yun's economic thought, praised Chen Yun so lavishly that some accused him of promoting a cult of personality. Since 1949, Deng Liqun said, Chen Yun's policy proposals have all been correct. What went wrong during the Great Leap? Others failed to follow Chen Yun's advice. And what is wrong now? People are not sufficiently adhering to Chen Yun's words of wisdom. It is essential to carry out readjustment thoroughly.[19]

The balancers also jumped on the story of the collapse of an oil rig in the Gulf of Bohai, accusing Yu Qiuli and Kang Shi'en of trying to cover up the incident, which had resulted in the deaths of seventy workers. Their alleged cover-up of the incident became a pretext for removing them from their administrative positions. In fact, as experienced professionals who knew they would be held responsible for their errors, Yu Qiuli and Kang Shi'en were more careful than the political leaders who had urged them to expand their projects. At the NPC meeting in February 1978, Yu Qiuli had warned that China would have difficulty increasing oil exports because no new oil had been discovered in recent years, and because even if it were discovered, it would take three years to move from discovery to production.[20] After the oil rig collapsed, Yu Qiuli gave a thorough explanation of how and why it had occurred. Even Li Xiannian, who remained close to Chen Yun, later acknowledged that Yu Qiuli had accepted responsibility for things for which he should not have been held accountable.[21]

Although Yu Qiuli was removed as director of the State Planning Commission, he was allowed to remain on the Politburo. Furthermore, Deng still had enough respect for Yu that he used his military connections to get Yu appointed as head of the Political Department of the PLA. But by late 1980, Chen Yun had made sure that those officials who were committed to tighter financial control over new projects and new construction had firm control over economic affairs.[22] Accordingly, one of Chen Yun's allies, Wang Bing-qian, became minister of finance.[23] And Yu Qiuli's replacement was Chen Yun's longtime ally Yao Yilin, who was widely respected for his administrative abilities as well as his knowledge of the economy.[24]

On October 28, 1980, Deng, responding to accusations that drawing up ten-year visions had led to the creation of wish lists without careful analysis, accepted Chen Yun's view that they stop drawing up ten-year visions. Long-term economic discussions would focus on the more careful process of draw-ing up five-year plans.[25]

In November 1980 China's economic growth rate targets for 1981 were set at a much lower rate, 3.7 percent, and capital construction allocations were reduced from 55 billion yuan to 30 billion yuan. When there were com-plaints that such restraints would waste valuable time, Chen retorted, "How much time have we wasted since the Opium War? Over a hundred years. Why is it such a big thing to wait three years to move ahead?" What had most delayed China's advances since 1949, he said, was leftist errors made while rashly pushing ahead.[26] Chen Yun was allowed to take firm control over guid-ing the drafts for the Sixth Five-Year Plan (1981–1985) and over bringing the budget and deficit under control.[27]

As 1980 came to a close, Chen and his balancers maintained a firm grip on China's economic policy. In late 1980, Chen delivered a major address sup-porting a stricter readjustment policy. On December 15, just as the series of nine Politburo meetings pushing Hua aside was coming to an end, Deng said, "I fully agree with Comrade Chen Yun's speech." Further, he said Chen's policy of readjustment had not been effectively implemented "because party members did not have a profound or unanimous understanding of the issues involved." To overcome this problem, they must "resolutely cast away unreal-istic ideas and overly ambitious targets."[28] In short, Hua Guofeng was blamed for the unrealistic plans, Deng and Chen Yun were united, and Deng sup-ported Chen Yun's efforts to undertake a more penetrating implementation of the readjustment policy.

Retrenchment created other problems: Deng had to explain to foreigners why China was breaking contracts for the importation of plants and equip-ment. Beijing had the power to handle disappointed local officials, but break-ing contracts with foreign companies affected foreign relations and raised long-term questions about the credibility of the Chinese government.

The problem proved especially troublesome for Sino-Japanese relations because nearly half of all the contracts with foreign companies were with Japanese companies; the Japanese business community, while controlled in its communications to China, was furious at the cancellation of signed agreements. As early as March 1979, when the first efforts were made to reduce purchases, some US$2.7 billion of Chinese contracts with Japan were frozen.[29] The postponement of the Baoshan Steel Plant, in particular, had a huge negative effect on many of the Japanese companies involved in the project. In late October 1980, just before China formally announced the postponement of its contracts, Yao Yilin, who had worked closely with the Japanese, was dispatched to Tokyo to prepare the Japanese for the impending announcement. But it fell to Deng Xiaoping to smooth things over with high-level Japanese leaders.

Deng could not avoid the loss of much of the goodwill that had followed his visit to Japan in October 1978. He did not engage in deep humble apologies as Japanese would have done under similar circumstances, but he acknowledged forthrightly that China lacked experience, that it had made mistakes, that it faced a serious situation whereby it could not afford to pay for all the things it had hoped to buy, and that it had not always made appropriate preparations to use the plants it had hoped to purchase. But, Deng reassured them, China was willing to provide compensation to the Japanese firms adversely affected, and it expected in the long run to resume its purchases as it grew and was better prepared.

On September 4, 1980, Deng gave his explanation to visiting Japanese Foreign Minister Ito Masayoshi.[30] The visit was followed on January 13, 1981 by an official letter to Baoshan Steel announcing cancellation of the second phase of the planned construction. The first senior Japanese to visit Deng after that letter was former foreign minister Okita Saburo, an "old friend" of China who arrived in February at the invitation of Gu Mu. When he met Deng, Deng acknowledged they had been overly optimistic about oil production. Okita was courteous and respectful, but he conveyed both the Japanese government's request for a full explanation and the stern message from Japanese businessmen that cancellation would tarnish China's reputation in the international business community.[31] After he returned to Japan, Okita explained that because of the Cultural Revolution, Chinese officials who might have been able to provide expertise in a timely way had been unable to do so.[32]

Deng's meeting with Okita was followed by several others. On March 18, Deng met with the highly respected Doko Toshio, the eighty-five-year-old, plain-living president of Japan's largest business association, Keidanren.[33] On April 4, Deng met with a delegation from the Sino-Japanese Friendship Association, headed by Furui Yoshimi.[34] And on April 14, he met with Prime Minister Ohira, who was making efforts to promote a Pacific community.[35] Deng conveyed the same basic message to all of these leaders: China lacked experience and it had made mistakes, but it intended to revive the contracts later.

Many Japanese firms swallowed the losses so as not to endanger their future business relations with China. Moreover, the Japanese government extended new loans to help continue the projects that had already begun. One central and innovative example of such support occurred when Okita Saburo became head of Japan's Overseas Economic Cooperation Fund (OECF), the government agency that gives financial aid to promote Japanese exports. In the first arrangement of its kind, whereby OECF gave funding to a second country so it could give aid to a third country, Okita arranged to lend money to Australia so it could ship iron ore and high-grade coal to Baoshan, thus resolving the key stumbling block in allowing the project to go forward. The first phase of the Baoshan project was resumed on a modest scale in the fall of 1981, and by the fall of 1982 the Baoshan construction site was buzzing with new activity.[36] When it was completed in May 1985 it became the first large modern steel plant in China, and the model for future plants.[37] Before it was built China produced less than one-quarter of the steel that Japan produced. Within thirty years, the Baoshan plant and those built in its likeness had helped China produce almost 500 million tons of steel per year, roughly five times the amount of steel produced in either Japan or the United States.[38]

Some thoughtful Chinese officials believed that Chen Yun provided a much-needed balance to an impatient Deng. It was unfortunate, they acknowledged, that China had barged ahead and then retreated just as it was beginning its modernization drive. But, they argued, Chen Yun's readjustment policy was seriously needed and some of the problems of the late 1980s could have been avoided had Deng initially listened more to Chen.

Although the readjustment policy ended with the 12th Party Congress in September 1982, one important policy that had jelled as part of the retrenchment effort still remained: birth control. Chen Yun had long believed that China's population was too large for its resource base. A party document of December 1978 acknowledged that grain consumption per capita was slightly less than it had been in 1957, and that the average annual per capita rural income was 60 yuan (at the exchange rate at the time, about US$39). Roughly 12 percent of the funds then used to pay for imports was used for grain.[39] When Mao was alive, despite some educational programs and the supplying of birth control devices, birth control made little headway. On December 20, 1980, however, as part of the overall readjustment policy, Li Xiannian sent a key document on implementing the birth control program to the State Planning Commission headed by Yao Yilin. On January 4, 1981, the resulting Document No. 1 ordered that officials "use legal, administrative, and economic measures to encourage couples to have but one [child]."[40] The one-child policy was implemented in the urban areas without qualification, but because the Chinese government lacked funds to provide benefits for the elderly in the countryside, officials allowed rural families whose first child was a girl to have a second child in the hope that it would be a son who could look after his parents in their old age.

No other society in the world has enforced such a stringent birth control policy. Paradoxically, the strong neighborhood associations in the city and countryside, which had been established by Mao, became the vehicle to enforce the new birth control policy, which Mao would have vehemently opposed. Once the one-child policy was introduced in the urban areas, most urban families chose to have only one child and few rural families had more than two.

On March 23, 1979, Deng had declared his strong support for the birth control policy, which Li Xiannian and others had helped put in place. In presenting the program to the public, as customary, Deng began with the broad picture, saying the policy was necessary to reduce grain imports and expand imports of foreign technology, and to attain a high average per capita income by the end of the century.[41] Deng reiterated the same message in several speeches that followed.[42] As he did with other controversial issues, Deng carefully avoided going out on a limb by advocating specific measures. Instead, he referred to the work of well-known scientists and statisticians, along with authoritative-sounding scientific analyses, that laid out the need for birth control. The policy introduced at the time of the readjustment policy was to continue not only for the rest of Deng's era, but in the decades after he stepped down.

Wan Li and Rural Reform

In 1978 China still did not have enough grain to feed its population. Collectivized agriculture, introduced in 1955 and later pushed to higher levels, had led to advances in irrigation, but it had also brought massive starvation. The downsizing of the scale of the collectives after the Great Leap and the increased supply of chemical fertilizer led to production increases, but grain shortages remained severe.

At the time of the Third Plenum, some officials were already advocating a further decrease in the size of the agricultural units, but the atmosphere among top leaders at the time firmly supported the continuation of collective agriculture: officials then pushed for improved management, better seeds, more fertilizer, and more farm machinery. At the Third Plenum, it was specifically forbidden for rural areas to contract agricultural production down to the household. Party officials in the collectives had a vested interest in retaining the collectives, so they were not willing to admit that collectivization had not been successful. Some party leaders even feared that if private land ownership were allowed, poor farmers would end up becoming tenants, landlords would return to exploit the tenants, and the pre-1949 rural problems would reappear. Some believed that the rural party organization would also be seriously weakened.

In 1962, before going to Mao with a proposal to assign the individual rural household responsibility for grain production, Chen Yun had asked Deng privately whether he would support such a proposal; Deng told him he would. But if Deng had advocated such a proposal in 1978, he would have been vulnerable to the same accusations leveled against him during the Cultural Revolution: "pursuing the capitalist road." So how did Deng find a way to permit experimentation with household farming while managing the political opposition? The breakthrough came under Wan Li in Anhui province.

In June 1977, at about the same time that Deng was allowed to return to work, Wan Li was appointed by Hua Guofeng as first party secretary of Anhui province.[43] Wan Li's predecessor in Anhui had stuck close to the Maoist vision of supporting large collectives; starvation was still widespread.[44] Anhui, an overwhelmingly rural province, was one of the poorest in the country: an estimated three to four million had starved to death during the Great Leap Forward.

In the first few weeks after his arrival in Anhui in August 1977, Wan Li visited all the major rural areas of the province and observed and talked with local officials.[45] He was shocked to see the extensive poverty. The towns were filled with emaciated people who lacked warm clothing and adequate housing. In some places, there were only crude structures made of mud instead of wooden tables. As Wan Li told his children, he could not help but ask why, so many years after the Communists had taken power, conditions could still be so bad.[46]

Even before Wan Li arrived in Anhui, the party had directed its Rural Policy Research Office to survey several counties in Anhui's Chu prefecture, where people were still dying of starvation, and to formulate recommendations for dealing with the food shortages. Wan Li, on the basis of their several months of study and his personal visits to the area, had guided the drafting of the "Provincial Party Committee Six-Point Proposal" for dealing with the rural problems in Anhui. The proposal recommended (1) that the production teams, depending on the circumstances and as long as production responsibilities were met, allow certain tasks in the fields to be assigned to a small work group or even to an individual, (2) that the autonomy of the production teams in making decisions be respected by higher levels, (3) that the quotas assigned to the production teams and individual members be reduced, (4) that the produce be distributed to members according to their work, not according to their need, (5) that decisions on the allocation of grain reflect the interests of the nation, the collective, and the individual, and (6) that team members be permitted to work on their own private plots and to sell the produce at local markets.[47] The document did not directly attack the almost sacred Dazhai collective model; it simply did not mention it. Wan Li knew that Chen Yonggui, the Dazhai hero who was still officially in charge of agriculture, would regard the six points as bourgeois.[48]

At the time of Wan Li's six-point proposal, national policy explicitly prohibited contracting down to the household and Wan Li could not oppose national policy. But when Deng saw the Anhui Party Committee's six-point proposal, produced under Wan Li's leadership, he, like a number of other officials, immediately affirmed the value of the experiment.[49] Deng said that where there is serious starvation in poor mountain areas, peasants should be allowed to find their own ways to avoid starvation. Leftists realized that Deng was giving permission to decentralize agricultural production down to the household in the poor mountain areas, but it was hard to argue against peasants' finding ways to avoid starvation.

In November 1977, Wan Li addressed an assembly of Anhui county party secretaries to discuss implementation of the six-point proposal. The assembly was large and official enough to reassure Anhui officials who were frightened that if they followed Wan Li and the political line were to change, they would be attacked for pursuing capitalism. Wan Li, standing firm, simply declared that "any methods or policies that interfere with the advancement of production are wrong." Instead, officials should rely on practice to determine which ways worked best, to give full play to creativity, and not to worry about making errors. Wan Li's conviction and his willingness to take personal responsibility, qualities he had displayed when ending the railway stoppages in Xuzhou in 1975, gave the officials a measure of confidence to move ahead.[50] Despite some lingering concerns, the policy was implemented, and in early 1978 Wan Li allowed local areas to continue to decrease the size of the agricultural units. In some places such as Fengyang county, where starvation remained widespread, production responsibility was contracted down to the household.[51]

A few weeks later, on February 1, 1978, the day after Deng arrived in Sichuan on his way from Myanmar to Nepal, Deng told Sichuan Party Secretary Zhao Ziyang about Wan Li's success in Anhui with the six-point proposal.[52] In fact, Zhao Ziyang had already begun permitting production teams to decentralize rural work to smaller units *(baochan dao zu)*, although this step had not been fully reported to Beijing. Deng encouraged Zhao to allow bold experiments similar to those of Wan Li, and Zhao complied, quickly developing a twelve-point program for decentralizing responsibility for agricultural production.[53] He declared that the basic accounting unit could be a small group, but he did not go as far as Wan Li; he did not allow the responsibility to be passed down to the household.[54]

By the fall of 1978, officials in Anhui, cheered by the successful midyear harvests produced by the smaller work groups, reported their successes, setting off arguments with those who supported large-scale cooperatives. At a meeting of the National Agricultural Economic Association held in Suzhou in the fall of 1978, an official from the Anhui Agricultural Policy Research Office had the courage to say that one should not blindly follow the Dazhai model and that the government should not launch so many political movements that interfered with local economic initiatives.[55] But on the other side, Chen Yonggui, still vice premier in charge of agricultural affairs, accused Wan Li of secretly promoting individual household farming. Newspaper articles, too, denounced Wan Li for opposing Dazhai and for restoring capitalism. But Wan Li had gained confidence from the successful harvests in the areas that had tried decentralized work assignments and he was rapidly winning support within the party. In November 1978, when criticized by Chen Yonggui, Wan Li, living up to his reputation for bravery, replied: "You say you are speaking from the Dazhai experience; I say Dazhai is an ultra-leftist model. . . . You go your way and I'll go mine. . . . Don't impose your views on me and I won't impose mine on you. As for who is right and who is wrong, let's see which way works best."[56]

Until he fell from power, Hua Guofeng continued to support the Dazhai model and to advocate improving agricultural production by introducing new seeds, more chemical fertilizers, as well as water pumps, tractors,
and other machinery. His goal was within five years to have a large tractor
in every brigade and a small tractor in every production team.[57] The eighteen large-scale fertilizer plants that had been approved in 1975 (when Deng
was at the helm) were in full production by 1978. Hua continued building
large chemical fertilizer factories, and by 1982 twice as much chemical fertilizer was available throughout the country as in 1978. Electric power in the
countryside doubled between 1978 and 1982 as well. But Hua's expectations
about these initiatives' positive effects on agriculture proved wildly optimistic. And although Deng did not object to Hua's efforts to introduce more and
better industrial products to help agriculture, he also believed that a successful Chinese agricultural system would require spurring the enthusiasm of
peasants by decentralizing rural production.

The Third Plenum in December 1978 continued to support the Dazhai
model, creating concern among Anhui officials that they might be vulnerable to later attack.[58] Although Chen Yonggui was replaced as vice premier in
charge of agriculture shortly after the Third Plenum, his replacement Wang
Zhenzhong still supported the Dazhai model, and in the spring of 1979 the
new vice premier for agriculture wrote a letter to Hu Jiwei, editor of the *People's Daily*, asking him to help put a stop to the decentralization of production
teams. A series of articles was published that opposed further decentralization
and most members of the Politburo were still too cautious to take a different
stance.[59]

In this atmosphere, Wan Li had serious doubts about whether his toler-
ance for further decentralization would be supported at higher levels. At a
meeting on June 18, 1979, Wan Li took Chen Yun aside and asked his views.
Chen said to Wan privately, "I support you with both hands." Wan Li also
asked Deng his views. Deng, not yet ready to support him publicly, replied,
"You don't need to engage in debates, just go ahead, that's all. Just seek the
truth from facts."[60] As the debate heated up, Wan Li was buoyed by the quiet
support from Deng and Chen Yun. At a meeting in Beijing, when a vice minister of agriculture attacked the practice of contracting down to the household, Wan Li shot back: "You are a *feitou da er*" (fat head and big ears—in
other words, like a pig). "You have plenty to eat. The peasants are thin because they do not have enough to eat. How can you tell the peasants they
can't find a way to have enough to eat?"[61]

After Anhui enjoyed a very successful midyear harvest in 1979 in areas where contracting down to the household was being implemented, Wu Xiang, a former New China News Agency reporter who had spent time in Anhui, was encouraged by high officials in Beijing to publicize those successes. In 1992, when looking back at his actions from 1979 to 1981, Deng recalled that he was aware many people were then opposed to contracting down to the household and had even labeled it "capitalism," but rather than attack them he had waited until the results were proven; gradually people recognized that the new strategy was working, and within several years, the experiments became national policy.[62] Indeed, by the end of 1979, some estimated that half of the production teams in the country were distributing work down to small groups and one-quarter had made contracts with households.

In early 1980, Wan Li, seeking Hu Yaobang's support, told Hu that it wouldn't work to have people at lower levels surreptitiously practicing contracting down to the household: instead they needed the full support of the top party leaders. Wan Li thus suggested to Hu Yaobang that they convene a meeting of provincial party secretaries to give clear public support for the policy.[63]

It was only at this time, before the meeting of provincial secretaries, that Deng gave permission to allow the decentralization of rural production down to the household. On May 31, 1980, Deng called in Hu Qiaomu and Deng Liqun to express his support for contracting down to the household and to tell them to publicize his views. Many local areas moved quickly to allow household production, but even then some local officials remained unaware of Deng's position. Deng's request to his two writers in effect marked the end of the collective agriculture that had been launched with Mao's famous speech of July 31, 1955. At that time, Mao had proclaimed: "Throughout the Chinese countryside a new upsurge in the socialist mass movement is in sight. But some of our comrades are tottering along like a woman with bound feet. . . . The tide of social reform in the countryside—in the shape of cooperation—has already been reached in some places. Soon it will sweep the whole country."[64]

In his talk to Hu Qiaomu and Deng Liqun on May 31, 1980, Deng avoided Mao's dramatic appeal. He said:

> Now that more flexible policies have been introduced in the rural areas, the practice of fixing farm output quotas on a household basis has been adopted in some localities where it is suitable. It has proved quite effec-

tive and changed things rapidly for the better. Fixing output quotas on a household basis has been adopted in most of the production teams in Feixi county, Anhui province, and there have been big increases in production. . . . Some comrades are worried that this practice may have an adverse effect on the collective economy. I think their fears are unwarranted. . . . Some comrades say that the pace of socialist transformation had been too rapid. I think there is some ground for this view. . . . If the transformation had advanced step by step, with a period of consolidation followed by further development, the result might have been better. . . . It is extremely important for us to proceed from concrete local conditions and take into account the wishes of the people.[65]

Deng, acutely aware of opposition among party conservatives, made his argument not to a large audience where there was certain to be unsympathetic critics, but only to his two writers, who then spread the message to the broader public.

Four years after Mao gave his rousing speech, tens of millions of peasants were starving, and twenty-five years after his speech, the collectives were dissolved. By contrast, four years after Deng's cautious, reasoned explanation to his writers, most of China's farming was being done by individual households, and agricultural production was rising rapidly. Twenty-five years after Deng's speech, the system he installed was still going strong.

Personnel changes accompanied the change in policy. At the Fifth Plenum of the 11th Party Congress in early 1980, when Deng brought in his own team headed by Hu Yaobang and Zhao Ziyang to lead the country, Wan Li became a vice premier, director of the State Agricultural Commission, and the member of the party Secretariat in charge of agriculture. As head of the State Agricultural Commission, Wan Li, with Deng's permission, could extend the model of household production nationwide. In August 1980 the leaders opposing contracting down to the household—Hua Guofeng, Chen Yonggui, and Wang Renzhong—were formally relieved of their posts as premier and vice premiers, respectively, and the media began criticizing the ultra-leftism of the Dazhai model.

In the summer of 1980 Wan Li began to prepare the formal document supporting the new policy, which was to be issued in late September. At a meeting of first party secretaries to discuss rural issues, Wan Li called on Du Runsheng, the highly respected agricultural specialist who had been head of the Secretariat of the Rural Work Department and also head of the Rural Development Institute on agricultural policy. After Du made a presentation analyzing the results in Anhui, the provincial secretaries expressed varying views. Some of the strongest opposition came from Heilongjiang, where the larger fields were suitable for dry land crops and greater mechanization, and where it was not easy to divide the land down to the household. Some of those areas chose not to contract down to the household.

There also were differing views on what form household farming should take. In the end, the way that was chosen, "contracting down to the household," retained public ownership of the land and allowed local officials to assign a certain production quota to each individual household. In the contract with the household, village officials specified which crops the household had to cultivate and how large the quota turned over to the government should be. In the contract, the local officials agreed to supply the land and machinery to the household and in return, after the harvest, the household would turn over a certain amount of grain and other crops. If a household no longer had enough able-bodied people to work the land, village leaders could reassign the land to other households. The term *baochan dao hu,* "contracting production responsibility down to the household," was suggested by Du Runsheng; compared to some expressions, this term reassured conservatives that there was still a local unit that was assigning responsibility.[66] From the perspective of the Beijing authorities, the system ensured that national needs for grain, cotton, and other crops would be met by the sum of the contracts with the farm households. Farm households had the freedom to grow crops in their own way, and once they had turned over the goods in their contracts, any remaining produce could be used by the family or sold in markets.

Based on papers and discussions at the meeting of provincial officials, Wan Li had his staff prepare Directive No. 75, which was issued on September 27, 1980.[67] The document was carefully crafted. It permitted local collectives to assign responsibility for production down to the household in especially poor areas in order to avoid starvation. By October 1981 over half the production teams in the country had chosen some form of contracting down to the household. And by the end of 1982, 98 percent of rural households were listed as having some form of contracts with the production team.[68]

In 1982, the communes, which had been established in 1958 to mobilize peasants for large public-works projects and large-scale collective farming, were abolished. The highest of the three levels in the collective structure (commune, brigade, and team), the communes had originally combined economic and political functions in a single organization. After they were abolished, their political functions were taken on by the town or a large administrative village government, and the commune's workshops and other economic units became independent "collective" enterprises.

Meanwhile, the doubling of chemical fertilizer production between 1978 and 1982 and the 20 percent increase in the procurement price of grain in 1979 assisted the improvement of grain production and the growth of rural income, albeit less than the shift to contracting production down to the household.[69] From 1978 to 1982, peasant income roughly doubled.[70]

Some observers have argued that the idea of decentralizing production down to the household was invented by peasants, but in fact many officials knew about the idea and some had been considering it ever since the beginning of collectivization. It would be more accurate to say that when peasants were given a choice between collective or household farming, they overwhelmingly chose the household. Gradually officials who had doubts about household agriculture were won over. At the 13th Party Congress in 1987, the constitution was revised to guarantee the right to contract down to the household for the indefinite future.[71]

It took several years after de-collectivization and the introduction of household agriculture to make adjustments in supply and demand and to stabilize an effective national system of production and sale of agricultural crops. For several years agricultural specialists drew up documents each year dealing with such issues as rural organization, machinery, and other inputs to aid rural production. The documents were published in early January each year as central government Document No. 1. In Document No. 1, 1982, contracting down to the household and similar programs were all declared "socialist." The ideological battle was over.

After household farming was introduced, grain production continued to rise rapidly. Indeed, as early as 1984 grain production surpassed 400 million tons, compared to 300 million tons in 1977. After 1981, the growth in the grain supply led the government to encourage farmers to diversify into vegetables, fruits, and industrial crops. Official estimates of per capita grain consumption rose from 1977 to 1984 from 195 kilograms to 250 kilograms, and consumption of pork, beef, poultry, and eggs increased even more sharply.[72]

The government had been completely unprepared for the huge grain harvest of 1984. As a result, there was not enough warehouse space to store the grain, and some local governments, lacking sufficient funds to purchase all the grain that had been produced, had to give the farmers paper IOUs. Before then, the government, fearing urban unrest, since 1978 had not passed on to the urban consumer the increase in prices paid to the farmers for rice.

This subsidy was a strain on the government budget, and after 1984 the costs were passed on to the urban consumer. On January 1, 1985, the government announced that it was no longer obligated to buy grain produced by the farmers. Because farmers planting their fields in 1985 worried that they might not get full payment for rice, they planted smaller rice crops and grain production consequently dropped 28 million tons, or about 7 percent (which was still 60 million tons more than that produced in 1980, when household farming first began to take hold). It took several years after the 1985 adjustments for grain production to recover to the 1984 levels and to put rural production on an even keel, but by 1989 grain output had surpassed the 1984 peak, and it continued at high levels thereafter.[73] By then, there was sufficient rice production so that the government abolished grain rationing and consumers could buy all the rice they needed.

Contracting down to the household was not a panacea for all rural problems. Some areas, especially those in the Northeast where the large dry fields, instead of rice paddies, produced wheat, sorghum, or other grains, the farmers used tractors that could plow more land than that farmed by a single family. Some of those areas chose to retain collective agriculture. Under the collective system, the more successful production teams had been able to provide some care for the elderly and infirm residents who did not have families to look after them. With the end of collective agriculture, it was difficult to provide local community welfare. The twenty-five years of collective agriculture had had devastating consequences, especially where it was carried to extremes, but rural collectivization had also made it easier to expand irrigation and to develop a strong local party structure grounded in the collective—a party structure that did not entirely disappear with the introduction of household production.[74]

In addition to ending grain shortages and raising peasants' income, household production allowed for the expansion of industrial crops such as cotton, flax, and tobacco. In 1981 China was the fourth largest importer of cotton, and four years later it was exporting cotton. Rural families, motivated to work hard, could meet their agreed-upon grain-production targets and release their young adults to work in rural industry. Farmers selling produce in towns and cities, too, improved the quality and quantity of food for urban consumers. Even officials who had opposed the abolition of collective agriculture found that their wives and children were pleased with the expanded choices and improved quality of vegetables, fruit, chicken, and pork in the urban markets. In the 1980s, as refrigeration and transport improved, the varieties of vegetables, meat, and fruit continued to grow rapidly. Hundreds of millions of rural peasants were lifted above the poverty line. Increased rural incomes provided outlets for expanding light industry. Yet most peasants, except for those on the outskirts of the urban areas, on average remained far poorer than urban residents and their health care and education lagged.

Deng continued to follow the adjustments in rural policy each year after the transition to household production was completed in 1981, but not with the same intensity and personal involvement as from 1978 to 1981, when he had personally supervised the process of de-collectivization. By allowing Wan Li to tell local rural officials they could allow peasants to do what was necessary to solve the problem of starvation and then publicizing the successful results, Deng had accomplished his goal: relieving China's grain shortage. Deng had no ideological commitment to household farming. He allowed it because it solved the grain problem and the problem of rural livelihood. To reach this goal, he had to de-collectivize agriculture. He accomplished that politically difficult task without a debilitating split in the party and without personally becoming a target of attack by conservative officials. The popular enthusiasm for the results of rural reforms, both among peasants who enjoyed more freedom and income and among urban consumers who enjoyed more varieties of food supplies, greatly strengthened public support for further reforms.

Township and Village Enterprises

In a talk with a Yugoslav official in June 1987, Deng recalled, "In the rural reform our greatest success—and it is one we had by no means anticipated— has been the emergence of a large number of enterprises run by villages and townships. They were like a new force that just came into being spontaneously."[75] Deng did not launch the township and village enterprises (TVEs) experiment, but it fit his philosophy: when something works, support it. It also dovetailed with the recommendations of researchers in Zhao's think tanks: continue the economic planning structure but allow markets to expand as long as they do not interfere with the plans.

When communes were abolished in 1982, the small commune workshops and commercial stores automatically became enterprises under the jurisdiction of the recently reestablished towns and villages. Commune industrial workshops had relied on manual labor and primitive machinery, almost all of which, except for tractors and water pumps, was made locally. Because the transportation systems were so rudimentary, commune enterprises had to repair their own tractors and maintain the water pumps used to irrigate the rice paddies. Some commune workers wove reeds into baskets; others forged metal in small iron foundries and with lathes shaped simple plows, discs, and harrows to be pulled by water buffalos, small tractors, or teams of young peasants. Many towns had simple food-processing plants for husking rice, making soy sauce, drying fruit, or pickling vegetables. Some communes had simple brick kilns, where they made low-quality bricks, and cement factories, where they crushed rocks and added sand to make simple cement for local use. Some villages had sewing machines for making or repairing clothes. People in towns in hilly and mountainous areas gathered herbs and roots to make simple Chinese medicines, and many built pits where they created organic or in some cases simple chemical fertilizers.[76]

Although TVEs were not planned, conditions were in fact ripe for their growth. When commune workshops became TVEs with the abolition of the communes, they not only gained some independence from commune management, but they were no longer bound by the geographical area of the commune. They were free to produce goods that they could sell wherever they wanted. Unlike state factories, they had the flexibility to adapt to demand, and unlike independent businesses that were still restricted to having no more than seven employees, they were considered "collectives" and thus ideologically acceptable, with no limit on size. Farm workers who had little incentive to become more efficient when working for the production team had a great incentive to be more efficient when farming the land allocated to their household. Fewer workers were needed to farm the land and more rural youth were available to work in the TVEs. And with the increased production of industrial crops like cotton, flax, and tobacco, the TVEs could turn the harvested crops into cotton goods, canvas, cigarettes, and other products.

Furthermore, the growth of TVEs was fueled by the investment flowing in from the outside. Throughout the 1980s, more than half of the production of the TVEs was taking place in the five coastal provinces of Guangdong, Fujian, Zhejiang, Jiangsu, and Shandong.[77] Investment in these provinces and the technology came from Hong Kong, Taiwan, and overseas Chinese (see Chapter 14). Many of the towns and villages in Guangdong brought in foreign technology and partnered with local officials in creating increasingly modern factories producing for global markets. In short, as Du Runsheng said, when the communes were abolished and the government and enterprises were separated, the former commune enterprises could begin to act like economic animals, responding to the needs of the market. By the mid-1980s, under pressure from the government to be more efficient, some state enterprises even subcontracted out to the TVEs to help them meet their production plans.

Compared to state-owned enterprises, the TVEs had many advantages. State enterprises, including all enterprises in basic industries, transportation, utilities, and national defense, produced a given quota of goods according to the annual plan, with a fixed number of personnel whose salaries were set by grade. Materials were bought and sold at prices that were set by bureaucrats to reflect the priorities of the plan. In short, state-owned enterprises had no flexibility, but the TVEs were completely flexible in adapting to market conditions. Furthermore, state enterprises were expected to supply many benefits for all their employees: housing, welfare, medical care, and schooling. The TVEs could draw on young labor and avoid the higher pay and extensive welfare payments that went to an older workforce. In 1978, 28.3 million people were employed in commune enterprises; in 1992 when Deng stepped down, the TVEs employed 105.8 million people. In 1978, the value of production in commune enterprises was reported to be 49 billion yuan; in 1992 when Deng stepped down, the value of TVE production was reported to be 1798 billion yuan, almost fifty times as much.[78] In 1978 commune enterprises comprised 9 percent of China's industrial output, but by 1990 the TVEs comprised 25 percent and by 1994, 42 percent.[79]

The TVEs began to draw materials and labor from state enterprises. In the Yangtze delta area, for example, engineers working in state factories who produced goods according to annual plans as part of their regular weekday jobs moonlighted on weekends in TVEs in Wuxi, Suzhou, and Kunshang, not far west of Shanghai, that were far more efficient than the regular state factories.

By the late 1980s, Chen Yun had become upset that the TVEs were consuming materials needed for state enterprises, that small TVEs were wasting fuel and other resources that could be used more efficiently by state enterprises, and that competition from the leaner TVEs was making it more difficult for state enterprises to operate in the black and to provide for their older staff and retirees. As a result, the balancers in state planning and finance began to demand stricter supervision over the TVEs so they would not drain too many resources and labor away from the state enterprises.

Individual Household Enterprises

Although the TVEs were independent of the government, they were still under the supervision of local party officials. Since the TVEs were considered "cooperatives," they were easier for the Communist conservatives to accept than "private enterprises" that were owned by individuals. Yet there was tremendous pent-up demand for the services and products that such individually owned businesses typically offered. After collectivization in 1955–1956, urban private businesses had been eliminated, but when the reforms began in the 1970s people were eager for restaurants, neighborhood shops, repair shops, and stores with all kinds of goods. Deng and his colleagues knew there was a need for small private enterprises in the urban areas, but how would they win acceptance from conservative officials to allow such businesses to restart?

The answer lay in the urgency of finding employment for young people to curb urban unrest. By 1978, there were several hundred million people who were underemployed and yet, because socialist societies theoretically eliminated "unemployment" (shiye), even the term "unemployment" was then too sensitive to be used. If urban youth did not have work, they were "waiting for assignment" (daiye). And although rationing in the early years after 1977 had made it difficult for unauthorized youth to return to the cities, as peasants in the countryside increasingly sold off their surplus in the markets, urban families found ways to feed the returned youth without ration coupons, and more youth began seeping back into the urban areas—where they could not find jobs. Also, beginning in 1977, once youth in the countryside who passed the university examinations were allowed to return to study, the envious who were left behind in the countryside began to find ways to trickle back into the cities.

In 1978 and 1979, an estimated 6.5 million youth returned to urban areas from the countryside.[80] By the early 1980s, an estimated 20 million intellectual youth and workers, largely former urban residents, had also moved back to the cities. With the state budget under great strain, state enterprises lacked the funds to hire them. By 1979 reports of increasing crime among youth "waiting for employment" grew more worrisome to the political leaders. So just as Deng had used the danger of starvation as leverage to permit peasants to "find their own solution," in 1979 he used the danger of increasing crime among urban youth to convince other leaders to let them form getihu (individual household enterprises).[81] As long as they relied on their own labor and did not exploit the labor of others, they would still be considered workers, not capitalists, and so, Deng said, they should be allowed to open a shop, repair station, or some other "household enterprise." By early 1980, then, small markets and food stalls began to appear in cities and towns.

But how should one draw the line between heads of household enterprises and capitalists? In volume 4 of Das Kapital, Marx describes the case of an employer who had eight employees and was exploiting the labor of others. Practical Beijing politicians, then, suggested that as long as the household had no more than seven employees and the household head himself (or herself) worked, the leader of the household enterprise would be classified as a "worker."

Once they were permitted, household enterprises proliferated like bamboo shoots after a spring rain: stalls sprang up in towns and cities offering haircuts; repairs of shoes, knives, and bicycle tires; drinks or prepared foods; and handicrafts or manufactured goods. In some areas, such shops were allowed to be open only in the evenings and became "night stalls." In July 1981, the State Council issued regulations to guide the development of household enterprises, and local communities began to regulate where they could be located and required them to be licensed. The revival of urban services, like the revival of household agriculture, proved enormously popular, both to those who now had a way to earn a living and to the consumers who now had access to needed services and products.

By 1982 it was discovered that some household enterprises were hiring eight or even more workers, and a debate ensued. Deng asked what people were afraid of—that it would harm socialism?[82] He used simple examples to make his case. If a farmer has three ducks, he has no problem, but if he gets a fourth duck, is he a capitalist? Still, the issue of where to draw the line on how many employees a private businessperson could hire remained so sensitive that the final answer required the personal involvement of Deng and Chen Yun. Deng said to Chen Yun that if they publicly discussed the issue, people would be afraid that the policy allowing private enterprise could be changed, so he suggested that they "let it continue for a couple years, then see how it's working" *(kan yi kan)*. Although some enterprises were reluctant to grow so large that they would be noticeable, others continued to expand. Meanwhile, Deng continued to avoid public statements, a strategy that allowed private enterprises to grow in a way that would not alarm conservative officials. At the 13th Party Congress in 1987, party officials officially permitted individual household enterprises to hire more than seven employees. Deng had scored another victory by using his basic approach to reform: Don't argue; try it. If it works, let it spread.

16

Accelerating Economic Growth and Opening

1982–1989

By 1982 the success of Chen Yun's retrenchment policy had, paradoxically, given Deng a much stronger case for promoting a policy that Chen Yun would not have approved: rapidly accelerating China's growth. In 1980 the budget deficit stood at 11.7 percent of revenue, but by 1982 it had dropped to 2.6 percent. In 1980 foreign reserves were only US$4 billion but by 1982 they had risen to US$14 billion. In addition, in 1982 the grain harvest was 354 million tons, up 9 percent over the previous year, and the actual rate of economic growth was 7.7 percent, nearly double the 4 percent projected rate.[1]

Deng and Chen Yun Disagree on the Growth Rate, 1981–1983

By 1981, Deng's effort to be patient with Chen Yun's readjustment policy that slowed growth rates was wearing thin. Deng had already begun talking about quadrupling industrial and agricultural output by the year 2000. When at one meeting he asked how fast China would have to grow to quadruple GNP growth from 1980 to 2000, Hu Yaobang, who had already done the calculations, immediately responded: 7.2 percent per year.[2] Yet in 1981 the economy grew at only a 5.2 percent rate. Chen Yun, Yao Yilin, and the cautious planners who controlled the planning apparatus had restricted outlays of investment for construction.

Deng wanted to avoid an open split with Chen Yun, but with Hua Guofeng removed, Deng no longer needed Chen's cooperation in political struggles, and he began to push harder for modernization and economic expansion. When Deng diplomatically raised the question of whether it was useful to have the large disparity between plan rates and actual growth rates that China then had, Chen Yun answered that it was all right for production to surpass planned goals. In fact, in his view it was better to have low goals that were surpassed than to set higher goals: because officials at lower levels were so eager to charge ahead, if higher goals were set, these officials would push beyond what the economy could bear. The result would be a shortage of supplies and inflation, and soon chaos would break out and growth would be stymied.

At the end of 1980, while discussing annual plans for 1981, Chen Yun's ally Yao Yilin had said that the highest possible growth target was 4 percent, though they could strive to achieve 5 percent—and over the long term the most they could grow was 6 percent a year. Hu Yaobang, making every effort to defend Deng's goals, countered by saying that if that were the case, all of their discussions about quadrupling growth by 2000 were meaningless.[3] At the 4th Session of the National People's Congress (NPC) in December 1981, just when the Sixth Five-Year Plan (1981–1985) and the annual plan for 1982 were being considered, disagreements over the speed of growth were so serious that the NPC did not pass an annual budget, nor did it spell out a precise growth target for the Sixth Five-Year Plan.[4]

In December 1982, when the Shanghai delegation to an NPC meeting visited Chen Yun at his winter residence in Shanghai, Chen described his view with an analogy used by Huang Kecheng: the economy "is like a bird. You can't hold it in your hand but have to let it fly. But it might fly away, and that is why you need a cage to control it." To those who wanted a more open economy with faster growth, Chen Yun's "bird cage economics" became the symbol for outdated thinking that stymied market growth. Chen Yun would later explain that what he meant by controls were macroeconomic controls; the cage could be an entire province, the whole country, or in some cases an area even larger than the single nation.[5] This qualification, however, did not stop his critics.

Although Chen Yun's critics sometimes sounded as if he were opposed to all reforms, this was not the case. Chen supported the enterprise reform that Zhao Ziyang had pioneered in Sichuan, which gave businesses increased responsibility for their own profits and losses. He agreed that Beijing should allow enterprises more freedom to buy materials and sell commodities. He had not opposed rural contracting down to the household, and he supported efforts to decentralize controls over commerce and industry, giving lower-level officials more freedom to push ahead. He was willing to support some price flexibility, so that some of the smaller items then under planning could be taken off the plan and be exchanged on markets. He, too, wanted economic vitality.[6] But he felt responsible for keeping the planning system in good order, for seeing that key industries received the resources they needed, and for ensuring that inflation did not get out of control. On these issues he could be adamant.

The documents issued by the 12th Party Congress (September 1–11, 1982) and by the NPC meetings that followed (November 26–December 10, 1982) reflected the widening gap between Deng and Chen Yun over the targeted speed of growth for China. Most of the documents at the party congress were prepared by the cautious planners. But at Deng's insistence, the congress also took on the goal of quadrupling (*fan liang fan,* literally "doubling twice") the gross value of industrial and agricultural production by the end of the century. Deng firmly reiterated that it was not good to have a planned rate so much lower than the actual rate.[7] As a disciplined Communist, Chen Yun did not criticize publicly Deng's plan for quadrupling the economy by 2000, but he also did not endorse it. He reiterated that economic construction over the next twenty years should be divided into two decades, the first to lay the foundation with moderate growth, and then a second decade of more rapid growth.[8]

The revised Sixth Five-Year Plan (1981–1985), approved at the NPC meeting, represented a victory for the cautious planners. The annual growth target for the five years was set at 4 to 5 percent. Capital construction for the period would be US$23 billion, essentially no increase over the Fifth Five-Year Plan, with an emphasis on energy and transport. And spending on education, science, culture, and health care would increase.

Hu Yaobang believed that one of the ways he could best contribute to modernization was to travel the country giving encouragement to local officials. He listened to their problems and tried to cut through the obstacles to growth. And based on his visits to the countryside, Hu became convinced that local areas had the capacity to grow faster. In response to Chen Yun's argument that China should grow slowly in the 1980s to build a base for more rapid growth in the 1990s, Hu Yaobang said that current leaders should do as much as possible in the 1980s so as not to leave unrealistic goals for those who would lead the economy in the 1990s. In the eyes of Chen

Yun and his cautious planner allies, and even to Zhao Ziyang, Hu Yaobang, in his efforts to be supportive to local officials, was too willing to create exceptions to the rules and not sufficiently concerned about curbing inflation.

Hu Yaobang's local visits put him on a collision course with Chen Yun. Although the two men had worked well together to reverse verdicts and although Hu remained deferential, Chen Yun was increasingly critical of Hu Yaobang. At a meeting to discuss annual plans on January 12, 1983, Deng again noted that the sixth Five-Year Plan beginning in 1981 still projected an annual growth rate of 3 to 4 percent, but that the actual growth rate was more than twice as high.

Year	1978	1979	1980	1981	1982	1983
GDP growth	11.7%	7.6%	7.8%	5.2%	9.1%	10.9%

Source: Jinglian Wu, *Understanding and Interpreting Chinese Economic Reform* (Mason, Ohio: Thomson/South-Western, 2005), p. 362.

Deng asked again if it were appropriate to have such a big gap between the plan and actual performance, and the planners answered that there was no problem.[9] In typical Deng fashion, he then both avoided confrontation and enabled his own strategy to prevail. Without publicly criticizing Chen Yun and the party's decision, he did not restrain local officials from finding ways to expand more rapidly, nor did he keep Hu Yaobang from traveling to the local areas. Once again, Deng had been confronted by a party consensus with which he disagreed and his approach was vintage Deng: "Don't argue, just push ahead."

Conceptualizing Reform: Zhao Ziyang

Chen Yun agreed in 1980 that Zhao Ziyang should be given a staff to examine the economic issues of the new era, which he realized were different from the period when he had set up the planning system (for more on Zhao, see Key People in the Deng Era, p. 743). When Zhao arrived in Beijing, he accepted the readjustment policies of Chen Yun, and Chen Yun in turn supported Zhao's efforts to allow enterprise managers more autonomy and to contract responsibility for rural production down to the household. In a more general sense, too, Chen Yun appreciated Zhao's efforts to "speak with a Beijing accent," to give up his years of thinking like a provincial leader and focus on the national economy as a whole.

Zhao preferred to avoid political struggles; as premier he did not interfere in the work of Chen Yun and the cautious planners in guiding the daily work of economic planning. Instead Zhao and his think tanks, working outside the regular bureaucracy, concentrated on the big issue of how to guide the transition from a relatively closed economy to a more open one. It was natural that after they had been in Beijing for two or three years, Zhao, with help from his staff, had begun to formulate views about new directions for the economy and that Deng would turn to Zhao for guidance. As Deng became impatient with the slow pace of growth under Chen Yun and the cautious planners, he began turning away from Chen Yun and toward Zhao Ziyang and his think tanks for guidance on basic economic policy. Zhao was at the forefront in working with Japanese advisers, as well as the economists and economic officials around the world who had been assembled by the World Bank to conceptualize how China should undertake the transition. To date, no socialist country had successfully—and without serious disruptions—made the shift from a planned economy to a sustained open, market-based economy. Thus when World Bank officials and leading economists from around the world came to China, their most important meeting was with Zhao. Although Zhao did not have formal university training, foreigners were impressed with his knowledge, his intellectual curiosity, his ability to grasp new ideas, and his analytic abilities.[10] When he visited Beijing in 1988, the famous American economist Milton Friedman expected a half-hour session with Zhao, but the discussion with Zhao, Friedman, and an interpreter alone lasted two full hours. Friedman said about Zhao, "He displayed a sophisticated understanding of the economic situation and of how the market operated." Friedman described the meeting as "fascinating."[11]

One of Zhao's think tanks that played a key role in rural reforms was the small (thirty member) China Rural Development Research Group. It had its origins in a discussion group of bright university graduates who had a deep knowledge of the situation in the countryside from their years "rusticating" there during the Cultural Revolution. In November 1981, it became an independent institute under the Agricultural Economics Institute of the Chinese Academy of Social Sciences.[12] Later it would be incorporated into the Research Center for Rural Development under the State Council, where it did the staff work in the policy formulation for contracting down to the household and later the basic drafting of the yearly Document No. 1 of the Central Committee, which adjusted agricultural policy.[13]

Another think tank was the System Reform Commission *(Tizhi gaige wei-yuanhui)*, which was established to consider fundamental system reforms. Because it could recommend bureaucratic reorganization, some bureaucrats were nervous about what it might propose. It began as a small group under the Chinese Academy of Sciences studying system reform; in 1981, it was reorganized as the System Reform Office and placed under Zhao; and in March 1982, it was renamed the System Reform Commission and raised to ministerial level. By 1984, under the direction of Premier Zhao Ziyang, it was employing around one hundred officials.[14] Bao Tong, a loyal and studious official, originally assigned to Zhao by the Organization Department of the party, began to function in effect as Zhao's chief of staff.

Those who worked under Zhao at the think tanks had great respect and admiration for him. They appreciated his lack of pretense, his informal style, his openness to ideas from people of any rank, and his skill in moving from ideas to practical policies that would move the country forward.

Learning from Abroad

On June 23, 1978, after listening to a report by the Ministry of Education on plans to send students abroad, Deng said he wanted to increase the number of students going abroad to the tens of thousands. Deng believed that for China to modernize quickly, it had to learn about and adapt ideas that were working overseas. The Soviets, who feared a "brain drain," were reluctant to let their promising scholars and students go abroad. Mao had closed the doors with the West. Even Chiang Kai-shek had worried about rapidly losing some of his smartest young people. But Deng never worried about a brain drain. As a result, no developing country other than Japan and South Korea could compare with Deng's China in the scope and depth of its efforts to learn the secrets of modernization from advanced countries. And China, with its huge population, quickly surpassed those two countries in the scale of its learning from abroad.

Deng sent officials abroad on study tours, he invited in foreign specialists, he set up centers to study foreign developments, he encouraged efforts to translate foreign information into Chinese—all on a huge scale. Unlike Japanese and South Korean leaders, who worried that their domestic companies might be overwhelmed by foreign competition, Deng encouraged foreign companies to set up modern factories in China to help train Chinese managers and workers. He made good use of the ethnic Chinese who lived abroad and could assist in understanding developments overseas. But above all he encouraged young people to go abroad to study. During the three decades, from 1978 to 2007, more than a million Chinese students studied abroad, and by the end of those three decades about a quarter of them had already returned to China.[15] In learning about foreign economic developments, Deng allowed Zhao to meet the economists; he preferred to talk with scientists and successful business leaders like Y. K. Pao, Matsushita Konosuke, and David Rockefeller, to collect their ideas on how China could progress. He also met foreigners involved in national economic planning, like Okita Saburo and Shimokōbe Atsushi of Japan. Beginning in early 1979, every few days a report written by senior Chinese scholars was published outlining key foreign developments that were important for the Chinese economy: these were known as *Jingji cankao ziliao* ("economic reference materials"). When delegations went abroad they wrote reports about what they learned, and the reports were then made available to Chinese leaders.

In China's effort to study foreign economic experiences, no institution played a role that could compare in importance with that played by the World Bank, and in no other country did the World Bank play a role as large as it did in China.[16] In 1980, when mainland China replaced Taiwan as the Chinese member of the World Bank, the president of the bank, Robert McNamara, visited Beijing to pave the way in developing the new relationship. McNamara, declaring that the World Bank would not be a truly World Bank without China, resisted pressures from the U.S. government to slow the entry of China into the bank. This independence on McNamara's part gave Chinese officials, who at the time were still worried about nations using China for their own purposes, more confidence that the World Bank did not represent the interests of any single country.

When McNamara met Deng, Deng told him that in its future dealings with the World Bank, ideas would be much more important for China than money. He said that modernization in China was inevitable, but with the cooperation of the World Bank, China could grow faster. And when McNamara and Deng went on to discuss the selection of the chief representative for the bank in China, Deng stated that he didn't care where that person was from; he simply wanted the best person for the job.[17]

After Deng's meeting with McNamara, China's relations with the World

Bank moved ahead quickly; just one month later, on May 15, 1980, China was formally voted into member status. Most member countries of the World Bank had joined in 1945 when the bank was founded, and the World Bank's knowledge of each member country had developed gradually. But because China was such a large country with no previous relationship with the bank until it replaced Taiwan, to make loans to China the bank first needed a much better understanding of the Chinese economy. In October 1980, the World Bank did something it had never done for any other country: it assembled and dispatched to China for a three-month study tour a team of thirty experts composed of many of the world's leading specialists on the Chinese economy, as well as agronomists, engineers, and specialists on health and education. A counterpart team of Chinese experts worked with them; one on the Chinese team was Zhu Rongji (later, premier), who volunteered to accompany them because he saw it as a learning opportunity.

Deng's personal endorsement helped overcome the fear among Chinese team members that they might later be accused of passing on secrets to foreigners. To enhance trust and reduce suspicions of hidden motives, the World Bank team while in China held no meetings to which the Chinese counterpart members were not invited. These Chinese team members, along with their superiors in Beijing, were entrusted with the daunting task of opening up their country; they were eager to think through the unique issues that China needed to face. The World Bank team, aware of its historic role in the opening of China and its special opportunity to learn about China, sought to establish a good long-term professional relationship. This was by far the largest country study the World Bank had ever undertaken. The bank, not then yet as large and bureaucratic as it later became, provided great leeway for its team to adapt to local needs. Edwin Lim, a Mandarin-speaking Philippine-Chinese with a Harvard Ph.D. in economics and World Bank experience in Southeast Asia and Africa, was appointed the bank's chief economist on China shortly after McNamara's visit. He served as the de facto head of the World Bank team on the ground in 1980; beginning in 1985, when the bank opened its Beijing office, and until 1990 he was the first head ("Resident Representative") of the World Bank in China. Lim described the special relationship between China and the World Bank in the 1980s as "made in heaven."[18]

During the three months in late 1980 when World Bank team members were in China, they talked with Chinese officials in charge of the economy and visited local sites. Team members, although hosted by the Ministry of

Finance, met officials in all major economic ministries, including both the "builders" and the "balancers." Officials from the State Planning Commission and State Statistical Bureau played important leadership roles on the Chinese team. The Chinese team had not been trained in Western economic theory, but its members all had experience in managing planned development. The Western specialists, many of whom had worked in other developing countries, tended, like their Chinese hosts, to pay more attention to what was happening on the ground in the institutional settings than to the theoretical explanations offered by academic economists.

Upon its return, the World Bank team, drawing on the joint study in China, wrote a report on the history of the Chinese economy since 1949, describing Chinese policies and endeavoring to distinguish which areas would and would not be amenable to policy changes. The three-volume report was discussed with the Chinese as soon as it was completed in March 1981, and in June, it was presented to the board of the World Bank to provide perspective as the bank made decisions about its first loan to China. The report was read by Zhao Ziyang and other high-level party officials, as well as by Chinese specialists—after approval by the Chinese authorities, it was published for general circulation.

A central issue from the beginning was how to keep the Chinese economy functioning while making the transition to a more open system that had fewer controls. The bank report suggested that more attention should be paid to the use of prices to promote both more efficient investment decisions and greater flexibility in promoting foreign trade. It recommended allowing more internal migration to make possible greater efficiency in the use of labor. But it also advocated that changes in prices and other reforms should not be made too quickly; the team did not recommend comprehensive rapid market liberalization or privatization. For the Chinese, participation in the study gave them an opportunity to understand the perspective of economics professionals with development experience from around the world and to look at the Chinese structure afresh.

Given Deng's emphasis on training, it is not surprising that the first grant China negotiated with the World Bank after becoming a member was for assistance in higher education. In addition, the World Bank set up specific programs to help train Chinese specialists who would work on various economic issues. In this, China cooperated with the bank's Economic Development Institute, which sponsored courses each year to train personnel. The bank also helped establish, with funding by UNDP (United Nations Development Programme) and later the Ford Foundation, a program to train Chinese economists for one year at Oxford University. Between 1985 and 1995 nearly seventy economists were trained in the program, most of whom later held key positions guiding the Chinese economy; the Ford Foundation also supported study in the United States by Chinese economists. As a further aid to China, the World Bank used its incomparable network of contacts with economists around the world to respond to Chinese requests to meet with specialists in various areas.

In the early 1980s, the Chinese officials responsible for adapting their economic system had initially looked to Eastern Europe for reform models. First they fixed their attention on Yugoslavia, but by 1983 their interest had focused on Hungary's "comprehensive reforms" that linked together all the plans in the various sectors. Two Chinese delegations visited Hungary to study its reform programs, and Hungary sent a team to China to explain its reforms. Those familiar with Hungarian issues suggested that China make wider use of economic controls to replace administrative controls, further decentralize authority to the localities, and permit more diverse forms of ownership. Like the Japanese, the Hungarians were using a kind of "indicative planning" in which targets were set; they had stepped away from mandatory planning strategies that required specifying ahead of time precisely which inputs were needed from a broad range of sectors.[19] Yet at the same time, some Chinese officials were beginning to have doubts about the applicability of East European models to the complex problems they faced.

In August 1982, in response to a Chinese request, the World Bank assembled at Moganshan (Mount Mogan, in Zhejiang province) leading specialists from Eastern Europe and elsewhere who had the theoretical perspective and practical experience to discuss overall problems in the reform of socialist systems. The Chinese side was headed by Xue Muqiao; leading East European economists from Poland, Czechoslovakia, and Hungary, including Włodzimierz Brus, presented their views. The discussions and post-meeting visits by foreign consultants to local areas in China greatly strengthened doubts about the suitability of the Eastern European reforms as models for China. The Eastern Europeans had concluded that if they only carried out partial reforms it would build up resistance to future reforms; therefore, they had to leap to full-scale reforms all at once. In China the rural reforms were already having a positive, seemingly irreversible effect so it was not necessary to try to leap to full-scale reforms all at once. After the conference, as the Eastern Europeans traveled to various localities in China, they came to agree with their

Chinese hosts that the Eastern European model of introducing bold reforms all at once would not work in China because of its huge size and great variations in conditions. The only realistic way for China to proceed was to open markets and decontrol prices step by step, and then to allow gradual adjustments. The views of the conference participants were passed on to Zhao Ziyang, who agreed with their conclusions, and then on to Deng, who supported Zhao's views about reforming step by step rather than all at once.

When A. W. Clausen, who replaced McNamara as president of the World Bank in 1981, visited Beijing in 1983, Deng told Clausen that he had found the World Bank's 1981 report interesting and useful. He then invited the World Bank to assess the feasibility of his goal of quadrupling output by 2000. The issue of speed seemed central to Deng; he wanted to grow as fast as possible, but to avoid the dangers of the Great Leap and because he was concerned that as before Chinese officials might be excessively optimistic, he wanted to hear outside opinions. Deng expressed his desire for the World Bank to undertake another study, one that would consider alternative options based on global experience to realize this goal over the next two decades. In response to Deng's request, the bank sent a second comprehensive mission to China in 1984, again led by Edwin Lim. On the basis of research by Chinese collaborators, World Bank staff members, and consultants, the World Bank published a report in 1985 that played an important role in shaping the Seventh Five-Year Plan (1986–1990).[20] The World Bank study confirming that quadrupling economic output in two decades was feasible undoubtedly reassured Deng. The World Bank concluded that China could reach the goal either by concentrating on industrial production or by promoting more balanced development of other sectors, including services; China chose to concentrate on industry.

In 1984, another Moganshan conference of young and middle-aged economists, but without World Bank participation, considered issues such as price reform. The conference conclusions supported a dual-price system—that is, one set of prices for items on the state plan and another set of prices that would be more responsive to market changes. State-owned enterprises that met their quotas would be allowed to sell whatever other products they could make at market prices. As a result, many enterprises would likely orient their practices to the market, while still relying on set prices to provide some stability during the transition to increased use of markets. Some World Bank officials criticized the dual-price system because it created opportunities for officials at state companies to purchase goods at state prices and then to make a quick profit by selling them in the market at higher prices. Higher-level Chinese officials, however, felt confident that they could keep the corruption under control with administrative punishments.[21]

In 1985, following Deng's political successes, Chinese officials again asked the World Bank to assemble experts for some guidance about making the transition from a controlled economy to one where markets played a still larger role. The Chinese and foreign experts assembled for a week on a ship, the *Bashanlun,* where they engaged in intensive formal and private discussions as the vessel passed the Three Gorges on its way from Chongqing to Wuhan. Among the Westerners assembled by the World Bank was Nobel laureate James Tobin, who discussed the possibility of using macroeconomic measures, especially regulating demand, to control markets. Włodzimierz Brus and János Kornai, who was in China for the first time, spoke of Eastern European problems in adapting a central planning system. By the end of the conference, Chinese participants, already doubtful about the appropriateness of Eastern European models for China, were thoroughly convinced that the structural problems in socialist economies—such as the "soft budget constraints" that permitted firms to survive even with low performance and cycles of overproduction—were systemic problems in planning systems. This marked the end of the use of Eastern European reform models and greater acceptance of the role of markets.

The central issue, not well understood by Chinese before the conference, was how to introduce other monetary and fiscal controls that could regulate the markets, avoiding the extremes of cycles that Chinese had previously thought were endemic in capitalist systems. Tobin, in particular, helped convince the Chinese that they could use macroeconomic controls to keep a market system within bounds. The Chinese economists left the meeting with an increased readiness to continue expanding the role of markets in China while introducing macroeconomic controls.

Since inflation had become severe by the time of the conference, the Chinese quickly worked to apply the main lesson learned from the conference: how to use macroeconomic controls to tame it. Premier Zhao Ziyang read the conference report, accepted the conclusions, and was in charge of implementing them, with Deng's blessing.

In the early 1980s, while Chinese leaders were exploring the experiences of Eastern Europe and making use of World Bank advisers, they were also studying Japanese experiences. Although Japan was a member of World Bank, Japanese efforts to work with China were generally done bilaterally and were conducted on a larger scale than China's relations with any other country. Although China was also interested in the Taiwan and South Korea experiences in modernization, mainland China did not have direct relations with them until the late 1980s so their experiences in the early 1980s did not play a major role in shaping Chinese views.

Following Deng's visit to Japan in October 1978, Okita Saburo, who was also an economic planner experienced in helping Asian countries with their economic development, arrived in China in January 1979 to discuss with Gu Mu plans to set up a Japanese advisory group and, more broadly, to consider the role that Japan might play in China's development. Okita, born in Dalian, Liaoning province, had studied engineering and had played a central role in Japan's Economic Stabilization Board, which had guided the Japanese economy after World War II as the country moved away from wartime economic controls and struggled with severe shortages. After 1955 the Economic Stabilization Board was absorbed into the Japanese Economic Planning Agency, which provided indicative planning for the Japanese economy. Okita arranged with Gu Mu that he would lead a Japanese team of experienced bureaucrats to hold a series of annual meetings with Chinese officials, led by Ma Hong, as Chinese officials were making the transition away from tighter controls over the economy. When Prime Minister Ohira visited China in December 1979, Okita, then foreign minister, accompanied him. Deng jokingly asked Okita if he could still continue as an adviser to China even though he was foreign minister. Indeed, the joint meetings did end briefly while Okita was foreign minister, but they resumed in July 1980 after he left office. The Japanese advisory team that joined Okita included Shimokōbe Atsushi, former leader of the National Land Agency, who told the Chinese how the Japanese government had helped promote regional expansion in a balanced, sustainable way by building institutions and ensuring that necessary resources were available.[22] The advisory group continued to meet with Chinese economic officials until 1992.

The two Chinese organizations built on the Japanese model in early 1979 were a Quality Control Association and an Enterprise Management Association. They established training programs in Beijing for regional officials, who in turn set up training programs for factory managers in their respective regions on industrial management, introducing ideas they had learned from Japan.[23] It is difficult, of course, to measure the effect of such training programs, but for factory managers and workers who had been operating at a very slow pace, these models and Chinese officials' strong encouragement that they follow them did stimulate greater efficiency and the improvement of quality controls.

In the 1980s, Japanese gave more aid and built more industrial plants in China than did citizens from any other country. The Japanese factories built in China set standards by which China measured its progress in achieving efficient industrial production. For the study of modern science, the Chinese looked overwhelmingly to the United States. But more new machinery to build assembly lines in Chinese factories came from Japan than from anywhere else. Prime Minister Ikeda's income-doubling plan for the 1960s became the inspiration for Deng's goal of quadrupling the gross value of industrial and agricultural output in the 1980s and 1990s. And from 1974 on, Deng met more delegations from Japan than from any other nation.

Delegations of Chinese economic officials visiting Japan also had been impressed with how consumer demand had become the driver of factory production, leading to a reduced role for state wholesalers as distributors of industrial products. As a result, Chinese factories producing consumer goods were directed to consult directly with local commercial outlets about which products consumers wanted to buy.[24]

Chinese officials were especially impressed with how Japan's Ministry of International Trade and Industry (MITI) analyzed what was needed in each sector for Japanese firms to have the resources and technology to compete in world markets—and then let the firms themselves lead the way in creating the products that would lead to rapid growth for the country as a whole. During his visit to Japan, Deng had marveled at not only the amount of planning that goes on within Japanese enterprises, but also how the planning was much more flexible and responsive to market changes than was the planning in China. MITI gave encouragement and support to leading companies, which then competed fiercely for market share.

China's readjustment policy of 1980–1981, which resulted in the cancellation of many contracts with Japanese companies, had slowed down cooperation between Japanese companies and their Chinese counterparts (see Chapter 15). But by 1982 when the most difficult readjustment steps had been completed, Sino-Japanese relations had revived. In late May and early June 1982, Zhao Ziyang visited Japan not only to seek further Japanese investment and technological advice, but also to restore Japanese interest in the Chinese economy.[25] The Japan External Trade Organization (JETRO) under MITI had several offices in China that conducted research on the Chinese economy, helped Japanese companies locate sectors where there were business opportunities, and provided training to Chinese managers and technicians in various industrial sectors.

By the mid-1980s huge changes were occurring because of the introduction of imported machinery. What might be called "handicraft heavy industry," with bare-backed men throwing coal into steel furnaces and other men with heavy hammers pounding into shape the molten metal, was replaced by the Baoshan modern oxygen furnace with continuous casting and electronic controls. When modern assembly lines replaced men using lathes to shape machinery parts one by one, overall industrial output took off. Midlevel Chinese managers in joint-venture firms with foreign partners also contributed to the surge, by learning how to use modern electronic controls and by implementing the latest management techniques. Some of these managers used the skills they learned in foreign firms to start Chinese firms. And as computers were introduced in the West in the 1980s, they spread quickly to Chinese firms.

The cumulative effect of the new machinery and the new systems introduced by firms based in Japan, Europe, Hong Kong, and (beginning in the late 1980s) Taiwan had at least as much of an influence on economic growth as the system reforms introduced by Beijing officials. The new opening had, in effect, brought about an imported industrial revolution, information revolution, and consumer revolution.

Deng's Economic Offensive, 1984

When the economy was doing well, Deng had the political support needed to speed up reform and opening. But when the economy encountered problems such as inflation, Chen Yun and his cautious balancers gained the political leverage to enable them to tighten the reins on planning and inflationary pressures. In 1982 and 1983 as the economy began to grow more rapidly, and inflation was under control, the atmosphere favored Deng. Not only was grain production going up, but textile production, an important part of consumer industry, increased so markedly that cloth rationing was ended. Per capita rural incomes, according to official figures, rose from 134 yuan in 1978 to 355 yuan in 1984.[26]

At a Central Party Work Conference, held June 26 to June 30, 1983, Deng spoke out strongly in favor of increasing rates of investment more than the rates advocated by Chen Yun and the State Planning Commission.[27] In December 1983, impatient with the cautious planners, Deng said that one cannot anticipate scientifically exactly what will happen. If one thought only about stability, it would be hard to make progress. That is, if the Chinese did not have the spirit to break new paths *(chuangjin)*, then they would not be able to quadruple the output of the economy.[28]

In the favorable atmosphere, Deng was ready to expand the opening of other coastal areas. In January 1984 he traveled to Guangdong and Fujian, where he announced that the policy supporting special economic zones (SEZs) had proved a success (see Chapter 14). The TV cameras conveying the impressive construction that was taking place in Shenzhen to the rest of China laid the basis for public acceptance of the opening of other coastal areas later in the year.

In May 1984, the State Council issued the official document "On Regulations for Further Expanding the Autonomy of State-Owned Enterprises." The development of plans to grant more autonomy to state enterprises was done largely by Zhao's staff at the think tanks. The document advanced the use of macroeconomic controls, including prices and taxes, to control economic activities. Zhao, a longtime advocate of granting greater flexibility to enterprises, also expanded further their freedom to engage in the markets once their official quotas were met.

In June 1984 Deng began using the term "socialism with Chinese characteristics," a grand but marvelously vague expression that perfectly fit Deng's basic approach: stretch the acceptable ideological framework to allow the country to pursue policies that worked. Deng used the term to promote his goal of expanding markets and launching comprehensive reforms in the areas of industry, commerce, science, and education.[29] Following the 1984 Moganshan conference of economists (held September 3 to September 10), the state enterprises, using the dual-track price system, were allowed to expand the use of market prices. Consequently executives increasingly focused their energies on markets, which offered their firms more profits, and in this way learned about markets even while the planning system still provided a measure of stable output for the economy.[30] In the ongoing tug-of-war between reformers and conservatives, the reformers who wanted to expand the role of the market were making progress.

In the entire Deng era, the peak of popular support for Deng was reached on National Day, October 1, 1984, when Peking University students lined the streets and unfurled a banner that read, "Xiaoping, ni hao" (hello, Xiaoping), an informal, friendly greeting. The crowds lining the streets spontaneously joined in with "Xiaoping, ni hao." These words and this scene were in sharp contrast to the orchestrated reverential "Long live Chairman Mao" slogans that the Red Guards had shouted seventeen years earlier in response to orders from above. Instead, these students were spontaneously expressing the sentiments of people throughout the country who felt grateful to Deng for ending the disorder of the Cultural Revolution, for solving the grain shortage, for improving their lives, and for providing leadership that at last put China on the right path. Just a week earlier, Deng had concluded an agreement for the peaceful return of Hong Kong.

Less than three weeks after National Day, Deng, taking advantage of the momentum, was able to get approval at the Third Plenum of the 12th Party Congress to pass the "Decision on the Reform of the Economic Structure," the most comprehensive statement of Chinese economic reform to date. The declaration included a broad theoretical explanation as well as an outline of the measures that would pave the way for an overall expansion of markets. The decision incorporated Deng's term "socialism with Chinese characteristics" and stated that the fundamental difference between socialism and capitalism is not whether the economy is planned or unplanned but whether there is public ownership. The goal of socialism is not egalitarianism but common prosperity. Zhao, who had guided the drafting of this document, achieved what Deng was seeking, a clear explanation of why socialism could encompass market reforms.

The "Decision on the Reform of the Economic Structure" announced that pricing by the state would gradually be reduced and the role of the market in pricing would be increased.[31] The document gave a great boost to officials in various ministries who wanted greater flexibility. In his speech to the plenum in support of the document, Deng admitted that others had done the hard work in preparing the document and refining the wording, but that he approved of all parts of the final document. Deng said that the most important statement in the document was the phrase "respecting knowledge and talented people." He repeated the basic argument for opening, saying that Chinese history shows that it makes great progress only when the country is open (a statement that became the basis for a television series that had an extraordinary, though controversial, effect when it appeared in June 1988: River Elegy (Heshang).[32] Deng then acknowledged that some problems inevitably arise from opening, but he expressed confidence that they could be solved.[33]

At the 1984 Third Plenum, Chen Yun did not publicly criticize the "Decision on the Reform of the Economic Structure," but as Deng began pushing for faster growth and market reforms the tensions between the two became more intense. In meetings during 1984, Chen Yun objected to the excessive 33 percent increase in capital construction, the 15 percent rise in GNP, and the 9 percent rise in the retail price index, the highest since the start of the reforms.[34] Indeed the inflation produced deep anxiety among the public.[35]

The expansion of markets also required some adjustment to the government's system for collecting revenue. In October 1984 the Chinese government, after trying some experiments, introduced a new nationwide system of taxes to replace the prior reliance on profit remittances for taxation *(ligaishui)*. Under the old system, the government assigned factories overall production targets and taxes; there was no economic incentive to increase efficiency. Under the new system, by contrast, each enterprise was completely responsible for its own profits and losses; after remitting its taxes, managers could retain the after-tax profit, thus providing local enterprises with incentives to become more efficient. Both private and state firms, as well as joint ventures with foreign firms, were eligible. Initially, however, the managers lacked sufficient experience to make the system work smoothly. During the first several years, there was no increase in central government revenues.[36]

The data announced at the end of 1984 were deeply disturbing to Chen Yun. At an enlarged Politburo meeting on February 18, 1985, held while Deng was away in Guangdong, Chen Yun denounced the large budget deficits, the excessive use of foreign currency reserves, and the failure to keep tight controls over spending. He concluded that the policy of giving primacy to the plan over the market was not outdated.[37] He used the data at the end of the year to pull back Deng's latest bold charge ahead. Provincial leaders were called to a series of urgent meetings that resulted in the curtailing of large-scale construction, the tightening of bank credits, and tighter controls on wage increases and the use of foreign exchange.[38] With the high inflation by Chinese standards, even Zhao Ziyang moved to tighten controls and constrain investments. Finally Deng too, responding to the atmosphere, joined in the effort to reduce the overheating of the economy.[39]

As he had done in the early 1980s, Chen Yun again used his position as head of the party's Central Commission for Discipline Inspection to restrain the experiments in Guangdong and Fujian. He and his allies publicized cases of smuggling, laundering of foreign exchange, gambling, and pornography. Chen Yun was also aware that various ministries in Beijing were illegally investing funds in the SEZs, making it more difficult to enforce party discipline.[40]

As part of this effort to curtail excesses, Hu Qiaomu traveled to Fujian, where he criticized provincial officials for recreating foreign enclaves like the nineteenth-century treaty ports. Yao Yilin went to Shenzhen, where he complained that there had already been too many "blood transfusions" of state funds into Shenzhen; he said that it was time to "pull the needle."[41] In addition, during the summer of 1985 the Central Commission for Discipline Inspection published a report on an automobile scandal in Hainan where local officials had abused their special privileges to import vehicles for development in order to sell the vehicles on the mainland at great profit.[42] And Gu Mu announced that China would give priority to only four of the fourteen new coastal development zones—those around Shanghai, Tianjin, Dalian, and Guangzhou.[43] Even Deng was constrained by the more critical mood toward the SEZs; he qualified the statements on SEZ policy that he had issued in early 1984, saying that if the SEZs proved unsuccessful, they should be regarded simply as experiments.[44]

In a speech at a national conference convened September 18–25, 1985, in order to set the basic policies for the Seventh Five-Year Plan (for the years 1986 to 1990), Chen Yun declared that the growth-rate target for the economy should be no more than 6 or 7 percent (roughly half the growth rate of 1984 and 1985), even if the actual growth might be somewhat higher. He added that the township and village enterprises (TVEs) should be restrained from taking away resources needed by state enterprises and he warned that if they were not constrained, China could suffer serious energy shortages and transportation bottlenecks.[45]

On the defensive because of the new atmosphere, Deng protected his ideological flank by opposing bourgeois liberalization and advocating the strengthening of "education" so that officials would better resist corruption and injustice. Deng said he fully supported the Seventh Five-Year Plan growth target of 7 percent, which was agreed to unanimously by the Standing Committee of the Politburo. In fact, Deng was not upset at this figure for he knew that given the rapid growth during the last two years, if the country continued to grow by 7 percent per year until 2000, it would easily meet his target of quadrupling GNP between 1980 and 2000.[46] Some of Deng's critics still complained, however, that it would have been better had Deng not been so exuberant in 1984; that way they could have avoided the inflation and corruption that accompanied the overheated Chinese economy.

Panic and Backlash over Inflation, 1988

Just as Chen Yun's readjustment policy of 1980–1981 brought the economy under control and paved the way for Deng to speed up growth and reform, so too did Chen Yun's retrenchment policies of 1985–1986 again bring the economy under control and pave the way for Deng to barge ahead. In February 1987, when setting guidelines for the 13th Party Congress to be held that fall, Deng, in direct contradiction to what Chen Yun had been urging, directed that "[In the past] we said that in a socialist economy planning was primary. We should not say that any longer."[47] In talks with various foreign leaders in 1987 Deng made it clear that he wanted to leave a legacy of further market opening before he retired.

In his major address at the 13th Party Congress in October 1987, Zhao Ziyang, with Deng's approval, used the expression "primary stage of socialism." It was again a marvelous concept that allowed Zhao and Deng to say to conservatives that they were upholding socialism and had not given up the goal of achieving a higher stage of socialism. They did add, however, that the higher stage could be postponed for as long as a century. The new concepts, "planning should no longer be primary" and the "primary stage of socialism," provided a framework for continued movement to a market economy. Zhao declared that "commodity exchange" should be conducted according to the "law of value," with prices increasingly determined by value; if goods were in short supply, prices would be higher. Private enterprises were explicitly allowed to employ more than seven people. Zhao added that in the future, shareholders would receive cash dividends. While Zhao was still speaking, Chen Yun walked out of the hall, which reformers took to be his way of avoiding a public fight while making it clear what he thought of Zhao's speech.[48]

In early 1988, Deng decided to move boldly to remove price controls on more goods. As he explained in mid-May to O Jin U, defense minister of North Korea, Chinese standards of living had risen and the public could absorb some price increases.[49] At its meeting later that month (May 30 to June 1), the Politburo, under strong pressure from Deng, endorsed a comprehensive plan for price and wage reforms. Deng, who had been briefed for years on the importance of price reform, realized that market prices were critical for achieving a market-led economy. He explained to his colleagues that "it is better to endure short-term pain than to endure long-term pain." Deng had been told over the years that if prices were to rise, they would do so only temporarily: market forces would cause other suppliers to enter the market and the prices would come down.

Deng was also concerned with growing corruption, and one of the main structural causes of the corruption was the dual-price system that enabled some officials to acquire goods at low state prices and sell them at much higher market prices. Ending state prices would eliminate that cause of corruption.[50] Thus the bold warrior Deng charged ahead to decontrol prices, declaring that price reforms should be completed within three to five years. In July, price controls were removed from alcohol and tobacco, causing prices to rise more than 200 percent.[51] But this did not stop Deng from barging ahead.

Deng's economic advisers warned that the timing was not right for price reform because many goods, already under inflationary pressures, were in short supply.[52] Before lifting the price controls, supplies had to be ready so that prices would not skyrocket. Deng was undeterred. At a Politburo meeting at Beidaihe (August 15–17, 1988), there were heated discussions about removing price controls. In the end, Deng prevailed and the Politburo endorsed his plan of comprehensive removal of price controls. Immediately after the meeting, on August 19, the decision was announced in the *People's Daily*. As soon as the editorial appeared, the urban public, already straining to cope with inflation, panicked. People rushed to withdraw bank deposits and buy supplies wildly to guard against future price increases. Stores sold out of goods, and the public took to the streets in demonstrations.

Deng was keenly aware that changing party decisions weakens party authority, and since becoming preeminent leader, he had stoutly resisted announcing publicly any changes in decisions. But at this point, Deng had no choice. The public mood was overwhelming. Deng accepted the August 30 decision of the State Council to withdraw the plan for removing price controls. This reversal of party policy represented the most dramatic retreat of a reform measure since Deng had mounted the stage in December 1978.

Deng's decision to announce plans for large-scale price reforms proved to be perhaps the most costly error of his career. His assessment of the long-term needs was correct. To move to a market economy, prices at some point needed to be released. In the 1990s, Zhu Rongji would lift price controls, but he did so when inflationary pressures were lower and the public, by then more accustomed to moderate price increases, was more accepting. Zhu managed to avoid a hard landing and his policies were judged a great success.

Deng had erred in his short-term assessment of the public mood. He was mistaken in his estimate that the rise in the standard of living would enable the public to accept the freeing of prices. At age eighty-three, he no longer mingled with the public and was out of touch with the mood of the Chinese people. Deng's family had played a role in sensitizing Deng to public sentiments, but their contacts were largely with families of other high officials who were more insulated from inflationary pressures than were ordinary salaried workers.

Deng's mistake led not only to a loss of popularity with the public, but also to a loss of power within high-level party circles. His ability to move boldly and expect compliance was greatly reduced. But Deng the soldier had long learned to regroup after his troops had suffered losses. On September 12, 1988, Deng called Zhao Ziyang, Li Peng, Hu Qili, Yao Yilin, Wan Li, Bo Yibo, and Qiao Shi—a mixture of reformers and cautious planners—to his home to discuss price reforms. He acknowledged, "Right now things don't seem in good order. There are all kinds of problems such as inflation. Prices are rising so some adjustments have to be made. Nevertheless, in our effort to stem inflation and keep prices down, we must on no account jeopardize the policies of reform and opening. . . . We have to maintain a proper rate of growth."[53] Deng had little choice but to yield on lifting price controls, but he made clear that he remained fully committed to the overall reform agenda.

The public reaction to the freeing of prices also weakened Zhao Ziyang. Although he had not agreed with the decision to remove price controls at that time, he had earlier made the case for freeing prices and he had allowed inflationary pressures to rise more rapidly than Chen Yun had believed wise. From studying the experiences of other countries, he believed that economies could grow rapidly with some inflationary pressures. But inflation had risen far more rapidly than at any time since 1949. The official retail price index was 18.5 percent higher in 1988 than it was in 1987. And the official retail price index in the second half of 1988 had risen 26 percent over the previous year; many economists believed that other measures would have shown inflation to be much higher.[54]

The cautious planners had disagreed completely with Zhao's decisions in 1987 and early 1988 that had permitted inflation to rise so rapidly. At the Third Plenum of the 13th Party Congress (held September 26–30, 1988), Zhao Ziyang was criticized for policies that had allowed inflation to grow out of control earlier in the year. Zhao accepted responsibility for his errors: he acknowledged that some assumptions guiding policy earlier in the year were wrong and that the problem of inflation had not been resolved due to the overheated economy and excess aggregate demand.[55] Some thought he should have been removed from his post as party general secretary. He managed to remain as general secretary, but he was given some instructions from Chen Yun about economic policy. On October 10, 1988, Chen pointedly told Zhao Ziyang that there should never be fiscal deficits; too much currency was in circulation. In addition, there should always be balanced development of the economy, otherwise chaos would ensue.[56] The warning seemed stern, but, unlike Chen's criticism of Hu Yaobang in 1983, it was not delivered at a large public meeting. Power over economic decisions was then handed to Li Peng, who in November 1987 had been made acting premier and in March 1988 became premier. Needless to say, the relationship between Zhao, a committed reformer who believed in moving to markets, and Li Peng, who was carrying out Chen Yun's retrenchment policies, was not an easy one.

Although Zhao acknowledged errors, he was not ready to be the pawn completely sacrificed to protect the king. He did not announce in a prominent public way that the responsibility for the decision to free up price controls was his. Knowledgeable party officials reported that though Deng continued to support Zhao as general secretary of the party, relations between Zhao and Deng were strained because Deng was held responsible by both high-level party officials and the public for taking the lid off prices.

Following the public panic of August and the weakening of the power of Deng and Zhao, the cautious planners quickly regained control of economic policy. On September 24, 1988, the State Council promulgated a document stating that the focus of work for the next two years would be "improving the economic environment." No one familiar with Chen Yun's readjustment policies of 1979–1981 could have been surprised by the economic policies of 1988 when the cautious balancers took control. No new price adjustments were approved in 1988. Enterprises and work units were told not to raise prices. The People's Bank of China, which had been paying interest rates far below inflation rates, guaranteed that if necessary, deposits would be raised in value to keep pace with inflation. Localities were told to scale back capital construction.[57] Investments were cut back and price controls tightened. Bank credit was stringently controlled and loans to TVEs were suspended. In the 1990s Zhu Rongji would manage to bring inflation under control with a soft landing, but in late 1988 Chen Yun was as bold in stopping inflation as Deng had been in removing price controls. Not surprisingly, in late 1988 there was a hard landing, as we see from declines in growth during the subsequent years:

	Growth (%)	Retail Price Index (%)	Consumer Price Index (%)
1988	11.3	18.5	18.8
1989	4.1	17.8	18.0
1990	3.8	2.1	3.1

Source: National Statistics Bureau, cited by Jinglian Wu, *Understanding and Interpreting Chinese Economic Reform* (Mason, Ohio: Thomson/South-Western, 2005), p. 369.

Due to the combination of economic controls and political decisions between 1988 and 1990, the GNP growth rate fell from 11 percent in 1988 to 4 percent in 1989, and the industrial growth rate fell from 15 percent to 5 percent. By the last quarter of 1990, the increase in the retail price index had dropped to 0.6 percent.[58] Consumer spending remained sluggish, unemployment mounted, and signs of unrest appeared in many cities. Planners still aimed to narrow the budget deficit, but because of the lower tax base, the budget deficit actually grew. Yet despite these unsettling economic indicators, for three years after the outbreak of opposition to the lifting of price controls, Deng could not muster support within the party to challenge Chen Yun's contraction policies.

Chinese and Soviet Reforms: A Comparison

The socialist planning system, which was first introduced into the Soviet Union and later into China to help late-developing countries catch up with the early industrializing areas, enabled China to accumulate capital and channel resources into high-priority areas. As it had earlier in the Soviet Union, this planning system allowed China to develop heavy industry in the 1950s. In the 1970s, however, the economies of both countries had fallen far behind those of countries with more open, competitive systems. Yet by 1991, when communism fell apart in the Soviet Union and Eastern Europe, China could boast average growth of 10 percent a year since 1978. What had enabled China to outperform the Soviet Union and Eastern Europe in the 1980s?

China had many advantages over the Soviet Union. It had a long coastline that made ocean transport less expensive and far easier to expand than land transport. As a source of capital and knowledge, mainland China could call on a pool of some 20 million Chinese émigrés and their descendants who in the previous two centuries had left mainland China for Hong Kong, Taiwan, Southeast Asia, and the West. Moreover, the vast potential mainland Chinese market encouraged many businesspeople around the world to offer help so that they might eventually access this pool of one billion customers. Political motives played a part as well: after China began its opening in 1978, many Western countries, eager to wean China away from the Soviet Union, were willing to be generous to China in terms of passing on capital and technology and in welcoming students and visitors.

Geography and ethnic homogeneity also played important roles in China's success. The boost in enthusiasm and agricultural output from dividing collective rice paddy fields could not be duplicated in the Soviet Union, where the large dry fields could be better farmed with large tractors. It was also easier to unify a country like China, in which 93 percent of the population came from the same ethnic group, than a country where over half the population came from diverse ethnic groups. The Soviet Union had expanded to a broad geographical area within the previous century by annexing minority groups that were either actively or passively resistant to Soviet authority. China, by contrast, had ruled most of its geographical area for over two millennia and was not overextended by occupying other countries resistant to its leadership.

Chinese leaders, too, had a confidence that came from the country's long history as the center of civilization, whereas Soviet leaders had long been aware that the USSR lagged far behind the Western European countries. And finally, China's neighbors—Japan, South Korea, Taiwan, Hong Kong, and Singapore, which shared some common cultural characteristics—had recently made the transition to become rich modern countries that could serve as models for China.

But whatever intrinsic advantages China might have enjoyed, at key points Deng made choices different from those made by his Soviet counterparts, choices that proved to be far more successful in stimulating economic growth.[59] First, he maintained the authority of the Communist Party. In the Soviet Union, Gorbachev hoped to develop a new system of governance by abolishing the monopoly of power by the Soviet Communist Party. But Deng never wavered in his faith that the Chinese Communist Party, originally modeled after the Soviet Communist Party, should be retained as the sole governing structure in China. In Deng's view, only the party could provide the core of loyalty, discipline, and commitment that was needed to provide stable leadership for the country. His belief that China needed to be led by a single ruling party was shared by all three of the other major Chinese leaders in the twentieth century—Sun Yat-sen, Chiang Kai-shek, and Mao Zedong.

Yet Deng was also realistic about changes that needed to be made: he knew that the party he had inherited in 1978 was bloated with dead wood and unable to provide the leadership needed for modernization. He was convinced that many senior Communist Party officials, especially those who had risen during the political struggles of the Cultural Revolution, were useless in providing leadership for modernization. He did not expel many of them outright from the party, since doing so would have been disruptive, polarized the party, and distracted attention from dealing with the real problems the country faced. But he did quietly push them out of the most important positions, giving their jobs to those who could provide leadership for modernization. Indeed, Deng took great care to select able officials for the top positions, and he encouraged lower-level leaders to do the same. Once selected, these teams of leaders were given considerable leeway to make progress.

Deng advanced step by step, rather than with a "big bang." After 1991, Russia had followed the advice of economists who recommended opening markets suddenly, with a "big bang." In contrast, Deng, with the advice of experts brought in by the World Bank, accepted the view that a sudden opening of markets would lead to chaos. He understood what many Western economists who took institutions for granted did not: that it was vitally important to take the time to build national institutions with structures, rules, laws, and trained personnel adapted to the local culture and local conditions. China did not have the experience, rules, knowledgeable entrepreneurs, or private capital needed to convert suddenly to a market economy. Deng knew that it had taken many decades in nineteenth-century Japan and later in the other East Asian economies to build institutions appropriate to catch up with the West. He could not suddenly disband China's existing state enterprises without causing massive unemployment, a result that would have been politically and socially unsustainable. So he allowed Chen Yun and others to keep the old system functioning to provide a stable economic base while he permitted markets to grow, people to gain experience, and institutions to adapt to a more open economy. Deng did not impose the new structures—household agriculture, TVEs, or private enterprises. Instead, he let the local areas try out these experiments, publicizing any successes to allow other areas to adapt them to their own circumstances.

Underpinning all of Deng's strategies was a commitment to opening China fully to ideas and trade with the outside world. Soviet leaders had been cautious about allowing foreign businesspeople and foreign businesses to establish enterprises in the Soviet Union, and were worried about sending large numbers of Soviet students abroad. Deng knew China would face huge adjustment problems from changes wrought by outsiders and from returning students, but he firmly believed that nations grow best when they remain open. Unlike some of his colleagues who feared that China would be overwhelmed by foreigners and foreign practices, Deng was confident that the Communist Party was strong enough to control them. He strongly supported sending officials and students abroad, translating foreign books and articles, and welcoming foreign advisers and businessmen to China. He was prepared to face criticism from those who feared that Chinese lifestyles and interests would be adversely affected by foreign competition. He believed competition from foreign companies would not destroy the Chinese economy but rather stimulate Chinese businesses to become stronger. He also did not worry if a substantial percentage of those who went abroad did not return, for he believed that they too would continue to help their motherland.

The process that propelled China's dramatic opening in the 1970s and 1980s did not begin with Deng Xiaoping. Instead Mao first began to open the country after clashes with the Soviet Union in 1969, and both Zhou Enlai and Hua Guofeng continued his initiative. But Deng was unique in that he pushed the doors open far wider—to foreign ideas, foreign technology, and foreign capital—than his predecessors, and he presided over the difficult process of expanding the opening despite the disruptions it caused. Radiating his deep confidence in China's potential and maneuvering skillfully through political obstacles, he set the stage for a new era in Chinese history. With Deng at the helm, the Chinese people were willing to swallow their pride, admit their backwardness, and keep learning everything they could from abroad.

17

One Country, Two Systems: Taiwan, Hong Kong, and Tibet

Throughout China's imperial history, as dynasties declined, territory along the country's long borders would begin to slip away from central control, only to be reclaimed and fortified by the bold warriors who founded the next dynasty. In the 1890s, as the Qing, China's last dynasty, was declining, Li Hongzhang, a Chinese official facing much stronger Western powers, was forced to sign the "unequal treaties," which gave the Western nations control over territory along the Chinese coast. After China lost the Sino-Japanese War (1894–1895), Li signed away Taiwan to Japan, and in 1898, he signed the lease passing Hong Kong's New Territories to the British. For yielding China's rights to foreigners, Li was regarded as a traitor, and indeed he became one of the most vilified officials in Chinese history. Mao Zedong, like the strong warriors before him who had founded China's great dynasties, regained most of China's territory lost by the late Qing—Shanghai, Qingdao, and elsewhere—but he was unable to recover possession of Taiwan and Hong Kong. That task would fall to Deng.[1]

Unlike emperors before him, Mao had access to radios, movies, the press, and a modern propaganda structure to marshal public support for patriotic goals. He was particularly successful in mobilizing Chinese youth, who were outraged at the past humiliations of their great civilization. Once Communist leaders had fanned the flames of nationalism to build support for their struggle, no Chinese leader—certainly not Deng Xiaoping—could consider betraying that popular sentiment. Indeed, when he took command, Deng Xiaoping regarded regaining Taiwan and Hong Kong as among his most sacred responsibilities.

Deng also worked to firm up control over areas inside China's borders. Many of China's borders to the north, west, and south were mountainous regions where minorities were eking out an existence even closer to subsistence level than were the peasants on the flatlands. Most minority groups lacked the scale, the organization, and the foreign support to challenge Beijing's efforts to control them. But Tibet was different. More than a millennium earlier Tibetans had claimed a geographical area almost as large as China, and as Tibetan territory had contracted over time, small communities of Tibetans had remained behind in several Chinese provinces. Tibetans had temples and monasteries that could become centers for resistance to Chinese rule. In Deng's era, they were supported by a large, politically active community of exiles in India who remained hostile to China. Above all, Tibetans had the leadership of the Dalai Lama, who inspired a worldwide following beyond that of any other Asian leader.

To regain Taiwan and Hong Kong, and to keep Tibet firmly under Chinese rule, Deng, like other Chinese leaders, was prepared to use armed force if necessary, but he much preferred to expand and maintain control through peaceful means. To gain the cooperation of local people and avoid the use of force, he was willing to grant considerable autonomy. In January 1979, immediately after becoming preeminent leader, Deng announced a policy that proclaimed Chinese sovereignty and ultimately control over Taiwan and Hong Kong, yet also granted a high degree of local independence. The essence of the policy had already been enunciated by Zhou Enlai, but in 1982 under Deng, it was elaborated on and systematized as the "one country, two systems" policy. As part of this policy, Hong Kong and Taiwan would be allowed to keep their very different social systems in place for half a century or even longer. Deng was also willing to grant considerable autonomy to Tibet and to allow it to retain much of its own culture.

Seeking Reunification with Taiwan

Even after he learned that the United States would continue selling arms to Taiwan despite normalization of U.S.-China relations, Deng remained determined to reunite Taiwan with the mainland while he was at the helm.[2] The importance of regaining Taiwan did not derive from geostrategic considerations. Instead, the island, which was ruled by China's bitter enemies, was a painful reminder that the Communists had yet not finished their civil war. Even more galling, Taiwan stood as a towering symbol of the century of humiliation inflicted by the imperialists who had taken parts of China.

In his New Year's message on January 1, 1979, the day China and the United States officially established diplomatic relations and only weeks after he became the preeminent leader, Deng made clear how important he considered regaining Taiwan. He listed his three overall goals: (1) achieving the four modernizations, (2) normalizing U.S.-China relations, and (3) setting an agenda for the return of Taiwan to the mainland.[3] A few days later, he told a delegation of U.S. senators led by Senator Sam Nunn that the use of Chinese force for regaining Taiwan could not be ruled out, for that would be like tying one's hands behind one's back and it would make impossible any peaceful resolution of the Taiwan question.[4] Deng's logic was easy for the Chinese to understand. In their view, without U.S. support, Taiwan would choose to unite with the mainland to avoid being overrun militarily; thus the United States, by maintaining its ties to Taiwan, was blocking this peaceful resolution of the Taiwan issue. In January 1980, when Deng spelled out his major goals for the next decade, again one of them was regaining Taiwan.[5] At the time of normalization talks he expected, as did Ambassador Leonard Woodcock, that Taiwan would become part of the mainland within several years.

A historical parallel gave Deng particular hope for realizing his plans. In 1683, some twenty-two years after Koxinga, with the remnants of Ming troops, had fled to Taiwan after being defeated by the newly established Qing dynasty, Koxinga's grandson, then the ruler of Taiwan, had agreed that Taiwan would again become part of mainland China. Deng hoped that his classmate in Moscow, President Chiang Ching-kuo, son of Generalissimo Chiang Kai-shek who had fled to Taiwan in 1949 after being defeated by the newly established Communist government, would follow that precedent. In a 1979 New Year's letter addressed to their Taiwan compatriots, China's National People's Congress (NPC) declared that if Taiwan were to rejoin the mainland, China would respect the island's status quo. Deng also told Senator Nunn's delegation that if Taiwan did rejoin the mainland, it could keep its own social system for as long as a thousand years. Taiwan would have to take down its flags, but it could even keep its own army.[6] When he was informed of Deng's proposal, however, Chiang Ching-kuo was defiant: he repeated his intention to increase the military budget, build up his fighting forces, and eventually retake the mainland.[7] In addition, he continued to maintain that his "Republic of China" on Taiwan represented all of China, and that the members of his Legislative Yuan represented all of China's provinces.

The U.S. Congress further complicated the situation when, on April 10, 1979, it passed the Taiwan Relations Act, which gave encouragement to Chiang Ching-kuo. The act was designed in part to adjust a variety of agreements with Taiwan on trade, exchanges, and other fields, steps that were needed since officially Taiwan no longer represented the government of all of China. Yet the content and spirit of the Taiwan Relations Act went beyond these updates to reflect the sentiment of many in Congress who were critical of normalization with the mainland. In normalization discussions, Congress had been kept in the dark, and Kissinger and Brzezinski, preoccupied with relations with China, had given little consideration to the security of Taiwan nor had they fully anticipated the strength of political support in the United States for Taiwan.[8] The insulting way that Chiang Ching-kuo in December 1978 had been awakened in the middle of the night to be told that normalization was to be announced a few hours later added to Congressional determination to help Taiwan. Members of Congress, some of whom had received generous financial contributions from Taiwan sources or had connections with American companies selling arms to Taiwan, complained that the normalization process had been no way to treat loyal friends in Taiwan. The act sought to rectify these slights by committing the United States to supply the necessary military weapons for Taiwan to defend itself, and it stated that any effort to resolve the Taiwan Strait issue by other than peaceful means would be a matter of grave concern to the United States.

The spirit of the Taiwan Relations Act made sense in U.S. politics: the United States was being loyal to its ally. But it was out of keeping with the spirit of the normalization discussions with China, and some contended even with the letter of the Shanghai Communiqué of 1972, in which the U.S. government acknowledged that "all Chinese on either side of the Taiwan Strait maintain there is but one China and that Taiwan is part of China." Issues that later became important to members of Congress—Taiwan as a beacon of democracy, respect for human rights, and rule of law—were not then discussed because Taiwan was still under martial law and exercised repressive measures to control the opposition, practices for which human rights activists then criticized Taiwan and would, on a far larger scale, later criticize the mainland.

Passage of the Taiwan Relations Act infuriated Deng, who was also criticized by other high Chinese officials for not having been tougher on the United States when he negotiated normalization. He was not concerned with the question of whether the Taiwan Relations Act was technically legal; he was worried about its political impact. The act made his deeply felt political mission of finishing the civil war against the Guomindang and regaining control over Taiwan—a mission for which he had fought for so many years and had seen tens of thousands of his troops die—far more difficult, and perhaps even impossible during his lifetime. Deng objected particularly to the clause that specified that the United States would supply Taiwan with "enough defensive arms to maintain a sufficient self-defense capability." This U.S. commitment to provide military aid had destroyed Deng's leverage for persuading Taiwan to voluntarily rejoin the mainland.

What more could Deng do to increase the possibility of reaching an agreement with Taiwan? In addition to showing his "feisty" side through diplomatic channels, Deng invited members of the U.S. Congress to China, where he could present China's views directly. On April 19, 1979, Deng told Senator Frank Church, chairman of the Senate Foreign Relations Committee, that the Taiwan Relations Act did not acknowledge that there was only one China. The act, Deng added, contained clauses designed to assist in the defense of Taiwan, which violated the most basic premise of the normalization of relations. (Deng later stated that the Taiwan Relations Act was an even greater problem than the sale of arms itself.[9]) Deng also pushed to isolate the people of Taiwan as much as possible. He supported lobbying other countries to keep Taiwan out of regional and international organizations, and he vowed to shut out of the mainland market any foreign company that traded with Taiwan.

Even more disturbing to Deng than the Taiwan Relations Act was the presidential campaign of Ronald Reagan, who vowed to treat Taiwan "with dignity," including seeking to establish formal relations with Taiwan. On August 22, Reagan's running mate, vice presidential candidate George H. W. Bush, traveled to Asia to meet an infuriated Deng Xiaoping. James R. Lilley, who accompanied Bush (and later served as U.S. ambassador to China), called their discussion a "particularly unpleasant meeting." Bush tried to reassure China that Reagan would not carry out a two-China policy, but during the meeting, Deng's aides brought him up-to-date news dispatches, including a report of a press conference in which Reagan had said that Taiwan was a country and that the United States should restore diplomatic relations with it and supply whatever it needed to defend itself. Deng complained: "He did it again."[10] He went on to say, "On more than one occasion, Reagan has said he supports official relations with Taiwan. . . . No matter what one's views and positions are on other international issues, if Reagan's remarks and the Republican platform should be carried out, this is bound to damage Sino-U.S. relations." Deng also announced that if the Republicans continued to support Taiwan, he would be forced to stand up for the "interests of one billion

Chinese." As much as Bush tried to soften the U.S. stance, Lilley reported, "Deng was unmollified."[11]

After Reagan's election, the close bond between China and the United States that had been created during Deng's visit two years earlier gave way to growing Chinese discomfort, as President Reagan nurtured warmer relations with Taiwan and sold more advanced weapons to the island. Deng sought to build even closer relations with the United States; he wanted the Americans' help with China's four modernizations. But he considered the Taiwan issue sufficiently important that he was prepared to downgrade relations with the United States if it officially recognized Taiwan. Deng was absolutely steadfast on the issue. As one American diplomat said at the time, dealing with China then was like pulling apart a clam with one's bare hands.

On January 4, 1981, shortly before Reagan's inauguration, Deng laid down a marker when he met Republican Senator Ted Stevens and Anna Chennault—the ethnic Chinese widow of General Claire L. Chennault, the U.S. Flying Tiger hero who had piloted for China in World War II. Knowing that Anna Chennault was a friend of Taiwan and a member of the Reagan inaugural committee, Deng warned her of the serious consequences for U.S.-China relations if the United States were to encourage Taiwan independence. Deng told his visitors that he wanted to see U.S.-China relations develop, but that China was concerned about some things Reagan had said. Deng said he realized that some things a candidate says before an election are different from what he does after he is elected. But he wanted to clarify his position given comments in an American paper asserting that as long as the United States took an anti-Soviet stance, China needed American help. While acknowledging that China was indeed poor and weak, as the paper had claimed, Deng stated that the remaining comments were false: China, he said, had become independent by its own power, it was not a supplicant, and it would stand up for its views—it would not swallow the Taiwan issue if the United States took a firmly anti-Soviet stance. He further warned that if Reagan were to send a private representative to Taiwan, China would regard this as a formal government decision, a violation of the Shanghai Communiqué as well as a violation of the communiqué on the establishment of diplomatic relations. If these delicate relationships were not handled properly, Deng said, China was prepared to return not to the U.S.-China relations of the 1970s but to the adversarial relations of the 1960s. He was absolutely determined not to allow Reagan to reach agreements with Taiwan that would make it more difficult in the long run to regain the island, and he let his visitors know unequivocally that China would be watching carefully what Reagan said and did.[12]

The fear that President Reagan would treat Taiwan as a country was reduced when China's ambassador to Washington, Chai Zemin, was able to attend Reagan's inauguration ceremony. Chai had threatened not to take part if the invited representatives from Taiwan were to attend, and in the end they did not, a development that the Chinese took as a positive sign.[13] But Deng remained deeply concerned about Reagan's relations with Taiwan.

Deng then tried to develop a package of carrots for Taiwan that would make improving relations with the mainland more attractive. China drew up a new document describing China's policy toward the island. After showing British Foreign Secretary Lord Carrington a draft in March 1981, this document, written under the direction of Liao Chengzhi, was formally presented to the public in the speech given by Marshal Ye Jianying on September 30, 1981, the day before China's National Day. Marshal Ye was chosen because he had many friends in the Guomindang dating back to his early days at the Whampoa Military Academy during the Communist-Guomindang United Front. Marshal Ye's "nine-point proposal" included the following proclamations:

- Talks should be held between the Communist Party and the Guomindang;
- The two sides should facilitate trade, air travel, shipping, tourism, and mail between the mainland and Taiwan;
- People from Taiwan are welcome to invest in and carry on business in the mainland;
- After reunification, Taiwan can enjoy a high degree of freedom and maintain its own army; and
- Taiwan's current social and economic system, including private companies and private property, will remain.[14]

Taiwan did not respond to this overture, however, and relations between China and the Reagan administration remained tense. Knowing it would be fruitless to use military means against a Taiwan that was backed by American power, Deng continued to use the one tool he had, the threat that China would reduce and even end its cooperation with the United States. When told that the United States was prepared to sell some weapons to China, Deng responded that China would not accept such a deal if it meant that the United States would upgrade the weapons it sold to Taiwan.

Reagan's secretary of state Alexander Haig, accepting an invitation from Deng, arrived in Beijing in June 1981. On June 16, Deng told Haig what he had told others: although China wanted relations with the United States to develop smoothly, the sale of weapons to Taiwan, if it was not handled properly, could cause Sino-U.S. relations to stagnate or even regress.[15] Furthermore, he complained to Haig that when China had agreed to normalization, it was told that military sales to Taiwan would be reduced, but the United States had still not done this. In particular, China wanted the United States to stop all sales of military aircraft to the island. Deng was ready to break off relations with the United States if the United States did not reduce arms sales. Haig, convinced that the United States would have to comply in order to ensure Chinese cooperation against the Soviet Union, reassured Deng that for the foreseeable future the United States would continue to sell Taiwan only "carefully selected defensive weapons."[16]

Three days after Deng had forcefully presented his views to Haig, President Reagan met with Singapore's prime minister Lee Kuan Yew, whom he had invited to Washington to discuss relations with Taiwan and China. In answer to Reagan's question, Lee Kuan Yew said he believed that the security of Taiwan did not require the proposed sale of U.S. FX-15 fighter jets. At the end of their discussion, Reagan asked Lee Kuan Yew to carry the message to Taiwan President Chiang Ching-kuo that it would be difficult to supply all of Taiwan's requests and that President Chiang should not press for high-tech weapons at the moment, but that he, President Reagan, would not let Chiang down. A few days later, Lee delivered the message to President Chiang.[17]

Meanwhile, Deng and his colleagues kept up the pressure on the United States. A few weeks after the Haig visit, Arthur Hummel, then dean of the State Department China specialists and U.S. ambassador to Beijing, was handed by Chinese diplomats a démarche saying that if the United States continued to sell weapons to Taiwan, there would be grave consequences for strategic cooperation. In an interview with a Hong Kong newspaper in late August, Deng again warned that Beijing was prepared to let the relationship deteriorate, and in October at the North-South Summit meeting in Cancun, Mexico, Premier Zhao Ziyang told President Reagan that although China wanted to cooperate in efforts against the Soviet Union, the Taiwan issue remained an obstacle to such cooperation. Also while at Cancun, Foreign Minister Huang Hua told Secretary of State Haig that the Chinese wanted a specific date when the level of arms sales to Taiwan would not exceed the number or quality sold during the Carter administration. He also wanted such arms sales to be reduced each year until, within a specified period, they would end altogether. And the following week, Foreign Minister Huang Hua passed along Deng's request that the United States not conclude any agreement on weapons sales to Taiwan before U.S.-China discussions on military cooperation were completed. The United States accepted Deng's request, and Haig replied to Huang Hua that although the United States could not agree to a cut-off date for arms sales to Taiwan, arms sales would be "restrained and selective" and they would not exceed those during the Carter administration.[18]

To convey Beijing's continuing frustration at the failure of the United States to reduce arms sales, Premier Zhao Ziyang not only rebuffed President Reagan's invitation to go to the United States to celebrate the tenth anniversary of the 1972 Shanghai Communiqué; he did not even respond to Reagan's letter. Following the Chinese aphorism of killing the rooster to warn the monkey, China downgraded relations with the Netherlands for selling two submarines to Taiwan. In January 1982, the United States sent Assistant Secretary of State John Holdridge to Beijing to head off a further deterioration in relations.[19] Although at first Holdridge's delegation was received very coolly, the Chinese became more cordial when Holdridge announced that the United States had decided not to sell FSX aircraft to Taiwan. But Holdridge had his own mandate: he had been told to seek a broader agreement with Beijing on the framework of relations before the United States would decide which weapons systems to sell—or not sell—to Taiwan. He had brought a draft agreement for this framework, but the Chinese considered the initial draft too vague and unresponsive to their concerns. Instead, Beijing demanded that for talks to continue, the United States had to forgo any new transfer of arms to Taiwan.[20] The lines had been drawn. And in the early months of 1982 the Chinese press continually attacked the United States for interfering in the Taiwan issue, which the Chinese regarded as a domestic Chinese affair.

Hoping to break the tension, President Reagan suggested that Vice President George H. W. Bush, who had managed to retain cordial relations with Deng and other leading Chinese officials, visit Beijing while on a trip to Asia. The Chinese did not respond at first; only after Bush had visited several Asian capitals did they notify the United States that Bush would be welcome. During his first several days in Beijing, Bush found the Chinese to be adamant on arms sales to Taiwan. Then Deng invited Bush in for a talk. At one point in the conversation, Deng suggested that he and Bush step into a nearby room for a fifteen-minute conversation with only Ambassador Arthur Hummel and the interpreters present. The small group remained for an hour, during which time Bush and Deng reached an informal understanding that would eventually be incorporated into a formal document on the limiting of U.S. arms sales to Taiwan. Deng knew that he had achieved the best he could hope for: the United States did not stop arms sales to Taiwan, but it placed limits on the sales—and as U.S. sales declined, Deng could be optimistic that in the long run Taiwan would be incorporated as part of China. After their conversation, the invectives stopped and the mood lightened.[21] Deng, who for more than a year had behaved like a stern, truculent soldier lecturing American officials, again became a good-humored partner.[22]

The understanding that emerged from the Deng-Bush conversation became the basis for detailed negotiations between Ambassador Hummel and his counterparts and was incorporated into the "United States-China Joint Communiqué on United States Arms Sales to Taiwan (August 17, 1982)." The agreement, which put a lid on weapons sales to Taiwan, specified that the United States "has no intention of infringing on Chinese sovereignty and territorial integrity, . . . or pursuing a policy of 'two Chinas' or 'one China and one Taiwan.'" It specified that arms sales to Taiwan "will not exceed, either in qualitative or in quantitative terms, the level of those supplied in recent years . . . and that it intends to reduce gradually its sales of arms to Taiwan, leading over a period of time to the final resolution."[23] To calm Taiwan and members of Congress who objected, President Reagan invited thirty senators and representatives for a briefing to persuade them why the agreement did not undercut Taiwan.

When the August 17 communiqué was issued, Deng invited Ambassador Hummel to an informal meeting where he exuded goodwill and congratulated him on achieving the historic agreement. This communiqué became, along with the Shanghai Communiqué of February 27, 1972, and the normalization communiqué of January 1, 1979, one of the three fundamental documents underpinning U.S.-China relations.[24] From then until the Tiananmen tragedy of June 1989, it provided a stable basis for the Sino-American relationship. It also paved the way for President Reagan to make a six-day visit to China in late April 1984, when he became the first president to visit China since the establishment of formal diplomatic relations in 1979. During Reagan's trip, Deng and Reagan met for three hours of friendly conversation. After explaining the Chinese position on Taiwan, Deng asked Reagan to consider the Chinese point of view and not simply be wagged by the tail of Chiang Ching-kuo.[25] Reagan, pleased with the visit, remarked that Deng "didn't seem like a Communist."[26]

In the mid-1980s, Deng still had a thin reed of hope for resolving the reunification issue before he "went to meet God": his personal relationship with Chiang Ching-kuo, his classmate at Sun Yat-sen University in Moscow in 1926. When he met Lee Kuan Yew on September 20, 1985, Deng, aware that Lee had seen Chiang recently and that Chiang's diabetes had become serious, asked Lee if Chiang had made any arrangements for his succession. When Lee replied that he could not say who would eventually replace Chiang, Deng said that he feared that after Chiang's death, there would be chaos in Taiwan as forces there attempted to join with parties in the United States and Japan in a quest for independence. Deng then asked Lee to convey his regards to Chiang and to convey his suggestion that the two meet soon. Within a month, Lee flew to Taiwan carrying Deng's message. But Chiang, who retained bitter memories of his many years of dealing with the Communists, said he could not trust them. He declined the invitation to meet.[27] Thereafter Deng, already eighty-one years old, had little reason to hope that he would be able to resolve the Taiwan problem. All he could do was to block any move Taiwan made toward independence, thus paving the way for his successors to regain control of the island.

Two years later, in 1987, Chiang Ching-kuo, on his deathbed, abolished the long-standing martial law and legalized political opposition parties, thus creating the basis for the democratization of Taiwan. He also allowed residents of Taiwan, for the first time, to visit their relatives on the mainland, not by direct travel, but rather by transfer through Hong Kong. As people from Taiwan began to visit with relatives on the mainland they also started new businesses there. It was difficult to distinguish between those who had relatives and those who did not, and soon all Taiwanese were allowed to visit the mainland. Deng welcomed the visitors from Taiwan and their business ventures, seeing both as possible steps toward eventual reunification, even if not in his lifetime. As he observed, "If we can't reunify China right away, we will do it in a century; if not in a century, then in a millennium."[28]

Resuming Sovereignty over Hong Kong

On May 25, 1975, Deng accompanied Mao to a meeting with Edward Heath, who had served as British prime minister from 1970 to 1974. Mao, making it clear that the time to resolve the Hong Kong issue had not yet arrived, pointed to Deng and other younger comrades sitting there and said, "The issue is for them to deal with."[29]

From the time he returned to work in 1977, Deng took a deep interest in Hong Kong affairs. But when he visited Guangdong with Marshal Ye that year, the focus of their discussions was not resumption of sovereignty, but how Hong Kong could help China in its drive to modernize. Deng realized that China could benefit greatly from Hong Kong's assistance in the areas of finance, technology, and management, and that China would want Hong Kong to remain prosperous even after it resumed sovereignty. The immediate task was to reduce the fear and ill will of the Hong Kong business community resulting from the Red Guards' attacks during the Cultural Revolution. The Red Guards had not only pursued relatives of Hong Kong residents living on the Chinese side of the border; they had invaded Hong Kong itself, terrorizing citizens and arousing public resentment against Mao's leadership.[30]

In April 1978 Deng set up a Hong Kong and Macao Affairs Office under the State Council with a leading small group headed by Liao Chengzhi. Liao was an excellent choice for the assignment. His family home was in a village near Huizhou, less than fifty miles from Hong Kong. Moreover, he had deep roots in Hong Kong as well as in Japan: he had lived in Hong Kong during the late 1940s, and his cousin was the wife of the chief justice of Hong Kong.

One of Liao's initial assignments was to prepare for and host the first conference on Hong Kong and Macao since the end of the Cultural Revolution. The conference, which lasted nearly a month, focused on eliminating the radical "ultra-leftist" policies that had alienated Hong Kong people. The emphasis initially was on improving relations between China and the business community in Hong Kong and Macao.

In referring to Hong Kong, it was long Beijing's practice to say *Gang-ao* (Hong Kong–Macao), almost as if it were a single word. But to Deng and other Chinese leaders, Macao, the Portuguese colony across the Pearl River delta from Hong Kong, was small and relatively unimportant; the economic dynamism was in Hong Kong, and in effect Macao was already under mainland control, even though the lease to Portugal did not officially expire until 1999. Twice, in 1967 and 1974, Portugal had offered to return Macao to China, and Beijing had concluded an agreement with Portugal outlining plans for its return. Beijing, however, fearing the decision might negatively affect the volatile mood in Hong Kong, had kept that agreement a secret and publicly stated that it was not yet ready for Macao's return. To Deng, "Hong Kong–Macao" meant Hong Kong.

Throughout the Cold War from 1949 to 1978, Hong Kong had been China's most important window to the world. The British colonial government allowed Communists and the Guomindang in Hong Kong to co-exist, even spy on each other there, so long as they refrained from open warfare and allowed the British colonial government to maintain law and order.[31] Beijing used Hong Kong as a place to earn foreign currency, import technology, and gain information about the world. Until 1978, however, the window was open only a crack, and the mainland's relations with Hong Kong were highly restricted. China could have cut off the water and food shipments to Hong Kong, but it chose not to, even during the Cultural Revolution. In the 1960s the Soviets, tired of hearing Chinese accusations of revisionism, terrorized the people of Hong Kong by arguing that if China were so anti-revisionist, it could prove it by overrunning the imperialist colony on its doorstep. Beijing responded that Hong Kong was a historical problem that would be dealt with at the proper time. In essence, Beijing chose to "keep a long-term perspective and make full use of Hong Kong."[32]

Deng wanted to prepare carefully before dealing with the issue of "resuming sovereignty" over Hong Kong, and in 1978 he had not yet begun to develop a roadmap for doing so. For the moment, Deng would offer little more than a general reassurance that China would keep Hong Kong prosperous. On August 19, 1978, however, Liao Chengzhi, following Deng's lead, reassured a group of Hong Kong visitors that Hong Kong could keep its present system for a long time and that China would not conduct mass campaigns in Hong Kong.[33]

In November 1978, even amidst the fervid activity of his visits to Southeast Asia and his preparations for becoming China's preeminent leader, Deng took time to welcome the Hong Kong shipping magnate Y. K. Pao, who was then the best-known and perhaps richest Hong Kong businessman.[34] Deng grew to appreciate not only Pao's success, but also his first-hand knowledge of world business matters, his shrewd observations of the world political leaders whom he had met, his frank appraisals of the mood of Hong Kong businessmen, his pragmatism, and his sincerity in wanting to help with China's modernization. No other family outside the mainland developed as close a relationship with Deng and his family as the Y. K. Pao family.[35] In November 1978 the two men focused their discussion on the role Hong Kong businesspeople might play in creating a modern China.

In December 1978 Li Qiang, China's foreign trade minister, was dispatched to Hong Kong to explore how Hong Kong might help China's modernization efforts, particularly in Guangdong. While visiting Hong Kong, Li announced for the first time that China would accept foreign investments and would welcome loans. Li also invited Governor Murray MacLehose to visit Beijing. Deng knew that Governor MacLehose was a Chinese-speaking official, highly respected in London, who had good working relations with Communist representatives in Hong Kong, and he knew that the fate of Hong Kong after 1997 would eventually require careful consultation with the British.[36] The oral invitation to MacLehose was followed by a formal written invitation, the first letter to a Hong Kong governor by a Chinese minister. Governor MacLehose recognized the historical importance of this gesture, commenting, "It was a serious initiative, against the background of the modernization program. Everyone agreed: of course I should go."[37] (For more on the role of Hong Kong in the four modernizations, see Chapter 14.)

Deng had taken an interest in Hong Kong ever since his ship had stopped there in 1920 on its way to France, and he had become more familiar with it in the months he spent there while assigned to lead urban uprisings in Guangxi from 1929 to 1931.[38] Deng knew the basic colonial history: that the island of Hong Kong had been ceded to Great Britain by treaty after the Opium War in 1842; that Kowloon, the tip of the mainland, had been ceded by treaty in 1860; and that the ninety-nine-year lease to Great Britain for the New Territories north of Kowloon would expire in 1997. Like other Chinese patriots, he regarded all three "unequal treaties" as invalid because they had been forced on China when it was too weak to resist.

From 1949 to 1978, the Communists had maintained organizations within Hong Kong and had a small following of ordinary citizens.[39] Suspicions abounded between the Communists and all others, including the Guomindang, British, and Americans, but most Hong Kong residents, frightened of possible consequences, avoided all politics like the plague. The branch of the Communists' New China News Agency (NCNA) in Hong Kong published newspapers, magazines, and books; sent back secret as well as public reports on Hong Kong and the outside world; and housed officials assigned from the Ministry of Foreign Affairs. The Hong Kong branch of the Bank of China handled mainland financial interests. China Resources conducted business on behalf of China's Ministry of Foreign Trade and Chinese regional governments. China also had its own retail outlets, its own intelligence organizations, left-wing schools, and labor unions in Hong Kong. In reports to

Beijing, all these organizations exaggerated the support for communism in Hong Kong, thus causing Deng and other officials to underestimate the extent to which ethnic Chinese residents in Hong Kong were in fact content with British rule. In fact, most residents feared what China, having just undergone the Cultural Revolution, might do to Hong Kong.[40]

By the time Governor Sir Murray MacLehose met Deng in Beijing on March 24, 1979, some British diplomats had begun to suspect that they would have to give up sovereignty in 1997, for once the lease on the New Territories had ended and those areas were returned to China, the remainder of Hong Kong would not be viable as an independent administrative unit. Yet how could the Beijing government—fresh from the Cultural Revolution, with no experience governing a modern capitalist city, and with a record of ending all private business in the mainland in the early 1950s—possibly provide the wise leadership required to keep Hong Kong stable and prosperous? Not only the foreign businesspeople in Hong Kong, but also the ethnic Chinese living there had serious doubts. Hong Kong government officials and many ordinary citizens hoped that even if Britain gave up sovereignty in 1997, China would still allow British officials to continue to administer Hong Kong.[41]

British officials en route to Beijing knew that Deng would want to talk about what Hong Kong could do to help China's modernization. But to their surprise, Deng, in his opening remarks to Governor MacLehose, mentioned the issue of Hong Kong's eventual fate. He declared that a negotiated settlement should be based on the premise that Hong Kong was a part of China, but that for a considerable period of time, into the next century, Hong Kong could continue its capitalist system while China practiced socialism.[42] Although it would be three years before Deng formally presented his "one country, two systems" policy, the outlines of it were presented to Governor MacLehose at this initial meeting.

MacLehose and his fellow China specialists realized that if they raised with Deng the issue of possible British administration after 1997, they would be courting an outburst. They thus decided to approach the issue indirectly, by raising the problem of how to assure those signing fifteen-year leases that those agreements would still be valid after 1997. In the same vein, MacLehose mentioned the concerns of Hong Kong investors about making new loans, mortgages, and other investments when it was unclear what would happen after 1997. MacLehose suggested changing the wording of official documents, which specified that the leases would expire after 1997, to "as long as the Crown administers the territory." Cradock, who accompanied MacLehose, records that Deng apparently did not understand the difference between the fifteen-year business leases and the ninety-nine-year government lease for the New Territories as a whole.[43] In any case, Deng avoided expressing an opinion on the leases, but he did say that investors should put their hearts at ease.[44] In response to British expressions of concern that mainland officials would be assigned to Hong Kong, Deng answered immediately that China would take measures to avoid the problem.

When MacLehose returned to Hong Kong, he did not publicly announce the details of his discussions in Beijing. But he did pass on Deng's reassuring message that China would not damage the interests of investors. Hong Kong residents were enormously relieved to hear this, which reinforced the impression of the more open mood in China and the reports in the Hong Kong media of Deng leading China on a more pragmatic path after the Third Plenum. Over the next year, Hong Kong real estate and stock prices rose dramatically.[45]

During the following months a number of high-ranking British officials flew to Beijing for discussions with Deng and other Chinese officials, and Hua Guofeng visited Britain in November 1979. All the British officials conveyed to their Chinese counterparts the same basic message: it was essential to make an early decision about Hong Kong. But Deng was not yet ready to begin negotiations; instead he simply reiterated what he had told MacLehose in early 1979—that Hong Kong could keep its own system after 1997 and that China would protect the rights of investors.[46]

An important breakthrough for Deng in dealing with Hong Kong occurred when the December 1980 Politburo meetings resolved the historical issues of Mao and the fate of Hua. This development meant that Deng no longer had to worry about conservative opposition to allowing Hong Kong to remain as a capitalist city for half a century after China resumed sovereignty. After he installed his new team of Hu Yaobang and Zhao Ziyang, Deng had reason to feel confident that his administration could acquire the capacity to govern a modern capitalist city.

In early 1981, then, Deng was ready for negotiations over the future of Hong Kong to begin. After Reagan became president in 1981, Deng knew he could not make swift progress on Taiwan. And by focusing on Hong Kong, patriotic youth who might have protested against the weak Chinese government's failure to make progress on Taiwan's return could turn their attention to the struggle to regain sovereignty over Hong Kong, where Deng had all the leverage he needed to succeed. China had so many troops on its side of the border that the small garrison of British troops in Hong Kong could not provide meaningful resistance. China also controlled Hong Kong's water and food supplies. Moreover, by early 1981 China had already established working relationships with Y. K. Pao and other Hong Kong business leaders. And the one country, two systems policy, prepared originally to deal with Taiwan, could be adapted easily to provide the framework for relations with Hong Kong. Success in reassuring Hong Kong people might even reduce the fears of a wary Taiwanese public about its reunification with the mainland.

In March 1981, the Hong Kong and Macao Affairs Office called a meeting in Beijing to discuss the future of Hong Kong.[47] At the meeting, Deputy Foreign Minister Zhang Wenjin conveyed Deng's views that if they did not take back Hong Kong, they would not be able to face their ancestors, the billion people in China, their descendants, and the people in the third world. Once Zhang had communicated Deng's views, the issue was resolved, for no one dared to suggest that China would consider allowing Britain to administer Hong Kong after the lease on the New Territories ran out.[48]

It was unlikely that Britain would send troops to defend Hong Kong, but Britain was just then considering sending troops to the Falklands and China could not rule out the possibility that the British might do the same in Hong Kong. Deng, always prepared for the worst-case scenario, resolved the question of how China would respond if Britain sent troops. In September 1982, a week before Prime Minister Margaret Thatcher arrived in Beijing, Deng met with Li Xiannian and others and told them that as a last resort China was prepared to use force to secure Hong Kong.

Once Deng had made a firm decision to resume full sovereignty, Chinese officials began preparing drafts for internal discussions about how the Chinese might govern the colony after 1997. Deng, too, read the reports on Hong Kong and began hosting more leaders from the Hong Kong business community. For instance, when the pro-Beijing Hong Kong businesspeople who were members of the NPC attended NPC meetings in Beijing, Deng invited them for special sessions in which they exchanged views on Hong Kong.[49]

Deng, like other Chinese officials, worried that in the years between 1979 and 1997 Britain might leave behind "poison pills" that would complicate the problems of governing after China resumed sovereignty in 1997. Britain might try to drain Hong Kong's assets by allowing British companies to engage in large public works projects, leaving the government in debt. It might lease so much of the land that it would leave little for the Chinese to earn income from after 1997. The British might increase the salaries of government officials, which would make it difficult for China to balance the budget after 1997. At the time, Deng did not anticipate what he and others would later consider another poison pill, the weakening of government power by "democratic" reforms.

Beijing's basic stance on the future of Hong Kong was presented at a United Front Work Conference held from December 21, 1981, to January 6, 1982. Preliminary negotiations began as soon as the conference ended, when on January 6, 1982, Foreign Minister Humphrey Atkins met with Premier Zhao Ziyang. At this meeting, for the first time, Beijing was ready to begin negotiations and discuss concrete issues. Zhao told Atkins that Hong Kong would remain a free port and a commercial and financial center, and China would ensure its continued prosperity. At the end of the visit, it was announced that in return for Hua Guofeng's visit to Britain in November 1979, Prime Minister Margaret Thatcher would visit China in the fall of 1982 as the two sides began to negotiate in earnest.[50] In March 1982 Deng formally approved the basic proposal developed at the January conference and forwarded it to the party center.

Over the next months, Deng joined in many discussions on Hong Kong, including meetings with some twelve different individuals and groups, among them Y. K. Pao and Henry Fok, another businessman long friendly with mainland China.[51] In talks with British officials, Deng vowed that political power after 1997 would be in the hands of the people of Hong Kong. Always focused on training successors, Deng requested that during the remaining fifteen years, Hong Kong leaders in business, education, and culture suggest the names of promising "patriotic" Hong Kong young people who could begin immediately preparing for responsible positions in various fields after 1997, thereby ensuring a smooth handover and continued stability and prosperity.[52] One of Deng's key visitors from Hong Kong was Rayson Huang, vice chancellor (in effect the president) of Hong Kong's leading institution of higher learning, Hong Kong University, which would play a role in preparing future officials.

When Deng welcomed former prime minister Edward Heath to Beijing on April 6, 1982, Deng, drawing on a twelve-point plan presented at the January meeting, was very specific: Hong Kong would remain a free port and a global financial center. It would be ruled by Hong Kong people, including the British and others. It would be led by the bourgeoisie and would include people from all social classes. It would be called "Hong Kong, China," but there would be no change in business practices. As Deng explained to Heath, "In our Chinese constitution, there is a provision that we can establish special administrative regions with rules separate from the rest of the country."[53]

Prime Minister Thatcher Visits China

Prime Minister Margaret Thatcher arrived in Beijing on September 22, 1982, shortly after her decisive June victory in the Falklands War. The victory had buoyed her confidence, leading her to intimidate Edward Youde and other advisers who did not forcefully explain how impossible it was to hope that Deng might allow the British to retain sovereignty over Hong Kong after 1997. Two leading China specialists in the Foreign Office, Percy Cradock and Alan Donald, did try to make clear Deng's determination and avoid a confrontation.[54] But the confident "iron lady" mistakenly considered the Chinese refusal to consider British sovereignty after 1997 as merely a negotiating position.[55] Thatcher's first meeting in Beijing was with Premier Zhao Ziyang. But even before he met her, Zhao told Hong Kong reporters that of course China would resume sovereignty, and that the handover would not affect Hong Kong's prosperity and stability. By going first to the press with the basic message that he would later present to Thatcher, Zhao was signaling that those views were non-negotiable. When Deng met Prime Minister Thatcher, he conveyed the same message.[56]

On the morning of September 24, Deng Xiaoping, the "steel factory," met Thatcher, the "iron lady," in a two-and-a-half-hour session. Thatcher later described the session as abrasive, but British officials who attended the session testify that Thatcher's reports of a confrontation with Deng were greatly exaggerated and that a sense of confrontation derived only from her press presentations after the meeting and the Chinese reaction. British participants in the session reported that Thatcher delivered her comments with eloquence and charm, but said that in spite of herself, she was impressed with Deng's almost limitless authority.[57] In his opening statement, Deng declared that China would resume sovereignty in 1997, that it would maintain Hong

Kong's prosperity, and that China hoped to have Britain's cooperation.[58] Thatcher, however, countered that from Britain's perspective, Hong Kong was British by virtue of three agreements, all of which were valid according to international law and could be altered only by mutual agreement. She said that over the 150 years the British had learned how to administer Hong Kong and did it well. Moreover, she asserted, only after arrangements had been made to preserve Hong Kong's stability and prosperity could the issue of sovereignty be addressed, and only a British administration could guarantee such stability and prosperity: without such an assurance from the British, businesspeople would be no longer willing to invest. Yet Thatcher did make one concession—if satisfactory arrangements could be made regarding Hong Kong's administration, she would consider making recommendations to Parliament on the issue of sovereignty. They should, therefore, begin discussions in diplomatic channels to see if a satisfactory agreement could be reached.

Deng categorically rejected her proposal.[59] He said there were three major issues: sovereignty, how China would administer Hong Kong to preserve prosperity after 1997, and how the Chinese and British governments together could avoid major disturbances before 1997. Deng said: "On the questions of sovereignty, China has no room to maneuver. To be frank, the question is not open to discussion." He said he would not be like Li Hongzhang, who had infamously signed the unequal treaties. Sovereignty meant full sovereignty. To preserve Hong Kong's prosperity after 1997, the current political system and most of Hong Kong's laws would remain in effect. In addition, China would consult extensively with people in Hong Kong and devise policies that would benefit investors, including British investors. But there was a limit to how far he would bend to please the British government or business community. If the British were to put up serious resistance or remove significant funds from Hong Kong before the 1997 handover, Deng warned, China would "reconsider the timing and manner of recovery." He did indicate that he wanted to work with Britain and agreed that the two sides should immediately begin consultations through diplomatic channels.[60] But, he added, if they did not reach satisfactory agreements for the transition within two years, China would announce its policy unilaterally.[61] Among foreign diplomats in Beijing, it was widely known that Deng Xiaoping often used a spittoon to emphasize a point; observers noted that during his meeting with Thatcher, he used one frequently.[62]

After her meeting with Deng, as she descended the outside steps, Prime Minister Thatcher, distracted by a correspondent's question, slipped and fell to her knees. The scene was caught by television cameras, shown on the Hong Kong evening news, and replayed many times thereafter on Hong Kong television. The pictures conveyed the impression that Thatcher, shaken by Deng's tough stance, was kowtowing and was only saved from a bad fall by Cradock, who happened to be standing next to her.[63]

Later, when Thatcher spoke of Deng, she remained positive in her view of him. He had been blunt but not rude. At the farewell banquet Thatcher hosted in Beijing, Premier Zhao was the guest of honor; Deng had chosen instead to attend a banquet for Kim Il Sung. In her speech at the banquet with Zhao, Thatcher was more conciliatory, saying that the conversations had given her clearer insight into Chinese affairs. "Seeing for one's self," she said, using the Chinese maxim, "is a hundred times better than hearing from others."[64]

The bland communiqué on the Thatcher-Deng meeting, drafted by representatives of the two sides, stated, "The leaders of the two countries held far-reaching talks in a friendly atmosphere on the future of Hong Kong. Both leaders made clear their respective positions on the subject. They agreed to enter talks through diplomatic channels following the visit with the common aim of maintaining the stability and prosperity of Hong Kong."[65] Unlike Deng, Thatcher took pride in Britain's historical role in Hong Kong and believed in the legitimacy of the treaties. In a BBC interview before leaving China, she said, "If one party to a treaty or a contract says, 'I cannot agree to it, I am going to break it,' you cannot really have a great deal of confidence that any new treaty they make will be honored." China specialists in the British Foreign Office cringed when she repeated these comments at a press conference in Hong Kong, for they knew that these words would dampen the goodwill with China that they had been working to build. As they expected, China complained, strongly. In the week after the Thatcher visit, the Hong Kong stock market fell 25 percent, and by the end of October, the Hang Seng Stock Index, which had registered 1,300 in June, had fallen to 772.[66]

After the Thatcher visit, negotiations were delayed because the Chinese insisted that a negotiated settlement be concluded on the assumption of full Chinese sovereignty after 1997—a condition that Thatcher would not accept. Then came the Chinese warning: in late February 1983, the British were told that the Chinese had nearly completed a draft of their unilateral plan for Hong Kong after 1997. In effect, if there were no negotiations, the Chinese would announce their own plan for Hong Kong's future by September 1984.[67] Ambassador Cradock in Beijing and Governor Youde in Hong

Kong became so worried that the Chinese would present their unilateral plan for action to the NPC in June 1983 that they flew back to London to talk with Thatcher in early March. The Hong Kong stock market had dropped to a new low, and even Thatcher by then had become convinced that the Chinese would not yield on sovereignty. To break the deadlock, Cradock suggested that Thatcher write a letter to Premier Zhao in which she would repeat a statement that she had made in Beijing, but using slightly different language: if arrangements satisfactory to the people of Hong Kong were made, she "would be prepared to recommend to Parliament the transfer of sovereignty." Thatcher concurred, and the letter was sent on March 9, 1983. But because the letter did not meet the Chinese demand for an agreement about sovereignty before any discussions would begin, China did not immediately respond. Only after two months did China agree to proceed with negotiations. As Deng later explained to Hong Kong delegates to the NPC meeting, he had relented on the order of the agenda items so as to let the British out of an embarrassing situation. The agreed agenda for further negotiations was: first, arrangements for stability and prosperity after 1997; next, plans for the period before 1997; and finally, sovereignty. The first meeting was held on July 12, some ten months after Thatcher's visit.[68]

To prepare for the negotiations, to form liaisons with prominent Hong Kong people, and to train officials to take over Hong Kong after 1997, Deng concluded that Beijing needed to send to Hong Kong higher-level party officials than those who were currently serving there. The top official sent to Hong Kong should be given considerable freedom to engage in open discussions with influential people in Hong Kong and report directly to the highest levels in Beijing. Deng needed someone who had an insider's understanding of Beijing, who could meet Hong Kong leaders as an equal, and who had the confidence to report fully and frankly to the mainland's top leaders. One candidate he had in mind was Xu Jiatun.

While Deng and his family were spending the 1983 Spring Festival in Shanghai, he paid a visit to nearby Jiangsu, where provincial party secretary Xu Jiatun showed him around. Before the visit, Deng had not known Xu well, although in 1975 when Deng was carrying out consolidation throughout the country, Xu played a key role in carrying out consolidation first in Nanjing and then in all of Jiangsu. When Deng met Xu during Spring Festival 1983, they were scheduled for a twenty-minute session in which Xu was to report on developments in his province. In fact, Deng and Xu talked for two hours. Under Xu's leadership, Jiangsu had doubled its GNP over the previous six years; at the time of their meeting it was enjoying the highest combined output of industrial-agricultural production in the country. As a coastal province next to Shanghai, Jiangsu carried on international trade, and Xu was on the forefront in allowing markets to develop, causing some cautious economic planners in Jiangsu to complain about Xu to Chen Yun. In fact, Chen Yun had urged that Xu Jiatun be removed from Jiangsu—but Deng, who could see that he was a bold reformer, had kept him on.

Within a few weeks after Deng's Spring Festival meeting with Xu, Hu Yaobang, who was responsible for appointing high-level officials and who knew of Deng's high regard for Xu, proposed to Deng that Xu be assigned to the new position in Hong Kong. Deng agreed and in April 1983 Hu notified Xu that he would be transferred to Hong Kong and given overall responsibility for China's relations with Hong Kong in preparation for the transition in 1997.[69] On June 30, 1983, just after the first round of Sino-British talks, Xu Jiatun was officially named party secretary of the Hong Kong–Macao Work Committee of the Chinese Communist Party and assigned to Hong Kong. One of Xu's major responsibilities was to select influential Hong Kong people to be invited to Beijing where they would have an opportunity to meet Deng.[70]

Xu, in preparation for taking up his new position, visited the leaders in Beijing with whom he would be dealing on the Hong Kong issue—Li Xiannian, Zhao Ziyang, Hu Yaobang, Yang Shangkun, Wan Li, Ji Pengfei, and Hu Qili, as well as Deng. He found them all acutely aware that the Hong Kong Communist organization would need dramatic changes in order to lead Hong Kong's transition. The organization was composed largely of Cantonese locals who were accustomed to repeating leftist slogans and had been criticizing Hong Kong business and government leaders for decades. Members of the group had little ability to think imaginatively about Hong Kong's future. Even so, Xu would eventually ceatively transform the Hong Kong Communist Party into a group that nurtured imaginative, pro-Beijing apprentices who would be ready by 1997 to supervise their native Hong Kong. Although these leaders-in-training were not necessarily party members, they were ready to cooperate with the new Communist elite.

In Beijing, meeting with various officials before taking up his new post, Xu met Liao Chengzhi, but unfortunately Liao died on June 10, just before Xu took up his post. Thereafter, Deng announced that Li Xiannian and Zhao

Ziyang would be responsible for guiding Hong Kong affairs. Managing the daily work on Hong Kong issues would be former foreign minister Ji Pengfei in Beijing and Xu Jiatun in Hong Kong.

In Hong Kong, Xu's official title was head of the Hong Kong branch of the NCNA. In public he was addressed by that title, but it was an open secret that his power came from being head of the Hong Kong–Macao branch of the Chinese Communist Party. His arrival in Hong Kong attracted great interest, for he was the highest-ranking Communist ever to be assigned there. In the past, the head of Hong Kong's NCNA had always been a local Cantonese with a Ministry of Foreign Affairs background. Xu's first language was Mandarin and his appointment showed that Hong Kong was now considered by top party leaders an issue of national importance.[71]

Before Xu left Beijing for Hong Kong, he was told by Nobel Prize winner Yang Zhenning, who spent winters in Hong Kong and had close contacts with intellectuals there, that he needed to upgrade China's understanding of Hong Kong. Xu responded by hiring Yang Zhenning's younger brother, Zhenhan, to head a small independent think tank in Hong Kong to help identify and explain to Chinese officials economic and intellectual trends in Hong Kong. Xu also brought scholars from the Chinese Academy of Social Sciences to Hong Kong to improve Beijing's understanding of the territory and its place in the world economy.

Xu arrived in Hong Kong just before the second round of negotiations with Great Britain was to begin, and his first order of business was to help the Chinese negotiators in Beijing understand the local situation in preparation for the next round of talks. At first, many people in Hong Kong, suspicious that Xu was trying to tighten Communist control over Hong Kong, were wary of him, but Xu's openness and genuine desire to understand Hong Kong helped win them over. His basic message was that China would resume control after 1997, but there was no need to worry, for things would remain the same.[72] "What comes after 1997?" went the popular Hong Kong riddle of the time. Answer: "1998." Xu visited schools, banks, and corporations, and spoke frequently at meetings, celebrations, sporting events, poor neighborhoods, and public institutions of all kinds. He became in effect a shadow governor (indeed, informally he was called "governor"). At his headquarters of the NCNA, Xu selected promising local people to join his staff, which grew in number from about one hundred to about four hundred. He divided them up and assigned them to become acquainted with the various departments of the Hong Kong government and each of the district offices in the New Territories. While helping to keep Xu abreast of developments in all areas, they served, during the fifteen years before the handover, as apprentices, a veritable "government in training."[73] It was assumed that those who proved themselves would occupy important positions after 1997.

After his first three months in Hong Kong, Xu went to Beijing to report to Zhao Ziyang and Li Xiannian on the mood in Hong Kong, the local economy, and the quality of Communist officials there. His observations surprised the leadership in Beijing. The local Communists in Hong Kong, long accustomed to passing on what Beijing wanted to hear, had been repeating the mantra that the residents of Hong Kong were opposed to the imperialists and were eagerly awaiting liberation by the mainland. Even Hong Kong business-people, who were always eager to win Beijing's favor, would report how enthusiastic the people of Hong Kong were about the prospect of Communist leadership. Xu, however, bravely relayed the unpleasant truth: he reported that the people of Hong Kong had a deep mistrust of the Communist Party and sometimes felt doomed.[74] He also described the dominant view of Chinese businesspeople in Hong Kong, which was that they respected British administration and the rule of law and doubted that Beijing would be able to provide good leadership. Moreover, many businesspeople in Hong Kong who had fled the mainland soon after 1949 felt they could never again trust the Communists. They had seen how the Communists in the 1950s had betrayed their promises to work with businesspeople who had cooperated with them, by attacking them and appropriating their businesses.[75] Disturbed by Xu's reports, Li Xiannian responded by saying that Beijing's top priority should be to win over the Hong Kong public.[76]

Xu's report was sobering, but it did not change Deng's overall plan for the resumption of sovereignty. After an unproductive second round of talks, China published its twelve-point plan, thus reminding the British negotiators that if an agreement were not reached by September 1984, the Chinese would be ready with their unilateral plans. Deng met former prime minister Edward Heath on September 10, 1983, after the third round of negotiations that remained deadlocked. Deng told Heath that Britain's tactic would not work: he would never allow the British to continue the administration of Hong Kong in return for agreeing to Chinese sovereignty there. Deng expressed the hope that Prime Minister Thatcher and her government would act wisely and not cut off the road to cooperation, since nothing would stop

China from resuming sovereignty over Hong Kong in 1997. Deng also said he hoped that during the next round of talks Britain would change gears and work with China in making plans that would ensure a smooth handover.[77]

After the fourth round of talks that also made no progress, the value of the Hong Kong dollar plummeted to its lowest in history. Panic buying cleaned out supermarkets, and large amounts of capital began to flow from Hong Kong to overseas destinations; families that could afford it bought residences in Canada and elsewhere. Many observers considered it the most serious crisis in Hong Kong since World War II. Cradock, with Thatcher's permission, suggested that on a conditional basis they explore what the Chinese proposed they would do after 1997. At the fifth round of negotiations the Chinese were pleased that the British showed some flexibility, but the Chinese still suspected that the British were engaging in a tactical ploy; little progress was made.[78]

At the sixth round, Cradock explained that the British were genuine in their wish to explore what China would do after 1997; if satisfactory arrangements could be made, Britain would be prepared to give up administration after 1997. This proved to be the turning point in the negotiations. After the sixth round, the Communist press stopped the attacks on the British position. It was now the Chinese turn to present its plans, but at the seventh round the Chinese were not yet ready with new proposals. Beginning with the eighth round on January 25–26, 1984, the talks became more productive. The British side presented a more detailed analysis of how they governed the complex global city, and the Chinese side incorporated a large part of the analysis into their papers.[79] As the discussions proceeded without any specific agreement about sovereignty, it became increasingly clear that the Chinese would take over sovereignty after 1997.

After the twelfth round of talks, Foreign Secretary Geoffrey Howe flew to Beijing, where on April 18, 1984, he had a two-hour talk with Deng. Deng pressed hard on some basic concerns, such as how to prevent British companies and the British government from taking capital out of Hong Kong and how to prevent the British government from leasing out large areas of land. Deng suggested that they set up a joint structure to monitor developments in Hong Kong before 1997, and that a liaison group among leaders in Beijing, London, and Hong Kong be established to work through any problems. Deng made it clear to Howe that although the government system would not be changed after 1997, Chinese troops would definitely be stationed in Hong

Kong.[80] But he also made some procedural concessions in hopes of reaching an agreement by September, with ratification by Britain's Parliament and China's NPC to follow. On April 20, when he stopped in Hong Kong after Beijing, Howe publicly acknowledged for the first time what had already become clear to the politically savvy Hong Kong public: "It would not be realistic to think in terms of an agreement that provides for continued British administration in Hong Kong after 1997." Although the Hong Kong reaction was solemn and some expressed surprise, the city's business community was hugely relieved that the uncertainty had been resolved.[81]

The details of Deng's message had apparently not been made clear to everyone, however. On May 25, 1984, when Deng met with the Hong Kong delegates to the NPC meeting, Xu Jiatun told him that some Chinese officials were giving out information that was not in line with Deng's policies. Geng Biao, former minister of defense, had told Hong Kong reporters that no Chinese troops would be stationed in Hong Kong after 1997. Deng was furious. He immediately called in the Hong Kong delegates to the NPC as well as Hong Kong reporters to clear up any possible misunderstandings. Deng exclaimed: "Geng Biao has been talking nonsense! What has been said about the question of stationing troops in Hong Kong is not the view of the party center. Troops will be stationed in Hong Kong. It is part of Chinese territory. Why shouldn't we station troops in Hong Kong?"[82] Deng immediately went on TV to make his views absolutely clear. He said that after 1997 China would station troops in Hong Kong to provide security. The popular press in Hong Kong, which had seen Deng as a pragmatic moderate, became unnerved by his forceful announcement, but the issue gradually disappeared. In 1997 China did indeed send troops but they rarely left their barracks and their presence never aroused great attention.

In 1984, as Hong Kong awaited announcement of the Joint Declaration, three members of the Hong Kong Executive Council flew to Beijing to express the concerns of many Hong Kong residents about the ability of the Chinese to govern the territory. When Deng met them on June 23, 1984, he opened the meeting by telling them he warmly welcomed them as individuals and encouraged them to walk around and enjoy Beijing. Deng's implication was clear: he did not accept the Hong Kong Executive Council as having any formal authority in deciding the future of Hong Kong. Some Hong Kong and British politicians had been trying to create a "three-legged stool," with representatives from Hong Kong as well as Britain and China, but Deng, concerned that this might complicate and slow down the negotiations, made it clear that the negotiations were between Great Britain and Beijing.

At the meeting, when Sze-yuen Chung, head of the Hong Kong Executive Council, expressed doubts about the capacity of lower-level Communist officials to manage the complex problems of Hong Kong, Deng snapped back that this view amounted to saying that only foreigners can govern Hong Kong. Such an attitude reflects, he said, the influence of colonial mentality. Deng continued by telling the group that they should seek a better understanding of the Chinese people and of the People's Republic of China. He assured them that Hong Kong's capitalist system would be in place for fifty years, and he added that a patriot is one who respects the Chinese nation, supports China's resumption of sovereignty, and does not want to hurt prosperity and stability in Hong Kong. He said it did not matter if one believes in capitalism, feudalism, or even slavery. He noted as well that there were thirteen years left before resumption of sovereignty and that officials in Beijing were just as concerned about stability during these years as were the members of the Hong Kong Executive Council. After Deng's comments about the colonial mentality, the three representative of the Executive Council did not argue. One of them, Maria Tam, even volunteered that she, too, was a Chinese.[83]

To avoid the risk of Britain siphoning away Hong Kong's wealth and causing problems in its remaining years, Deng had proposed a joint committee of China, Britain, and Hong Kong to deal with problems before 1997. British officials, concerned about their ability to govern effectively during their last years, rejected such a dispersal of power. In July 1984 Vice Foreign Minister Zhou Nan proposed to Cradock and Anthony Galsworthy an alternative: a joint Sino-British Liaison Committee, without power, to promote communication. Both sides agreed, and the two sides moved on to draft the final document. The Sino-British Joint Declaration on the Question of Hong Kong was reached after twenty-two rounds of negotiations held from July 12, 1983, until September 6, 1984.

When Deng met Foreign Secretary Geoffrey Howe on July 31, 1984, a formal agreement on the Joint Declaration was in sight. Deng, who had just returned well tanned from his summer vacation at Beidaihe, was ebullient. For 140 years Chinese patriots had been trying to resume sovereignty over Hong Kong but had always failed. Deng had accomplished it peacefully with British cooperation, albeit with China making good use of its leverage. Deng even had good words to say about Thatcher; he said the agreement was "an example to the world for settling questions between states, left over from the past. . . . General de Gaulle brought an end to French colonial rule. Now we can say that Prime Minister Margaret Thatcher will bring an end to British colonial rule." In meetings to celebrate the Joint Declaration, Deng joked that he was impressed to be surrounded by so many knights of the realm. A British official recorded Deng's comments: "We have concluded that we can trust the British people and the British government. Please convey to your Prime Minister that we hope she will come to sign the agreement and to your Queen our hope that she will come to visit China." The British official added that Deng was not just amicable, but even warm and courtly.[84] One day later, the two sides formally agreed to establish the Liaison Group that would meet alternately in Beijing, Hong Kong, and London.

Howe then flew from Beijing to Hong Kong, where he broke the news of the agreement's completion. To the Hong Kong public he declared that although the administration of Hong Kong would transfer to China after 1997, they had been able to ensure that Hong Kong would continue its same social and economic systems; he had in hand legally binding documents that would ensure Hong Kong's continued autonomy. The media reaction, both in Hong Kong and London, was overwhelmingly favorable, and the public, relieved that the period of uncertainty had ended, believed that the detailed agreement created a strong foundation for a stable, prosperous Hong Kong. On the day Howe made his announcement in Hong Kong, the local stock market enjoyed its largest one-day gain since the Thatcher visit had depressed the market two years earlier.[85]

After long hours of hammering out the details—work that was done by teams led by a British diplomat, David Wilson, and a Chinese foreign ministry official, Ke Zaishuo—on September 26, Ambassador Richard Evans and Vice Foreign Minister Zhou Nan formally signed the final document. In an annex, the Chinese spelled out in considerable detail their twelve-point plan for keeping on the foreign and local officials who had worked for the British government. They also agreed to retain existing laws, the judiciary, the international financial center, shipping arrangements, and the educational system. China agreed that these basic provisions would remain unchanged for fifty years and that Britain would be responsible for Hong Kong until 1997.[86] On October 3, Deng welcomed the Hong Kong delegates who came to Beijing to celebrate National Day and reassured them that Beijing's policies would not change.[87] And on December 18, 1984, Prime Minister

Thatcher arrived in Beijing. The next day, in a brief ceremony, she and Premier Zhao signed the Joint Declaration on behalf of their two governments.[88]

With the Joint Declaration in place, the Chinese turned their attention to creating the "Basic Law," which in effect would be the constitution for the Special Administrative Region of Hong Kong after 1997. This underlying law spelling out the future relationship between Beijing and the Special Administrative Region was drafted by a Chinese committee of thirty-six people from the mainland and twenty-three people from Hong Kong. Xu Jiatun was responsible for selecting the representatives from Hong Kong, and in the interest of winning over those who might resist Communist leadership, he chose prominent mainstream Hong Kong people who represented different constituencies and diverse views. On the closing day of the first plenary session of the drafting committee, Deng Xiaoping showed his support by meeting with the members and other officials and posing for group photos.[89]

In the deliberations at the ten plenary sessions held over the next several years to draft the Basic Law, there were discussions on all major issues— the nature of the chief executive and to whom he would report, how the Legislative Council would be formed, whether Hong Kong would possess a Court of Final Appeals, and the relationship between the courts and the executive. The drafters were a highly diverse group with very different views and different fears who managed to work together because they all believed deeply in their common interest in maintaining the stability and prosperity of Hong Kong. Many Hong Kong Chinese businesspeople proved no more eager for Western-style democracy than were party leaders in Beijing. But the Hong Kong public was concerned enough about what the Communists might do that many Hong Kong drafters supported Martin Lee, an outspoken Hong Kong lawyer, who sought more legal guarantees. In particular, the Hong Kong representatives wanted assurances that the decisions of the Hong Kong High Court, which enjoyed a high reputation for integrity, could not be overturned by political leaders in Beijing. To enhance public confidence about the outcome of these and other decisions, Chinese leaders agreed to brief reporters from both mainland China and Hong Kong after each plenary session.[90]

Xu Jiatun had warned Deng and other high-level leaders in Beijing that the Hong Kong public had doubts about Communist rule, but the tremendous outpouring of support for British rule in the weeks after the death of

Governor Youde on December 5, 1986, still surprised them. Youde had been a hard-working popular governor, and in his death he came to symbolize the best of the British public servants in Hong Kong. He had kept peace in turbulent times, while people were being killed and starved on the other side of the border, and he symbolized the British officials who had provided a fair system of government that brought great prosperity to the colony. Several hundred thousand people took to the streets of Hong Kong to mourn Governor Youde and to commemorate the other British officials who had served the territory. Many Hong Kong citizens wondered whether the officials after 1997 would serve Hong Kong as well.

Deng was aware that the mood in Hong Kong was volatile. In 1987, when Hong Kong's fears were at a high point, Deng, in an effort to calm the people, personally, and without notes, addressed the fourth plenary session of the Basic Law Drafting Committee. As an attendant brought in a spittoon, Deng began by saying, "I have three vices. I drink, I spit, and I smoke."[91] He said that China would not waver in its commitment to socialism and to the Communist Party, for without that commitment China could lose the momentum for its economic growth, which would in turn be bad for Hong Kong. Yet China, he said, also remained committed to continued reform and opening. In Hong Kong, the basic political and administrative policies would not change for fifty years. He added that Hong Kong had been operating under a system different from that of Britain and the United States, so it would not be appropriate to adopt a fully Western system with three separate branches of government. He then articulated the kind of personal freedoms the public should expect: After 1997, China would still allow people in Hong Kong to criticize the Communist Party but if they should turn their words into action, opposing the mainland under the pretext of democracy, then Beijing would have to intervene. Troops, however, would be used only if there were serious disturbances.[92] Deng's speech provided the kind of straight talk that the people of Hong Kong were hoping for. It eased their concerns, even as it effectively ended all discussion of establishing three separate branches of government.[93]

A final vote on the draft of the Basic Law was held at the eighth plenary session, which was convened in Guangzhou on February 16, 1989. Members were asked to vote on each of the 159 articles. Several of the original members had died, but each of articles was signed by at least 41 of the 51 drafters present. The next day, Deng Xiaoping met with the drafting committee to congratulate them on their success. He called their document a "creative masterpiece."[94] On February 21, 1989, this draft of the Basic Law was released to the public.[95]

During the discussions, the two leading pro-democracy members on the drafting committee, Martin Lee and Szeto Wah, tried without success to ensure that the chief executive and the members of the Legislative Council would be democratically elected by the public. In the end, however, the Standing Committee of the NPC retained its final authority to interpret the Basic Law, and Beijing had the right to appoint the chief executive, to station troops, and to decide on issues that affected foreign relations and national defense. Hong Kong was given the right to retain its system of government for at least fifty years. It was to remain an open port, issue its own currency, permit free speech, including criticism of the Communist Party, and maintain its court system with local laws and the right to make final decisions—as long as they did not interfere with China's security or foreign relations. To the advocates of full democracy for Hong Kong, Martin Lee and Szeto Wah, the Basic Law betrayed the people of Hong Kong. To the leaders in Beijing, however, the "one country, two systems" formula gave far more autonomy to Hong Kong than any central government in the West had given to any local area under its rule.[96] After the Basic Law was announced, it was received warmly in both China and Hong Kong.

Only four months after the signing, however, the optimism in Hong Kong was destroyed by the news of the tragedy in Tiananmen Square. To Hong Kong people, the specter that they would soon be ruled by a regime that could shoot its own people on the streets was terrifying. On June 4, 1989, out of sympathy for the students protesting for freedom in Beijing and out of concern for their own future, an estimated one million of Hong Kong's five million people took to the streets. The demonstrations were far larger than any in the history of Hong Kong. After June 4, thousands of Hong Kong people who could afford it purchased foreign property, sent their children abroad to study, and took out foreign citizenship. Sino-British relations, which had been proceeding smoothly prior to June 4, deteriorated rapidly.[97] Even those working for China's NCNA in Hong Kong were swept up in the protests, and Xu Jiatun did nothing to punish the protestors.[98] When Hong Kong's leading businessmen, Y. K. Pao and Li Ka-shing, visited a resolute Deng in Beijing shortly after June 4, Deng did not make any concessions. He said China had to meet the toughness of the British government with its own toughness.[99]

In January 1990 Xu Jiatun was replaced by Zhou Nan. Xu had passed the usual retirement age of seventy, but more importantly he had defended the Hong Kong people who had criticized Beijing's handling of the demonstrations in Tiananmen Square; also, he was known to be close to Zhao Ziyang, who had been placed under house arrest in the aftermath of the Tiananmen crackdown. Despite all his past successes in bringing Beijing and Hong Kong together, after the Tiananmen tragedy the gap between the views of Beijing officials and Hong Kong residents was too great for Xu Jiatun to bridge.

Zhou Nan, who had worked on the Hong Kong issue as an English-speaking foreign ministry official, was on a much tighter leash. He dutifully expressed Beijing's messages in a rigid and nasty manner. Zhou Nan was as unpopular in Hong Kong as Xu Jiatun had been popular. After several weeks, Xu fled to the United States, where he sought asylum and wrote his memoirs. Many NCNA staff members in Hong Kong who, like Xu, had sympathized with the protestors, were replaced by newly assigned foreign affairs specialists from the mainland.

A secret visit to Beijing shortly after June 4, 1989, by Percy Cradock, the great problem-solver of Sino-British relations, helped avoid a rupture between Great Britain and China, just as a secret visit by Brent Scowcroft at the time helped contain the damage to U.S.-China relations. Despite the strains from the Tiananmen tragedy, frequent close contact between Qian Qichen, China's minister of foreign affairs and Politburo member, and Douglas Hurd, the British foreign secretary, helped overcome an impasse on the Basic Law that had become the main focus of the dispute: the number of publicly elected members. At the ninth and final plenary session of the Basic Law Committee, held from February 13 to 17, 1990, several months after the Tiananmen tragedy, the drafting committee took a final vote on the Basic Law, and on April 4, 1990, it was approved by the NPC.[100]

Before the Tiananmen tragedy, Britain and China had made a joint effort to put in place what they called a "through train," a political structure that would continue smoothly after 1997. In 1992, the year Deng stepped down from politics, the British assigned Chris Patten, a leading politician, as the new governor of Hong Kong. David Wilson, who had been governor from 1987 to 1992, was, like his predecessors, a diplomat specializing on China. After the tumult from the Tiananmen tragedy, Wilson had managed to protect projects like the new Hong Kong airport, which Chinese officials had criticized, while quietly expanding the range of elections and supporting advocates of more freedoms. Despite the tense environment, he had maintained professional working relations with his Chinese counterparts.

Chris Patten took an entirely different approach.[101] He chose not to pay a visit to China before taking up his post and as governor was an outspoken advocate for increasing freedom and the number of popularly elected officials. He did not accept the views of senior foreign office officials like Percy Cradock, who believed that Patten was overlooking some of the understandings between China and Great Britain. He had highly adversarial relationships with Chinese officials throughout his tenure. In 1997, when the Chinese took charge, they undid Patten's reforms, charging that through Patten Britain had introduced democratic reforms at the end of British rule, hoping to force China to follow rules that Britain itself had not followed during its 150 years of governing Hong Kong. Patten's admirers claimed that he did his best to express the desires of the Hong Kong people and to fight valiantly for more freedoms, and that in the process he gave them an experience in democracy that continued to serve as a beacon after 1997. Critics in both Hong Kong and Beijing, however, charged that Patten had been self-serving; that he returned to Britain as a popular politician who had gained stature fighting for freedom, whereas those who stayed in Hong Kong had to deal with the turmoil that he had created between Hong Kong and China.

Some Hong Kong residents argued that Patten had derailed the "through train," for the increases in democracy that he introduced did not remain after 1997. But from a broader perspective, there was a "through train" despite the controversies created by Patten's rule. The system that Deng set in place, through the Joint Declaration and Basic Law, was implemented as Deng said it would be. China kept Deng's promise to allow Hong Kong's capitalist and legal systems to continue without interruption and to allow Hong Kong people to rule Hong Kong. Mainland cities became more like Hong Kong than the other way around. Residents of Hong Kong could continue to criticize publicly the Communist Party and publish newspapers, magazines, and books banned elsewhere in China. Hong Kong increased rather than decreased the number of officials elected by popular voting. Hong Kong set a high standard for freedoms and legal protections, serving as a refuge for many who choose to live there and as a benchmark for many who live on the mainland. After the handover, Hong Kong remained, as before, a cosmopolitan, prosperous city that valued free speech and respect for law.

Deng often said that he hoped to live to see the handover of Hong Kong, but he died on February 19, 1997, four months before China resumed sovereignty. Had Deng been alive on June 30, 1997, he would undoubtedly have taken pride in his role in creating and implementing the one country, two systems policy—a policy that brought Hong Kong back as part of China, even if it retained a different system. Deng would also have agreed with Foreign Minister Qian Qichen's description of that day: "It was raining the whole day of the handover ceremonies, but I am sure that all Chinese in the world felt this was a refreshing shower, washing away China's humiliation."[102]

Containing Tibet's Drive for Autonomy

When Deng became the preeminent leader of China in late 1978, he sought to improve relations between the leaders in Beijing and the Tibetans. To achieve this, he tried to reestablish relations with the one person he thought might make that possible, the Dalai Lama, who was then living in Dharamsala, India, with some 80,000 exiles. Deng set a low hurdle for resuming relations: on November 28, 1978, just three days after Hua Guofeng yielded to the new atmosphere at the Central Party Work Conference, Deng told Arch Steele, an American journalist long known for communicating Chinese Communist views to the outside world, that "The Dalai Lama may return but he must return as a Chinese citizen. . . . As for high-level people in Taiwan and Tibet, we have just one request: that they love the country."[103] During that same month, to assist his efforts to reach out to the Dalai Lama, Deng ordered the release of a number of Tibetan prisoners.

Deng knew that it was impossible to remove entirely the tensions between Tibetans and the Han majority, but he wanted to return to the relatively peaceful relations that had existed between Beijing and the Tibetans before 1956. During that pivotal year, the introduction of the "democratic reforms" in Tibetan areas in Sichuan had ignited pockets of resistance that spread into Tibet proper in 1958 and festered until 1959, when some of the most militant Tibetans marched across the mountains into northern India, where they settled in Dharamsala.

In the 1950s Mao had achieved relatively good relations with the Tibetans by allowing the Dalai Lama, who turned sixteen in 1951, to have a remarkable degree of freedom in ruling Tibet. In minority areas, with some 7 percent of the population, Mao had been willing to go slower in gaining control than in the rest of the country, where the Han majority lived. He was willing to be even more patient with the Tibetans than with other minority groups in the hopes of gaining the positive cooperation of the Dalai Lama and other Tibetan leaders in eventually establishing a socialist structure. Even when the Dalai Lama fled with his followers in 1959, Mao ordered Chinese troops not to fire on them, in the hopes of eventually gaining the Dalai Lama's cooperation.

In May 1950, after Chinese troops had taken over the eastern portion of Tibet proper (later known as the Tibetan Autonomous Region), Mao had invited Tibetan leaders to Beijing where, with Han officials, they arrived at a seventeen-point agreement that accepted Chinese political control over Tibet, but allowed a measure of autonomy for Tibetans to practice their own religion, keep their monasteries, use their own language, and maintain their own customs.[104] The agreement had established a framework whereby Tibetans accepted Chinese sovereignty but the Chinese granted for an unspecified period of time the right of the Tibetan government of the Dalai Lama to continue administrating Tibet proper, where roughly half of the four million Tibetans in China lived. Mao had agreed that in Tibet proper changes to Tibetan society and religion would come only when the Tibetan religious and aristocratic elite and masses agreed that it was time to implement them. After the seventeen-point agreement, the Tibetans, led by the Dalai Lama, were still able to collect taxes, adjudicate disputes, use their own currency, and even maintain their own army; the Communists had control of foreign affairs, military affairs, and border controls. Until a socialist structure would be introduced, the system in the 1950s had many features of that which had existed from 1720 to 1910 when under Chinese suzerainty, the Tibetans essentially ruled Tibet while the Chinese government was responsible for foreign affairs.

In 1954–1955 the Dalai Lama traveled to Beijing to attend the 1st NPC meeting and while in Beijing he met Mao and other leaders and developed a warm and cordial relationship with them. Mao and the other Chinese leaders treated the Dalai Lama with great respect because he was not only a great religious leader but also the head of the Tibetan government with which Beijing had signed a formal agreement. During that time, the Dalai Lama agreed to establish a Preparatory Committee for a Tibet Autonomous Region that he would head. The Dalai Lama also agreed to reduce the Tibetan army to only 1,000 and to end the use of Tibet's own currency, although in the end the size of the Tibetan army was not reduced and Mao gave permission for Tibet to continue using its own currency. In most areas of China, China had introduced preparatory governments in 1948–1950, and within a year or two established regular governments. On April 16, 1956, the Dalai Lama, who had returned from Beijing to live in Lhasa, had welcomed with a grand celebration a delegation from Beijing that would help establish a temporary government structure, which was expected to become a regular government within two to three years.[105]

China's problems with Tibetans erupted after 1955 when provincial leaders throughout China were told to accelerate the collectivization of agriculture. Mao said that "democratic reforms," including collectivization, would be implemented among minority peoples if conditions seemed right, but they were not yet to be implemented in Tibet itself. The two million Tibetans outside Tibet proper were largely living in Sichuan, Yunnan, Qinghai, and Gansu. The leaders of Sichuan put together a plan not only to collectivize agriculture rapidly, but also to start "democratic reforms" in Sichuan's Tibetan and other minority areas. Collectivization that was launched in the Tibetan areas in Sichuan at the beginning of 1956, including the taking over of some monasteries, quickly precipitated a serious and bloody uprising in Sichuan's Tibetan areas, especially among the Khampa Tibetans, who constituted a large portion of Tibetans in Sichuan. The uprising was bloody because virtually every family in the Khampa Tibetan areas in Sichuan, where blood vengeance and raiding were endemic, had modern firearms and knew how to use them. After initial successes, the Khampas were overwhelmed by the much stronger PLA; in 1957–1958, they fled to Tibet proper with their guns. In 1957 at the height of the Cold War, the CIA began to train a small number of Khampas in Colorado and then dropped them back into Tibet to collect intelligence.[106] Beijing directed the Dalai Lama to send the Khampas back to Sichuan, but the Dalai Lama refused. India had earlier invited the Dalai Lama to settle in India, and in March 1959 he led many of the most militant Tibetans across the mountains into India. Other Tibetans followed over the next two to three years.

After becoming the preeminent leader in 1979, Deng faced a more daunting problem in gaining the positive cooperation of the Tibetans than Mao had faced in the 1950s. More Han Communist officials had been sent into Tibet to tighten controls after 1959, arousing local resistance. In most parts of China, Red Guards were seen as revolutionary youth, but in Tibet, where they trashed temples and monasteries and destroyed works of art, they were seen as Han youth destroying Tibetan culture.

After 1979, in Tibet as elsewhere, Deng sought to make amends for the damages done by the Cultural Revolution. Deng understood the deep religious respect Tibetans had for the Dalai Lama as their spiritual leader. He knew the Dalai Lama was seen by Tibetans as the incarnation of the Bodhisattva of Compassion, and hence a god. After the thirteenth Dalai Lama died, in 1937 a two-year-old had been identified as the incarnation, thus becoming the Fourteenth Dalai Lama. He was well trained in Tibetan culture and would become a deeply religious and learned man. In 1978 Deng hoped that through Tibetan intermediaries he could build a relationship with the Dalai Lama, reach some accommodation, and reduce the antagonism between Communist officials and Tibetans.

In the 1950s and 1960s Deng had personally been deeply involved in Tibetan issues. In 1951, the Communist troops sent to gain military control over Tibet were from the Southwest, a region then led by Deng Xiaoping, and the Northwest. Tibetan forces were weak and there was little armed resistance. As secretary general in the 1950s Deng was also involved in carrying out Mao's more "lenient" policy in Tibet proper as well as the more forceful policy imposing collectivization among Tibetans in Sichuan and elsewhere.

In 1978 Deng had many reasons for trying to reduce hostilities between the Han majority and the Tibetan minority. A calmer relationship could strengthen Tibetan ties to China and form a bulwark against possible Soviet penetration into Tibet. It could lessen the risk that a revolt by one minority group against the Chinese could stir up resistance by other minority groups. It would reduce the drain on national resources caused by the continuing conflicts with Tibetans. Above all, perhaps, at the time when Deng wanted to establish good relations with Western countries to help with modernization, it would ease foreign complaints about Chinese treatment of Tibetans. When Deng met President Gerald Ford in December 1975, Ford asked about the Dalai Lama. When Deng met George H. W. Bush on September 27, 1977, Bush not only took a special interest in Tibet and the fate of the Dalai Lama, but also asked to visit Tibet—and because Bush was an "old friend of China," Deng gave special permission for Bush to travel there.[107]

In late 1978, when Deng began to reach out to the Dalai Lama's intermediaries, the 80,000 Tibetans who had settled in India were among the Tibetans most alienated from Chinese rule; they were a diverse group that did not easily reach agreement, but as a group they were less willing to compromise on important issues than many of the Tibetans who remained in China. Moreover, since the Chinese did not permit Tibetans within China to organize to represent their interests, the exile community in Dharamsala in northern India spoke on behalf of all Tibetans and took a strong stand against China.

The best channel for Deng to reach the Dalai Lama was through the Dalai Lama's Mandarin-speaking second-oldest brother, Gyalo Thondup. Deng's meeting with him was arranged by Li Jusheng, the second in command of the NCNA in Hong Kong, who had been meeting with him for several weeks. When Deng met Gyalo Thondup, he told him he hoped that the Dalai Lama might return to China, take a look at Tibet, and, if he wished, remain in China. If he preferred, the Dalai Lama could first send his representatives to observe the situation in China; as Deng admitted to Gyalo Thondup, China had some political work to do before the Dalai Lama returned.[108]

On March 17, 1979, a few days after Deng's meeting with Gyalo Thondup, the NCNA announced, "The Tibetan Autonomous Region legal organs have decided to be generous in treating all those who took part in the Tibetan uprising [of 1959]."[109] On the same day, after a meeting of the four prefectures in Tibet, it was announced that many verdicts against Tibetan officials dating from the Cultural Revolution would be reversed. In promoting reconciliation, Deng relied on reports of Communist officials in Tibet, and was unaware of the seriousness of the Tibetan resistance and the powerful influence of the Dalai Lama around the world. When Deng met Vice President Walter Mondale in August 1979, he told him, "As for the matter of the Dalai Lama this is a small matter. . . . It is not a very important question because the Dalai Lama is an insignificant character." Deng went on to say that it was an illusion for the Dalai Lama to think of having an independent state.[110]

At that time Deng had some reason to be hopeful that the Tibetan situation was improving. After he met Gyalo Thondup, it was arranged for the Dalai Lama to send a delegation of Dharamsala exiles to Tibet to observe the situation and to meet with local officials. In the following months, two more delegations from Dharamsala visited China. It turned out that the Chinese officials advising Deng had vastly underestimated the alienation of the Tibetans against the Han and the resistance that would be stimulated by the visit of Tibetans from Dharamsala. When one of the Tibetan exile delegations visiting Qinghai province was greeted by exuberant crowds of Tibetans expressing support for the Dalai Lama, Beijing officials were shocked and embarrassed. Hoping to avoid further unpleasant surprises, the Chinese officials immediately asked the first party secretary of Tibet, the Han former general Ren Rong, what they might expect when the delegation visited Lhasa. Ren Rong predicted there would be no problem. But in Lhasa there was an even larger outpouring of support for the Dalai Lama.

As a result of his misstep, Ren Rong was fired by Hu Yaobang who directed that Ren leave Tibet so he would not undermine efforts to establish good relations with Tibetans. Ren Rong was replaced by another former Han general, Yin Fatang, who soon became Deng's man in Tibet. Yin had spent some two decades in Tibet and was sufficiently committed to the building of Tibet that he remained there and helped build schools after he retired as party secretary.

The visits of these three delegations backfired. Deng had been led to believe that under Communist leadership, Tibet had achieved enough stability and economic growth since 1959 that the delegations from the exile community would be favorably impressed by the conditions they saw in Tibet. But they were not. On the contrary, they became vocal critics of Chinese treatment of Tibetans.

Despite the seriousness of the problems revealed during the visits of the three delegations, Deng still endeavored to bridge the gap with the Tibetans. He continued the policy of repairing Tibetan temples and other cultural objects. Deng directed Hu Yaobang, the newly appointed general secretary, and his deputy, Wan Li, to lead a major delegation to Tibet to try to restore better relations between the Han and the Tibetans.

After a few months of preparation, Hu and his delegation of eight hundred people arrived in Tibet on May 22, 1980, ready to celebrate on the next day the twenty-ninth anniversary of the signing of the seventeen-point agreement that had launched Mao's moderate policy toward Tibet in 1951. After spending a week observing conditions and talking with local officials, Hu Yaobang gave a dramatic speech in front of five thousand mostly Tibetan local officials. In his speech, "Strive to Build a United, Prosperous and Civilized New Tibet," Hu said, "Our party has let the Tibetan people down. We feel very bad . . . the life of the Tibetan people has not notably improved. Are we not to blame?" Hu then spelled out six tasks: (1) let Tibetans be the masters of their own lives, (2) relieve and reduce their economic burdens, exempting Tibetans from agricultural and livestock taxes for three to five years, (3) contract responsibility for agricultural production down to the small group, (4) make great efforts to develop agriculture and animal husbandry, (5) promote education and begin planning for a university in Tibet, and (6) strengthen the unity of the Tibetan and Han people by sending most of the Han officials in Tibet to other parts of China and by cultivating more local Tibetan officials.[111]

Hu's speech represented a bold effort to change the relationship between Beijing and Tibetans. After Hu's speech, there were rounds of enthusiastic applause for Tibet's new hero, Hu Yaobang. Hu was obviously sincere: he was honest about the damages done to Tibet, he accepted responsibility on behalf of the party for the suffering inflicted on Tibetans, and he outlined ways to do better in the future. Until he was dismissed in 1987, Hu continued to believe in a conciliatory policy toward Tibet.

Before Hu Yaobang's trip, PLA factories, located in several provinces where Tibetans lived, held a monopoly on producing felt hats, leather boots, and other goods prized by Tibetans. In the years after Hu Yaobang's 1980 trip, the PLA monopoly was broken and local civilian companies under Tibetan leadership were allowed to make these products. Some progress was also made in promoting Tibetan officials and in improving the lives of the Tibetan people. In 1978, 44.5 percent of the officials in Tibet were Tibetan; in 1981, the figure reached 54.4 percent; and in 1986, 60.3 percent.[112] Monasteries were permitted to recruit small numbers of monks, the Tibetan language was formally permitted, and opposition to religious prayers, pilgrimages, and ceremonies was dropped.

Within a year after Hu Yaobang's yeoman attempts to resolve the Tibetan issue, however, his efforts ended in failure. They failed because Hu Yaobang aroused the resistance of Han officials both in Tibet and in Beijing and because his efforts were still not enough to satisfy the Tibetans. Deng, constrained by Han officials, and the Dalai Lama, constrained by the militant community of exiles in Dharamsala, could not bridge the gap.

To the Han officials trying to keep order in Tibet, Hu Yaobang's policies were seen as an attack on them for being too severe with the Tibetans. Some Han officials were reassigned to other locations to make way for local Tibetan officials, and the Han who remained mostly objected to Hu Yaobang's policies; when they were ordered not only to learn the Tibetan language but also to listen to the views of the Tibetan people, they had difficulty maintaining the authority to keep political order. Han officials in Tibet responsible for security remained especially concerned about the Tibetan monasteries, which, with their newly increased freedoms, became hotbeds of Tibetan nationalism and centers for organizing Tibetan resistance. (According to figures in the late 1950s there were some 150,000 monks among a population of over two million in Tibet proper.) Wary officials in Beijing—like the Han officials in Tibet—were outspokenly critical of Hu for not recognizing the dangers of the Tibetan "separatists" who were supported by foreigners.[113]

Adding to the strain, the Tibetan exiles in Dharamsala were making demands for a level of autonomy that would be even greater than that Taiwan was being offered. They demanded a different political system in Tibet from that in the rest of China. They also asked for the creation of a "Greater Tibet," which would bring all Tibetan areas in China into one new political autonomous region. These demands went far beyond what even the more lenient officials in Beijing considered reasonable; thus the talks led nowhere.

In the 1980s, the Communists granted Tibetans far more autonomy than in the 1950s. Local people were permitted to use their local language, local dress, and send substantial numbers of delegates to people's congresses. The Communists allowed local people to have more children than the Han majority. Locals could enter high schools and universities with a lower cutoff score than that required of the Han majority. But real power over important decisions was placed in the hands of Han Communist officials in Lhasa, who received their directions from Beijing.

The second irreconcilable difference stemmed from the Tibetan demand that the boundaries of Tibet be extended to include the Tibetan minority areas in other provinces. In the seventh century, Tibetans had controlled an area almost as large as China, and ever since there had been small communities of Tibetans in the provinces of Sichuan, Qinghai, Gansu, and Yunnan. Even the most lenient Chinese refused to consider yielding such a large expanse of territory to the Tibetans.

On March 23, 1981, the Dalai Lama, after reviewing reports by his three groups of emissaries who had observed the conditions of Tibetans in China and after the Hu Yaobang visit, wrote a cordial letter to Deng, saying, "We must try to develop friendship between Tibetans and Chinese in the future through better understanding." But he also observed, "In reality, over 90 percent of the Tibetans are suffering both mentally and physically, and are living in deep sorrow. These sad conditions have not been brought about by natural disasters, but by human actions."[114] It took some time for Beijing to decide how to respond.

Beijing officials waited some four months, until July 27, 1981, when Hu Yaobang met with Gyalo Thondup in Beijing to convey Beijing's response to the Dalai Lama's March letter. In his 1980 mission to Tibet, Hu Yaobang had been allowed considerable leeway in trying to win the goodwill of Tibetans. But this meeting was different: he was under instructions to convey China's new policy that would put a tighter lid on Tibetan separatist activities. Hu specified to Gyalo Thondup the conditions under which the Dalai Lama would be welcomed to Beijing: The Dalai Lama could enjoy the same political status and living conditions as before 1959. He would live in Beijing, not Tibet, but he could visit Tibet. He would be made a vice chairman of the NPC and of the Chinese People's Political Consultative Conference.

The Tibetans understood that accepting this offer would give the Dalai Lama honor and some religious freedom, but that political power would still be firmly in the hands of the Chinese—so they rejected it. The Dalai Lama chose not to return to China. Deng's effort to form a closer, more positive relationship on both sides had failed. But neither Deng nor the Dalai Lama wanted to create a sharp break in relations. In October 1981, the Dalai Lama sent a negotiating team for further discussions. It too was unable to bridge the gap, but it avoided an open break between the Dalai Lama and Chinese leaders.[115]

After the failure to bridge the gap in 1981–1982, Deng put the Tibetan issue on the back burner until 1984, when expanded support for markets in the nation suggested a new vision for dealing with Tibetan problems: economic growth and increased linkages, including market linkages, between Tibet and other provinces. From February 27 to March 6, 1984, four years after the First Tibet Work Forum (and on the heels of Deng's announcement in Guangdong about the correctness of the special economic zone policies), Beijing held the Second Tibet Work Forum, which affirmed the further opening of Tibet. Until then, there had been only a trickle of tourists and outside merchants allowed into Tibet, but after the forum, merchants were allowed to go into Tibet and market their wares, with few constraints. Deng hoped that by linking Tibetans to the national economy and accelerating the growth rate in Tibet, support for the government would increase, just as it had elsewhere. In fact, Deng made Tibetan economic development high on the list of national priorities. Richer provinces were encouraged to send financial assistance, and officials knowledgeable about the economy were sent to help promote Tibetan development, thereby strengthening the links between Tibet and other provincial governments.

In 1985, as part of a related effort intended to reduce the risk of separatism, about four thousand very bright Tibetan middle-school students were sent to other provinces to take advantage of greater educational opportunities and to become more connected to the rest of the country. In 1984, talks were held between Beijing and the Tibetan exile community but they made no progress.

With the failure of these talks, the Dalai Lama tried to break the stalemate with Beijing by appealing for support in the West, which would put pressure on Beijing. He sent responsible young Tibetans abroad to make the case for Tibet. Lodi Gyari, for example, was sent to Washington where he was to spend several decades promoting the Tibetan cause. But none of these young emissaries compared in influence with the Dalai Lama himself. The Dalai Lama had learned English and could inspire a Western audience with his deep spirituality, a quality that many Westerners felt was missing from their own materialistic daily lives. They saw him as a man of peace fighting for the freedom of his people against oppressive Chinese. No other Asian leader had developed such a dedicated following of Westerners. The Dalai Lama's prominence enabled Tibetans, who constituted only 0.3 percent of the total population of China, to attract great attention from the Western world, far more than any other minority group in China, including those far more numerous. But despite widespread foreign support for the Dalai Lama, no foreign government formally recognized Tibet. Meanwhile, the Chinese regarded him as someone who made occasional high-sounding promises about being ready to accept Chinese sovereignty but was unwilling to make agreements that he would follow. They came to believe he had no negotiating room, given the constraints of the unruly extremist band of 80,000 exiles in India. The Han Chinese public, informed about Tibet through the Communist propaganda apparatus, believed that the Tibetans were ungrateful despite generous financial assistance from the Chinese government. As tensions grew and Han officials in Tibet tightened controls, Tibetans regarded the Han as oppressive and anti-Tibetan.

Monks in Tibet, buoyed by the Dalai Lama's success in gaining support from Europeans, members of the U.S. Congress, human rights activists, and foreign nongovernmental organizations (NGOs), were emboldened to press for greater autonomy. On September 27, 1987, less than one week after the Dalai Lama's first speech to the U.S. Congressional Human Rights Caucus on September 21, a demonstration of monks in Lhasa turned into a riot. Many Tibetans had become overly optimistic that, with Western support, they could force the Chinese government to back down. On the contrary, Beijing officials tightened their controls. In June 1988, in a speech to the European Parliament at Strasbourg, the Dalai Lama repeated his view that

Tibetans should be able to decide on all affairs relating to Tibet—within months, in December 1988, another serious riot occurred in Lhasa. And the awarding of the Nobel Peace Prize in 1989 to the Dalai Lama emboldened monks within Tibet to revive their resistance activities, which again led Communist Party leaders to tighten their controls.

Chinese leaders, frustrated by the growing resistance of Tibetan monks as a result of the Dalai Lama's success abroad, have used whatever leverage they have with foreign groups to isolate the Dalai Lama. Some foreigners have yielded to Chinese pressures, but overall, Chinese efforts have increased foreign attention to the Dalai Lama and strengthened foreign criticism of China. In Tibet, the growing resistance of monks caused Chinese officials to fortify their security forces and to exercise stricter control over monasteries.

Chinese officials have complained that foreign assistance from human rights groups is motivated by a desire to weaken China. And when foreigners criticize the Chinese for failing to give the Tibetans more autonomy, some Chinese officials snap back that their policies have been more humane than those the United States used in assimilating and destroying its own Native American communities.

Both Deng and the Dalai Lama, while unable to resolve their differences, tried to avoid all-out conflict. In early 1988 Beijing released several monks who were being held for their political activities. And in April 1988, China announced that if the Dalai Lama were willing to give up his efforts to achieve independence, he could live in Tibet. The Dalai Lama continued to say that he accepted Chinese sovereignty and that he wanted a peaceful solution that gave Tibetans more freedom.

In January 1989, Deng sent to Tibet a new provincial party secretary, Hu Jintao, to try to control the unrest. Hu talked with various Tibetan leaders, but his basic goals echoed Deng's: support economic growth, expand education in Mandarin, strengthen outside linkages, co-opt some Tibetans, and keep tight control over separatist activities. Riots again broke out in Tibet in the spring of 1989 at the same time that students were demonstrating in Beijing; in response, Hu Jintao declared martial law.

In early 1989, after the death of the Panchen Lama (another Tibetan religious leader) with the second-largest following among Tibetans, there was a brief moment of hope. The Dalai Lama, in his role as religious leader, was invited to go to Beijing for the memorial services. Beijing's assumption was that the Dalai Lama was generally more flexible than the Tibetan exile community and that Deng and the Dalai Lama might be able to begin some useful discussions during his visit. But the exile community in Dharamsala, recognizing that Beijing leaders were trying to pull the Dalai Lama closer to Beijing, convinced the Dalai Lama that he should not attend. After this refusal, Deng and later his successors gave up trying to work with the Dalai Lama and the gridlock continued. Some observers felt that the Dalai Lama missed a great opportunity to make progress in bridging the gap. Since then, although the Dalai Lama has sent representatives from time to time for discussions in China, neither side has yielded on the basic points of contention.

By the middle of the 1980s a tragic cycle had emerged that continues to this day: The Dalai Lama's popularity abroad emboldens local Tibetans to resist, leading to a crackdown by Beijing. When foreigners learn of the crackdown, they complain, emboldening Tibetans to resist, and the cycle continues. But the Tibetans and Han Chinese both recognize there is a long-term change that began with the opening of Tibet to outside markets in the mid-1980s and the input of economic aid to Tibet: an improvement in the standard of living and a decline of economic autonomy. In the 1950s outsiders settling in Tibet were mostly Han party officials and troops sent in by Beijing. After the mid-1980s settlers from the outside were overwhelmingly merchants who went to take advantage of economic opportunities generated by inputs of Chinese economic assistance to Tibet; many were members of Hui or other minorities from nearby poor provinces. Almost no outsiders settled in Tibetan villages but by the late 1990s, outsiders were already threatening to outnumber Tibetans in Lhasa.[116] With more Tibetan youth learning Mandarin and receiving a Chinese education to further their careers, both Tibetans and Chinese see that the long-term trend is toward Tibetans absorbing many aspects of Chinese culture, and becoming integrated into the outside economy, while not giving up their Tibetan identity and loyalty.

Since Deng sent Hu Yaobang to Tibet in 1980, there has been no serious effort to reach a positive agreement between Tibetans and Beijing. The gridlock remains between Tibetan exiles determined to establish a greater Tibet that possesses genuine autonomy, and leaders in Beijing convinced that economic growth and expanded Tibetan participation in Chinese schools and culture will draw Tibet toward greater integration into the national economy and culture. The standoff between foreigners who want to help Tibetans gain more autonomy and Beijing leaders, who feel increasingly optimistic about their power to block such efforts as China rises, also continues.

18

The Military: Preparing for Modernization

When Deng returned to work in mid-1977, he worked with Marshal Ye Jianying and other senior officials to lay the groundwork for modernizing China's military. Yet scarcely a year later, this effort was postponed when Deng concluded that China's national security was under serious threat and the country had to begin immediate preparations for military action in Vietnam. When the war with Vietnam ended in March 1979, Deng judged that the risk of imminent military conflict was sufficiently low that he could continue to hold off on large-scale investments in modern military hardware and concentrate instead on the civilian economy. Deng did resume, however, the improvements to the military that he had begun in 1975: downsizing the forces; bringing in new, better-educated recruits; and strengthening overall discipline and training. This way, by the time he retired, China would have not only a stronger economic base but also a smaller, better-trained military force, one better prepared to use the modern weaponry that would be acquired after he left the stage.[1]

In 1977, Deng remained publicly deferential to Hua Guofeng, who was chairman of the Central Military Commission (CMC). But in fact, Marshal Ye and Deng, vice chairmen of the CMC, were in charge of China's military affairs. Hua had once been minister of public security, but aside from modest service with the guerrillas during World War II, and as a political commissar in the People's Liberation Army (PLA) after the Lin Biao affair, he had not served in the military and was unprepared for military leadership. He did not compare with Deng or Marshal Ye in terms of military experience, knowledge, or the respect accorded them by high-level military officials. So when

Hua was officially pushed aside and Deng became chairman of the CMC in June 1981, it merely gave official recognition to the man who, with Marshal Ye, had in fact been leading the military since mid-1977.[2] There was no change in military policy.

Deng was forthright in recognizing the problems that China faced in its military. Deng said, "None of us, including the veteran comrades, is sufficiently capable of directing modern wars. We must recognize this fact."[3] Deng knew that China had fallen far behind in military technology and needed to adapt its strategies to cope with its main adversary, the Soviet Union. He knew that the assignment of military officials to civilian positions in the Lin Biao period had diverted attention from military issues.

What troubled him about military affairs during his eighteen months out of power was not that the Gang of Four had built up a solid following, for only in the Political Department under Zhang Chunqiao had they established real roots. What troubled him during his years out of office was that two years of valuable time that could have been used to restructure and improve the PLA had been wasted. During 1976 the military leaders whom Deng and Marshal Ye had put in place in 1975 could not reach Deng and Ye's earlier goal of reducing the number of personnel in the PLA by 26 percent by the end of the year; instead, the number of personnel was reduced by only 13.6 percent.[4] After Mao's death, Deng spoke frankly about the problems of the PLA that had arisen on Mao's watch, even if he blamed them not on Mao but on Lin Biao.

In 1977 Deng's combination of responsibilities—in the military, science, technology, education, and foreign affairs—made it natural for him to focus on upgrading science and technology in the military. Two years earlier, he had advocated elevating education and training to the level of national strategic importance, but at the time he did not have the chance to implement it. Now, at a CMC forum on August 23, 1977, Deng repeated the message and underlined its importance. By elevating education and training, he meant not only teaching discipline and politics, but also making military leaders understand what would be required to improve their specialized technical knowledge and to carry out military exercises in preparation for battling an enemy with modern technology.[5]

In 1977 Deng and Marshal Ye were heirs to a group of Chinese military leaders, led by Peng Dehuai, who had tried in the 1950s to create a more professional military but had never received the full mandate from Mao to achieve this goal.[6] Peng Dehuai had hoped to receive technological help from the Soviet Union. Deng understood the West's reluctance to share cutting-edge military technology, but he maintained the hope that he could at least obtain civilian technological help from the West that would indirectly aid military modernization and, without giving up Chinese independence, even receive some military technology.

To achieve their goal of creating a professional military that would gradually acquire modern equipment, Deng and Marshal Ye first needed to replace those who had grown "lax, conceited, extravagant, and lazy," develop a system for retiring aged officers, and provide a framework for downsizing. Meanwhile, they also needed to prepare for a great expansion of military training and new military exercises to ensure that the leaner military could operate effectively in battle.[7]

Deng and Marshal Ye aimed to select a team of officials in each unit who were committed to remaking the PLA into a more modern force. Deng wanted to recruit young people with higher educational levels, including some college graduates, who could better absorb the new technology as it was developed. To select these promising young people, he introduced recruitment standards that included performance on written examinations.

Military academies would be central for upgrading training. These academies, Deng said, should employ outstanding teachers who not only had high academic qualifications, but also were willing to familiarize themselves with actual battle conditions and whose work ethic would be an example for their students.[8] When he spoke to the CMC on August 23, 1977, Deng said that historically, troops had been tested in battle and promoted on the basis of their battle performance. "Now that we are not at war," he asked, "how are we to test our officials, raise their level, and improve the quality and combat effectiveness of our troops? How else, if not through education and training?"[9]

Like the Meiji leaders of Japan who had concluded that modernization was not just about learning technology but also about gaining "enlightenment," Deng realized that effective modernization of the military required new perspectives and a broad base of knowledge. Consequently, a small group of talented young recruits in the PLA were taught foreign languages and sent abroad in the first wave of Chinese young people to study overseas. Instead of studying specialized military topics, they focused on broader subjects such as management, science, technology, and international relations.

Meanwhile, downsizing the bloated, outdated Chinese military structure was a first priority. By December 1977, new plans for troop reductions had been prepared, and the CMC had approved a "plan concerning the readjustment of the structure of the military tables of organization" *(guanyu jundui bianzhi tizhi de tiaozheng),* which described the desired structure for a more modern military. On March 20, 1978, at a forum sponsored by the General Political Department of the PLA, Deng announced plans to transfer 500,000 PLA officers to civilian positions.[10]

On January 2, 1979, in his first talk to the military after becoming pre-eminent leader at the Third Plenum, Deng bluntly told a CMC-sponsored forum of high-level officers:

> The military is in bad shape . . . the problem is not because of any par-
> ticular bad person. It is because the system is bloated, and people glide
> over things. . . . People say that it is not convenient to get certain things
> done while in a single unit there are five or six tables of officers playing
> mahjong. . . . Our army's reputation has gotten worse. . . . Some com-
> rades don't want to retire and become advisers. . . . I would like to set an
> example by becoming an adviser, but it is not now possible. I hope to
> become an adviser in 1985. Really, I am not kidding. What's wrong
> with it? You can live a few years longer. If you don't have a secretary or a
> car, you can still have a chair. . . . As for rejuvenating our army, some
> people agree in principle, but oppose it in the concrete.[11]

Deng's progress in getting rid of the bloating was remarkable. When Deng began the process in 1975, there were 6.1 million troops; by 1979 the numbers were reduced to 5.2 million, by 1982 to 4.2 million, and by 1988 to 3.2 million.[12] The process of downsizing was interrupted in late 1978 by preparations for the attack on Vietnam, and after the attack was over, by the maintenance for several years of troops who took part in skirmishes along the border with Vietnam.

Deng's Attack on Vietnam, February 17–March 16, 1979

By the summer of 1978, the growing cooperation between Vietnam and the Soviet Union led Chinese officials to worry that the Vietnamese military might use the dry season, when they could move their motorized vehicles, to attack Cambodia. Vietnam had already overrun Laos in July 1977, and the dry season would begin in December.

Deng had been telling Americans that to stop Soviet advances one had to show a willingness to fight. Cambodia was a client state of China and if China did not make a strong response to an invasion of Cambodia, then the Soviets and Vietnamese would gain confidence that they could expand toward Thailand and on to the Straits of Malacca, giving them access to the Indian Ocean in the west and the Pacific in the east. If the Vietnamese were to invade Cambodia, the Soviets were likely to send in more men and military equipment to assist in the invasion. Deng firmly believed that if Vietnam invaded Cambodia, China had to make a strong response.

Cambodian leader Pol Pot, who by the summer of 1978 had begun to realize the seriousness of the Vietnamese threat, asked Deng to send Chinese "volunteers" to Cambodia to resist the invasion of the Vietnamese, as Mao had done in Korea to resist the invasion of the South Koreans and the Americans. Deng was ready to cooperate with Pol Pot despite the atrocities he had committed against his own people and the vehement opposition these acts had caused in the West because Deng judged him to be the only Cambodian leader capable of offering significant resistance to Vietnam.

But Deng chose not to send troops to Cambodia; he was convinced that China would get bogged down in an expensive campaign and lose control over events in the region. Deng preferred a "quick decisive campaign," like the one China had successfully conducted along the Indian border in 1962. With a brief thrust into Vietnam he would demonstrate that the costs to Vietnam and the Soviet Union for continued expansion would be unacceptably high.

Many high Chinese officials, military and civilian, had doubts about the wisdom of attacking Vietnam. Some were concerned that just as China was beginning its modernization drive, it would be unwise to divert China's scarce resources, which were sorely needed for building modern industries. Some worried that Chinese troops were not properly prepared. Others opposed in principle an attack on a fraternal Communist country. Some worried that an attack would heighten long-term Vietnamese hostility to China.

Other officials feared that the Soviet Union and its massive military forces might be drawn into the conflict. Deng personally believed that because the Soviets were then in the final stages of negotiating the Startegic Arms Limitation Treaty (SALT) II with the United States, they would be reluctant to disrupt the negotiations by engaging in a land war in Asia.[13] But the risks were great and Deng solicited the views of other senior Chinese leaders about possible Soviet intervention. After a careful assessment of the issue, Chen Yun noted that the Soviet divisions along the northern Chinese border, the most likely locus for attacking China, were seriously undermanned; any attack on

China would require diverting forces from Europe, which would take more than a month to complete. Chen concluded that if the war were very brief, the chance of Soviet intervention was extremely low.

After hearing Chen Yun's assessment, Deng announced that the Chinese attack would last no longer than its attack on India in 1962 (thirty-three days). It would be a ground war and no aircraft would be used.[14] Deng knew that Vietnamese pilots were then much better trained than Chinese pilots and that the Chinese did not have airfields close to Vietnam. Furthermore, avoiding an air war reduced the chances that the Soviets might be drawn in. But Deng was still sufficiently concerned about a possible Soviet response that an estimated 300,000 Chinese civilians were pulled back from Yili in the north near the Soviet border, and intelligence officials were ordered to monitor closely all Soviet troop movements.[15]

Deng encountered widespread opposition from other members of the CMC who felt that Chinese troops were not prepared for the war. The PLA had not yet recovered from the Cultural Revolution disruptions; discipline was poor and training inadequate. Except for the more than 1,100 border skirmishes by 1978 with Vietnam, no Chinese had fought in a war since the Indian border clashes of 1962. The Vietnamese troops, in contrast, were battle hardened from decades of war against the French, the South Vietnamese, and the Americans. They also possessed modern Soviet military equipment, and the Soviets had been providing Vietnam with significant economic aid for construction since the Americans were defeated in Vietnam in 1975.[16]

In the end, Deng's authority and his conviction about the need for a strong response to the Soviet-Vietnamese threat won out over those who had doubts about attacking Vietnam. Some officials in Beijing are convinced that Deng launched the attack and provided detailed direction during the war so he could personally gain tight control over the military as he was coming to power. Others believe that Deng, aware that the United States had supplied technology freely to Japan and South Korea because they were allies, wanted to show the United States that in invading Vietnam, China had drawn a sharp line against the Soviets and was in no danger of restoring close relations with the Soviets. Although there is no firm evidence to prove exactly how Deng weighted these various considerations, Deng was clearly passionately upset at Vietnamese ambitions and deeply concerned about the risks of Soviet expansion in the region.

The Guangzhou and Kunming military regions and the Chinese General

Staff had been discussing the possible need to expand their forces along the border, but they did not begin planning for the attack on Vietnam until the CMC meeting in September 1978.[17] The CMC meeting opened with briefings by the intelligence department of the General Staff on the increasing number of skirmishes between Chinese and Vietnamese forces along the border. The two nearby military regions, Guangzhou (Guangdong) and Kunming (Yunnan), were directed to prepare scenarios for an attack on Vietnam. On November 23, senior officers from the air force, navy, and General Staff operations and intelligence departments convened a week-long meeting. After this meeting, all commands in the Northeast, North, and Northwest went on a full-scale alert to watch for possible Soviet military reaction.

By November, Chinese troops, coming from ten of the eleven military regions but mostly from the Kunming and Guangzhou regions, had begun to position themselves near Vietnam. The Chinese border with Vietnam stretched 797 miles, roughly half of which was along the Yunnan border, under the Kunming Military Region, and half along the Guangxi border, under the Guangzhou Military Region. Chinese troops, deployed along the entire border, served under the leadership of General Xu Shiyou in a single front. The troops moved toward the Vietnamese border at night, as they had during the civil war and the Korean War, to catch the enemy by surprise. According to a U.S. estimate, as many as 450,000 Chinese troops took part in the war, including those who provided support on the Chinese side of the border; the Vietnamese estimated that 600,000 Chinese troops were involved.[18]

On December 8, the CMC ordered the Guangzhou and Kunming military regions to be ready for an attack on Vietnam by January 10, and on December 11 the commander of the Guangzhou Military Region, Xu Shiyou, prepared to deploy his troops. Soon thereafter, on December 21, Xu set up military headquarters in Nanning, Guangxi, close to Vietnam, where he and his staff worked out concrete plans for the attack.[19]

Meanwhile, the CMC, anticipating a Vietnamese invasion of Cambodia, called a forum on December 20 during which military leaders closely monitored Vietnamese developments and supervised planning for their attack. On December 25, as expected, the Vietnamese did invade Cambodia with an estimated 120,000 troops; twelve days later they captured Phnom Penh.

In addition to managing the military preparations for the attack on Vietnam, Deng also managed the diplomatic relations. He briefed Lee Kuan Yew in November and President Carter in January 1979 of his plans. On his way back to China in early February, Deng stopped in Japan to inform the Japanese that he was planning to attack Vietnam and to discourage them from providing financial or other aid to Vietnam. While in Tokyo, he also told Ambassador Mike Mansfield, whom he knew influenced U.S. Congressional views, what he had told Lee Kuan Yew and Carter—that the Vietnamese and Soviets were planning to surround China and that China would attack to teach the Vietnamese a lesson.[20]

In the weeks before his attack on Vietnam, Deng had been busy with the Central Party Work Conference, the Third Plenum, the normalization of relations with the United States, and the assumption of responsibilities as preeminent leader, but he still took time to guide military and diplomatic preparations. Once the attack began, he was deeply involved in the daily military operations. John Lewis and Xue Litai, after reviewing the evidence on Deng's role in the attack on Vietnam, conclude, "The strategic thinking behind the assault was his as was the determination of the war's objectives and scale. He chose his top warriors as the field commanders, mobilized the relevant provinces to support the fighting, approved the details of the operation, and gave the order to launch the attack. This was Deng's war."[21] Deng continued to provide overall leadership throughout the operations; some said he was familiar with Chinese movements down to the platoon level.[22]

Like many Chinese commanders, Deng thought in terms of an annihilation campaign. Just as in the Huai Hai campaign when the troops aimed to annihilate Guomindang troops north of the Yangtze River, so in the quick thrust into Vietnam he hoped to annihilate a major part of the Vietnamese army in a quick, decisive campaign that would set back by many years Vietnam's ability to threaten China. This strategy came as no surprise to Vietnamese military officials, who had worked closely with the Chinese to fight American forces: they quickly pulled back their main forces from the Chinese border to the area around Hanoi, leaving in place their forces in Cambodia. To repulse the Chinese, the Vietnamese assigned local troops and militia who knew the terrain and the local people.

The Chinese would attack during the dry season in Vietnam but after the ice had begun to melt on the Ussuri River; that way, the Soviets could not use the ice bridge to cross the border to attack China from the north.[23] During its February 9 to February 12 meeting, the CMC made the final decision to attack, and on February 13 Deng met with his Cambodian ally, Prince Sihanouk. On February 16, only seventeen hours before the attack was launched, Hua Guofeng chaired a meeting at which Deng informed high-level Beijing officials of the final plans.[24] Since Hua Guofeng's footprint was clear in the preparations for the war, he would be in no position to criticize Deng if serious problems were to arise.

At dawn on February 17, some 200,000 Chinese troops launched their assault into Vietnam at twenty-six sites stretching out across the entire border. Before the attack, the Chinese had led raids at many points along the long border, forcing the Vietnamese to disperse their troops. The Chinese concentrated their forces where they had superior numbers and sought to gain control over the hills overlooking five provincial capitals—Lang Son, Cao Bang, Lao Cai, Ha Giang, and Lai Chao—which they expected to capture within several days.

Deng launched the invasion at a strategically opportune time for China: less than three weeks after concluding his triumphant tour of the United States and his stopover in Japan. Because of Deng's visit, the Soviets worried that the United States might be giving intelligence aid to China, and that if the Soviets were to act, the United States might support China. Brezhnev even phoned Carter to seek assurances that the United States was not giving tacit support to China's invasion of Vietnam. But even after Carter gave his assurances, Brezhnev's doubts were not eased.[25]

As soon as Chinese forces thrust into Vietnam, they found Vietnamese resistance to be unexpectedly effective. Chinese officers were unprepared and panicked. The invading Chinese troops had been given specific assignments, but they lacked the intelligence and communications from higher levels to adapt quickly. Coordination between troops was poor and Chinese supply lines were stretched so far that some soldiers had to be sent back into China to bring in supplies. The Chinese used artillery to support troop advances, and they tried to concentrate troops where they outnumbered the local resistance. But unlike during the anti-Japanese and civil wars, when the PLA could rely on assistance by local residents, in Vietnam the local people provided information and logistical support to the opposing Vietnamese forces.

The Chinese had expected to take all five provincial capitals in one week, but they did not capture Lang Son until three weeks after the fighting began. Indeed, the heaviest fighting took place around Lang Son, where the Chinese concentrated their forces to gain control of the mountain pass leading south to Hanoi, to show the Vietnamese they could threaten the Vietnamese capital. Chinese forces were sufficiently large and determined that they did indeed take all five provincial capitals, despite casualty numbers that were far higher than for the Vietnamese. Estimates are that as many as 25,000 Chinese were killed and 37,000 wounded during the fighting.[26]

As soon as the Chinese took Lang Son on March 6, the Chinese declared victory and began withdrawing. As they withdrew, they destroyed as much of the Vietnamese infrastructure as possible. Deng had pledged that the fighting would not last longer than the thirty-three days of attack on India in 1962, and the withdrawal from Vietnam took place on March 16, twenty-nine days after the invasion began.[27]

In the publicity that followed the invasion, both at home and abroad, Chinese called their assault a "defensive counteroffensive." They argued that they were responding to the many Vietnamese incursions across the border in 1978 and that their thrust into Vietnam was a form of self-defense. For officers stationed along the border who had defended against the Vietnamese incursions, and for their military superiors, it was not difficult to understand the need to "counterattack." Other Chinese officials shared Deng's anger at the Vietnamese for mistreating and expelling ethnic Chinese despite China's warnings. Yet some high Chinese military officials never expressed support for the war.

Deng claimed that China had taught the Vietnamese a lesson, but Western military analysts who examined the war reported that in fact it was the battle-tested Vietnamese who taught the Chinese a lesson.[28] As the military analysts pointed out, the war exposed many weaknesses in the Chinese military, in addition to its lack of modern weaponry. China's rush to war between November and February meant that its preparations were inadequate. Command and control functions were weak. In particular, the command posts of the two military regions fighting in Vietnam were poorly coordinated, with lower-level units given targets but no knowledge of what other lower-level units were doing. The PLA was not proud of its military performance; some commanders complained they should have been allowed to go all the way to Phnom Penh to complete their victory. And although they didn't make their views public, many top Chinese military officials, including Marshal Ye and Su Yu, opposed the whole idea of the war, feeling that the danger of encirclement had not been so great as to warrant the attack.[29] The public also had its doubts: some posters on Democracy Wall in Beijing pointed to the poor showing of Chinese troops, and some even criticized Deng for pursuing the war.[30]

But within party circles and in visits with foreigners, Deng explained that the Chinese had accomplished their announced military goals—the capture of the five provincial capitals—and, more importantly, their overall strategic aim. That is, they had shown both the Soviet Union and Vietnam that the costs of additional Soviet expansion in the region would be unbearably high. As Lee Kuan Yew commented, "The Western press wrote off the Chinese punitive action as a failure. I believe it changed the history of East Asia. The Vietnamese learned that China would attack if they went beyond Cambodia on to Thailand. The Soviet Union did not want to be caught in a long drawn-out war in a remote corner of Asia."[31] As it turned out, the Soviet invasion of Afghanistan nine months later quickly proved to be such a burden on the Soviet Union that the risk of Soviet expansion into Southeast Asia after that would have been very low, even if China had not attacked Vietnam.

Chinese military officials tried to downplay the costs of the campaign, but the total budget for defense expenditures in 1979 was 22.3 billion yuan, much higher than the previous year or the next year; the burdens on local areas near the Vietnamese border made the costs of the war even higher. Western analysts estimated that the cost of matériel alone was 5.5 billion yuan.[32] Diplomats were concerned about a different sort of cost: that the attack would make it difficult for China to take a principled stand when it complained of a Western country interfering in the internal affairs of another. Domestic criticisms about failure in Vietnam were not publicized, and in the early 1990s when China and Vietnam normalized relations they agreed not to discuss past conflicts.[33] In the official three-volume collection of Deng's talks on military matters, there are twenty-six selections from his talks during 1978 and 1979, but only a few passing references to China's attack on Vietnam—not one of his talks deal with it directly.[34] Some Chinese have called the attack on Vietnam "China's last war." Given the lack of public discussion, it might better be called "China's forgotten war."

There is no record of Deng expressing any doubt about the wisdom of the attack on Vietnam. But after the war, Deng did use the army's poor performance to fortify the efforts he had been making since 1975 to retire ineffective senior officers, strengthen discipline, expand military training, and recruit better-trained officers. He also directed the PLA to analyze carefully the weaknesses that had become apparent during the war. The PLA would eventually point to many of the issues noted by U.S. military analysts: the poor quality of Chinese intelligence before and during the war, the lack of communication among units, the poor quality of equipment, and the inability of the PLA leadership to provide overall coordination.[35]

After the war, Deng directed that the Chinese army keep large numbers of troops along the Vietnamese border to skirmish with the Vietnamese. As Deng told visiting U.S. officials such as Senator Henry M. ("Scoop") Jackson, he was wearing the Vietnamese down to reinforce the lessons he had taught them about their excessive ambitions.[36] Over the next several years, selected units from at least fourteen Chinese armies (at the corps level) were rotated through the Laoshan area on the Chinese side of the border.[37] At times as many as 800,000 Vietnamese soldiers were stationed in the north to be ready for a Chinese assault. Given the relative populations of China and Vietnam, roughly twenty to one, Vietnamese efforts to protect their border over that next decade were a heavy drain on resources.

Meanwhile, China used these continuing border skirmishes—and occasional larger conflicts involving entire Chinese divisions—to train its troops. By the 1980s units from most of the infantry armies in China had been rotated to the Vietnam border to take part in the border skirmishes. As military analysts noted, assigning Chinese troops to fight against some of the most experienced ground troops in the world provided excellent combat training. The presence of large numbers of Chinese troops also made the Soviets cautious about sending additional aid to the Vietnamese.

Vietnam's threat to the weaker Southeast Asian countries reinforced their willingness to cooperate with China to reduce the threat. Vietnamese aggressive behavior led Southeast Asian countries to strengthen the Association of Southeast Asian Nations (ASEAN).[38] In 1984 when the Vietnamese seized a critical pass leading from Cambodia into Thailand that could have endangered Thailand, the Chinese launched their biggest attack since 1979 and the Vietnamese retreated.[39] Deng's thrust into Vietnam in 1979 and his continuing harassment of Vietnamese along their common border gave other Southeast Asian countries greater confidence to resist Vietnam's ambitions, knowing that the Chinese would help them as they had helped Cambodia and Thailand.

As in the board game of *weiqi* (*go* in Japanese), Deng tried to prevent the Soviets and Vietnamese from controlling space and encircling China, while trying to gain control himself over key locations. In 1984 he fought hard to control the key area that would block Vietnam from entering Thailand and continuing on to the key Straits of Malacca. In Deng's view, by the early 1980s the danger of encirclement had been removed.

Vietnam's occupation of Cambodia and the continued skirmishes with China along the border did lead the Vietnamese to become overstretched. Deng had already seen this possibility when he welcomed Vice President Mondale to Beijing. He explained to U.S. Vice President Walter Mondale in August 1979, "Vietnam is not yet in enough of a difficult position to accept a political solution. Perhaps later, when the difficulties the Vietnamese are facing increase to an unbearable extent, then the time would be appropriate for them to accept."[40] He told Mondale that Vietnam had a double heavy burden of occupying Cambodia while supporting 600,000 to one million troops near the Chinese border and that sooner or later, the Vietnamese would realize that the Soviet Union could not meet all their requests.

Deng's comments proved prescient: by 1988, Vietnam had withdrawn half of its troops from Cambodia, and the next year it pulled out its remaining forces. Vietnam had failed to achieve its ambitions to dominate Southeast Asia. By the time Deng retired, Vietnamese no longer threatened Southeast Asian countries and instead began pursuing friendly ties with them. In the early 1980s Vietnamese threats to the region had led Southeast Asian countries to strengthen ASEAN, but paradoxically, by the early 1990s Vietnam itself was seeking better relations with ASEAN and was welcomed as a member in 1995.

Reducing the Soviet Threat

Mao had declared that war was inevitable, and Deng had on some occasions repeated Mao's words. But after the PLA returned from its attack on Vietnam, Deng had reason to be more optimistic: the risks of China going to war with the Soviet Union were low and he had lowered them further. Even earlier, in his December 1977 address to a plenary session of the CMC, Deng had said that because the Soviet Union was still working on extending its strategic deployments and because the United States was on the defensive, "it is possible to win a delay in the outbreak of war."[41] What had become clear during China's attack on Vietnam was that with China prepared to defend its interests in Southeast Asia, the Soviet Union had become more cautious about risking a confrontation with China in Southeast Asia. The Soviet Union had enough to do in Eastern Europe, along its long border with China, and in Afghanistan where its involvement would lead to an invasion nine months after Deng's war with Vietnam. And because China had just normalized relations with the United States, a Soviet leader could not be certain that the United States would stand idly by if the Soviet Union were to attack China.

Having discouraged the Soviet Union from rushing to build bases in Vietnam by showing Chinese resolve, Deng moved next to further reduce tensions with the Soviet Union so that he could concentrate on economic development.[42] Immediately after his brief war with Vietnam, Deng instructed Foreign Minister Huang Hua "to hold negotiations with the Soviet Union on unsolved questions and on improving the state-to-state relationships and to sign related documents."[43] Scarcely two weeks after the Chinese withdrawal from Vietnam, Foreign Minister Huang Hua met with the Soviet Ambassador Yuri Scherbakov in Beijing to propose a new series of discussions to normalize relations between China and the Soviet Union.[44] From April through mid-October, 1979, there were five meetings between Chinese and Soviet deputy foreign ministers to help improve the climate between the two powers. During these meetings, China expressed its wish to discuss both obstacles to normal relations as well as trade and scientific and cultural exchanges between the two nations.[45]

On August 29, 1979, before a Chinese delegation was to leave for the Soviet Union, Deng directed that the delegation should convey to the Soviets that there were two requirements to improving relations: the Soviets should withdraw their troops from Outer Mongolia, and they should not assist Vietnam in the occupation of Cambodia. Deng also proposed that the two sides agree not to station troops in areas along the border. He directed Wang Youping that the Chinese delegation should not show any weakness and should avoid being in a hurry to reach an agreement. Long-distance marathons, he said, are fine.[46]

From September 25 to December 3, 1979, the Chinese delegation carried on negotiations with its counterparts in Moscow. The Soviets did not budge on the two issues on which Deng insisted that the Chinese remain firm. Yet the discussions, the first series of talks between the Soviets and the Chinese in twenty years, were conducted in a friendly manner and the Soviets were cordial hosts. The two sides agreed that the Soviets would send a delegation to Beijing to follow up on the discussions.[47]

The Soviet invasion of Afghanistan that followed within weeks after the meetings in Moscow delayed the dispatch of the Soviet delegation to Beijing, but it also reduced even further the risk that the Soviets would attack the Chinese. Shortly after the Soviet invasion, Deng added a third requirement before China could normalize relations with the Soviet Union: the Soviets must withdraw from Afghanistan. It would take almost a decade before the overstretched Soviet Union was ready to agree to the three conditions for full normalization, but for that Deng was in no hurry. He had achieved his short-term goal of reducing the risk of conflict with the superpower that he now considered the most dangerous, thus allowing China to concentrate on civilian economic development.[48] In March 1980, in a major address on the military situation, he said, "After calmly assessing the international situation, we have concluded that it is possible to gain a longer period free from war than we had thought earlier."[49] Soon afterward, Deng became more specific, saying that China should be able to avoid the risk of war for a decade or two.[50]

Deng's efforts to reduce tensions made it easier for the Soviets to do the same. On March 24, 1982, Brezhnev gave a speech in Tashkent recognizing China as a socialist country and expressing a desire to improve relations. Deng responded quickly to this overture, directing Foreign Minister Qian Qichen to convey a favorable reaction to the speech.[51] Deng concluded that the Soviet Union, which was burdened by its effort to match U.S. military advances and its occupation of Afghanistan, felt it was in its strategic interest to ease tensions with China. When Brezhnev died a few months later, on November 10, 1982, Deng instructed Foreign Minister Huang Hua to attend Brezhnev's funeral, in another gesture of fraternity with the Soviet Union.[52]

In addition to negotiating with the Soviet Union, Deng also sought to reduce the risk of Soviet and Vietnamese advances by involving the United States. Deng knew that the United States was then in no mood to engage in a land war in Asia; what better way to ensure that the Soviets would not dominate the seas near Vietnam than to have a large American oil company conduct oil explorations there? After January 1979, as part of its economic readjustment, China had cut back on its plans to work with international oil companies. A Chinese petroleum delegation visiting the United States signed only one contract, on March 19, 1979, with ARCO, the only U.S. firm that had proposed prospecting for oil between Hainan Island and Vietnam. China gave ARCO exclusive exploration rights in an area in the South China Sea, less than thirty minutes from Vietnam by air. With a major U.S. oil company prospecting in nearby waters, Deng had reason to expect the Soviet Union would be cautious about making use of port facilities in Vietnam. China signed the contract three days after Chinese troops withdrew from Vietnam.

Deng also made sure that U.S.-China security cooperation came to the attention of the Soviet Union. When U.S. planes carrying equipment to monitor nuclear weapons movements in the Soviet Union arrived for a stop at the Beijing airport, the Chinese had the plane dock next to a Soviet Aeroflot plane, making it clear to the Soviets what equipment was arriving; when the equipment was transferred and flown to Xinjiang near the Soviet border, the Chinese also made no effort to camouflage it. The hope was that the Soviets would pause before risking a fight that might also involve the United States.

Military Cooperation with the United States

Deng never gave any indication that he ever considered forming a military alliance with the United States, for like Mao before him, he wanted China to remain completely independent on security matters. But he did seek U.S. cooperation in acquiring more modern military technology. Indeed, when Deng met President Carter in January 1979, he brought up the issue of the possible transfer of military technology from the United States. Although Carter did not welcome the idea while China was preparing to attack Vietnam or was actively involved in battle, after Deng withdrew Chinese forces from Vietnam, talks about such cooperation warmed. Deng did not display any urgency, but he raised the issue of sharing military technology at every opportunity. The Americans took notice: when Deng spoke to Vice President Mondale in late August 1979, he expressed his disappointment that the United States had decided not to supply China with high-speed computers, and Mondale replied that the United States was preparing lists of technology that could be transferred to China but not to the Soviet Union.[53]

Following Mondale's very successful visit, the United States decided to send Secretary of Defense Harold Brown to Beijing for discussions on security issues. Planning for this trip helped to advance the agenda for technology transfers, for although the United States would not sell weapons to China, it would consider on a case-by-case basis the transfer of military equipment— and the Soviet invasion of Afghanistan in December 1979 lent support to those who wanted to intensify U.S. cooperation with China as a way of putting pressure on the Soviet Union. By the time Secretary Brown arrived in Beijing in January 1980, the Chinese had studied American procedures and learned the range of technology the United States was considering for transfer. They handed to the American side a list of the technology they sought, which permitted a business-like examination of concrete cases. To highlight the favorable consideration given to U.S. technology transfer to China, Brown gave the example of Landsat-D (a satellite that collected information on natural resources), which was then being supplied to China but not the Soviet Union. During this meeting, although there were advances in cooperation, the Chinese were reluctant to rely on the U.S. security umbrella. They still

By the time Geng Biao had completed his visit to the United States, technical exchanges were under way and there was a broader basis for cooperation on strategic issues. As a result of these discussions, later arrangements were made to send to the United States delegations of Chinese officers from the military academies as well as specialists in military logistics. In return, high-level U.S. army and navy officers would visit China.[56] During the 1980s there was rapid growth in military-to-military contacts, including exchanges of visits between the U.S. secretary of defense and the Chinese minister of defense, service chief visits, technology transfers and arms sales to China, and exchanges of academic specialists and training delegations. Although these interactions did not compare to the level of military exchanges that the United States had with Japan and South Korea, the two sides did develop very good working relations. The exchanges ended abruptly following the Tiananmen tragedy of 1989, however, and in the decades afterward were not fully restored.

Postponing Military Modernization

When Deng believed that the likelihood of war with the Soviet Union was reduced, he directed China's resources not toward military modernization but toward the other three modernizations, and, in particular, toward the priorities Chen Yun advocated—agriculture and light industry. Modernizing the military could wait. As he explained on March 19, 1979, three days after Chinese troops returned from Vietnam, to a meeting of the Military Commission on Science and Technology (*Kexue jishu zhuangbei weiyuanhui*), "It appears that at least for ten years there will not be a large-scale war in the world. We don't need to be in such a hurry. Now the number of troops is too large. We have to cut back. . . . We don't need to prepare all things. We need to pick a small number of projects and focus on them."[57] Deng took a long-term perspective, but perhaps he underestimated how long it would take China, despite its rapid growth, to modernize. He spoke of achieving modernization by 2000.

High-level military officials were less patient. Many had been waiting since the 1950s to acquire modern military equipment, and had been frustrated first by the Great Leap and the Cultural Revolution, and now because of Deng's new focus on the civilian economy. Deng had to explain over and over again to disappointed officers why it was in the national interest first to develop the civilian economy and then to modernize the military. Given his extensive military background, Deng was probably the only leader of his time with the authority, determination, and political skill to keep these officers from launching serious protests against this policy.

During the critical period in 1979 and early 1980, Deng remained chief-of-staff, surrounded by generals unhappy with the prospect of early retirement and with the news that the development of new weapons systems would be postponed. Yang Dezhi, who succeeded Deng as chief-of-staff, inherited responsibility for explaining why military modernization had to take a back seat to improvements in the civilian economy. As Yang acknowledged, "The broad masses of commanders and soldiers . . . are longing for rapidly changing our economic backwardness and the backwardness of our military technique and equipment. . . . Such feelings are completely understandable. However, it will . . . not be possible to achieve very great progress in the modernization of our national defense."[58] Geng Biao, who served briefly as defense minister, and Zhang Aiping, whom Deng appointed as defense minister in 1982 (and who had directed military science and technology policy since 1975), also had to explain Deng's strategy to disgruntled officers. In March 1983 Zhang put it very directly: "The military has to take the needs of other sectors into account and to carry out . . . strict budgeting within the scope allowed by the limited amount of funds."[59]

Throughout the 1980s, then, the Chinese government decreased the proportion of the budget going to the military. Although China's data are incomplete because income from military enterprises or extra-budgetary income is not included, according to official figures, Chinese military expenditures were 4.6 percent of GNP in 1979 when the reforms began, but declined continuously to 1.4 percent of GNP by 1991.[60] During the 1980s China's purchase of foreign arms was one-sixth the amount of Vietnam's purchases and one-half the amount of Taiwan's purchases, even though China's population was roughly twenty times that of Vietnam and fifty times that of Taiwan.[61] Moreover, given the inflation rate of nearly 100 percent from 1980 to 1989, U.S. analysts estimate that the nominal increase in the defense budget of about 30 percent translated into a decrease in actual funds available for the military during the decade.[62]

Deng's Military Team

Chinese Communist leaders have all repeated that the party commands the gun, but in a crucial power struggle, as Mao and Deng understood, allegiances among key military leaders would be critical. Deng sought both formal institutional and personal control over the military. He did not strenuously object to not being named premier, but it was important to gain institutional control over the military. After Hua was pushed aside in December 1980, Deng became chairman of the party's CMC; the post gave him unrivaled institutional control over military affairs. In 1987 Deng gave up his positions as vice chairman of the party and vice premier, but he remained chairman of the CMC until the fall of 1989, when he passed the position on to Jiang Zemin.

In selecting high officials for party and government posts, Deng sought the best person for the job, regardless of where they were from, whom they knew, or who recommended them. For high military positions, he wanted able people, but personal loyalty was also critical. In the military, the strongest bonds of loyalty were among those who had served in the same field army during the civil war. Just as Lin Biao had chosen for the highest military positions many officers from his Fourth Field Army, in 1980, when Deng was able to select his own officials in various military sectors, five of the eleven military-region commanders were comrades from his Second Field Army, including Qin Jiwei in the critical Beijing region.[63] Deng continued to rely on his former underlings throughout his tenure as China's top military leader. Of the six military members on the CMC in the late 1980s, half were from the Second Field Army. These included Defense Minister Qin Jiwei and director of the General Political Department Yang Baibing. Of the other three military positions on the CMC, one seat each went to someone who had served in the third or fourth field armies.[64] Of the seventeen full generals that Deng commissioned in 1988, ten were from the Second Field Army.

For key military positions, others chosen who had not served in the Second Field Army still had personal ties of loyalty to Deng. After Hua was finally removed as head of the CMC (in December 1980), Deng appointed Yang Shangkun as secretary general of the CMC. Yang, also from Sichuan and only three years younger than Deng, had worked closely with Deng from 1956 to 1966 when Yang was head of the party General Office and Deng was party general secretary. Yang had the ready confidence to communicate easily with Deng. In September 1982 Yang was promoted to first vice chairman of the CMC, in charge of daily work. He was a good manager and in effect became an extension of Deng on the CMC, representing Deng's views and reporting to Deng the views of other CMC members. Deng's confidence that Yang could manage military matters freed him to concentrate on other issues.

In February 1980, after Deng had completed the transition and named his own people, he resigned as chief-of-staff and passed the job of managing the PLA's daily affairs to Yang Dezhi, who had commanded the forces of the Kunming Military Region during the attack on Vietnam and had proved very loyal to Deng. In 1982 Deng appointed Zhang Aiping as minister of defense, and because the ministry had been reduced in power after Lin Biao's plane crash in 1971, he also named him to the critical position of deputy secretary general of the CMC. While serving under Deng in 1975, Zhang had been very effective in organizing plans for the modernization of military technology. His strategic sense of high-tech military weapons development and strong management skills made him the right person to help China sort out its priorities and lay the groundwork for the development of high technology.

Expanding the Range of Defense Strategies

The defense strategy that Deng inherited from Chairman Mao rested heavily on a combination of two extremes: "People's War" and nuclear weapons. The "People's War," whereby local people were mobilized to harass and wear down a better-equipped occupying army, had been well-adapted to the long-term Japanese occupation during World War II. It had also helped discourage the Soviets from long-term occupation when they had thrust into China in 1969, and indeed it was still a way of discouraging another Soviet assault, making the low likelihood of such an attack even lower. Lacking a broad economic base, Mao could not hope to modernize the military in all areas, so he concentrated his resources on those he considered to be the most critical: rockets and nuclear weapons (China first exploded an atomic bomb in 1964 and a thermonuclear device in 1967).[65] He would leave his successors with a small nuclear arsenal that could not compare in number or sophistication with that of the U.S. or Soviet nuclear arsenals, as well as a modest rocket and satellite capacity (China launched its first satellite in 1970).[66] Research on missiles, satellites, and submarines generally had been protected during the Cultural Revolution.[67] Even so, during the Cultural Revolution China made only modest progress in military technology, and it fell far behind the United States and the Soviet Union, each of which had invested heavily to keep pace with the other.

By the time Deng came to power, Soviet advances in long-range aircraft and rocketry made the "third front" factories that Mao had moved inland, away from China's borders, vulnerable to attack. But Deng, like Mao before him, believed that the threat of a People's War as well as nuclear weapons reduced the likelihood that China would be attacked, even by an enemy with far superior military technology.[68] Yet China needed to adapt to Soviet technical advances. Deng directed that the Chinese military should begin making preparations to fight a "People's War under modern conditions," a concept that Su Yu, hero of the Huai Hai campaign and then in charge of planning for advanced weaponry, had begun to develop in 1977. At a conference in the fall of 1980, Chinese military leaders began to develop a consensus around strategic guidelines that would provide a more active defense than passively luring the enemy deep into Chinese territory.[69] In June 1981 Song Shilun, commandant of the Chinese Academy of Military Science, spelled out in some detail the meaning of "under modern conditions." In the case of a full-scale military invasion, the Chinese would respond, as in the Mao era, with a People's War, wearing down the enemy. But Song explained that additional responses were needed because China could not abandon its cities, and because modern technology required longer supply lines, defense of industrial sites, more coordination between ground and air forces, and more specialization. Therefore, (1) the PLA would use positional warfare to stop the enemy before it penetrated deeply into China, (2) China would use not only infantry but also combined arms, including planes, to resist the enemy, (3) China would prepare to protect longer logistic lines than those in the immediate locality of the fighting, and (4) the army would turn over its political tasks—which in Mao's day had been handled by military political commissars—to civilians so it could concentrate on military tasks. Deng did not formulate this analysis, but he supported these efforts by the PLA to reorient its existing doctrine, structure, and training, as well as its recruitment programs, to fit these "modern conditions."[70]

When the reform and opening began, China had not yet taken part in the complex discussions and calculations about how to prevent nuclear war that had preoccupied specialists in the United States and Soviet Union. By the mid-1980s, however, Chinese graduate students and young research scholars who went abroad to study strategic thinking in the West were returning home and beginning to introduce these new more sophisticated calculations. After developing nuclear weapons, the Chinese had always planned on retaining a second-strike capacity. But now the discussions widened. Instead of focusing only on People's War and nuclear attack, the Chinese began to consider the possibility of limited nuclear attacks and tactical nuclear weapons, which might prevent a war from escalating into an all-out nuclear conflict.[71]

Deng inherited from the Mao era a navy that was small and completely outdated. In 1975 when Deng was at the helm under Mao, the navy under Su Zhenhua's command had submitted a new development plan. After 1978, as foreign trade, and especially as imports of oil, hard coal, and iron ore began to pick up, Chinese planners became more concerned with ensuring the safety of China's sea lanes. China also began to expand energy exploration in the South China Sea as well as in the Bohai Gulf, thus necessitating protection of exploration in disputed territories.[72] But as China began to consider developing capacities to respond to these new challenges, Deng urged restraint. In a talk to naval officers in July 1979, Deng still placed limits on naval development plans, explaining that the navy's role was defensive, to protect the waters near China, and that China did not have any ambitions to become a dominant power.[73]

Even in high-priority military sectors—missiles, satellites, and submarines—the emphasis remained on developing technology rather than large-scale production, with the hope that if the need arose, China could produce more weaponry quickly. China tested its first intercontinental ballistic missile (ICBM) in 1980 and began deployment shortly thereafter. Work had begun on a nuclear-powered submarine in 1958, and in 1982 China successfully tested its first submarine-launched ballistic missile.[74] Deployment of such systems continued on a modest scale during Deng's era.[75] Research and production developed much more rapidly after Deng's era, in response to President Lee Teng-hui's 1995 efforts to bring about Taiwan's independence.

After 1984, as the Soviet Union became increasingly bogged down in Afghanistan and overstretched in its attempts to keep up with U.S. military advances, the CMC formally concluded what Deng had personally determined much earlier, that the risk of an all-out war with the Soviet Union was low. In a speech to the CMC in 1985 Deng summed up his views on global threats saying, "We have changed our view that the danger of war is imminent." He said only the two superpowers could launch a major war, and they were not a concern; because both have "suffered setbacks and met with failures, neither dares to start a war."[76] It followed that Deng could continue to keep down military expenditures to channel resources to advance the civilian economy.

While the risks of all-out war with the superpowers had decreased, Deng and his colleagues judged that the risk of small-scale wars had increased as the bipolar world was being replaced by a multipolar world. Japan, India, Vietnam, South Korea, and Europe had strengthened their economic and military presence on the world stage. The PLA, therefore, should focus its planning and training efforts on the possibility of small local wars on China's periphery, which were more within China's military capacity than fighting an all-out war with a superpower. Each of China's military regions, which with the downsizing of military forces had by then been consolidated from eleven to seven, was to adapt its planning and preparations to the nature of the potential adversary, as well as to the geography and climate of their border areas. The military in turn appealed for more funds to develop key technologies required for local wars, such as tanks, artillery, aircraft avionics, and command and control systems. As they made their plans, the strategists had in mind Deng's penchant for rapid, decisive strikes. Strategists studied carefully other nations' experiences using such strategies, particularly Britain's operations during the Falklands War and Israel's invasion of Lebanon. By responding quickly, other nations and world opinion would not have time to influence the outcome.[77]

Toward a Smaller, Better-Trained Force

On March 12, 1980, shortly after launching his administration, Deng presented an overview of military issues to the Standing Committee of the CMC. He said that the military was confronted with four issues: (1) reducing "bloatedness," (2) reforming the organizational structure, (3) improving training, and (4) strengthening political and ideological initiatives. "Unless we reduce 'bloatedness,' we won't be able to raise the army's combat effectiveness and work efficiency. . . . Our policy is to reduce manpower and use the money thus saved to renew equipment. If some of the savings can be used for economic construction, so much the better. . . . The main purpose of our streamlining is to reduce the number of unnecessary non-combatants and of personnel in leading and commanding organs—mainly officials."[78]

Party leaders had long considered establishing a mandatory retirement age for high-level party and military leaders, but it had not yet been established. Deng continued, "We must have a retirement system. . . . Since the army has to fight, the retirement age for military officials should be lower than for civilians."[79] Retirement was a sticky issue. Officers had no term limits and because of their "contributions to the revolution," they felt a sense of entitlement. Although Deng gave final approval for all important military decisions, no military issue would take more of his personal time and energy than the downsizing of the senior military leadership. As Deng explained, "Most armies around the world don't spend much on personnel. They spend most of their funds on equipment. We have a very bad situation. We spend too much on personnel. We have too many people directing things and not many people to fight."[80] The issue of retirement would come up in virtually all his meetings with military officers during his years as paramount leader.

Throughout the 1980s, Deng continued the efforts he began in 1975 to get officials to draw up new tables of organization with reduced numbers, then to implement the policies and plug all the loopholes that creative officers would invent to evade the policy. He encouraged civilian units to find places for both senior retirees and ordinary enlisted men completing their terms of service. To make retirement more appealing, he allowed high officials to retain many of the perquisites they had in the military—housing, the use of cars, access to medical treatment, and even substantial income. After he established the Central Advisory Commission in 1982, many of the senior military leaders were honored with membership, and retired.

At an enlarged June 1985 meeting of the CMC assembled to promote a reduction in the size of the PLA by one million, some had argued that such a reduction would shrink military capacity, leaving China vulnerable in a conflict. Deng answered them by saying that in the event of war it was important to reduce the size of the military to engage in efficient military operations.[81] Deng would, however, retain a large reserve force of veterans who could be called on in case of conflict. The large-scale troop reduction began in 1985, and it was basically completed in 1988. From 1980 to 1989 local civilian institutions were pressed to find civilian positions for some 1,540,000 military officers who retired.[82] But the end of rural collectivization in 1982 had eliminated many positions that typically had provided opportunities for demobilized servicemen.[83] To help with post-mobilization employment, Deng suggested that the army should do more to train people for jobs that would enable them later to play a role in the civilian economy.[84]

To find employment opportunities for soldiers being discharged, Deng proposed special training courses. In March 1980 he told the Standing Committee of the CMC, "I suggest that training courses of various kinds be run for those officials whose posts are eliminated. What kind of training? To prepare them for the professions and trades they will enter."[85] Deng also continued the work he had begun in 1975 of reopening and expanding military academies and military training institutes. At the pinnacle stood the National

Defense University, opened in September 1985 to train promising officers. In his address to the enlarged meeting of the CMC in March 1980, Deng reminded his audience that he considered training so essential that it should be considered of strategic importance. "In the absence of war," he said, "training is the only way to improve the army's quality." Still, by comparison with the U.S. and USSR militaries, Chinese training programs for preparing troops for high-tech war remained at an early stage of development.[86]

Commercializing Military Production and Services

When Deng became preeminent leader, he was acutely aware that both the civilian defense industries that produced most of the equipment used by the military, and the military enterprises that were directly under military control, were drains on the government budget, inefficient, and incapable of producing weapons and equipment that could match those produced by the advanced military powers. Deng therefore worked to close down inefficient plants and to improve supervision at others to increase efficiency.

To achieve these goals, Deng encouraged both the civilian defense industries and the military's own factories to produce more civilian goods that could compete in open markets. He began promoting this strategy even before the Third Plenum when he declared that China should depart from the inefficient Soviet model of strictly separating military and civilian production.[87] The new policy helped to satisfy the pent-up consumer demand for basic consumer goods, reduce burdens on the state budget, and provide continued employment for personnel who might otherwise have been laid off.

The competitive pressures on these factories were reflected in factory closings: from 1979 to 1982, nearly half of the factories in the civilian defense sector either closed down or operated at greatly reduced capacity.[88] Those that remained open during the late 1980s were successful in expanding into civilian production, especially consumer electronics but also products as diverse as pianos, refrigerators, washing machines, baby carriages, hunting rifles, and even passenger aircraft.[89] To enable the defense industries to better respond to the markets, many companies were allowed to become profit-seeking corporations independent of ministry control.[90] In 1978, 92 percent of the value of the goods in civilian state enterprises in the defense sector was produced for the military and 8 percent for the civilian economy. By 1982, military production in these factories had dropped to 66 percent and by 1992, when Deng stepped down, it had dropped to 20 percent.[91]

In addition, Deng urged the military itself to make available some of its facilities and technology for the civilian economy. For example, on November 1, 1984, in a talk to a forum called by the CMC to discuss the military's role in the civilian economy, Deng suggested that military airports could be opened for civilian use and naval ports could be used for both civilian and military purposes. As the new policy took hold, military units turned mess halls into commercial restaurants, guest houses into commercial hotels, supply centers into stores, and military hospitals into military-civilian hospitals that accepted paying civilian patients. Between 1985 and 1990 the value of production by PLA enterprises increased by an estimated 700 percent.[92]

Another area that offered opportunities for diversification away from military-only purposes was agriculture. State farms run by the military were encouraged to diversify their products and, after the creation of markets, to sell some of their produce in local food markets. Because the military had access to a considerable amount of land, it could also rent out land to developers and other government units or to enterprises for a fee—or even become a stakeholder in these new enterprises. As foreign firms began seeking sites to set up factories, many military farms supplied some of their valuable real estate in exchange for equity in joint ventures that drew on Western technologies.[93]

When the military shifted to civilian-related business activities, officers had a chance to improve their military units' housing, medical care, and recreational facilities. Those who were being retired were assisted with housing and given other benefits. Even the situation for ordinary soldiers improved when their military units made profits.[94] These new sources of income helped to make military officers and servicemen stakeholders in Deng's reforms.

One of the biggest problems Deng faced was in adapting inland civilian and military factories to the new market economy. It was almost impossible to turn factories deep in inner China, with such high transport costs, into profitable enterprises that could compete in open markets with those along the coast. In 1978, more than half of defense industrial production was located in inner China, in the "third front" factories that Mao had moved inland to reduce vulnerability to foreign attack. Now that China had developed peaceful relations with other countries, some factories, or at least parts of factories, were allowed to relocate to the coast where they could not only reduce transport costs, but also make better use of foreign technology and management strategies as well as commercial opportunities.[95] For example, inland factories producing electronic products for the military established branches in Shenzhen to produce radios, TVs, calculators, and other electronic equipment for consumers both at home and abroad. Doing so gave them faster access to foreign technology as well as to civilian markets, as well as the opportunity to transfer new technologies to any remaining inland factories.

In 1978 China's military technology was far more advanced than its civilian technology, but Deng took an interest both in how technology could be "spun off" from military to civilian uses and how it could be "spun on" from advanced global civilian technology to Chinese military uses. Deng took great interest, for example, in learning how Japan, immediately after World War II, had begun converting its military industry to civilian industry.[96] But he also learned from Japan's experience in making good use of "spin on." On June 28–29, 1978, he suggested that China should learn from Japan's handling of shipbuilding after World War II: it made great advances in civilian shipbuilding by transforming the production processes, which then enabled Japan not only to sell ships, but also to build more modern ships for the navy.[97]

In 1982, following the 12th Party Congress, large parts of the PLA were converted to civilian status and given opportunities to earn money in the marketplace—a move that helped reduce the size of the PLA after 1985. The large military railway and engineering construction units, for instance, were placed under the Ministry of Railways and the Capital Construction Corps. And the civilian construction companies that played the key role in transforming Shenzhen from a rural town to a large city within a decade were largely formed from former military construction units that had been demobilized.

Prior to these changes it was rather easy to engage in science and technology planning, but the complexities due to the opening to global civilian technology required new broader coordination. In 1982 a new organization, the Commission for Science, Technology, and Industry for National Defense, was established to provide some overall coordination of planning for the rapid changes in civilian and military technology. And in 1986, the "863 program" was established as a new cooperative program between civilians and the military for the development of advanced technology.[98]

The commercialization of military operations in the 1980s was a messy, confusing process that created nightmares for some bureaucrats trying to coordinate the process. But in the end it brought many of the benefits that Deng had intended. It eased the demands on the government budget, helped meet pent-up consumer demand, assisted firms in becoming more efficient, improved living conditions for both officers and ordinary soldiers, provided employment opportunities for those discharged from military service, and enabled the advances in civilian technology and efficiency to be used to improve military production. Even so, it was just a start. Although Deng's redirection of the national defense industries and military enterprises led to some progress in the 1980s, the process of relocating from inner China to the coastal areas, of overcoming the bureaucracy, and of upgrading personnel would require several decades to complete.

Despite all the advantages of the commercialization of military activities, the mixing of military and private affairs also created opportunities for corruption and greed that detracted from the spirit of dedication to the military mission. Many military leaders became concerned not only about illegal profiteering, but also about the erosion of the patriotic fighting spirit due to the new preoccupation with making money. After several years of struggling with these problems, lower-level military units were forbidden to engage in commercial activities. Higher-level, specialized commercial activities continued, however, and although many PLA businesses failed, some joint ventures spawned in the early years of reform became successful enterprises, with a few later emerging as world-class international businesses.

A Foundation for a Modern Military

The Persian Gulf War of 1991 showed leaders how much military technology in other countries had advanced in the 1980s and just how far behind China had fallen while Deng was restraining the military budget and channeling resources to the civilian economy. Yet by keeping the risk of conflict low, Deng succeeded in promoting rapid economic growth without sacrificing the nation's security.

In 1995, however, Deng's successors, confronted with a real possibility that President Lee Teng-hui might declare an independent Taiwan, decided the risk was sufficiently great that China must be prepared militarily not only to attack Taiwan but also to deter the United States from supporting Taiwan in the event of a conflict. China would raise the cost of U.S. involvement by endeavoring to deny American ships, planes, and troops the access they would need to defend Taiwan. Since 1995, under Jiang Zemin's concerted drive for military modernization, the increase in the military budget has been far greater than the increase in GNP. Chinese military modernization was soon extended beyond denying Americans access to Taiwan; because China was dependent on sea lanes for its energy, it began to develop a navy and to aim to become a top military power overall. Deng did not begin that process nor did he plan for his successors to build up a modern military. But he left his successors with a smaller, better-educated military force; a better understanding of the requirements for modern warfare; and a stronger civilian economic and technical base that his successors could build on to modernize China's military.

19

The Ebb and Flow of Politics

On August 18, 1980, a Chinese citizen gave one of the most biting and comprehensive criticisms of Chinese officials made during the entire Deng era. In scathing terms, he accused them of abusing power; divorcing themselves from reality and the masses; spending time and effort putting up impressive fronts; indulging in empty talk; sticking to rigid ways of thinking; overstaffing administrative organs; being dilatory, inefficient, and irresponsible; failing to keep their word; circulating documents endlessly without solving problems; shifting responsibility to others; assuming the airs of mandarins; reprimanding and attacking others at every turn; suppressing democracy; deceiving superiors and subordinates; being arbitrary and despotic and practicing favoritism; offering bribes; and participating in other corrupt practices. The citizen? Deng Xiaoping.[1] Like Mao, he was seeking to ensure that officials maintained the support of the people.

When Deng gave this speech in August 1980, Communist parties in Eastern European countries were losing popular support. A month before his speech, Poland's labor union, Solidarity, had launched Poland's largest and longest-lasting strike. Many Chinese leaders, initially sympathetic with Solidarity, thought it was reasonable for workers to have their own organization. But they also worried about what would happen if Chinese workers went out on strike. Deng and Hu Yaobang, trying to reassure Chinese officials who worried about similar disruptions, said that Chinese leaders, unlike Eastern European leaders, did not have to bend to unpopular demands from the Soviet Union. Furthermore, the reforms in China beginning with the Third Plenum were popular with the working people.[2] Nonetheless, Deng and Hu Yaobang were sufficiently concerned that they decided that to reduce the risk of such problems in China, they should expand freedoms, provide opportunities for people to voice legitimate complaints against Chinese officials, and make an effort to resolve the problems causing these complaints.

Deng's speech of August 18, 1980 was a high point of Deng's efforts to grant more freedoms. In the speech, he gave a positive evaluation of democracy. He did not go so far as to advocate voting, nor did he suggest changing the role of the Communist Party. In fact, he criticized Western democracy, using the well-known code words "bourgeois thinking," "ultra-individualism," and "anarchism." But Deng aimed his sharpest criticism at "feudalism"—the code word for leftism—and its vicious attacks on those who spoke out. His appeal for more freedoms and for party leaders to listen to criticism aroused expectations among intellectuals who even years later pointed to this speech as a beacon of hope.

Within weeks after the speech, as the Polish situation dragged on, the atmosphere in high Chinese party circles began to change. Leaders started to worry that Deng had given too much encouragement to protestors and that events in China could quickly spin out of control, as they had in Poland. A long letter from Hu Qiaomu to General Secretary Hu Yaobang, written scarcely a month after Deng's speech, helped crystallize support for a firmer response to disorder. Hu Qiaomu's letter also reflected the views of Chen Yun, the former union leader who had helped organize demonstrations in Shanghai but had told workers in the Jiangxi Soviet that because the proletariat was in charge, one of the major responsibilities of the labor union was to increase production. In his letter, Hu Qiaomu warned that an independent labor union could enable dissidents to unite and cause great difficulties.

Hu Yaobang, who was more sympathetic to independent worker organizations in China, did not respond to Hu Qiaomu's letter. He continued to believe that the real lesson from Poland was that China should speed up reform and opening.[3] But the tide had already turned. On October 9, two weeks after Hu Qiaomu sent his letter, the party Secretariat distributed it, in a slightly revised form, to various units. Wang Renzhong, conservative head of the Propaganda Department, also sent out a directive saying that discussion of Deng's August speech should end. And on December 25, 1980, at the closing session of the Central Party Work Conference, Deng, backpedaling, declared that they should proceed cautiously with political reforms.[4]

Deng's reactions to the 1980 Polish strikes resembled Mao's reactions to the Hungarian and Polish uprisings in 1956. First, allow more open criticism to help correct some of the worst features of the bureaucracy and to win over those critics who felt some changes were needed. But if hostility to the party threatened party control, clamp down. Having noted how Mao's virulent anti-rightist campaign in 1957 had destroyed the support of intellectuals, Deng in 1980 tried to walk a fine line between curbing expressions of freedom and retaining intellectuals' active support for modernization.

Deng did not engage in a full-blown campaign against intellectuals as Mao had (with Deng's help) in 1957. Still, it was clear that Deng was clamping down. In his December speech, Deng did not directly disavow anything he said in his August speech and he continued to use the term "democracy" positively, but he insisted also on "democratic centralism," meaning that once a party decision was made, party members were expected to carry it out. In addition, after Hu Qiaomu's letter was distributed, Deng was careful not to appear as permissive as he had in his August speech, and he reiterated the importance of following the "four cardinal principles." Deng did not give up the idea of undertaking political reform, but he would only bring it up again when he judged the time to be ripe. That time would not arrive until 1986.

The Retirement of Senior Officials

In his speech of August 18, 1980, Deng took up another very divisive issue: "The primary task [of older comrades] is to help the Party organizations find worthy successors . . . [who will] take the 'front-line' posts while the older comrades give them the necessary advice and support."[5] There was then no retirement age, and many senior officials were dragging their feet in the search for successors. Having been removed during the Cultural Revolution for almost a decade during the peak of their careers, they believed that they had sacrificed themselves for the cause of the party and now had only a few brief years left to play the roles they had long hoped for. Furthermore, these senior officials were reluctant to give up not only the power but also the perquisites of office: housing, access to a chauffeur-driven car, a staff of assistants, a seat at important meetings, and fancy banquets.

At this point, the party had not developed an overall policy on retirement for high-level officials. Managing the issue of retirement at lower levels was not a problem: the higher-level officials established the rules and made the lower levels implement them. The problem was how to deal with the retirement of high-level leaders in Beijing. The party leaders were able to reach a consensus on the need for general rules regarding their retirement. But the devil was in the details—how to deal with the retirement of each of the top several hundred leaders given that China was entering a critical period during which these senior officials were needed to train and cultivate the next generation of leaders.

In his speech of August 18, Deng laid out a proposed solution: the creation of a high-level Central Advisory Commission (CAC) that would bestow on senior officials honor and the perquisites of their positions. Senior officials had no difficulty discerning that Deng meant "honor without power." In July 1975, he had proposed a similar solution to the problem of military retirement. In effect, the senior members of the Politburo Standing Committee would be transferred to the CAC as core members.

At the time, Deng was himself planning to retire within the next several years. Several days after his August speech, when journalist Oriana Fallaci asked if he was going to give up his post of vice premier, Deng replied, "I will not be the only one to resign. All other comrades of the older generation are giving up their concurrent posts. . . . Previously . . . there was life tenure in leading posts. . . . [This] institutional defect . . . was not evident in the sixties because we were then in the prime of life . . . it would be better for us old comrades to take an enlightened attitude."[6]

A few weeks later, Deng would express his exasperation that the older generation did not take an "enlightened attitude." On December 25, at the end of a ten-day conference to begin preparations for the Sixth Plenum and the 11th Party Congress, Deng complained, "In the past year the Central Committee has repeatedly emphasized that veteran officials should make the selection and training of middle-aged and young officials their first and most solemn duty. If we fail to do other work well, naturally we ought to make self-criticisms; but if we fail to do this work well, we will have made a mistake of historic magnitude."[7]

In 1982 the CAC was formally established and Deng hoped that the members would give up their regular positions. Membership required forty years of party membership and leadership experience. Deng Xiaoping served as the first chairman, with the special right to take part in meetings of the Standing Committee of the Politburo.[8] All 172 members appointed were allowed to retain their full salaries, ranks, and perquisites, but they were to cease serving on regular decision-making bodies.[9] Deng announced that the CAC would remain in existence for ten to fifteen years. He explained that it was created because the members had special revolutionary experience that would be needed during the transition period.

Deng's effort to give honor and perquisites without power was only partially successful. Many senior officials, including Chen Yun, Wang Zhen, and Song Renqiong, became members of the CAC, but also retained their previous positions. After they retired, Zhao Ziyang recorded that during the 1980s he and Hu Yaobang were like secretary generals, in effect office managers, since power throughout the decade was still in the hands of Deng, Chen Yun, Li Xiannian, and "the six-person small group" (Bo Yibo, Peng Zhen, Deng Yingchao, Song Renqiong, Yang Shangkun, and Wang Zhen). Deng was paramount, but he simply did not have the absolute power required to force all the others to retire. In fact, in March 1982, in response to pressure from senior officials, it was announced that because of the size of the party and the country and for the sake of stable leadership, it was necessary for "a few dozen old comrades to remain in the central leading posts of the Party and the State."[10] But Deng did establish the principle that the CAC would come to an end when these revolutionary veterans passed from the scene. In the future, too, all positions would have term limits. As planned, the CAC was abolished in 1992. It had given its members honor and it had reduced but not entirely eliminated their power until Deng himself fully stepped down in 1992.

"Unrequited Love" and Cultural Limits

In July 1981, Hu Qiaomu and Deng Liqun asked Deng for his judgment on whether the recently completed movie *Unrequited Love* should be made available to the general public. The movie, which was based on a very popular drama, was brought to Deng's attention because it was controversial and had the potential of being one of the biggest hits in years. The screenplay, *Bitter Love (Kulian)*, which had appeared in the magazine *October (Shiyue)* in September 1979, told of an artist who had been forced to flee China during the Japanese occupation. After leading a good life abroad, he decided in 1949 to return to China to help his motherland. For having gone abroad, he was always considered suspect and punished, but he continued to dedicate himself to his country. When the artist's daughter wished to go abroad, the artist was reluctant to grant his permission. In frustration, she said to her father, "You love the motherland, but does your nation love you?" Shortly after this conversation, the artist, when attempting to flee from the Red Guards who hounded him, collapsed and died. In the movie version that Deng reviewed, the father, while reflecting on his daughter's question as he trudged along in the snow, fell and died, leaving his body in the shape of a big question mark set against the white snow.

After viewing the movie, Deng declared that it "gives the impression that the Communist Party and the socialist system are bad." He acknowledged that the movie was well done, which, he said, made it all the more dangerous: "The movie vilifies the party to such an extent that one wonders what has happened to the author's party spirit."[11] Deng's decision provided a guideline for propaganda officials trying to make difficult distinctions among the many stories of suffering during the Cultural Revolution.[12] What should be prohibited is what reflects badly on the party as a whole and what should be permitted is what reflects badly only on certain individuals.

In his effort to create a better atmosphere than that which had existed during Mao's era, Deng allowed the author of the play, Bai Hua, to remain in the party, even though he was criticized. At the time, Deng also allowed Liu Binyan, a popular investigative journalist who had written vivid firsthand accounts of corrupt officials, to remain a party member. Even Hu Qiaomu, the keeper of orthodoxy, said that documents coming from Beijing should drop the expression "literature in service of politics," which had alienated so many intellectuals. Hu Qiaomu substituted "literature in service of the people and in service of socialism," an expression that expanded the range of acceptable writing.[13]

But among the endless number of stories that were written about the past, it was impossible to draw a sharp line between those that were permissible and those that were not. Disagreements continued to rage. Less than two weeks after Deng's attack on *Unrequited Love,* at a Forum on Problems on the Ideological Battlefront called by the Propaganda Department, Deng Liqun and Hu Qiaomu tried to build on the momentum created by Deng's decision on *Unrequited Love* to build a stronger bulwark against literature criticizing communism and the Communist Party. At that same meeting, however, Zhou Yang, who had been cultural czar in the 1950s, gave a rousing speech in favor of literary diversity that was enthusiastically received by the audience. After his personal suffering in the Cultural Revolution, Zhou Yang was now emerging as the champion of a literature that, as cultural czar, he would have criticized twenty-five years earlier. At this forum, Zhou Yang rhetorically asked whether it was better for culture to be like a stagnant pond or the roaring Yangtze. His answer: better to have the roaring Yangtze, even if it did carry a little sediment.

The enthusiastic support of the audience for Zhou Yang placed Hu

Qiaomu, who acknowledged that there were differences among comrades, in a difficult position. But he persisted in saying that it was important to resist "bourgeois liberalization," a term that he, Deng Liqun, and Deng Xiaoping himself would use throughout the 1980s to criticize those leaders whom they considered too enamored with the freedoms in the West.[14]

Wang Zhen Tightens Up the Party School, 1982–1983

For Chinese youth and many intellectuals, the winds of freedom that they felt from the West after 1978 were exhilarating. But high-level officials disagreed among themselves about how much freedom could be given to the public (many of whom had suffered from political attacks), given that no one wanted to return to the chaos of the period before 1949 or of the Cultural Revolution. Hu Yaobang, the high official most sympathetic to intellectuals who wanted more freedoms and to local officials who wanted more flexibility, was under constant pressure from conservatives who were worried about the consequences of leniency. Deng, though always ready to enforce discipline when he deemed it necessary, continued to support Hu Yaobang, even when attacked by conservatives.

One important battleground was the Central Party School. After December 1978, Hu Yaobang had little time to devote to the Central Party School as its de facto president, but the staff that he supported there and the spirit of free inquiry that he encouraged continued to nurture promising young officials. Scholars in the theory section of the school enjoyed high regard for their role in preparing the article "Practice Is the Sole Criterion for Judging Truth" and for criticizing the "two whatevers." Three scholars—Wu Jiang, Sun Changjiang, and Ruan Ming—buoyed by the respect they enjoyed and with the support of the deputy head of the school, Feng Wenbin, continued to push for additional freedom of expression, much to the consternation of senior party officials, who feared an erosion of party discipline and principles. Wang Zhen and Chen Yun were particularly upset with the criticisms of the party that flourished in the permissive atmosphere, which had been reported to them by Deng Liqun after he had visited and lectured at the Central Party School. In August 1981, the party Central Organization Department sent a team to the school to investigate the three scholars. Chen Yun wrote a letter to the head of academic training at the school declaring that just as the Whampoa Military Academy had turned out disciplined young military officers, so too he hoped the Central Party School would train disciplined party officials, not those who encourage criticism of the party.

When the question of a new president of the Central Party School arose in 1981, Hu Yaobang supported the appointment of Xiang Nan, an enlightened, well-educated party official who later became party secretary of Fujian province. Chen Yun, however, supported the appointment of Wang Zhen as a way to rein in permissiveness at the school.[15] Progressive party members were outraged by the possibility of a man whom they regarded as crude, rustic, and ill-informed about the wider world leading some of the country's most enlightened scholars.[16] Nevertheless, Deng Xiaoping approved the appointment and Wang Zhen took over the Central Party School in 1982.

Upon assuming power at the school, Wang immediately removed Feng Wenbin and expelled Wu Jiang, Ruan Ming, and Sun Changjiang. Ruan Ming was permitted to migrate to the United States, where he wrote about his dismissal in great detail.[17] Sun Changjiang was appointed to a faculty position at a lesser university, Shoudu Teachers University—a move that Chen Yun supported. (Sun once joked that he was thankful that Wang Zhen sent him to the smallest university, not the largest elementary school.[18]) And Wu Jiang was transferred to the Chinese Academy of Social Sciences (CASS).

Apart from cleaning out faculty who were considered too permissive, Wang Zhen played no role at the school. Instead, Chen Yun, who despite his political conservatism believed in high educational standards, arranged for Jiang Nanxiang, a well-educated intellectual, to become the new de facto head of the school. Jiang upheld the school's intellectual standards while placing limits on the free expression of ideas. Overall, the attack on faculty members and redirection of intellectuals were understood as indirect criticisms of Hu Yaobang, who had created the freer atmosphere in the first place.

Wang Zhen and Chen Yun also supported efforts to establish firmer control over the Propaganda Department. Chen Yun had claimed that the leadership of the party would not survive if it could not do two things well: economic work and propaganda work. Wang Zhen and Chen Yun regarded Wang Renzhong, head of the Propaganda Department after Hu Yaobang, as sufficiently conservative, but he did not prove to be an effective leader. On March 23, 1982, then, Deng Xiaoping appointed Deng Liqun to replace him.

Much as Mao in 1975 had supported the Gang of Four to keep strict ideological control while he allowed Deng to provide overall executive leadership, so in 1982 Deng assigned Deng Liqun to hold in check criticisms of the party, while allowing Hu Yaobang to continue directing party activities.[19] Although Deng Xiaoping was not concerned about maintaining ideological orthodoxy per se, he was determined to avoid having permissiveness lead to the publication of articles and stories that disparaged the role of the party.

Chen Yun's Criticism of Hu Yaobang

Another battleground was over the flexibility that Hu Yaobang was granting to local officials—a struggle that came to a head with Chen Yun's attack on Hu Yaobang on March 17, 1983. In January 1983, while Zhao Ziyang was on a month-long trip to eleven African countries, Hu Yaobang had assumed some of Zhao's responsibilities in supervising the government. Hu's style, however, was much more freewheeling than Zhao's. For instance, when Hu, aware of coal shortages, traveled to local areas that mined coal, he encouraged the people to do all they could to increase their production. He had not considered what would happen when people turned to strip mining, causing great environmental damage, nor did he anticipate that private mine owners would often fail to take elementary safety precautions, leading to many mining accidents. In the eyes of the cautious planners, Hu Yaobang was an undisciplined populist who did not adequately consider the broader consequences of his actions and did not take seriously the national economic plans that they had so carefully crafted.

When Chen Yun heard reports of Hu Yaobang's lack of regard for the economic plans, he was livid. On March 14, Chen reported his views to Deng.[20] The very next day Deng called in Hu Yaobang, Zhao Ziyang, and Hu Qiaomu to complain of Hu Yaobang's lax leadership.[21] And on March 17, 1983, during a joint meeting of the Standing Committee of the Politburo and the party Secretariat, Zhao Ziyang, without mentioning Hu Yaobang by name, criticized harshly Hu's activities, which he argued had interfered with disciplined control of the economy. Despite Zhao Ziyang's later protestations to the contrary, allies of Hu Yaobang were convinced that Zhao went far beyond what could be considered necessary criticism.[22]

At that same March 17 meeting, Chen Yun made ten points:

1. The readjustment policy had been very successful and without it the economy would be in serious trouble.
2. The years until 2000 should be divided into two ten-year periods, with the first dedicated to building a solid base, without which the economy would be in trouble.

3. It is possible to temporarily use bank loans or the sale of gold to make up for budget deficits, but such budget deficits cannot be allowed to continue.

4. One must take seriously the reports of the ministries and commissions that present an overview of the economy.

5. It is incorrect to say that 156 projects in the First Five-Year plan went astray.

6. Gold reserves purchased in 1973–1974 following consultation with Li Xiannian were not excessive. (The decision to purchase this gold, made by Chen Yun earlier that year, was later considered a very wise decision since gold greatly increased in value over the following decade.)

7. The Planning Commission must acquire capital from the various ministries and regions and invest it in high-priority projects.

8. The party Secretariat and the State Council must both supervise and discuss economic issues, but overall economic leadership should fall under the party's Central Finance and Economics Leadership Small Group.

9. The wild use of capital investment funds in too many projects must be curtailed.

10. The party Secretariat (then under Hu Yaobang) may carry on research, but it must change its methods and show regard for the overall situation.

As soon as Chen Yun concluded, Deng, visibly upset by Chen Yun's attack on Hu Yaobang, whom he then still supported, concluded the meeting, saying that from then on, the party's Central Finance and Economics Leadership Small Group, led by Zhao, would be in charge of all economic work. Others should not interfere.[23]

Although Chen Yun's ten points all concerned keeping the economy under control, the last several points constituted a powerful attack on Hu Yaobang, and indirectly an attack on Deng's policies of trying to promote overly rapid growth. On the same day, Deng Liqun, without authorization, leaked the contents of Chen Yun's speech to the press. The next day, Deng Xiaoping called in Deng Liqun to criticize him for this violation of party discipline, but the damage had been done: Hu Yaobang's authority in the party had been weakened, to the extent that some officials wondered if Hu would remain in his post much longer.[24] Other officials who worked with Hu Yaobang and shared his views about expanding freedom of expression were furious at Deng Liqun.

Hu Yaobang was in a difficult position. The presence of more than one "popo" ("mother-in-law," the senior woman running the household) in Beijing made it difficult for Hu Yaobang to have real control over party organs. Hu had formal power and, with Deng's support, he still presided over meetings and gave directions on daily work. But he chose to spend much of his time away from Beijing, traveling around the country to encourage local officials and trying to clear up obstacles to modernization. During his years in office, Hu visited a total of 1,703 counties, more than 80 percent of all counties in the country, and 173 of the nation's 183 prefectures. His plan to visit the remaining ten prefectures was aborted only when he was removed from office in January 1987.[25]

Meanwhile, it was impossible to keep the heated differences between Chen Yun and Deng from key members of their staffs, and rumors of dissonance spread to the Hong Kong press. Deng could not have been pleased to have his chief assistant attacked in such a devastating way that his authority for carrying out his work was weakened.[26] And Chen Yun, who had supported Hu Yaobang's appointment as general secretary, could not have been pleased by Hu Yaobang's greater responsiveness to Deng and Deng's policies than to his own. But both party leaders knew that an open break would unleash powerful attacks from others, which would be devastating to the party, so they refrained from going public with their feud.

The Attack on Spiritual Pollution and the Reaction

In early 1983 outspoken liberal theorists were again promoting philosophical perspectives to expand the range of intellectual freedom, causing conservatives to worry that the authority of the Communist Party itself was being challenged by those who believed in principles higher than loyalty to the party. In January 1983, Wang Ruoshui, deputy editor of the *People's Daily*, wrote, "Socialist humanism . . . means resolutely discarding the 'all-round dictatorship' and cruel struggle in the ten-year period of internal disorder . . . doing away with the cult of the personality which deifies an individual and belittles the people, and upholding the principle that all men are equal before the truth and the law and that a citizen's personal freedom and dignity are inviolable."[27] Soon thereafter, at the Central Party School's celebration of the one hundredth anniversary of Karl Marx's death on March 7, Zhou Yang added his voice, arguing that alienation can exist not only in capitalist society but even in socialist society, when officials abuse their power and there is a lack of democracy and rule of law. Both Hu Qiaomu and Deng Liqun tried unsuccessfully to block Zhou Yang's speech from publication, but it was printed in the *People's Daily* on March 16 and had an enormous impact.[28] The idea that humanism and alienation were universal principles represented to Deng and other Chinese leaders a fundamental challenge to the ultimate authority of the party. Western notions of a transcendental God that could criticize the earthly rulers were not part of Chinese tradition.

Deng Xiaoping did not rush to stop all discussions of humanism and alienation, but by September 1983 he had concluded that the loose atmosphere had to be tightened. He asked Hu Qiaomu to prepare a speech taking a tougher line against those views that he labeled "spiritual pollution."[29] Deng acknowledged that problems do exist in socialist society but he declared that according to Marxism, "alienation" refers to the feelings of workers when their labor is exploited for the benefit of capitalists, so such a problem did not exist in socialist society. Deng's main targets were those who were attacking the authority of the Communist Party.[30]

Deng Liqun had criticized Hu Yaobang for putting patriotism before the Communist Party, but Deng Xiaoping personally did not choose between the two. Had Deng expressed his own personal assessment, he might have said that over the span of centuries, patriotism will be longer-lasting but that at least for many decades nothing could replace the party; it was absolutely essential to give full support to the party. Some young intellectuals who had suffered from the Cultural Revolution, Deng Xiaoping said, were now hiding out, engaging in clandestine activities and trying to settle accounts. Some who were filled with unscrupulous ambition would have to be removed from their positions and expelled from the party. The underlying problem? "Party discipline has been lax so that some bad people have been shielded." Deng's solution was that ideological workers should help educate people to "assess the past correctly, to understand the present, and to have firm faith in socialism and the leadership by the Party."[31] Officials in Beijing were aware that Deng's comments, like those of Chen Yun in March, contained implicit criticism of Hu Yaobang, who had been pushing to expand the range of freedom for intellectuals.

On October 12, 1983, at the Second Plenum of the Twelfth Central Committee, Deng Xiaoping expanded the criticism into a nationwide political campaign against spiritual pollution. As much as Deng felt reluctant to resort to political campaigns, which could upset the pace of work and antagonize all those threatened with criticism, he still found it difficult to curb "spiritual pollution" without a political campaign. This was the first political campaign to be launched since Deng had mounted the political stage in 1978. Still, to avoid the extremes of the earlier political campaigns, he began by warning: "The ruthless methods used in the past—the over-simplified, one-sided, crude, excessive criticism and merciless attacks—must never be repeated."[32]

Despite his warnings, some officials assigned to carry out the campaign inevitably resorted to the intimidating attacks with which they were familiar. But some sympathetic officials tried to soften the criticisms. When a group of bureau chiefs met to discuss how to campaign against humanism and against the idea that there could be "alienation" under socialism, Du Runsheng, a key adviser on rural issues, asked the group if they knew the meaning of "alienation." When most confessed that they were not too clear about it, Du asked how, then, could they ever expect peasants to understand what alienation means. It is ridiculous, Du said, to try to carry on such a campaign in the countryside. Wan Li, too, argued that the campaign should not be carried out in rural areas. Zhao Ziyang pleaded that the campaign not be allowed to interfere with the economy. Fang Yi argued that it should not be allowed to interfere with scientific areas. And Yu Qiuli, then head of the Political Department of the PLA, quickly stopped the campaign from reaching the army. These officials succeeded in restricting the scope of the campaign. After scarcely a month, Deng, trying to balance his sense of a need to set limits to criticisms of the party with the widespread opposition to political campaigns, allowed the campaign to wind down. On January 3, 1984, Hu Qiaomu gave a lengthy authoritative statement on alienation that essentially ended the campaign but left in place the boundaries limiting free expression.[33]

In the minds of many intellectuals, Deng Liqun was the person responsible for the campaign. As a result, he was placed on the defensive and underwent a self-criticism; he was accused of initiating another anti-rightist campaign.[34] Hu Deping, eldest son of Hu Yaobang, and Deng Pufang, eldest son of Deng Xiaoping, like other intellectuals, criticized Deng Liqun for carrying the campaign further than Deng Xiaoping had intended. Deng Liqun made it clear that Deng Xiaoping made the decision to launch the campaign. His refusal to protect his leader was not soon forgotten: at Deng Xiaoping's funeral some fifteen years later, Deng Pufang made it clear that Deng Liqun would not be welcome. Hu Qiaomu, under pressure from the outspoken intellectuals, later went so far as to say the anti-spiritual-pollution campaign was a mistake. Indeed, Deng Liqun, realizing that the struggle against spiritual pollution had not achieved its goals, told Hu Qiaomu a year later, on March 14, 1984, that "the struggle against spiritual pollution will be a long-lasting one."[35]

Deng chose to be relatively lenient in 1984–1985 to ease the burden on intellectuals, who were still stung by the aborted campaign. For instance, Wang Ruoshui, a scholar admired by many intellectuals for his strong convictions and courage, was allowed to continue to write about humanism, and even after being attacked in January 1984, he published in Hong Kong a defense of his position. He would not be purged from the party until late 1984.

Other writers, buoyed by Deng's leniency in curbing the campaign against spiritual pollution, reached a new peak of confidence during the Fourth Congress of the Chinese Writers Association, held from December 29, 1984, to January 5, 1985. The organizers of the congress had the courage not to invite Hu Qiaomu or Deng Liqun, who was still director of the Propaganda Department. At the congress, Hu Yaobang dutifully presented the official point of view that placed limits on free expression, but his attendance alone gave a measure of confidence to the participants. Conservatives, predictably, were outraged that he attended and failed to stop the outspoken criticisms. The bold writers elected as president of the congress someone who had been criticized by both Hu Qiaomu and Deng Liqun—Ba Jin, a leading novelist in the 1930s. The famous investigative reporter Liu Binyan, a former rightist and one of the most outspoken critics of the party's treatment of intellectuals, was elected senior vice president. Liu used the forum to criticize those who had attacked him during the campaign against spiritual pollution.

In assessing the overall importance of the meeting, the writer Xia Yan declared the congress to be the writers' Zunyi conference. Just as Mao had achieved independence from Soviet domination at Zunyi in January 1935, so too were Chinese writers breaking away and declaring their independence.[36] Such statements infuriated the conservatives. Although many of those present at the writers' congress were members of the Communist Party, Li Xiannian, upon hearing about the gathering from his son-in-law, Liu Yazhou, a PLA writer who had attended, denounced it as an anti-party meeting. Hu Qiaomu and Deng Liqun, too, were incensed by the rebellious spirit of the writers; Deng Liqun called the congress a "mess." On January 2, 1985, while the conference was still in session, Deng Xiaoping, informed of developments at the congress, summoned Hu Yaobang for a private talk. Following that talk with Deng, Hu Yaobang gave a speech at the close of the congress that was far more critical of the prevailing atmosphere than his earlier speech had been.[37]

Deng Xiaoping was furious about the audacious challenge to party authority that had occurred at the writers' congress. From Deng's perspective, Hu Yaobang was earning the goodwill of intellectuals by being an overly permissive official who failed to enforce party discipline. Moreover, Hu Yaobang's permissiveness made it appear that Deng Xiaoping was an arbitrary, overly strict authoritarian.[38]

Meanwhile, in an effort to achieve some common ground between the conservatives and intellectuals, Hu Qiaomu assisted Hu Yaobang in writing a speech for delivery at a February 8, 1985, party Secretariat meeting devoted to the party's handling of newspaper work.[39] Although the speech was basically conservative, in the draft Hu Qiaomu tried to balance the ideas of the intellectuals with those of the conservatives. He wrote that spiritual pollution should be opposed, but that the expression "spiritual pollution" should be rarely if ever used.[40] Deng Xiaoping was reportedly upset at Hu Qiaomu's change of tone and for backing down from placing limits on challenges to the authority of the party.[41]

In March 1985, during this atmosphere of greater freedom, leading investigative journalist Liu Binyan, who three decades earlier had been labeled a rightist, published *The Second Kind of Loyalty*, in which he contrasted party members who automatically accept orders from higher party officials with party members with a conscience who serve the ideals of the party. Liu Binyan's book hit a deep nerve among those who had agonized about whether to carry out party policy during the Great Leap and the Cultural Revolution. It also had a tremendous influence on idealistic Chinese youth who sought independence from the party. Deng, who always believed in the importance of party discipline, regarded Liu's message as a challenge to party leadership, and as a result in 1987 Liu was expelled from the party. Yet unlike Mao, Deng was not vindictive. In 1988 he allowed both Liu Binyan and Wang Ruoshui to go abroad. In addition, Deng Xiaoping, fully aware of how much Deng Liqun had done to alienate intellectuals, had him removed as head of the Propaganda Department in July 1985. He was replaced by Zhu Houze, who until then had been provincial party secretary in his home province of Guizhou.[42]

Even though Zhu Houze did not have full control of the Propaganda Department because there were still many conservatives there, his appointment was a great victory for those who sought more freedom. Officials familiar with the Propaganda Department commented that usually when a person becomes the head of the department, he becomes conservative because his job is to maintain party orthodoxy—but there was one exception: Zhu Houze. Zhu Houze's new approach, which he publicized as the three relaxations—more permissive, tolerant, and magnanimous (*kuan song, kuan rong, kuan hou*)—encouraged those party members who wished to express variant opinions.

Although Zhu Houze had suffered before and during the Cultural Revolution, because of his success in developing the backward province of Guizhou, he had been selected as a promising provincial official to attend the second year-long class at the Central Party School after it reopened in 1978 under the direction of Hu Yaobang (a Central Party School classmate of Zhu Houze's, Hu Jintao, would become the top leader of China in 2002). In his new position in Beijing, Zhu supported the appointment of Wang Meng, a well-known, open-minded creative writer, as minister of culture.[43] Deng Liqun and other conservative theorists believed that Zhu Houze was creating an even larger mess by granting more freedoms to people like Fang Lizhi, Wang Ruowang, and Wang Ruoshui.[44] They feared that the end result would be chaos. Outspoken intellectuals, meanwhile, were as pleased and enthusiastic with Zhu Houze's efforts as Deng Liqun and his fellows were dismayed.

Deng Xiaoping continued to attempt the almost impossible task of curbing criticism of the party without thoroughly alienating intellectuals. At the National Party Representatives Conference, held September 18–23, 1985, Deng compared the positive strength of socialism with bourgeois selfishness.[45] He said that by preserving community ownership of rural land and state ownership of enterprises, China could "eliminate the greed, corruption, and injustice that are inherent in capitalism and other forms of exploitation. . . . We must firmly oppose any propaganda in favor of bourgeois liberalization, that is, in favor of the capitalist road."[46] But he still tried to prevent all-out attacks on intellectuals. He stated, "We should follow the policy of letting a hundred flowers bloom and uphold the freedoms guaranteed by the Constitution and the laws of the state. With regard to erroneous ideological tendencies, we should follow the policy of persuasion and education and refrain from political movements and 'mass criticism.'"[47]

Preparing for Succession, 1985

By 1985, Deng, endeavoring to settle the issue of high-level successions that had been dragging on for some time, proposed holding the 13th Party Congress in 1985 instead of waiting until the 1987 scheduled date. When others strongly objected to altering the regular schedule of a party congress, Deng instead convened a special "National Party Representatives Conference" from September 18 to 23, 1985, which enabled the party to announce key retirements and appointments of potential successors. With 992 officials in attendance, the conference was almost as large as a party congress.[48] Because the conference did not have the formal authority to select members of the Central Committee, the Fourth Plenum was held on September 16, just before the start of the conference, to accept the resignations. On September 24, immediately after the closing of the conference, the Fifth Plenum officially announced the new appointments. The issue of Deng's succession was not discussed publicly but it was already in the air on May 10, four months before the party conference, when Hu Yaobang was interviewed by Lu Keng, a former rightist who had become deputy editor of the Hong Kong semi-monthly *The Masses (Baixing)*.

After the interview appeared, Deng asked Qiao Shi to convey Deng's displeasure to Hu Yaobang. Deng complained to Qiao Shi that Hu was trying to appear as if he were an enlightened leader.[49] Moreover, when Lu Keng had asked Hu Yaobang "While Deng is still healthy, why doesn't he simply pass on the leadership of the Central Military Commission [CMC] to you?" instead of completely quashing any implication that he was thinking of taking over from Deng the key position that would make him the leader of the third generation, Hu had responded that Deng could resolve military issues with one phrase, whereas for Hu it would take five phrases.[50]

Deng had let Hu Yaobang know he was thinking of retiring, but he did not want others pushing him to retire. He would retire at his own pace. He knew that Hu Yaobang had lost the support of Chen Yun and other conservatives for being too spontaneous without giving full consideration to balanced overall planning. In their view, Hu was winning the favor of intellectuals by being overly permissive and leaving the task of constraining them to others. He was derided in private by his adversaries as the "cricket"—"small, wily, rail-thin, and constantly jumping around."[51] Hu's supporters had thought that Hu might indeed be appointed head of the CMC at the National Party Representatives Conference, but Hu did not receive the appointment.[52] As Deng later told Yang Shangkun, "If I have made an error, the error is in misjudging Hu Yaobang."[53]

Although there was no explicit discussion of succession at the National Party Representatives Conference, it appeared to many attendees that Deng had decided by then that Zhao Ziyang, fifteen years his junior (compared to Hu who was eleven years his junior), was a leading candidate. Zhao had done well with the urban economic reforms, he had not alienated the conservative leaders, and he had the poise of a leader. It was rare for Deng to praise other officials publicly, but when he met with several writers at the National Party Representatives Conference, Deng openly praised Zhao Ziyang, especially his support of the four cardinal principles.[54]

At the Fourth Plenum preceding the National Conference, a total of some sixty-four senior full and alternate members of the Central Committee, roughly one-fifth of the total membership, including nine members of the Politburo, announced their retirement. Of the sixty-four, sixty-one were over sixty-seven years of age. One was Marshal Ye Jianying, a member of the Standing Committee of the Politburo. Because no replacement was named, Standing Committee membership was reduced from six to five, leaving Deng, Chen Yun, Li Xiannian, Hu Yaobang, and Zhao Ziyang.

In choosing new officials for high positions, two key considerations were age and educational level. The process of selection was conducted with great care by the Politburo and the party Secretariat over several months, beginning in May 1985. Of the sixty-four new members of the Central Committee, 76 percent were college graduates and their average age was just over fifty. The Politburo had in effect replaced senior officials with their younger, better-educated followers. Yao Yilin was close to Chen Yun; Hu Qili to Hu Yaobang; Tian Jiyun to Zhao Ziyang; Qiao Shi to Peng Zhen; and Li Peng to his adopted mother, Deng Yingchao.[55]

Among the younger new senior officials were Li Peng, then fifty-seven years old, and Hu Qili, then fifty-eight, who were considered potential candidates for premier and general secretary, respectively. Li Peng, trained in hydraulic engineering, did become acting premier in November 1987 and full premier in March 1998. Hu Qili, trained in physics at Peking University and a successful first party secretary in Tianjin from 1980 to 1982, was brought back to Beijing to be director of the party's General Office and party secretary of the Secretariat. He was fluent in English and very cosmopolitan.[56] After graduating in 1951, he had served for five years as the Communist Youth League party secretary at Peking University and beginning in 1977 as deputy party secretary at Tsinghua University, which had just reopened.

Among the younger officials selected as alternate members of the Politburo were Jiang Zemin and Hu Jintao. After 1985, they could attend Politburo meetings, and assuming they continued to be deemed promising and made no serious mistakes, they would be candidates for even higher positions at a later time.

Deng urged the new members of the Central Committee and the other new leaders to study the spirit of the senior officials who had built the party, united the country, and were now working hard for the four modernizations. He asked them to serve the Chinese people, to speak only the truth, to work realistically, to draw a sharp line separating public and private interests, to read Marxist theory, and to study changing circumstances and adapt accordingly.[57] In effect, the new leaders became apprentices to the senior leaders, to be cultivated and tested for potential advancement to higher positions.

One person who almost lost out at the time was Deng Liqun, whom intellectuals blamed for the campaign against spiritual pollution (although some acknowledged that Deng Xiaoping was ultimately responsible). Shortly after the National Party Representatives Conference, Deng Xiaoping approved a notice, distributed on September 28, 1985, announcing that Deng Liqun would no longer head the Research Office of the party Secretariat. The assumption among politically astute intellectuals was that he was being held responsible for the unpopular political campaign. Ordinarily, it was expected that the Politburo Standing Committee members would have been notified before such a move; in this case they were not.[58] But within half an hour after the notice was distributed, it was rescinded, presumably by Chen Yun. In fact, it would be two years before Deng Liqun's Research Office was finally abolished; meanwhile, Deng Liqun remained in office.

Political Reform, 1986–1987

On June 10, 1986, at a meeting with Zhao Ziyang, Yu Qiuli, Wan Li, and others, Deng spoke of three major issues to deal with: agriculture, foreign currency, and political reform. It was the first time he had talked of political reform since 1980. Deng said, "Early in 1980 it was suggested that we reform the political structure, but no concrete measures to do so were worked out. Now it is time for us to place political reform on the agenda. Otherwise, organizational overlapping, overstaffing, bureaucratism, sluggishness, endless disputes over trifles, and the repossession of powers devolved to lower levels will retard economic restructuring and economic growth." He added that the number of official organizations and personnel had to be reduced so as to decrease the heavy burdens on the state budget.[59]

At last, the time seemed right. The *Bashanlun* conference of 1985 had marked the end of the basic study of economic system reform, and some changes in the political system were needed to mesh with the new economic system. In 1980, Deng and his fellow officials had been worried about the risk of demonstrations like those sweeping Eastern Europe. In 1986, they were worried about the new wave of democratic demonstrations in Asian countries following the "people power" movement that had driven out President Marcos earlier that year and had led Chiang Ching-kuo to announce, three months prior to Deng's meeting in June, that he was undertaking a study of political reform. Was it not wise to show the public, at home and abroad, that the mainland was just as open as Taiwan?

In dealing with protests, Deng, like other Chinese Communist leaders, tried to maintain tight control while alleviating the cause of the complaints. As news of demonstrations spread abroad, Deng continued to explain to the Chinese public that the socialist system of public ownership was superior to bourgeois democracy; he pointed to the capitalists' exploitation of workers and to the difficulties of making timely decisions in countries where there was a separation of powers among the executive, legislative, and judicial branches. But Deng also was determined to stay ahead of the popular movements by introducing timely political reform. He therefore directed that China undertake serious study of political systems to determine which systems endure for the long term, which systems collapse, and why.

It was logical to select as head of the study group for political system reform a person who would have a major role in implementing future political reform. If Hu Yaobang were to be Deng's successor, he would have been the logical choice to lead the study group, but by May 1986 Deng had already told Hu Yaobang that he would step down as chairman of the CMC after the 13th Party Congress, to be held in the fall of 1987. When Hu Yaobang responded as expected, saying he would step down as general secretary, Deng told Hu he could continue working, but in a lesser role. Deng explained that it was too early to determine whether Hu might become chairman of the CMC or chairman of the state.[60]

By then, Zhao Ziyang had already been assigned overall responsibility for preparing the documents for the 13th Party Congress; many anticipated that there was a good chance that during the congress he would become the top leader for the daily work of the party. In September 1986, when Deng gave Zhao the responsibility to study political reform, the assumption was that he might well be given responsibility to implement it in the future. The selection of Zhao was also appropriate because with his think tanks he had already managed research into various economic systems. Zhao's experience in guiding the study of economic reform made it appropriate for him to consider the political reforms needed to gear in with the economic changes.

On June 28, 1986, at a meeting of the Standing Committee of the Politburo, Deng directed that in preparation for the 13th Party Congress to be held a year later, the party Secretariat should draw up a plan for a year-long study of political system reform and then suggest a program for action. "Without political reform," he cautioned, "economic reform cannot succeed."[61] His staff was to prepare initial drafts of documents by July 1987 to be discussed at the Seventh Plenum that would meet in August or September; that way, the final draft could be announced at the 13th Party Congress.[62]

In setting the stage for the study of political reform, Deng stressed the desirability of separating the functions of the party from those of the government, an idea that he had supported as early as 1941.[63] Indeed, the overlapping system in place had emerged by the 1950s as a way of dealing with the reality that some high government officials who remained after the Communist takeover were not members of the party: in essence, a Communist Party unit had been established in each major government unit to ensure party control. By the 1980s, however, virtually all government officials in important positions were party members, so many felt it was no longer necessary to have party supervision. Moreover, many observed that the extra layer of party supervision made it virtually impossible for the heads of a ministry or province to coordinate in a responsive, flexible way the activities of their respective units. Clearly it was time to streamline the political system.[64]

In mid-September 1986, then, at Deng's direction, Zhao Ziyang set up the Central Committee Small Group on Political System Reform (*Zhongyang zhengzhi tizhi gaige yantao xiaozu*), with Hu Qili, Tian Jiyun, Bo Yibo, and Peng Chong as members. The group was given a staff and an office named the Political Reform Office, and Zhao wrote a letter to Politburo Standing Committee members Deng, Chen Yun, Li Xiannian, and Hu Yaobang with a proposed list of members. In his letter, in accordance with Deng's directives, Zhao laid out the goals of political reform: to contribute to modernization and long-term stability. Bao Tong, who had proved to be an able assistant ever since 1980 when he had been assigned by the Organization Department to work for Zhao, was named head of the office.[65]

Although Deng had presented a relatively narrow focus for what he wanted from political reform, he gave Zhao Ziyang a broad mandate to study different political systems and to listen to diverse groups of experts within China.

rejected U.S. proposals for additional consultations or ship visits and did not accept a telephone hotline between the two countries.[54]

Secretary Brown explained to Deng that a number of Soviet actions during the previous year had been viewed negatively by the U.S. public and that the United States was now spending more on defense, strengthening its Pacific fleet and deploying more forces to the Middle East. Deng, who in May 1978 had complained to Brzezinski that the United States was not doing enough to counter Soviet moves, expressed approval to Secretary Brown in January 1980 that the United States was now responding more vigorously to the Soviet threat. But, Deng said, "It would have been better if this could have been done even earlier, . . . My personal judgment is that for a long time the West has not offered an effective response to actions of the Soviet Union." He had no objections to treaties, he said, but they were of little value in restraining the Soviets: "There is only one way to cope with the Soviet Union." What was required was a demonstration of force. During the meeting, Deng touched on other issues as well. He was pleased that the United States was now offering assistance to Pakistan, a move he had been advocating for some time. He believed that other nations should help turn Afghanistan into a quagmire for the Soviet Union, just as he had helped to bog down Vietnam along the border. And he coyly reminded Brown of China's interest in buying fighter planes, saying, "I will not mention the purchase of F-15 or F-16 aircraft any more," but, he added, "the scope of technology transfer is too narrow."[55]

Geng Biao, vice premier and secretary general of the CMC Standing Committee, was selected to make the return visit to Washington. Geng Biao had served in the Chinese military during the Jiangxi Soviet period, the Long March, World War II, and the civil war. He had served as an ambassador (in Scandinavia, Pakistan, and Myanmar) between 1950 and 1965, longer than any other Chinese diplomat. In Washington in May 1980, he met President Carter and Vance's replacement as secretary of state, Edmund Muskie, but his main host was Secretary Brown. He and Secretary Brown worked to devise ways in which the United States and China could respond effectively to the Soviet threat if it expanded in a southeast direction, from the Middle East to the Indian Ocean and to Southeast Asia. Reflecting the views of Deng and other Chinese leaders, Geng Biao reported that China had successfully tied down some 600,000 Vietnamese troops along the border, which had both weakened Vietnamese capacity to control Cambodia and prevented Vietnam from controlling the Straits of Malacca.

Wu Guoguang, a former *People's Daily* writer who became one of the staff members in the group and later wrote his Ph.D. thesis at Princeton on the political reform efforts in China in 1986–1987, has noted the differences of emphasis between Deng's and Zhao's views of political reform. Deng wanted to achieve efficient administration with highly motivated staff members, whereas Zhao was willing to consider a broader reduction in the party's role in economic and social units. Yet even Deng's narrower focus required that those studying political reform consider ways to raise the morale of staff members, and as the members of the group explored this issue, they inevitably considered mechanisms to ensure that underlings could express their views.[66]

Between November 1986 and April 1987 the group organized over thirty symposia with various officials and experts.[67] Although the final draft of its report required approval by Deng, Zhao Ziyang and Bao Tong could select the specialists to participate in the meetings. They chose experts who were knowledgeable about political reform in the Eastern European countries, Western political history, and the Chinese political structure before and after 1949. The group examined the role of the party, the government, and the National People's Congress (NPC), and heard the views of local officials dealing with various issues in their localities. The group cabled Chinese embassies around the world to collect information on other political systems. And the New China News Agency (Xinhua) and various Communist organizations in Hong Kong assisted in collecting information on political practices throughout the world. Although many foreign experts earlier had been invited to discuss economic system reform, none were asked to discuss the sensitive issue of political reform.

Among the speakers at the symposia, there were differing visions of what "political reform" might entail. The term naturally attracted hopeful intellectuals and students, who followed Deng's call to review broad issues about political systems. Even if they took care to reiterate Deng's emphasis on efficiency, intellectuals like Yan Jiaqi, head of the Institute of Political Science at CASS, raised questions far beyond efficient administration. Bao Tong was careful to quote Deng when he made public statements in order to show he was acting within his mandate, but it became clear that both Bao Tong and Zhao Ziyang believed strongly that the party should withdraw from its close supervision of government, businesses, and academic institutions. In fact, they argued, by doing so the party could exert even stronger overall leadership.[68] Just as the government could guide the economy indirectly by macroeconomic controls, so the party could withdraw from daily administration and still provide overall guidance.

In January 1987, after the student demonstrations were curtailed, Hu Yaobang fell, and the campaign against bourgeois liberalization began, Beijing's political atmosphere turned more conservative. Zhao responded to the chill in the air by inviting Hu Qiaomu and Deng Liqun to the meetings of the Small Group on Political System Reform, thus ensuring that the orthodox senior members would have their views well represented in the discussions.[69] The new atmosphere constrained but did not stop the discussions on political reform. On February 4, 1987, Zhao Ziyang proposed expanding the independent role of trade unions to give them more leeway in representing the interests of workers. Even Bo Yibo, who remembered the period before and immediately after 1949 when labor unions had been encouraged to assume more power in order to restrain capitalist trends, could foresee a future in which the party would turn again to independent unions to constrain entrepreneurs in the new free market economy. Researchers also discussed the possibility of encouraging the NPC to change from a body that issued rubber stamps to one that held meaningful discussions representing different views.[70]

In his talk with President Paul Biya of Cameroon in March 1987, Deng said a political system was sound if it contributed to political stability, national unity, and higher living standards, and continued development of the productive forces.[71] There was no mention of expanding freedoms or seeking to hear the voices of the public. Yet when he met Zhao Ziyang on April 28, 1987, Deng made it clear that despite the ongoing attack on bourgeois liberalization, he wanted to continue considering political reforms. Zhao, concerned about the tighter political atmosphere, requested that Deng permit the reprinting of Deng's speech from August 1980, which showed his support for political reform, and Deng agreed.

When he read Zhao's semi-final draft of his political report for the forthcoming party congress, Deng was more specific in rejecting the broader demands for freedom as advocated by intellectuals: "The main goal of our reform is to guarantee the efficiency of the executive organs without too many other interferences. . . . Do not yield to the feelings for democracy. . . . Democracy is only a means [to an end]. Democracy should be talked about in connection with legality. Only through the law will we have a stable environment."[72] The heady hopes of many intellectuals in late 1986 that they could make a real breakthrough in changing the political system were not to be realized in 1987. After reviewing Deng's comments, Zhao gave a speech on May 13 on plans for the 13th Party Congress. His remarks signaled the end of the campaign against bourgeois liberalization and made it clear that the party congress would include a proposal for political reform. But at least for the time being, political reform did not include steps to expand democratic practices.

The Student Movement and the Fall of Hu Yaobang

In the spring of 1986, Chinese television footage of the "people power" demonstrations in the Philippines that drove the corrupt President Marcos and his wife Imelda from office and ignited student demonstrations all over East Asia was fueling student protests in China as well. In early 1980 there were 3.5 million television sets in China, but by the beginning of 1985, with the explosion of television production, there were already over 40 million.[73] In 1986 Chinese TV viewers were aware of developments both within and outside China, including the news that in Taiwan in September 1986 Chiang Ching-kuo had allowed the legal existence of an opposition party. The effect of the foreign student movements and Taiwan elections was electric: Chinese students began calling for "people power" and for Western-style democracy.

The 1986 demonstrations were the first large student demonstrations in China since April 1976, when students had taken to the streets to honor Zhou Enlai and support Deng Xiaoping. On May 29, 1987, some weeks after these Chinese student demonstrations subsided, Zhao Ziyang explained to Singapore's Deputy Prime Minister Goh Chok Tong that when China opened up, its students, who had had no previous contact with the outside world, could not judge what was good or bad. When they saw that the United States and Japan were more advanced, some came to the wrong conclusion, advocating total Westernization for China, without understanding that this was not possible in China where conditions were so different. Zhao admitted that it was not surprising some students had come to this conclusion, because the socialist system before 1978 did have its failures. But Zhao blamed the loosening of party controls for the demonstrations.[74] He did not mention the name of the official who was considered responsible for this loosening: Hu Yaobang.

Throughout the twentieth century most Chinese student movements had begun in Beijing; in 1986, however, it began in universities in Anhui's capital, Hefei, and nearby Nanjing and Shanghai—that is, wherever the internationally famous astrophysicist Fang Lizhi, vice president of the University of Science and Technology in Hefei, spoke. Fang was a dynamic, powerful speaker who energized the crowds wherever he appeared with his radical message. For example, at Tongji University in Shanghai on November 18, 1986, Fang Lizhi said, "Not a single socialist country has succeeded since the end of World War II." He continued, stating that the current Chinese government was a modern form of feudalism. He described to the audiences how European scientists in the Middle Ages had courageously broken loose from the bounds of dogmatic traditions; he ridiculed Mao for praising the wisdom of the uneducated; and he berated Hu Qiaomu, saying Hu's comments would be welcome if he understood astrophysics, otherwise he should refrain from speaking out. At a public meeting in Anhui, former Anhui party secretary Wan Li, one of the most liberal of the top leaders, tried to curb Fang Lizhi, saying he had already granted Fang Lizhi enough democracy. But Fang Lizhi fired back that Wan Li had not been chosen to be vice premier by the people, so he had no right to decide how much democracy to allow.

It would have been easy for the party to crack down early on Fang Lizhi had he been an ordinary intellectual. But Fang was a brilliant scientist who had become an exemplar of the kind of intellectual China was attempting to cultivate. Fang had entered the physics department of Peking University at age sixteen and became the youngest full professor in China. In late summer 1986 he had just returned from spending several months as a scholar at the Princeton Institute of Advanced Studies. Everywhere Fang Lizhi appeared, he attracted enthusiastic followers. It was not yet the era of the Internet, but listeners sent tapes and transcripts of his speeches to friends elsewhere. On December 4, 1986, after a speech at the University of Science and Technology, student demonstrations exploded in number and scale.

In a session Hu Yaobang chaired of the party Secretariat on December 8, Hu made an effort to mollify the students, admitting that conditions in the universities needed improvement—an admission that conservatives later criticized as being too soft on the demonstrators. The next day, on the anniversary of the December 9, 1935, patriotic student demonstrations, students took to the streets in Wuhan, Xi'an, and Hefei. When coverage of the demonstrations was blocked on Chinese television, students listened avidly to Voice of America and the BBC, which broadcast the news.

When launching his four modernizations, Deng had warned that some would get rich first, but in the view of most students, the people getting rich first were the least deserving—greedy individual entrepreneurs and corrupt officials—not the morally upright government employees working in the national interest after years of hard study. Students often lived in poor conditions, crowded eight to a small room. Able students who had sacrificed for years to be among the very small percentage to pass the examinations to enter good schools were outraged that the children of high officials received better opportunities and lived in a grander style because of their connections.[75] Furthermore, university graduates were then not yet free to choose jobs; they were assigned jobs by the state based in part on reports compiled by the political guides who lived with the students. Many students felt they had no choice but to ingratiate themselves to these political guides, who often appeared to them to be arbitrary, arrogant, and poorly educated.[76]

After Fang Lizhi lit the spark to rouse students, demonstrations spread to Beijing and some 150 other cities. Local leaders were held responsible for keeping the movement under control. On December 18, when demonstrations expanded in Shanghai, Mayor Jiang Zemin appeared before a mass audience. As he began speaking, some students heckled him and others remained inattentive, so he stopped speaking and asked some of them to come up to podium to express their views. After a number of students responded, Jiang said that the students did not fully understand the differences between the West and China and what they had heard about democracy came only from translations. They should learn more about democracy directly from the sources. He then proceeded to recite by memory the Gettysburg Address in English, a feat that impressed many of the students. Over the next few days, as students busied themselves with examinations and the Shanghai municipal authorities decreed that all public demonstrations required permits, the student demonstrations in Shanghai tapered off without incident.[77] Jiang Zemin won high marks from top leaders in Beijing, who admired his ability to end the demonstrations without conflict.

On December 27, Deng Liqun, Wang Zhen, Hu Qiaomu, Peng Zhen, Bo Yibo, Yu Qiuli, and Yang Shangkun were summoned to Deng's home to report on the student movement. The situation, they reported, was very serious.[78] For Deng and other party elders who believed that Hu Yaobang had serious weaknesses, his inability to control the student movement was the last straw. In Deng's view, it was best to act immediately, both on the student movement and on Hu Yaobang's leadership. Deng had not waited until the 12th Party Congress to push aside Hua Guofeng, and now he chose not to wait until the 13th Party Congress to push aside Hu Yaobang.

Deng was aware that pushing Hu aside would create problems because of Hu's widespread public support. His dismissal would raise questions about

Deng's wisdom in originally choosing Hu, just as Mao's split with Lin Biao had caused some to doubt Mao's judgment for trusting Lin Biao so deeply in the first place. Deng also knew that no one could surpass Hu in his dedication to reform and in his ability to inspire enthusiastic supporters among intellectuals and local officials. Deng had been considering removing Hu Yaobang at least since May 1986 when he had asked Deng Liqun his views on Hu and Zhao Ziyang. What Deng could not foresee, however, was the turmoil that Hu's dismissal would cause after Hu's death just two years later.

On December 30, 1986, Deng summoned Hu Yaobang, Zhao Ziyang, Wan Li, Hu Qili, Li Peng, and others and announced to them that it was necessary to end the permissiveness toward the student movement. He told them, "When a disturbance breaks out in a place, it is because the leaders there didn't take a firm clear-cut stand. . . . It is essential to adhere firmly to the Four Cardinal Principles; otherwise bourgeois liberalization will spread unchecked." Hu Yaobang, aware that he was being held responsible for this lack of a "clear-cut stand," knew that it was time to submit his resignation.

Deng went on to criticize Fang Lizhi:

I have just read Fang Lizhi's speeches. He doesn't sound like a Communist Party member at all. He should be expelled. . . . In developing our democracy . . . we cannot simply copy bourgeois democracy. . . . People in power in the United States . . . actually have three governments . . . the people in the three governments often pull in different directions, and that makes trouble. We cannot have such a system. . . . The struggle against bourgeois liberalization will last for at least 20 years. Democracy can develop only gradually, and we cannot copy Western systems. Bourgeois liberalization means rejection of the Party's leadership; there would be no center around which to unite our one billion people.[79]

On January 1, 1987, a *People's Daily* editorial stressed the importance of the four cardinal principles and attacked bourgeois liberalization, thus preparing the public for the criticism of Hu Yaobang for failures on both counts. The next day, on January 2, Hu Yaobang formally submitted his resignation as general secretary. Deng Xiaoping contacted Zhao Ziyang, Bo Yibo, Yang Shangkun, Wan Li, and Hu Qili, all senior leaders, and they agreed to accept his resignation. Deng then named them to a committee that would lead planning for the 13th Party Congress and told them to organize immediately "party life meetings" (in effect, closed-door struggle sessions) for January 8, before Hu Yaobang was to be criticized openly.[80] Supporters of Hu Yaobang later complained that using "party life meetings" to criticize Hu violated regular party procedures because the dismissal of such a high-level person required approval first by the Politburo, then by a plenum of the Central Committee, and finally by a party congress. Deng chose instead to let the "party life meetings" build the case against Hu before presenting it to an enlarged meeting of the Politburo.

From 1982 to 1986 the first document of each year (Document No. 1) from the party Secretariat was devoted to agriculture, but the Document No. 1 released on January 6, 1987, to all party members instead summarized the key points in Deng Xiaoping's directives on the student demonstrations. Deng said the struggle against bourgeois liberalization was critical to the future of the country and that people must take a firm stand. Those who refused to respond to "education" would be dealt with severely.[81] Within days, the demonstrations came to a halt, with no reports of any deaths.[82]

On January 6, Deng also met with Hu Yaobang to break the news that "party life meetings" were being held to criticize him. In organizing the meetings, Deng had directed party officials to use "soft treatment."[83] The case against Hu Yaobang, Deng said, was not so serious as to warrant characterizing it as a struggle between two lines of thought or as an attack on factionalism, and the meetings should not be an occasion for personal vilification.[84] Yet, given Hu Yaobang's widespread following among high-level liberal party officials, local officials, and intellectuals, Deng believed that to counter Hu's considerable influence a detailed, well-documented case needed to be presented. Hu's most persistent critic, Deng Liqun, was asked to prepare a detailed criticism. Meanwhile, Zhao Ziyang met with Hu Yaobang to tell him that he would be allowed to remain on the Politburo, but he should be mentally prepared for the criticism session that would begin the next day. Zhao also advised Hu that if student demonstrations were to continue, he should take a strong public stance against them.[85]

From January 10 to January 15, some twenty to thirty top party officials, with Bo Yibo as chair, criticized Hu Yaobang in the "party life meetings" that Deng had called. Neither Deng or Chen Yun, too senior to engage in the fray, took part, and Li Xiannian, who disapproved of the removal of Hu Yaobang, absented himself by staying in Shanghai. Some said that if Marshal Ye had not died (on October 22, 1986), he would have protected Hu Yaobang and never have allowed such criticism sessions to take place.

At the opening session, Hu Yaobang presented his self-criticism. He acknowledged his responsibility in failing to follow Deng's directions to stop the student demonstrations. "Since November 1986 Deng three times passed on directions . . . about the student disturbances which were the biggest in ten years." In addition, aware of the specific issues for which he would be criticized, Hu Yaobang gave a serious response to each, admitting his errors, but also trying to defend himself:

- Concerning his failure to uphold the four cardinal principles: "I did speak out some and did grasp some matters, but I failed to seriously grasp the basic principles."
- On bourgeois liberalization: "I didn't believe the problem was so serious and I felt that if I did my work well, the problem would take care of itself."
- Regarding spiritual pollution: "After Comrade Xiaoping spoke out, I did not take correct steps in a timely fashion to stop some incorrect thinking and behavior."
- On preparing officials to be successors: "The party center and especially several old revolutionaries have repeatedly asked me to prepare the successor generation, to promote boldly those with virtue, ability, and experience. I have firmly supported this. In promoting and assigning officials, for decades I have never made myself the center. We have always gone through collective discussions. I have not chosen people with personal connections to me or supported small circles . . . but I still made some mistakes."
- On meeting with foreigners: "One must be especially prudent. Some branches responsible for receiving foreign guests asked me to see Lu Keng. I did not refuse. That was an error. In talking with him . . . I did not firmly enough refute some things he said."
- Concerning ideology: "The main reason for my errors is that after the Cultural Revolution, in the battle over 'ideology,' I always wanted stability and feared disorder. I focused on preventing 'leftists' and not enough on preventing 'rightists.' . . . Some matters of secondary importance I elevated to too high a place. . . . After I was in office for a long time, I became overly excited and impetuous. . . . I did not calmly listen to other people's opinions."
- Regarding approving too many things from below: "I have never approved anything that is outside my jurisdiction."[86]

Hu Yaobang was completely unprepared for the force of the attacks that followed. He later said that had he known the "party life meetings" would take such a turn, he would not have submitted his resignation or engaged in such a thorough self-criticism.[87]

Deng Liqun's detailed criticisms of Hu Yaobang took up the entire morning of January 12 and half of the following morning, a total of more than five hours. Deng Liqun spelled out Hu's "errors," meeting by meeting. He said that Hu's biggest failure was not giving more attention to the four cardinal principles and to the struggle against spiritual pollution. He had failed to unify the party; he primarily had used people who agreed with him; and he had not consulted sufficiently with senior leaders concerning key personnel appointments.[88]

On January 15, Zhao Ziyang made his criticisms of Hu. Later, in interviews and tapes that he made after he was placed under house arrest in 1989, Zhao would take special pains to show that although he had differences with Hu, he had been no more critical than was required, and that he and Hu had agreed about the need for reform and had worked together. He said he had "not thrown stones after Hu fell in the well."[89] In his criticism on January 15, Zhao said that although Hu was generous and did not bear grudges, he had weak points. "He enjoyed expressing new and different ideas and surprising people, amazing people with new feats. He did not accept organizational restraints. . . . If his authority were larger, problems would have been even greater. . . . Why was he so tolerant toward wild people like Liu Binyan and Wang Ruowang? Perhaps he wanted to create an image, at home and abroad, of being enlightened." Zhao continued, "Comrade Hu Yaobang doesn't respect discipline. If conditions were to change and Comrades Deng Xiaoping and Chen Yun were no longer with us, I couldn't continue working with him, I would resign. It doesn't matter what the Standing Committee decides, or what the party congress decides, or what was decided before, whatever he wanted to do, he just did."[90] Hu was shocked to hear these words; he had not expected Zhao to be so critical. Hu's friends, too, felt Zhao had indeed "thrown stones after Hu fell in the well."[91]

On the morning of January 15, at the end of the "party life meetings," Hu Yaobang presented a closing self-criticism in which he accepted responsibility for all his errors. But he also asked for continued investigations of whether he was truly overly ambitious and part of a faction. After the meetings ended, Hu was observed on the steps of the meeting hall, dejected and crying.[92]

On January 16, the opening day of the more formal enlarged Politburo meeting that included seventeen members of the CAC, Chen Yun, who had not attended the "party life meetings," expressed his views. He said that he had fully supported the decision to promote Hu Yaobang to general secretary in 1980, but in 1980–1981 he had observed that the Secretariat under Hu did not function well. At meetings, Hu would go through the motions of having each of over one hundred ministry-level units submit its report without resolving the key issues. In addition, Hu simply rushed around from one locality to another. In one week he visited twenty-two counties, without really concentrating on the major issues that he should have pursued more deeply. He also did not hold regular meetings of the Politburo and its Standing Committee, even though to practice party democracy, one had to hold regular meetings. Chen continued, saying that after he had criticized Hu in March 1983, he had hoped Hu would correct his errors, but apparently Hu did not fully understand. In selecting officials, one should draw on talented people from everywhere, but Hu only selected people from his own circles. In selecting officials, one should consider both "virtue" and "talent," but "virtue" (loyalty to the party) should come first. Nevertheless, Chen Yun stressed that it was important for the party to follow legal procedures in removing Hu.[93]

Hu Yaobang was relieved of his duties as general secretary, without going through formal procedures. Zhao Ziyang remained as premier but also took Hu's place as acting general secretary. Zhao Ziyang told others that he did not want to be general secretary and that he was more suited to be premier, but some knowledgeable observers were convinced that Deng Xiaoping had no other senior allies appropriate for the position who would have been approved by the other senior leaders. There was indeed widespread agreement that Zhao had done a good job with the economy, and his appointment as acting general secretary was accepted without great controversy. These decisions were formally approved later at the next Central Committee plenum and then at the 13th Party Congress. Hu would retain his party membership, his membership on the Central Committee, and, on paper, temporarily remain on the Politburo; in fact, however, he was completely sidelined.

Some progressive party members worried that with the dismissal of Hu, the conservatives might gain control and slow down China's reform and opening. But the "group of five" who continued to lead the daily work of the party—Zhao Ziyang, Yang Shangkun, Bo Yibo, Wan Li, and Hu Qili —were all close to Deng Xiaoping and responsive to his leadership.[94] Both Deng and Zhao insisted that the reform and opening would continue unchanged.[95]

On January 17, Hu Yaobang's secretary told his family that Hu was physically and emotionally exhausted, that he was resting in a building in Zhong-nanhai, and that he had requested that his family members not visit him. Two weeks later, Hu Yaobang walked through the special passage from Zhong-nanhai to his home located several minutes away. He asked his assistant to collect his speeches, reports, and other documents from the last ten years; he then stayed home for three months to read through these documents, con-cluding in the end that he had made no errors of principle. While at home, he also watched TV and reread passages from the complete works of Marx and Lenin. He rarely met visitors and took little part in party activities, al-though he did attend the celebrations surrounding the founding of the PLA, the Seventh Plenum, and the 13th Party Congress.

On January 19, the party center issued Document No. 3, listing the rea-sons for Hu Yaobang's removal:[96] (1) He resisted the party's efforts to oppose spiritual pollution and bourgeois liberalization, giving rise to demands for total Westernization and the creation of student turmoil, (2) He failed to support fully the four cardinal principles, and attacked only the left but not the right, (3) In economic work, he encouraged accelerated growth and con-sumption, causing the economy to spin out of control, (4) In political work, he frequently violated legal procedures, (5) In foreign affairs, he spoke out of turn and said things he should not have said, such as inviting three thousand youth from Japan without making adequate preparations, and (6) He fre-quently disobeyed party resolutions and spoke without authorization by the party center.[97]

Document No. 3 also contained a summary of Hu's self-criticism. In his self-criticism, Hu acknowledged that he had made grave errors that caused great damage to the party, the nation, and the people. He did not say, how-ever, that his ideological permissiveness had led to spiritual pollution, bour-geois liberalization, or student demonstrations. Document No. 3 went on to note that in the future, senior leaders such as Deng, Chen Yun, and Li Xian-nian, if still in good health, should supervise other officials, meaning the general secretary and the premier. During March and May, supplements to Document No. 3 were issued, spelling out more details of Hu's period of leadership.[98]

In the opinion of many liberal officials, it was a tragic injustice that Hu Yaobang, who had worked so hard for the country, who was so selfless, and whose policies could have worked, ended his service humiliated by people whom he had served with such dedication.[99] Other officials who had worked with Deng, however, believed that if Hu had remained in office, public order would have collapsed, for Hu lacked the firmness necessary to maintain the authority of the state and the party. They were thankful that Deng had managed and orchestrated the removal of Hu Yaobang without damaging the party, which remained unified at the top and which continued on with Deng's reforms. After Hu Yaobang's death two years later, the wide differences between these two views would emerge again, with more tragic results.

In February 1987, at the time of the Spring Festival when friends would traditionally visit each other, Hu Yaobang and his wife visited the Deng home and exchanged pleasantries. When Deng asked Hu if he had thought through his problems, Hu did not answer. Deng also invited Hu to play bridge on several occasions. Hu politely declined all but one time: on December 30, 1987, exactly one year after learning about his dismissal, Hu accepted Deng's invitation.[100] At the memorial service for Hu Yaobang in April 1989, Deng would extend his hand to Hu's widow, Li Zhao, but she refused to shake it, saying instead, "It's all because of you people."[101]

Opposing Bourgeois Liberalization, 1987

As Hu Yaobang was being removed, Deng initiated an orchestrated effort to firm up party discipline that he felt had grown lax under Hu. Deng tried to reduce Hu Yaobang's influence by publicizing his "errors" and removing some of his followers who had been protected by Hu even though they criticized the party. Deng also aimed to counter the broader appeal of Western ideals such as humanism, freedom, and democracy that in his view were being used to challenge the ultimate authority of the party.

At the January 16 enlarged Politburo meeting that Deng himself had attended, it was announced that China would undertake a campaign to criticize bourgeois liberalization. At the same time, Deng announced that China would continue the all-around reform and opening to the outside. On the eve of the Chinese New Year, January 28, the government released Document No. 4, "Notification Concerning Some Issues Related to the Current Opposition to Bourgeois Liberalization," which outlined the campaign that was beginning to unfold.[102]

Intellectuals whom Hu Yaobang had protected—Fang Lizhi, Liu Binyan, and Wang Ruowang—were expelled from the party, and in March, Zhu Houze was removed as head of the Propaganda Department. Liu Binyan defended himself by saying that his investigative reporting criticizing some party officials was not an attack on the party, but some high officials concluded that his criticisms and his appeals for a "higher kind of loyalty" to humane ideals had caused people to form a negative impression of the party.[103] Many others, including the head of the Institute of Political Science of CASS, Yan Jiaqi, and several university administrators who were party members, were not attacked in the press but were criticized behind closed doors.[104] To avoid a large negative response from intellectuals, Deng announced that the campaign was to be limited to those within the party,

Many seasoned high-level party officials who worked under Hu—like Zhu Houze, Wu Mingyu, Yu Guangyuan, and Ren Zhongyi—remained firmly convinced that Fang Lizhi, Wang Ruowang, and Liu Binyan were never threats to peace, that the demonstrations could have been resolved through discussions, that more openness would have strengthened, not weakened, the country, and that Deng had overestimated the threat to stability and had overreacted.

Deng tried to tighten the discipline of senior party officials responsible for the media and urged them to defend socialist ideals. On March 29, the party center issued a document on rectification work in newspapers and publications, and in article after article and broadcast after broadcast there were criticisms of bourgeois liberalization *(fan zichan jieji ziyouhua),* including Western thinking that promoted individualism and decadence.[105] The media also praised patriotism and extolled Chinese creativity and scientific successes.[106]

Deng Liqun played the key role in promoting the campaign against bourgeois liberalization. Zhao Ziyang, by contrast, managed to limit the negative impact of the campaign on economic units by saying that the anti–bourgeois liberalization criticism should not interfere with the economy and that the public was tired of political campaigns. At a conference promoting the campaign, held from April 6 to April 12, Deng Liqun criticized bourgeois liberalization on such a broad scale that he aroused the ire of many people attending the conference. Zhao Ziyang's assistant Bao Tong obtained copies of Deng Liqun's speech and Zhao forwarded them to Deng Xiaoping. Deng Xiaoping reacted as Zhao Ziyang and Bao Tong had hoped: he agreed that Deng Liqun had gone too far, alienating too many intellectuals and liberal officials. Some liberal party members feared that Deng Xiaoping was considering Deng Liqun as a possible successor to Hu Yaobang. Deng Xiaoping's reaction at this moment marked a turning point both in the campaign and in Deng Xiaoping's support for Deng Liqun.

Assured that Deng Xiaoping was behind him, on May 13, 1987, Zhao Ziyang gave a speech that both implicitly criticized Deng Liqun and in effect marked the end of the campaign against bourgeois liberalization. A few weeks later, on July 7, Deng Xiaoping also did not object when Zhao abolished the Research Office of the party Secretariat that Deng Liqun had earlier used as his base to support party orthodoxy. This change in the political atmosphere that strengthened Zhao and weakened Deng Liqun paved the way for Zhao to prepare for a more enlightened agenda at the 13th Party Congress.[107]

On July 10, Li Rui, who had worked briefly as a secretary to Mao Zedong in the 1950s, sent a letter to Deng Xiaoping containing a detailed critique of Deng Liqun. Li Rui reported that during the Yan'an period Deng Liqun had inappropriately used his position to investigate Li Rui in order to repeatedly interview Li Rui's wife, whom he then courted. Li went on to criticize Deng Liqun for his attacks on good officials.[108]

But while Deng Liqun was under fire, Zhao too was feeling some heat from conservatives who saw him as a threat to conservative economic and political policies. Zhao later recalled that although he had relatively good relations with the conservatives until that point, after Zhao eliminated Deng Liqun's base (the Research Office under the Secretariat), his relations with Chen Yun and Li Xiannian suffered.[109] Zhao also reported that after the 13th Party Congress these conservative leaders feared that Zhao might use his leadership mandate at the congress to pursue "political system reform."[110]

The 13th Party Congress: Zhao Ziyang Takes Charge

Aware that Mao, like many emperors, had caused great damage by remaining in office until his death, Deng was determined to establish a new pattern in which top leaders served with term limits and then retired. In Deng's case, however, retirement would have a caveat attached. Even after the 13th Party Congress, as Zhao Ziyang revealed to Gorbachev in May 1989, there was a secret agreement among high-level leaders that although Deng had retired, he retained the right to have the final say on important matters.

Senior officials in Deng's age cohort knew that when Deng retired, they would be expected to retire as well. In 1985, when Deng began referring to his possible retirement, a number of senior officials urged him to remain on. Like authoritarian rulers in other countries where the timing and procedure for succession are not clearly specified, Deng and his peers had reason to suspect that some impatient younger officials were preparing for, or at least eagerly awaiting, their retirement, perhaps even before they were ready. On November 11, 1986, at a small group meeting convened to plan for the 13th Party Congress, Hu Qili mentioned that Deng and a large group of senior officials would be retiring. When Bo Yibo heard him say this, his face reddened and he said, "So you want us all to die sooner?"[111] Hu Qili politely responded that he hoped they would continue on. Wang Zhen, not known for hiding his feelings, was in effect speaking for other officials when, in another incident, he exploded at Hu Yaobang for preparing for the retirement of the senior officials.[112]

At the 13th Party Congress, held October 25 to November 1, 1987, Deng gave up all his party and government positions, resigning from the Central Committee, the Politburo, and its Standing Committee. He retained his positions as chairman of the CMC and as chairman of the State Military Commission.[113] Other senior leaders had no choice but to retire from their official positions as well. Chen Yun was allowed to replace Deng as head of the CMC, and responsibility for front-line leadership was passed to Zhao Ziyang.

The 13th Party Congress was Zhao's congress. Deng knew that for a successor to exercise effective leadership, he needed considerable room to maneuver. Unless Deng judged that there was an emergency, Zhao would be in charge. After removing Hu Yaobang, Deng gave Zhao a relatively free hand to plan for and later lead the 13th Party Congress. Zhao's speech on May 13 thus marked not only the end of the campaign against bourgeois liberalization, but also the beginning of Zhao's leadership during the half-year of concentrated planning for the congress.[114] To prepare the Western public for the changes, on September 25, 1987, Zhao made himself available for an interview with U.S. anchorman Tom Brokaw that showed Zhao in the spotlight and comfortable with his new position as the front-line leader of China, a promotion that was to be formalized at the party congress the following month.[115]

Although Zhao was in charge, he operated within the parameters that Deng had established. He supported the four cardinal principles and he opposed bourgeois liberalization. He expressed a commitment to further opening to the outside and to economic reform. Deng had long supported a sharper separation of powers between the party and government and Zhao toed this line. Even so, Zhao was given considerable leeway, since Deng and even Chen Yun understood that under Zhao's leadership the economy and the political system would continue to evolve.

On May 29, 1987, two weeks after Zhao was given the green light, he told Singapore Deputy Prime Minister Goh Chok Tong that he was preparing an outline for political reform, to be presented at the 13th Party Congress, with the long-term goal of "building socialism with a high degree of democracy." That process, Zhao admitted, would require political stability and would take a long time to accomplish. The changes would be introduced step by step, province by province. Zhao said that in the future the party would not interfere with government affairs and that within the party there would be a high degree of democracy.[116]

To take account of opinions at various levels, the document went through eight drafts. On September 27, after reviewing the document, Deng, determined not to micromanage, simply said, "I read it, I have no objections. It is well-written" *(kanle, mei yijian, xie de hao)*. Under Zhao's direction, it was presented to the 13th Party Congress under the banner "Building and Institutionalizing Socialist Democratic Politics." On the eve of the congress, Deng made a brief statement showing that he fully supported it.[117]

Like Deng, Zhao sought to avoid contentious arguments. The congress documents supported continued reform and opening while avoiding concrete details that might arouse controversy. Zhao chose as his theme "the primary stage of socialism," the first time this concept was introduced at a large party gathering. It had the virtue of allowing ideologues to cling to the mantra that China would eventually move to socialism, while allowing those who believed in markets the freedom to do what was needed to develop productive forces. When asked how long the primary stage would last, Zhao said, "It will be at least 100 years . . . [before] socialist modernization will have been in the main accomplished."[118]

In effect, Zhao postponed the higher stage of socialism indefinitely; he put a stop to those who hoped that, after a brief consolidation, the party would again advance toward a higher stage of socialism. At the 13th Party Congress the new term for the economic system, "a planned market economy," reflected the growing importance of markets, in contrast to earlier party documents that declared planning to be primary. The state was to regulate the market, and the market was to guide enterprises; the role of detailed mandatory planning would continue to decline. Markets would be developed in labor services, technology, information, and real estate. The long-range goal, Zhao said, was "to build a socialist political system with a high degree of democracy and a complete set of laws, a system that is effective and full of vitality." The report provided direction for continued reform:

1. Party and government roles would be kept separate, and the party would play a smaller role in guiding government affairs. The party

committee at any given level would no longer designate a full-time secretary who holds no government post and merely supervises government work.

2. More powers would be delegated to lower levels.
3. In government units, responsibilities would be specified and overlapping reduced.
4. Promotions, demotions, rewards, and punishments would be based on performance, and rights to training, wages, welfare, and retirement would be guaranteed by law.
5. On issues of relevance to the local population, the government would consult with local authorities and inform the public of the results.
6. To strengthen "socialist democracy," various organizations for women, labor, and other groups would be encouraged as a way of presenting the views of their constituencies. The autonomy of minority nationalities would be enhanced, and great efforts would be made to train officials from among them.
7. The socialist legal system would be strengthened.[119]

The congress also approved some procedural changes. In order to stay better informed, the Central Committee would hold plenums twice a year instead of once a year. Key decisions at Politburo meetings would be reported by the media rather than kept secret. Party organizations would be reduced in factories, schools, hospitals, and firms, allowing these local organizations to have greater leeway in making decisions about their own operations.

In the months prior to the congress, Zhao had overall responsibility for personnel changes, but in fact the senior officials still played an important role in selection. The new members of the Standing Committee, Zhao, Li Peng, Hu Qili, Qiao Shi, and Yao Yilin, were not extremists. Yao Yilin, who was widely recognized as a very able administrator, was strongly supported by Chen Yun. But Hu Qili and Qiao Shi firmly backed reforms, thus assuring Zhao of a majority of reformers on the Standing Committee. Like the National Party Representatives Conference two years earlier, the selection criteria emphasized educational achievement, successful leadership experience, and relative youth. After the personnel changes, the average age of Politburo members dropped by five years.

For the first time in party history, more candidates for the Central Committee were listed than were selected, thus weeding out the least popular candidates and ensuring that all those selected in the voting had at least a minimum level of support from the other members. In the first round of voting at the congress, ten more candidates for the Central Committee were listed than there were available slots, and the ten receiving the least number of votes therefore did not become members. Deng Liqun was one of the ten not selected.[120] This represented a thorough rebuff to Deng Liqun and reflected widespread sympathy for Hu Yaobang.[121] With Deng Liqun off the Central Committee and his main work unit, the Research Office under the Secretariat, abolished, Zhao, unlike Hu Yaobang, would escape being hounded by the country's most persistent conservative watchdog.

The 13th Party Congress avoided a sharp split between conservatives who feared change and reformers who dreaded stagnation. The two most controversial officials who had aroused opposition as representatives of the opposite poles, General Secretary Hu Yaobang and his critic Deng Liqun, had been removed, making it easier for centrists to pull together a coalition for continued market reforms and modest advances in the political system. In effect, the goalposts for the debate between the conservatives and the reformers had been moved in the years prior to the congress toward more openness, more freedom of expression, and more market reform—and Zhao managed at the 13th Party Congress to move them again, even though the struggle continued. Deng Xiaoping had successfully pushed aside Hu Yaobang, whom he regarded as too permissive, without destroying party unity at the top. He had reason to hope that as he stepped down, Zhao Ziyang, who adhered to Deng's four cardinal principles and was advancing Deng's economic and political agendas, would be effective in guiding China to the next stages of reform.

Challenges to the Deng Era

1989–1992

20

Beijing Spring

April 15–May 17, 1989

From April 15 to June 4, 1989, as the whole world watched in fascination, hundreds of thousands of young Chinese took to the streets of Beijing and other Chinese cities.[1] In the early days after Hu Yaobang's untimely death on April 15, the demonstrators were mostly innocent youth seeking to pay their respects to their departed hero and to the democracy that he had supported. When they first started gathering, they expressed respect for the Communist Party and paraded in an orderly fashion so that they would not disturb traffic; initially, they had no political agenda. As the demonstrations grew larger and the demands became louder and more radical in content, however, tensions between the demonstrators and the authorities escalated. The clashes culminated on June 4, 1989, when troops restored order by shooting unarmed civilians on the streets of Beijing.

Deng was then eighty-four years old and he did not come out to the streets to meet the demonstrating students nor did he manage the daily details of the party's response. But behind the scenes, he remained focused on the unfolding drama and was the ultimate decision-maker. He had little sympathy with the demonstrators, who had benefited from the reform and opening that he had helped to create and from the political stability that underpinned the economic growth, a stability they were now threatening.

Deng sought to avoid in China what was occurring in Eastern Europe as political leaders were yielding to citizens' demands and losing control. Initially, Deng tried to avoid bloodshed, which he knew would only inflame the demonstrators. But from the beginning he believed that firmness was required, and after Hu Yaobang's funeral he became more directly involved in supervising the party's response to the demonstrators. He was prepared to ensure that officials carried out whatever steps he considered necessary to restore order.

Before June 4, no one—party leaders, intellectuals, or student leaders—proved able to stop the mounting chaos. Party leaders' efforts to gain control were frustrated by splits in their own leadership, disagreements about how much freedom China could then manage, the differing perspectives between senior officials who had fought in the Chinese revolution and students accustomed to more comfortable lives, the insecurity of the urban residents who were worried about inflation and jobs, the massive scale of the demonstrations, the inability of the student leaders to control their own movement, the sympathy of the Chinese public and foreigners for the demonstrators, and Chinese troops' lack of experience in crowd control.

The student movements that senior leaders had taken part in before 1949 were well organized, with thought-through plans and agenda, and by 1949, the student leaders had worked together for many years. Students in the late 1960s had experience as Red Guards. But the tight controls in the decade before 1989 had prevented the growth of an independent organized student movement. In 1989 the students who came together did not have any experience in organizing. Articulate orators emerged as leaders, but, lacking organization, an agenda, and procedures for ensuring compliance, they had no basis for negotiating with political leaders on behalf of other students.

Urban residents did not join in restraining the demonstrators, for they sympathized with their complaints. Even some older intellectuals who tried to keep the students from taking radical actions in fact admired the students for boldly expressing views that they themselves, beaten down by years of political pressures, were afraid to express. What began as an unplanned peaceful outpouring of mourning for Hu Yaobang was transformed into parades, political forums, campouts, angry protests, hunger strikes, and clashes that spiraled out of control.

Student demonstrators wanted improvements in their living conditions and they were upset that they were receiving fewer economic rewards for their ability and hard work than were uneducated entrepreneurs. But they had learned from the failure of the student movement in 1986 that it was important to win widespread public support for their cause. So in 1989, instead of complaining about their miserable living conditions, they used slogans that resonated with the citizenry—democracy, freedom, and a more humane and accountable party with upright officials who were dedicated to the public good.

The demonstrations were spurred on by and played out before global television audiences who were moved by the tender, heartfelt appeals of Chinese youth. Foreign reporters in China, who in their work had long been hounded by Chinese officials who policed their activities and arrested any sources who dared to speak out, listened eagerly to the students' demands. Before April 15, most students had been afraid to talk openly with foreign reporters, but as they grew bolder over the course of the spring, foreign reporters gave voice to their hopes for a more democratic society, winning them sympathy throughout the world.

For their part, students were buoyed not only by the enormous support at home and abroad, but also by the failure of the government's initial efforts to curb the demonstrations. When masses of students broke through police cordons, students and foreign observers alike became unrealistically hopeful that the government would eventually yield to their cause. At the time, the students could not have imagined that the political leaders would eventually resort to armed force and that the People's Liberation Army (PLA) would shoot unarmed citizens on the streets of Beijing.

Chinese leaders, for their part, could see that foreign attention and support encouraged the protestors. They found it difficult to believe that Chinese citizens could be that angry at the leadership and found it easy to believe that the protests were being controlled behind the scenes by domestic and foreign "black hands." Stories and rumors of such "black hands" circulated widely among high officials and were used by the conservatives to push Deng to take stronger action.

The Death of Hu Yaobang

Shortly after returning to Beijing from a winter holiday in the south, Hu Yaobang attended a Politburo meeting on April 8. During the first hour of the meeting, he had a sudden, severe heart attack and collapsed. Rushed to the hospital, he seemed to be recovering when suddenly, early on the morning of April 15, he passed away. The news was made public on the seven o'clock evening television news. On the following day, an official obituary was read on television and printed in the newspapers. The shock was universal. Hu's death had been completely unexpected and attracted enormous sympathy, even among hardliners.[2] Deng Liqun, Hu's most vocal critic and the one who had led the attack on Hu in January 1987, now praised him. He later wrote that Hu had not engaged in plots and that he had been completely aboveboard and bore no grudges. Deng Liqun later claimed that, in contrast, Zhao Ziyang had engaged in plots and attacked people.[3]

The Chinese public had long been inspired not only by Hu's enthusiasm and personal warmth, but also by his integrity and dedication to the party. He was the hope of the intellectuals, for whom he had fought so valiantly, and he was their symbol of the good official—a man with high ideals who was free of any trace of corruption. As the longtime general secretary of the Communist Youth League, Hu had always identified with young people, whom he cultivated and whose interests he promoted. Yet Hu was coldly ejected from office in 1987 amid accusations that he had been soft on the 1986 student demonstrators.

The 1989 demonstrations represented an implicit criticism of Deng Xiaoping's unwillingness to do more to promote democracy and to support Hu Yaobang's efforts. Hu Yaobang's friends felt that Hu had been criticized unfairly and they reported that he had felt deeply wounded, especially by the criticism from Deng, whom he had served so loyally. After being removed in 1987, Hu had ceased watching television and lost weight.[4] Many believed he died from sheer disappointment, a martyr for the cause of freedom and democracy. But many of those who took part in the demonstrations were not concerned about Hu Yaobang personally; instead, they regarded him as a useful rallying point for expanding their efforts to increase freedom and democracy. Indeed, many intellectuals regretted that they had been submissive in 1986 when the student movement was so easily defused. They were now determined to stand stronger.

As students invoked the memory of Hu Yaobang to advance the cause of freedom and democracy, the parallels between the April 5, 1976, demonstrations (to mourn Zhou Enlai) and the April 1989 demonstrations (to mourn Hu Yaobang) were striking enough to inspire the demonstrators and to worry the Chinese leaders. The demonstrations in 1989 were taking place in the very same place as the April 1976 "Tiananmen Incident." Like Zhou Enlai, Hu Yaobang had fought to protect the people and had died a tragic death. In both 1976 and 1989, the public was outraged that a man whom they revered had not been treated with more respect. In 1976 the demonstrators had taken advantage of the occasion to attack the Gang of Four. Now, was it not possible to use the occasion to criticize Deng Xiaoping and Premier Li Peng? By the fall of 1978, too, those arrested in the spring of 1976 had been rehabilitated and called patriotic. In the same way, was it not possible that the demonstrators in 1989 would later be called patriotic as well? Among those Chinese who hoped for a more humane government, Hu Yaobang had replaced Zhou as the great hero of the time.

Sources of Unrest

In the spring of 1989, political disagreements among high-level leaders, particularly Zhao Ziyang and Li Peng, as well as the gradual withdrawal of Deng from involvement in leading daily affairs, led to conflicting signals and confusion. This uncertain environment allowed serious sources of social unrest to fester and intensify at lower levels. Most Chinese students in the late 1980s were less concerned about political freedoms than about their personal freedoms, such as the ability to choose their own jobs and to escape from their "political guides." After already having proved their talent and dedication by preparing for the difficult university entrance examinations, they felt entitled to pursue whatever jobs they wanted. But in 1989, with a shortage of trained graduates in key industries and government offices, government policy still mandated that graduates be assigned their jobs. Since one's job assignment was based in part on what the political guides who lived with the students wrote in the "little reports" in each student's secret records, the political guides became the symbol of government surveillance. The political guides were rarely as well educated as the students on whom they were reporting; some were suspected of favoritism and flaunted their authority to influence a student's future. Many cosmopolitan, independent-minded students detested the constant worry about pleasing them. "Freedom," to them, meant eliminating these political guides and being able to choose their jobs and careers on their own. The students actually spent little time discussing election systems.

Intellectuals, both young and old, were also still angry about the 1983 campaign against spiritual pollution and the 1987 campaign against bourgeois liberalization. The popular Chinese television documentary *River Elegy*, which had been broadcast for a short time in the late 1980s (until the conservatives were able to end it), caught the mood of many intellectuals when it criticized the Yellow River—a symbol of traditional China—and praised the Blue Ocean that had brought innovative foreign ideas and modern practices to China's shores.[5]

For the general public, a major worry was inflation. Party and government workers, state enterprise employees, and others with fixed salaries were furious to see rich private businesspeople flaunting their material wealth and driving market prices higher, threatening the ability of salaried workers to pay for their basic food and clothing needs. The problem was exacerbated by corruption: township and village enterprise workers were enriching themselves by siphoning off needed materials and funds from state and public enterprises; independent entrepreneurs were making fortunes, in part due to government loopholes; and "profiteering officials" were finding ways to use society's goods to line their own pockets as the incomes of law-abiding officials stagnated.[6] Migrants beginning to stream into the cities also contributed to the inflation problem.

Official indices, which underestimate the actual changes, showed consumer prices in Beijing between 1987 and 1988 rising more than 30 percent, terrifying families that were dependent on fixed salaries and for over three decades had expected stable prices. Frugal families that had been able to put aside some savings for old age and future illness were distressed to note the drop in the value of their savings. As prices continued to rise and officials threatened to lift more price controls, anger turned to panic.

Government employees on fixed salaries had been taught that they were working for the public good. It was thus outrageous that the least moral people in Chinese society, those working for themselves and those willing to exploit public resources for personal benefit, were now able to afford expensive restaurants, better housing, stylish clothes, motorcycles, and even cars or vans. No city had as large a concentration of public salaried officials or university students who expected to live on fixed salaries after graduation as Beijing. They believed that government enterprises should use more of their income to offer employees higher salaries or at least better welfare services. In the excitement of the spring of 1989, some government employees were sufficiently outraged that they were willing to run the risks of joining the demonstrations with signs bearing the names of their government units. But even for the general public, the student slogans opposing inflation and corrupt officials tapped a deep reservoir of outrage.

When the Chinese public talked about "corrupt officials," they did not mean those who disobeyed laws, for the concept of legality was not that strong. They meant those who used their positions or their personal contacts for benefits that others sought but did not have. Protesting students, furious at "profiteering" officials, demanded that these officials' incomes and expenses be revealed, along with the number of villas they owned and the sources of their children's money.[7] In 1966 many children of high officials had joined the Red Guards against those who had "taken the capitalist road," but in 1989 few children of high officials joined the protestors. Instead they were under attack, along with their parents, for the privileges they enjoyed as a result of turning their powerful positions into sources of profit in the new market economy.

For employees in state enterprises, even more frightening than inflation was the fear that their "iron rice bowls"—their secure jobs and benefits— might be at risk as state enterprises became subject to market forces. The government had already begun to pressure state enterprises that were losing money to cut their costs. Some firms were even permitted to go bankrupt, creating near-panic among their employees. The stakes were extremely high for workers because China lacked a national social security system and a national health program. Sizable state enterprises, much like U.S. military bases, were not just economic units but total societies that provided subsidized housing, medical care, and even education for workers' children. For the workers in state enterprises, to lose a job was to lose everything. The prospect of free markets that could put state enterprises out of business was terrifying.

In the expanding economy of the mid-1980s, many rural migrants were streaming into Beijing and other urban areas to work—especially in construction where machinery was not yet widely available and large numbers of laborers were needed. But the tight readjustment policies that had begun in late 1988 took away dramatic numbers of job opportunities for these laborers, and many of those who were laid off struggled to remain in the cities, where they observed profiteering officials and entrepreneurs displaying their newfound wealth. In short, to many, the results of the drastic new changes wrought by market forces were deeply upsetting.

But in addition to those sources of discontent, many people wanted more than freedom of movement. They were tired of living in fear of being criticized and punished for "political errors." The calls for freedom and democracy, and the celebration of Hu Yaobang, tapped into a desire to be liberated from the surveillance and criticism sessions of the intrusive state.

From Mourning to Protesting, April 15–22

In the evening of April 15, within hours after the announcement of Hu Yaobang's death, the walls of Peking University were full of posters mourning his passing.[8] The next day, April 16, an estimated eight hundred students marched to the foot of the Monument to the People's Heroes in the center of Tiananmen Square to lay memorial wreaths. The police did not interfere with the mourners who marched from their universities to pay their respects.

As more students began assembling in the square, the mourning began to take on more political overtones. Early in the morning of April 18, several hundred students went across Tiananmen Square to the Great Hall of the People to deliver to the Standing Committee of the National People's Congress (NPC) several demands, including allowing more freedom and democracy, ending the campaign against burgeois liberalization, reversing the decision to punish the 1986 protesters, and publicizing the incomes of party leaders and their children. That night, around 11 p.m., several thousand angry protestors walked the few hundred yards from Tiananmen Square to the Xinhua Gate at Zhongnanhai, the seat of the party and government. There they continued to shout and demand that they be allowed to enter. Despite requests to leave, they refused and the crowd persisted until 4 a.m., when police finally forced their dispersal. This marked the first time since the Communists' 1949 takeover of the government that protestors had demanded access to Zhongnanhai. As Li Peng noted, April 18 was the day the tone of the demonstrations changed from one of mourning to one of protest.[9]

The rowdy shouting at Xinhua Gate could easily be heard within Zhongnanhai, and high-level officials soon realized the seriousness of the situation. Li Peng, who had rushed back from Japan as soon as he was notified of Hu Yaobang's death, disagreed with Zhao Ziyang about what should be done. Li Peng told Zhao that they needed to respond firmly. But Zhao Ziyang, who as general secretary remained in charge, believed that it was better not to provoke the students, and that as long as there was no hitting, smashing, looting, or destruction of property, the leadership would be wise not to take any strong actions.[10]

By April 21, the demonstrations had grown in size and speakers in the square had begun calling for more democracy.[11] In their efforts to calm the students, Li Tieying, head of the State Education Commission, directed university officials to carry on normal campus activities and to restrain the student demonstrations. A regiment of troops was sent into Zhongnanhai as a precaution against the danger that students might break through the gates. The *People's Daily* announced that demonstrations were banned and warned students "not to mistake the regime's forbearance for weakness." But the officials had badly miscalculated, and the students, flaunting their power, refused to quiet down. On April 22, the day of Hu's funeral, an estimated 200,000 people listened attentively to the twenty-minute memorial service as it was broadcast on loudspeakers in the square. Hu Yaobang was given an honorable memorial service in the Great Hall of the People, and his body was taken to Babaoshan, the burial place for high officials. After the memorial service, three student representatives kneeled on the steps of the Great Hall of the People and waited some three hours to talk with Li Peng. They later complained that they had been encouraged to believe that Li or another high official would meet with them, although Li Peng and other officials claimed that Li was unaware of this.[12] At the time, Li Peng did not agree to meet any groups of students for fear that it would give the student organizations a legitimacy he refused to grant. He also worried that doing so would weaken the official student organizations sponsored by the party, over which the party had more control.

Li Peng and Deng's April 26 Editorial

Deng Xiaoping did not take any steps to curb the students when they were mourning Hu Yaobang. Whatever criticisms Deng had of Hu Yaobang during his last years in office, Hu was still considered a dedicated official who had made a contribution to reform and opening. Deng knew that the students would become incensed if their mourning were curtailed, just as the April 1976 protesters had become inflamed when their attempts to mourn Zhou Enlai's passing were blocked. But as soon as the period of mourning ended, Deng was ready to issue a warning to the students, and at this point Li Peng, who favored taking a hard line, temporarily replaced Zhao Ziyang in managing the demonstrations.

Zhao Ziyang's trip to North Korea had long been scheduled to begin on April 23, the day after Hu's funeral. Zhao reports that when he met Deng shortly before departing for North Korea, Deng told him that he should still make the trip and that when he returned, he would be promoted to head the Central Military Commission, a sign that at the time Deng still expected Zhao to be his successor. Right on schedule, then, Zhao left for Pyongyang from the Beijing train station on April 23.[13] Li Peng, to dampen talk of conflict with Zhao, saw him off at the station. Zhao told Li that in his absence he should feel free to call a Politburo meeting.

Zhao Ziyang and others had hoped that after Hu Yaobang's funeral the crowds would disperse, but they did not. On the day Zhao left Beijing, despite the ban on forming student organizations, students from twenty-one universities met to form what they called a "United Students' Association," which decided that in 1986 students had given up the protests too easily; the current group of students would be more steadfast. Reversing their earlier announcement that the students would return to classes after May 4, the student organizers declared that the boycott of classes would continue for an indefinite period.[14]

After Zhao left the country, Li Peng, who was then in charge, realized the weight of his responsibility. He consulted with Yang Shangkun, who advised that in view of the seriousness of the situation they should report to Deng. That very evening, Li Peng and Yang Shangkun communicated to Deng their view that the protests required firm and swift action. Li Peng said that students were criticizing Deng Xiaoping personally, and that there were other troubling developments: scuffles at Xinhua Gate of Zhongnanhai, the report that 60,000 students were still boycotting classes, the obstruction of traffic, and the reports of "black hands" who wanted to bring down the Communist Party and the socialist system all signaled serious problems.[15] Deng agreed that the demonstrators should be warned of the gravity of their actions. From then on, Deng became deeply involved in decision-making about how to respond to the demonstrators.

The next day, Li Peng called a meeting of the Politburo to hear reports by Chen Xitong and Li Ximing, the Beijing municipal officials responsible for monitoring developments in the capital. Some observers have argued that the two men, worried about the danger of being held responsible if something were to go wrong, exaggerated the gravity of the demonstrations and so misled Deng about the actual situation. But other officials believed that the developments were indeed serious and that Li and Chen were reporting accurately on what was happening in Tiananmen Square.

At 10 a.m. on April 25, Deng met Li Peng and Yang Shangkun in his home to hear their report of the situation. Li Peng wrote in his diary that by April 23 Deng had already decided that a firm warning was needed.[16] After listening to their report, Deng said that the turmoil had to be stopped— that in other Communist countries where protests had been tolerated, such as Poland, party authority had simply collapsed. Chinese leaders therefore needed to be clear and firm in ending the turmoil and in bringing things under control. Deng then said an authoritative editorial warning the students of the dangers should be released immediately. Party leaders in the region were to be told to remain firm, and party and administrative leaders in the universities were to be directed to quiet things down.[17]

Deng personally directed what he felt the editorial should include and as usual with important decisions, he prepared his comments carefully. Hu Qili was put in charge of preparing the editorial and the master drafter Hu Qiaomu edited the final version. The editorial was broadcast that very same night and appeared the next day, April 26, in the *People's Daily*.[18] It praised the majority who had mourned Hu Yaobang, but it also accused some of the mourners of making improper statements and engaging in inappropriate actions. According to the editorial, protestors were attacking the leadership of the Communist Party and the socialist system, going so far as to form illegal organizations to try to seize power from the government-approved student associations. They were engaging in strikes and causing turmoil *(dongluan)* to overthrow the leadership of the Communist Party and using the banner of democracy to undermine Chinese-style democracy. If such turmoil went unchecked, there would be chaos. The struggle was serious, and all illegal organizations were to be disbanded and unlawful parades banned, immediately. Any persons fabricating rumors would be investigated for criminal liability.[19]

Li Peng and his allies were counting on the editorial to intimidate and subdue the students; after all, the serious accusations articulated in the editorial constituted an open threat by the government that many student leaders would be arrested. But to Deng's dismay, the plan backfired. Instead of backing down, the student leaders dug in their heels and recruited massive numbers of additional students to join them. In his diary Li Peng wrote that the April 26 editorial had succeeded, but reports from the square concluded that it had only served to inflame the students. University presidents and administrators, who were more in touch with the student mood than Li Peng, felt that the editorial had removed the basis for dialogue that might have led to a peaceful resolution of the student grievances. In their view, the April 26 editorial was too harsh.[20] At age eighty-four, Deng went out less, talked to fewer people, and no longer had a keen sense of the public mood. Had Zhou Enlai been alive, some officials believed, he could have reached an understanding with the students. But in April 1989 no leader had both the authority to offer a solution and the ability to bridge the communication gap between the senior revolutionaries and the youth. Even Zhao Ziyang, who later advocated dialogue with the students and a retraction of the April 26 editorial, had been aloof and at the time was not seen by the students as a sympathetic ally. Students accused his sons of corruption and criticized him for playing golf.

With the appearance of the April 26 editorial, the battle lines were drawn. The leaders of the demonstrations identified Deng Xiaoping and Li Peng as their enemies. The demonstrations grew, to the extent that they easily broke

through the line of police who had been told to be restrained in their response, for fear of causing bloodshed.[21] Meanwhile, the officials would not
budge. Deng would not retract the editorial for fear of weakening the party's
authority. And although Li Peng and other officials overcame their initial
reluctance to meet the students, while meeting with them the officials held
their line and failed to calm the situation. For instance, when Yuan Mu, State
Council spokesperson, and He Dongchang, vice minister of the State Education Commission, met with forty-five students on the afternoon of April 29,
Yuan Mu refused to admit that corruption was a serious problem and denied
the existence of any censorship. Students left angrier than ever.[22]

Sympathy for the students was so widespread that Li Peng had difficulty
retaining support of lower-level officials for the crackdown. Hu Qili, the Politburo Standing Committee member who supervised propaganda work, explained to his fellow officials that many newspaper reporters were upset because their articles about what was actually happening in the square were not
being published. University officials who were told to quiet down the demonstrations dutifully passed along the message to the students, but for many
their hearts were not in it.[23] Li Peng could not even count on the official media to support him. For several days no newspapers of any kind appeared. On
one national television station, reporters describing what was taking place in
the square were interrupted, and for a brief time the picture went dark and
the voiceover simply stopped. One day, an announcer said, "There is no news
today."[24] After June 4, the head of the Propaganda Department and the editor of *People's Daily*, who were considered too sympathetic to the students,
were both removed from their positions.

The Li Peng–Zhao Ziyang Split, April 29–May 12

Under the strain of the growing popular demonstrations against the government and party, high-level officials became polarized between those who
feared chaos and believed tighter control was necessary, and those who believed they should be more accommodating to the student demands. Li Peng
was the symbol and rallying point for the former, and Zhao Ziyang for the
latter. Li Peng's diary is filled, day after day, with criticisms of Zhao Ziyang;
he notes that by the fall of 1988 Deng was already dissatisfied with Zhao's
handling of the economy, his political softness in failing to give strong support for the campaign against bourgeois liberalization, and his reluctance to
accept full responsibility for the rampant inflation and the public's reaction
to the lifting of price controls.[25] Zhao, by contrast, stated the problems be-

came worse after he left for North Korea and Li Peng reported to Deng on the ominous threats from the demonstrations.[26] Deng, the other party elders, and the security forces all supported Li Peng. Zhao, who after returning from North Korea advocated that the April 26 editorial be retracted, won the support of the intellectuals, reformers, students, and the general public.

Li Peng and Zhao made a serious effort to avoid displaying their differences in public. Just as Li Peng had dutifully seen Zhao off at the train station on April 23, so too did he dutifully welcome him back home on April 30. But their personal differences, rivalries, and the pull of separate constituencies were far stronger than their desire to cooperate with one another. Tensions between the two had been escalating since the summer of 1988 as the economic problems mounted and Zhao was held responsible for China's high inflation. At the time, Zhao officially kept his position as head of the Finance and Economics Leadership Small Group, but control of China's economic bureaucracy, which formerly had also rested with Zhao, shifted to Li Peng. The overlapping responsibilities became a battleground between Zhao the reformer and Li Peng the cautious planner.

Li Peng, a sober official, was trained originally as a hydraulic engineer and was known to be a responsible and effective administrator. He held special status as the son of a revolutionary martyr and as one of the many godsons of Zhou Enlai and his wife, Deng Yingchao. Li Peng, in fact, had to have had a high level of ability to have attended a very selective program to study advanced science in the Soviet Union, but among leaders he was not renowned for his brilliance. He was unassertive in offering independent ideas and he was thoroughly loyal, hard-working, and dedicated—ready to carry out the wishes of the senior leaders, no matter how unpopular their message. Li's dour, careful nature was in sharp contrast to the warm and sympathetic Hu Yaobang or the more aloof but gentlemanly and analytical Zhao Ziyang. Because Li Peng found it hard to hide his disdain for the student protestors, his encounters with them did more to incite them than to quell their anger.

On April 25, when Deng laid out to Li Peng his views on the importance of publishing an editorial, the summary of Deng's comments was sent to Zhao in Pyongyang where in a secluded room, surrounded by a black curtain, he read Deng's message. Zhao immediately wired back, "I completely agree with the policy decision of Comrade Xiaoping with regard to the present problem of turmoil."[27] In his diary, Li emphasizes that Zhao had approved of the editorial, though in reality he had only approved of Deng's comments, upon which the editorial was eventually based.

Once Zhao returned from his trip to North Korea, he quickly concluded that the battle lines between the party and the students were so sharply drawn that there was little hope for reconciliation without retracting the editorial. At one point he even agreed to take full responsibility for the April 26 editorial if it could be withdrawn.[28] Zhao, who knew Deng well, must have realized that the prospects of getting Deng to withdraw the editorial were very slight. Indeed, Deng, who believed that indecision and reversing decisions could only weaken party authority, refused to consider a retraction. On the student side, Zhao did what he could to ease the tension. He tried to reassure the students that they would not be punished by stressing that the vast majority of them were patriotic; he also encouraged them to leave the square and return to their classrooms.

On May 1, just two days after he returned from Pyongyang, Zhao chaired a Politburo Standing Committee meeting to discuss how to respond to the anticipated demonstrations on the seventieth anniversary of the May 4, 1919, protests. Zhao advocated adapting to the changed times by issuing a statement stating that the party supported increasing democracy and transparency in political life. Li Peng, however, argued that the government's primary emphasis should be on stability. He criticized the illegal organizations and the spreading of rumors. If the young people got their way, he insisted, China would take a huge step backward. Zhao countered that although China did need stability, the students' slogans—which advocated upholding the Constitution, promoting democracy, and opposing corruption—were also the positions of both the party and the government.[29]

In contrast to the stern, disapproving, and disciplinarian tone of Li Peng's pronouncements, Zhao's attitude was that of an understanding parent giving advice to children who were basically good. On May 3 and May 4, in two important public addresses, Zhao laid out the larger case for responding positively to the student demands. On May 3, at a conference celebrating the anniversary of the May Fourth movement, Zhao said that just as seventy years earlier the demonstrators had promoted science and democracy, the current demonstrators should also stress the essential roles of science and democracy in the modernization of China. He emphasized the importance of stability and Deng's four cardinal principles, but he also declared that "the vast numbers of youth . . . hope to promote democracy and call for punishing people who . . . are guilty of corruption. This is also the exact intention of our party."[30] As always, party leaders attempted to present a united front. Zhao's speech was so skillfully worded that it was difficult for the conservatives to find any criticism.

In his speech to the annual meeting of the Asian Development Bank on May 4, Zhao also made an effort to reassure foreign investors that China's social and economic systems were not disintegrating into turmoil and that the student demonstrations would soon be brought under control. Unlike Zhao's May 3 speech, which had been sent to other leaders for comments before delivery, this speech was not vetted by other officials, since Zhao was not required to clear in advance a presentation to an economic institution like the Asian Development Bank. Even so, Zhao faced criticism later for not sending the speech to senior party leaders for review before he delivered it.[31] This carefully worded speech, written by Bao Tong, was also broadcast to the students. In it Zhao acknowledged that there were problems with corruption in the party, problems that he attributed to imperfections in the socialist legal system and to a lack of openness and democratic supervision. He reiterated that the students were patriotic.[32] The students were calmed by Zhao's speech; afterward the numbers demonstrating in the square fell off sharply.

By this time, the Hong Kong press had picked up on the difference in tone between Zhao's speech and Li Peng's conversations with the students, and began speculating about conflicts between the two. A July 6 report to the NPC on the "counter-revolutionary rebellion" by Chen Xitong, the Beijing municipal official allied with Li Peng who was presenting reports to the top officials on the demonstrations, claimed Li Peng was ready to be tough while Zhao was trying to be more understanding. Chen Xitong joined the allies of Deng and Li Peng in criticizing Zhao's May 4 speech; like the others, he said that it departed from the message of the April 26 editorial. Chen stated that many grassroots officials like himself who had been attempting to control the unruly students felt that they had been betrayed by Zhao's speech. These officials had been trying to get the students to back down, but in their eyes Zhao was far too sympathetic. Chen Xitong also claimed that many intellectuals, encouraged by Zhao's speech, had begun speaking out more openly, causing a new wave of demonstrations and promising more turmoil.[33] Zhao's followers felt that Li Peng and his allies were making their task of winning the cooperation of the students more difficult.

Preparing for Gorbachev and the Hunger Strike, May 13–May 24

Gorbachev's visit to Beijing on May 15–18 marked a historic turning point in Sino-Soviet relations and a personal triumph for Deng Xiaoping. The three-decades-long estrangement of the world's largest Communist powers was coming to an end and normalized relations were in sight. In the early 1980s, Deng had summarized the conditions necessary for China to resume normal relations with the Soviet Union: the Soviets had to pull out of Afghanistan and remove their troops from China's northern border area, and the Vietnamese had to leave Cambodia. Deng's earlier view that the Soviet Union was overextended and would need to readjust its foreign policy had proved correct. Gorbachev had agreed to all of the conditions and was coming to Beijing on Deng's terms. The event would be one of the capstones to Deng's career. In his triumph, Deng was prepared to be the gracious host, welcoming the press from around the world to the celebration.

As Gorbachev's arrival approached, reporters and photographers from around the globe assembled in Beijing in large teams to cover the event. American TV anchorman Dan Rather, who rarely went abroad, appeared, as did other Western celebrities. Not surprisingly, then, Deng was ready to try almost anything to clear Tiananmen Square before Gorbachev's arrival. After Zhao's speech on May 4, when students began returning to their campuses, there was reason to be hopeful. Moderate students from the Beijing area had voted with their feet and returned to their classrooms. Yet more radical locals and students who had traveled from distant regions persisted in camping out in the square.

On the morning of May 13, two days before Gorbachev was scheduled to arrive, radical student leaders, desperate to keep their dwindling movement alive and confident that they would not be arrested while Gorbachev was in Beijing, announced a novel addition to the Chinese protest tradition: a hunger strike to start that very afternoon. Over a thousand students marched to Tiananmen, where they stated that they would not eat until the government met their demands. The students declared, "We do not want to die. We want to live and live fully. . . . But if the death of a single person or of several people will enable a greater number of people to live better or if these deaths can make our homeland stronger and more prosperous, then we have no right to live on in ignominy."[34]

Most hunger strikers did drink liquids and some pretended to fast but in fact ate solid food. Others took no food or water and before long, fainted. Their readiness to die elevated their struggle above practical politics and gave them a moral superiority with the public. The pictures of hunger strikers on television evoked sympathy both at home and abroad. Some viewers who had blamed the students for interrupting Beijing traffic began to sympathize with those who were ready to sacrifice their lives, seeing them not as troublemak-ers but as heroic victims. Government officials, aware that any deaths from hunger could inflame the public, were restrained in dealing with the strikers. None of the students were attacked or arrested, and the government supplied buses to shelter them when it rained, provided toilet facilities, and assigned government workers to help clean up the square. Sympathetic medical work-ers treated those who were fainting and moved the more serious cases to nearby hospitals. According to official statistics, between May 13 and May 24, some 8,205 hunger strikers were taken to hospitals.[35] With such good medical attention, none of the students died, but the risk of death added drama to the demonstrations.

The hunger strike caught party leaders completely by surprise. On May 13, the day the hunger strike began, a worried Deng Xiaoping met with Zhao Zi-yang and Yang Shangkun. Deng declared that the movement had dragged on for too long; he wanted the square cleared before Gorbachev's arrival. When Deng inquired about the mood of the public, Zhao replied that the vast ma-jority of students were aware that the honor of their nation was at stake and would be unlikely to disrupt the welcoming ceremony. The pressure was on Zhao to ensure that Beijing would remain quiet during Gorbachev's visit, and he was given considerable leeway to do whatever he thought necessary to clear the square.

On May 14, several well-known Chinese intellectuals, aware of how im-portant it was to empty the square before Gorbachev arrived and fearing a vi-olent confrontation, did their best to mediate the dispute. Twelve of China's most famous writers and commentators, including Dai Qing, Liu Zaifu, and Yan Jiaqui, issued an announcement criticizing the government's treatment of the students and failure to publish the truth about the movement. In an attempt to reach a reconciliation, they advocated that the government recog-nize the independent student organizations. But they also urged the students remaining in the square to return to their universities.[36] They pleaded with the students: "Democracy is erected gradually . . . we must be completely clear-headed . . . we beg that you make full use of the most valuable spirit of the student movement, the spirit of reason, and temporarily leave the Square."[37]

Instead of personally appearing in front of the students, Zhao sent Yan Mingfu in his stead. Yan, head of the United Front Work Department, met with the students on May 16. As one of the party secretaries in the Secretar-iat, Yan was sympathetic to the students' demands. Desperate to reach an agreement, Yan spoke frankly with them about the split within the party; he urged them to leave the square to protect Zhao. He promised to meet them again the next day and assured them that if they returned to their campuses, they would not be punished. Yan Mingfu went so far as to offer himself as a hostage to guarantee their protection.[38] His efforts, however, failed.

Although the hunger-striking students were demonstrating for democracy, they did not practice majority rule among themselves. As Wuer Kaixi, a bold student leader, explained, they had made a pact that if any one student wanted to stay in the square, the movement would continue.[39] The students remained well-behaved, and when the Chinese flag was raised, they stood up in respect and sang the national anthem. But the enormous outpouring of sympathy from the citizenry had strengthened their determination not to yield. When it became obvious that the students were not going to leave, Yan Mingfu, who understood what this would mean for Zhao's career and had some intimations of what it could mean for the country, was seen in tears.[40]

Gorbachev Visits Beijing, May 15–18

By May 15, the day of Gorbachev's arrival, the crowds in support of the students had again grown. At about 1 a.m. on May 16—the day Deng was scheduled to meet Gorbachev—the government made a last-ditch effort to clear the square. Loudspeakers in the square broadcast that the government was beginning a dialogue with the student representatives. The official message urged the students to consider China's national interest, end their hunger strike, and return to their universities. The students listened under banners they had made welcoming Gorbachev, whom they regarded as a political reformer worthy of China's emulation. One banner read, "We salute the ambassador of democracy."[41] But they refused to leave the square and more crowds assembled to support them. The government had no choice but to cancel the planned welcoming ceremonies in the square. Instead, a small ceremony was held at the heavily guarded airport, and the meeting between Deng and Gorbachev was held inside the Great Hall of the People, which the demonstrators also tried to crash into, breaking a window in the process.

These changes of venue amid the distractions caused by the hunger strike were humiliating to Deng and the other senior officials who were unable to bring order to their own capital. Yet the meeting between Deng and Gorbachev went smoothly. No Chinese leader had been more centrally involved in the quarrels with the Soviet Union than Deng. He had supervised the drafting of the nine anti-Soviet letters in the early 1960s and he had represented China in the quarrels with Mikhail Suslov in 1963. But Deng personally had also laid the basis for the improvement of relations immediately after his attack on Vietnam in 1979 and in 1985, when he had asked visiting Romanian leader Nicolai Ceauşescu to convey to the Soviet leaders the Chinese conditions for normalization of relations. Negotiations between Soviet and Chinese diplomats had continued until February 1989, when the two sides agreed on the wording of a joint communiqué that ended the Vietnamese occupation of Cambodia and announced the timing of the visit by Gorbachev to Beijing to launch a new era of friendly relations between the two nations.[42]

Deng was careful to keep U.S. officials informed so that improvements in relations with the Soviet Union would not come at the expense of relations with the United States. No sooner had the two sides worked out the agreement than Deng, on February 26, 1989, met with President George H. W. Bush. During their meeting Deng assured Bush, who was making a quick trip to China after the Japanese emperor's funeral, that China's improved relations with the Soviet Union would not affect its good relations with the United States. Deng began by tracing the history of Sino-Soviet relations, making it clear that conditions were now very different and that there was no danger that China would develop a close relationship with the Soviet Union similar to that in the 1950s. China, he explained, would continue to seek closer relations with the United States because it was in China's strategic interests to do so.[43] In May, on the eve of the Gorbachev visit, Deng sent Wan Li to reassure U.S. and Canadian officials, including President George H. W. Bush on May 23, that the meeting with Gorbachev would not be at the expense of relations with the United States and Canada. And after the visit, Deng arranged to send Foreign Minister Qian Qichen to inform the U.S. government about the discussions.

Foreign Minister Qian Qichen, who sat in on Deng's two-and-a-half-hour discussion with Gorbachev on May 16, reported that Deng was in good spirits, even exuberant, as he healed the breach with the Soviet Union on his terms. Deng and Gorbachev were both reformers; Deng at eighty-four was at the end of his career and Gorbachev at fifty-eight was at the beginning of his. Deng proved disarming when talking about the previous tensions with the Soviet Union. He acknowledged that he had been personally involved in the ideological debates with the Soviet Union, but described the arguments on both sides as "all empty words."[44] He confessed that "we do not believe that our views were always correct." Speaking from memory and without notes, Deng then gave a clear, detailed account of the ups and downs in Sino-Soviet relations. The problems, he said, stemmed from the fact that the Soviet Union did not always treat China as an equal. But he also said that the Chinese would never forget the Soviet Union's assistance in laying the industrial foundations for the new China. Deng agreed to end the past disputes and focus on the future, so that China could enjoy friendly relations with its neighbors. Gorbachev had been well briefed on the historical background; he spoke carefully and expressed support for Deng's view that, as neighboring countries, the two should strive to develop a friendly relationship.[45]

Deng made a thorough and forward-looking presentation to Gorbachev, but at the time he seemed uncharacteristically tense. While on camera during the banquet honoring Gorbachev, Deng, hands shaking, let a piece of dumpling drop from his chopsticks.[46] That same day, some two hundred hunger strikers had been rushed to Beijing hospitals for emergency care and there were still some 3,100 hunger strikers left in the square.[47] Deng could not easily forget the worsening situation.

When he met Zhao Ziyang later in the afternoon of May 16, Gorbachev said that he had already met with Deng, but now that he was meeting with General Secretary Zhao, all agreements could become official. Zhao explained that Deng was still acting in an official capacity; China still needed Deng's wisdom and experience and "therefore the First Plenary Session of the 13th Party Congress in 1987 made the solemn decision that we still need Comrade Deng Xiaoping at the helm when it comes to the most important questions."[48] When Deng learned about Zhao's statement, he was upset. Zhao's supporters later explained that it was natural that Zhao should try to correct Gorbachev's impression because in fact his meeting with Deng had been official. Zhao later said he was trying to protect, not harm, Deng's image.[49] In his diary, however, Li Peng offered a different view: he admitted that Zhao's comments were accurate but he felt that raising them in this context was Zhao's way of laying blame on Deng for the economic problems in 1988 and for the decisions that had led to the worsening of the student demonstrations.[50] Indeed Deng, like Li Peng, interpreted Zhao's comments as blaming him for the recent problems.[51]

The world press, assembled in Beijing to cover the reconciliation between China and the Soviet Union, found the student movement spellbinding; indeed, the dramatic events on the square quickly eclipsed the Gorbachev visit as the center of media attention. For foreign reporters, it was impossible not to get caught up in the idealism and enthusiasm of the students, who were far more open than Chinese had previously dared to be. With a vast international audience watching, the students grew even more confident that the PLA would not attack. Some, recognizing an opportunity to present their case to the world, assigned English-speaking demonstrators to the outside columns of the marchers, so they could tell the world about their desire for freedom and democracy and the need to end high-level corruption. A few persistent foreign reporters, trying to maintain balance, reported that most students in fact knew little about democracy and freedom and had little idea about how to achieve such goals.[52]

During the Gorbachev visit, the number of students in the square grew daily. On May 18, the Ministry of State Security estimated that despite the rain, some 1.2 million people were in Tiananmen Square.[53] Protests had spread to other major cities as well, and an estimated 200,000 students, from as far as several days' train ride away, had descended upon Beijing. Some students, feeling entitled on moral grounds, demanded free railway passage like the Red Guards had received during the Cultural Revolution. At the last minute, Gorbachev's press conference, originally scheduled to be held in the Great Hall of the People, was moved to the Diaoyutai Guest House because his motorcade could not pass through the square.[54] Vast numbers of reporters, however, skipped the press conference altogether to remain at Tiananmen Square.

The Gorbachev visit marked a turning point not only in Sino-Soviet relations, but in the student movement as well. Until then Deng had hoped that the students would heed the call for patriotism and leave Tiananmen Square before the arrival of Gorbachev. For Deng, the end of the Sino-Soviet rift on Chinese terms was too big of an occasion to consider abandoning Tiananmen Square as the site of the welcoming ceremony. But the students were unwilling to back down. Deng did not want to spoil the Gorbachev visit by sending in troops that would have clashed with students. But after the students had been so brazen as to refuse to leave Tiananmen Square during Gorbachev's stay, Deng concluded they had gone too far. He was ready to bring in the troops.

21

The Tiananmen Tragedy

May 17–June 4, 1989

As Deng moved ahead with plans to bring in the troops and declare martial law, Zhao and a group of liberal officials made a final desperate effort to avoid a violent crackdown. At 10 p.m. on May 16, after a meeting with Gorbachev, Zhao chaired an emergency Politburo Standing Committee meeting where he reiterated his view, supported only by Hu Qili, that there would be no peaceful resolution unless the party retracted the April 26 editorial. Outside the Politburo, a group of retired liberal officials on the Central Advisory Commission—including Li Chang, Li Rui, Yu Guangyuan, and Du Runsheng—gathered to make final arrangements for releasing a declaration that the student movement should be declared patriotic. And early the next morning, with his back to the wall, Zhao called Deng's office, hoping that if he could meet privately with Deng, he might be able to persuade him not to bring in the troops. Zhao was told to come in the afternoon. But when he arrived, he learned that he would not be meeting Deng alone; other members of the Standing Committee would be present. Clearly Deng was not about to accept his views.[1]

Martial Law and Zhao's Departure, May 17–20

Even before Gorbachev arrived in Beijing, Deng had begun considering contingency plans in case the demonstrators did not clear the square. On April 25, the same day he decided to publish the editorial warning the demonstrators, Deng put the People's Liberation Army (PLA) on alert. By the beginning of May, all military leaves had been canceled.[2] Later, after the Gorbachev visit had ended and the most prominent members of the foreign media had left, Deng was ready to make his move. On May 17 at 4 p.m., Deng assembled the members of the Politburo Standing Committee (Zhao Ziyang, Li Peng, Qiao Shi, Hu Qili, and Yao Yilin) as well as Yang Shangkun, Deng's liaison with the Central Military Commission (CMC), to decide on the next steps. All the participants were allowed to express their views. Zhao explained that the situation was serious; there were still as many as 300,000 to 400,000 people protesting daily. He believed that unless they retracted the harsh April 26 editorial, the students would not voluntarily evacuate the square.[3]

After listening to others' opinions, Deng said that a solution to the nation's problems had to begin in Beijing because any turmoil in the capital would have an influence on the whole country. They needed to be firm. In Hungary, for example, national leaders had made concessions that had only led to further demands. If Chinese leaders were to yield again, China would be finished. In Shanghai, Deng added, Jiang Zemin had successfully restored order in 1986 by taking a tough, top-down approach, closing down the *World Economic Herald* for failing to follow directions (which had helped calm student demonstrations there). Deng believed that a similar steely resolve was needed now. But at present, Deng concluded, the police in Beijing were insufficient to restore order: troops were needed. These troops would have to be moved in quickly and decisively, and for the time being, plans for their deployment needed to remain secret.[4] When some in the room expressed worries that foreigners would react negatively to any use of force, Deng replied that swift action was required and the "Westerners would forget."[5]

Li Peng and Yao Yilin immediately supported Deng's views, and although Hu Qili raised some concerns, only Zhao Ziyang clearly disagreed. When Zhao spoke up, he was reminded that the minority must follow the lead of the majority. Zhao replied that as a party member he accepted this, but he still had some personal reservations.[6] As general secretary, Zhao realized that he would be expected to announce the imposition of martial law and then to oversee its implementation. He feared that the decision to bring in the military, even if unarmed, would only inflame the conflict.

Immediately after the meeting with Deng, Zhao asked his assistant, Bao Tong, to prepare his letter of resignation. Zhao knew that he could not bring himself to implement martial law and that this decision would mean the end of his career, but he also was confident that his decision would place him on the right side of history. At the dinner table with his family, he told his wife,

Liang Boqi, and daughter, Wang Yannan, that he planned to resign and that his decision would be hard on all of them. The family then phoned Zhao's sons in Macao and Hainan with the same message. They all understood and accepted what he was about to do.[7]

That evening Zhao had the awkward responsibility of chairing a Politburo Standing Committee meeting, without Deng, to discuss how to implement Deng's decision to carry out martial law. At the meeting Zhao announced that he could not implement the decision to introduce martial law. Acknowledging that his career was over, he said his time was up.

The next morning Zhao Ziyang arrived in Tiananmen Square at about 5 a.m. to express his concern for the students. Accompanied by Li Peng, who was now monitoring his movements, Zhao, speaking into a handheld microphone, said, "We have come too late. . . . No matter how you have criticized us, I think you have the right to do so." Zhao was shown on television around the world, trembling, with tears in his eyes. He explained that he too had once been young and had taken part in demonstrations without regard for the consequences. He then encouraged the students to give up their hunger strike and look after their health, so they could take an active part in the four modernizations.[8] Some listeners interpreted Zhao's message as a warning that he could no longer help protect the students. This would be his last public appearance.

After forcing this split on May 17, Zhao was not kept informed of meetings to plan for martial law and he refused to make the public announcement on its imposition. On May 19 Zhao wrote a letter to Deng, trying once again to persuade him to soften the April 26 editorial, even though by then he knew it had virtually no chance of success. His letter was never answered.

When Yang Shangkun first learned about Zhao's letter of resignation, he asked Zhao to withdraw it so as not to reveal to the public an open split within the leadership—even though Deng, upset about Zhao's appearance in the square, felt that such a split may have already become apparent. Zhao refused to chair the meeting to announce the imposition of martial law, but he did agree to withdraw his letter; instead of resigning he requested a three-day leave due to physical exhaustion.[9] During those three days, martial law was to be introduced.

On May 28 Zhao wrote a letter to Deng, attempting to explain his remarks to Gorbachev that had so angered Deng. On the same day, Zhao was put under house arrest. His assistant Bao Tong was arrested and later moved to Qincheng Prison for high-level inmates. Although Deng lived for eight more years, he never answered Zhao's letter and the two never again met.

From May 24 to May 26, the party center in Beijing hosted provincial first party secretaries, many governors, and leaders from Hong Kong and Macao to explain the reasons for introducing martial law and to seek their support.[10] The procedures for making a formal case against Zhao, however, took place after June 4. Having observed the results of Hu Yaobang's confession in 1987, Zhao refused to confess, saying he had done nothing wrong. Under house arrest, he was given comfortable living conditions, but his visitors were strictly limited and his own visits outside were tightly controlled until his death in 2005.[11]

Plans for carrying out martial law moved quickly after Deng's meeting with the members of the Politburo Standing Committee on May 17. The CMC held an enlarged meeting the next morning, and Yang Shangkun announced the decision to introduce martial law. That afternoon, the CMC held a working meeting to finalize the details for implementation: Gorbachev was to leave Beijing on the morning of May 19 and that evening 50,000 troops would begin moving in quickly, arriving in Tiananmen Square the morning of Saturday, May 20.[12] At 10 p.m. on May 19, Li Peng spoke to a large gathering of high-level party, government, and military officials to inform them of the movement of troops. The following morning, at 9:30 a.m., Li Peng announced that martial law would begin at 10:00 a.m.[13] Yang Shangkun instructed the military commanders that their soldiers were not to fire, even if provoked. Most of the soldiers did not even carry weapons.

The Failure of Martial Law, May 19–22

Deng and the military leaders were so confident that the troops would reach their destination quickly and without incident that the soldiers were not briefed on what to do if they encountered resistance. They were not even given maps of alternate routes in case their paths were blocked. Meanwhile, by the afternoon of the May 19 the students were beginning to learn that soldiers in tanks, trucks, and armored vehicles were entering the outskirts of the city. The mood among students in the square was tense and fearful as they anticipated that the troops would arrive before dawn. Some Beijing students returned to their universities, but the more radical students, as well as those students who had come to Beijing from some distance (the Ministry of Railways reported that some 56,000 students had arrived in Beijing by rail between 6 p.m. May 16 and 8 a.m. May 19), hunkered down and braced for the worst.[14]

Neither the students in the square nor the high officials anticipated what happened next: the people of Beijing overwhelmed and completely stalled the 50,000 troops coming in from the north, east, south, and west, on six major and several minor routes. In his May 20 diary entry Li Peng simply noted: "We had not expected great resistance" and he then went on to record that troops everywhere had been stopped. Some troops had tried to enter Tiananmen Square by subway, but the subway entrances were blocked. Some had attempted to come in by suburban trains, but people lay on the tracks. In one instance, two thousand troops coming from some distance managed to arrive at the train station, but as soon as they got off the train, they were surrounded and unable to move.[15] Cell phones were not yet available, but people used regular phones to call acquaintances, and those with walkie-talkies set themselves up at key crossings to warn of the arrival of troops so that people could swarm to attempt to stop them. People organized motorcycle corps to speed ahead and carry news of the troops' movements as they entered Beijing. Some officials blame Zhao Ziyang's assistant Bao Tong for leaking to the student protesters the plans for how and where the troops would arrive, but even if Bao Tong were a brilliant organizer, he could not have been able to alert or organize the vast throngs that took to the streets.

That night a full moon lit up the city. Foreign news people observed massive numbers of people coming from all directions, joining crowds totaling hundreds of thousands in the streets of Beijing. Correspondents reported that the entire city became involved in the demonstrations, beyond anything ever before witnessed in the city. There was not only widespread sympathy for the students, but also overwhelming opposition to martial law.[16] Before dawn the next morning, at 4:30 a.m., student-controlled loudspeakers in Tiananmen Square triumphantly announced that the troops had been blocked in all directions and were unable to reach the square. Demonstrators in the square cheered.

The soldiers, mostly rural youth who were less educated and less sophisticated than the university students, were unprepared for what they encountered. Foreign correspondents reported that many of them appeared bewildered. They had been briefed not to respond to taunts and not to cause bloodshed, and they obeyed. Few soldiers carried weapons. Students quickly organized themselves to address the truckloads of stalled troops, trying to convince them of the justice of the student cause—their desire for more freedoms and an end to corruption. Bystanders with access to printing machines quickly printed and passed out leaflets opposing martial law. Some soldiers, with little knowledge and preparation, appeared sympathetic to the students' appeals.[17]

In his diary entry of May 22, Li Peng acknowledged that the troops were unable to move for fifty hours. He also reports that Deng was worried that the "soldiers' hearts may not be steady" *(junxin buwen)*. For Deng, this became the crucial issue. Would the soldiers maintain order when so many young people opposed them? Might the soldiers be influenced by the students and lose their determination to impose discipline? Some soldiers appeared weary and hungry.[18]

At 7 a.m. on Monday, May 22, the troops were ordered to withdraw. As they began to leave, however, confusion reigned. Some residents thought the troops were merely maneuvering to find alternate routes to the center of the city and so they continued to block their movements. In any case, by May 24 the troops had disappeared and withdrawn to the outskirts of the city, where they remained. Martial law had not officially ended, but as the troops departed, the demonstrators began to celebrate their victory.[19] Never since 1949—not even during the Cultural Revolution—had so many people in Beijing spontaneously demonstrated against the party leadership. Deng now confronted a mass movement that Mao would have been proud of, if only it had not been directed at his very own Communist Party.

Deng Prepares for Armed Force, May 22–June 3

Immediately after May 20, while allowing the troops to retreat temporarily, Deng directed Yang Shangkun to prepare tanks, armored vehicles, trucks, and armed men in sufficient numbers to overcome all resistance. By this point, the top leaders in Beijing had become acutely worried about the steadiness of the troops and high officials in the face of civilian opposition. On May 20, eight retired generals who had not been consulted about the imposition of martial law sent Deng a statement opposing the use of force. Deng and Yang Shangkun dispatched two top military leaders to visit each of these generals individually to explain the reasons for the imposition of martial law.[20]

Over the next few days, Li Peng led an effort to garner the support of high officials throughout the country. Li Peng's diary for days after May 20 is filled with reports of phone conversations to local leaders across the country in which he relayed what had happened, asked for their approval, and recorded their declarations of support for the decisions of the Beijing leadership. By May 21, Li Peng had reported that leaders of twenty-two provincial-level units had expressed their support for martial law.[21] For his part, Deng remained busy consulting with other senior Chinese leaders to ensure their support. In the crisis, Chen Yun supported Deng, saying it was important to remain firm and not back down.[22] Deng met also with Li Xiannian, Qiao Shi, Peng Zhen, and other elders to make sure there were no splits in the top leadership.

In mid-May Wan Li was traveling in North America. Fearing that he might support Zhao, central party leaders notified him not to return directly to Beijing but to return first to Shanghai. On May 26 at 3 a.m., Wan Li arrived at the Shanghai airport, where he was met by Jiang Zemin and Ding Guan'gen, an alternate member of the Politburo, who briefed him on the situation. On the next day, Ding Guan'gen gave Wan Li a more complete briefing based on orders from Beijing, and Jiang Zemin gave Wan a package of documents prepared in Beijing that explained why Zhao was being pushed aside.[23] Although Wan had spoken favorably of democracy while in North America, after he returned to Shanghai, Wan, ever the loyal party member, expressed support for Deng's policies.[24] Only then was he given permission to return to Beijing.

Deng Readies a New Leadership Structure

Even before martial law was imposed on May 20, Deng was busy considering the new leadership structure that would be announced to the public immediately after order was restored. Deng first took time to reaffirm the decisions of the 13th Party Congress, convened in 1987, before announcing the dismissal of Zhao, for he wanted to make clear to the public that decisions introduced by Zhao would continue: markets would not only remain open but would be expanded. Projects then being carried out by foreign companies, even the large controversial project planned for Yangpu in Hainan (led by the Japanese trading company Kumagaigumi), would continue. It was also announced that there would be a vigorous effort to deal with the problem of official corruption.[25]

In his effort to regain public support, Deng wanted new leaders who were not identified with the Tiananmen crackdown to be introduced right after the troops took over the square. By May 19, the day before martial law was imposed, Deng, Chen Yun, and Li Xiannian had already chosen Jiang Zemin as general secretary; they planned to announce his appointment immediately after the Fourth Plenum.[26] Deng had praised Jiang Zemin for his decisive action in skillfully closing down the *World Economic Herald* without causing a big reaction. From 1983 to 1985, Jiang had also served as minister of the Ministry of Electronics Industry and had given briefings to Deng in 1985. Deng, Chen Yun, and Li Xiannian had come to know Jiang well during their winter visits to Shanghai, where Jiang, as first party secretary, had hosted them. He had already served for three years as one of the younger members of the Politburo, so he was also familiar with central party issues. Moreover, Jiang had the combination of firmness, commitment to reform, knowledge of science and technology, and experience in dealing with foreign affairs that Deng considered important for leading China.

Deng, Chen Yun, and Li Xiannian also considered the new membership of the Standing Committee of the Politburo. Li Ruihuan, party secretary in Tianjin, another effective, reform-minded leader, would be placed on the Standing Committee in charge of propaganda—replacing Hu Qili, who now seemed too close to Zhao. Song Ping, an experienced and popular official who had dealt with difficult organizational issues, was to be added at the suggestion of Chen Yun. And Li Peng, who had proved to be firm in carrying out Deng's wishes, would remain as premier, along with Yao Yilin as vice premier. The new appointments were to be announced immediately and would become official at the next Central Committee plenum.[27] Zhao Ziyang would leave the Politburo. Although he did not accuse Zhao of factionalism, Deng said that like Hu Yaobang, Zhao had worked only with a small circle of people.[28]

Having made his decisions about the new leadership, Deng met with the two continuing members of the Standing Committee, Li Peng and Yao Yilin. It would have been only human if the two were upset at being passed over for the top position of general secretary, so Deng patiently explained to them the need for new faces to maintain national order. He also encouraged them to take practical steps against corruption to show the public that the party leaders were serious about dealing with the problem. At the meeting, Deng explained that Jiang Zemin and the other new leaders would need to take dramatic steps in their first few months of power to show their commitment to reform. Deng believed Jiang should not bring his personal staff with him to his new position; instead he urged everyone to unite around Jiang Zemin and form a strong leadership team.[29] Once that new leadership team was in place, Deng would announce his intention to retire completely. He would retain some influence even without any titles, but Jiang Zemin, without the personal authority of the revolutionary leaders, would need authority conferred by official titles in order to lead the country.

Jiang Zemin was unaware of many of these high-level discussions about his future role. Li Peng telephoned Jiang and, without explaining why, told him to fly to Beijing immediately. When Jiang arrived, Li Peng told him that Deng wished to see him. Deng then notified Jiang of his official selection as paramount leader. In Beijing, Jiang consulted individually with the other two top leaders, Chen Yun and Li Xiannian, and began at once to prepare for his new responsibilities.

Jiang Zemin's background made him an appealing choice for leader of the second generation. Born in 1926, Jiang had proved his high intellectual ability by passing the examinations to enter Yangzhou Middle School and later to enter Jiaotong University, one of the top engineering universities in the country. While pursuing his education, he learned some English and also some Russian, which he used during the two years when he was an exchange student in the Soviet Union. He also learned some Romanian. Jiang's uncle, a Communist revolutionary martyr, became Jiang's adopted father after Jiang's own father died when he was thirteen, a turn of events that gave Jiang a personal revolutionary history. Jiang joined the underground Communist Party before 1949. Beginning in 1980, as party secretary and a member of the leading group on foreign investment, under Gu Mu, he gained experience in reform and opening. During his six years as party leader in a Changchun automobile factory (one of China's largest), Jiang also acquired a solid grounding in heavy industry. He became mayor of Shanghai in 1985, party secretary of Shanghai the following year, and a member of the Politburo in 1987.

In selecting their successors, top Chinese leaders were partial to those who came from families of party revolutionaries, especially martyrs, for in a crunch they could be counted on to remain absolutely dedicated to the party. Deng wanted someone thoroughly committed to and knowledgeable about reform, as Jiang had proved he was. He also wanted someone who was firm and skilled at handling crises, as Jiang had been during the 1986 student demonstrations and in closing the *World Economic Herald*. In addition, Deng was looking for someone who could maintain good relations with a variety of people; while in Shanghai and Beijing, Jiang had shown that he could get along with other officials. Indeed, beneath his jovial exterior, Jiang was a smart and mature political manager. Although he never worked in the party structure in Beijing, he used his three years on the Politburo to familiarize himself with party leaders and central party affairs, becoming known as someone who could effectively manage political issues.[30]

The Hardcore Students Persist, May 20–June 2

Immediately after the failure of the troops to establish martial law in Beijing on May 20, more and more people flocked back to the square, buoyed by the mood of popular support and outraged at the imposition of martial law. Although some students had grown weary or intimidated and returned to their campuses, they were replaced by new arrivals from the provinces, who continued to flood in.

On the night of May 29, the Goddess of Democracy, a huge styrofoam statue modeled after the American Statue of Liberty, was placed facing the portrait of Mao and unveiled in a ceremony that attracted enormous attention at home and abroad.[31] The statue had been made by students from the Central Academy of Fine Arts in three rushed days and carted on pedicabs, piece by piece, to Tiananmen Square. Intended to provide a lasting reminder of the cause of Chinese democracy, it would be smashed to pieces in the cleaning up of the square after June 4.

Meanwhile, the tenor of the movement had begun to change. Railway officials estimated that during the period there had been some 400,000 one-way trips to or from Beijing, but by May 30 more people were leaving than arriving.[32] Many of the protestors worried about punishment and wanted to bargain for clemency. By late May, like the Propaganda Department they were opposing, the student leaders began trying to limit the access of reporters to ordinary demonstrators so that they could control the message reaching the public. The message itself was hard to control because the students were not united and because those who emerged as leaders tended to be bold orators who could sway a crowd rather than strategists with a long-term, unified program; the students could not agree on a course of action. In an effort to have at least a minimum of unity, those who remained in the square took the following oath: "I swear to devote my life and my loyalty to protect to the death Tiananmen Square, the capital Beijing, and the republic."[33]

The Crackdown, June 3–4

There is no evidence to suggest that Deng showed any hesitation in deciding to send armed troops to Tiananmen Square. At 2:50 p.m. on June 3, he gave the order to Chi Haotian to do whatever was necessary (*yong yiqie de shouduan*) to restore order. Melanie Manion, a perceptive Western scholar who was there at the time, explained Deng's rationale. In her view, it was "highly probable that even had riot control measures cleared the streets on June 3, they would not have ended the protest movement. . . . The protestors would have retreated only temporarily, to rally in even greater force at a later date . . . the force used on June 4 promised to end the movement immediately, certainly, and once and for all."[34] Deng's family reported that despite all the criticism he received, he never once doubted that he had made the right decision.[35] Many observers who saw the dwindling numbers in Tiananmen Square toward the end of May believe it may have been possible to clear it without violence. But Deng was concerned not only about the students in the square but also about the general loosening of authority throughout the country, and he concluded that strong action was necessary to restore the government's authority.[36]

Two years would pass before the Soviet Union was to collapse, but by 1989 Deng had become convinced that Soviet and Eastern European leaders had not done enough to preserve state and party power. In Poland on April 4, 1989, as a result of the roundtable talks, the labor union Solidarity had taken political control, the presidency had been made an elective office, and the Communist Party had been dissolved. By coincidence, the Polish election was held on June 4, the same day that Chinese troops took over Tiananmen Square. Jiang Zemin, who had studied in the Soviet Union, later praised Deng for having moved boldly to keep China from falling apart as had the Soviet Union.[37]

In total, some 150,000 troops were positioned on the outskirts of Beijing.[38] They had arrived mostly by rail, but ten planeloads of soldiers from the more distant military regions of Chengdu and Guangzhou also arrived on June 1. In case more troops were needed, the Guangzhou airport sold no tickets for six days starting on May 31. Troops had come from five of the seven military regions, but commanders of all the military regions had recorded their approval of the military effort to control the square, so there was no danger that some regions might later express after-the-fact opposition to the suppression of the students. For better or worse, they were in this together.

For the crackdown itself, military strategists, in an effort to prevent roads from being blocked, as early as May 26 started sending small groups of soldiers to infiltrate the neighborhoods of Beijing. Secrecy was key. Some arrived in unmarked trucks, with their weapons hidden. Others came in street clothes, on foot or on bicycles, in groups of three to five, so as to avoid drawing attention. Some stationed near key intersections wore sunglasses and dressed like street toughs. Others were allowed to wear uniforms but appeared to be groups of joggers, out for their regular exercise.[39] For several days they continued entering in small numbers, but on Friday, June 2, the number of soldiers arriving increased. In particular, a large group of soldiers gradually assembled inside the Military Museum four miles west of Tiananmen, which would become an important staging area for troops and equipment. Many especially well-trained troops began to pass through the underground tunnels to position themselves inside the Great Hall of the People, adjacent to Tiananmen Square, where they could be counted on to help clear the square in a disciplined manner. Other soldiers in civilian clothes were located at additional key points around the city, where they could provide intelligence about roadblocks and about any movements by the demonstrators.

On May 19, when the troops had first tried to impose martial law, they had moved at night believing (incorrectly) that people would be in bed, but masses of people swarmed the streets, aided by the light of a full moon. On this second attempt, military leaders chose the night of June 3, the darkest night of the lunar month. The date also seemed promising because if order could be established on June 4, a Sunday, most of the disruption would occur during the weekend, not on a normal work day.

On June 3, Deng acknowledged that once order had been reestablished in Tiananmen Square and Beijing at large, it would take additional months or even years to change people's minds. He was in no hurry and felt no need to blame those who had joined the hunger strike, demonstrated, or petitioned. He told the troops to target only those who were breaking the law and trying to subvert the nation. The logic of the crackdown, he told them, was that China needed a peaceful, stable environment in order to continue its reform and opening, and to modernize the country.

In explaining his rationale for sending in the troops, Deng acknowledged that political reform was needed, but he was firm about maintaining the four cardinal principles: upholding the socialist path, supporting the people's democratic dictatorship, maintaining the leadership of the Communist Party, and upholding Marxist–Leninist–Mao Zedong Thought. If the demonstrations and the pasting up of posters continued, he said, there would not be enough energy left to get things done. He said that leaders should explain their decision to restore order and persuade all levels that it was correct to take action against the protesters.[40]

In the days before June 3, students began to get some hint of troop movements, but they had no idea how many soldiers had already infiltrated the center of Beijing. Moreover, most students could not imagine that their protests would lead to shooting. On several occasions before June 3, the students had voted whether or not to continue to occupy the square. The majority always voted to stay, for most of those who advocated leaving simply voted with their feet. Yet in the days before June 4, some student leaders, fearing punishment, tried to bargain with the government, saying that as a condition for leaving the square they should be guaranteed that they would not be punished and that the student organizations would be given official recognition.[41] They received no such guarantees.

On the night of June 2, word spread on the streets of Beijing that some troops were entering Beijing. Demonstrators and their allies sent the word out, and many PLA vehicles were blocked, overturned, or even set on fire as the troops tried to make their way through the city. Meanwhile, government officials pushed ahead. On the afternoon of June 3, Qiao Shi called an emergency meeting to discuss the final plans for clearing the square. Yang Shangkun presented the plans to Deng, and Deng quickly approved them.[42] The leaders had expected some resistance from demonstrators on June 2, but they had underestimated the strength of the opposition: Chen Xitong reported that people "surrounded and beat soldiers. . . . Some of the rioters even seized munitions and military provisions. Offices of the Central Government and other major organs came under siege." Li Peng was so distraught at the scale and determination of the resistance that for the first time he used the term "counterrevolutionary riot," indicating that those resisting would be treated like enemies. He declared, "We have to be absolutely firm in putting down this counterrevolutionary riot in the capital. We must be merciless with the tiny minority of riot elements. The PLA martial law troops, the People's Armed Police, and Public Security are authorized to use any means necessary to deal with people who interfere with the mission."[43]

On June 3, the commanders of the various group armies met at the headquarters of the Beijing Military Region to go over the details of their assault plan. Three waves of soldiers in motorized vehicles would enter Beijing. In each wave troops would move in from the north, south, east, and west. The first wave would move from the third and fourth ring roads between 5:00 p.m. and 6:30 p.m.; the second between 7:00 p.m. and 8:00 p.m.; and the third between 9:00 p.m. and 10:30 p.m. Some of the earlier trucks would not contain weapons, but two waves of armed soldiers would follow the three earlier waves; one would set out at about 10:30 p.m. and another after midnight.[44] The soldiers were to clear the square before dawn.

The launch proceeded as planned. At 6:30 in the evening on June 3, an emergency announcement was made on radio and TV that workers should remain at their posts and citizens should stay at home to safeguard their lives. Chinese state television (CCTV) broadcast these emergency announcements nonstop, while loudspeakers made the same announcements in the square.[45]

The announcements did not say specifically that troops were moving in, however, and since the government had already issued many other warnings, many people did not attach sufficient weight to the phrase "safeguard your lives."

On June 2 and June 3, the student protesters used tactics they had developed since May 19. Few had walkie-talkies, but they did make good use of motorcycles to spread the word of troop movements. Several hundred motorcyclists, known as the "Flying Tigers," made themselves available to speed from one site to another, warning of troop movements, so that the people had time to set up new roadblocks. When the roadblocks forced the lead trucks to stop, people rushed to slash tires or simply to let the air out, thus bringing the trucks to a halt. Then the people cut wires or ripped out parts of the engines and began taunting and throwing bricks and stones, and in some cases assaulting the soldiers on the back of the trucks. These roadblocks proved effective in some cases, stopping not only the first wave of trucks, but also later waves that could not get around the first group of disabled vehicles.[46]

The greatest resistance and the greatest violence on the night of June 3 and the early morning of June 4 took place on a main street four miles west of Tiananmen Square, near Muxidi Bridge and next to tall apartment buildings where retired high-level officials lived. At about 9:30 p.m., troops from the 38th Group Army reached Muxidi, where they found several thousand civilians gathered to resist any advance. Buses were stretched across the road at Muxidi Bridge, blocking further movement by armored vehicles. The PLA first tried firing tear gas and rubber bullets, which had little effect; people responded by boldly throwing rocks and other objects at the troops. An officer used a bullhorn to order the crowds to disperse, but to no avail. The 38th Group Army that had approached from the west, like the Guomindang turncoats who had joined the PLA during the Chinese civil war, were under special pressure to prove their loyalty: their commander, Xu Qinxian, had excused himself, saying that medical problems made it impossible for him to lead his troops. At about 10:30 p.m. the troops near Muxidi Bridge began firing into the air and throwing stun grenades but there were no deaths.

By 11:00 p.m. the troops, still unable to advance, began firing live weapons directly at the crowds (using AK-47 automatic rifles that can fire ninety shots per minute). As people were shot, others carried the wounded to the side of the battle area and took them to ambulances, or put them on bicycles or pedicabs to rush them to nearby Fuxing Hospital. PLA trucks and armored cars also began charging ahead at full speed, running over anyone who dared to stand in their path.[47] Even after they began shooting with live rounds, using deadly force against their countrymen, it took the troops some four hours to advance the four miles eastward from Muxidi to Tiananmen.[48]

At Tiananmen Square, troops did not arrive in sizable numbers until after midnight, but some police and plainclothes military were already in place, having arrived several hours earlier. At 8 p.m., lights lit up the square and the adjacent Chang'an Boulevard that runs east of the square, and by 9 p.m., this boulevard was mostly deserted. In armored vehicles and tanks, the troops began to move toward the square. Several miles out, as they approached from the east, some rifle shots hit the windows of buildings where foreign photographers and reporters were located; the troops were warning them to keep away from the windows, where they might take pictures of killings near the square. Foreigners were also stopped by plainclothes officers, who told them to get off the streets so that they would not get hurt and warned them not to take photographs of military action. Many photographers had their cameras and film confiscated.[49]

An estimated 100,000 demonstrators were still in Tiananmen Square just before the troops began to move in. By 1 a.m. on Sunday, June 4, soldiers had begun arriving from every direction. Around the edges of the square, on Chang'an Boulevard and at the Great Hall of the People, soldiers opened fire on civilians who had begun taunting, throwing bricks, and refusing to move. The protestors had not expected that the troops would fire real bullets, but when some died and when wounded protesters were carried away, the remaining people panicked.

By 2 a.m., only several thousand people remained in the square. Student leader Chai Ling announced that those who wanted to leave could leave, and those who wanted to stay could stay. Hou Dejian, a popular singer from Taiwan who along with several well-known intellectuals had entered the square on May 27 for what they all thought would be the final days of the occupation, took the microphone to warn those still there that armed troops were now pressing into the square.[50] Hou said that those listening had proved that they were not afraid to die, but that there had already been enough bloodshed; those remaining should withdraw peacefully without leaving behind anything that could be used as a weapon.

At about 3:40 a.m., as the soldiers approached, Hou Dejian and three others met with the martial law troops to negotiate a peaceful exit from the square. After a brief discussion, the PLA officer agreed. At 4 a.m. the lights went out in the square. Hou Dejian returned to the microphone shortly thereafter to announce their agreement and told those who remained to evacuate immediately. Some three thousand persons hurriedly followed Hou out of the square. At 4:30 a.m. troops and military vehicles moved forward, and the students who stayed behind retreated toward the southwest. At 5:20 a.m., only about two hundred defiant demonstrators remained. They were forced out by the troops and by 5:40 a.m., just before dawn, as ordered, the square was completely clear of demonstrators.[51]

Some observers reported that people were shot in the square, but government spokesmen denied that anyone had been shot in the square between 4:30 and 5:30 a.m.—implicitly acknowledging that some may have been shot before or after that time.[52] The government also did not deny that people were killed on Chang'an Boulevard, adjacent to the square. Many have tried to determine the number of people killed during that night, but estimates vary widely. Official Chinese reports a few days after June 4 stated that more than two hundred were killed, including twenty soldiers and twenty-three students, and that about two thousand were wounded.[53] Li Peng told Brent Scowcroft on July 2 that 310 had died, including some PLA soldiers and thirty-six students.[54] Ding Zilin, the mother of one of those killed, later tried to collect the names of all those killed that night, and as of 2008 she had collected almost three hundred names. Li Zhiyuan, chief political commissar of the 38th Group Army, reported that in addition to the killed and wounded soldiers, some sixty-five trucks and forty-seven armed personnel carriers were destroyed, and another 485 vehicles were damaged.[55] The most reliable estimates by foreign observers who have carefully studied the event are that somewhere between 300 and 2,600 demonstrators were killed and that several thousand were wounded. Some initial foreign reports of tens of thousands killed were later acknowledged to have been greatly exaggerated. Timothy Brook, a Canadian scholar then in Beijing, drawing on estimates by foreign military attachés and data from all eleven major Beijing hospitals, reported that at those hospitals there were at least 478 dead and 920 wounded.[56] Some believe that the number of deaths may have been higher than the numbers documented at these hospitals, however, because some families, fearing long-lasting political punishment for the wounded or themselves, would have sought treatment for their loved one, or disposed of his or her body, outside of regular channels.[57]

For several days after clearing the square, the PLA and the police cleaned up the area that had been trashed during the demonstrations, crushing the

Goddess of Democracy in the process. There were a few scuffles with local citizens, but following the bloody crackdown, an uneasy calm returned to the square and to Beijing.

Student leaders of the demonstrations were rounded up and arrested: some were detained briefly, others were placed in jails. Even some prominent intellectuals like Dai Qing, who had been in the square encouraging the students to withdraw, were arrested and jailed. Deng personally decided on a seven-year sentence for Bao Tong, Zhao Ziyang's assistant; but after serving his seven years, he has remained under strict surveillance. Other subordinates of Zhao's were jailed and after more than twenty years some demonstrators had still not been released. Some student leaders, including Chai Ling and Wu'er Kaixi, and intellectual leaders such as Yan Jiaqi and Chen Yizi, with the help of an "underground railroad" of safe houses and brave friends, managed to escape from the country. Wang Dan, however, was jailed for several years before being released and exiled to the West, where he continued his studies.

The Hothouse Generation and a Postponement of Hope

The students and older intellectuals who took part in the 1989 demonstrations—like intellectuals throughout Chinese history—felt a deep sense of responsibility for the fate of their country. They were, however, a hothouse generation, with little experience outside their schools and universities. Unlike the students of the late 1940s, they had not spent years building an organization to attain power. Unlike the students of the early 1980s, they had not been tempered by political campaigns, struggles during the Cultural Revolution, or work in the countryside. They were the ablest students of their generation, but they had been tested by examinations instead of experiences—they were the sheltered beneficiaries of academic reform in the best middle schools and universities of the country.

Moreover, these students had grown up at a time in Chinese history that offered no space for independent political activists to organize and test their ideas. The demonstrators were not members of political organizations, but a part of crowds with changing leaders and loosely affiliated participants. Those who rose to take high positions in the movement did so not by displaying superior judgment and strategic planning, but through their spontaneous oratory and bravado. Those who remained in the square harbored the illusion that their national leaders would recognize their patriotism and their high morals, talk with them, take their concerns as legitimate, and deal with the issues they were raising.[58]

This hothouse student generation resembled Sun Yat-sen's description of China in the 1920s: like a sheet of loose sand. Zhao Ziyang's opponents blamed him for inciting the students and directing their spears at Deng. Zhao's supporters, in turn, blamed his rivals for provoking the students to embarrass Zhao. Both Zhao's supporters and his opponents may have tried to direct the student protestors, but in fact they had little ability to do so. The Chinese students marched to their own drummers. Even the students' own leaders could only incite the protesters gathered in the square, not control them.

After June 4, students and their families mourned those who had been killed or injured. They also mourned the loss of hope that a more open, moral China would emerge in the near future. Student leaders, considering what to do after June 4, acknowledged to one another that they had been naïve in challenging the nation's leaders and in expecting them to give up their power. Students of this generation, as well as the following generations, took away from their tragic experience the lesson that direct confrontation with the leadership would likely cause a reaction so forceful that it was not worth the costs.

The Chinese students after June 4, then, unlike their counterparts in the Soviet Union and Eastern Europe, stopped attacking the Communist Party. Many students came to believe that progress could only be achieved by slowly building a base, by improving the economic livelihood of more people, by improving people's understanding of public issues, and by gradually developing experience in democracy and freedom. Even some students who were not members of the Communist Party acknowledged that the leaders had been in danger of losing control over the country, and that only the party could maintain the stability necessary to promote economic growth. Many believed that despite the corrupt and self-serving officials, the Communist-led program that had brought about the reform and opening policies—and with them, the improved livelihood of the people—was preferable to any likely alternative. They hoped that after decades of stability and economic growth, a stronger base for a freer society could develop. In the meantime, the vast majority of student activists simply gave up promoting collective action and instead concentrated on pursuing their own careers.

Many intellectuals and even some high-level party officials believed that the decision to fire on innocent people was unforgivable and that sooner or later the party would have to reverse its evaluation of the movement. Although such a change seems unlikely while those who played an active role in deciding to use force are still alive, there has been a softening of the government's position. Within two decades after the crackdown, many of those imprisoned were released and the opprobrium of having taken part was gradually reduced as the events first called a "counterrevolutionary rebellion" *(fangeming baoluan),* became a "riot" *(baoluan),* then "political turmoil" *(zhengzhi dongluan),* and finally, the "1989 storm" *(1989 fengbo).*

The Power of the Tiananmen Image

All of us who care about human welfare are repulsed by the brutal crackdown on June 4, 1989. The tragedy in Tiananmen Square evoked a massive outcry in the West, far greater than previous tragedies in Asia of comparable scale elicited.[59] For instance, on February 28, 1947, as the Guomindang took over Taiwan, the Guomindang general Chen Yi killed off thousands of the most prominent local leaders so as to eliminate any local leader who might have resisted the Guomindang. In Taiwan the incident embittered relations between "locals" and "outsiders" for decades, but it received little attention abroad. In 1980, too, Korean president Chun Doo Hwan led a bloody crackdown during which he slaughtered far more people than were killed in Beijing in 1989 in order to eliminate local resistance in Kwangju. Yet the Kwangju events were not covered by Western television, and global condemnation of the South Korean leaders did not compare with the condemnation of the Chinese leaders after the Tiananmen tragedy.

In his comparative analysis of these incidents, American scholar Richard Madsen tackles this question of why Western audiences became so emotionally involved in the Tiananmen tragedy and suggests that the answer has to do with the way the events unfolded dramatically in real time on television, as well as how the students came to be identified with Western ideals. In short, Madsen concludes that the crackdown in Beijing struck a nerve because it was interpreted as an assault on the American myth that economic, intellectual, and political freedoms will always triumph. Many foreigners came to see Deng as a villainous enemy of freedom who crushed the heroic students who were standing up for what they believed in.[60]

During the Cultural Revolution, there was no comparable foreign media access in China, even though the raw brutality that occurred then affected far greater numbers of people than did the events of June 4. Paradoxically, Deng Xiaoping's efforts to open China to the foreign press made it possible for foreign correspondents to report to the world about his crackdown in Tiananmen Square.

Before the spring of 1989, foreign reporters in China had been highly restricted in their movements and in their access to the Chinese people. Chinese officials, too, under pressure from above not to give away "state secrets," rarely talked to the press and when they did, they were guarded. Until April 1989, when reporters began meeting with dissidents who wanted to pass on their message, they had to meet secretly so as not to get the activists in trouble.

For foreign correspondents trying to see behind the curtain, then, the Beijing Spring provided a unique opportunity. Indeed, for most foreign reporters in Beijing, covering the student demonstrations from April 15 through June 1989 was the most exciting time of their careers. During this period, they worked to the limits of their physical endurance under adverse circumstances to capture the yearning for freedom and democracy and were given air time and print space to report the exciting drama in their home media.

Meanwhile, the Chinese students were as eager for their views to reach wider audiences as the reporters were to broadcast them. For reporters, as for students, the obvious depth of support for the students from the older citizens of Beijing made it difficult to imagine that the government would fire on its own people. Many reporters later criticized themselves for being so caught up in the excitement that they, like the students whom they were covering, had failed to see the lurking dangers and to prepare Western audiences for the consequences.

By the end of May, Western TV viewers and newspaper readers had so thoroughly identified with the students fighting for democracy that the bloody finale was perceived as a crackdown on "our" students, who stood for what "we" stand for. The Goddess of Democracy statue brought home to Americans in particular the apparent yearning for all that the Statue of Liberty represents. In the eyes of Western viewers, heroic young demonstrators were being gunned down by brutal dictators. And when the reporters saw the students they had come to know being battered and killed, they were so viscerally moved that they tended to exaggerate the horrors. Some reported that as many as five thousand or ten thousand demonstrators were killed. After June 4, the story that China was on the brink of civil war continued in the

Western press even though by June 9, when Deng had met with the leaders from all the military regions, it was clear to objective observers that the situation had stabilized.[61]

To Chinese leaders straining to keep control over events, the foreign media that could be seen or heard by hotel staff and residents of southern cities near Hong Kong, as well as by Chinese people overseas, became "black hands" fomenting the disturbance. Indeed, many Chinese eagerly sought the reports of Voice of America, the BBC, and CNN. Professional Chinese journalists envied the freedom of Western journalists to report events as they saw them and tried to stretch their own range of freedom in the stories they wrote.

In the aftermath of the Tiananmen incident, businesspeople, scholars, and U.S. government officials who believed that U.S. national interests required working with the Chinese government were vulnerable to criticism for cooperating with the "evil dictators" in Beijing. As the Cold War was coming to a close, many outspoken U.S. liberals were arguing that our policies should reflect our values, that we should not coddle dictators but instead should stand on the side of democracy and human rights. And what better way to display Western commitments to these ideals than to condemn those responsible for the Tiananmen crackdown? After June 4, then, Deng Xiaoping was confronted not only by disaffected youth and urban residents in China, but also by Western officials who espoused the same values as the Chinese demonstrators.

What If?

A tragedy of such enormous proportions, one that caused such extensive human suffering and was witnessed around the world, led all those who care about the welfare of humankind to ask how such a catastrophe might have been avoided. Those looking for an immediate cause of the tragedy point to the decision by Deng Xiaoping to use whatever means necessary to clear the square. Deng's critics argue that if he had not taken such a firm stance against the "turmoil" on April 26, 1989, if he had been more willing to listen to the students, or if he had used all the nonviolent means at his disposal, the square could have been cleared without such violence and loss of life. Critics of Zhao Ziyang argue that if he had given less encouragement to the students and had been more resolute in dealing with them, and if he had been less concerned about his personal image as an enlightened leader, the ultimate tragedy could have been avoided. Critics of Li Peng claim that if he had not been so stubborn in refusing to talk with the students and to understand their concerns, so quick to condemn them, so determined to promote the editorial of April 26 that branded them as perpetrators of "turmoil," and so rigid in his disdain for and lack of sympathy for them, the tragedy might not have occurred. Critics of Chen Xitong and Li Ximing say that had they not exaggerated the gravity of the situation and the extent of foreign involvement in their reports to Deng and other senior officials, the senior leaders, including Deng, would not have felt compelled to respond so strongly.

Critics of the student leaders say that had they not been so vain, displayed such an exaggerated sense of personal importance, and refused to consider the dangers they were creating, the tragedy would not have occurred. Some suggest, too, that if the students and the other Beijing residents had not stopped the troops on May 20 that were trying to bring order by peaceful means, the regime could have avoided the shootings that followed two weeks later. For their part, Chinese critics of Westerners argue that if Westerners had not fanned the flames of student protest and if the foreign "black hands" had not tried to destroy Chinese communism and the socialist system, the demonstrations would never have gotten out of hand.

Those who look for deeper causes point to the decisions by Deng and Zhao Ziyang to allow inflation to rise in 1988 and to lift price controls on consumer products, arousing the anger and anxiety of the citizenry. Others complain about the arbitrary exercise of power and privilege by those in high positions who intimidated the public, exercised unnecessarily tight controls over personal lives, and gave unfair advantages to their friends and relatives. Some conservatives blame the market reforms that went too far by encouraging greed and contributing to official corruption. Others believe that Deng's failure to move the country faster toward democracy and to support Hu Yaobang in 1986 was the ultimate cause of the conflagration. Deng did believe that officials at the "commanding heights" have a responsibility to make decisions and that although they should listen to constructive opinions, in the end they must do what they feel is necessary for the long-term success of the country. If Deng had done more to experiment with voting methods, to weaken the bonds of authoritarian leadership, to introduce the rule of law, and to punish corrupt officials, some say, the country could have progressed faster and avoided the challenge from the students.

Other officials, who admire Deng's handling of the Tiananmen demonstrations, believe that in late May 1989, once the situation in Tiananmen Square began spinning out of control, the strong actions taken by Deng represented the Chinese people's only chance for keeping their nation together. Many officials believe that once Deng was unable to bring order by introducing martial law without firing on the crowds, he had no choice but to do what he did to keep the country united. When many Chinese people compare Deng's response to the Beijing student uprising with those of Gorbachev and his Eastern European counterparts to their own versions of the Beijing Spring, they believe the Chinese people and the Chinese nation today are far better off. They are convinced that given its early stage of development, China could not have stayed together had the leadership allowed the intellectuals the freedom they sought. They acknowledge the seriousness of the tragedy of 1989, but they believe that even greater tragedies would have befallen China had Deng failed to bring an end to the two months of chaos in June 1989.

As much as we scholars, like others concerned about human life and the pursuit of liberty, want to find clear answers that explain the causes of that tragedy, the truth is that none of us can be certain what would have happened had different courses of action been taken. Nor is it possible, only two decades after these events, to make a final judgment on the long-run impact of Deng's decisions. If Chinese people in the decades ahead acquire more freedom, will the path to that freedom be less tortuous than that taken in the former Soviet Union, and will the events of the spring of 1989 have been a major factor? We must admit that we do not know.

What we do know is that in the two decades after Tiananmen, China enjoyed relative stability and rapid—even spectacular—economic growth. Small-scale protests have occurred in large numbers and the leaders have been nervous about the danger of larger outbreaks, but in the first two decades after Tiananmen China avoided any large-scale turmoil. Today hundreds of millions of Chinese are living far more comfortable lives than they were living in 1989, and they enjoy far greater access to information and ideas around the world than at any time in Chinese history. Both educational levels and longevity have continued to rise rapidly. For these reasons and others, Chinese people take far greater pride in their nation's achievements than they did in the previous century.

We also know that the yearnings of Chinese people for more personal freedom and for a more representative government remain deep. Popular discontent due to government corruption has if anything grown since 1989. Many

Chinese worry that without more independent media and a more independent judicial system, it will be difficult to make progress in controlling corruption. And clearly many Chinese leaders who believe Deng was correct in linking rapid economic growth to increased popular support are worried about the ultimate "what if": what if they fail to make progress in solving these problems before the pace of growth slows?

22

Standing Firm

1989–1992

After June 4, 1989, the mood in Beijing was grim. Deng faced a public more alienated from the party than at any time since Communist rule began. By May 20 it had become clear that the government had lost the support of both its urban residents and its youth, and leaders feared the government might not survive. The use of force on June 4 intimidated the public into compliance, but it had only deepened the chasm between the party and the people. The morale of the military was also low; soldiers felt anything but heroic for having killed innocent civilians to help the party retain power, and recruitment was down. The support for Deng and the Communist Party after the inflation of 1988, the death of Hu Yaobang, and the use of armed troops to clear Tiananmen Square was at a low point, far from the exhilarating high point of 1984.

Deng believed that to regain the support of the public, the party desperately needed to keep the economy growing quickly, but the cautious conservatives who had gained control over economic policy after the inflation of 1988 were holding down growth. The challenges to Communist leadership in the Soviet Union and Eastern Europe, too, had made many Chinese wonder if communism had a future in China.

At the same time, Western human rights groups and Chinese students abroad were supporting dissidents in China, and Western politicians were imposing sanctions against China. For the Westerners, the killing of innocent students protesting for freedom and democracy in Beijing was a far worse crime than the decisions of their countries that had brought about the deaths of many more civilians in Vietnam, Cambodia, and elsewhere. Western human rights groups began lecturing Chinese about freedom and regard for human life. High-level Western officials stopped visiting China, and restrictions were placed on the export of technology, especially military technology. Foreign trade and tourism suffered. The drama of the Tiananmen tragedy had so captivated the West that Western TV stations played and replayed pictures of the smashing of the Goddess of Democracy, the carrying out of bloody corpses, and the lone youth trying to stop a tank—images that only strengthened the anti-Chinese mood among foreign governments. Foreign support for dissidents and foreign sanctions against China would not easily dissipate.

Deng believed that foreign support for demonstrators and the imposition of sanctions against China made it far more difficult to maintain control in China. He knew that foreign criticism would win some followers within China. Yet at this critical juncture, as he was both cracking down and bracing for the impact of foreign sanctions, Deng reaffirmed the importance of remaining open. A few days before June 4, when he was readying the PLA to do what he considered necessary to restore order, he said: "We should open to the outside world instead of closing our doors—open wider than before."[1] To regain the trust of the people, he said, he and others must achieve concrete results, investigate quickly, and punish prominent cases of corruption, no matter who is involved. He reiterated that the third generation of leaders must continue the policy of reform and opening.[2]

Addressing the PLA Generals, June 9, 1989

For several days after June 4, Deng and the leadership remained preoccupied with rounding up those whom they considered responsible for the "turmoil" and cleaning up the city to restore order. Deng did not appear in public, and rumors quickly spread that the leaders were badly split and even that the government was in danger of falling apart. On June 9 Deng broke his silence by addressing the generals who had led the crackdown. Parts of his address were presented on TV, giving the public its first glimpse of a high-level leader since the crackdown. Deng expressed his appreciation to the generals for the crucial role they had played in restoring order. He also used the occasion to tell the public that they, too, should be grateful to the military for its contribution and that the government was stable and its policy would remain unchanged.

Deng began by expressing his sorrow over the deaths of the soldiers and police who had died while heroically defending the interests of the party and the people during the struggle. He said that given the global atmosphere and the environment in China, such conflict was inevitable. It was fortunate, Deng said, that the conflict had occurred when many experienced senior military leaders—men who had the strength and courage to resolve the issue—were still around. He acknowledged that some comrades did not understand the need for their action, but he expressed confidence that eventually they would come to support the effort. Difficulties arose, Deng claimed, because some bad people who had mixed with students and onlookers had the ultimate goal of overthrowing the Communist Party, demolishing the socialist system, and establishing a bourgeois republic that would be the vassal of the West. Deng asked, "What should we do from now on? . . . In my opinion, we should continue to follow unswervingly the basic line, principles and policies we have formulated."[3] He also repeated the importance of the four cardinal principles: upholding the socialist path, supporting the people's democratic dictatorship, standing behind the leadership of the Communist Party of China, and upholding Marxism–Leninism–Mao Zedong Thought.[4]

Talking to Party Leaders

One week later, on June 16, Deng told leading members of the Central Committee that because he personally was withdrawing from his active role, a new third generation of leaders should complete the work of putting down the "rebellion." They should use the rebellion to call attention to past errors and correct them, but in his view, the basic principles had to remain unchanged. "Only socialism can save China, and only socialism can develop China. Economic development should not slow down. . . . We should do some things to demonstrate that our policies of reform and opening to the outside world will not change but will be further implemented."[5] Deng reaffirmed as well the correctness of the party's strategic goal of quadrupling the economy between 1980 and 2000 and making China a moderately developed country by the middle of the twenty-first century.

Foreigners in Beijing who heard Deng's address said that his tone was one of calm confidence; he showed no sign of regret for the actions he had taken and no sense of panic about what might develop.[6] Deng appeared to believe that the show of force on June 4 had quieted the opposition, enabling the party and the PLA to establish firm control; indeed, he claimed that the military action had won for China a decade or two of stability. Deng's consistency and firm hand reassured many who were worried that China might fall into chaos.

Deng displayed confidence that China, which had experienced nearly complete isolation during the 1950s and 1960s, could withstand the foreign sanctions after 1989. Politics change quickly in democratic countries, he said, and the strict sanctions would not last longer than several years. He believed that foreign businesspeople would pressure their governments to improve relations so that they could once again have access to the Chinese market, and that foreign governments too would again recognize the need for China's cooperation. China should remain firm, encourage its foreign friends to lift sanctions, and be prepared to make good use of every future opportunity.

Deng's estimate proved correct: in November 1990, when U.S. Secretary of State James Baker sought Chinese cooperation to pass a UN Security Council resolution pressuring Iraq to withdraw from Kuwait, he negotiated an agreement whereby President Bush would meet Qian Qichen in exchange for China's support.[7] Although most sanctions remained in place after this agreement, it was a breakthrough step in restoring working relations between China and the United States.

After his two public talks in June, Deng rarely appeared in public again, and rumors of his illness or death became so persistent that newspapers were forced to print occasional denials. In fact, Deng attended the Fourth Plenum in mid-June, met President Bush's representative Brent Scowcroft in early July, and then went to Beidaihe, the summer resort for high officials.[8]

The Fourth Plenum, June 23–24, 1989

Members of the Central Committee assembled three weeks after the Tiananmen tragedy for the Fourth Plenum of the 13th Party Congress. There they affirmed that all the moves taken to control the turmoil during the previous two months had been necessary and proper; indeed, the plenum report praised Deng and the senior leaders for the roles they had played in the time of crisis, and praised the troops and armed police for their support. The plenum also formalized changes in the top official roster. Zhao Ziyang was removed from all his posts; Jiang Zemin was named general secretary of the party; and Song Ping and Li Ruihuan were promoted to join Jiang Zemin, Li Peng, Yao Yilin, and Qiao Shi as members of the Standing Committee of the Politburo. The new leadership vowed to continue the same path forged by Deng and his colleagues. In his speech at the plenum, Jiang Zemin reaffirmed his commitment to the goals of the December 1978 Third Plenum of the 11th Party Congress: reform, opening, and the promotion of economic development.[9]

Yet the big question remained: How would Deng bridge the gap between the expectations of the many Chinese who wanted more freedom, and the unyielding determination of the party elders who felt tight control was needed to preserve order? Deng's strategy would come as no surprise to those who knew him well: he aimed to promote economic growth and strengthen "political education." That is, he did not respond to the calls of intellectuals for Western-style democratic reforms; rather he sought to persuade the public that the current system was the most appropriate for China at that time.

Passing the Baton to Jiang Zemin

Deng had given a great deal of thought to what it would take for a successor to maintain unity and keep China on the path of reform and opening. In light of the public reaction to the tragedy of June 4, Deng was pleased that they chose someone who had not been involved in the crackdown and could appeal to the public for a fresh start. Although Jiang Zemin had arrived in Beijing before June 4, Deng made sure that Jiang's reputation would be unsullied by Tiananmen by taking personal responsibility for bringing order to Beijing and by making sure Jiang's appointment was not announced until June 24, after he was formally voted party general secretary at the Fourth Plenum.[10] By waiting until then to announce his successor, Deng also demonstrated to the party and the public that he was passing the baton with a firm hand, following proper procedures, and not rushing hastily to put a successor in place. The party elders seemed to agree with the need for a strong central figure; although in 1978 they had been reluctant to give Deng many titles for fear that doing so might allow power to become too centralized, in 1989 they readily gave Jiang Zemin the titles so he could acquire the authority necessary to become an effective national leader.

In the weeks after June 4, Deng had reason to be pleased with Jiang Zemin's performance. Jiang learned quickly and established good relations with the party elders who had selected him, including Chen Yun and Li Xiannian as well as Deng. He showed sound political instincts and made good use of the advice of Zeng Qinghong, a well-connected political insider who had worked under Jiang as vice party secretary in Shanghai and had accompanied him to Beijing to serve as vice head of the party's General Office. For many years

Zeng Qinghong's father, Zeng Shan, had engaged in party organization and security work, and Zeng Qinghong knew from him many of the inside stories about party personnel; his mother, Deng Liujin, had been in charge of the Yan'an kindergarten that many of the current leaders had attended as children. Zeng made good use of his personal network to assist Jiang in his political maneuvering in Beijing. There was no way Jiang Zemin could match the sure-footed Deng Xiaoping, who could draw on his decades of firsthand experience in Beijing and his vast background knowledge of his colleagues. So instead Jiang deferred to Zeng and other knowledgeable subordinates to manage the details of these relationships.

On the morning of August 17, 1989, while still at Beidaihe, Deng summoned Yang Shangkun and Wang Zhen to tell them that he planned to pass his remaining position as chairman of the Central Military Commission (CMC) on to Jiang Zemin in November at the Fifth Plenum.[11] Party leaders understood that this move would represent the transfer not only of control over the military, but also of overall responsibility for China.

After Deng and others had returned from Beidaihe, on September 4, Deng summoned the top party leaders—Jiang Zemin, Li Peng, Qiao Shi, Yao Yilin, Song Ping, Li Ruihuan, Yang Shangkun, and Wan Li—to his home to discuss his retirement plans. Deng began the meeting by reminding them that, as he had often declared in the past, one of his final responsibilities would be to establish a mandatory retirement system, so that aged officials would automatically pass on their responsibilities to younger leaders. Deng expressed the view to his assembled colleagues that the lack of a mandatory retirement age had been a critical weakness in the system, not only in Mao's later years but in imperial days as well. (Some of his critics might have added that they admired his decision to retire and it would have been even better had he done it a few years earlier.) Deng said that if he were to die while still holding his position, his loss might create international difficulties; it would be better to pass on the position while he was still healthy. Even so, he felt he could continue to play a role in meeting those foreign guests whom he knew personally.

Deng directed that at the next party congress, scheduled for 1992, the Central Advisory Commission should also be abolished. The commission, then headed by Chen Yun, had been established as a temporary institution "to take advantage of the wisdom of the generation of revolutionary leaders." Deng announced that when he retired at the Fifth Plenum in November, the party retirement procedures, like those for other parts of the government, should be kept simple.[12] Deng then gave his valedictory message: it was important for both the Chinese public and foreigners to understand that Chinese leaders remained committed to reform and opening to the outside world. His successors should maintain the authority of the party center and the State Council, for without it, in times of difficulty, China would not be able to solve its problems.[13]

Deng added an injunction to his successors about how to respond to continued Western sanctions and possible attacks: "First," he said, "we should observe the situation coolly. Second, we should hold our ground. Third, we should act calmly. Don't be impatient. It is no good to be impatient. We should be calm, calm, and again calm, and quietly immerse ourselves in practical work to accomplish something—something for China."[14]

Later, on the same day that he met with senior officials, Deng sent a personal letter to all Politburo members with the following message:

> The core leadership headed by Comrade Jiang Zemin . . . has been working very efficiently. After careful consideration, I should like to resign my current posts while I am still in good health. . . . This will be good for the Party, the state, and the army. . . . Since I am an old citizen and a veteran party member who has worked for decades for the communist cause and for the independence, reunification, development, and reform of the country, my life belongs to the Party and the country. After my retirement I shall continue to be devoted to their cause. . . . As the reform and opening to the outside world have only just begun, our task is arduous and our road will be long and tortuous. But I am certain that we shall be able to surmount all difficulties, and that one generation after another will advance the cause pioneered by the first generation.[15]

Deng was determined to continue the scientific exchanges and flow of new technologies into China. Knowing that Americans of Chinese ancestry had strong patriotic sentiments and would keep their ties to China despite foreign sanctions following the Tiananmen tragedy, Deng invited Nobel Prize winner Lee Tsung-Dao to visit Beijing. Press releases about Deng's conversations with Lee, on September 16, amounted to a public announcement of Deng's retirement. Deng knew that ever since June 4, the public had been on edge, worried about the fate of the country. He also remembered that when Mao had pulled back after the difficulties of the Great Leap Forward and rumors began to spread that he was sick or dead, pictures appeared in the press purportedly showing Mao swimming in the Yangtze. Similarly, no matter how concerned Deng was about China's difficulties after June 4, in the pictures taken with Lee Tsung-Dao, Deng conveyed a carefree, reassuring image to the world. Photos released to the public show Deng standing in the water off the beach at Beidaihe. And in a well-publicized interview, Deng told Lee: "Recently I began to swim for an hour every day in the sea at Beidaihe. I don't like indoor pools; I like to swim in an expansive natural setting." He confessed that recent events in China had been sobering, but he went on to say, "I am certain that after the recent disturbances, China will be even more successful in its drive for modernization and in reform and opening to the outside world."[16] Deng's underlying message came through loud and clear: he remained optimistic about China's future, and despite the criticism from foreign politicians, China still had a door through which international science and technology could enter.

At the Fifth Plenum on November 7, Deng passed the chairmanship of the CMC to Jiang Zemin. Yang Shangkun became first vice chairman, with his half-brother, Yang Baibing, replacing him as CMC secretary general. The Politburo commended Deng for his great contributions to the second-generation leadership.[17] After the plenum ended on November 8, Deng arrived at the Great Hall of the People to pose for pictures with his former colleagues. One by one, they came forward to shake his hand. He then returned home for a retirement banquet with his family, prepared by his cook of thirty years. Two days later, the *People's Daily* featured the letter that Deng had sent to Central Committee members: "I thank our comrades for their understanding and their support. I sincerely thank all of you for accepting my request to retire. I sincerely thank all my comrades."[18] The Berlin Wall fell on the day of Deng's retirement, but in China his retirement passed without incident.

A year after Deng passed the baton to Jiang, Singapore's Prime Minister Lee Kuan Yew similarly named his own successor, Goh Chok Tong. Thereafter, Lee exercised great restraint so as not to interfere with the work of his successor, but he said that he remained the "goalkeeper" and if problems arose, he would feel responsible to do whatever was necessary to maintain Singapore's success. Similarly, Deng told Nobel Prize winner Lee Tsung-Dao: "My chief desire is to retire completely, but if there are disturbances, I shall have to intervene."[19]

After he passed the mantle to Jiang, Deng no longer had responsibility for giving final approval on important matters. At eighty-five, he was moving more slowly, his hearing had further deteriorated, he rested more, and he had trouble maintaining the intense concentration for which he had been famous until two or three years earlier.[20] After June 1989 Deng did not dominate the political scene by framing the issues, setting overall policy, gaining compliance, making the final decisions, or controlling what went into the media. But he did continue to have crucial meetings with important foreigners, and on the big questions of overall strategy, he could still exert influence—a power that he was prepared to use fully if the need arose.

Keeping the U.S. Door Open

Immediately after the June 4 incident, President George H. W. Bush tried to do something no American leader had yet done with a Chinese Communist leader—he tried to telephone Deng Xiaoping. Bush also immediately announced the suspension of military sales and high-level official contacts with China. He offered humanitarian and medical assistance to anyone in China who had been injured in the Tiananmen tragedy. On June 5, Bush also met with Chinese students living in the United States to offer them political asylum and show his support for the suffering of their fellow students in China. Yet in contrast to U.S. public opinion, and especially the newspaper editorials that supported severe sanctions, Bush said that he did not want to punish the Chinese people for the actions of the Chinese government. Knowing the difficult history between the United States and China, Bush wanted to avoid any confrontation that would make it more difficult to restore a healthy U.S.-China relationship in the future. Continued contacts, he declared, would in the long run strengthen pressures within China calling for greater freedoms. Several years later, when reflecting on the events of 1989, Bush said, "Had I not met the man [Deng], I think I would have been less convinced that we should keep relations with them going after Tiananmen Square."[21] The timing of Bush's term as head of the U.S. Liaison Office in Beijing (from September 26, 1974, to December 7, 1975) had proved fortuitous: Bush had taken up his assignment soon after Deng had replaced Zhou Enlai in meeting with foreign leaders and he left Beijing just as Deng was again pushed aside by Mao. James Lilley, Bush's China specialist who became ambassador to Beijing after Bush became president, observed that Bush and Deng "established an unusual chemistry in the 1970s based in part on each man's perception that the other would be a future leader of his country."[22] In fact, Lilley concluded that when Mao, Zhou Enlai, Nixon, and Kissinger were passing from the scene, Deng and Bush sustained the working relationship between the two countries that the earlier leaders had built. Their relationship was relaxed and friendly: on December 6, 1975, at the farewell luncheon that Deng gave in Bush's honor as he departed Beijing to head the CIA, Deng joked with him: "Have you been practicing your spying here in China?"[23] Bush believed in personal diplomacy, and he would send Deng occasional notes; Deng did not reciprocate these personal approaches, but he was always ready to meet with Bush in person.[24]

The relationship between the two men had continued after Deng became the preeminent leader. When Deng traveled to the United States in January 1979, he had requested a private meeting with Bush in Houston, during which Deng told Bush of his still-secret plans to attack Vietnam. While Deng was in Texas, Bush also invited him to his mother's home. Later, when President Reagan would try to formalize relations with Taiwan, Deng and Vice President Bush helped keep the relationship between the United States and the mainland on track. Indeed, when relations between the two countries grew very tense, a Deng-Bush meeting had enabled the two countries to turn a difficult corner, thus opening the way for the August 1982 communiqué that stabilized relations.[25] Later, when Bush decided to run for president, his wife, Barbara, traveling in Asia, was sent to Beijing to tell Deng personally of her husband's intention. And in February 1989, Deng gave Bush a frank account of the improvements in Sino-Soviet relations as China prepared for Mikhail Gorbachev's visit.[26] Some years later when Bush was asked on TV who was the greatest leader he had ever met, after first replying that no one in particular stood out, he added that Deng Xiaoping was a very special leader.

Yet in June 1989, when Bush tried to phone Deng, Deng would not accept the call. It was not the practice of Chinese leaders to answer phone calls from foreign leaders. Therefore, on June 21, 1989, Bush sent Deng a handwritten note:

I write this letter with a heavy heart. I wish there were some way to discuss this matter in person, but regrettably this is not the case. First, I write in a spirit of genuine friendship, this letter coming as I'm sure you know from one who believes with a passion that good relations between the United States and China are in the fundamental interests of both countries. . . . I write you asking for your help in preserving this relationship that we both think is very important. . . . I ask you . . . to remember the principles on which my young country was founded. Those principles are democracy and freedom. . . . Those principles inevitably affect the way Americans view and react to events in other countries. It is not a reaction of arrogance or of a desire to force others to our beliefs but of simple faith in the enduring value of those principles and their universal applicability.[27]

Bush went on to explain that that as president of the United States he could not avoid imposing sanctions. "When there are difficulties between friends, as now, we must find a way to talk them out. . . . Sometimes in an open system such as ours it is impossible to control all leaks; but on this particular letter there are no copies, not one, outside of my own personal file."[28] In his letter, Bush proposed that he send a personal envoy to Beijing.

The day after Bush sent his letter, he received a response from Deng Xiaoping saying that he was prepared to receive a special emissary. Bush—aware that the U.S. public would be upset at the dispatch of an envoy so soon after June 4—kept the mission secret; even the U.S. embassy in Beijing was not informed. (China, for its part, had no difficulty keeping the visit secret.) U.S. National Security Adviser Brent Scowcroft and Deputy Secretary of State Lawrence Eagleburger flew to Beijing, where they met Deng on July 2. Just before the meeting, Deng had told Li Peng and Qian Qichen that in their meetings with the Americans, they should only talk about principles, not specifics; China wanted to improve relations with the United States, but the Chinese leaders were not afraid of the Americans or of sanctions. Diplomats should keep this in mind.[29]

The Americans who accompanied Scowcroft reported that Deng greeted Scowcroft and Eagleburger cordially, saying, "The reason I have chosen President Bush as my friend is because since the inception of my contact with him, I found that his words are trustworthy. . . . He doesn't say much in terms of empty words or words that are insincere."[30] But Deng was still tough as nails, and deadly serious, in his assessment of U.S.-China relations. With respect to June 4, he said that it was "an earthshaking event, and it is very unfortunate that the United States is too deeply involved in it . . . the various aspects of U.S. foreign policy have actually cornered China. . . . The aim of the counterrevolutionary rebellion was to overthrow the People's Republic of China and our socialist system. If they should succeed in obtaining that aim, the world would be a different one. To be frank, this could even lead to war." Deng then accused the United States of siding with those trying to overthrow the Chinese government and said that the U.S. press was exaggerating the violence and interfering with China's internal affairs.

Deng regarded Bush's decision to send the two envoys as a good decision. "It seems that there is still hope to maintain our original good relations. . . . I believe that is the hope of President Bush. It is also the hope shared by me. However, a question of this nature cannot be solved by two persons from the perspective of being friends." Differences between the two countries were caused, Deng said, by the United States, which "on a large-scale has impinged upon Chinese interests. . . . It is up to the person who tied the knot to untie it. . . . It is up to the United States to cease adding fuel to the fire." Deng went on to explain that the People's Republic of China was founded as a result of twenty-two years of war, with over 20 million lives lost, and no force could substitute for the Chinese Communist Party in governing China. This was a stern message from someone who felt that the fate of his country was at risk and that continuing U.S. support for Chinese protestors had contributed to that risk.

In his response, Scowcroft reiterated that President Bush believed in maintaining good relations with China; it was in the U.S. national interest to do so. Bush also wanted Deng to understand the political constraints on the American president at the time.[31] Deng replied by asking Scowcroft to "convey my feelings to my friend, President Bush . . . that no matter what should be the outcome of the discussions between our two governments on this issue, if he would continue to treat me as his friend, I would also like to do that."[32] Scowcroft attempted to explain why the United States harbored such strong feelings about personal freedom—but he didn't get far. Deng concluded the meeting by saying that he did not agree with much of what Scowcroft had said, and that "with regard to concluding this unhappy episode in the relations between China and the United States . . . we have to see what kind of actions the United States will take."[33] And then, Scowcroft reports, Deng took his leave.

One of the casualties in U.S.-China relations at this time was the continuation of U.S. agreements to supply military equipment to China. Between 1983 and 1989, as anti-Soviet allies, the Chinese and Americans militaries had worked out arrangements whereby the United States sold China avionics equipment, missiles, and torpedoes. The biggest single item was a radar system for the F-8 fighter plane; the Chinese also purchased Sikorsky Black Hawk helicopters. This package represented a significant amount of money at China's early stage of economic development. After 1989, because U.S. sanctions prevented the sale of parts to China, including parts for the Sikorsky helicopters, the Chinese were unable to use much of the equipment they had already paid for.

Between 1989 and 1993, there were virtually no contacts between senior U.S. and Chinese military officials. The contacts were resumed in 1993, but the level of trust between the two never returned to the earlier high of 1983–1989. In fact, after 1989 the Chinese turned to the Soviet Union to purchase the SU-27 fighter jet and to Israel for other military equipment and supplies. China was reluctant to buy any important piece of military equipment from the United States.[34]

At the G-7 economic summit in France that began on July 14, 1989, a month after the Tiananmen tragedy, the main question was not whether to impose sanctions on China, but rather how harsh the sanctions should be. Compared to other leaders, President Bush and Japanese prime minister Sō-suke Uno favored milder sanctions. President Bush did support withholding new World Bank loans to China and approved of giving permanent residency to Chinese students in the United States, but he opposed stronger measures that he feared might lead to a rupture in overall Sino-U.S. relations.[35]

On July 28, 1989, Bush again wrote to Deng, repeating his desire to maintain their working relationship. Responding to Deng's view that the United States had "tied the knot," Bush wrote that he believed it was China's actions that had created the problem. On August 11, Deng replied cordially to Bush, expressing appreciation for his efforts to maintain and develop relations, but repeated that it was the United States that had imposed sanctions and had infringed on China's interests and dignity. Deng then expressed the hope that the situation would soon be changed.[36] In his reply to Deng, Bush, aware that China was sensitive to U.S. contacts with the Soviet Union, suggested that after the Bush-Gorbachev meeting on Malta on December 1, Scowcroft could fly to Beijing to brief Deng and Jiang Zemin on the meeting.

Meanwhile, because the United States and Japan had decided not to send high officials to China, Deng welcomed a host of former U.S. officials. He met Leonard Woodcock, who served as a messenger for U.S. Democrats, and he saw both former president Richard Nixon and Henry Kissinger, who served, in effect, as go-betweens with the Bush administration. In Japan there was no strong opposition party or former politicians who could serve as good messengers, so Deng met leaders of the Japanese business community who were in close contact with the Japanese government. When these visitors came to Beijing, Deng encouraged them to work with his successor, Jiang Zemin, but he still led the key discussions.

In October 1989 Deng met former president Nixon, accompanied by President Carter's China hand, Michel Oksenberg. Nixon made a forceful statement about why Americans were responding strongly to the June 4 crackdown, but the two sides also explored ways to break the deadlock. Deng said that China was in a weak position and could not take the initiative; the United States, he insisted, was in a strong position and should take the first steps.[37]

Less than two weeks later, on November 10, the day after Deng officially resigned and the Berlin Wall fell, Deng met former secretary of state Henry Kissinger and assured him that China's policy of reform and opening would be continued. He also gave Kissinger a letter to carry back to President Bush suggesting a diplomatic package whereby (1) China would allow Fang Lizhi, the dissident astrophysicist who had taken refuge in the U.S. embassy, to travel to the United States, (2) the United States would lift some of its sanctions against China, (3) the two sides would endeavor to sign one or two major economic cooperation projects, and (4) Jiang Zemin would visit the United States.[38] A few months later, in May 1990, Bush announced that he was granting China most-favored-nation trading status and that the Chinese had permitted Fang Lizhi to exit the U.S. embassy and leave the country.[39]

By the time Scowcroft and Eagleburger met Deng for a second time on December 10, some progress had been made. Scowcroft was instructed to publicly announce the current visit, and on December 18, CNN broke the news of the earlier secret visit.[40] For many Americans who remained deeply distressed by the events of June 4, it was a moral outrage that representatives of the U.S. government would fly secretly to a nation led by Communists who had just shot unarmed advocates of democracy in the streets, especially since the Bush administration had already announced there would be no high-level visits.[41] But for Bush and Scowcroft, who thought in terms of the fate of nations and the intricate personal relationships between national leaders, the trip had helped avoid a rift with China and so was clearly in the strategic, cultural, and economic interests of the United States.[42]

During the second visit, Deng told Scowcroft and Eagleburger that it was good that they were visiting Beijing, for without strong U.S.-China relations it would be difficult to preserve peace and stability in the world. He continued, saying that it was not China that threatened the United States but rather U.S. policies that threatened China: moreover, if there were more turmoil in

China, it would be terrible for the entire world. With his disarmingly light touch, Deng also asked Scowcroft to tell Bush that there is a retired old man in China who believes in the importance of the relationship and that both sides must find a way to resolve their problems.[43] Immediately following the visit, the United States announced it would sell China three communication satellites and would support World Bank loans to China for humanitarian purposes. And shortly thereafter, in early January, China announced that it was lifting martial law in Beijing and that 573 detainees from the spring of 1989 were to be released.[44]

Following these initial overtures, U.S.-China discussions reached a stalemate for about a year. Foreign Minister Qian Qichen complained that the United States had lost interest in negotiating with China. Scowcroft, in turn, noted that Chinese leaders were no longer being flexible. But both sides agreed that the cause of the stalemate was the turmoil in Eastern Europe and the Soviet Union.

Communism Collapses in Eastern Europe and the Soviet Union

The political upheaval from 1989 to 1991 in the Soviet Union and Eastern Europe—in addition to the demonstrations in Beijing in the spring of 1989—caused not only foreigners but also many Chinese to wonder if the Chinese Communist Party would survive. Many Westerners, exhilarated by the collapse of the Berlin Wall, the ending of Communist Party rule in Eastern European countries, and the dissolution of the Soviet Union, hoped that supporters of democracy in China would succeed in ending Communist rule in China. Meanwhile, the Chinese leaders, maneuvering to keep their domestic problems under control, were again and again embarrassed that their media reports to the Chinese public were overtaken by unanticipated events in Eastern Europe and the Soviet Union. Chinese officials were kept better informed than the Chinese public through the daily translations of the Western media in *Reference News (Cankao ziliao)*.

Particularly devastating to the Chinese and to Deng personally was the growing mass movement in Romania against China's friend Nicolai Ceauşescu and his wife that culminated on December 25, 1989, with their execution. Ceauşescu was the only Eastern European leader to order troops to fire on civilians, and no Chinese leader could avoid seeing the parallels with the recent military action in Beijing just seven months earlier. Indeed, the sudden turn of events in Romania that led to his execution caused Chinese leaders to wonder if they were immune to the fate of Ceauşescu, who had earlier expressed approval of Beijing's June 4 crackdown.

The level of concern can perhaps be measured by the extent to which the Chinese public was kept in the dark about the turmoil in Romania. When Ceauşescu ordered his troops to fire on civilians on December 17, 1989, the Chinese press did not report his action, but four days later simply reported that Ceauşescu had declared a state of emergency in order to protect socialism from terrorist activities. When it became more difficult to avoid reporting on the huge Romanian clashes, the Chinese press only acknowledged that some windows in the office of the New China News Agency (Xinhua) in Bucharest had been shattered by bullets. And on December 27, two days after Ceauşescu had been executed, the *People's Daily* noted in a single sentence on the lower part of page 4: "Romanian television announced on December 25 that the Romanian Special Military Court had condemned Ceauşescu and his wife to death and had carried out the sentence."[45] Brent Scowcroft, who was in Beijing at the time, said that Chinese leaders who had frequently praised Ceauşescu as proof that communism could survive a liberal onslaught panicked when they heard about the events in Romania.[46]

For Deng, the execution of Ceauşescu was particularly disturbing. Ceauşescu had pinned the golden star of the Socialist Republic of Romania, Romania's highest award, on Deng during his visit to China in October 1985. As early as July 1965, when China still had some links with the Warsaw Pact, Deng and Ceauşescu had shared their views on how to achieve their common desire to gain greater independence from the Soviet Union and the Warsaw Pact. Ceauşescu had been allowed to address mass audiences during his visits to China in 1982 and 1985. And it was during Ceauşescu's 1985 visit that Deng had asked him to convey to Gorbachev the conditions for improving Sino-Soviet relations, paving the way for Gorbachev's visit to Beijing in 1989.[47] The *People's Daily* in early September 1989 quoted from an interview with Ceauşescu in which he declared, "Cooperation between Communist parties and socialist countries should be made stronger than ever before."[48] Meanwhile, *Referenced News* contained detailed translations of Western reports—reports not available to the general public—that described growing opposition to Ceauşescu.[49]

In December, after the seriousness of the Romanian opposition was exposed, Deng temporarily withdrew from public meetings. According to the official chronology of Deng's activities *(Deng Xiaoping nianpu)*, he attended six meetings in the first half of December, but did not go to any meetings from December 17, when Ceauşescu ordered firing into the crowds, until January 18 (when Deng met Hong Kong business leader Lee Ka-shing).[50] Thus it fell to Jiang Zemin, on December 21, 1989, in the midst of the Romanian crisis, to meet with Hong Kong reporters to calm the worries of Hong Kong residents, who had been in a state of panic since June 4 about what might happen in just eight years when Hong Kong was to revert to mainland rule. Jiang's approach, like Deng's, was to show calm in a tense situation; he explained why the situation in China was fundamentally different from that in Eastern Europe. The founding of the Chinese Communist regime in 1949, he noted, was the result of the victory of the Chinese army, not the Soviet army. China was not surrounded by capitalist nations, and it had been improving the livelihood of its people. Jiang explained that martial law had been introduced in China not to deal with unruly students, but to preserve order. Like Deng in 1957, Jiang affirmed that democracy is a worthy target and that the amount of democracy achieved will depend on the political steadiness of the situation in China.[51]

From 1989 until the end of 1991, when the Soviet Union collapsed, Beijing officials who supervised propaganda work found it difficult to manage the incoming news from Eastern Europe and the Soviet Union. Despite great efforts to hide, tone down, delay, or slant the news, ultimately they were frequently embarrassed by events that made it impossible for them to maintain their credibility. On June 4, 1989, the very day that Deng's troops put down the demonstrators in Tiananmen Square, Polish citizens were voting for a democratically elected parliament, the first such election in an Eastern European Communist country since the Soviet occupation began shortly after the end of World War II. But the *People's Daily* waited until June 10, the day after Deng's address to military leaders, before it notified the Chinese public of the election. Even then it did not disclose how overwhelmingly the opposition party candidates had defeated the Communist Party's candidates. And although earlier, in the mid-1980s, Beijing's media had cheered Woyciech Jaruzelski as he clamped down on the popular trade union Solidarity, when Jaruzelski was overthrown in November 1989, Beijing's officials, horrified, did not immediately report the news to the Chinese people.[52]

During late September and early October 1989, while tens of thousands of East Germans were seeking asylum in West Germany, Chinese newspapers continued to praise East Germany. On October 7, for example, when massive protests broke out in East Germany (on the fortieth anniversary of Communist rule), the *People's Daily* not only ignored them, but misleadingly reported that "the East German people are now strengthening their unity under the leadership of the party." Such efforts to shield the Chinese public from the truth of what was happening in Eastern Europe would only come back to bite the leadership of Beijing, however, when on November 11 the Berlin Wall was torn down and the *People's Daily* could not hide the news.[53]

In February 1990, as the Soviet party plenum discussed giving up the party's monopoly over political power, the *People's Daily* printed nothing. Instead, on the day the plenum ended, without mentioning the Soviet Union, the *People's Daily* announced, "In China, without the strong leadership of the Chinese Communist Party, new turmoil and wars would surely arise, the nation would be split, and the people, not to mention state construction, would suffer." The following day the paper carried the news that the Moscow plenum had agreed to give up the party's monopoly of power.[54] As the Soviet Union was falling apart, some Chinese intellectuals were as joyful as many Westerners. Some even repeated to trusted friends one of the great Chinese slogans of the 1950s when China was introducing Soviet-style industrialization, now used with a very different connotation: "The Soviet Union's today is our tomorrow."

After he resigned in late 1989, Deng did not take an active role in dealing with the issues of Eastern Europe and the Soviet Union, but he could not escape the consequences of those developments. From 1989 to 1992, he tried to reinforce popular confidence that the Chinese Communist Party was different from that in Eastern Europe or the Soviet Union, and that it would prevail. He did not predict what would happen in the Soviet Union or in Eastern Europe, but by late 1989 Deng began using phrases like "whatever happens in the Soviet Union or Eastern Europe" to lead off statements about how China was different. Convinced that rapid growth was key to keeping the support of the people, Deng also frequently reiterated the importance of adopting policies that would continue economic progress.

On one particularly sensitive occasion, August 20, 1991, the day after conservatives in the Soviet Union had engineered a coup and while they were still holding Gorbachev under house arrest in a dacha in Crimea, Deng called a meeting of the leading power holders in China—including Jiang Zemin, who had just returned from Moscow; Yang Shangkun; and Li Peng—to strengthen their determination to work together and avoid splits. Deng reiterated that China, despite its turmoil, would be able to resist foreign pressures because of its successful reform and opening. He acknowledged that China might seem to advance in waves, with times of rapid progress followed by periods of adjustment. He also noted that the great changes in the world had given China an opportunity to move forward, but that if China failed to grasp this opportunity, other countries would move ahead while China fell behind. Finally, Deng reassured his comrades that emphasizing economic growth did not mean that China was forgetting Marx, Lenin, and Mao.[55]

On October 5, 1991, a few weeks after Estonia, Latvia, and Lithuania split with the Soviets, setting off the process that led to the final dissolution of the Soviet Union, Deng came out to welcome Kim Il Sung, leader of North Korea, one of the few remaining Communist countries. Deng conveyed to Kim that China remained firmly committed to economic reform and opening but also steadfast in its commitment to the four cardinal principles. To illustrate the need for communism in China, Deng said that when China had suffered floods that year, no other country could have solved the problem; China had dealt with the floods effectively because of the leadership of the Communist Party.[56] On October 26, 1991, Deng again pronounced his belief in the party system, telling the Thai prime minister, Chatichai Choonhavan, that "no one can shake China's determination to build socialism, a socialism that is adapted to our own conditions."[57]

Despite Chinese leaders' slowness in reporting to the public the changes in the Soviet Union and Eastern Europe, China's foreign policy adapted quickly to the new realities. When the Baltic republics declared their independence China immediately recognized them; and after December 25, 1991, when Soviet president Mikhail Gorbachev announced his resignation and the Russian flag replaced the Soviet flag at the Kremlin, China quickly granted diplomatic recognition to Russia and the other independent states.[58]

In attempting to explain what had gone wrong in the Soviet Union, Deng asserted that the Soviet Union had failed to institute economic reforms in a timely manner and that the top Soviet leaders had not firmly supported the Communist Party. Instead, Soviet leaders had become caught up in an arms race with the United States, a contest that had led to wasteful spending that did not improve the lives of ordinary people. Soviet leaders had enjoyed a good life, but the Soviet people had not. During the difficult period after the Tiananmen tragedy and through the period of the collapse of the Soviet Union, Deng continually repeated the mantra "observe calmly, hold one's ground, respond soberly, and get some things done" *(lengjing guancha, wenzhu zhenjiao, chenzhuo yingfu, yousuo zuowei).*[59]

Whatever doubts Deng may have personally had about the fate of China after June 4, 1989, there is no record that he ever expressed any doubts about the ability of the Chinese Communist Party to surmount the difficulties presented by the collapse of communism in Eastern Europe and the Soviet Union. In public, Deng displayed a quiet confidence that the Chinese Communist Party would survive and eventually prevail, and that the economy would continue to grow. He recalled that he had been personally criticized and had lost his position three times, yet each time had returned. He had seen his troops lose battles yet win ultimate victory. He had seen China reverse itself after both the Great Leap Forward and the Cultural Revolution. Not many world leaders, under such circumstances, could have displayed the toughness, the resilience, and the sheer confidence that Deng exuded in public in the three years after June 4.

Impatience with Conservative Economic Policies, 1989–1991

The atmosphere within the party did not allow Deng to reverse the conservative economic policies that had been put in place to quell the inflation and public panic that had followed the lifting of price controls in 1988. Yet Deng passionately believed that only rapid economic growth would maintain the public support necessary to avoid the fate of Eastern Europe and the Soviet Union. The austerity program that had officially begun on September 26, 1988, at the Third Plenum of the 13th Party Congress was vintage Chen Yun. To end inflation, the government had lowered growth targets and spending flows, reduced the money supply, centralized and tightened financial controls, and endeavored to eliminate financial deficits. In addition, in an effort to appeal to a public that was fed up with corruption, government spokesman Yuan Mu announced that the austerity program would be expanded to include a moratorium on construction of luxurious office buildings, auditoriums, and guest houses.[60]

Xue Muqiao, an experienced adviser on economic matters, provided the overall rationale for the "consolidation" *(zhengdun)* policies of the austerity program. He explained that after 1984, administrative controls over the economy—through pricing, taxation, and credit allocations—had been weakened before new institutional and macroeconomic controls had been put in place. With the decentralization of controls, local governments and enterprises, including township and village enterprises, had expanded investments too rapidly, causing shortages of raw materials and energy, as well as bottlenecks in the inadequate infrastructure. The result was inflation, and to avoid having it get out of hand, tight controls were introduced.[61] At a planning conference in late 1989, Premier Li Peng loyally promoted the austerity program, saying that the party should concentrate on raising quality standards, improving the circulation of goods, and strengthening party controls over the political and ideological spheres. He argued that even with the austerity program, the party would continue to promote reform. Industrial plant managers would still make key decisions about technology and production, and China would maintain its policy of opening to the outside.[62]

The attack by Western countries on the Chinese political leadership after June 4 led to a reaction against Western "capitalist countries" and "bourgeois thinking"—and against the opening of markets.[63] Deng Liqun, the conservative ideologue who had been pushed aside in 1987, again began to criticize bourgeois liberalization and spiritual pollution. Chen Yun's associates argued that the excessive opening of markets had led to a loss of discipline and to the student demonstrations. And Jiang Zemin drew on the skills of the keeper of orthodoxy, Hu Qiaomu, to draft his speech for the July 1991 seventieth anniversary of the Chinese Communist Party.[64]

The conservative policies introduced since 1988 had helped to curb inflationary pressures, tighten controls over investment, and balance budgets. And it was expected that at the end of the 1989–1992 period, once the readjustment had been completed, reforms—including price reform, separation of enterprise management from ownership, tax reform, and banking reform—could be reintroduced at a modest pace.[65] But the sanctions by Western countries after June 4, 1989, had further restricted Chinese growth even as economic officials continued to pursue cautious economic policies. Even Jiang Zemin, who tried to maintain good personal relations with Deng, felt compelled on economic policies to act in accord with the dominant atmosphere, which now was more aligned with Chen Yun and his cautious approach. Consequently, the GNP growth rate fell from 11.2 percent in 1988 to 3.9 percent in 1989. To prevent political unrest given this precipitous fall, workers in state enterprises in the big cities did not lose their jobs and their wages remained intact. In smaller towns and administrative villages, however, nearly 20 million industrial workers lost their jobs in 1989 and 1990.[66] At the time, Deng desperately wanted to speed up growth to maintain public support, but he lacked enough support in the party to do so.

Patriotic Education

After the immediate crises in the weeks following June 4, Deng and other leaders began to deal with the larger problem of alienation among Chinese youth toward their government and the Communist Party. When he discussed the problems that had led to June 4, Deng referred to the failure to provide youth with "education," by which, like Mao, he meant political education. Yet Deng's idea of education did not focus on "ideology," which he considered too rigid; instead he endeavored to provide civic and moral training. After June 4, 1989, what would this mean?

The collapse of communism in Eastern Europe and the USSR had revealed that youth in the Communist world had lost faith in Marxism-Leninism, the socialist economy, and Communist orthodoxy. Deng and his fellow party elders realized that political training in Marxism-Leninism or even Maoism could no longer be expected to appeal to the sensibilities of Chinese youth. Nor, even if Deng had personally supported it, would class struggle against the landlord and bourgeois classes resonate with the youth as it had at the height of the Mao era.

What should replace Marxism-Leninism and Maoist ideology to win the hearts and minds of China's youth? The answer seemed obvious: patriotism.[67] Patriotic education that emphasized the history of the century of humiliation by foreign imperialists had been the main theme of propaganda in the 1940s, and it had never disappeared. It had, however, played only a secondary role as China had built up socialism beginning in the 1950s, and it had languished in the 1980s as Deng tried to build closer relations with the West. Yet after 1989, when Western countries were imposing sanctions, there was a widespread patriotic reaction against foreign sanctions. To many Westerners, sanctions on China were a way of attacking Chinese leaders who used force on June 4, but to Chinese people the sanctions hurt all Chinese. Patriotic "education" linked nationalism to the Communist Party, as the Communists in World War II appealed to patriotism and nationalism to rally support against the Japanese. Conversely, criticism of the Communist Party was ipso facto unpatriotic.[68]

The timing was right for such a shift in ideology. During the Deng era there was, as the scholar Benjamin Schwartz has pointed out, a "progressive reclaiming of Chinese history." Under Deng, the historical figures criticized by Mao for representing the exploitative landlord and bourgeois classes were gradually recast as having been "progressive for their time." That is, during the Deng era it became easier to study Chinese history in a more objective way; historical figures once vilified as class enemies emerged as human beings who possessed admirable, or at least understandable, qualities. In the late 1980s, even Chiang Kai-shek, the arch-enemy of the civil war, began to be treated more sympathetically, although to be sure his achievements paled by comparison with Mao's.[69] In the aftermath of 1989, then, the Propaganda Department used this trend to encourage young people to take pride in Chinese history.[70]

As one Chinese intellectual describing the layers of Chinese thinking discerned, even in the 1980s when Chinese were attacking their own traditions and worshipping Western things, "beneath the rebellious message . . . throbs the impatient heart of a full-blooded new generation with an urgent sense of mission to reassert the pride of being Chinese."[71] Even without Chinese patriotic education, by the late 1980s many Chinese had realized that when China first opened to the outside after 1978, the Chinese people had over-glamorized the West (as some propaganda officials put it, some Chinese youth "thought the Western moon was larger than the Chinese moon"). But as China began to grow rapidly and modernize, the Chinese naturally began to take more pride in their country.

The sanctions imposed by foreign countries and the criticism of foreigners that followed June 4 provided Deng and his colleagues with a useful vehicle for enhancing this patriotism. Within weeks after the Tiananmen tragedy, Deng began emphasizing his patriotic message. The Propaganda Department skillfully publicized anti-Chinese statements by foreigners that caused many Chinese, even students who advocated democracy, to feel outraged. The efforts by foreign countries to keep China out of the GATT (General Agreement on Tariffs and Trade, which in 1994 was replaced by the World Trade Organization) were publicized so as to focus Chinese anger on the prejudices of foreigners toward China. The refusal by foreign countries to supply modern technology was framed as an effort to unfairly prevent the Chinese from sharing in the fruits of modernization. Foreign criticism of China for its treatment of Tibetans, Uighurs, and other minority groups was presented to the Chinese public as part of an organized effort by foreign powers to weaken China. The West's support for Taiwan and resistance to China's claims to the islands in the South China Sea and the East China Sea were also offered up to the public as examples of efforts to keep China down. These stories and others had their intended effect. In the years after 1989, students who had shouted slogans against the government for corruption and for not granting more democracy and freedom began supporting the government and the party by shouting slogans against foreigners, who they felt were unfairly criticizing China.

One issue that was particularly successful in arousing the patriotism of youth was the clever publication of comments by foreigners who, due to the events of 1989, opposed allowing Beijing to host the 2000 Olympics. When President Yang Shangkun's announcement to the International Olympic Committee in 1990 that China wanted to host the 2000 Olympics was met with resistance abroad, Chinese youth were outraged. Youth who had opposed their government in 1989 were now passionately supporting their government's claims that China was being mistreated by other countries.

Among these efforts to teach patriotism, nothing was more effective than the revival of anti-Japanese propaganda that had promoted Chinese patriotism during World War II. When Japanese politicians visited the Yasukuni Shrine to Japanese fighters in World War II or when extreme right-wing politicians denied the Nanjing Massacre, even when these events received no publicity in Japan, their comments would receive play in Chinese media, stirring up strong anti-Japanese sentiments and support for Chinese political leaders.

By late 1991, too, the Propaganda Department had developed a more systematic approach to teaching patriotic education—through textbooks, lectures, and media guides. In November 1991, it issued a document entitled "Fully Using Cultural Relics to Conduct Education in Patriotism and Revolutionary Traditions." It then issued a "Circular on Carrying out Education in Patriotism in Primary and Secondary Schools throughout the Country by Films and Television." In both these documents, the focus was on educating those too young to have experienced the war against Japan or the civil war.

In the aftermath of the Tiananmen tragedy, Deng criticized foreign countries for imposing sanctions, and there is no record that before he stepped down in 1992 he opposed the efforts by the Propaganda Department to stir up patriotism, even with its anti-foreign slant. The danger that China might fall apart, as the Soviet Union and Eastern European countries were falling apart, required a serious effort to win back the support of China's youth, and patriotism, along with economic growth and expanded economic opportunities, was part of the solution. But the stirring up of anti-foreign sentiment went far beyond what Deng encouraged, and it became even stronger after he stepped down. As foreign countries reduced their sanctions in the 1990s, China had to balance this anti-foreign patriotism with efforts to revive the good relations with other countries that Deng had fostered since 1977.

23

Deng's Finale: The Southern Journey

1992

A generation earlier, in 1965, Mao had been unhappy with the "bourgeois" policies of Beijing over which he did not have full control. Unable to get his views aired in the central party newspaper, the *People's Daily,* he published them in Shanghai's *Wenhui bao;* the next day the article also appeared in the Shanghai party newspaper, the *Liberation Daily.* Then Mao, seventy-one years old, journeyed on his special train to the southern cities of Hangzhou, Shaoshan, and Wuhan, where he lit the fire that launched the Cultural Revolution in 1966.

This series of events would be echoed in 1991 when Deng found himself unhappy with the conservative economic policies of Beijing, policies over which he did not have full control. Unable to get his views published in the *People's Daily,* he had them published in another paper, Shanghai's *Liberation Daily.* But the fire did not take in 1991, so in 1992 a determined Deng ignited a bigger fire. He took a southern journey at age eighty-seven in his special train to Wuhan, Shenzhen, Zhuhai, and Shanghai, where he successfully lit the fire for further market opening and faster growth.

The panic over inflation in 1988, the near collapse of the Beijing government after the failure of martial law in May 1989, and the news of continuing failures in the Soviet Union and Eastern Europe had created in Beijing an atmosphere of near desperation and heightened tensions. Chen Yun remained the magnet for cautious planners and Deng remained the magnet for the bold advocates of further opening and faster growth. In the late 1970s and the early 1980s the "builders" were largely central government officials trying to bring in new plants and technology. By the end of the 1980s, local governments along the coast had built up their own wealth and provided a larger base of support that Deng could appeal to against the cautious planners.

The cautious planners under Chen Yun who believed that the failure to control inflation in 1988 was responsible for the tragedy of 1989 became even more determined to set the country on what they considered the only safe path. Deng, who felt that Communist rule would be in danger if the country did not grow rapidly, became equally adamant in his view that only more rapid growth and opening could keep the popular support necessary for China to survive. The fear of collapse heightened the tensions.[1]

Deng's Failures, 1990–1991

On his winter vacation in Shanghai from January 21 until February 13, 1990, Deng was already working to gain the political leverage he needed to overcome the conservative economic policies. In Shanghai, he talked to local leaders about their visions for a huge development project in Pudong.[2] Shanghai leaders, he knew, were itching to be permitted to develop Pudong, if only Beijing would approve. Pudong included a vast area of some 188 square miles within Shanghai, conveniently located near the mouth of the Yangtze River. At the time it was largely rural and thus easy to develop, even though earlier in the century Sun Yat-sen had broached the idea of developing it into a large port. Local officials hoped that it would become the financial center of China.[3] Even though Shanghai had been held back by the central government, there was substantial growth of industry in the area around the Yangtze River delta, including not only Shanghai but also nearby Jiangsu and Zhejiang.

Deng, who was thinking strategically about what might enhance Chinese economic growth, knew that Shanghai was large enough and contained enough talent that any growth there would have an immediate and positive influence on national growth, not only in the nearby provinces of Zhejiang and Jiangsu, but also for the hundreds of millions of people living in areas all along the Yangtze River.[4] Deng had first experienced the dynamism of Shanghai when he spent a week there in 1920 on his way to France; a decade later he had spent several months working in the Shanghai underground; and in 1949 he had been in charge of the Communist takeover there. When he visited the city for his winter "vacation" in the late 1980s, he could feel the vibrant population's pent-up energy waiting to be released. Even officials far less perceptive than Deng were fully aware that Shanghai leaders, proud of the city's preeminence as the cosmopolitan business center of Asia in the 1930s when Hong Kong was still a minor city, had bristled in the early 1980s when the provinces of Guangdong and Fujian were given the green light to move ahead and Shanghai was not. Shanghai leaders made no effort to hide their view that Shanghai had far higher levels of education, science, technology, and industry than any city in either Guangdong or Fujian. Shanghai leaders, with full support of the public, would be great allies in Deng's efforts to speed up growth.

In 1984, as a part of the opening of the fourteen coastal cities, Shanghai had been given some leeway to develop, but from 1984 to 1990, it had still received little assistance from the central government, and the city had scarcely begun to realize its potential. In Guangdong it was relatively easy to get foreign businesses to invest: erecting a completely new plant on undeveloped land entailed a large but manageable cost. But remaking the large old industries in Shanghai required an initial outlay of capital that only the government could provide. Shanghai leaders, upset that their city was required to make such a heavy contribution to the national budget while receiving so little help, had long been urging Beijing to change its policies. Some leaders in Beijing's ministries were sympathetic to investing more in Shanghai, for they were beginning to fear that they were losing control over Guangdong, where financial resources came largely from outsiders and not from the Chinese government. If Beijing were to supply capital to Shanghai, national planners would be able to maintain greater control there than they had been able to achieve in Guangdong.

While spending his winter "vacation" in Shanghai in 1988 and 1989, Deng had talked with Jiang Zemin and his replacement as Shanghai party secretary, Zhu Rongji. Deng had known Zhu in Beijing earlier, when Zhu had been deputy head of the State Economic Commission, and Deng recognized that he was a rare talent who combined bold political leadership skills, a strategic understanding of how to improve the economy, and an unusual confidence in pursuing reforms. In January–February 1990 Deng met with Zhu and other Shanghai party, government, and military leaders to discuss how to spark local growth.[5]

In February 1990, immediately after returning to Beijing, Deng told Premier Li Peng: "I have already retired, but there is one thing I must tell you about, that is the development of Shanghai's Pudong. You must give it more attention."[6] Two weeks later, on March 3, 1990, Deng called in Jiang Zemin,

Yang Shangkun, and Li Peng to lecture them on the international situation and the domestic economy: "Why do the people support us? Because over the last ten years our economy has been developing. . . . If the economy stagnated for five years or developed at only a slow rate—for example, at 4 or 5 percent, or even 2 or 3 percent a year—what effects would be produced? This would be not only an economic problem but also a political one." Deng continued: "We must analyze problems from an overall, strategic point of view and work out concrete measures. . . . We should do some research to determine which localities have the most favorable conditions and promise the best economic returns. . . . It is of prime importance to develop Shanghai. That city is a trump card."[7]

Alas, in 1990, Beijing leaders were not moved by teacher Deng's lecturing nor by the desires of Shanghai leaders to accelerate growth. They were then guided more by the master cautious planner Chen Yun who had grown up in Qingpu on the outskirts of Shanghai and had frequently returned to observe the situation there; he enjoyed special authority within the party on Shanghai-related issues. Chen Yun had opposed the establishment of a special economic zone (SEZ) in Shanghai, not only because of the risks to the nation's established heavy industry and tax bases, but also because as someone who had worked there in the 1920s and 1930s, he was acutely aware of the worst evils of capitalism and the "comprador mentality" of Shanghai businesspeople, who were all too willing, in Chen's view, to subordinate themselves to foreigners. Chen Yun thus feared a return of the foreign settlements. Deng, however, had no patience for Chen's hesitation. Although he did not attack Chen Yun by name, in February 1990 when he stated that Shanghai lagged behind Guangdong, insiders knew he was expressing frustration at Chen Yun's resistance to opening Shanghai.[8]

On December 24, 1990, on the eve of the Seventh Plenum (December 25–30), which was to review the drafts of the next five-year plan and the ten-year vision, Deng again called in Jiang Zemin, Yang Shangkun, and Li Peng to give them some lessons about accelerating growth. Stressing the vital importance of doubling the economy by 2000, he told his successors not to be afraid of taking risks.[9] Deng repeated that if China did not grow fast enough, its stagnant economy would become a political problem—and the austerity program, aggravated by foreign sanctions, was slowing economic growth. Deng passionately argued that China had to overcome the conservative policies to avoid the fate of the USSR and Eastern Europe.[10] But Deng's lessons had little effect. Despite his entreaties, the Seventh Plenum was still dominated by strict conservatives who were more afraid of an overheated economy than of slower growth.

On January 28, 1991, Deng took his special train to Shanghai where he remained until February 20, taking his winter rest while again trying to light the fire of economic growth. After being briefed by Zhu Rongji, he visited aeronautic and automobile factories and the construction site for the Nanpu Bridge, which would soon become the third longest suspension bridge in the world.[11] Deng reiterated what he had said in 1990: that he had made a mistake in not opening up Shanghai in 1979, when he had opened the four SEZs, and that he should have taken advantage of the great intellectual resources of Shanghai. He emphasized the importance of developing Pudong not only for the city itself but for the entire Yangtze River basin. Finance, Deng explained—carefully avoiding using the charged word "capital"—is at the core of a modern economy; if China is to acquire an international status in finance, the entire nation would have to rely on Shanghai.[12]

In 1991 Deng's spark again failed to light a prairie fire. His picture was shown on national television as he, Yang Shangkun, and Li Xiannian greeted Shanghai leaders on New Year's Eve, but there was still no mention of Deng's efforts to speed up Shanghai's development.[13] Deng's views did not even appear in the *People's Daily.* In 1991 Deng did, however, have two smaller successes. Deng garnered enough support to bring Zhu Rongji to Beijing to serve as vice premier. He also succeeded in getting several articles published in a Shanghai newspaper, albeit under a pseudonym. During March and April 1991 Shanghai officials allowed the Shanghai newspaper *Liberation Daily* to compile Deng's earlier comments in Shanghai into a four-part series. The articles did not reveal Deng's connection and simply appeared under the name "Huangfu Ping" (or "Shanghai Commentary," "Huang" after the Huangpu River that flows through the city and "fu ping" which also can imply "fuzhu Deng Xiaoping," or "to assist Deng Xiaoping").[14] The first Huangfu Ping article was published on March 3. The commentary criticized "some comrades" who said that markets were capitalist. The article stated that planning and markets are simply two different means of deploying available resources; neither one is the hallmark of either socialism or capitalism. Political insiders speculated who was behind the Huangfu Ping articles, but initially only a handful of people realized that it was Deng.

The Central Propaganda Department mobilized the *People's Daily* and *Guangming Daily* to refute the Huangfu Ping articles. At the opening ceremony of Shanghai's impressive Nanpu Bridge in November 1991, Premier Li

Peng, speaking on behalf of the conservative leadership in Beijing, publicly criticized the Huangfu Ping articles, saying that they provided the misleading impression that the political mood in Beijing had changed.[15]

In 1991, party officials began preparing for the 14th Party Congress, to be held in late 1992. Deng made it clear that if Jiang Zemin promoted faster growth and greater opening, he would support him; if not, he would back other party leaders. Yet the other leaders were also constrained by the prevailing atmosphere. After Zhu Rongji became vice premier in Beijing, for example, Premier Li Peng, who had dutifully followed the conservative policies of his seniors, felt pressure from Deng who wanted Zhu to take over responsibility for guiding the economy. But Li resisted this pressure, and in 1991 Zhu had no choice but to follow the current cautious policies.

Chen Yun and Deng avoided carrying out their struggle in public, but their respective supporters publicly expressed their views on their behalf. In October 1991, President Yang Shangkun used the occasion of the eightieth anniversary of the 1911 revolution to argue for bolder reform and wider opening.[16] An article by Deng Liqun, arguing for the other side, in the *People's Daily* on October 23, 1991, warned that class struggle was acute and there was a danger of "peaceful evolution"—that is, the gradual replacement of communism by capitalism—which, he argued, was just what some liberals were hoping for.[17] In late 1991, as officials prepared for the forthcoming congress, the battle lines were clearly drawn. When at the Eighth Plenum (November 25–29, 1991) the conservatives still had the upper hand, Deng took his usual approach: instead of wasting time arguing, he chose to act to build support.

Deng's Southern Tour, January–February 1992

When Deng's special train pulled out of the Beijing station on January 17, 1992, no other central party leaders, not even Jiang Zemin, were notified: the trip had been arranged entirely by the police forces within the People's Liberation Army (PLA). As far as other leaders in Beijing knew, and as far as the local hosts in the south had been told, Deng, his wife, and four children—all except Deng Zhifang, the youngest—as well as their spouses and children, seventeen persons in all, were going on a "family vacation" with some leisurely sightseeing as they traveled south. And who would oppose a family vacation for the ancient patriarch?

The first stop on Deng's southern tour was Wuhan, a major rail junction in central China where the 1911 revolution had started. Deng arrived at the Wuchang train station on the morning of January 18, 1992, where he was met by Hubei party secretary Guan Guangfu and Governor Guo Shuyan, as was fitting for Deng's eminence, even if on a family vacation. Deng remained on the platform only twenty minutes, but that proved ample time for him to vent his spleen: "When I turn on the television, all I see is meetings. There are too many meetings, the reports are too long, the speeches are too long, the content is too repetitious. . . . You should do more and talk less. . . . For the 4th National People's Congress [NPC] [1974], Zhou [Enlai] . . . ordered that there be no more than 5,000 characters in his speech. I got the speech down within those limits. . . . [now] there are more documents than there are hairs on a cow." He told the story of the provincial secretary who returned from a week in the countryside only to find such a huge mountain of papers that he got a headache.[18] Long opposed to empty talk, long reports, and meetings without careful preparation, Deng had once declared, "If you don't have something to say, keep your mouth shut . . . the purpose of meetings and talks is to solve problems."[19] After his opening blast, Deng got to his main point: "Whoever is against reform must leave office." Although he was talking to a local audience in Wuhan and his words were not recorded in the public press, Deng's comments received quick attention from Jiang Zemin. Two days later, Jiang told fellow officials that China should quicken the pace of reform, revive the open-door policy, and reduce the number of meetings.[20]

That same afternoon, when Deng's train stopped at the station in Changsha, Hunan, Deng spent ten minutes greeting Xiong Qingquan, first party secretary of Hunan, and other provincial officials. At first, Deng seemed buoyant as he received reports of a good harvest despite the natural disaster in 1991, but teacher Deng still had some basic lessons to give: he instructed Secretary Xiong that Hunan "should be bolder in carrying out reform and opening. . . . Speed up economic development."[21]

The morning of January 19, Deng stopped briefly in Guangzhou, where provincial officials joined him for an eleven-day inspection tour to the two most vibrant SEZs, Shenzhen and Zhuhai. Local officials had scarcely a week's notice to prepare for Deng's visit by walking through all the places Deng would visit to ensure their security and by arranging the necessary facilities, including spittoons. Officials had only been told that they should prepare to welcome Deng for a family vacation, but by the time he arrived, they had already received detailed reports from officials whom he had met in

Wuhan and Changsha; they understood that this was not an ordinary family outing.[22]

Guangdong party secretary Xie Fei, deputy provincial secretary general Chen Kaizhi, and a small number of other provincial officials joined local Shenzhen officials in guiding Deng through the city. Some of the local officials who welcomed him had also helped host him in 1984 when he came to affirm the success of the SEZs. After arriving at his guest house and taking a ten-minute rest, Deng, Xie Fei, and the others took a walk in the adjoining garden. Deng Nan, Deng's daughter, reminded her father that he had written some thoughts when they visited this same spot eight years earlier. Deng responded by reciting from memory his words at the time—"Shenzhen's development and experience prove that our policy of establishing the Special Economic Zones was correct"—which brought cheers from his delighted hosts who considered him their greatest booster, unlike other Beijing officials who were trying to restrain their investments.

Deng preserved his strength by touring only three hours each morning, then eating meals with his family, napping, and resting in the afternoon. On one tour of local areas, when the family saw a sign with the characters "Shenzhen" copied from Deng's own handwriting, Deng Nan remarked, "You should collect interest; you should have intellectual property rights." Deng laughed.[23] Later, when they saw bamboo trees brought from Chengdu at the Xinhua Botanical Gardens, Deng teased his local guides, saying that they should pay Sichuan province for intellectual property rights.[24] The joke had a deep resonance for Deng: everyone knew that Deng had complained to Westerners about China having to pay large sums for intellectual property rights, and that Deng had reminded the Westerners that China had not charged other countries for borrowing Chinese inventions such as gunpowder and the printing press. But Deng also knew that China needed to adapt to the new international order. When visiting a Shenzhen factory making compact discs, Deng inquired whether they had bought the rights from the foreign countries and reminded the factory managers, "You must abide by international rules on intellectual property rights."[25]

Everywhere in Guangdong, Deng was surrounded by admiring, grateful fans. Although initially, in 1982–1983, he had not defended the SEZs, by 1984 he was praising them when they were under heavy attack from the conservatives in Beijing. It is said of the residents of Guangdong that if they have a green traffic light, they go ahead; if they have a yellow traffic light, they go ahead, only faster; and if they have a red light, they simply go around it. In 1992, however, the Cantonese were worried about the red and yellow lights coming from Beijing and badly wanted to see some green lights. Deng was now supporting their cause, further opening and rapid growth; in turn they became cheerleaders for the cause he was promoting on his southern journey.

Following official guidance from Beijing on arrangements for a "family vacation," Deng had taken only one reporter and one photographer, and he held no press conferences. Yet by the time he started touring Shenzhen, an estimated fifty to sixty photographers had gathered to watch him enjoying his "family vacation"; many even brought tape recorders to ensure that they caught every word.[26]

Deng, brimming with enthusiasm as he viewed the skyline of the tall buildings, then still rare in China, inspected the new technologies, in which he displayed a detailed interest, and listened to briefings by local officials. Officials told Deng that Shenzhen, which in 1984 had an average annual per capita income of 600 yuan, had raised this to 2,000 yuan by 1992. He could only have felt cheered by the prospect that such momentum would help realize his dreams for faster growth. While traveling to spur future growth, Deng enjoyed the rich harvest from the seeds he had planted with his reform and opening policies.

Large numbers of ordinary citizens, tipped off through leaks about his arrival, were waiting when Deng exited factories and office buildings. As he descended from Shenzhen's fifty-three-story World Trade Center, where he had viewed scenes of the vast new construction from the revolving restaurant at the top, an especially large crowd gathered to clap and cheer.[27] Although he had acquired a well-deserved reputation for not being talkative, Deng was, with the help of his daughter Deng Rong—who repeated loudly into his ears what his deafness would not allow him to hear directly—fully engaged in conversations with local officials and appreciative onlookers. To many officials in Beijing, Deng was viewed as a stern commander, but the crowds in Shenzhen cheerily greeted "uncle Deng" (shushu hao) (and, for younger people, "grandpa Deng," yeye hao), whom they found warm, witty, approachable, and eager to soak in all the latest developments.

In the privacy of the car, however, Deng furiously criticized the conservatives back in Beijing. He asked the accompanying officials, all of whom were sympathetic with his purpose, not to repeat in public what he said in private. But even in public, he expressed his fear that the leftist policies could have dire consequences and even destroy socialism.[28] He cautioned: "China should maintain vigilance against the right but primarily against the left."[29] In frank talks with local officials, Deng countered his critics who said that the SEZs were capitalistic and controlled by foreigners by saying that only a quarter of the investment came from foreigners. Moreover, Deng said, China had political control over all foreign-owned firms, so it could be certain that they served Chinese interests. Instead of worrying about the current level of foreign involvement, Deng advised, China should increase foreign investment and form more joint ventures: foreign firms pay Chinese taxes and provide local workers with jobs and wages.[30]

Sessions with local officials and retired uncle Deng were far more casual than the Beijing party meetings Deng had taken part in. Deng was relaxed and informal, and as he made humorous comments, local leaders often chimed in. Deng was giving one of his last lessons, urging officials to be bolder and to try harder. He repeated the lessons he had been giving everywhere: continue reform and opening, keep a lean government, train young people, talk less, and do more. On the bus returning to his guest house after visiting the World Trade Center, Deng repeated many of his basic points: Planning is not the same as socialism, and markets are not the same as capitalism. There is planning under capitalism and there are markets under socialism. Socialism is not poverty. In following the socialist path, everyone can become rich, and toward this end the places that get rich first should turn over more taxes, which then can be used to assist less-developed areas. But the situation cannot be equalized too quickly—people should not "eat out of the same pot"—for this would destroy the people's enthusiasm. Deng again urged his listeners to experiment, to take risks, and to not be afraid of making mistakes; when you make them, just correct them.[31]

Deng exhorted Shenzhen to catch up within twenty years with the four little dragons of Hong Kong, Singapore, South Korea, and Taiwan. "Society in Singapore," he said, "is quite orderly. They manage things very strictly. We ought to use their experience as a model. And we ought to manage things even better than they do." After being briefed about graft and corruption in Shenzhen, Deng replied, "You have to use a two-fisted approach. With one hand, you grab reform and opening. With the other, you grab every kind of criminal behavior. You have to have a firm grip with both hands."[32]

On January 23, after five days in Shenzhen, Party Secretary Li Hao told Deng of his plans for reorganizing, redistricting, and expanding the legal system. Deng, as if he were still in charge of the country, declared that he approved of all these ideas and encouraged Li to carry them out boldly. Al-though many officials back in Beijing were critical of Shenzhen for moving ahead too rapidly, Deng's parting words to Li Hao were "speed up growth and reform." Li Hao's reply? "We'll definitely speed things up."[33] Deng's next stop was Zhuhai, and the first party secretary of Zhuhai, Liang Guangda, came to Shenzhen to escort the Deng family and the provincial officials dur-ing the hour-long boat ride across the mouth of the broad Pearl River to his city. As the boat passed by the remains of a Qing dynasty customs house, Deng again passed on the essence of his departing message: China had been humiliated by the foreign imperialists, but that era had passed: "Those who are backward get beaten. . . . We've been poor for thousands of years, but we won't be poor again. If we don't emphasize science, technology, and educa-tion, we will be beaten again."[34]

Guangdong party secretary Xie Fei and Liang Guangda were fully aware of Deng's concerns about the growing economic inequalities; they knew he had long urged that those who get rich first should help others along. During the boat trip, Deng was told that the bustling Pearl River delta area was already doing a great deal to help the poorer mountainous areas in the northern and western parts of the province. Deng replied that the progress since the reform and opening was due to the creativity of local people, who were willing to experiment, and the ability of the government to notice what was working and pass the ideas on to the rest of the country.[35]

Just as Macao was smaller and less bustling than Hong Kong, so Zhuhai, adjacent to Macao, was smaller and less bustling than Shenzhen. From Zhu-hai's revolving restaurant at the top of its twenty-nine-story trade center, as in Shenzhen, Deng and his family gazed at the tall buildings under construc-tion. Deng warmed to the crowds in Zhuhai just as he had in Shenzhen. In one factory in Zhuhai, observers estimated that Deng shook more than one hundred hands; on the streets he was restrained by police to keep him from mingling with the crowds and shaking even more hands.

In questioning local residents, Deng tried to gauge how quickly the growth in the coastal urban areas was spreading to the more remote areas, and to in-fer what future development might mean for the people. He could already see many signs that consumer goods—bicycles, sewing machines, radios, watches, and other manufactured items—were beginning to spread to the rural areas.[36] He was pleased to hear that migrants from poor areas had found opportunities for employment along the coast. He was also encouraged by reports of eager young people who had gone abroad to study but then returned to help build their motherland. He was told that some factories, led by entrepreneurial Chinese, were already approaching world technological standards. He praised local leaders' success in using markets to further the cause of socialism, and credited socialism in turn for aiding in that success: he said that capitalism could not match the socialist system in terms of focusing on talent to make things happen quickly. He also noted that if not for the progress from 1984 to 1988, things would not have gone so smoothly in China during the difficult years from 1989 to 1992.

During the car ride from Zhuhai to Guangzhou, Deng stopped for a few minutes in the two counties just north of Zhuhai, Zhongshan and Shunde, that were flourishing from the rapid spillover of the dynamism of the SEZs to the nearby areas. After an hour-long meeting with provincial leaders in Guangzhou, Deng boarded his train to Shanghai, with a brief stop in Yingtan, located in eastern Jiangxi province.[37]

Upon his arrival in Yingtan, Deng was again received at the train station by local officials who briefed him about the excellent harvests of the past year and their progress in responding to the floods. Deng praised their efforts but also declared that they needed to plant more trees to prevent erosion, which causes flooding. Deng also said that officials should try to go faster, be bolder, and open up even further. At this point, Deng Nan chimed in to say that her father had been preaching this message during the entire trip. She added that her father cared a lot about Jiangxi, where he had served in the Jiangxi Soviet some sixty years earlier and where he had spent three-and-a-half years during the Cultural Revolution. In fact, during much of the trip, Deng reminisced about his experiences in Ruijin and Huichang counties in 1931.[38] Deng Nan reminded her father that on February 19, 1973, after his years of "rustication" in the countryside during the Cultural Revolution, the family had boarded the train to Beijing at that same Yingtan station. Now from Yingtan they boarded the train to Shanghai and by the time they arrived, the seeds for further opening that Deng planted in Guangdong were beginning to bear fruit.

The Breakthroughs

Deng had failed in 1990 and 1991 to get the country back on the fast track to reform and opening, but in 1992 he made a dramatic breakthrough thanks to the Hong Kong press and to a meeting he held in Zhuhai.

Following protocol, Deng held no press conferences, but once word got out that he was in Shenzhen, eager Hong Kong reporters and photographers crossed the border in large numbers to cover his trip. On January 22, three days after Deng arrived in Shenzhen, the Hong Kong newspaper *Ming bao* broke the news of his visit as well as his message about speeding up reform. It also reported that Yang Shangkun was accompanying Deng in Shenzhen. Perceptive Hong Kong readers instantly perceived that Deng's trip south was more than an ordinary family outing.

The editors of leftist publications in Hong Kong, remembering that many staff members had been fired for supporting the June 4 protests, were jittery about covering Deng's visit and message. Nonetheless, the next day, January 23, they, along with Hong Kong television stations, also reported the news of Deng's trip to Shenzhen. And because Chinese propaganda officials were unable to block the reception of Hong Kong television in nearby mainland areas, millions of residents in southern Guangdong watched parts of Deng's Shenzhen visit on Hong Kong television.

Beijing propaganda officials who took the side of the cautious planners were faced with a hard choice: to ignore Deng's trip despite gradual seepage of information into southern China and elsewhere, or to acknowledge the trip while trying to weaken Deng's assault on those who took a more conservative stance on reform and opening.[39] Meanwhile, Deng's allies, local officials in southern China who wanted permission to grow faster, were willing to take risks to get Deng's message out.

Given the attention that Deng had received in Shenzhen and Zhuhai, it was difficult for the conservative media managers to ignore Deng's trip, but they tried. On February 3, Beijing television showed Deng and Yang Shangkun giving New Year's greetings to Shanghai leaders, without even mentioning his trip to Shenzhen and Zhuhai or his push for more reform. On the same day, the English-language *China Daily* showed a photo of Yang Shangkun and Deng that had been taken in Shenzhen, but it did not provide a date for the picture. And on February 4, the editors of Shanghai's *Liberation Daily*, which was controlled by the Communist Party in Shanghai, cleverly managed to both avoid mentioning the southern trip and to carry a front-page article praising Deng's effort to emancipate the mind, already enshrined from the Third Plenum, which could be seen as a boost for the large new projects they sought for their city.[40] But by that time, the local press in Guangdong and Shanghai was itching to spread word of Deng's trip, and with knowledge of Deng's journey so widespread in southern Guangdong, there was no way Beijing propaganda officials could prevent others from knowing its purpose.

In Zhuhai, Deng held a meeting ostensibly for military planning that turned up the heat under Jiang Zemin. He repeated the message he gave in Wuhan: "Whoever is opposed to reform must leave office. . . . Our leaders look like they're doing something, but they're not doing anything worthwhile."[41] The meeting Deng attended in Zhuhai on "military planning" was chaired by Qiao Shi, one of the six members of the Standing Committee of the Politburo. Since Qiao Shi was in charge of domestic security matters, it was appropriate for him to call such a meeting. But Qiao Shi was also regarded by many as having the qualities needed to be a top leader and as a potential rival to Jiang Zemin, so this meeting had the potential to be about China's leadership. Even more ominously for Jiang, attending the meeting were President Yang Shangkun, vice chairman of the Central Military Commission (CMC); General Liu Huaqing, another vice chairman of the CMC; and Yang Shangkun's half-brother General Yang Baibing, who was head of the PLA Political Work Department and secretary general of the CMC. Although all these officials were concerned with security, they also all agreed with Deng about the need to speed up reform.[42]

The Zhuhai meeting is not mentioned in books on the southern tour published in mainland China, nor is it noted in the official chronology of Deng's life, *Deng Xiaoping nianpu*. This omission is understandable, for Communist Party leaders do not want inner-party tensions to be revealed in public. But news of the meeting leaked from participants and from observers in Zhuhai and was, in effect, confirmed by the reactions of Jiang Zemin in the weeks following the meeting. The strong representation of military leaders made it clear that if necessary, the high-level military brass was willing to support a new leader.

Jiang Zemin Responds

Jiang Zemin, eager to get precise news of the Zhuhai meeting, persuaded Jia Qinglin, first party secretary of Fujian, to give him a tape of the meeting; not long thereafter it was announced that Jia Qinglin had been appointed to the Politburo. And although it was not customary for Jiang to phone Deng on New Year's, on February 3, 1992, five days after Deng left Zhuhai, Jiang Zemin phoned Deng to wish him a happy New Year. As Jiang later acknowledged, the phone call was no accident.[43] Jiang thereafter began to tilt more boldly toward reform.

Deng arrived in Shanghai on January 31 for three more weeks of vacation, when at a more leisurely pace than in the SEZs he viewed Pudong's development and edited the draft of his speeches in Shenzhen and Zhuhai.[44] He also toured the recently completed Nanpu Bridge and the construction site of the huge Yangpu Bridge.[45] While repeating his "self-criticism" for not making Shanghai an SEZ earlier, he also suggested that by starting now, Shanghai could use its advantage as a latecomer to learn from Guangdong's experience, allowing it to do things even better.

Meanwhile, a team of writers, under the direction of Zheng Bijian, a former secretary to Hua Guofeng and Hu Yaobang, prepared a systematic summary of Deng's speeches in Shenzhen and Zhuhai. They first received a preliminary summary of 20,000 to 30,000 characters prepared by Guangdong officials from the trip and then boiled it down in successive drafts to 7,000 characters by going through several drafts with Deng. The report, which had a more official ring than Deng's original pithy comments during the tour, was completed before Deng left Shanghai.[46]

Chen Yun was in Shanghai while Deng was there, but Deng did not arrange a meeting with him. President Yang Shangkun and Shanghai Party Secretary Wu Bangguo, however, went in person to pay their Chinese New Year's respects to Chen Yun.[47] A seasoned leader like Chen Yun had no trouble understanding all the political nuances of Deng's efforts. He also knew that Deng's efforts to speed up reform enjoyed strong support within the military and that plans for the development of Pudong had the enthusiastic backing of the Shanghai Party Committee.

For over a decade, Deng, so busy with his work, had never gone shopping, but one morning, he visited Shanghai's No. 1 Department Store, which boasted the highest sales of any retail establishment in China. There he could see the brisk sales of a wide range of consumer goods. The scene stood in striking contrast to the meager offerings of bare basics on the shelves that had greeted customers only fourteen years earlier, when his reforms began, and it could have only reinforced his pride in China's progress.[48] With the help of his daughter Deng Rong, he bought some pens as presents for his grandchildren.

When Deng boarded the train to return to Beijing, he had reason to hope that the southern journey was accomplishing its purpose and that Jiang Zemin would now speed up growth and reform.[49] Indeed, from February 20, the day Deng departed Shanghai for Beijing, until March 6, staff members of the *Shenzhen Daily* were sufficiently optimistic about Deng's ultimate victory that they dared to publish a series of eight articles on the southern tour.[50] Although Beijing propaganda leaders tried to prevent copies of these articles from making their way to Beijing, they could not stop copies of the paper reaching audiences throughout China, including in the capital.

By mid-February, several days before Deng returned to Beijing, Jiang Zemin was already saying publicly that he supported Deng's calls for further reform.[51] From the reports he had received from Zhuhai, Jiang realized that Deng was determined to remove him if he did not boldly promote reform and opening. Jiang could see from Deng's visit to the south that he had attracted a great deal of support from key leaders in Beijing and from local leaders. Later Jiang acknowledged that by then he had concluded that Deng's views would prevail and that he, Jiang, would be wise to support them.[52]

When Zheng Bijian's summary of Deng's speeches in the SEZs was completed, Jiang Zemin obtained the Politburo's approval for circulating the draft to small groups of top officials. The summary was less provocative than Deng's spontaneous comments on the ground, but it was nonetheless strong and direct. When party leaders became aware of the public attention paid to Deng's trip in the south and read the report, they realized that despite his age, Deng was exerting himself on a determined crusade and that his base of support was rapidly expanding.[53] Leaders in Shanghai, Guangdong, and elsewhere who wanted to move faster toward open markets, increasingly optimistic about the outcome, rallied behind Deng. Even without Deng's southern journey, the gradual easing of foreign sanctions and the conservatives' success in reducing inflationary pressures would have led Chinese leaders to increase growth targets. But Deng's tour and its success in converting Jiang Zemin enabled the change to begin sooner and continue at a faster pace than otherwise would have been possible.

Even as Jiang was beginning to come around to Deng's point of view, the national press lagged behind in publicizing Deng's trip and Deng's message. On February 20, the day before Deng returned to Beijing, the conservative bi-monthly *Contemporary Trends of Thought (Dangdai sichao)*, in a last-ditch effort to promote the cautious planners' views, published an article by Deng Liqun that undoubtedly reflected the views of Chen Yun. The article stated that the major danger was not from the left but from the right. "People who stubbornly cling to their liberal beliefs are using anti-leftism as a pretext to oppose the Communist Party leadership and the socialist system. . . . Unless we fight back . . . the result of course would be a disastrous proliferation of all kinds of anticommunist ideas."[54]

But the tide had turned. After this article appeared, the voices of the conservatives grew weaker as Jiang Zemin and his colleagues began to prepare the public for their endorsement of Deng's call to accelerate growth. On February 21, the day Deng returned to Beijing, a *People's Daily* editorial, drawing on Zheng Bijian's summary, was entitled, "Be Bolder in Reform."[55] The editorial still made no mention of Deng's southern tour, which had already dominated the Hong Kong media for a month. A week later, however, on February 28, high officials in Beijing released Document No. 2, based on Deng's speech a week earlier, and distributed it to a broad group of high-level party officials. Like most official documents, it was carefully written and well-organized, but lacked the vehemence and freshness of Deng's original talks. Titled "A Notice about Passing on and Studying Comrade Deng's Important Talks," it was circulated to all members of the Central Committee and selected other groups, such as the two thousand students and faculty at the Central Party School.[56]

By the March 9–10 Politburo meeting, when all fifteen members of the Politburo met to discuss Document No. 2, opinion had jelled to support the document. Deng had pushed hard, building on his base of support by local officials. He had made use of the Hong Kong press and mobilized PLA supporters. But he also was also riding a wave of good news about the economy. Not only was inflation under control, thanks to Chen Yun's efforts, but industry had begun to grow, exports were strong, and foreign countries were beginning to relax their sanctions. The climate for expansion had greatly improved.

At the Politburo meeting, President Yang Shangkun began the discussion by forcefully backing the document, and Jiang Zemin followed by expressing full support for Deng's efforts and admitting that he had been too lax in promoting reform.[57] The Politburo unanimously endorsed the basic message of Deng's trip to the south—accelerate the pace of reform and opening—and agreed that the message would be the centerpiece of the 14th Party Congress to be held at the end of that year. Deng later agreed that Document No. 2 would be the final document in his three-volume *Selected Works*. The essence of his advice was no surprise to those who had followed Deng's words and deeds: be bolder in reform and opening to the outside.

From the March Politburo meeting on, the approved summary of Deng's statements on the southern journey became the new guideline for official policy. On March 11, the day after the Politburo meeting and almost two months after Deng had begun his southern journey, the New China News Agency (Xinhua) finally officially broke the news to the public about Deng's southern journey, and offered an accompanying editorial stating that people needed to be more daring in reform and opening. It took until March 31, however, before the *People's Daily* would finally fall into line, publishing its own detailed report of the trip.

The Changed Atmosphere

As news of the trip was fully reported and policies began to change, Deng's talks became known as the *nanxun tanhua* (talks from the southern tour). The term *nanxun* was used in imperial times to refer to the grand inspection tours of emperors to the south (to the Yangtze River area, not as far south as Deng went). But in order to remove the connotation that Deng was acting like an emperor, the trip was officially given a more neutral term, *nanfang tanhua* (talks from the south).

Conservative officials, aware of the widespread support for Deng's message, reluctantly approved the documents reporting Deng's message. At the annual meeting of the NPC that opened on March 20, the overall political atmosphere among the delegates reflected the forward momentum created by Deng's southern journey.[58] Intellectuals and military leaders took advantage of the changed mood to mount criticisms of leftism in their respective units. On March 23, Yang Baibing announced that the army would protect and support reform, a clear warning to those who dragged their feet.

In late May, the party center issued Document No. 4, designed to implement Deng's policies. The document announced the opening of five inland cities along the Yangtze River as well as nine border cities, and stated that all thirty provincial and prefectural capital cities would enjoy the same privileges as the SEZs.[59]

In the several months after the southern journey, Deng did not meet with Jiang to tell him how to conduct further reform and opening, nor did he express clear support for Jiang. Indeed, Jiang Zemin reported that he felt Deng was still testing him, and that the implicit threat remained: if Jiang did not fully support reform, Deng, with the backing of the military, might try to have him replaced by Qiao Shi.

Jiang was determined to pass Deng's final examination. In public appearances during the spring, Jiang became a strong advocate of further reform and opening. And he carefully crafted a speech that he delivered on June 9 to the graduating class of senior provincial- and ministerial-level students at the Central Party School.[60] In his speech—entitled "Deeply Understand and Implement Comrade Deng Xiaoping's Important Spirit, Make Economic Construction, Reform and Opening Go Faster and Better"—Jiang Zemin both presented a comprehensive overview of what was required to implement the spirit of Deng's southern journey and summarized Deng's contributions since the 1978 Third Plenum. Jiang said that they should accelerate the pace of reform, reaching a growth rate of as high as 9 to 10 percent a year. (At the time, the official goal in the five-year plan, as presented by Li Peng at the NPC meeting, was still 6 percent a year.) Jiang said they should move boldly, taking lessons from the advanced practices of the capitalist countries; there was no need to discuss whether the reforms were called capitalist or socialist. Moreover, Jiang packaged these ideas under a term he expected Deng would welcome: a "socialist market economy."[61]

On June 12, three days after this major address, Jiang Zemin, the hopeful young leader, asked the master if he approved of the term "socialist market economy," which clearly was intended to replace Chen Yun's "planned socialist market economy." Deng, to Jiang's relief, said that he had liked Jiang's speech, adding, "Actually, Shenzhen has a socialist market economy." Jiang had passed the test. Then, as if he were still the final decision-maker, Deng told Jiang Zemin to circulate his Central Party School speech for internal comment and, if the reaction were favorable, to use it as the theme for the 14th Party Congress. Not surprisingly, the reaction was favorable.

Chen Yun, the elder statesman of the cautious conservatives but also a disciplined party member who always supported party policy, accepted the unanimous Politburo decision to accelerate reform and opening. During his long winter vacation in Shanghai during the early months of 1992, Chen had observed the progress in Pudong and talked to the Shanghai officials overseeing its development. On April 26, 1992, the day before his return to Beijing, Chen, upon hearing reports from Shanghai Party Secretary Wu Bangguo and Mayor Huang Ju on Pudong, not only approved their efforts to enliven Shanghai but also told them to become even bolder.

About three months later, in his July 21 eulogy for his longtime colleague Li Xiannian, who had died a month earlier, Chen Yun acknowledged that he and Li Xiannian had never visited the SEZs, but he said they both acknowledged such experiments were necessary: "We must learn from our experience with them in order to make them a success." He declared that he was impressed with Shenzhen's modern construction and with its great success in increasing exports much faster than imports. He added, "Economic development in China is much larger in scale and more complicated than in the past, and many measures that were effective in the past are no longer applicable to the current situation of reform and opening up. The new situation requires us to learn more and to continuously explore and solve new problems."[62] Chen Yun had fought tenaciously to keep inflation low and to keep the planning system running smoothly. In 1992, thanks to his retrenchment policies since 1988, inflation was under control and exports were rising, overcoming the effects of the sanctions. By then, as his career was drawing to a close, Chen Yun acknowledged that China was entering a new and more complex era. In effect, he was giving his vote of confidence to the next generation of leaders, who would move China along a path different from that which he had pursued with such intensity.

By the summer, Deng had consolidated his victory. Local officials were allowed to make higher rates of investment, they could expand their foreign trade, and the experiments from the coast were extended inland. Deng could give more attention to other issues China would face in the decades ahead. On July 24, after reading through the drafts of the documents prepared for the forthcoming party congress, Deng raised several other issues to consider: the structure of rural life, his own personal role in China's development, the governing system, and national security.

On rural policy, Deng acknowledged that contracting down to the household and the abolition of communes had been necessary to motivate China's farmers and other rural workers. But as new agricultural technologies were acquired or developed, the tiny household farms could not afford to upgrade on their own; at some point, a larger collective organization would be required. Deng advised government leaders not to hurry this process but wait until individual farmers took the initiative to change the system.

In considering his legacy, Deng said leaders should not exaggerate his personal role, but describe it as it was. The process of developing reform and opening was so large and complex that no single individual or small group of leaders could think of everything. No one had thought deeply beforehand about relying on township and village enterprises, for example, yet they had become essential to China's development. China's success since 1978 had come from the experiences of large numbers of people. His own role was simply to try to put developments into an overall package and present them to a broader audience.

On the issue of governance and freedom, Deng said that the concept of "democratic centralism" was still the "most rational system" and should remain the country's basic governing principle. Leaders should find ways to encourage people to express their opinions, but once a decision is made, people should follow the collective decision.

Deng also addressed the issue of China's security. He said that the balance of power among nations was undergoing great changes and that it was important to study these changes carefully. In the current situation, he believed that China could continue to reduce the size of its military, but it was important to raise the quality of military personnel and to be prepared if necessary to defend the country with increased fighting capacity.[63]

Deng read over Jiang Zemin's proposed address for the 14th Party Congress and approved it. The essence of the speech was the message from Deng's southern journey: accelerate reform and opening.

The 14th Party Congress, October 12–18, 1992

The 14th Party Congress featured the usual carefully prepared documents on present and future policy, but above all it was a public tribute to Deng and the success of his policies—in effect, his retirement celebration. The main address, Jiang Zemin's political report, was filled with praise for Deng and his policies, which were to set the course for China for the next five years—the building of a "socialist market economy." To be sure, Jiang's speech reflected some compromise with the conservatives: instead of projecting growth of 10 percent per year as Deng had originally proposed, he set the goal of 8 or 9 percent growth. Still, this was a much greater rate than the 6 percent that Li Peng had announced earlier that year.[64]

Jiang not only praised Deng Xiaoping as the architect of China's reform and opening, he also elevated Deng's views into what would become "Deng Xiaoping theory" (Deng Xiaoping lilun). The informed public knew that Deng was a pragmatist, not an ideologue; unlike many top leaders in the Communist world, he had not considered it necessary to be a theorist to make his claim to the highest office. But for Jiang Zemin, elevating Deng's views to a theory strengthened their importance, making them comparable to "The Thought of Mao Zedong" and making it as easy to focus on the four modernizations as on making revolution.

Deng was credited with promoting the concept of "socialism with Chinese characteristics" and using the phrase "primary stage of socialism." Deng's "theories" had accomplished exactly what Deng had hoped they would: they provided ideological justification for adopting pragmatic policies that supported the continued expansion of markets. Jiang also reiterated Deng's view that it was not necessary to ask if something was called "capitalism" or "socialism." Public ownership was to be the chief form of ownership, but efforts to allow state enterprises to become more independent economic units would continue. Shareholding was to be introduced on an experimental basis, and markets were to be expanded, not only for commodities but also for capital, technology, labor, information, and housing. Science and technology were to be considered not simply as a productive force but as the primary productive force.[65] In short, the congress represented a ringing affirmation of Deng's fundamental views. Mao's fundamental beliefs—class struggle and continuing the revolution—had begun to weaken even before he had passed away and when he died, they died with him. By contrast, Deng's basic policies, which resonated with the economic needs and wishes of the people, continued to guide policy-making for decades.

At the congress, only three years after the Tiananmen tragedy, Jiang, like Deng, gave more weight to stability than to political reform. At the 14th Party Congress, Jiang did not even mention the possibility of separating the party from business enterprises and administrative structures as Zhao Ziyang had proposed during the previous congress. Like Deng, Jiang used harsh words to condemn the "counterrevolutionary rebellion" of 1989. Yet he maintained that the main threat came not from the right but from the left.[66]

Although Deng's spirit pervaded the 14th Party Congress, he did not attend the meetings until the concluding session. At that point, Deng entered the hall, went over to Jiang Zemin, and for some twenty minutes stood beside him while television cameras captured the images of the two together; Deng was passing the mantle to Jiang and the news was transmitted throughout China and to the world.[67] Jiang Zemin had vigorously affirmed continued reform and opening, and now Deng was showing that he fully supported him. From that moment on, Jiang no longer had to look over his shoulder to see if Deng approved; the baton had been passed to the man whom Deng and others now referred to as the "nucleus" of the party's third generation.[68]

Shortly before the 14th Party Congress, Deng had pushed the Yang brothers, longtime allies who had joined him on the southern journey, to retire.[69] Deng appointed their replacement, the seventy-seven-year-old Liu Huaqing, who was to follow the lead of Jiang Zemin, and of Jiang's ally Zeng Qinghong.[70] Jiang Zemin had long considered the Yang brothers, who were senior to him, as rivals who constrained his behavior. Deng earlier told Jiang: "When Mao was in charge and spoke, the issues were settled. When I was in charge and spoke, the issues were settled. My mind will be at ease if when you speak, the issues will be settled."[71] Deng was close to the Yang brothers, but for him a strong united national leadership was more important than personal friendship. He was doing everything he could to give Jiang the full authority he needed with a team he could command to provide effective national leadership.

Compared to Mao's chosen successors who were arrested or pushed aside shortly after his death, Deng's chosen successors continued to lead China for two decades. At the 15th Party Congress in 1997, Jiang Zemin was reelected for another term and served a full ten years beyond the two years remaining in the term of the deposed Zhao Ziyang. Despite some of Deng's misgivings before the spring of 1992, Jiang proved successful in uniting the country and guiding it during the very difficult years after the Tiananmen tragedy, when he faced skeptical citizens and restrictive foreign sanctions. He steadily pursued Deng's policy of reform and opening and proved to be an excellent political manager. Considering the uncertainties after the Tiananmen tragedy and the collapse of communism throughout Eastern Europe and the Soviet Union, Jiang's success in steering a steady course was a remarkable accomplishment.

In June 1992 the proven economic leader whom Deng had brought to Beijing in 1991, Zhu Rongji, became head of the newly established Economic and Trade Office, which emerged as the most powerful organization overseeing economic work.[72] Later, at the NPC meeting in March 1993 when government appointments were announced, Zhu became first vice premier while Li Peng was reappointed premier. Because Li Peng had played a major role in clamping down on the June 4 demonstrations, as long as he was premier, Deng did not have to worry about the possibility of a reversal of the verdict on those demonstrations. Zhu Rongji was enormously successful in managing the economy, especially in overcoming inflationary pressures without causing a hard landing like that which had occurred in 1988–1989. At the 15th Party Congress in 1997, Zhu Rongji became premier.

The man Deng selected as the youngest member of the Standing Committee of the Politburo at the time of the 14th Party Congress, Hu Jintao, became the heir apparent after Jiang. At the time of the congress he was fifty years old, eight years younger than any other member. Hu managed to keep the support of other senior leaders and was later selected at the 16th and 17th Party Congresses to serve two five-year terms as head of the fourth generation of leaders. The people chosen by Deng as successors were thus confirmed by the three party congresses after 1992.

As Deng had planned, the 14th Party Congress also marked the end of lifetime appointments. The Central Advisory Commission, which had provided a formal channel for that special generation of revolutionary heroes to express their opinions—and so had eased their transition from active duty into retirement—was officially abolished. Not only Deng but the entire senior generation, including Deng's rival Chen Yun, stepped down. In the future, all appointments, including those of the highest-level political leaders, would be term appointments. The officials selected for other key positions in 1992 were selected according to Deng's personnel policy—that is, people who performed well in their posts would rise step by step to higher positions.

The Politburo members selected in 1992 were completely in tune with Deng's policies. The two government ministers selected for the Politburo were both concerned with foreign affairs and ready to promote continued opening to the outside—Foreign Minister Qian Qichen and Minister of Foreign Trade Li Lanqing. And before 1992, one Politburo member had represented an inland province, but in 1992 he was dropped and all five members of the new Politburo who had held provincial-level appointments were from the coastal provinces that had prospered under Deng's open policies: Xie Fei from Guangdong, Chen Xitong from Beijing, Wu Bangguo from Shanghai, Tan Shaowen from Tianjin, and Jiang Chunyun from Shandong. The officials from Beijing who remained on the Politburo were also all from coastal areas, including Qiao Shi, Yang Baibing, and Liu Huaqing, the three who had joined Deng Xiaoping in Zhuhai in crafting strategy during the southern journey. These senior leaders were old enough to remember the failures of the Great Leap Forward. They had risen to important positions in the early 1960s and had suffered during the Cultural Revolution. After 1978, they emerged as committed reformers, determined to devote their last years to overcoming the misguided policies and promoting modernization.

By contrast, Jiang Zemin's subordinates who later became the leaders of the fourth generation were not revolutionary heroes, but rather good students who had grown up in the system established by Deng and the others of his generation. They had been born during the war years, but they received their schooling after 1949 under the Communist leadership. They came of age too late to have had the opportunity to study in the Soviet Union or Eastern Europe but too early to have pursued advanced education in the West. Yet even though they were in school before subjects like Western law, economics, and business administration were introduced, they began learning these subjects after coming to office, through documents, meetings, and short-term training courses. They were able, broad-gauged technocrats, mostly trained in engineering, who accepted the system and wanted to make it work. As a group, they were noted for being responsible, for enjoying good relations with their peers and subordinates, and for not challenging their superiors. They had not been tested in grave crises and they were not prepared to challenge the system. Instead they worked pragmatically and competently within the framework that Deng and his generation had built.

The Fruits of the Southern Journey

In line with the policies laid down at the 14th Party Congress and the NPC meeting of March 1993 that supported growth targets of 8 or 9 percent, more local investment and construction was permitted. In the several years after Deng's 1992 southern journey, China achieved some of the fastest growth rates the world has known, on a scale never seen before. Indeed, from 1992 to 1999 China, with the world's largest population, grew more than 10 percent per year.

	1991	1992	1993	1994	1995
GDP growth (%)	9.2	14.2	13.5	12.6	10.5
Consumer Price Index (%)	3.4	6.4	14.7	24.1	17.1

Source: National Bureau of Statistics, cited in Jinglian Wu, *Understanding and Interpreting Chinese Economic Reform* (Mason, Ohio: Thomson/South-Western, 2005), p. 373.

Following the Tiananmen tragedy, from 1989 to 1991 foreign direct investment in China stagnated at $4 billion per year; from 1992 to 1999, however, with China's policy of opening to the West and the gradual easing of foreign sanctions, it averaged more than $35 billion per year. The rapid growth led to a new round of overheating and inflationary pressures, but by 1995 Zhu Rongji was able to bring these pressures down with a soft landing.

A decision to grant selected companies the right to interact directly with foreign companies was a great boon to the expansion of foreign trade. Before then, exporters and importers had to buy and sell through state trading firms, making it difficult for them to adapt quickly to opportunities in foreign markets. Furthermore, the state trading firms could not manage the rapid expansion of foreign trade. Gradually, however, designated Chinese firms were allowed to deal directly with foreign companies, and the number of designated firms grew. Housing construction also took off with new initiatives introduced by the reformers. Before 1995, housing was assigned by work units or by city officials. After 1995, as the government opened the housing market, families of state employees were allowed to purchase their homes at subsidized prices. With the creation of a private real estate market and opportunities for profit from the building of homes, new homes were built at a dizzying pace.[73]

Deng's southern journey did not silence cautious planners and conservative ideologues, but it again moved the goalposts for what was considered possible; even the most easily alarmed planners gradually began accepting, however grudgingly, a larger role for markets and foreign trade. With so many people benefiting from markets at home and abroad, the policies of reform and opening became irreversible. There was no way China could close the doors it had opened after 1978.

Remembering Deng

In the last decades of the twentieth century, the continuing revolution in China consumed many of its heroes. Deng himself had three ups and three downs, but in his last years, he was more fortunate than any of his fellow leaders, many of whom had met sad and even tragic ends. After April 5, 1976, Mao was faced with the reality that the masses in Beijing had rejected his Cultural Revolution and class struggle and preferred Zhou Enlai's four modernizations. Zhou Enlai died knowing that he was still being criticized by Chairman Mao and by the party to which he had dedicated his life. Liu Shaoqi died under house arrest, the target of criticism, without receiving adequate medical treatment. Hu Yaobang, after being heartlessly dismissed from office, was rejected by his fellow leaders during the remaining two years of his life. Zhao Ziyang died under house arrest, officially shunned and permitted to meet only a few selected visitors. Hua Guofeng, when pushed aside, was humiliated. Marshal Ye did retire happily to pleasant familiar surroundings in his native province, but he was no longer completely comfortable with developments in Beijing.

Deng knew that his handling of the 1989 Tiananmen demonstrations would be regarded by many as a permanent blot on his career. In both China and abroad, many felt that in June 1989 he had become overly concerned with maintaining civil order, and that it was unforgivable for him to have allowed the shooting of innocent people on the streets. They believed he had not done enough to advance the cause of democracy when he had the opportunity. He had not resolved the fundamental problems of corruption and inequality. Deng's defenders, by contrast, admired his courage for boldly taking responsibility to do what was necessary to hold the nation together.

Regardless of their views on the Tiananmen tragedy, however, many admired his determined effort, at age eighty-seven, to embark on the southern journey as a way of ensuring that China stayed on the course of rapid reform and opening. Indeed, Deng lived his last years knowing that his chosen successors were following the policies he had initiated, and that these policies were helping China to advance. He spent these years with his family, honored by his party and nation. He had guided China through a difficult transition from a backward, closed, overly rigid socialist nation to a global power with a modernizing economy. If there is one leader to whom most Chinese people express gratitude for improvements in their daily lives, it is Deng Xiaoping. Did any other leader in the twentieth century do more to improve the lives of so many? Did any other twentieth-century leader have such a large and lasting influence on world history?

Deng said he wanted to be remembered as he really was. He wanted to be well thought of, but he did not want to be celebrated with the grandiosity accorded to Mao Zedong. Unlike Chairman Mao who compared himself with the great emperors, Deng did not consider himself to be a "son of heaven." He asked only to be remembered as an ordinary earthly being, as a "son of the Chinese people."

Deng's last public appearance was on New Year's 1994. After that his health deteriorated and he no longer had the strength to take part in meetings. He died on February 19, 1997, shortly after midnight, at age ninety-two, from complications of Parkinson's disease and a lung infection.[74] He had asked that his funeral be simple and frugal. Mao's body had been embalmed and put on display in the specially erected Chairman Mao Memorial Hall, where it was viewed by the public. In contrast, there would be no memorial hall for Deng. On February 25, some ten thousand selected party members assembled at the Great Hall of the People for a memorial service. Jiang Zemin fought back tears as he delivered the eulogy.[75] The service was broadcast on television, and reports on Deng's life dominated the media for the following several days. In line with Deng's wishes, his corneas were donated for eye research, his internal organs donated for medical research, and his body cremated. The box with his cremated remains was draped with the flag of the Chinese Communist Party. On March 2, 1997, his ashes were scattered in the sea.

Deng's Place in History

24

China Transformed

When Deng stepped aside in 1992 he had fulfilled the mission that had eluded China's leaders for 150 years: he and his colleagues had found a way to enrich the Chinese people and strengthen the country. But in the process of achieving this goal, Deng presided over a fundamental transformation of China itself—the nature of its relation with the outside world, its governance system, and its society. After Deng stepped down, China continued to change rapidly, but the basic structural changes developed under Deng's leadership have already continued for two decades, and with some adaptations, they may extend long into the future. Indeed, the structural changes that took place under Deng's leadership rank among the most basic changes since the Chinese empire took shape during the Han dynasty over two millennia ago.

The transformation that took place in the Deng era was shaped by the highly developed Chinese tradition, by the scale and diversity of Chinese society, by the nature of world institutions at the time, by the openness of the global system to sharing its technology and management skills, by the nature of the Chinese Communist Party, and by the contributions of large numbers of creative and hard-working people. But it occurred at a time of transition, in which the top leader was granted considerable freedom by others to guide the political process and make final decisions. And it was shaped by the role that leader, Deng Xiaoping, personally played. To be sure, the ideas underlying this sea change came from many people, and no one fully anticipated how events would play out. Deng did not start reform and opening; they began under Hua Guofeng before Deng came to power. Nor was Deng the architect with a grand design for the changes that would take place under his rule; there was in fact no clear overall design in place during this era.

Rather, Deng was the general manager who provided overall leadership during the transformation. He helped package the ideas and present them to his team of colleagues and to the public at a pace and in a way they could accept. He provided a steady hand at the top that gave people confidence as they underwent dramatic changes. He played a role in selecting and guiding the team that worked together to create and implement the reforms. He was a problem-solver who tried to devise solutions that would work for the various parties involved both within China and in foreign countries. He helped foster a strong governing structure that could stay in control even as the Chinese people struggled to adapt to the new and rapidly evolving situation on the ground. He played a leading part in guiding the process of setting priorities and creating strategies to realize the most important goals. He explained the policies to the public in a straightforward way by describing the overall situation they faced and then what concrete measures were needed to respond. When controversies arose, he played a major role in making the final decisions and managed the process so as to minimize cleavages that would tear the country apart. He supported the effort to provide incentives and to offer hope based on realistic enough goals that people were not later sorely disappointed. He supported the effort to give enough freedom to specialists—scientists, economists, managers, and intellectuals—so they could do their work, but placed limits on their freedom when he feared that the fragile social order might be undone. And he played a central role in improving relations with other major countries and in forming workable relationships with their leaders. In all of his work, Deng was guided by his deep conviction that employing the world's most modern practices in science and technology, and most effective management techniques, would lead to the greatest progress for China—and that the disruptions that occurred from grafting these practices and techniques onto a Chinese system were manageable and worth it for the Chinese people as a whole.

It is difficult for those in China and abroad who became adults after Deng stepped down to realize the enormity of the problems Deng faced as he began this journey: a country closed to fundamentally new ways of thinking; deep rifts between those who had been attacked during the Cultural Revolution and their attackers; proud military leaders who were resistant to downsizing and budget reductions; public animosity toward imperialists and foreign capitalists; an entrenched, conservative socialist structure in both the countryside and the cities; a reluctance by urban residents to accept over 200 million migrants from the countryside; and dissension as some people continued to live in poverty while others became rich.

But Deng also had enormous advantages as he assumed responsibility for the overall management of China's transformation. He took over a functioning national party and government in a country that Mao had unified. He had many experienced senior officials who shared his view that deep changes were needed. He came to power when there was an open world trading system and other countries were willing to share their capital, technology, and management skills and to welcome China into international institutions.

Deng also had an impressive array of personal qualities that enabled him to guide China's transformation. It is doubtful that anyone else then had the combination of authority, depth and breadth of experience, strategic sense, assurance, personal relationships, and political judgment needed to manage China's transformation with comparable success. What, then, is the nature of the transformation that Deng helped guide?

From the Center of Asian Civilization to a Single Nation of the World

During imperial times, China was never a global power or even an active participant in global affairs. It was a regional Asian power. In the "Chinese world order" that guided China's relations with other countries before the Opium War, the smaller political entities around China's periphery paid ceremonial tribute to the emperor of the "Central Kingdom," China. These other political entities thereby acknowledged the superiority of Chinese civilization over the surrounding areas. In exchange, China agreed that these political entities outside China could remain autonomous and live in peace.[1]

Rarely did a Chinese emperor take any interest in extending China's reach beyond the Asian mainland. For a brief time during the fifteenth century, Chinese emperors did allow the construction of oceangoing vessels, and Admiral Zheng He led seven voyages overseas that stretched as far as the Middle East and the east coast of Africa. But subsequent emperors not only prohibited such lengthy voyages; they also prevented the building of oceangoing vessels. For them it was difficult enough to manage affairs within China's long borders without linking China to lands beyond its shores. In 1793, when the British envoy Lord McCartney arrived in China and proposed the opening of trade, Emperor Qianlong famously replied, "We possess all things. I . . . have no use for your manufactures."[2]

Later, after the Opium Wars of 1839–1842 and 1856–1860, European powers forced China to grant them access to a number of ports along the coast, but the Chinese government took virtually no initiative to extend its reach beyond its land borders in Asia. China as a nation did not adapt effectively to the challenge as the Industrial Revolution brought new power to Western nations. Because of China's weak response, stronger imperialist powers from the West dominated relations with China and even dominated industry and trade along the China coast.

Mao, at the time of the Korean War, ended the role of imperialists by closing the country to contact with the West. After that time, China began to play a role in the Communist world and for a brief time in the 1950s and 1060s played a part in the affairs of the third world. Its role in the Communist world greatly declined after it broke off relations with the Soviet Union in 1960. Before 1978 the Chinese government still had only limited involvement in affairs beyond its borders. For a long period during the Cultural Revolution, for example, China had only one ambassador abroad, stationed in Egypt.

Although Mao had begun to open China to the West after the clashes with the Soviet Union in 1969, and the People's Republic did take over the China seat in the United Nations in 1971, during Mao's lifetime China was open barely a crack. After Mao died, Hua Guofeng was receptive to efforts to open the country, but it was left to Deng Xiaoping to open the country and lead China to take an active part in international affairs. It was not until Deng's era that government leaders had both the vision and the political strength to overcome the sour memories of the imperialist era and develop a lasting and positive new pattern of relations with other nations whereby China was a part of the new world order that had emerged after World War II.

Under Deng's leadership, China truly joined the world community, becoming an active part of international organizations and of the global system of trade, finance, and relations among citizens of all walks of life. China became a member of the World Bank and of the International Monetary Fund (IMF). China began to play an active role in World Health Organization activities, as well as the endeavors of all important international organizations in every sphere. And although it would take nearly a decade after Deng stepped down before China was admitted to the World Trade Organization, preparations for China's entry began under Deng.

During the early years of China's participation in international organizations, as China was learning how these organizations actually functioned, China was still a very poor nation, and China's efforts first focused on defending its own interests. It was left for Deng's successors, who realized the benefits of the international system for China, to begin to think about what

China could do as a stakeholder in the international system and global institutions to strengthen those organizations. Before China joined institutions like the World Bank and the IMF, some participants worried that China's participation would be so disruptive that they would have trouble functioning. In fact China's participation has strengthened those organizations even as it has represented its own interests; it has abided by the rules of the organizations.

When Deng became preeminent leader in 1978, China's trade with the world totaled less than $10 billion; within three decades, it had expanded a hundredfold. At the same time, China was encouraging the United States to accept a few hundred Chinese students; by a decade after Deng's death, an estimated 1.4 million students had studied abroad and some 390,000 had already returned to China.[3] By 1992 the nation had already come a long way toward playing an active role in global intellectual conversations as well as in the global trading system. The basic breakthrough was achieved during Deng's period as paramount leader.

During Deng's era, to adjust to its new global role, China went through wrenching internal changes that Chinese leaders called *"jiegui,"* or linking tracks, drawing on the term used in the 1930s for the linking together of Chinese railways of different gauges. In the 1980s Chinese used the term to describe the adjustments that China was making to take part in international organizations and in global systems of all kinds.

In the early years after 1978, when China was beginning to link up with international organizations, it greatly expanded the specialized organizations that were in effect a buffer in dealing with the outside world. Foreign enterprises in China were located in special areas like the special economic zones (SEZs), and the overall system for dealing with foreign enterprises erected artificial walls that kept foreigners from close contact with China as a whole. Foreigners in China worked with special foreign affairs offices located in local governments, in universities, and in large companies. Foreign affairs service bureaus, for example, handled domestic employees who worked for foreigners. To capture more foreign currency, which China was desperately short of, foreigners were encouraged to spend "foreign-exchange certificates" (which they received in exchange for their homeland's currency) at special "friendship stores" where they could buy goods made abroad that ordinary Chinese were not allowed to purchase. State trading firms handled much of the buying and selling of goods with foreigners, and a large proportion of foreigners who bought Chinese goods did so at the semi-annual Canton trade fair. The

Chinese Foreign Ministry played a large role in supervising Chinese government activities dealing with foreigners at these specialized "go-between" institutions, which were staffed by Chinese officials trained in foreign languages and familiar with foreign practices.

In the late 1980s, however, China's relations with the outside world had already begun to expand rapidly beyond these specialized institutions. Foreigners' travel was no longer restricted to certain areas, and more Chinese firms could deal with foreign firms directly. The practices that began with the SEZs and spread to fourteen coastal areas in 1984 had started to spread to the entire country. So many foreigners were coming to China that the specialized "foreign affairs offices" could no longer manage all their affairs; the specialized institutions for dealing with foreigners mostly remained, but their activities were more often limited to routine official data collecting.

Before Deng stepped down, Chinese institutions of all kinds began to link their tracks, to adapt to foreign practices. Firms that were involved in international trade had to learn foreign legal, accounting, and organizational methods.[4] Universities and high schools that sent their graduates abroad began to create training programs to prepare their students for the entrance examinations and other procedures required to gain admittance at foreign institutions. Chinese athletic coaches began to focus on preparing the best athletes for competition in international sports contests. Tourist facilities built to meet international standards spilled over to handle both domestic and foreign travelers. Products initially produced for export were increasingly made available to domestic consumers. And just as the United States after World War II expanded its academic and research institutions to underpin its role as a global power, so too under Deng did China's academic and research institutions expand greatly, deepening Chinese understanding of world affairs.

Deng advanced China's globalization far more boldly and thoroughly than did leaders of other large countries like India, Russia, and Brazil. The process has continued after the Deng era, but the basic breakthroughs were achieved by the time Deng stepped down.

Rule by Party Leadership Teams

Although the Chinese Communist Party had begun the transition from a revolutionary party to a ruling party in 1956, Mao soon led it once again into revolution. By contrast, after 1978, with the return of senior officials, the dismissal of revolutionaries not suited for governing, and the recruitment of new leaders, Deng guided the transition to a party that focused on governing the country.

The U.S. system of separating the executive, legislative, and judicial branches of government was devised by leaders concerned about an excess concentration of power. The system devised by Mao, but fundamentally revised by Deng and his colleagues, was created to deal with the opposite problem—providing unified leadership in the midst of chaos, confusion, deadlocks, inaction, and widely varied local areas. Deng and his colleagues also believed, unlike the Americans, that basing final decisions on the overall political judgments of top leaders would serve the interests of the country better than basing them on the evaluations of an independent judiciary in which laws determine what actions are permitted. They believed that a system that allows a legislative body to make laws without having the responsibility for implementing them is not as effective as concentrating law-making and implementation in one body.

The United States was formed by independent states that retained independent powers. China for centuries had been a centralized government with control over regional governments. Mao had further centralized these powers so that they extended deeply throughout the country. But Deng pulled back on the governing structure that tried to penetrate everywhere. Instead of setting tight rules that local areas had to follow, he established a system in which governing teams, selected by the next higher level, were given considerable independence as long as they managed to bring rapid growth.

The core governing structure in Beijing that Deng established is, as under Mao, centered around the Politburo and the Secretariat. It is linked to local areas through a network of party leadership teams *(lingdao banzi)* that is present in every locality and at every level of every major office of government. Each leadership team is responsible not only for directing the work of the Communist Party at its level, but also for overseeing the government office (or economic or cultural unit) under it. The team is expected to make judgments about broad overall issues and see to it that work within its jurisdiction makes an overall contribution to the four modernizations.

The higher levels of the party pass down rules for how the leadership teams should conduct their work and they send down endless numbers of directives to each level. They also hold meetings with lower levels, sometimes by inviting the lower-level leaders to attend higher-level meetings, but also by sending higher-level officials on inspection tours of the lower levels. When officials at the higher level consider an issue very important, they can and do intervene. But it is difficult for them to monitor all developments at the lower levels, so the team ordinarily has considerable freedom in guiding the work at its level.

The key leverage that Beijing has over the provinces is the power to appoint and dismiss the members of the leadership team. Team members commonly serve a term of several years, but they can be dismissed at any time by leaders at the next higher level. The several members of a party leadership team are given responsibility for different sectors and are judged not only by how well they manage their respective sectors, but also by how well the entire team and the unit it supervises perform. In Deng's era and in the decades after Deng, those judgments were based overwhelmingly on how much the team contributed to China's overall economic growth. Over the years, secondary criteria have become more important for judging the performance of the teams, criteria that include the training of the next generation of officials, environmental protection, managing disturbances, and responding to emergencies.[5]

Like Deng, Deng's successors believe that a sense of commitment to the overall goals of the nation can be achieved by the proper selection, training, and supervision of officials. Because officials at the next level down have a great deal of freedom over how they do their work, the selection and training of the members of a team are done with considerable care. At each level, younger officials judged likely to excel because of their overall intellectual ability, reliability under stress, mature judgment, ability to work well with colleagues, and dedication to serving the party and the country are picked for special training, mentoring, and testing.

Indeed, considerable time is spent mentoring officials at every level. A mentor's role is to suggest to younger, lower-level officials how they should enhance their performance and skills. The most promising young officials are allowed to accompany their superiors to various high-level meetings and to take part in informal gatherings at party retreats. They are also permitted to attend classes at the party schools, with those judged with the most potential for national leadership positions taking courses at the Central Party School in Beijing, and those considered likely nominees for provincial or urban official positions taking leadership courses at the party schools in their respective regions. Not all party members, who numbered 37 million when Deng ascended the stage, shared the camaraderie that developed among those selected to attend retreats with higher officials and to become students at the party schools. Those who attended party schools not only got to know each other as well as those who attended the party school before and after, but also became acquainted with those higher-level officials who would visit the party schools and, with the help of evaluations by party school officials, make recommendations about their future positions. Although officials in the Organization Department kept personnel files and could make recommendations, the members of the party leadership team at each level made the final decisions about who should be promoted in their jurisdiction.

There is a danger in allowing local leaders so much freedom. The system that Deng founded, which endures today, emphasizes results more than following rules and helps nurture officials who have a broad vision in evaluating issues, who are entrepreneurial, and who support rapid growth. Without tight supervision from above, however, many of these officials have found ways not only to enrich China, but also to enrich themselves and their friends while alienating others in their locality.

Deng Xiaoping did not introduce the system of party leadership teams, but he stabilized it, professionalized the work the teams did, and changed the key criteria for judging officials from contributions to political campaigns to contributions to economic growth. This basic structure has been continued by his successors.

The Modern Meritocracy

By the time Deng stepped down, young party officials had to prove their ability by first passing examinations to the better high schools and better universities. Deng's focus on meritocracy has deep roots in China, which was the first country in the world to select officials on the basis of their performance on examinations. Beginning in 605 c.e., during the Sui dynasty, China had used written examinations as the chief criterion for determining which aspiring candidates were qualified to become government officials. But from the time when the imperial examinations ended, in the year after Deng was born, until Deng ascended the stage, China had not had the combination of stability and leaders' political determination to reestablish a national meritocratic basis for selecting officials. When Mao was alive it was impossible to use educational achievement as the major criterion for selecting officials. Many of those who had made contributions to the Communist cause and emerged in high positions simply had not had any opportunity for university training during the chaotic war and revolution years of the 1930s and 1940s. Furthermore, Mao considered political commitment ("redness") a more important qualification than expertise, and he favored peasants and workers over candidates from the "bad classes" (landlord and capitalist families), who were generally better educated. For this reason, examinations were not the main criterion for selecting and promoting officials. Indeed, many of the officials after 1949 were veterans from the Communist armies or guerrilla forces who were barely literate. If examinations had been held, they and their children would not have outperformed the children from the "wrong social classes" who had received better formal training. After Mao's death, Deng boldly dismissed a "good class background" as a criterion for selecting officials; instead he strictly relied on qualifications as measured by entrance examinations. Under new guidelines that Deng introduced in 1977, many children and grandchildren of those once labeled as belonging to the "bad classes" passed examinations, gained admission to the best universities, and became officials.

In fact, Deng established a system of highly competitive meritocratic examinations at each level, from elementary school through university to officialdom. His goal was not to produce social equality but to sift out the ablest and provide them with the best education possible. Examinations were given for entrance to elementary school, junior middle school (the equivalent of grades seven to nine in the United States), senior middle school (grades ten to twelve), and college, and those who made it into the most competitive schools were given the best teachers and facilities.

The unified examination system that Deng introduced in 1977 for universities was not only specifically for future officials. It was a system for selecting the ablest young people for large organizations in all walks of life. But all those selected as officials had first proved themselves in examinations at each educational level. Even among those who became officials, the ablest from the best universities would get jobs in the central government, whereas those who had gone to less competitive universities would start out at lower levels in the bureaucracy. As the number of university graduates rapidly increased in the late 1980s and beyond, additional exams became important for selecting government servants from among university graduates. Once selected as an official, however, one rose through the system not primarily by taking further examinations but on the basis of work performance. This system has been continued under Deng's successors.

In the mid-1980s, many ambitious and energetic young people sought success by "jumping into the rough waters" (xia hai) of business. Yet despite these attractive career alternatives, the position of "official" remains highly valued, not only for the power and the economic security it provides, but also because of the deep respect Chinese have for those judged to have great ability and a commitment to public service. Deng thus left his successors with a meritocratic system for choosing officials that accords with the same principle of selection by examination as in imperial times. But the system he left his successors is completely different in content and structure from imperial times. Furthermore, Deng's system extends the principle of meritocratic selection to include not only the identification of promising officials, but also the selection and training of talented people in many walks of life.

An Open, Urban, National Society

From the dawn of Chinese history until the 1990s, China was predominantly a rural society with strong regional differences in dialect and culture. Before 1949, China's poor transportation systems meant that most goods were produced and consumed within walking distance from a local market town and many people spent most of their lives within that area.[6] Mao's tight controls over population movement slowed the modest amount of migration that occurred before 1949. At his death in 1976 the population remained more than 80 percent rural, and life in the countryside was dominated by the local village, family, and collective, with little contact with the outside world. In the Mao period, even large urban work units *(danwei)*—such as government offices, factories, schools, universities, and military bases—were located within relatively self-sufficient compounds, many of which were gated so that any visitors would have to report to the gatekeeper before entering. These closed communities supplied the basic needs of the employees and their families: housing, food, care and education of children, medical care, and welfare. It was difficult for residents to obtain any of these services outside their work units; like rural dwellers, most of these residents lacked opportunities to find alternative work and had little choice but to heed the authorities of their respective units. The limited mobility, the dependence on authorities within the village or urban work unit, and the limited communications with the outside world led to stagnation. Mao trumpeted a revolutionary ideology, but the controls on movement that he imposed further solidified a closed, "feudal" society.

By the time Deng retired, the new economic opportunities created by economic growth and the mobility that he had allowed had put China well on its way to becoming an urban rather than a rural society. During the Deng era, an estimated 200 million people migrated to towns and cities, movement that has since continued at a rapid pace. It is estimated that by 2015, scarcely two decades after Deng's retirement, an estimated 700 million people, more than half the population, will be urban. By the time Deng stepped down, more than 90 percent of households owned television sets, which instantly brought urban culture to the countryside. Youth returning from coastal areas to visit their families in the villages also brought with them the latest fashions, utensils, electric appliances, and food they had come to know in the cities.[7] In short, even rural areas had begun to become urban in culture.

After the reforms began in 1978, urban leaders of Chinese cities, fearing that a torrent of rural migrants could overwhelm urban services and food supplies, still preserved the urban household registration system that had long restricted access to urban services such as housing, employment, and schooling for children. In the early 1980s when grain and edible oil rations were at barely more than subsistence level, there was not enough food to support those people from the countryside who had entered the cities and were trying to live surreptitiously there with relatives or friends. After 1983, however, as food supplies grew, the government began allowing people to move to the cities even without an urban household registration. By then, too, the export industries on the coast could absorb vast numbers of rural youth who were migrating to the area to find a better life. Throughout Chinese history, as a result of wars and famines, millions of people had relocated, but never before on a scale like that which took place in the decades after 1978.

Even during Mao's days, despite the lack of mobility, the entire population had come to share a deep layer of common national culture. By the late 1960s many urban households owned radios, and those that lacked radios, both in the countryside and the cities, could listen to loudspeakers that broadcast national news and music. More of the population could see movies, which brought a shared national culture, and the entire population learned the same slogans and songs from the political campaigns. Elementary schools grew rapidly in number, so that by the time Mao died, roughly 80 percent of the young adults could be considered literate.

The continuing expansion of the educational system under Deng enabled most youth in the 1980s to complete not only elementary school but also junior high school. The rapid diffusion of television in the late 1980s, and the introduction of national channels that broadcast standard news in Mandarin, greatly expanded the public's common base of information. By the time Deng stepped down, the widespread use of standard Mandarin, not only in schools and public offices, but also in state enterprises, stores, and educational institutions, made it possible for a substantial majority of Chinese to communicate with one another using the standard Mandarin pronunciation *(putonghua)*. The spread of transportation systems during the Deng era also made it possible to distribute industrial goods to a larger geographical area and therefore to increase the scale of production for domestic as well as foreign markets. Before the 1980s, there were few brand names in China, but by the time Deng retired, manufactured goods with national and international brand recognition were beginning to spread throughout the country.

With the opening of the closed urban living compounds and the mixing of populations from different areas, local differences declined and were replaced by more shared national culture. Before 1978, people ate local dishes as a matter of course. Just as in the Western world in the late twentieth century when certain dishes that had once been national dishes—like pizza, donuts, bagels, and sushi—became international dishes, so too in China during the 1980s and 1990s did many regional dishes become popular nationwide. Southerners learned to eat steamed buns made from wheat, which had long been standard fare in northern cuisine; and northerners learned to eat rice, which had long been a staple of southern cuisine. Similarly, some of the best regional operas, which had previously been viewed mostly by local people, were now presented to national audiences. After Deng stepped down, the greater mobility of the Chinese population, and the diffusion of cell phones, computers, and the Internet, helped to spread this national culture. The Chinese, like people elsewhere, maintain loyalties to their own village, town, county, dialect group, or province. Members of minority groups have always identified with others of their group. But during the Deng period the growth of a truly national culture and greater awareness of foreign cultures greatly strengthened identification with the nation as a whole.

When Deng retired, a substantial number of youth who had spent several years working in the coastal areas returned to their hometowns, bringing with them not only new goods from the coast, but also new ideas and styles that enabled them to establish their own enterprises and to set new standards for the hinterland. This process further hastened the rapid spread of an urban national culture. Even though the inland residents had far less money to spend, they still acquired products not long after inhabitants of the coastal areas, often by creating less expensive imitations. Not surprisingly, then, more costly items like automobiles spread inland far more slowly than did smaller consumer products—but by the end of the Deng era, even they were beginning to trickle into inner China. But when Deng stepped down in 1992, the construction of rural housing that met global standards of modest comfort had scarcely begun, and the quality of elementary schooling in rural areas still lagged far behind that in the better urban schools.

The transformation of rural to urban society and the growth of a stronger national culture derived not from any plan of Deng or his colleagues. Deng did try to break down regional loyalties within the military so that soldiers would serve commanders from other regions. He did promote the teaching of Mandarin so people from one locality could communicate with men and women from other areas of China. But the growth of urban society and a national culture derived less from conscious planning and more from the new urban opportunities and the appeal of city life to so many rural youth. Once these changes began occurring, however, officials involved in planning adjusted to the changing realities. They began to reorganize the administration of local areas, allowing cities to expand their administrative reach to include surrounding rural counties and allowing towns and counties to restructure as they became cities.

Paradoxically, the open mobility that began with the Deng era had a far more revolutionary influence on the structure of society than the so-called Mao revolution that had imposed rigid social barriers. The transition from a predominantly rural to a predominantly urban society and the spread of a common national culture are among the most fundamental changes that have occurred in Chinese society since the country's unification in 221 B.C.

The Wild East

When China began opening in the 1980s, there were virtually no rules in place for food and drugs, product and workplace safety, working conditions, minimum wages, or construction codes.[8] In the early 1980s, if an enterprising person found empty Coke bottles and filled them with a liquid of a similar color, there was no law against selling them as bottles of Coca Cola or some similar beverage. In the nineteenth century, in the United States and Europe, the rules and laws designed to protect the public by placing limits on what companies could do in pursuit of profits had evolved slowly. The situation in China under Deng was reminiscent of the rapacious capitalism of nineteenth-century Europe and the United States, when there were no anti-trust laws and no laws to protect workers. In China, when the markets suddenly exploded in the 1980s, there was no way to immediately enact a comprehensive set of rules and laws adapted to Chinese conditions; nor was it possible to train officials right away to implement and enforce such rules and laws. In some ways the situation in China during the Deng era was also similar to the nineteenth-century American West before there were local laws and courts. Like gun-slinging sheriffs in dusty, out-of-the-way towns, Chinese officials responsible for local markets, in the absence of a well-developed court system, defined the law on their own.

One advantage of the Wild East, from the view of local officials and businesspeople, was that the small number of leaders in charge could make decisions far more rapidly than leaders in countries where more elaborate legal systems required "due process." By the time Deng retired, rules and laws had been introduced in virtually every major sector of the economy by young Chinese legal scholars trained in the West, but implementation by local officials lagged behind because many saw the rules as too complicated and not in keeping with their personal interests. In some areas like international trade, where the Chinese worked closely with foreign partners, the Chinese partners adapted quickly to the use of international rules and laws. As economic relations expanded from small groups of people who knew one another personally and shared understandings, to larger groups that included links with regional, national, and even international partners, some rules and laws were needed so that agreements would hold up and inspire confidence among all parties.

It was difficult for Deng to create a more flexible, dynamic economy in China when after the Cultural Revolution so many were worried about being accused of allowing capitalist practices. Deng understood that if officials were too strict in enforcing the rules, it would be difficult for China's economy to take off. Deng, as usual, was more interested in producing results than in following some precise process. He believed some corruption was unavoidable. As he said, "When you open the door, flies will get in." He wanted officials who dared to move boldly and he was willing to pay the price of allowing in some flies. Some of Deng's children have been accused of using their connections for personal purposes, but there is no evidence suggesting that Deng ever sought personal wealth for himself or for his family.

Deng knew, too, that if local officials were actively to support reforms and entrepreneurial activities, they had to be given some opportunity to improve their own living conditions. Reforms had all too often been stalled or even overturned in the Soviet Union and Eastern Europe by bureaucrats who could not see how their personal interests would be served by the reforms.

Deng wanted officials committed to reform and to the public good, so he allowed some local officials to get rich first if they brought economic success to their locality. Deng valued the importance of preserving the authority of local party officials in the eyes of the local public. To call attention publicly to the errors of officials who were otherwise making solid contributions to modernization ran the risk, in Deng's view, of making their jobs more difficult. But Deng made no effort to protect officials who upset the public, and he was ready to deal severely with any officials who were criticized by local citizens for rampant disregard of the public good. The death penalty has been used in China more frequently than in many countries to warn others who might be tempted to engage in similar criminal activities.

Opportunities for personal gain in the Wild East are almost endless. Officials who control access to land often receive gifts when they distribute permits for land use. When government enterprises are "privatized," employees of the unit sometimes acquire shares in the enterprise at prices well below market prices. Leaders of state firms have been allowed to sell products on the market once they meet their targets, and they have often devoted considerable energy to such buying and selling. Trucks available after being used by a work unit for its core responsibilities have been allowed to transport and sell goods at a profit to improve the living conditions of the members of the unit. As a popular saying goes, in Mao's days, people were *"xiang qian kan"* (looking to the future), but since Deng's time they are *"xiang qian kan"* (with the same pronunciation)—looking for money.

The system Deng left his successors did not maintain a sharp separation between the private and public realms. Among local officials there was widespread variation in views about how much to accept from the businesses they supervised: New Year's presents? Introductions to jobs for relatives and friends? "Red envelopes" containing cash and, if acceptable, then how much cash? Opportunities for children to enter better schools or study abroad? Official cars or trucks for private use? The public, without an independent judiciary, is often reluctant to risk challenging local power holders who serve their own interests. China has only weak protections for those who are moved from their property to make way for construction projects, and businesses can work with government officials to take over property quickly with at best modest compensation to those who were previously living on or otherwise using that land. From the view of Chinese leaders, such links between local governments and builders are not necessarily improper and may allow enterprises to jumpstart their production and so more quickly provide employment for local residents.

Those who complain about corruption find it upsetting that officials and their family members flaunt public goods acquired through their connections or privileges, such as fancy banquets, cars, sumptuous clothing, or upscale homes. Candidates who have worked hard to pass examinations and to fulfill their work responsibilities become indignant when they see people whom they regard as less able promoted to higher positions or receiving more privileges because of their special connections.

Urban construction and the creation of public spaces in China are proceeding at a far faster pace than in most other countries. In cities like Guangzhou and Lanzhou, for example, within several years' time the government has been able to remove all the old structures for tens of miles along the river to make way for parks. At the peak of subway building, some large cities like Guangzhou and Beijing constructed an average of one entirely new subway line per year for several successive years. In just five years, new campuses at universities like Nanchang University or East China Normal University have sprung up with facilities for ten thousand students, including administration buildings, classroom buildings, auditoriums, dormitories, apartment projects for faculty and administrators, athletic facilities, and park-like campus spaces. Given these dramatic success stories, it is perhaps no surprise that in the view of Deng and his successors, the legal rights of individuals who had formerly occupied the land should not stand in the way of what they consider to be good for the greatest number of people.

China is not unique in the weak protection it has been giving to foreign patents and foreign copyrights. Similar problems have been found in Japan, South Korea, Taiwan, and other countries that have sought to make use of the newest technologies from abroad. Some Chinese companies have been careful to honor Western patents and copyrights, making payments and using foreign technologies in ways that do not violate their patents. But many Chinese enterprises have not exercised such care, and some Chinese once employed by foreign companies have started their own companies, sometimes illegally making use of the technology they had learned while on the job. Even Hong Kong, which is far stricter about enforcing laws than is mainland China, has found it difficult to prevent the pirating of songs and movies; the copied CDs, DVDs, and discs have sold at a fraction of the price of the patented products and so offer a hefty profit margin to those who engage in such illegal practices. When criticized and pressured by foreign companies and foreign governments for violating copyright laws, the Chinese government has on occasion closed down the enterprises and smashed the machines making the copies. Not long thereafter, however, other Chinese entrepreneurs have been found brazenly producing similar copies in other locations.

Conditions for Chinese workers, including work hours, environmental conditions on the factory floor, and safety standards, have often not been better than some terrible Western working conditions at the early stage of the nineteenth-century Industrial Revolution. Some entrepreneurs have taken advantage of the lack of effective regulations concerning working conditions to give their workers only cramped dormitory spaces in which to live, and to offer them little in the way of safe working environments or quality standards.[9] For tens of millions of rural Chinese youth, life in the factories in the coastal areas, as hard as it is and as poorly as they are paid, is far better than the grinding poverty they knew in the countryside. They have thus been willing to work long hours and even to hold back complaints for fear of being fired.

Factories built with Western and Japanese capital and managed by foreigners, while taking advantage of the cheap labor, have generally offered better working conditions than local enterprises. In many foreign factories, the spaces are well-lit with good air circulation, and in warmer climates, summer temperatures are kept well below the sweltering heat outside. In such factories, standards related to the number of hours in a workday, working conditions, and worker safety have been gradually introduced, and progress has been made in overcoming the most serious abuses. In these factories, too, some youth from poor areas learn the basics of modern living, including regular hours, cleanliness and hygiene, and discipline.[10]

Large numbers of foreign firms have built factories in China. By 2000, the largest branch of the U.S. Chamber of Commerce outside the United States was in Shanghai, and the Japanese Chamber of Commerce there, which was the largest Japanese Chamber of Commerce outside of Japan, was more than twice the size of the U.S. Chamber. Moreover, the numbers of Americans, Japanese, and Europeans in Shanghai pale in comparison with the number of Taiwanese businesspeople who are there. Why have so many businesspeople from abroad been flocking to a country where rules are not fully developed and where patents receive only limited legal protection? They have been attracted by the sheer dynamism of the place: the speed with which decisions can be made and implemented without the burden of complex legal procedures, and the quick pace of growth in markets of enormous scale. Although some foreign entrepreneurs have complained that they have been taken advantage of by their Chinese partners and by local Chinese government officials, others have found that the unusual combination of some legal protections, relationships with reliable problem-solving local officials, and the possibility of appealing to higher authorities has created sufficiently promising opportunities that they are willing to take on whatever risks are involved.

Challenges for Deng's Successors

As a result of Deng's transformation, in the several decades after Deng left the stage, his successors have been confronted by a series of challenges that are likely to remain in the decades ahead. These challenges include:

PROVIDING UNIVERSAL SOCIAL SECURITY AND HEALTH CARE. During Deng's era, those employed by the government, including the large state enterprises, had their health care and welfare benefits provided by the work unit, but such employees made up only a small proportion of the population.[11] The government budget was far too small to provide retirement, health, and other welfare benefits for everyone. Toward the end of the 1980s, as the role of markets increased, those with large incomes could afford good medical treatment and provide for their own welfare needs. But vast numbers of Chinese people were still not offered health care and welfare benefits.

Deng's successors have found that those who lack these benefits have become more vocal. The increased mobility of the population requires protections that a single work unit cannot provide, and the government budget and numbers of well-trained medical professionals are not yet sufficient to meet the growing demand. With the abolition of the rural collective, there is no rural unit to provide first aid and elementary public health services. With the privatization of housing and the pressure placed on state enterprises to compete in a more open-market environment, even the welfare provided by large work units is not always adequate. The challenge for Chinese leaders, then, is to expand the number of qualified medical personnel, upgrade facilities, and develop a system of health care and social security that protects the entire population, including the people living in poverty in remote areas—all within the constraints of the national budget.[12] And because it will take many decades to develop a system that meets these goals, an additional challenge is to distribute the resources and facilities that are currently available in a way that appears fair and reasonable.[13]

REDEFINING AND MANAGING THE BOUNDARIES OF FREEDOM. Perhaps the most troubling problem that Deng faced was setting boundaries of freedom that would satisfy the demands of the intellectuals and general public and at the same time enable leaders to maintain public order. After the Tiananmen tragedy, the public has generally been afraid to demand more freedoms, but such intimidation will not last forever. In the meantime, the growth in the number of publications and the dramatic expansion of Internet and mobile phone use have made it vastly more difficult for the party to control the spread of ideas officials judge to be dangerous.

Deng's successors fear, just as Deng had, that tolerating the expression of divergent views will unleash a torrent of public expressions of hostility, which will again, like in 1989, lead to demonstrations that disrupt public order. The challenge for government leaders is to find boundaries that people find reasonable enough to accept, and then find ways to enforce these accepted boundaries. Given the growing sophistication of modern communications and the creativity of those who seek to evade controls, can government leaders find a way to shape public perceptions and prevent turmoil?

CONTAINING CORRUPTION. During his tenure, Deng had advocated punishment for prominent cases of corruption, but he also was willing to look the other way when local officials quietly bent the rules in order to promote the four modernizations and accelerate economic growth. The problem for Deng's successors is that officials at every level have found ways to receive incomes beyond their regular salaries. Public officials, medical doctors, and employers often receive "red envelopes" with money. Officials who grant permits for land acquisitions for new projects and for construction receive not only direct payments, but also shares in the company, property at below market price, lavish dinners, and luxurious cars. Officials, both in the military and civilian institutions, make payments to superiors who make promotion decisions. And young people pay the army recruiter to be allowed to join the military. The challenge for high-level officials is that such practices are now so widespread, and so many officials or members of officials' families are involved, that tackling the problem is extremely difficult.

PRESERVING THE ENVIRONMENT. In Deng's era, poverty was so widespread and the desire for economic growth so strong that economic growth took precedence over preventing pollution—although Deng did take a personal interest in promoting reforestation and expanding park areas. Since Deng's time, however, as industry has expanded greatly, and as environmental concerns such as coal smoke, water shortages, river pollution, acid rain, environmentally related health problems, and contaminated food have grown along with public consciousness about them, officials are confronted with how to change those practices that cause serious environmental damage. Some of the most difficult problems have arisen in poor areas where mining and the use of coal and other resources cause great environmental damage but the economic pressures to continue these practices are great. How too will China respond to complaints from other countries now that it is the largest emitter of greenhouse gases, the number of motor vehicles on Chinese roads is growing by several million each year, and the growth of heavy industry is likely to increase the use of coal?

MAINTAINING THE GOVERNMENT'S LEGITIMACY TO RULE. Mao achieved his legitimacy to rule by winning the civil war, expelling the foreign imperialists, and unifying the country. Deng gained legitimacy by bringing about order after the chaos of the Cultural Revolution, by dealing pragmatically with the serious issues facing the country, and by achieving rapid economic growth. How will Deng's successors establish their own legitimacy in this new age?

Deng's successors are under pressure for not being more successful in stopping China's widespread corruption and for not doing more to resolve the problems of inequality. And it may be even harder in the future to combat these problems: given global economic fluctuations, China faces the potential of an economic slowdown before a substantial portion of the population has had the chance to enjoy the benefits of the earlier rapid growth period. To prepare for this possibility, Chinese leaders will have to look beyond fast economic growth for legitimacy and accelerate progress on some of the issues that the public is most concerned about: reducing corruption and inequality, providing a reasonable level of universal medical care and welfare, and finding a way to show that public opinion is being respected in the selection of officials.

China as a Superpower: Deng's Legacy

China's extraordinarily rapid growth, which began under Deng and further accelerated with his departing final effort, his southern journey, has raised the question of how China will behave as the size of its economy rivals that of the United States. What would Deng do if he were alive?

Concerning territorial disputes, Deng believed in setting them aside and allowing wiser people to resolve them peacefully, at a later time. The big picture to him was not to get excited about border issues; what was important was to maintain overall good relationships with other countries.

Deng believed that it was in China's interest to have harmonious relations with its neighbors and to concentrate on peaceful development. He strengthened relations with Europe beginning with a quick trip to France in 1974 and a state visit the following year. He not only improved relations with Japan in 1978 and made the first visit in history by a Chinese leader to Japan, but he also supported the development of cultural relations so there would be a stronger positive relationship between the two nations overall. He normalized relations with the United States and made a triumphant visit to America to strengthen U.S.-China relations. He opened trade with South Korea and paved the way for normalization of relations that followed shortly after his southern journey. One of his crowning achievements was to restore normal relations with the Soviet Union in 1989 after thirty years of strained relations. In short, he improved China's relations with every major nation.

Deng, as the first Chinese leader to address the UN General Assembly in 1974, said that China would never become a tyrant and that if it ever oppressed and exploited other nations, the world, and especially the developing countries, should expose China as a "social imperialist" country and, in cooperation with the Chinese people, overthrow the Chinese government. In August 1991, upon receiving the news that Soviet leader Gennady Yanayev had staged a coup against Gorbachev, Wang Zhen sent a telegram to the party center proposing that they lend support for Yanayev's coup. Deng replied *"taoguang yanghui, juebu dangtou, yousuo zuowei."*[14] (Incorrectly translated by some Westerners as "avoid the limelight, don't take the lead, bide your time." What it means is "avoid the limelight, never take the lead, and try to accomplish something.") In Deng's view, China should not get involved in other countries' domestic affairs.

In the years after Deng, as China gained strength, some Chinese security specialists, as well as some of their American counterparts, debated whether once China became strong it should continue biding its time or take a more forceful stance. After some months of debate in 2010–2011, during which time some Chinese leaders were ready to behave more aggressively, the debate was resolved in favor of China continuing to maintain harmonious relations with other countries. One cannot predict how future generations of Chinese leaders will respond to the issue, but there is no question what Deng would say if he were still alive. He would say that China should never behave like a hegemon that interferes in the internal affairs of another nation. Rather, it should maintain harmonious relations with other countries and concentrate on peaceful development at home.

Key People in the Deng Era

Chen Yun

The careers of Deng Xiaoping and Chen Yun were deeply intertwined since the early 1930s, when they both served in the Communist underground in Shanghai under Zhou Enlai.[1] Since then, and until 1980, they had generally been allied on the same side in inner-party struggles. The two had gone together in 1953 to ask Mao Zedong to blow the whistle on Gao Gang in an effort to prevent what would have been the biggest split in the party in the 1950s. Chen Yun and Deng had also both been pushed aside but not destroyed by Mao in the mid-1960s. But beginning in 1981–1982, fissures began to appear in the two leaders' long relationship. Deng and Chen Yun began to disagree over the speed of growth and after 1984, when Deng began pushing urban reform as well as faster growth, their differences became sharper. They each became spokesmen for broader groups of high-level party officials, becoming known as "two tigers on one mountaintop."

Chen Yun and Deng continued to work with each other for the good of the party and they both endeavored to keep their differences from becoming public, but these differences became the basic fault lines of the intra-party politics of the 1980s, especially after 1984. Chen Yun remained more concerned about barging ahead too quickly; he was less willing to take risks, more determined to prevent inflation, more sympathetic to the Soviet Union, less ready to form deep ties with the capitalist countries, less willing to expand the role of markets, and more determined to follow regular party procedures. Deng was more prepared to experiment, to work outside the party framework, to open widely to the West, and to move boldly. In crossing the river, Chen Yun and Deng both searched for stepping stones, but Chen Yun wanted to make sure each stepping stone was secure before putting any weight on it.

Chen Yun enjoyed deep respect within the party, not only because of his extraordinary economic successes, but also because of his long service in high positions, his contribution in helping Mao to be accepted by the Soviet Union in the mid-1930s,

717

his work to build up the Chinese personnel system in Yan'an, his role in establishing the Communist urban administration system as the Communist armies occupied certain areas on the way to conquering the whole country, and his efforts to restrain Mao from the excesses of the Great Leap Forward. Although some considered him too conservative and cautious, he was generally respected for his political judgment, his independent analytic abilities, and his principled dedication to the party. High-level officials who worried that Deng might charge ahead too rapidly without consulting other high officials looked to Chen Yun for support, while in the late 1980s those who wished to experiment boldly with markets regarded Chen Yun as an adversary. Even if Deng had wanted to push Chen Yun aside, it is doubtful that he could have done so. As frustrating as they sometimes found each other after 1984 as their paths continued to diverge, they managed to coexist.

In sharp contrast to Deng, who came from a landlord family, Chen Yun was born into poverty. His father died when he was two, his mother died two years later, and then he was cared for by his maternal grandmother, who died when he was seven. He then lived with his mother's brother until age fourteen, when a teacher arranged that he be apprenticed to the Commercial Press in Shanghai, where he worked in the printing plant and then became a shop clerk.

The Commercial Press, the largest publisher of scholarly books in China, was a center of Chinese intellectual life, and Chen Yun took advantage of the opportunity to educate himself. He read books, attended lectures, and joined in discussions about the outside world. As he made estimates of how much the capitalists at the top of the Commercial Press earned, he calculated how much the capitalists were exploiting the workers. His calculations resonated with the Communist explanation of imperialism. His formative years were as a shop clerk in Shanghai and he never lost his passion against imperialists or his fear that the evil capitalists he observed there might someday return. On May 30, 1925, when British police fired into Shanghai crowds and killed several Chinese, Chen Yun joined in the demonstrations and, before the end of the year, at age twenty, he had joined the Communist Party. He gave speeches and wrote articles about how China was suffering from imperialism and how workers were suffering at the hands of capitalists.

In 1927 when the Guomindang split with the Communists, Chen Yun was forced to go underground, often changing aliases and locations. Under Zhou Enlai, he was also responsible for the assassination of Guomindang officials who might have killed Communists. Unlike Deng, who had spent five years in a capitalist country, Chen Yun, repulsed by the capitalism he saw in Shanghai during the 1920s, never spent any time in a capitalist country and later did not take part in meetings with Western leaders.

In 1928, after the split between the Communists and Guomindang, the Comintern representatives from the Soviet Union advised the Chinese Communists that they must rely on the workers because intellectuals, who overwhelmingly came from landlord and bourgeois families, were not a reliable base for the revolutionary movement. Since China at that time had such a miniscule industrial workforce and almost no workers with sufficient education to provide leadership, the Chinese Communist Party sorely needed bright "workers" in its leadership. Chen Yun, already a labor leader and well educated from the environment at the Commercial Press, was chosen and then rapidly promoted. In fact, although he was a year younger than Deng, for over two decades, beginning in 1931 when he became a member of the Central Committee, Chen ranked much higher in the party than Deng.

In 1933 in Jiangxi, Chen Yun, the only high official from a "worker background," was soon promoted to membership on the Politburo Standing Committee, making him one of the top seven leaders of the Chinese Communist Party. On the eve of the famous Zunyi conference in 1935 on the Long March, Chen Yun participated in the key meeting that increased the number of participants to take part at Zunyi, with more people supporting Mao, thus paving the way for Mao to gain the upper hand at Zunyi. After the Zunyi conference, the small group of Chinese Communists, to maintain Comintern support, needed someone to reestablish connections with the Comintern in Shanghai and to report to it on their leadership changes. Chen Yun, who was able to disguise himself as a local merchant speaking the local Shanghai dialect, was selected by party leaders to report to the Comintern in Shanghai. When he arrived there, however, the situation was dangerous: he could easily have been recognized by the many former Communists who were then siding with the Guomindang. He was thus advised to take a freighter right away to Vladivostok, from where he would make his way to the Comintern in Moscow to report to the Soviet leaders on developments at the Zunyi conference—in particular, the rise of Mao Zedong. He remained in Moscow for two years.

Unlike Deng, who was in Moscow under the New Economic Policy (NEP), Chen Yun was there after Stalin had built a socialist structure and had established the Soviet five-year plans. Deng had traveled to the Soviet Union as a student, but Chen Yun went as a high official who interacted with Soviet leaders and even met Stalin. After leaving Moscow he spent half a year in Xinjiang, where he attempted to build up a regular transport route between the Soviet Union and China (an effort that failed due to the power of local warlord Ma Bufang and his cavalry).

Later, in the early 1950s when Chen Yun was playing a leading role in Chinese economic planning, he enjoyed good relations with the Soviet advisers who helped him put in place China's First Five-Year Plan. In contrast to Deng, who led the Chinese side in the quarrel with the Soviets in the early 1960s, Chen Yun maintained good relations with Soviet leaders. After Chen Yun joined Mao in Yan'an in the 1930s, he was put in charge of the Organization Department. Since the situation in Yan'an was more stable than that in the Jiangxi Soviet, he was able to develop files on party members, and because the Organization Department was then responsible for the personal lives of party members, including family connections and marriages,

Chen knew a great deal about all the important Communist leaders. Chen Yun was active in recruiting intellectual youth from the cities; although he acknowledged the need to weed out Guomindang spies, he found it difficult to attack many of his own recruits in the rectification campaign: instead he reported sick, spent months recuperating, and was replaced by Peng Zhen who vigorously pursued the campaign. Chen Yun was then reassigned to work on economic affairs, drawing on his experience at the Commercial Press where he had handled accounts and traveled as a salesman. A key responsibility was breaking the economic blockade the Guomindang had imposed; his solution was to make it profitable for outside merchants to make money in their own currency by buying and selling opium and other products from the Communists. After his success in breaking the blockade, he was given responsibility for the overall development of the economy in the Northwest (where Yan'an is located).

After World War II, Mao sent Chen Yun and other high-level Communist officials to the Northeast (then known as Manchuria). There they were to take advantage of the region's proximity to the Soviet Union, as well as the industrial machinery left behind there by the Japanese, to build a base from which to fight the civil war. As the Communist base area in the Northeast expanded, Chen Yun helped guide the development of the regional economy. And after the Communist troops won military battles in the Northeast, Chen worked to organize a network of grain and other supplies from the Northeast to serve the Communist army as it moved south.

When the Communist troops took over their first city, Harbin, economic stability was critical, so Chen Yun, with experience in economic affairs, was given responsibility for managing the transition to Communist rule, including ensuring that local facilities continued to operate. This required him to cooperate with many officials who had served under the Guomindang. When Communist troops took over an even larger city, Shenyang, Chen Yun was again put in charge of bringing the city administration under Communist rule. He was sufficiently successful in guiding this difficult process that the Shenyang takeover became a model for Communist takeovers of other cities as the troops swept south and west, unifying the country.

When the Communists established their capital in Beijing, Chen Yun, having brought economic order to the Northeast, was placed in charge of the national economy. His most pressing problem was the rampant inflation that had never been tamed during the decades that the warlords had struggled for power and that had spun out of control after World War II. Chen Yun used strong administrative punishments to force businesspeople to stop raising prices, and when they refused, he made use of the market: he took goods out of the warehouses and flooded the market, forcing prices down precipitously and devastating the resistant merchants. Through a combination of administrative controls and use of the market, by 1952 the Communists, under Chen Yun's leadership, had achieved what the Guomindang and the warlords for decades had been unable to accomplish: they brought inflation under control.

Chen Yun's next assignments were to develop a socialist economic planning system—which also entailed taking control of supplies of key goods—and then, in 1955–1956, to nationalize large enterprises and direct the collectivization of smaller enterprises and the countryside. His efforts brought the entire economy under socialist planning. Starting in the 1950s and until the Great Leap Forward, Chen Yun managed to unify a national system of collecting grain that ensured the collection of sufficient grain from the countryside to supply the urban areas. This advance, along with the introduction of industrial projects from the Soviet Union, enabled the Chinese economy to grow rapidly until the 1958 Great Leap, when Mao cast aside the cautious Chen Yun, derailed the planning apparatus, and destroyed the economy. When the disaster persisted, Mao recalled Chen Yun to lead the recovery effort. In the early 1960s, Chen Yun once again brought order to the economy. Why is it, Mao once asked, that only Chen Yun seems able to make the economy successful?

Chen Yun was a sober, cautious person of delicate disposition who, in times of stress, especially when criticized by Mao, complained of a heart condition and took weeks and even months off to recuperate. In 1962, when Mao criticized him for suggesting the possibility of contracting rural production down to the household, Chen Yun was so devastated that he could not speak for two weeks and recovered very slowly. Mao once said that Chen Yun was so frightened that if a leaf falls, he is afraid it will land on his head. Chen was also a private man who seldom met visitors and who often ate by himself.

Unlike Deng, who wanted to read fifteen newspapers and many reports each day, Chen read the *People's Daily* from cover to cover and had an assistant bring him daily just the five most important daily reports, which he read with great care. His experiences as a shop clerk in keeping accounts and as a planner in keeping track of each item and then seeing the system derailed reinforced his natural carefulness. Unlike Deng, who believed that the troops might lose an opportunity if they waited until everything was carefully investigated and all the desired information was collected, Chen Yun's favorite saying was "exchange views, compare, go over the issues again and again" (*jiaohuan, bijiao, fanfu*). As the father of Chinese economic planning who spent years putting the details in place, Chen Yun had an understandable attachment to the system that had once worked and a determination not to let anyone ruin his painstaking handiwork, which had already been destroyed once, during the Great Leap Forward.

Although Chen Yun possessed higher qualifications that dated back earlier than Deng's, he was not seriously considered for the top position in the party. He had virtually no military experience, he had had no contact with the West that would be important for the new era, and he was sickly. Chen Yun was far more imaginative and flexible in his thinking than his critics acknowledged, but he lacked the bold leadership style that Deng used to rally people behind him. Chen Yun also had little experience leading an independent unit or locality. After Mao's death, Chen Yun himself declared that Deng was the only person appropriate to be the top leader of the party.

Deng and Chen Yun both survived epic struggles in an age of revolutionary heroes. Each would have been less than human had he not taken pride in his own achievements, beyond the pride of ordinary bureaucrats who rose to high positions in a stable organization. After 1979, when Deng received international adulation, with his picture on the cover of *Time* magazine as the "man of the year," Chen Yun allowed Deng Liqun to present a series of talks at the Central Party School so lavish in praise of Chen Yun that they compared his contributions in the economic sphere with Mao Zedong's in the political sphere, without giving comparable praise to Deng Xiaoping. The *Selected Works of Chen Yun* was rushed to press even before publication of the *Selected Works of Deng Xiaoping*. Although Deng and Chen Yun never split openly, it is understandable that their relationship had an edge to it, as they became the magnets for two opposing views on China's modernization: that China should move more boldly or that China should avoid taking dangerous risks.

Deng Liqun

Deng Liqun (no relation to Deng Xiaoping)—head of the Political Research Office of the party Secretariat after 1980 and leader of the Propaganda Department from 1983 to 1985—was not one of China's highest-ranking officials. His influence, however, greatly exceeded his rank, and not simply because he supervised the influential, twice-daily intelligence briefs that came from the party Secretariat to the top officials; helped draft many of Deng's speeches; and employed on his staff Mao's daughter Lina; Chen Yun's wife, Yu Ruomu; and one of Chen Yun's secretaries. Deng Liqun was also influential because he was fearless in expressing his views, knowledgeable about theory, and was supported by Chen Yun and Wang Zhen, whose opinions he often voiced. He was ready to accept a job loss, a prison sentence, or even heavy physical labor to do what he regarded as correct. Well-organized and skilled at strategic maneuvering, Deng Liqun also protected and looked after his subordinates, who in turn became appreciative and devoted followers.

Deng Xiaoping found Deng Liqun useful for curbing intellectuals critical of the party. Because Deng Liqun was smart, fearless, frank, and helpful in speechwriting, and because he was not an official with line responsibilities, Deng Xiaoping could interact with him more easily than with officials who had line responsibilities. Deng solicited his views more often than those of other officials in more important positions. With powerful conservative support, Deng Liqun dared to attack not only intellectuals but also General Secretary Hu Yaobang. In fact, he became Hu's chief critic, voicing the despair of the senior conservatives who believed Hu was allowing too much freedom and not adequately defending the authority of the party. Deng Liqun strongly advocated the importance of maintaining party discipline and he did not hesitate to attack intellectuals and officials who criticized the party. Intellectuals advocating more freedom were convinced that Deng Liqun exercised a pernicious influence, provoking senior officials into cracking down unnecessarily on freedoms. After the death of Kang Sheng, who was secretive and devious, the official whom intellectuals and liberal officials most hated was Deng Liqun.

Deng Liqun was born in Guidong county, Hunan province, in 1915. He was officially classified as a rich peasant, but his family home, which had stood for more than three hundred years, had more than twenty rooms. Deng Liqun's father had passed the imperial civil-service examination although he never became an official; after the failed 1898 reforms, he founded the first Western-style school in his home area. An elder brother of Deng's had been chairman of the Hunan Provincial Government under the Guomindang and a member of the Guomindang Central Committee. Deng Liqun went to Beiping (renamed Beijing when it became the capital) to study at an American missionary school and in the fall of 1935 passed the exam to enter Peking University, where he enrolled as an economics major. Before finishing his first year, however, shortly after the December 9 anti-Japanese demonstrations, he left the university and set out for Yan'an.[2]

In Yan'an, Deng Liqun joined the Communist Party in 1936, and later was attached to the Marxist-Leninist Academy and carried on secret investigative work. When Deng Liqun was surreptitiously investigating Li Rui, who was criticized during the Yan'an rectification campaign, Deng interviewed Li Rui's wife whom he then courted, even while ostensibly continuing the investigation; the two eventually ran off together, an act for which Deng Liqun later made a self-criticism.

During the civil war, Deng Liqun was sent to the Northeast where he met Chen Yun and served in a variety of positions, including director of the Political Research Office of the Liaodong Provincial Committee. In the summer of 1949 Deng Liqun was assigned to Xinjiang, where he became head of the Propaganda Department and secretary general of the Xinjiang branch of the Communist Party.[3] He worked closely with General Wang Zhen, who had been sent to Xinjiang to pacify the region. When Mao Zedong, who was then seeking the cooperation of the minority groups, found out that General Wang had started minority reforms too early and had killed massive numbers of Uighurs, he became furious. At that point, Deng Liqun notified Mao that it was not Wang Zhen but he, Deng Liqun, who had made the decision to wipe out so many locals who might have resisted Communist rule. For his bravery in defending Wang Zhen and exposing his own role, Deng Liqun lost his job; it would take some time before he again rose in the hierarchy. But he did win the undying support of Wang Zhen, who shared with Deng Liqun a strong sense of *yiqi,* a code of brotherly honor and loyalty among some brotherhoods. After reading the popular book *Water Margin* and virtually all of the traditional tales of knights-errant. Deng Liqun developed a deep belief in *yiqi* that he maintained throughout his life.[4]

After Xinjiang was pacified, Deng Liqun went to Beijing where he worked under the supervision of Liu Shaoqi in the party General Office, then directed by Yang Shangkun. He helped to draft party documents and later joined the staff of the party journal *Red Flag*. When Liu Shaoqi was attacked during the Cultural Revolution, his top two secretaries roundly denounced him, but Deng Liqun, then his third secretary, again moved by *yiqi,* refused to criticize him. As punishment, Deng Liqun was attacked and sent to a "May 7 Cadre School" for reeducation and labor. After serving his time, he chose to remain at the May 7 cadre school for another year before returning to Beijing, so that he could devote himself to mastering Marxist-Leninist theory.

After returning to Beijing, in 1975 Deng Liqun was invited by Hu Qiaomu to become the seventh and final senior member of Deng Xiaoping's Political Research Office. When Deng Xiaoping was criticized later in the year, his closest associates were told to join in the criticism. Virtually all of them did, with the exception of Deng Liqun. Deng Liqun was prepared to go to prison for taking this stand, but he only lost his job. Moreover, soon after Deng Xiaoping returned to work in 1977, Deng Liqun became one of the insiders who drafted his speeches.[5] And in June 1980, Deng Liqun became head of the Research Office of the party Secretariat, where he put out daily intelligence briefs that were circulated to the highest-level officials, collected research materials for leaders, conducted his own research, produced four journals, and wrote theoretical works.[6]

Staff writers like Deng Liqun followed directives from Deng Xiaoping, Chen Yun, and others, but as knowledgeable specialists on party history and theory, they had an opportunity to help shape the documents. Given the respect that others had for Hu Qiaomu and Deng Liqun as guardians of party orthodoxy, higher-level officials dared not argue that the documents and speeches the two men supervised violated party theory and precedent.

Deng Liqun was neither a "knee-jerk" conservative nor an impulsive nationalist. He and his son Deng Yingtao both specialized in rural economics at Peking University and were early advocates of rural reform. In the early stages of the rural reform, Deng Liqun advocated a larger role for the market. When he returned from a study tour in Japan, immediately after Deng Xiaoping's visit there in October 1978, Deng Liqun was full of praise for Japanese efficiency and quality standards, as well as for the Japanese spirit and organizational methods. But Deng Liqun supported Chen Yun's cautiousness about giving up the planned economy. Moreover, in 1980 Deng Liqun gave a series of lectures at the Central Party School on the economic views of Chen Yun that seemed to encourage a cultish reverence for Chen himself. Thereafter, Chen Yun always strongly supported Deng Liqun.

Decades of Communist propaganda extolling workers and peasants did not fully erase the disdain that Deng Liqun, who attended Peking University and was from a prominent family, felt toward someone like Hu Yaobang, who left school at the age of fourteen and lacked poise. Chen Yun, Wang Zhen, and other conservatives believed Deng Liqun would make an excellent party general secretary, and liberal officials had no doubts that he nourished such ambitions. Deng Liqun denied that he had ever sought such a post, but he did not disguise his disdain for Hu Yaobang, which he displayed with a vigor that went beyond mere objective analysis.

Hu Qiaomu

Hu Qiaomu, former secretary to Mao Zedong, master drafter (*bi ganzi*, "a pen") of official documents, and the most authoritative party historian, enjoyed higher rank and greater prestige than Deng Liqun.[7] Hu was a brilliant scholar of extraordinary breadth. As an official, he felt responsible for preserving the authority of the party and the orthodoxy of party statements. As a scholar, he read broadly and continued to learn. As a friend, he could be very considerate of those who wished to express diverse views, advising them how to make their views acceptable to the top leaders. As the defender of orthodoxy, he could attack intellectuals who criticized the party. As a competitor, he could put down rivals as the most authoritative voice on party orthodoxy and as the master writer.

Hu had personal relationships with many of the top leaders that dated back to when he worked in Yan'an as a secretary to Mao. As a member of the Communist Youth League, he automatically became a member of the Communist Party in 1936. In the early years after 1949, Mao had used Hu as the guardian of the official party view by appointing him to supervise publication of the *People's Daily*. Drawing on his personal knowledge of Mao's papers as well as party documents, in 1951 Hu wrote the official thirty-year history of the party, establishing himself as the top party historian. He was also one of the editors of the four volumes of Mao's *Selected Works*.

Although Hu Qiaomu was far more familiar with theory and party history than were other top officials, he was more cautious than Deng Liqun about injecting his own views. Even so, Hu sometimes took liberties when recording leaders' spontaneous statements, in order to give their writings a consistency with party theory, history, and terminology. Top leaders knew of his talent, his encyclopedic knowledge of party history, and also his sensitivities, and thus sought his assistance to give legitimacy to their actions. Deng Xiaoping, for instance, drew on Hu Qiaomu's talents to provide leadership for his Political Research Office, and he continued to call on him to provide the unchallenged ideological perspective that would enable Deng to write speeches and documents that expressed his own viewpoints but were, after Mao's death, invulnerable to any criticism that they strayed from party orthodoxy.

Unlike Deng Liqun, who had a strong sense of righteousness and was ready to endure punishment out of his sense of *yiqi*, Hu Qiaomu was pliable and concerned about keeping good relations with whoever was in power. Hu was quick to show his allegiance to whomever he thought held power, but he did not always have a good sense of current politics. In 1975, Hu supported Deng Xiaoping, but in the 1976 campaign to criticize Deng, he cooperated in criticizing him. (When Deng returned to power, Hu asked Deng Liqun to take his letter of apology to Deng, but Deng Xiaoping, aware that Hu had not passed on any deep secrets, said there was no problem and without looking at the letter sent it back.[8]) Then, when Zhao Ziyang became premier, Hu Qiaomu was not only quick to visit him but also went so far as to question the usefulness of Deng's speech on the four cardinal principles, a speech that Hu himself had drafted for Deng.

Hu passed the entrance examination in physics at Peking University but studied history instead. At Zhejiang University he studied English and other European languages and European literature and history. He could also draw on his vast knowledge of party history, science, economics, and philosophy, some of which he had picked up from his readings in Chinese, Russian, and Western languages. In Yan'an, he had helped to draft the first document of "Resolution on Some Questions of History," and it was understandable that Deng would turn to him in 1980–1981 to be a key drafter of a second document, "Resolution on Certain Issues in the History of Our Party since the Founding of the People's Republic of China," which evaluated the history of the party under Mao. Somewhat paradoxically given his role as the keeper of party orthodoxy, Hu Qiaomu could see the value of many of the contradictory readings he digested, and he never developed a fully consistent point of view. Indeed, in private he could at times express positions that were more liberal than those of many of his critics, and during the Cultural Revolution he was attacked by the radicals and later by the Gang of Four. But in his public role as the chief guardian of orthodoxy, with the weighty responsibility of preserving the authority of the party, he often joined in the attacks on liberals.

Hu Qiaomu could write quickly under pressure. He had a large group of writer-researchers who checked historical documents for precedents, pulled together current information, and wrote initial drafts, but he usually did the final editing of important documents and speeches, thereby providing an overall consistency and an authoritative tone that balanced different perspectives. With his deep knowledge of party history, he was rarely questioned when he judged whether something was consistent with party tradition. Hu was intense and dedicated, but also moody. He could be dogmatic in defending party orthodoxy against any rivals and prickly in defending himself against any challengers to his role as the top writer in the party.

Hu Yaobang

Hu Yaobang joined the Communist Youth League and the Red Army at age fourteen.[9] He was so completely dedicated, spontaneous, and enthusiastic; so willing to exert himself with every ounce of his energy; so willing to go the extra mile for comrades who had suffered, that in the late 1980s perhaps no high-level leader had more devoted admirers than Hu. Indeed, Hu Yaobang was beloved as the conscience and heart of the party. When Hu was removed from office in 1987, many party members—even those who were not close to him—believed that he, like Zhou Enlai, had been treated unfairly. In his speeches, Hu was so bubbly, so completely open and obviously genuine, that no other Chinese leader could move an audience as he did. Listeners were deeply affected, for instance, when he recounted how he felt when under attack during the Cultural Revolution or when in 1932 he had been sentenced to execution, a fate he escaped when a fellow official interceded on his behalf.[10]

Even some of Hu's admirers acknowledge that he lacked the poise and gravitas normally expected of top officials. When he gave speeches, with arms flailing in animated gestures, he appeared to some like an inexperienced youth; critics disparagingly called him "the cricket." In his taped memoirs, Zhao Ziyang acknowledged that Hu was an idealistic, committed reformer, but argued that because Hu had never held a top position with overall responsibility for a local area, he couldn't appreciate fully the importance of political stability and unity.[11] In fact, Hu had held such a position when he served briefly as first party secretary in Shaanxi province (November 1964–June 1965); while there, conservative officials criticized him for putting too much emphasis on production and for protecting officials instead of giving full support to the class struggle. Hu was never a military commander, but some officials said that if he were, he would be like a bold general ready to lead his troops into battle, rather than a brilliant strategist who could weigh all the factors and determine the appropriate plans.

From 1952 to 1966, when Hu was head of the Communist Youth League, his task was to encourage young people, to help them enjoy political work so they would want to dedicate themselves to the party and the country. He did not have Deng's weighty responsibilities: to make overall decisions for the nation, to keep order, and to defend China from the outside. Even admiring subordinates acknowledged that Hu Yaobang was not a well-organized office manager, nor did he manage to protect his subordinates from attacks by others. His loudest critics said that Hu often spoke too long and too spontaneously without taking enough care to consider all the implications. Former subordinates report that Hu took far more care to familiarize himself with policies and to follow them than his critics acknowledged, but he was inclined to grant freedom to intellectuals and leeway to lower-level officials who wanted to resolve problems in their own ways. When Australian prime minister Robert Hawke asked Hu's deputy Hu Qili how he felt when Hu Yaobang began to speak without notes, Hu Qili replied, "terrified."[12]

Born in 1915 to a Hakka farm family in Liuyang county, Hunan, Hu, a top student, was encouraged by his left-leaning teachers to take part in patriotic activities. At age fourteen, he left school, crossed the eastern border of his province into Jiangxi, and made his way to the Jiangxi Soviet. He took part on the Long March as one of the "little red devils," the dedicated youth who served the older soldiers. In Yan'an, he was one of Mao's favorites. After his youth work, Mao placed Hu in the Political Department of the PLA. During the civil war, Hu was a low-ranking political commissar in He Long's Second Front (later the First Field) Army, which took the northern route into Sichuan. Deng came to know Hu in 1950 when Hu served under him as a party secretary in northern Sichuan (at the time Deng, who was party secretary of the Southwest Bureau, was headquartered in Sichuan). When officials from the six large regions were transferred to Beijing in 1952 and Deng was assigned to the party center, Hu was named first secretary of the Communist Youth League.

Hu sometimes joked with visitors that Deng had selected him for leadership because, at four feet eleven inches, he was the only official shorter than Deng.[13] But Deng had many good reasons to choose Hu Yaobang. During his many years in the Jiangxi and Yan'an soviets, Hu had enjoyed good relationships with other top leaders. Moreover, Deng knew that Hu Yaobang learned quickly and studied hard, possessed boundless energy, and was completely dedicated to reform: he was ready to do whatever was necessary to get the country moving. Recognized as one of the ablest officials of his generation, Hu had been effective as first secretary of the Communist Youth League from 1952 to 1966, a decade of which overlapped with Deng's tenure as general secretary of the party. Hu was also effective in the early 1960s when he served in Hunan as party secretary of Xiangtan prefecture and in the mid-1960s as provincial party secretary of Shaanxi and party secretary of the Northwest Region. In early 1967 when the Red Guards made a list of Deng's supporters who should be criticized, the first name on the list was Hu's.[14]

After returning to work in July 1975, Hu rallied the dispirited scientists whose help was badly needed to promote modernization. At the Central Party School in 1977–1978, too, he inspired officials preparing to rejuvenate the party and the government after the Cultural Revolution. After being appointed head of the Organization Department in December 1977, Hu was tireless in his efforts to reverse the verdicts on officials who had been falsely accused during the Cultural Revolution. He also provided theoretical leadership by promoting the influential essay "Practice Is the Sole Criterion for Judging Truth." At the Central Party Work Conference held before the Third Plenum in December 1978, Hu played a major role in coordinating issues among the different groups, promoting a consensus on personnel appointments, and helping prepare speeches for all three principal speakers—Hua Guofeng, Ye Jianying, and Deng Xiaoping.[15] Hu thus had a broad general knowledge of all aspects of party work, having worked in the military and in leadership positions in the party's propaganda and organization departments.

When he became general secretary, Hu initially enjoyed the support of all key officials. He had maintained good relations with Hua Guofeng since 1962–1964 when they had worked together as provincial leaders in Hunan. He had strong backing from Marshal Ye, a fellow Hakka, who had known him since the Yan'an period. Chen

Yun, too, had known Hu in Yan'an when Hu was head of the Organization Department in the army's Political Department while Chen Yun was head of the overall Organization Department of the party. In 1978 Chen Yun worked closely with Hu Yaobang in reversing verdicts and in 1980 he supported Hu Yaobang's appointment as party chairman.[16] At the time of the 12th Party Congress in 1982 when the title of "party chairman" was abolished, Hu Yaobang became general secretary.

Mao had made full use of people like Zhou Enlai and Kang Sheng, who felt vulnerable to criticism and would do almost anything to avoid it. Hu Yaobang did not have the same vulnerabilities, but in contrast to Deng Xiaoping, who always remained confident, poised, and authoritative, Hu, lacking comparable confidence, endeavored to prove that he deserved to be in high leadership circles.[17] He liked reading and read widely in theory, history, and literature, and he worked hard to prove that he had the theoretical background to be a worthy high-level leader. In busy times, he slept in his office in Zhongnanhai rather than return to his home, even though it was within easy walking distance.[18]

Hua Guofeng

Hua Guofeng, like many leaders of his generation, joined the party as an anti-Japanese patriot. He had completed elementary school and three years of middle school. Originally named Su Zhu, he took the name Hua Guofeng (meaning "Chinese vanguard against the Japanese") when he joined the Communist Party in 1938 at age seventeen, just after the Communists' Eighth Route Army established its headquarters in his home province of Shanxi. After joining the party, he was assigned to help recruit soldiers for the military and to find others who would serve as guerrillas in the militia in their local villages. He also helped recruit and cultivate young people to become party members. In the years of fighting from 1937 to 1949 he took part in guerrilla activities and worked with the regular army but he never joined the army. He ended the civil war as a local county party leader, like Zhao Ziyang and Wan Li, at the same time, in their respective provinces.

In 1949, as the advancing Communist army took over the country, Hua was sent to Hunan province, first as party secretary in Xiangying county and then, in 1951, to Xiangtan county, Mao's home county. In 1952 he rose to be head of the government office of Xiangtan prefecture, which included twelve counties, and deputy party secretary; in 1955 he became party secretary of Xiangtan prefecture. In Xiangtan where he strongly supported collectivization, he came to the attention of Mao Zedong on one of Mao's visits to his home area. In 1956 Hua was promoted to the provincial level where he first worked in educational and cultural affairs, then headed the provincial United Front and in 1958 the Hunan province economics small group. He became deputy governor in 1958. In the fall of 1959, Hua became one of Hunan's provincial party secretaries. In 1964 he played a role in developing the industries that had moved inland to Hunan from the coastal areas to escape the possibility of foreign attack.

In the summer of 1959, Hua accompanied Mao on a visit to his home county. At the time, China had no air conditioning and Hua, concerned about the heat and Mao's safety, reportedly stood guard all night so that the windows in Mao's bedroom could remain open. Under Hua's leadership, Mao's home in Xiangtan in effect became a national shrine and Hua helped build the area around it into a tourist site. In Mao's hometown, Shaoshan, Hua also supervised the development of an irrigation project.

By early 1967 Hua was already the second-highest official in Hunan and at the 9th Party Congress in April 1969 he was elected a member of the Central Committee. In 1970 he became provincial first party secretary. In short, Hua was a generalist who rose step by step within the hierarchy with experience in all major civilian sectors: agriculture, industry, finance, culture-education, and science and technology.[19]

The month after Lin Biao's crash in 1971, Mao assigned Hua to be first political commissar of the Hunan Provincial Military Region to help ensure that Lin Biao's followers did not dominate the military in the region. Hua's experience on the Politburo from 1973 to 1976 gave him a broad introduction to national policy issues and a chance to get to know other high-level officials. He had no experience in foreign policy and had never served in the regular army. At the January 1975 NPC he was promoted to vice premier and minister of public security. Hua did not stand out as a brilliant leader, but Mao found him to be a strong and reliable supporter of his political campaigns and Hua rose after each major political campaign. But unlike Mao the romantic revolutionary, Hua acquired a reputation as one who investigated problems firsthand and then solved problems pragmatically.

Ji Dengkui

In 1975, Ji Dengkui, at age fifty-two, was one of the youngest of the vice premiers and was considered a possible candidate for an even higher position.[20] In 1952 when Mao was touring Henan, he had been dissatisfied with the vague, general answers he was receiving from local officials—until he talked with Ji Dengkui, then a twenty-nine-year-old party secretary in a factory producing machinery for a coal mine. In his explanations, Ji Dengkui was very concrete, clearly well-informed, and, unlike most officials who were intimidated when talking to Mao, not afraid to answer directly. Mao asked Ji a series of questions—if he had joined in the intense criticisms of other people, whether others had done the same to him, whether he had killed other people, and whether he had committed errors in killing others. Ji answered "yes" to all the questions while providing examples. Mao had expected to talk with Ji for ten to fifteen minutes, but, impressed with his answers, he instead invited Ji to join him on the train to Wuhan, where they talked for four hours. An able official, Ji Dengkui had risen steadily in the Henan party structure and was considered more skilled than a Hunan rival who was about the same age, Hua Guofeng. Every time Mao visited Henan, he asked to speak with Ji. It is estimated that Mao talked with Ji on over fifty occasions. In the wake of the Great Leap Forward, when Mao asked whether the problems were serious, Ji explained that he and several members of his family had suffered from malnutrition due to policy errors. When Mao asked how long it would take to recover from the Great Leap, Ji said if things went well, it would take two to three years; if they did not go well, three to five years. Mao publicly contrasted Ji's views, which later proved correct, with those of Chen Yun, who said it would take a decade. From that point on, Ji did not have good relations with Chen Yun. Though Ji suffered at the outset of the Cultural Revolution, his career rebounded quickly and by 1970 Mao had appointed him to the State Council.

Shortly before the civil war began in 1946, Deng Xiaoping had met Ji and Ji's friend Zhao Ziyang, both then district party secretaries in Henan, in the border region under Deng's direction. Thereafter, Ji studied for one year in Moscow and then was assigned to Henan, working under the No. 1 Ministry of Machine Building. Deng was familiar with Ji's abilities and supported Ji's assignment to work in Zhejiang. Ji Dengkui had the necessary qualifications for guiding the government's work in the factious province: experience, skill, and support from high-level leaders.

Li Xiannian

Li Xiannian, who after the Third Plenum ranked just below Deng Xiaoping and Chen Yun in the Chinese power structure, had a remarkable ability to get along with many different and even opposing leaders, including Mao and his rival Zhang Guotao, Mao and Zhou Enlai, Hua Guofeng and Deng, and Deng and Chen Yun. Ever since arriving in Beijing in 1954, Li had worked on economic affairs.[21] Born into a poor peasant family in eastern Hubei, he joined the Communist Party in 1927 and after the Guomindang and Communists split, he took part in guerrilla activities in the E-Yu-Wan (Hubei, Henan, Anhui) base. Later he joined the forces of Zhang Guotao, who then commanded far more troops than Mao. Zhang, recognizing Li's abilities, promoted him to the rank of political commissar in one of the regiments of his Fourth Front Army.[22] On the Long March, when the Fourth Front Army under Zhang separated from Mao's forces and took the western route, it suffered devastating defeats at the hands of local warlord forces, particularly the cavalry of Ma Bufang. Li Xiannian led some 1,500 of these soldiers, now emaciated, through China's Northwest until the four hundred survivors reached Xinjiang. There they were met by Chen Yun—who arranged food and medical care until the men were nursed back to health. Li then went on to Yan'an. After Mao's split with Zhang Guotao, Li Xiannian was extremely careful to show his complete loyalty to Mao and to avoid any possible dubious activities.

In the latter part of the civil war, Li moved forces placed under his command to the Central Plain region, not far from his native village in Hubei. When Deng and

Liu Bocheng marched to the nearby Dabie Mountains, their troops encountered serious hardships and Li, making use of his local contacts, helped provide them support: for his efforts, he was promoted to deputy commander of the Liu-Deng forces. After the Communist victory in 1949, Li Xiannian remained in Hubei as provincial party secretary. Over the next several years, he held a variety of high positions in Wuhan City, Hubei province, and in the party's Central-South Bureau, where he worked with Lin Biao.

In Wuhan, Li worked on economic issues, and in 1954, when Deng gave up his position as minister of finance, Li was brought to Beijing as Deng's replacement, serving concurrently as vice chairman of the Finance and Economics Commission of the State Council, under the direction of Chen Yun. At the plenum immediately following the 8th Party Congress in 1956, Li became one of the seventeen members of the Politburo. Unlike Chen Yun, he took an active role in foreign affairs, greeting foreign delegations and making a number of trips abroad. In 1972, for example, he accompanied President Nixon on his visit to the Great Wall. Foreigners remembered Li as warm and affable, and it was clear that he was devoted to his professional work. In addition, he did not express strong opinions and avoided taking political stands that favored one leader against another. Li was a survivor, always able to move with the political winds.

During the Cultural Revolution, Li was kept on by Zhou Enlai to serve as first deputy head of the *yewuzu,* with overall responsibility for the economy. From 1966 to 1970 the economic disruptions were so severe that no party meetings were held to discuss annual or multiyear economic plans; Li's job was to keep the economy functioning despite the political disruptions. After 1970, however, Li Xiannian was able to revive the planning process. Li was acceptable to the senior officials, for he had been a senior official under Zhou Enlai and he did not rise because of the Cultural Revolution. Yet he was also acceptable to those who rose during the Cultural Revolution, for he had also worked closely with them as a member of the *yewuzu.* In 1975, when Deng was in charge of the country but still on a leash from Mao, Li played a key role in helping Deng gain control over the railroads and the steel industry. At the end of 1975 when Mao began to harbor doubts about Deng, Li joined wholeheartedly in the criticisms of Deng. But in 1976 when the criticism against Deng expanded, Li was also criticized and in Mao's last months, from February to September 1976, Li voluntarily stepped aside so that Hua Guofeng could lead the daily work of the government.

Immediately after Mao's death, Hua Guofeng sent Li Xiannian to talk with Marshal Ye Jianying about how to respond to the Gang of Four. And after Deng's removal from early 1976 until 1978, when he held the post of vice premier under Hua Guofeng, Li was in charge of the daily work of the government. During these years, he played a central part in decisions to import chemical fertilizer and artificial fiber plants and, beginning in 1978, in arranging further imports of foreign factories with members of the "petroleum faction." In mid-1978 Li Xiannian, working under Hua Guofeng, played key roles in developing the ten-year economic vision, making arrangements for delegations to travel abroad, and importing large numbers of foreign factories and assembly lines. At an economic conference in the summer of 1978, to which Chen Yun was not invited, Li Xiannian kept Chen Yun informed.

After the Third Plenum, when Chen Yun complained about the careless and overly optimistic planning by Hua Guofeng, Li Xiannian, as the responsible official under Hua, was implicated. He managed to keep his position, but he was placed on the defensive. He undertook a self-criticism for his overly optimistic assessments and passed on overall responsibility for guiding the Chinese economy to his former mentor, Chen Yun, who had helped nurse him back to health in Xinjiang more than two decades earlier. In March 1979, Li Xiannian and Chen Yun sent a joint letter to the party center asking that a new Finance and Economics Commission be established under the direction of Chen Yun, with Li as his deputy.

No matter how much Li cooperated with Deng, he could not completely shed his past thinking or his personal connections with those leaders who had remained in office during the Cultural Revolution. Many of the reforms introduced after 1978 were, inevitably, critical of the policies that Li had supported during the Cultural Revolution and of the organizations in which he had worked. He had, for example, supported the Dazhai and Daqing models that Deng and other reformers considered inappropriate for the era. His relations with Zhao Ziyang, who was pushing ahead with an agenda to open markets far more widely, were at best awkward. But his special relations with Chen Yun, as his rescuer in the 1930s, and with Deng, whom he had assisted during the difficult days in the Dabie Mountains—along with his seniority, adaptability, and general competence—were sufficient to allow him to remain in a high position. Among the post-1978 reformers, he was relatively conservative. Also, Li did not fully support Deng in pushing aside Hua Guofeng. His views were closer to those of his old superior Chen Yun than to those of Deng. Like Chen Yun, Li never visited the SEZs, even though he had supported the establishment of a ship-demolition facility in Shekou, which became a small corner of the Shenzhen SEZ.

Li was flexible enough to join Deng's reform team, but he was not a full-fledged dedicated reformer himself. Even so, he had seniority, knowledge, and experience useful to Deng and the more committed reformers, and he did not challenge their leadership.

Mao Yuanxin

At the beginning of 1976, Mao Zedong's nephew Mao Yuanxin was only thirty-six years old, but he was already a provincial party secretary in Liaoning where he had aligned himself firmly with the radicals (although not with the Gang of Four). He was easily the brightest, most knowledgeable, and experienced young relative of Mao Zedong. He was forceful and confident, and Mao already had a close relationship with him.[23]

Mao Yuanxin's father, Mao Zemin, a dedicated Communist and younger brother of Mao Zedong, was killed in 1943 by a Xinjiang warlord, Sheng Shicai. Mao Zedong's second son, Anqing, was mentally ill. When Mao's eldest son, Anying, was killed in the Korean War, Mao, lonely for a son, invited his high-school-age nephew Yuanxin to live with him, which he did for several years. At the time, Mao did not discuss politics with him, but he talked to him about Chinese history and classical literature. Yuanxin grew attached to his uncle but he did not get along with Jiang Qing, whom he considered hysteric and unreasonable. For several years, he did not talk to her. Yuanxin passed the entrance examination to Tsinghua University but transferred to Harbin Military Engineering University, the favorite for children of high military officers. He was still a student when the Cultural Revolution broke out and he became a leader of a rebel faction.

At the beginning of the Cultural Revolution Mao Yuanxin was sympathetic to the senior officials, but after Mao took him aside and explained the problems with these senior officials, Yuanxin became more radical. The first time Mao was interested in hearing Yuanxin's views on political issues was in 1968 when Yuanxin, then a twenty-nine-year-old official in Liaoning, went to Beijing at his uncle's request. Mao asked him detailed questions about the political situation in the Northeast. When his nephew responded, Mao was impressed with his detailed understanding. After 1969, when the PLA tried to unify the different factions, Mao Yuanxin developed a good working relationship with Zhou Enlai, who was supervising this effort. Indeed, Mao Yuanxin played a central role in resolving the differences between the two most powerful leaders in the Northeast, Chen Xilian and Song Renqiong.

In 1973, when Mao Yuanxin was already a party secretary in Liaoning, a university applicant, Zhang Tiesheng, passed in a blank sheet of paper for his entrance examination, explaining that he had been working in the fields and did not have time to study. Yuanxin, finding the case emblematic and an opportunity to back the workers, supported him and the case received national attention. Mao Yuanxin thus had established radical credentials when Mao invited him to Beijing to serve as his liaison with the outside.

Ren Zhongyi

Although he had never lived in Guangdong before 1980 and had visited only once, Ren played such a central role in guiding Guangdong to use to the hilt its special role in experimenting with new systems that he remained there after his retirement in 1985 until his death in 2005. A committed reformer who had excelled as a provincial leader, Ren was a natural choice to lead Guangdong. From 1978 to 1980 Ren was first party secretary of Liaoning, then one of China's most industrialized provinces and far more industrialized than Guangdong. While in Liaoning he had advocated that the province be made into a SEZ. Ren first met with Deng in 1977 before taking up his post in Liaoning, and he was one of Deng's escorts in the Northeast in September 1978 as Deng lit the sparks for reform. In a fall 1978 article in the Liaoning provincial party journal, Ren was among the first provincial leaders to endorse Deng's reform goals and to criticize the "two whatevers." At the Central Party Work Conference in late 1978, Ren was chairman of the Northeast group, in which Chen Yun brought up historical questions that Hua had not acted on.[24]

For his position in Guangdong, Ren was recommended by Premier Zhao Ziyang, who had known Ren as a fellow provincial first party secretary and who shared his views about the need for reform. Because of his longtime service in Guangdong, Zhao had a special interest in developments there.

Ren was a charismatic leader who lit up a room upon entering it. Even in his last years when he walked with a cane and after several operations for cancer, he had a sparkling sense of humor. He joked that after he had his stomach removed he had *"wusuo weiju"* (literally, "nothing to fear," with *wusuo weiju* also a homonym for having "no stomach"), and that, having lost sight in one eye, he could *"yimu liaoran"*— "understand a situation with one glance," but literally "see with one eye."

Born in 1914 near Tianjin, in Wei county, Hebei province, Ren held responsible positions starting in his youth. As a patriotic student at Zhongguo University in Beiping, where he studied political economy for three years, he took part in the December 9, 1935, student movement of patriotic young Chinese students opposed to the Japanese military advances. He then joined the party in 1936 and became a branch secretary with responsibility for over fifty members. He was long known as one of the more progressive intellectuals in the party. Attracted to the ideals of a new people's democracy that supported cooperation among different social classes, he was disturbed by the criticism of dedicated young intellectuals during the Yan'an period.[25]

During World War II, Ren joined the guerrilla forces constantly on the move along a Japanese-held railway. He later became head of the political cadre school in the sixth column of the Eighth Route Army in the Taixi region of western Shandong. He became a vice mayor of Dalian in 1949 and, at age thirty-eight, the first party secretary of Harbin in 1953. He was criticized for his rightist tendencies but was always protected by his superiors, who admired him for his outstanding leadership abilities. In the years before the Cultural Revolution, he was not only party secretary of Harbin, but also a party secretary of Heilongjiang province. During the Cultural Revolution he was "dragged out," paraded with a dunce cap, and criticized more than five hundred times, once for over six hours, for being a rightist and the person most willing to "take the capitalist road" in Harbin. He was sent to the countryside, where he lived for two years in a cow shed and worked as a manual laborer.

Ren's fortunes changed again as the Cultural Revolution was winding down. He was made first party secretary in Heilongjiang and then, in 1978, when the reformers were returning to high positions, he became first party secretary of Liaoning province, where he was given the task of overcoming the tide of leftism in the province under Chen Xilian and Mao's nephew, Mao Yuanxin.

Decades earlier, when Tao Zhu had headed south to lead Guangdong in 1951, he brought with him thousands of northerners who did not mix well with the locals. By contrast, in 1980 when Ren went to Guangdong, he brought a single staff assistant, Lei Yu. By 1980 localism was no longer a threat to central control. Ren Zhongyi followed the advice of Marshal Ye and made good use of the local Guangdong officials who had been recently released by Xi Zhongxun: they in turn were grateful to Ren for providing them an opportunity to provide their services. Ren was close to Hu Yaobang and defended intellectuals within the party. After he retired, he was bold enough to ask publicly why the party could not experiment with political zones, as it had with economic zones.

Ren was known for his ability to make good strategic decisions, especially in situations where there were not yet rules and one had to judge how much higher-level officials would permit. In these difficult circumstances, Ren was widely revered not only for doing what was necessary to promote reform and growth, but for accepting any criticism and protecting those under him who implemented the new procedures. Ren spent his first few months in Guangdong traveling throughout the province, observing conditions, talking with local officials, and reading reports. To promote rapid economic growth, he concentrated on constructing key bridges, roads, and electric power stations. He also encouraged officials under him to be flexible and courageous in attracting industrial investment. As he told his subordinates regarding possible political criticism from Beijing, "If something is not explicitly prohibited, then move ahead. If something is allowed, use it to the hilt."[26]

Wan Li

Like Zhao Ziyang, Wan Li first came to Deng's attention in 1946, when Deng was responsible for Communist activity in the mountainous border region of Jin-Ji-Lu-Yu (Shanxi, Hebei, Shandong, and Henan).[27] Deng had noticed that in certain areas the troops were much better supplied with food and other necessities than elsewhere. When he investigated, he found that Wan Li had helped mobilize local people to gather grain and other supplies and transport them to the frontline troops fighting under his and Liu Bocheng's command. During the civil war, in the absence of regular rail and truck transport, Wan Li was responsible for mobilizing some 1.4 million transport workers to move weapons and supplies, some on carts pulled by donkeys or oxen and much on people's backs or hanging from carrying poles across their shoulders. Wan Li was always a pragmatic, straightforward strong person who wanted to get things done for the good of the people.

Twelve years younger than Deng, Wan Li came from a poor peasant family in Dongping county, located in mountainous western Shandong (famous as the hideout for the rebels in the legend *Water Margin*). In 1933 after his father's death, due to his mother's hard work and sacrifice, Wan was able not only to complete local schools but also to continue his studies in nearby Qufu, at No. 2 Normal School where, in 1936, he became a member of the Communist Party.[28] After graduation, he taught in a modern comprehensive elementary school, where he secretly recruited patriotic youth to join the party. Within a few years Wan Li became head of the party committee in his native county. He was slightly senior to Zhao Ziyang, who was a county party secretary in the neighboring province of Hebei, but in the same border region. There were then twenty-four Communist Party members in Wan Li's county, ten of whom had been personally recruited by Wan. Wan Li rose to be deputy party secretary of Yunxi prefecture, comprising several counties, and a political commissar of a branch district of the PLA *(jun fenqu zhengwei)*. During the civil war, Wan Li served with the forces led by Deng and Liu Bocheng that later became the Second Field Army. As the Communist armies advanced westward and officials were assigned to manage the transition to Communist rule in various areas, Wan Li was briefly assigned to be deputy head of the Nanjing Municipal Finance and Economics Commission and head of the Nanjing Construction Bureau.

In 1950, when Deng became party secretary of the entire Southwest Bureau, Wan Li was made deputy head of the Ministry of Industry in the region, where he was responsible for expanding industrial production. At the time, there was very little industry in the Southwest, and the priorities for new industrial projects favored China's Northeast and the coastal areas. Wan Li's job was to see that the few facilities available in the Southwest were running and that the factories received their needed supplies. Wan Li developed a clear understanding of what was necessary to complete construction projects, and he proved to be a firm disciplinarian, good at mobilizing people to get the job done. After he moved to Beijing, in November 1952, he became deputy minister of construction. After 1956, while concurrently serving as vice mayor and vice party secretary of Beijing, Wan supervised major building projects in Beijing, most notably those around Tiananmen Square, including the Great Hall of the People and the Museum of Chinese History and the Musaum of the Chinese Revolution. For his success in completing these projects, he was praised highly by Chairman Mao.

Trained at a teachers' college and having taught briefly himself, Wan Li enjoyed interacting with intellectuals and was even friendly with some of the dissident scholars. Among high-level officials, he was one who favored allowing more intellectual freedom.

Deng valued Wan Li's capacity to organize and complete large projects. In 1975, after Deng assigned Wan Li to be minister of railways, Deng was pleased with Wan's success in ending the bottlenecks and ensuring the smooth flow of rail transport. In June 1977, Hua Guofeng appointed Wan Li as first party secretary of Anhui province, where the starvation was among the worst in the country. Wan Li, known to be especially sympathetic to the unfortunate, traveled around the province to observe the situation firsthand. After Deng became paramount leader, he encouraged Wan Li to implement whatever policies worked best to eradicate the starvation.

Wan Li was comfortable meeting foreign leaders and, as an accomplished tennis player, was allowed to play with foreign dignitaries like Prime Minister Robert Hawke of Australia and George H. W. Bush when he was the head of the U.S. Liaison Office in Beijing. He also enjoyed bridge. Even before 1952 when they were neighbors in Sichuan, Deng invited Wan Li to play bridge, and after going to Beijing in 1952, they often played together. Typically, they would each have a professional bridge player as a partner and an informal trainer; though Wan Li and his partner sometimes won, Wan acknowledged that Deng won more often and was the better bridge player. They continued to play bridge together throughout the 1980s. But even when they met to play cards, they did not talk about personal matters. Deng was Wan's superior, and Wan Li never thought of Deng as an intimate friend.[29]

Wang Hongwen

Wang Hongwen first came to Mao's attention when Mao saw him on television in July 1967, leading three thousand Shanghai workers in a Communist struggle session. A year earlier, Wang Hongwen, then just thirty-one and a security official at a Shanghai cotton mill, had attacked those taking the "capitalist road" in his factory.[30] On November 9, 1966, Wang was elected leader of the Shanghai Workers' Revolutionary Rebels General Headquarters, and within weeks he was playing a role in the takeover of the Shanghai party and government. In February 1967, he became vice head of the Shanghai Revolutionary Committee, which later became the core of the restructured Shanghai government.[31] By the time Mao saw him on television, then, Wang, poised and tall, was leading Shanghai's largest workers' faction. When Mao asked Shanghai party leader Zhang Chunqiao about Wang, Zhang provided Mao with a brief introduction and Mao liked what he heard.

Wang met Mao's criteria for leadership. He was young and a strong rebel leader. He was also from a peasant family, had served in the military in Korea, and was officially categorized as a worker. Zhang Chunqiao, aware of Mao's high opinion of Wang, allowed Wang to lead the delegation from Shanghai to take part in the 9th Party Congress in April 1969. Mao first met Wang when Wang led a Shanghai delegation to Beijing to take part in the October 1, 1969, National Day celebrations.[32]

Immediately after Lin Biao's crash on September 13, 1971, Wang Hongwen was summoned to Beijing where he was dispatched back to Shanghai to arrest Lin's closest followers.[33] Wang Hongwen did this very successfully, strengthening Mao's favorable impression of him.[34] A year later, on September 7, 1972, Mao had Wang transferred to Beijing and personally received him. Mao, aware that Wang had a low-level educational background, assigned him to read theoretical works, including Marx and Lenin. Mao also suggested that Wang read the story of Liu Penzi in the *Houhan Shu* (History of the Later Han Dynasty). Liu Penzi was a cowherd who at age fifteen was suddenly catapulted to become emperor, but because he was totally unprepared, he was quickly pushed aside. The message was obvious: Wang Hongwen should study and become better prepared than Liu Penzi, and Mao would observe his development.[35] On December 28, 1972, at a conference of the party committee of the Beijing Military Region, Wang was appointed to a prominent position. At that meeting, Ye Jianying and Zhou Enlai spoke of the need to help prepare Wang for a leadership role.[36] Thereafter, under Mao's direction, Wang Hongwen was assigned to spend at least two hours a day reading works on Marxism-Leninism and Mao Zedong Thought.

In March 1973 Wang Hongwen, then head of the Shanghai Revolutionary Committee, in effect the Shanghai government, began attending Politburo meetings, along with Hua Guofeng and Wu De, whom Mao also was observing as potential leaders.[37] In May, Wang Hongwen was put in charge of planning for the 10th Party Congress, forthcoming in August 1973. At that congress, Wang Hongwen, a scarcely known youth, suddenly was catapulted into the position of vice chairman of the party, ahead of both Kang Sheng and Ye Jianying. Although Wang Hongwen made serious efforts to play the role Mao assigned him, he was not respected by other high-level party officials and by mid-1975 Mao had removed him from his major responsibilities.

Xi Zhongxun

In 1934, Xi Zhongxun, then just twenty-one years old, was already a high official under Gao Gang and Liu Zhidan in the small Communist base area in Shaanxi province that had welcomed Mao Zedong and his troops when they arrived exhausted from the Long March. Mao came to regard Xi Zhongxun as very promising, and Xi rose rapidly to become a party secretary in the Northwest Bureau. Xi remained in the Northwest throughout the anti-Japanese war and the civil war.

In 1950, when Peng Dehuai, who had been the top leader in the Northwest Bureau, went off to lead the Chinese troops fighting in the Korean War, Xi Zhongxun briefly served as the bureau's top leader, at the same time that Deng was the top leader of the Southwest Bureau. Later that year, Xi was brought to Beijing to be head of the Central Propaganda Department and in 1953, he was named secretary general of the Administrative Council (later renamed the State Council). In 1959 he became a vice premier as well as secretary general of the State Council.

In 1962, Liu Zhidan's sister-in-law published a novel about Liu Zhidan, glorifying him and describing how he had been mistreated by Mao. Mao suspected Xi Zhongxun of being behind the publication of the novel and as a result demoted him to deputy head of a factory in Loyang. Xi was psychologically wounded by the attacks and was depressed until 1978, when his case was reversed and he was allowed to leave Luoyang and take up a position in Guangdong where he played a critical role in preparing Guangdong to become the nation's experimental area and in negotiating with Beijing officials. His son Xi Jinping in 2011 was selected as the leading candidate for president of China beginning in 2012.

Ye Jianying

Mao knew he could count on Marshal Ye to unify the military after Lin Biao's plane crash in 1971 because of his ability to grasp the big picture, his good judgment, his loyalty, and his lack of personal ambition.[38] He had kept the confidence of Mao ever since the Long March when he had switched his loyalty from Mao's rival Zhang Guotao. Mao said of Ye that "on big issues, he was never muddled" *(dashi bu hutu)*; he played a central role not only in restructuring the army after Lin Biao's crash but in arresting the Gang of Four, assisting Hua Guofeng after Mao's death, and in the return of Deng in 1973 and 1977. Marshal Ye avoided managing things himself and preferred to pass responsibility to others. He did not express strong opinions but was ready to give advice.

A gregarious person, Marshal Ye was known for his ability to win and keep the confidence of people from widely varied backgrounds. During the Cultural Revolution, Ye chose to be on the sidelines rather than get involved in disputes; he was not in an important position at the time of the Cultural Revolution and therefore was not targeted for serious attack. Ye often said *"ban jun ru ban hu"*—serving a lord is like serving a tiger—he knew political involvement was dangerous and preferred to be on the sidelines.

Born in 1897, Ye graduated from Yunnan Military Academy. He also served with Zhou Enlai on the staff of the Whampoa (Huangpu) Military Academy when Lin Biao was a student. Ye took part in the Nanchang and Guangzhou uprisings of 1927, but of the ten military leaders selected to be a marshal in the army, he was the only one who lacked experience leading men into battle. Battle commanders did not consider him one of their own, but they respected him for his long years as a high-level military leader when he was a negotiator and adviser. Ye worked closely with Zhou Enlai during the war years from 1937 to 1949, bringing detailed knowledge of the military situation to negotiations with the Guomindang and with foreigners.

Ye was born in Mei county in mountainous northern Guangdong, the informal Hakka capital that produced many generals and many emigrants. Ye's grandfather had worked as a miner in Malaya, and Ye spent several months in Malaya with his family members who were in business there. Ye was thus far more cosmopolitan than most military leaders. From 1949 to 1952, when Ye was first party secretary of the South China Bureau (including Guangxi and his native province, Guangdong), the South China Bureau was under the Central-South Bureau, headed by Lin Biao. He therefore knew personally many of the top officials who served under Lin. This special relationship served him well in keeping the loyalty of Lin Biao's close associates after Lin Biao's crash. On October 3, 1971, then, scarcely two weeks after Lin Biao's failed escape, Mao and Marshal Ye formed a new structure, "Office of the Central Military Commission," and replaced Lin's followers with members whom they knew were loyal to Mao. The following day, Mao held a meeting of the office *(junwei bangong huiyi)* to launch a campaign to contain the influence that Lin Biao might have had on leaders of the PLA.[39] In February 1972, Ye chaired a meeting that systematically reviewed Lin's errors and issued new directives for the armed forces. Several days after the meeting, under Ye's editorial direction, documents were released spelling out the mistakes made during Lin Biao's twelve years of leadership and the content and procedures to be used in carrying out the consolidation campaign within the PLA.[40]

Marshal Ye continued to enjoy the goodwill of Chairman Mao, and after Mao's death played a key role in arresting the Gang of Four. He then served as a kingmaker, a respected elder, who helped advise Hua Guofeng. He also played a key role in paving the way for Deng's return in 1977, but later did not support Deng's effort to push Hua aside. After Hua was pushed aside, Marshal Ye retired and spent his last years in his native Guangdong.

Yu Qiuli

During the Long March, Yu Qiuli traveled for 192 days with an arm that had been mangled in battle before finally reaching a medical station where it was amputated. He was known for his grit and determination, but also for his resourcefulness.[41] Deng knew Yu Qiuli and his reputation for completing assignments under difficult circumstances. In 1949 Yu marched into Sichuan with the First Field Army, and at the end of 1949 he was assigned first to work in western Sichuan and then to handle logistics as head of rear services in the Southwest Military Region, where Deng was head of the region's military as well as head of the Southwest Bureau. Yu Qiuli, who remained in the military, was reassigned to Beijing shortly after Deng was transferred to Beijing in 1952. In April 1961, when Deng visited the Daqing oilfield, Yu Qiuli had already left the site, but Deng was fully briefed on his work by Yu's former right-hand man Kang Shi'en. Deng was in close contact with Yu Qiuli when they worked together on plans for the "third front": the development of industry and military resources in China's western interior, where they would be insulated from any foreign attack. Unlike Deng who kept more regular hours, Yu Qiuli was a micromanager who put in long hours, going over plans with work associates to make sure that jobs were completed. When problems arose, Yu Qiuli immersed himself until they were solved.

Yu Qiuli skyrocketed to national attention in December 1963 when Mao publicly called him a national hero for his role in creating the Daqing oilfield in the early 1960s. Because oilfields were generally in remote areas protected by the military and because petroleum was essential to military transport, the military was centrally involved in oil exploration and production. As the Soviets withdrew their specialists and stopped supplying petroleum in 1960, it was essential for China to develop its own oilfields. The most promising field was Daqing, in remote Heilongjiang province. China lacked the proper equipment, roads, vehicles, electricity, and trained manpower needed to develop Daqing. At the worksite, workers as well as officials lived in tents and, later, mud housing that they built. Yu Qiuli, as minister of the petroleum industry (a position he had held since 1958), personally went to Daqing where he became the local party secretary, in effect the project manager. He slept on site, and proved to be a resourceful and determined leader. In 1960 when Yu first went to Daqing, Daqing produced 9 percent of the nation's total petroleum. In 1963, after Yu developed Daqing, this ratio had shot up to 46 percent.[42]

In December 1964, Mao, disgusted with the usual cautious balancers who guided planning work, made Yu Qiuli deputy head and secretary general of the State Planning Commission, despite protests by Yu and, even more, by his cautious planner critics who complained that Yu had little background in overall planning work. Mao responded, "Is he only a fierce and daring general *(mengjiang)?* The Ministry of the Petroleum Industry also does planning."[43] Yu was also put in charge of the "Little State Planning Commission," an inner leading group within the State Planning Commission. There Yu guided the development of the Third Five-Year Plan, even though the cautious planners did not share Mao's high regard for Yu. In 1965, with the outbreak of the Vietnam War, Mao directed that the plan focus on national defense needs, including moving defense-related industries farther inland. Yu Qiuli and his project managers relocated these "third front" factories under adverse circumstances. When Yu was attacked by Red Guards, Zhou Enlai arranged for him to be brought to live in Zhongnanhai, safe from the Red Guards but away from his family. In 1970 he was promoted again, to be director of the State Planning Commission.

After Lin Biao's death in September 1971, because of the high regard for Yu in the Rear Services Department of the PLA, he was brought back to the military to ensure that those in the rear services who had been close to Lin Biao were removed. In 1972, when prospects for importing new technologies appeared to be more promising, Yu Qiuli played a role in arranging for China to acquire them. In 1975 Yu visited Japan to lay the groundwork for importing Japanese steel technology. And when Deng was elevated to first vice premier in January 1975, he worked closely with Yu, who not only continued on as director of the State Planning Commission but also became a vice premier. In August 1977 when Deng returned to work, Yu Qiuli was elevated to Politburo membership. Although Chen Yun and the cautious planners used the collapse of an oil platform in the Gulf of Bohai as an excuse for removing Yu from head of the State Planning Commission, Deng arranged for Yu to return to the military as head of the Political Department of the PLA.

Zhao Ziyang

In 1989 Zhao Ziyang became known to the world for his willingness to be punished rather than to send in troops to end the demonstrations in Tiananmen Square.[44] In 1986 Zhao had supervised the high-level study of political reform, but before 1989 he was not known as a strong advocate of freedom and democracy. Foreign leaders knew Zhao as someone with an excellent grasp of international economic issues. And Deng wanted him as premier because he was a brilliant, committed reformer and an experienced official with keen analytic abilities who was able to guide the introduction of Deng's bold economic reforms. In 1980, whereas central government officials were accustomed to operating within the existing framework and had not yet introduced reforms, Zhao was a proven provincial leader who had already begun to experiment with new approaches. In Sichuan, with Beijing's permission, he had experimented with granting more autonomy to industrial enterprises and allowing the rural collectives to divide work responsibilities among smaller-sized groups. No other provincial leader could then compare with Zhao Ziyang in these respects.

After the Communists took over the country in 1949, Deng never worked directly with Zhao, but he had long known of his reputation as a proven provincial leader. Deng first met Zhao in 1946 when Zhao, then twenty-seven, was party secretary in Hua county, Henan province, and district party secretary for several of the surrounding counties. Hua county was then under the jurisdiction of the Jin-Ji-Lu-Yu (Shanxi, Hebei, Shandong, and Henan) Border Region that Deng headed. After Deng went to Beijing in 1952, he became familiar with the role that Zhao, then in his early thirties, was playing as vice provincial party secretary in Guangdong province, and he followed Zhao's progress as he rose to be provincial secretary of Guangdong in 1965. In 1975 Deng chose Zhao to be first party secretary of Sichuan, the most populous province and a region close to Deng's heart: it was Deng's home province, and Deng had been responsible for the area in 1949–1952.

When Deng returned to work in 1977 and began thinking seriously of the next generation of Chinese leaders, he supported including Zhao as an alternate member of the Politburo, which at that time had seventeen regular members. This position would entitle Zhao to attend Politburo meetings and to become familiar with affairs at the party center. But Zhao needed some convincing to take on the job. In January 1978, in a stopover in Sichuan on the way to Nepal, Deng had an opportunity to talk with Zhao about their visions of reform. Zhao explained that it was exciting to "ride the tiger" close to the center of power, but it was also risky. He knew many officials had been destroyed in the process—Lin Biao, Liu Shaoqi, and also Tao Zhu, Zhao's longtime mentor and supporter in Guangdong. Tao had been brought to Beijing by Mao on the eve of the Cultural Revolution to be fourth in command, but then, caught in the currents of the Cultural Revolution, had been attacked and incarcerated: in 1969 he died without receiving proper medical attention. Deng, however, pushed Zhao to go to Beijing to take part in the new reform era, and at the beginning of 1980, Zhao finally agreed.

Born in Henan in 1919 into a rich landlord family, Zhao Ziyang was a natural leader. He was an inspired visionary who always displayed confidence and an easy charm. He attended Kaifeng No. 1 Junior Middle School and Wuhan Senior Middle School. Had he been in United States at the time, he might have attended an American prep school and an Ivy League college (a route that two of his grandchildren later took), where, without effort, he would have been an excellent student and a student leader. By 1938, Zhao was already Communist Party secretary in his native Hua county in Henan. After the civil war ended, Zhao, at age thirty-two, was selected by Tao Zhu, the newly appointed first party secretary in Guangdong, to be his right-hand man. Thus in 1951, while Hu Yaobang, one of the promising young officials in the Southwest, was guiding land reform in northern Sichuan, Zhao Ziyang was guiding land reform in northern Guangdong.

From 1951 to 1965 Tao Zhu gave Zhao a variety of leadership responsibilities and by 1965, when Tao was busy as first party secretary of the Central-South Bureau, Zhao in Guangdong became the youngest provincial first party secretary in the country. He was one of the officials who, after criticism in the Cultural Revolution, returned relatively early: in 1972 he became secretary of the Inner Mongolian Autonomous Region Revolutionary Committee, and in 1974 he returned as first party secretary of Guangdong. Ambitious local leaders commonly cultivated good relations with higher-ups (*la guanxi*) to make their way up the hierarchy. Zhao, however, who was fully backed by Tao Zhu, rose without having to engage in political maneuvering and never became a political wheeler dealer. If Hu Yaobang was moved by his heart and his conscience, Zhao Ziyang was cerebral, with a great ability to grasp foreign practices and to conceive new programs.

Though not as effusive as Hu, Zhao also became a complete favorite of his underlings because of his informality and his easy give-and-take, his readiness to listen to ideas without regard to the status of the speaker, and his quick grasp of a strategy's implications. Although not a political infighter, he displayed a sense of noblesse oblige to the nation as a whole. He was personally privileged but he worked hard to look after the interests of the poor, the students, and the intellectuals. During the Great Leap Forward, for instance, he stretched national policy to deal with the food shortages.[45] When U.S. ambassador Leonard Woodcock, a former union leader representing the great capitalist nation, first met Zhao, who was representing the proletariat class in Communist China, Woodcock said to an aide after the meeting, "Did you see his hands? That guy has never worked a day in his life."[46]

Though Zhao was pleasant and cordial, some fellow officials considered him somewhat aloof and ready to look out for himself. At the beginning of the Cultural Revolution, subordinates who were told by Zhao to resist the Red Guards were upset that Zhao himself quickly handed over to the Red Guards the keys to his office.

In the 1950s, all provincial leaders were deeply involved in rural issues, and Mao recognized in Zhao someone very knowledgeable about agriculture. But even more relevant to Zhao's later work in the reform era was his early experience guiding Communist organizations that operated in the market economy of Hong Kong—including the Bank of China, China Resources (which managed work in Hong Kong for the Chinese economic ministries), New China News Agency (Xinhua), department stores, "patriotic" schools, and labor unions. These organizations reported to Beijing, but they also reported to Guangdong, so through his work with them, Zhao became familiar with the market climate in Hong Kong. Beginning in 1957, too, Guangdong hosted a semiannual trade fair that attracted foreign businesspeople, which gave Zhao a far deeper understanding of the foreign business world than was possible for party secretaries in other provinces.

In 1980 Zhao arrived in Beijing as a well-respected provincial leader, not as a member of the Beijing old-boy club. He had become more familiar with Beijing affairs as an alternate member of the Politburo in August 1977 but he did not become a full member until September 1979. Unlike most officials, who had worked together in Beijing for many years, he did not have established friendships among those working in the Zhongnanhai offices or courtyards. Nor had he taken an active role in Beijing politics and maneuvering. His children, who had lived in the provinces, did not know the children of other high officials through school and social activities. His family suffered not only during the decade of the Cultural Revolution, but also after 1989, when on the eve of the Tiananmen tragedy Zhao was purged and put under house arrest, with no gestures of support offered from Beijing's top political families.

After becoming premier in 1980, Zhao, in addition to guiding the daily work of all branches of government and meeting foreign officials, was responsible for changes in government policy and organization. Earlier, Zhou Enlai had brilliantly managed the work of the government, mastering massive amounts of detailed information, but in his day, policies came from Mao and he did not have to guide a fundamental reorientation of the government. Zhao Ziyang, by contrast, spent much of his time working with think tanks and people then outside of the regular bureaucracy—such as the Economic System Reform Commission and the Research Center for Rural Development—to determine which foreign ideas and practices could be grafted onto existing Chinese institutions. Zhao's responsibility for conceiving new structures worried some bureaucrats who feared Zhao might be reorganizing them out of a job.

Chinese Communist Party
Congresses and Plenums

1956–1992

8th Party Congress, Sept. 15–27, 1956
First plenum: Sept. 28, 1956
Second plenum: Nov. 10–15, 1956
Third plenum: Sept. 20–Oct. 9, 1957
Fourth plenum: May 3, 1958

**8th Party Congress, 2nd Session,
May 5–23, 1958**
Fifth plenum: May 25, 1958
Sixth plenum: Nov. 28–Dec. 10, 1958
Seventh plenum: Apr. 2–5, 1959
Eighth plenum: Aug. 2–16, 1959
Ninth plenum: Jan. 14–18, 1961
Tenth plenum: Sept. 24–27, 1962
Eleventh plenum: Aug. 1–12, 1966
Twelfth plenum: Oct. 13–31, 1968

9th Party Congress, Apr. 1–14, 1969
First plenum: Apr. 28, 1969
Second plenum: Aug. 23–Sept. 6, 1970

10th Party Congress, Aug. 24–28, 1973
First plenum: Aug. 30, 1973
Second plenum: Jan. 8–10, 1975
Third plenum: July 16–21, 1977

11th Party Congress, Aug. 12–18, 1977
First plenum: Aug. 19, 1977
Second plenum: Feb. 18–23, 1978
Third plenum: Dec. 18–22, 1978

Fourth plenum: Sept. 25–28, 1979
Fifth plenum: Feb. 23–29, 1980
Sixth plenum: June 27–29, 1981
Seventh plenum: Aug. 6, 1982

12th Party Congress, Sept. 1–11, 1982
First plenum: Sept. 12–13, 1982
Second plenum: Oct. 11–12, 1983
Third plenum: Oct. 20, 1984
Fourth plenum: Sept. 16, 1985
National Party Representatives
   Conference: Sept. 18–23, 1985
Fifth plenum: Sept. 24, 1985
Sixth plenum: Sept. 28, 1986
Seventh plenum: Oct. 20, 1987

13th Party Congress, Oct. 25–Nov. 1, 1987
First plenum: Nov. 2, 1987
Second plenum: Mar. 15–19, 1988
Third plenum: Sept. 26–30, 1988
Fourth plenum: June 23–24, 1989
Fifth plenum: Nov. 6–9, 1989
Sixth plenum: Mar. 9–12, 1990
Seventh plenum: Dec. 25–30, 1990
Eighth plenum: Nov. 25–29, 1991
Ninth plenum: Oct. 5–9, 1992

14th Party Congress, Oct. 12–18, 1992

Abbreviations

ASEAN	Association of Southeast Asian Nations
CAC	Central Advisory Commission
CAS	Chinese Academy of Sciences
CASS	Chinese Academy of Social Sciences
CMC	Central Military Commission
IMF	International Monetary Fund
JETRO	Japan External Trade Organization
MITI	Ministry of International Trade and Industry (Japan)
NCNA	New China News Agency (Xinhua)
NPC	National People's Congress
PLA	People's Liberation Army
SEZ	special economic zone
TVE	township and village enterprise

Notes

Abbreviations for Notes

CYNP	Zhonggong zhongyang wenxian yanjiushi (Central Chinese Communist Party Literature Research Office), ed., *Chen Yun nianpu: 1905–1995* (A Chronology of Chen Yun: 1905–1995), 3 vols. (Beijing: Zhongyang wenxian chubanshe, 2000)
CYZ	Zhonggong zhongyang wenxian yanjiushi (Central Chinese Communist Party Literature Research Office), ed., *Chen Yun zhuan* (A Biography of Chen Yun), 2 vols. (Beijing: Zhongyang wenxian chubanshe, 2005)
DNSA	Digital National Security Archive (Proquest in cooperation with the National Security Archive), The George Washington University, Washington, D.C.
DXPCR	Rong Deng, *Deng Xiaoping and the Cultural Revolution: A Daughter Recalls the Critical Years* (Beijing: Foreign Languages Press, 2002)
DXPJW	*Deng Xiaoping junshi wenji* (Collection of Deng Xiaoping's Military Writings), 3 vols. (Beijing: Junshi kexue chubanshe and Zhongyang wenxian chubanshe, 2004)
DXPNP-1	Zhonggong zhongyang wenxian yanjiushi (Central Chinese Communist Party Literature Research Office), ed., *Deng Xiaoping nianpu (1904–1974)* (A Chronology of Deng Xiaoping [1904–1974]), 3 vols. (Beijing: Zhongyang wenxian chubanshe, 2009)
DXPNP-2	Zhonggong zhongyang wenxian yanjiushi (Central Chinese Communist Party Literature Research Office), ed., *Deng Xiaoping nianpu: Yi jiu qi wu– yi jiu jiu qi* (A Chronology of Deng Xiaoping: 1975–1997), 2 vols. (Beijing: Zhongyang wenxian chubanshe, 2004)
DXPSTW	Yu Guangyuan, *Deng Xiaoping Shakes the World: An Eyewitness Account of China's Party Work Conference and the Third Plenum (November–December 1978)* (Norwalk, Conn.: EastBridge, 2004)

DXPWJHD	Waijiaobu dang'anguan (Ministry of Foreign Affairs Archives), ed., *Weiren de zuji: Deng Xiaoping waijiao huodong dashiji* (The Tracks of the Great Man: A Chronicle of Deng Xiaoping's Foreign Affairs Activities) (Beijing: Shijie zhishi chubanshe, 1998)
FBIS	Foreign Broadcast Information Service
Guoshi, vol. 8	Shi Yun and Li Danhui, *Zhonghua renmin gongheguo shi: Di 8 juan, Nanyi jixu de "jixu geming": Cong pi Lin dao pi Deng, 1972–1976* (The History of the People's Republic of China, vol. 8: The Difficulties Continuing the "Continuous Revolution": From Criticizing Lin to Criticizing Deng, 1972–1976) (Hong Kong: Dangdai Zhongguo wenhua yanjiu zhongxin, Zhongwen daxue, 2008)
Guoshi, vol. 10	Xiao Donglian, *Zhonghua renmin gongheguo shi: Di 10 juan, Lishi de zhuangui: Cong boluan fanzheng dao gaige kaifang* (History of the People's Republic of China, vol. 10: The Turning Point of History: From Bringing Order out of Chaos to Reform and Opening) (Hong Kong: Dangdai Zhongguo wenhua yanjiu zhongxin, Zhongwen daxue, 2008)
JPRS	Joint Publications Research Service
LPLSRJ	*Li Peng liusi riji* (Li Peng's June 4 Diary), unpublished manuscript, available in the Fairbank Collection, Fung Library, Harvard University
LWMOT	Carter Administration China Policy Oral History Project, Leonard Woodcock and Michel Oksenberg Tapes, Walter P. Reuther Library Archives, Wayne State University
LZQ	Cheng Zhongyuan and Xia Xiangzhen, *Lishi zhuanzhe de qianzou: Deng Xiaoping zai 1975* (The Prelude to the Historical Turning Point: Deng Xiaoping in 1975) (Beijing: Zhongguo qingnian chubanshe, 2003)
Memcon	Memorandum of Conversation
MZDZ	Zhonggong zhongyang wenxian yanjiushi (Central Chinese Communist Party Literature Research Office), ed., *Mao Zedong zhuan, 1949–1976* (A Biography of Mao Zedong, 1949–1976), 2 vols. (Beijing: Zhongyang wenxian chubanshe, 2003)
SWCY	Chen Yun, *Selected Works of Chen Yun,* 3 vols. (1926–1949, 1949–1956, 1956–1994) (Beijing: Foreign Languages Press, 1988, 1997, 1999)
SWDXP-2	Deng Xiaoping, *Selected Works of Deng Xiaoping, 1975–1982* (Beijing: Foreign Languages Press, 1984)
SWDXP-3	Deng Xiaoping, *Selected Works of Deng Xiaoping, 1982–1992* (Beijing: Foreign Languages Press, 1994)
TP	Liang Zhang, comp., and Andrew J. Nathan and Perry Link, eds., *The Tiananmen Papers* (New York: Public Affairs, 2001)
WNZEL	Gao Wenqian, *Wannian Zhou Enlai* (Zhou Enlai in His Later Years) (Carle Place, N.Y.: Mingjing chubanshe, 2003)
WYDXP	Yu Guangyuan, *Wo yi Deng Xiaoping* (Recalling Deng Xiaoping) (Hong Kong: Shidai guoji chuban youxian gongsi, 2005)

YJYNP	Zhongguo renmin jiefangjun junshi kexueyuan (Academy of Military Sciences of the Chinese People's Liberation Army), ed., *Ye Jianying nianpu, 1897–1986* (A Chronology of Ye Jianying, 1897–1986), 2 vols. (Beijing: Zhongyang wenxian chubanshe, 2007)
YJYZ	Fan Shuo and Ding Jiaqi, *Ye Jianying zhuan* (Biography of Ye Jianying) (Beijing: Dangdai Zhongguo chubanshe, 1995)
YJZGJSK	Fan Shuo, *Ye Jianying zai guanjian shike* (Ye Jianying at the Critical Time) (Shenyang: Liaoning renmin chubanshe, 2001)
ZGGCDLD	Zhonggong zhongyang dangshi yanjiushi (Central Chinese Communist Party History Research Office), *Zhongguo gongchandang xin shiqi lishi dashiji, 1978.12–2002.5* (A Chronological History of the Chinese Communist Party in the New Period, December 1978–May 2002) (Beijing: Zhonggong dangshi chubanshe, rev. ed., 2002)

Preface

1. *SWDXP-3,* p. 307.

Introduction

1. Some earlier writings on Deng use the Wade-Giles transliteration of his name: Teng Hsiao-p'ing. Throughout this book I use the standard pinyin transliteration of his name, Deng Xiaoping, which is the name he used from 1931 until his death in 1997. Deng's father gave him the name Xiansheng, but at the suggestion of the teacher in his family school, his name was changed to Deng Xixuan, which was also the name he used in his school years and in France. In the Soviet Union he was known as "Krezov" but at Sun Yat-sen University as "Ivan Sergeevich Dozorov." He took the name "Xiaoping" after returning to China in 1927. Some thought the name appropriate since he was short *(xiao)* and his head was flat *(ping)*. He took various pseudonyms at different stages while he was in the underground from 1927 to 1931.

2. Interview with a British diplomat who accompanied MacLehose, March 2001.

3. As with many aphorisms associated with Deng's name, this one was not coined by Deng. The first record of Deng's use of this expression was March 22, 1966. See *DXPNP-2,* 2:1902.

4. *MZDZ,* 2:1674.

5. Benjamin I. Schwartz, *In Search of Wealth and Power: Yen Fu and the West* (Cambridge: Belknap Press of Harvard University Press, 1964). For a basic introduction to Chinese imperial history and for references to other works, see John King Fairbank, ed., *The Chinese World Order: Traditional China's Foreign Relations* (Cambridge: Harvard University Press, 1968); John King Fairbank and Merle Goldman,

China: A New History, 2d exp. ed. (Cambridge: Harvard University Press, 2006); Jonathan D. Spence, *The Search for Modern China* (New York: W. W. Norton, 1990); Paul A. Cohen, *China Unbound: Evolving Perspectives on the Chinese Past* (Stanford, Calif.: Stanford University Press, 2002); Denis Twitchett and John King Fairbank, eds., *The Cambridge History of China* (New York: Cambridge University Press, 1978–); and Gungwu Wang, *To Act Is to Know: Chinese Dilemmas* (Singapore: Times Academic Press, 2002). For work incorporating recent scholarship on the Qing, the last dynasty, see also Mark C. Elliott, *Emperor Qianlong: Son of Heaven, Man of the World* (New York: Longman, 2009); R. Kent Guy, *Qing Governors and Their Provinces: The Evolution of Territorial Administration in China, 1644–1796* (Seattle: University of Washington Press, 2010); William T. Rowe, *China's Last Empire: The Great Qing* (Cambridge: Belknap Press of Harvard University Press, 2009). For Sun Yat-sen, see Marie-Claire Bergère, *Sun Yat-sen* (Stanford, Calif.: Stanford University Press, 1998). For Chiang Kai-shek, see Jay Taylor, *The Generalissimo: Chiang Kai-shek and the Struggle for Modern China* (Cambridge: Belknap Press of Harvard University Press, 2009). For the Chinese revolution, see Lucian Bianco, *Origins of the Chinese Revolution, 1915–1949* (Stanford, Calif.: Stanford University Press, 1971). And for Mao Zedong, see Philip Short, *Mao: A Life* (New York: Henry Holt and Co., 1999). For Mao's writings and speeches, see Stuart R. Schram, ed., *Mao's Road to Power: Revolutionary Writings, 1912–1949* (Armonk, N.Y.: M. E. Sharpe, 1992–2005), 10 projected volumes, 7 volumes published to date, 1912–1941.

6. Notes from the meeting were provided to me by a participant, Merle Goldman.

1. From Revolutionary to Builder to Reformer

1. At the time of Deng Xiaoping's birth, the small village of Paifang was called Yaopingli, within the larger administrative village of Wangxi Xiang. Later these names were changed to Paifang village and Xiexing town. See *DXPNP-1,* 1:1, August 22, 1904.

2. Deng's daughter Deng Rong (Maomao) writes about the family background in *Deng Xiaoping: My Father* (New York: Basic Books, 1995). This section also draws on two trips to Guang'an county that included visits to Deng's home and local museums, interviews with local historians, as well as interviews with Deng Rong, 2002–2006.

3. *DXPNP-1,* 1:5, 1915.

4. Ibid., 1:7, October 17–18, 1919.

5. Geneviève Barman and Nicole Dulioust, "Les années Françaises de Deng Xiaoping," *Vingtième Siècle: Revue d'histoire,* no. 20 (October–December 1988): 19; *DXPNP-1,* 1:10, October 19, 1920. Deng Rong also describes her father's study and work experience in France in her book *Deng Xiaoping: My Father,* pp. 58–79.

6. *DXPNP-1,* 1:11, January 12, 1921.

7. Ibid., 1:12, April 2, 1921.

8. Ibid., 1:17, February 17–19, 1923.

9. Ibid., 1:17–18, March 7, 1923.

10. Ibid., 1:19, June 11, 1923, and 1:20, February 1, 1924.

11. Ibid., 1:19, July 13–15, 16, 1924.

12. Marilyn Levine, *The Guomindang in Europe: A Sourcebook of Documents* (Berkeley, Calif.: Institute of East Asian Studies, University of California, 2000), pp. 90–93; Barman and Dulioust, "Les années Françaises de Deng Xiaoping," 30; interviews with Marilyn Levine, n.d.

13. Barman and Dulioust, "Les années Françaises de Deng Xiaoping," 34.

14. For a description of the life and activities of the Chinese students in France, see Marilyn A. Levine, *The Found Generation: Chinese Communists in Europe during the Twenties* (Seattle: University of Washington Press, 1993); Geneviève Barman and Nicole Dulioust, "The Communists in the Work and Study Movement in France," *Republican China* 13, no. 2 (April 1988): 24–39; and Deng Rong, *Deng Xiaoping: My Father.*

15. Alexander Pantsov and Daria Alexandrovna Spuchnik, "Deng Xiaoping in Moscow: Lessons from Bolshevism," trans. Steven I. Levine, on deposit in the Fairbank Collection, Fung Library, Harvard University. Pantsov and Spuchnik were given full access to the files of the Soviet party archives pertaining to Chinese students in the Soviet Union. Also interviews with Alexander Pantsov, n.d.

16. Pantsov and Spuchnik, "Deng Xiaoping in Moscow."

17. Ibid., p. 12.

18. Ibid., p. 11.

19. Ibid.

20. Deng Rong, *Deng Xiaoping: My Father.*

21. Teng Hsiao Ping [Deng Xiaoping], "Economic Reconstruction in the Taihang Region," in Stuart Gelder, ed., *The Chinese Communists* (Westport, Conn.: Hyperion Press, 1946), p. 201.

22. Interviews with party historians in the Taihang area, n.d.

23. Jay Taylor, *The Generalissimo: Chiang Kai-shek and the Struggle for Modern China* (Cambridge: Belknap Press of Harvard University Press, 2009).

24. Zhonggong zhongyang wenxian yanjiushi Deng Xiaoping yanjiu zu (Central Chinese Communist Party Literature Research Office, Research Team on Deng Xiaoping), ed., *Deng Xiaoping zishu* (Deng Xiaoping in His Own Words) (Beijing: Jiefangjun chubanshe, 2005), p. 1.

25. For a detailed description of this process, see Ezra F. Vogel, *Canton under Communism* (Cambridge: Harvard University Press, 1969).

26. *DXPNP-1,* 2:1065.

27. See, for example, ibid., 2:1133, September 16, 1953.

28. Vladislav M. Zubok, "Deng Xiaoping and the Sino-Soviet Split, 1956–63," *Cold War International History Project Bulletin,* no. 10 (1997): 152–162; Jian Chen, "Deng Xiaoping and Mao's 'Continuous Revolution' and the Path toward the Sino-Soviet Split: A Rejoinder," *Cold War International History Project Bulletin,* no. 10 (1997): 162–182.

29. For Deng's role in the various activities related to the 8th Party Congress, see *DXPNP-1,* 2:1249–1250, August 17, 1955; 2:1261, October 14, 1955; 2:1271, February 6, 1956; 2:1303–1318, August 10–September 28, 1956. The congress documents are found in *Eighth National Congress of the Communist Party of China* (Peking: Foreign Languages Press, 1956), pp. 1–390.

30. *Khrushchev Remembers: The Last Testament,* trans. and ed. Strobe Talbott (Boston: Little, Brown, 1974), p. 253.

31. Ibid., p. 281.

32. Jasper Becker, *Hungry Ghosts: Mao's Secret Famine* (New York: Free Press, 1996); Frank Dikötter, *Mao's Great Famine: The History of China's Most Devastating Catastrophe, 1958–1962* (New York: Walker, 2010); Yang Jisheng, *Mubei: Zhongguo liushi niandai da jihuang ji shi* (Tombstone: Record of the Famine in China During the 1960s), 2 vols. (Hong Kong: Tiandi tushu youxian gongsi, 2008).

33. Interviews with Deng Rong, 2002–2006.

34. Zubok, "Deng Xiaoping and the Sino-Soviet Split, 1956–63," 152–162; Chen, "Deng Xiaoping and Mao's 'Continuous Revolution' and the Path toward the Sino-Soviet Split," 162–182.

35. Roderick MacFarquhar and Michael Schoenhals, *Mao's Last Revolution* (Cambridge: Belknap Press of Harvard University Press, 2006).

2. Banishment and Return

1. *DXPCR,* pp. 108, 117.

2. Ibid., pp. 106–115. See also the author's notes from a visit to the factory and discussions with local people at the factory, November 2008.

3. *DXPCR,* pp. 133–147.

4. Ibid., pp. 148–154.

5. Ibid., p. 185.

6. A contrast with Chen Yi was made by Ji Chaozhu, who served as interpreter for both Deng and Chen. Interviews with Ji Chaozhu, April 2002, November 2006, and April 2009.

7. Interviews with Li Shenzhi, March 2001 and January 2002.

8. *DXPCR,* pp. 120–132; Wu Meng, Xiong Cheng, and Li Xiaochuan, "Deng Xiaoping zai Jiangxi Xinjianxian de rizi" (Deng Xiaoping's Days in Xinjian County of Jiangxi Province), *Bainianchao,* no. 1 (2003), reprinted in Yang Tianshi, ed., *Deng*

Xiaoping xiezhen (A Portrait of Deng Xiaoping) (Shanghai: Shanghai cishu chuban-she, 2005), p. 55; and interviews with Deng Rong, 2002–2006.

9. *DXPCR,* p. 179.

10. Interview with Deng Lin, July 2007.

11. Interviews with Deng Rong, 2002–2008.

12. *DXPCR,* p. 103.

13. Ibid., p. 181.

14. Ibid., pp. 140–145.

15. Ibid., pp. 191–194; interview with Shen Zaiwang, one of Li Jingquan's children who took part in the visit, December 2007.

16. Interview with Deng Lin, July 2007.

17. Maomao [Deng Rong], *Wo de fuqin Deng Xiaoping: "Wen ge" sui yue* (My Father Deng Xiaoping: The Cultural Revolution Years) (Beijing: Zhongyang wenxian chubanshe, 2000), p. 223.

18. Benjamin Yang, *Deng: A Political Biography* (Armonk, N.Y.: M. E. Sharpe, 1998), pp. 215, 267. Yang was Pufang's classmate at Peking University.

19. Interviews with Deng Rong, 2002–2006.

20. *DXPCR,* p. 244.

21. *Guoshi,* vol. 8, p. 197.

22. Zhonggong zhongyang wenxian yanjiushi Deng Xiaoping yanjiu zu (Central Chinese Communist Party Literature Research Office, Research Team on Deng Xiaoping), ed., *Deng Xiaoping zishu* (Deng Xiaoping in His Own Words) (Beijing: Jiefangjun chubanshe, 2005), p. 125.

23. *DXPCR,* p. 192.

24. Philip Short, *Mao: A Life* (New York: Henry Holt, 2000), pp. 588–599.

25. On Deng being instructed not to send more letters, see *DXPCR,* p. 187. For more on the letter he did send, see *DXPCR,* pp. 182–184. For an account of the Lin Biao affair and the events before and after the crash, see Harrison E. Salisbury, *The New Emperors: China in the Era of Mao and Deng* (Boston: Little, Brown, 1992), pp. 275–306. See also Frederick C. Teiwes and Warren Sun, *The Tragedy of Lin Biao: Riding the Tiger during the Cultural Revolution, 1966–1971* (Honolulu: University of Hawaii Press, 1996). Teiwes and Sun emphasize that Lin Biao originally had wanted to stay out of politics, that it was Mao who brought Lin into politics, that Lin did not depart from Mao's policies, and that the tensions in the year before Lin's death were due to Mao's initiatives to weaken Lin's control.

26. *DXPCR,* p. 184.

27. Mao's personal physician, Li Zhisui, reports that Mao's "physical decline after the Lin Biao affair was dramatic . . . he became depressed. He took to his bed and lay there all day. . . . [He lay] in bed for nearly two months." See Zhisui Li, with the editorial assistance of Anne F. Thurston, *The Private Life of Chairman Mao: The Mem-*

oirs of Mao's Personal Physician (New York: Random House, 1994), pp. 542–543. For an account of Mao's growing suspicions of Lin Biao in the year before the crash, see Short, *Mao: A Life,* pp. 588–599.

28. *MZDZ,* 2:1610, 1616–1618. On Mao's medical condition, see Li, with the editorial assistance of Thurston, *The Private Life of Chairman Mao.*

29. *WNZEL,* pp. 356–357. Mao's doctor reports, "As always when adversity sent him to bed, Mao was thinking through a new political strategy." See Li, with the editorial assistance of Thurston, *The Private Life of Chairman Mao,* p. 543.

30. Interviews with Zhou's interpreter Ji Chaozhu, April 2002, November 2006, and April 2009.

31. *DXPCR,* pp. 191–192.

32. Ibid.

33. *WNZEL,* pp. 363–364.

34. *DXPCR,* p. 242.

35. *MZDZ,* 2:1621.

36. *WNZEL,* p. 362.

37. Ibid., pp. 356–357.

38. Ibid., pp. 359–368.

39. Frederick Teiwes and Warren Sun, *The End of the Maoist Era: Chinese Politics during the Twilight of the Cultural Revolution, 1972–1976* (Armonk, N.Y.: M. E. Sharpe, 2007), p. 59.

40. Teiwes and Sun document Zhou's decision to doctor a picture taken of Zhou shaking President Nixon's hand by removing the picture of the interpreter, Ji Chaozhu, and replacing it with a picture of Wang Hairong, Mao's trusted relative who was in fact not a competent interpreter. See Teiwes and Sun, *End of the Maoist Era,* pp. 29–30.

41. *WNZEL,* pp. 356–358.

42. John Holdridge, personal communication, n.d.

43. *DXPCR,* pp. 192–193; *WNZEL,* pp. 364–368.

44. Maomao, *Wode fuqin Deng Xiaoping,* p. 222.

45. *DXPCR,* pp. 198–200.

46. Ibid., pp. 201–202.

47. *Deng Xiaoping tongzhi de xin: Yi jiu qi er nian ba yue san ri* (Comrade Deng Xiaoping's Letter of August 3, 1972), unpublished document available in the Fairbank Collection, Fung Library, Harvard University.

48. *DXPCR,* pp. 209–210.

49. *Guoshi,* vol. 8, p. 202.

50. *MZDZ,* 2:1650.

51. *Guoshi,* vol. 8, p. 202.

52. *DXPCR,* pp. 214–239.

53. Shu Huiguo, "Hongse dadi weiren xing" (The Travels of the Great Man in the

Red World), in Zhonggong zhongyang wenxian yanjiushi (Central Chinese Communist Party Literature Research Office), ed., *Huiyi Deng Xiaoping* (Remembering Deng Xiaoping), 3 vols. (Beijing: Zhongyang wenxian chubanshe, 1998), 3:199. Deng said, "Wo hai keyi gao 20 nian."

54. *DXPCR*, pp. 242–243. Although Jiang Qing later claimed that she had not initially opposed Deng's return and had supported him (Teiwes and Sun, *End of the Maoist Era*, pp. 180, 202), party historians support Deng Rong's view that Jiang Qing had resisted his return. See *MZDZ*, 2:1650.

55. *WNZEL*, pp. 504–505; *DXPCR*, pp. 246–247.

56. *DXPCR*, pp. 242–243.

57. *DXPNP-1*, 3:1973, March 28, 29, 1973.

58. Ibid., 3:1973, March 29, 1973.

59. *DXPCR*, pp. 244–246. For the Sihanouk banquet, see *DXPWJHD*.

60. *DXPWJHD*, pp. 71–81; *DXPNP-1*, 1:1974–1990.

61. *WNZEL*. The English version is much abbreviated. See Wenqian Gao, *Zhou Enlai: The Last Perfect Revolutionary; A Biography* (New York: PublicAffairs, 2007).

62. Interview with Zhang Hanzhi, English teacher and one of his interpreters, who first met Mao in 1963, October and December 2006. See also Gao, *Zhou Enlai*, pp. 237–240.

63. Interview with Zhang Hanzhi, October 2006.

64. This account draws heavily on *WNZEL* and the English translation, Gao, *Zhou Enlai*. For a decade Gao had been deputy head of a unit in the Central Chinese Communist Party Literature Research Office. Critics have argued that some of Gao's interpretations go beyond the data and that there are other, more plausible explanations. Gao claims, for example, that Mao lit firecrackers to celebrate Zhou's death, but it is common for firecrackers to go off during the New Year's festivities; this could have been the reason that firecrackers were going off.

65. *WNZEL*.

66. *DXPCR*, p. 210.

67. *MZDZ*, 2:1655.

68. Barbara Barnouin and Changgen Yu, *Ten Years of Turbulence* (New York: Kegan Paul International, 1993), pp. 248–249.

69. *DXPCR*, pp. 252–254; Richard Evans, *Deng Xiaoping and the Making of Modern China* (New York: Viking, 1994), pp. 196–197.

70. *MZDZ*, 2:1661.

71. Teiwes and Sun, *End of the Maoist Era*, p. 97.

72. *MZDZ*, 2:1654. For a fuller account of the congress, see ibid., pp. 93–109.

73. *DXPNP-1*, 3:1976–1977.

74. *MZDZ*, 2:1661.

75. Evans, *Deng Xiaoping and the Making of Modern China*, p. 197.

76. Patrick Tyler, *A Great Wall: Six Presidents and China; An Investigative History*

(New York: PublicAffairs, 1999), pp. 159–164; William Burr, ed., *The Kissinger Transcripts: The Top Secret Talks with Beijing and Moscow* (New York: New Press, 1998), pp. 124–128.

77. Tyler, *A Great Wall*, pp. 168–169. See also Burr, *The Kissinger Transcripts*, pp. 166–169. The meeting between Kissinger and Mao is on pp. 179–199.

78. DNSA, CH00277, Kissinger and Zhou Enlai, November 11, 1973. Many of the meetings recorded in the DNSA are also available in Burr, *The Kissinger Transcripts*.

79. DNSA, CH00278, November 12, 1973; DNSA, CH00284, November 14, 1973.

80. Kissinger's own later accounts of these visits are contained in Henry Kissinger, *Years of Renewal* (New York: Simon and Schuster, 1999), pp. 136–166. Many of the documents with commentary are published in Burr, *The Kissinger Transcripts*.

81. *WNZEL*, p. 461.

82. Ibid., p. 502.

83. Many officials criticized during the Cultural Revolution felt deep resentment toward those, including Zhou, who continued to cooperate with Mao. Deng remarked to Kissinger that "though Zhou had undoubtedly eased the fate of many, he had never actually tried to reverse the policies which had caused the suffering in the first place." See Kissinger, *Years of Renewal*, p. 160.

84. *WNZEL*, p. 472; Gao, *Zhou Enlai*, pp. 242–247.

85. *WNZEL*, pp. 505–506; Gao, *Zhou Enlai*, p. 247. (Warren Sun questions whether he joined the CMC at that time or a year later.)

86. *DXPNP-1*.

87. Salisbury, *The New Emperors*, p. 296.

88. Evans, *Deng Xiaoping and the Making of Modern China*, p. 197.

89. *WNZEL*, pp. 473–474.

90. Teiwes and Sun, *End of the Maoist Era*, pp. 131–139; ibid., pp. 473–474, 531–533.

91. Gao, *Zhou Enlai*, pp. 256–259, 262.

92. *WNZEL*, pp. 531–533.

93. Ibid., pp. 506–507, 527–528.

94. *DXPCR*, pp. 264–265.

95. Interview with Zhang Hanzhi, December 2006. Zhang married Foreign Minister Qiao Guanhua in 1973 after the death of Qiao's first wife.

96. *DXPCR*, pp. 264–265.

97. Ibid., pp. 266–268.

98. Interview with Jiang Changbin, Central Party School, January 2002.

99. Kissinger, *Years of Renewal*, p. 164.

100. Ibid., pp. 869–886.

101. Ibid., p. 868.

102. Ibid., p. 164.

103. Ibid., pp. 163–164.

104. Ibid., p. 163.

105. Interview with Shi Yanhua, Deng's interpreter during the trip, December 2007.

106. Interviews with Zhang Hanzhi, wife of Qiao Guanhua and an interpreter for the delegation, October and December 2006.

107. *DXPCR*, pp. 268–270.

108. *DXPWJHD*, pp. 88–117.

109. Deng's interview with the delegation of American university presidents, November 14, 1974. I am indebted to Merle Goldman, who took part in the delegation, for sharing her notes.

110. *LZQ*, p. 1.

111. Ibid., pp. 1–16.

112. *DXPCR*, p. 274.

113. See Short, *Mao: A Life*, p. 618.

114. *WNZEL*, pp. 528–530.

115. Ibid. See also *DXPCR*, pp. 276–277; *Guoshi*, vol. 8, pp. 377–409.

116. *DXPCR*, p. 281.

117. Evans, *Deng Xiaoping and the Making of Modern China*, pp. 202–203.

118. *DXPCR*, pp. 275–280.

119. *WNZEL*, pp. 501–509.

3. Bringing Order under Mao

1. *LZQ*, p. 25; Zhang Hua, *Deng Xiaoping yu 1975 nian de Zhongguo* (Deng Xiaoping and China in 1975) (Beijing: Zhonggong dangshi chubanshe, 2004).

2. *WNZEL*.

3. Ibid.

4. Interview with party historians with access to the letters exchanged between Mao and Jiang Qing, n.d.

5. *LZQ*, p. 178.

6. Zhou Enlai, "Report on the Work of the Government," January 13, 1975, in *Documents of the First Session of the Fourth National People's Congress of the People's Republic of China* (Peking: Foreign Languages Press, 1975).

7. *LZQ*, pp. 44–45; interview with Nancy Tang, April 2002.

8. *DXPNP-2*, February 1, 1975.

9. *DXPNP-2*, May 29, 1975. See also *LZQ*, pp. 45–47.

10. Zhang Hua, *Deng Xiaoping yu 1975 nian de Zhongguo*, pp. 70–74.

11. *DXPNP-2*, January 25, 1975; *SWDXP-2*, pp. 13–15.

12. Jonathan D. Pollack, "Rebuilding China's Great Wall: Chinese Security in the

1980s," in Paul H. B. Godwin, ed., *The Chinese Defense Establishment: Continuity and Change in the 1980s* (Boulder, Colo.: Westview, 1983), pp. 3–20; Paul H. B. Godwin, "Mao Zedong Revised: Deterrence and Defense in the 1980s," in Godwin, ed., *The Chinese Defense Establishment,* pp. 21–40; June Teufel Dreyer, "Deng Xiaoping: The Soldier," *The China Quarterly,* no. 135 (September 1993): 536–550.

13. *DXPNP-2,* January 25, 1975; *DXPJW,* 3:4–6, January 19, 1975.

14. *LZQ,* pp. 424–425; *DXPNP-2,* January 12, 1975.

15. *DXPJW,* 3:1–3.

16. Deng Xiaoping, "Dangqian junshi gongzuo de jige wenti" (Some Issues in Our Current Military Work), January 14, 1975, key points in Deng's response after hearing reports from staff members in the General Staff Department, ibid., 3:1–3; Deng Xiaoping, "Guofang gongye jundui zhuangbei gongzuo de jidian yijian" (Some Opinions on the National Defense Industry and Work on Military Equipment), May 4, 1975, in response to reports of the Standing Committee of the CMC, ibid., 3:20–25; Deng Xiaoping, "Yao jianli yange de kexue guanli he keyan shengchan zhidu" (We Must Establish Strict Scientific Management and a System for Scientific Production), May 19, 1975, a talk to the Standing Committee of the CMC in response to reports of the Science and Technology Commission and the No. 7 Ministry of Machine Building (missiles), ibid., 3:26–27.

17. William Burr, ed., *The Kissinger Transcripts: The Top Secret Talks with Beijing and Moscow* (New York: New Press, 1998), p. 308. For the context of the talks and the memoranda of the conversations, see pp. 265–321.

18. *LZQ,* p. 398.

19. For example, at a forum of the General Staff, Deng explicitly stated that there was no hurry to prepare the troops for battle. See *DXPJW,* 3:9.

20. Ibid., 3:9–13.

21. *LZQ,* pp. 404–405; *DXPNP-2,* January 19 and 25, 1975; *DXPJW,* 3:6–8; *SWDXP-2,* pp. 27–28.

22. *DXPJW,* 3:1–3.

23. *LZQ,* pp. 407–408.

24. Ibid., pp. 415–417.

25. Ibid., p. 416.

26. *DXPJW,* 3:26–27, May 19, 1975.

27. *LZQ,* pp. 408, 412–415.

28. Ibid., p. 94.

29. Ibid., pp. 107–108; *DXPNP-2,* May 19, 1975.

30. Interviews with Zhang Xingxing, deputy director of the Institute for Contemporary China Research, 2006.

31. Harrison E. Salisbury, *The New Emperors: China in the Era of Mao and Deng* (Boston: Little, Brown, 1992), p. 334.

32. *LZQ,* pp. 55–56.

33. Salisbury, *The New Emperors,* pp. 333–334. Salisbury interviewed Wan Li on October 7, 1987.

34. Wang Lixin, *Yao chimi zhao Wan Li: Anhui nongcun gaige shilu* (If You Want Rice, Find Wan Li: The True Record of Rural Reform in Anhui) (Beijing: Beijing tushuguan chubanshe, 2000), p. 22.

35. *LZQ,* pp. 57–59.

36. Ibid., pp. 54–56.

37. *LZQ,* pp. 57–61.

38. The Chinese terminology for provincial secretaries (the highest party positions in the province) changed frequently and varied from province to province. Generally, before 1982 there were several provincial party secretaries in each province, one of whom was designated "first party secretary." Sometimes the other party secretaries were numbered in order, sometimes they were listed as deputy party secretaries, and sometimes they were called secretaries of the provincial party Secretariat. Those other provincial secretaries were each responsible for a sector *(xitong),* such as political-legal, industry-transport, commerce-trade, or education-culture. Often the changes in title do not reflect changes in responsibility. Even Chinese authors do not always use the correct title. After the 12th Party Congress in 1982, which gave new emphasis to collective leadership, the term "first secretary" was gradually dropped in most provinces and by 1985 was no longer in use. One secretary, however, was still given the overall top responsibility. In the English edition of this work, I refer to the top provincial party secretary as "first party secretary" regardless of the era and refer to the others simply as provincial party secretaries.

39. *LZQ,* p. 62.

40. *SWDXP-2,* pp. 16–19. Tang Tsou, in his review of Deng's *Selected Works,* writes that there are very few changes from the original texts. See Tang Tsou, "Review: The Historic Change in Direction and Continuity with the Past," *The China Quarterly,* no. 98 (April 1984): 320–347.

41. *LZQ,* pp. 58, 67–68.

42. Ibid., pp. 64, 68.

43. *DXPCR,* pp. 298–299.

44. *LZQ,* pp. 68–69.

45. Ibid., pp. 69–70.

46. Ibid., p. 70.

47. *DXPCR,* p. 299.

48. *LZQ,* pp. 70–71.

49. Ibid., pp. 71, 77.

50. *DXPNP-2,* March 22, 1975; *LZQ,* pp. 73–74.

51. *DXPNP-2,* April 18–26, 1975.

52. *LZQ,* pp. 81–84.

53. Ibid., pp. 429–445, 465.

54. Ibid., p. 456.

55. Ibid., pp. 76, 82, 126.

56. Ibid., pp. 113–114.

57. Ibid., p. 125.

58. Ibid., pp. 118–120.

59. Ibid., pp. 126–133.

60. Ibid., pp. 142–153.

61. Ibid., p. 125.

62. Ibid., pp. 147–149.

63. Ibid., pp. 150–152.

64. *DXPNP-2,* May 21, 1975.

65. *DXPNP-2,* May 29, 1975.

66. *LZQ,* pp. 163–166.

67. Ibid., p. 166.

68. Ibid., p. 169.

69. Ibid., pp. 169–170.

70. Ibid., pp. 443–465; Frederick Teiwes and Warren Sun, *The End of the Maoist Era: Chinese Politics during the Twilight of the Cultural Revolution, 1972–1976* (Armonk, N.Y.: M. E. Sharpe, 2007), pp. 245–251, 274–282; Keith Forster, *Rebellion and Factionalism in a Chinese Province: Zhejiang, 1966–1976* (Armonk, N.Y.: M. E. Sharpe, 1990); interview with Ji Humin, son of Ji Dengkui, October 2007.

71. *LZQ,* p. 445.

72. Ibid., pp. 445–446.

73. Ibid., p. 446.

74. From an interview conducted by Cheng Zhongyuan, in *LZQ,* p. 454.

75. Ibid., p. 465.

76. *DXPNP-2,* April 18–26, 1975.

77. Ibid., April 18, 1975.

78. Ibid., April 27, 1975.

79. Ibid., May 3, 1975.

80. Ibid., May 27, June 3, 1975.

81. Ibid., July 12–17, 1975; *DXPWJHD,* May 12 to May 18, 1975.

82. Interview with Jacques Chirac, *China Daily,* August 23, 2004.

4. Looking Forward under Mao

1. *LZQ,* pp. 202–203; *WYDXP,* p. 5.

2. *SWDXP-2,* pp. 24–26.

3. *LZQ,* pp. 537–540.

4. Ibid., p. 208.

5. Material from this section on the Political Research Office comes from interviews with Yu Guangyuan, a senior member of the Political Research Office, and Zhu Jiamu, party secretary of the theory group of the Political Research Office. See also *WYDXP.* For biographical information on Hu Qiaomu, see Key People in the Deng Era, p. 725.

6. *LZQ,* p. 213.

7. Ibid., pp. 204–208.

8. Ibid., pp. 212–213.

9. *DXPNP-2,* July 13, July 18, and August 8, 1975, p. 69n; ibid., pp. 213–215.

10. It held meetings in 1975 on June 29; July 23; August 26; September 13, 19, 25, and 26; October 10, 14, and 24; and November 10, 15; as well as on January 17, 1976.

11. *LZQ,* pp. 233–272; Frederick Teiwes and Warren Sun, *The End of the Maoist Era: Chinese Politics during the Twilight of the Cultural Revolution, 1972–1976* (Armonk, N.Y.: M. E. Sharpe, 2007), pp. 324–339.

12. *LZQ,* pp. 241–243.

13. *DXPNP-2,* September 20, 1975.

14. *SWDXP-2,* pp. 41–44.

15. For a listing of differences in the two drafts, see *LZQ,* pp. 265–266.

16. Ibid., pp. 252–256.

17. Ibid.; *DXPNP-2,* December 25, 1975.

18. *LZQ,* pp. 242–243. Some concessions were made to localities with higher incomes; they were permitted to spend more. See pp. 239–241.

19. Ibid., pp. 353–357.

20. Ibid., p. 353.

21. Ibid., pp. 353–357.

22. Ibid., pp. 222–224.

23. Ibid., p. 367.

24. Ibid., pp. 364–365.

25. Ibid., pp. 366–367.

26. Ibid., pp. 374–380; *WYDXP,* pp. 68–70.

27. *LZQ,* pp. 371–374.

28. Ibid., pp. 381–386.

29. Ibid., p. 390.

30. Ibid.

31. Ibid., pp. 389–392.

32. Ibid., pp. 390–392.

33. Ibid., pp. 392–394; Wu De, *Wu De koushu: Shinian fengyu jishi; Wo zai Bei-*

jing gongzuo de yixie jingli (Wu De Oral History: A Record of the History of Ten Years of Storms; Some Personal Experiences) (Beijing: Dangdai chubanshe, 2004), pp. 166–173; *WYDXP*, pp. 94–97.

34. *LZQ*, pp. 226–232.

35. Ibid., p. 275.

36. Ibid., pp. 282–286.

37. Ibid., pp. 274–282, 341. The recorded talk with Jiang Qing, with some later editing by Mao, is included in his published talks of November 15, 1975, available in *Jianguo yilai Mao Zedong wengao* (Manuscripts by Mao Zedong since the Founding of the State), 13 vols. (Beijing: Zhongyang wenxian chubanshe, 1987–1998), 13:447–449.

38. *LZQ*, pp. 343–346.

39. Ibid., pp. 291–298. The text of the letter is reprinted on pp. 295–296.

40. The background to his eye operation is explained by Mao's doctor. See Zhisui Li, with the editorial assistance of Anne F. Thurston, *The Private Life of Chairman Mao: The Memoirs of Mao's Personal Physician* (New York: Random House, 1994), pp. 604–605.

41. *LZQ*, pp. 296–298.

42. Ibid., pp. 329–339.

43. Ibid., p. 273.

44. Ibid., pp. 339–341.

45. Ibid., pp. 471–473.

46. This was the conclusion of the scientists on the National Academy of Sciences delegation, of which I was a member.

47. "Di sanji po bing" (Part 3: Breaking the Ice), in Zhongyang wenxian yanjiushi Hunan shengwei, Hunan dianshi tai (Hunan Television, Hunan Provincial Committee, Central Chinese Communist Party Literature Research Office), *Daxing dianshipian "Deng Xiaoping shi zhang"* (Large-Scale Television Series "Deng Xiaoping in Ten Parts") (Hunan Provincial Television, 2004).

48. *LZQ*, pp. 473–474.

49. Ibid., pp. 477–478, 495.

50. Ibid., pp. 478–480.

51. Ibid., pp. 480–482, 488–490.

52. Ibid., pp. 490–496.

53. Merle Goldman, the China specialist who accompanied the delegation, kindly showed me the notes from the meeting.

54. *LZQ*, p. 498; *SWDXP-2*, pp. 45–47.

55. *LZQ*, pp. 581–582.

56. Ibid., pp. 499–502.

57. Ibid., pp. 499–502, 506.

58. For a more detailed account of the *Water Margin* issue, see Merle Goldman, *Chinese Intellectuals: Advise and Dissent* (Cambridge: Harvard University Press, 1981).

59. *LZQ,* pp. 507–512; *Guoshi,* vol. 8, pp. 577–580. According to this last account, Lu Di, rather than Mao, initiated the discussion and the recording of Mao's views, and it was Yao Wenyuan and Jiang Qing, rather than Mao, who promoted the public discussion. At the very least, however, Mao allowed the public discussion to take place and was aware of its political significance.

60. *LZQ,* pp. 512–517.

61. *WNZEL,* p. 565.

62. For various accounts of the *Water Margin* campaign, see Teiwes and Sun, *End of the Maoist Era,* pp. 363–374; Merle Goldman, "The Media Campaign as a Weapon in Political Struggle: The Dictatorship of the Proletariat and *Water Margin* Campaign," in Godwin C. Chu and Francis L. K. Hsu, eds., *Moving a Mountain: Cultural Change in China* (Honolulu: University Press of Hawaii, 1979), pp. 191–202; Barbara Barnouin and Changgen Yu, *Ten Years of Turbulence: The Chinese Cultural Revolution* (New York: Kegan Paul International, 1993), pp. 283–285.

63. Wenqian Gao, *Zhou Enlai: The Last Perfect Revolutionary; A Biography* (New York: PublicAffairs, 2007), p. 166.

64. *LZQ,* pp. 512–517.

65. View of Mao Yuanxin from my interview with an official familiar with Mao Yuanxin's views, January 2006.

66. For various accounts of this struggle, see *MZDZ,* 2:1753–1755; *DXPCR,* pp. 350–351; Teiwes and Sun, *End of the Maoist Era,* pp. 388–399; Jiaqi Yan and Gao Gao, *Turbulent Decade: A History of the Cultural Revolution* (Honolulu: University of Hawaii Press, 1996), pp. 471–473; Roderick MacFarquhar and Michael Schoenhals, *Mao's Last Revolution* (Cambridge: Belknap Press of Harvard University Press, 2006), pp. 404–407; *LZQ,* pp. 560–563.

67. *Guoshi,* vol. 8, p. 406.

68. *MZDZ,* 2:1754.

69. Ibid.

70. This section draws on interviews in January 2006 with an official in a position to know Mao Yuanxin's situation, as well as *MZDZ,* 2:1752–1758; *DXPCR,* pp. 350–355; Teiwes and Sun, *End of the Maoist Era,* pp. 374–381, 399–410; *LZQ,* pp. 560–579; *Guoshi,* vol. 8, pp. 592–598; *DXPNP-2,* November 1–November 28, 1975.

71. Interview with an official in a position to know, January 2006. See also Teiwes and Sun, *End of the Maoist Era,* p. 517.

72. *DXPCR,* p. 361.

73. *DXPNP-2,* January 1, 2, 1976; Teiwes and Sun, *End of the Maoist Era,* p. 516.

74. In 1980, in evaluating historical issues, Chen Yun, Ye Jianying, and others feared that it would diminish Mao's reputation if Yuanxin were simply passing on Mao's views. Yuanxin agreed to accept responsibility for influencing Mao and was given better treatment than he otherwise would have received. Interview with party historian familiar with the documents, December 2008.

75. For a discussion of the Chaoyang model, see Teiwes and Sun, *End of the Maoist Era*, p. 340.

76. This section draws on an interview with a party historian who has had access to many of the relevant archives, January 2006.

77. *DXPCR*, p. 351.

78. Interviews in January 2006 with an official in a position to know Mao Yuanxin's situation. *MZDZ*, 2:1754–1755; *DXPCR*, pp. 352–353.

79. *DXPCR*, p. 362; *DXPNP-2* lists the visit simply as early November.

80. *DXPCR*, p. 352.

81. *DXPNP-2*, November 1, 2, 1975; *MZDZ*, 2:1755.

82. *MZDZ*, 2:1755–1756.

83. Ibid., 2:1756.

84. David S. Zweig, "The Peita Debate on Education and the Fall of Teng Hsiaop'ing," *The China Quarterly*, no. 73 (March 1978): 140–159.

85. *DXPNP-2*, November 17, 1975.

86. Ibid., November 20, 1975; *DXPCR*, p. 361.

87. Bo Yibo, *Ruogan zhong da juece yu shijian de huigu* (Recollections on Certain Major Policies and Events), 2 vols. (Beijing: Zhonggong zhongyang dangxiao chubanshe, 1991), 2:1249.

88. *DXPCR*, p. 366.

89. Patrick Tyler, *A Great Wall: Six Presidents and China; An Investigative History* (New York: PublicAffairs, 1999), p. 226. In this work, Liu Bei is incorrectly referred to as Liu Pu.

90. Henry Kissinger, *Years of Renewal* (New York: Simon and Schuster, 1999), pp. 890–891.

91. *LZQ*, p. 574.

92. *DXPCR*, pp. 364–365; *LZQ*, pp. 575–576; *DXPNP-2*, November 24, 1975; interview with Nancy Tang, April 2002.

93. *LZQ*, pp. 576–577; *DXPCR*, p. 365.

94. *LZQ*, pp. 583–586.

95. Ibid., pp. 579–580; see also Wu De, *Wu De koushu*, pp. 194–199.

96. *LZQ*, pp. 579–582.

97. A tape of Deng's speech is still in the party archives. The account presented here is based on Cheng Zhongyuan's summary, which in turn is based on a transcript of the tape. See *DXPNP-2*, December 20, 1976.

98. *DXPCR,* pp. 367–368.

99. *LZQ,* pp. 571–579.

100. Memcon of meetings between Deng and Kissinger, DNSA, CH00366, CH00367, CH00369, and CH00373, October 20–22, 1975.

101. Analysis, highlights of Secretary Kissinger's meeting with Mao, DNSA, CH00368, October 22, 1975; Memcon, meeting between Kissinger and Mao, DNSA, CH00372, October 17, 1975; DNSA, CH00398, December 3, 1975.

102. Ibid.

103. Memcon, meeting between Gerald Ford, Henry Kissinger, and Deng Xiaoping, DNSA, CH00398, December 3, 1975.

104. Mao's meeting with Ford, DNSA, CH00395, December 2, 1975; Memcon, meeting between Gerald Ford and Deng Xiaoping, DNSA, CH00396, December 2, 1975; DNSA, CH00398, December 3, 1975; Memcon, meeting between Gerald Ford, Henry Kissinger, and Deng Xiaoping, DNSA, CH00399, December 4, 1975; *DXPNP-2,* December 1–5, 1975; Kissinger, *Years of Renewal,* pp. 886–894; Tyler, *A Great Wall,* pp. 215–219.

105. Report by George Bush, DNSA, CH00402, December 9, 1975.

106. DNSA, CH00402, December 9, 1975.

107. *DXPNP-2,* January 1, 2, 1976.

108. *LZQ,* pp. 420–422.

5. Sidelined as the Mao Era Ends

1. *DXPNP-2,* January 8, 1976.

2. On Mao's comment to Wang Dongxing, see *WNZEL,* pp. 7–8, 602–604.

3. Jiaqi Yan and Gao Gao, *Turbulent Decade: A History of the Cultural Revolution* (Honolulu: University of Hawaii Press, 1996), p. 482.

4. *DXPNP-2,* January 5, 1976.

5. Ibid., January 9, 1976.

6. For Zhou's relations with Mao in his last years, see *WNZEL.*

7. Wu De, *Wu De koushu: Shinian fengyu jishi, Wo zai Beijing gongzuo de yixie jingli* (Wu De's Oral History: A Record of the History of Ten Years of Storms, Some Personal Experiences) (Beijing: Dangdai chubanshe, 2004), pp. 203–204.

8. Roger Garside, a British diplomat who served in Beijing from 1976 to 1979, and David Zweig, a Canadian exchange student, both Chinese-speaking, were at Tiananmen Square much of the time during these several days. See Garside, *Coming Alive: China after Mao* (New York: McGraw-Hill, 1981).

9. Wu De, *Wu De koushu,* p. 203.

10. On the prohibition against wearing black armbands, see ibid., p. 204.

11. Garside, *Coming Alive,* pp. 10–13.

12. *DXPNP-2,* January 12, 1976.

13. Chaozhu Ji, *The Man on Mao's Right: From Harvard Yard to Tiananmen Square, My Life inside China's Foreign Ministry* (New York: Random House, 2008), p. 285; interview with Ji Chaozhu, April 2002.

14. *DXPNP-2,* January 15, 1976; Ji, *The Man on Mao's Right,* p. 285.

15. Garside, *Coming Alive,* pp. 12–13.

16. *DXPNP-2,* January 14, 1976.

17. *DXPCR,* p. 372.

18. *DXPNP-2,* January 20, 1976.

19. Interview with party historians, n.d.

20. *DXPCR,* pp. 372, 380–388; Frederick Teiwes and Warren Sun, *The End of the Maoist Era: Chinese Politics during the Twilight of the Cultural Revolution, 1972–1976* (Armonk, N.Y.: M. E. Sharpe, 2007), pp. 414–415.

21. *DXPNP-2,* January 20, 1976.

22. Ibid., January 21, 1976. p. 146.

23. Ibid., January 21, 1976, January–April 1976.

24. *Renmin ribao* (People's Daily), January 26, 1976.

25. *DXPNP-2,* January 21, 1976.

26. Ibid., February 2, 1976.

27. *DXPCR,* pp. 380–388; *DXPNP-2,* January 15, 21, February 2, 1976.

28. Teiwes and Sun, *End of the Maoist Era,* pp. 443–447.

29. *LZQ,* p. 584.

30. *DXPNP-2,* February 2, 1976.

31. Ibid., February 25–early March 1976.

32. Garside, *Coming Alive,* pp. 18–24.

33. Ibid., pp. 110–115; David S. Zweig, "The Peita Debate on Education and the Fall of Teng Hsiao-p'ing," *The China Quarterly,* no. 73 (March 1978): 154.

34. *DXPNP-2,* March 26, 1976.

35. Wu De, *Wu De koushu,* pp. 204–206.

36. Garside, *Coming Alive,* p. 115.

37. On Deng telling his family not to go to Tiananmen Square, see *DXPNP-2,* late March–early April 1976.

38. Zweig, "The Peita Debate on Education and the Fall of Teng Hsiao-p'ing," 154–158; Garside, *Coming Alive,* pp. 125–128.

39. Garside, *Coming Alive,* pp. 125–126.

40. Wu De, *Wu De koushu,* pp. 207–211.

41. *DXPNP-2,* April 5, 1976.

42. Wu De, *Wu De koushu,* pp. 210–214. Garside reports that it was 6:30 p.m. when the announcement was broadcast and 9:35 p.m. when the floodlights went on and the militia marched out from the Forbidden City where they had assembled (Garside, *Coming Alive,* pp. 128–135). After the Gang of Four was arrested, Wu De

made many self-criticisms for slandering Deng, but also defended himself by saying that on April 5 he had no choice but to obey Chairman Mao and the Politburo. Although some reported that much blood had been spilled on April 5, three later investigations of the incident, including investigations in hospitals, crematoria, and elsewhere, produced no evidence that anyone had died as a result of the crackdown. Wu De explains that there is some confusion in Zhonggong zhongyang dangshi yanjiushi (Central Chinese Communist Party History Research Office), *Zhonggong dangshi dashi nianbiao* (Chronology of Major Events in the History of the Chinese Communist Party) (Beijing: Renmin chubanshe, 1987), because the results of the two Politburo meetings on April 4 and April 5 are lumped together as if they had both been held on April 4 and because some of the criticisms that the Gang of Four expressed at the meetings are not recorded. See Wu De, *Wu De koushu,* pp. 218–221.

43. Interview with Zhang Hanzhi, October 21, 2006.

44. Interview with an official familiar with Mao Yuanxin's views, January 2006.

45. *DXPNP-2,* April 6, 1976.

46. *WNZEL,* p. 308.

47. Since even high-ranking Chinese did not know Deng's whereabouts, rumors spread among foreigners that Deng had fled to Guangzhou, where he was being protected by his old friend and supporter General Xu Shiyou, head of the Guangzhou Military Region from January 1974 to February 1980. These rumors were reported not only in Hong Kong papers, but also by some Western analysts. See Garside, *Coming Alive,* p. 140; and Harrison E. Salisbury, *The New Emperors: China in the Era of Mao and Deng* (Boston: Little, Brown, 1992), p. 367. Deng's daughter later corrected this misunderstanding.

48. *DXPNP-2,* April 7, 1976; Wu De, *Wu De koushu,* pp. 216–218.

49. Zweig, "The Peita Debate on Education and the Fall of Teng Hsiao-p'ing," 158.

50. *MZDZ,* 2:1778.

51. Mao's doctor, Li Zhisui, reports that Mao wrote these words for Hua on April 30. See Zhisui Li, with the editorial assistance of Anne F. Thurston, *The Private Life of Chairman Mao: The Memoirs of Mao's Personal Physician* (New York: Random House, 1994), p. 5.

52. *DXPNP-2,* April 7, 9, 1976.

53. Ibid., July 7, September 9, 1976.

54. Ibid., September 9, 1976.

55. Wu De, *Wu De koushu,* p. 197.

56. Teiwes and Sun, *End of the Maoist Era,* p. 390.

57. *DXPNP-2,* September 9, 1976.

58. Roxane Witke, *Comrade Chiang Ch'ing* (Boston: Little, Brown, 1977), p. 449. For general accounts of the background and process of the Gang of Four's arrest, see *Guoshi,* vol. 8, pp. 647–716; Wu Jianhua, "Fensui 'sirenbang' cehua shishi guocheng"

(The Plan to Overthrow the "Gang of Four" and the Process of Its Implementation), *Zhonghua ernu*, nos. 10 and 11 (2001), reprinted in Li Haiwen, *Zhonggong zhongda lishi shijian qinli ji (1949–1980)* (Memories of Personal Experiences during the Important Historical Events of the Chinese Communist Party [1949–1980]), 2 vols. (Chengdu: Sichuan renmin chubanshe, 2006), 2:248–281; *YJZGJSK*; and Wu De, *Wu De koushu*. For English accounts, see Yan and Gao, *Turbulent Decade*, pp. 519–528; Teiwes and Sun, *End of the Maoist Era*, pp. 536–594; and Richard Baum, *Burying Mao: Chinese Politics in the Age of Deng Xiaoping* (Princeton, N.J.: Princeton University Press, 1994), pp. 40–45.

59. *YJZGJSK*, pp. 363–364; Li, with the editorial assistance of Thurston, *The Private Life of Chairman Mao*, pp. 3–30, 615–625; and interview with Ji Humin, son of Ji Dengkui, October 2007.

60. *YJZGJSK*, p. 367.

61. Ibid., pp. 369–370.

62. Yan and Gao, *Turbulent Decade*, p. 524; Cheng Zhongyuan, Wang Yuxiang, and Li Zhenghua, *1976–1981 nian de Zhongguo* (China from 1976 to 1981) (Beijing: Zhongyang wenxian chubanshe, 2008), pp. 4–5; Teiwes and Sun, *End of the Maoist Era*, pp. 551–594.

63. *YJZGJSK*, p. 368. Western and Chinese scholars have different views as to whether Hua or Ye took the initiative and who played a more important role. While Hua was in office, the Chinese press emphasized his role, but after he was removed, the same press emphasized the role of Ye. Clearly both played a significant part. For a discussion of the issue, see Teiwes and Sun, *End of the Maoist Era*, pp. 536–594.

64. *YJZGJSK*, pp. 377–380.

65. Garside, *Coming Alive*, p. 154, and Salisbury, *The New Emperors*, p. 274, present unverified reports that Mao Yuanxin made a run for it and was captured when trying to board a plane for the Northeast, but Fan Shuo, who had access to more party documents, does not mention such rumors, which also appeared in Hong Kong journals *Ming bao* and *Zhengming*, along with dramatic versions of the capture of Jiang Qing, summarized by Garside, *Coming Alive*, pp. 152–167. These too have not been verified by party historians. See also Teiwes and Sun, *End of the Maoist Era*, p. 580.

66. Teiwes and Sun, *End of the Maoist Era*, p. 582.

67. Roderick MacFarquhar, *The Politics of China: The Eras of Mao and Deng*, 2d ed. (New York: Cambridge University Press, 1997), p. 312.

68. For the background of the workers' militia, see Elizabeth J. Perry, *Patrolling the Revolution: Worker Militias, Citizenship, and the Modern Chinese State* (Lanham, Md.: Rowman and Littlefield, 2006).

69. Cheng Zhongyuan, Wang Yuxiang, and Li Zhenghua, *1976–1981 nian de Zhongguo*, pp. 11–14; Teiwes and Sun, *End of the Maoist Era*, pp. 582–590.

70. Garside, *Coming Alive*, pp. 154–167.

71. *DXPNP-2,* October 21, 1976; Garside, *Coming Alive,* pp. 165–166.

72. Teiwes and Sun, *End of the Maoist Era,* pp. 586–587.

73. *DXPNP-2,* October 26, 1976.

74. Ibid., October 1976, after the smashing of the Gang of Four.

75. *DXPCR,* pp. 440–441.

76. *DXPNP-2,* October 7, 10, 1976, quoted in Baum, *Burying Mao,* p. 43.

77. *DXPNP-2,* December 7, 12 13, 14, 24, 1976.

78. Ibid., p. 154, sometime after December 24, 1976.

6. Return under Hua

1. U.S. Dept. of State, "Ambassador Gates' Discussion in Peking," DNSA, doc. CH00407, Secret, Action Memorandum, April 22, 1976.

2. An insightful analysis of the two years under Hua can be found in Cheng Meidong, "1976–1978 Zhongguo shehui de yanhua: Jianlun Hua Guofeng de shiqi zhengzhi huanjing de biandong yu shiyijie sanzhong quanhui de zhaokai" (The Evolution of Chinese Society, 1976–1978: A Second Discussion of Changes in the Political Environment during the Period of Hua Guofeng and the Opening of the Third Plenary Session of the Eleventh Central Committee), *Xuexi yu tansuo,* no. 6 (2008): 32–41. I am indebted to Warren Sun for providing evidence of Hua's support for reform.

3. At other levels and in other sectors, such as the economic sector, personal authority remained strong. See, for example, Andrew G. Walder, *Communist Neo-Traditionalism: Work and Authority in Chinese Industry* (Berkeley: University of California Press, 1986).

4. Biographers of Ye Jianying claim that he had the primary role in planning the arrest of the Gang of Four. In assessing the views of party historians who give more credit to Ye and those who give more credit to Hua, however, Frederick Teiwes and Warren Sun give great credit to Hua: he was the person in charge and took the initiative. See Teiwes and Sun, *The End of the Maoist Era: Chinese Politics during the Twilight of the Cultural Revolution, 1972–1976* (Armonk, N.Y.: M. E. Sharpe, 2007), pp. 591–594. A similar conclusion can be found in Akio Takahara, "Gendai chugokushi no saikento: Kakokuho to Toshohei, soshite 1978-nen no kakkisei ni tsuite" (A Reexamination of Modern Chinese History: On the Epoch-making of Hua Guofeng and Deng Xiaoping in 1978), *Toa,* no. 495 (September 2008): 32–40.

5. See, for example, Yu Guangyuan, "Wo dui Hua Guofeng de yinxiang" (My Impression of Hua Guofeng), *Lingdao wencui,* no. 16 (August 2008): 68–70.

6. There have been various translations of the "two whatevers." I have followed the official translation used in *SWDXP-2,* p. 137.

7. Interview with Cheng Zhongyuan, October 2005.

8. *DXPNP-2*, October 1976, after the arrest of the Gang of Four.

9. Richard Baum, *Burying Mao: Chinese Politics in the Age of Deng Xiaoping* (Princeton, N.J.: Princeton University Press, 1994), p. 43.

10. *YJYNP*, December 12, 1976.

11. Shen Baoxiang, *Zhenli biaozhun wenti taolun shimo* (The Complete Story of the Discussion on Practice Is the Sole Criterion for Testing Truth) (Beijing: Zhongguo qingnian chubanshe, 1997), pp. 331–332.

12. Interview with Cheng Zhongyuan, October 2005.

13. *CYZ*, 2:1447–1450.

14. Teiwes and Sun, *End of the Maoist Era,* pp. 238–240.

15. Cheng Meidong, "1976–1978 Zhongguo shehui de yanhua," 34.

16. Cheng Zhongyuan, Wang Yuxiang, and Li Zhenghua, *1976–1981 nian de Zhongguo* (China from 1976 to 1981) (Beijing: Zhongyang wenxian chubanshe, 2008), p. 43.

17. Ibid., p. 44.

18. *CYZ*, 2:1447–1448; *CYNP*, March 17, 1977. Chen Yun presented the same message to the Shanghai delegation. See *CYNP*, March 13, 1977; Cheng Zhongyuan, Wang Yuxiang, and Li Zhenghua, *1976–1981 nian de Zhongguo*, p. 44; *DXPNP-2*, March 10–20, 1977; and Shen Baoxiang, *Zhenli biaozhun wenti taolun shimo*, p. 4.

19. Cheng Zhongyuan, Wang Yuxiang, and Li Zhenghua, *1976–1981 nian de Zhongguo*, pp. 44–45. See also *DXPNP-2*, March 10–20, 1977.

20. *CYNP*, March 17, 1977.

21. *DXPNP-2*, March 10–20, 1977; Cheng Zhongyuan, Wang Yuxiang, and Li Zhenghua, *1976–1981 nian de Zhongguo*, pp. 45–46.

22. *DXPNP-2*, April 7, 1977.

23. Deng presented a more complete version of these views to the Third Plenum of the Tenth Central Committee on July 21, 1977. See his "Mao Zedong Thought Must Be Correctly Understood as an Integral Whole," *SWDXP-2*, pp. 55–60.

24. *DXPNP-2*, April 10, 1976.

25. Ibid., after April 10, 1976.

26. For example, Li Desheng, "Weida de zhuanzhe, lishi de biran: Huiyi shiyijie sanzhong quanhui de zhaokai" (A Great Turning Point, The Inevitability of History: Recollections on the Opening of the Third Plenary Session of the Eleventh Central Committee), in Yu Guangyuan et al., *Gaibian Zhongguo mingyun de 41 tian: Zhongyang gongzuo huiyi, shiyijie sanzhong quanhui qinliji* (The Four Days That Changed the Fate of China: A Record of My Experience at the Central Work Conference of the Third Plenary Session of the Eleventh Central Committee) (Shenzhen: Haitian chubanshe, 1998), p. 230.

27. Cheng Zhongyuan, Wang Yuxiang, and Li Zhenghua, *1976–1981 nian de Zhongguo*, p. 46.

28. *DXPNP-2*, May 24, 1977; *SWDXP-2*, May 24, 1977, pp. 51–52.

29. "Zhongfa shiwu hao—Deng Xiaoping zhi Hua Guofeng de liangfeng xin yi (yijiuqiqi nian wuyue sanri yi Deng Xiaoping you Wang Dongxing zhuan Hua Guofeng de xin)" (Document No. 15, letter from Deng Xiaoping to Hua Guofeng, passed on by Wang Dongxing on May 3, 1977), unpublished document, available in the Fairbank Collection, Fung Library, Harvard University.

30. *DXPNP-2*, April 10, 1977.

31. Cheng Zhongyuan, Wang Yuxiang, and Li Zhenghua, *1976–1981 nian de Zhongguo*, pp. 44–45; see also *DXPNP-2*, March 10–20, 1977.

32. *DXPNP-2*, May 12, 1977.

33. Ibid.

34. *DXPJW*, 3:53–87.

35. *DXPNP-2*, May 24, 1977; *SWDXP-2*, pp. 53–54.

36. Deng Liqun, *Shierge chunqiu, 1975–1987: Deng Liqun zishu* (Twelve Springs and Autumns, 1975–1987: Deng Liqun's Autobiography) (Hong Kong: Bozhi chubanshe, 2006), pp. 86–96.

37. *DXPNP-2*, July 16–21, 1977; Cheng Zhongyuan, Wang Yuxiang, and Li Zhenghua, *1976–1981 nian de Zhongguo*, p. 47.

38. Cheng Zhongyuan, Wang Yuxiang, and Li Zhenghua, *1976–1981 nian de Zhongguo*, pp. 47–48; *DXPNP-2*, July 16–21, 1977; *SWDXP-2*, pp. 55–60.

39. Cheng Zhongyuan, Wang Yuxiang, and Li Zhenghua, *1976–1981 nian de Zhongguo*, pp. 47–48; *DXPNP-2*, July 16–21, 1977.

40. *DXPNP-2*, July 30, 1977; communication from someone present, n.d.

41. Shen Baoxiang, *Zhenli biaozhun wenti taolun shimo*, p. 10.

42. "Closing Address at the 11th National Congress of the Communist Party of China," in *The Eleventh National Congress of the Communist Party of China* (Peking: Foreign Languages Press, 1977), pp. 189–195.

43. *DXPNP-2*, July 23, 1977.

44. *SWDXP-2*, p. 81.

45. *DXPNP-2*, October 10, 1977.

46. *SWDXP-2*, p. 61.

47. Ibid., p. 54; *DXPNP-2*, May 24, 1977.

48. *DXPNP-2*, July 23, 1977.

49. Ji Weiqing, "Jiaoyu zhanxian tuifan 'sirenbang' liange guji qianhou" (Two Ideas on the Educational Front before and after the Overthrow of the "Gang of Four"), *Yanhuang chunqiu*, no. 5 (2003): 40–42. For an overview of his 1977 efforts to promote education, see Xia Xingzhen, "Deng Xiaoping yu jiaoyu zhanxian de boluan fanzheng" (Bringing Order out of Chaos on the Educational Front), *Dangdai Zhongguo shi yanjiu*, no. 4 (2004): 50–58.

50. *SWDXP-2*, p. 84.

51. *DXPNP-2,* July 27, 1977.

52. Ibid., August 1, 1977.

53. Ibid., July 29, 1977.

54. Ibid., August 4, 1977. See also his speech on August 9, 1977; the English version is in *SWDXP-2,* pp. 61–71.

55. *SWDXP-2,* p. 81.

56. Ibid., pp. 81–82.

57. Cheng Zhongyuan, Wang Yuxiang, and Li Zhenghua, *1976–1981 nian de Zhongguo,* pp. 55–56; "Di sanji po bing" (Part 3: Breaking the Ice), in Zhongyang wenxian yanjiushi, Hunan shengwei, and Hunan dianshi tai (Hunan Television, Hunan Provincial Committee, and Central Chinese Communist Party Literature Research Office), *Daxing dianshipian "Deng Xiaoping shi zhang"* (Large-scale Television Series "Deng Xiaoping in Ten Parts") (Hunan Provincial Television, 2004).

58. *SWDXP-2,* p. 81.

59. "Di sanji po bing."

60. Cheng Zhongyuan, Wang Yuxiang, and Li Zhenghua, *1976–1981 nian de Zhongguo,* pp. 56–77.

61. Ibid., p. 57.

62. This follows the social patterns in Japan, South Korea, Taiwan, and other East Asian countries, where examinations played a similar role. See, for example, Ezra F. Vogel, *Japan's New Middle Class: The Salary Man and His Family in a Tokyo Suburb* (Berkeley: University of California Press, 1963), pp. 40–67; Thomas P. Rohlen, *Japan's High Schools* (Berkeley: University of California Press, 1983); Denise Potrzeba Lett, *In Pursuit of Status: The Making of South Korea's "New" Urban Middle Class* (Cambridge, Mass.: Asia Center, Harvard University, 1998).

63. *SWDXP-2,* pp. 64–65.

64. *DXPNP-2,* September 19, 1977, p. 204.

65. Much of Deng's thinking is spelled out in his August 8, 1977 speech on science and education; see *SWDXP-2,* pp. 61–71.

66. *LZQ,* pp. 223–230.

67. *SWDXP-2,* pp. 98–111.

68. *DXPNP-2,* July 23, 1977.

69. For an overview of the Central Party School and other party schools, see David Shambaugh, "Training China's Political Elite," *The China Quarterly,* no. 196 (December 2008): 827–844.

70. Interview with Sun Changjiang, August 2006. See also Ma Licheng and Ling Zhijun, *Jiaofeng: Dangdai Zhongguo sanci sixiang jiefang shilu* (Crossing Swords: A Record of Three Emancipations of the Mind in Contemporary China) (Beijing: Jinri Zhongguo chubanshe, 1998), pp. 49–61.

71. The literal translation for *shijian shi jianyan de weiyi biaozhun* is "experience is the sole criterion for testing truth."

72. Interview with Sun Changjiang, August 2006; Shen Baoxiang, *Zhenli biao-zhun wenti taolun shimo;* Michael Schoenhals, "The 1978 Truth Criterion Contro-versy," *The China Quarterly,* no. 126 (June 1991): 243–268.

73. Shen Baoxiang, *Zhenli biaozhun wenti taolun shimo,* pp. 107–108; Party His-tory Research Center, comp., *History of the Chinese Communist Party: A Chronology of Events, 1919–1990* (Beijing: Foreign Languages Press, 1991), May 11, 1978.

74. Schoenhals, "The 1978 Truth Criterion Controversy," 252–260; Shen Bao-xiang, *Zhenli biaozhun wenti taolun shimo.*

75. Shen Baoxiang, *Zhenli biaozhun wenti taolun shimo,* p. 122.

76. Ibid., pp. 127–129; *DXPNP-2,* July 22, 1978.

77. Ma Licheng and Ling Zhijun, *Jiaofeng,* p. 41.

7. Three Turning Points

1. Paul A. Cohen, *Between Tradition and Modernity: Wang T'ao and Reform in Late Ch'ing China* (Cambridge: Council on East Asian Studies, Harvard University, 1987).

2. "Li Xiannian zhuan" bianxiezu (Editorial Group for the Biography of Li Xian-nian), ed., *Li Xiannian zhuan: 1949–1992* (A Biography of Li Xiannian: 1949–1992), 2 vols. (Beijing: Zhongyang wenxian chubanshe, 2009), 2:1049; Nina P. Halpern, "Learning from Abroad: Chinese Views of the East European Economic Experience, January 1977–June 1981," *Modern China* 11, no. 1 (January 1985): 77–109.

3. Deng Xiaoping, *South China Elites Weekly,* August 17, 2004, quoted in Edwin C. Lim, "Xuyan: Zhongguo gaige kaifang guochengzhong de duiwai sixiang kaifang" (Preface: Thoughts on Opening to the Outside during the Process of China's Reform and Opening), in Wu Jinglian, ed., *Zhongguo jingji 50 ren kan sanshi nian: Huigu yu fenxi* (Fifty Chinese Economists Look at the Thirty Years: Reflections and Analysis) (Beijing: Zhongguo jingji chubanshe, 2008).

4. Li Xiangqian and Han Gang, "Xin faxian Deng Xiaoping yu Hu Yaobang deng sanci tanhua jilu" (Newly Discovered Record of Three of Deng Xiaoping's Talks with Hu Yaobang and Others), *Bainianchao,* no. 3 (1999): 4–11, reprinted in Xie Chuntao, ed., *Deng Xiaoping xiezhen* (A Portrait of Deng Xiaoping) (Shanghai: Shanghai cishu chubanshe, 2005), p. 192.

5. *DXPSTW,* pp. 55–56.

6. See Jinglian Wu, *Understanding and Interpreting Chinese Economic Reform* (Mason, Ohio: Thomson/South-Western, 2005), pp. 17–30, for a Chinese econo-mist's view of the Eastern European reforms.

7. Xinhua General Overseas News Service, March 9 to April 6, 1978.

8. Gu Mu, "Xiaoping tongzhi lingdao women zhua duiwai kaifang" (Comrade Xiaoping Led Us to Grasp Reform and Opening), in Zhonggong zhongyang wen-

xian yanjiushi (Central Chinese Communist Party Literature Research Office), ed., *Huiyi Deng Xiaoping* (Remembering Deng Xiaoping), 3 vols. (Beijing: Zhongyang wenxian chubanshe, 1998), 1:155–156; see also Gu Mu, "Xiaoping lingdao women zhua kaifang" (Xiaoping Led Us to Grasp Opening), *Bainianchao,* no. 1 (1998): 4–11, reprinted in Yang Tianshi, ed., *Deng Xiaoping xiezhen* (A Portrait of Deng Xiaoping) (Shanghai: Shanghai cishu chubanshe, 2005), pp. 203–204.

9. Zhang Gensheng, "Ting Gu Mu tan qinli de jijian dashi" (Listening to Gu Mu Speak about Some of the Big Events That He Personally Experienced), *Yanhuang chunqiu,* no. 1 (2004): 3–5.

10. Xu Ai, "Bu kan bu zhidao: Fang yuan guojia qinggongbu buzhang Yang Bo" (Don't See, Don't Know: An Interview with Yang Bo, the Former Minister of the Ministry of Light Industry), in Song Xiaoming and Liu An, eds., *Zhuixun, 1978: Zhongguo gaige kaifang jiyuan fangtanlu* (Tracking Down 1978: A Record of Interviews on the Beginning of China's Reform and Opening) (Fuzhou: Fujian jiaoyu chubanshe, 1998), p. 539.

11. Xinhua General Overseas News Service, May 2 to June 7, 1978.

12. Xu Ai, "Bu kan bu zhidao," p. 540.

13. "Li Xiannian zhuan" bianxiezu, *Li Xiannian zhuan,* 2:1050–1054.

14. Gu Mu, "Xiaoping lingdao women zhua kaifang," pp. 203–204.

15. Xinhua General Overseas News Service, May 2 to June 7, 1978.

16. Cheng Zhongyuan, Wang Yuxiang, and Li Zhenghua, *1976–1981 nian de Zhongguo* (China from 1976 to 1981) (Beijing: Zhongyang wenxian chubanshe, 2008), pp. 263–266.

17. Cui Ronghui, "Gaige kaifang, xianxing yi bu: Fang yuan Guangdong sheng shengwei shuji Wang Quanguo," in Song Xiaoming and Liu An, *Zhuixun, 1978: Zhongguo gaige kaifang jiyuan fangtanlu,* p. 558.

18. Xu Ai, "Bu kan bu zhidao," p. 541.

19. Ibid., p. 541; Cui Ronghui, "Gaige kaifang, xianxing yi bu," p. 558.

20. Cui Ronghui, "Gaige kaifang, xianxing yi bu," p. 559.

21. Gu Mu, "Xiaoping tongzhi lingdao women zhua duiwai kaifang," p. 156.

22. Zhang Gensheng, "Ting Gu Mu tan qinli de jijian dashi," 3.

23. Cheng Zhongyuan, Wang Yuxiang, and Li Zhenghua, *1976–1981 nian de Zhongguo,* p. 70; Xiao Donglian, "1979 nian guomin jingji tiaozheng fangzhen de tichu yu zhenglun: Da zhuanzhe jishi zhiyi" (The Proposal and Debate over the 1979 Economic Readjustment Policy: The First Big Turning Point), *Dangshi bolan,* no. 10 (2004): 4–10.

24. Xiao Donglian, "1979 nian guomin jingji tiaozheng fangzhen de tichu yu zhenglun."

25. Gu Mu, "Xiaoping tongzhi lingdao women zhua duiwai kaifang," pp. 156–157.

26. *DXPNP-2,* September 20, 1978.

27. Xiao Donglian, "1978–1984 nian Zhongguo jingji tizhi gaige silu de yanjin: Juece yu shishi" (The Process of Conceptualizing Thinking on China's Economic Restructuring from 1978 to 1984: Decision-making and Implementation), *Dangdai Zhongguo shi yanjiu*, no. 9 (2004): 59–70; *DXPSTW*, pp. 53–61.

28. *DXPNP-2*, September 20, 1978.

29. Chen Yun, *Chen Yun wenxuan* (Selected Works of Chen Yun), 3 vols., 2d ed. (Beijing: Renmin chubanshe, 1995), 3:235.

30. Ibid., 3:252.

31. Su Tairen, ed., *Deng Xiaoping shengping quan jilu: Yige weiren he tade yige shiji* (The Entire Record of Deng Xiaoping's Life: A Great Man and His Century), 2 vols. (Beijing: Zhongyang wenxian chubanshe, 2004), 2:625.

32. At the time, many localities still had "revolutionary committees," that is, government offices that included many local officials who were military careerists and some civilian officials who had also been given concurrent military titles.

33. Su Tairen, *Deng Xiaoping shengping quan jilu*, 2:623–624.

34. Wang Enmao [then first party secretary of Jilin province], "Jueding Zhongguo mingyun de 'gongzuo zhongdian zhuanyi'" (Determine the Fate of China's "Shift in Focus"), in Yu Guangyuan et al., *Gaibian Zhongguo mingyun de 41 tian: Zhongyang gongzuo huiyi, shiyijie sanzhong quanhui qinli ji* (The 41 Days That Changed the Fate of China: A Record of My Experience at the Central Work Conference of the Third Plenary Session of the Eleventh Central Committee) (Shenzhen: Haitian chubanshe, 1998), pp. 204–206; *SWDXP-2*, pp. 137–139.

35. Li Desheng, "Weida de zhuanzhe, lishi de biran: Huiyi shiyijie sanzhong quanhui de zhaokai" (A Great Turning Point, the Inevitability of History: Recollections on the Opening of the Third Plenary Session of the Eleventh Central Committee), in Yu Guangyuan et al., *Gaibian Zhongguo mingyun de 41 tian*, pp. 231–235.

36. *DXPSTW*, p. 131; Yu's original book in Chinese is Yu Guangyuan, *1978: Wo qinli de naci lishi zhuanzhe; Shiyijie sanzhong quanhui de taiqian muhou* (1978: My Experience at that Historical Turning Point; Behind the Curtain of the Third Plenary Session of the Eleventh Central Committee) (Beijing: Zhongyang bianyi chubanshe, 1998). Li Xiangqian and Han Gang, "Xin faxian Deng Xiaoping yu Hu Yaobang deng sanci tanhua jilu," pp. 190–200.

37. *DXPSTW*; see also Zhu Jiamu, *Wo suo zhidao de shiyijie zhong sanzhong quanhui* (What I Know about the Third Plenary Session of the Eleventh Central Committee) (Beijing: Zhongyang wenxian chubanshe, 1998), pp. 46–181.

38. *DXPNP-2*, p. 415, end of October; Su Tairen, *Deng Xiaoping shengping quan jilu*, 2:625.

39. Li Xiangqian and Han Gang, "Xin faxian Deng Xiaoping yu Hu Yaobang deng sanci tanhua jilu," pp. 129–148; *DXPSTW*, pp. 128–148.

40. *SWDXP-2*, pp. 167–168.

41. *DXPSTW*, pp. 18–22.

42. Ibid., pp. 29–32.

43. This information is from my meetings with Southeast Asian officials with whom Deng interacted during his visit to the region.

44. Zhu Jiamu, "Hu Qiaomu zai shiyijie sanzhong quan huishang" (Hu Qiaomu at the Third Plenary Session), in Yu Guangyuan et al., *Gaibian Zhongguo mingyun de 41 tian*, p. 304; *DXPSTW*, p. 21.

45. *SWDXP-2*, pp. 65–72.

46. *DXPSTW*, p. 24.

47. Ibid., pp. 23–28.

48. Ibid., pp. 51–53.

49. Yu Guangyuan et al., *Gaibian Zhongguo mingyun de 41 tian; DXPSTW*, pp. 39–42.

50. Wang Quanguo, "Shiyijie sanzhong quanhui yu Guangdong de gaige kaifang" (The Third Plenary Session of the Eleventh Central Committee and Reform and Opening in Guangdong), in Yu Guangyuan et al., *Gaibian Zhongguo mingyun de 41 tian*, pp. 198–203.

51. This information is drawn from discussions with Ye Xuanji, who was working with his uncle Ye Jianying during this time. See also his article "Ye shuai zai dishiyijie sanzhong quanhui qianhou: Du Yu Guangyuan '1978: Wo qinli de naci lishi da zhuanzhe' yougan" (Marshal Ye before and after the Third Plenary Session of the Eleventh Central Committee: Feelings from Reading Yu Guangyuan's '1978: My Experience from that Historical Turning Point'), *Nanfang zhoumo*, October 30, 2008, D23, at http://www.infzm.com/content/19143/0, accessed March 17, 2010. Yu Guangyuan was one of Deng's speechwriters and took careful notes on the discussions, but he was not aware of the November 11 meeting.

52. Qian Jiang, "Zhang Wentian yuan'an shi zenyang pingfan de" (How the Unjust Case of Zhang Wentian Was Reversed), *Zongheng*, no. 2 (2001): 4–6. As early as June 25, Deng Xiaoping had already read the report on the sixty-one cases. When Deng read the report, he said that these cases had to be resolved, but in fact they were not resolved until the Central Party Work Conference six months later. The question of whether these sixty-one had been too cooperative with the Guomindang in order to secure their release from prison in April 1936 had already been decided by party leaders and they had been declared innocent. But in March 1967 Lin Biao, Kang Sheng, and Jiang Qing again declared them renegades.

53. *DXPSTW*, pp. 63–65. See also the Chinese original: Yu Guangyuan, *1978: Wo qinli de naci lishi zhuanzhe*, pp. 77–79.

54. *DXPSTW*, p. 70.

55. Ibid., pp. 71–72.

56. Yu Guangyuan, *1978: Wo qinli de naci lishi zhuanzhe*, pp. 85–86.

57. Ibid., pp. 90–91.

58. *YJYNP*, November 10–15, 1978, pp. 1155–1156; November 12–13, 1978, p. 1156.

59. *DXPSTW,* pp. 72–76.

60. Ibid., pp. 46–51, 74–76, 78–79, 166.

61. Yu Guangyuan, *1978: Wo qinli de naci lishi zhuanzhe,* p. 86.

62. *DXPSTW,* pp. 80–90, 108. See also the original: ibid., pp. 115–125.

63. *DXPSTW,* pp. 163–165.

64. *DXPNP-2,* December 28, 1978.

65. *DXPSTW,* pp. 39–46.

66. Wu Xiang, "Wan Li tan shiyijie quanhui qianhou de nongcun gaige" (Wan Li on Agricultural Reform before and after the Third Plenary Session of the Eleventh Central Committee), in Yu Guangyuan et al., *Gaibian Zhongguo mingyun de 41 tian,* pp. 286–287.

67. Liang Lingguang, "Yici hua shidai de zhongyang huiyi" (A Landmark Central Meeting), in Yu Guangyuan et al., *Gaibian Zhongguo mingyun de 41 tian,* pp. 273–274.

68. Ren Zhongyi, "Zhuixun 1978 nian de lishi zhuangui" (Pursuing the Historical Turning Point in 1978), in Yu Guangyuan et al., *Gaibian Zhongguo mingyun de 41 tian,* p. 216.

69. *DXPSTW,* p. 127.

70. Zhu Xueqin, "Sanshi nianlai de Zhongguo gaige, you liangge jieduan" (There are Two Stages to the Thirty Years of Chinese Reform), *Nanfang dushi bao,* December 16, 2007.

71. *YJYNP,* p. 1157, mid-November 1978.

72. Ibid., November 27, 1978.

73. Ibid., November 25, 1978; *DXPSTW,* pp. 76–78 contains the text of Deng's remarks.

74. *DXPSTW,* p. 78.

75. This discussion of preparations for Deng's speech and the quotations from Deng's comments come from ibid., pp. 129–148. In this discussion I have also drawn on interviews with Yu Guangyuan. See Yu Guangyuan, *Wo yi Deng Xiaoping* (Recalling Deng Xiaoping) (Hong Kong: Shidai guoji chuban youxian gongsi, 2005); also Han Gang, "Yifen Deng Xiaoping zhengui shougao de faxian" (The Discovery of a Precious Deng Xiaoping Manuscript), *Bainianchao,* no. 4 (1997): 4–6, reprinted in Yang Tianshi, ed., *Deng Xiaoping xiezhen* (A Portrait of Deng Xiaoping) (Shanghai: Shanghai cishu chubanshe, 2005), pp. 186–189; Li Xiangqian and Han Gang, "Xin faxian Deng Xiaoping yu Hu Yaobang deng sanci tanhua jilu," pp. 190–200.

76. *DXPSTW,* pp. 185–190.

77. Ibid., pp. 129–143.

78. "Emancipate the Mind, Seek Truth from Facts and Unite as One in Looking to the Future," *SWDXP-2,* pp. 150–163.

79. *DXPSTW,* pp. 132–139.

80. Ibid., pp. 168–172; Liang Lingguang, "Yici hua shidai de zhongyang huiyi," p. 175.

81. Robert D. Novak, *The Prince of Darkness: 50 Years Reporting in Washington* (New York: Crown Forum, 2007), pp. 324, 326.

82. Ren Zhongyi, "Zhuixun 1978 nian de lishi zhuangui," pp. 215–216.

83. *DXPSTW,* pp. 205–207.

8. Setting the Limits of Freedom

1. Roger Garside, *Coming Alive: China after Mao* (New York: McGraw-Hill, 1981).

2. Ibid.

3. Ibid., pp. 237, 243–244.

4. Ibid., p. 241.

5. Ibid.

6. Ibid., pp. 196–197; Robert D. Novak, *The Prince of Darkness: 50 Years Reporting in Washington* (New York: Crown Forum, 2007); Merle Goldman, "Hu Yaobang's Intellectual Network and the Theory Conference of 1979," *The China Quarterly,* no. 126 (June 1991): 223.

7. Goldman, "Hu Yaobang's Intellectual Network," pp. 223–225, 237, 243–244.

8. Ibid., pp. 220–221.

9. Hu Jiwei, "Hu Yaobang yu Xidan minzhu qiang," at http://www.shufa.org/bbs/viewthread.php?tid=85030, accessed August 6, 2010.

10. Interview with Yu Guangyuan, January 2001.

11. Reprinted in Garside, *Coming Alive,* p. 247.

12. Ibid., p. 255.

13. Ibid., pp. 431–434.

14. Interview with Yu Guangyuan, January 2001.

15. Garside, *Coming Alive,* pp. 231–233; see also pp. 263–284.

16. Ibid., p. 257.

17. Ibid., pp. 257–259.

18. Observed by a Western scholar, n.d.

19. Garside, *Coming Alive,* p. 259.

20. Zhu Jiamu, "Hu Qiaomu zai shiyijie sanzhong quan huishang" (Hu Qiaomu at the Third Plenary Session of the Eleventh Central Committee), in Yu Guangyuan et al., *Gaibian Zhongguo mingyun de 41 tian: Zhongyang gongzuo huiyi, shiyijie sanzhong quanhui qinli ji* (The 41 Days That Changed the Fate of China: A Record of My Experience at the Central Work Conference of the Third Plenary Session of the Eleventh Central Committee) (Shenzhen: Haitian chubanshe, 1998), p. 308.

21. Interview with Yu Guangyuan, January 2001.

22. Deng Liqun, *Shierge chunqiu, 1975–1987: Deng Liqun zishu* (Twelve Springs and Autumns, 1975–1987: Deng Liqun's Autobiography) (Hong Kong: Bozhi chubanshe, 2006), p. 133.

23. Shen Baoxiang, *Zhenli biaozhun wenti taolun shimo* (The Complete Story of

the Discussion on Practice Is the Sole Criterion for Testing Truth) (Beijing: Zhongguo qingnian chubanshe, 1997), pp. 321–325. For accounts of the Theory Work Conference, see Sheng Ping, ed., *Hu Yaobang sixiang nianpu: 1975–1989* (A Chronology of Hu Yaobang's Thought: 1975–1989), 2 vols. (Hong Kong: Taide shidai chubanshe, 2007), 1:293–315; 1:341–347; Zheng Zhongbing, ed., *Hu Yaobang nianpu ziliao changbian* (Materials for a Chronological Record of Hu Yaobang's Life), 2 vols. (Hong Kong: Shidai guoji chuban youxian gongsi, 2005), 1:355–367, 1:385–387; *Guoshi*, vol. 10, pp. 69–82; Merle Goldman, *Sowing the Seeds of Democracy in China: Political Reform in the Deng Xiaoping Era* (Cambridge: Harvard University Press, 1994), pp. 47–61; Cheng Zhongyuan, Wang Yuxiang, and Li Zhenghua, *1976–1981 nian de Zhongguo* (China from 1976 to 1981) (Beijing: Zhongyang wenxian chubanshe, 1998), pp. 273–356.

24. Shen Baoxiang, *Zhenli biaozhun wenti taolun shimo*, p. 328.

25. The full text of the speech is in Zheng Zhongbing, *Hu Yaobang nianpu ziliao changbian*, 1:355–367.

26. Goldman, "Hu Yaobang's Intellectual Network," 229–237; Shen Baoxiang, *Zhenli biaozhun wenti taolun shimo*, pp. 323–327.

27. Shen Baoxiang, *Zhenli biaozhun wenti taolun shimo*, pp. 370–371.

28. Sheng Ping, *Hu Yaobang sixiang nianpu: 1975–1989*, 1:306; *Guoshi*, vol. 10, p. 67; interview with Wang Ruoshui, November 2001.

29. Sheng Ping, *Hu Yaobang sixiang nianpu: 1975–1989*, 1:306; *Guoshi*, vol. 10, p. 67.

30. Shen Baoxiang, *Zhenli biaozhun wenti taolun shimo*, pp. 342–347.

31. Ibid., pp. 321–333. The text of part of his speech is on pp. 321–323.

32. Goldman, *Sowing the Seeds of Democracy in China*, pp. 50–54.

33. Goldman, "Hu Yaobang's Intellectual Network," 229–235.

34. Shen Baoxiang, *Zhenli biaozhun wenti taolun shimo*, pp. 367–370.

35. *Guoshi*, vol. 10, pp. 65–74.

36. Sheng Ping, *Hu Yaobang sixiang nianpu: 1975–1989*, 1:322–324.

37. *DXPNP-2*, March 16, 1979.

38. Ming Ruan, *Deng Xiaoping: Chronicle of an Empire* (Boulder, Colo.: Westview, 1994), p. 56.

39. *DXPNP-2*, March 27, 1979.

40. *SWDXP-2*, p. 177.

41. *SWDXP-2*, pp. 179–181.

42. Deng Liqun, *Shierge chunqiu*, pp. 136–139. (Ye Jianying was unimpressed with Deng's speech; see p. 137.)

43. "Hu Yaobang tongzhi zai dangde lilun gongzuo wuxu huishang de jiesu yu" (Hu Yaobang's Words at the Closing Meeting of the Theory Work Conference), April 3, 1979. Extracts published in Sheng Ping, *Hu Yaobang sixiang nianpu: 1975–1989*, pp. 345–347.

44. Deng Liqun, *Shierge chunqiu*, pp. 138–139.

45. Goldman, "Hu Yaobang's Intellectual Network," 236–237.

46. *Guoshi*, vol. 10, pp. 165–247.

47. Deng Liqun, *Shierge chunqiu*, pp. 135–137.

48. Ibid., pp. 155–156.

49. See Goldman, *Sowing the Seeds of Democracy in China*; and Merle Goldman, *From Comrade to Citizen: The Struggle for Political Rights in China* (Cambridge: Harvard University Press, 2005).

9. The Soviet-Vietnamese Threat

1. Formally Deng took over responsibility for foreign affairs on March 10, 1978, but immediately after returning to work, he was in charge of meeting Cyrus Vance and dealing with concerns related to the United States, which was considered China's most important foreign policy issue.

2. Hua Huang *Huang Hua Memoirs* (Beijing: Foreign Languages Press, 2008).

3. George Bush and Brent Scowcroft, *A World Transformed* (New York: Knopf, 1998), p. 93.

4. Huang, *Huang Hua Memoirs*, p. 289.

5. Nayan Chanda, *Brother Enemy: The War after the War* (San Diego: Harcourt Brace Jovanovich, 1986), p. 259.

6. Robert S. Ross, *The Indochina Tangle: China's Vietnam Policy, 1975–1979* (New York: Columbia University Press, 1988), p. 67; Jian Chen, "China and the First Indo-China War, 1950–54," *The China Quarterly*, no. 133 (March 1993): 85–110.

7. Henry J. Kenny, "Vietnamese Perceptions of the 1979 War with China," in Mark A. Ryan, David M. Finkelstein, and Michael A. McDevitt, eds., *Chinese Warfighting: The PLA Experience since 1949* (Armonk, N.Y.: M. E. Sharpe, 2003), p. 218.

8. *DXPWJHD*, April 18, 19, 22, 23, 1965.

9. Kuan Yew Lee, *From Third World to First: The Singapore Story, 1965–2000* (New York: HarperCollins, 2000), p. 661. For the total aid program, see Junshi kexueyuan junshi lishi yanjiusuo (Military History Research Office of the Academy of Military Sciences), *Zhonghua renmin gongheguo junshi shiyao* (Outline of the Military History of the People's Republic of China) (Beijing: Junshi kexue chubanshe, 2005), pp. 549–570. U.S. sources vastly underestimated the number of Chinese forces in Vietnam during America's Vietnam War. One estimate, for example, was 50,000. See Kenny, "Vietnamese Perceptions of the 1979 War with China," p. 217; Donald S. Zagoria and Sheldon W. Simon, "Soviet Policy in Southeast Asia," in Zagoria, ed., *Soviet Policy in East Asia* (New Haven, Conn.: Yale University Press, 1982), pp. 153–173.

10. Jian Chen, *Mao's China and the Cold War* (Chapel Hill: University of North Carolina Press, 2001), pp. 221–229.

11. William J. Duiker, *Ho Chi Minh* (New York: Hyperion, 2000), pp. 541, 550.

12. Chen, *Mao's China and the Cold War,* pp. 229–237.

13. M. Taylor Fravel, *Strong Borders, Secure Nation: Cooperation and Conflict in China's Territorial Disputes* (Princeton, N.J.: Princeton University Press, 2008), pp. 276–287.

14. Chanda, *Brother Enemy,* pp. 13–18; Ross, *The Indochina Tangle,* pp. 64–65.

15. *DXPWJHD,* September 22–25, 1975.

16. Ibid., September 25, 1977.

17. Ross, *The Indochina Tangle,* pp. 67–68.

18. Chanda, *Brother Enemy,* pp. 134–135; Kenny, "Vietnamese Perceptions of the 1979 War with China," pp. 26–28, 222–223; Ross, *The Indochina Tangle,* p. 67.

19. Chanda, *Brother Enemy,* p. 28.

20. Ross, *The Indochina Tangle,* p. 75.

21. See, for example, Lee Kuan Yew's account of his seven hours of discussions with Hua Guofeng in May 1976; Lee, *From Third World to First,* pp. 642–650.

22. Chanda, *Brother Enemy,* pp. 27–28.

23. Ross, *The Indochina Tangle,* p. 68.

24. Ibid., p. 127; Chanda, *Brother Enemy,* pp. 88–89.

25. Ross, *The Indochina Tangle,* pp. 128–129.

26. Chanda, *Brother Enemy,* pp. 187–188, 240–245.

27. Ross, *The Indochina Tangle,* pp. 130–131.

28. Chanda, *Brother Enemy,* p. 189.

29. Lee, *From Third World to First,* p. 661.

30. Fan Hongwei, "Zhou Enlai yu Miandian huaqiao" (Zhou Enlai and the Burmese Overseas Chinese), *Dangdai Zhongguo shi yanjiu,* no. 1 (2008): 31–37.

31. See Wayne Bert, "Chinese Policy toward Burma and Indonesia: A Post-Mao Perspective," *Asian Survey* 25, no. 9 (September 1985): 963–980; Bertil Lintner, "Burma and Its Neighbors," in Surgit Mansingh, ed., *Indian and Chinese Foreign Policies in Comparative Perspective* (New Delhi: Radiant Publishers, 1998); Tian Zengpei, *Gaige kaifang yilai de Zhongguo waijiao* (Chinese Foreign Policy since the Reform and Opening) (Beijing: Shijie zhishi chubanshe, 2005), pp. 70–72; *DXPWJHD,* January 26–31, 1978; William R. Heaton, "China and Southeast Asian Communist Movements: The Decline of Dual Track Diplomacy," *Asian Survey* 22, no. 8 (August 1982): 779–800.

32. Xinhua News Service, February 4, 6, 1978.

33. Ibid., February 6, 1978.

34. *DXPNP-2,* April 18–26, 1975, pp. 36–37.

35. Don Oberdorfer, *The Two Koreas* (New York: Basic Books, 1997), p. 96.

36. Dae-Sook Suh, *Kim Il Sung: The North Korean Leader* (New York: Columbia University Press, 1988), pp. 262, 391, n26.

37. *DXPWJHD,* August 7, 1977.

38. Ibid., September 8–13, 1978; *DXPNP-2,* September 8–13, 1978.

39. *DXPNP-2,* September 12, 1978.

40. Pan Jingguo, ed., *Gongheguo waijiao fengyunzhong de Deng Xiaoping* (Deng Xiaoping in the Storm of Foreign Policy of the Republic) (Ha'erbin: Heilongjiang chubanshe, 2004), p. 379.

41. Chanda, *Brother Enemy,* p. 318; Ross, *The Indochina Tangle,* p. 208.

42. Ross, *The Indochina Tangle,* pp. 207–208.

43. Ibid., p. 208.

44. *DXPWJHD,* October 3, 1978.

45. Ibid., March 29–April 1, 1978.

46. Xinhua News Service, March 30, 1978.

47. *Facts on File World News Digest,* July 21, 1978.

48. Chanda, *Brother Enemy,* p. 325.

49. Xinhua News Service, November 9, 1978.

50. *DXPWJHD,* November 5–9, 1978; Xinhua News Service, November 9, 1978; Chanda, *Brother Enemy,* pp. 325–326; Lee, *From Third World to First,* p. 662.

51. Heaton, "China and Southeast Asian Communist Movements," 785.

52. Xinhua News Service, November 9, 1978.

53. Lucian W. Pye, *Guerrilla Communism in Malaya: Its Social and Political Meaning* (Princeton, N.J.: Princeton University Press, 1956).

54. Heaton, "China and Southeast Asian Communist Movements," pp. 786–790.

55. *Facts on File World News Digest,* November 24, 1978.

56. Xinhua News Service, November 10, 11, 1978.

57. Ibid., November 12, 1978.

58. Chanda, *Brother Enemy,* p. 325.

59. Stephen Leong, "Malaysia and the People's Republic of China in the 1980s: Political Vigilance and Economic Pragmatism," *Asian Survey* 27, no. 10 (October 1987): 1109–1126.

60. Xinhua News Service, November 12, 1978.

61. Lee, *From Third World to First,* pp. 662–665; also discussions with Singapore officials, November 2004.

62. Lee, *From Third World to First,* pp. 660–662; also discussions with Singapore officials, November 2004.

63. Discussions with Singapore officials, November 2004.

64. Lee, *From Third World to First,* p. 667.

65. Ibid., p. 668.

66. Ibid.

67. Discussions with Singapore officials who took part in meetings with Deng, November 2004.

68. Lee, *From Third World to First,* pp. 668–669.

69. Ross, *The Indochina Tangle,* p. 154.

10. Opening to Japan

1. The expression "anti-hegemony," which the Chinese used frequently, was first introduced to Premier Zhou Enlai by Henry Kissinger. See Henry Kissinger, "The China Connection," *Time,* October 1, 1979.

2. Pei Hua, ed., *ZhongRi waijiao fengyunzhong de Deng Xiaoping* (Deng Xiaoping amid the Currents of Sino-Japanese Foreign Relations) (Beijing: Zhongyang wenxian chubanshe, 2002), pp. 50–54.

3. Ibid., pp. 47–50.

4. See Sunao Sonoda, *Sekai Nihonai* (World, Japan, Love) (Tokyo: Shinchosha, 1981), pp. 174–185, for Sonoda's recollections.

5. For Huang Hua's account of the negotiations in the context of Sino-Japanese relations, see Hua Huang, *Huang Hua Memoirs* (Beijing: Foreign Languages Press, 2008), pp. 308–342.

6. Brzezinski reported that he had stopped in Tokyo in May 1978 after his visit to Beijing and impressed upon the Japanese that the United States favored an "expeditious conclusion of the treaty." He reports that the Japanese shortly thereafter "acceded" to the treaty. Zbigniew Brzezinski, *Power and Principle: Memoirs of the National Security Advisor, 1977–1981,* rev. ed. (New York: Farrar, Straus, Giroux, 1985), p. 218. The Japanese had already decided to move ahead with the treaty in March, but the issue was not resolved until July. When Fukuda met Vance and Carter in Washington on May 2 and 3, they also discussed these issues. See Pei Hua, *ZhongRi waijiao,* pp. 65–66.

7. Kazuhiko Togo, *Japan's Foreign Policy 1945–2003: The Quest for a Proactive Policy,* 2d ed. (Leiden: Brill, 2005), pp. 134–135; Pei Hua, *ZhongRi waijiao,* p. 80.

8. Chae-Jin Lee, *China and Japan: New Economic Diplomacy* (Stanford, Calif.: Hoover Institution Press, 1984), pp. 26–27.

9. Togo, *Japan's Foreign Policy,* pp. 134–135.

10. George R. Packard, *Edwin O. Reischauer and the American Discovery of Japan* (New York: Columbia University Press, 2010).

11. A Japanese book devoted entirely to Deng's visit to the emperor records this part of the visit in great detail. See Nagano Nobutoshi, *Tennō to Tō Shōhei no akushu: Jitsuroku Nitchū Kōshō hishi* (The Handshake between the Emperor and Deng Xiaoping: The Secret History of Sino-Japanese Relations) (Tokyo: Gyōsei Mondai Kenkyūjo, 1983).

12. The authoritative Chinese source on the visit of Deng to Japan is Pei Hua, *ZhongRi waijiao,* pp. 115–209.

13. Ibid., p. 120.

14. Ibid., pp. 121–122.

15. Ibid., p. 122.

16. Ibid., p. 125.

17. Huang, *Huang Hua Memoirs,* pp. 333–334; ibid., pp. 137–140.

18. Huang, *Huang Hua Memoirs,* pp. 334–335.

19. Pei Hua, *ZhongRi waijiao,* p. 126.

20. Ibid., pp. 147–148.

21. Ibid., p. 182.

22. Ibid., p. 151.

23. Ibid., pp. 150–153.

24. Ibid., pp. 154–155.

25. Ibid., pp. 150–155.

26. Ibid., pp. 156–159.

27. Ibid., p. 202.

28. Ibid., pp. 165–174.

29. Ibid., pp. 165–172.

30. Ibid., pp. 165–174.

31. Interview with Matsushita Konusuke, June 1979.

32. Matsushita Konusuke, *Matsushita Kōnosuke wa kataru: Jōnetsu ga nakereba hito wa ugokan* (Matsushita Speaks Out: Without Passion No One Works for You) (Tokyo: Kodansha, 1985), p. 137; Pei Hua, *ZhongRi waijiao,* pp. 194–197.

33. Interview with Akira Chihaya (then chairman of New Japan Steel and of the China Committee of Keidanren) and Hanai Mitsuyu, October 2004. Hanai was living in Manchuria at the end of World War II, when, at age thirteen, he left home and joined the PLA in northern Jilin. He remained in the PLA until after 1949, then attended People's University in Beijing. In 1957 Hanai returned to Japan and in 1962 he was hired by Yawata, where he worked as an interpreter, continuing after Yawata was merged into New Japan Steel.

34. Ibid.

35. Interview with Hanai Mitsuyu, Akira Chihaya, and Sugimoto Takashi, October 2004. In the 1980s Sugimoto was a Chinese-language interpreter and negotiator for New Japan Steel in China during the Baoshan negotiations. See also Pei Hua, *ZhongRi waijiao,* pp. 174–178.

36. Pei Hua, *ZhongRi waijiao,* p. 164.

37. Deng Liqun, *Shierge chunqiu, 1975–1987: Deng Liqun zishu* (Twelve Springs and Autumns, 1975–1987: Deng Liqun's Autobiography) (Hong Kong: Bozhi chubanshe, 2006), pp. 190–195; Deng Liqun, "Fang Ri guilai de sisuo" (Pondering the Return from the Visit to Japan), *Jingji guanli,* no. 3 (March 15, 1979): 7–14.

38. "Dai ikkai kakuryoo kaigi, Gaimushoo Ajia Kyoku Chuugoku ka" (The First Joint Cabinet Meeting), unpublished document, Chinese Section, Asian Bureau, Japanese Ministry of Foreign Affairs, Tokyo. The second cabinet meeting was held December 14–17, 1981.

39. Lanqing Li, *Breaking Through: The Birth of China's Opening-Up Policy* (New York: Oxford University Press, 2009), pp. 318–324.

11. Opening to the United States

1. Memcon, Carter with Huang Zhen, 2/8/77, vertical file, China, box 40, Jimmy Carter Library, Atlanta; Memo, Michel Oksenberg to Zbigniew Brzezinski, no. 17, "The Road to Normalization" (nine-page summary of the negotiations written shortly after negotiations were completed), vertical file, China, Jimmy Carter Library, also available in the Fairbank Collection, Fung Library, Harvard University.

2. Memcon, Secretary Vance's meeting with Huang Hua, 8/24/77, vertical file, China, Jimmy Carter Library. For various accounts of the discussions leading up to and including normalization talks, see Cyrus Vance, *Hard Choices: Critical Years in America's Foreign Policy* (New York: Simon and Schuster, 1983), pp. 75–83; Jimmy Carter, *Keeping Faith: Memoirs of a President* (Fayetteville: University of Arkansas Press, 1995), pp. 190–197: Zbigniew Brzezinski, *Power and Principle: Memoirs of the National Security Advisor, 1977–1981* (New York: Farrar, Straus, Giroux, 1983); Robert S. Ross, *Negotiating Cooperation: The United States and China, 1969–1989* (Stanford, Calif.: Stanford University Press, 1995); Patrick C. Tyler, *A Great Wall: Six Presidents and China: An Investigative History* (New York: PublicAffairs, 1999); Jimmy Carter, Zbigniew Brzezinski, and Richard N. Gardner, "Being There," *Foreign Affairs* 78, no. 6 (November–December 1999): 164–167; Brent Scowcroft and Patrick Tyler, "Safe Keeping," *Foreign Affairs* 79, no. 1 (January–February 2000): 192–194; James Mann, *About Face: A History of America's Curious Relationship with China from Nixon to Clinton* (New York: Alfred Knopf, 1999); Richard H. Solomon, *U.S.-PRC Political Negotiations, 1967–1984: An Annotated Chronology* (Santa Monica, Calif.: Rand, 1985), which was originally classified but later declassified; Richard H. Solomon, *Chinese Negotiating Behavior: Pursuing Interests through "Old Friends"* (Washington, D.C.: United States Institute of Peace Press, 1999); Nicholas Platt, *China Boys: How U.S. Relations with the PRC Began and Grew* (Washington, D.C.: New Academia, 2009); and Jeffrey T. Richelson, project director, *China and the United States: From Hostility to Engagement, 1960–1998* (Alexandria, Va.: Chadwyck-Healey, 1999). For an account of the issues concerning Taiwan, see Nancy Bernkopf Tucker, *Strait Talk: United States–Taiwan Relations and the Crisis with China* (Cambridge: Harvard University Press, 2009) and Alan D. Romberg, *Rein in at the Brink of the Precipice: American Policy toward Taiwan and U.S.-PRC Relations* (Washington, D.C.: Henry L. Stimson Center, 2003). In reconstructing the events of this chapter, I have talked with officials, including President Carter, Walter Mondale, Zbigniew Brzezinski, Stapleton Roy, Chas Freeman, Richard Solomon, Win Lord, Michel Oksenberg, and Nicholas Platt. I also talked with Chinese foreign minister Huang Hua and with Chinese interpreters Ji Chaozhu, Nancy Tang, Zhang Hanzhi, and Shi Yanhua. In addition, I have relied on the Carter Administration China Policy Oral History Project (LWMOT) for which Michel Oksenberg and Leonard Woodcock, after leaving office, met for thirty-nine sessions from the fall of 1981 through the summer

of 1982 to record and preserve for history their account of the normalization process. The records from these sessions are now deposited at the Wayne State University Library and in some of Woodcock's private papers, to which I had access courtesy of his widow, Sharon Woodcock.

3. Memcon, Meeting of Teng Xiao-ping and Secretary Vance, 8/24/77, vertical file, China, Jimmy Carter Library; Vance, *Hard Choices,* p. 82.

4. Solomon, *Chinese Negotiating Behavior.*

5. *DXPWJHD,* August 24, 1977.

6. Quotations are from *DXPNP-2,* August 24, 1977.

7. Vance, *Hard Choices,* p. 82; Solomon, *U.S.-PRC Political Negotiations, 1967–1984,* p. 62.

8. *DXPWJHD,* August 24, 1977.

9. Vance, *Hard Choices,* pp. 82–83; Ross, *Negotiating Cooperation,* pp. 110–111.

10. *DXPNP-2,* August 24, 1977.

11. Robert S. Ross, *The Indochina Tangle: China's Vietnam Policy, 1975–1979* (New York: Columbia University Press, 1988); *Renmin ribao* (People's Daily), November 26, 1975.

12. Memcon, Meeting of Teng Xiao-ping and Secretary Vance, 8/24/77, vertical file, China, Jimmy Carter Library; *DXPWJHD,* September 17, 1977.

13. Tyler, *A Great Wall,* pp. 249–250.

14. Cable, Brzezinski to Ambassador Woodcock, 11/18/77, Brzezinski Collection, Geo file, "Brzezinski's Trip [11/19/77—5/14/78]," box 9, Jimmy Carter Library.

15. Interview with Jimmy Carter, April 2009, and various discussions with Stapleton Roy and Woodcock's widow, Sharon Woodcock. Much of the story is available in Ross, *Negotiating Cooperation,* pp. 126–132. For a discussion of the Brzezinski-Vance rivalry, see Tyler, *A Great Wall,* pp. 237–239.

16. Memo, Michel Oksenberg to Zbigniew Brzezinski, "Impressions on our China Policy to Date," 8/23/78, Jimmy Carter Library, also available in the Fairbank Collection, Fung Library, Harvard University; Michel Oksenberg, "A Decade of Sino-American Relations," *Foreign Affairs* 61, no. 11 (Fall 1982): 184.

17. Interview with Stapleton Roy, who helped brief Congressional leaders, October 2008.

18. Memcon, Meeting of Zbigniew Brzezinski and Vice Premier Teng Hsiao P'ing, 5/25/78, vertical file, China, Jimmy Carter Library.

19. Memo, Cyrus Vance to the President on "Next Moves on China" Woodcock's Approach, 6/13/78, NSA Staff Material, Far East-Armacost, "Armacost Chron. File [6/14–6/30/78]," box 7, Jimmy Carter Library.

20. Although secrecy was tightly controlled on the U.S. side, a small number of government officials in Washington were involved in some of the discussions, including Richard Holbrooke, Harry Thayer, Roger Sullivan, James Lilley, Charles Neuhauser, and David Shambaugh.

21. Memcon, Dr. Brzezinski's meeting with Foreign Minister Huang Hua, May 21, 1978, 9:52 a.m. to 1:20 p.m., vertical file, China, Jimmy Carter Library; Solomon, *U.S.-PRC Political Negotiations, 1967–1984,* p. 64; Brzezinski, *Power and Principle,* p. 212. Brzezinski writes he told Huang Hua that peace in the Far East depended on continued U.S. credibility, which he took as a way of explaining delicately that the United States reserved the right to continue selling arms to Taiwan. In December, however, the Chinese expressed surprise that the United States was planning to continue selling arms to Taiwan. See the record of their conversation as well as Tyler, *A Great Wall,* pp. 254–255.

22. Carter, *Keeping Faith,* p. 200.

23. Brzezinski, *Power and Principle,* pp. 213–214.

24. *DXPWJHD,* May 21, 1978.

25. Oksenberg to Brzezinski, "The Road to Normalization."

26. Quotations are from Memcon, Meeting of Zbigniew Brzezinski and Vice Premier Teng Hsiao P'ing, 5/25/78.

27. Brzezinski, *Power and Principle,* p. 215.

28. *DXPWJHD,* May 22, 1978.

29. Ibid., August 6, 2005.

30. Solomon, *U.S.-PRC Political Negotiations, 1967–1984,* pp. 65–69.

31. *SWDXP-2,* pp. 98–111.

32. *DXPNP-2,* July 10, 1978.

33. Kathlin Smith, "The Role of Scientists in Normalizing U.S.-China Relations: 1965–1979," in Allison L. C. de Cerreno and Alexander Keynan, eds., "The Role of Scientists in Mitigating International Discord," *Annals of the New York Academy of Sciences* 866 (December 1998): 120; interview with Anne Keatley Solomon, the National Academy of Sciences staff official responsible for coordinating the visit, December 2005; Richard C. Atkinson (a member of Press's delegation), "Recollection of Events Leading to the First Exchange of Students, Scholars, and Scientists between the United States and the People's Republic of China," at http://www.rca.ucsd.edu/speeches/Recollections_China_student_exchange.pdf, accessed March 22, 2011. I was a member of the Committee on Scholarly Communication with the People's Republic of China (CSCPRC) for several years and traveled to China with the first delegation of scientists in May 1973. The Chinese scientists were subdued by the Cultural Revolution but hopeful, even though the relationship did not begin to blossom until 1978. In mid-October 1978, Zhou Peiyuan, the de facto president of Peking University, led a delegation of Chinese scholars to the United States to follow up on Deng's request to send scholars to the United States for further study. Due to the poor education during the Cultural Revolution, the number did not reach seven hundred in the first year and many of those who did go were not properly prepared in English. The U.S. government planned to manage exchanges through a government program as they did with exchanges with the Soviet Union, but Zhou Peiyuan, who had received a Ph.D. from the University of Chicago, made personal

contacts with scholars on the West Coast before traveling to Washington, D.C., and found ample private arrangements that did not require formal government relations (interview with Anne Keatley Solomon, December 2005); Atkinson, "Recollection of Events"; see also Memo, Frank Press to the President, 10/16/78, Staff Offices Collection: Science and Technology Adviser, Jimmy Carter Library.

34. Interview with President Jimmy Carter, April 2009.

35. LWMOT, tape 15, p. 25.

36. Ross, *Negotiating Cooperation,* p. 159.

37. Vance to Woodcock, 6/28/78, Brzezinski Collection, box 9, doc. 4, China, Alpha Channel [2/72–11/78], Jimmy Carter Library.

38. Woodcock to the White House, 7/25/78, Brzezinski Collection, box 9, doc. 4, China, Alpha Channel [2/72–11/78], Jimmy Carter Library.

39. His autobiography is Huang Hua, *Qinli yu jianwen: Huang Hua huiyilu* (History as I Witnessed It: The Memoirs of Huang Hua) (Beijing: Shijie zhishi chubanshe, 2007). The English translation is Hua Huang, *Huang Hua Memoirs* (Beijing: Foreign Languages Press, 2008).

40. Vance, *Hard Choices,* p. 117.

41. Memcon, USLO Peking, "Transcript of CODEL Wolff Meeting with Teng Hsiao-píng," 7/10/78, vertical file, China, box 40, Jimmy Carter Library.

42. Interview with Stapleton Roy, October 2008.

43. Richard Holbrooke and Michel Oksenberg to Ambassador Woodcock, 9/7/78, vertical file, China, box 40, doc. 24, Jimmy Carter Library.

44. Memcon, "Summary of the President's Meeting with Ambassador Ch'ai Tsemin," 9/19/78, vertical file, China, box 41, Jimmy Carter Library.

45. Memcon, Summary of Secretary Vance's Meeting with Foreign Minister Huang Hua, 10/3/78, vertical file, China, Jimmy Carter Library.

46. Ross, *Negotiating Cooperation,* pp. 134–136.

47. Interview with Stapleton Roy.

48. Robert D. Novak, *The Prince of Darkness: 50 Years Reporting in Washington* (New York: Crown Forum, 2007), pp. 324–332; *DXPWJHD,* November 27, 1978.

49. Leonard Woodcock to Cyrus Vance and Zbigniew Brzezinski, "Sixth Session: December 4 Meeting with Han Nianlong," Brzezinski Collection, Alpha box 9 cont. [12/78–1/79], docs. 3A, 4A, 5, and 6, Jimmy Carter Library.

50. Ross, *Negotiating Cooperation,* pp. 136–137.

51. Solomon, *U.S.-PRC Political Negotiations, 1967–1984,* p. 71; ibid., pp. 136–137.

52. Leonard Woodcock to Cyrus Vance and Zbigniew Brzezinski, "My Meeting with Teng Xiaoping December 13," Vertical File, China, box 40, Jimmy Carter Library.

53. Ibid.

54. LWMOT, tape 19, p. 8.

55. Leonard Woodcock to Cyrus Vance and Zbigniew Brzezinski, "To the White House Immediate," 12/14/78, vertical file, China, box 40, Jimmy Carter Library.

56. Ibid.

57. LWMOT, tape 18, p. 28.

58. Cable, Woodcock to Vance and Brzezinski, 12/15/78, "Full Transcript of December 15 Meeting with Teng," vertical file, China, box 40, Jimmy Carter Library.

59. Ibid.

60. This comment and all other quotes from the meeting are from Leonard Woodcock to Cyrus Vance and Zbigniew Brzezinski, "Full Transcript of December 15 meeting with Teng," 12/15/78, vertical file, China, box 40, Jimmy Carter Library.

61. Carter, *Keeping Faith*, p. 205.

62. Telephone Record, Peking to Secretary of State, 1/11/79, vertical file, China, Jimmy Carter Library.

63. Memo, Vance to Carter, 1/26/79, Scope Paper for the Visit of Vice Premier Deng Xiaoping of the People's Republic of China, January 29–February 5, 1979, vertical file, China, Jimmy Carter Library.

64. Observation by Richard Solomon who attended the ceremony, personal communication, November 2010.

65. Don Oberdorfer, "Teng and Khrushchev," *The Washington Post*, February 5, 1979, A1.

66. Chaozhu Ji, *The Man on Mao's Right: From Harvard Yard to Tiananmen Square, My Life inside China's Foreign Ministry* (New York: Random House, 2008).

67. Orville Schell, *"Watch Out for the Foreign Guests!" China Encounters the West* (New York: Pantheon, 1980).

68. Carter, *Keeping Faith*, p. 214.

69. Michel Oksenberg, "I Remember Deng," *Far Eastern Economic Review*, March 6, 1977, 35; Brzezinski, *Power and Principle*, pp. 405–406.

70. Brzezinski, *Power and Principle*, p. 406.

71. Carter, *Keeping Faith*, p. 207.

72. Ibid., pp. 209–210.

73. *DXPNP-2*, January 24, 1979.

74. Letter, Carter to Deng, Brzezinski Collection, China, Pres. Meeting w/ Deng Xiaoping, box 9, Jimmy Carter Library.

75. Carter, *Keeping Faith*, pp. 211–213; Brzezinski, *Power and Principle*, pp. 409–410.

76. Brzezinski, *Power and Principle*, pp. 412–415.

77. Solomon, *U.S.-PRC Political Negotiations, 1967–1984*, p. 76.

78. Carter, *Keeping Faith*, p. 211; Brzezinski, *Power and Principle*, p. 407. A list of attendees at the state banquet, including some twenty-two members of Congress, may be found in the *New York Times*, January 30, 1979.

79. Carter, *Keeping Faith*, p. 213.

80. Ibid., p. 212; *The Washington Post,* November 1, 1979; *The New York Times,* January 30, 1979.

81. On communications between Nixon and Carter, see "Staff Office on Chinese Normalization" Collection, box 34A, Jimmy Carter Library.

82. LWMOT, tape 21, p. 7.

83. Brzezinski, *Power and Principle,* p. 407; Tyler, *A Great Wall,* p. 275.

84. Memcon, Mondale and Deng in Beijing, 8/28/79, Vertical File, China, box 41, Jimmy Carter Library.

85. Solomon, *U.S.-PRC Political Negotiations, 1967–1984,* p. 76.

86. Tip O'Neill, *Man of the House: The Life and Political Memoirs of Speaker Tip O'Neill* (New York: Random House, 1987), pp. 306–307.

87. Arthur Hummel and David Reuther in Nancy Bernkopf Tucker, ed., *China Confidential: American Diplomats and Sino-American Relations, 1945–1996* (New York: Columbia University Press, 2001), p. 329; Carter, *Keeping Faith,* p. 213.

88. I was one of those in attendance on the occasion. Jan Berris, vice president of the National Committee on U.S.-China Relations, kindly shared documents and memories of the occasion as well.

89. Don Oberdorfer, "Teng, Tired but Satisfied, Leaves U.S.," *The Washington Post,* February 6, 1979, A12.

90. Karen Elliott House, "Teng to Return to China with Assurances of U.S. Economic, Political Cooperation," *Wall Street Journal,* February 5, 1979, 6.

91. Donald Anderson, Chinese-speaking State Department official who accompanied the Deng delegation around the country, in Tucker, *China Confidential,* p. 330; *New York Post,* January 29, 1979.

92. Fox Butterfield, "Teng Inspects Boeing 747 Factory," *New York Times,* February 6, 1979, A1.

93. Oberdorfer, "Teng and Khrushchev."

94. Richard L. Strout, *Christian Science Monitor,* February 5, 1979.

95. Harry F. Rosenthal, Associated Press, Atlanta, February 1, 1979.

96. *Atlanta Constitution* and *Atlanta Journal,* February 1, 2, 1979.

97. LWMOT, tape 22, p. 6.

98. Schell, *"Watch Out for the Foreign Guests,"* p. 124.

99. *Houston Post,* February 3, 1979.

100. Oberdorfer, "Teng and Khrushchev."

101. Associated Press, Seattle, February 5, 1979.

102. LWMOT, tape 22, p. 14.

103. Carter, *Keeping Faith,* p. 207. The fuller diary was later published as Jimmy Carter, *White House Diary* (New York: Farrar, Straus, and Giroux, 2010).

104. Carter, *Keeping Faith,* p. 207.

105. Ibid., p. 216.

106. From Don Oberdorfer, who covered both their tours as a newsman. See Oberdorfer, "Teng and Khrushchev"; Richard L. Strout, *Christian Science Monitor,* February 5, 1979.

107. Smith, "The Role of Scientists in Normalizing U.S.-China Relations."

108. David M. Lampton, *A Relationship Restored: Trends in U.S.-China Educational Exchanges, 1978–1984* (Washington, D.C.: National Academy Press, 1986), pp. 30–32.

109. Harry Thayer and Arthur Hummel, in Tucker, *China Confidential,* pp. 326–328. These issues and the concern with China's human rights record were also raised in a *Christian Science Monitor* editorial of January 29, 1979.

110. Interview, February 2008, with Shi Yanhua, one of Deng's English-language interpreters and later China's ambassador to Luxemburg, and Ji Chaozhu, Deng's interpreter on the trip to the United States, November 2006 and April 2009.

12. Launching the Deng Administration

1. *Guoshi,* vol. 10, pp. 194–204.

2. *DXPNP-2,* July 11, 1979.

3. Among scholars, Warren Sun was the first to call attention to the political significance of the climb up Yellow Moutain.

4. *SWDXP-2,* pp. 197–201.

5. For example, Deng Liqun, *Shierge chunqiu, 1975–1987: Deng Liqun zishu* (Twelve Springs and Autumns, 1975–1987: Deng Liqun's Autobiography) (Hong Kong: Bozhi chubanshe, 2006), p. 157.

6. Interviews with Deng's daughter, Deng Rong, 2002–2006.

7. *SWDXP-2,* pp. 197–201.

8. *DXPNP-2,* September 5–October 7, p. 553. For Hu Yaobang's full speech at the conclusion of the forum on October 5, 1979, see Zheng Zhongbing, ed., *Hu Yaobang nianpu ziliao changbian* (Materials for a Chronological Record of Hu Yaobang's Life), 2 vols. (Hong Kong: Shidai guoji chuban youxian gongsi, 2005), 1:412–421.

9. Deng Liqun, *Shierge chunqiu,* pp. 150–152.

10. LWMOT, tape 29, pp. 7–8.

11. Xinhua General Overseas News Service, September 30, 1979, pp. 1–22.

12. Ibid., pp. 6–7.

13. Ibid., p. 2.

14. Ibid., p. 6.

15. Deng Liqun, *Shierge chunqiu,* p. 160.

16. An excellent discussion of the issues related to preparing the report on party history is contained in *Guoshi,* vol. 10, pp. 249–258.

17. Deng Liqun, *Shierge chunqiu,* p. 160.

18. LWMOT, tape 31, pp. 16–17.

19. *DXPNP-2,* late October 1979, p. 574.

20. Ibid., October 12, 1979, p. 566; November 10, 1979, p. 578.

21. *SWDXP-2,* pp. 225–226.

22. Ibid., p. 251.

23. Ibid., pp. 241–242.

24. Ibid., p. 242.

25. Ibid., p. 233.

26. Ibid., pp. 253–254.

27. Ibid., pp. 252–257.

28. Interview with Edwin Lim, August 2009. Lim was head of the China desk at the World Bank in the early 1980s and head of the Beijing Office of the World Bank in the first years after it was established.

29. *SWDXP-2,* pp. 260–261.

30. Ibid., pp. 260–265.

31. Ibid., pp. 280, 281.

32. Ibid., pp. 273–283.

33. *DXPNP-2,* February 28, 1980, and May 17, 1980. For broader background on the reversal of verdicts, see *Guoshi,* vol. 10, pp. 258–267.

34. The record of his meetings in Japan is found in "Hua Guofeng sori jun nichi: shuno kaidan ni okeru" (Premier Hua Guofeng's Visit to Japan: Concerning the Summit Conversation), May 27–29, 1980 (China Section, Asia Bureau, Japanese Ministry of Foreign Affairs), declassified, on file in the Japanese Ministry of Foreign Affairs.

35. The text of the final document is "Resolution on Certain Questions in the History of Our Party since the Founding of the People's Republic of China," June 27, 1981, *Beijing Review,* no. 27 (July 6, 1981).

36. Oriana Fallaci, "Deng: Cleaning Up Mao's 'Feudal Mistakes,'" *Washington Post,* August 31, 1980; *SWDXP-2,* August 21, 23, 1980, pp. 326–334.

37. *DXPNP-2,* October 25, 1980.

38. *SWDXP-2,* pp. 290–292; Deng Liqun, *Shierge chunqiu,* pp. 160–162.

39. *SWDXP-2,* p. 295.

40. Ibid., pp. 295–297; Deng Liqun, *Shierge chunqiu,* pp. 164–166.

41. A detailed summary of the views of many officials is contained in *Zhongzhi jiguan taolun lishi jueyi (cao'an) jianbao* (Summary of the Discussion on the Resolution on Party History in the Organs directly under the Party Center [draft]), unpublished document available in the Fairbank Collection, Fung Library, Harvard University.

42. Deng Liqun, *Shierge chunqiu,* pp. 103–104; *SWDXP-2,* pp. 289–290.

43. *Resolution on CPC History (1949–81)* (Beijing: Foreign Languages Press, 1981), pp. 28, 32.

44. Deng Liqun, *Shierge chunqiu*, p. 165.

45. Deng acknowledged his own errors in this general way, but he did not give concrete examples except when under pressure to do so.

46. *SWDXP-2*, pp. 342–349.

47. Qian Qichen, "Yici ji bu xunchang de tanhua" (A Very Unusual Interview), in Zhonggong zhongyang wenxian yanjiushi (Central Chinese Communist Party Literature Research Office), ed., *Huiyi Deng Xiaoping*, 3 vols. (Beijing: Zhongyang wenxian chubanshe, 1998), 1:35–41.

48. "Zhengfu gongzuo baogao" (Government Work Report), in Zhonggong zhongyang wenxian yanjiushi (Central Chinese Communist Party Literature Research Office), ed., *Sanzhong quanhui yilai zhongyao wenjian huibian* (Beijing: Renmin chubanshe, 1982), June 18, 1979, 1:198–222.

49. Deng Liqun, *Shierge chunqiu*, pp. 166–169; Gaimusho Ajia Kyoku, Chugokuka, May 27–29, 1980 (China Section, Asia Bureau, Japanese Ministry of Foreign Affairs), declassified, on file in the Japanese Ministry of Foreign Affairs.

50. *SWDXP-2*, June 22, 1981, pp. 306–308.

51. Deng Liqun, *Shierge chunqiu*, p. 169; ibid., p. 297.

52. *SWDXP-2*, pp. 304–305; Deng Liqun, *Shierge chunqiu*, p. 196.

53. "Hu Yaobang zai zhongyang zhengzhiju huiyishang de fayan" (Hu Yaobang Speech to the Politburo Meeting), November 19, 1982, in Zhonggong zhongyang wenxian yanjiushi, *Sanzhong quanhui yilai zhongyao wenjian huibian*, 2:735–747.

54. Interview with someone close to Mao Yuanxin, January 2006.

55. Deng Liqun, *Shierge chunqiu*, pp. 169–171.

56. Ibid.

57. Richard Baum, *Burying Mao: Chinese Politics in the Age of Deng Xiaoping* (Princeton, N.J.: Princeton University Press, 1994), pp. 116–117.

13. Deng's Art of Governing

1. *SWDXP-2*, p. 329.

2. From an examination of Deng by Dr. Samuel Rosen, an ear, nose and throat specialist. The information is from David Shambaugh, November 2010.

3. Carol Lee Hamrin, "The Party Leadership System," in Kenneth G. Lieberthal and David M. Lampton, eds., *Bureaucracy, Politics, and Decision Making in Post-Mao China* (Berkeley: University of California Press, 1992), pp. 95–124. For lists of members of the party Central Committee, Politburo, and Politburo Standing Committee, see the annual *China Directory, in Pinyin and Chinese* (Tokyo: Radiopress, 1979–present). For an overall summary of the functioning of these institutions, see Kenneth Lieberthal, *Governing China: From Revolution through Reform*, 2d ed. (New York: W.W. Norton, 2004). For more recent developments, see Richard McGregor, *The Party: The Secret World of China's Communist Rulers* (New York: Harper, 2010).

4. For the concept of *xitong* (vertical functional hierarchy), see A. Doak Barnett, with a contribution by Ezra F. Vogel, *Cadres, Bureaucracy, and Political Power in Communist China* (New York: Columbia University Press, 1967). Also see Lieberthal, *Governing China.*

5. See Hamrin, "The Party Leadership System," pp. 95–124.

6. Interviews with Wu Mingyu, one of Deng's bridge partners, August 2006, July 2007.

7. Interviews with Deng's daughter, Deng Rong, 2002–2006.

8. Interviews with people who served under Deng; Ezra F. Vogel, "From Friendship to Comradeship: The Change in Personal Relations in Communist China," *The China Quarterly*, no. 21 (January–March 1965): 46–60.

9. Wang Wenqing and Liu Yiding, "Gaige kaifang chuqi de renshi zhidu gaige: Fang yuan guojia renshiju juzhang Jiao Shanmin" (Reform of the Personnel System at the Beginning of the Period of Reform and Opening: An Interview with Former Chief of the Personnel Bureau Jiao Shanmin), *Bainianchao*, no. 5 (2007): 42–47. Jiao Shanmin was head of state personnel at the time.

10. This is an observation by Leonard Woodcock; see LWMOT.

11. *SWDXP-2,* p. 97.

14. Experiments in Guangdong and Fujian

1. *Guoshi,* vol. 10, p. 760.

2. *DXPNP-2,* November 8, 18, 20, 1977; *Guoshi,* vol. 10, p. 760.

3. *Guoshi,* vol. 10, p. 760.

4. Ibid.

5. See Ezra F. Vogel, *Canton under Communism: Programs and Politics in a Provincial Capital, 1949–1968* (Cambridge: Harvard University Press, 1969).

6. Yang Shangkun, *Yang Shangkun huiyilu* (Recollections of Yang Shangkun) (Beijing: Zhongyang wenxian chubanshe, 2001); Yang Shangkun, *Yang Shangkun riji* (Yang Shangkun's Diary), 2 vols. (Beijing: Zhongyang wenxian chubanshe, 2001).

7. Yang Jisheng, *Zhongguo gaige niandai de zhengzhi douzheng* (Political Struggles during the Period of China's Reform) (Hong Kong: Excellent Culture Press, 2004), pp. 235–236; Xi Zhongxun zhuzheng Guangdong bianweihui (Editorial Committee for Xi Zhongxun in Power in Guangdong), *Xi Zhongxun zhuzheng Guangdong* (Xi Zhongxun in Power in Guangdong) (Beijing: Zhonggong dangshi chubanshe, 2007).

8. For Gu Mu's summary of some of the key events in setting up the zones, see Gu Mu, "Xiaoping lingdao women zhua kaifang" (Xiaoping Led Us to Grasp Opening), *Bainianchao*, no. 1 (1998): 4–11. Reprinted in Yang Tianshi, ed., *Deng Xiaoping xiezhen* (A Portrait of Deng Xiaoping) (Shanghai: Shanghai cishu chubanshe, 2005), pp. 204–211.

9. *Guoshi,* vol. 10, p. 764.

10. Zhonggong zhongyang wenxian yanjiushi (Central Chinese Communist Party Literature Research Office), ed., *Huiyi Deng Xiaoping*, 3 vols. (Beijing: Zhongyang wenxian chubanshe, 1998), 2:383; "Let's call them special zones. In the past, Shaan-Gan-Ning was called a special zone! There was no money, but the center enacted some policies to make a breakthrough and to hew a path" *(Haishi jiao tequ hao. Guoqu Shaan-gan-ning jiu jiao tequ ma! Meiyou qian, zhongyang gei xie zhengce, you nimen chu chuang. Sha chu yi tiao xue lu), DXPNP-2,* p. 510.

11. Interview with Yang Li, later vice governor of Guangdong, who took part in the delegation, December 1987.

12. Following the issuance of Document No. 50 on July 15, a series of circulars by the government and Central Committee were issued on Guangdong, Fujian, and the SEZs. Document No. 27, addressing theoretical questions, was issued on July 19, 1981, Document No. 17, on crimes and smuggling, was issued on March 1, 1982, and Document No. 50, confirming the role of the SEZs, was issued on December 3, 1982. All were issued under the direction of Gu Mu. See Lawrence Reardon, ed., "China's Coastal Development Strategy, 1979–1984 (I)," *Chinese Law and Government* 27, no. 3 (May–June 1994) and "China's Coastal Development Strategy, 1979–1984 (II)," *Chinese Law and Government* 27, no. 4 (July–August 1994).

13. *DXPNP-2*, April 17, 1979; Gu Mu, "Xiaoping tongzhi lingdao women zhua duiwai kaifang" (Comrade Xiaoping Led Us to Grasp Reform and Opening), in Zhonggong zhongyang wenxian yanjiushi, *Huiyi Deng Xiaoping*, 1:157–158. For Deng's later account of this, see *SWDXP-3*, June 12, 1987, pp. 236–237.

14. Reardon, "China's Coastal Development Strategy, 1979–1984 (I)," pp. 19–44.

15. Ibid., pp. 45–58.

16. Sebastian Heilmann, "From Local Experiments to National Policy: The Origins of China's Distinctive Policy Process," *China Journal*, no. 59 (January 2008): 1–30.

17. Ou Dajun and Liang Zhao, "Deng Xiaoping jingji tequ lilun" (Deng Xiaoping's Theory on Special Economic Zones), *Dangdai Zhongguo shi yanjiu*, no. 4 (2004): 41–49.

18. Gao Bowen, "Ershi shiji bashi niandai yanhai diqu jingji fazhan zhanlüe de xuanze jiqi xiaoying" (The Choice of Economic Development Strategy in China's Coastal Regions in the 1980s and Its Effects), *Dangdai Zhongguo shi yanjiu*, no. 4 (2005): 92–100.

19. Xu Maohui and Xu Weisheng, "Deng Xiaoping quyu jingji xietiao fazhan sixiang xingcheng de tiaojian" (Deng Xiaoping's Thoughts on the Conditions for the Formation of Coordinated Regional Economic Development), *Dangdai Zhongguo shi yanjiu*, no. 4 (2004): 80–85.

20. China Data Center, *National and Provincial Statistics* (Ann Arbor: University of Michigan, various years).

21. Gu Mu, *Gu Mu huiyi lu* (Recollections of Gu Mu) (Beijing: Zhongyang wenxian chubanshe, 2009), p. 256.

22. Reardon, "China's Coastal Development Strategy, 1979–1984 (I)," pp. 21–32.

23. Zhonggong zhongyang wenxian yanjiushi, *Huiyi Deng Xiaoping*, 2:383.

24. Wang Shuo, "Teshi teban: Hu Yaobang yu jingji tequ" (Special Issues, Special Procedures: Hu Yaobang and the Special Economic Zones), *Yanhuang chunqiu*, no. 4 (2008): 37.

25. Christine Loh, *Underground Front: The Chinese Communist Party in Hong Kong* (Hong Kong: Hong Kong University Press, 2010), pp. 152–153.

26. Reardon, "China's Coastal Development Strategy, 1979–1984 (I)," p. 22.

27. These observations are based on my field work in Guangdong in the 1980s and 1990s. In 1980 I was there for two months. In the early 1980s, I took several field trips, and from 1985 through the 1990s I made at least one field trip per year. In 1986, I spent six months in Guangdong and had a chance to travel to each of the prefectures and to visit enterprises in some thirty counties. See Ezra F. Vogel, *One Srep Ahead in China: Guangdong under Reform* (Cambridge: Harvard University Press, 1989).

28. Reardon, "China's Coastal Development Strategy, 1979–1984 (II)," pp. 32–33.

29. Lu Di, "Weiren de danshi he xionghuai: Ji Ren Zhongyi huiyi Deng Xiaoping" (The Courage, Insight, and Cherished Memory of the Great Man: Remembering Ren Zhongyi's Recollections of Deng Xiaoping), *Bainianchao*, no. 8 (2008): 18–19; *Guoshi*, vol. 10, pp. 771–772.

30. For a description of the influence of the growing wealth on families, including their new consumption patterns, see Charlotte Ikels, *The Return of the God of Wealth: The Transition to a Market Economy in Urban China* (Stanford, Calif.: Stanford University Press, 1996).

31. Rachel Murphy, *How Migrant Labor Is Changing Rural China* (New York: Cambridge University Press, 2002); Leslie T. Chang, *Factory Girls: From Village to City in a Changing China* (New York: Spiegel and Grau, 2008).

32. *CYNP,* December 12, 1981.

33. *SWCY,* 3:303.

34. Ibid., 3:307.

35. Ibid., 3:303.

36. Wang Shuo, "Teshi teban," pp. 36–37.

37. Guan Shan, "Ren Zhongyi tan Deng Xiaoping yu Guangdong de gaige Kaifang" (Ren Zhongyi on Deng Xiaoping and the Reform and Opening in Guangdong), *Yanhuang chunqiu*, no. 8 (2004): 8–17. Interviews with Du Ruizhi, July 17 and November 11, 2006. Du Ruizhi, also a member of the Guangdong Provincial Party Committee at the time, attended meetings with Ren Zhongyi, both in Guangdong and Beijing.

38. Guan Shan, "Ren Zhongyi tan Deng Xiaoping," pp. 8–17.

39. Reardon, "China's Coastal Development Strategy, 1979–1984 (I)," pp. 46–58; Discussions with Lawrence Reardon, translator and editor of these documents.

40. *CYNP,* January 5, 1982, p. 287; *DXPNP-2,* January 5, 1982, p. 796.

41. *DXPNP-2,* January 18, 1982.

42. Guan Shan, "Ren Zhongyi tan Deng Xiaoping," p. 10.

43. Wang Shuo, "Teshi teban," p. 38; see also Lu Di, "Weiren de danshi he xionghuai," pp. 16–22.

44. *CYNP,* January 25, 1982, pp. 289–290. The English excerpt from the speech replaces the phrase "get out of the cage" with "come out boldly"; *SWCY,* 3:307.

45. Hence the heading of the section, *er jingong* (literally, "twice entering the palace"). The reference is drawn from a Beijing opera in which a Ming official, once jailed for breaking the law, is released, again commits a crime, and then is called back to the palace and again sent to jail.

46. *CYNP,* February 11–13, 1982. Although I interviewed Ren Zhongyi several times after he retired, he never mentioned the meetings in Beijing nor did he complain about Beijing's pressure. He said only that he had tried to do his best to carry out the party's wishes and to deal with the smuggling and corruption. Information about Ren's summons to Beijing comes from publications by other officials.

47. Guan Shan, "Ren Zhongyi tan Deng Xiaoping," p. 14; interviews with Du Ruizhi, July 2006 and November 2006.

48. Yang Jisheng, *Zhongguo gaige niandai de zhengzhi douzheng,* pp. 238–242; Guan Shan, "Ren Zhongyi tan Deng Xiaoping," pp. 11–12.

49. Gu Mu, "Xiaoping lingdao women zhua kaifang," p. 206.

50. Wang Shuo, "Teshi teban," p. 39.

51. For an account of the case that received the most attention, the Hainan Island car scandal, see Vogel, *One Step Ahead in China.*

52. Lu Di, "Weiren de danshi he xionghuai," p. 20.

53. Ibid.

54. Dong Fureng, ed., *Zhonghua renmin gongheguo jingji shi* (An Economic History of the PRC), 2 vols. (Beijing: Jingji kexue chubanshe, 1999), p. 138.

55. *DXPNP-2,* January 22 to February 17, 1984; *SWDXP-3,* February 24, 1984, p. 61.

56. *DXPNP-2,* January 22 to February 24, 1984.

57. Ibid., February 14, 1984.

58. Ibid., February 24, 1984; *SWDXP-3,* pp. 61, 64–65.

59. Reardon, "China's Coastal Development Strategy, 1979–1984 (II)," pp. 49–66.

60. Ibid., pp. 49–66.

61. Gu Mu, "Xiaoping tongzhi lingdao women zhua duiwai kaifang," 1:152–174.

62. Notes from my attendance at the games.

15. Economic Readjustment and Rural Reform

1. As told to Timothy Stratford in late 1990, commercial minister-counselor in the U.S. embassy in Beijing, 1989–1992.

2. One account of the differences between the planners and the builders can be found in Chen Zhiling, "Yao Yilin," in Zhonggong dangshi renwu zhuan yanjiu hui (Research Committee on Chinese Communist Biographies), ed., *Zhonggong dangshi renwu zhuan* (Biographies of Chinese Communist Personalities) (Beijing: Zhongyang wenxian chubanshe, 2000), 72:1–120.

3. Kenneth Lieberthal and Michel Oksenberg, *Policy Making in China: Leaders, Structures, and Processes* (Princeton, N.J.: Princeton University Press, 1988), p. 45.

4. Dorothy J. Solinger, "The Fifth National People's Congress and the Process of Policy Making: Reform, Readjustment, and the Opposition," *Asian Survey* 22, no. 12 (December 1982): 1238–1275; Hua Kuo-Feng, "Unite and Strive to Build a Modern Powerful Socialist Country!" *Peking Review* 21, no. 10 (March 10, 1978): 24–26.

5. Jinglian Wu, *Understanding and Interpreting Chinese Economic Reform* (Mason, Ohio: Thomson/South-Western, 2005); Wu Li, ed., *Zhonghua renmin gongheguo jingjishi, 1949–1999* (An Economic History of the People's Republic of China, 1949–1999), 2 vols. (Beijing: Zhongguo jingji chubanshe, 1999), 1:773; Barry Naughton, *Growing Out of the Plan: Chinese Economic Reform, 1978–1993* (New York: Cambridge University Press, 1995), p. 67; Thomas Rawski, "Reforming China's Economy: What Have We Learned?" *China Journal*, no. 41 (January 1999): 139–156.

6. The Chinese term *guihua*, ordinarily translated as "plan," is different from *jihua*, though it is also translated as "plan." I translate the term "ten-year *guihua*" as "ten-year economic vision" because it lays out the goals, similar to the economic "visions" issued by Japan's MITI. The five-year and annual plans *(jihua)*, unlike the *guihua*, specify where the inputs are to come from and precisely where the funds and resources will be used. The ten-year economic vision is drawn up by a separate section of the State Planning Commission.

7. Naughton, *Growing Out of the Plan*, pp. 70–71.

8. *CYNP,* December 10, 1978; *SWCY,* 3:237–239.

9. *DXPNP-2*, pp. 465–467, January 6, 1979; Xiao Donglian, "1979 nian guomin jingji tiaozheng fangzhen de tichu yu zhenglun" (The Proposal and Debate over the 1979 Economic Readjustment Policy: The First Big Turning Point), *Dangshi bolan*, no. 10 (2004): 4–10.

10. Denis Fred Simon, "China's Capacity to Assimilate Foreign Technology: An Assessment," in U.S. Congress, Joint Economic Committee, *China under the Four Modernizations: Selected Papers*, 2 vols. (Washington, D.C.: Government Printing

Office, 1982), 1:523; Chae-Jin Lee, *China and Japan: New Economic Diplomacy* (Stanford, Calif.: Hoover Institution Press, 1984), pp. 47–49.

11. *CYNP,* March 14, 1979; March 21–23, 1979; *SWCY,* 3:248–254. The full text can be found in Zhonggong zhongyang wenxian yanjiushi (Central Chinese Communist Party Literature Research Office), ed., *Sanzhong quanhui yilai zhongyao wenjian huibian* (Major Documents since the Third Plenum), 2 vols. (Beijing: Renmin chubanshe, 1982), 1:109–147.

12. Dong Fureng, ed., *Zhonghua renmin gongheguo jingji shi* (An Economic History of the PRC), 2 vols. (Beijing: Jingji kexue chubanshe, 1999), 2:8; Barry Naughton, *The Chinese Economy: Transitions and Growth* (Cambridge: MIT Press, 2007).

13. Gene Tidrick and Chen Jiyuan, eds., *China's Industrial Reform* (New York: Oxford University Press, 1987), p. 2.

14. Deng Liqun, *Shierge chunqiu, 1975–1987: Deng Liqun zishu* (Twelve Springs and Autumns, 1975–1987: Deng Liqun's Autobiography) (Hong Kong: Bozhi chubanshe, 2006), p. 143. Deng Liqun attended the meeting and was one of the drafters of the report. For an account of the Wuxi conference, see Joseph Fewsmith, *Dilemmas of Reform in China: Political Conflict and Economic Debate* (Armonk, N.Y.: M. E. Sharpe, 1994), pp. 62–68.

15. Deng Liqun, *Shierge chunqiu,* p. 144.

16. Dong Fureng, *Zhonghua renmin gongheguo jingji shi,* 2:8–9.

17. For a summary of the process of allowing the provinces to "eat in separate kitchens" (by splitting the kitchen, as brothers often did when the parents died), see Susan L. Shirk, *The Political Logic of Economic Reform in China* (Berkeley: University of California Press, 1993), pp. 162–175.

18. Fewsmith, *Dilemmas of Reform,* pp. 92–96.

19. Rong Sheng, "Deng Liqun tan Chen Yun jingji sixiang" (Deng Liqun on Chen Yun's Economic Thinking), *Zhengming,* no. 32 (May 1, 1981): 43–44, translated in JPRS: *China Report, Political, Sociological and Military Affairs,* no. 200 (JPRS 78410), June 29, 1981, pp. 35–40.

20. Wu Li, *Zhonghua renmin gongheguo jingjishi, 1949–1999,* 1:776.

21. Benkan teyue jizhe (Special Correspondent), "Gaige chuqi de gongye xue Daqing huodong: Fang Yuan Baohua tongzhi" (Learning from Daqing about Industry at the Beginning of Reform: An Interview with Comrade Yuan Baohua), *Bainianchao,* no. 8 (2002): 9. For an account of Kang Shi'en, see Wen Houwen, *Kang Shi'en zhuan* (A Biography of Kang Shi'en) (Beijing: Dangdai Zhongguo chubanshe, 1998).

22. Fewsmith, *Dilemmas of Reform,* pp. 100–109.

23. Quanguo renda changweihui bangongting yanjiushi (Research Division of the General Office of the Standing Committee of the NPC), *Zhonghua renmin gongheguo renmin daibiao dahui wenxian ziliao huibian, 1949–1990* (Collection of Materials on

the National People's Congresses of the People's Republic of China, 1949–1990) (Beijing: Zhongguo minzhu fazhi chubanshe, 1991), p. 785.

24. Fewsmith, *Dilemmas of Reform,* p. 100.

25. *CYZ,* pp. 1561, 1600.

26. *CYNP,* November 28, 1980. Deng supported Chen in his comments on economic work on October 4, 1979; *DXPNP-2,* October 4, 1979; *SWDXP-2,* pp. 201–208.

27. *CYNP,* December 16, 1980; *SWCY,* 3:275–280; Dong Fureng, *Zhonghua renmin gongheguo jingji shi,* 2:25.

28. *SWDXP-2,* pp. 350–368. On November 28, Deng also gave a speech strongly supporting Chen Yun's readjustment policy. See *CYNP,* November 28, 1980, and *DXPNP-2,* November 28, 1980.

29. Lee, *China and Japan,* pp. 49–50.

30. *DXPNP-2,* September 4, 1980.

31. Lee, *China and Japan,* p. 62; Ryosei Kokubun, "The Politics of Foreign Economic Policy-Making in China: The Case of Plant Cancellations with Japan," *The China Quarterly,* no. 105 (March 1986): 19–44; *DXPNP-2,* p. 712, February 12, 1981. See also various discussions with Okita Saburo, August 1983.

32. Okada Takahiro, "Interview with Okita Saburo," *Chuo Koron* (April 1981): 116–121; Saburo Okita, *Saburo Okita: A Life in Economic Diplomacy* (Canberra: Australia-Japan Research Centre, Australian National University, 1993), pp. 118–121.

33. Lee, *China and Japan,* p. 64; *Renmin ribao* (People's Daily), March 13, 14, 15, 1981; *DXPNP-2,* p. 722, March 18, 1981.

34. *DXPNP-2,* April 4, 1981.

35. Ibid., April 14, 1981.

36. The developments at Baoshan are presented in Lee, *China and Japan,* pp. 30–75.

37. Personal communication with Sugimoto Takashi, a Chinese-speaking official of Shin Nippon Steel Company who spent several years in China negotiating the steel plant imports with the Chinese, November 2004.

38. World Steel Association, "World Steel in Figures, 2009," at www.worldsteel. org, accessed April 13, 2011.

39. Roger Garside, *Coming Alive: China after Mao* (New York: McGraw-Hill, 1981), p. 366.

40. Susan Greenhalgh, *Just One Child: Science and Policy in Deng's China* (Berkeley: University of California Press, 2008), p. 229.

41. *DXPNP-2,* March 23, 1979.

42. *SWDXP-2,* p. 173, March 30, 1979; ibid., July 28, 1979; Greenhalgh, *Just One Child,* p. 357n6.

43. Ling Zhijun and Ma Licheng, *Hu Han: Dangjin Zhongguo di 5 zhong shengyin* (Shouts: Five Kinds of Sounds in Today's China) (Guangzhou: Guangzhou chubanshe, 1999), pp. 72, 78.

44. Wang Lixin, *Yao chimi zhao Wan Li: Anhui nongcun gaige shilu* (If You Want Rice, Find Wan Li: The True Record of Rural Reform in Anhui) (Beijing: Beijing tushuguan chubanshe, 2000), p. 28.

45. Wu Xiang et al., "Wan Li tan shiyijie sanzhong quanhui qianhou de nongcun gaige" (Wan Li on Agricultural Reform before and after the Third Plenary Session of the 11th Central Committee), in Yu Guangyuan et al., *Gaibian Zhongguo mingyun de 41 tian: Zhongyang gongzuo huiyi, shiyijie sanzhong quanhui qinli ji* (The 41 Days That Changed the Fate of China: A Record of My Experience at the Central Work Conference of the Third Plenary Session of the 11th Central Committee) (Shenzhen: Haitian chubanshe, 1998), p. 281; Dali L. Yang, *Calamity and Reform in China: State, Rural Society, and Institutional Change since the Great Leap Famine* (Stanford, Calif.: Stanford University Press, 1996); and William L. Parish, ed., *Chinese Rural Development: The Great Transformation* (Armonk, N.Y.: M. E. Sharpe, 1985). For an overall summary of the changes in rural policy, with particular attention to the role of think tanks, see Fewsmith, *Dilemmas of Reform*, pp. 19–56.

46. Many years later, Wan Li's daughter, Wan Shupeng, still cringed as she talked about the starving people she saw when she went with her father to the poorer rural areas in Anhui. Interview with Wan Shupeng, October 2003; Wu Xiang et al., "Wan Li tan shiyijie sanzhong quanhui qianhou de nongcun gaige," pp. 281–289. See also Liu Changgen and Ji Fei, *Wan Li zai Anhui* (Wan Li in Anhui) (Hong Kong: Kaiyi chubanshe, 2001); Wan Li, *Wan Li wenxuan* (Selected Works of Wan Li) (Beijing: Renmin chubanshe, 1995); Zhonggong Anhui shengwei dangshi yanjiushi (Research Office of the Anhui Province Party Committee on Party History), ed., *Anhui nongcun gaige koushushi* (An Oral History of Agricultural Reform in Anhui) (Beijing: Zhonggong dangshi chubanshe, 2006).

47. Wu Xiang et al., "Wan Li tan shiyijie sanzhong quanhui qianhou de nongcun gaige," p. 283.

48. Liu Changgen and Ji Fei, *Wan Li zai Anhui*, pp. 80–82.

49. Ibid., p. 83.

50. Ibid., p. 80.

51. Wu Xiang et al., "Wan Li tan shiyijie sanzhong quanhui qianhou de nongcun gaige," pp. 284–286.

52. *DXPNP-2*, January 31, February 1, 1978.

53. Du Xingyuan (who was then Zhao Ziyang's deputy in Sichuan), "Minyi ru chao, lishi jubian" (Waves of Historic Changes in Public Opinion), in Yu Guangyuan et al., *Gaibian Zhongguo mingyun de 41 tian*, pp. 218–223; Liu Changgen and Ji Fei, *Wan Li zai Anhui*, p. 83.

54. *Renmin ribao* (People's Daily), January 31, 1979, and *China News Analysis*, no. 1149 (March 2, 1979), in Jürgen Domes, *Socialism in the Chinese Countryside: Rural Societal Policies in the People's Republic of China, 1949–1979* (London: C. Hurst, 1980), p. 102.

55. Liu Changgen and Ji Fei, *Wan Li zai Anhui*, p. 89.

56. Ling Zhijun and Ma Licheng, *Hu Han*, p. 81.

57. Domes, *Socialism in the Chinese Countryside*, pp. 81–106.

58. Liu Changgen and Ji Fei, *Wan Li zai Anhui*, pp. 96–97.

59. Ibid., pp. 144, 155, 163.

60. Ibid.

61. Interview with Yao Jianfu, who attended the meeting, April 2009.

62. Tong Huaiping and Li Chengguan, *Deng Xiaoping baci nanxun jishi* (Record of Deng Xiaoping's Eight Southern Journeys) (Beijing: Jiefangjun wenyi chubanshe, 2002), p. 281.

63. Wu Xiang et al., "Wan Li tan shiyijie sanzhong quanhui qianhou de nongcun gaige," p. 288.

64. Mao Zedong, *The Question of Agricultural Co-operation* (Peking: Foreign Languages Press, 1956).

65. *SWDXP-3*, pp. 314–316; *DXPNP-2*, May 31, 1980.

66. Interview with Yao Jianfu, a staff member at the center under Du Runsheng, April 2009. The system was sometimes referred to as "the responsibility system" *(chengbao zhi)*. A similar system was used in Hungary in the mid-1960s.

67. Wu Xiang et al., "Wan Li tan shiyijie sanzhong quanhui qianhou de nongcun gaige," p. 289; Liu Changgen and Ji Fei, *Wan Li zai Anhui*, pp. 178–179; Yang Jisheng, *Deng Xiaoping shidai: Zhongguo gaige kaifang ershinian jishi* (The Age of Deng Xiaoping: A Record of Twenty Years of China's Reform and Opening), 2 vols. (Beijing: Zhongyang bianyi chubanshe, 1998), 1:187–188.

68. Wu Li, *Zhonghua renmin gongheguo jingjishi, 1949–1999*, 2:838–840.

69. On the doubling of chemical fertilizer production, see State Statistical Bureau, *Statistical Yearbook of China 1985* (Oxford: Oxford University Press, 1985), p. 339. On the 20 percent increase in the procurement price of grain in 1979, see Zhang-Yue Zhou, *Effects of Grain Marketing Systems on Grain Production: A Comparative Study of China and India* (New York: Food Products Press, 1997), p. 33.

70. Yang Jisheng, *Deng Xiaoping shidai*, 1:188; Parish, *Chinese Rural Development*.

71. See Wu Xiang et al., "Wan Li tan shiyijie sanzhong quanhui qianhou de nongcun gaige," pp. 287–288.

72. State Statistical Bureau of the People's Republic of China, *Statistical Yearbook of China, 1987* (Beijing: China Statistical Information & Consultancy, 1988); Ross Garnaut and Ma Guonan, "China's Grain Demand: Recent Experience and Prospects to the Year 2000," in Ross Garnaut, Guo Shutian, and Ma Guonan, eds., *The*

Third Revolution in the Chinese Countryside (New York: Cambridge University Press, 1996), pp. 38–62.

73. Dong Fureng, *Zhonghua renmin gongheguo jingji shi*, 2:116; Wu Li, *Zhonghua renmin gongheguo jingjishi, 1949–1999*, 2:1506.

74. Interview with Du Runsheng, a leader in agricultural policies since the 1950s and deputy director of the State Agricultural Commission under Zhao Ziyang, September 2006.

75. *SWDXP-3*, p. 234, June 12, 1987. For a discussion of TVEs, see Naughton, *Growing Out of the Plan*, pp. 137–169; and Wu, *Understanding and Interpreting Chinese Reform*, pp. 118–138.

76. For accounts of rural industry on the eve of the breakup of the communes, see American Rural Small-Scale Industry Delegation, *Rural Small-Scale Industry in the People's Republic of China* (Berkeley: University of California Press, 1977); Jon Sigurdson, "Rural Industrialization in China," in U.S. Congress, Joint Economic Committee, *China, a Reassessment of the Economy: A Compendium of Papers Submitted to the Joint Economic Committee, Congress of the United States, July 10, 1975* (Washington, D.C.: Government Printing Office, 1975), pp. 411–435. I also had the opportunity to visit many TVEs in Guangdong during 1987–1988 as a guest of the Guangdong Provincial Economic Commission. In 1960 Mao had directed that rural areas should have five small industries: iron and steel, hydroelectric power, farm implements, cement, and chemical fertilizer. But after the retrenchment from the Great Leap Forward very few rural areas had iron and steel factories.

77. Justin Yifu Lin, Fang Cai, and Zhou Li, *The China Miracle: Development Strategy and Economic Reform* (Hong Kong: Published for the Hong Kong Centre for Economic Research and the International Center for Economic Growth by the Chinese University Press, 1996), p. 190.

78. Wu Li, *Zhonghua renmin gongheguo jingjishi, 1949–1999*, 2:1520–1521.

79. Lin, Cai, and Li, *The China Miracle*, p. 189.

80. Naughton, *Growing Out of the Plan*, p. 90.

81. See, for example, Charlotte Ikels, *The Return of the God of Wealth: The Transition to a Market Economy in Urban China* (Stanford, Calif.: Stanford University Press, 1996); Willy Kraus, *Private Business in China: Revival between Ideology and Pragmatism* (Honolulu: University of Hawaii Press, 1991).

82. Deng Liqun, *Shierge chunqiu*, pp. 558–587.

16. Accelerating Economic Growth and Opening

1. Barry Naughton, *Growing Out of the Plan: Chinese Economic Reform, 1978–1993* (New York: Cambridge University Press, 1995).

2. The meeting is recorded as having taken place on August 26. See Sheng Ping, ed., *Hu Yaobang sixiang nianpu: 1975–1989* (A Chronology of Hu Yao-

bang's Thought: 1975–1989), 2 vols. (Hong Kong: Taide shidai chubanshe, 2007), pp. 537–538.

3. *DXPNP-2*, July 17, 1980. Sheng Ping, *Hu Yaobang sixiang nianpu: 1975–1989*, pp. 537–538.

4. Yizi Chen, "The Decision Process behind the 1986–1989 Political Reforms," in Carol Hamrin and Suisheng Zhao, eds., *Decision-Making in Deng's China: Perspectives from Insiders* (Armonk, N.Y.: M. E. Sharpe, 1995), p. 138.

5. Zhu Jiamu, Chi Aiping, and Zhao Shigang, *Chen Yun* (Beijing: Zhongyang wenxian chubanshe, 1999), p. 186.

6. Deng Liqun, *Xiang Chen Yun tongzhi xuexi zuo jingji gongzuo* (Learn from Comrade Chen Yun to Do Economic Work) (Guangdong: Zhonggong zhongyang dangxiao chubanshe, 1981), p. 93.

7. Zhongguo renmin gongheguo shigao weiyuanhui (Committee on Historical Manuscripts of the People's Republic of China), ed., *Deng Liqun guoshi jiangtan lu* (A Record of Deng Liqun's Talks on the History of the Country), 7 vols. (Beijing: n.p., 2000), 7:204–205.

8. *CYNP*, November 4, 1982.

9. Zhongguo renmin gongheguo shigao weiyuanhui, *Deng Liqun guoshi jiangtan lu*, 7:247.

10. Interviews with Edwin Lim, August 2008, Ross Garnaut, June 2001, and Laurence Lau, March 2007. Lim, of the World Bank, met Zhao more frequently than any other Westerner. Ross Garnaut, Australian ambassador to Beijing from 1985 to 1988, is a professional economist who worked with Prime Minister Robert Hawke in liberalizing the Australian economy. Laurence Lau had been professor of economics at Stanford and was later vice chancellor at the Chinese University of Hong Kong.

11. Milton and Rose D. Friedman, *Two Lucky People: Memoirs* (Chicago: The University of Chicago Press, 1999), p. 543.

12. Joseph Fewsmith, *Dilemmas of Reform in China: Political Conflict and Economic Debate* (Armonk, N.Y.: M. E. Sharpe, 1994), pp. 34–41.

13. For a discussion of these think tanks, see ibid. I have also conducted interviews with Du Runsheng (September 2006), Lu Mai (August 2006), Yao Jianfu (August 2006), and Deng Yingtao (October 2003).

14. Zhonggong zhongyang dangshi yanjiushi (Central Chinese Communist Party History Research Office), *Zhongguo gongchandang xin shiqi lishi dashiji, 1978.12–2002.5* (A Chronological History of the Chinese Communist Party in the New Period, December 1978–May 2002), rev. ed. (Beijing: Zhonggong dangshi chubanshe, 2002), March 18, 1982.

15. Meng Zhen, "Chuguo liuxue 30 nian" (Thirty Years of Foreign Study), *Renmin ribao haiwai ban* (People's Daily Overseas Edition), June 26, 2008, 6.

16. Deng also supported China's entry into the International Monetary Fund (IMF), which led to better linkages between China and the international financial

community. On October 25, 1981, Deng met with the chairman of the IMF, Jacques de Larosière, and expressed approval for cooperation; *DXPNP-2*, October 25, 1981.

17. Edwin Lim, "Learning and Working with the Giants," in Indermit S. Gill and Todd Pugatch, *At the Frontlines of Development: Reflections from the World Bank* (Washington, D.C.: World Bank, 2005), pp. 89–119; Edwin Lim, "Xuyan: Zhongguo gaige kaifang guochengzhong de duiwai sixiang kaifang" (Preface: Thoughts on Opening to the Outside during the Process of China's Reform and Opening), in Wu Jinglian, ed., *Zhongguo jingji 50 ren kan sanshi nian: Huigu yu fenxi* (Fifty Chinese Economists Look at the Thirty Years: Reflections and Analysis) (Beijing: Zhongguo jingji chubanshe, 2008); Pieter Bottelier, "China and the World Bank: How the Partnership Was Built," working paper 277, Stanford Center for International Development, April 2006; Robert McNamara, *Oral History Recording*, October 3, 1991, pp. 16–18, as related by Edwin Lim, interview, August 2009. For a broader context of China's negotiations on participation in the IMF and the General Agreement on Tariffs and Trade (GATT) as well as the World Bank, see Harold K. Jacobson and Michel Oksenberg, *China's Participation in the IMF, the World Bank, and GATT: Toward a Global Economic Order* (Ann Arbor: University of Michigan Press, 1990).

18. The mission was officially headed by Shahid Husain, regional vice president for East Asia at the World Bank, but work on China, including the team in China, was headed by Edwin Lim. See Jacobson and Oksenberg, *China's Participation in the IMF, the World Bank and GATT.*

19. Fewsmith, *Dilemmas of Reform,* p. 130.

20. Edwin Lim et al., *China, Long-Term Development Issues and Options: The Report of a Mission Sent to China by the World Bank* (Baltimore: Published for the World Bank by the Johns Hopkins University Press, 1985). The report includes specialized volumes on education, agriculture, energy, transport, economic projections, and the economic structure.

21. Fewsmith, *Dilemmas of Reform,* p. 137. This Moganshan conference was held September 3 to September 10, 1984.

22. Saburo Okita, *Saburo Okita: A Life in Economic Diplomacy* (Canberra: Australia-Japan Research Centre, Australian National University, 1993), pp. 112–123; discussions with Shimokōbe Atsushi, August 1991.

23. Deng Liqun, *Shierge chunqiu, 1975–1987: Deng Liqun zishu* (Twelve Springs and Autumns, 1975–1987: Deng Liqun's Autobiography) (Hong Kong: Bozhi chubanshe, 2006), pp. 125–126. In visits to Chinese factory floors in 1987–1988, I observed many posters in factories outlining key principles and giving ratings to various groups based on their performance in following the Japanese examples.

24. Ibid., pp. 125–126, 156.

25. Chae-Jin Lee, *China and Japan: New Economic Diplomacy* (Stanford, Calif.: Hoover Institution Press, 1984), p. 138; Okita, *Saburo Okita: A Life in Economic Diplomacy.*

26. Dong Fureng, ed., *Zhonghua renmin gongheguo jingji shi* (An Economic History of the PRC), 2 vols. (Beijing: Jingji kexue chubanshe, 1999), 2:152–153.

27. *CYNP,* June 30, 1983; *DXPNP-2,* June 30, 1983.

28. *DXPNP-2,* December 22, 1983.

29. Ibid., June 30, 1984; *SWDXP-3,* pp. 72–75.

30. Naughton, *Growing Out of the Plan.*

31. Zhonggong zhongyang wenxian yanjiushi (Central Chinese Communist Party Literature Research Office), ed., *Shierda yilai zhongyao wenxian xuanbian* (Selection of Important Documents since the 12th Party Congress), 3 vols. (Beijing: Renmin chubanshe, 1986), 2:610–619; Deng Liqun, *Shierge chunqiu,* pp. 545–557; Fewsmith, *Dilemmas of Reform,* pp. 137–138.

32. Xiaokang Su and Luxiang Wang, *Deathsong of the River: A Reader's Guide to the Chinese TV Series "Heshang"* (Ithaca, N.Y.: East Asia Program, Cornell University, 1991).

33. *SWDXP-3,* pp. 90–99.

34. Jinglian Wu, *Understanding and Interpreting Chinese Economic Reform* (Mason, Ohio: Thomson/South-Western, 2005), pp. 357–369; Dong Fureng, *Zhonghua renmin gongheguo jingji shi,* 2:310–311.

35. Wu, *Understanding and Interpreting Chinese Economic Reform,* p. 357.

36. Barry Naughton, "False Starts and Second Wind: Financial Reforms in China's Industrial System," in Elizabeth J. Perry and Christine Wong, eds., *The Political Economy of Reform in Post-Mao China* (Cambridge, Mass.: Council on East Asian Studies, Harvard University, 1985), pp. 223–252; David Bachman, "Implementing Chinese Tax Policy," in David M. Lampton, ed., *Policy Implementation in Post-Mao China* (Berkeley: University of California Press, 1987), pp. 119–153; Penelope B. Prime, "Taxation Reform in China's Public Finance," in U.S. Congress, Joint Economic Committee, *China's Economic Dilemmas in the 1990s: The Problems of Reforms, Modernization and Interdependence* (Washington, D.C.: Government Printing Office, 1991; and Armonk, N.Y.: M. E. Sharpe, 1992), pp. 167–185.

37. *CYNP,* February 18, 1985.

38. Dong Fureng, *Zhonghua renmin gongheguo jingji shi,* 2:311–312; Wu, *Understanding and Interpreting Chinese Economic Reform,* pp. 363, 949–952.

39. *DXPNP-2,* January 23, 1985.

40. Interviews with Guangdong officials, n.d.

41. Fewsmith, *Dilemmas of Reform,* p. 152; Richard Baum, *Burying Mao: Chinese Politics in the Age of Deng Xiaoping* (Princeton, N.J.: Princeton University Press, 1994), pp. 181–182.

42. Ezra F. Vogel, *One Step Ahead in China: Guangdong under Reform* (Cambridge: Harvard University Press, 1989), pp. 291–294.

43. Fewsmith, *Dilemmas of Reform,* p. 153.

44. *DXPNP-2,* June 29 and August 1, 1985.

45. *SWCY,* 3:340–344; *CYNP,* 3:383–384.

46. *SWDXP-3,* pp. 144–150.

47. Ibid., p. 203.

48. Ziyang Zhao, *Prisoner of the State: The Secret Journal of Zhao Ziyang,* trans. and ed. Bao Pu, Renee Chiang, and Adi Ignatius (New York: Simon and Schuster, 2009), pp. 122–123.

49. *SWDXP-3,* pp. 257–258, May 19, 1988.

50. Ibid.

51. Dong Fureng, *Zhonghua renmin gongheguo jingji shi,* 2:316.

52. Wu Guoguang, *Zhao Ziyang yu zhengzhi gaige* (Political Reform under Zhao Ziyang) (Hong Kong: Taipingyang shiji yanjiusuo, 1997), pp. 526–531.

53. *SWDXP-3,* pp. 271–272; *DXPNP-2,* September 12, 1988.

54. Wu, *Understanding and Interpreting Chinese Economic Reform,* p. 368.

55. Fewsmith, *Dilemmas of Reform,* p. 228.

56. *CYNP,* October 10, 1988.

57. Zhonggong zhongyang wenxian yanjiushi (Central Chinese Communist Party Literature Research Office), ed., *Shisanda yilai zhongyao wenxian xuanbian* (Selection of Important Documents since the 13th Party Congress), 3 vols. (Beijing: Renmin chubanshe, 1991–1993), 1:253–255.

58. Dong Fureng, *Zhonghua renmin gongheguo jingji shi,* 2:321–322; Wu, *Understanding and Interpreting Chinese Economic Reform,* p. 369.

59. For a fuller statement of many of these differences, see William H. Overholt, *The Rise of China: How Economic Reform Is Creating a New Superpower* (New York: W.W. Norton, 1993), pp. 32–45.

17. One Country, Two Systems

1. For an account of China's territorial disputes, see M. Taylor Fravel, *Strong Borders, Secure Nation: Cooperation and Conflict in China's Territorial Disputes* (Princeton, N.J.: Princeton University Press, 2008).

2. For general background on Taiwan and the issues between China and the United States, see Ralph Clough, *Island China* (Cambridge: Harvard University Press, 1978); Nancy Bernkopf Tucker, *Taiwan, Hong Kong and the United States, 1945–1992: Uncertain Friendships* (New York: Twayne, 1994); Robert S. Ross, *Negotiating Cooperation: The United States and China, 1969–1989* (Stanford, Calif.: Stanford University Press, 1995); Richard C. Bush, *Untying the Knot: Making Peace in the Taiwan Strait* (Washington, D.C.: Brookings Institution Press, 2005); Michel Oksenberg, "Taiwan, Tibet, and Hong Kong in Sino-American Relations," in Ezra F. Vogel, ed., *Living with China: U.S.-China Relations in the Twenty-first Century* (New York: W.W. Norton, 1997), pp. 53–96; Alan D. Romberg, *Rein in at the Brink of the Precipice: American Policy toward Taiwan and U.S.-PRC Relations* (Washington,

D.C.: Henry L. Stimson Center, 2003); and Nancy Bernkopf Tucker, *Strait Talk: United States–Taiwan Relations and the Crisis with China* (Cambridge: Harvard University Press, 2009).

3. *DXPJW,* 3:141, January 1, 1979.

4. Ibid., 3:151, January 9, 1979.

5. Ibid., 3:164–166, January 16, 1980.

6. *DXPNP-2,* January 9, 1979; Robert Cottrell, *The End of Hong Kong: The Secret Diplomacy of Imperial Retreat* (London: John Murray, 1993); Carter Administration China Policy Oral History Project, Leonard Woodcock–Michel Oksenberg Tapes (LWMOT), tape 19, p. 21. Michel Oksenberg and Leonard Woodcock, after leaving office, met for thirty-nine sessions from the fall of 1981 through the summer of 1982 to record and preserve for history their account of the normalization process.

7. Robert A. Madsen, "Chinese Chess: U.S. China Policy and Taiwan, 1969–1979," Ph.D. thesis, Trinity College, Oxford University, 1999, pp. 274–275.

8. Tucker, *Strait Talk,* p. 108.

9. Conversation with former British prime minister Edward Heath, *DXPNP-2,* September 10, 1983.

10. Tucker, *Strait Talk,* pp. 132–133.

11. James Lilley with Jeffrey Lilley, *China Hands: Nine Decades of Adventure, Espionage, and Diplomacy in Asia* (New York: PublicAffairs, 2004), pp. 218–220. See also John H. Holdridge, *Crossing the Divide: An Insider's Account of Normalization of U.S.-China Relations* (Lanham, Md.: Rowman and Littlefield, 1997), pp. 197–198.

12. *SWDXP-2,* pp. 371–372; *DXPJW,* 3:181–185.

13. Holdridge, *Crossing the Divide,* pp. 199–201.

14. NCNA, September 30, 1981.

15. *DXPNP-2,* June 16, 1981.

16. Ross, *Negotiating Cooperation,* p. 182.

17. Kuan Yew Lee, *From Third World to First: The Singapore Story, 1965–2000* (New York: Harper Collins, 2000), pp. 527–531.

18. Ross, *Negotiating Cooperation,* pp. 184–185; Holdridge, *Crossing the Divide,* pp. 211–215; Alexander M. Haig, Jr., *Caveat: Realism, Reagan, and Foreign Policy* (New York: Macmillan, 1984); Patrick Tyler, *A Great Wall: Six Presidents and China: An Investigative History* (New York: PublicAffairs, 1999).

19. Holdridge, *Crossing the Divide,* pp. 211–215; Ross, *Negotiating Cooperation,* pp. 186–187.

20. Holdridge, *Crossing the Divide,* pp. 215–222.

21. Ibid., pp. 222–226. Holdridge accompanied George H. W. Bush on this trip.

22. For similar interpretations, see ibid., p. 240; Ross, *Negotiating Cooperation,* pp. 190–258.

23. The detailed negotiations on the agreement were conducted between Ambas-

sador Hummel and his Chinese counterparts in Beijing. On the Chinese side, they were sent to Deng for approval.

24. Holdridge, *Crossing the Divide,* pp. 230–241; Ross, *Negotiating Cooperation,* pp. 189–200. These three communiqués are reprinted in Ross, *Negotiating Cooperation,* pp. 265–272 and Holdridge, *Crossing the Divide,* pp. 263–279.

25. *DXPNP-2,* April 26, 1984.

26. Interview with U.S. Defense Department official Eden Woon, December 2008.

27. Lee, *From Third World to First,* pp. 677–679.

28. Qi Pengfei, *Deng Xiaoping yu Xianggang huigui* (Deng Xiaoping and the Return of Hong Kong) (Beijing: Huaxia chubanshe, 2004), p. 66.

29. Ibid. For work on Hong Kong more generally, see Zong Daoyi et al., eds., *Zhou Nan kou shu: Shenzai ji feng zhou yu zhong* (Zhou Nan's Oral History: In the Middle of Heavy Rains and Strong Winds) (Hong Kong: Sanlian shudian, 2007), pp. 265–267. For discussions on Hong Kong I am especially indebted to Sir David Wilson, Sin Por Shiu, and Dalena Wright for sharing their deep knowledge of developments in Hong Kong.

30. Qi Pengfei, *Deng Xiaoping yu Xianggang huigui,* p. 56.

31. Christine Loh, *Underground Front: The Chinese Communist Party in Hong Kong* (Hong Kong: Hong Kong University Press, 2010).

32. Sin Por Shiu, "The Macao Formula and an Assessment of the Sino-British Negotiations over Hong Kong," unpublished paper, Kennedy School of Government, Harvard University, May 2006; Steve Shipp, *Macau, China: A Political History of the Portuguese Colony's Transition to Chinese Rule* (Jefferson, N.C.: McFarland, 1997).

33. Qi Pengfei, *Deng Xiaoping yu Xianggang huigui,* pp. 56–57.

34. Ibid., p. 248.

35. Interview with Edgar Cheng, son-in-law of Y. K. Pao, who often accompanied Y. K. Pao on visits with Deng, November 2008.

36. Documents written later stress the consistency and continuity of Deng's policy; some even suggest that he had already decided about the return of Hong Kong. But no documents issued at the time support such a view. The issue was not yet settled.

37. Cottrell, *The End of Hong Kong,* pp. 38–40.

38. Qi Pengfei, *Deng Xiaoping yu Xianggang huigui,* pp. 65–66.

39. Xu Jiatun, the highest Communist official in Hong Kong, reports that in 1983 there were 6,000 party members in Hong Kong. See Jiatun Xu, "Selections from Serialized Memoirs," *Lianhebao,* translated in JPRS-CAR, 93-050, 93-070, 93-073, 93-091, 94-001, 94-010, 94-016, and 94-017, 1993–1994, and later published as Xu Jiatun, *Xu Jiatun Xianggang huiyilu* (Xu Jiatun's Reminiscences of Hong Kong), 2 vols. (Taipei: Lianjing chubanshe, 1993).

40. This is clear in the writings of Xu Jiatun, who dared to give Beijing a more accurate view of Hong Kong opinion in the early 1980s. Xu Jiatun, *Xu Jiatun Xianggang huiyilu.*

41. Sin Por Shiu, "The Macao Formula," pp. 14–15.

42. Cottrell, *The End of Hong Kong,* pp. 54–55.

43. Percy Cradock, *Experiences of China* (London: John Murray, 1994).

44. Cottrell, *The End of Hong Kong,* p. 56.

45. Ibid., p. 57.

46. *DXPNP-2,* April 3, 1981.

47. Xu, "Selections from Serialized Memoirs."

48. Qi Pengfei, *Deng Xiaoping yu Xianggang huigui,* p. 70; Sin Por Shiu, "The Macao Formula," p. 21.

49. Cottrell, *The End of Hong Kong,* pp. 66–67.

50. Ibid., pp. 67–68.

51. Sin Por Shiu, "The Macao Formula," p. 22. See also *DXPNP-2,* May 21, June 2, September 24, 1982.

52. Qi Pengfei, "Deng Xiaoping yu Xianggang 'hou guodu shiqi' de zhong ying waijiao douzheng" (Deng Xiaoping and Hong Kong: The Sino-British Diplomatic Struggle over the Post-Transition Period), *Dangdai Zhongguo shi yanjiu,* no. 4 (2004): 59–71.

53. *DXPNP-2,* April 6, 1982.

54. Interview with Sir Alan Donald, political adviser in Hong Kong, 1974–1977, ambassador in Beijing, 1988–1991, and undersecretary in London in charge of planning for the Thatcher visit in 1982, November 2007.

55. Ibid.

56. Frank Ching, *Hong Kong and China: "One Country, Two Systems"* (New York: Foreign Policy Association, 1996), pp. 11–12; Cottrell, *The End of Hong Kong,* pp. 85–86.

57. Cradock, *Experiences of China,* p. 179. In her memoirs, Thatcher describes the session with Deng as a dramatic confrontation; see Margaret Thatcher, *The Downing Street Years* (New York: HarperCollins, 1993). The diplomats present, however, report that both sides gave careful, unemotional presentations that were well within the bounds of normal diplomatic discussions.

58. Cottrell, *The End of Hong Kong,* pp. 87–88.

59. Ibid., p. 88; interview with Sir Alan Donald.

60. *SWDXP-3,* pp. 23–25.

61. Cottrell, *The End of Hong Kong,* p. 89.

62. Ibid., p. 87.

63. Ching, *Hong Kong and China,* p. 11; interview with Sir Alan Donald.

64. Cottrell, *The End of Hong Kong,* pp. 91–92.

65. Ibid., p. 89.

66. Ibid., pp. 94, 97.

67. Ibid., pp. 99–102.

68. Ibid., pp. 101–107; Mark Roberti, *The Fall of Hong Kong: China's Triumph and Britain's Betrayal* (New York: J. Wiley, 1994), p. 64; interview with Sir Alan Donald.

69. Xu Jiatun, *Xu Jiatun Xianggang huiyilu*, 1:1–12.

70. Cottrell, *The End of Hong Kong*, pp. 113–114.

71. Xu Jiatun, *Xu Jiatun Xianggang huiyilu*, 1:3; Xu Jiatun, *Xu Jiatun huiyi yu suixiang lu* (Xu Jiatun's Reminiscences and Record of His Random Thoughts) (Brampton, Ont.: Mingjing chubanshe, 1998).

72. Cottrell, *The End of Hong Kong*, pp. 113–114.

73. Roberti, *The Fall of Hong Kong*, p. 155.

74. Xu, "Selections from Serialized Memoirs," *Lianhebao*, May 14, 1993, translated in JPRS-CAR, 93-056, July 16, 1993.

75. Ibid., May 27, 1993, translated in JPRS-CAR, 93-050, July 16, 1993. The local pun was that private business was the "United Nations," because the term for United Nations *"lianheguo"* could mean linked, amalgamated, or nationalized, i.e., appropriated.

76. Xu Jiatun, *Xu Jiatun Xianggang huiyili*, 1:12–28.

77. *DXPNP-2*, September 10, 1983.

78. Cottrell, *The End of Hong Kong*, pp. 129–132; Ching, *Hong Kong and China*, pp. 19–20.

79. Cottrell, *The End of Hong Kong*, pp. 132–146.

80. *DXPNP-2*, April 18, 1984, pp. 970–971.

81. Cottrell, *The End of Hong Kong*, pp. 148–153.

82. Xu, "Selections from Serialized Memoirs," *Lianhebao*, June 1, 1993, translated in JPRS-CAR, 93-070, September 21, 1993; Roberti, *The Fall of Hong Kong*, pp. 92–93; *DXPNP-2*, p. 978, May 25, 1984.

83. Zong Daoyi et al., *Zhou Nan koushu*, pp. 263–269; *SWDXP-3*, June 22–23, 1984, pp. 68–71.

84. Cottrell, *The End of Hong Kong*, pp. 154–174.

85. Ibid., pp. 163–174; Ching, *Hong Kong and China*, p. 27.

86. The text of the Joint Statement and the annex are included in Ching, *Hong Kong and China*, pp. 81–96, and in Cottrell, *The End of Hong Kong*, pp. 205–223.

87. *DXPNP-2*, October 3, 1984, pp. 988–989; *SWDXP-3*, October 3, 1984, pp. 80–84.

88. Cottrell, *The End of Hong Kong*, pp. 106–109, 199–204; Roberti, *The Fall of Hong Kong*, pp. 125–126.

89. *DXPNP-2*, July 5, 1985; Roberti, *The Fall of Hong Kong*, pp. 145–148.

90. Li Hou, *Bainian quru shide zhongjie: Xianggang wenti shimo* (The End of the Hundred Years of Humiliation: The Hong Kong Issue from Beginning to End) (Beijing: Zhongyang wenxian chubanshe, 1997), pp. 170–171.

91. Roberti, *The Fall of Hong Kong,* pp. 191–192.

92. *SWDXP-3,* pp. 214–220; Li Hou, *Bainian quru shide zhongjie,* pp. 172–173.

93. Li Hou, *Bainian quru shide zhongjie,* p. 185.

94. *SWDXP-3,* p. 340.

95. Li Hou, *Bainian quru shide zhongjie,* p. 198.

96. Roberti, *The Fall of Hong Kong,* pp. 280–291; ibid., pp. 166–207.

97. Qichen Qian, *Ten Episodes in China's Diplomacy,* foreword by Ezra Vogel (New York: HarperCollins, 2005), pp. 254–255.

98. Xu, "Selections from Serialized Memoirs," *Lianhebao,* September 3, 1993, translated in JPRS-CAR, 94-015, March 8, 1994.

99. *DXPNP-2,* January 18, 1990.

100. Qian, *Ten Episodes in China's Diplomacy,* pp. 257–260; Li Hou, *Bainian quru shide zhongjie,* pp. 205–207.

101. For Patten's account, see Chris Patten, *East and West: China, Power, and the Future of Asia* (New York: Times Books, 1998).

102. Qian, *Ten Episodes in China's Diplomacy,* p. 279.

103. *DXPNP-2,* November 28, 1978. For works on Tibet during this period, I have found to be most useful the following books: Melvyn C. Goldstein, *The Snow Lion and the Dragon: China, Tibet, and the Dalai Lama* (Berkeley: University of California Press, 1997); Tashi Rabgey and Tseten Wangchuk Sharlho, *Sino-Tibetan Dialogue in the Post-Mao Era: Lessons and Prospects* (Washington, D.C.: East-West Center, 2004); Dan Zeng, ed., *Dangdai Xizang jianshi* (A Simple History of Contemporary Tibet) (Beijing: Dangdai Zhongguo chubanshe, 1996); and Tsering Shakya, *The Dragon in the Land of Snows: A History of Modern Tibet since 1947* (New York: Columbia University Press, 1999). I am indebted to Melvyn Goldstein for many discussions in which he selflessly tried to educate a China specialist about matters on Tibet. See also Chen Weiren, "Hu Yaobang yu Xizang" (Hu Yaobang and Tibet), in Su Shaozhi, Chen Yizi, and Gao Wenqian, eds., *Renmin zhong de Hu Yaobang* (Hu Yaobang in the Hearts of the People) (Carle Place, N.Y.: Mingjing chubanshe, 2006), pp. 166–185; Wang Lixiong, *Tianzang: Xizang de mingyun* (Sky Burial: The Fate of Tibet) (Mississauga, Ont.: Mingjing chubanshe, 2006); Barry Sautman and June Teufel Dreyer, eds., *Contemporary Tibet: Politics, Development, and a Disputed Region* (Armonk, N.Y.: M. E. Sharpe, 2006); and Robert Barnett and Shirin Akiner, eds., *Resistance and Reform in Tibet* (Bloomington: Indiana University Press, 1994). A letter from the Dalai Lama to Deng and Jiang Zemin on September 11, 1992, summarizing his views on relations with China since 1979, is contained in Andy Zhang, *Hu Jintao: Facing China's Challenges Ahead* (San Jose, Calif.: Writer's Club Press, 2002), appen-

dix 5, pp. 133–148. For an account of Western images of Tibet, see Orville Schell, *Virtual Tibet: Searching for Shangri-la from the Himalayas to Hollywood* (New York: Metropolitan Books, 2000).

104. Melvyn C. Goldstein, *The History of Modern Tibet,* vol. 2: *The Calm before the Storm, 1951–1955* (Berkeley: University of California Press, 2007), pp. 98–99.

105. Dan Zeng, *Dangdai Xizang jianshi,* pp. 132–146.

106. John Kenneth Knaus, one of the CIA officials, describes the program in *Orphans of the Cold War: America and the Tibetan Struggle for Survival* (New York: PublicAffairs, 1999).

107. *DXPNP-2,* December 1–5, 1975, September 27, 1977.

108. Ibid., March 12, 1979.

109. Ibid., March 17, 1979.

110. Memcon, Summary of the Vice President's Meeting with People's Republic of China Vice Premier Deng Xiaoping, 8/27/79, vertical file, China, Jimmy Carter Library, Atlanta.

111. Zheng Zhongbing, ed., *Hu Yaobang nianpu changbian* (Materials for a Chronological Record of Hu Yaobang's Life), 2 vols. (Hong Kong: Shidai guoji chuban youxian gongsi, 2005), May 21, 22, 1980, 1:482–483.

112. Shakya, *The Dragon in the Land of Snows,* p. 126.

113. Deng Liqun, *Shierge chunqiu, 1975–1987: Deng Liqun zishu* (Twelve Springs and Autumns, 1975–1987: Deng Liqun's Autobiography) (Hong Kong: Bozhi chubanshe, 2006), pp. 207–208.

114. Goldstein, *The Snow Lion and the Dragon,* p. 67.

115. Ibid., pp. 69–71.

116. Xiaojiang Hu and Miguel A. Salazar, "Market Formation and Transformation: Private Business in Lhasa," in Sautman and Dreyer, *Contemporary Tibet,* pp. 166–190; June Teufel Dreyer, "Economic Development in Tibet under the People's Republic of China," in Sautman and Dreyer, *Contemporary Tibet,* pp. 128–151; also Xiaojiang Hu, "The Little Shops of Lhasa, Tibet: Migrant Businesses and the Formation of Markets in a Transitional Economy," Ph.D. thesis, Department of Sociology, Harvard University, 2003.

18. The Military

1. I am grateful for the advice of specialists on the Chinese military: Kenneth Allen, Dennis Blasko, John Corbett, Andrew Erickson, David Finklestein, Taylor Fravel, Paul Godwin, the late Ellis Joffe, John Lewis, Nan Li, David Shambaugh, Eden Woon, Larry Wortzel, and Xue Litai. For a general overview of the Chinese military, see James C. Mulvenon and Andrew N. D. Yang, *The People's Liberation Army as Organization* (Santa Monica, Calif.: Rand, 2002). For a broad perspective

on Chinese strategic thinking, see Michael D. Swaine and Ashley J. Tellis, *Interpreting China's Grand Strategy: Past, Present, and Future* (Santa Monica, Calif.: Rand, 2000). For a general account of Chinese defense in the 1980s, see Paul H. B. Godwin, ed., *The Chinese Defense Establishment: Continuity and Change in the 1980s* (Boulder, Colo.: Westview Press, 1983). For general works on the Chinese military, see David Shambaugh, *Modernizing China's Military: Progress, Problems, and Prospects* (Berkeley: University of California Press, 2002); and Andrew Scobell, *China's Use of Military Force beyond the Great Wall and the Long March* (New York: Cambridge University Press, 2003).

2. *DXPNP-2*, July 23, 1977; Zhi Shaozeng and Lei Yuanshen, "Zhongyang junshi weiyuanhui (Central Military Commission)," in Zhongguo junshi baike quanshu bianshen weiyuanhui (Editorial Review Board for the Chinese Military Encyclopedia), ed., *Zhongguo junshi baike quanshu* (China Military Encyclopedia), vol. 3 (Beijing: Junshi kexue chubanshe, 1997).

3. *SWDXP-2*, p. 74.

4. *DXPJW*, 3:62–69, August 23, 1977; *LZQ*, pp. 417–419.

5. *DXPJW*, 3:53–72, August 23, 1977.

6. See Ellis Joffe, *The Chinese Army after Mao* (Cambridge: Harvard University Press, 1987); Harlan W. Jencks, *From Muskets to Missiles: Politics and Professionalism in the Chinese Army, 1945–1981* (Boulder, Colo.: Westview, 1982).

7. See Liu Huaqing, *Liu Huaqing huiyilu* (Reminiscences of Liu Huaqing) (Beijing: Jiefangjun chubanshe, 2004).

8. *SWDXP-2*, pp. 75–78.

9. Ibid., p. 73.

10. *DXPJW*, 3:95, March 20, 1978.

11. Ibid., 3:144–149, January 2, 1979.

12. Compiled from Ji You, *The Armed Forces of China* (London: I.B. Taurus, 1999); http://www.chinatoday.com/arm/index.htm, accessed September 30, 2010; "The 'Inside Story' on the Reduction in the Size of the PLA," *Wen Wei Po* (Hong Kong), April 29, 1987; Ellis Joffe, "Radical Reforms Underway," *Financial Times*, December 9, 1985; John D. Friske, ed., *China Facts and Figures Annual, vol. 17 (1993)* (Gulf Breeze, Fla.: Academic International Press, 1993), p. 61.

13. Harlan W. Jencks, "China's 'Punitive' War on Vietnam: A Military Assessment," *Asian Survey* 20, no. 10 (October 1980): 965–989. For the Vietnamese view of the war, see Henry J. Kenny, "Vietnamese Perceptions of the 1979 War with China," in Mark A. Ryan, David M. Finkelstein, and Michael A. McDevitt, eds., *Chinese Warfighting: The PLA Experience since 1949* (Armonk, N.Y.: M. E. Sharpe, 2003), pp. 217–240; Edward C. O'Dowd, ed., "People's Liberation Army Documents on the Sino-Vietnamese Conflict, 1979 (I)," *Chinese Law and Government* 42, no. 5 (September–October 2009): 3–100; and Edward C. O'Dowd, ed., "People's

Liberation Army Documents on the Third Indochina Conflict, 1979 (II)," *Chinese Law and Government* 42, no. 6 (November–December 2009): 3–116. For an analysis of the political views about the war, see Scobell, *China's Use of Military Force,* pp. 119–143.

14. Edward C. O'Dowd, "The Last Maoist War: Chinese Cadres and Conscripts in the Third Indochina War, 1978–1981," Ph.D. thesis, Princeton University, 1994, p. 132.

15. In his speech at the conclusion of the war, Deng said the issue they had been most concerned about in planning the war was the possible Soviet reaction, but they judged the chances of Soviet entry to be very slight. See "Deng Xiaoping zai Zhong-Yue bianjing zuozhan qingkuang baogao huishang de jianghua" (Deng Xiaoping's Speech at the Meeting to Report on the Situation on the Sino-Vietnamese Border), March 16, 1979, unpublished speech available in the Fairbank Collection, Fung Library, Harvard University.

16. John Wilson Lewis and Litai Xue, *Imagined Enemies: China Prepares for Uncertain War* (Stanford, Calif.: Stanford University Press, 2006), pp. 127–133.

17. Xiaoming Zhang, "Deng Xiaoping and China's Decision to Go to War with Vietnam," *Journal of Cold War Studies* 12, no. 3 (Summer 2010): 3–29.

18. O'Dowd, "The Last Maoist War," pp. 99, 106–109, 171.

19. Ibid. For an overview of the war, see Edward C. O'Dowd and John F. Corbett, Jr., "The 1979 Chinese Campaign in Vietnam: Lessons Learned," in Laurie Burkitt, Andrew Scobell, and Larry M. Wortzel, eds., *The Lessons of History: The Chinese People's Liberation Army at 75* (Carlisle, Penn.: Strategic Studies Institute, U.S. Army War College, 2003), pp. 353–378.

20. Communication from Mark Mohr, October 2007, then a State Department official and the only one present with Mansfield during the meeting except for the Chinese ambassador Huang Hua and the interpreter Ji Chaozhu.

21. Lewis and Xue, *Imagined Enemies,* p. 127.

22. *DXPNP-2,* late December 1978, January 2, 1979.

23. Michael Leifer, "Kampuchia, 1979: From Dry Season to Dry Season," *Asian Survey* 20, no. 1 (January 1980): 33–41.

24. King Chen, "China's War against Vietnam, 1979: A Military Analysis," occasional paper, University of Maryland School of Law, 1983, pp. 1–33; Kenny, "Vietnamese Perceptions of the 1979 War with China."

25. Elizabeth Wishnick, *Mending Fences: The Evolution of Moscow's China Policy from Brezhnev to Yeltsin* (Seattle: University of Washington Press, 2001), p. 63.

26. Xiaoming Zhang, "China's 1979 War with Vietnam: A Reassessment," *The China Quarterly,* no. 184 (December 2005): 866–867.

27. Kenny, "Vietnamese Perceptions of the 1979 War with China," p. 228; O'Dowd, "The Last Maoist War," pp. 114–132.

28. O'Dowd, "The Last Maoist War," pp. 165–166. The weaknesses are also detailed in Lewis and Xue, *Imagined Enemies,* pp. 132–133; Zhang, "China's 1979 War with Vietnam," pp. 869–874.

29. Interviews in Beijing, Fall 2006.

30. I am indebted to Michael Lampton who was in China at the time and made these observations.

31. Kuan Yew Lee, *From Third World to First: The Singapore Story, 1965–2000* (New York: HarperCollins, 2000), pp. 669–670.

32. James C. Mulvenon, *Soldiers of Fortune: The Rise and Fall of the Chinese Military-Business Complex, 1978–1998* (Armonk, N.Y.: M. E. Sharpe, 2001), p. 53. Defense expenditures increased roughly 10 percent each year. But in 1979, because of the attack on Vietnam, they increased by 55.9 billion yuan, approximately 40 billion yuan more per year than average, which was then about one-quarter of the total military budget. In 1978, defense expenditures were 167.8 billion yuan; in 1979, 222.7 billion yuan; and in 1980, 193.3 billion yuan. Additional costs of the Vietnam War were borne by the southern provinces of Guangdong, Guangxi, and Yunnan. Data are from the June 21, 1979 Report on the Final State Accounts for 1978 and the Draft State Budget for 1979 by Finance Minister Zhang Jingfu at the Second Session of the 5th National People's Congress, available in "Quarterly Chronicle and Documentation," *The China Quarterly,* no. 79 (September 1979): 661–663, and the August 30, 1980, Report on Financial Work by Finance Minister Wang Bingqian to the Third Session of the 5th National People's Congress, available in "Quarterly Chronicle and Documentation," *The China Quarterly,* no. 84 (December 1980): 799–802.

33. M. Taylor Fravel, *Strong Borders, Secure Nation: Cooperation and Conflict in China's Territorial Disputes* (Princeton, N.J.: Princeton University Press, 2008), p. 217.

34. *DXPJW,* vol. 3.

35. For an account of PLA lessons learned, see O'Dowd and Corbett, Jr., "The 1979 Chinese Campaign in Vietnam: Lessons Learned," pp. 353–378.

36. Senator Jackson visit on February 16, 1978 (communication from Dwight Perkins, who was part of the delegation, October 2010).

37. O'Dowd, "The Last Maoist War," p. 101.

38. Zhang, "China's 1979 War with Vietnam," pp. 867–888.

39. O'Dowd, "The Last Maoist War," pp. 179–184.

40. Meeting with Vice President Mondale, August 27, 1979; Memcon, Summary of the Vice President's Meeting with People's Republic of China Vice Premier Deng Xiaoping, 8/27/79, vertical file, China, Jimmy Carter Library, Atlanta.

41. See *SWDXP-2,* p. 90.

42. He made such statements on many occasions; for example, on January 16, 1980, at a party center meeting of officials. See *DXPJW,* 3:165.

43. Hua Huang, *Huang Hua Memoirs* (Beijing: Foreign Languages Press, 2008), p. 294.

44. Shen Zhihua, ed., *Zhong Su guanxi shigang, 1917–1991* (A Historical Outline of Sino-Soviet Relations, 1917–1991) (Beijing: Xinhua chubanshe, 2007), pp. 406–407.

45. Robert S. Ross, *Negotiating Cooperation: The United States and China, 1969–1989* (Stanford, Calif.: Stanford University Press, 1995), p. 172.

46. Shen Zhihua, *Zhong Su guanxi shigang, 1917–1991,* p. 408.

47. Ibid., pp. 408–411.

48. *SWDXP-2,* p. 242, January 16, 1980.

49. Ibid., p. 284, March 12, 1980.

50. Zhang Xingxing, "Zhongguo jundui dacaijun yu xin shiqi jingji jianshe" (The Great Reduction in Chinese Military and Economic Construction in the New Era), *Dangdai Zhongguo shi yanjiu* 13, no. 1 (January 2006): 21–28; see also Huang, *Huang Hua Memoirs,* p. 291.

51. As mentioned earlier, Deng was willing to take initiatives to reduce the risk of conflict but he still insisted that in order to resume full normal relations, the Soviet Union would have to leave Afghanistan and withdraw its troops near the Chinese border, and Vietnam would have to leave Cambodia. Conditions for this did not ripen until the late 1980s. See Qichen Qian, *Ten Episodes in China's Diplomacy,* foreword by Ezra Vogel (New York: HarperCollins, 2005), pp. 1–31.

52. Ibid., pp. 13–14.

53. Memcon, Summary of the Vice President's Meeting with People's Republic of China Vice Premier Deng Xiaoping, 8/27/79, vertical file, China, Jimmy Carter Library.

54. Memcon, Secretary of Defense Harold Brown to the President, 1/8/80, National Security Archive, Brzezinski Material, Far East, Brown (Harold) Trip file, box 69, Jimmy Carter Library.

55. Ibid.

56. Memcon, Meeting between Secretary of Defense and Vice Premier Geng Biao, 5/29/80, National Security Archive, Brzezinski Material, Far East, Geng Biao Visit file, box 70, Jimmy Carter Library; Memcon, Meeting between Secretary of Defense Dr. Harold Brown and Vice Premier of the People's Republic of China, Geng Biao, 5/27/80, National Security Archive, Brzezinski Material, Far East, Geng Biao Visit file, box 70, Jimmy Carter Library; Memo, Brzezinski to Carter, Summary of Dr. Brzezinski's Conversation with Vice Premier Geng Biao of the People's Republic of China, 5/29/80, National Security Archive, Brzezinski Material, Far East, Geng Biao Visit file, box 70, Jimmy Carter Library.

57. *DXPJW,* 3:154–155, 168–174.

58. Joffe, *The Chinese Army after Mao,* pp. 58–59.

59. Ibid., pp. 60–61.

60. Information Office, State Council, *2008 nian Zhongguo guofang* (Chinese National Defense in 2008) (Beijing: January 2009), appendix 5, at http://www.gov.cn/jrzg/2009-01/20/content_1210075.htm, accessed April 9, 2011.

61. William H. Overholt, *The Rise of China: How Economic Reform Is Creating a New Superpower* (New York: W.W. Norton, 1993), pp. 340–344.

62. Robert J. Skebo, Gregory K. S. Man, and George H. Stevens, "Chinese Military Capabilities: Problems and Prospects," in U.S. Congress, Joint Economic Committee, *China's Economic Dilemmas in the 1990s: The Problems of Reforms, Modernization and Interdependence* (Washington, D.C.: Government Printing Office, 1991 and Armonk, N.Y.: M. E. Sharpe, 1992), p. 665.

63. Cheng Li and Scott Harold, "China's New Military Elite," *China Security* 3, no. 4 (Autumn 2007): 79. For a general work on political succession, see Michael D. Swaine, *The Military and Political Succession in China: Leadership, Institutions, Beliefs* (Santa Monica, Calif.: Rand, 1992). For an introduction to the importance of the field army connections, see the comprehensive early study by William W. Whitson, with Chen-hsia Huang, *The Chinese High Command: A History of Communist Military Politics, 1927–71* (New York: Praeger, 1973).

64. Cheng Li and Lynn White, "The Army in the Succession to Deng Xiaoping: Familiar Fealties and Technocratic Trends," *Asian Survey* 33, no. 8 (August 1993): 772.

65. Morton H. Halperin, *China and the Bomb* (New York, Praeger, 1965).

66. Evan A. Feigenbaum, *China's Techno-Warriors: National Security and Strategic Competition from the Nuclear Age to the Information Age* (Stanford, Calif.: Stanford University Press, 2003).

67. In 1975, however, Deng had to resolve factional fighting in the No. 7 Ministry of Machine Building that was responsible for missiles and the space industries. See ibid.; also *LZQ*, pp. 87–112.

68. Feigenbaum, *China's Techno-Warriors*. For an account of Chinese behavior concerning its borders, see Fravel, *Strong Borders, Secure Nation*.

69. M. Taylor Fravel, *Active Defense: Exploring the Evolution of China's Military Strategy* (Princeton, N.J.: Princeton University Press, forthcoming).

70. Ellis Joffe, "People's War under Modern Conditions: A Doctrine for Modern War," *The China Quarterly*, no. 112 (December 1987): 555–571; Harlan W. Jencks, "People's War under Modern Conditions: Wishful Thinking, National Suicide or Effective Deterrent?" *The China Quarterly*, no. 98 (June 1984): 305–319; Paul H. B. Godwin, "Mao Zedong Revisited: Deterrence and Defense in the 1980s," in Godwin, *The Chinese Defense Establishment: Continuity and Change in the 1980s*, pp. 21–40. See also U.S. Department of State, Bureau of Intelligence and Research, "Chinese Military Reforms: Social and Political Implications," Confidential Intelligence Report 1205-AR, December 6, 1985, available in DNSA.

71. Joffe, *The Chinese Army after Mao,* pp. 85–86; Godwin, "Mao Zedong Revisited."

72. Joffe, "People's War under Modern Conditions," 568–569; John Wilson Lewis and Litai Xue, *China's Strategic Seapower: The Politics of Force Modernization in the Nuclear Age* (Stanford, Calif.: Stanford University Press, 1994); Alexander C. Huang, "The PLA Navy at War, 1949–1999: From Coastal Defense to Distant Operations," in Ryan, Finkelstein, and McDevitt, *Chinese Warfighting,* pp. 241–269.

73. *DXPJW,* 3:161, July 29, 1979.

74. Joffe, "People's War under Modern Conditions," 565.

75. The details of the programs to develop the nuclear-powered submarine and the submarine-launched ballistic missile are described in Lewis and Xue, *China's Strategic Seapower.*

76. *SWDXP-2,* p. 132.

77. Skebo, Man, and Stevens, "Chinese Military Capabilities: Problems and Prospects," pp. 663–675.

78. *SWDXP-2,* p. 284, March 12, 1980.

79. Ibid.

80. *DXPJW,* 3:179, October 15, 1980.

81. *SWDXP-2,* pp. 131–133.

82. Zhang Xingxing, "Zhongguo jundui dacaijun yu xin shiqi jingji jianshe," p. 7.

83. Richard Baum, *Burying Mao: Chinese Politics in the Age of Deng Xiaoping* (Princeton, N.J.: Princeton University Press, 1994), pp. 121–124.

84. *SWDXP-3,* pp. 104–105, November 1, 1984; *DXPNP-2,* p. 1012.

85. *SWDXP-2,* p. 285, March 12, 1980.

86. Ibid. For a general account of military education during the 1980s, see William R. Heaton, "Professional Military Education in the People's Republic of China," in Godwin, *The Chinese Defense Establishment,* pp. 121–137. Dennis J. Blasko, Philip T. Klapakis, and John F. Corbett, Jr., "Training Tomorrow's PLA: A Mixed Bag of Tricks," *The China Quarterly,* no. 146 (June 1996): 488–524.

87. *DXPJW,* 3:130.

88. Lewis and Xue, *China's Strategic Seapower,* p. 100.

89. Mulvenon, *Soldiers of Fortune,* pp. 91–104.

90. John Frankenstein and Bates Gill, "Current and Future Challenges Facing Chinese Defence Industries," *The China Quarterly,* no. 146 (June 1996): 394–427.

91. Tai Ming Cheung, *Fortifying China: The Struggle to Build a Modern Defense Economy* (Ithaca, N.Y.: Cornell University Press, 2009), p. 76. See also Frankenstein and Gill, "Current and Future Challenges Facing Chinese Defence Industries," 394–427.

92. Cheung, *Fortifying China,* p. 57. The overall trends in this period are on

pp. 50–77. In fact, monitoring these activities, especially lower-level units, was difficult, so there are no precise figures.

93. Ezra F. Vogel, *One Step Ahead in China: Guangdong under Reform* (Cambridge: Harvard University Press, 1989).

94. Mulvenon, *Soldiers of Fortune*, pp. 59–63.

95. Barry Naughton, "The Third Front: Defence Industrialization in China's Interior," *The China Quarterly*, no. 115 (September 1988): 382.

96. Ibid.; Cheung, *Fortifying China*, pp. 60–63.

97. *DXPNP-2*, June 28–29, 1978.

98. Cheung, *Fortifying China*, pp. 52–100.

19. The Ebb and Flow of Politics

1. *SWDXP-2*, p. 326.

2. Ming Ruan, *Deng Xiaoping: Chronicle of an Empire* (Boulder, Colo.: Westview, 1994), pp. 93–94.

3. Zheng Zhongbing, ed., *Hu Yaobang nianpu ziliao changbian* (Materials for a Chronological Record of Hu Yaobang's Life), 2 vols. (Hong Kong: Shidai guoji chuban youxian gongsi, 2005), September 24, 1980, 1:497.

4. Ruan, *Deng Xiaoping*, pp. 91–103; "Implement the Policy of Readjustment, Ensure Stability and Unity," *SWDXP-2*, pp. 350–368.

5. *SWDXP-2*, p. 320. For background on this issue and its implementation, see Melanie Manion, *Retirement of Revolutionaries in China: Public Policies, Social Norms, Private Interests* (Princeton, N.J.: Princeton University Press, 1993), esp. pp. 48–49.

6. *SWDXP-2*, p. 347.

7. Ibid., p. 356.

8. Richard Baum, *Burying Mao: Chinese Politics in the Age of Deng Xiaoping* (Princeton, N.J.: Princeton University Press, 1994), p. 145.

9. Manion, *Retirement of Revolutionaries in China*, pp. 55–56; ibid., pp. 144–145.

10. *Hongqi* (Red Flag), no. 6 (1982): 5, quoted in Wolfgang Bartke and Peter Scheier, *China's New Party Leadership: Biographies and Analyses of the Twelfth Central Committee of the Chinese Communist Party* (Armonk, N.Y.: M. E. Sharpe, 1985), p. 26.

11. Deng Liqun, *Shierge chunqiu, 1975–1987: Deng Liqun zishu* (Twelve Springs and Autumns, 1975–1987: Deng Liqun's Autobiography) (Hong Kong: Bozhi chubanshe, 2006), p. 208; Yang Jisheng, *Deng Xiaoping shidai: Zhongguo gaige kaifang ershinian jishi* (The Age of Deng Xiaoping: A Record of Twenty Years of China's Reform and Opening), 2 vols. (Beijing: Zhongyang bianyi chubanshe, 1998), 2:479–480; *SWDXP-2*, p. 384, also pp. 373–376, 383–386; Richard Kraus, "Bai Hua: The

Political Authority of a Writer," in Carol Lee Hamrin and Timothy Cheek, eds., *China's Establishment Intellectuals* (Armonk, N.Y.: M. E. Sharpe, 1986), pp. 185–211. For some of the text of the play, see Michael S. Duke, *Blooming and Contending: Chinese Literature in the Post-Mao Era* (Bloomington: Indiana University Press, 1985); Merle Goldman, *Sowing the Seeds of Democracy in China: Political Reform in the Deng Xiaoping Era* (Cambridge: Harvard University Press, 1994), pp. 88–112; W. J. F. Jenner, "1979: A New Start for Literature in China?" *The China Quarterly,* no. 86 (June 1981): 274–303.

12. For some of this literature, see Jinhua Lu et al., *The Wounded: New Stories of the Cultural Revolution, 77–78* (Hong Kong: Joint Publishing, 1979); Perry Link, ed., *Stubborn Weeds: Popular and Controversial Chinese Literature after the Cultural Revolution* (Bloomington: Indiana University Press, 1983); Perry Link, ed., *Roses and Thorns: The Second Blooming of the Hundred Flowers in Chinese Fiction, 1979–80* (Berkeley: University of California Press, 1984); Binyan Liu, *People or Monsters? And Other Stories and Reportage from China after Mao* (Bloomington: Indiana University Press, 1983). For accounts placing these stories in context, see Link's introduction to these three volumes and Merle Goldman, *Chinese Intellectuals: Advise and Dissent* (Cambridge: Harvard University Press, 1981). See also Goldman, *Sowing the Seeds of Democracy.* For an account of the role of the writer and the context in which he wrote, see Perry Link, *The Uses of Literature: Life in the Socialist Chinese Literary System* (Princeton, N.J.: Princeton University Press, 2000).

13. Link, *Stubborn Weeds,* pp. 21–23.

14. Ruan, *Deng Xiaoping,* pp. 116–117.

15. Ibid., pp. 120–121.

16. Ibid.

17. Ibid. Also interviews with Ruan Ming, 1993–1994.

18. Yang Jisheng, *Deng Xiaoping shidai,* pp. 177–179; interview with Sun Changjiang, August 2006.

19. Ruan, *Deng Xiaoping,* pp. 121–130.

20. *DXPNP-2,* March 14, 1983.

21. Ibid., March 15, 1983; Ziyang Zhao, *Prisoner of the State: The Secret Journal of Zhao Ziyang,* trans. and ed. Bao Pu, Renee Chiang, and Adi Ignatius (New York: Simon and Schuster, 2009), pp. 115–116.

22. Ruan, *Deng Xiaoping,* pp. 129–130; Deng Liqun, *Shierge chunqiu,* pp. 256–258; *CYNP,* March 17, 1983.

23. *CYNP,* March 17, 1983.

24. Deng Liqun, *Shierge chunqiu,* pp. 258–259.

25. Sheng Ping, ed., *Hu Yaobang sixiang nianpu: 1975–1989* (A Chronology of Hu Yaobang's Thought: 1975–1989), 2 vols. (Hong Kong: Taide shidai chubanshe, 2007), November 1986, 2:1293.

26. Ibid., 2:1215.

27. Quoted in Goldman, *Sowing the Seeds of Democracy*, p. 117.

28. Ibid., pp. 119–120.

29. Ibid., pp. 270–272.

30. *SWDXP-3*, pp. 47–58; ibid., pp. 122–127.

31. *SWDXP-3*, pp. 47–58.

32. Ibid., p. 57; Deng Liqun, *Shierge chunqiu*, pp. 274–275.

33. Ruan, *Deng Xiaoping*, p. 135; Binyan Liu, *A Higher Kind of Loyalty: A Memoir by China's Foremost Journalist* (New York: Pantheon, 1990), p. 173; Goldman, *Sowing the Seeds of Democracy*, pp. 121–128; Deng Liqun, *Shierge chunqiu*, pp. 269–312.

34. Deng Liqun, *Shierge chunqiu*, p. 338.

35. Ibid., pp. 315, 336–343.

36. Goldman, *Sowing the Seeds of Democracy*, pp. 137–165; ibid., pp. 320–322.

37. *DXPNP-2*, January 2, 1985; Goldman, *Sowing the Seeds of Democracy*, p. 138.

38. Sheng Ping, *Hu Yaobang sixiang nianpu*, 2:1310.

39. Ibid., 2:1080–1086.

40. Deng Liqun, *Shierge chunqiu*, pp. 320–322, 346–347.

41. Ibid.

42. Ibid., pp. 336–343.

43. Interviews with Zhu Houze, August 2006 and September 2006.

44. Deng Liqun, *Shierge chunqiu*, p. 370.

45. Ibid. Deng Liqun writes that Deng Xiaoping had Hu Qiaomu prepare this speech, but friends of Hu Yaobang who edited his papers report that Deng Xiaoping said Hu Qiaomu made an error in opposing spiritual pollution and that he would make his own revisions to the speech and not ask Hu Qiaomu to revise it. See Sheng Ping, *Hu Yaobang sixiang nianpu*, 2:1085.

46. *SWDXP-3*, pp. 146, 148.

47. Ibid., p. 148.

48. Zheng Zhongbing, *Hu Yaobang nianpu ziliao changbian*, September 18, 1985, 2:1042–1045.

49. Sheng Ping, *Hu Yaobang sixiang nianpu*, 2:1310.

50. Ibid., 2:1113, 1303–1310; the full interview is in 2:1110–1116. See also Deng Liqun, *Shierge chunqiu*, pp. 445–446.

51. Report from Don Keyser, February 2010, then on the staff of the American embassy, Beijing.

52. Baum, *Burying Mao*, pp. 187–188.

53. Sheng Ping, *Hu Yaobang sixiang nianpu*, January 16, 1987, 2:1310.

54. Deng Liqun, *Shierge chunqiu*, p. 347.

55. "Younger People Elected to Party Central Committee," Xinhua, September

22, 1985; Daniel Southerland, "China Replaces 91 in Party Committee: Move Seen Strengthening Deng's Control," *The Washington Post,* September 22, 1985, A17.

56. Interviews with Australian Prime Minister Robert Hawke (who traveled with Hu Qili in Australia), June 2001 and November 2002.

57. *DXPNP-2,* September 18, 1985, pp. 1078–1080.

58. Deng Liqun, *Shierge chunqiu,* p. 365.

59. *SWDXP-3,* p. 163; *DXPNP-2,* June 10, 1986.

60. Sheng Ping, *Hu Yaobang sixiang nianpu,* May 1986, 2:1212; January 16, 1987, 2:1311.

61. *SWDXP-3,* p. 167; *DXPNP-2,* June 28, 1986.

62. Wu Guoguang, *Zhao Ziyang yu zhengzhi gaige* (Political Reform under Zhao Ziyang) (Hong Kong: Taipingyang shiji yanjiusuo, 1997), pp. 21, 27–35.

63. Yizi Chen, "The Decision Process behind the 1986–1989 Political Reforms," in Carol Lee Hamrin and Suisheng Zhao, eds., *Decision-Making in Deng's China: Perspectives from Insiders* (Armonk, N.Y.: M. E. Sharpe, 1995), p. 135; Guoguang Wu, "Hard Politics with Soft Institutions: China's Political Reform, 1986–1989," Ph.D. thesis, Department of Politics, Princeton University, 1995, ch. 2. Wu Guoguang, who came to the United States in the spring of 1989, was a member of Zhao's office staff, which included Yan Jiaqi and Chen Yizi. See Guoguang Wu and Helen Lansdowne, eds., *Zhao Ziyang and China's Political Future* (London: Routledge, 2008).

64. On September 13, 1986, when Deng met with leading members of the Finance and Economics Leadership Small Group, Zhao Ziyang, Yao Yilin, Tian Jiyun, and others, to discuss economic issues and prepare for the 13th Party Congress, Deng reiterated that they should separate government duties from party responsibilities, decentralize authority, and streamline government functions. He said that the party should deal with the discipline of party members, but legal issues should be left to the government. See *DXPNP-2,* September 13, 1986; *SWDXP-3,* p. 179; Zhonggong zhongyang wenxian yanjiushi Deng Xiaoping yanjiu zu (Central Chinese Communist Party Literature Research Office, Research Team on Deng Xiaoping), ed., *Deng Xiaoping zishu* (Deng Xiaoping in His Own Words) (Beijing: Jiefangjun chubanshe, 2005), pp. 200–201.

65. Wu, "Hard Politics with Soft Institutions," ch. 2.

66. Ibid.; Wu Guoguang, *Zhao Ziyang yu zhengzhi gaige.*

67. Ibid.

68. Wu Guoguang, *Zhao Ziyang yu zhengzhi gaige.*

69. Deng Liqun, *Shierge chunqiu,* p. 480.

70. David Bachman, "Differing Visions of China's Post-Mao Economy: The Ideas of Chen Yun, Deng Xiaoping, and Zhao Ziyang," *Asian Survey* 26, no. 3 (March 1986): 293–321.

71. *SWDXP-3*, p. 213.

72. Wu, "Hard Politics with Soft Institutions," ch. 2, n100.

73. Data on television ownership are from Link, *The Uses of Literature*, p. 35; and Robin Munro, "Political Reform, Student Demonstrations and the Conservative Backlash," in Robert Benewick and Paul Wingrove, eds., *Reforming the Revolution: China in Transition* (Chicago: Dorsey, 1988), p. 71. Munro was a reporter in China at the time.

74. Interviews with Singapore officials, October 2004. See also Yang Jisheng, *Zhongguo gaige niandai de zhengzhi douzheng* (Political Struggles during the Period of China's Reform) (Hong Kong: Excellent Culture Press, 2004), pp. 317–326.

75. Wu, "Hard Politics with Soft Institutions"; Wu Guoguang, *Zhao Ziyang yu zhengzhi gaige*. For research on social conditions at the time, see chapters by Deborah Davis, Thomas B. Gold, Gail Henderson, Charlotte Ikels, Richard Madsen, and Andrew Walder in Deborah Davis and Ezra F. Vogel, eds., *Chinese Society on the Eve of Tiananmen: The Impact of Reform* (Cambridge: Council on East Asian Studies, Harvard University, 1990); Ezra F. Vogel, *One Step Ahead in China: Guangdong under Reform* (Cambridge: Harvard University Press, 1989), p. 403.

76. See Stanley Rosen, "The Impact of Reform Policies on Youth Attitudes," in Davis and Vogel, *Chinese Society on the Eve of Tiananmen*, p. 292.

77. Benedict Stavis, *China's Political Reforms: An Interim Report* (New York: Praeger, 1988), pp. 89–107. Stavis was at Fudan University, Shanghai, from September 1986 to January 1987 at the time when these incidents were taking place.

78. Sheng Ping, *Hu Yaobang sixiang nianpu*, December 27, 1986, 2:1297; Zheng Zhongbing, *Hu Yaobang nianpu ziliao changbian*, 2:1179.

79. *SWDXP-3*, pp. 194–197; *DXPNP-2*, December 30, 1986.

80. Zheng Zhongbing, *Hu Yaobang nianpu ziliao changbian*, January 2, 1987, 2:1182; Sheng Ping, *Hu Yaobang sixiang nianpu*, January 2, 1987, 2:1302.

81. Sheng Ping, *Hu Yaobang sixiang nianpu*, January 6, 1987, 2:1302.

82. See Stavis, *China's Political Reforms*, pp. 90–96. See also Goldman, *Sowing the Seeds of Democracy*, pp. 194–203; Sheng Ping, *Hu Yaobang sixiang nianpu*, 2:1279, 1301.

83. Sheng Ping, *Hu Yaobang sixiang nianpu*, January 10, 1987, 2:1306.

84. Zheng Zhongbing, *Hu Yaobang nianpu ziliao changbian*, 2:1182.

85. Ibid., January 9, 1987, 2:1182.

86. Sheng Ping, *Hu Yaobang sixiang nianpu*, January 10, 1987, 2:1303–1304.

87. Zheng Zhongbing, *Hu Yaobang nianpu ziliao changbian*, 2:1195–1196.

88. The full text of Deng Liqun's criticisms is in Deng Liqun, *Shierge chunqiu*, pp. 417–445.

89. Yang Jisheng, *Zhongguo gaige niandai de zhengzhi douzheng*, pp. 568–622, extracts translated in Qiren Mei, ed., "Three Interviews with Zhao Ziyang," *Chinese*

Law and Government 38, no. 3 (May–June 2005); Zong Fengming, *Zhao Ziyang: Ruanjinzhong de tanhua* (Zhao Ziyang: Captive Conversations) (Hong Kong: Kaifang chubanshe, 2007); Zhao, *Prisoner of the State*, pp. 176–182.

90. Zheng Zhongbing, *Hu Yaobang nianpu ziliao changbian*, January 15, 1987, 2:1185.

91. Deng Liqun, *Shierge chunqiu*, pp. 447–448.

92. Zheng Zhongbing, *Hu Yaobang nianpu ziliao changbian*, January 16, 1987, 2:1186.

93. Sheng Ping, *Hu Yaobang sixiang nianpu*, January 16, 1986, 2:1307–1309.

94. Wu, "Hard Politics with Soft Institutions," ch. 2, n101.

95. Zheng Zhongbing, *Hu Yaobang nianpu ziliao changbian*, January 16, 1987, 2:1187–1188; *ZGGCDLD*, January 16, 1987, p. 224.

96. Document No. 3 is printed in Sheng Ping, *Hu Yaobang sixiang nianpu*, 2:1313–1314.

97. Ibid., January 19, 1986, 2:1313–1314.

98. Zheng Zhongbing, *Hu Yaobang nianpu ziliao changbian*, 2:1189–1190; ibid., 2:1313–1314, 1319–1320.

99. Interviews with Zhu Houze (August 2006, September 2006), Wu Mingyu (August 2006, July 2007), Yu Guangyuan (February 2003, October 2003, and June 2005), and Li Rui (February 2006, August 2006, and July 2007).

100. Man Mei, *Sinian yiran wujin: Huiyi fuqin Hu Yaobang* (Longing without End: Memories of My Father, Hu Yaobang) (Beijing: Beijing chubanshe, 2005), p. 473; Zheng Zhongbing, *Hu Yaobang nianpu ziliao changbian*, 2:1190–1195.

101. Du Daozheng, *Du Daozheng riji: Zhao Ziyang shuoguo shenme hua* (Du Daozheng Diary: What Zhao Ziyang Said) (Hong Kong: Tiandi, 2010), p. 151.

102. James Tong, ed., "Party Documents on Anti-Bourgeois Liberalization and Hu Yaobang's Resignation," *Chinese Law and Government* 21, no. 1 (Spring 1988): 29–38.

103. *ZGGCDLD*, January 13, 1987, p. 224.

104. Stavis, *China's Political Reforms*, pp. 111–128; Goldman, *Sowing the Seeds of Democracy*, pp. 214–225; Baum, *Burying Mao*, p. 209.

105. Sheng Ping, *Hu Yaobang sixiang nianpu*, March 29, 1987, 2:1319.

106. Goldman, *Sowing the Seeds of Democracy*, pp. 204–214.

107. Baum, *Burying Mao*, pp. 211–215; ibid., pp. 225–232.

108. Deng Liqun, *Shierge chunqiu*, pp. 467–468; interviews with Li Rui, February 2006, August 2006, and July 2007.

109. Du Daozheng, *Du Daozheng riji*, p. 160.

110. Ibid., pp. 173–174.

111. Sheng Ping, *Hu Yaobang sixiang nianpu*, November 11, 1986, 2:1290.

112. Ibid., January 16, 1987, 2:1306.

113. *SWDXP-3*, p. 395, n117.

114. For Deng Liqun's view of the May 13 speech, see Deng Liqun, *Shierge chunqiu*, pp. 459–460.

115. Anthony J. Kane, "1987: Politics Back in Command," in Anthony J. Kane, ed., *China Briefing, 1988* (New York: Asia Society, 1988), p. 11.

116. Interviews with Singapore officials in October 2004; *DXPNP-2*, May 29, 1987.

117. Chi Huang, "Deng's Ideas on Political Restructuring," *Beijing Review* 30, no. 39 (September 29, 1987): 14–15.

118. Ziyang Zhao, "Advance along the Road of Socialism with Chinese Characteristics," *Beijing Review* 30, no. 45 (November 9–15, 1987): xv–xxi. For an account of the political reforms written shortly after the congress, see Tony Saich, "Reforming the Political Structure," in Benewick and Wingrove, *Reforming the Revolution*, pp. 27–47.

119. Saich, "Reforming the Political Structure," pp. 27–47.

120. Wu, "Hard Politics with Soft Institutions," ch. 2; Deng Liqun, *Shierge chunqiu*, pp. 472–473.

121. Deng Liqun, obviously wounded, goes into the background in great detail in his book *Shierge chunqiu*, pp. 467–478.

20. Beijing Spring

1. The two accounts by high-level officials are Ziyang Zhao, *Prisoner of the State: The Secret Journal of Zhao Ziyang*, trans. and ed. Bao Pu, Renee Chiang, and Adi Ignatius (New York: Simon and Schuster, 2009), a translation based on the tapes Zhao recorded after he was under house arrest; and Li Peng's diary covering this time period, *LPLSRJ*, available in the Fairbank Collection, Fung Library, Harvard University. Among the most useful works on the Spring 1989 movement are Michel Oksenberg, Lawrence R. Sullivan, and Mark Lambert, eds., *Beijing Spring, 1989, Confrontation and Conflict: The Basic Documents* (Armonk, N.Y.: M. E. Sharpe, 1990), esp. Melanie Manion, "Introduction: Reluctant Duelists," pp. xiii–xlii; Suzanne Ogden et al., eds., *China's Search for Democracy: The Student and Mass Movement of 1989* (Armonk, N.Y.: M. E. Sharpe, 1992); Minzhu Han, ed., *Cries for Democracy: Writings and Speeches from the 1989 Chinese Democracy Movement* (Princeton, N.J.: Princeton University Press, 1990); Orville Schell, *Mandate of Heaven: A Generation of Entrepreneurs, Dissidents, Bohemians, and Technocrats Lays Claim to China's Future* (New York: Simon and Schuster, 1994); Binyan Liu, with Ming Ruan and Gang Xu, *Tell the World: What Happened in China and Why* (New York: Pantheon, 1989); Tony Saich, ed., *The Chinese People's Movement: Perspectives on Spring 1989* (Armonk, N.Y.: M. E. Sharpe, 1990); Long Bow Group, *The Gate of Heavenly Peace,*

video recording produced and directed by Richard Gordon and Carma Hinton (San Francisco: NAATA/CrossCurrent Media, 1996); Mike Chinoy, *China Live: Two Decades in the Heart of the Dragon* (Atlanta: Turner Publishing, 1997); Tang Tsou, "The Tiananmen Tragedy," in Brantly Womack, ed., *Contemporary Chinese Politics in Historical Perspective* (New York: Cambridge University Press, 1991); Richard Baum, *Burying Mao: Chinese Politics in the Age of Deng Xiaoping* (Princeton, N.J.: Princeton University Press, 1994); Melinda Liu, "Beijing Spring: Loss of the Mandate of Heaven," in David and Peter Turnley, *Beijing Spring* (New York: Stewart, Tabori & Chang, 1989), pp. 44–172; Jonathan Unger, ed., *The Pro-Democracy Protests in China: Reports from the Provinces* (Armonk, N.Y.: M. E. Sharpe, 1991); Dingxin Zhao, *The Power of Tiananmen: State-Society Relations and the 1989 Beijing Student Movement* (Chicago: University of Chicago Press, 2001); James Lilley with Jeffrey Lilley, *China Hands: Nine Decades of Adventure, Espionage, and Diplomacy in Asia* (New York: PublicAffairs, 2004), pp. 297–392 (Lilley arrived in China on May 2, 1989, to be U.S. ambassador, and remained until May 1991). For a careful examination of the available documentation, see Robert L. Suettinger, *Beyond Tiananmen: The Politics of U.S.-China Relations, 1989–2000* (Washington, D.C.: Brookings Institution Press, 2003); the U.S. government's "Tiananmen Papers" containing declassified government documents, available through the National Security Archive, and with a guide, is included in the electronic briefing book Michael L. Evans, ed., "The U.S. 'Tiananmen Papers': New Documents Reveal U.S. Perceptions of 1989 Chinese Political Crisis," a National Security Archive Electronic Briefing Book, June 4, 2001, at http://www.gwu.edu/~nsarchiv/NSAEBB/NSAEBB47/, accessed March 16, 2010. A bibliography of publications during the first year after June 4 by Tony Saich and Nancy Hearst can be found in Saich, *The Chinese People's Movement*, pp. 190–196. The most comprehensive collection of materials, including a detailed chronology, is Liang Zhang, comp., and Andrew J. Nathan and Perry Link, eds., *The Tiananmen Papers* (New York: Public Affairs, 2001) (*TP*). The documents were collected by Chinese reformers and passed on to a compiler to publish in the West. Some of the documents are clearly authentic, but questions have been raised about the authenticity of other documents, particularly those reporting meetings of eight senior leaders and those summarizing phone calls. Deng Rong, daughter of Deng Xiaoping, reports that her father discussed personnel issues in one-on-one meetings to get the views of each person rather than in larger groups, as described in these volumes. The Chinese edition (Zhang Liang, ed., *Zhongguo "liusi" zhenxiang* [June 4: The True Story], 2 vols. [Hong Kong: Mingjing chubanshe, 2001]) is more complete than the English edition. On p. 988 of the Chinese edition, the term *"Hanguo"* is used for South Korea, but in fact mainland publications did not use that term until 1992 when China normalized relations with South Korea; before that it used the term *Nan chaoxian*. Because Taiwan and Hong Kong in 1989 used the term *Hanguo*, this raises a question about the legitimacy of at least some of the documents. The fact that the meetings of eight leaders are not mentioned by Li Peng or Zhao Ziyang in their confidential accounts of high-level politics at the time or by any of the official chronologies raises questions about whether such meetings actually took place, but it is possible that there are classified documents of such meetings that have not yet been released and that even Li Peng and Zhao Ziyang were unaware of them. Alfred L. Chan raises questions about the authenticity of the Tiananmen Papers in an exchange with Andrew Nathan, "The Tiananmen Papers Revisited," *The China Quarterly*, no. 177 (March 2004): 190–214. Nathan and Link have done a careful job of editing and checking the English translations; since this is a convenient collection, I make use of many of the documents, but I have not used the reported meetings of the eight senior leaders or reports of phone calls since questions have been raised about their authenticity.

2. *TP*, p. 21.

3. Deng Liqun, *Shierge chunqiu, 1975–1987: Deng Liqun zishu* (Twelve Springs and Autumns, 1975–1987: Deng Liqun's Autobiography) (Hong Kong: Bozhi chubanshe, 2006), pp. 466–467.

4. Li Rui, "Hu Yaobang qushiqian de tanhua" (Conversation with Hu Yaobang Shortly before He Died), in Zhang Liqun et al., eds., *Huainian Yaobang*, 4 vols. (Hong Kong: vols. 1–2: Lingtian chubanshe, 1999; vols. 3–4: Yatai guoji chuban youxian gongsi, 2001), 4:277–278.

5. A particularly insightful account of Chinese intellectuals at the time is Perry Link, *Evening Chats in Beijing: Probing China's Predicament* (New York: Norton, 1992). No foreigner had deeper contacts among Chinese intellectuals than Link, who has excellent Chinese-language skills and was living in Beijing in 1988–1989. A collection of popular views of the time is Perry Link, Richard Madsen, and Paul G. Pickowicz, eds., *Unofficial China: Popular Culture and Thought in the People's Republic* (Boulder, Colo.: Westview, 1989). Bette Bao Lord, wife of U.S. Ambassador Winston Lord, also met with many of the intellectuals advocating democracy. At a January 2009 meeting to commemorate the thirtieth anniversary of normalization, Ambassador Lord told me there was such widespread support for the students, including from members of the Chinese press, that it was difficult not to get caught up in the hope that the regime would make some changes to allow more democracy. In retrospect, Lord said, they underestimated the determination of the top leaders to crack down.

6. Dong Fureng, ed., *Zhonghua renmin gongheguo jingji shi* (An Economic History of the PRC), 2 vols. (Beijing: Jingji kexue chubanshe, 1999), 2:348.

7. Ogden et al., *China's Search for Democracy*, pp. 57–58, 87–88.

8. Nicholas D. Kristof and Sheryl WuDunn, *China Wakes: The Struggle for the Soul of a Rising Power* (New York: Times Books, 1994), p. 78.

9. *LPLSRJ*, April 18, 1989.

10. Ibid., April 18, 19, 20, 1989.

11. Liu, Ruan, and Xu, *Tell the World What Happened in China and Why*, p. 9.

12. Interview with Yao Jianfu, November 2006; Ogden et al., *China's Search for Democracy*, pp. 95–96, and Oksenberg, Sullivan, and Lambert, *Beijing Spring, 1989*, pp. 27–28, are based on reports by students who were unaware that NPC members met with the petitioners. See also Baum, *Burying Mao*, pp. 248–249; Saich, *The Chinese People's Movement*, pp. 165–166.

13. As reported by Yang Jisheng in an interview with Zhao Ziyang on December 16, 1993. See Yang Jisheng, *Zhongguo gaige niandai de zhengzhi douzheng* (Political Struggles during the Period of China's Reform) (Hong Kong: Excellent Culture Press, 2004), extracts translated in Qiren Mei, ed., "Three Interviews with Zhao Ziyang," *Chinese Law and Government* 38, no. 3 (May–June 2005). This was reported as well by Zhao Ziyang's close work associate Sun Changjiang in "Zhao Ziyang koushu yu Hu Yaobang guanxi" (Zhao Ziyang on His Relations with Hu Yaobang), *Dongxiang*, no. 5 (2006): 28–32. Also see Zhao, *Prisoner of the State*, pp. 6–7.

14. *TP*, p. 55; Oksenberg, Sullivan, and Lambert, *Beijing Spring, 1989*, p. xvi. There are no official records of the number of people in the square at various times, and there are very different estimates regarding the size of the crowds, the exact time of day that events occurred, and the number of universities represented in the association. I have used as estimates of the size of the crowds the near consensus of several observers.

15. *LPLSRJ*, April 23, 1989.

16. Ibid.

17. Ibid., April 24, 1989.

18. Ibid., April 25, 1989; *TP*, pp. 78–79; Larry M. Wortzel, "Review: *Quelling the People*," *Australian Journal of Chinese Affairs*, no. 31 (January 1994): 125; Timothy Brook, *Quelling the People: The Military Suppression of the Beijing Democracy Movement* (Stanford, Calif.: Stanford University Press, 1998), pp. 39–40; Kristof and WuDunn, *China Wakes*, p. 79.

19. *Renmin ribao* (People's Daily) editorial, April 26, 1989; Domestic Radio 0930 GMT, FBIS, April 25, 1989, pp. 23–24.

20. *TP*, pp. 76, 80–81.

21. Saich, *The Chinese People's Movement*, p. 167; Long Bow Group, *The Gate of Heavenly Peace*.

22. *TP*, pp. 95–96.

23. Ibid., pp. 86–95.

24. Interview with Liu Binyan, June 1989.

25. *LPLSRJ*, April 23, 1989.

26. Zhao, *Prisoner of the State*, pp. 5–9.

27. *TP*, p. 74.

28. Zhao, *Prisoner of the State*, pp. 8–14.

29. Ibid., pp. 100, 107–108.

30. Reprinted in Oksenberg, Sullivan, and Lambert, *Beijing Spring, 1989,* pp. 244–251.

31. It is not required that presentations to a foreign audience be cleared by other leaders, but given the tensions at the time, Zhao's failure to consult with others heightened the sense that he was not acting in accordance with the will of the other members of the Politburo Standing Committee. According to *TP,* p. 108, Zhao had in fact distributed a draft to the members of the Politburo Standing Committee on May 1.

32. Reprinted in Oksenberg, Sullivan, and Lambert, *Beijing Spring, 1989,* pp. 254–256.

33. Reprinted in ibid., pp. 69–70.

34. *TP,* p. 154.

35. Brook, *Quelling the People,* p. 37.

36. Ogden et al., *China's Search for Democracy,* pp. 215–217.

37. For the statement and signatories, see Han, *Cries for Dem*ocracy, pp. 207–208. For analysis, see Tsou, "The Tiananmen Tragedy," p. 308.

38. David Zweig, "The Hunger Strike: From Protest to Uprising," in Ogden et al., *China's Search for Democracy,* pp. 194–195, especially n29; *TP,* p. 176.

39. *TP,* p. 202.

40. Interview with Yao Jianfu, November 2006.

41. Lilley, *China Hands,* p. 301.

42. Qichen Qian, *Ten Episodes in China's Diplomacy,* foreword by Ezra Vogel (New York: HarperCollins, 2005), pp. 1–31.

43. George Bush and Brent Scowcroft, *A World Transformed* (New York: Knopf, 1998), pp. 91–96; *DXPNP-2,* February 26, 1989.

44. Shen Zhihua, who examined the documents carefully, concludes that this was what Deng actually said to Gorbachev. The official record of the meeting reports that Deng said that the original arguments included "some empty words."

45. Qian, *Ten Episodes in China's Diplomacy,* pp. 29–31.

46. Tsou, "The Tiananmen Tragedy," p. 306.

47. *TP,* p. 173.

48. Oksenberg, Sullivan, and Lambert, *Beijing Spring, 1989,* p. 261.

49. Zhao, *Prisoner of the State,* pp. 35–44.

50. *LPLSRJ,* May 16, 1989.

51. Zhao, *Prisoner of the State,* p. 48.

52. Discussion with Wang Dan and other leaders of the student movement, August 2007.

53. *TP,* p. 194.

54. Ibid., pp. 163–175.

21. The Tiananmen Tragedy

1. Ziyang Zhao, *Prisoner of the State: The Secret Journal of Zhao Ziyang,* trans. and ed. Bao Pu, Renee Chiang, and Adi Ignatius (New York: Simon and Schuster, 2009), p. 27.

2. Timothy Brook, *Quelling the People: The Military Suppression of the Beijing Democracy Movement* (Stanford, Calif.: Stanford University Press, 1998), p. 34.

3. Zhao, *Prisoner of the State,* pp. 27–28.

4. *LPLSRJ,* May 17, 1989, available in the Fairbank Collection, Fung Library, Harvard University.

5. James Lilley with Jeffrey Lilley, *China Hands: Nine Decades of Adventure, Espionage, and Diplomacy in Asia* (New York: PublicAffairs, 2004), p. 309.

6. Zhao, *Prisoner of the State,* pp. 28–29; Li Peng's accounts of these meetings relate the events from the view of one who was critical of Zhao's reluctance to do what was necessary to restore order; see *LPLSRJ,* May 17, 18, 19, 1989.

7. Zhao, *Prisoner of the State,* pp. 25–34; interviews with Zhao's daughter, Wang Yannan, October 2006, July 2007.

8. From Beijing TV Service, reported in FBIS, May 19, 1989, pp. 13–14, reprinted in Michel Oksenberg, Lawrence R. Sullivan, and Mark Lambert, eds., *Beijing Spring, 1989, Confrontation and Conflict: The Basic Documents* (Armonk, N.Y.: M. E. Sharpe, 1990), pp. 288–290; Mike Chinoy, *China Live: Two Decades in the Heart of the Dragon* (Atlanta: Turner Publishing, 1997), p. 217; Brook, *Quelling the People,* pp. 42–43.

9. Zhao, *Prisoner of the State,* pp. 27–34.

10. *TP,* p. 277.

11. Zhao, *Prisoner of the State,* pp. 48–87.

12. *LPLSRJ,* May 18, 1989.

13. Ibid., May 19, 20, 1989.

14. *TP,* p. 222.

15. *LPLSRJ,* May 20, 1989.

16. Sandra Burton in an interview with Amy Zegert. I am deeply indebted to Amy Zegert, who granted me access to the twenty-three interviews she conducted for the Shorenstein Center, Kennedy School of Government, Harvard University, with correspondents who covered Beijing in 1989.

17. Brook, *Quelling the People,* pp. 48–78. Brook had been in Beijing before June 4 and returned after June 4 to carry out extensive interviews about the role of the military. For a review of this book by a U.S. military attaché in Beijing at the time, see Larry M. Wortzel, "Review: *Quelling the People,*" *Australian Journal of Chinese Affairs,* no. 31 (January 1994): 123–126.

18. *LPLSRJ,* May 22, 1989.

19. Brook, *Quelling the People,* pp. 43–77.

20. *TP,* p. 265.

21. *LPLSRJ,* May 21, 1989.

22. Ibid., May 19, 25, 1989.

23. *TP,* pp. 277–279, 291.

24. Ibid., p. 305.

25. *LPLSRJ,* May 31, 1989.

26. Ibid., May 19, 1989.

27. *TP,* pp. 297, 308–314.

28. *LPLSRJ,* May 31, 1989.

29. *TP,* pp. 323–328. An alternate translation of Deng's explanation is found in Oksenberg, Sullivan, and Lambert, *Beijing Spring, 1989,* pp. 333–338.

30. Robert Lawrence Kuhn, *The Man Who Changed China: The Life and Legacy of Jiang Zemin* (New York: Crown, 2004). Though this is not a scholarly work, it is mostly accurate in the information it reports.

31. Brook, *Quelling the People,* pp. 87–88.

32. *TP,* p. 319.

33. Ibid., pp. 288–289.

34. Melanie Manion, "Introduction: Reluctant Duelists," in Oksenberg, Sullivan, and Lambert, *Beijing Spring, 1989,* p. xl.

35. Interview with his daughter, Deng Lin, July 2007.

36. When I met with Liu Binyan during the last week of May, he predicted a bloody incident because he believed that Deng wanted to intimidate the public.

37. Interview with Jiang Zemin, November 2006.

38. Brook, *Quelling the People,* pp. 73–74, 80.

39. Ibid., pp. 89–91.

40. *TP,* pp. 359–362.

41. Ibid., pp. 353–354.

42. *LPLSRJ,* June 3, 1989.

43. *TP,* pp. 368–369.

44. Brook, *Quelling the People,* pp. 108–113.

45. *TP,* pp. 368–371; Andrew Scobell, *China's Use of Military Force: Beyond the Great Wall and the Long March* (New York: Cambridge University Press, 2003), pp. 150–151.

46. *TP,* p. 365; Brook, *Quelling the People,* pp. 114–120.

47. Brook, *Quelling the People,* pp. 121–122.

48. Ibid., pp. 114–130; *TP,* pp. 372–377.

49. Brook, *Quelling the People,* pp. 118–120.

50. Ibid., p. 94.

51. Long Bow Group, *The Gate of Heavenly Peace,* video recording, produced and

directed by Richard Gordon and Carma Hinton (San Francisco: Distributed by NAATA/CrossCurrent Media, 1996); ibid., p. 145; *TP,* pp. 377–382, 389–391. Although there is consistency in these accounts, there are varying estimates as to precisely when things occurred.

52. Brook, *Quelling the People,* pp. 133–148.

53. *TP,* pp. 383–385.

54. George Bush and Brent Scowcroft, *A World Transformed* (New York: Knopf, 1998), p. 109.

55. Brook, *Quelling the People,* p. 130.

56. Ibid., p. 161.

57. Ibid., pp. 151–169.

58. Many of the leaders are presented on film in Long Bow Group, *The Gate of Heavenly Peace,* which was carefully researched over many years.

59. For this section, I have drawn on the interviews of reporters by Amy Zegert, but she should not be held responsible for any of my interpretations here. For CNN coverage, see Chinoy, *China Live.*

60. Richard Madsen, *China and the American Dream: A Moral Inquiry* (Berkeley: University of California Press, 1995), pp. 1–27.

61. *New York Times* correspondents Kristof and WuDunn reported, for example, "Those killings [June 4] may have marked the beginning of the end of Communist rule in China." See Nicholas D. Kristof and Sheryl WuDunn, *China Wakes: The Struggle for the Soul of a Rising Power* (New York: Times Books, 1994).

22. Standing Firm

1. *SWDXP-3,* May 31, 1989, p. 289.

2. Ibid., p. 291.

3. Ibid., p. 299, June 9, 1989.

4. Ibid., pp. 294–299.

5. Ibid., pp. 302–303, June 16, 1989.

6. Timothy Brook, *Quelling the People: The Military Suppression of the Beijing Democracy Movement* (Stanford, Calif.: Stanford University Press, 1998), pp. 196–197.

7. Qichen Qian, *Ten Episodes in China's Diplomacy,* foreword by Ezra Vogel (New York: HarperCollins, 2005), pp. 143–146; George Bush and Brent Scowcroft, *A World Transformed* (New York: Knopf, 1998), p. 414.

8. *DXPNP-2,* July 16, 1989.

9. Ibid., June 23–24, 1989.

10. Robert Lawrence Kuhn, *The Man Who Changed China: The Life and Legacy of Jiang Zemin* (New York: Crown, 2004), p. 173.

11. *DXPNP-2,* August 17, 1989.

12. Ibid., September 4, 1989; *SWDXP-3,* pp. 305–311. He added that as for his burial, the simpler the better.

13. *DXPNP-2,* September 4, 1989; *SWDXP-3,* pp. 305–311.

14. *SWDXP-3,* p. 311.

15. Ibid., p. 313.

16. *DXPNP-2,* September 16, 1989.

17. Ibid., November 6–9, 1989.

18. Rong Deng, *Deng Xiaoping: My Father* (New York: Basic Books, 1995), pp. 1–5.

19. *SWDXP-3,* p. 315.

20. Observation of Michel Oksenberg, who accompanied President Nixon when he met with Deng in October 1989. This was Oksenberg's fourteenth and final time to sit in on meetings with Deng. See Michel Oksenberg, "I Remember Deng," *Far Eastern Economic Review,* March 6, 1997, 35.

21. George Bush, *The China Diary of George H. W. Bush: The Making of a Global President* (Princeton, N.J.: Princeton University Press, 2008), p. 461.

22. James Lilley with Jeffrey Lilley, *China Hands: Nine Decades of Adventure, Espionage, and Diplomacy in Asia* (New York: PublicAffairs, 2004), p. 378.

23. Bush and Scowcroft, *A World Transformed,* p. 93.

24. Personal communication from Ambassador Stapleton Roy, November 2010.

25. John H. Holdridge, *Crossing the Divide: An Insider's Account of Normalization of U.S.-China Relations* (Lanham, Md.: Rowman and Littlefield, 1997), pp. 225–226; Lilley, *China Hands,* pp. 222–223, 378.

26. Bush and Scowcroft, *A World Transformed,* pp. 91–99. See also Perry Link, *Evening Chats in Beijing: Probing China's Predicament* (New York: Norton, 1992), pp. 29–38; Robert L. Suettinger, *Beyond Tiananmen: The Politics of U.S.-China Relations, 1989–2000* (Washington, D.C.: Brookings Institution Press, 2003), pp. 24–28.

27. Bush and Scowcroft, *A World Transformed,* pp. 98–102. See also Bush, *China Diary of George H. W. Bush;* Lilley, *China Hands.*

28. Bush and Scowcroft, *A World Transformed,* p. 102.

29. Qian, *Ten Episodes in China's Diplomacy,* pp. 131–146.

30. Bush and Scowcroft, *A World Transformed,* p. 106.

31. Ibid., pp. 106–111; *DXPNP-2,* July 2, 1989; Qian, *Ten Episodes in China's Diplomacy,* pp. 131–139. For an account of the effects of Tiananmen on U.S.-China relations, see Suettinger, *Beyond Tiananmen.*

32. Bush and Scowcroft, *A World Transformed,* pp. 106–107.

33. Ibid., p. 109. See also a report of the trip in Suettinger, *Beyond Tiananmen,* pp. 79–83.

34. Interview with Eden Woon, Defense Department official who played a central role in these negotiations, December 2008.

35. Bush and Scowcroft, *A World Transformed,* p. 128.

36. Ibid., p. 157.

37. *DXPNP-2,* October 31, 1989; "The United States Should Take the Initiative in Putting an End to the Strains in Sino-American Relations," *SWDXP-3,* p. 321; Suettinger, *Beyond Tiananmen,* p. 81.

38. *DXPNP-2,* November 10, 1989.

39. Lilley, *China Hands,* pp. 358–362.

40. Suettinger, *Beyond Tiananmen,* p. 100.

41. Richard Madsen, *China and the American Dream: A Moral Inquiry* (Berkeley: University of California Press, 1995).

42. Bush and Scowcroft, *A World Transformed,* p. 157.

43. *DXPNP-2,* December 10, 1989; "Sino-U.S. Relations Must Be Improved," *SWDXP-3,* pp. 338–339.

44. Suettinger, *Beyond Tiananmen,* pp. 100–101.

45. Quoted in ibid., p. 51.

46. Bush and Scowcroft, *A World Transformed,* p. 179.

47. Qian, *Ten Episodes in China's Diplomacy; DXPNP-3,* October 9, 1985; James A. R. Miles, *The Legacy of Tiananmen: China in Disarray* (Ann Arbor: University of Michigan Press, 1996), pp. 46–48.

48. Zhou Rongzi, "Qi'aosaisiku he Mengbotuo biaoshi zhichi Zhongguo pingxi fan'geming baoluan" (Ceauçescu and Mobutu Express Support for China's Counter-revolutionary Rebellion), *Renmin ribao* (People's Daily), September 23, 1989, 3.

49. Miles, *Legacy of Tiananmen,* pp. 47–48.

50. *DXPNP-2,* pp. 1303–1306.

51. "Jiang Zemin and Li Ruihuan Interviewed by Hong Kong Journalists," BBC *Summary of World Broadcasts,* FE/0650/B2/1, December 30, 1989.

52. Miles, *Legacy of Tiananmen,* p. 41. This and the following paragraphs draw heavily on the work of Miles, who was in Beijing at the time closely following Chinese reactions to developments in the USSR and Eastern Europe. For a somewhat dispassionate Chinese account of developments in Eastern Europe and the USSR, see Huang Hong, ed., *Ying daoli: Nanfang tanhua huimou* (The Hard Truth: Looking Back on the Southern Journey) (Ji'nan: Shandong renmin chubanshe, 2002), pp. 3–38.

53. Huang Hong, *Ying daoli,* pp. 44–46.

54. Miles, *Legacy of Tiananmen,* pp. 59–60.

55. *DXPNP-2,* August 20, 1991; *SWDXP-3,* pp. 356–357; Kuhn, *The Man Who Changed China,* pp. 206–207.

56. *DXPNP-2,* October 5, 1991.

57. *SWDXP-3,* p. 318.

58. Qian, *Ten Episodes in China's Diplomacy,* pp. 170–171, 174–177.

59. Chen Guoyan, "Deng Xiaoping dui dong'ou de zhanlüe fangzhen ji qi yiyi" (Deng Xiaoping's Strategic Policy toward Eastern Europe and Its Significance), in Wang Taiping and Zhang Guangyou, eds., *Deng Xiaoping waijiao sixiang yanjiu lunwenji* (A Collection of Essays on Research on Deng Xiaoping's Foreign Policy Thought) (Beijing: Shijie zhishi chubanshe, 1996), pp. 270–275; Qian, *Ten Episodes in China's Diplomacy,* pp. 172–174.

60. "Regulations on Construction of Expensive Buildings Issued," Xinhua General Overseas Service, September 25, 1988. For an overview of the official steps and analysis supporting austerity, see Wu Li, ed., *Zhonghua renmin gongheguo jingjishi, 1949–1999* (An Economic History of the People's Republic of China, 1949–1999), 2 vols. (Beijing: Zhongguo jingji chubanshe, 1999), 2:983–1010.

61. Xue Muqiao, "Laoji lishi jingyan, jianjue zhixing zhili zhengdun de fangzhen" (Clearly Remember the Historical Experience, Resolutely Implement the Policy of Rectification), *Renmin ribao* (People's Daily), December 18, 1989, 6.

62. Xinhua Domestic Broadcast in Chinese, December 26 1989, in FBIS, January 3, 1990, pp. 12–18.

63. Suettinger, *Beyond Tiananmen,* pp. 120–125.

64. Richard Baum, *Burying Mao: Chinese Politics in the Age of Deng Xiaoping* (Princeton, N.J.: Princeton University Press, 1994), p. 337.

65. See, for example, *Guangming ribao,* December 9, 1989, in FBIS, January 4, 1990, pp. 27–28.

66. Simon Long in the Economist Intelligence Unit, May 1992, quoted by Miles, *Legacy of Tiananmen,* pp. 62, 326.

67. The Chinese term for patriotism, *aiguozhuyi,* literally means "love for the country." Since China officially is composed of many ethnic groups (*minzu,* sometimes translated as nationalities), China did not use the term *minzuzhuyi,* which is translated as nationalism but literally means "love for one's nationality."

68. Suisheng Zhao, "A State-Led Nationalism: The Patriotic Education Campaign in Post-Tiananmen China," *Communist and Post Communist Studies* 31, no. 3 (September 1998): 287–302; Paul A. Cohen, *China Unbound: Evolving Perspectives on the Chinese Past* (New York: Routledge Curzon, 2003), pp. 166–169 and n181, n182; Parks Coble, "China's 'New Remembering' of the Anti-Japanese War of Resistance, 1937–1945," *The China Quarterly,* no. 190 (June 2007): 394–410; Suisheng Zhao, *A Nation-State by Construction: Dynamics of Modern Chinese Nationalism* (Stanford, Calif.: Stanford University Press, 2004), pp. 213–247.

69. Coble, "China's 'New Remembering,'" pp. 400–402.

70. For an account of the nuances of how writers responded to the clues from above, see Perry Link, *The Uses of Literature: Life in the Socialist Chinese Literary System* (Princeton, N.J.: Princeton University Press, 2000), pp. 68–81.

71. Shuqing Zhang, "Marxism, Confucianism, and Cultural Nationalism," in Zhiling Lin and Thomas W. Robinson, eds., *The Chinese and Their Future: Beijing, Taipei, and Hong Kong* (Washington, D.C.: The AEI Press, 1994), pp. 82–109.

23. Deng's Finale

1. Joseph Fewsmith, *China since Tiananmen: From Deng Xiaoping to Hu Jintao*, 2d ed. (New York: Cambridge University Press, 2008).

2. *DXPNP-2*, January 20, 1990; January 26, 1990; February 13, 1990.

3. Victoria Wu, "The Pudong Development Zone and China's Economic Reforms," *Planning Perspectives* 13, no. 2 (April 1998): 133–165; Zhongyang wenxian yanjiushi keyanbu tushuguan (Library Department on Scientific Research of the Central Chinese Communist Party Literature Office), ed., *Deng Xiaoping rensheng jishi* (A Record of the Life of Deng Xiaoping), 3 vols. (Nanjing: Fenghuang chubanshe, 2004), 3:2019–2052.

4. Tong Huaiping and Li Chengguan, *Deng Xiaoping baci nanxun jishi* (Record of Deng Xiaoping's Eight Southern Journeys) (Beijing: Jiefangjun wenyi chubanshe, 2002), pp. 214–216, 220. Another account is in Zhongyang wenxian yanjiushi keyanbu tushuguan, *Deng Xiaoping rensheng jishi*.

5. *DXPNP-2*, January 26, 1990.

6. Tong Huaiping and Li Chengguan, *Deng Xiaoping baci nanxun jishi*, p. 216.

7. *SWDXP-3*, pp. 342–343; *DXPNP-2*, March 3, 1990.

8. *DXPNP-2*, Febuary 13, 1990.

9. *SWDXP-3*, December 24, 1990, pp. 350–352.

10. Robert Lawrence Kuhn, *The Man Who Changed China: The Life and Legacy of Jiang Zemin* (New York: Crown, 2004), p. 205.

11. Tong Huaiping and Li Chengguan, *Deng Xiaoping baci nanxun jishi*, pp. 204–222; Huang Hong, ed., *Ying daoli: Nanfang tanhua huimou* (The Hard Truth: Looking Back on the Southern Journey) (Ji'nan: Shandong renmin chubanshe, 2002), pp. 127–149.

12. *SWDXP-3*, pp. 353–355.

13. *DXPNP-2*, February 10, 1991; February 12, 1991; February 14, 1991.

14. Ibid., February 15, 1991; March 2, 1991; March 22, 1991; and April 12, 1991; Huang Hong, *Ying daoli*, pp. 130–136.

15. James A. R. Miles, *The Legacy of Tiananmen: China in Disarray* (Ann Arbor: University of Michigan Press, 1996), pp. 78–83; Suisheng Zhao, "Deng Xiaoping's Southern Tour: Elite Politics in Post-Tiananmen China," *Asian Survey* 33, no. 8 (August 1993): 748–749.

16. Fewsmith, *China since Tiananmen*, p. 54.

17. Ibid., p. 55.

18. Tong Huaiping and Li Chengguan, *Deng Xiaoping baci nanxun jishi*, p. 226.

19. Ibid., p. 226. The comment is from a talk delivered on February 29, 1980.

20. Ibid., pp. 227–228.

21. Ibid., pp. 228–229.

22. Interview with Chen Kaizhi, who accompanied Deng on the trip, and other local officials, October 2003.

23. Tong Huaiping and Li Chengguan, *Deng Xiaoping baci nanxun jishi*, pp. 231–232.

24. Ibid., p. 243.

25. Miles, *Legacy of Tiananmen*, pp. 96–97.

26. Interview in October 2003 with Chen Kaizhi, who was deputy secretary general of Guangdong at the time of the Deng visit and responsible for making the arrangements for the trip to Shenzhen and Zhuhai. See also Cen Longye, ed., *Yueai wujia* (Priceless Experience and Love) (Beijing: Zuojia chubanshe, 2001), pp. 182–190. Figures about cameras and tape recorders are from Zhao, "Deng Xiaoping's Southern Tour," 750. For another account of the trip see Huang Hong, *Ying daoli*, pp. 150–190.

27. Tong Huaiping and Li Chengguan, *Deng Xiaoping baci nanxun jishi*, pp. 234–235.

28. Interview with an official who rode with Deng, November 2003, in Guangzhou.

29. *SWDXP-3*, pp. 362–363.

30. Tong Huaiping and Li Chengguan, *Deng Xiaoping baci nanxun jishi*, p. 232; Kuhn, *The Man Who Changed China*, p. 212.

31. Tong Huaiping and Li Chengguan, *Deng Xiaoping baci nanxun jishi*, pp. 240, 245–246.

32. Ibid., pp. 232–233.

33. Ibid., pp. 246–248.

34. Cen Longye, *Yueai wujia*, p. 186.

35. Tong Huaiping and Li Chengguan, *Deng Xiaoping baci nanxun jishi*, pp. 248–249.

36. Ibid., pp. 251–253.

37. *DXPNP-2*, January 29, 1992.

38. Tong Huaiping and Li Chengguan, *Deng Xiaoping baci nanxun jishi*, pp. 279–282.

39. Miles, *Legacy of Tiananmen*, p. 95.

40. Ibid., p 95; Zhao, "Deng Xiaoping's Southern Tour," 749; Tong Huaiping and Li Chengguan, *Deng Xiaoping baci nanxun jishi*, p. 286.

41. Kuhn, *The Man Who Changed China*, pp. 212–213.

42. Miles, *Legacy of Tiananmen*, pp. 95–96; Zhao, "Deng Xiaoping's Southern Tour," 749; Kuhn, *The Man Who Changed China*, p. 213.

43. Kuhn, *The Man Who Changed China*, p. 214.

44. Deng had gone to Shanghai in 1985, where he had had a chance to see the initial progress following both his 1984 visit and his decision to open up the fourteen coastal cities, but in the winter of 1986 he went instead to Guilin and Chongqing. In 1987 he remained in Beijing because of the turmoil over the dismissal of Hu Yaobang. See *DXPNP-2*, January 31, 1985; January 24, 1986; January 31, 1986; February 10, 1988; February 23, 1988; January 21, 1989; February 16, 1989; January 20, 1990; and February 13, 1990.

45. Ibid., February 7, 1992.

46. Interview with Chen Kaizhi, October 2003.

47. *CYNP,* February 3, 1992.

48. I visited the store in 1973 when it displayed only simple cotton clothing and thermos bottles.

49. Tong Huaiping and Li Chengguan, *Deng Xiaoping baci nanxun jishi*, pp. 285–294; *DXPNP-2*, February 21, 1992.

50. For listings of the Hong Kong, Shenzhen, and foreign coverage, see Huang Hong, *Ying daoli*, pp. 192–200; Fewsmith, *China since Tiananmen*, p. 242, n65.

51. Chen Maodi, "Jiang Zemin kaocha Shanghai shi qiangdiao quandang yao shizhong buyu quanmian guanche dangde jiben luxian jinyibu jiefang sixiang jiakuai gaige kaifang bufa" (During his visit to Shanghai Jiang Zemin stresses party must unswervingly implement the party's basic line to emancipate the mind and to speed up the pace of reform and opening), *Renmin ribao* (People's Daily), January 20, 1992, 1. Kuhn, *The Man Who Changed China*, pp. 214–215.

52. Kuhn, *The Man Who Changed China*, p. 214.

53. Ibid., pp. 213–214.

54. February 20, 1992, as quoted by Miles, *Legacy of Tiananmen*, p. 101.

55. Zhao, "Deng Xiaoping's Southern Tour," 750; Miles, *Legacy of Tiananmen*, pp. 100–101; Huang Hong, *Ying daoli*, p. 195.

56. An authoritative summary of the document may be found in *DXPNP-2*, February 28, 1992. The final version of the revision of Deng's talks in Shenzhen and Zhuhai is in *SWDXP-2*, pp. 358–370.

57. Miles, *Legacy of Tiananmen*, pp. 99–100, n50.

58. Ibid., p. 102.

59. Huang Hong, *Ying daoli*, p. 237; Fewsmith, *China since Tiananmen*, p. 62.

60. Kuhn, *The Man Who Changed China*, pp. 219–220.

61. Zhonggong zhongyang wenxian yanjiushi (Central Chinese Communist Party Literature Research Office), ed., *Shisanda yilai zhongyao wenxian xuanbian* (Selection of Important Documents since the 13th Party Congress), 3 vols. (Beijing: Renmin chubanshe, 1991–1993), 3:2055–2089.

62. *SWCY,* 3:370.

63. *DXPNP-2*, July 23–24, 1992.

64. Tony Saich, "The Fourteenth Party Congress: A Programme for Authoritarian Rule," *The China Quarterly,* no. 132 (December 1992): 1141–1142; Richard Baum, *Burying Mao: Chinese Politics in the Age of Deng Xiaoping* (Princeton, N.J.: Princeton University Press, 1994), pp. 364–368.

65. Saich, "The Fourteenth Party Congress," 1142–1146.

66. Ibid., 1146–1148.

67. Kuhn, *The Man Who Changed China,* p. 222.

68. For example, *DXPNP-2,* January 22, 1993.

69. Wu Guoguang, *Zhulu shiwuda: Zhongguo quanli qiju* (Toward the 15th Party Congress: Party Game in China) (Hong Kong: Taipingyang shiji yanjiusuo, 1997).

70. Kuhn, *The Man Who Changed China,* p. 223; Fewsmith, *China since Tiananmen,* pp. 67–68.

71. Zhu Jianguo, "Li Rui tan 'Jiao Guobiao taozhao,' tonggan shi huang nan jue yuan" (Li Rui on "Jiao Guobiao's Crusade": The Pain of Isolation of the First Emperor), at http://www.newcenturynews.com/Article/gd/200710/20071005150035.html, accessed August 16, 2010.

72. Saich, "The Fourteenth Party Congress," 1154.

73. Ding Lu, "China's Institution Development for a Market Economy since Deng Xiaoping's 1992 Nanxun," in John Wong and Yongnian Zheng, eds., *The Nanxun Legacy and China's Development in the Post-Deng Era* (Singapore: World Scientific, 2001), pp. 51–73.

74. *DXPNP-2,* February 19, 1997.

75. Ibid., February 25, 1997; Jim Lehrer, host, "Transcript on Deng's Legacy, February 25, 1997," *On Line Focus,* at http://www.pbs.org/newshour/bb/asia/february97/deng_2–25.html, accessed March 5, 2010.

24. China Transformed

1. John K. Fairbank, ed., *The Chinese World Order: Traditional China's Foreign Relations* (Cambridge: Harvard University Press, 1968); Thomas J. Barfield, *Perilous Frontier: Nomadic Empires and China* (Cambridge, Eng.: Basil Blackwell, 1989); Paul Cohen, *China Unbound: Evolving Perspectives on the Chinese Past* (New York: Routledge Curzon, 2003).

2. Quoted in E. Backhouse and J. O. P. Bland, *Annals and Memoirs of the Court of Peking* (Boston: Houghton Mifflin, 1914).

3. Linda Jacobson and Dean Knox, "New Foreign Policy Actors in China," SIPRI (Stockholm International Peace Research Institute) Policy Paper no. 26 (September 2010), p. 22.

4. On the international trading system in particular, see Edward S. Steinfeld, *Playing Our Game: Why China's Rise Doesn't Threaten the West* (New York: Oxford University Press, 2010).

5. For general works on the Communist Party see Richard McGregor, *The*

Party: The Secret World of China's Communist Rulers (New York: HarperCollins, 2010); Yongnian Zheng, *The Chinese Communist Party as Organizational Emperor* (London and New York: Routledge, 2010).

6. See G. William Skinner, "Marketing and Social Structure in Rural China," parts 1, 2, and 3, *Journal of Asian Studies* 24, no. 1 (November 1964): 3–44; 24, no. 2 (February 1965): 195–228; 24, no. 3 (May 1965): 363–399.

7. See Rachel Murphy, *How Migrant Labor Is Changing Rural China* (New York: Cambridge University Press, 2002), and Leslie T. Chang, *Factory Girls: From Village to City in a Changing China* (New York: Spiegel and Grau, 2008), on bringing urban advances back to the villages.

8. For works on law, see Stanley B. Lubman, *Bird in a Cage: Legal Reform in China after Mao* (Stanford, Calif.: Stanford University Press, 1999); Randall Peerenboom, *China's Long March toward Rule of Law* (New York: Cambridge University Press, 2002); Jianfu Chen, *Chinese Law: Context and Transformation* (Boston: Martinus Nijhoff, 2008).

9. See Anita Chan, *China's Workers under Assault: The Exploitation of Labor in a Globalizing Economy* (Armonk, N.Y.: M. E. Sharpe, 2001); Chang, *Factory Girls.*

10. Ezra F. Vogel, *One Step Ahead in China: Guangdong under Reform* (Cambridge: Harvard University Press, 1989). For some of the abuses in the system, drawing on exposures within China, see Chan, *China's Workers under Assault.*

11. See Martin King Whyte, *Small Groups and Political Rituals in China* (Berkeley: University of California Press, 1974); Gail E. Henderson and Myron S. Cohen, *The Chinese Hospital: A Socialist Work Unit* (New Haven: Yale University Press, 1984); Andrew G. Walder, *Communist Neo-Traditionalism: Work and Authority in Chinese Industry* (Berkeley: University of California Press, 1986).

12. See Deborah S. Davis, *The Consumer Revolution in Urban China* (Berkeley: University of California Press, 2000); Scott Rozelle and Jikun Huang, "The Marketization of Rural China: Gain or Pain for China's Two Hundred Million Farm Families?" in Jean C. Oi, Scott Rozelle, and Xueguang Zhou, eds., *Growing Pains: Tensions and Opportunity in China's Transformation* (Stanford, Calif.: Walter H. Shorenstein Asia-Pacific Research Center, Stanford University, 2010), pp. 57–85.

13. Martin King Whyte, *Myth of the Social Volcano: Perceptions of Inequality and Distributive Justice in Contemporary China* (Stanford, Calif.: Stanford University Press, 2010).

14. Interview with Communist Party historian Shen Zhihua, December 2010.

Key People in the Deng Era

1. A longer presentation about Chen Yun, including fuller sources, is in Ezra F. Vogel, "Chen Yun: His Life," *Journal of Contemporary China* 24, no. 45 (November 2005): 751–759.

2. Deng Liqun, *Shierge chunqiu, 1975–1987: Deng Liqun zishu* (Twelve Springs

and Autumns, 1975–1987: Deng Liqun's Autobiography) (Hong Kong: Bozhi chu-banshe, 2006), pp. 540–552.

3. Chu Feng and Lu Wenhua, "Sulian yu Xinjiang de heping jiefang" (The So-viet Union and the Peaceful Liberation of Xinjiang), *Dangshi zonglan,* no. 3 (2005): 53–55.

4. Interviews with Cheng Zhongyuan, who has been responsible for working with Deng Liqun in sorting out his papers and writing his history, July 2006.

5. Immediately after the Third Plenum in 1978, Hu Qiaomu was assigned to oversee the drafting of party documents; Deng Liqun worked under him in the Po-litical Research Office. See Deng Liqun, *Shierge chunqiu.*

6. See ibid., pp. 213–215.

7. This information on Hu Qiaomu relies in part on Liu Zhonghai, Zheng Hui, and Cheng Zhongyuan, eds. *Huiyi Hu Qiaomu* (Remembering Hu Qiaomu) (Bei-jing: Dangdai Zhongguo chubanshe, 1994); and Hu Qiaomu, *Zhongguo gongchan-dang de sanshi nian* (Thirty Years of the Chinese Communist Party) (Beijing: Renmin chubanshe, 1951).

8. Hu Qiaomu's criticisms of Deng Xiaoping in 1976 are reprinted in a volume by one of his co-workers; see Feng Lanrui, *Bie youren jianxing lunan: 1980 niandai qianhou Zhongguo sixiang lilun fengyun ji qita* (It Is an Unusually Difficult Journey to Travel: The Precarious Situation for Theoretical Thought Before and After the 1980s) (Hong Kong: Shidai guoji, 2005), pp. 38–83.

9. Sheng Ping, ed., *Hu Yaobang sixiang nianpu: 1975–1989* (A Chronology of Hu Yaobang's Thought: 1975–1989), 2 vols. (Hong Kong: Taide shidai chubanshe, 2007); Zheng Zhongbing, ed., *Hu Yaobang nianpu ziliao changbian* (Materials for a Chronological Record of Hu Yaobang's Life), 2 vols. (Hong Kong: Shidai guoji chuban youxian gongsi, 2005); Zhang Liqun et al., *Hu Yaobang zhuan* (Biography of Hu Yaobang), 2 vols., unpublished ms., available in the Fairbank Collection, Fung Library, Harvard University; and a collection of his friends' recollections, in Zhang Liqun et al., eds., *Huainian Yaobang,* 4 vols. (Hong Kong: vols. 1–2: Lingtian chu-banshe, 1999; vols. 3–4: Yatai guoji chuban youxian gongsi, 2001).

10. His daughter Man Mei, a medical doctor, has written—with the help of party historians—a detailed history of her father; see Man Mei, *Sinian yiran wujin: Huiyi fuqin Hu Yaobang* (Longing without End: Memories of My Father, Hu Yaobang) (Beijing: Beijing chubanshe, 2005); Zhong Mei Yang, *Hu Yao Bang: A Chinese Biog-raphy* (Armonk, N.Y.: M. E. Sharpe, 1988); separate interviews with Hu's two sons, Hu Deping and Hu Dehua, both in July 2007; Sheng Ping, *Hu Yaobang sixiang nianpu;* Zheng Zhongbing, *Hu Yaobang nianpu ziliao changbian;* Zhang Liqun et al., *Hu Yaobang zhuan;* and Zhang Liqun et al., *Huainian Yaobang.*

11. Ziyang Zhao, *Prisoner of the State: The Secret Journal of Zhao Ziyang,* trans. and ed. Bao Pu, Renee Chiang, and Adi Ignatius (New York: Simon and Schuster, 2009).

12. Interview with Robert Hawke, November 2002.

13. Interview with Frank Gibney, November 2005.

14. Printing Committee of the Canton Area Workers Revolutionary Committee, *Thirty-three "Leading Counterrevolutionary Revisionists,"* March 1968, translated into English in *Current Background,* no. 874 (March 17, 1969); "Disclosure of Teng Hsiao-ping's Dark Scheme to Form a 'Petofi Club,'" *Tung Fang Hung* [Dongfang Hong], no. 20 (February 18, 1967), translated into English in *Survey of China Mainland Press,* no. 3903 (March 21, 1967): 1–6; Qinghua daxue Jinggangshan bingtuan "Meihuaxiao" zhandou zu ("Smiling Plum Blossom" Struggle Group of the Jinggangshan Corps of Qinghua University), ed., *Chumu jingxin: Deng Xiaoping yanxinglu* (Eye to Eye with Something Frightening: A Record of Deng Xiaoping's Words and Deeds) (Beijing: Qinghua daxue Jinggangshan bingtuan "Meihuaxiao" zong dui yin, 1967), p. 21.

15. *DXPSTW,* pp. 105–112, 207–208.

16. *LZQ,* pp. 359–361.

17. Interview with Hu's son, Hu Dehua, in their home just outside Zhongnanhai, July 2007.

18. Ibid.

19. Michel Oksenberg and Sai-cheung Yeung, "Hua Kuo-feng's Pre–Cultural Revolution Hunan Years, 1949–66: The Making of a Political Generalist," *The China Quarterly,* no. 69 (March 1977): 3–53.

20. Information in this section is from an interview with Ji Humin, son of Ji Dengkui, October 2007.

21. For a more detailed official account of Li Xiannian's life, see "Li Xiannian zhuan" bianxiezu (Editorial Group for the Biography of Li Xiannian), ed., *Li Xiannian zhuan: 1949–1992* (A Biography of Li Xiannian: 1949–1992), 2 vols. (Beijing: Zhongyang wenxian chubanshe, 2009).

22. Chang, Kuo-t'ao [Zhang Guotao], *The Rise of the Chinese Communist Party: The Autobiography of Chang Kuo-t'ao,* 2 vols. (Lawrence: University Press of Kansas, 1971–1972), pp. 188–189.

23. This biographical overview draws on discussions in January 2006 with an official familiar with Mao Yuanxin's thinking.

24. Guan Shan, "Ren Zhongyi tan Deng Xiaoping yu Guangdong de gaige kaifang" (Ren Zhongyi on Deng Xiaoping and the Reform and Opening in Guangdong), *Yanhuang chunqiu,* no. 8 (2004): 8. This discussion draws on several visits with Ren after he retired and with officials around him. Ren was modest about his own achievements, and the evaluation of his successes comes from others who served under him. Even after he retired, Ren did not complain about the party or other officials: criticisms of their roles come from officials who served with him.

25. Li Rui, "Li Chang he 'yierjiu' neidai ren" (Li Chang and the December 9 Generation), *Yanhuang chunqiu,* no. 4 (2008): 1–4.

26. Interview with Ren Zhongyi, December 2005.

27. The biographical information in this section on Wan Li is drawn from Liu Changgen and Ji Fei, *Wan Li zai Anhui* (Wan Li in Anhui) (Hong Kong: Kaiyi chubanshe, 2001); Harrison E. Salisbury, *The New Emperors: China in the Era of Mao and Deng* (Boston: Little, Brown, 1992); as well as interviews with Wan Li's daughter, Shupeng, October 2003, and with Prime Minister Robert Hawke of Australia, June 2001 and November 2002

28. Interview with Wan Shupeng, Wan Li's daughter, October 2003.

29. Ibid.

30. Elizabeth J. Perry, *Shanghai on Strike: The Politics of Chinese Labor* (Stanford, Calif.: Stanford University Press, 1993), pp. 256–257.

31. Barbara Barnouin and Changgen Yu, *Ten Years of Turbulence: The Chinese Cultural Revolution* (New York: Kegan Paul International, 1993), p. 248.

32. *Guoshi*, vol. 8, p. 95.

33. Xu Jingxian, *Shinian yimeng: Qian Shanghai shiwei shuji Xu Jingxian wenge huiyi lu* (A Dream of Ten Years: A Record of the Recollections of the Cultural Revolution by Xu Jingxian, the Former Party Secretary of Shanghai) (Hong Kong: Shidai guoji chuban youxian gongsi, 2003), pp. 276–282, reported in Frederick C. Teiwes and Warren Sun, *The End of the Maoist Era: Chinese Politics during the Twilight of the Cultural Revolution, 1972–1976* (Armonk, N.Y.: M. E. Sharpe, 2007), p. 95.

34. *Guoshi*, vol. 8, p. 206.

35. Ibid., pp. 206–207.

36. Barnouin and Yu, *Ten Years of Turbulence*, pp. 248–249.

37. Richard Evans, *Deng Xiaoping and the Making of Modern China* (New York: Viking, 1994); Parris H. Chang, "Political Profiles: Wang Hung-wen and Li Tehsheng," *The China Quarterly*, no. 57 (March 1974): 124–128; Philip Short, *Mao: A Life* (New York: Henry Holt, 2000), pp. 608–609.

38. For general background on Ye, see *YJYZ*. An early summary of Ye's career until 1965 and before the release of new materials about his background is contained in Donald W. Klein and Anne B. Clark, *Biographic Dictionary of Chinese Communism, 1921–1965*, 2 vols. (Cambridge: Harvard University Press, 1971), 2:1004–1009. Also interviews with Ye's son Ye Xuanlian, April 2002, and his nephew Ye Xuanji, December 2008 and September 2009.

39. *DXPCR*, p. 190; *YJYZ*, pp. 605–606.

40. *YJYZ*, p. 608.

41. This section on Yu Qiuli draws from Lei Li, *Lishi fengyunzhong de Yu Qiuli* (Yu Qiuli in the Winds of History) (Beijing: Zhongyang wenxian chubanshe, 2005); interview with Yu Qiuli's daughter, Yu Xiaoxia, December 2008; ibid.; Teiwes and Sun, *The End of the Maoist Era*; *LZQ*.

42. Kenneth Lieberthal and Michael Oksenberg, *Policy Making in China* (Princeton, N.J.: Princeton University Press, 1988), pp. 175–181. National publicity dis-

torted the story of Daqing, calling attention to heroic, ordinary workers finding and digging the site and neglecting the expertise of Kang Shi'en and others. But the basic story of Yu Qiuli going down to the front lines and overseeing the development was confirmed by later scholars who debunked much of the later success of the Dazhai Brigade.

43. Lei Li, *Lishi fengyunzhong de Yu Qiuli*, p. 15.

44. In addition to the works cited earlier, I have relied on interviews with Zhao's daughter, Wang Yannan, who lived with her parents during the sixteen years that Zhao was under house arrest, October 2006 and July 2007. I have also drawn from my August 2006 interviews with Du Daozheng, who knew Zhao since Guangdong days and helped bring the tapes to Hong Kong, and my December 2006 interview with Zong Fengming, a friend from Zhao's youth who wrote *Zhao Ziyang: Ruanjinzhong de tanhua* (Zhao Ziyang: Captive Conversations) (Hong Kong: Kaifang chubanshe, 2007) and who visited Zhao more often than anyone else during his years of house arrest.

45. Ezra F. Vogel, *Canton under Communism: Programs and Politics in a Provincial Capital, 1949–1968* (Cambridge: Harvard University Press, 1969) (the Wade-Giles transliteration is used; see index entries under Chao Tzu-yang). See also David L. Shambaugh, *The Making of a Premier: Zhao Ziyang's Provincial Career* (Boulder, Colo.: Westview, 1984).

46. Interview with Woodcock's aide, William McCahill, U.S. embassy official who accompanied Woodcock at the meeting, October 2003. Zhao is reported to have worked in a machine shop in Xiangzhong Mechanics Factory in Hunan for several years during the Cultural Revolution.

Index

Praise for *MARILYN MONROE*

"This is a book that wound up teaching me a great deal about Hollywood, the social history of California, the movie business, the trials of female actors in American show business, and the life of a woman who has been so mythologized that often the real woman is obscured from actual view. Donald Spoto has accomplished what I would have thought was impossible: he has made me into a Marilyn Monroe fan after all these years."

—Erica Jong, *Washington Post Book World*

"Immensely readable, this book lacks sensationalism and is more scrupulously researched and better written than all those previous hack jobs."

—*New Statesman* (London)

"[Spoto] offers a welcome challenge to the muckraking, unsubstantiated tales that have been published in the years since the actress' demise in 1962."

—*Free Press* (Columbus, Ohio)

"Spoto puts new life into the tradition of biography, and his book is fresh and important. His life of Monroe does much to remind us that biography is a branch of history."

—*London Sunday Telegraph*

"[Spoto] has researched Monroe's life quite brilliantly and his riveting book comes up with the facts, pure and simple."

—*Birmingham Post* (London)

"[A] well-written and well-researched work."

—*Arkansas Democrat Gazette*

"[*Marilyn Monroe*] digs behind the usual drivel to celebrate a woman of warmth, wit, and considerable resources, all backed up with Spoto's renowned research, objectivity, and evident admiration. [An] inspired biography that will endure longer than most."

—*Empire* (UK)